HERITAGE STUDIES 1

Teacher's Edition

Third Edition

FREE
Lesson Plan Overview
now available at
bjupress.com/resources

bju press
Greenville, South Carolina

Note
The fact that materials produced by other publishers may be referred to in this volume does not constitute an endorsement of the content or theological position of materials produced by such publishers. Any references and ancillary materials are listed as an aid to the student or the teacher and in an attempt to maintain the accepted academic standards of the publishing industry.

HERITAGE STUDIES 1 Teacher's Edition
Third Edition

Authors
Eileen Berry
Gina Bradstreet
Ann Larson

Project Editor
Carolyn Cooper

Bible Integration
Bryan Smith

Permissions
Sylvia Gass
Lilia Kielmeyer
Kristin Villalba

Project Coordinators
Amy Johnson
Kendra Wright

Page Layout
Bonnijean Marley

Designer
Michael Asire

Cover Design
Elly Kalagayan

Cover Illustration
Ben Schipper

Cover Photography
Craig Oesterling

p. viii: Digital Vision/Getty Images; Getty Images/Digital Vision/Thinkstock

National Council for the Social Studies, Expectations of Excellence: Curriculum Standards for Social Studies (Washington, DC: NCSS, 1994) (pages 196–99)

Unless otherwise specified, all poems and rhymes are original works by BJU Press authors.

ISBN 978-1-60682-222-7 (Teacher's Edition with CD)

15 14 13 12 11 10 9 8 7 6 5

Contents

Goals

Strengthen knowledge of God and encourage Christian growth

- Reveal God's wisdom, omnipotence, sovereignty, and benevolence through the study of the history of the world (Psalm 19:1; Romans 1:20).
- Encourage evaluation and rejection of false philosophies.
- Promote discipline in the student's approach to and performance of responsibilities.
- Reinforce that all people need to trust Christ for salvation (John 3:16–18).

Develop interest in history, geography, citizenship, economics, and culture

- Emphasize God's plan for the individual, the family, and the nation.
- Emphasize the student's role in his expanding environment: family, community, state, and country.
- Encourage the student to make wise decisions and become a responsible Christian citizen.
- Teach practical skills, such as reading maps and charts, sequencing events, and working with timelines.

Present a balanced overview of American heritage

- **American history**—the study of America's past
  - Appreciate and comprehend the past as it relates to the present.
  - Recognize the significance of events.
  - Distinguish God's leading in historical events.
  - Examine the record of God's dealing with man.
- **Geography**—the study of the earth's surface and how it is used
  - Read and interpret maps and other geographic representations and tools to acquire and report information.
  - Demonstrate the wise use of natural resources to God's glory (Genesis 1:28).
  - Praise God for creating the world (Genesis 1:1).
- **Citizenship**—the study of government and civic responsibilities
  - Examine the Christian's responsibility to the government.
  - Identify the Christian's responsibility toward his community, state, and country.
- **Economics**—the study of how people use resources to meet their needs
  - Recognize that people everywhere have needs and wants.
  - Acknowledge that the physical environment affects the way people live and work.
- **Culture**—the study of the way of life of a group of people
  - Demonstrate how historians rely on primary sources to learn about the past.
  - Explain that landforms, climate, and resources influence the way of life of a group of people.
  - Express the need for worldwide missions (Acts 1:8).

Promote an understanding and an ability to discern connections between events

- Provide opportunities to use several skills, such as making decisions and inferring relationships.
- Teach cause-and-effect relationships to explain historical events.

Organize information in chronological order

- Understand how daily life has changed over time.
- Explore events in historical order to see progression and connections between events.

Build silent and oral reading habits that further fluency

At the beginning of the year, you may choose to read the text to the students prior to discussion. The goal, however, is that the students learn to read the text independently. Even small sections of silent, independent reading will help the students gain confidence. As the year progresses and their skills improve, students will be able to read more independently.

Reading for information is an important skill for the students to learn. The introductory questions or directives are designed to help the students find important information in the text.

Feature Pages

Additional reference selections called feature pages will include vocabulary that may be unfamiliar to the students. Encourage the students to follow along as you read or invite ready readers to read aloud for the class.

Vocabulary Words

Introduce new vocabulary words before reading a section. Write the word for display and pronounce it for the students. As the text is read, remind the students to look for the vocabulary word in bold print.

The students should demonstrate an understanding of the vocabulary words. It is not intended that these words and their definitions be memorized.

Content Words

Some Student Text pages will include content words that the students may not have learned to read yet. Guide the students in decoding the words before the reading of that page.

Online Resources

Visit bjupress.com/resources for links to enhance the lessons. (*Note:* Though these links have been carefully selected, check to ensure that the links are current and evaluate all material before presentation.)

Instructional Materials

Student Text

The student text is a colorful, easy-to-read presentation of social studies that integrates Bible, citizenship, culture, economics, geography, and history. Beginning with the framework of God's redemptive plan, the book includes an age-appropriate study of citizenship and government and then covers United States history from Native Americans to the Plymouth Colony. The final chapter contrasts the past and the present, noting changes that have taken place in the way we live. Each chapter includes a poem; engaging artwork, maps, graphs, and photos; Quick Check questions; and an extended hands-on activity to enhance learning. A Picture Glossary, a Geogloss, an atlas, and an index are included at the back of the book.

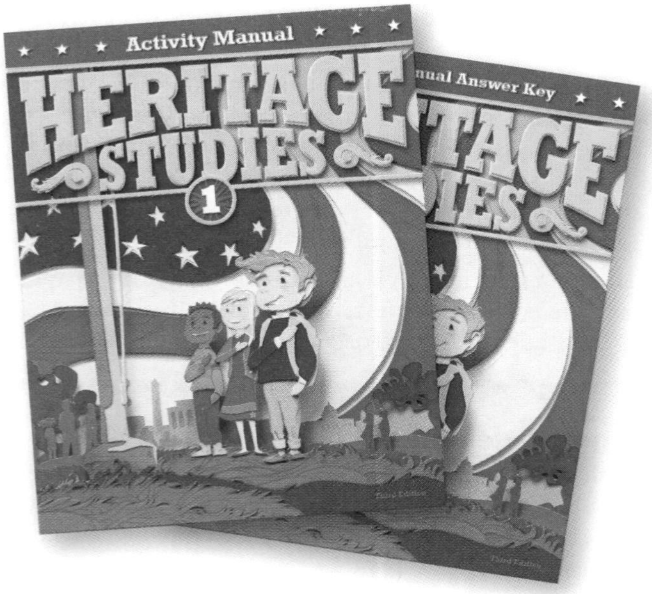

Activity Manual

Heritage Studies 1 Activity Manual contains full-color pages to review and enrich the lessons, including reinforcement, map skills, study skills, Bible connections, and chapter reviews. Answers are located in the Activity Manual Answer Key. The Answer Key is available in two formats: the Teacher's Toolkit CD and a printed copy that may be purchased separately.

Teacher's Edition

Heritage Studies 1 Teacher's Edition is the foundation of the program. This manual contains 90 lessons and coordinates all the instructions and activities. Each lesson identifies objectives, explains vocabulary, gives ideas for discussion, and offers hands-on activities. Reduced student text pages with answers to the student text questions appear with each lesson. Review games help prepare students for assessments. The Picture Glossary, the Geogloss, and the alignment of *Heritage Studies 1* with national standards are located in the appendix.

Teaching Visuals

The large teaching visuals are full-color charts that may be used as instructional aids. They include maps, diagrams, illustrations, and photos enlarged for classroom use. Some are die-cut or designed to be cut apart and used for class activities.

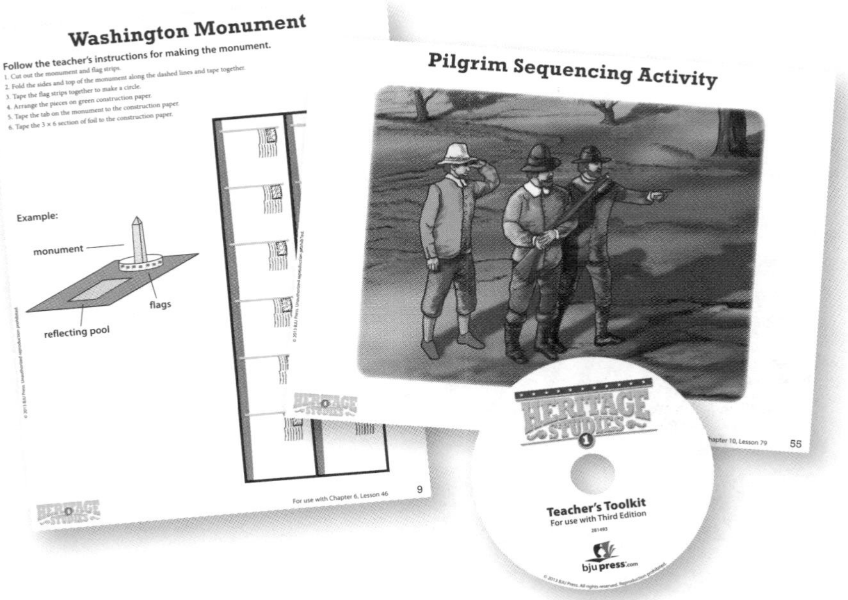

Teacher's Toolkit CD

The Teacher's Toolkit CD, located inside the back cover of this Teacher's Edition, includes the Activity Manual Answer Key, teaching visuals, maps, and instructional aids and activities.

Tests

Heritage Studies 1 Test Packet provides one age-appropriate test per chapter, covering the most important concepts taught in the lessons. These tests are optional and can serve as the objective part of an evaluation of a student's progress. The most effective tests are an outgrowth of the teaching process. Accordingly, these tests should not replace the teacher's individual assessment of a student's understanding and application. The tests can be adjusted in accordance with the teaching emphasis and direction as well as the student's maturation level. The teacher may find it necessary to eliminate some items or provide additional test items. An Answer Key is available separately.

United States of America

Because these materials emphasize United States history and citizenship (community government, state government, and national government), the readers in most cases are addressed as though they were in the context of the United States. If you are using these materials in a country other than the United States, you may choose to adapt as necessary. One possible adaptation would be to compare United States culture, symbols, and traditions with those of the country where you live.

Lesson Features

Chapter Opener

Discuss a poem that introduces the chapter topic.

Prepare students for chapter content by analyzing a photo.

Objectives

Understand the outcome of instruction in terms of the students' behavior.

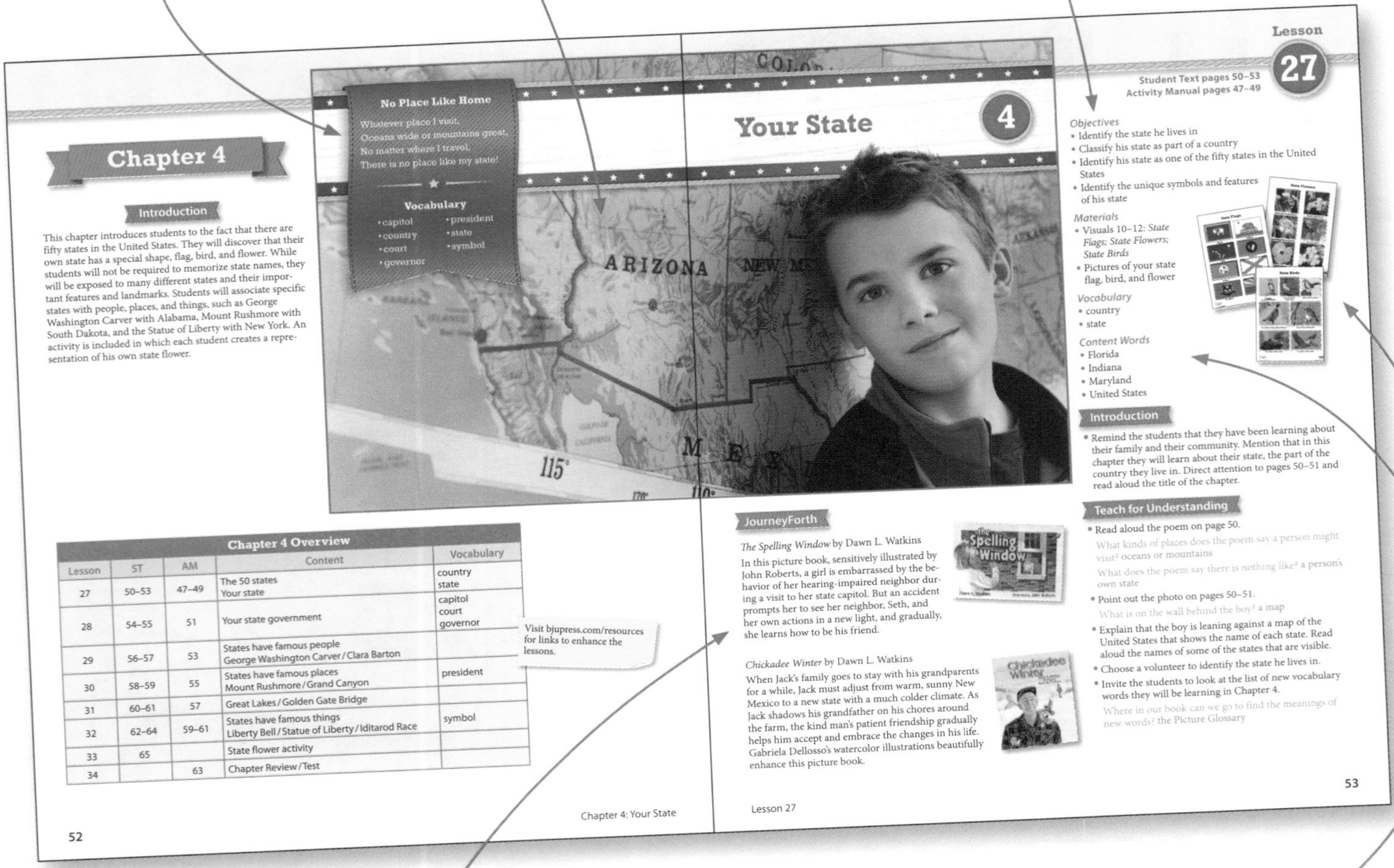

Chapter 4

Introduction

This chapter introduces students to the fact that there are fifty states in the United States. They will discover that their own state has a special shape, flag, bird, and flower. While students will not be required to memorize state names, they will be exposed to many different states and their important features and landmarks. Students will associate specific states with people, places, and things, such as George Washington Carver with Alabama, Mount Rushmore with South Dakota, and the Statue of Liberty with New York. An activity is included in which each student creates a representation of his own state flower.

No Place Like Home

Whatever place I visit,
Oceans wide or mountains great,
No matter where I travel,
There is no place like my state!

Vocabulary

- capitol
- country
- court
- governor
- president
- state
- symbol

Your State 4

Chapter 4 Overview

Lesson	ST	AM	Content	Vocabulary
27	50–53	47–49	The 50 states Your state	country state
28	54–55	51	Your state government	capitol court governor
29	56–57	53	States have famous people George Washington Carver / Clara Barton	
30	58–59	55	States have famous places Mount Rushmore / Grand Canyon	president
31	60–61	57	Great Lakes / Golden Gate Bridge	
32	62–64	59–61	States have famous things Liberty Bell / Statue of Liberty / Iditarod Race	symbol
33	65		State flower activity	
34		63	Chapter Review / Test	

Visit bjupress.com/resources for links to enhance the lessons.

52 Chapter 4: Your State

JourneyForth

The Spelling Window by Dawn L. Watkins

In this picture book, sensitively illustrated by John Roberts, a girl is embarrassed by the behavior of her hearing-impaired neighbor during a visit to her state capitol. But an accident prompts her to see her neighbor, Seth, and her own actions in a new light, and gradually, she learns how to be his friend.

Chickadee Winter by Dawn L. Watkins

When Jack's family goes to stay with his grandparents for a while, Jack must adjust from warm, sunny New Mexico to a new state with a much colder climate. As Jack shadows his grandfather on his chores around the farm, the kind man's patient friendship gradually helps him accept and embrace the changes in his life. Gabriela Dellosso's watercolor illustrations beautifully enhance this picture book.

Lesson 27

Lesson 27

Student Text pages 50–53
Activity Manual pages 47–49

Objectives
- Identify the state he lives in
- Classify his state as part of a country
- Identify his state as one of the fifty states in the United States
- Identify the unique symbols and features of his state

Materials
- Visuals 10–12: *State Flags; State Flowers; State Birds*
- Pictures of your state flag, bird, and flower

Vocabulary
- country
- state

Content Words
- Florida
- Indiana
- Maryland
- United States

Introduction

- Remind the students that they have been learning about their family and their community. Mention that in this chapter they will learn about their state, the part of the country they live in. Direct attention to pages 50–51 and read aloud the title of the chapter.

Teach for Understanding

- Read aloud the poem on page 50.
  What kinds of places does the poem say a person might visit? oceans or mountains
  What does the poem say there is nothing like? a person's own state
- Point out the photo on pages 50–51.
  What is on the wall behind the boy? a map
- Explain that the boy is leaning against a map of the United States that shows the name of each state. Read aloud the names of some of the states that are visible.
- Choose a volunteer to identify the state he lives in.
- Invite the students to look at the list of new vocabulary words they will be learning in Chapter 4.
  Where in our book can we go to find the meanings of new words? the Picture Glossary

53

JourneyForth Books

Suggest books with a biblical worldview for readers of varying abilities and interests.

Vocabulary/Content Words

Develop students' understanding of vocabulary and content words.

Materials

Determine which materials need to be gathered in advance of the lesson.

Other Features

Promote higher-level thinking skills through interactive learning strategies such as questioning, demonstrating, and discussing.

Apply integrated Bible truths and principles.

Assess students' understanding of the main concepts by asking the question given at the end of each lesson.

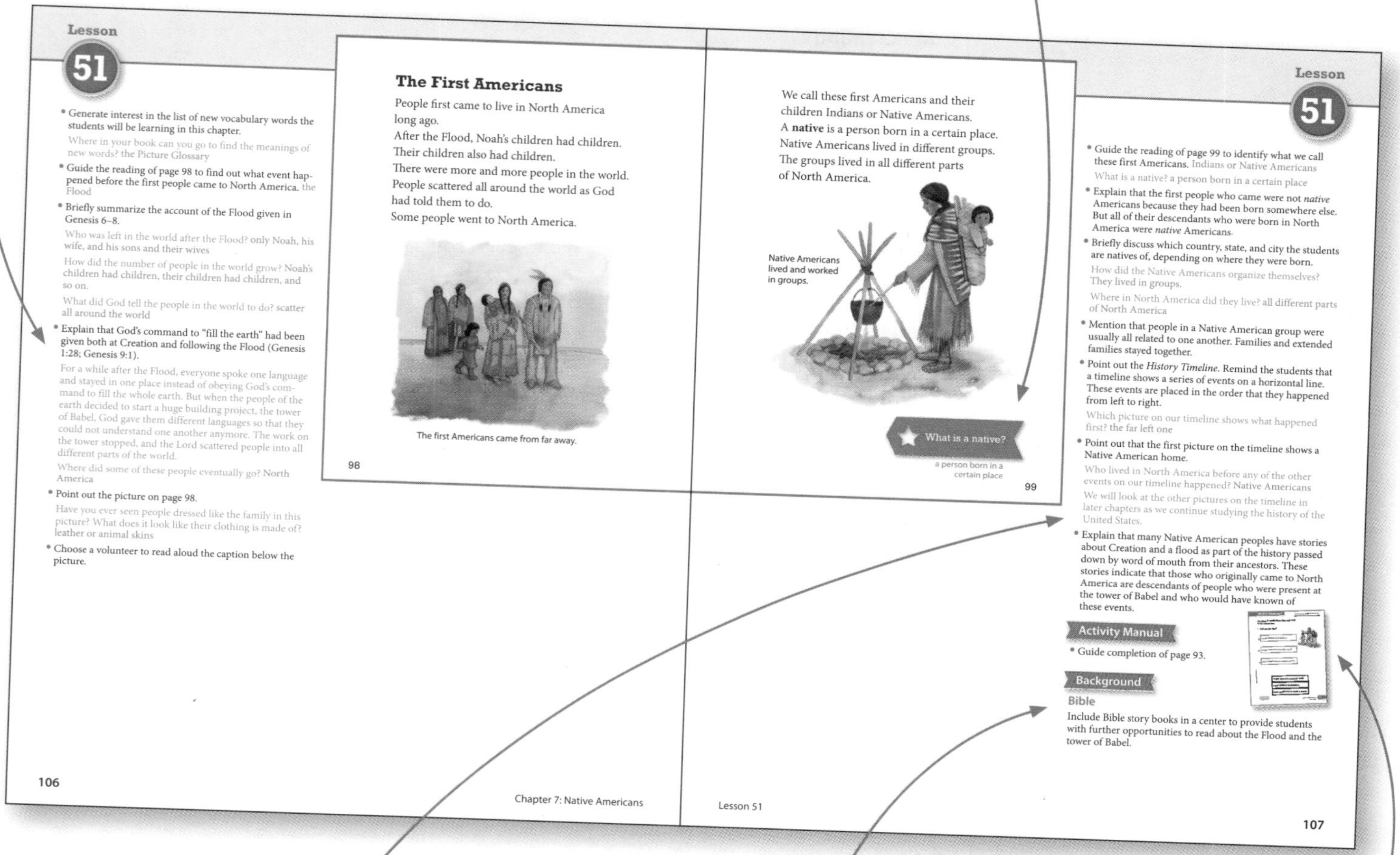

Lesson 51

- Generate interest in the list of new vocabulary words the students will be learning in this chapter.

  Where in your book can you go to find the meanings of new words? the Picture Glossary
- Guide the reading of page 98 to find out what event happened before the first people came to North America. the Flood
- Briefly summarize the account of the Flood given in Genesis 6–8.

  Who was left in the world after the Flood? only Noah, his wife, and his sons and their wives

  How did the number of people in the world grow? Noah's children had children, their children had children, and so on.

  What did God tell the people in the world to do? scatter all around the world
- Explain that God's command to "fill the earth" had been given both at Creation and following the Flood (Genesis 1:28; Genesis 9:1).

  For a while after the Flood, everyone spoke one language and stayed in one place instead of obeying God's command to fill the whole earth. But when the people of the earth decided to start a huge building project, the tower of Babel, God gave them different languages so that they could not understand one another anymore. The work on the tower stopped, and the Lord scattered people into all different parts of the world.

  Where did some of these people eventually go? North America
- Point out the picture on page 98.

  Have you ever seen people dressed like the family in this picture? What does it look like their clothing is made of? leather or animal skins
- Choose a volunteer to read aloud the caption below the picture.

The First Americans

People first came to live in North America long ago.
After the Flood, Noah's children had children.
Their children also had children.
There were more and more people in the world.
People scattered all around the world as God had told them to do.
Some people went to North America.

The first Americans came from far away.

98

We call these first Americans and their children Indians or Native Americans.
A **native** is a person born in a certain place.
Native Americans lived in different groups.
The groups lived in all different parts of North America.

Native Americans lived and worked in groups.

What is a native?

a person born in a certain place

99

Lesson 51

- Guide the reading of page 99 to identify what we call these first Americans. Indians or Native Americans

  What is a native? a person born in a certain place
- Explain that the first people who came were not *native* Americans because they had been born somewhere else. But all of their descendants who were born in North America were *native* Americans.
- Briefly discuss which country, state, and city the students are natives of, depending on where they were born.

  How did the Native Americans organize themselves? They lived in groups.

  Where in North America did they live? all different parts of North America
- Mention that people in a Native American group were usually all related to one another. Families and extended families stayed together.
- Point out the *History Timeline*. Remind the students that a timeline shows a series of events on a horizontal line. These events are placed in the order that they happened from left to right.

  Which picture on our timeline shows what happened first? the far left one
- Point out that the first picture on the timeline shows a Native American home.

  Who lived in North America before any of the other events on our timeline happened? Native Americans

  We will look at the other pictures on the timeline in later chapters as we continue studying the history of the United States.
- Explain that many Native American peoples have stories about Creation and a flood as part of the history passed down by word of mouth from their ancestors. These stories indicate that those who originally came to North America are descendants of people who were present at the tower of Babel and who would have known of these events.

Activity Manual

- Guide completion of page 93.

Background

Bible

Include Bible story books in a center to provide students with further opportunities to read about the Flood and the tower of Babel.

106 Chapter 7: Native Americans Lesson 51 107

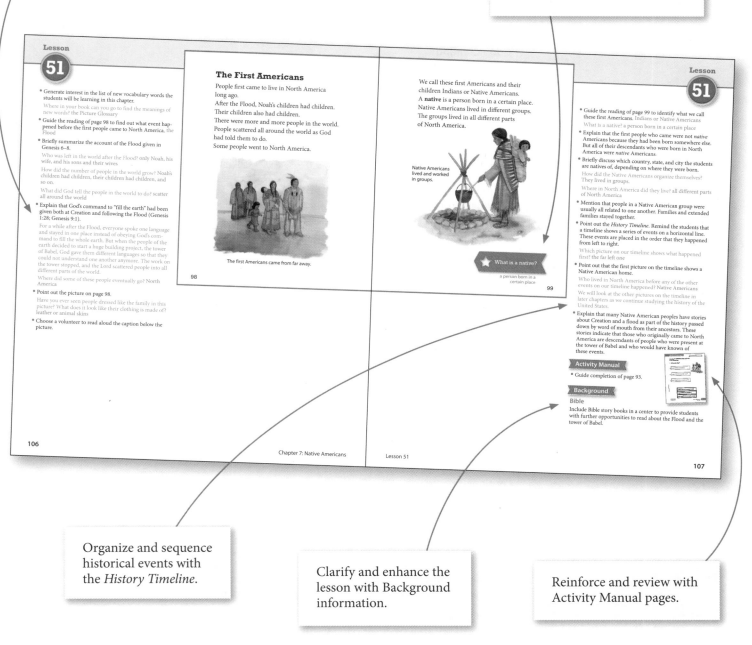

Organize and sequence historical events with the *History Timeline*.

Clarify and enhance the lesson with Background information.

Reinforce and review with Activity Manual pages.

Enhance students' curiosity and awareness by using pictures, graphs, and maps.

Enrich students' knowledge by incorporating cross-curricular and optional activities.

Lesson Plan Overview

Chapter 1: God's World

Lesson	Teacher's Edition	Student Text	Activity Manual	Content Objectives & Christian Worldview
1	xxii–3	2–5		**Introduction** • Identify major topics of social studies • Infer meaning from pictures by interpreting the clues they contain • Interpret a poem's figurative language • Identify components of the textbook
2	4–7	6–9	1	**God's Creation** • Explain from the Bible why people are important • Affirm that God is the Creator of the world • Identify specific features of God's creation • Identify the way in which God created the world
3	8–9	10–11	3	**God Created Animals and People** • Affirm that God created all the animals • Identify unique features that God gave to each species • Affirm that God created people • Summarize the special instructions that God gave Adam and Eve • Explain from the Bible why people are different from animals
4	10–11	12–13	5	**Sin and a Savior** • Defend the truth that God's creation was very good • Explain the rule that God gave to Adam and Eve • Define *sin* and explain the consequences of Adam and Eve's disobedience • Contrast what the world was like before sin with what it was like after sin • Summarize God's plan of salvation
5	12–13	14–15	7	**Introduction to Maps** • Explain from the Bible why people have moved into different parts of the world • Identify the purpose of a map • Locate water and land on a map • Identify on a map places where people live
6	14–15	16–17	9	**Continents and Oceans** • Identify the large land areas on a map as the seven continents • Name the continent where he lives • Identify the four large oceans on a map • Name the oceans near North America
7	16–17	18–19	11	**Cardinal Directions and the Globe** • Identify the four cardinal directions on a map • Recall that a globe is a representation of the earth • Compare the shape of the earth to a ball • Locate the continents and oceans on a globe
8	18	19		**Continents and Oceans on a Map** • Locate continents and oceans on a map • Explain why Jesus wants Christians to go to every continent
9	19–20	20–21	13	**World Culture and Hudson Taylor** • Name things that people do differently around the world • Identify Hudson Taylor as a man who was led by God to tell people in China about Jesus • Explain why Hudson Taylor dressed and ate like people in China • Affirm that God loves all the people of the world
10	21		15	**Review and Test**

Chapter 2: Your Family

Lesson	Teacher's Edition	Student Text	Activity Manual	Content Objectives & Christian Worldview
11	22–25	22–25	17–19	**Introduction** • Affirm that God is the one who puts families together • Define a family • Identify the first two children born on earth
12	26–27	26–27	21	**Roles of Family Members** • Identify the different roles that family members fill • Compare and contrast the first family with a modern family • State where God wants families to live
13	28–29	28–29		**Families Work and Play Together** • Explain how family members work together to help each other • Identify ways families play together
14	30		23	**Graphing the Number of People in Families** • Visualize differences in families by completing a graph
15	31–32	30–31	25	**Family Rules** • Define *rules* • Distinguish rules that prohibit behavior from rules that demand behavior • Identify the basic rules that God gives to families • Explain how God helps us keep His rules
16	33–34	32–33	27	**Needs and Wants** • Distinguish between *needs* and *wants* • Explain the role that choices play in spending money • Classify church involvement as a need and not a want
17	35			**Making a Timeline** • Visualize how people grow and change by completing a timeline with photos
18	35		29	**Review and Test**

Chapter 3: Your Community

Lesson	Teacher's Edition	Student Text	Activity Manual	Content Objectives & Christian Worldview
19	36–39	34–37	31	**Introduction** • Identify people and places in a community • Describe his community • Name goods that his family uses • Identify goods that people make, grow, or sell
20	40–41	38–39	33	**Service Jobs** • Identify a service job as a job helping others • List people in service jobs • Identify paying jobs and volunteer jobs • Name a way that his family could serve others
21	42–43	40–41	35	**Places in a Community** • Distinguish community places where people work and visit • Associate places with the community where they are found • Associate the jobs people do with the places where they work
22	44–45	42–43	37	**Recycling and Caring for Natural Resources** • Explain how God intends for people and places in a community to be cared for • List ways to care for God's world by recycling • Apply Genesis 1:26–28 to the work of keeping natural resources clean
23	46–47	44–45	39	**Government Workers** • Define the role of a mayor • List the duties of the government • Explain that the government is made up of workers • Explain from the Bible why Christians should obey the law
24	48–49	46–47	41	**Benjamin Franklin** • List ways Benjamin Franklin made his city a better place • List ways he can make his city a better place • Compare Philadelphia then and now
25	50–51	48–49	43	**Maps** • Locate parts of a map: title, map key, cardinal directions • Locate places on a map using cardinal directions • Explain the purpose of a map key
26	51		45	**Review and Test**

Chapter 4: Your State

Lesson	Teacher's Edition	Student Text	Activity Manual	Content Objectives & Christian Worldview
27	52–55	50–53	47–49	**Introduction** • Identify the state he lives in • Classify his state as part of a country • Identify his state as one of the fifty states in the United States • Identify the unique symbols and features of his state
28	56–57	54–55	51	**State Government Leaders** • Summarize how state leaders are chosen • Explain the state governor's main job • Explain the function of a state capitol • Explain the role of judges in state courts
29	58–59	56–57	53	**States Have Famous People** • Associate famous people with states • Summarize the contributions of George Washington Carver • Summarize the contributions of Clara Barton
30	60–61	58–59	55	**States Have Famous Places (1)** • Associate famous places with states • Explain the significance of Mount Rushmore • Associate the Grand Canyon with the greatness of God
31	62–63	60–61	57	**States Have Famous Places (2)** • Associate famous places with states • State facts about the Great Lakes • State facts about the Golden Gate Bridge
32	64–66	62–64	59–61	**States Have Famous Things** • Associate famous things with states • Explain the significance of the Liberty Bell • Explain the significance of the Statue of Liberty • Associate the state of Alaska with dog-sled racing
33	67–68	65		**State Flower** • Create a representation of his state flower
34	69		63	**Review and Test**

Chapter 5: Your Country

Lesson	Teacher's Edition	Student Text	Activity Manual	Content Objectives & Christian Worldview
35	70–73	66–69	65	**Introduction** • Define the meaning of the word *country* • Explain why the United States is called the Land of the Free • Locate the United States on a globe • Name the countries that border the United States
36	74–75	70–71	67	**The American Flag and the Pledge** • Identify the flag as a symbol of the United States of America • Name the colors in the American flag • Explain why the phrase *under God* is important in the pledge to the American flag • Explain why people make a pledge to their country
37	76–77	72–73	69	**United States Symbols** • Explain why the bald eagle was chosen as a symbol of the United States • Identify "In God We Trust" as the motto of the United States • Identify "The Star-Spangled Banner" as the official song of the United States
38	78–79	74–75	71	**"America the Beautiful"** • Analyze the hymn "America the Beautiful" • Name some of the landforms found in America • Explain the importance of asking God's grace for our country
39	80–81	76–77	73	**Government of the United States** • Identify the president as the leader of the United States • Explain why the Constitution is important • Identify the role of a judge • Explain what a citizen is
40	82–83	78–79		**Elections** • Explain why an election is held • List the steps of a voting campaign • Explain why voting is important
41	84–85		75	**Voting Activity** • Participate in a classroom election
42	85		77	**Review and Test**

Chapter 6: Your Country's Capital

Lesson	Teacher's Edition	Student Text	Activity Manual	Content Objectives & Christian Worldview
43	86–89	80–83	79	**Introduction** • Locate Washington, DC, on a map • Classify Washington, DC, as an important city • Identify the United States Capitol • Associate the Capitol with government workers
44	90–91	84–85	81	**The White House** • Identify the White House as the home of the president and his family • Locate the White House in Washington, DC • Explain why people visit the White House
45	92–93	86–87	83	**The Washington Monument** • Name the tallest monument in Washington, DC • List reasons that a monument was built to honor George Washington • Associate George Washington's birthday with the celebration of Presidents' Day
46	94–95			**Washington Monument Activity** • Assemble a model of the Washington Monument • Locate the Capitol, the White House, and the Washington Monument on a map of Washington, DC
47	96–97	88–89	85	**Map Activity** • Locate the Capitol, the White House, the Washington Monument, and the World War II Memorial on a map of Washington, DC • Define *veteran* • Explain the importance of Veterans Day
48	98–99	90–91	87	**The Lincoln Memorial** • Describe the Lincoln Memorial • Locate places on a map of Washington, DC • Identify Abraham Lincoln as a president • Associate Abraham Lincoln's birthday with the celebration of Presidents' Day
49	100–102	92–95	89	**Cardinal Directions** • Use cardinal directions to locate places on a map • Locate places on a map of Washington, DC • Explain the significance of the Fourth of July holiday
50	103		91	**Review and Test**

Chapter 7: Native Americans

Lesson	Teacher's Edition	Student Text	Activity Manual	Content Objectives & Christian Worldview
51	104–7	96–99	93	**The First Americans** • Trace the series of events (the Flood, the tower of Babel, and the scattering of people around the world) that brought the first people to North America • Identify the meaning of the term *Native Americans* • Affirm that Native Americans lived in North America before Europeans came • Sequence events on a timeline
52	108–9	100–101	95	**Native American Culture** • Locate on a map of North America areas where Native Americans lived • Identify Native American groups as tribes • Make cultural distinctions among Native American tribes • Associate Native American culture with specific religious beliefs • Evaluate Native American religious beliefs in light of biblical teaching
53	110–11	102–3	97	**The Kiowa Tribe** • Associate the Kiowa tribe with the plains • Explain the significance of the buffalo to the Kiowa culture • Identify distinctive elements of Kiowa culture
54	112–13	104–5	99	**The Hopi Tribe** • Associate the Hopi tribe with the desert of the Southwest • Identify distinctive elements of Hopi culture • Infer ways that the location of the Hopi affected their culture
55	114–15	106–7	101–3	**The Tlingit Tribe** • Associate the Tlingit tribe with the Northwest Coast • Identify distinctive elements of Tlingit culture • Infer ways that the location of the Tlingit tribe affected their culture
56	116–17	107		**Canoe Activity** • Make and decorate a Native American canoe
57	118–19	108–9	105	**Native American Artifacts** • Distinguish artifacts from modern objects • Infer the function of Native American artifacts • Explain how artifacts help us understand history
58	119		107	**Review and Test**

Chapter 8: Christopher Columbus

Lesson	Teacher's Edition	Student Text	Activity Manual	Content Objectives & Christian Worldview
59	120–23	110–13	109	**Introduction** • Recall facts about Columbus's early life that influenced his decision to explore • Explain why people wanted to explore and go to Asia • Explain why the traditional routes to Asia made travel difficult
60	124–25	114–15	111	**Maps** • Contrast the differences in the beliefs about the size of the earth that were popular in Columbus's day • Explain the differences between maps used long ago and those used today
61	125			**Mapmaking** • Participate in a map-making activity • Explain how a map gives information
62	126–28	116–18	113	**Planning the Voyage** • Identify the events that led to the funding of Columbus's plan to sail west
63	129–31	119–21	115	**Columbus Discovers the New World** • Summarize the voyage taken by Columbus and his crew • Affirm that God used the voyage to change the world • Recognize the chronological indicators on a timeline • Explain that Columbus's discovery of land happened in 1492
64	132–33	122–23	117	**Ships Long Ago and Columbus Day** • Compare ships made long ago with modern ships • Explain why Columbus Day is important
65	134			**Columbus Play** • Recall facts about Columbus by participating in a play
66	135		119	**Review and Test**

Chapter 9: Jamestown

Lesson	Teacher's Edition	Student Text	Activity Manual	Content Objectives & Christian Worldview
67	136–39	124–27		**Introduction** • Recognize why the Europeans came to the New World • Locate the Old World and the New World on a map • Contrast the appearance of the Native American and the English man
68	140–41	128–29	121–23	**Why the English Came** • Explain why the English came to settle Jamestown • Locate an ocean, a coast, a river, and a harbor on a map • Locate Jamestown on a map
69	142–43	130–31	125	**Meeting the Woodland People** • Affirm that Native Americans lived in America before the English came • Identify Native Americans as Woodland tribes • Dramatize the concern of the Woodland people about the arrival of the English • Conclude that God wanted Jamestown to be a lasting English settlement
70	144–45	132–33	127–29	**Building a Settlement** • Create a map of the school library • Interpret a map key • Infer the importance of God and the Bible at Jamestown from looking at a map of Jamestown • Sequence a list of three events
71	146–49	134–37	131	**Life at Jamestown** • Classify needs and wants • Conclude that John Smith was a wise leader of Jamestown • Differentiate trade items between the Native Americans and the colonists
72	150–51	138–39	133	**The Woodland People** • Identify items made from natural resources • List goods made from things found in the woods • Assemble a wigwam
73	152–53	140–41	135	**Pocahontas** • Differentiate between Woodland culture and English culture • Dramatize the story of Pocahontas's interactions with the English
74	154–55	142–43	137	**The Settlement Grows** • Differentiate between Woodland culture and English culture • Describe the different family roles • Explain the importance of women and families in the survival of Jamestown • List good leadership qualities
75	156–57		139	**Review and Test**

Chapter 10: Plymouth

Lesson	Teacher's Edition	Student Text	Activity Manual	Content Objectives & Christian Worldview
76	158–61	144–47	141	**Introduction** • Explain why the Pilgrims came to America • Express in role-play the control that the king of England had over churches in England • Compose a prayer of thanks to God for the Pilgrims who came to America
77	162–64	148–50	143–45	**The *Mayflower*** • Read a diagram to identify parts of the *Mayflower* • Describe what life was like for the Pilgrims while traveling on the *Mayflower*
78	165–67	151–53	147	**The Voyage to the New World** • Identify ways God cared for the Pilgrims on the *Mayflower* • Trace the route of the Pilgrims' voyage to the New World • Explain why the Mayflower Compact was written • Use cardinal directions
79	168–69	154–55	149	**Plymouth** • Recognize that *Of Plymouth Plantation* was written by a Pilgrim • Affirm that the Pilgrims prayed to God • Sequence the events after the Pilgrims landed at Plymouth
80	170–71	156–57	151	**The Pilgrims and the Woodland People** • Conclude from the Pilgrims' friendship with the Woodland people that God was caring for the Pilgrims • Write a peace treaty
81	172–73	158–59	153	**Squanto** • Follow directions to plant a simulated garden • List proofs of God's providence in the life of Squanto
82	174–75	160–61	155	**The First Thanksgiving** • Use the textbook to find answers • Compare the Pilgrim culture with today's culture using a Venn diagram • Explain why the Pilgrims held a Thanksgiving feast
83	176			**First Thanksgiving Activity** • Dramatize the first Thanksgiving
84	177		157	**Review and Test**

Chapter 11: Today and Long Ago

Lesson	Teacher's Edition	Student Text	Activity Manual	Content Objectives & Christian Worldview
85	178–81	162–65	159	**Introduction** • Contrast the past with the present • Identify ways to learn about the past • Identify a specific event in his life that occurred in the past • Explain how God's command to fill and care for the earth leads to change
86	182–83	166–67	161	**Timeline of Communication** • Explain how communication has changed over time • Identify the order of inventions for communication on a timeline
87	184–85	168–69	163	**Tools from the Past** • Identify tools used in the past • Explain how tools help get work done
88	186		165	**Changes in Children's Clothing over Time** • Explain how children's clothing has changed over time
89	187–88	170–71	167	**The Future** • Identify the things that will remain the same in the future • Affirm that God is in control and does not change
90	189		169	**Family History Day Activity / Optional Review and Test** • Participate in "Family History Day"

Heritage Studies 1 from a Christian Worldview

God wrote a completely accurate history in the Bible. The Bible presents us with a view to examine history as we read and learn about it. This biblical view is called a **Christian worldview**.

What Is Our Place in God's World?

God made humans to declare His glory by being like Him. He has made each of us in His image (Genesis 1:26–27). In the **Creation Mandate** (the first command of God found in Genesis 1:28), God calls us to imitate His deeds. God is the infinite ruler of the universe, and people are to be finite rulers of His earth. As people have attempted to live out the Creation Mandate, they have created a way of living that includes language, religion, government, customs, and the arts. This way of living is people's culture.

Tragically, shortly after Creation, people sinned. Adam and Eve disobeyed and failed to exercise the dominion given to them (Genesis 3:6). However, God did not abandon His image bearers. At that time God promised to redeem the world to Himself, principally by sending His own Son into the world to save His people from sin (Genesis 3:15). The story of the human race is the story of God's redemptive acts to rescue His people and destroy His enemies.

Why Teach Heritage Studies 1?

Heritage Studies 1 is part of a developmental social studies program used to teach history, geography, government, economics, and culture skills, as well as a knowledge of God and Christian character. History is the record of the past acts of God and humans on earth from Creation to the present. It records mankind's attempts to live out the Creation Mandate in a fallen world. Heritage Studies 1 focuses on a small but important part of this study—the United States and the country's interaction in world events. History is an account of good and evil, of great advances for God's work of redemption, and of human sin and suffering.

Why should first graders be taught about the accounts of evil in history? We believe there are at least three important reasons for studying the good as well as the evil.

To Learn Lessons for Life

In studying events from the past, right and wrong choices and their consequences can be seen. The main lesson that should be learned from these choices is that people should trust God and obey His Word. As the student studies and applies lessons from these events, he gains not only knowledge, but more importantly, wisdom.

To Understand Cultural Identity

Studying Heritage Studies 1 will help the student understand who he is as an American. Many Americans possess very little knowledge of their society's past. Because of this, they do not understand the values that have shaped our nation's story in order to preserve what is good about the past. They also lack the ability to critically evaluate the current conditions of our nation.

As this course is taught, special attention should be given to how Americans have valued freedom. Freedom is a condition in which people may make their own choices without fear of harm. Freedom can be a good thing (1 Corinthians 7:21, 23; Romans 6:17–22). However, the kind of freedom that a Christian should value is limited by God's Word (Genesis 2:16–17; Psalm 2:10–12; 9:17). Often, freedom has been understood as freedom to do whatever one wants, even if it means disobeying God and harming others. A good society protects the people's freedom to live according to God's commands.

To See God at Work

The Bible teaches that redemption in Jesus Christ is the goal of history. God has planned and directed all events in order to establish Christ's kingdom on earth (1 Corinthians 15:28; Ephesians 1:10–11). As the events of the past are taught, regularly ask students how God may be using these events to carry out His work of redemption.

Understanding how God has been at work will give the student hope for the future. In particular, it will provide an understanding of how God may use him in his own life. Throughout history, Christians were and still are being used by God. A student cannot change the fallen world by himself. But he can, by God's grace, do much good.

Chapter 1

Introduction

The students will be introduced to the major topics of social studies and will explore the various features of their book. The first part of the chapter gives an overview of Creation, the Fall, and Redemption as the basis for the study of history. The second part covers basic map skills, introduces the seven continents and the four oceans, discusses different world cultures, and presents a brief biography of Hudson Taylor. The students will participate in an interactive floor map activity to help them recognize the continent shapes.

To Learn

To learn is to go sailing
To a new and distant shore.
To learn is to meet people
I have never met before.

History

Geography

2

Chapter 1 Overview				
Lesson	ST	AM	Content	Vocabulary
1	2–5		Topics of social studies	
2	6–9	1	God's creation of the world	
3	10–11	3	God's creation of animals and people	
4	12–13	5	The Fall God's plan for redemption	Savior
5	14–15	7	Water and land on a map	map
6	16–17	9	Continents and oceans	continent ocean
7	18–19	11	Cardinal directions The globe	directions globe
8	19		Floor map activity	
9	20–21	13	Different world cultures Hudson Taylor	
10		15	Chapter Review / Test	

Visit bjupress.com/resources for links to enhance the lessons. (*Note:* Though these links have been carefully selected, check to ensure that the links are current and evaluate all material before presentation.)

To learn is to find treasure
In a place I'd never look.
To learn is to grow wiser
As I travel through my book.

Economics

Culture

Citizenship

3

Lesson 1 Student Text pages 2–5

Objectives

- Identify major topics of social studies
- Infer meaning from pictures by interpreting the clues they contain
- Interpret a poem's figurative language
- Identify components of the textbook

Introduction

- Read aloud the poem on pages 2–3. Tell the students that the author of the poem is Eileen Berry. The author is the person who wrote the poem. Encourage the students to notice how some words in the poem make them imagine pictures in their minds.

What is this poem about? learning

How does the poem make learning sound exciting and fun? It compares learning to sailing or finding treasure.

How is learning like traveling to a new place? We find out things we have never seen or known before.

Can you think of a way you might meet a new person in your Heritage Studies book? by reading about someone's life

What happens to a person as he learns? He grows wiser.

Teach for Understanding

- Point out the first picture on page 2 and read the word *History.*
- Explain that history is the study of what happened in the past.

What is behind the boy and his grandfather? a statue; the Statue of Liberty

This statue was built long ago. It is an important part of our country's past. We will learn more about it later in our book.

- Read the word *Geography* above the second picture. Explain that geography is the study of places on the earth.

What is the girl in the picture looking at? a map

What do you think she could learn by looking at a map? where places are

- Read the word *Economics* beside the picture on page 3.

What is the boy in the picture doing? putting coins in a piggy bank

What do you think the word *economics* has to do with? money

Economics is the study of the way people use goods and money.

- Read the word *Culture* above the picture on page 3.

How would you describe the girl's clothing? bright, colorful; the parasol, flowers, and dress style are different from what we normally wear.

The girl is wearing the traditional style of dress in her country. Culture is the way of life of a certain group of people. A people's culture is based on what they think about God and what they think He wants them to do.

- Read the word *Citizenship* above the last picture.

Why is the girl's hand over her heart? She is saying the pledge to the American flag.

Citizenship is the study of how we can help and appreciate the country we live in.

Optional Activities are provided in some lessons.

Activity

Economics

Pass around a coin bank. Discuss the purpose of the slot and how to get money out of the bank. Ask the students whether they have ever saved money in a bank like the boy in the picture is doing. Discuss reasons for saving money and what kinds of things we might use money for.

Lesson

1

- Read the first sentence on page 4.

  This is a picture of the Contents page of our book. What do you think it shows us? chapter titles; the page numbers where each chapter begins

  Where would you find this page in our book? in the front

- Direct the students to turn to the Contents page. Read some of the titles. Invite students to tell which chapters they would be most excited to learn about.
- Read the second sentence on page 4.

  Flip through the pages in your book. Do you see lots of pictures? Why are pictures important in a Heritage Studies book? They show the people, places, and events we are learning about.

Clarify and enhance the lesson with information from the Background section.

Background

Bible

As we study different aspects of social studies, we come to a better understanding of God, of our world, and of our responsibilities in that world. Mastering the various academic disciplines God created is a way of obeying His command in Genesis 1:28 to have dominion over the earth.

Reading the Student Text

At the beginning of the year, you may choose to read the text to the students prior to discussion. The goal, however, is for the students to learn to read the text independently. Even small sections of silent, independent reading will help the students gain confidence. As the year progresses and their skills improve, students will be able to read more independently.

Reading for information is an important skill for the students to learn. The introductory questions or directives are designed to help the students find important information in the text.

Chapter Poems

The poem on each chapter opener page has been written by Eileen Berry. As you discuss the poems in the first lesson of each chapter, read the title and tell the students who the author is.

Eileen Berry works as an author at BJU Press, where she has contributed stories, poems, and nonfiction to a variety of educational materials. She also teaches a course in Writing for Children at Bob Jones University. She is the author of several children's books and numerous song lyrics for children and adults.

Exploring Our Book

Learn new things.

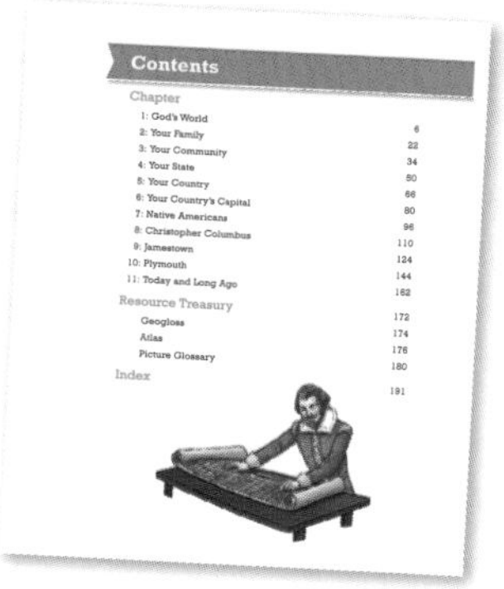

Enjoy pictures.

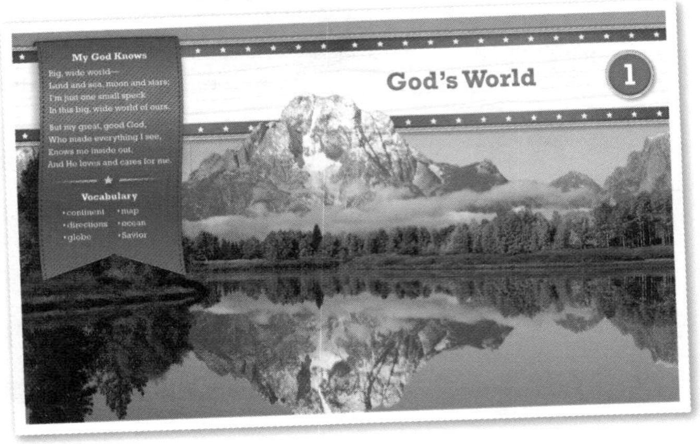

4

JourneyForth

Books

The trade division of BJU Press, JourneyForth Books, produces books with a biblical worldview for readers of varying abilities and interests.

Wait and See by Dawn L. Watkins

Take an imaginative look at some of the animals God has created. Written in fanciful poetry and illustrated with Suzanne R. Altizer's beautiful photographs, this concept book will help children learn to observe details.

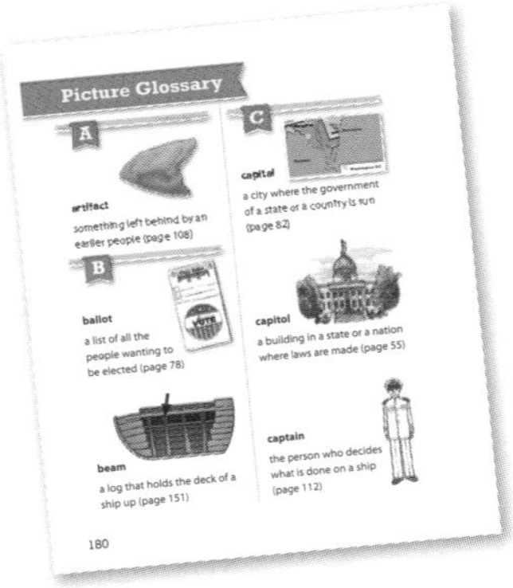
Picture Glossary

A

artifact
something left behind by an earlier people (page 108)

B

ballot
a list of all the people wanting to be elected (page 78)

beam
a log that holds the deck of a ship up (page 151)

C

capital
a city where the government of a state or a country is run (page 82)

capitol
a building in a state or a nation where laws are made (page 55)

captain
the person who decides what is done on a ship (page 112)

180

Read new words.

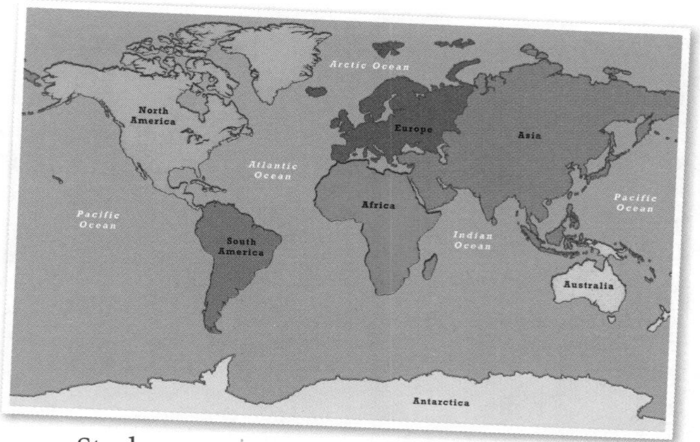

Study a map.

5

- Read the first sentence on page 5.

  This is a page from the Picture Glossary in the back of your book. What do you think is in a glossary? new words and their meanings

- Direct the students to turn to the Picture Glossary.

  Do you see any words you already know? How do the pictures in the glossary help you? The pictures give clues to the meanings of words.

  What else does the glossary tell? page numbers where the words are found

  We will learn many new words as we go through our book.

- Read the second sentence on page 5.

  This is a map of the whole world. How does the whole world fit in such a small space? Elicit that a map is smaller than the actual place it represents.

  Flip through your book again. Do you see any more maps? We will learn many new ways to find information on a map.

Background

Cover Art

The art on the cover of *Heritage Studies 1* was created with artistic paper manipulation called paper sculpture. The concept was drawn as if it were going to be painted. The various shapes that make up the drawing were then cut out of colored paper. These shapes were then reassembled to form the image. During this step of the paper-sculpture process, the shapes are layered or cut-through to add interest. Paper sculpture may include painted patterns to give additional texture. To create the idea of depth, some paper shapes have been supported off the background surface using foam or cardboard. Provide an opportunity for the students to create their own paper sculpture.

Mumsi Meets a Lion by Kim Stegall

This richly detailed picture book takes children to the continent of Africa and immerses them in the world of Mumsi, a Samburu boy from Kenya. On a dark forest path one night, Mumsi meets a lion, and he must remember the important lesson his parents have taught him. Accompanied by Kimberly Batti's vivid illustrations, this story brings the sights and sounds of Kenyan culture to life.

Haiku on Your Shoe by Eileen M. Berry

This early chapter book tells the story of a cross-cultural friendship between Jeremy and the new boy from Japan who joins his class. Comparing the effort of friendship to thawing ice and melting marshmallows, Jeremy's mother encourages him to show Christian love to Taka by taking an interest in the arts of his culture—paper-folding and Japanese poems. Instructions for two simple crafts are included at the end of the book.

Lesson

2

Student Text pages 6–9
Activity Manual page 1

Objectives

- Explain from the Bible why people are important
- Affirm that God is the Creator of the world
- Identify specific features of God's creation
- Identify the way in which God created the world

Introduction

- Direct attention to the Contents page.

  We are ready to start Chapter 1 of our Heritage Studies book. What is the title of Chapter 1? God's World

  On what page does Chapter 1 begin? page 6
- Instruct the students to turn to the opener for Chapter 1.

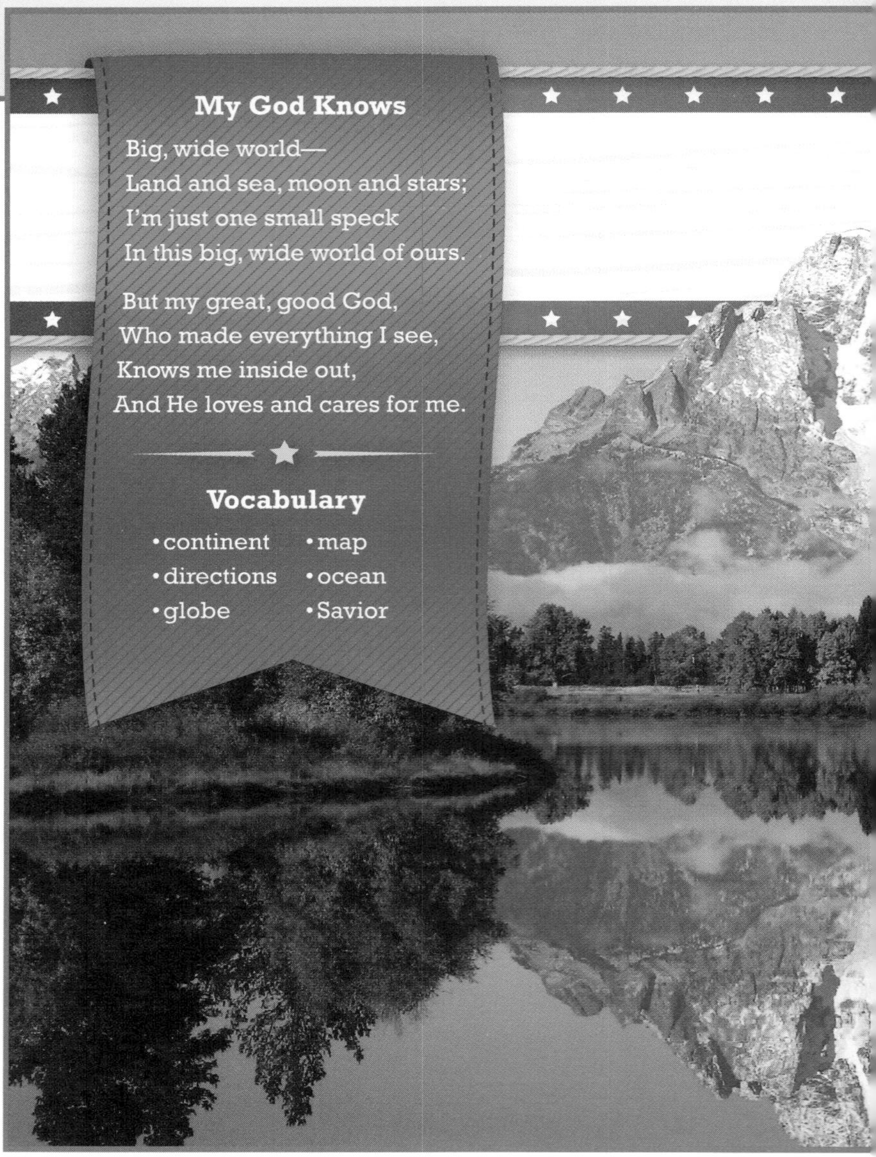
My God Knows
Big, wide world—
Land and sea, moon and stars;
I'm just one small speck
In this big, wide world of ours.
But my great, good God,
Who made everything I see,
Knows me inside out,
And He loves and cares for me.
Vocabulary
•continent
•map
•directions
•ocean
•globe
•Savior

God's World

1

Teach for Understanding

- Point out the chapter title at the top of page 7.

  What is the title of Chapter 1? God's World
- Generate interest in the photo on pages 6 and 7.

  What does this picture show about God's world? how beautiful and big it is; it has mountains, trees, and lakes.

  What time of year is it in the photo? fall How do you know? The leaves are turning orange, yellow, and red.
- Read aloud the poem "My God Knows."

  Name some things the poem says about God. He is great and good, He made everything we see, He knows us inside out, and He loves and cares for us.

  How does the speaker in this poem feel when he looks at the world? like a small speck

  A speck is like one little piece of dust we can hardly see. Does God see us as small specks? No, He knows us, loves us, and cares for us. We are important to Him.
- Point out the vocabulary words the students will learn in this chapter. Explain that the meanings of these words can be found in the Picture Glossary at the back of the book.

Lesson

2

- Guide the reading of page 8 to find out when God made the world. in the beginning

  What did God make the world out of? nothing

  How did God make it? by speaking
- Draw attention to the picture on page 8. Explain that this is similar to how our world looks from space.
- Guide the reading of page 9 to find out what else God made. everything in the world: light, sky, land, sea, flowers, trees, sun, moon, and stars

  What things do you see in the picture that God made? sky, land, sea, tall trees, tiny flowers, sun

  Where in the Bible do we find the story of God's creation? Genesis 1

  Why do you think we start our study of history (the past) with God's creation of the world? That is how and when the history of our world began.
- Emphasize that the Bible tells us the truth about things in the past that no one was there to see. Explain that we accept the Bible's words by faith. Only by accepting God's words by faith are we able to understand the world we live in (Hebrews 11:3). [BAT: 8b Faith in the power of the Word of God]

God Made the World

In the beginning God made the world.
God made it out of nothing.
He just spoke.
Then the world was there.

8

God made everything in the world.
He made light.
He made the sky.
He made the land and the sea.
He made tiny flowers and tall trees.
He made the sun, the moon, and the stars.

★ How did God make the world?

God just spoke.

9

Activity Manual

- Read aloud the directions for page 1. Encourage the students to look at the picture on page 9 in their Student Texts if they need ideas for drawing things God made. Invite the students to show their pictures and tell about what they have drawn.

Activity

God's World

Invite the students to bring in photos of places they have been that show the beauty of God's world. Demonstrate the activity using a personal example. Provide an opportunity for the students to show and tell about their experiences.

Background

Creation

Read aloud the Creation account in Genesis 1. Point out that God made everything in the world in only six days.

Lesson 3

Student Text pages 10–11
Activity Manual page 3

Objectives
- Affirm that God created all the animals
- Identify unique features that God gave to each species
- Affirm that God created people
- Summarize the special instructions that God gave Adam and Eve
- Explain from the Bible why people are different from animals

Introduction

- Briefly review that God made the world out of nothing by just speaking.

  What are some things in the world that God made? light, sky, land, sea, trees, grass, flowers, sun, moon, and stars

  Today we will read about some other very important things that God made.

Teach for Understanding

- Guide the reading of page 10 to find out what else God made. animals

  What animals are named on this page? fish, birds, cats, rabbits, deer, and bugs
- Point out the picture of each animal.

  Do any of these animals look exactly alike? no

  Which two animals on the page look most alike? the two fish

  How are even the fish different from each other? They are two different sizes and colors.
- Discuss how different each kind of animal looks. Emphasize the variety of God's creation. Every animal was specially designed for the purposes God has for it.

God Made Animals

God made animals.
He made shiny fish and bright birds.
He made big cats.
He made quick rabbits.
He made shy deer.
He made little bugs.

10

Lesson 3

God Made People

God made people too.
God made a man.
The man was Adam.
God made a woman.
The woman was Eve.
God told them to have children.
He told them to care for His world.

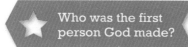

Who was the first person God made?

Adam

11

- Guide the reading of page 11 to find out the last thing God made. people

  What two kinds of people did God make? man and woman

  Who did God make first? the man What was the man's name? Adam

  What was the woman's name? Eve

  What did God tell the man and the woman to do? have children

  What special job did God give the man and the woman? to care for His world
- Explain that the man and the woman were different from everything else God created. They were made in the "image of God." God made them to think, understand, and love. God could talk with them in a way that He could not talk with the animals. He told them to take care of everything else He had made, including the animals. Because people are made in God's image, they are important to God. We should also be important to one another, and we should treat others with respect and care because every person bears God's image.
- Choose a volunteer to tell what Adam and Eve are doing to care for God's world in the picture on page 11. taking care of the animals

Activity Manual

- Emphasize that God still expects people to take care of His world today. Discuss ways we can take care of God's world. Guide completion of page 3.

Activity

Animals

Invite the students to bring stuffed animals to display in the classroom. Discuss the variety in the animal kingdom, and point out the creativity and wisdom of God's design.

Background

Bible

Read the Creation account of man and woman from Genesis 2:7, 18–24.

Lesson

4

Student Text pages 12–13
Activity Manual page 5

Objectives

- Defend the truth that God's creation was very good
- Explain the rule that God gave to Adam and Eve
- Define *sin* and explain the consequences of Adam and Eve's disobedience
- Contrast what the world was like before sin with what it is like after sin
- Summarize God's plan of salvation

Vocabulary

- Savior

Introduction

- Remind the students that God made the world out of nothing and created everything in it, including animals and people. Read Genesis 1:31.

  What does this verse say about the world God had made? It was very good.

Teach for Understanding

- Guide the reading of page 12 to find out what God's world was like when He created it. perfect; it had nothing bad in it.
- Remind the students that God had given Adam and Eve the special job of taking care of His world.

  Does this mean that Adam and Eve could do whatever they wanted with God's world? No; elicit that they had to take care of God's world in the way He had planned. They had to obey God's rules.

  What rule did God give Adam and Eve? They could not eat from one tree.

  What happened to change God's perfect world? Adam and Eve broke the rule. They sinned and ate from the tree.

  What is sin? anything we do that is wrong and goes against God's plan for us
- Draw attention to the picture on page 12. Remind the students that up until the time that they sinned, Adam and Eve had been living in the beautiful Garden of Eden.

  Why do Adam and Eve look so sad in the picture? They had to leave the garden because of their sin; they were sorry they had sinned.

Sin and a Savior

God's world was perfect.
It had nothing bad in it.
God gave Adam and Eve one rule.
They could not eat from one tree.
Adam and Eve broke the rule.
They sinned.
Then God's world was no longer perfect.

12

Many lessons include some questions that extend beyond the information given in the Student Text. It is not intended that all students know the answers to these questions. They are meant to guide your discussion as you build upon previous exposure.

But God had a plan.
He would send a **Savior** one day.
This Savior would be perfect.
He would save people from their sin.

Who did God plan to send?

a Savior

13

- Guide the reading of page 13 to find out what God's plan was. to send a Savior

  What is a Savior? someone who saves

  Who is the Savior God planned to send? Jesus Christ

  How was Jesus different from every other person who ever lived? Possible answers: He was God's Son; He was perfect; He never sinned.

  What did Jesus come to save us from? our sin

  Why is there a picture of Jesus on the cross? His death on the cross was God's plan. By dying He paid the penalty for our sin.

  Did Jesus stay dead?
  No, He rose from the dead.

Activity Manual

- Guide completion of page 5.

Background

Bible

Read Romans 5:8 and 19. Explain that Adam's sin brought the penalty of death and eternity in hell on every person that would be born after him. Mention that the death of God's Son, Jesus Christ, made it possible for us to be saved from sin's penalty and spend eternity ruling with Him on earth (Revelation 22:5).

Lesson

5

Student Text pages 14–15
Activity Manual page 7

Objectives
- Explain from the Bible why people have moved into different parts of the world
- Identify the purpose of a map
- Locate water and land on a map
- Identify on a map places where people live

Vocabulary
- map

Introduction

- Review what happened to change God's world so that it was no longer perfect. Adam and Eve sinned.

  What was God's wonderful plan to deal with the problem of sin? He would send a Savior, Jesus Christ.

Teach for Understanding

- Tell about a missionary or someone you know who lives in another country.
- Invite students to tell about anyone they know who lives in a different country.
- Guide the reading of page 14 to find out whose plan it was for people to live all over the world. God's

  How did the number of people in the world grow after Adam and Eve? They had children, their children had children, and so on.

  Why are there people all over the world today? People moved to many different places around the world.
- Briefly review the story of the tower of Babel (Genesis 11). Explain that after God changed people's languages, people scattered all over the world. People separated into different places so that those who spoke the same language could be together.
- Draw attention to the pictures on page 14.

  Why do you think the children in the pictures are dressed differently from each other? They are all from different parts of the world.
- Explain that the girl on the left is wearing traditional clothing of Africa, the boy on the horse is wearing the traditional dress of Mongolia in northern Asia, and the boy on the right is wearing a traditional American baseball uniform.

People in the World

God wanted people to live in every part of the world.
Adam and Eve had children.
Their children had children.
People moved to many different places.
Now people live all over the world.

14

Background

Introducing Vocabulary Words

Introduce new vocabulary words before reading a section. Write the word for display and pronounce it for the students. As the text is read, remind them to look for the vocabulary word in bold print.

The students should demonstrate an understanding of the vocabulary words. It is not intended that these words and their definitions be memorized.

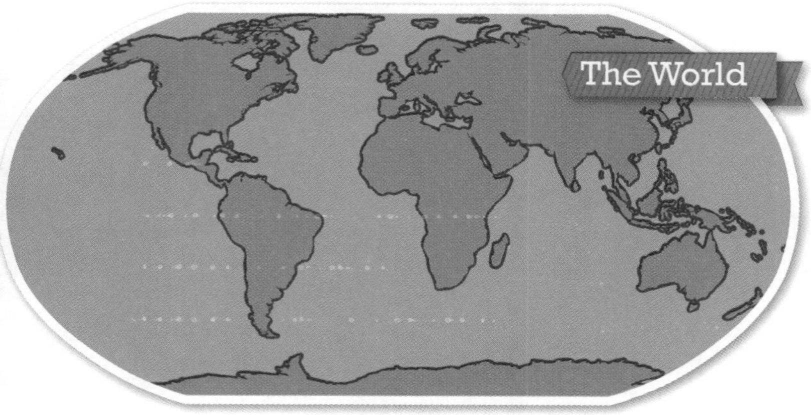

God's world has water and land.
Look at the **map**.
A map is a drawing that shows
where places are.
The blue color shows water.
The green color shows land.
People live in almost all the green places.

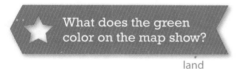

★ What does the green color on the map show?

land

15

Lesson

5

- Guide the reading of page 15 to learn what is pictured on the page. a map of the world

  What is a map? a drawing that shows where places are
- Choose a volunteer to read the title on the map. The title is found on the red ribbon. The World

  What do the blue places on the map show? water

  What do the green places show? land

  In which places on the map do people live? almost all the green parts

  Where do people iive—on land or on water? on land
- Instruct the students to point to a place on the map where people live.

Activity Manual

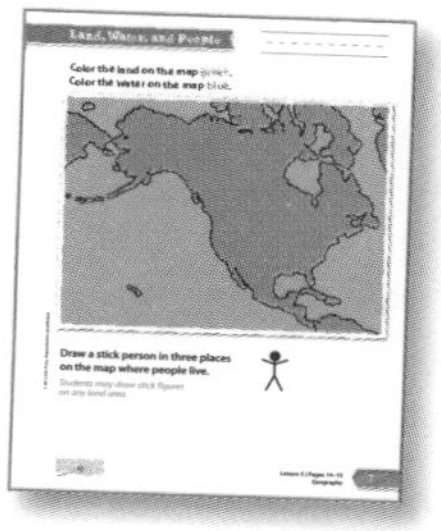

- Read aloud the directions for page 7. Encourage the students to consider whether their stick figures should go on the parts of the map they color blue or the parts they color green. Guide completion of the page.

Lesson 6

Student Text pages 16–17
Activity Manual page 9

Objectives
- Identify the large land areas on a map as the seven continents
- Name the continent where he lives
- Identify the four large oceans on a map
- Name the oceans near North America

Materials
- Visuals 1–4: *Continents*

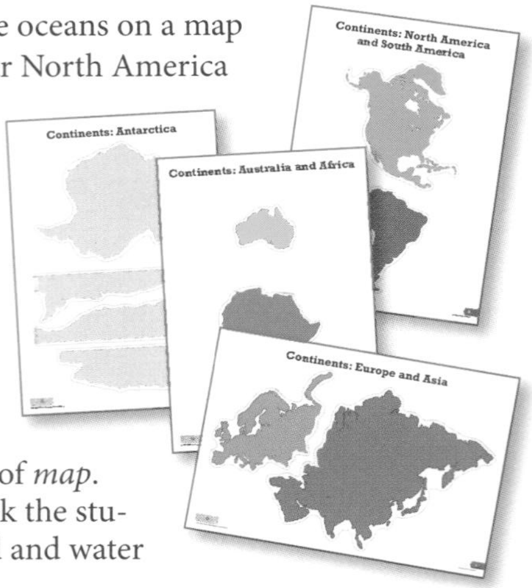

Continents: North America and South America
Continents: Antarctica
Continents: Australia and Africa
Continents: Europe and Asia

Vocabulary
- continent
- ocean

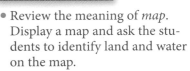

Introduction

- Review the meaning of *map*. Display a map and ask the students to identify land and water on the map.

Teach for Understanding

- Invite the students to turn to pages 16–17 to see another map of the world.

  How is this map different from the one on page 15? possible answers: bigger; more colors on it; names of places are given
- Guide the reading of page 16 to find out what the large pieces of land are called. continents

  How many continents are there? seven

  On this map, how can you tell each continent apart? Each continent is a different color.
- Count together the colored pieces of land on the map to find all seven continents. Repeat the names of each continent together.

  Which continent do you live on? possible answer: North America
- Locate North America on the map.
- Display the prepared visuals in a row by attaching them to the board one by one. Repeat the name of each continent together as you display it.

  Let's see if we can arrange these continents the way they are arranged on the map.

  Which continent is North America?
- Encourage the students to guide you in arranging the continents as they are on the map. Invite them to repeat a continent's name after you, and then choose a volunteer to come and point out where it should go as you re-create the map.

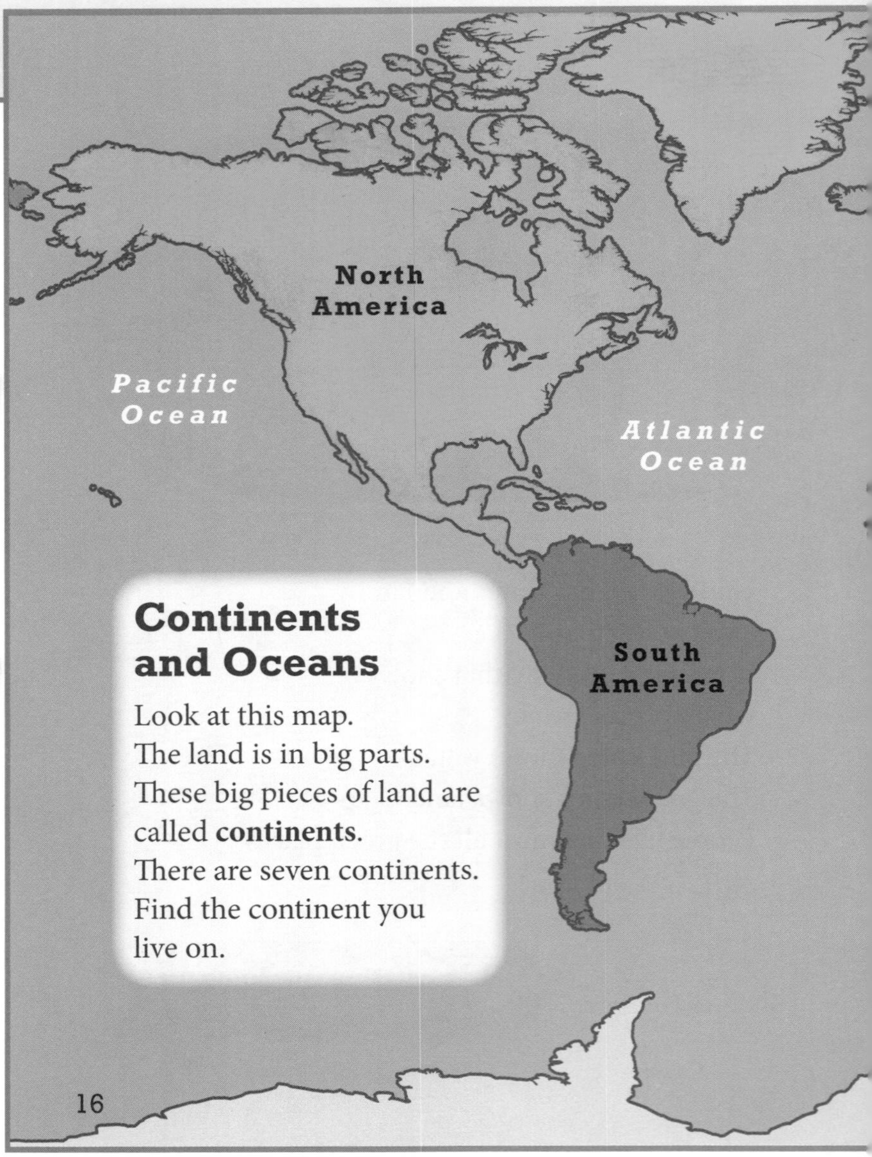

North America
Pacific Ocean
Atlantic Ocean
South America
Continents and Oceans
Look at this map.
The land is in big parts.
These big pieces of land are called continents.
There are seven continents.
Find the continent you live on.
16

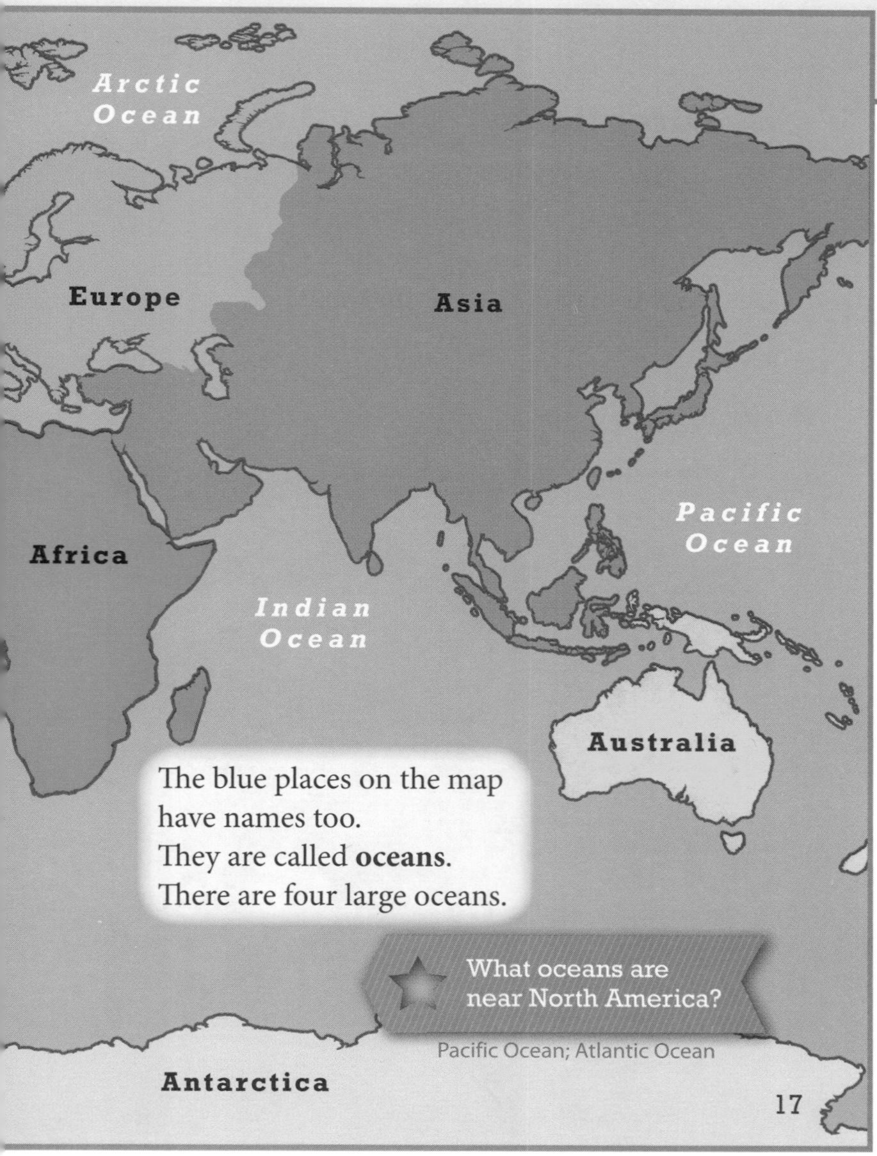
Arctic Ocean
Europe
Asia
Africa
Pacific Ocean
Indian Ocean
Australia
The blue places on the map have names too.
They are called **oceans**.
There are four large oceans.
What oceans are near North America?
Pacific Ocean; Atlantic Ocean
Antarctica
17

- Guide the reading of page 17 to find out what the blue places on the map are. oceans
- Explain that an ocean is a large body of water.

  How many different oceans are there? four
- Repeat the names of the oceans together.

  Why is the Pacific Ocean shown twice on the map? Elicit that the earth is round and that the blue places on the far west and far east edges of this map are both part of the same ocean.

  Which two oceans are near North America? Pacific Ocean and Atlantic Ocean
- Mention that the students might have seen one of these oceans on a trip to the beach.

Activity Manual

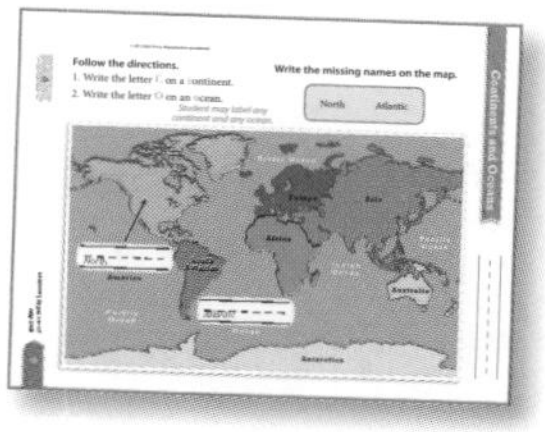

- Read aloud the directions for page 9. Review the name *North America* and the names of the two oceans surrounding it. Guide completion of the page.

Activity

Continents

Allow the students to arrange the continents independently, using the map in their book as a guide.

Lesson

7

Student Text pages 18–19
Activity Manual page 11

Objectives
- Identify the four cardinal directions on a map
- Learn that a globe is a representation of the earth
- Compare the shape of the earth to a ball
- Locate the continents and oceans on a globe

Materials
- A globe

Vocabulary
- directions
- globe

Introduction

- Review the meanings of *continent* and *ocean* and the number of each.

  Where can we see the seven continents and four oceans all spread out in a drawing? on a world map

- Review the names and locations of the continents and oceans from the map on pages 16 and 17.

Teach for Understanding

- Guide the reading of page 18 to find out the names of the four directions. north, south, east, and west

  What is the purpose of directions? to point us to places

- Point out the yellow cross on the map. Explain that the points of the cross are pointing to the four different directions on a map.

  What continent is pictured on this map? North America

  Which side of North America would be its west coast on this map? the left side

  Put your finger on the map in the blue area west of North America. Which ocean is this? the Pacific Ocean

  Which side of North America would be its east coast? the right side

  Put your finger on the map in the blue area east of North America. Which ocean is this? the Atlantic Ocean

- Point out that below North America is the tip of another continent in a lighter shade of green.

  What continent is this? South America

  Put your finger on North America. Look at the yellow cross. In what direction would you move your finger to put it in South America? south

Directions

A map shows **directions**.
Directions point us to places.
North, south, east, and west are directions.
On this map north is at the top.
South is at the bottom.
East is on the right.
West is on the left.

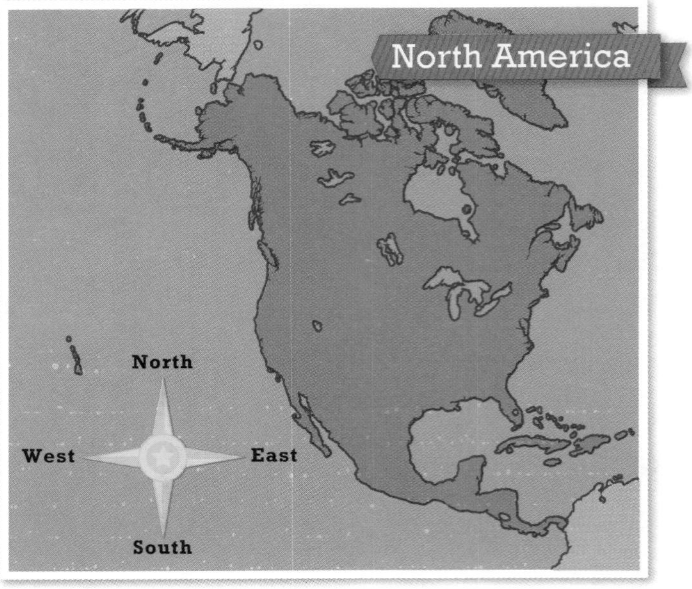

18

The Globe

The earth looks like this from space.

This is a **globe**.
A globe shows the shape of the world.
A globe is shaped like a ball.
You can turn a globe to see different places.
You can find the seven continents and the four oceans.

Can you find your continent on a globe?

Activity

19

- Guide the reading of page 19 to find out what is pictured at the top of the page. a girl looking at a globe

  What does a globe show? the world as it is actually shaped

  What is a globe shaped like? a ball

  Where would we have to be to see the world shaped like a ball or a globe? in space
- Display the globe. Show how to turn the globe to see different places on it.

  What can you find on a globe? the seven continents and the four oceans
- Choose a student to point to North America on the globe. As time allows, choose students to find other continents and oceans on the globe.

Activity Manual

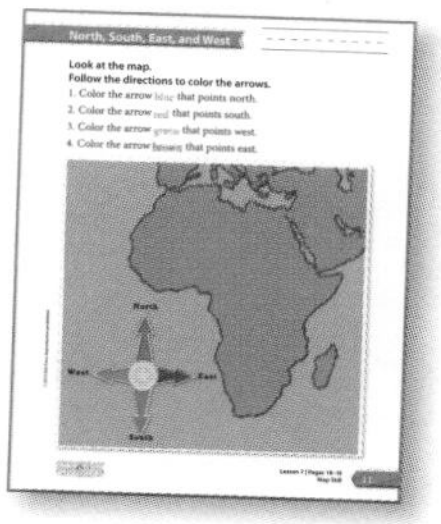

- Read aloud the directions for page 11. Review the four cardinal directions on a map or on the globe. Guide completion of the page.

Activity

Cardinal Directions

Provide additional practice with cardinal directions using the globe or the continent visuals. Instruct the students to place a finger on a certain continent and then move it north, south, east, or west as you direct them. When you say "stop," ask a student to identify the continent or ocean his finger is resting on. Continue until each student has had a turn to answer.

Lesson

8

Chapter Activity
Student Text page 19

Objectives
- Locate continents and oceans on a map
- Explain why Jesus wants Christians to go to every continent

Materials
- A world floor map prepared for the activity

The floor map introduced in this lesson will be referenced in later chapters. You may also use the map throughout the semester for additional reinforcement activities that fit your schedule.

Introduction

- Read Matthew 28:19–20, explaining that this was one of the last things that Jesus told His disciples while He was on earth.

Where does Jesus want Christians to go to tell people the good news of the gospel? to all the world

There are people all over the world who need to hear about Jesus. God loves people all over the world and wants them to know Him. Some Christians learn other languages and travel by boat or plane across the oceans to tell people in other parts of the world about Jesus.

Teach for Understanding

- Prepare a floor map using the picture on page 19 as a guide. The continent cutouts may be attached to a length of blue fabric, felt, or plastic. They may also be used as stencils to draw continents or to cut continent shapes from a contrasting color of fabric.
- Place the map on the floor with the students seated around it. Identify each of the seven continents and the four oceans on the map.
- Sing together the "Continent Song" to the tune of "London Bridge." Point to each continent as you sing its name.

  Europe, Asia, Africa,
  Australia, Antarctica,
  North and South America,
  All for Jesus.
- Choose seven students to stand on each of the seven continents as they are named in the song. Sing slowly to give them time to step onto the continents. Continue singing until each student has had a turn.
- Sing the song slowly several more times, inviting volunteers to point to the various continents as the class sings.

Activity

Different Places, Different Ways

The people in the world are not all alike.
Not all people do things the same way.
People in different places have different ways.

Some people dress like this.

Some people eat food like this.

Some people live in homes like this.

God loves people in every part of the world.

What is one thing people do in different ways? ★

dress; food; homes

0

Student Text pages 20–21
Activity Manual page 13

Objectives

- Name things that people do differently around the world
- Identify Hudson Taylor as a man who was led by God to tell people in China about Jesus
- Explain why Hudson Taylor dressed and ate like people in China
- Affirm that God loves all the people of the world

Materials

- Objects from other countries or cultures
- The world floor map prepared in Lesson 8

Content Word

- famous

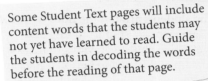

Some Student Text pages will include content words that the students may not yet have learned to read. Guide the students in decoding the words before the reading of that page.

Introduction

- Show the objects you brought from another country or culture. Discuss how they are alike or different from objects the students use or have in their homes.

Teach for Understanding

- Guide the reading of page 20 to find out something that people in another part of the world often do differently.
  possible answers: dress differently; eat different foods; live in different kinds of homes
- Explain that many women in India wear saris like this one. A sari is a long piece of fabric draped around the body.
- Explain that the food pictured is sushi, a popular food in Japan and other parts of Asia. Usually sushi is made of sour-tasting rice and fish, often wrapped in seaweed.
  Have you ever eaten sushi? Answers will vary.
- Explain that the type of thatched-roof home pictured is found in parts of Africa and Asia and on some islands.
  What does it look like the roof is made of? possible answer: dried grass
- Point out that our ways of doing things are not necessarily better than the ways of people in other parts of the world. Explain that we can learn and grow by learning about other cultures.
  Does God's love for a person change depending on the part of the world he lives in? No, God loves people all over the world just the same.
- Conclude the discussion by asking the question on page 20.

Lesson

9

- Read page 21 to find out what continent Hudson Taylor lived on. Europe

  To which continent did God lead Hudson Taylor? Asia
  What part of Asia did he go to? China

  What did God want Hudson Taylor to do in China? tell people about Jesus Christ

  How did Hudson Taylor change his ways in China? He dressed like Chinese people and ate Chinese food. Why did he make these changes? to be more like the Chinese so that he could be their friend and tell them about Jesus

  What good thing happened because Hudson Taylor was willing to go to China? Many people in China trusted Jesus as their Savior.

- Gather the students around the floor map. Explain that Hudson Taylor took a ship from England to China. With your finger, trace Hudson Taylor's route from England around the tip of Africa and between Asia and Australia to China. Review the names of all the different continents he sailed near.
- Sing the "Continent Song" together. Invite children to point to the various continents on the map as you sing their names.

  Europe, Asia, Africa,
  Australia, Antarctica,
  North and South America,
  All for Jesus.

Activity Manual

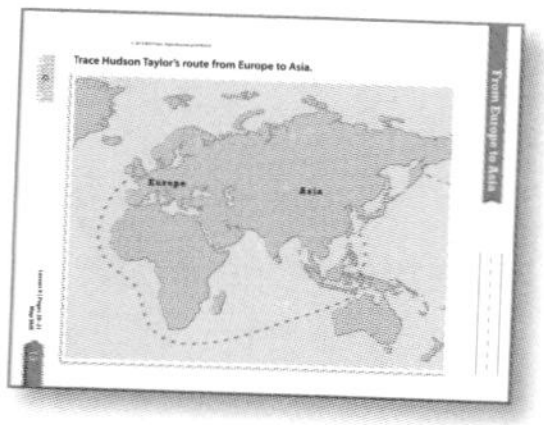

- Guide completion of page 13.

Activities

Culture

Distribute samples of Asian trail mix or another type of Asian snack. Discuss how it is different from American snack foods.

Geography

Guide a review of Hudson Taylor's route from England to China on the floor map. Invite students to walk the route that he sailed or trace it with their finger.

Famous People

Hudson Taylor

Hudson Taylor lived in Europe.
God led him to another continent.
God led him to go to China in Asia.
Hudson Taylor told people in China about the Savior, Jesus Christ.
But Chinese people had different ways.
So Hudson Taylor changed his ways.
He dressed like the people of China.
He ate their food.
Many people in China trusted Jesus.

2

Feature pages will include vocabulary that may be unfamiliar to the students. Encourage the students to follow along as you read, or invite advanced readers to read aloud for the class.

Lesson 10

Chapter Review
Activity Manual page 15

Objective
- Recall concepts and terms from Chapter 1

Review

- Draw attention to the poem on Student Text page 6. Invite a student to read it aloud. Instruct the other students to stand and stretch out their arms wide on the words *Big, wide world*. Instruct them to hold their thumb and pointer finger up to their eye on the words *one small speck*. Discuss the difference between the size of God's world and the size of a person.

  Does a person's size matter when it comes to God's love and care? No, God loves and cares for each person, even the smallest individual in His creation.
- Draw attention to the Picture Glossary. Invite students to read the meanings of the vocabulary words *continent, directions, globe, map, ocean,* and *Savior*.
- Review Chapter 1 by playing "Around the World." Choose two students at a time to answer a question from the material in this chapter. Lay the prepared continents (Visuals 1–4) on the floor around the classroom. Place a student at each continent. Direct one student to stand beside the student at North America, and both listen as you ask a question. The student who answers the question correctly first wins that round and moves on to South America. The student who loses remains on that continent while the game continues. Continue until each student has had at least one opportunity to compete. You may review any or all of the material during this lesson.

Activity Manual

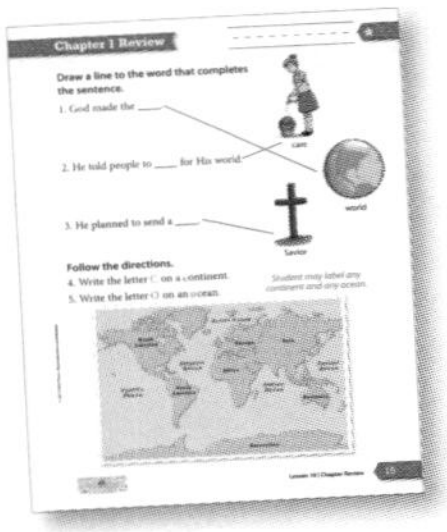

- Guide completion of page 15.

Chapter 1 Test

- Administer Test 1.

Background

Tests

These tests can serve as the objective part of an evaluation of a student's progress. The most effective tests are an outgrowth of the teaching process. Accordingly, these tests should not replace the teacher's individual assessment of a student's understanding and application.

The tests can be adjusted in accordance with the teaching emphasis and direction as well as the student's maturation level. The teacher may find it necessary to eliminate some items and/or provide additional test items.

Chapter 2

Introduction

This chapter will compare Adam and Eve's family to families today. The student will learn about roles in the family, how families work and play together, and why rules are important in a family. He will learn how to distinguish wants from needs and learn what it means to save and spend wisely. The student will make a timeline and a family tree.

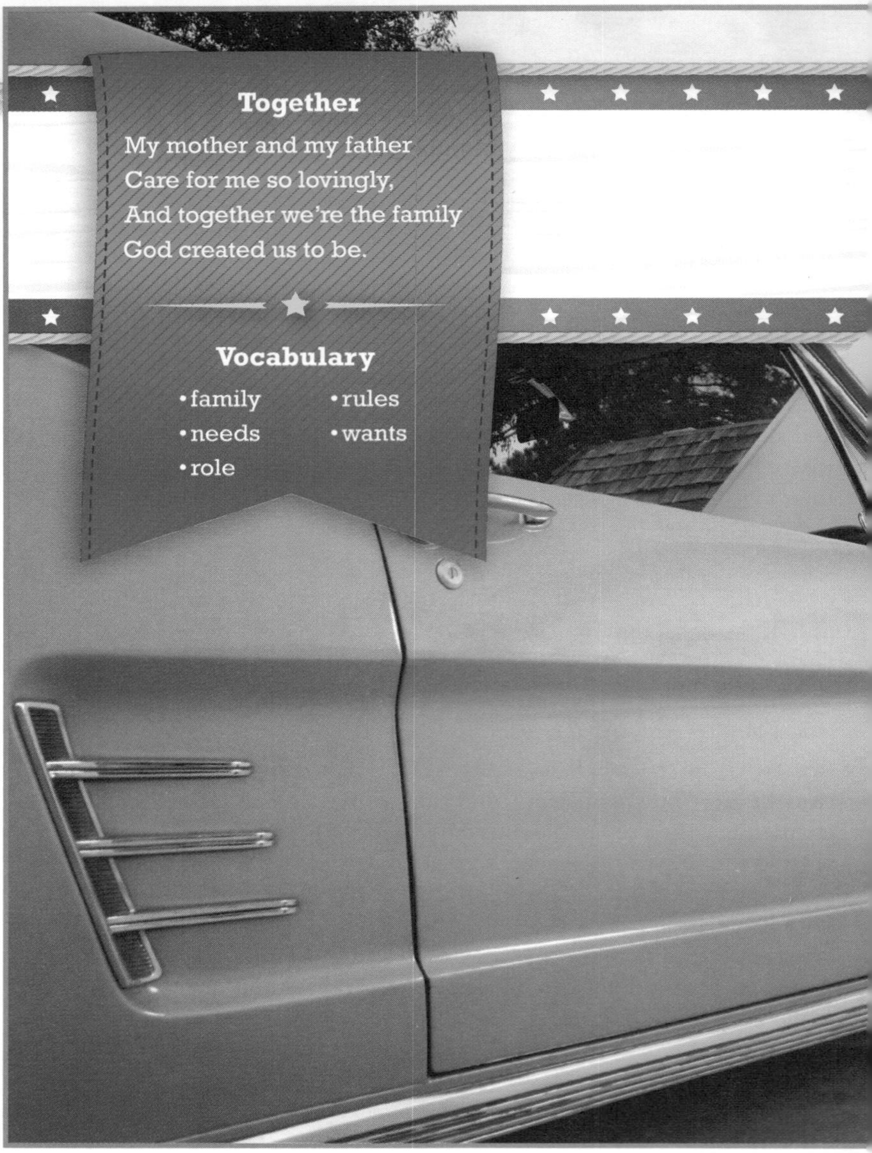

Together

My mother and my father
Care for me so lovingly,
And together we're the family
God created us to be.

Vocabulary

- family
- needs
- role
- rules
- wants

Ask the parents to send in copies of four photos of their child to be used for a timeline activity in Lesson 17. The photos should show the child as a baby, a toddler, and a preschooler and should include a recent photo.

Chapter 2 Overview

Lesson	ST	AM	Content	Vocabulary
11	22–25	17–19	The first family	family
12	26–27	21	Roles in a family God's plan for the family	role
13	28–29		Working and playing together	
14		23	The student's family	
15	30–31	25	God's rules for families Obeying your parents Family Bible reading and church attendance	rules
16	32–33	27	Needs and wants How families use money	needs wants
17			Timeline activity	
18		29	Chapter Review / Test	

Visit bjupress.com/resources for links to enhance the lessons.

Your Family

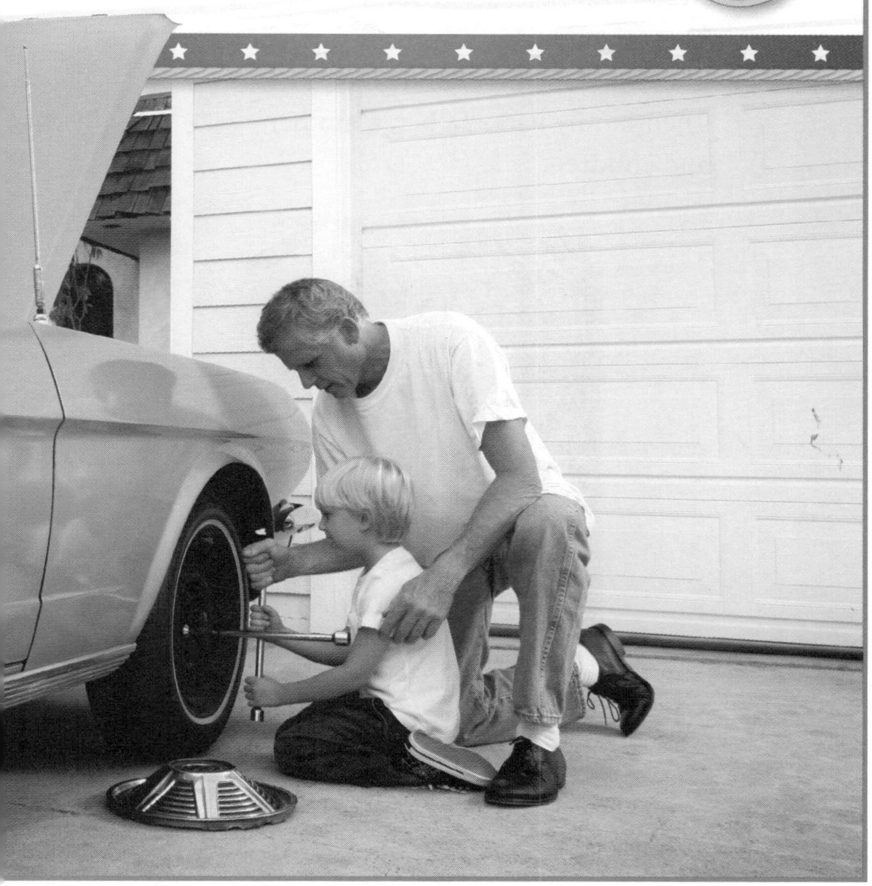

Lesson 11

Student Text pages 22–25
Activity Manual pages 17–19

Objectives
- Affirm that God is the one who puts families together
- Define a family
- Identify the first two children born on earth

Materials
- Visual 5: *Family Tree*

Vocabulary
- family

Content Words
- Abel
- Cain

Introduction

- Direct attention to the Contents page.

  We are ready to begin Chapter 2 of our Heritage Studies book. What is the title of Chapter 2? Your Family

  On what page does Chapter 2 begin? page 22

Teach for Understanding

- Point out the picture for the opener of Chapter 2. Ask a volunteer to read the title of the chapter.

  What is the title of Chapter 2? Your Family

  Who is in this photo? a boy and a man
- Invite students to describe what they think the man and the boy are doing. The father may be showing his son how to change a tire.

  Does this car look like your family car? Answers will vary.
- Encourage the students to comment on the picture. Elicit that since the car is an older car, perhaps the father is repairing it.
- Read aloud the poem "Together." Encourage the students to notice something about a family as they listen. [Bible Promise: H. God as Father]

  What is this poem about? a family

  Who cares for children in a family? the father and the mother

  Who puts a family together? God
- Point out the vocabulary words the students will learn in this chapter. Explain that the meanings of these words can be found in the Picture Glossary at the back of the book.

JourneyForth

Little Bear's Surprise by Kathleen Allan-Meyer

Discouraged that he has trouble cutting out hearts and squeezing glue bottles, Little Bear gives up on the idea of making valentines for his family. Then he has an idea for an even better surprise to show his love for them. Elaine Garvin's charming illustrations in this picture book will delight young readers.

Little Bear's Crunch-a-Roo Cookies by Kathleen Allan-Meyer

Another Little Bear picture book illustrated by Elaine Garvin, this is a story of how Little Bear and his mother work together to develop his skills in being a good friend. A recipe for Little Bear's famous cookies is included.

Grandpa's Gizmos by John Menken

Grandpa Winslow has all kinds of gizmos in his backyard, including windsocks, bottles, kites, and other objects that spin and sway in the wind. In this picture book illustrated by Tim Davis, a boy enjoys a special time with his grandfather while learning how the wind works.

Lesson

11

- Guide the reading of page 24 to find out who began the first family. Adam and Eve

  Who did God make first? Adam
- Write the names *Cain* and *Abel* for display. Guide the students as they decode the names.

  Who were Cain and Abel? Adam and Eve's sons; Cain and Abel were the first children born on earth.
- Draw attention to the picture on page 24. Explain that this is how an artist drew Adam and Eve.

  We don't have pictures of the people mentioned in the Bible because there were no cameras when they were alive. This picture shows how we think Adam and Eve may have looked.

  What people make up a family? a father, a mother, and children

  God planned for the first family to have children. Then He wanted those children to get married and have children. God's plan for most people is to marry, have families, and fill the earth.

Be sensitive to children who might have nontraditional family circumstances.

The First Family

Adam and Eve began the first **family**.
God made Adam first.
Adam and Eve had two sons.
They named their sons Cain and Abel.
They were the first family.
Their family had a father, a mother,
and children.

God made Eve to help Adam.

24

Eve cooked the food.

Adam plowed the land.

Abel took care of the sheep.

Cain planted a garden.

Who was in the first family?

Adam, Eve, Cain, Abel

25

- Direct attention to the picture of Adam at the top of page 25.

  What is Adam doing? plowing the land

  What do you think Adam will do next? possible answer: plant some seeds

  What kind of tool is Adam using? possible answer: a homemade tool

  Adam did not have modern tools to use. God gave him wisdom to make his own tools.
- Read the caption aloud.
- Direct attention to the picture of Eve.

  What is Eve doing? making bread

  Why did Eve not go to a grocery store to buy bread? There were no grocery stores long ago.
- Read the caption aloud.
- Direct attention to the picture of Cain.

  What is Cain holding in the picture? a basket of vegetables

  How do you think Cain helped his family? He grew vegetables for them to eat.
- Read the caption aloud.
- Direct attention to the picture of Abel.

  What is Abel doing? holding a lamb

  How did Abel help his family? He cared for the sheep.

  Each member of the family helped in some way.
- Read the caption aloud.
- Conclude the discussion by asking the question on page 25.
- Display Visual 5. Guide a discussion about a family tree.

Activity Manual

- Guide completion of pages 17–19.

Background

Bible

Adam and Eve's children did not have grandparents because God created Adam and Eve and they did not have parents. Read Genesis 1:26–27 and Genesis 2:20–23.

Culture

Display Visual 5. Explain that a family tree has names and sometimes pictures of family members. The oldest family members are at the top of the family tree, and the youngest family members are at the bottom.

Lesson

12

Student Text pages 26–27
Activity Manual page 21

Objectives

- Identify the different roles that family members fill
- Compare and contrast the first family with a modern family
- State where God wants families to live

Vocabulary

- role

Introduction

- Guide a review of the first family.

Teach for Understanding

- Guide the reading of page 26 to find out the meaning of the word *role.* the special part each person plays in a family

  What did God plan for everyone? to live in a family

  What do fathers and mothers do for their children? care for them
- Write *father, mother,* and *children* for display. Ask students to identify the roles of each family member. List them under the words as the students dictate.
- Point out the picture on page 26.

  What is the father teaching his daughter to do? fish
- Invite students to tell about one thing their fathers have taught them to do.

Families

God planned for you to live in a family.
He wants you to have a father and a mother.
Each family member has a **role**.
A role is the special part each person plays in a family.
Fathers and mothers care for their children.
Everyone in a family works together.

This dad is teaching his little girl how to fish.

26

This is the first family.

This is a family today.

God had a plan.
He wanted families in every part of the earth.
Families can be found everywhere.

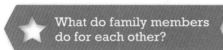

What do family members do for each other?

They care for each other and work together.

27

- Draw attention to the first picture on page 27.

  Read the caption silently and find out who this family is. the first family

- Choose a volunteer to read the caption aloud.
- Draw attention to the picture of the other family. Ask a student to read the caption aloud.

  Is this a family from Bible times? no How do you know? possible answer: the way they are dressed; their clothes

  How many children are in this family? three

  In what ways are these two families alike? There are children in each family; each family has a mother and a father.

  In what ways are the two families different? Possible answers: They are wearing different clothes. The first family has two sons. The other family has two girls and a boy.

  Where does God want families to live? in every part of the earth

- Explain that God's plan was for families to spread throughout the earth. Read Genesis 1:27–28.

  Where can families be found today? everywhere

- Conclude the discussion by asking the question on page 27.

Activity Manual

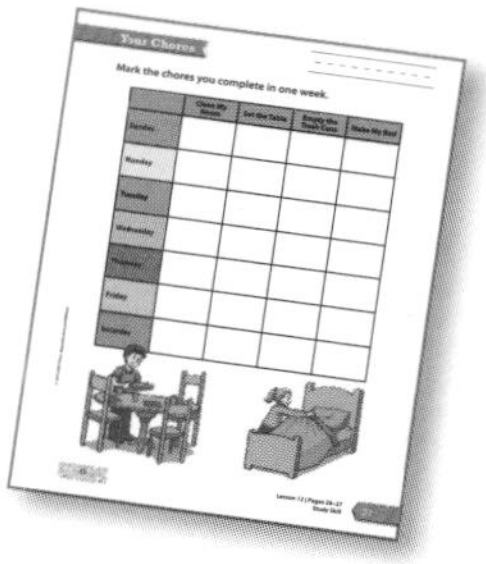

- Encourage the students to track their chores this week. Explain the Job Chart on page 21 for the students to complete at home.

Activity

Bible

Guide a discussion about the differences between the lives of the first family and families today.

Lesson

13

Student Text pages 28–29

Objectives

- Explain how family members work together to help each other
- Identify ways families play together

Introduction

- Guide a review of family roles.

Teach for Understanding

- Guide the reading of page 28 to find out about work and play in a family.

  How can family members help each other? Possible answers: A parent can teach a child to ride a bike. A child can help clear the table after a meal. An older child can hold a younger child's hand while crossing a street.
- Invite students to describe other activities family members can do together.
- Ask students to tell about someone in their family who works away from home. Then allow students to tell about family members who have a job that allows them to work from home.
- Direct the students to read silently the caption below the picture on page 28.

  What is this family doing together? clearing away fallen leaves
- Ask several students to tell about a job their family does together. Invite them to tell what part they like most about working together as a family. [BAT: 2e Work]

Families Work and Play

Families help each other.
They also have fun together.
Some people in a family work in the home.
Some people work away from home.

Working together is fun.

28

This family likes to play games inside.

This family likes to play outside.

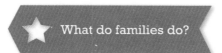

★ What do families do?

They work and play together.

29

- Draw attention to the picture at the top of page 29.
- Choose a volunteer to read the caption aloud.

  What is this family doing together? playing a game indoors
- Invite students to tell about indoor games they like to play with their family.
- Draw attention to the picture at the bottom of the page.
- Choose a volunteer to read the caption aloud.

  What is this family doing together? playing basketball outside
- Encourage students to name activities their families enjoy doing outside.
- Conclude the discussion by asking the question on page 29.

Lesson
14 Activity Manual page 23

Objective
- Visualize differences in families by completing a graph

Materials
- Visual 5: *Family Tree*

Introduction
- Review some ways a family works and plays together.

Teach for Understanding
- Guide a discussion about how families differ in the number of people in the family.
- Ask several students to tell how many people are in their family.
- Draw a graph with four columns labeled *3, 4, 5,* and *6.* Graph the number of people in each family represented by the students in the class.
- Direct students with three people in their family to stand. Place one tally mark under the column labeled *3* for each student standing.
- Continue until each student's family is represented under a heading.
- Examine the graph together and make observations about the results.
- Display Visual 5. Guide a discussion about grandparents and family trees. Invite several children to tell the names of some of the people who would be on their family tree.

Activity Manual
- Guide completion of page 23.

Activity
Family Bracelet
Provide a chenille wire and blue, red, yellow, white, green, and orange beads for each student.

Write the following for display.

Dad: blue	Brother: yellow
Mom: red	Grandparent: green
Sister: orange	Yourself: white

Direct the students to string one bead for each member of their family onto a chenille wire. Assist each student as he fastens the completed wristband around his arm.

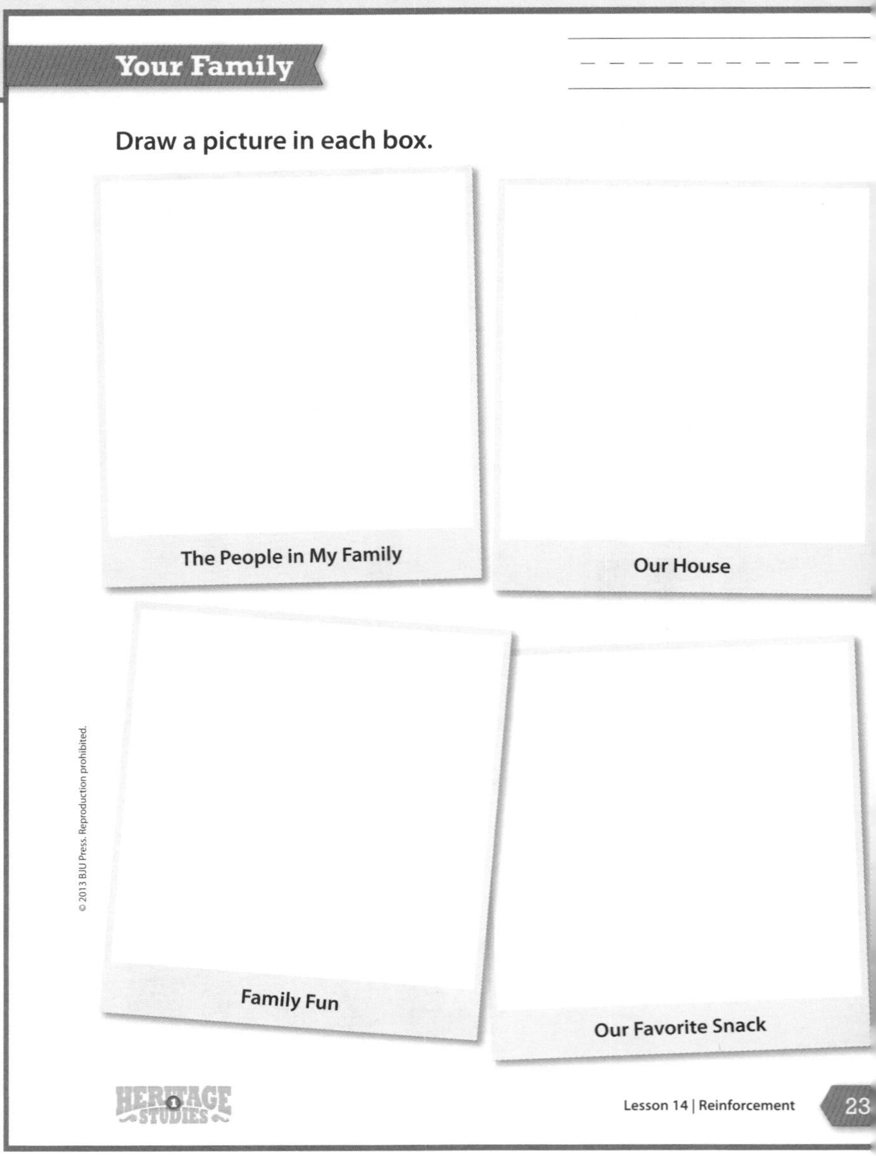
Your Family

Draw a picture in each box.

The People in My Family

Our House

Family Fun

Our Favorite Snack

© 2013 BJU Press. Reproduction prohibited.

HERITAGE STUDIES

Lesson 14 | Reinforcement 23

Family Rules

Families have **rules**.
God gives rules to families.
The Bible says to obey your mom and dad.
Rules let you know what you must do.
Rules let you know what you should not do.
Following rules protects you.

KITCHEN RULES
1. Put your dishes in the dishwasher.
2. Wipe up your spills.

Rules help everyone in a family get along.

Lesson 15

Student Text pages 30–31
Activity Manual page 25

Objectives

- Define *rules*
- Distinguish rules that prohibit behavior from rules that demand behavior
- Identify the basic rules that God gives to families
- Explain how God helps us keep His rules

Materials

- Visual 5: *Family Tree*

Vocabulary

- rules

Introduction

- Use Visual 5 to guide a review of a family tree.

Teach for Understanding

- Guide the reading of page 30 to find out the meaning of the word *rules*. They let you know what you must do and what you should not do.

  Who gives rules to families? God Where does God give these rules? in the Bible

  Can children and parents obey God's rules all on their own? No, they need God's help.

  How does God help people obey His rules? He offers all people salvation from sin. How does a person receive God's salvation? A person needs to turn away from his sin and trust in Jesus to save him from sin. God saves all people who trust in His Son.
- Point out that once a person is trusting in Jesus, God helps him obey through reading the Bible and going to church.

  How does attending church as a family help a family? The entire family can learn the truths of the Bible together. If the family members are trusting in Jesus, God will help them obey and get along.
- Explain that God does all things well. He knows what is best for families. [BAT: 2a Authority]

  What does the Bible say about obeying parents? Obey your parents.

  Your parents love you and know what is best for you. They want you to grow up to love and obey God.

  The Bible tells a husband to love and provide for his family. A wife is to obey and honor her husband. Children are to obey their parents.

  What two things do rules let you know? what you must do and what you should not do
- Invite students to give examples of how following rules can protect them. Elicit that rules for drivers keep many people from being involved in accidents. Following rules at a pool can keep you from drowning.
- Encourage students to identify a rule that directs them to do something and one that directs them not to do something.

  What is a rule that protects you from harm? Possible answer: Do not cross a street if a car is coming.
- Draw attention to the whiteboard at the bottom of page 30. Choose a student to read the caption and the rules written on the board.

  Do these rules tell you what you must do or what you should not do? what you must do

  How do rules help family members get along? Rules let you know what you should do.
- Invite several students to describe rules their families follow at mealtimes.

Lesson

15

- Guide the reading of page 31 to find out what families do to show their love to God. They read the Bible and attend church.

  How can we learn about God? by reading the Bible
- Guide a discussion about how great God is.

  What does the Bible teach you about how to treat your parents? love and obey them

  What are the families in the pictures doing to grow as Christians? reading the Bible and going to church
- Explain that attending church as a family helps a family learn the truths of the Bible together. Learning Bible truths together will help each family member obey and get along.
- Conclude the discussion by asking the question on page 31.

Activity Manual

- Guide completion of page 25.

Activity

Guest Speaker

Invite a police officer to discuss with the students how laws make a community safe.

Background

Bible

Read Ephesians 6:1 aloud. Explain that sometimes it is hard to obey your parents, but God will help you if you will ask Him to. You should obey right away with a good attitude. [BAT: 2a Authority]

Families Love God

The Bible teaches you about God. It teaches you to love and obey your mom and dad.

This family reads the Bible.

This family goes to church.

How do rules help you?

Rules protect you and help family members get along.

31

Needs and Wants

Everyone has needs.
Needs are things a family must have to live.
A family needs things like food, clothes, and shelter.

This mom has cooked a meal for her family.

Each person in a family needs love and care.
People work to get money.
Families use money to buy things they need.

32

Student Text pages 32–33
Activity Manual page 27

Objectives
- Distinguish between *needs* and *wants*
- Explain the role that choices play in spending money
- Classify church involvement as a need and not a want

Vocabulary
- needs
- wants

Introduction

- Guide a review of rules.

Teach for Understanding

- Guide the reading of page 32 to find the different needs a family has.

  What are needs? things a family must have to live

  Who has needs? everyone

  God has promised to supply all our needs.

  What are examples of things a family needs? food, clothes, shelter, love, and care

  What do people have to do to get money? work

  What do families use the money to get? things they need

- Draw attention to the picture on the page.

  What is the family doing? eating a meal

Lesson 16

- Draw attention to the picture on page 33.

  What is the man in the picture doing? cutting a board

  What is being built? a building
- Guide the reading of the page to find out how families use money. They use money to buy things they want.

  What are wants? things people would like to have
- Write *wants* and *needs* for display as column headings.
- Guide the students as they suggest words to fill each column (examples of needs: clothes, food, shelter; examples of wants: a puzzle, a bike, a vacation).

  Do most people have everything they want? no

  How do families decide how to spend their money? by making choices
- Draw for display an apple, a house, a toy, a bike, and a church.

  If a family can spend their money on only three things, which three of these things should they spend money on?
- Choose a volunteer to circle three of the pictures. Emphasize that having a church is a need and not a want.

  How do churches get built? People give money so the building can be built and the preacher can preach.

  Is it important for families to give money to their church? Yes, it is very important. It is something that families need to do.

Activity Manual

- Direct the students to cut out the pictures on page 27 and then glue them in the correct boxes.

This dad builds houses.

Families also buy some things
they want.
Wants are things people would
like to have.
But people cannot have all they
want.
They must make choices about
how to spend their money.
Families give money to God's work.
Be thankful for your family.

What things do all people need?

food, clothes, shelter, love, care

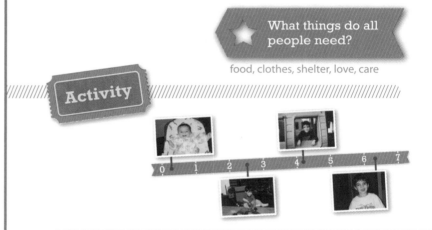

Activity

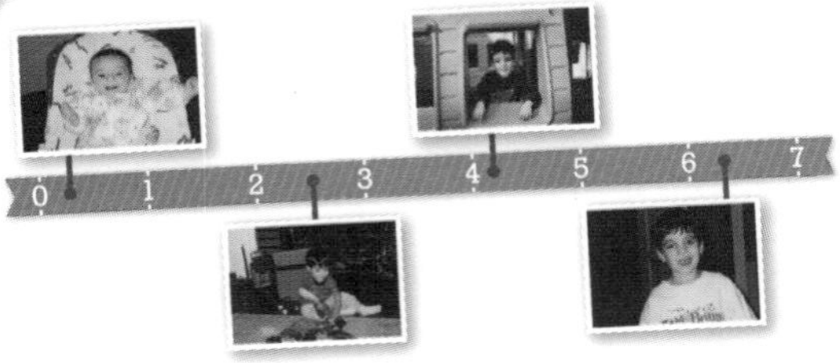

Lesson 17

Chapter Activity

Objective
- Visualize how people grow and change by completing a timeline with photos

Materials
- *Timeline* (Teacher's Toolkit CD)
- 4 timeline photos of each student
- A completed timeline

Photos are available on the Teacher's Toolkit CD for students who do not have any.

Introduction
- Guide a review of needs and wants and how families spend money.

Activity

- Generate excitement about making a timeline using the photos the students brought.
- Distribute the timelines. Direct the students to cut apart and tape the pieces together.
- Explain that the numbers on the timeline represent ages. Direct the students to arrange their pictures from when they were youngest to when they were oldest.
- Assist the students as they glue the pictures of themselves onto the timeline.
- Direct each student to draw a line from the age he is in the picture to the picture.
- Display the timelines in the classroom.

Lesson 18

Chapter Review
Activity Manual page 29

Objective
- Recall concepts and terms from Chapter 2

Review
- Draw attention to the poem on page 22. Choose several students to take turns reading it aloud. After each reading allow a volunteer to share one thing his mother or father does to care for him.
- Guide a review of the Chapter 2 vocabulary by inviting the students to look up each word in the Picture Glossary.
- You may choose to review Chapter 2 by playing "My Growing Family." Divide the students into two teams. One student from each team will compete to answer a question from the material in this chapter. The student who answers the question correctly will make a tally mark for his team. Continue until each student has had at least one opportunity to compete. You may review any or all the material during this lesson.

Activity Manual
- Guide completion of page 29.

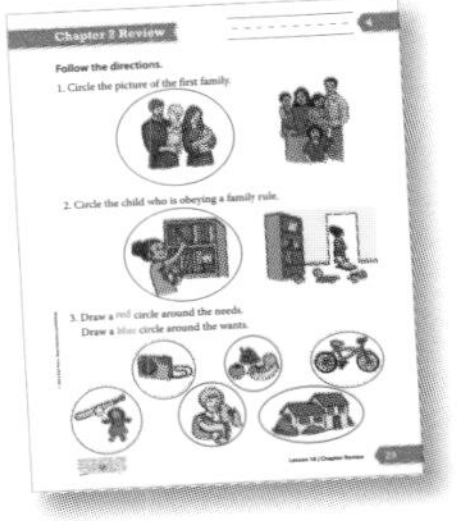

Chapter 2 Test
- Administer Test 2.

Chapter 3

Introduction

In this chapter the students will study people and places in their community. They will learn about community jobs that help people and jobs that provide goods. They will become aware of their role in the community. They will find out that government is ordained by God, and therefore they should be obedient to that authority. They will study about Benjamin Franklin, who made the city of Philadelphia a better place to live. The students will have the opportunity to dress up as community workers and be in a community parade.

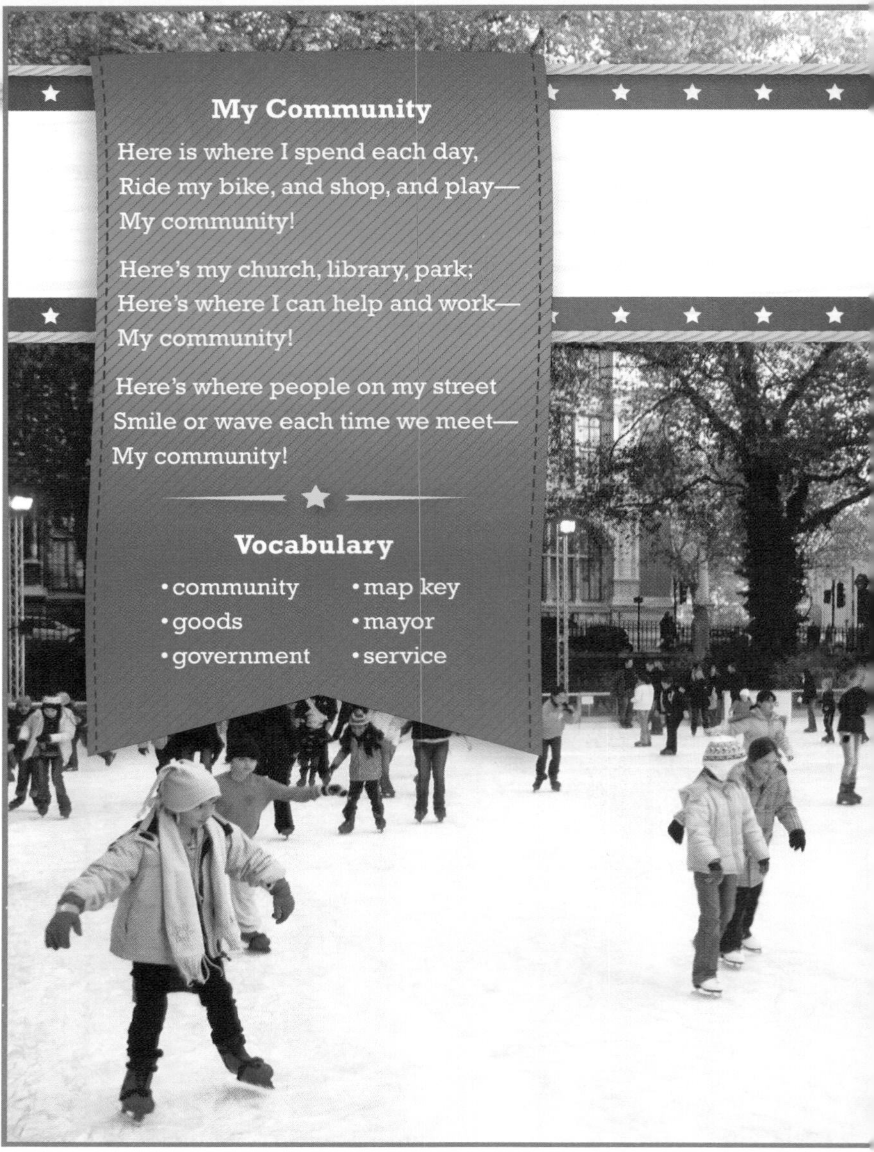

My Community

Here is where I spend each day,
Ride my bike, and shop, and play—
My community!

Here's my church, library, park;
Here's where I can help and work—
My community!

Here's where people on my street
Smile or wave each time we meet—
My community!

Vocabulary

- community
- goods
- government
- map key
- mayor
- service

Chapter 3 Overview				
Lesson	**ST**	**AM**	**Content**	**Vocabulary**
19	34–37	31	People and places in a community Goods that people make, grow, or sell	community goods
20	38–39	33	Service jobs help others Paying jobs and volunteer jobs	service
21	40–41	35	Places where people work in a community Places people visit in a community	
22	42–43	37	God intends for us to help people in the community Recycle items to care for God's world	
23	44–45	39	The role of a mayor Duties of the government Christians should obey the law	government mayor
24	46–47	41	Benjamin Franklin made his city a better place Compare Philadelphia then and now	
25	48–49	43	Map skills	map key
26		45	Chapter Review and Activity / Test	

Send home the *Community Parade Parent Letter* (Teacher's Toolkit CD) in preparation for the Chapter Activity in Lesson 26.

Visit bjupress.com/resources for links to enhance the lessons.

Student Text pages 34–37
Activity Manual page 31

Your Community 3

Objectives
- Identify people and places in a community
- Describe his community
- Name goods that his family uses
- Identify goods that people make, grow, or sell

Materials
- Visual 6: *Communities*

Vocabulary
- community
- goods

Introduction

- Direct attention to the Contents page.

  We are ready to begin Chapter 3 of our book. What is the title of the chapter? Your Community

  On what page does Chapter 3 begin? page 34

Teach for Understanding

- Generate interest in the photo on pages 34 and 35.

  What are the people in this picture doing? ice-skating

  Where are the people ice-skating? in a city How do you know? There are city buildings in the picture.

  What kinds of people are ice-skating? grownups and children

  Many families like to ice-skate. Ice-skating is an activity that can be enjoyed by many people in a community.
- Read aloud the poem "My Community."

  What activities does the poem say you do in a community? ride a bike, shop, play, help, work

  What are some places the poem says are in a community? church, library, park
- Guide a discussion about other activities children might do in their community.

  Do you think the speaker in the poem lives in a friendly community? yes How do you know? People on his street smile and wave.
- Point out the vocabulary words the students will learn in this chapter. Remind them that the meanings of these words can be found in the Picture Glossary at the back of their book.

JourneyForth

Rodney Robbins and the Rainy-Day Pond by Kim Stegall

In this picture book, a young boy and his elderly neighbor team up to solve the problem of an unwanted pond in their community. Bruce Day's lively illustrations add extra sparkle to this mischievous tale.

Looking for Home by Eileen M. Berry

In this early chapter book, Liz and Micah befriend Grandma Jan, a new neighbor in their apartment community who misses her farm in the country. Humor, love, kindness, and sympathy cross the generations in this heartwarming story of homesick neighbors who come together in their quest for new homes and for real treasure, the kind that lasts forever.

Lesson

19

- Display the vocabulary word *community*. Invite a volunteer to read the word aloud.
- Read the section title. Point out the picture on page 36. Explain that the family in the picture is at a yard sale.

  A yard sale is a community activity.
- Guide the reading of the page to find out what makes a community. people living or working together

  Who makes up a community? people living near your family; people working near where your family lives
- Guide a discussion of the communities that the students live in. Remind the students that their family lives in a community.
- Display Visual 6. Discuss urban and rural communities.

  An urban community may have tall buildings and lots of traffic. Rural communities may have fields and open pastureland.
- Display the vocabulary word *goods*. Invite a volunteer to read the word aloud.

  We will find out that the word *good* has a different meaning than "fine" or "excellent."

Your Community

Your family lives in a **community**.
People that live near your family make a community.
People working near where your family lives are a part of your community.
People living or working together make a community.

36

Many people in a community work.
Farmers grow food. Foods are **goods**.
Goods are things people make, grow, or sell.
Some people make goods we need.
Other people sell goods we use.

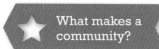

We buy food.
Foods are goods.

The man sells tires. Tires are goods.

What makes a community?

people living or working together

37

Lesson 19

- Draw attention to the pictures on page 37. Choose volunteers to read the captions.

  The fruits and vegetables in the store are goods people buy. The man is selling a tire. Tires are goods.

- Guide the reading of page 37 to find out what goods are.

  What are goods? things people make, grow, or sell

  What kinds of goods are in the picture with the girl and her mother? food; fruit

  The man in the next picture is replacing a used tire with a new tire. What are the goods that he sells? tires

- Guide a discussion about people in the community making things, growing food, and selling goods that people in the community need. Your community may be known for making something special such as cars or growing a certain kind of fruit like oranges.
- Conclude the discussion by asking the question on page 37.

Activity Manual

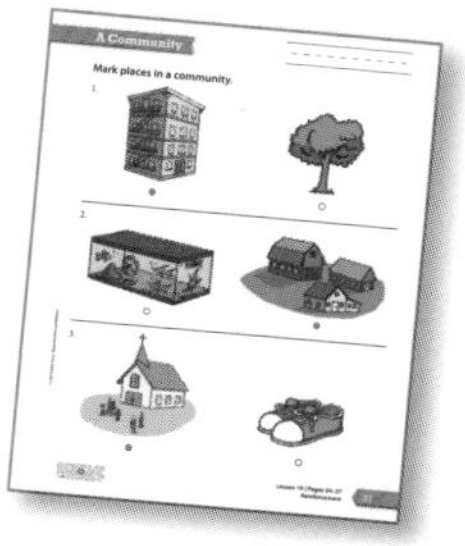

- Guide completion of page 31. Demonstrate how to mark the answer bubble completely.

Activities

Goods

Make a list of goods that you use every day. Write for display as the students dictate (examples: paper, milk, gas, clothes).

Communities

Collect pictures of communities, including contrasting places such as a tribal village and a houseboat community. Allow students to decide which picture goes with their community. Discuss how the contrasting communities differ.

Places in Your Community

Tell the students about a place in your community and then invite them to tell about special places in their own communities.

Background

Economics

People use goods provided by vendors, stores, farmers, and businesses in the community. Goods are things that people use every day. Goods can be things that you need or want. People make or grow goods. People buy and sell goods.

Lesson

20

Student Text pages 38–39
Activity Manual page 33

Objectives

- Identify a service job as a job helping others
- List people in service jobs
- Identify paying jobs and volunteer jobs
- Name a way that his family could serve others

Materials

- Visuals 6–7: *Communities; Community Service Jobs*
- A piece of wrapped candy for each student

Vocabulary

- service

Content Word

- letter carrier

Introduction

- Use Visual 6 to review urban and rural communities.
- Invite two volunteers to serve the class the treat. Mention that in this lesson we will learn about people who serve.

Teach for Understanding

- Read the section title. Draw attention to the pictures on page 38. Display the term *letter carrier.*
- Point out that the teacher is using sign language to teach deaf children.

  The lady carrying the mail is called a *letter carrier*. How is she helping the community? She is delivering the mail.

  How are the medics serving? They are ready to help when needed.
- Guide the reading of page 38 to find out the meaning of the word *service*. something that helps people

  How does a doctor serve others? by helping people in the community with health needs

  How does a police officer keep you safe? by keeping traffic moving or rescuing someone who needs help

  How does a pastor help in the community? by caring for people in the community
- Explain that these kinds of people serve the community. Many people serve a community by helping others. Discuss other people who serve in the community, such as dentists, hairdressers, and fitness trainers.
- Invite volunteers to act out either their father's or their mother's job. Guide the students as they determine whether the jobs are service jobs.
- Display Visual 7.

  Which job is a service job? both jobs

Your Community Helpers

A doctor helps people stay well.
A police officer helps to keep you safe.
A pastor serves the community too.
A **service** is something that helps people.
Community helpers serve people.

This teacher uses hand signs to teach.

A letter carrier delivers the mail.

These medics are ready to help the community.

38

- Explain that some service jobs are paid with money. Other service jobs are called volunteer jobs and are not paid with money.

  The woman serving food to the children is doing a service job. That person is paid. The man and woman are volunteering to help needy people. They are not paid.
- Discuss examples of people in your community who do service jobs for pay and others who do service jobs as volunteers.

Activity

Jobs

Display a T-chart similar to the example below. Invite students to identify the jobs their parents do. Guide the student as he decides whether his parent has a service job or another type of job.

Jobs	
Service Job	Other Job
nurse	truck driver

God wants you to serve people
in a special way.
You can offer to help people
in your community.
The Bible says to serve one another
with love.

Galatians 5:13

By love serve one another.

The man tells children about Jesus.

A family serves people with no home.

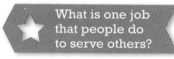

What is one job that people do to serve others?

Answers will vary.

39

- Guide the reading of page 39.
- Direct attention to the pictures on the page. Choose volunteers to read aloud the captions.

  What service job is the family in the picture doing? serving food

  What service job is the man in the picture doing? telling children about Jesus

  These people are not being paid for doing these jobs. They are volunteers. Christians sometimes do volunteer jobs to show Christ's love for others.
- Ask a volunteer to read the Bible verse on the page. Remind the students that Galatians is a book in the Bible. Explain that the verse commands Christians to serve others with love. [BAT: 2b Servanthood]

  What example can you find on the page of someone serving with love? The man is giving his time to serve the children in the community; he receives no pay. The family is serving homeless people in the community; they are not being paid.
- Mention that there are many service jobs. Encourage the students to tell about a paid service job they might want to do someday.
- Invite other students to tell about a volunteer job that they might want to do.
- Conclude the discussion by asking the question on page 39.

Activity Manual

- Invite a student to read the verse about serving. Guide completion of page 33.

Activities

Guest Speaker

Invite a pastor or a volunteer worker to visit the classroom to describe how he serves people in the community.

Volunteering

Encourage children to volunteer to help elderly people in the church, neighborhood, or community. (*Note:* Remind the students to ask parental permission as they look for ways to help.)

Working Together

Make a community chain using construction-paper strips. Instruct each student to write his name on a strip of paper. Work together to link the chain. Explain that every link (person) plays an important part in the chain (community).

Lesson 21

Student Text pages 40–41
Activity Manual page 35

Objectives
- Distinguish community places where people work and visit
- Associate places with the community where they are found
- Associate the jobs people do with the places where they work

Materials
- Visuals 6–8: *Communities; Community Service Jobs; Community Places*

Content Word
- museum

Introduction

- Use Visuals 6 and 7 to review types of communities.

There are many jobs that people do in your community. These jobs represent different places in a community.

Teach for Understanding

- Generate interest in places in a community.

Every community is a little different. Communities are made up of people and places. Some of the places are where people work or do a service. A hospital, a store, and a fire department are places where people work in your community. The park, the library, and the beach are places people visit in your community. A church, a school, and a museum are places people go to learn.

- Read the section title and the caption below the picture on page 40.

What kind of place do you see in the picture? a flower shop

Can you tell whether this shop is on a street or inside a mall? on a street How do you know? The shopkeeper and flowers are on the outside of the shop.

- Allow volunteers to describe a flower shop in their community.
- Guide the reading of the page to find out the different places in a community.
- Display Visual 8. Lead a discussion about the different places in a community.

What types of places would you find in an urban or a city community? Answers may include subway stations, skyscrapers, stores, and restaurants.

What types of places would you find in a rural or a country community? Answers may include a dairy farm, a feed store, and a horse ranch.

Your Community Places

People work in many different places
in your community.
A farmer may sell apples from his truck.
The lady next door may cut hair in a shop.
Also, people visit many different places
in your community.
You may like to eat a snack at the bakery.
You may visit a park or the library.

This lady works at a flower shop in her community.

40

- Draw for display a Venn diagram with two ovals. Entitle the diagram *Different Places in Communities*. Label the first oval *My Community*. Label the second oval *Your Community*.
- Write places in your community under *My Community*. Ask a student to name places in his community. Write the places under *Your Community*. Adjust the list when both communities share the same places. Allow several students to identify places in their communities. Follow the example.

Different Places in Communities

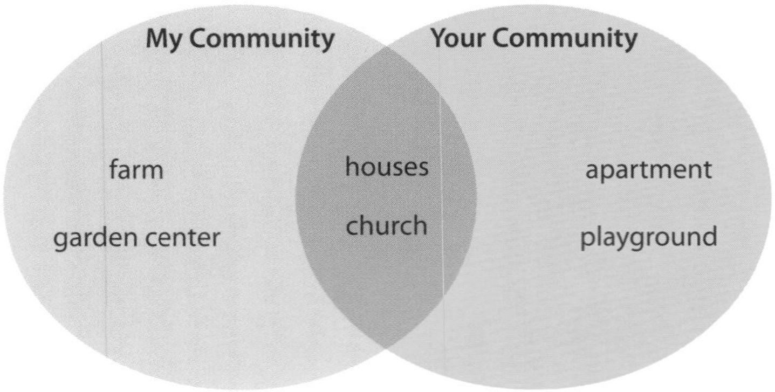

A family works at the church.

Families play at the park.

A boy learns at the museum.

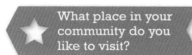

What place in your community do you like to visit?

Answers will vary.

41

- Guide the reading of page 41 to find places in a community. a church, a park, and a museum
- Draw attention to the pictures. Invite a volunteer to read the captions.

  Where in the community is the family working? at a church

  Where in the community is the boy learning? at a museum

  Where in the community are the grandfather and grandson playing? at a park
- Conclude the discussion by asking the question on page 41.

Activity Manual

- Guide completion of page 35.

Activities

Community Chart

Display a T-chart similar to the following example. Make a list of places in the community. Encourage the students to identify the people who work there.

Community Chart	
Places	**People**
library	librarian
hospital	doctor
school	teacher

Communities

Provide age-appropriate magazines for the students to use to make a community collage. Direct the students to cut out and glue pictures that they would find in either an urban community or a rural community. Encourage the students to title the collage.

Community Visual

Prepare a visual presentation of your community using pictures of each child in front of a place in the community. Invite each student to tell about his picture. (*Note:* Ask the parents to send in pictures of their children.)

Lesson

22

Student Text pages 42–43
Activity Manual page 37

Objectives

- Explain how God intends for people and places in a community to be cared for
- List ways to care for God's world by recycling
- Apply Genesis 1:26–28 to the work of keeping natural resources clean

Materials

- Visual 8: *Community Places*

Content Word

- recycle

Introduction

- Use Visual 8 to review people and places in a community.

Teach for Understanding

- Read the section title.

  People are responsible to care for places in the community. Everyone must do his part to keep neighborhoods and communities clean. People should take care of the places where they live, work, and play. A good goal is to leave a place as clean as or cleaner than it was when you arrived.

- Direct attention to the picture on page 42.

  How are these children caring for the community? They are picking up trash.

  Do you think these children put the trash on the ground? no

  How do you think the trash got there? from thoughtless or careless actions; from people not caring for the community

  God wants us to care for the community. The Bible tells us to do good to all men (Galatians 6:10).

- Guide the reading of page 42 to find out who and what God wants you to care for in your community. people and places

  Families are responsible to take care of the people living in their homes. Families are also responsible to care for people and places in their community.

- Explain that people in your community are your neighbors.

  God wants families to care for their neighbors. The Bible account of the Good Samaritan shows how he cared for his neighbor.

- Retell the story of the Good Samaritan from Luke 10. In the Bible a neighbor is a fellow human being. Today a neighbor is the person who lives next door. The Bible principle is the same since the person who lives next door is a fellow human being.

Helping in Your Community

Your family is part of a community.
You are part of a community.
God wants you to help other people
in your community.
God wants you to take care of the place
where you live.
God's plan is that you care for others
and for the community.

42

Who does the Bible say are your neighbors? people that we meet or people that have a need

What does the Bible say about caring for your neighbors? You should care about your neighbors, those in the community.

- Encourage students to tell of ways they have helped or could help their neighbors. Elicit ideas such as helping a neighbor get the mail, visiting a neighbor, inviting a neighbor to church, giving out a gospel tract, making a card, and helping take a meal to a needy neighbor. (*Note:* Remind the students to ask parental permission as they look for ways to help.) [BAT: 5a Love]

Background

Bible

In Luke 10 a lawyer asked Jesus, "Who is my neighbor?" Jesus told him the account of the Good Samaritan. A man was overtaken by thieves and left to die. A priest and a Levite passed by the beaten man and did not stop to help him. A man from Samaria stopped, cleansed the man's wounds, took him to an inn, and cared for him. Jesus implied that the Samaritan was a neighbor to the man who fell among thieves. Christians are to follow the Samaritan's example.

You can help keep the lake and land clean.

You can help people who live near you.

Many communities recycle paper.

How can you help your community?

Answers will vary.

43

- Guide the reading of page 43 to find out how to care for resources that God has created in the community.

  God has created natural resources for us to use. Natural resources, such as land and water, are things we use that God has created. We are responsible to keep the land and the water clean.

- Direct attention to the pictures on the page. Choose volunteers to read aloud the captions.

  How is the boy caring for the land and the water? He is throwing the bottle away. He is not littering.

  One way we can keep the land and water clean is by not littering.

  How is the girl helping her neighbor? She is picking up the paper.

- Introduce the pictograph.

  This graph is called a pictograph. The title of the pictograph is at the top of the graph.

- Direct the students to put their finger on the title. Invite a volunteer to read the title of the pictograph.

  What does the graph show? a paper drive; collecting papers

  Communities have paper drives to collect newspapers and magazines to be reused or recycled. This helps keep the community clean and provides a way to reuse papers that would have been thrown away.

- Choose volunteers to read the names of the places where papers were collected for the paper drive. Then direct the students to locate the small box (graph key) that shows 1 picture = 1 paper.

  The box is a key to reading the graph. Each picture stands for one magazine or newspaper that was collected.

  Count each picture on the graph.

- Read the data.

  How many magazines or newspapers did the fire station collect? 3 the store? 4 the church? 3

  Which place collected the most papers? the store; Todd's Store

- Read the caption under the graph.

  What does *recycle* mean? *Recycle* means to reuse something that is old or to use something old to make something new.

- Conclude the discussion by asking the question on page 43.

Activity Manual

- Guide completion of page 37.

Activity

Recycle

Provide bins in the classroom to collect plastic bags, paper, and cans for recycling.

Background

Bible

Christians are responsible to keep natural resources clean. This is implied in the idea that God created people to rule over the earth (Genesis 1:26–28). Christians should rule over the earth by setting a good example that promotes the health of other people. We exercise dominion over the earth by showing love to our neighbors when we do our part to keep the earth clean.

Recycling

Recycling is an important practice. It provides a way to reuse things that we no longer need. Recycling is a way to make something new from something old (e.g., plastic bags, paper, aluminum cans, glass).

Lesson

23

Student Text pages 44–45
Activity Manual page 39

Objectives
- Define the role of a mayor
- List the duties of the government
- Explain that the government is made up of workers
- Explain from the Bible why Christians should obey the law

Materials
- A sign with the word *mayor* on it

Vocabulary
- government
- mayor

Introduction

- Guide a discussion about a nearby city.

  What is the name of a city near where you live? Is the city big? Who works in a city?

Teach for Understanding

- Display the vocabulary words. Guide the students as they locate the words in the Picture Glossary. Pronounce each word and read the definition.
- Read the section title on page 44. Direct attention to the picture.

  Who do you think the man is behind the stand? Answers may vary.

  Why do you think the people are clapping? Answers may vary.
- Guide the reading of the page to find out who the leader of a city is. the mayor

  Communities are made of many people. Several communities form a city. People in cities and communities need leaders to guide them. Leaders help make laws or rules to live by. The mayor is a leader of a city. He has help making the laws. Other people make sure the laws are obeyed.

  Which person in the picture could be the mayor? the man standing behind the American flag

  Who are the other people? the mayor's helpers
- Explain that a mayor helps make laws, makes the community better, and oversees city divisions such as the police, fire, and education departments.
- Invite a volunteer to read aloud the caption.
- Choose a student to be the mayor of the classroom. Place the sign on his desk.
- Guide the mayor as he states a law he would make for the class.
- Allow several students the opportunity to be mayor.

Your Community Leaders

Many communities near each other make a city.
A city has leaders.
The leader of a city is a **mayor**.
The mayor helps make laws.
He works to make the community better.

The mayor works for the community.

44

A community helper clears the street.

A city worker keeps the community safe.

All the city workers form the city **government**.
The government workers serve the people of the community.
These workers care for the people.
They make the city a better place to live.

Who is the leader of a city?

the mayor

45

- Guide the reading of page 45 to find out what a government is. workers serving the people of the community
- Introduce the map of the United States in the Resource Treasury in the back of the book (pages 178–79). Point out the United States, the state you live in, and the area where your city is. Use the map as you explain the leaders of each.

  The leader of the United States government is the president. Your state's leader is the governor. The leader of your city is the mayor. People in the community choose the mayor and his helpers by voting. The mayor and his helpers are citizens of the community where they live. They work together to make the city and the community better places to live. Mayors attend community activities such as fairs, parades, and holiday events. The mayor can help make laws that keep people safe. Citizens living in the community must obey the laws.

  Who are the mayor's helpers? the city workers or government workers

  Name two city or government workers. Answers may vary.
- Explain that every Christian should obey the law and those in authority. God's Word tells us to obey authorities like the mayor. Christians are to obey the laws that the city government makes. God established government to provide order and justice (Romans 13; 1 Peter 3).

- Choose a volunteer to read the caption beside each picture. Discuss how each of these city workers makes the city a better place to live.

  How is the man in the snowplow making the community a safer place? He is clearing snow from the roads so that people can travel safely.

  What kind of job does the lady in the next picture have? She is a police officer. How do you know? She is wearing a uniform and standing by a police car. What does a police officer do? helps people obey the laws; makes the community a safer place to live

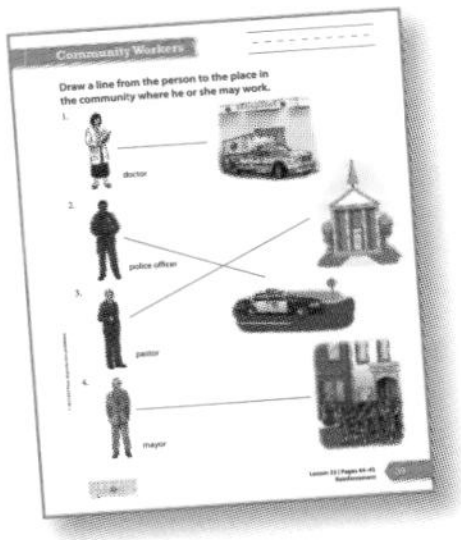

Activity Manual

- Guide completion of page 39.

Activity

Guest Speaker

Invite a city official to discuss his duties with the students.

Background

Government

City government is the smallest form of government. The city government is made of elected and appointed officials. The officials represent people in the communities. The mayor works with the officials or city council to make laws and decisions for the good of the citizens. Citizens make the government work by voting for the leadership. The community is an important part of city government.

Authority

God commands Christians to obey the law and submit to authority (1 Peter 3:13–17). Christians should have an attitude of respect for the government. Government leaders are God's ministers whether or not they are Christians. God has established government to provide order and justice.

Lesson

24

Student Text pages 46–47
Activity Manual page 41

Objectives

- List ways Benjamin Franklin made his city a better place
- List ways he can make his city a better place
- Compare Philadelphia then and now

Introduction

- Prepare a chart titled *The Community*. Label the column headings *People* and *Places*. Ask questions such as the following to review people and places in a community. Complete the columns as the students dictate.

  Who are people in a community? mayor, police officer

  What is a place in a community? church, store

Teach for Understanding

- Read the section title. Guide the reading of page 46 to find out how Benjamin Franklin helped his community long ago.

  When did Benjamin Franklin live? long ago In what city did he live? Philadelphia

- Explain that Benjamin Franklin worked to make Philadelphia a better city. Mr. Franklin established the first library, started a fire department, set up the postal service, and opened the first hospital. He served the people in his community.
- Display a word web with *Ben Franklin* written in the center oval. Draw four ovals originating from the center oval.
- Direct students to find a sentence on this page that tells how Benjamin Franklin helped the city of Philadelphia. Select a student to read the sentence aloud.
- Write in each oval an organization Benjamin Franklin started (library, fire department, post office, hospital).

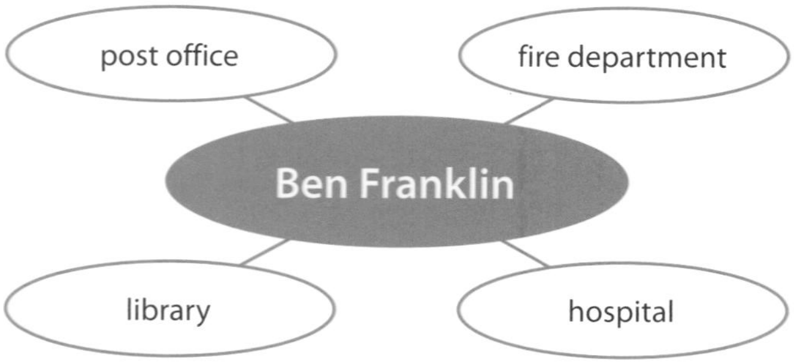

  Benjamin Franklin served his community and his country in many other ways.

- Use the Background information about Benjamin Franklin as you point out the pictures of Mr. Franklin on this page.

Famous People

A Community Long Ago

Long ago Ben Franklin lived in the city of Philadelphia.
Mr. Franklin worked to make his city better.
He enjoyed serving the people.
Mr. Franklin started the first library.
He began a fire department in his city.
Ben Franklin started the first post office.
He also set up a hospital to help the sick.

Benjamin Franklin

Mr. Franklin liked to read.

46

- Make a human web by placing a student in the center of the room. Direct students who answer the question to stand around the first student and place a hand on his shoulder.

  What things can (student's name) do to make his community a better place? talk to people about Jesus; pick up litter; follow rules or laws; recycle

- Direct attention to the chart on page 47. Read the title of the chart.

  The title *Comparing Philadelphia* means that we will find how the items on the chart are the same and how the items on the chart are different.

  What does *then* mean? a time in the past What does *now* mean? the present time

- Explain that this chart pictures things in the past and things in the present.

  Benjamin Franklin was interested in people learning to read and write. Children who lived during the time of Mr. Franklin used a hornbook in school.

- Direct the students to locate the picture of the hornbook.

  Look across the chart to find what many children use in school nowadays. computers

Then and Now

Comparing Philadelphia	
Then	Now
 Hornbook	 Computer
 Water pump	 Fire truck
 Franklin's library	 City library

47

- Direct the students to point to the water pump.

  Long ago fire departments used a water pump to put out fires. The fire department in the city of Philadelphia used water pumps similar to this one. Look across the chart to find what fire departments use now. fire trucks
- Follow a similar procedure for the library.

  Ben Franklin began the first library in the city of Philadelphia.
- Compare things that are the same (books, shelves, people) and things that are different (children, teacher) in the two libraries.

Activity Manual

- Guide completion of page 41. Compare the printing press with the printer, the Franklin stove with a modern-day stove, and a 1700s desk with a modern desk.

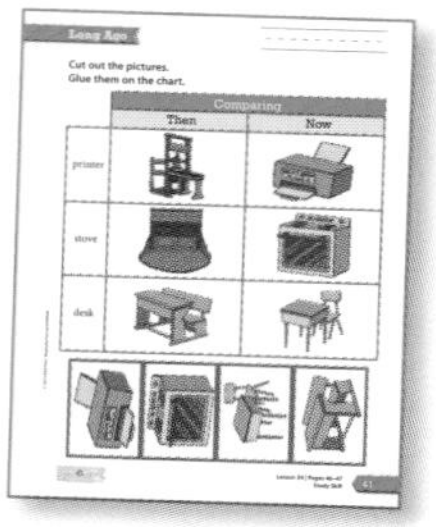

Background

Benjamin Franklin

Benjamin Franklin was an outstanding citizen. He diligently served his community and his country as clerk of the Pennsylvania Assembly, chief delegate to the Albany Congress, and representative to France. He served on the Pennsylvania Supreme Council. He desired to make life better for mankind by starting a library, fire department, post office, and hospital. Ben Franklin was a well-known writer and printer. He educated people through his printing and writing of the *Pennsylvania Gazette* and *Poor Richard's Almanac*. He began an academy that is now the University of Pennsylvania. He was a scientist and an inventor. He invented the Franklin stove, and his payment was the satisfaction of knowing that many homes were warm. Benjamin Franklin is probably most famous for his experiments with electricity. He served his community through his writings, inventions, and aid to mankind. Benjamin Franklin helped form the new government in America and signed both the Declaration of Independence and the Constitution.

The Hornbook

The hornbook was used for reading during the colonial period. It consisted of paper containing the letters of the alphabet mounted on wood and protected by a thin layer of transparent horn.

The Water Pump

The water pump was used to pump water on fires. It was not very efficient and pumped only small amounts of water at a time.

The First Library

Benjamin Franklin established the first library. In the library he displayed stuffed snakes and fossils.

The Franklin Stove

The Franklin stove was like a fireplace for cooking and heating inside the home.

Primary and Secondary Sources

The water pump in the picture is a primary source. The hornbook in the picture is a secondary source because it is a reproduction. Franklin's library picture is a secondary source since it is an artist's rendition. Compare these sources, make inferences, and draw conclusions. Invite students to evaluate these sources and then explain how they are different and how they are similar to the computer, fire truck, and library that they see today.

Lesson

25

Student Text pages 48–49
Activity Manual page 43

Objectives
- Locate parts of a map: title, map key, cardinal directions
- Locate places on a map using cardinal directions
- Explain the purpose of a map key

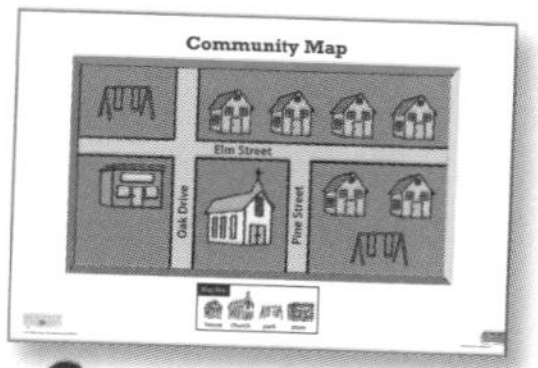

Materials
- Visual 9: *Community Map*
- The world floor map prepared in Lesson 8

Vocabulary
- map key

Introduction

- Review the map terms on pages 15–18.

  What is a map? a drawing that shows where places are

  What are the names of the four directions? north, south, east, west
- Gather the children around the floor map. Display the prepared continents. Repeat the name of each continent together as you display it.
- Instruct students to place each continent on the map. Choose a volunteer to re-create the map.
- Direct attention to the Atlas on pages 176–77.
- Guide the students as they make changes on the map to match the Continents and Oceans map.
- Sing together the "Continent Song" to the tune of "London Bridge." Point to each continent as you sing its name.

  Europe, Asia, Africa,
  Australia, Antarctica,
  North and South America,
  All for Jesus.

Teach for Understanding

- Read the section title. Guide the reading of page 48 to find out what a map key is. a box near the map that shows what the pictures mean
- Display Visual 9 to introduce the map.

  Maps are important for locating places. Maps have titles that tell what the map is about.
- Draw attention to the corresponding map in the student text. Direct the students to put their finger on the title of the map.
- Invite a volunteer to read the title of the map.

  This map is a picture of a community. What do you see on the map? houses, swing sets, a church, a building Do you think there are only two swing sets in the community? Could the swing sets mean something else? On the map a swing set could represent a place where children play, such as a playground or a park.

Finding Your Community

The map shows places in the community.
It is a drawing that shows where places are.
The box below the map is the **map key**.
The map key shows what the pictures mean.

Community Map

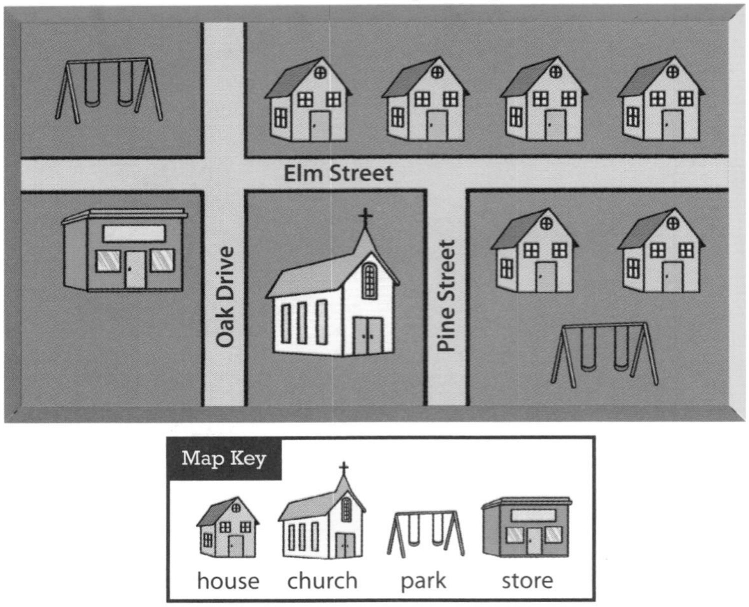

48

- Point out the map key. Explain that the map key tells what the pictures mean. Explain the key.

  There is one picture for each type of building or place. A map key gives important information about reading a map.

  How many churches are in this community? 1 how many houses? 6 how many parks? 2

  What do you think the building represents? a store How do you know? The key says that the building is a store. Without the key we would not know what the building was.
- Review cardinal directions: north, south, east, and west.

  The four different colors that border the map represent the four directions.
- Instruct the students to point to each border color as you say it.

  The red border is north.
  The yellow border is east.
  The blue border is south.
  The purple border is west.

  Place your finger at the top of the map on the road between the playground and the house. You are at the north part of the map. Now, move your finger straight down the street. What direction did you move? south

Families living and working together make
a community.
Communities near each other form a city.
The mayor is the leader of the city.
Community leaders work for the government.
People working together make a community
a good place to live.

Activity

49

Put your finger on the street between the playground and the store. You are at the west part of the map. Move your finger on the street across the map. What direction did you move? east

- Discuss the picture at the top of page 49 of the urban and rural communities coming together.
- Guide the reading of the page and review key ideas from the chapter.

Activity Manual

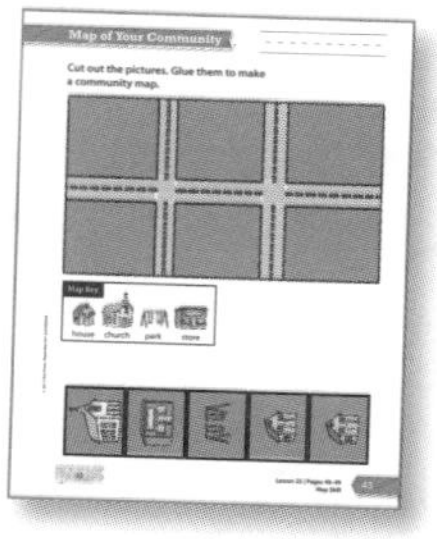

- Guide completion of page 43.

Activities

Map

Guide the students as they draw a map of the route they take from home to church. Title the map *Map to Church*, and include a map key.

Online Mapping

Use an online mapping program to locate your school or home. Discuss the aerial view as you point out surrounding landmarks.

Lesson 26

Chapter Review and Activity
Activity Manual page 45

Objective

- Recall concepts and terms from Chapter 3

Materials

- *Community Worker Worksheet* (Teacher's Toolkit CD)
- *Community Parade Parent Letter* (Teacher's Toolkit CD)
- *Community Worker Hats* (Teacher's Toolkit CD)
- Paper plates with centers cut out

Review

- Direct attention to the poem on page 34. Encourage the students to march around the room to the rhythm of the poem as you read it out loud.
- Guide a review of the Chapter 3 vocabulary by inviting the students to look up each word in the Picture Glossary.
- Review Chapter 3 by playing "A Community Parade." Direct each student to dress up like someone in a community. Encourage him to tell who he is and what part he has in the community. Allow the children to parade through the classroom or a nearby neighborhood as time allows. (*Note:* The worksheet on the Teacher's Toolkit CD provides information for this activity and serves as a review for the student.)

Activity Manual

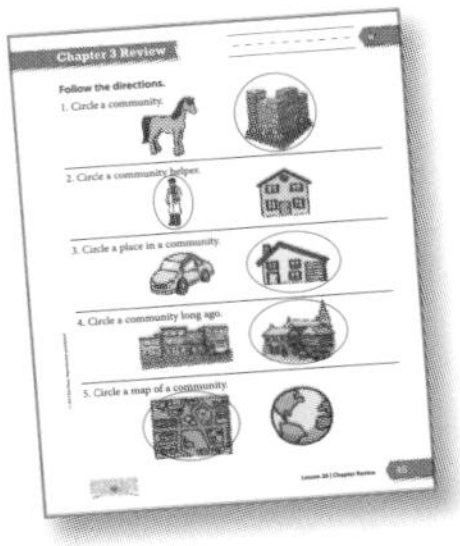

- Guide completion of page 45.

Chapter 3 Test

- Administer Test 3. (*Note:* The test introduces students to answer bubbles. Remind the students to fill in the answer bubbles completely.)

Chapter 4

Introduction

This chapter introduces students to the fact that there are fifty states in the United States. They will discover that their own state has a special shape, flag, bird, and flower. While students will not be required to memorize state names, they will be exposed to many different states and their important features and landmarks. Students will associate specific states with people, places, and things, such as George Washington Carver with Alabama, Mount Rushmore with South Dakota, and the Statue of Liberty with New York. An activity is included in which each student creates a representation of his own state flower.

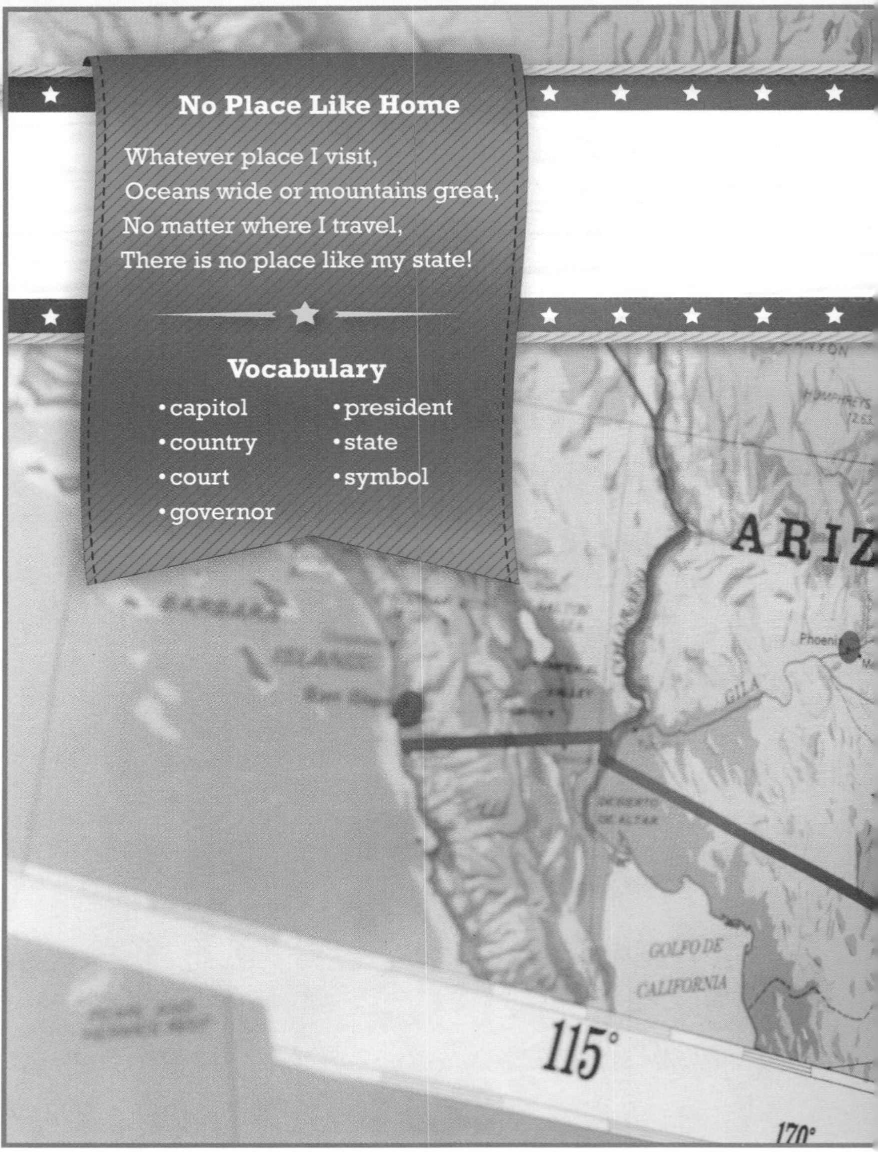

No Place Like Home

Whatever place I visit,
Oceans wide or mountains great,
No matter where I travel,
There is no place like my state!

Vocabulary

- capitol
- country
- court
- governor
- president
- state
- symbol

Chapter 4 Overview				
Lesson	**ST**	**AM**	**Content**	**Vocabulary**
27	50–53	47–49	The 50 states Your state	country state
28	54–55	51	Your state government	capitol court governor
29	56–57	53	States have famous people George Washington Carver / Clara Barton	
30	58–59	55	States have famous places Mount Rushmore / Grand Canyon	president
31	60–61	57	Great Lakes / Golden Gate Bridge	
32	62–64	59–61	States have famous things Liberty Bell / Statue of Liberty / Iditarod Race	symbol
33	65		State flower activity	
34		63	Chapter Review / Test	

Visit bjupress.com/resources for links to enhance the lessons.

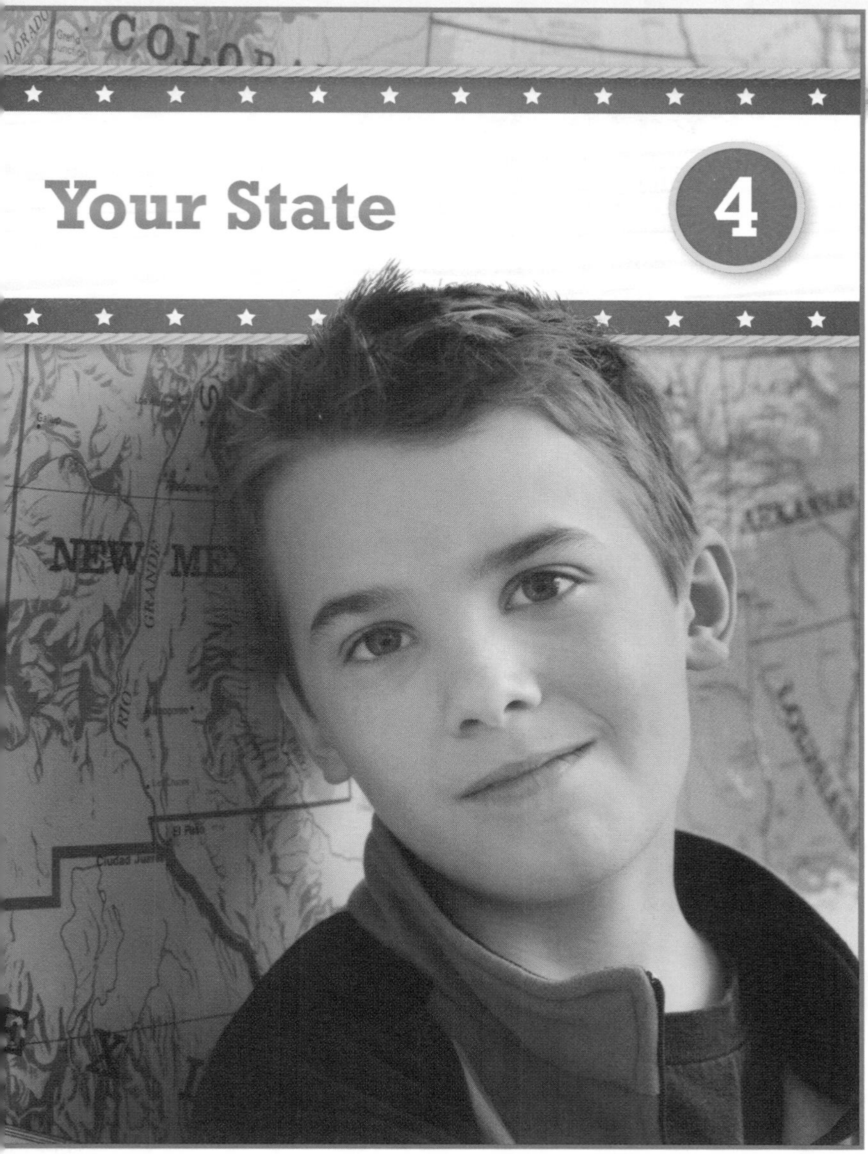

Student Text pages 50–53
Activity Manual pages 47–49

Objectives

- Identify the state he lives in
- Classify his state as part of a country
- Identify his state as one of the fifty states in the United States
- Identify the unique symbols and features of his state

Materials

- Visuals 10–12: *State Flags; State Flowers; State Birds*
- Pictures of your state flag, bird, and flower

Vocabulary

- country
- state

Content Words

- Florida
- Indiana
- Maryland
- United States

Introduction

- Remind the students that they have been learning about their family and their community. Mention that in this chapter they will learn about their state, the part of the country they live in. Direct attention to pages 50–51 and read aloud the title of the chapter.

Teach for Understanding

- Read aloud the poem on page 50.

  What kinds of places does the poem say a person might visit? oceans or mountains

  What does the poem say there is nothing like? a person's own state
- Point out the photo on pages 50–51.

  What is on the wall behind the boy? a map
- Explain that the boy is leaning against a map of the United States that shows the name of each state. Read aloud the names of some of the states that are visible.
- Choose a volunteer to identify the state he lives in.
- Invite the students to look at the list of new vocabulary words they will be learning in Chapter 4.

  Where in our book can we go to find the meanings of new words? the Picture Glossary

JourneyForth

The Spelling Window by Dawn L. Watkins

In this picture book, sensitively illustrated by John Roberts, a girl is embarrassed by the behavior of her hearing-impaired neighbor during a visit to her state capitol. But an accident prompts her to see her neighbor, Seth, and her own actions in a new light, and gradually, she learns how to be his friend.

Chickadee Winter by Dawn L. Watkins

When Jack's family goes to stay with his grandparents for a while, Jack must adjust from warm, sunny New Mexico to a new state with a much colder climate. As Jack shadows his grandfather on his chores around the farm, the kind man's patient friendship gradually helps him accept and embrace the changes in his life. Gabriela Dellosso's watercolor illustrations beautifully enhance this picture book.

Lesson

27

- Guide the reading of page 52.

  What larger area is your community a part of? a state

  What is a state? a part of a country

  What is a country? a land with its own people and laws
- Point out the American flag in the classroom and repeat the first line of the pledge together: "I pledge allegiance to the flag of the United States of America."

  What is our country's name? the United States of America

  How many states does our country have? fifty

  What is the name of our state?
- Point out the photo on page 52. Choose a volunteer to try to sound out the name of the state.
- Read aloud the caption.

  Which state is this sign welcoming drivers to? Montana

  What does the sign show that you might find in the state of Montana? possible answer: mountains

  What is unusual about the shape of the sign? It is shaped like the state.
- Invite the students to turn to page 176. Explain that this section of the book is called the Atlas, which means a collection of maps. Draw attention to pages 178–79 in the Atlas. Explain that this is a map of the United States showing all fifty states. Point out your own state. Draw an outline of the state for display, explaining that each state has its own shape.
- Point out Montana on the United States map.

You Live in a State

Your community is a part of a **state**.
A state is a part of a **country**.
A country is a land with its own people and laws.
Our country is the United States of America.
There are fifty states in the United States.
You live in one of these states.

A state sign welcomes you to a state.

52

Your state has a flag.
It has a special bird.
It has a special flower.
It has its own shape.
No other state is quite like yours.

Maryland state flower

Indiana state bird

Florida state flag

What state do you live in?

Answers will vary.

53

Lesson 27

- Guide the reading of page 53.

  What other special things does each state have? a flag, a bird, and a flower
- Read aloud the name of each state in the captions. Point out the state flag of Florida. Explain that state flags have special colors and symbols on them that represent that state.

  What does Florida's flag say on the bottom of the circle? In God we trust.
- Display Visual 10. Identify the state each flag represents, and compare ways the flags differ from each other.
- Display the picture of your state flag, and discuss its unique features.
- Point out the state flower of Maryland on page 53.

  This is a black-eyed Susan. It is the special flower of the state of Maryland. What is our state flower?
- Display Visual 11. Identify the state each flower represents, and compare ways the flowers differ from each other. Explain that a state flower is usually one that is commonly found in that state or grows well there.
- Display the picture of your state flower, and discuss its unique features.
- Point out the state bird of Indiana on page 53.

  What kind of bird is this? a cardinal

  What is our state bird?
- Display Visual 12. Identify the state each bird represents, and compare ways the birds differ from each other. Explain that a state bird is one that lives in that state. However, sometimes a state bird is an endangered species that is rarely seen.
- Display the picture of your state bird, and discuss its unique features.

Activity Manual

- Read aloud the directions for page 47. Guide the students as they locate their state on the map and complete the page.
- Display the picture of your state bird. Guide completion of page 49.

Activity

Sing

Introduce a song about the states to help the students recognize the names of the fifty United States. At this grade level, the students should not be required to memorize all the state names.

Lesson

28

Student Text pages 54–55
Activity Manual page 51

Objectives
- Summarize how state leaders are chosen
- Explain the state governor's main job
- Explain the function of a state capitol
- Explain the role of judges in state courts

Materials
- Visual 13: *Justice, Liberty, and the Bible*
- A picture of your state governor for display

Vocabulary
- capitol
- court
- governor

Introduction

- Review the name of the state where you live, its flower and bird, and what its flag looks like.

Teach for Understanding

- Guide the reading of page 54.

  Who chooses a state's leaders? the people who live in the state

  Who is the leader of a state? a governor
- Display the picture of your state governor and introduce him or her to the students. Explain that this governor was chosen by people who voted in an election. Most adults who live in a state may vote.

  What does a state governor do? leads the state and works with the people who make laws
- Point out the photos of governors on page 54 and read aloud the caption.

  What does the Bible tell us God wants us to do for our leaders? pray for them
- Read aloud 1 Timothy 2:1–2.

  What kind of life does the Bible say we will have when our leaders keep order and lead well? quiet; peaceful

  According to this verse, how can we help our leaders lead well? by praying for them
- Lead in a brief prayer for your government leaders.

Your State Has Leaders

People in a state choose their government leaders.
Your state has a **governor**.
The governor leads your state.
He works with the people who make laws.

God wants you to pray for your leaders (1 Timothy 2:1–2).

54

Your state has a **capitol** building.
Laws are made at the capitol.
Your state also has **courts**.
Judges in courts use laws to settle problems.
They decide what is just and right.

Who leads a state?

a governor

55

- Guide the reading of page 55. Point out the picture of the state capitol.

  What happens at the building called the capitol? Laws are made.

  What is flying at the top of the capitol building in the picture? flags

- Explain that the upper flag is the American flag and the lower flag is a state flag.

  What do judges do in courts? They use laws to settle problems.

- Point out the picture of the judge and explain that judges need to be honest people who can be trusted.

  What does a judge decide when he deals with a problem? He decides what is just and right.

  How do we know what is just and right? by reading the Bible

- Display Visual 13. Point out the photo of the Moses statue and explain that this statue has stood on the roof of the New York Appellate Courthouse for many years. Explain that the statue shows Moses holding the two tablets with the Ten Commandments on them.

  For many, many years people everywhere in our land have recognized that the Bible is our source for what is just and right. Some judges in our country are Christians who read the Bible and try to follow it when making decisions.

- Conclude the discussion by asking the question on page 55.

Activity Manual

- Guide completion of page 51.

Lesson

29

Student Text pages 56–57
Activity Manual page 53

Objectives
- Associate famous people with states
- Summarize the contributions of George Washington Carver
- Summarize the contributions of Clara Barton

Content Words
- Alabama
- Clara Barton
- George Washington Carver

Introduction

- Review the meanings of *country* and *state.*

  How many states are in our country? fifty

Teach for Understanding

- Point out the photo and the state shape on page 56. Explain that this is the shape of Alabama on a map. Guide the reading of the page to find out what famous person lived in Alabama. George Washington Carver

  What does it mean to be famous? well-known

  Into what kind of life was George Washington Carver born? He was born a slave.
- Explain that being a slave means that a person is owned by someone else and spends his time working for his owner.

  What did Dr. Carver learn how to do as he grew up? to read, write, draw, and farm
- Explain that George Washington Carver's owners taught him these skills, but not all slaves were allowed to learn these things. Later Carver had the opportunity to go to school. Emphasize that God planned to use Carver in a special way, and He ordered Carver's life so that he received the skills he needed. [Bible Promise I. God as Master]

  What do we remember George Washington Carver for? We remember him for finding many uses for plants and for teaching farmers to use plants wisely.
- Explain that Dr. Carver was an inventor who found many new uses for the peanut and the sweet potato. He helped farmers take better care of their soil by planting different crops each year instead of the same one over and over again.

States Have Famous People

Famous people lived in some states.
This state was home to a famous man.
His name was George Washington Carver.
Dr. Carver was born a slave.
He learned to read, write, draw, and farm.
Dr. Carver found many ways to use plants.
He taught farmers to use plants wisely.

56

This state was home to a famous woman.
Her name was Clara Barton.
Miss Barton was a brave nurse.
She cared for men who had been hurt in battles.
She helped families find missing men.
She started the American Red Cross.
The Red Cross still cares for people today.

How did Dr. Carver and Miss Barton help people?

taught people to use plants wisely; cared for men hurt in battle

57

- Point out the photo and the state shape on page 57. Explain that this is the shape of Maryland. Guide the reading of the page to find out what famous person lived in Maryland. Clara Barton

  What job did Miss Barton have? She was a nurse.

  Who did she care for? men who had been hurt in battles

- Explain that Miss Barton brought clothing, food, medicine, and other supplies to soldiers who were wounded on battlefields. Miss Barton had been a teacher before she nursed soldiers, and she learned that some of the men she cared for had been her students.

  What did Clara Barton do for families? helped them find soldiers who were missing

  What was the name of the organization Miss Barton started? the American Red Cross

  Is there still a Red Cross organization in America today? yes

Activity Manual

- Guide completion of page 53.

Background

George Washington Carver

George Washington Carver was born in Missouri, but he spent most of his adult life in Tuskegee, Alabama, working in connection with the Tuskegee Institute for African-American students. During his years there, he discovered hundreds of new uses for the peanut, the sweet potato, and other plants. He also studied soil conservation and taught Southern farmers how to rotate their crops to enrich the nutrients in the soil. He died at Tuskegee Institute in 1943.

Clara Barton

Clara Barton was born in 1821 in Massachusetts, and she began helping soldiers during the American Civil War. She often risked her life to stay with soldiers in dangerous areas until their medical needs could be cared for. Miss Barton was introduced to the Red Cross organization on a visit to Switzerland. She became the major influence in forming the American Red Cross in the early 1900s. She died at her home in Maryland in 1912, but her work lives on. The Red Cross continues to participate in relief work during disasters, wars, and other emergency situations.

Lesson 30

Student Text pages 58–59
Activity Manual page 55

Objectives
- Associate famous places with states
- Explain the significance of Mount Rushmore
- Associate the Grand Canyon with the greatness of God

Vocabulary
- president

Content Words
- Arizona
- Grand Canyon
- Rushmore
- South Dakota

Introduction

- Review that each person in our country lives in one of the fifty states. Some states have famous people.

Teach for Understanding

- Point out the photo and the state shape on page 58. Explain that this is the shape of South Dakota. Guide the reading of the page to find out what famous place is in South Dakota. Mount Rushmore

  What can you see carved in the rock on Mount Rushmore? four faces of United States presidents

  What is a president? a leader of our country

  Do you recognize any of the presidents' faces in the photo of Mount Rushmore? Answers will vary.

- Explain that the faces are George Washington, Thomas Jefferson, Theodore Roosevelt, and Abraham Lincoln.

  Do you think these faces are bigger or smaller than the actual faces of the presidents? bigger

  Each face measures about sixty feet in length. This is about the size of ten men stacked on top of one another.

  What does Mount Rushmore make us think of? great men who helped make our country great

States Have Famous Places

This state has a famous place.
The place is called Mount Rushmore.
You can see four faces in the rock.
They are faces of United States **presidents**.
A president is a leader of our country.
Mount Rushmore makes us think of great men.
These men helped make our country great.

58

This lesson introduces students to the Geogloss, a visual glossary of geographical terms included in the Resource Treasury at the back of the book. The Geogloss displays terms and pictures the various land features being described.

This state has a famous place too.
The place is called the Grand Canyon.
Many people go to see the tall cliffs
and the river.
The Grand Canyon is made of rock.
The Grand Canyon makes us think
of our great God.

★ What is the Grand Canyon made of?

rock

59

- Point out the photo and the state shape on page 59. Explain that this is the shape of Arizona. Guide the reading of the page to find out what famous place is in Arizona. the Grand Canyon
- Explain that a canyon is an enormous hole, or chasm, in the ground.

  What can people see at the Grand Canyon? tall cliffs and a river
- Turn to pages 174–75 in the Resource Treasury at the back of the book. Explain that the Geogloss shows pictures of various land features. Assist the students in locating *cliff*. Explain that a cliff is a steep rock face that drops off from a high point.
- Return to page 59.

  What is the Grand Canyon made of? rock

  What does the Grand Canyon make us think of? our great God Why? God caused the Grand Canyon to be formed, and its huge size shows His greatness.

Activity Manual

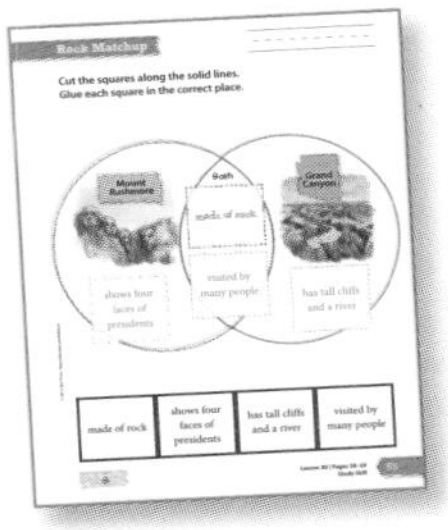

- Read aloud the headings on the Venn diagram, and point out how it organizes information in its different sections.
- Guide completion of page 55.

Activity

Show and Tell

Invite any students who have visited Mount Rushmore or the Grand Canyon to show pictures of their visit and tell about their experience.

Background

Mount Rushmore

Sculpted by Gutzon Borglum, the faces on Mount Rushmore were completed in 1941. They are sixty feet tall and look down from a cliff five hundred feet in the air.

The Grand Canyon

Many creation scientists believe that the Grand Canyon formed as a result of the Flood. Huge amounts of rapidly moving water from the Flood could have formed the canyon in no more than a few months.

Lesson 31

Student Text pages 60–61
Activity Manual page 57

Objectives
- Associate famous places with states
- State facts about the Great Lakes
- State facts about the Golden Gate Bridge

Content Words
- California
- Michigan

Introduction

- Review the two famous places you have discussed so far and mention the names of the states where they are found.

  Today we will learn about other states that have famous places.

Teach for Understanding

- Point out the photo and the state shape on page 60. Explain that this is the shape of Michigan. Guide the reading of the page to find out what famous place is in Michigan. the Great Lakes
- Turn to the Geogloss (pages 174–75), and assist the students in locating *lake*. Explain that a lake is a large inland body of water.
- Return to page 60.

  How many Great Lakes are there? five

  How do people use the lakes? They fish and sail on them.

  What are the people in the photo doing on the lake? boating or kayaking
- Point out that the shape of the state has two parts.

  What does the lower part look like? a hand
- Guide the students in comparing their right hands to the shape of Michigan's Lower Peninsula.

This state also has a famous place.
The place is called the Great Lakes.
There are five deep lakes around this state.
People fish and sail on the lakes.
The land is in two parts.
Look at your right hand.
The lower part of the state looks
like your hand.

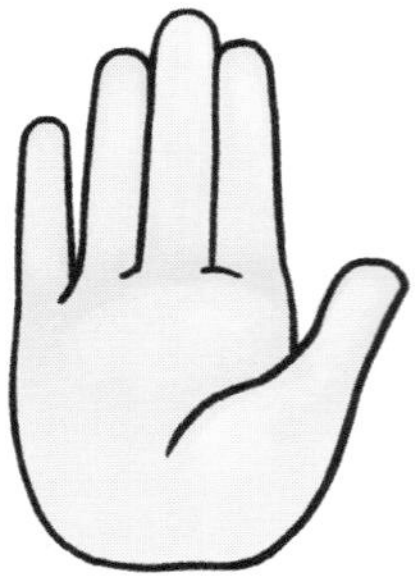

60

This state has a famous place.
It is a huge bridge.
The Golden Gate Bridge is very long.
Cars drive across a bay on the bridge.

★ How many Great Lakes are there?

five

61

- Point out the photo and the state shape on page 61. Explain that this is the shape of California. Guide the reading of the page to find out what famous place is in California. the Golden Gate Bridge

  Is a bridge usually built across land or water? water
- Explain that the bridge crosses the San Francisco Bay, a body of water that flows into the Pacific Ocean.
- Assist the students as they locate *bay* in the Geogloss. Explain that a bay is a broad part of a sea or a lake partly surrounded by land.

  Compare the pictures of the lake and the bay. How is a bay different from a lake? A lake is completely surrounded by land, and a bay is only partly surrounded by land.
- Return to page 61.

  What words tell about the size of the Golden Gate Bridge? *huge; very long*

  What is the bridge used for? Cars drive across the bay on it.

  What time of day is it in the photo of the bridge? nighttime
- Point out the lights on the bridge in the photo. Explain that many people think the Golden Gate Bridge is one of the most beautiful bridges in the world.

Activity Manual

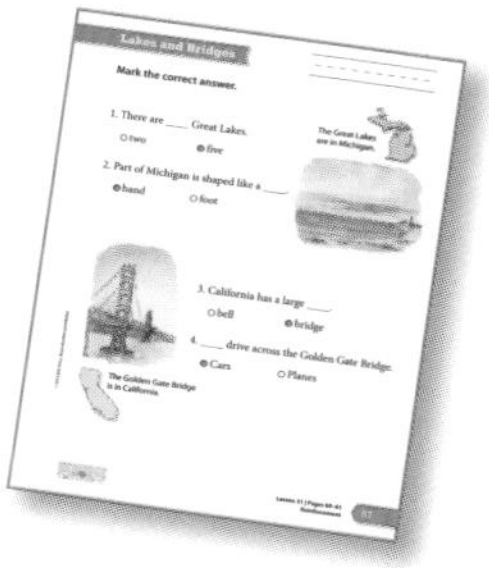

- Guide completion of page 57. Remind the students to fill in the answer bubbles completely.

Background

The Great Lakes

The five Great Lakes include Superior, Michigan, Huron, Erie, and Ontario. The lakes cover almost 95,000 square miles. Together they form the largest system of freshwater lakes in the world, about one-fifth of the world's freshwater supply.

The Golden Gate Bridge

The Golden Gate Bridge is painted a bright shade of orange called orange vermilion. It is 1.7 miles long and 90 feet wide. Construction of the bridge lasted about four years and cost $35 million dollars. It was completed in 1937.

Lesson 32

Student Text pages 62–64
Activity Manual pages 59–61

Objectives
- Associate famous things with states
- Explain the significance of the Liberty Bell
- Explain the significance of the Statue of Liberty
- Associate the state of Alaska with dog-sled racing

Materials
- Visual 13: *Justice, Liberty, and the Bible*

Vocabulary
- symbol

Content Words
- Alaska
- freedom
- liberty
- New York
- Pennsylvania
- statue

Introduction

- Review the name of your state, and locate it together on the United States map on Atlas pages 178–79. Review the names of other states you have discussed in this chapter. Point out some of these states on the map.

Teach for Understanding

- Point out the photo and the state shape on page 62. Explain that this is the shape of Pennsylvania. Guide the reading of the page to find out what famous thing is in Pennsylvania. the Liberty Bell

  Is the Liberty Bell old or new? old How do you know? It was made long ago.
- Display Visual 13. Point out the crack in the Liberty Bell. Mention that the bell has been damaged and remade several times.

  In what year was the Liberty Bell rung? 1776
- Explain that the original Liberty Bell hung in a government building, the Pennsylvania State House. Historians believe it was rung to call people together for a reading of the Declaration of Independence, an important document that announced our country's decision to be free of the king of England's rule.
- Read aloud Leviticus 25:10. Explain that part of this verse appears on the top of the Liberty Bell: "Proclaim liberty throughout all the land unto all the inhabitants thereof." Point out the verse at the top of the bell.

  The Liberty Bell is a symbol. What is a symbol? something that stands for something else

  What is the bell a symbol of? freedom

States Have Famous Things

Some states have famous things.
This state has a famous bell.
The Liberty Bell was made long ago.
The bell was rung in 1776.
The Liberty Bell is a **symbol** of freedom.
A symbol stands for something else.

62

- Explain that a symbol is often an object that makes us think of something we cannot see or touch.

  Freedom is an idea, something we cannot see or touch but only think about in our minds. When people see the Liberty Bell, it reminds them that our country is free.

This state also has a famous symbol.
It is called the Statue of Liberty.
The statue is of a tall lady.
She wears a crown.
She holds a torch up to the sky.
People see the statue and remember
that our country is free.

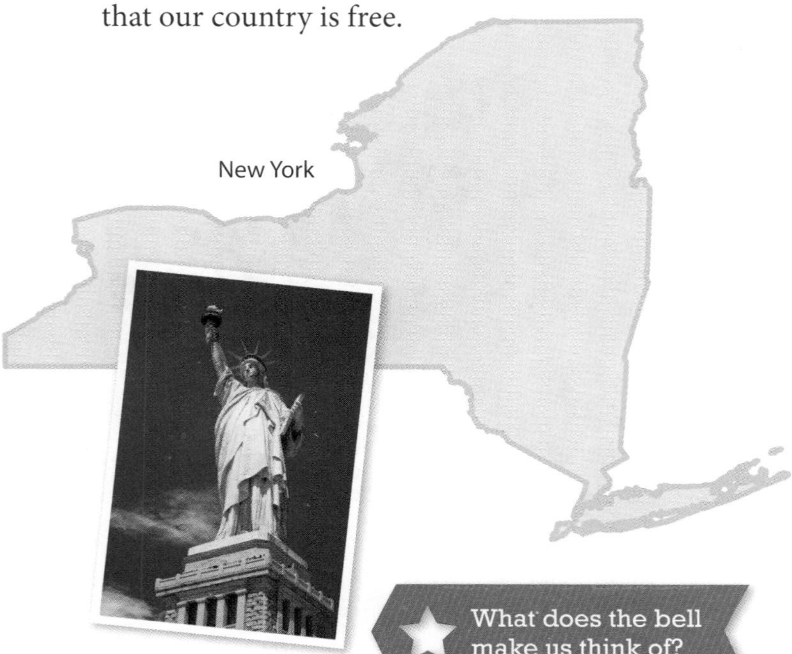

What does the bell make us think of?

our freedom

63

- Point out the photo and the state shape on page 63. Explain that this is the shape of New York. Guide the reading of the page to find out what famous thing is in New York. the Statue of Liberty

  What does the statue look like? It is a tall lady wearing a crown and holding a torch up to the sky.
- Explain that a torch is an old-fashioned type of lamp that used a flame to produce light.
- Mention that people often refer to the statue as "Lady Liberty." The statue stands on Liberty Island in New York Harbor. It was a gift to the United States of America from the country of France.

  What do people remember when they see the statue? that our country is free

  How is the Statue of Liberty like the Liberty Bell? They are both symbols of our country's freedom.

Background

The Liberty Bell

The Liberty Bell hung in the Pennsylvania State House in 1776. It is traditionally thought to have been rung to call Philadelphia citizens to a public reading of the newly completed Declaration of Independence. The original bell has been recast several times and is now on display at the Liberty Bell Center in Pennsylvania's Independence National Historical Park.

The Statue of Liberty

The Statue of Liberty was given to the United States by the people of France in 1886. The statue holds a torch in one hand and a tablet representing the law in the other. She wears a seven-pronged crown. A broken chain lies at her feet. Because of the statue's closeness to Ellis Island, where United States immigration began being handled in the late 1800s, the statue has come to represent America's freedom to the oppressed around the world.

Lesson

32

- Point out the photo and the state shape on page 64. Explain that this is the shape of Alaska. Guide the reading of the page to find out what famous thing is in Alaska. a famous dog-sled race
- Explain that this special race is called the Iditarod Trail Sled Dog Race, or simply the Iditarod. It is held once a year in Alaska.

  What is the weather like in Alaska? cold and snowy

  How do you know that the special race is a long race? Dogs pull the sleds many miles.

  What do you think the dogs that pull the sleds have to be like? possible answers: strong; fast; able to endure cold weather

  Does the photo show just one dog pulling the sled? No, a team of dogs is pulling the sled.

  How is the winner of the race decided? The fastest dogs win.

Activity Manual

- Guide completion of page 59.
- Guide completion of page 61. Display the finished pictures.

Activity

Literature

Read a book about Balto, the leader of the sled dog team that completed the famous medicine run to Nome.

Background

The Iditarod Trail Sled Dog Race

The Iditarod Trail Sled Dog Race was first held to commemorate an event in which sled dogs played an important role. In 1925, the village of Nome, Alaska, suffered an epidemic of diphtheria. Diphtheria serum needed to be taken to Nome from Anchorage, a city more than 1,000 miles away. Because of the rough terrain, the only way to carry the serum was by dog sled. A relay of dog sleds was able to complete the remarkable journey in just six days. The route those mushers and their teams took was known as the Iditarod Trail. Today the Iditarod Trail Sled Dog Race follows roughly the same route in memory of the great race to save lives long ago.

This state is cold and snowy.
This state has a famous race.
It is a special dog sled race.
Dogs pull sleds many miles in the snow.
The fastest dogs win.

64

Bible

Emphasize that freedom is a great privilege that comes with responsibility. Living in a free country does not mean that a person can do exactly as he likes. Freedom can be used for good, but it can also be used to justify irresponsible or sinful behavior. Christians who have been given the privilege of freedom must use that freedom for godly purposes. Discuss ways that people might use freedom to do something wrong or ways they might use it to do something godly.

Every state has something important about it. Every state is special.

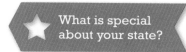

What is special about your state?

Answers will vary.

Activity

65

Chapter Activity
Student Text page 65

Objective

- Create a representation of his state flower

Materials

- Visuals 10–12: *State Flags; State Flowers; State Birds*
- A picture of your state flower for display
- Construction paper and other materials for creating a representation of your state flower, such as chenille wire, fabric scraps, tissue paper, and seeds

Lesson

33

Introduction

- Display Visuals 10–12. Review the fact that each state has its own special flag, flower, and bird.

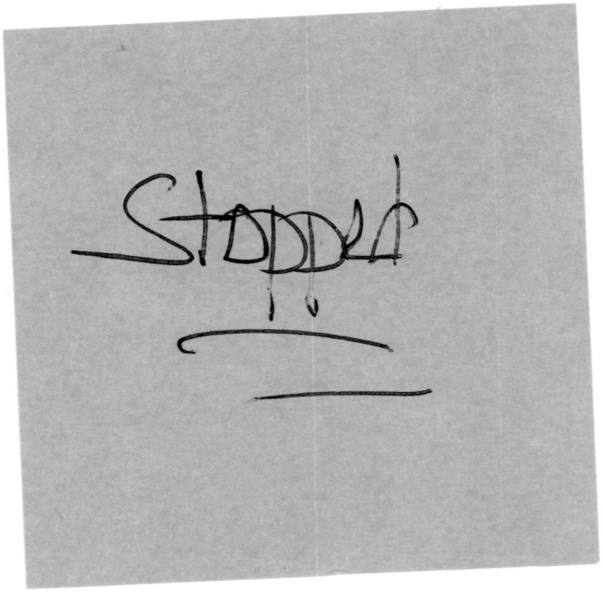

Teach for Understanding

- Guide the reading of page 65. Briefly discuss what is special or important about your state.
- Point out the photo on page 65 of an art project showing the state flower of Kansas. Ask whether anyone knows the name of the flower. sunflower

  What is the name of our state's special flower?
- Display the picture of your state flower, and point out some of the features that make it unique from other flowers.
- Assist the students as they create their flowers. Encourage them to be creative; all the flowers do not need to look exactly alike.

Activity

Chapter Review
Activity Manual page 63

Objective

- Recall concepts and terms from Chapter 4

Materials

- *Landmark Cards* (Teacher's Toolkit CD) Prepare a set for each student.

Review

- Draw attention to the poem on page 50. Decide together on motions to represent the words *oceans*, *mountains*, *travel*, and *my state*. Recite the poem as a class with everyone doing the motions together.
- Invite students to read the meanings of the vocabulary words from the Picture Glossary.
- Review Chapter 4 by playing "Landmark Match." Give each student a set of Landmark Cards and instruct him to cut them apart. Ask questions to review the various landmarks, such as, "Which landmark holds up a torch?" "Which landmark makes a noise?" "Which landmark has four noses?" Encourage the students to answer the questions by holding up the correct card.

Activity Manual

- Guide completion of page 63, reading the directions as the students progress through the page.

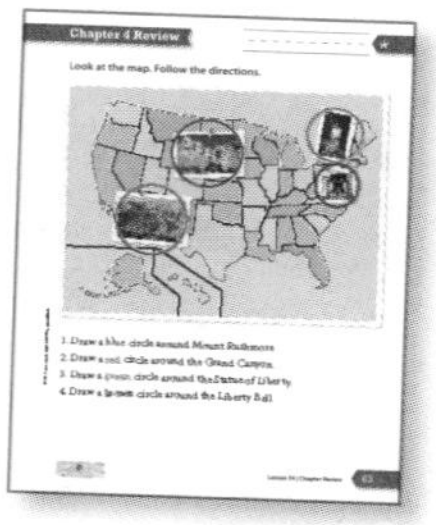

Chapter 4 Test

- Administer Test 4.

Chapter 5

Introduction

This chapter introduces the students to their country. They will learn about America's symbols. The students will enjoy pictures that show the geography of their country. They will learn facts about the president, the Constitution, and the rights and duties of citizens. The last lesson will allow the students to participate in an election.

Fireworks

Kaboom! Crackle-pop!
Big bursts of bright light—
Glowing sky-spiders
Trailing down through the night.

Kaboom! Sizzle-bang!
What a show up above!
A grand celebration
For the land that we love.

Vocabulary

- ballot
- citizen
- election
- motto
- pledge
- right
- vote

Chapter 5 Overview				
Lesson	ST	AM	Content	Vocabulary
35	66–69	65	Definition of a country The United States' neighbors	
36	70–71	67	The American flag The pledge to the American flag	pledge
37	72–73	69	The bald eagle "In God We Trust" "The Star-Spangled Banner"	motto
38	74–75	71	"America the Beautiful" The geography of the United States of America	
39	76–77	73	The president and the White House The Constitution Citizenship Rights	citizen right
40	78–79		Elections Voting	ballot election vote
41		75	Voting activity	
42		77	Chapter Review/Test	

Visit bjupress.com/resources for links to enhance the lessons.

Lesson 41 includes a class election. You may choose to use some of the suggestions in the lesson in earlier lessons.

Your Country 5

JourneyForth

Roses on Baker Street by Eileen M. Berry

In this picture book, Danae's missionary family moves from France to America for a year of furlough, and all the things that have meant "home" to Danae are missing—stone walls, church bells, roses, . . . and a best friend. What does Papa mean, she wonders, when he tells her to look for roses here in America? Vivid illustrations by John Roberts help bring this heartwarming story to life.

A King for Brass Cobweb by Dawn L. Watkins

In this early chapter book, Chipmunk goes in search of a king for the land of Brass Cobweb. He meets many animals and encounters many dangers on his journey, but among all his new acquaintances, he cannot find one who is brave and wise and true. He returns home thinking he has failed, only to discover that he has succeeded brilliantly. Detailed color illustrations and pencil sketches by Holly Hannon enrich this thought-provoking story about the qualities of a good leader.

Lesson 35

Student Text pages 66–69
Activity Manual page 65

Objectives

- Define the meaning of the word *country*
- Explain why the United States is called the Land of the Free
- Locate the United States on a globe
- Name the countries that border the United States

Materials

- A globe
- The world floor map prepared in Lesson 8

Content Words

- Canada
- Mexico

Introduction

- Direct attention to the Contents page.

  We are ready to begin Chapter 5 of our book. What is the title of the chapter? Your Country

  On what page does Chapter 5 begin? page 66

Teach for Understanding

- Draw attention to the picture on pages 66–67. Choose a volunteer to read the title of the chapter.

  What do you see in the picture? fireworks

  What holiday celebration includes fireworks? July 4
- Encourage the students to tell about fireworks displays they have seen.
- Read aloud the poem "Fireworks."

  What words in the poem describe the sound of the fireworks? *kaboom, crackle-pop, sizzle-bang*

  What other words did the author use to describe fireworks? *big bursts of bright light; glowing sky-spiders trailing down through the night*

  Why do you think people use fireworks to celebrate the birth of their country? Answers will vary, but elicit that fireworks are pretty and loud and fun to watch.

  You will learn what makes a country as you read the chapter.
- Draw attention to the vocabulary words the students will learn in this chapter. Remind the students that the words can be found in the Picture Glossary.

Lesson

35

- Guide the reading of page 68 to find out the name of our country. the United States of America

  What is a country? a land with its own people and laws

  Most of the people in a country speak the same language.

  How many states are in the United States of America? fifty

  What is the United States called? the Land of the Free

  To be free means that we can make our own choices as long as we do not hurt anyone.

  What is an example of hurting others? hitting them; stealing from them
- Use some of the Background information about freedom to extend the discussion.

  Some people live in countries that do not allow them to worship God. They do not have many choices or rights. You should be thankful to live in a free country.
- Use the world floor map to review the names of the continents.
- Choose a volunteer to point to the continent that has the United States on it.
- Choose a volunteer to find the United States on a globe.
- Draw attention to the picture on page 68.

  Which country are the children pointing to? the United States
- Choose a volunteer to read the caption aloud.

The United States of America

Your country is called the United States of America.
A country is a land with its own people and laws.
There are fifty states in the United States.
The United States is called the Land of the Free.

Here is the United States on a globe.

68

Background

Fireworks

Fireworks were first used to celebrate the Fourth of July in 1776. The next year was the first official celebration of America's independence. Americans used cannons, bonfires, guns, and fireworks. July 4 was declared a federal holiday in 1941. Fireworks are a part of most Independence Day celebrations today.

Government

Throughout the history of the world, there have been groups of people united by their common descent, customs, and language. The United States is different from most countries. From the beginning, people with different ethnicities, languages, and customs have been part of the United States. What has made the United States a single nation is its ideas. Chief among these is freedom. Americans have always valued their freedom.

Freedom

Freedom is the condition in which a person can make his own choices without fear of harm, provided his choices do not harm others or diminish their choices. Freedom has become an empty concept in society because people cannot agree on what harm is or what it means to diminish the choices of others. Many non-Christians think it is harmful to teach children they are sinners and that they need Jesus to save them. But Christians believe it is harmful not to teach these things.

Freedom can be a good thing. But everyone must agree on what harm is. The only right way to know what harm is, is to let God tell us. God knows what harm is, and we must let the Bible guide us in our choices. Freedom is good only if the Bible is used to show us when we are free to do something and when we are not.

Bible

Genesis 11:1–9 tells about people who sinned by wanting to exalt themselves at the tower of Babel. God changed the language of the people from one language to many languages. New nations were formed as the people reorganized themselves by common language.

Canada is the country north of the United States.
Mexico is the country south of the United States.

America's Neighbors

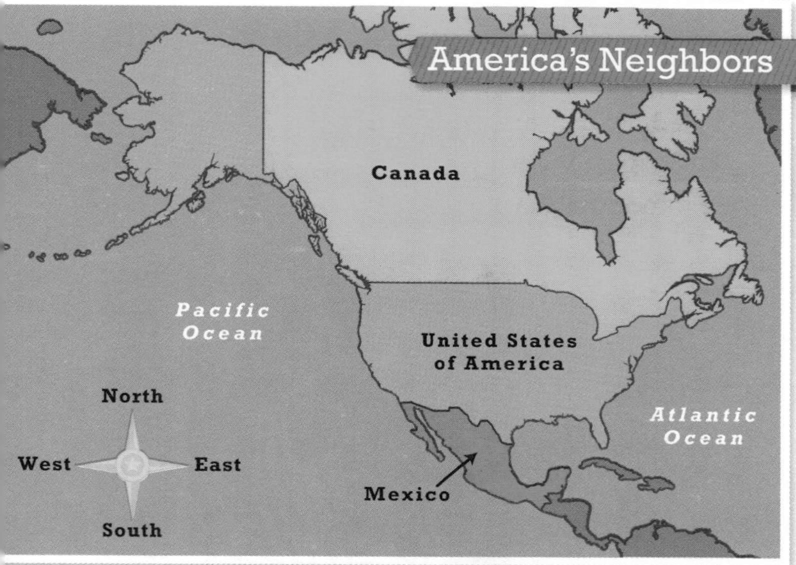

What is a country?

a land with its own people and laws

69

- Draw attention to the picture on page 69. Point out the United States on the map.

  Canada and Mexico are neighbors of the United States.

  What is the name of the country located north of the United States? Canada
- Mention several facts about Canada such as the following: Canada is the second largest country in the world. Citizens of Canada speak English and French. Canada has mountains, plains, forests, lakes, and rivers.

  What is the name of the country located south of the United States? Mexico
- Mention several facts about Mexico such as the following: Mexicans speak Spanish. They produce beautiful music. Mexico has mountains, deserts, rain forests, and deep canyons.
- Conclude the discussion by asking the question on page 69.

Activity Manual

- Guide completion of page 65.

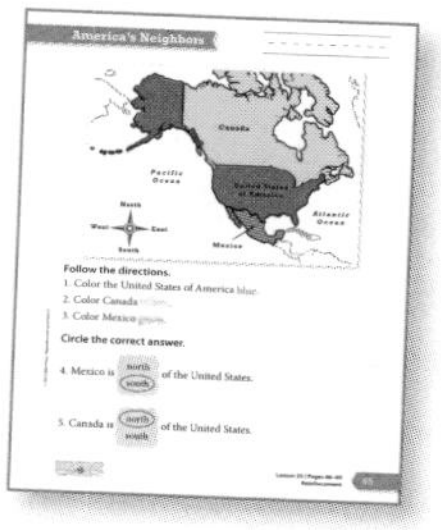

Lesson

36

Student Text pages 70–71
Activity Manual page 67

Objectives

- Identify the flag as a symbol of the United States of America
- Name the colors in the American flag
- Explain why the phrase *under God* is important in the pledge to the American flag
- Explain why people make a pledge to their country

Materials

- Visual 14: *The American Flag and the Pledge*

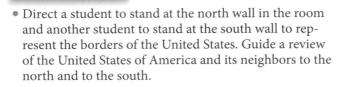

Vocabulary

- pledge

Content Word

- reminds

Introduction

- Direct a student to stand at the north wall in the room and another student to stand at the south wall to represent the borders of the United States. Guide a review of the United States of America and its neighbors to the north and to the south.

Teach for Understanding

- Guide the reading of page 70 to find out the meaning of the word *pledge.* a promise

  What is one symbol of the United States of America? the American flag

  What colors are in the American flag? red, white, and blue

  What do the stars on the American flag stand for? the fifty states

  What does the pledge remind you of? ideas important to our country

  What are some of those ideas? Answers might include that Americans believe in God and that Americans have liberty.

- Choose a volunteer to read aloud the caption beside the picture.

  Why is the flag being flown? It is Flag Day.

  Does your family own an American flag? How often does your family fly the American flag?

Your Country's Flag

The American flag is a symbol of the United States of America.
Symbols stand for things that are important.
The American flag is red, white, and blue.
Each star stands for one of the fifty states.
You say a pledge to the flag.
A **pledge** is a promise.
The pledge reminds you of the ideas that are important to your country.

Many Americans fly a flag on Flag Day.

70

The Pledge

I pledge allegiance to the flag
of the United States of America,
and to the republic for which
it stands,
one nation under God,
indivisible,
with liberty and justice for all.

What is a pledge?

a promise

71

- Instruct the students to follow the words on page 71 as you read the pledge together.
- Draw attention to the picture on the page.

  What are the children in the picture doing? saying the pledge to the American flag
- Introduce Visual 14.
- Explain that the government of the United States of America is called a republic. People in a republic choose others to make laws for them.

  What do you think "one nation" means? Americans work together to solve problems. They do not let problems divide them.
- Ask the students what they think it means to be a nation "under God." Elicit that it is similar to saying, "I live under my parents' rules."

  That means that your parents are in charge, and you are supposed to do what they say. So "under God" means that the nation believes in God and wants to be ruled by Him.
- Conclude the discussion by asking the question on page 71.

Activity Manual

- Guide completion of page 67.

Background

Flag Etiquette

When pledging to the American flag, you should stand at attention facing the flag and put your right hand over your heart. Men should remove their hats and hold them in their right hands over their hearts. The American flag should be flown higher than lesser flags.

Flag Day

Bernard J. Cigrand was a teacher who loved the American flag. He and others wanted to have a national holiday to honor the flag. They worked for many years to get the holiday. In 1949 President Truman signed an act of Congress designating June 14 as Flag Day.

Lesson 37

Student Text pages 72–73
Activity Manual page 69

Objectives

- Explain why the bald eagle was chosen as a symbol of the United States
- Identify "In God We Trust" as the motto of the United States
- Identify "The Star-Spangled Banner" as the official song of the United States

Materials

- Visual 15: *America's Symbols*
- Several coins

Vocabulary

- motto

Content Words

- "The Star-Spangled Banner"

Introduction

- Guide a review of the American flag. Invite several students to demonstrate pledging to the flag.

Teach for Understanding

- Guide the reading of page 72 to find out which bird is a symbol of the United States of America. the bald eagle
- Direct attention to the picture of the bald eagle. Choose a volunteer to describe the eagle.
- Read aloud the caption.
- Point out the picture of the bald eagle on Visual 15.

  Why was the bald eagle chosen as the symbol of the United States? It is strong and free like Americans.
- Point out the picture of the motto on the visual.

  What is a motto? an important saying

  What is the motto of the United States of America? "In God We Trust"

  What do you think the motto means? The United States of America believes in God.
- Direct attention to the coin. Read aloud the caption.

  What is this coin called? a penny
- Invite a student to move his finger across the motto on the penny.
- Distribute the coins you brought. Direct the students to find the mottoes on the coins.
- Mention that the American flag and the Statue of Liberty are also symbols of America.

Symbols of Your Country

The United States has many other symbols.
Your country has a **motto**.
A motto is an important saying.
"In God we trust" is the motto of the United States.

The motto is printed on your country's money.

The bald eagle is a symbol of your country.
An eagle is strong and free.

72

"The Star-Spangled Banner" is your country's song.
It is sung before sports games and at concerts.
People should stand when they hear "The Star-Spangled Banner."
They also put their hand over their heart.
Men and boys take off their hats.

"The Star-Spangled Banner"

What is a motto?

an important saying

73

- Guide the reading of page 73 to find the name of our nation's song. "The Star-Spangled Banner"

  When is "The Star-Spangled Banner" usually sung? before sports events and at concerts

  What should you do when you hear "The Star-Spangled Banner"? Stand and put your hand over your heart. Men and boys should take off their hats.
- Draw attention to the picture.

  What song is written on the sheet music? "The Star-Spangled Banner"
- Conclude the discussion by asking the question on page 73.

Activity Manual

- Guide completion of page 69.

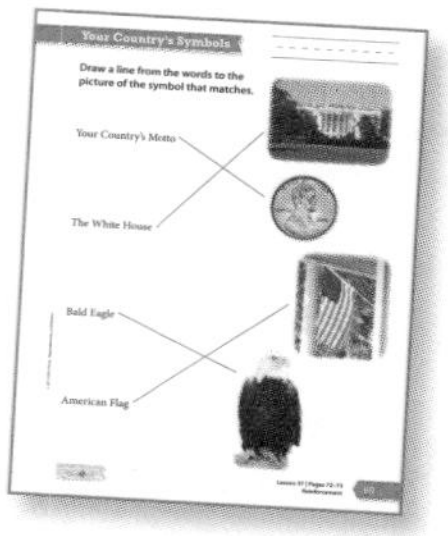

Background

"The Star-Spangled Banner"

Just before the British attack on Baltimore in 1814, lawyer and poet Francis Scott Key and Colonel John Skinner went out to a British ship to try to get Key's friend released from the British. Although the British agreed to release the friend, the men were forced to stay on the ship until the attack on Baltimore was over.

During the attack, the men could see Fort McHenry and the large American flag flying above it. Suddenly, the shelling stopped, and the sun began to rise. Key looked over to the fort and saw that the flag was still flying. He was inspired to write a poem about the flag and the battle. That poem became our national anthem. The flag that Key saw that morning is preserved today in the Smithsonian Institution.

Lesson

38

Student Text pages 74–75
Activity Manual page 71

Objectives

- Analyze the hymn "America the Beautiful"
- Name some of the landforms found in America
- Explain the importance of asking God's grace for our country

Materials

- Visuals 15–16: *America's Symbols; Geography of the United States*
- A recording of "America the Beautiful"

America's Symbols
Geography of the United States

Introduction

- Use Visual 15 to review the symbols of the United States of America.

Teach for Understanding

- Direct attention to page 74.

  The name of this lesson is the name of a song. The song "America the Beautiful" speaks of the geography of America.
- Play the recording of "America the Beautiful." Direct the students to follow along in their books as they listen. Sing together as you play the song again.
- Find two words on the page that describe the geography of America. *mountain* and *plain*
- Direct the students to turn to the Geogloss (pages 174–75) to find a mountain and a plain.
- Discuss the pictures on page 74.

  What kind of crop is growing in the field? wheat

  Can you think of other kinds of crops grown in fields? possible answers: corn, tomatoes, pumpkins, cotton

  Large fields of grains and other crops are grown in the middle part of the United States.

  What colors do you see in the picture of the mountains? pink, green, purple

America the Beautiful

O beautiful for spacious skies,
For amber waves of grain,

For purple mountain majesties
Above the fruited plain!

74

Background

"America the Beautiful"

Katherine Lee Bates was a teacher, poet, and author of several books. She wrote "America the Beautiful" in 1893 as she was taking a long trip to the state of Colorado. Some people think she thought of the poem while visiting Pike's Peak and then wrote it down later. Samuel Augustus Ward, composer and organist, wrote the melody used for the song in 1882. "America the Beautiful" was one of the songs considered for the national anthem.

America! America!
God shed His grace on thee,
And crown thy good with brotherhood
From sea to shining sea!
Do you live near an ocean or a mountain?
ocean or mountain or both or neither
75

- Point out the picture on page 75.

  What do you see in the picture? ocean waves, rocks, and a beach

- Encourage students to identify some landforms and bodies of water found in your state.
- Conclude the discussion by asking the question at the bottom of the page.
- Discuss each picture on Visual 16.

  Why do you think it is important for a country to have God's divine help? so God can protect the country from sin and bad times

  What are some bad times that we would want God to protect us from? possible answers: war, tornadoes, sickness

Activity Manual

- Guide completion of page 71.

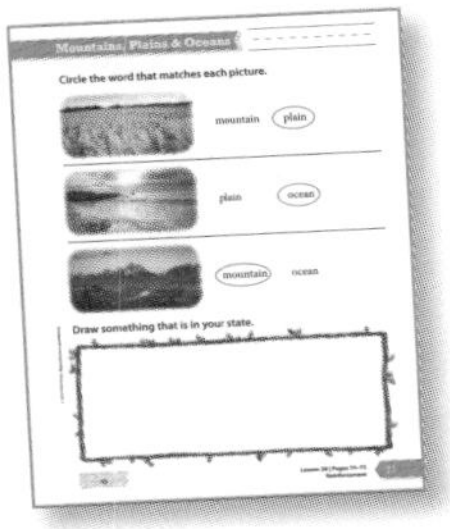

Lesson

39

Student Text pages 76–77
Activity Manual page 73

Objectives
- Identify the president as the leader of the United States
- Explain why the Constitution is important
- Identify the role of a judge
- Explain what a citizen is

Materials
- Visual 16: *Geography of the United States*

Vocabulary
- citizen
- right

Content Words
- Constitution
- lawmakers

Introduction
- Use Visual 16 to review the geographic features of the United States.

Teach for Understanding
- Guide the reading of page 76 to find out what the leader of our country is called. the president

  Where does the president live? in the White House

  Who else lives in the White House? the president's family

  The White House is located in Washington, DC.

  Who makes new laws? lawmakers

  Why does the United States have laws? to ensure justice; to make sure that its citizens are safe and treated fairly
- Guide a discussion about what is not safe or fair.

  Who helps decide whether or not people are following the laws? a judge
- Point out the picture on page 76.

  The Constitution is a set of laws telling the government what it can and cannot do.

  The government can hold elections, make laws, and protect its citizens from danger. The government cannot put people in jail for no reason or tell people they cannot go to church.

  The Constitution keeps the government doing what it should do, and it keeps the government from doing what it should not do.

  The Constitution does not give all the laws in our country. It just tells us the kinds of laws that are allowed.

  Which leaders must follow the Constitution? the president, lawmakers, and judges

Your Country's Leaders

The president is the leader of your country.
He lives with his family in the White House.
Lawmakers make new laws.
Laws help keep the country safe.
A judge decides if people are following the laws.
The Constitution is a set of laws.
The president, lawmakers, and judges must follow the Constitution.

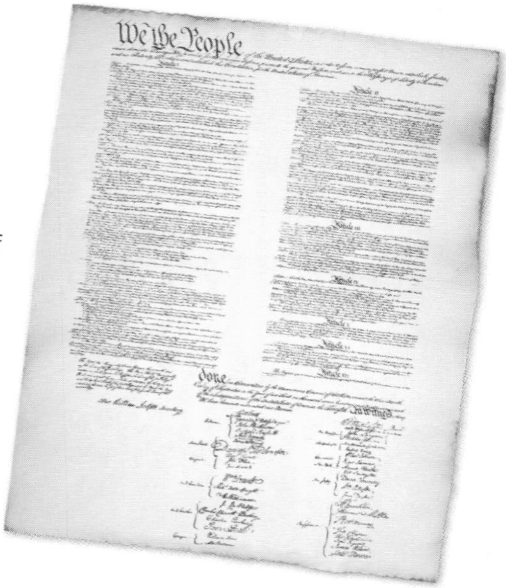

The Constitution of the United States of America

76

Citizens

A **citizen** is a member of a country.
You are a citizen of the United States of America if you are born here.
A person from another country can also become a citizen of the United States.
Citizens of a country have rights.
A **right** is something you are free to do.
Citizens also have a duty to their country.
Good citizens follow the laws of their country.
Laws make a country a better place to live.

New citizens of the United States

What is a citizen?

a member of a country

77

- Guide the reading of page 77 to find out what a citizen is. a member of a country

  How did you become a citizen of the United States? by being born in the United States or by being born to a citizen of the United States

- Include Background information about becoming a citizen as you discuss the picture.

  Can people from other countries become citizens of the United States? yes

  The picture shows people who are becoming new citizens of the United States.

- Discuss rights and citizenship. [BAT: 8b Faith in the power of the Word of God]

  What is a right? something you are free to do

  Rights also protect citizens from things like having their house or car searched without a good reason.

  What duty do Christian citizens of the United States have to their country? They must follow the laws of God and the Bible and obey the country's laws.

  Some people believe that God and the Bible should not be part of how we make laws or how judges make decisions. But all people are sinful. Only God is good and right. If we want our laws to be just and our decisions to be good, God must be part of lawmaking. Judges should pray for help, and lawmakers should read the Bible to know how to make good laws.

  What makes a country a better place to live? laws

- Conclude the discussion by asking the question on page 77.

Activity Manual

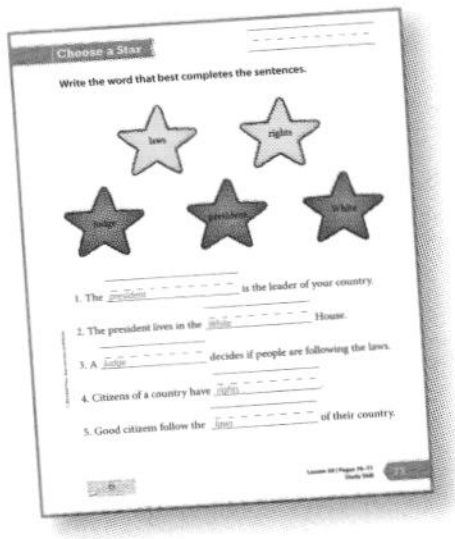

- Guide completion of page 73.

Background

The Constitution

The Constitution is the highest law in the country. All other laws come from the Constitution. The Constitution creates the Presidency, Congress, and the Supreme Court. The Constitution can be changed by an amendment. Among the amendments is a list of the rights of citizens of the United States. The first ten amendments are called the Bill of Rights.

Becoming a Citizen

In order to become a citizen of the United States, a person must have been a lawful permanent resident for three to five years, must be eighteen years old, must maintain continuous residence for five years, must be physically present in the United States for three to five years, must be a person of good moral character for three to five years, must demonstrate an elementary level of English, and must have knowledge and understanding of the fundamentals of the history and the government of the United States.

Lesson

40

Student Text pages 78–79

Objectives
- Explain why an election is held
- List the steps of a voting campaign
- Explain why voting is important

Materials
- *Class Ballot* (Teacher's Toolkit CD)

Vocabulary
- ballot
- election
- vote

Introduction

- Guide a review of the president, the Constitution, judges, citizens, and rights.

Teach for Understanding

- Guide the reading of page 78 to find out why a country has elections. to choose its leaders

  What does it mean to vote? to choose

  Why is it important to choose leaders wisely? so the leaders who are chosen are the ones who will do a good job
- Direct attention to the picture of the yard sign.

  Why do people who are trying to win an election give speeches and put signs on the roadsides and in yards during elections? They want people to vote for them.

  What is the first step in the voting process? People give speeches.

  What is the next step in the voting process? voting

  What is a ballot? a list of all the people wanting to be elected
- Direct attention to the ballot and explain how it is used.

  What happens after the voting is completed? All the votes are counted.

Elections

An **election** is held to choose new leaders.
Citizens choose or **vote** for their leaders.
They need to choose wisely.

Step 1: People give speeches.
They put their signs here and there.
They want people to vote for them.

Step 2: Citizens use a **ballot** to vote.
The ballot is a list of all the people who want to be elected.

Step 3: All the votes are counted.

This sign is in a yard.

78

Step 4: The people with the most votes become the new leaders.

The United States of America is the country God has given you to live in.

God wants you to be a good citizen of your country.

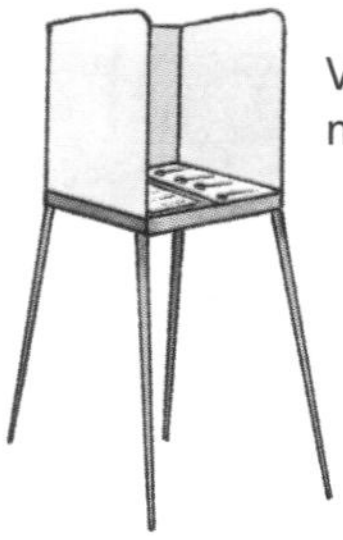

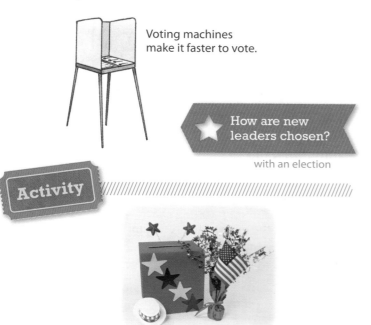

Voting machines make it faster to vote.

How are new leaders chosen?

with an election

Activity

79

- Guide the reading of page 79 to learn another step in the election process. Those with the most votes become the new leaders.
- Draw attention to the voting machine. Choose a student to read the caption aloud.

  You should be thankful for the country you live in and try to be a good citizen.
- Draw attention to the picture of the voting box.

  You will be taking part in an election in the next lesson.
- Conclude the discussion by asking the question on page 79.

Lesson 41

Chapter Activity
Activity Manual page 75

Objective
- Participate in a classroom election

Introduction

- Guide a review of the voting process.

Activity

Select the activities you would like to include for this lesson. You may prefer to extend the activity over several days. Choose two puppets or stuffed animals to run for "Puppet President."

Book

Materials
- *Duck for President* by Doreen Cronin and Betsy Lewin

Read the book aloud to the students to prepare them for the class election.

Voter Registration

Materials
- A 3 × 5 card for each student

Instruct each student to write his name, draw a picture of himself, write his birthday as his identification number, and include anything else of importance about himself on the card.

Posters

Materials
- Poster board or heavy paper

Choose partners to make posters for one of the puppets or stuffed animals.

Campaign Rally

Preparation
- Write a speech for each puppet or stuffed toy listed on the ballot.
- Display the posters.

Allow time for the puppets to present their speeches to the students.

Activity

Absentee Ballots

Materials

- *Class Ballot* (Teacher's Toolkit CD) Prepare 2–3 copies for each child.

Explain what an absentee ballot is. Give each child two ballots to take home. Instruct the students to explain the election to family members at home and ask them to complete an absentee ballot for the election and send it back to you.

Election

Materials

- *Class Ballot* (Teacher's Toolkit CD) Prepare a copy for each child.
- A box
- A class list

Invite a student to be a poll worker. Instruct him to sit at a desk and look at each voter's registration card and put a check by his name on the class list.

Direct each student to complete his ballot and drop it into the ballot box. Count the votes and absentee votes to determine the winner.

Acceptance Speech

Preparation

- Prepare a medal for the winner of the election. Hang the medal on a piece of string or yarn (optional).

Announce the winner of the election and place the medal around his neck. Allow the puppet to make an acceptance speech announcing "no homework for the night."

Activity Manual

- Guide completion of page 75.

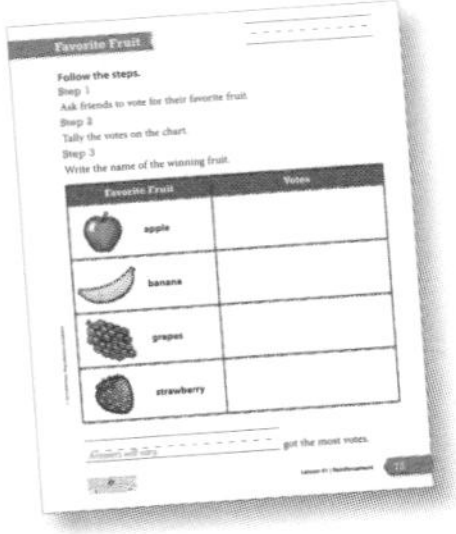

Chapter Review
Activity Manual page 77

Objective

- Recall concepts and terms from Chapter 5

Materials

- Star stickers or cutouts

Review

- Direct attention to the poem on page 66. Assign various groups of students to read the words *kaboom*, *crackle-pop*, and *sizzle-bang*. Then read the poem aloud, pausing for each group to shout their line when it is their turn.
- Guide a review of the Chapter 5 vocabulary by inviting the students to look up each word in the Picture Glossary.
- You may choose to review Chapter 5 by playing "American Stars." Ask a question from the material in this chapter. Award a star to the student who stands first and correctly answers the question. Allow each student to earn only one star in order to give everyone in the class the opportunity to participate. You may review any or all of the material during this lesson.

Activity Manual

- Guide completion of page 77.

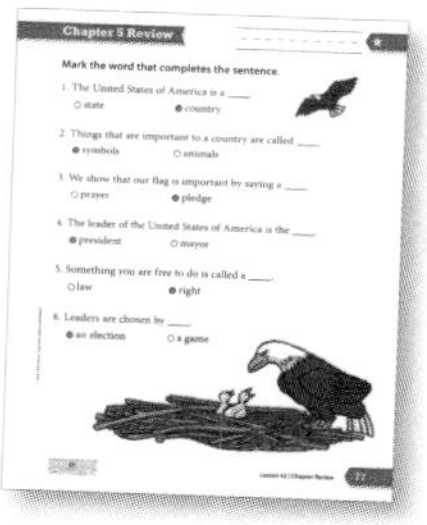

Chapter 5 Test

- Administer Test 5.

Chapter 6

Introduction

This chapter introduces students to the capital of the United States, Washington, DC. The students will learn to recognize buildings and monuments in the capital city. Students will study about important people and holidays associated with the monuments. An interactive map of Washington, DC, will be used to review the cardinal directions and locate monuments.

Star City

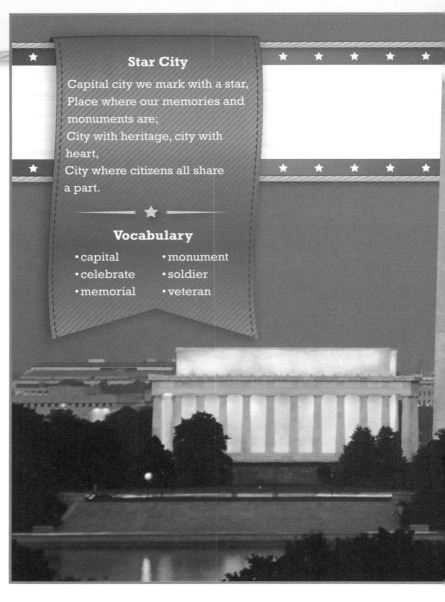

Capital city we mark with a star,
Place where our memories and monuments are;
City with heritage, city with heart,
City where citizens all share a part.

Vocabulary

- capital
- celebrate
- memorial
- monument
- soldier
- veteran

Chapter 6 Overview				
Lesson	**ST**	**AM**	**Content**	**Vocabulary**
43	80–83	79	Washington, DC, map study Capital of the United States, Washington, DC	capital
44	84–85	81	The White House, home of the president People who visit the White House	
45	86–87	83	The Washington Monument President George Washington Presidents' Day	celebrate monument
46			Washington Monument Activity	
47	88–89	85	The World War II Memorial Veterans Day	memorial soldier veteran
48	90–91	87	The Lincoln Memorial President Abraham Lincoln	
49	92–95	89	Independence Day Fourth of July parade in Washington, DC	
50		91	Chapter Review / Test	

Visit bjupress.com/resources for links to enhance the lessons.

Your Country's Capital 6

Prepare the *Landmarks in Washington, DC* visual by taping together Visuals 17 and 18. Punch out the five die-cut pieces from Visual 19 to be mounted on the map as directed in the lessons.

The interactive map will be used in each lesson of this chapter. The landmark pieces will be positioned and removed daily to reinforce the building shapes and building locations on the map.

Lesson 43

Student Text pages 80–83
Activity Manual page 79

Objectives

- Locate Washington, DC, on a map
- Classify Washington, DC, as an important city
- Identify the United States Capitol
- Associate the Capitol with government workers

Materials

- Visuals 17–19: *Landmarks in Washington, DC*
- A classroom map of the United States

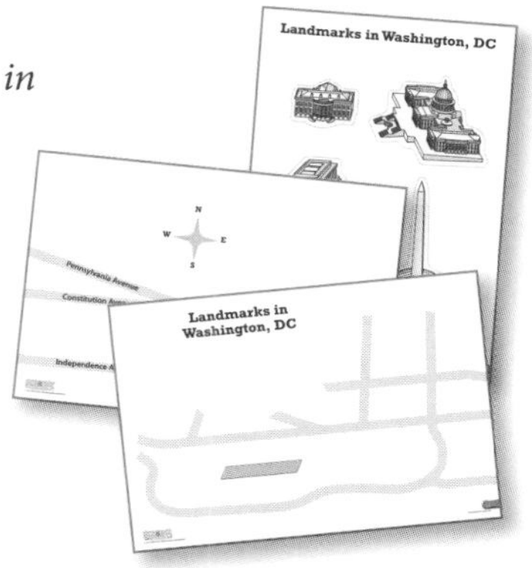

Vocabulary

- capital

Content Word

- Washington, DC

Introduction

- Direct attention to the Contents page. Read aloud the title of the chapter.

  We have been learning a lot about our state and our country.

- Ask a student to name the state he lives in.
- Point out the capitol building on page 55. Remind the students that each state has a capitol building. Generate interest in learning about the country's Capitol in Washington, DC.

Teach for Understanding

- Direct attention to the picture on pages 80–81. Choose a volunteer to read the title of the chapter.

  What does this picture show? buildings at night

  The picture is the capital city of the United States of America, Washington, DC. We will learn about these buildings in this chapter.

- Read aloud the poem "Star City."

  On a map a capital city is represented by a star.

- Point out Washington, DC, on a classroom map.
- Generate interest in the vocabulary words the students will learn in this chapter. Remind the students that the words can be found in the Picture Glossary.
- Display the word *capital*. Instruct the students to find the word *capital* in the Picture Glossary. Choose a volunteer to read the definition. Follow the same procedure with the word *capitol*.

  What vowel in the last syllable is different in the spelling of these two words? *a* and *o* What is the difference in the meaning of the two words? *Capital* is a city; *capitol* is a building.

Lesson 43

- Mention that the capitol building pictured in the glossary has a dome, or a rounded top.

  The words *capitol* and *dome* both have an *o* in them. Remembering the *o* in *dome* will help you spell *capitol* correctly.

- Read the section title on page 82. Point out the aerial view of Washington, DC. Explain that an aerial photo looks as if it were taken from an airplane. Invite students to identify things they see in the picture.
- Guide the reading of the page.
- Prepare a word web. Write *Washington, DC* in the center oval. Ask questions from the reading to complete the word web.

  What do we call the city of Washington, DC? the capital; the capital city of the United States of America

  What kind of city is it? an important city in America

  Which government is run in Washington, DC? the United States government

  Who works in Washington, DC? many government leaders

  What can people visit in Washington, DC? special buildings

Washington, DC

The **capital** of the United States of America is Washington, DC.
It is a very important city in America.
The United States government is run here.
Many government leaders work here.
You can visit many special buildings in the capital city.

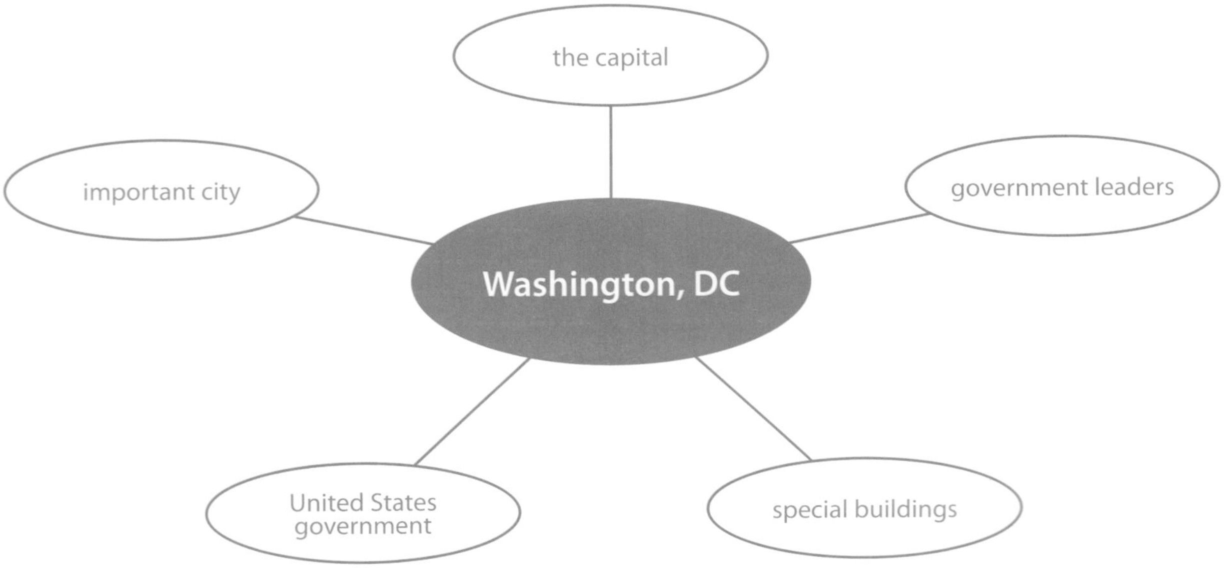

The Capitol Building

The United States Capitol Building
is in Washington, DC.
The Capitol is the building
where lawmakers work.
Lawmakers use the Constitution
to make laws for the country.

United States Capitol

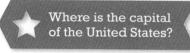

Where is the capital of the United States?

Washington, DC

83

- Read the title on page 83. Point out the photo of the United States Capitol Building.

  On the previous page we read about our country's capital city, Washington, DC. On this page we will read about our country's Capitol Building, the United States Capitol.

- Guide the reading of the page.

  In what building do the government leaders, or lawmakers, work? the United States Capitol

  What important set of laws is used in our country? the Constitution

- Display the map (Visuals 17–18) and the Capitol landmark from Visual 19. Point out the main streets in Washington, DC, as you introduce the map.

  There are many special buildings in the capital city. The United States Capitol Building is located on the east side of the city between Pennsylvania Avenue and Independence Avenue. It is on a hill called Capitol Hill.

- Guide a student as he locates and positions the Capitol Building on the map.
- Conclude the discussion by asking the question on page 83.

Activity Manual

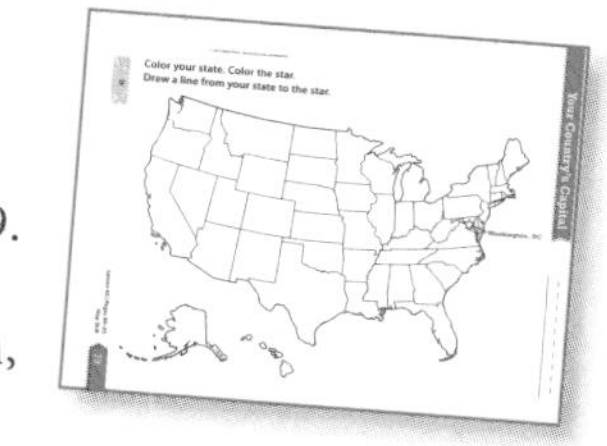

- Assist the students as they find their state on the map on page 79. Direct the students to color their state and the star for Washington, DC. Instruct them to draw a line from their state to the capital of the United States as they complete the page.

Background

The Capital

The capital city was planned by Pierre Charles L'Enfant. L'Enfant used the compass rose to plan the city in a north, south, east, and west grid pattern. When you stand on the steps of the United States Capitol today, you can look west and see the Washington Monument. The plan was later perfected by Andrew Ellicott and Benjamin Banneker.

The capital city is located between Virginia and Maryland. *DC* stands for the District of Columbia, named after Christopher Columbus.

The Capitol

The original designer of the Capitol was William Thornton. George Washington chose Thornton's plan because of its simplicity and beauty. Construction of the Capitol began in 1793. The building was first used in 1800. It has been rebuilt and remodeled as needs have changed over the years. It is made of marble. It is 289 feet high, and it has 540 rooms. The Statue of Freedom stands on top of the dome. Today the Capitol houses the Senate and House of Representatives.

Inside the Capitol is the Congressional Prayer Room. This room is set apart for government leaders to pray for the country and important decisions they are making. In the room is a stained-glass window of George Washington kneeling in prayer. Around him are words from the Bible: "Preserve me, O God: for in thee do I put my trust" (Psalm 16:1). [BAT: 6b Prayer]

"In God we trust" is inscribed in both house chambers.

Lesson

44

Student Text pages 84–85
Activity Manual page 81

Objectives

- Identify the White House as the home of the president and his family
- Locate the White House in Washington, DC
- Explain why people visit the White House

Materials

- Visuals 17–19: *Landmarks in Washington, DC; Capitol, White House*

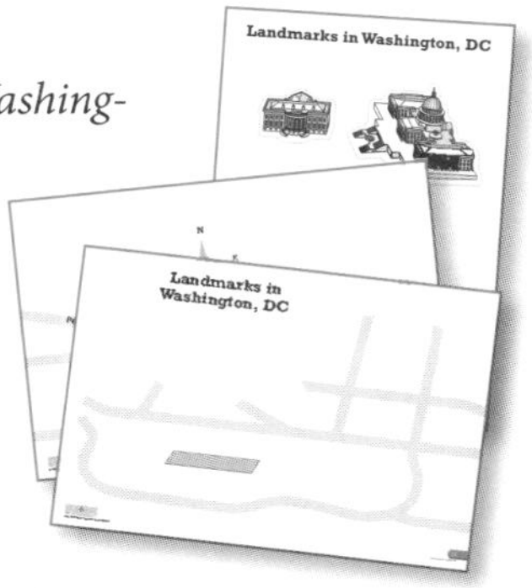

Introduction

- Display the map (Visuals 17–18) and the Capitol landmark from Visual 19.

  The title of the map tells what the map is about. This map is about landmarks, important buildings or monuments in Washington, DC.

  What city is shown on this map? Washington, DC

  What is special about Washington, DC? It is the capital of the United States.

  What building do our lawmakers work in? the Capitol
- Invite a student to place the Capitol on the map.

Teach for Understanding

- Direct attention to page 84. Choose a volunteer to read the title. Direct attention to the photo.

  What house is pictured on the page? the White House
- Invite a volunteer to read the caption.

  What does the caption tell you about the White House? Many people visit the White House.

  Who are the people in the picture? visitors
- Guide the reading of the page. Explain that the president of the United States is the leader of the United States of America. While he is president, he lives in the White House.

  Who lives in the White House with the president? his family

  Who can visit the White House? people from all over the world; students from the classroom
- Ask the students why they think people visit the White House. Point out that the White House is a very beautiful building.

  Many people from around the country and around the world come to see the building. Other people come hoping to get a glimpse of one of the most powerful men in the world, the president.
- Display the White House landmark from Visual 19. Point out the White House on page 84. Compare the two images.

The White House

The president's house is in Washington, DC.
It is called the White House.
The president and his family live there.
People from all over the world visit
the White House.
You can visit it too.

Many people visit the White House.

84

  Do the buildings look exactly the same? no
- Guide a comparison of the two images to determine how they are different.

  Does the front of your house look exactly like the back of your house? The north face of the White House is pictured in your book. It has a square porch. The south face of the White House is on the visual. It has a rounded porch. The White House has two faces, or fronts.
- Instruct a volunteer to locate and position the White House on the map.

  The south face of the White House is located on Pennsylvania Avenue.

  Trace your finger from the Capitol along Pennsylvania Avenue. Place the White House on the map.

  The yellow cross on the map is a compass rose. It shows the directions north, south, east, and west.

  What does the *N* stand for on the compass rose? north
- Follow the same procedure with the directions south, east, and west.

  What building is on the east side of the map? the Capitol

  What building is on the north side of the map? the White House

Children in the White House

The president's children have favorite foods.
Sasha Obama likes ice cream.
The president's children can have a pet.
Young Ted Roosevelt had a bird named Eli.
Children can play hide-and-seek in the 132 rooms of the White House.
Little John Kennedy liked to hide under the desk in the president's office.

Sasha Obama

Ted Roosevelt Jr.

John Kennedy Jr.

★ Where does the president live?

the White House; Washington, DC

85

- Direct attention to page 85. Invite a student to read the title.

  What will you read about on this page? children in the White House

  What do all these children have in common? Their father was the president; they lived in the White House.

- Read the names of the children. Guide the reading of the page.

  The children who live in the White House have favorite foods, own pets, and like to play just as you do.

  What kind of food does Sasha Obama like? ice cream What is your favorite ice cream?

  Who had a pet named Eli? Ted Roosevelt Jr. What kind of pet was Eli? a bird Do you have a pet?

  Who liked to play hide-and-seek in the White House? John Kennedy Jr. Where did he like to hide? under his father's desk Where do you like to hide when you play hide-and-seek?

  Do you think these are the only children who have lived in the White House? No, many presidents' children have lived in the White House.

- Conclude the discussion by asking the question on page 85.

Activity Manual

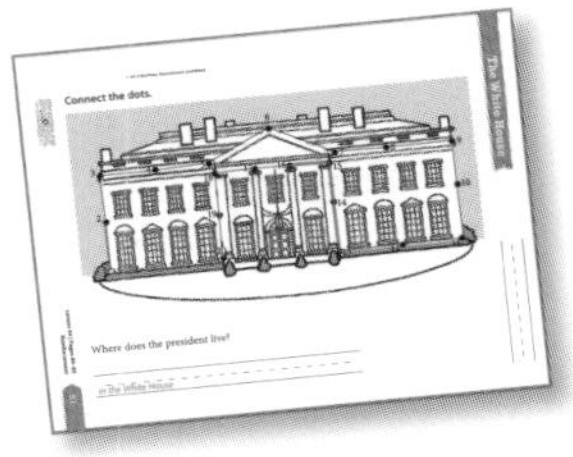

- Guide completion of page 81. Mention that the front of the White House faces north. Ask a student whether the porch on this page is round or square.

Background

The White House

The White House is a symbol of the president. It has been the home of the president since 1800. The president is called Mr. President, and his wife is often called the First Lady. The president and his family have special gatherings, celebrate birthdays, and spend holidays in the White House.

The Oval Office is the room in which the president works. It is named for its oval shape. Each president redecorates the office to suit his personal tastes. The Oval Office is often used by the president when he addresses the people of the United States. He entertains foreign leaders there. (*Note:* In the student text, President Kennedy is pictured working in the Oval Office.)

The White House has 132 rooms with 35 bathrooms, 412 doors, 147 windows, 28 fireplaces, 8 staircases, and 3 elevators. A tennis court, track, swimming pool, movie theater, and bowling lane are also inside the house.

Tours of the White House are by request through a member of Congress. Requests must be made in advance. All White House tours are free. People who are not citizens must go through their embassy.

About the Photo

The photo of Sasha Obama was taken on Father's Day when President Barak Obama took his two daughters, Malia and Sasha, to an ice-cream shop in Washington, DC.

Lesson 45

Student Text pages 86–87
Activity Manual page 83

Objectives

- Name the tallest monument in Washington, DC
- List reasons that a monument was built to honor George Washington
- Associate George Washington's birthday with the celebration of Presidents' Day

Materials

- Visuals 17–20: *Landmarks in Washington, DC*; *Capitol, White House, Washington Monument*; *President George Washington*

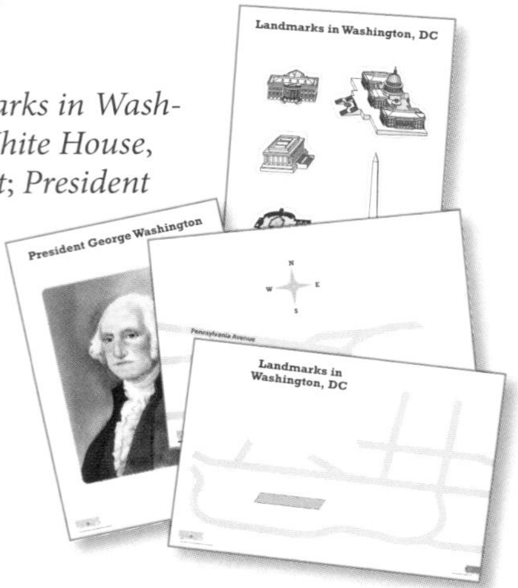

Vocabulary

- celebrate
- monument

Content Word

- countrymen

Introduction

- Display the map (Visuals 17–18).

  What city is shown on this map? Washington, DC

  What is special about Washington, DC? It is the capital of the United States.

  What building do our lawmakers work in? the Capitol

- Invite a student to place the Capitol on the map. Direct another student to place the White House in position.

  What building does the president live and work in? the White House

Teach for Understanding

- Direct attention to pages 86–87. (*Note:* The buildings pictured here are the National Museum of Natural History, the Washington Monument, and the Capitol.)

  A monument can be a stone or a metal statue that stands for an important person or an important event in the past. In Washington, DC, monuments have been built that remind us of presidents and other important people. Some of these people fought in wars. These monuments can also be called memorials because they help us remember people and times in the past.

- Instruct the students to read the title on page 86 and look at the picture and predict what the page is about.
- Guide the reading of the page. Display the Washington Monument landmark from Visual 19.

  What is a monument? something built that stands for a person in the past

  What is the tallest monument in Washington, DC? the Washington Monument

  What is the Washington Monument made of? stone

The Washington Monument

A **monument** is something built that stands for a person in the past.
The Washington Monument is the tallest monument in Washington, DC.
It is made from stone.
There are fifty American flags around the bottom of the monument.
The Washington Monument reminds us of a great man, George Washington.

What is the tallest monument in Washington, DC?

the Washington Monument

86

How many American flags surround the monument? fifty

What great man does the monument remind us of? George Washington

Background

The Washington Monument

The Washington Monument stands in the mall area of Washington, DC, between Constitution Avenue and Independence Avenue. It is the tallest monument in the city.

The Washington Monument was built in honor of the first president, George Washington. Construction of the monument was completed in 1884. It is about 555 feet tall and weighs 81,120 tons. The walls are made of white marble, which was quarried mostly from Maryland. There are 896 steps from the ground floor to the top of the monument. From a window at the top, you can see over the city. The Washington Monument stands tall and grand but is very simple and stately in design like the man, George Washington.

The Latin phrase *Laus Deo*, "Praise be to God," is inscribed on the top of the monument. Other Scripture references are carved in blocks along the stairway: "Holiness to the Lord" (Exodus 28:36), "Search the Scriptures" (John 5:39), and "The memory of the just is blessed" (Proverbs 10:7).

George Washington
The American people loved George Washington.
It is said that he was "first in war, first in peace, and first in the hearts of his countrymen."
God gave us a wise man to be the first president of the United States.
America **celebrates** his birthday in February on Presidents' Day.
87

- Direct attention to page 87. Choose a volunteer to read the title.

  The Washington Monument was built to honor George Washington.

- Guide the reading of the page to find out why a monument would be built in his honor.
- Write *George Washington* for display. Write the word *first* three times under the name.

  George Washington

  First *in war*

  First *in peace*

  First *in the hearts . . .*

- List the three ways that George Washington was first as students dictate.
- Explain that "first in war" refers to the fact that George Washington led the first army. "First in peace" is a reference to his being the first president of the United States of America. The country had peace after war. And he was loved by Americans: "first in the hearts of his countrymen."
- Guide a discussion of George Washington using Visual 20.

  George Washington lived in his family home called Mount Vernon. He loved his family, his home, and his country. He was a soldier, a writer of the Constitution, and the country's first president. He is known as the Father of our Country.

- Direct attention to the map (Visuals 17–18). Choose a volunteer to point to the Capitol and then place the Washington Monument on the map.

  Pretend that you are standing on the steps of the Capitol and looking west. You would be able to see the Washington Monument rising tall in front of you several blocks away. If you were standing on the south face of the White House looking south, you would also be able to see the Washington Monument.

- Direct attention to the map on pages 94–95. Instruct the students to respond to the questions you ask by pointing to the answer on the map.

  What is the title of the map? *Landmarks in Washington, DC*

  Point to the yellow cross on the map. The cross is called a compass rose.

  What do the letters *N*, *S*, *E*, and *W* represent? north, south, east, and west

  Point to the north part of the map. What building is there? the White House

  What monument is south of the White House? the Washington Monument

  What building is east of the Washington Monument? the Capitol

- Conclude the discussion by asking the question on page 86.

Activity Manual

- Guide completion of page 83.

Background

George Washington

Henry Lee eulogized George Washington with these famous words: "First in war, first in peace, and first in the hearts of his countrymen." George Washington was the first commander-in-chief of the Continental army. Lord Cornwallis surrendered to Washington at Yorktown, thus ending the Revolutionary War and bringing peace to the country. Washington was elected the first president of the United States under the Constitution. He was born on February 22, 1732, and died on December 14, 1799.

Presidents' Day

The federal holiday designated to commemorate Washington's birthday is commonly known as Presidents' Day. Although George Washington was born on February 22, Presidents' Day is celebrated on the third Monday in February. Many Americans also honor Abraham Lincoln on Presidents' Day. In some states all presidents are honored on Presidents' Day.

Lesson

46 Chapter Activity

Objectives

- Assemble a model of the Washington Monument
- Locate the Capitol, the White House, and the Washington Monument on a map of Washington, DC

Materials

- Visuals 17–19, 21: *Landmarks in Washington, DC*; *Capitol*, *White House*, *Washington Monument*; *Compass Rose*
- *Washington, DC* (Teacher's Toolkit CD)
- *Washington Monument* (Teacher's Toolkit CD)
- A sheet of green construction paper
- A 3 × 6 section of foil
- A completed model of the Washington Monument prepared for the activity

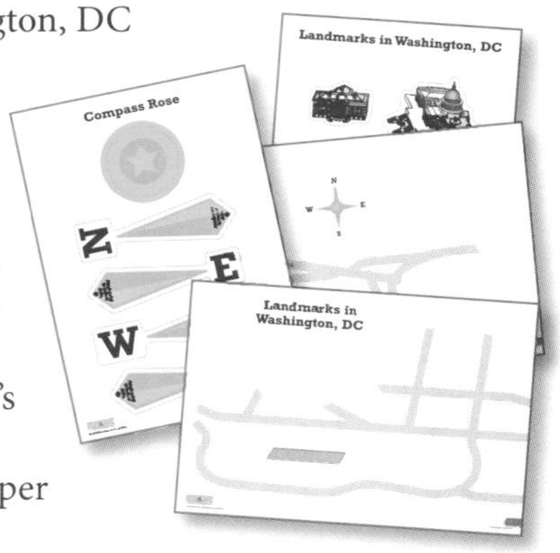

Introduction

- Display the map (Visuals 17–18) and the Capitol, White House, and Washington Monument landmarks from Visual 19.

  What is the title of this map? *Landmarks in Washington, DC*

  What is special about Washington, DC? It is the capital of the United States.

  What symbol gives directions? the yellow cross, or compass rose

- Give the die-cut pieces from Visual 21 to four students. Direct the students to stand at four points in the room. Invite students to identify the abbreviation for each of the four directions (north, south, east, and west).

You may designate the front of the classroom as north, or you may find actual north and use that point as a reference. The activity is intended for practice using the compass rose.

Activity

- Ask a student to identify the building where lawmakers work. the Capitol Choose a volunteer to place the Capitol on the Washington, DC, map.

  If you stand on the Capitol steps and look west, what tall monument can you see? the Washington Monument

- Direct another student to place the Washington Monument on the map.

  What special house is north of the Washington Monument? the White House

  Why is this house special? The president lives and works in the White House.

- Invite a student to affix the White House to the map.

Teach for Understanding

- Direct attention to the map on pages 94–95.

  The area around the Washington Monument is commonly called the Mall. There are several monuments in the mall area. There is also a pool of water there. The blue rectangle on the map represents the water commonly called the Reflecting Pool. The pool shows, or reflects, the image of the Washington Monument.

- Display the model of the Washington Monument that you prepared.

> The model pictured on page 94 is intended for demonstration purposes. It is not made to scale.

- Conclude the activity by reading the poem "Washington, DC" from the Teacher's Toolkit CD.

Background

The National Mall

The National Mall is a national park in downtown Washington, DC. The Mall includes the area from the Lincoln Memorial to the Capitol. The National Park Service cares for the buildings and monuments within the park or mall area.

The Lincoln Memorial Reflecting Pool reflects the Lincoln Memorial and the Washington Monument. It is located between the two. The pool is 2,029 feet long and 167 feet wide and has a depth of approximately 18 inches.

Lesson 47

Student Text pages 88–89
Activity Manual page 85

Objectives
- Locate on a map of Washington, DC, the Capitol, the White House, the Washington Monument, and the World War II Memorial
- Define *veteran*
- Explain the importance of Veterans Day

Materials
- Visuals 17–19: *Landmarks in Washington, DC; Capitol, White House, Washington Monument, World War II Memorial*

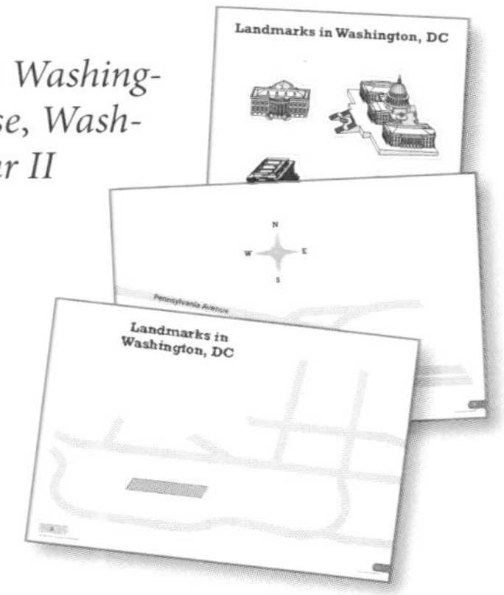

Vocabulary
- memorial
- soldier
- veteran

Content Word
- armed forces

Introduction

- Display the map (Visuals 17–18) and the Capitol, White House, and Washington Monument landmarks from Visual 19. Invite students to point to the answer on the map.

  What part of a map tells what the map is about? the title

  What is the title of this map? *Landmarks in Washington, DC*

  What shows directions on a map? the yellow cross or compass rose

  What are the four letters on the compass rose and the directions they represent? *N*, north; *S*, south; *E*, east; *W*, west

  What is the building where lawmakers work? the Capitol

  What tall monument is west of the Capitol? the Washington Monument

  What monument honors President George Washington? the Washington Monument

  What special house is north of the Washington Monument? the White House

  Why is this house special? The president lives and works in the White House.

Teach for Understanding

- Direct attention to page 88. Read the title and discuss the picture.

  This is a picture of the World War II Memorial.

  A memorial is something built that helps us remember a person or an event from the past. World War II was a war fought years ago to protect America from its enemies.

World War II Memorial

A **memorial** helps you remember people or times from the past.
The World War II Memorial reminds you of the many **soldiers** who served in that war.
These soldiers loved America and helped to keep their country safe.

88

What is a soldier? a person who serves in a war

This page tells us about how we remember the soldiers who fought in World War II.

- Guide the reading of the page.

  What does the World War II Memorial remind us of? the many soldiers who served in that war

  Who loved their country and helped to keep it safe? soldiers

Background

The World War II Memorial

The World War II Memorial honors Americans who served during World War II. It has fifty-six granite pillars representing the states, United States territories, and Washington, DC. The two arches represent war operations in the Pacific and the Atlantic. A fountain is in the middle of the pillars. The memorial is located between the Washington Monument and the Reflecting Pool. It opened in 2004.

Veterans Day

On November 11, America celebrates Veterans Day.

A **veteran** is someone who has served our country in the armed forces.

America honors war veterans with parades on this special day.

A veteran from World War II

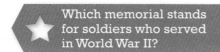

Which memorial stands for soldiers who served in World War II?

the World War II Memorial

89

- Direct attention to page 89. Invite a student to read the title and another student to read the caption.

  Who is in the picture? a veteran from World War II

  All veterans from World War II are older like this man, but not all veterans are this old. Some veterans fought in later wars. Veterans can be any age over 18. Veterans are men and women who have served in the armed forces. *Armed forces* is the name for all the men and women who fight on the land, on the sea, and in the air.
- Guide the reading of the page.

  What do Americans celebrate on November 11? Veterans Day Who do we honor on Veterans Day? veterans; those who have served in the armed forces

  Why do Americans have parades on Veterans Day? to honor veterans, or those who served in the armed forces
- Explain the importance of celebrating Veterans Day.

  When we celebrate Veterans Day, we show veterans that we are thankful for their willingness to die if necessary for their country. We can also thank God for keeping our country safe.

- Direct attention to the map (Visuals 17–18).

  The World War II Memorial is between the Washington Monument and the Reflecting Pool.
- Direct a volunteer to place the World War II Memorial on the map.
- Conclude the discussion by asking the question on page 89.

Activity Manual

- Guide completion of page 85.

Background

Veterans Day

Veterans Day is celebrated on November 11 to honor those who have served in the military both in wartime and in peacetime. On that day we thank the men and women who are still alive for their service, and we acknowledge those who have died. Every veteran has made a sacrifice for our country.

The idea of having a day to honor our veterans began in 1919 when President Wilson made November 11 a day to honor veterans of World War I, calling it Armistice Day. In 1938 the name of the day was changed to Veterans Day to include American veterans of all wars.

Although no Scripture is engraved on the World War II Memorial, in Governor Tim Pawlenty's dedication speech on June 9, 2007, he quoted from the Bible.

> In the Scripture, the Lord asks, "Whom shall I send? And who will go for us?"
>
> Isaiah responded by saying, "Here am I, send me!"
>
> In the defining moments of this glorious nation, our character, our resolve, and our collective soul have been tested.
>
> In those moments, the country has asked: Who shall we send? And who will go for us?
>
> Our heroes, the brave men and women in our United States military, always answer that call by saying: Here am I, send me.
>
> We thank God for these heroes, and we pray that each of us has the courage to live a life worthy of their legacy.

Lesson 48

Student Text pages 90–91
Activity Manual page 87

Objectives
- Describe the Lincoln Memorial
- Locate places on a map of Washington, DC
- Identify Abraham Lincoln as a president
- Associate Abraham Lincoln's birthday with the celebration of Presidents' Day

Materials
- Visuals 17–19, 21–22: *Landmarks in Washington, DC*; *Capitol*, *White House*, *Washington Monument*, *World War II Memorial*, *Lincoln Memorial*; *Compass Rose*; *President Abraham Lincoln*

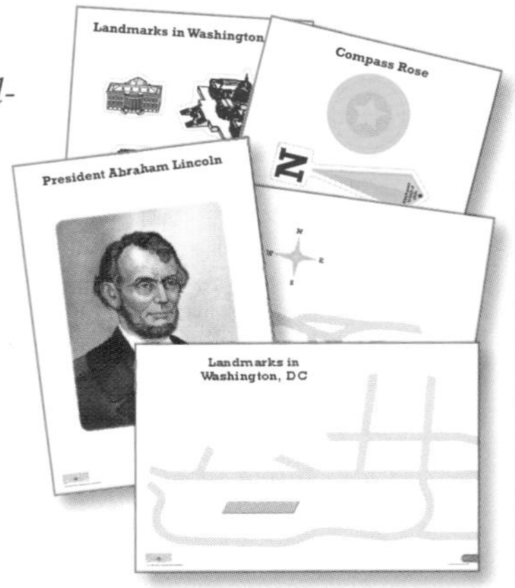

Content Word
- giant

Introduction

- Use the visuals to review Washington, DC, landmarks. Then give the compass rose pieces from Visual 21 to four students. Explain that students will make a room map to show Washington, DC. Establish the front of the room as north (or find true north). Instruct the student with the piece labeled *N* to stand at the north point. Direct the other three students to align themselves properly in the room to form a compass rose. Ask each student to tell whether he is standing at the south, east, or west point of the room.
- Distribute the landmark visuals: the Capitol, the White House, the Washington Monument, and the World War II Memorial. Direct the student holding the Washington Monument to find his place in the room. (*Note:* The Washington Monument is in the center of the four students representing the cardinal directions.) Guide each student as he finds his place on the room map.

  Which building is closest to the north point? the White House

  Which building is closest to the east point? the Capitol

  Which monument is south of the White House? the Washington Monument

  Which memorial is west of the Washington Monument? the World War II Memorial
- Choose volunteers to move north, south, east, and west among the monuments as you give directions.

Teach for Understanding

- Read the title on page 90. Discuss the picture of the Lincoln Memorial. Explain that this memorial honors President Abraham Lincoln.

Lincoln Memorial

The Lincoln Memorial honors President
Abraham Lincoln.
The stone building is very large.
The huge statue of President Lincoln is inside.
He is sitting in a big chair.
He looks like he is thinking.
You feel small when you look at the giant
statue of Mr. Lincoln.

90

- Encourage the students to notice words that describe the size of the Lincoln Memorial as they read the page.
- Prepare a word wheel with space to write descriptive words. Write *Lincoln Memorial* in the center of the wheel. Ask questions from the reading to complete the word wheel.

  What words describe the stone building? *very large*

  What words describe the statue of President Lincoln? *huge; giant*

  What word describes the chair that Mr. Lincoln is sitting in? *big*

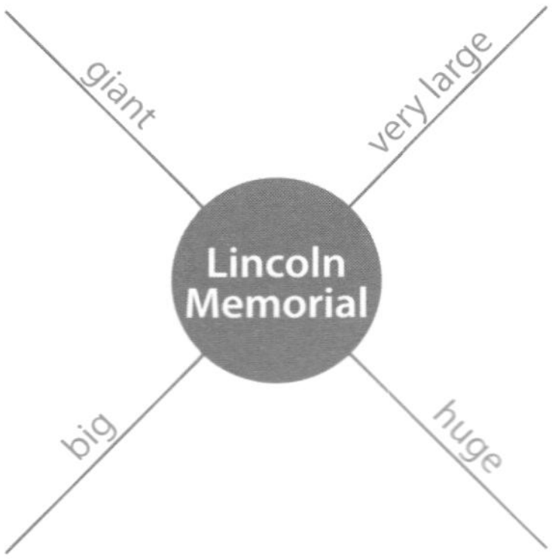

Abraham Lincoln

Abraham Lincoln was the sixteenth president of the United States.
He grew up in a log cabin.
He loved to read.
People trusted Mr. Lincoln because he was honest.
He is called Honest Abe.

What memorial honors President Lincoln?

the Lincoln Memorial

91

- Direct attention to page 91. Ask a student to read the title.

  Will this section be about the Lincoln Memorial? no What is the difference between this title and the title on page 90? Page 90 is about the memorial. Page 91 is about the person, Abraham Lincoln.
- Instruct students to read the page silently.
- Adapt the word wheel to describe Abraham Lincoln.
- Ask students to read aloud the sentences that name things about Mr. Lincoln to complete the word wheel. sixteenth president; grew up in a log cabin; loved to read; called Honest Abe

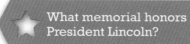

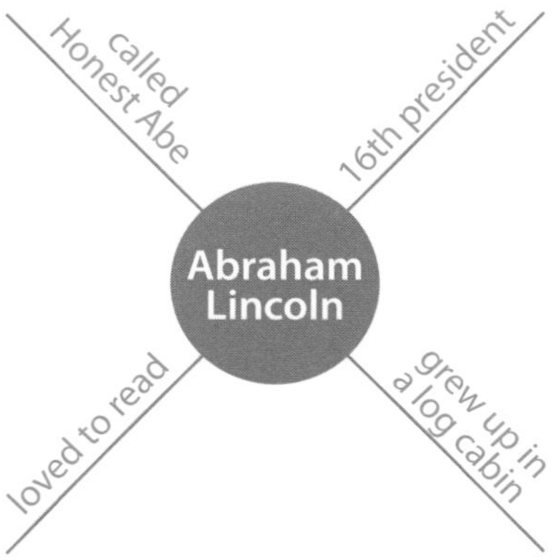

Which sentences tell you that he was known for telling the truth? "People trusted Mr. Lincoln because he was honest. He is called Honest Abe."

- Direct attention to the map (Visuals 17–18).

  The Lincoln Memorial is west of the World War II Memorial beside the Reflecting Pool.
- Invite a student to place the Lincoln Memorial landmark on the map.
- Introduce Visual 22.

  Abraham Lincoln's birthday is February 12. Many people honor him on the third Monday in February, which is often called Presidents' Day.
- Conclude the discussion by asking the question on page 91.

Activity Manual

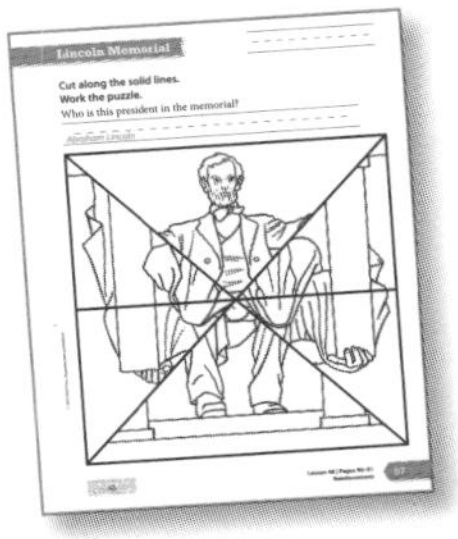

- Guide completion of page 87.

Background

The Lincoln Memorial

The sculpture of Lincoln seated in a chair is 19 feet tall and 19 feet wide and weighs 175 tons. It is made of 28 separate blocks of white marble. Lincoln's kind face looks down at all who enter the building.

The temple-like building is constructed of marble and limestone. Thirty-six columns surround the memorial, representing the states in the Union at the time of Lincoln's death. The building is about 190 feet long, 119 feet wide, and almost 100 feet high. Paintings of Lincoln's life are on the walls, as well as inscriptions of Lincoln's Gettysburg Address and his Second Inaugural Address.

These words in Psalm 19:9 from Lincoln's Second Inaugural Address are inscribed on the walls: "the judgments of the Lord are true and righteous altogether."

Abraham Lincoln

Abraham Lincoln was born on February 12, 1809, in Kentucky. His home state is Illinois. He married Mary Todd, and they raised four children, Robert Todd Lincoln, Edward Lincoln, Willie Lincoln, and Tad Lincoln. Only Robert Todd lived to adulthood.

Abraham Lincoln loved reading and was self-educated. He was a storekeeper, lawyer, state legislator, and United States representative before becoming president. As president during the Civil War, Lincoln ended slavery. The Gettysburg Address is his most famous speech. President Lincoln was assassinated by actor John Wilkes Booth and died on April 15, 1865, at the age of 56.

Lesson

49

Student Text pages 92–95
Activity Manual page 89

Objectives

- Use cardinal directions to locate places on a map
- Locate places on a map of Washington, DC
- Explain the significance of the Fourth of July holiday

Materials

- Visuals 17–19, 21: *Landmarks in Washington, DC*; *Capitol, White House, Washington Monument, World War II Memorial, Lincoln Memorial; Compass Rose*
- *Landmarks in Washington, DC* (Teacher's Toolkit CD)

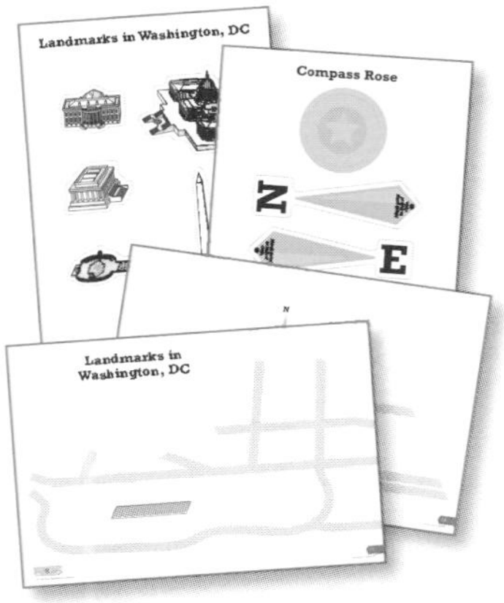

Content Word

- England

Introduction

Chapter 6 has been a study of buildings, monuments, and memorials located in our capital city, Washington, DC. We have also studied people and holidays as they are related to these special places. Today we will look at another holiday and review the map of Washington, DC.

Teach for Understanding

- Direct attention to page 92. Read the title.

What is a parade? possible answer: people dressed in costumes, marching bands, fire trucks, and famous people going through a town while people are watching and cheering

Independence Day is a special day when Americans celebrate the day that men in this country signed a paper called the Declaration of Independence. The paper declared that the colonies would separate from England. The Declaration declared independence. That day is called Independence Day, or the Fourth of July.

- Guide the reading of page 92.

How is Independence Day celebrated in Washington, DC? with a parade

What does the Fourth of July parade celebrate? America's freedom from England

On what day do we celebrate Independence Day? July 4

Who is in the top picture? soldiers marching in a parade

What building are they marching in front of? the Capitol

Who is marching in the bottom picture? boys dressed in costumes and carrying flags

The boys dressed in colonial costumes are marching in front of the Jefferson Memorial.

What is another name for Independence Day? the Fourth of July

Independence Day Parade

A parade takes place in Washington, DC, on July 4. The parade celebrates America's freedom from England.

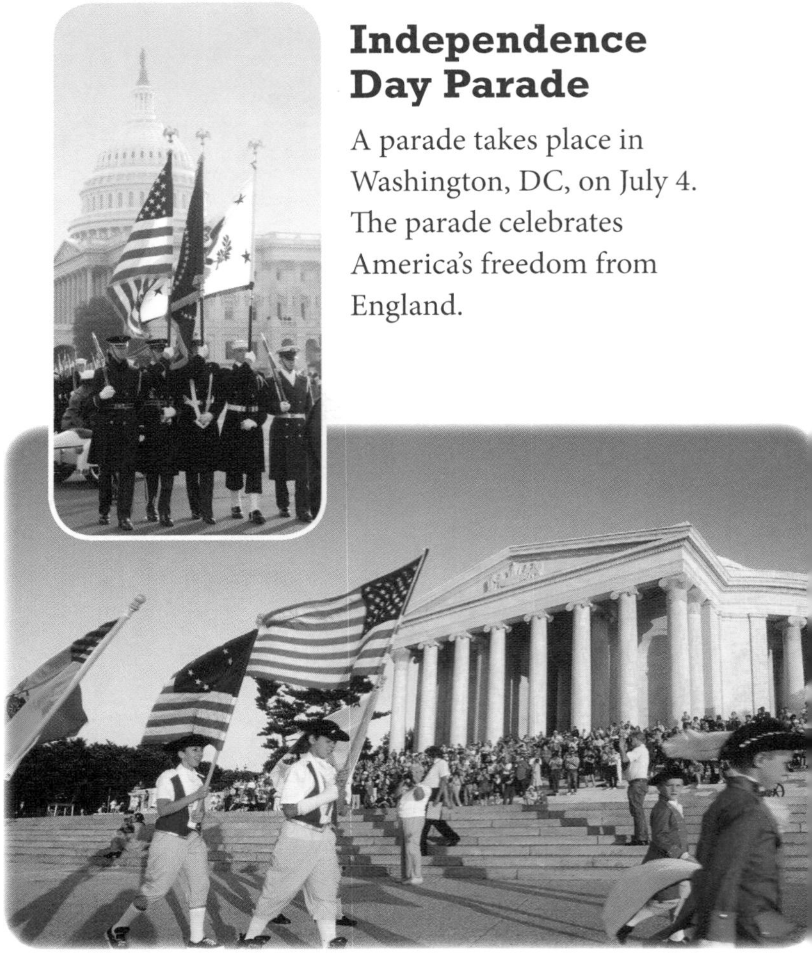

92

Background

About the Photo

The top photo on page 92 shows the color guard representing all branches of the United States Armed Forces marching past the United States Capitol in the Washington, DC, Independence Day parade.

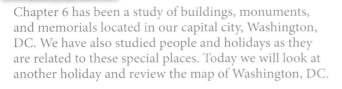

On July 4, 1776, a paper was signed saying that America was free from England. Our country celebrates this freedom with parades and fireworks.

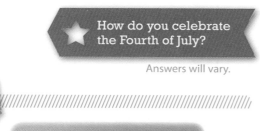

How do you celebrate the Fourth of July?

Answers will vary.

Activity

93

- Guide the reading of page 93.

  What was signed on July 4, 1776? a paper saying America was free from England

  How do we celebrate this freedom? with parades and fireworks
- Conclude the discussion by asking the question on the page.

Lesson 49

Activity Manual

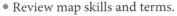

- Instruct the students to cut out the four parade figures on page 89.
- Direct attention to pages 94–95 (or use the map from the Teacher's Toolkit CD). Instruct the students to use the parade figures to locate directions and places on the Washington, DC, map. The figures are Uncle Sam, a drum major, a flag girl, and a cowboy.
- Review map skills and terms.

  What is the title of the map? *Landmarks in Washington, DC*

  Place a parade figure next to the map key. This map key is different. It has numbers that show where the buildings are located on the map.

  Look at number 1 on the key. Read the word beside the number. Capitol Find the number 1 on the map. Put a parade figure near the number 1. What landmark is beside the number 1? the Capitol
- Follow the same procedure with each of the landmarks listed.
- Practice locating the cardinal directions.

  What symbol on the map shows directions? the yellow cross, or compass rose
- Distribute the pieces of the compass rose from Visual 21 to four students. Direct them to read the letter and explain what the letter represents.
- Ask students to place figures on the map as you direct.

  Place the drum major on the north part of the map.

  Place the flag girl on the south part of the map.

  Place Uncle Sam on the east part of the map.

  Place the cowboy on the west part of the map.

  Move a figure from the Washington Monument east toward the Capitol.

  Move a figure from the Washington Monument south toward the bottom of the map.

  Move a figure from the Washington Monument north toward the White House.

  Move a figure from the Washington Monument west toward the Lincoln Memorial.

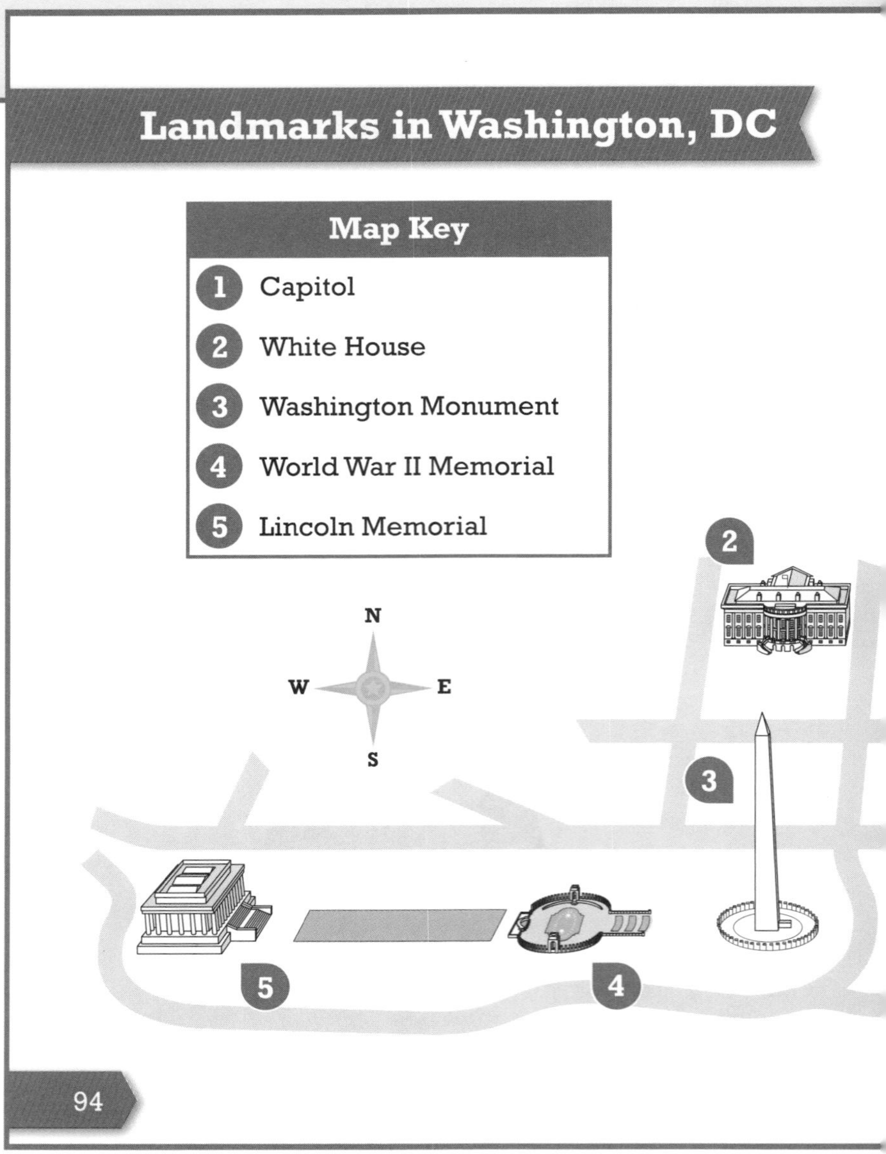

- Read the street names on the map. Ask students to place figures as you direct.

  Move a figure west to east along Constitution Avenue.
- Use the figures to continue locating places and directions. To conclude the activity, invite students to align the parade figures and march them around the streets of Washington, DC.
- Conclude the lesson by reading the poem "Star City" by Eileen Berry.

Star City

Eileen M. Berry

Capital city we mark with a star,
Place where our memories and monuments are;
Bustling with tourists and traffic and trains,
Cherry trees blooming in parks and on lanes.

City with heritage, city with heart,
City where citizens all share a part.
See all the flags—for our freedom they stand!
God by His grace has protected our land.

95

Lesson 50

Chapter Review
Activity Manual page 91

Objective

- Recall concepts and terms from Chapter 6

Materials

- Visuals 17–22: *Landmarks in Washington, DC*; *Capitol, White House, Washington Monument, World War II Memorial, Lincoln Memorial*; *President George Washington*; *Compass Rose*; *President Abraham Lincoln*
- Parade figures (Activity Manual page 89)

Review

- Direct attention to the Picture Glossary. Invite students to read the meanings of the vocabulary words.
- Review parts of the map. Engage students in actively using the map (Lesson 49).
- Guide the students as they identify places on the Washington, DC, map visual.
- Use the visuals to make a large-scale map of Washington, DC, in the classroom. Select students to represent the monuments, buildings, and compass rose. Allow other students to "parade" north and south, east and west as you direct. Encourage all students to actively participate in the map activity.
- Lead a review of the holidays: Presidents' Day, Veterans Day, and Independence Day. Play a Chapter Drill. Ask the students to find the page in Chapter 6 that tells about Veterans Day or Independence Day or the presidents who have a birthday celebrated in February.

Activity Manual

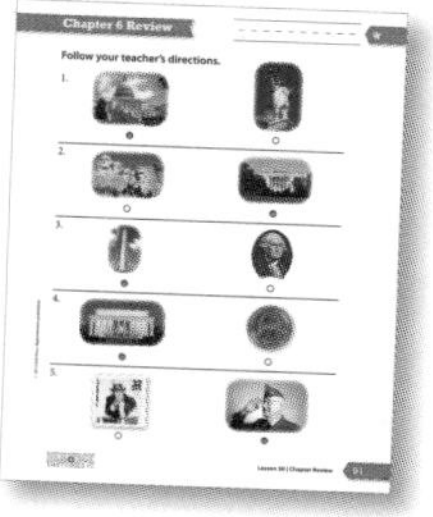

- Guide completion of page 91. Instruct the students to mark the answer bubble completely for each picture you say.

1. the United States Capitol Building
2. the White House, home of the president
3. a monument
4. a monument that honors President Lincoln
5. a man who served in a war

Chapter 6 Test

- Administer Test 6. Instruct the students to mark the answer bubble completely for each picture you say.

1. the United States Capitol Building
2. the White House, home of the president
3. a monument
4. a monument that honors President Lincoln
5. a man who served in a war

Chapter 7

Introduction

This chapter introduces the Native American people as the first Americans and briefly describes how they came to North America after the Flood. A map provides an overview of some of the Native American tribes in North America, their unique culture, and their religious beliefs. Then the chapter focuses in more detail on tribes from three different regions: the Kiowa of the Plains, the Hopi of the Southwest, and the Tlingit of the Northwest Coast. The chapter closes with a look at Indian artifacts and discusses what we can learn about Native American cultures from the things they left behind.

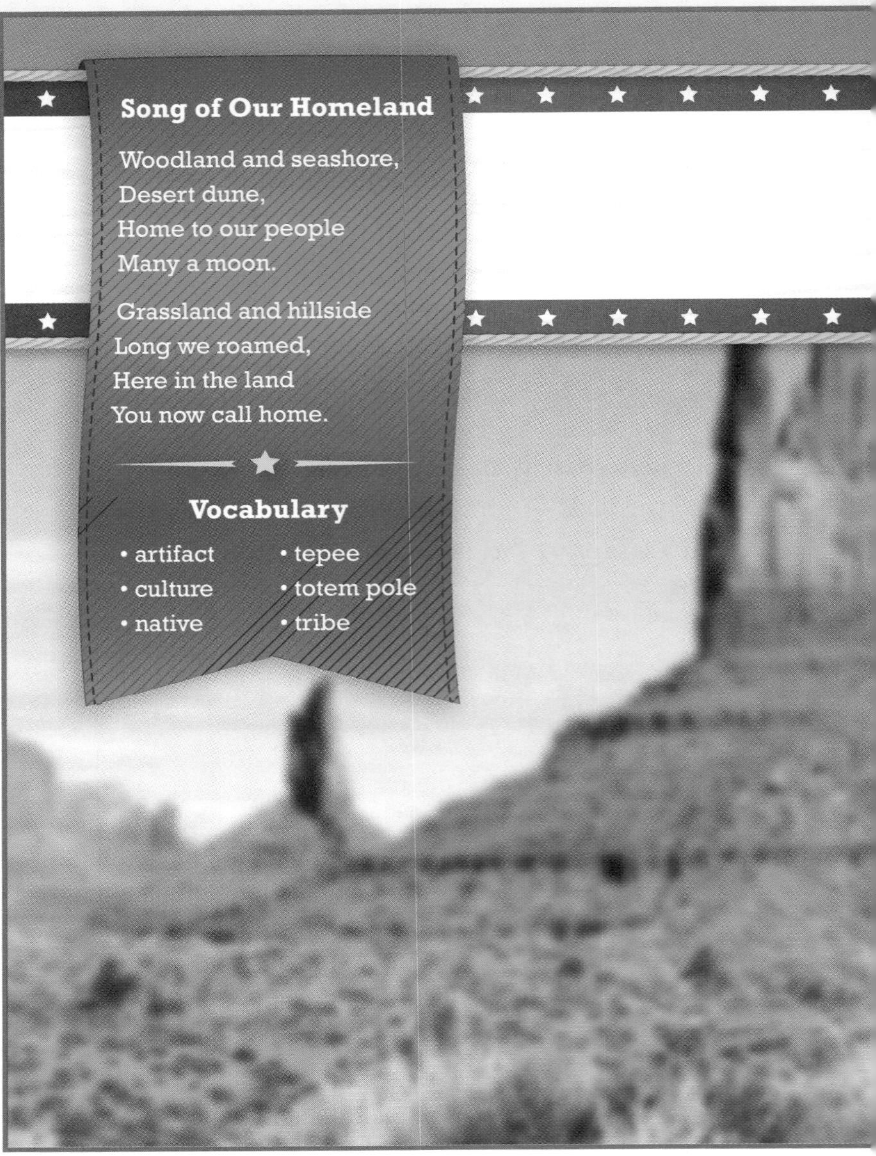

Song of Our Homeland

Woodland and seashore,
Desert dune,
Home to our people
Many a moon.

Grassland and hillside
Long we roamed,
Here in the land
You now call home.

Vocabulary

- artifact
- culture
- native
- tepee
- totem pole
- tribe

Chapter 7 Overview

Lesson	ST	AM	Content	Vocabulary
51	96–99	93	The first Americans Native Americans	native
52	100–101	95	Tribes and cultures (map) Native American religious beliefs	culture tribe
53	102–3	97	The Kiowa tribe	tepee
54	104–5	99	The Hopi tribe	
55	106–7	101–3	The Tlingit tribe	totem pole
56	107		Making a paper canoe	
57	108–9	105	Native American artifacts	artifact
58		107	Chapter Review / Test	

Visit bjupress.com/resources for links to enhance the lessons.

Native Americans

7

This lesson introduces the *History Timeline* (Visual 23). The timeline is a simple way to organize and sequence historical events, and it will help you illustrate relationships between the events pictured.

Student Text pages 96–99
Activity Manual page 93

Objectives
- Trace the series of events (the Flood, the tower of Babel, and the scattering of people around the world) that brought the first people to North America
- Identify the meaning of the term *Native Americans*
- Affirm that Native Americans lived in North America before Europeans came
- Sequence events on a timeline

Materials
- Visual 23: *History Timeline*

Vocabulary
- native

Content Words
- Flood
- Noah

Introduction

- Mount the *History Timeline* (Visual 23) at the students' eye level before beginning this chapter.
- Direct attention to pages 96–97. Read aloud the title of Chapter 7 and point out the photo.

In what kind of place is the girl in the picture standing? possible answer: desert; a rocky place

From looking at this photo, what do you think the chapter is going to be about? Accept any answer.

Teach for Understanding

- Read aloud the poem on page 96.

Name some of the places the poem mentions. woodland, seashore, desert, grassland, hillside

What words in the poem sound different from the way we speak? possible answer: *many a moon*

Who do you think is speaking in the poem? a Native American person

The Native American people you will learn about in this chapter spent much time outdoors and lived close to nature. They kept track of the passing of time by watching the moon's changing appearance.

Who do you think *you* refers to in the last line? all of us living here in the United States today

Why do you think the poem is called "Song of Our Homeland?" Possible answer: The speaker is emphasizing that these places in our country were his home before they were our home.

Do you think the speaker is happy or sad that things have changed for his people? sad

Lesson

51

- Generate interest in the list of new vocabulary words the students will be learning in this chapter.

  Where in your book can you go to find the meanings of new words? the Picture Glossary

- Guide the reading of page 98 to find out what event happened before the first people came to North America. the Flood

- Briefly summarize the account of the Flood given in Genesis 6–8.

  Who was left in the world after the Flood? only Noah, his wife, and his sons and their wives

  How did the number of people in the world grow? Noah's children had children, their children had children, and so on.

  What did God tell the people in the world to do? scatter all around the world

- Explain that God's command to "fill the earth" had been given both at Creation and following the Flood (Genesis 1:28; Genesis 9:1).

  For a while after the Flood, everyone spoke one language and stayed in one place instead of obeying God's command to fill the whole earth. But when the people of the earth decided to start a huge building project, the tower of Babel, God gave them different languages so that they could not understand one another anymore. The work on the tower stopped, and the Lord scattered people into all different parts of the world.

  Where did some of these people eventually go? North America

- Point out the picture on page 98.

  Have you ever seen people dressed like the family in this picture? What does it look like their clothing is made of? leather or animal skins

- Choose a volunteer to read aloud the caption below the picture.

The First Americans

People first came to live in North America
long ago.
After the Flood, Noah's children had children.
Their children also had children.
There were more and more people in the world.
People scattered all around the world as God
had told them to do.
Some people went to North America.

The first Americans came from far away.

98

We call these first Americans and their children Indians or Native Americans. A **native** is a person born in a certain place. Native Americans lived in different groups. The groups lived in all different parts of North America.

Native Americans lived and worked in groups.

What is a native?

a person born in a certain place

99

- Guide the reading of page 99 to identify what we call these first Americans. Indians or Native Americans

  What is a native? a person born in a certain place
- Explain that the first people who came were not *native* Americans because they had been born somewhere else. But all of their descendants who were born in North America were *native* Americans.
- Briefly discuss which country, state, and city the students are natives of, depending on where they were born.

  How did the Native Americans organize themselves? They lived in groups.

  Where in North America did they live? all different parts of North America
- Mention that people in a Native American group were usually all related to one another. Families and extended families stayed together.
- Point out the *History Timeline*. Remind the students that a timeline shows a series of events on a horizontal line. These events are placed in the order that they happened from left to right.

  Which picture on our timeline shows what happened first? the far left one
- Point out that the first picture on the timeline shows a Native American home.

  Who lived in North America before any of the other events on our timeline happened? Native Americans

  We will look at the other pictures on the timeline in later chapters as we continue studying the history of the United States.
- Explain that many Native American peoples have stories about Creation and a flood as part of the history passed down by word of mouth from their ancestors. These stories indicate that those who originally came to North America are descendants of people who were present at the tower of Babel and who would have known of these events.

Activity Manual

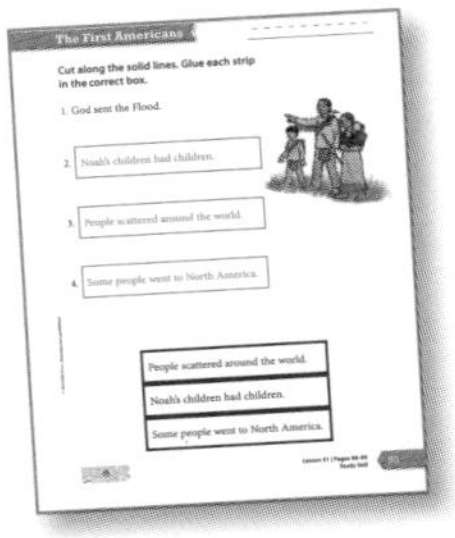

- Guide completion of page 93.

Background

Bible

Include Bible story books in a center to provide students with further opportunities to read about the Flood and the tower of Babel.

Lesson

52

Student Text pages 100–101
Activity Manual page 95

Objectives

- Locate on a map of North America areas where Native Americans lived
- Identify Native American groups as tribes
- Make cultural distinctions among Native American tribes
- Associate Native American culture with specific religious beliefs
- Evaluate Native American religious beliefs in light of biblical teaching

Vocabulary

- culture
- tribe

Content Words

- plains
- spirits
- worship

Introduction

- Invite a student to point to the first entry on the *History Timeline* as you review the events that first brought the Native American people to North America. Review the meaning of *native*.

Teach for Understanding

- Guide the reading of page 100 to find out what Native American groups were called. tribes
- Mention that a Native American tribe included people who were all related to one another and had a common culture.
- Point out the map on pages 100–101.

  What continent does the map show? North America

  What does the map tell you about where Native Americans lived? They lived all over the continent.

  In what kinds of areas did Native American tribes live? forests, plains, coasts, deserts
- Direct attention to the Geogloss on pages 174–75. Guide the students in locating in the Geogloss each of the areas mentioned on page 100. Help them infer the meanings of each geographical term from the Geogloss pictures.
- Return to the map on pages 100–101.

  What differences do you see in the homes pictured on the map? Possible answer: Homes in different parts of the continent have different shapes and are made of different materials.
- Explain that each Native American tribe made homes out of materials that were available where they lived. Homes were made of wood, grass, animal skins, and even blocks of snow.

Native American Groups

Some groups lived in the forests.
Some groups lived on the flat, grassy plains.
Some groups lived on the coasts.
Some groups lived in the dry, sandy deserts.
These groups were called **tribes**.
Each tribe of Native Americans had its own **culture**, or way of life.

100

What other differences do you see among the pictures? possible answers: different kinds of clothing; different activities

What is a tribe's culture? its way of life

The pictures show differences in each tribe's culture. In this chapter you will learn about the cultures of three Native American tribes. But all Native Americans had certain things in common.

Most Native Americans did not worship the true God.
They worshiped many spirits instead.
They thought these spirits lived in trees, rivers, wind, and rain.
These beliefs were a large part of their culture.
Many of the things they did were their way of trying to please the spirits.

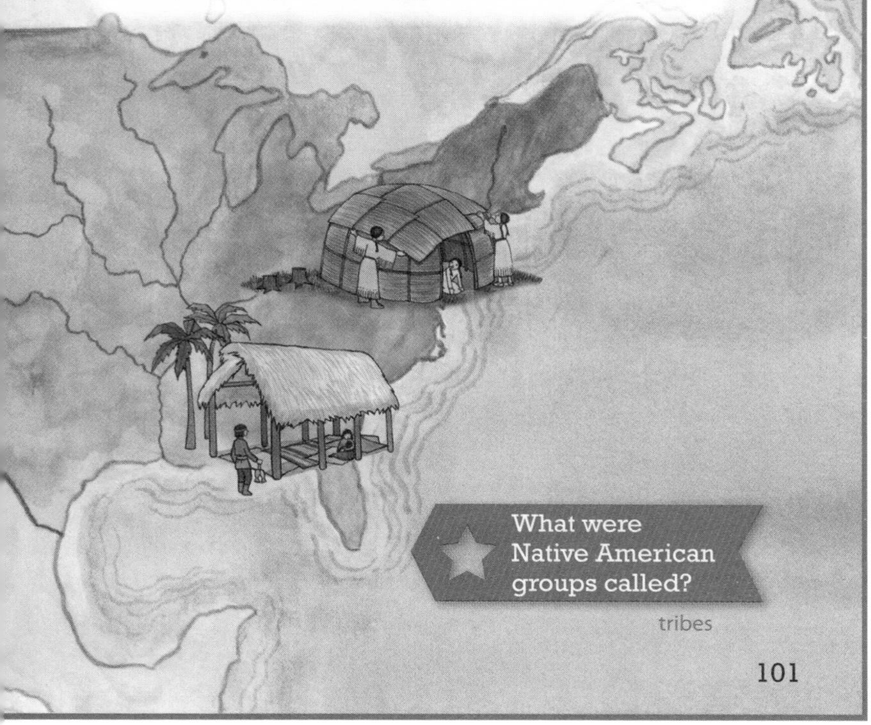

What were Native American groups called?

tribes

101

Lesson 52

- Guide the reading of page 101 to find out what most Native Americans believed about God. They did not worship the true God; they worshiped many spirits.
- Explain that Native Americans believed spirits had some of the powers that God has, such as control over the weather and natural events. But these spirits were not like the true God. They believed the spirits sometimes communicated with people.

  In what kinds of places did Native Americans think these spirits lived? in trees, rivers, wind, and rain

  Why do you think they tried to please these spirits? possible answer: so the spirits would do good things for them, such as protecting them or sending good weather for growing crops
- Remind the students that God is the one who created trees, rivers, wind, rain, animals, and all of nature. He is the one who controls them [Bible Promise I. God as Master]. He has given us all these things to use so we can meet our needs and help others.
- Read aloud Luke 4:8.

  According to the Bible, who is the only one we should worship? the Lord our God

Activity Manual

- Guide completion of page 95.

Background

Bible

Although the Native Americans did not know and worship the true God, it is important to remember that they were still created in God's image, that God loved them, and that He sent His Son to die for them. They were descendants of Adam and Eve, the first people whom God made to care for His earth and to fill it with more people. In this chapter we will see that the Native Americans cared for the earth in ways different from us and that we can learn many good things from them. Though their false religious beliefs often led them to do sinful things, there are also many good and productive aspects of their culture that we can appreciate and benefit from. Later we will see that God further demonstrated His love for these people by allowing many of them to hear the gospel through the witness of Europeans.

Lesson

53

Student Text pages 102–3
Activity Manual page 97

Objectives

- Associate the Kiowa tribe with the plains
- Explain the significance of the buffalo to the Kiowa culture
- Identify distinctive elements of the Kiowa culture

Materials

- Visual 24: *Buffalo*

Vocabulary

- tepee

Content Words

- buffalo
- Kiowa (KYE oh wuh)

Introduction

- Review the meaning of *tribe*. Invite students to tell about the family members they live with. Explain that if they lived in a tribe, many other relatives would live with them in the same community or even in the same house. Briefly discuss differences between living in a single family and living in a tribe.

Teach for Understanding

- Guide the reading of page 102 to find out where the Kiowa tribe lived. on the grassy plains in the middle of North America

  What did the Kiowa men do for a living? They were hunters.

  What animal did they hunt? the buffalo

- Display Visual 24, explaining that it shows buffalo on the plains. Point out that a buffalo is similar to a cow or an ox but with a much larger head and shoulders and a shaggy mane.

  The buffalo was very important to the Kiowa because they used it for many different purposes. Almost every part of the buffalo had some use—for food, clothing, housing, fuel, tools, weapons, toys, and religious objects. The Kiowa depended on the buffalo for survival.

  What did Kiowa people eat? buffalo meat

  Why did the people move often? They were following the buffalo herds.

- Point out the Kiowa hunters on horseback in the picture on page 102. Mention that Spanish settlers were the first to give the Native Americans horses. Horses allowed them to hunt much faster.
- Choose a volunteer to read aloud the caption below the picture.

  What did the Kiowa use buffalo skins for? shoes and clothes

People of the Plains

Some Native Americans lived on the grassy plains in the middle of North America.
One of these tribes was the Kiowa.
The Kiowa men were hunters.
They hunted the buffalo that grazed on the plains.
The Kiowa people ate buffalo meat.
They moved often, following the buffalo herds.

Kiowa people made clothes and shoes from buffalo skins.

102

Kiowa women cared for children, cooked, and kept the homes.
Kiowa homes needed to be easy to move.
Each Kiowa family set up wooden poles in a cone shape.
They covered the poles with buffalo hides.
The hides kept out the cold and the rain.
The Kiowa painted animals and other pictures on the hides.
These homes were called **tepees**.

Tepee poles and hides were easy to move.

Why did the Kiowa people move often?

They followed the buffalo herds.

103

- Guide the reading of page 103 to learn what Kiowa women did. cared for children; cooked; kept the homes

  Why was it important that Kiowa homes be easy to move? The Kiowa moved often, whenever the buffalo herds moved to a new place.

- Choose a volunteer to read aloud the caption beside the picture.

  How did the Kiowa people build their tepees? They set up wooden poles in a cone shape and covered them with buffalo hides.

  What part of the buffalo is the hide? its skin

- Explain that the Kiowa gave the buffalo skin a special treatment to preserve it and make it easier to shape. Hides were dried in the sun, pounded with animal fats or brains, and then salted or smoked. This process was called tanning.

  Why did the Kiowa use hides for coverings? The hides kept out the cold and the rain.

  What animals are painted on this tepee? buffalo, wolf or dog, birds

  If you were going to paint a tepee, how would you decorate it?

Activity Manual

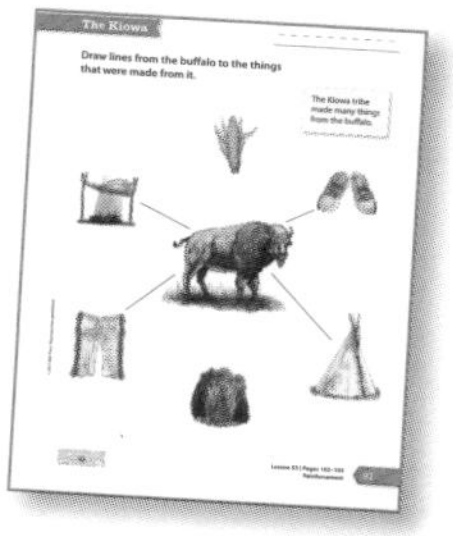

- Guide completion of page 97.

Activity

Tepee

Materials

- *Tepee* (Teacher's Toolkit CD)
- *Tepee Symbols* (Teacher's Toolkit CD)

Encourage each student to make and decorate his own tepee, using the pattern and symbols provided.

Background

Buffalo

Another name for the buffalo is the American bison. It is considered the largest land mammal in North America today. For hundreds of years, Native Americans used the buffalo with great resourcefulness, and large herds thrived on the plains. However, European settlers during the 1800s killed so many buffalo that the species nearly became extinct. Now that the buffalo is protected, there are thousands living in the United States, mostly in national parks and on reservations.

Lesson

54

Student Text pages 104–5
Activity Manual page 99

Objectives
- Associate the Hopi tribe with the desert of the Southwest
- Identify distinctive elements of the Hopi culture
- Infer ways that the location of the Hopi affected their culture

Content Words
- Hopi (HO pee)
- Southwest
- squash

Introduction

- Review information about the Kiowa from Lesson 53.
- Direct attention to the map on pages 100–101.

  Which picture on this map shows people from the Kiowa tribe? How can you tell? possible answers: tepees; location (the plains)
- Point out the region known as the Southwest on the map (the lower left corner). Explain that the land here is hot and dry, and much of it is desert. Direct attention to the picture of the Southwest tribe. Explain that the students will learn more about this Native American tribe in today's lesson.

Teach for Understanding

- Guide the reading of page 104 to find out what many Native Americans who lived in the Southwest did for a living. They were farmers.

  What made it difficult for crops to grow in the part of the country where they lived? It was a desert area that did not get much rain.

  What crops did they grow? corn, beans, and squash

  Why do you think they grew these particular crops? They grow well in dry weather.
- Direct attention to the picture on page 104.

  What is the Indian in this picture doing? weaving cloth
- Mention that the Southwest people colored the wool they wove with dyes made from desert plants and shrubs. Hopi men did most of the weaving.

  What other type of Hopi art is shown in the picture? clay pots

  What other craft did the Hopi make? handwoven baskets

People of the Southwest

Many Native Americans of the Southwest were farmers.
They lived in the hot desert where little rain fell.
But they knew how to grow corn, beans, and squash for food.
They also wove cloth and formed pots out of clay.
Many used dry grass and plants to make baskets.

104

Some Southwest people built homes high in the cliffs.
Their homes can still be seen today.
The Hopi tribe made homes of mud and bricks.
Many of their homes had two or three floors.
The Hopi climbed ladders to go from floor to floor.
On hot nights, they slept on the rooftops under the stars.

Hopi homes

Cliff homes

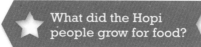

What did the Hopi people grow for food?

corn, beans, and squash

105

- Guide the reading of page 105 to learn where some of the early Southwest Indians built their homes. high in the cliffs

  Look at the photo of the cliff homes. Why do you think the people built their homes here? Possible answers: The rocks gave shelter from weather, and the high place was safe from enemies or wild animals.

  The people who built their homes in the cliffs were the ancestors, or people who came before, the Hopi.

  What were Hopi homes like? made of mud and bricks; had two or three floors with ladders between floors

  Why did the Hopi sometimes sleep on their rooftops? Possible answer: In hot weather it was too warm to sleep inside.

- Point out the photos of the Hopi homes.

  How are these homes different from the style of home you live in? Answers will vary.

Activity Manual

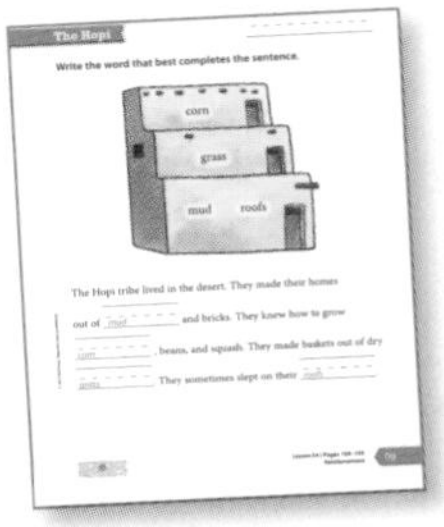

- Guide completion of page 99.

Activities

Culture

Prepare corn, beans, and squash for the students to sample. Popcorn, baked beans, blue or red corn chips, or cornbread would also make good Hopi snacks.

Science

The Hopi people grew several varieties of lima beans. Give each student a lima bean and a foam cup filled two-thirds full with soil. Show students how to poke the bean into the soil and water it. Place the cups in a sunny place and allow the children to observe the beans sprouting over the next several days. Lima beans will also germinate when placed against a damp paper towel in a plastic bag or jar and kept in a dark place.

Background

Hopi

The Hopi were an artistic people who were skilled at working with their hands. In addition to pottery, woven cloth, and baskets, they made jewelry out of beads and stones and fashioned kachina dolls out of wood. The Hopi believed in kachinas, or spirits, who had special powers over nearly all aspects of daily life. They portrayed these spirits as dolls, and men also wore masks and portrayed them in traditional dances.

Lesson

55

Student Text pages 106–7
Activity Manual pages 101–3

Objectives
- Associate the Tlingit tribe with the Northwest Coast
- Identify distinctive elements of the Tlingit culture
- Infer ways that the location of the Tlingit tribe affected their culture

Materials
- Visual 25: *Canoes*

Vocabulary
- totem pole

Content Words
- Alaska
- canoe
- carved
- Northwest
- sturdy
- Tlingit (TLIN git or KLIN kit)

Introduction

- Review information about the Hopi tribe from Lesson 54. Direct attention to the map on pages 100–101 and invite students to locate the Kiowa and the Hopi tribes.
- Point out the region known as the Northwest Coast on the map. Invite the students to look up the word *coast* in the Geogloss. Explain that this area is much colder than the Southwest, although not as cold as the Arctic lands farther north. Direct attention to the picture of the Indian from the Northwest tribe.

  What natural resource do you think this tribe could use? water; the ocean
- Explain that the students will learn more about this Native American tribe in today's lesson.

Teach for Understanding

- Guide the reading of page 106 to find out what the Native Americans on the Northwest Coast did for a living. They were fishermen.

  What kind of boats did they fish from? canoes

  What were their canoes made from? trunks of trees

  Why did the canoes need to be sturdy? They would be taken out on the sea.
- Display Visual 25 and briefly discuss the process of building a canoe. Explain that the Native Americans tried to choose the sturdiest trees so the canoes would be able to stand the rough ocean waves.

  The Northwest peoples made their canoes out of cedar wood. Often they would set fire to the felled trunk and burn the insides, and then scrape away the ash to hollow out the canoe.

  What did they hunt in the sea? fish, seals, and whales

People of the Northwest Coast

The Native Americans who lived along the Northwest Coast were fishermen.
They built sturdy canoes from the trunks of trees.
They took their canoes out on the sea.
They hunted fish, seals, and whales in the deep waters.

Northwest Coast Indians ate fish and whale meat.

106

- Choose a volunteer to read aloud the caption below the picture.

  What kind of sea creature are these Indians hunting? a whale

  What does the caption say the Northwest Coast Indians did with whale meat? ate it

One tribe, the Tlingit, lived on the coast of what is now Alaska.
Their homes needed to last through storms.
They built strong wooden homes.
They placed tall poles around the sides of their houses.
These **totem poles** were carved with pictures of people and animals.

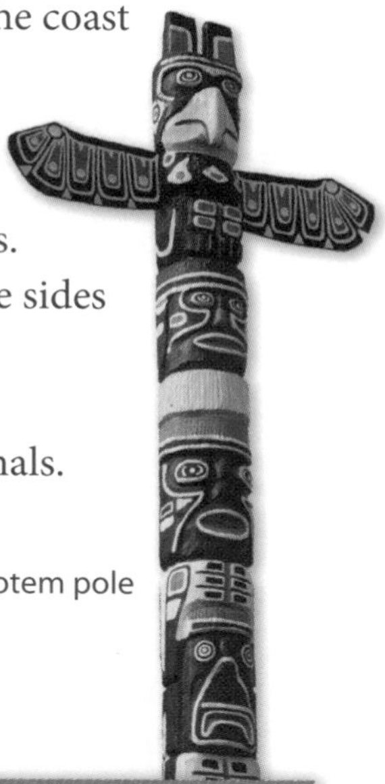

Totem pole

A Tlingit blanket

What did the Tlingit people place around their homes?
totem poles

Activity

107

- Guide the reading of page 107 to learn where the Tlingit tribe lived. on the coast of what is now Alaska

  Why did their homes need to be strong? They needed to last through storms.

  Which do you think would hold up better in a storm, a tepee or a wooden house? a wooden house
- Explain that the Tlingit homes were called plank houses because they were built from thick strips of wood called planks.

  What did the Tlingit people place around their homes? totem poles

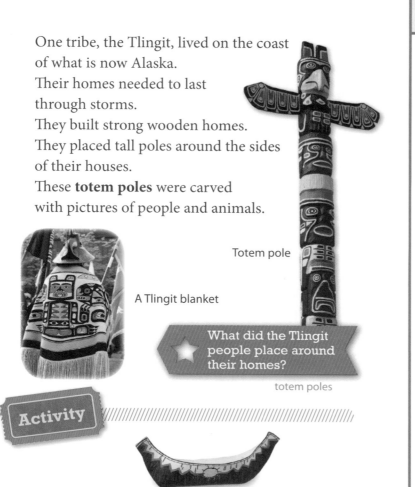

  What did the totem poles look like? They were tall and carved with pictures of people and animals.
- Direct attention to the photo of the totem pole. Explain that the faces on the totem pole were often a sort of "code" that told a history of the family who lived in the house.
- Point out the photo of the Tlingit blanket.

  Why do you think the man is wearing the blanket? possible answers: for warmth; for decoration
- Explain that the Tlingit people made blankets like these from wool and cedar bark.

Activity Manual

Materials
- *Totem Pole Faces* (Teacher's Toolkit CD)

- Guide completion of page 101.
- Guide completion of page 103. Allow the students to decorate their totem poles by drawing their own pictures, or provide the faces from the Teacher's Toolkit CD for them to cut out and glue in place.

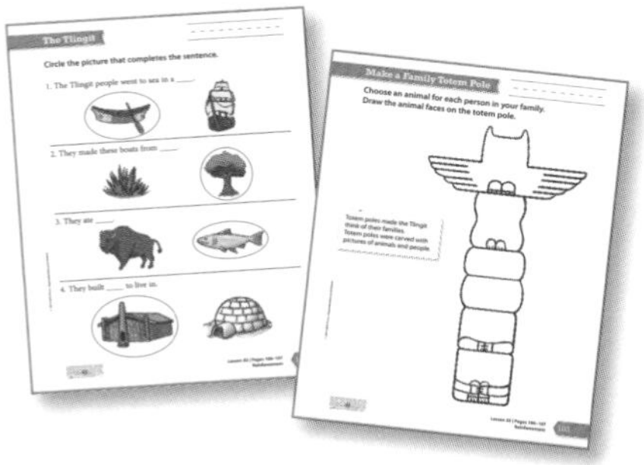

Activity

Culture

Act out the celebration of a Tlingit potlatch, or special feast. These feasts were held to celebrate marriages, to mark the completion of a house, or to accompany a funeral or other significant event. Arrange for the students to bring in finger foods and a blanket and hat to wear at the feast. Explain that a potlatch also included the giving of gifts. Encourage each student to make or bring from home a small gift to exchange with one other student at the potlatch.

Background

Tlingit

Tlingit canoes needed a special design and sturdy construction to be seaworthy. One canoe was usually shared by a large family group. It could take weeks or even months to make a canoe. Traditional songs and ceremonies usually accompanied the process of canoe making.

The Tlingit people's main food source was salmon. They used wooden traps, nets, spears, and poles with hooks to catch the fish. Salmon were not only eaten but also used for making oil. Herring and halibut were frequent catches as well.

Lesson

56

Chapter Activity
Student Text page 107

Objective

- Make and decorate a Native American canoe

Materials

- Visual 25: *Canoes*
- *Canoe* (Teacher's Toolkit CD)

Introduction

- Point out the photo of the canoe on page 107.

  Can you tell what this canoe is made of? paper

  What did the Tlingit make their canoes of? trunks of trees, specifically cedar wood

- Display Visual 25. Review the process of making a canoe.

  Which of the three tribes we have studied made sturdy canoes to take out on the sea? the Tlingit

  Today we will make and decorate paper canoes, although it will take us much less time than it did the Tlingit.

Teach for Understanding

- As you read aloud the following story about a Tlingit boy, ask the students to listen to find out what makes him happy.

  Sawak stood back admiring the sturdy form and beautiful carving of the new canoe. When he breathed in deeply, he could smell the sweet scent of cedar, the smell of the forest where he had played nearly every day since he was a tiny boy.

  "Father, when will you take the new canoe out on the sea?" Sawak asked.

  Father straightened up from the prow of the canoe, where he had been smoothing a rough area with a piece of bark. He looked at Sawak. "Tomorrow we will test the new canoe on the open sea."

  Sawak caught his breath at the word *we*. He spoke slowly, hardly daring to hope. "Father, do you mean that . . . my cousin Kashawan will go with you?"

  Father's dark eyes looked steadily into Sawak's. "No, my son. You will go." A hint of a smile creased the corners of his mouth.

  "I, Father?" Sawak tried to control the swirling joy he felt inside. Always he had watched the men go out in the canoes without

Activity

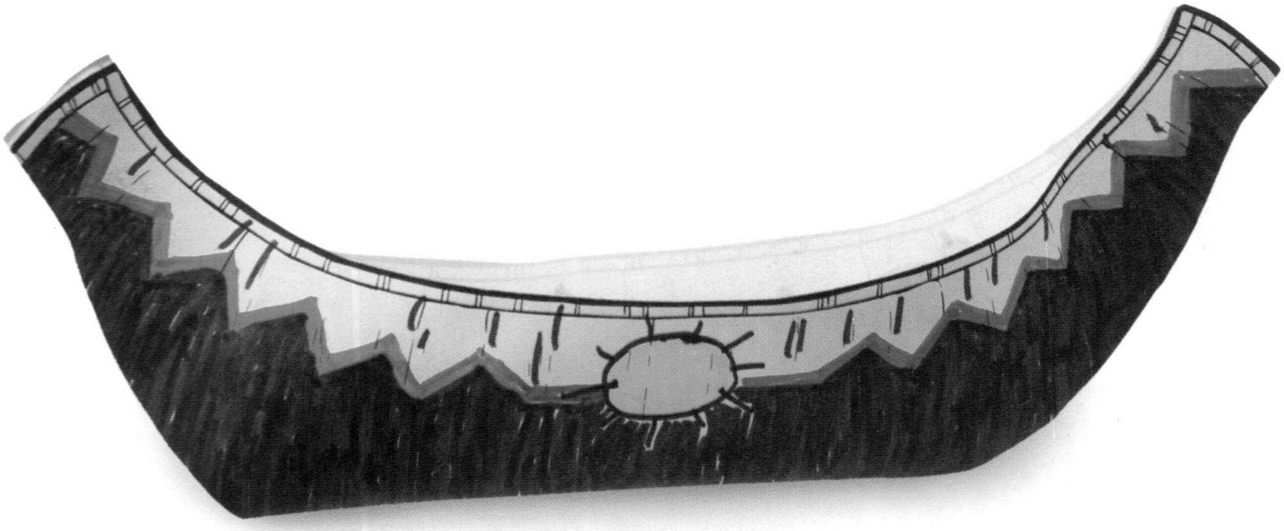

him. Always he had stayed at home to help his mother in the plank house. Always he had been too small.

"Yes, you, Sawak. You have worked very hard on this canoe. You have been up working at dawn and stayed at work by the light of the stars. You never complained. You have proven your skill, your strength, and your endurance. You are old enough to go.

"Tomorrow, wear your warm blanket that Mother made you. Bring your hat. It will be cold."

"Yes, Father."

Sawak waited until Father had walked away toward the firelight at the house. Then he hugged himself, jumped up and down, and let out a loud whoop in the darkness.

- Ask the following questions.

  Why was Sawak so happy at the end of the story? He was finally old enough to go out on the sea in the canoe.

  What might be the dangers of taking a canoe on the open sea? possible answers: storms or rough waves; sea creatures that could damage a canoe or harm someone who fell overboard

  What qualities did Father say Sawak had demonstrated that would be important when sailing? skill, strength, and endurance
- Distribute a copy of the canoe pattern to each student. Encourage him to color his canoe.
- Direct the students to cut out their canoes and to write their names on the back of their canoes.
- Demonstrate gluing the ends of the canoe together.
- Allow each student to retell the story to a partner, using his paper canoe and two pencils to represent Sawak and his father.
- Sing the following words to the tune of "Mulberry Bush" together to review the canoe-making process.

  (Pretend to chop down a tree with an ax.)
  This is the way we chop a tree, chop a tree, chop a tree,
  This is the way we chop a tree, making our canoe.

  (Pretend to hollow out a trunk.)
  This is the way we shape the trunk, shape the trunk,
  shape the trunk,
  This is the way we shape the trunk, making our canoe.

  (Pretend to shove a canoe out into the ocean.)
  This is the way we launch our boat, launch our boat,
  launch our boat,
  This is the way we launch our boat, putting out to sea.

  (Pretend to paddle a canoe, resting between each stroke.)
  This is the way we paddle and rest, paddle and rest,
  paddle and rest,
  This is the way we paddle and rest in our new canoe.

Lesson 57

Student Text pages 108–9
Activity Manual page 105

Objectives
- Distinguish artifacts from modern objects
- Infer the function of Native American artifacts
- Explain how artifacts help us understand history

Vocabulary
- artifact

Content Word
- arrows

Introduction

- Direct attention to the map on pages 100–101.

  Which three Native American tribes pictured on this map have we learned about? Kiowa of the Plains; Hopi of the Southwest; Tlingit of the Northwest Coast

  Today we will find out how we know so much about the way these people lived long ago.

Teach for Understanding

- Guide the reading of page 108 to find out what an artifact is. something a group of people left behind

  How has Native American culture changed in our world today? Most Native Americans live the way we do; they do not build tepees or wear animal skins anymore.

- Point out the photos of the Native American artifacts. Discuss each artifact's appearance and allow the students to speculate on what it was used for.

  What words would you use to describe these artifacts?

  Which ones would you have liked to wear or own?

- Choose a volunteer to read aloud the caption below the picture.

  How do these artifacts show us that Native Americans used things they found in God's world? Possible answers: The moccasins are made of leather (animal skin); the pendant is in the shape of a lizard; the lizard pendant is strung on a strip of leather or grass; the basket is made from some kind of dried grass or plant; the pottery is made of clay.

  Do you think the Native Americans liked beautiful things? yes

Activity

Visual Aids

Gather some Native American objects for the students to examine. Jewelry, leather fringe jackets or moccasins, arrowheads, clay pots, baskets, or dolls are common collectible items that might be easy to find.

Native American Artifacts

Today most Native Americans live the way we do.
Most do not build tepees or make shoes from animal skins.
But some Native Americans from long ago left things behind.
We call these things **artifacts**.

Most artifacts were made from things the Native Americans found in God's world.

108

- Guide the reading of page 109 to discover what artifacts can tell us about the lives of Native American children. Girls played with dolls; children played games with stone balls.

  How would a stone ball be different from a ball we use today? possible answers: heavier; might not be completely round

  How were beads used differently by Native Americans than they are in our culture? Both men and women wore them on jewelry and clothing.

  What were bone tools used for? building and farming

  What were used for hunting? stone arrows

- Point out the artifacts pictured on the page. Guide the students in identifying each artifact and discuss what it shows us about the way Native Americans lived.
- Explain that artifacts such as these are called *primary sources.* They are important to historians because they come directly from the people and the time period being studied. Primary sources are one of the best ways to learn about the past.
- Conclude the discussion by asking the question on page 109.

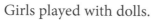

Girls played with dolls.
Both men and women wore beads.
Bone tools were used for building
and farming.
Stone arrows were used for hunting.
Stone balls were used in games.
Artifacts help us remember how
the first Americans lived.

How are these artifacts like things we use today?

Answers will vary.

109

Activity Manual

- Guide completion of page 105.

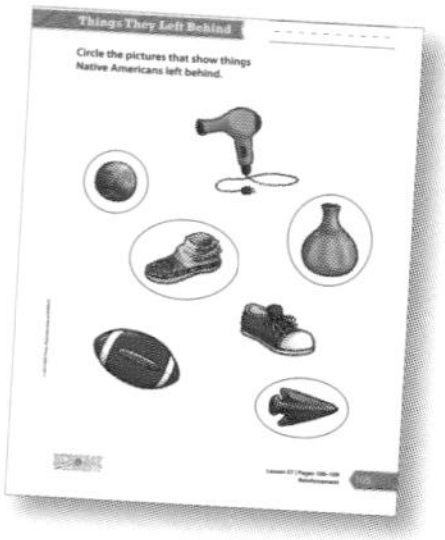

Background

Native American Words

Explain that another thing the Native Americans left behind was their language. Many of our words come from Indian words. The most familiar of these words are our state names, many of which come from tribal languages. Share any or all of the following state names and their meanings with the students. (*Note*: The following are generally accepted meanings.)

Alabama: thicket-clearers
Alaska: great land
Arizona: little spring
Arkansas: downstream people
Connecticut: long river
Illinois: great men
Kansas: people of the south wind
Massachusetts: large hill place
Minnesota: sky-tinted water
Missouri: big canoe people
Nebraska: flat water
North/South Dakota: allies
Ohio: beautiful or great river
Oklahoma: red people
Texas: friend
Utah: people of the mountains

Lesson 58

Chapter Review
Activity Manual page 107

Objective

- Recall concepts and terms from Chapter 7

Review

- Review the poem on page 96 by having the students read it aloud. Assign each line to a different student to read and encourage each reader to think about the sounds of the words and the pictures they describe.
- Draw attention to the Picture Glossary. Invite students to read the meanings of the vocabulary words.
- Review Chapter 7 by playing "Canoe Race." Divide the students into two teams and give each team one of the paper canoes created in Lesson 56. Direct each team to sit on the floor in a straight line as though they are riding in a canoe. Give the student at the end of each line a paper canoe. Alternately ask the student at the end of each line a question from the material in this chapter. If the student answers correctly, he passes his canoe forward to the person in front of him. If he answers incorrectly, he continues to hold the canoe. Continue moving up each line of students, alternately asking the next student in each line a question. Each line's paper canoe moves forward one student for each question correctly answered. The team whose paper canoe reaches the front of its line first wins.

Activity Manual

- Guide completion of page 107.

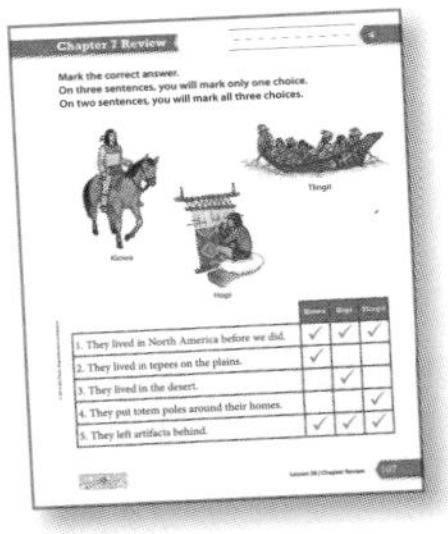

Chapter 7 Test

- Administer Test 7.

Chapter 8

Introduction

The students will learn about Christopher Columbus's early life, his sailing career, his plan to reach Asia by sailing west, the funding of his voyage, and his discovery of new lands to explore. They will make a map of the classroom as they learn about maps. A play about the life of Columbus and a game called "Voyage to an Island" will provide a review of the important events in the life of Christopher Columbus.

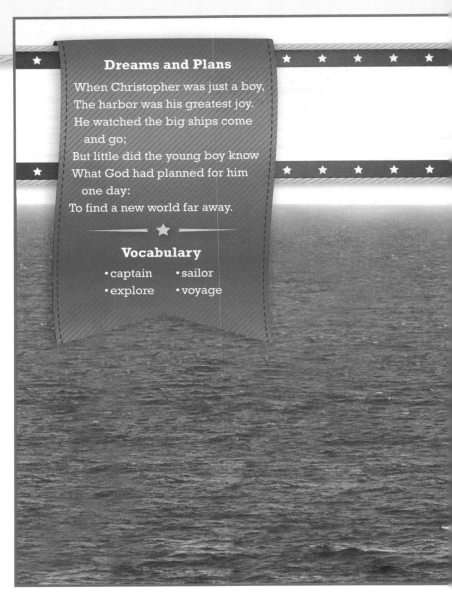

Dreams and Plans

When Christopher was just a boy,
The harbor was his greatest joy.
He watched the big ships come
and go;
But little did the young boy know
What God had planned for him
one day:
To find a new world far away.

Vocabulary

- captain
- sailor
- explore
- voyage

Chapter 8 Overview

Lesson	ST	AM	Content	Vocabulary
59	110–13	109	Facts about Columbus	captain explore sailor
60	114–15	111	Beliefs about the size of the earth Early maps	
61			A map-making activity	
62	116–18	113	Events leading to the funding of Columbus's voyage	voyage
63	119–21	115	Columbus's voyage Timeline	
64	122–23	117	Ships long ago and today Columbus Day	
65			A play about Columbus	
66		119	Chapter Review / Test	

Visit bjupress.com/resources for links to enhance the lessons.

Christopher Columbus

8

JourneyForth

Mice of the Herring Bone by Tim Davis

In this delightful fantasy, Charles and Oliver, two ordinary mice, find themselves in an extraordinary adventure, including pirate sea dogs, a ship full of cats, and a sunken treasure. This early chapter book presents life onboard an ancient frigate in a unique, engaging way.

Lesson 59

Student Text pages 110–13
Activity Manual page 109

Objectives

- Recall facts about Columbus's early life that influenced his decision to explore
- Explain why people wanted to explore and go to Asia
- Explain why the traditional routes to Asia made travel difficult

Materials

- A globe
- The world floor map prepared in Lesson 8

Vocabulary

- captain
- explore
- sailor

Content Words

- Africa
- Asia
- route

Introduction

- Direct attention to the Contents page.

  We are ready to begin Chapter 8 of our Heritage Studies book. What is the title of the chapter? Christopher Columbus

  On what page does Chapter 8 begin? page 110

Teach for Understanding

- Direct attention to the picture on pages 110–11. Invite a volunteer to read the title of the chapter.

  What do you see in the picture? a ship

  Do you think this ship looks like an old ship or a new one? old

  This ship looks like one that Columbus used. We call it a replica.

- Read aloud the poem "Dreams and Plans."

  What is the name of the boy? Christopher

  Where does Christopher like to play? at a harbor

  What does he watch the big ships do? come and go

  What would Christopher do in the future? find a new world

- Point out the vocabulary words and the meanings of the words in the Picture Glossary.
- Guide the students as they put the continents in place on the world floor map.

  Long ago a boy was born in Genoa, a city on the coast of what is now Italy. Italy is a country on the continent of Europe.

- Choose a volunteer to point out Europe on the floor map.

Lesson 59

- Guide the reading of page 112 to find out what a captain of a ship does. He decides what is done on the ship.

  Who lived in a large city near the sea? Christopher Columbus

  How do you think living by the sea made Columbus want to be a sailor? He watched the sailors at work on the ships, and he thought he would enjoy being a sailor like them.

- Direct attention to the picture on page 112.

  What did Columbus do when he grew up? sailed to many places; read many books; learned to draw maps

  Columbus did not have much education until he was older. He went to sea at an early age.

- Read aloud the following story about Christopher Columbus's adventures.

  "Christopher! Where is that boy?" Domenico Columbus looked at his wife. "As soon as he finishes his work, he's off to the docks. What is it about those ships that he likes so much?"

  Christopher's parents knew that their oldest son would not be happy staying at home. Christopher was just fourteen years old when he waved goodbye to his family and sailed away the first time. At first he worked as a cabin boy, helping the sailors and the captain of the ship. But soon he was a sailor himself.

  Christopher sailed from town to town on little ships. But he wanted more adventure. He went to work on a bigger ship. This ship sailed to places far away. But this time the ship did not sail very far before an enemy ship saw it. The enemy ship attacked, and the ship Christopher was on sank.

  Christopher clung to part of the ship. He kicked and paddled his way many miles to the shore. The shore Christopher reached was not part of his own country. Since he was hurt in the fight with the enemy ship, it took many days for Christopher to be well enough to travel again.

  When he began to feel better, Christopher thought about what he should do. He remembered that his brother Bartholomew lived nearby. Christopher went to live with his brother. He worked in Bartholomew's map-making shop. He learned to speak the language of this new country. He even learned to read this new language.

Christopher Columbus

Christopher Columbus lived in a large city
near the sea.
He dreamed of being the **captain** of a ship
someday.
A captain decides what is done on a ship.
When he grew up, Columbus sailed
to many places.
He read many books.
He learned how to draw maps.

112

People wanted to find a faster way to reach Asia by ship.
They wanted the gold and spices found there.
Columbus talked with many **sailors**.
Sailors do the work on ships.
Some of the sailors had seen land in the west that had not been explored.
To **explore** means to find out about a new place.

Route to Asia

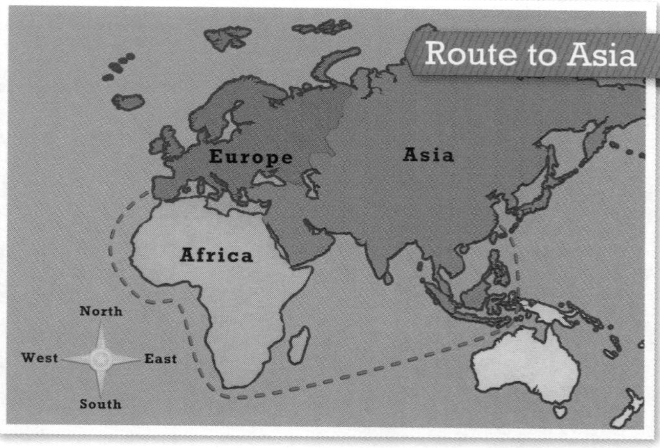

Ships sailed around Africa to get to Asia.

★ Who does the work on ships?

sailors

- Guide the reading of page 113 to find out what it means to explore. to find out about a new place

  Some people in Europe wanted to get rich by trading with other countries. They wanted gold and spices from Asia. Other people wanted to tell people in other lands about the Bible and God.

- Direct attention to the map. Choose a volunteer to read the caption.

  The routes traders took to get to Asia were very long.

  Put your finger on the map. Trace the path a ship would take around Africa to get to Asia. This route took many months to complete.

  What do sailors do on ships? the work

Activity Manual

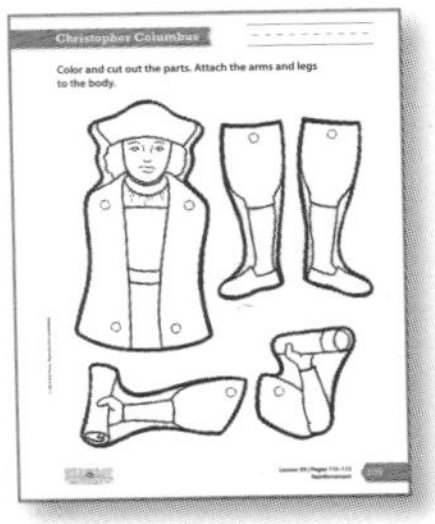

- Guide completion of page 109.

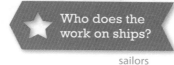

Background

Bible

It was not money and goods only that drove explorers such as Columbus to find a faster way to Asia. Columbus wanted to spread Christianity. How true and sincere he was in his beliefs we cannot know. But we do know that religion was more important to him than wealth and trade. Columbus said, "The beginning and the end of the enterprise was the increase and glory of the Christian religion" [William D. Phillips Jr. & Carla Rahn Phillips, *The Worlds of Christopher Columbus*, (New York: Cambridge, 1992), 169]. This is evidenced by the names Columbus gave the places he found: San Salvador (Holy Savior), Trinidad (Trinity), and Santa Cruz (Holy Cross).

Indies

Sources sometimes use the term *Indies* to refer to where Columbus planned to go. Using the term *Indies* necessitates an explanation about the two Indies: the East Indies and the West Indies. It is also important to note that Columbus did not even know that. He only knew the islands of Asia, or "the Indies," which included everything from the islands of the Indian Ocean to those all the way over to Japan. If you choose to use the term *Indies*, be sure to define the term and locate the islands that Columbus discovered. These are the islands that have collectively become known as the West Indies.

Lesson

60

Student Text pages 114–15
Activity Manual page 111

Objectives

- Contrast the differences in the beliefs about the size of the earth that were popular in Columbus's day
- Explain the differences between maps used long ago and those used today

Materials

- A globe
- The world floor map prepared in Lesson 8
- Several examples of current maps

Introduction

- Review the early life of Christopher Columbus.

Teach for Understanding

- Guide the reading of page 114 to find out what people in Columbus's day thought about the size of the earth. Some people thought the earth was a little smaller than it is, but Columbus thought it was much smaller.

  Columbus was wrong about the size of the earth.

  Which direction did Columbus think would take him to Asia faster? west
- Direct attention to the picture of the earth. Choose a volunteer to read the caption aloud.
- Display and discuss the maps you brought. Then display them for the students to examine more closely.

The First Maps

When Columbus lived, people did not know how large the earth really is.
Many people thought it was only a little smaller than it really is.
Columbus thought it was much smaller.
Columbus thought there might be a shorter, faster way to reach Asia by sailing west.

The earth is very large.

114

Background

Geography

That people in the 1400s thought the earth was flat is now recognized to be a myth. There is no evidence that Columbus had to argue against the idea of a flat earth. There is abundant evidence that people knew the earth was a sphere. There also is no evidence that Columbus's crew thought the earth was flat.

The issue was the size of the earth. Though most geographers thought the earth was about 23,000 miles in circumference, Columbus thought it was about 18,000 miles in circumference. The circumference of the earth at the equator is actually 24,901.55 miles. Although Columbus's calculations were wrong, God used him to lead Europeans to a continent they had not previously known about. Columbus is just one example of a person God used, despite his many flaws, to accomplish His own greater purposes.

- Guide the reading of page 115 to find out what the first maps were like. They did not show the entire world, only the parts men had explored.

  Men had not traveled to every part of the world yet.
- Choose a volunteer to read aloud the caption below the map.

  The first maps included only the continents that men had discovered.

  Which large continents are missing from the early maps? North America and South America
- Choose volunteers to point out each continent on the globe.
- Spread out the floor map and direct a student to arrange the continents in place. Then remove North America and South America.

  This is how the early maps looked. They were missing North America and South America because those continents had not been discovered yet.
- Conclude the discussion by asking the question on page 115.

The first maps were not like those used today. They showed only the land men had explored. People did not know that two continents lay between them and Asia.

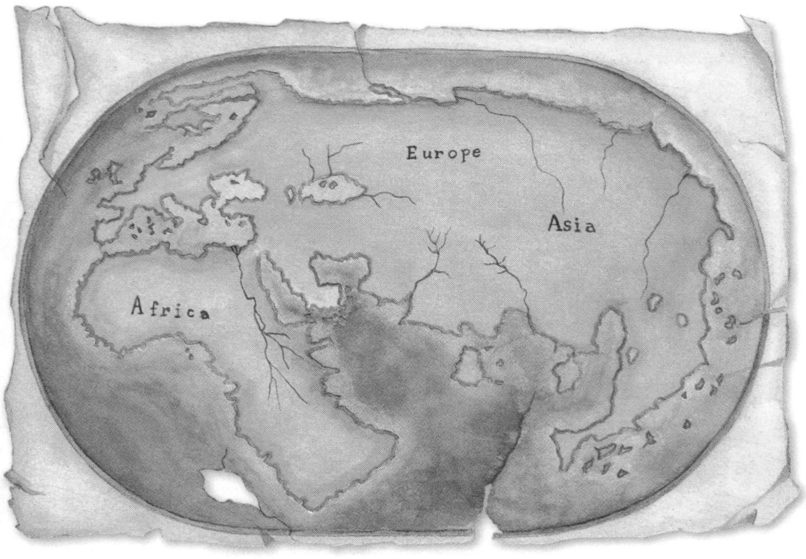

The first maps did not have North America or South America.

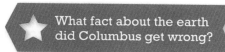

What fact about the earth did Columbus get wrong?

He thought the earth was much smaller than it really is.

115

Activity Manual

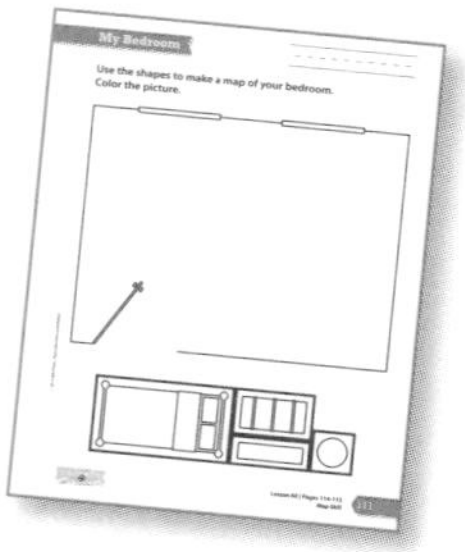

- Direct each student to cut out the bedroom furniture pictures and glue them in the box so they are arranged like his bedroom.
- Guide completion of page 111.

Background

Mapmaking

A cartographer is someone who enjoys studying and making maps. The first maps were made by painting on parchment paper. Those maps varied in quality, and since the maps were difficult to make, not many were produced. The oldest known maps are preserved on Babylonian clay tablets. Over time better tools and technology allowed cartographers to refine their skills.

The invention of the printing press led to the mass production of maps. Today cartographers make maps using computers with specialized software. Street-view maps are made possible by special cars mounted with many cameras that take 360-degree views of an area.

Objectives

- Participate in a map-making activity
- Explain how a map gives information

Materials

- A sheet of chart paper
- Blocks in various shapes and sizes
- A large sheet of paper for the background of the map with space at the bottom for a map key
- Several "jewels" hidden around the room

Introduction

- Guide a review of how early maps were different from those of today.

Teach for Understanding

- Invite students to tell how maps are helpful. Elicit that maps help you find where you need to go.

  If you wanted to make a map of this room, what would you include?
- List the students' suggestions on the chart paper as they respond.
- Place the large sheet of paper in an open space on the floor.
- Arrange the students on the floor so that each child can see the map background. Refer to the list as the students make the map.
- Guide the students as they determine which side of the paper will show the front of the room and which will show the back. Label the map with the words *front* and *back*.
- Choose a volunteer to draw the doorway on the map.
- Invite other students to place blocks on the map background to represent the objects on the list.

  Most maps have a map key. A map key helps you understand what each thing on a map is.
- Work together to complete a map key. Place one of each size block in the map key. Write a word to show what each kind of block represents.
- What can a visitor learn about our room by looking at the map we made? He can see how many objects are in the room and where they can be found.
- After the map is complete, place a small object on one of the blocks on the map.
- Choose a volunteer to identify what the block on the map represents in the room. If the student correctly identifies the place in the room represented by the block, allow him to go to that spot to find a jewel. Continue the activity until each jewel has been found.
- Leave the map set up for review in the next lesson.

Lesson

62

Student Text pages 116–18
Activity Manual page 113

Objective
- Identify the events that led to the funding of Columbus's plan to sail west

Materials
- Visual 26: *The* Niña, *the* Pinta, *the* Santa María

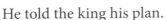

Vocabulary
- voyage

Content Words
- bought
- Ferdinand
- Isabella
- *Niña*
- *Pinta*
- Portugal
- *Santa María*
- Spain

Introduction

- Direct attention to the map of the classroom and lead a discussion to help students recall how they made it.

Teach for Understanding

- Guide the reading of page 116 to find out the meaning of the word *voyage*. a long trip to a place far away

  Columbus believed sailing west would be a faster way to get to Asia. He wanted to sail west to see if he was correct.

  What did Columbus need for the trip? money for ships and supplies; sailors

  Who did Columbus go to see? the king of Portugal
- Direct attention to the picture.

  What do you see in the picture? a man looking at a map; men unloading a boat; a ship in the harbor

A Visit to the King and Queen

Columbus began to plan a trip to Asia.
He thought he could get to Asia faster
by sailing west.
He would need things for the **voyage**.
A voyage is a long trip to a place far away.
Columbus needed money for ships and
supplies.
He would need to hire sailors.
Columbus went to see the king of Portugal.
He told the king his plan.

Columbus needed money for his voyage.

116

Background

Facts about Columbus's First Voyage

Food: hard biscuits, fish, bread, and salted meats
Pigs and chickens also provided meat and eggs.
Ships' Speed: 90–100 miles a day
The *Pinta* was the fastest ship, and the *Santa María* was the slowest ship.
Number of Men: about 120
Cooking: The cooking was done on a firebox using cooking pots.
Sleeping: The sailors slept on deck.
Navigational Aids: charts, hourglasses, sundials, compasses, almanacs

Columbus asked the king for money.
He said he would bring back gold and spices from Asia.
The king of Portugal did not want to help Columbus.
He thought Columbus was wrong about the size of the earth.
Columbus then went to see King Ferdinand and Queen Isabella of Spain.

Columbus asked the king and queen for help.

117

- Guide the reading of page 117 to find out why the king of Portugal refused to help Columbus. He thought Columbus was wrong about the size of the earth.

  What did Columbus ask the king? He asked for money so he could find a faster way to Asia.

  What did Columbus say he would bring back to the king? gold and spices

  Who did Columbus go to see next? King Ferdinand and Queen Isabella of Spain
- Choose a volunteer to read aloud the caption below the picture.

Lesson

62

- Guide the reading of page 118 to find out whether King Ferdinand and Queen Isabella decided to help Columbus with his exploration. yes

  Did the king and queen decide to help Columbus right away? No. It took them many years to decide to help Columbus.

  What did Columbus buy for his trip? He bought ships and food, and he hired sailors.

  Had Columbus's dream come true? Yes, he was finally a captain.
- Direct attention to the picture. Mention that these ships are replicas of Columbus's ships. Read the names of the ships and ask the students to repeat them after you.
- Introduce Visual 26.
- Conclude the discussion by asking the question on page 118.

Activity Manual

- Guide completion of page 113.

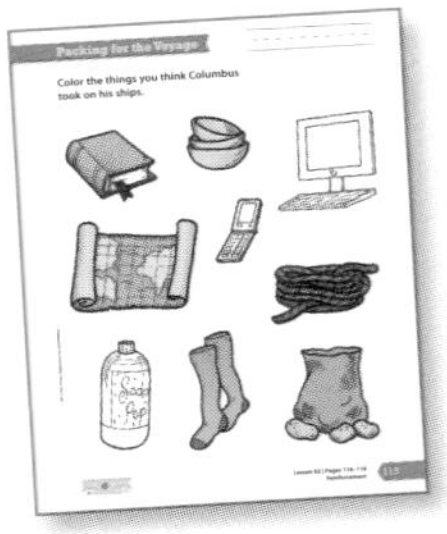

Background

Scurvy

Scurvy is a vitamin C deficiency. Humans have known about the disease since ancient Greek and Egyptian times. Scurvy is commonly associated with sailors who did not get enough vitamin C when on long voyages. Often they perished from the condition. A diet rich in vitamin C consists of fruits and vegetables such as citrus fruits (especially lemons, limes, and oranges), tomatoes, broccoli, green peppers, spinach, potatoes, and cabbage.

Columbus explained his plan to the king and queen.
They thought about what Columbus said.
Years later they decided to help him.
Columbus soon had three ships to use for his voyage.
He packed enough food to last a year.
He hired sailors to help on the ships.
His dream to be a captain had come true.

The *Niña*, the *Pinta*, and the *Santa María*

How many ships did Columbus use for his voyage?

three

118

A Long Voyage

The ships' sails were raised, and the voyage began.
The days were long and hard.
Weeks went by, but Columbus did not find land.
Some of the sailors began to grumble.
They did not want to keep going.

Some of the sailors wanted to turn back.

119

Lesson 63

Student Text pages 119–21
Activity Manual page 115

Objectives

- Summarize the voyage taken by Columbus and his crew
- Affirm that God used the voyage to change the world
- Recognize the chronological indicators on a timeline
- Explain that Columbus's discovery of land happened in 1492

Materials

- Visuals 23, 26–27: *History Timeline; The* Niña, *the* Pinta, *the* Santa María; *The Route Columbus Took*

Content Words

- claimed
- Indians

Introduction

- Invite two students to pretend to be King Ferdinand and Queen Isabella as you review the events from Lesson 62. Then invite a volunteer to be Christopher Columbus as he asks the king and queen to fund his voyage.

Teach for Understanding

- Display Visual 26.

  What are the names of the three ships Columbus used? the *Niña*, the *Pinta*, and the *Santa María*
- Use Visual 27 to explain the route that Columbus took.
- Guide the reading of page 119 to find out why some of the sailors on Columbus's ships began to grumble. The days were long and hard. They had not found land yet.

  How do you think Columbus felt after hearing the sailors grumble? discouraged
- Choose a volunteer to read aloud the caption below the picture.

Lesson

63

- Guide the reading of page 120 to find how Columbus responded to the grumbling of the sailors. He said he would turn back if they did not find land in three days.

  How soon did a sailor spot land? the next day

  How do you think Columbus felt when they saw land? happy; excited; thankful
- Choose a volunteer to read aloud the caption below the picture.

Columbus did not want to end the voyage yet.
He decided to turn back if they did not see land in three days.
The next day one of the men spotted land.
The sun was not up yet.
Most of the sailors were still sleeping.
"Land!" a sailor yelled. "Land!"

Columbus was happy to find land.

120

Background

Bible

God is in control of all of history. People can change the course of history with choices they do not fully understand. Columbus wanted to find a faster way to Asia in order to spread Christianity and increase wealth through trade. Columbus did not find Asia, but what he found did spread Christianity and increase wealth worldwide through trade. Wealth from trade came more from trade with the Americas than from trade with Asia. God did something great in 1492. Columbus was a tool God used. Columbus discovered America just before the Protestant Reformation began. God made Europe aware of a "New World" when they would need it most. When true believers in God were persecuted for their beliefs, they would have a place to flee.

The fact that Columbus found land was divine providence. His discovery opened North and South America to exploration and the spread of the gospel.

Columbus did not reach Asia by sailing west.
Though Columbus did not know where he landed, God did.
Columbus did not know he had found new lands to explore.
God used the voyage to change the world.

Columbus called the people he found Indians, and he claimed the land for Spain.

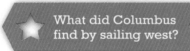

What did Columbus find by sailing west?

new lands to explore

121

- Guide the reading of page 121 to find out if Columbus found a faster route to Asia. He did not.

  Columbus thought he had reached the Indies. That's why he called the people Indians.

  Did Columbus know he had found new land to explore? no

  Was God surprised by the land Columbus found? no
- Explain that God used Columbus to open new lands to exploration and the spread of the gospel. [BAT: 5c Evangelism and missions]
- Choose a volunteer to read aloud the caption below the picture.
- Direct attention to the *History Timeline*. Remind the students that a timeline shows a series of events on a horizontal line, placed in the order that they happened from left to right.
- Point out the *Niña*, the *Pinta*, and the *Santa María* on the timeline near 1492.
- Review the Native American homes (before 1400) on the timeline to clarify the chronological order of the pictures.
- Conclude the discussion by asking the question on page 121.

Activity Manual

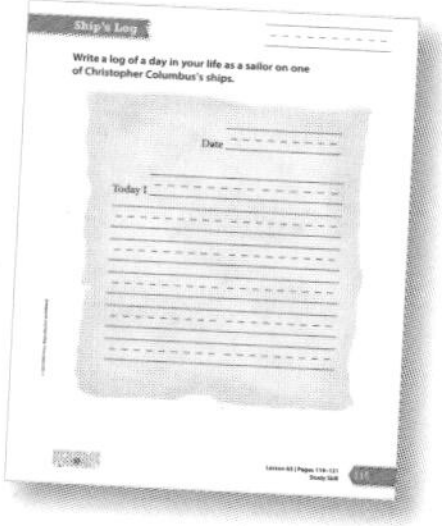

- Guide completion of page 115.

Activity

Miniship

Cut out a triangle from white paper or foam. Tape the triangle to a toothpick to make a sail. Press some clay into a walnut shell half. Push the end of the toothpick into the clay. Place the ship in a pan of water. Invite students to blow on the sail to move the boat.

Lesson 64

Student Text pages 122–23
Activity Manual page 117

Objectives
- Compare ships made long ago with modern ships
- Explain why Columbus Day is important

Materials
- Visual 28: *Christopher Columbus*

Introduction

- Review Columbus's voyage.

Teach for Understanding

- Guide the reading of page 122 to find out what was used to make ships long ago. wood

  Where does wood come from? trees

  What had to be done to the wood in order to build a ship? Boards had to be cut from the tree trunks.

  Which step in the process of building a ship do you see in the picture? The men are sawing logs, splitting boards, and carrying them to the men who are putting them together to build the ship.

  How did shipbuilders get the completed ship to the water? They rolled it to the water on a cart.
- Choose a volunteer to read aloud the captions.

  What are ships made from today? steel

Today and Long Ago

Ships

Long ago ships were made from wood.
The wood was cut and shaped by hand.
The ship was rolled to the water on a cart.

Boards were used to make the ship.

Today most ships are made from steel.

122

Columbus Day

Columbus Day is celebrated on the second Monday of October.
It is a day to remember Christopher Columbus and the land he found.
It is a day to remember what God did long ago.

Christopher Columbus

Activity

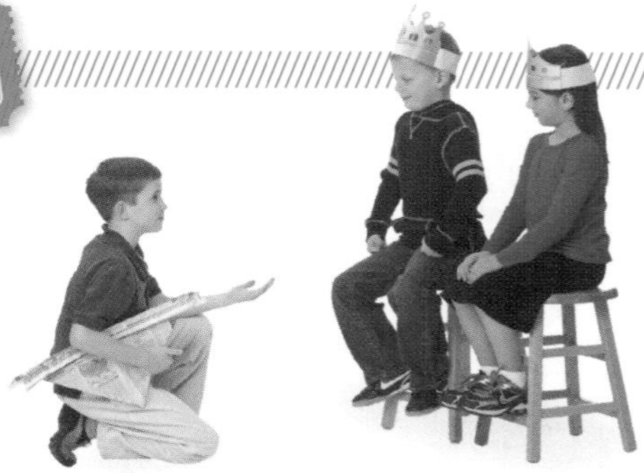

- Guide the reading of page 123 to find out what day is set aside for Columbus Day. the second Monday of October
- Display Visual 28 and discuss what the students have learned about Christopher Columbus.

  Why is Columbus Day important to us? It reminds us of Columbus and the land he found. It also reminds us of what God did through Columbus.
- Direct attention to the Activity picture. Generate excitement about acting out the story of Christopher Columbus in the next lesson.

Activity Manual

- Guide completion of page 117.

Lesson

65 Chapter Activity

Objective

- Recall facts about Columbus by participating in a play

Materials

- *Christopher Columbus Play* (Teacher's Toolkit CD)
- Props listed for each scene of the play
- Copies of each scene to give the students

Play

- Choose students to act out each scene. Give them a copy of the scene to use for practice.
- Instruct each student to mark his speaking and acting parts on the paper. Direct the students to read over their parts until they are familiar with them and to practice saying their lines aloud by practicing with other students in the scene. (*Variation:* Students in homeschool can perform the play as a reader's theater using the entire family.)
- Guide the students as they act out the play. You may also arrange to present the play for another group.

Activity

Lesson

66

Chapter Review
Activity Manual page 119

Objective

- Recall concepts and terms from Chapter 8

Materials

- *Ships* (Teacher's Toolkit CD)

Review

- Review the poem on page 110 by having students read it aloud. Choose one student to read the first three lines and another to read the last three lines. Encourage the students who are not reading to shade their eyes with their hands and pretend to be watching ships in the harbor.

  Why do you think the poem is called "Dreams and Plans"? The poem is about Christopher's dreams and God's plans.

  Does God have a plan for your life? yes
- Guide a review of the Chapter 8 vocabulary by inviting the students to look up each word in the Picture Glossary.
- Draw squares for display in a line, one square for each question you plan to use for the review. Attach the ships near the first square. Draw an island near the last square.

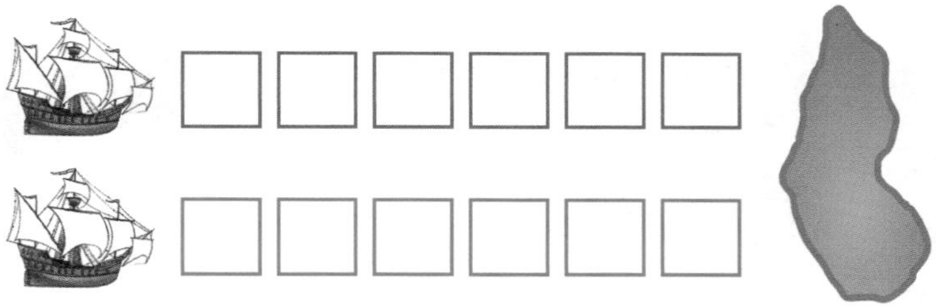

- You may choose to review Chapter 8 by playing "Voyage to an Island." Divide the students into two teams. Ask a question from the material in this chapter. Direct the student who correctly answers a question to move his team's ship one square closer to the island. The first ship to reach the island wins. You may review any or all of the material during this lesson.

Activity Manual

- Guide completion of page 119.

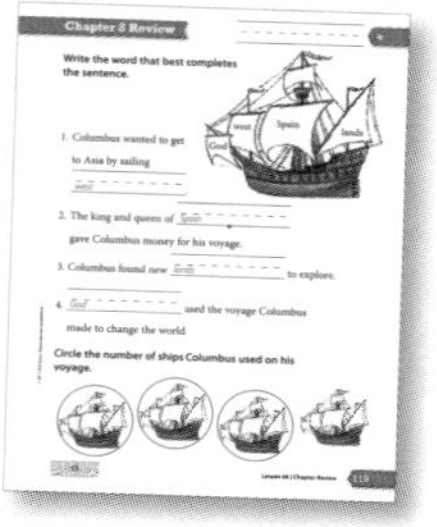

Chapter 8 Review

Write the word that best completes the sentence.

1. Columbus wanted to get to Asia by sailing west

2. The king and queen of Spain gave Columbus money for his voyage.

3. Columbus found new lands to explore.

4. God used the voyage Columbus made to change the world.

Circle the number of ships Columbus used on his voyage.

Lesson 66 | Chapter Review 119

Chapter 8 Test

- Administer Test 8.

Chapter 9

Introduction

This chapter continues the exploration theme of the previous chapter and then develops the establishment of the first permanent English settlement in the New World. It takes a look at the Native American point of view regarding the newcomers. Needs and wants become a major topic as the colonists learn to survive in America. God's sovereignty is the overarching premise in the existence of the settlement. God provides the needed friend in Pocahontas. Pocahontas accepts the Christian faith, which helps establish a peaceful existence for the colony for many years.

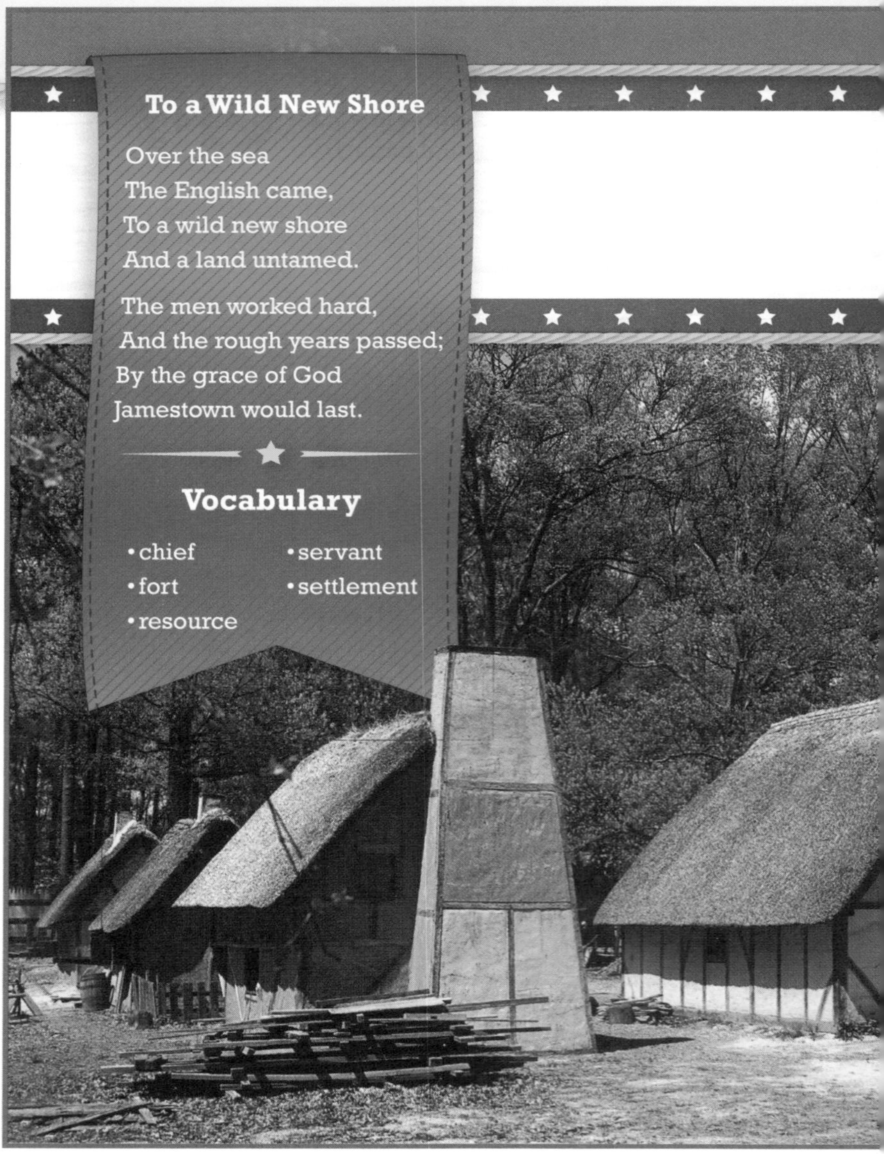

To a Wild New Shore

Over the sea
The English came,
To a wild new shore
And a land untamed.

The men worked hard,
And the rough years passed;
By the grace of God
Jamestown would last.

Vocabulary

- chief
- fort
- resource
- servant
- settlement

Chapter 9 Overview

Lesson	ST	AM	Content	Vocabulary
67	124–27		Locate on a map the Old World and the New World	
68	128–29	121–23	Explain why the English came to settle Jamestown	
69	130–31	125	Dramatize the concerns of the Woodland people and the arrival of the English	chief
70	132–33	127–29	Make a map with a key of the school library	fort settlement
71	134–37	131	Classify needs and wants of the Jamestown settlement	
72	138–39	133	Identify natural resources, listing things found in the woods	resource
73	140–41	135	Dramatize the story of Pocahontas	
74	142–43	137	Explain the importance of women and families to the growth of Jamestown	servant
75		139	Chapter Review / Test	

Visit bjupress.com/resources for links to enhance the lessons.

Jamestown 9

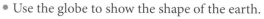

Lesson 67 Student Text pages 124–27

Objectives
- Recognize why the Europeans came to the New World
- Locate the Old World and the New World on a map
- Contrast the appearance of the Native American and the English man

Materials
- Visuals 1–4, 23, 29–30: *Continents,* including the aerial view of Antarctica; *History Timeline*; *The Old World and the New World Map*; *The Old World and the New World Men*
- A globe

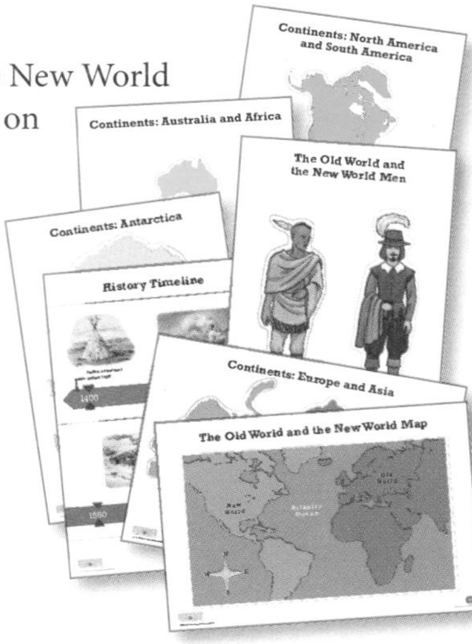

Introduction

Columbus thought that he had found a way to reach Asia. He did not know how big the earth was.

- Use the globe to show the shape of the earth.

  Columbus did not know he had found new lands to explore. He claimed the land for Spain. Many other men sailed west; they also found this New World. Other sailors and explorers claimed the land for their countries.
- Use the globe to review the continents and oceans. Use Visuals 1–4 and the optional Antarctica visual to review the names and shapes of the continents and the names of the oceans. Display the visuals in map form. Explain that the map is like the globe, but it is flat. Remove North and South America to review what the world looked like to Christopher Columbus. Remind the students that Columbus was most familiar with the continents of Europe, Asia, and Africa. Explorers who came after Columbus discovered that the continents of North and South America were not part of Asia but were a new world.
- Use the *History Timeline* to compare the Native Americans (before 1400) and Columbus (1492). Point out that the Native Americans lived in North and South America before Columbus set sail on his voyage.

Teach for Understanding

- Direct attention to the picture on pages 124–25. Ask a volunteer to read the title of the chapter.

  In Chapter 9, we will learn of other men who came to the New World.

  What do you see in the picture? old houses; fences

  The picture shows how the Jamestown settlement might have looked several hundred years ago. Today people visit the settlement to learn about the past.
- Read the poem aloud.

  In the poem, who crossed the sea? the English Who are the English? men from England

  Where were they sailing to? a new shore

  What words make you think no one lived there? *wild*; *new*

  What do you think "a land untamed" means in line 4? a land that has not been tamed or lived in

  The English did not know that the land had been used by Native Americans. The land had been tamed by the Native Americans many years earlier.

  Jamestown was a lasting settlement. Who made Jamestown last? God

  After reading the poem, what do you think this chapter is about? English people coming to Jamestown
- Point out the Jamestown Fort on the timeline and review the three dates that you have introduced (before 1400, 1492, and 1607).
- Remind the students that the vocabulary words can be found in the Picture Glossary.

Lesson

67

- Direct attention to the picture on page 126.

  Do you think the man in the picture lives today? no Why? His clothing, his hairstyle, and the map are old.

  The man in the picture worked for the Virginia Company. He was planning a trip to the New World.

- Invite a volunteer to read the title of the page. Guide the reading of the page.

  Men from many other countries came to the New World after Columbus landed there. Today we call this land North and South America.

  Some men from England wanted the riches from the Americas (North and South America). Other men wanted to tell the Native Americans about God and the Bible. Mapmakers soon made maps of the Old World (Europe, Africa, and Asia) and the New World called America.

  Was the land called America really a new world? no Who lived in America before the men from Europe came? Native Americans

Background

Early Explorers

Some early explorers include Christopher Columbus of Spain in 1492, John Cabot of England in 1497, and Jacques Cartier of France in 1534. Many explorers claimed land in the New World for the country that funded their exploration.

Sailing Across the Ocean

Many years had passed since Christopher Columbus had landed in the New World. English men heard about the New World too. They wanted some of the land called America. These men hoped to find gold and riches there.

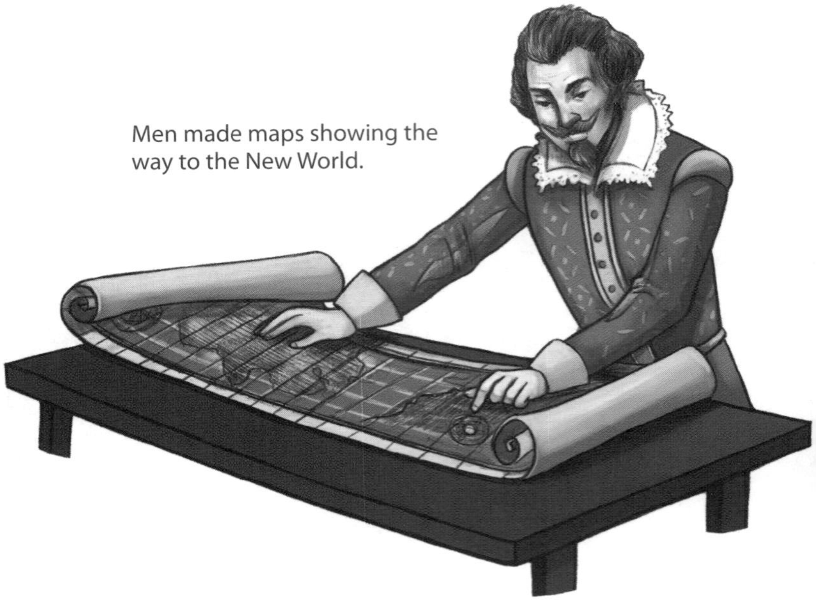

Men made maps showing the way to the New World.

126

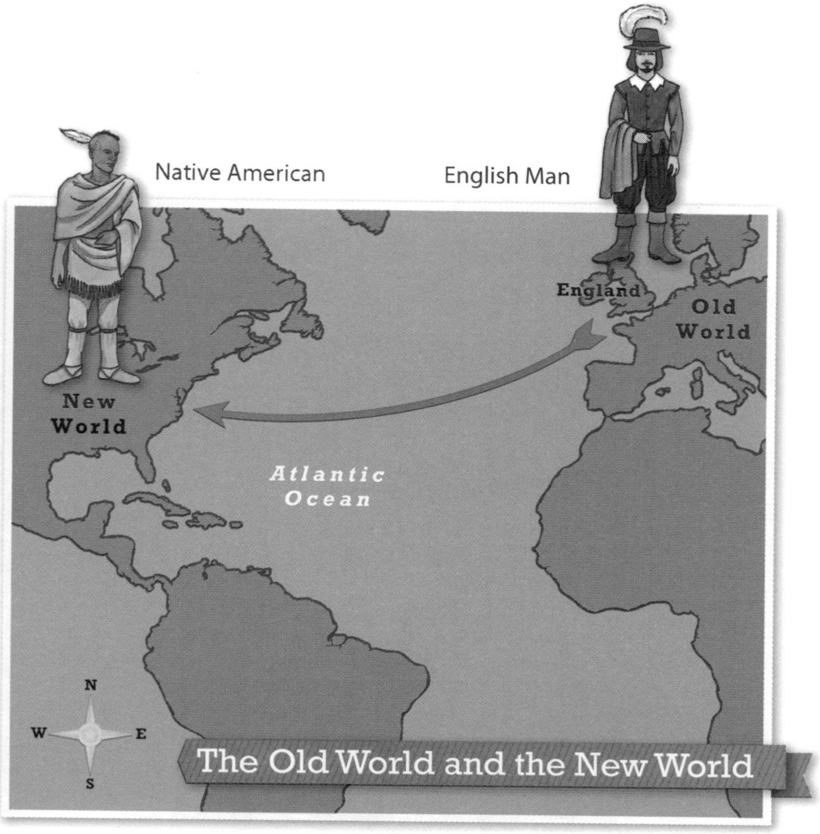

127

Lesson

67

- Direct attention to the map on page 127. Display Visual 29. Ask volunteers to point out parts of the map.

  What is the title of the map? The Old World and the New World

  What ocean is in the middle of the map? the Atlantic Ocean

  Use the compass rose to locate and identify the land area east of the Atlantic Ocean. the Old World

  Use the compass rose to locate and identify the land area west of the Atlantic Ocean. the New World

- Explain that during this time the known world included the Old World (Europe, Asia, and Africa) and the New World (the Americas: North and South America).
- Instruct the students to follow the red arrow on the map from the Old World to the New World.

  The English men sailed west across the Atlantic Ocean to reach the New World.

  Which man represents the Old World on this map? the English man

  Who represents the New World? the Native American

- Introduce Visual 30. Use the visual and page 127 to contrast the clothing of the Native American and the English man. Make a T-chart listing the differences the students suggest.

Compare the Native American and the English Man

Native American	English Man
feather in hair leather clothes no hair on face	feather in hat woven clothes beard

Lesson

68

Student Text pages 128–29
Activity Manual pages 121–23

Objectives

- Explain why the English came to settle Jamestown
- Locate an ocean, a coast, a river, and a harbor on a map
- Locate Jamestown on a map

Materials

- Visuals 29–30: *The Old World and the New World Map; The Old World and the New World Men*

Content Word

- coast

Introduction

- Use Visuals 29–30 to review the map and clothing of the Old World and the New World.

Teach for Understanding

- Direct attention to the picture on page 128. Read the names of the ships.

  The Virginia Company in England hired a crew of sailors to take men to the New World. The ships were named the *Susan Constant*, the *Godspeed*, and the *Discovery*. As you read, find out why men wanted to go to America.

- Guide the reading of the page.

  What kinds of people sailed to Virginia? rich men, workers, and boys

  What did the men want from the new land? Most wanted riches; a few wanted to tell others about Jesus.

  When the ship arrived on the coast of Virginia, Pastor Robert Hunt led the men in prayer, thanking God for their safe arrival in the New World. They sailed along the coast, or edge of the land, until they found a good place to build the settlement.

Three ships left England for the part of America called Virginia.
Many rich men and some workers and boys sailed in the ships.
Most of them wanted riches.
A few of them wanted to tell others about Jesus.
They arrived on the coast of Virginia in May of 1607.

The ships were named the *Discovery*, the *Susan Constant*, and the *Godspeed*.

128

The ships sailed up a river.
The men named it the James River
after their king, King James.
They called the place where they landed
Jamestown.

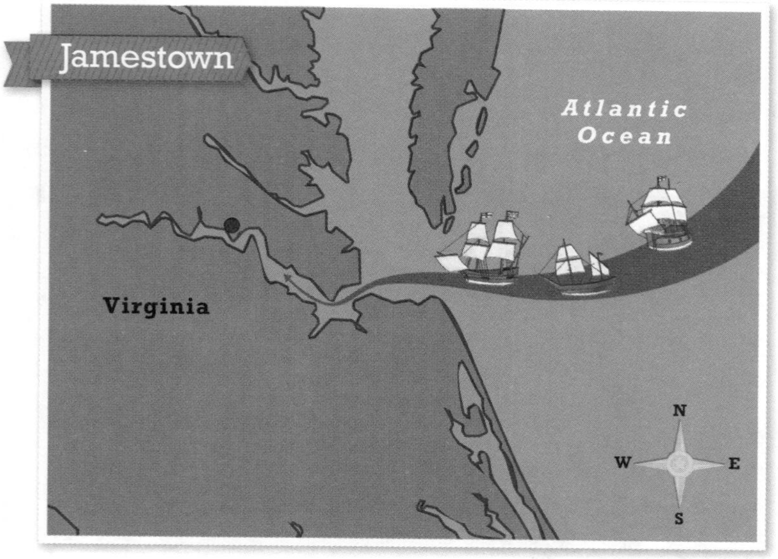

The dot (•) shows where Jamestown is.

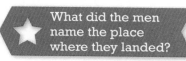

What did the men name the place where they landed?

Jamestown

129

- Guide the reading of page 129.

  What ocean did the ships sail across? the Atlantic

  What was the name of the river the ships sailed up? the James River

  Do you think the river was always named the James River? no

  Who was living in America before the English came? the Native Americans They would not have named the river after the king of England.

  What did the English name the land? Jamestown

  Who did they name the land and river after? their king; King James

  What is the title of the map? Jamestown

  The ships sailed across the Atlantic Ocean and then along the coast of Virginia. The English men chose the place to build a fort on a river where ships could easily harbor. They chose the river because of the fresh water for drinking. Because the land was free of large trees, a fort could be built quickly.

- Introduce geography terms by locating them on the map. Guide the students as they point to the Atlantic Ocean. Instruct each student to move his finger along the Virginia coast and down the James River to locate Jamestown (black dot on the map). Reinforce the terms *ocean*, *coast*, *river*, and *harbor* by finding them in the Geogloss on pages 174–75.
- Direct attention to Visual 29.

  A world map shows the big picture of the continents and oceans. But a world map does not show cities. Can you locate Jamestown on this map? no This map does not include cities.

- Compare the maps on pages 127 and 129.

  Can you locate Jamestown on the map on page 127? no

  Can you locate Jamestown on the map on page 129? yes Why? The map makes Jamestown bigger. It is easy to see.

  The purpose of this map is to zoom in on or show a close-up of the water and land area near Jamestown.

- Conclude the discussion by asking the question on page 129.

Activity Manual

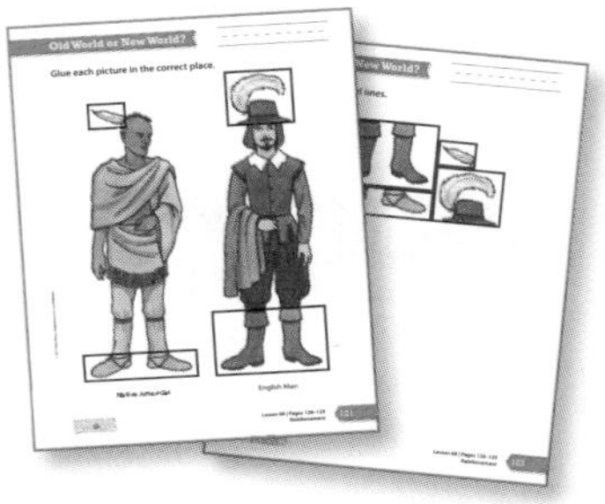

- Guide completion of pages 121–23.

Background

Place for a Settlement

When the *Susan Constant,* the *Godspeed,* and the *Discovery* arrived in Jamestown, it appeared to be a perfect place for a settlement. The position on the river would give the settlers protection from enemy ships coming up the James River. The native people lived miles away, and the Jamestown area was clear and vacant. The river would be ideal to harbor English ships. However, when summer came, the colonists realized that the area was a wetland that bred mosquitoes carrying malaria. The drinking water became salty and stagnant. The Woodland people became unfriendly. Consequently, the area did not have the best conditions for a successful settlement.

Lesson 69

Student Text pages 130–31
Activity Manual page 125

Objectives
- Affirm that Native Americans lived in America before the English came
- Identify Native Americans as Woodland tribes
- Dramatize the concern of the Woodland people about the arrival of the English
- Conclude that God wanted Jamestown to be a lasting English settlement

Materials
- A fur or leatherlike blanket
- Craft feathers

Vocabulary
- chief

Content Words
- copper
- powerful
- stranger

Introduction

- Direct attention to page 130. Read the title.
- Write the following letter headings as you introduce a *K-W-L* chart.

K: What do you *know*?
W: What do you *want to know*?
L: What have you *learned*?

K	W	L
first people to live in America		
lived in tribes		

- Complete the *K-W-L* chart as the students respond.
- Refer to Chapter 7 as you ask the question: "What do you know?"

What do you know about the Native Americans, or Woodland people? They were the first people to live in America; they lived in tribes.

- Continue with the second question: "What do you want to know?" The response to this question may not be limited to a specific lesson. The question is meant to stimulate thinking before reading. (*Note*: Column 3 will be completed at the end of the lesson.)

What do you want to know or learn about Native Americans?

Meeting the Woodland People

When English ships sailed up the river,
the Woodland people were watching.
These Native American people lived
in tribes in the woods.
Chief Powhatan was the leader
of the Woodland people.
He was the powerful ruler of many tribes.

A Woodland man
watched the ships
sail up the river.

130

Teach for Understanding

- Guide the reading of page 130. Pronounce the chief's name: Pow•HAT•an.

Which three ships does the first sentence refer to? the *Susan Constant*, the *Godspeed*, and the *Discovery*

What is the English name of the river? James River

Do you think the Native Americans called the river the James River? no
Why? Their leader was not King James.

Where did the Native Americans live? in the woods

The Woodland people depended on the woods to provide for them their everyday needs. They grew crops and hunted for food there. Their homes were in the woods too.

What were the smaller Native American groups called? tribes

Who was the leader of the Woodland tribes? Chief Powhatan

- Encourage students to tell what they think the Woodland man in the picture is thinking. Ask a volunteer what he might be thinking if he had been there.

Strangers had come to their land.
Some tribes did not want the English to live on their land.
Other tribes were friendly to the English men.
The chief was not sure what to think of these strangers.
But he let the English people stay.
The English men had guns, copper, and beads.
Chief Powhatan wanted these things.

Powhatan was the chief of many Woodland tribes.

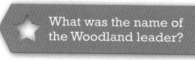

What was the name of the Woodland leader?

Chief Powhatan

131

- Direct attention to the picture on page 131. Invite a student to read the caption.

  Chief Powhatan is talking to the men in his tribe. He is seated above the other men because he is the chief.

  How are the men dressed? in leather or animal-skin clothing Is this the way you dress? no How is it different? Answers will vary.

  The men are sitting inside what is called a long house. The long house was a home and a place to meet. It was made of small trees covered with bark or animal skins.

  How is the long house different from your home? The walls are made of trees. The fire is in the middle of the long house. Men are sitting on the floor.

- Guide the reading of the page.
- Give the blanket you brought to a student to be the chief as the students act out the scene. Direct the chief to sit in a chair at the front of the room. Distribute feathers to several students to be members of the tribe. Arrange these students on the floor in front of the chief. Remind the students that the chief is powerful and must be respected. Allow the students to act out the page using their own words and ideas. Begin with the chief asking the question: "How do you feel about the strangers who have come to our land?"

- Conclude the activity by reviewing pages 130–31.

  God planned for Powhatan to befriend the English. The mighty Powhatan with his many warriors could have destroyed Jamestown. God wanted Jamestown to be a lasting English settlement.

  Why do you think God allowed Jamestown to last? Possible answers: God wanted the church to last. God wanted the Woodland people to hear about God. God wanted a Christian witness in Virginia.

- Complete the *K-W-L* chart by answering the question "What have you learned?" Possible answers: Powhatan was the chief of the Woodland people. Some tribes did not want the English to live on their land. Chief Powhatan befriended the people at Jamestown.
- Conclude the discussion by asking the question on page 131.

Activity Manual

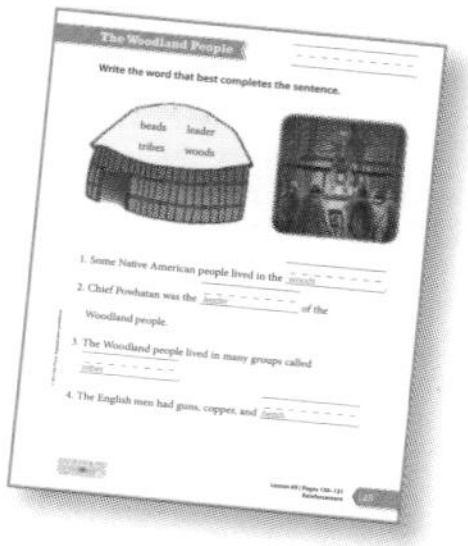

- Guide completion of page 125.

Background

Powhatan

The picture of Powhatan on page 131 is an artist's rendition of John Smith's original art piece created in 1612 (John Smith's Map of Virginia, published in 1612).

Chief Powhatan was nearly sixty years old when he met the colonists from Jamestown. Even though he was older, he was powerful, strong, and able to endure hard work. He was over six feet tall, which was much taller than the average Englishman.

Powhatan was the paramount chief of Virginia's Powhatan Indians. The Woodland people respected, honored, and obeyed him. Powhatan had supreme political and military power. About thirty tribes brought him furs, corn, and other valuables to show their allegiance. Powhatan and his warriors could have easily overtaken the small number of sickly colonists. The colonists were greatly outnumbered. The bow and arrow was more efficient than the matchlock weapons the colonists carried. Although leery of the colonists at first, Powhatan eventually came to trust them. He even allowed his daughter, Pocahontas, to marry an Englishman, John Rolfe.

God used Powhatan and his people to supply needed food to the men in Jamestown. God allowed Jamestown to survive and become the first lasting English settlement in the New World.

Lesson 70

Student Text pages 132–33
Activity Manual pages 127–29

Objectives

- Create a map of the school library
- Interpret a map key
- Infer the importance of God and the Bible at Jamestown from looking at a map of Jamestown
- Sequence a list of three events

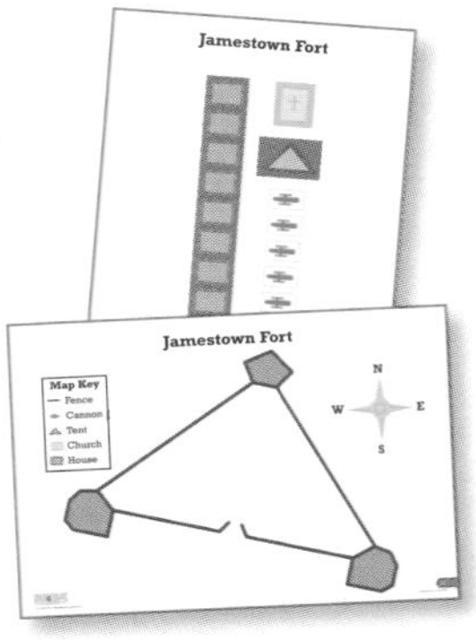

Materials

- Visuals 31–32: *Jamestown Fort* and prepared die-cut pieces
- 20–30 building blocks
- A sheet of poster board
- A picture of a chain saw

Vocabulary

- fort
- settlement

Content Word

- cannon

Introduction

- Create a map and a key of the school library, using the poster board as the base and the blocks as representations of the tables and shelves.
- Choose a volunteer to mark the front entrance of the library on the poster board. Invite the students to help you position the librarian's desk on the map.
- Direct several students to place blocks on the map to represent tables, shelves, and other furniture in the library. Title the map "Our Library."

  How can we show what each block on the map represents? with a map key
- Design the map key by placing and identifying a corresponding block for the librarian's desk, tables, shelves, and any other items on the map.

Teach for Understanding

After the men of Jamestown landed on the river's edge, they needed to build a fort to live in for protection.

If you were going to build a fort, what would you do first? Answers may vary.

- Direct attention to page 132. Invite a student to read the title. Guide the reading of the page.

  The men from Jamestown needed to build a fort. First they made a plan of the fort. It might have looked like a map. They needed to prepare the land by clearing trees and removing large rocks or fallen trees. Next they built the walls of the fort out of tall tree trunks. The walls would help protect them from their enemies. And last they built a church, a storehouse, and houses. The church was built so that the men could daily meet together to read the Bible, pray, and hear preaching.

  Do you think God, Jesus, and the Bible were important to the men of Jamestown? yes

  What did these men of Jamestown build to show how important it is to worship God? a church

Starting a Settlement

The leaders of Jamestown made a plan.
They would build a **fort**.
The fort would keep them safe.
The men cut the trees to clear the land.
Trees were used for the walls of the fort.
The fort was built in the shape of a triangle.
Houses, buildings, and a church were built inside the fort walls.
Jamestown Fort became the first English **settlement**.
A settlement is a group of people living in a new place.

This ax head was found in diggings at Jamestown.

Courtesy Preservation Virginia

The ax was used to chop trees for the fort.

132

- Point out the pictures at the bottom of the page. Select a student to read the captions.

  The men from Jamestown needed to chop down trees to use for the buildings and the log walls at the fort.
- Display the picture of a chain saw.

  Do you think the men used chain saws long ago to cut the trees? Answers may vary.

  Several hundred years after men came to Jamestown, people found in the ground objects that belonged to the men who built the Jamestown Fort. They did not find a chain saw, but they did find an ax head.
- Direct attention to the ax head.

  This ax head is over four hundred years old. It came from diggings at the Jamestown Fort. This ax head is called an artifact. An artifact is an object made by people from the past. An artist looked at the ax head artifact and

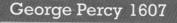

George Percy 1607

"The fifteenth of June we had built and finished our Fort, which was triangle wise."

Jamestown Fort

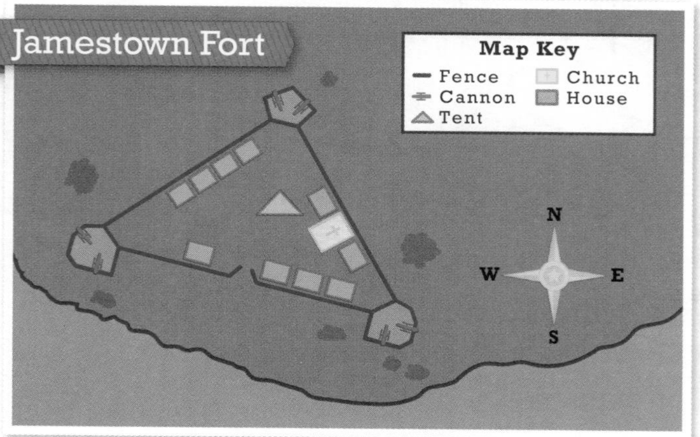

133

drew the ax head with a handle and placed it in the log. The artist thinks this is how the men from Jamestown used the ax head.

- Invite the students to comment about the picture and how real it looks.
- Direct attention to the picture of the Jamestown Fort and the map of Jamestown on page 133.

Were you at Jamestown when the fort was built? no

No one living today saw Jamestown being built. We know what Jamestown looks like because people have gone to the area near Jamestown, dug into the ground, and found parts of the fort. These people made pictures of what they found. It was much like the map on page 133. An artist studied these pictures and read old letters and books. The artist imagined how Jamestown might have looked four hundred years ago and then drew the picture on this page.

- Read the quotation on the page.

Who is the author of these words? George Percy

In what year did he write these words? 1607

The year 1607 was the year Jamestown was built. Mr. Percy was one of the men there.

What shape did Mr. Percy say the fort was built in? a triangle

What shape is the fort in the picture? a triangle

Do you think the artist could have used Mr. Percy's words when he drew the picture? yes

- Display Visual 31. Direct attention to the compass rose. Invite a student to point to north, south, east, and west on the map. Distribute the houses, cannons, tent, and church from Visual 32. Guide the students as they position each piece on the map as it is discussed.

What is the title of the map? Jamestown Fort

- Point out the map key.

What represents the fence or the fort wall? a brown line

What represents the tent? a gray triangle

- Direct a student to place the tent in the center of the fort.

What represents a house on the map key? a tan rectangle Place four houses to the west of the tent along the fort wall.

Place four houses south of the tent along the fort wall.

What represents the church on the map key? a gold rectangle with a cross

Place the church and two houses east of the tent along the fort wall.

Place two cannons in each corner of the fort.

Where is the door of the fort? at the space in the brown line; on the south wall

Activity Manual

- Guide completion of pages 127–29.

Background

Artifacts

Artifacts are used by historians as they gather information or clues about the life and times of people from the past. Images of artifacts in the text are designed to help students understand how people lived long ago.

Written Resources

Written resources are used by historians as they collect facts about early cultures. As you evaluate written sources, consider the point of view of the writer as well as the cultural norms of that day. The words of George Percy may help first graders grasp the fact that people really lived four hundred years ago and that they wrote about their experiences.

Lesson

71

Student Text pages 134–37
Activity Manual page 131

Objectives

- Classify needs and wants
- Conclude that John Smith was a wise leader of Jamestown
- Differentiate trade items between the Native Americans and the colonists

Materials

- Visual 30: *The Old World and the New World Men*
- A bottle of water, a bag of coins, a gemstone ring, a loaf of bread, a fur coat, and a photo of a house

Content Words

- argue
- iron

Introduction

- Display the English man and the Woodland man from Visual 30 as you play a review game. Instruct the students to answer each question by pointing to the correct figure.

  Who hoped to find gold and riches in the New World? the English men

  Who wanted guns, copper, and beads? the Woodland people

  Who called the place where they landed the ship Jamestown? the English men

  Who lived in groups called tribes? the Woodland people

  Who lived in the woods? the Woodland people

  Who lived in a settlement? the English men

Teach for Understanding

- Display the objects you brought. Invite students to choose the correct object as you ask each question.

  If you were really thirsty, would you need a bottle of water or lots of money? a bottle of water

  If you were really hungry, would you need a gemstone ring or a loaf of bread? a loaf of bread

  If you had no place to stay, would you need a house or a fur coat? a house

  You have made some wise choices—much better choices than some of the men who settled in Jamestown.

- Direct attention to page 134. Ask a student to read the title.

  As you read the page, look for things that would make the fort a good place to live.

- Guide the reading of the page.

  What needed to be done in Jamestown to make the fort a good place to live? The men needed to work, plant crops, and hunt for food. They needed a wise leader.

Living in a Settlement

Much work needed to be done to make
the fort a good place to live.
Everyone was needed to plant crops
and hunt for food.
But the rich men did not want to work.
They looked for gold but did not find it.

Jamestown Needs and Wants			
Needs	 food	 water	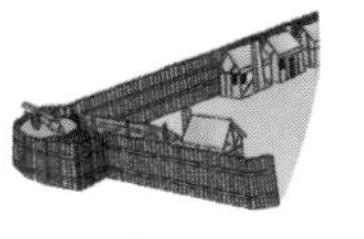 fort
Wants	 gold	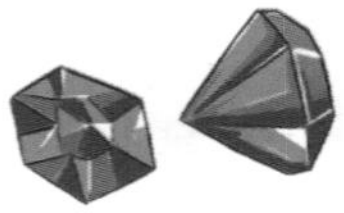 gems	 furs

The men argued with each other.
The settlement needed a wise leader.
Captain John Smith became the leader
of Jamestown.

134

- Direct attention to the chart. Discuss each item as either a need or a want.

  The men had made a long voyage across the ocean. They wanted gold, precious gems, and furs to take back to England. These things would make them rich.

- Guide a discussion about the scarcity of food, water, and shelter.

  There were no houses in Jamestown. Where would these men live? There were no grocery stores or restaurants in Jamestown. What would they eat? How would they get fresh water? There was no bottled water. What would they drink?

  The men had to make choices. Even though they were adults, many made wrong choices. They spent their time unwisely looking for riches.

  Captain John Smith became a wise leader in Jamestown. As you read the next page, notice where Captain Smith found wisdom.

2 Thessalonians 3:10

If any would not work,
neither should he eat.

Captain Smith used a truth from God's Word
to get the men to work.
If a man did not work, he could not eat.
All the men soon learned to work.
It was a hard job planting seeds in the dirt.
The crops did not grow well.
More food was needed for the men to live.

Captain Smith helped to plant a garden at the fort.

135

- Guide the reading of page 135.

  Where did Captain Smith find wisdom to lead the men of Jamestown? He used a truth from God's Word, the Bible.

- Invite a student to read the rule Captain Smith made.

  How many men do you think worked? all the men Was the work easy? no Did the crops grow well? no

  Did Captain Smith follow his own rule? yes

  Captain Smith worked the same as the other men.

- Point out the picture showing Captain Smith working alongside a man at Jamestown.

  Are the two men dressed the same? no How are they dressed differently? Answers will vary.

  The man in the armor is Captain Smith. He may have worn his armor so that he would be ready in case an enemy attacked.

Lesson

71

- Direct attention to page 136. Draw a T-chart for display. Label the columns *Captain John Smith* and *Woodland People*.

  Even though the men of Jamestown planted gardens, they still needed more food. They had money to buy food, but there were no places that sold food. The money had no value or worth in the New World because there was no place to spend it. As you read this page, find out some things that had value in the New World. What did Captain John Smith use instead of money to get the things the men in Jamestown needed?

Compare Things to Trade

Captain John Smith	Woodland People
glass beads	corn
copper	meat
iron	furs

- Guide the reading of the page. Complete the chart as the students respond.

  What did Captain Smith trade to get food? glass beads, copper, and iron

  What did the Woodland people trade to get the things they wanted? corn, meat, and furs

  What did the Woodland people value more than money? glass beads, copper, and iron
- Conclude the discussion by asking the question on page 136.

Captain Smith traded with the Woodland people.
He gave them glass beads, copper, and iron.
The Woodland people gave the settlers corn, meat, and furs.
The food they traded helped the men to live.
But some died from sickness.
Because Captain Smith was a wise leader, more men lived.

Captain Smith traded copper pots for food.

What did Captain Smith trade with the Woodland people?

beads, copper, and iron for food

136

Famous People

Captain John Smith

Captain John Smith loved to explore places far away.
He was a short man with red hair.
Captain Smith was a good leader and a skilled soldier.
While hunting for deer one day, he was taken by the Indians.
Chief Powhatan did not want John Smith to live.
But the chief's daughter begged for the captain's life to be saved.
Captain Smith made friends with the Woodland people.
He learned their way of life.
He learned to talk with them.
God used John Smith to make Jamestown a better settlement.

Captain John Smith

- Read about Captain John Smith on page 137.

  Who befriended Captain John Smith? Chief Powhatan's daughter

  List two things that Captain Smith did to make friends with the Woodland people. He learned their way of life. He learned to talk with them.

  Captain Smith was wise to learn about the Woodland culture.

- Direct attention to the statue of Captain John Smith.

  The statue of Captain John Smith stands in Jamestown today. Many people visit the statue that honors him.

  Pretend that your family is visiting Jamestown and you are standing at the statue with a little brother. What do you remember about Captain John Smith to tell your brother? Possible answers: John Smith became the leader of Jamestown. He was a wise leader. He used truth from God's Word to get the men to work. He worked and helped others. He traded with the Woodland people and learned their ways and their language. He was used of God to make Jamestown a better settlement.

Activity Manual

- Guide completion of page 131.

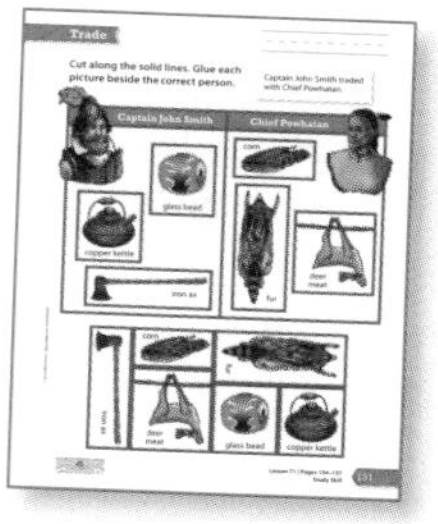

Background

John Smith

Captain John Smith joined the Virginia Company as an adventurer in colonizing the New World. Smith sailed on the *Susan Constant* to America. He was not originally the captain of the ship; he had been made a captain while fighting in Hungary for Austria. Smith was chosen by King James I to be one of the leaders in Jamestown. The weak leadership in the colony caused discontentment. The settlement was failing. Food was scarce, and there was no protection from the hostile Indians. Although he was not well liked, Smith was elected governor of the colony. Under his forceful leadership, all men were made to work. John Smith demanded that everyone work no matter what his background. He knew the importance of work and followed the teachings of 2 Thessalonians 3:10. Laws were passed requiring all the men to work each day, listen to sermons, and pray daily. They also prohibited them from stealing and blaspheming.

Relationships with the Indians eased as they respected Smith's daring and determined personality. He told Chief Powhatan, "I have but one God, I honour but one King; and I live not here as your subject, but as your friend."

The strong leadership of John Smith and the religious character of his laws saved the Jamestown settlement.

Lesson 72

Student Text pages 138–39
Activity Manual page 133

Objectives
- Identify items made from natural resources
- List goods made from things found in the woods
- Assemble a wigwam

Materials
- Items made from natural resources such as a wooden spoon, a woven basket, and stone or shell jewelry
- Manmade items such as a plastic spoon, a basket, and jewelry
- A table to frame a wigwam
- Towels or other fabric to cover the wigwam (*Note*: Encourage each child to bring a large towel to make the wigwam.)

Vocabulary
- resource

Introduction

When God made the earth, He gave us all that we need to live. The Native Americans wisely used natural resources that God gave them. From things in the woods, they made food, clothing, homes, and even decorations. The Woodland people had no stores to buy the things they needed. There were no factories to make the things they wanted. All the things they had were found in the woods or nearby rivers.

- Display the plastic and natural items that you have assembled. Invite students to select items made from plastic and items made from natural resources. Allow students to identify the natural object that each item is made from (e.g., wooden spoon—a tree).

Teach for Understanding

- Direct attention to page 138. Invite a student to read the title. Write the word *Woodland* for display.

  The Native Americans who lived in Virginia were the Woodland people.

  What two words make up the word *Woodland*? *wood* and *land*

  Where do you think these people lived? in the woods

  As you read the pages, look for resources or things the people used from the woods.

- Guide the reading of pages 138–39.

  Who lived in America before the English men settled in Jamestown? the Woodland people

  What did these people use to make their homes? trees

  What did the Woodland people use to make their clothes? deer hides; deerskins

Living in the Woods

The Woodland people lived in America long before men came from England.
Each Woodland family worked together.
Their homes were made from trees.
They made clothes from deer hides.
The men were hunters and fishers.
The women made mats, pots, and baskets.

138

How did these people get their food? by hunting, fishing, and gardening

What kinds of things did the Woodland people make? mats, pots, baskets, and clothes

- Direct attention to the Woodland village picture.

  The Woodland man in the picture is scraping and cleaning a deer hide. What could he do with the hide? make clothing, a blanket, or a covering for his home

  Another man has brought food to the village. What kind of food did he bring? fish

  What did the man use to catch the fish? a spear

  How do you think the spear was made? with a stick and an arrowhead or a sharp bone; something from the woods

  What is the woman in the picture doing? carrying a bowl of food

  The women made the bowls, baskets, and pots.

  Where did the women get materials to make things? from resources in the woods

  Baskets were made of grasses and tree bark. Pots were often made of clay or dirt and then baked to harden.

Boys practiced running and shooting bows and arrows.
Girls pulled weeds in the gardens and found sticks for the fire.
The family used the **resources** from the woods for food and to make homes and clothes.
Resources are things we find around us to use.

How is the little girl helping? She is gathering wood and sticks for the fire.

What is the boy doing? playing with a dog Is that something you would like to do?

- Instruct the students to look closely at the picture and point to something made from a tree that the Woodland people used to travel on the river.

Canoes were made from large trees. Men scraped the log with stone tools and then used fire to burn the inside of the log.

The Woodland people planted gardens because they lived in one place for long periods of time.

What plant is in the garden in the picture? corn

The Woodland people ate deer, rabbit, and other small animals that they hunted in the woods. They gathered berries from the woods. They also grew corn, squash, and other vegetables in gardens. Many lived close enough to a river to fish and gather shellfish such as clams.

- Describe the wigwams the Woodland people made using the resources God gave them.

The Woodland people lived in the forest. They prepared their village by clearing small trees and bushes from under the tallest trees. They used the small trees to make the wigwam homes. The trees were bent into a dome shape and pushed into the ground. The women placed grass mats or animal hides over the wood frame. They called their homes wigwams. Each part of the home was made from something they found in the woods. The Woodland people used the natural resources God gave them for food and shelter and for meeting their daily needs.

- Guide the students as they make one large wigwam or a village with several smaller wigwams using the table frame and towels to represent animal skins or grass mats.

Activity Manual

- Guide completion of page 133. Instruct the students to circle in blue the things the Woodland people used for food (fish, berries, shellfish, deer). Circle in red the things they made from a resource in the woods (canoe, home, clothing, basket).

Background

Woodland People

The Woodland tribes in Virginia belonged to Powhatan's chiefdom. Over thirty villages gave allegiance to Powhatan. A Woodland village could consist of thirty to a thousand people. Each village had a chief. These Woodland people lived for many years in the same area, moving only when the supply of wood or food diminished.

The Woodland people built semipermanent homes from the resources in the forest. To build a home, they used saplings to make a dome-shaped frame. The frame was covered with woven reed mats and animal hides. The smaller homes or wigwams might house a family. The larger homes or long houses would hold an extended family. A fire was kept burning in the home during cold months. An opening was made in the top of the wigwam for smoke to escape.

The Woodland people near Jamestown were farmers. The women planted corn, squash, and beans. The older boys kept watch of the garden from a raised hut. As they kept wild animals away from the crops, they practiced their archery skills. The women and girls tended the garden with crude tools made from deer antlers or stones. Other food sources in the woods were nuts, berries, and roots. Children often gathered the berries in season.

Important jobs for the men were protecting the tribe from enemies and providing meat. Men hunted and fished to supply the village with food. The deer was a primary source of food from the woods. The tribes used the meat for food, bones for tools, and hides for clothing, blankets, and covering their homes. The men and boys fished in the nearby rivers and the Chesapeake Bay. Boys often enjoyed diving for shellfish. They ate the meat inside the shell and made jewelry from the shell. The Native Americans used God's natural resources wisely.

Lesson

73

Student Text pages 140–41
Activity Manual page 135

Objectives

- Differentiate between Woodland culture and English culture
- Dramatize the story of Pocahontas's interactions with the English

Materials

- *The Woodland People and the English* (Teacher's Toolkit CD)
- *Pocahontas's Story* (Teacher's Toolkit CD)

Introduction

- Explain that a culture is a way of life.

  In this chapter we have been studying two very different cultures. What two cultures have we studied? the way of life of the Jamestown settlers and of the Woodland people

- Distribute the prepared Woodland and English pictures. Ask questions such as the following. Direct the student with the correct picture to stand and identify the culture and the object.

  What was used for water transportation? Woodland: canoe; English: ship

  What weapon was used in hunting? Woodland: bow and arrow; English: gun

  What items were used to trade? Woodland: corn; English: beads

  What kinds of homes did they live in? Woodland: wigwam; English: house

  What kind of clothes would princesses wear? Woodland: simple clothes made of deerskin; English: fancy clothes with fur trim and a crown

  What kind of clothes did people wear? Woodland: deerskin clothes; English: clothes from woven materials

  Where did people in the New World live? Woodland: woods; English: fort

  Who were the leaders of the people? Woodland: Powhatan; English: John Smith

  Who made up a family? In both cultures: dad, mom, and children

Teach for Understanding

- Generate interest in the lesson by asking questions such as the following.

  Would you like to be a princess? Or a prince? How do you think a princess would act? What things would she do? Do you think a prince would need to work hard?

- Direct attention to page 140. Ask a volunteer to read the title.

  We will read about an Indian princess. She is different from most princesses that you may know about. As you read the page, find out how this princess is different from a princess in a make-believe story.

- Guide the reading of the page. Direct attention to the picture and read the caption.

  Why do we call Pocahontas an Indian princess? Her father was Chief Powhatan.

  Did she sit on a throne and tell her servants what to do? No, she worked like other girls her age.

  In the picture, who is Pocahontas taking food to? the hungry men in Jamestown

- Explain that Pocahontas took corn to the starving men in the Jamestown settlement. She proved to be a good friend to Captain Smith and all the people in Jamestown.

  Some years later when Pocahontas was visiting a Woodland village, she was kidnapped by a sea captain. Her father, Powhatan, had captured some of Captain Argall's men and weapons. The captain wanted his guns and men returned. He thought he would be able to trade Pocahontas for them. Powhatan was not ready to return the men for several months. During this time Pocahontas learned the English way of life. A pastor taught her about the one true God. Pocahontas became a Christian. She chose to stay with the English people in Jamestown.

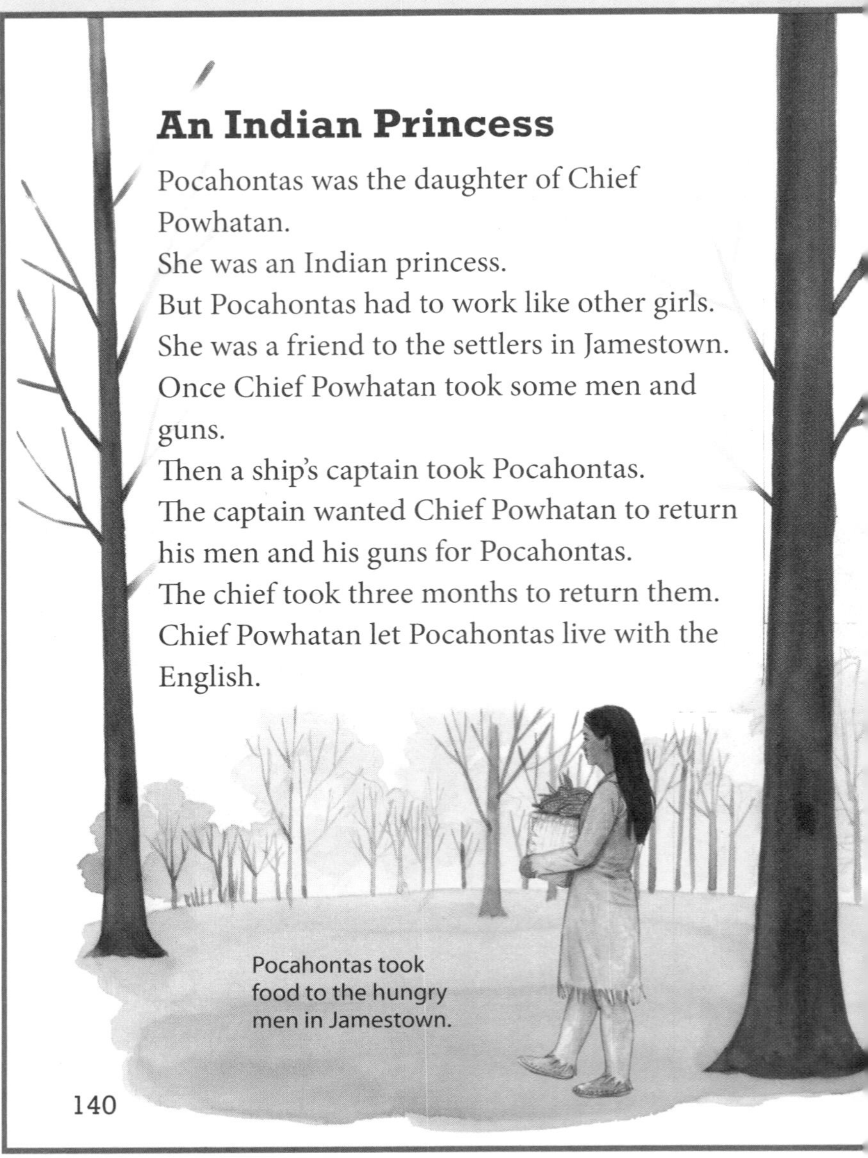

An Indian Princess

Pocahontas was the daughter of Chief Powhatan.
She was an Indian princess.
But Pocahontas had to work like other girls.
She was a friend to the settlers in Jamestown.
Once Chief Powhatan took some men and guns.
Then a ship's captain took Pocahontas.
The captain wanted Chief Powhatan to return his men and his guns for Pocahontas.
The chief took three months to return them.
Chief Powhatan let Pocahontas live with the English.

Pocahontas took food to the hungry men in Jamestown.

140

Pocahontas learned the English ways.
A pastor taught her about God.
She trusted in the true God.
Pocahontas loved a Christian man
from Jamestown.
John Rolfe and Pocahontas were married.
He took Pocahontas to visit England.
There the Indian princess met the
queen of England.

John Rolfe and Pocahontas were married in Jamestown.

Whom did Pocahontas trust in to become a Christian?

God

141

- Guide the reading of page 141. Direct attention to the picture and read the caption.

  Who did Pocahontas marry? John Rolfe

- Explain that John Rolfe was a Christian who had a great desire to see the Woodland people come to know the Lord.

  John Rolfe loved Pocahontas and her people. Because of the marriage of a Woodland woman (Pocahontas) and an English man (John Rolfe), there was peace between the Woodland people and the English.

  After some time Mr. Rolfe had a successful business in Jamestown. He was able to sell his crops in England. He took Pocahontas to England with him. She was able to see again her friend Captain John Smith, who had returned to England. Pocahontas also met King James and Queen Anne.

- Direct attention to the pictures on pages 140–41.

  Which picture shows Pocahontas dressed as an English woman? page 141

- Encourage the students to list some of the differences in the clothing. leather clothing; clothing made from woven material

  What do you think were some differences between Pocahontas's way of life in the woods and her way of life in the settlement? houses; clothing; manners

- Select several students to act out the story of Pocahontas as you reread the two pages. Distribute the prepared story pictures. Arrange the students with the signs in a line. Instruct Pocahontas to act out what you read as she passes in front of each person. (*Note*: You may discuss simple actions before you begin reading. Props are optional.) Example: Pocahontas and John Smith wave at each other as you read: "Pocahontas was a friend to the settlers."
- Conclude the discussion by asking the question on page 141.

Activity Manual

- Guide completion of page 135.

Background

Pocahontas

Pocahontas was eleven years old when the colonists arrived in Jamestown. She was attracted to the settlers, and they liked her. John Smith tells about a time when he lay across a stone ready to be beheaded by one of Powhatan's warriors. Pocahontas came to the rescue, begging her father to spare Smith's life. Smith owed the child his life and their friendship grew. The survival of Jamestown was due largely to the food Pocahontas provided to the settlement during the winter months.

In 1613 Captain Samuel Argall persuaded Pocahontas to come aboard his ship. Once she was aboard, he held her ransom. He wanted her father, Powhatan, to return the men and guns he had taken. However, Powhatan did not return the men or guns right away. Pocahontas was taken to Jamestown, where Reverend Alexander Whitaker taught her from the Word of God. She renounced the idols of her people and trusted in the one true God. She changed her name to Rebecca at her baptism.

In the spring of 1614, Pocahontas married a Christian man, John Rolfe. Her uncle and two brothers attended the wedding. Powhatan showed his approval by giving the newlyweds two dressed deerskins. Their marriage brought peace between the Woodland people and the colonists for many years.

Lesson

74

Student Text pages 142–43
Activity Manual page 137

Objectives

- Differentiate between Woodland culture and English culture
- Describe the different family roles
- Explain the importance of women and families in the survival of Jamestown
- List good leadership qualities

Materials

- *The Woodland People and the English* (Teacher's Toolkit CD)

Vocabulary

- servant

Introduction

- Select three pairs of the prepared pictures for each round of a memory game. Arrange the pictures face-down. Direct a student to turn over a picture and another student to turn over the matching picture. If the pictures are a match, instruct a third student to tell why. (*Example*: A canoe and a ship match because they are both forms of water transportation. The Woodland people used a canoe, and the English people used a ship.)

Teach for Understanding

- Direct attention to page 142. Ask a volunteer to read the title. Remind the students that a settlement is a group of people living together in a new place.
- Guide a discussion about the title and picture.

  What do you think the title means? Answers may vary.

  Look back in the chapter at the pictures. What is different about this picture? Answers may vary.

  What kinds of people are in this picture that are not in the other pictures in the chapter? an English woman, a girl, and a baby

  Find out how women changed the settlement.
- Direct the reading of the page.

  Two cultures or groups of people were brought together with the marriage of John Rolfe and Pocahontas.

  What two kinds of people were brought together? the Woodland people and the English people; the Old World and the New World

  The Rolfes were not the only married couple in Jamestown. The men living in Jamestown married the young women arriving on the ships from England. These men provided homes and food for their wives. Children were born, and the families made the settlement a better place to live.
- Sing the following words to the tune of "The Farmer in the Dell" as you play "The Settler in the Fort." Instruct the students to walk in a circle around the settler as they sing the first verse. At the end of the first verse, direct the settler to choose a wife. Follow the same procedure with each verse: the settler takes a wife, the wife takes a child, the child takes a dog, the dog takes a cow, the cow takes a pig, and the pig takes a chicken.

  The settler in the fort. The settler in the fort.

  Hi-ho, the derry-o. The settler in the fort.
- Explain that the family living in Jamestown had a father, a mother, and children.

  When women came to Jamestown, they wanted to have families. With the families came homes that would last. The family might have a dog to help watch for danger. Cows, pigs, and chickens would be kept for food. These farm animals were brought to the New World from England. They were not in Virginia before the English came.
- Direct attention to the picture on page 143. Read the caption.

  What is the man doing in the picture? stacking wood

  This man is a servant. He belongs to a rich man in Jamestown. Find out why a servant worked.
- Guide the reading of the page.

  Why is the servant working? He has no money.

The Settlement Grows

The Jamestown settlers and Woodland people had peace after Pocahontas and John Rolfe were married.

The settlement changed as women came to live in Jamestown.

Families were started, and children were born.

Families working together made the settlement a better place to live.

Families worked together in Jamestown.

142

Servants came to Jamestown with no money. After working seven years, they became free men.
More people came to Virginia.
They made laws themselves.
They formed a new government.
Jamestown was the first lasting English settlement.

The servant stacked wood.

Name two kinds of people that came later to Jamestown.

women and servants

Activity

143

Men who were poor and could not pay their way on the ships to the New World agreed to work for the person who paid their way. They worked as servants. After they worked for seven years, they became free.

Rich men, workers, and boys were first to come to Jamestown. Then women, children, and servants came. The settlement was growing into a large community of working people. Laws were needed to make the people safe. The people made their own government. The people in the settlement chose men to make laws for the good of all the people. Jamestown became a good place to live. More people came to settle in areas around Jamestown and in other parts of Virginia. Jamestown became the first lasting English settlement in the New World.

- Guide the students as they make laws for the Jamestown settlement, drawing ideas from the chapter. (*Examples*: If you don't work, you don't eat. All must work. All must plant gardens. Help those who are sick. Work together. All must attend church on Sunday.)
- Conclude the discussion by asking the question on page 143.

Activity Manual

- Guide completion of page 137.

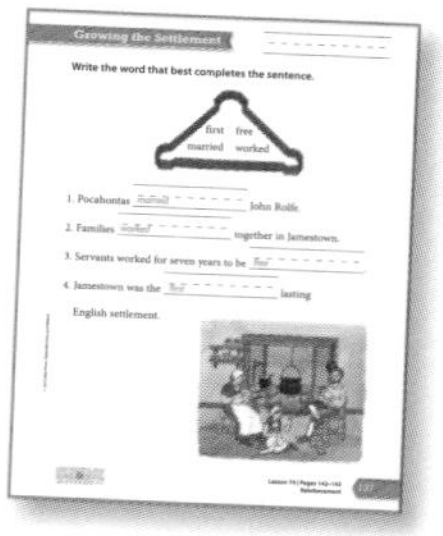

Background

Women in Jamestown

In 1608 small groups of women began coming to Jamestown. As more women lived in Jamestown, the men became responsible for the women and children. The men who were once irresponsible and quarrelsome became family men: husbands and fathers. This was necessary to make the settlement the kind of place that could face hardship, pull together, and endure. This is an example of what God says in Genesis 2:18: "It is not good that the man should be alone."

Indentured Servants

In 1619 a Dutch ship arrived in Jamestown with about twenty Africans. These were not slaves; they were indentured servants. They were men who wanted to come to America but who had no money. In order to pay their way, they agreed to serve the men who paid for their passage. After several years of service, the servant would be freed and given fifty acres to work himself. However, the practice of indentured servitude changed as years passed. Eventually some settlers decided that they needed Africans to serve for life, not just until their passage was paid for. This was the beginning of the practice of slavery in America.

Government

The Jamestown settlers were given the freedom to create their own government. In 1619 they formed the House of Burgesses. This assembly was composed of men elected by the settlers. They met regularly to pass laws to help the settlement. This was the first representative assembly in America. From this root would grow one of the most important institutions in American culture: the republican form of government.

Settlement

The English had many reasons to establish a colony in the New World. Their rival Spain had many settlements in the New World. England was concerned that Spain would surpass her in wealth and power in the New World.

Another concern was religion. Spain wanted to establish a Catholic empire. England, however, was Protestant and wanted the New World to be Protestant. One of the main goals for the English colony stated in the royal charter was the spread of Christianity among the Native Americans. Men like John Rolfe wanted "to convert and bring to the knowledge and true worship of Jesus Christ . . . [the] misbelieving people: . . . seeing they bear the Image of our heavenly Creator, and we and they come from one and the same mold."

Another English need was land. England's population was growing rapidly, and it needed more land to accommodate this growth. The New World held seemingly endless possibilities for the needed growth.

Lesson

75

Chapter Review and Activity
Activity Manual page 139

Objective

- Recall concepts and terms from Chapter 9

Materials

- Visuals 29–30: *The Old World and the New World Map; The Old World and the New World Men*
- *The Woodland People and the English* (Teacher's Toolkit CD)
- A container of puffed rice cereal with one candy ring, candy coins, and enough candy jewels for each child to have one piece (*Variation*: You may choose to use a container of sand with a ring, coins, and plastic jewels.)
- A plastic shovel

Activity

- Remind the students that an artifact is something a group of people left behind.

  In Jamestown today, people are digging up the ground where Jamestown was settled. These people are finding things the men from Jamestown left behind. They have found coins that look like copper pennies, blue glass beads that were traded with the Woodland people, and a special ring that belonged to William Strachey. William Strachey lived in Jamestown in 1609.

- Explain that the students will use the shovel to dig for artifacts in Jamestown. Allow each student to take a turn digging for a treasure.

Activity

Lesson 75

Review

- Reread the poem on page 124 to recap the chapter.

  Over what sea or ocean did the English sail? the Atlantic

  What was the wild shore or untamed land? Jamestown; Virginia; the New World

  What hard work did the men do? cleared the land; built a fort; planted gardens; protected the fort

  Who planned for Jamestown to last? God
- Invite a student to read the poem aloud, asking all the students to join him in reading the last line.
- Display Visual 29 to review parts of the map. Instruct students to identify the title and the compass rose.
- Review the parts of the Jamestown Fort using the map on page 133.
- Invite students to read the meanings of the vocabulary words using the Picture Glossary.
- Review Chapter 9 by playing a memory game with the prepared Woodland and English pictures.
- Guide the students as they tell about Woodland people and English people using the prepared pictures.

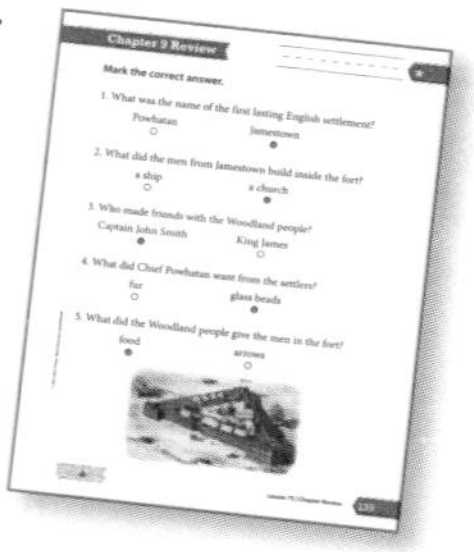

Activity Manual

- Guide completion of page 139. Instruct the students to mark the answer bubbles completely.

Chapter 9 Test

- Administer Test 9.

Chapter 10

Introduction

In Chapter 10 the students will follow the Pilgrims as they voyage across the Atlantic. But unlike the men from Jamestown, the Pilgrims sought religious freedom. In God's divine plan, the *Mayflower* was blown off course and landed in Plymouth, an uninhabited area. The students will learn that the Pilgrims wrote their own laws in the Mayflower Compact. After moving into newly built homes, they were greeted by a Native American who spoke English. The students will enjoy learning about the friendship that developed between the Pilgrims and the Woodland people, which culminated in a lasting peace treaty. The Pilgrims who survived the hardships of the long voyage, the first winter, and the deadly sickness gave thanks to God. The celebration became the first Thanksgiving and started the Thanksgiving holiday that Americans enjoy today.

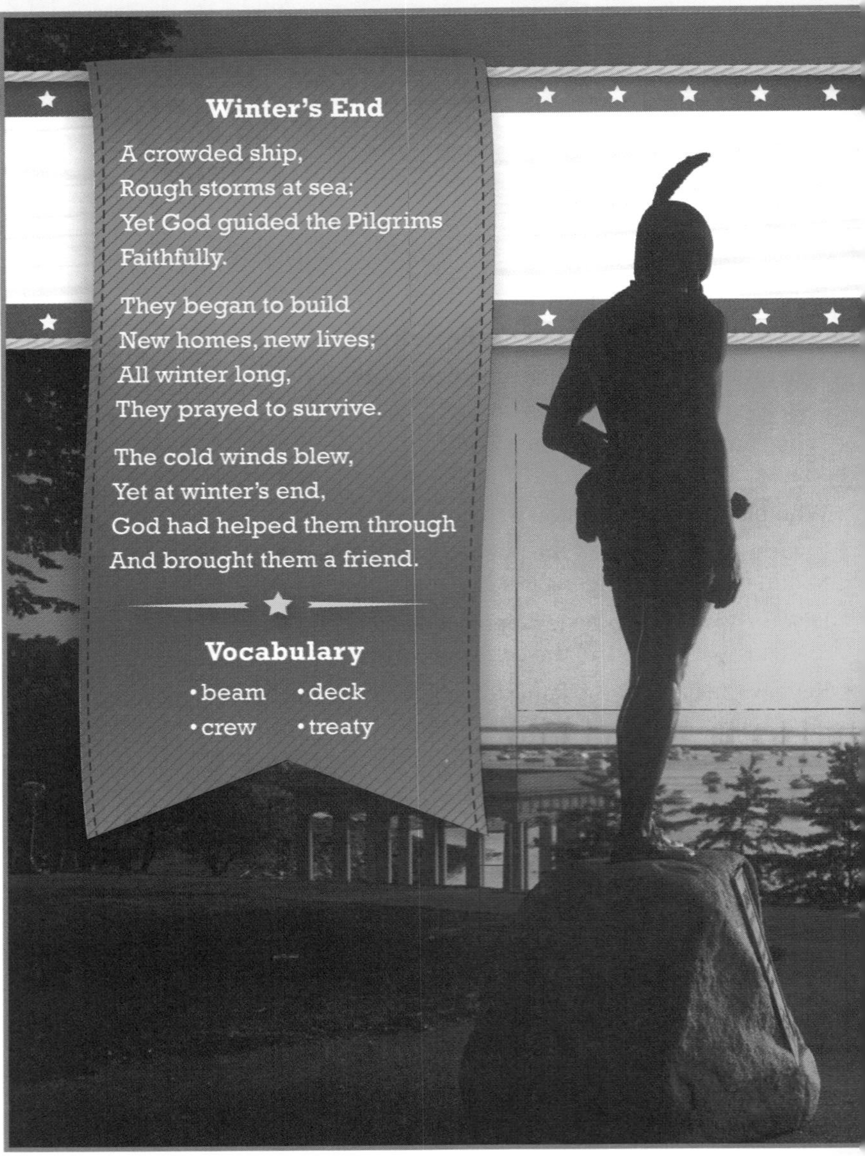

Winter's End

A crowded ship,
Rough storms at sea;
Yet God guided the Pilgrims
Faithfully.

They began to build
New homes, new lives;
All winter long,
They prayed to survive.

The cold winds blew,
Yet at winter's end,
God had helped them through
And brought them a friend.

Vocabulary

- beam
- deck
- crew
- treaty

Chapter 10 Overview				
Lesson	**ST**	**AM**	**Content**	**Vocabulary**
76	144–47	141	The Pilgrims came to America to worship and serve God	
77	148–50	143–45	Pretend that you are on the *Mayflower* sailing to the New World	crew deck
78	151–53	147	Trace the route of the Pilgrims' voyage to the New World	beam
79	154–55	149	The Pilgrims prayed when they reached the New World	
80	156–57	151	Write a peace treaty like the one the Pilgrims and Woodland people wrote	treaty
81	158–59	153	Learn that God worked through the life of Squanto	
82	160–61	155	Compare the Pilgrim culture with today's culture	
83			Act out the first Thanksgiving	
84		157	Chapter Review/Test	

Send a note to parents requesting that the children bring dress-up items for the Chapter Activity in Lesson 83.

Visit bjupress.com/resources for links to enhance the lessons.

Plymouth 10

Background

Pilgrim Memorial State Park

Pilgrim Memorial State Park honors the men and women who came to the New World in 1620 seeking a place to worship God. Plymouth Rock is within the shelter on the shore of Plymouth Harbor. It is a symbol of the faith of those who founded the first New England colony. The bronze statue of Chief Massasoit is a reminder of the friendship between the Woodland tribes and the Pilgrims. The Woodland people were instrumental in the survival of the Pilgrims.

Lesson 76

Student Text pages 144–47
Activity Manual page 141

Objectives

- Explain why the Pilgrims came to America
- Express in role-play the control that the king of England had over churches in England
- Compose a prayer of thanks to God for the Pilgrims who came to America

Materials

- Visual 23: *History Timeline*

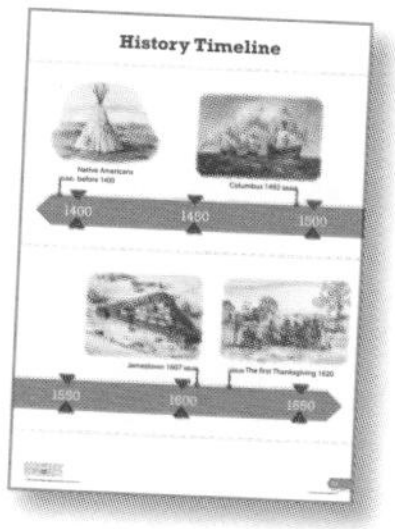

Introduction

- Direct attention to the Contents page. Read aloud the title of the chapter.
- Discuss the picture on pages 144–45.

What do you see in the picture? the statue of a Native American, water, and a monument or a building

The picture is of Plymouth Harbor where the Pilgrims' ship, the *Mayflower,* landed. The statue is of a Woodland chief who befriended the Pilgrims. In the shelter with the tall pillars is Plymouth Rock.

Teach for Understanding

- Read aloud the poem "Winter's End."

The Pilgrims are people who came to the New World to worship and serve God.

Who guided the Pilgrims through the storm? God

In what time of year did they build homes? winter

God helped the Pilgrims by sending a friend. Does the author of the poem tell the name of the friend? no

You will learn the name of that friend in this chapter.

Lesson

76

- Direct attention to the *History Timeline*. Review the events on the timeline. Guide a discussion as you introduce Plymouth.

  The president of the United States has made a new law. The law states that all people in the United States must go to the president's church. The president will be the head of the church. His ways will be taught in the church. No one will be allowed to go to a different kind of church.

- Ask the students what they think their family or pastor would do if this were true today.

  In the days of the Pilgrims, the king of England made rules like these.

  Do you think everyone in England liked the rules?

- Discuss additional Background information as time allows.

The Pilgrims in England

Some men from England sailed to the New World
to find riches.
Other people from England went to find a place
to worship God.
The king of England said that everyone must
worship in the Church of England.
But the Pilgrims wanted to worship God
in their own church.
They believed the Church of England was wrong.

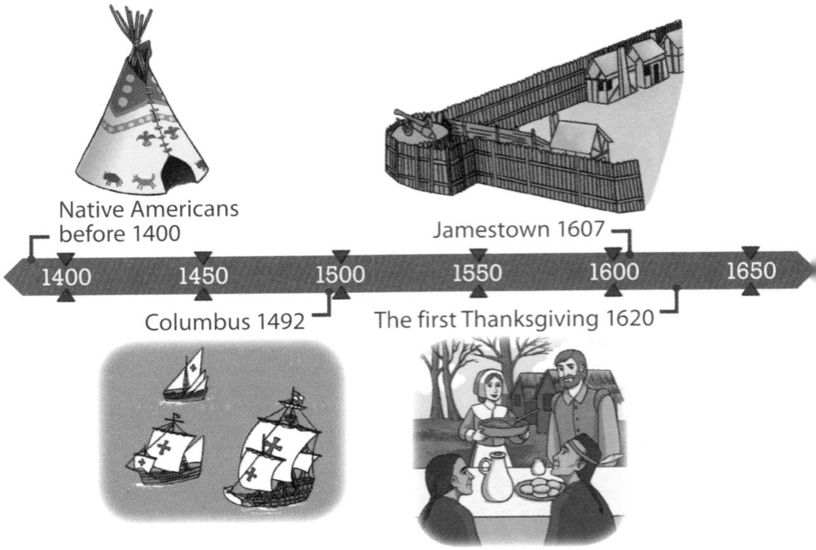

146

Background

Pilgrims

Pilgrims is a term William Bradford used to describe the Separatists as they left Leyden, Holland, to return to England to prepare for traveling to the New World. William Bradford wrote the following in his book *Of Plymouth Plantation*:

> So they lefte that goodly and pleasante citie [Leyden, Holland], which had been ther resting place near 12 years; but they knew they were pilgrimes, and looked not much on these things, but lift up their eyes to the heavens, their dearest cuntrie, and quieted their spirits.

The Separatists, or Pilgrims, did not like that the Church of England was governed by bishops who were appointed and led by the king. They believed that this was not a true church. They thought the people of God, led by God's Spirit, should choose their own church leaders.

The Separatists were distressed that the Church of England retained many of the ceremonies and teachings of the Catholic church. Since they did not feel that they could be right with God and attend the Church of England, they stopped attending those churches and started gathering in homes. However, because this was against the law, they moved to Holland where there was

The Pilgrims decided to go to America.
There they could worship the way God wanted them to.
There they could teach their children to love God and obey the Bible.

The Pilgrims were not happy in the Church of England.

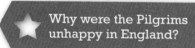

Why were the Pilgrims unhappy in England?

They could not worship the way God wanted them to.

147

Lesson 76

- Direct attention to pages 146–47. Invite a student to read the title and caption aloud. Guide the reading of the pages to find out why the Pilgrims went to the New World.

  Why did the Pilgrims sail to the New World? to worship God in their own church; to teach their children to love God and obey the Bible

  In our country today, your parents have the freedom to choose a church that follows the Bible. You are free to read the Bible and learn from God's Word. We need to thank God for the Pilgrims who came to America.
- Lead in a prayer of thanksgiving for our religious heritage.
- Conclude the discussion by asking the question on page 147.
- Encourage the children as they role-play a church service. Choose a student to be the pastor. Invite him to stand in the front of the "congregation" and read from his Bible. Direct a volunteer to act as the king who comes into the church service and announces that the people must worship as he says.

Activity Manual

- Encourage the students as they color the page to think of the Pilgrim families who came to America so that today their descendants can worship in the churches of their own choice.
- Guide completion of page 141. Discuss the similarities and differences between the clothing of a Pilgrim family and of a family today.

Activity

Guest Speaker

.Invite a pastor to tell about his ministry in the church.

religious freedom. But after twelve years, the Separatists longed for their English heritage and a home free of the vices of Leyden. They realized that they were just pilgrims in that land and longed for a better resting place. They wanted to worship and serve God in the way God wanted them to. They decided to move to the New World, where they could maintain both their English heritage and their desire to worship God without threats from the king of England.

Pilgrim Clothing

The Pilgrim clothing was much like that of other Europeans of that day. Unlike many pictures suggest, they did not wear all black. They had colorful clothing—blue, red, purple, and green.

Men and boys wore long linen shirts, baggy breeches that tied at the knee, stockings, shoes or boots, and a snug-fitting jacket. Hats were worn both inside and outside.

Women and girls wore fitted jackets and full-length skirts. Aprons were worn over the skirt. Most women wore a linen cap covering their hair. They also wore stockings and leather shoes.

Until the age of seven, boys and girls both wore shirt-like gowns, aprons, and caps. Stockings and shoes were similar to those of the adults.

Lesson

77

Student Text pages 148–50
Activity Manual pages 143–45

Objectives
- Read a diagram to identify parts of the *Mayflower*
- Describe what life was like for the Pilgrims while traveling on the *Mayflower*

Materials
- Visuals 33–34: *The Mayflower* and prepared die-cut pieces
- *Pilgrims' Voyage Story* (Teacher's Toolkit CD)
- A pennant or a length of fabric for a sail

Vocabulary
- crew
- deck

Content Word
- area

Introduction

- Direct attention to pages 146–47 as you ask the following question. Write the answers for display as the students dictate. Invite students to read the answers.

  Why did the Pilgrims want to leave England? to find a place to worship; to worship in their own church; to teach their children to love God and obey the Bible

Teach for Understanding

- Direct attention to the picture. Instruct the students to read the caption silently.

  What are the men doing on the ship? getting the *Mayflower* ready to sail

- Guide the reading of page 148 to find out what men who work on a ship are called. the crew

  Where are the Pilgrims going? Virginia

  The Pilgrims did not have a ship to sail across the Atlantic Ocean. They did not know how to sail a ship. They could not follow a map to the New World.

  Who did the Pilgrims hire to take them to the New World? a crew with a ship

  What was the name of the ship? the *Mayflower*

  Do you think the crew was looking for a place to worship God as the Pilgrims were? no These men were just doing their job.

The Pilgrims on the *Mayflower*

The Pilgrims planned to go to Virginia.
Virginia is part of America.
They hired a **crew** with a ship named the *Mayflower*.
A crew is the men that work on a ship.
The crew sailed the *Mayflower* across the ocean.

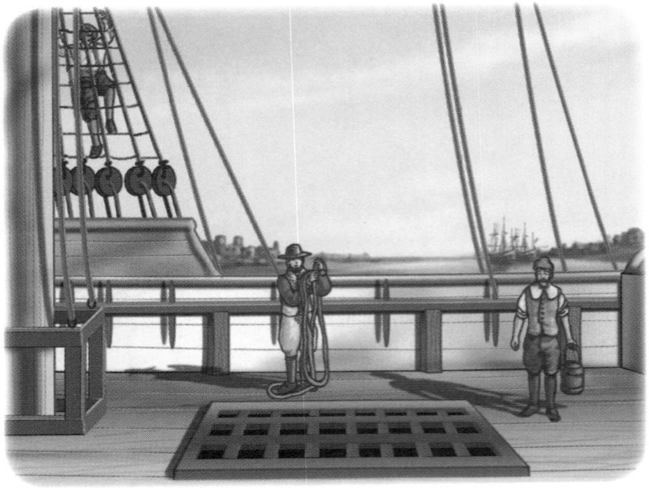

The crew is getting the *Mayflower* ready to sail.

148

The Pilgrims left
England for Virginia.

The Pilgrims lived on the middle **deck** of the *Mayflower*.
A deck is a floor of a ship.
The Pilgrims stayed in the small, dark area for many days.
Even the children ate, slept, and played there.

149

- Guide the reading of page 149 to find out where the Pilgrims stayed on the *Mayflower*. on the middle deck

  What is a deck? a floor of a ship

  What words describe the area where they stayed? *small* and *dark*

  Did the children go outside on the main deck? no How do you know? They ate, slept, and played on the middle deck.

Background

The Voyage

On the voyage to the New World, the ship was very crowded. It carried over one hundred passengers and a thirty-man crew. The Pilgrims (or Separatists), Puritans, and several children were the passengers. Living on the ship for sixty-six days was difficult for the Pilgrims. They ate biscuits, salted meat, and other foods that could be stored for long periods of time. Their belongings—tools, seeds, blankets, clothing, cookware, weapons, and Bibles—were kept in trunks. Rarely were they allowed to get fresh air or exercise on the main deck. Most of the passengers became seasick. Often they were thrown against the walls when heavy waves tossed the ship.

At first the sailors were not friendly to the Pilgrims. They made fun of them for saying prayers, singing hymns, and reading the Bible. However, by the end of the voyage, the sailors respected the Pilgrims for their strong faith in God.

Lesson

77

- Display Visual 33 and draw attention to the diagram of the *Mayflower* on page 150.

  How many decks can you count? three

  Describe what is happening on the main deck. Possible answer: The crew is working.

- Invite a student to place the sailor on the main deck.

  Who is living on the middle deck? the Pilgrims

- Ask a volunteer to place the Pilgrim boy on the middle deck.

  What do you see in the hold, or bottom deck? barrels and bags of things being stored

- Choose a student to place the barrels in the hold.
- Explain that the masts are the tall poles that hold the sails. On the masts are large crow's-nests often made of barrels. Members of the crew can get inside the nests. Crows were also kept in the nest.

  What do you think the crow's-nests are for? Because the crow's-nests are high on the mast, the men can see far away. Crows were kept in the nests.

  What do you think the sail does? catches the wind and moves the ship

- Give the sail pieces to volunteers to place on the masts.
- Invite the students to act out the Pilgrims' Voyage Story as you read it aloud, using the fabric or pennant you brought to represent the *Mayflower*.

Activity Manual

- Guide the students as they cut apart the pieces and glue them in place on pages 143–45.

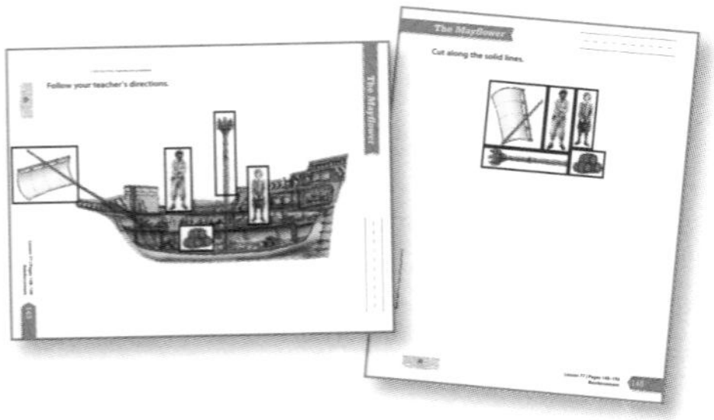

The *Mayflower*

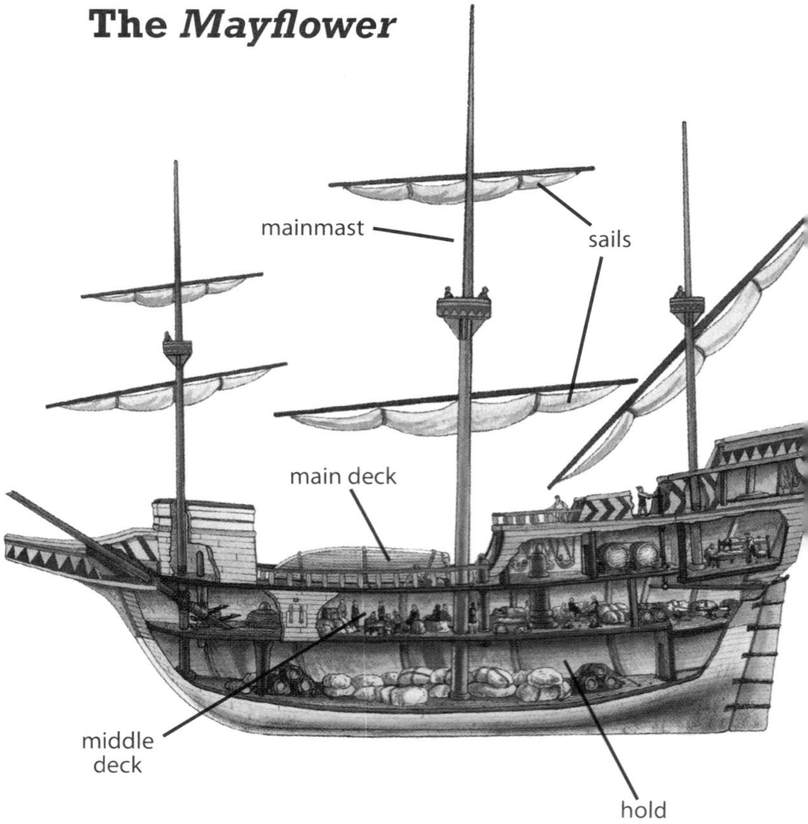

What was the name of the Pilgrims' ship?

the *Mayflower*

150

Background

The *Mayflower*

The *Mayflower* was a ninety-foot merchant or cargo ship. It used wind power from six sails to cross the Atlantic Ocean. Four of the sails hung from two tall masts. The other two sails were in the front and back of the ship. The crew worked the sails as officers shouted orders. Sails were rolled up during a storm. A crow's-nest was at the top of the mainmast. A sailor looked for land or danger from his place in the crow's-nest.

The ship had three decks. The crew (sailors and officers of the ship) lived and worked on the main deck. The passengers lived in the 'tween deck, or middle deck. The bottom deck, or cargo hold, was used to store supplies and barrels.

The master, or captain, of the *Mayflower* was Christopher Jones. He was in charge of navigating the ship. Simple tools such as the quadrant and cross staff were used to locate the position of the stars against the horizon to chart the route to the New World.

The Pilgrims' Voyage

The voyage on the *Mayflower* was not easy.
But God watched over the Pilgrims.
During a storm a **beam** on the ship cracked.
A beam is a log that holds the deck up.
A Pilgrim had packed a large iron screw.
The crew used the screw to fix the beam.
God knows all things.
He knew the Pilgrims would need that screw.

The *Mayflower* sailed safely through the storm.

151

Lesson 78

Student Text pages 151–53
Activity Manual page 147

Objectives
- Identify ways God cared for the Pilgrims on the *Mayflower*
- Trace the route of the Pilgrims' voyage to the New World
- Explain why the Mayflower Compact was written
- Use cardinal directions

Materials
- Visuals 33–34: *The Mayflower* and prepared die-cut pieces

Vocabulary
- beam

Introduction

- Instruct the boys to stand when the answer to the question you ask is *crew* and the girls to stand when the answer is *Pilgrims.*

  Who left England to worship God in their own church? the Pilgrims

  Who sailed the *Mayflower* across the ocean? the crew

  Who worked on the main deck? the crew

  Who lived on the middle deck? the Pilgrims

  Who ate and played in the dark? the Pilgrims
- Display Visual 33. Lead the students in identifying parts of the *Mayflower.* Distribute the die-cut pieces and direct the students to put the pieces in place as they locate the following:

  the area used for storing barrels the hold

  the area where the crew worked the main deck

  the area where the Pilgrims lived the middle deck

  the mainmast the pole in the center

  the sail the sail on the front of the *Mayflower*

Teach for Understanding

- Direct attention to page 151. Read the title and the caption.

  What do you think happened to the *Mayflower*? Elicit that the *Mayflower* sailed through a storm on the ocean.

  Do you think the Pilgrim children were afraid during this storm? Would you have been afraid if you were on the *Mayflower*?

  I think I would have been afraid. But I might have thought of the verse "What time I am afraid, I will trust in thee" (Psalm 56:3). God knew that even though the Pilgrims would go through many storms on the ocean, they would safely arrive in the New World.
- Guide the reading of the page to find out how God watched over the Pilgrims.

  Did God know about the storm? yes God knows all things.

  How did God provide for the repair of the cracked beam? A Pilgrim had brought a large screw with him. God knew the screw would be needed to repair the beam.
- Instruct the students to find sentences that show God cared for the Pilgrims. God watched over the Pilgrims. God knows all things. He knew the Pilgrims would need that screw.

Lesson 78

- Guide the reading of page 152 to find out where the Pilgrims landed. north of Virginia

  When the Pilgrims left England, they had planned to land in Virginia. Several storms blew the *Mayflower* off course. The ship landed in Plymouth instead. Plymouth did not have laws or a governor. The people on the *Mayflower* had to write their own laws to live by. They called the laws the Mayflower Compact, and they chose a governor to lead them.
- Choose a volunteer to read aloud the caption below the picture.

Storms had blown the *Mayflower* north,
near Plymouth.
The laws for the Virginia settlement
would not work there.
Now the Pilgrims needed to make new laws.
The laws were called the Mayflower Compact.
The laws in the Mayflower Compact honored
both God and the king of England.

The Mayflower Compact stated that the Pilgrims would tell others about God.

152

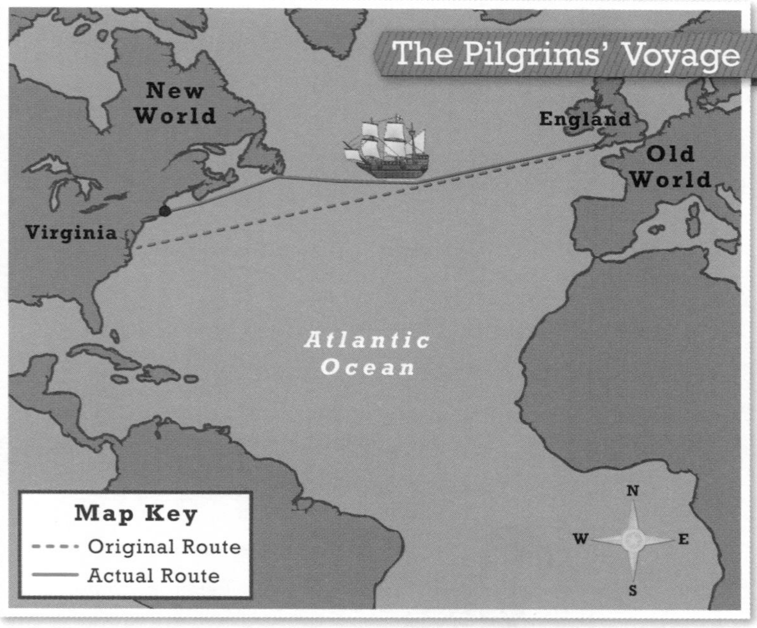

The dot (•) shows where Plymouth is.

Who watched over the Pilgrims during the voyage?

God

153

- Ask a volunteer to read the name of the map on page 153. *The Pilgrims' Voyage*
- Direct attention to the map key to find the routes to the New World. Instruct the students to follow each route with their finger as it is discussed.

  Which line shows the route the *Mayflower* should have taken? the dashed line

  Which line shows the route the *Mayflower* actually took? the solid line

  Why did the *Mayflower* take a different route? Storms blew the ship off course from the original route.
- Choose a volunteer to read the caption under the map.
- Direct the students to point to Plymouth.
- Guide the students in locating directions using the compass rose. Instruct them to use their finger to point out each location.

  Which ocean is in the middle of the map? the Atlantic Ocean

  Which direction did the *Mayflower* sail? mostly west
- Instruct the students to point to the following places on the map: the Old World, England, the New World, and Virginia.

  Is the Old World east or west of the Atlantic Ocean? east the New World? west Virginia? west

- Conclude the map study by asking the question on page 153.

Activity Manual

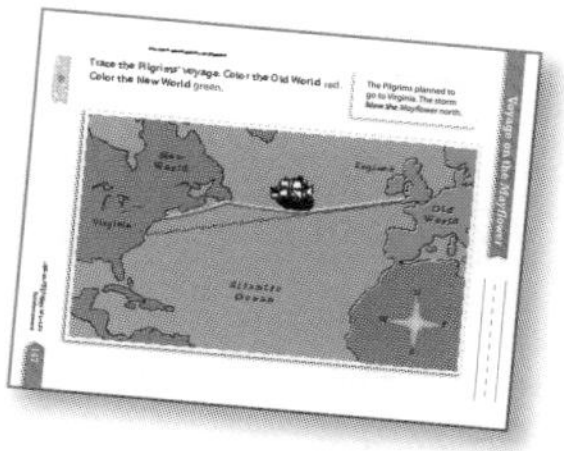

- Guide completion of page 147.

Background

The Providence of God

Captain John Smith surveyed the Virginia coast in 1616 and named the area Plymouth. This is the area where the *Mayflower* would later land.

The *Mayflower* was beaten by severe storms. In one of the storms, the main beam of the ship cracked. If the beam had completely broken, the ship would have sunk into the ocean. In the providence of God, the Pilgrims had brought a large iron screw with them, which was placed under the cracked beam. The screw kept the beam stable for the remainder of the voyage.

The Pilgrims' landing at Plymouth rather than Virginia was a great blessing. The storm blew the Pilgrims off course, which brought them great hardship, but the blessing was that they were able to develop their colony independent of the influence of Virginia. They established a colony in which they could worship and serve God as they believed He should be worshiped and served.

The Mayflower Compact

The laws for the Virginia Colony were not effective in Plymouth. To keep order, the colonists on the *Mayflower* established their own government in the Mayflower Compact. The colonists wanted to glorify God by giving allegiance to the king, ensuring the preservation of the colony, and advancing the Christian faith. They chose John Carver as their first governor. The Mayflower Compact was the first form of democratic government in the New World.

Lesson

79

Student Text pages 154–55
Activity Manual page 149

Objectives

- Recognize that *Of Plymouth Plantation* was written by a Pilgrim
- Affirm that the Pilgrims prayed to God
- Sequence the events after the Pilgrims landed at Plymouth

Materials

- Visuals 33–34: *The Mayflower* and prepared die-cut pieces
- *Pilgrim Sequencing Activity* (Teacher's Toolkit CD)
- Numbers 1–4 written on cards

Introduction

- Direct attention to the map on page 153. Review the cardinal directions. Trace the route to Plymouth.
- Display Visual 33. Use the visual to review the voyage to Plymouth.

Teach for Understanding

- Direct attention to page 154 and read the title.

  William Bradford was a Pilgrim. He made the voyage to Plymouth on the *Mayflower*. He wrote a book about the Pilgrims' journey. Since Mr. Bradford's book is about what he saw, his book is called a primary source. The words in the box on this page are taken from his book, *Of Plymouth Plantation*. These are Mr. Bradford's exact words.

- Invite a student to read the words. Explain that the pronoun *they* refers to the Pilgrims.

  What did the Pilgrims do when they landed in the New World? They fell on their knees.

  Why do you think they fell on their knees? to pray

  Which words mean that they prayed and gave thanks? "blessed the God of heaven"

  What is the Pilgrim doing in the picture? praying

- Ask the students to think of some things the Pilgrims might have prayed for when they reached the New World. Write for display as the students dictate. possible answers: safety, a new home, finding land, finding Plymouth
- Guide the reading of the page to find out what the Pilgrims did after they landed.

  What did the Pilgrims do first when they landed? They thanked God.

  What did some men do next? They left the ship to look for a place to build a settlement.

The Pilgrims in the New World

When the Pilgrims landed at Plymouth, they thanked God.
The men left the ship to look for a place to settle.
They found land that no one seemed to be using.
They decided that this land would be a good place for the Plymouth settlement.

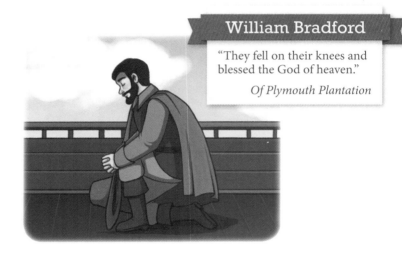

William Bradford

"They fell on their knees and blessed the God of heaven."

Of Plymouth Plantation

154

No one was living on the land at Plymouth. Because most of the land was clear, the Pilgrims could build homes. The cleared land was next to a harbor for the ship. It seemed to be a good place to build the settlement.

The men built houses on the new land.
The women and children stayed on the ship
until their homes were ready.
Some of the crew and the Pilgrims became sick.
The Pilgrims showed God's love.
They cared for each other and the crew.
After many weeks of building houses and a fort,
the Pilgrims moved to the land.

The Pilgrim woman showed God's love to the sick man.

Where did the women and children stay while houses were built?

on the *Mayflower*

155

- Guide the reading of page 155.

  While some men were building homes at Plymouth, others stayed on the ship. Some of the Pilgrims as well as the crew became sick.

  How did the Pilgrims show love for each other and the crew? The Pilgrims cared for each other and the crew members that were sick.

  What do you think the woman in the picture is doing? giving the sick man something to drink

  What sentence tells you how long it took to build the houses? "After many weeks of building houses and a fort, the Pilgrims moved to the land."

- Choose a volunteer to read aloud the caption below the picture.

- Arrange the prepared number cards across the front of the room. Divide the class into four groups. Display the sequencing pictures in random order. Give each group one picture. Encourage the members of each group to discuss their picture, including events that happened before and after the picture.
- Choose a volunteer to represent his group and stand in front of the room. Instruct the students to predict which picture will be first, second, third, and fourth, based on the order in which it happened. Reread pages 154–55, pausing each time a picture should be displayed.

  When the Pilgrims landed at Plymouth, they thanked God. Which picture shows this first event? the Pilgrims praying

- Continue this procedure until the four students are standing in the proper sequence with the number cards.

Activity Manual

- Guide completion of page 149.

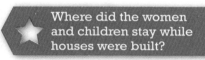

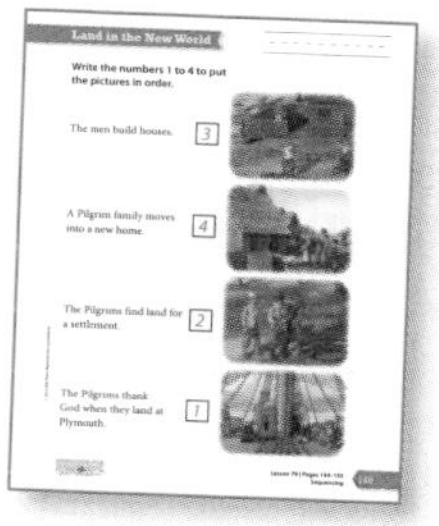

Background

William Bradford

William Bradford was a godly leader of the Pilgrims. He became governor after the death of John Carver and remained the governor of Plymouth Plantation for over thirty years. His book, *Of Plymouth Plantation*, gives much insight into the hardships and struggles of the Pilgrims. Bradford records God's faithfulness to a people desiring to serve Him.

William Bradford wrote the following in *Of Plymouth Plantation*:

> Being thus arrived in a good harbor and brought safe to land, they fell upon their knees and blessed the God of Heaven who had brought them over the vast and furious ocean, and delivered them from all the perils and miseries thereof, again to set their feet on the firm and stable earth, their proper element.

Plymouth

When the *Mayflower* arrived at Plymouth, the land was not inhabited. According to English common law, a man could legally occupy vacant land. This did not take into account that the Native Americans did not follow English common law. The land had been home to a Woodland tribe that had abandoned it some years earlier.

Although most of the people on the *Mayflower* survived the journey across the Atlantic Ocean, only half survived the first winter. Those who were healthy enough went ashore to help build homes. The crew, along with the women and children and the sick, were left onboard the *Mayflower* until the settlement was ready for them to move into.

Lesson

80

Student Text pages 156–57
Activity Manual page 151

Objectives

- Conclude from the Pilgrims' friendship with the Woodland people that God was caring for the Pilgrims
- Write a peace treaty

Materials

- *Pilgrim Sequencing Activity* (Teacher's Toolkit CD)
- Small rugs or carpet squares
- A sheet of parchment paper

Vocabulary

- treaty

Introduction

- Invite volunteers to hold the sequencing pictures in random order at the front of the classroom. Direct the students to arrange themselves in the proper sequence of events. You may reinforce the sequence by rereading pages 154–55.

Teach for Understanding

- Direct attention to page 156. Choose a volunteer to read the title.

  The Pilgrims moved from the *Mayflower* to their settlement at Plymouth. Life was difficult. They did not have much food. The winter was cold. But God cared for the Pilgrims.

- Guide the reading of the page to find out who came to visit the Pilgrims.

  In what way was the winter hard for the Pilgrims? They had little food, and many died.

  Who visited the Pilgrims? Samoset Who was Samoset? a Woodland man

  What surprised the Pilgrims about Samoset? that Samoset spoke English

  How do you think Samoset learned English? Answers may vary.

- Explain that Samoset spoke two languages: that of his Woodland tribe and English. Samoset learned English from English men who fished off the Atlantic coast.
- Direct attention to the map on page 153. Locate the waters along the coast of the New World. Explain that English men fished in these waters and traded with the Native Americans. They learned each other's languages so that they would be able to trade more effectively.

The Pilgrims and the Woodland People

The winter was hard for the Pilgrims.
They had little food, and many died.
One day a Woodland man visited
the settlement.
His name was Samoset.
The Pilgrims were surprised
when he spoke English.
He promised to bring his chief and
his friend Squanto to meet them.

Samoset spoke to the Pilgrims in English.

156

- Guide the reading of page 157. Explain that God in His care sent the Pilgrims a friend. Find the name of this friend. Squanto

  Samoset promised to return to the Plymouth settlement with two people. Who were the two people? his chief and his friend Squanto Which one could speak English: the chief or Squanto? Squanto

  Who trusted the Woodland people? the Pilgrims

  What did the Woodland people and the Pilgrims do to show their trust in each other? They made a peace treaty.

  What did the treaty promise? They would live in peace.

  Who lived in peace? the Woodland people and the Pilgrims

- Ask questions such as the following to generate interest in the picture. Explain that Governor Carver and Chief Massasoit are sitting on the floor of a newly finished Pilgrim home.

  What are the governor and chief sitting on? cushions on a green rug

  When a visitor comes to your house, would you ask him to sit on the floor? How do you think the artist knew to put cushions and a green rug in the picture? Answers may vary.

  Over four hundred years ago, a Pilgrim wrote about the day that the peace treaty was signed. An artist read about the cushions and green rug and drew them in this picture.

Soon the Pilgrims met the chief and Squanto.
Squanto spoke English too.
He also knew the English ways.
The Pilgrims trusted the Woodland people.
They made a peace **treaty**.
The treaty was a promise to live in peace.
The Woodland people and the Pilgrims lived in peace for many years.

God blessed the Pilgrims with peaceful friends.

157

- Point out that the Pilgrims and the Woodland people are meeting together to make a treaty.
- Instruct the students to find the word *treaty* in the Picture Glossary. Ask a volunteer to read the definition. a promise people agree to keep

  Chief Massasoit did not speak English. Governor Carver did not speak the language of the Woodland people. How do you think Chief Massasoit and Governor Carver are communicating with each other? Elicit that Squanto is interpreting.

  In the peace treaty the Pilgrims and the Woodland people agreed not to hurt each other. The treaty kept the peace for many years.
- Choose a volunteer to read aloud the caption below the picture.
- Encourage the students to role-play the peace talks as they sit on the rugs. Guide them in making a peace treaty for the classroom. Choose a volunteer to be the interpreter. Write on parchment paper as the students list ways to keep peace in the classroom (e.g., Keep your hands to yourself). Allow each student to sign the treaty. Display the classroom treaty for reference in Lesson 81.

Activity Manual

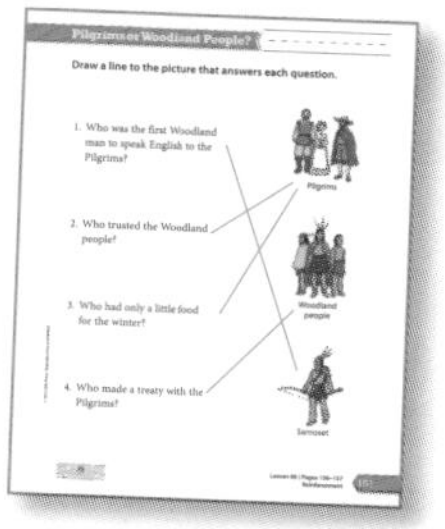
Pilgrims or Woodland People?
Draw a line to the picture that answers each question.
1. Who was the first Woodland man to speak English to the Pilgrims?
2. Who trusted the Woodland people?
3. Who had only a little food for the winter?
4. Who made a treaty with the Pilgrims?
Pilgrims
Woodland people
Samoset

- Guide completion of page 151. Explain that one picture will be used twice.

Background

Pilgrims

The Pilgrims' voyage to the New World took sixty-six days. Upon arriving, men explored the coast before choosing the Plymouth area for their settlement. As the winter weather allowed, they built homes so that families could move from the cold, damp *Mayflower* to land. The Pilgrims had a very rough first winter. Half of the people died from disease and poor living conditions. Despite the hardships they suffered, the Pilgrims were able to look at their situation as God's plan for them.

Peace Treaty

One day a Native American named Samoset walked boldly into the Plymouth settlement. Samoset welcomed the Pilgrims in broken English. He had learned English from fishermen on the coast. Samoset told the settlers of the Woodland tribe that had once lived there and had died of a disease. He promised to bring his friends Chief Massasoit and Squanto to meet the Pilgrims.

Samoset returned to the Plymouth settlement to introduce Chief Massasoit and Squanto to the settlers. Both Massasoit and the Pilgrims were reluctant at first. But eventually they met and exchanged gifts, which was the beginning of a lasting friendship.

Later Chief Massasoit and Governor Carver met to sign a peace treaty. The governor entered the house to the beat of a ceremonial drum and a trumpet. The signed treaty included these provisions.

1. They should not hurt each other.
2. If someone was hurt, the offender would be punished.
3. If anything was taken, it should be returned.
4. If an enemy should war against the settlement, the tribes would aid them; if an enemy should war against the tribes, the settlement would aid them.
5. They would do no wrong to each other.
6. When the tribes came to the settlement, they would leave their bows and arrows behind them.
7. King James would consider Massasoit his friend.

Lesson 81

Student Text pages 158–59
Activity Manual page 153

Objectives

- Follow directions to plant a simulated garden
- List proofs of God's providence in the life of Squanto

Materials

- Visuals 35–36: *Squanto's Garden* and prepared die-cut pieces
- The classroom peace treaty prepared in Lesson 80

Content Words

- bought
- bury
- kidnapped
- squash

Introduction

- Point out the classroom treaty as you review the meeting between the Woodland people and the people at the Plymouth settlement. Guide a review of pages 156–57.

  Why did it surprise the Pilgrims that Samoset could speak English? Samoset was a Woodland Indian.

  Did Chief Massasoit trust the Pilgrims? yes

  What did the chief do to show he trusted the Pilgrims? He signed a peace treaty.

  Do you think the treaty kept the peace? Yes, the Woodland people and the Pilgrims made a promise. They lived in peace for many years.

Teach for Understanding

- Guide the reading of page 158. Explain that God provided Squanto to help the Pilgrims survive in the New World. Squanto needed a place to live, and the Pilgrims needed to learn the Woodland people's ways.

  What Woodland man lived with the Pilgrims? Squanto

  What kinds of things did Squanto teach the Pilgrims? how to fish, hunt, plant, and bury fish in the soil

  What did Squanto do to show he was a friend to the Pilgrims? He lived with the Pilgrims and taught them how to live in the New World.

  The land at Plymouth was very different from the land in England. The weather was different too. Squanto knew how to plant seeds at Plymouth, and he knew the seasons. He had grown up there. God had prepared Squanto to help the Pilgrims.

- Generate interest in the picture on the page. Invite the students to read the caption silently.

  What is Squanto doing? showing the Pilgrims how to plant corn

  Squanto told the Pilgrims, "When the oak leaves are the size of a mouse's ear, it is time to plant corn."

Squanto lived with the Pilgrims in Plymouth.
He taught the Pilgrims how to hunt and fish.
He showed them how to plant corn, beans, and squash in a hill of dirt.
He taught them to bury a fish with the seeds to help the plants grow.
Squanto became a friend to the Pilgrims.

Squanto showed the Pilgrims how to plant corn.

Who helped the Pilgrims learn the ways of the Woodland people?

Squanto

158

What is an oak leaf? a leaf on an oak tree

How big is a mouse's ear? very small

Do you think people today look at an oak leaf to know when it is time to plant a garden? no

- Mention that deciding to plant a garden based on the size of an oak leaf was probably strange to the Pilgrims also.

  The Woodland people's culture, or way of life, was different from the Pilgrim way of life. The Pilgrims learned many good things from the Woodland people.

Famous People

Squanto

Squanto was born into a
Woodland tribe.
He loved his family and the
people in his tribe.
He ran through the woods
with the other boys.
And he helped gather
shellfish from the waters.
One day, a sea captain kidnapped Squanto.
The captain sold Squanto as a slave in Europe.
The man who bought Squanto told him
about Jesus.
Later God allowed Squanto to return home.
But his family and tribe had all died.
The Pilgrims settled where Squanto had lived.
They became his friends.
God knew the Pilgrims would need Squanto
to help them learn how to live in the New World.
God knows all things. He does all things well.

159

- Display Visuals 35–36. Explain that Squanto gave specific directions to the Pilgrims for planting seeds. It was important that the Pilgrims follow the directions in order for the plants to grow. Invite students to place the corresponding figures on the visual as you discuss the steps to planting Squanto's Garden.

  When the oak leaf is as big as a mouse's ear, begin planting.

  1. Place a small fish in the bottom of the mound of dirt.
  2. Place corn onto the mound.
  3. Wait for the corn to sprout.
  4. Plant the beans under the corn sprouts. The corn becomes the pole for the bean vines to climb.
  5. Plant the squash on the side of the dirt mound. The squash helps to prevent weeds and keeps the ground moist.
  6. Wait for the seeds to grow. Enjoy the mature plants.

- Guide the reading of page 159. Explain that Squanto had been born in America, was taken to Europe, and years later returned to America. This does not seem pleasant to us, but it was all in God's good plan.

Activity Manual

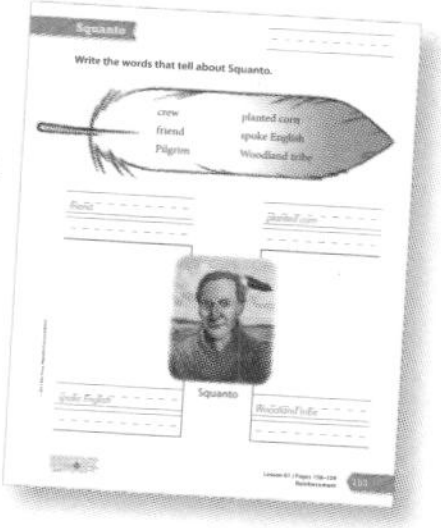

- Guide completion of page 153. Explain that the students will be writing words about Squanto around the picture. Some words will not be used.

Background

Squanto

Governor William Bradford said that Squanto was "a special instrument sent of God for their good, beyond their expectation." In God's providence Squanto had found a new home and helped the Pilgrims survive in the New World.

Squanto had been abducted from his Woodland home by the English in 1614. He lived in Europe for a time as a slave to Spanish monks. He also spent time in England, and an English explorer took him to New England, where he was taken in by Massasoit. Again, in God's providence, Squanto learned the English language and their culture. When he returned home, he had no family. While he had been away, his tribe had died from a disease. The Pilgrims had settled on the land where he was reared. Squanto embraced the Pilgrims, and they welcomed him. At his death Squanto requested prayer from William Bradford and gave his belongings to the English as remembrances of his love. Bradford felt a great loss when Squanto passed away.

Three Sisters Garden

Squanto used a method of gardening used by many Native Americans. The Three Sisters Garden was very different from gardens in England. The Three Sisters method used corn, beans, and squash. Planting was done in rounded hills of dirt. First, corn was planted in mounds. After the corn had sprouted, beans were planted. The bean grew up the corn stalk. Squash seeds were planted last. The squash provided ground cover that prevented weeds and kept the soil moist.

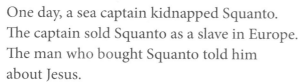

Lesson

82

Student Text pages 160–61
Activity Manual page 155

Objectives
- Use the textbook to find answers
- Compare the Pilgrim culture with today's culture using a Venn diagram
- Explain why the Pilgrims held a Thanksgiving feast

Materials
- Visual 37: *The First Thanksgiving*

Content Word
- harvest

Introduction

- Conduct a picture drill to review the Pilgrims' story. Invite the students to use their textbook to find a picture that answers each question. After most students have found the page, ask a student to identify the page number and answer the question.

  Why did the Pilgrims want to leave England? pages 146–47: They were unhappy with the Church of England.

  What was the name of the ship that the Pilgrims sailed on to the New World? pages 148–51: the *Mayflower*

  How did the Pilgrims show their love for God? page 154: through prayer; page 155: by caring for the sick

  Who made a peace treaty with the Pilgrims? page 157: the Woodland people

  Who became a friend to the Pilgrims? pages 158–59: Squanto

Teach for Understanding

At the end of the first year at the Plymouth settlement, the Pilgrims were very thankful. They had successfully crossed the Atlantic Ocean and landed at Plymouth. Homes had been built. They had learned a new way to plant seeds. Squanto had taught them to hunt and to fish. At harvest time plenty of food had been gathered from their gardens. It was time to show their thankfulness with a celebration.

- Guide the reading of page 160 to find out why the Pilgrims were thankful. God had kept His promise to supply their needs. God had blessed the Pilgrims with new land. God had sent Squanto. God had provided them with plenty of food.

The First Thanksgiving

God blessed the Pilgrims with a new land.
God sent Squanto to teach them.
At harvest time in the fall, there was plenty of food.
Because the Pilgrims were thankful, they held a harvest celebration.
The harvest celebration was the first Thanksgiving.

Philippians 4:19

God shall supply all your need.

160

- Read aloud Philippians 4:19. Explain how God met the Pilgrims' needs of shelter and food. Remind the students that God keeps His promises. Use Visual 37 as you lead the discussion.

  The Pilgrim leaders invited the Woodland people to join them in celebrating. When Chief Massasoit came to the celebration, he brought ninety men with him. The Pilgrims needed more food. The Pilgrims and Woodland men hunted for more deer and turkey. The Woodland people built small shelters to sleep in because the celebration lasted for several days.

  Much food was prepared for the feast. Some of the meat was cooked outside on an open fire. Other foods were cooked inside in a fireplace. The Pilgrims prepared many of the vegetables that they had grown, such as beans and squash. Some of the corn had been ground into flour like we use today to make bread. Children may have picked berries to sweeten the meal. Several meals were prepared during the three-day celebration. Most of the meals were eaten outside.

  During the day, children played leapfrog and other games, and the soldiers at the Plymouth settlement fired their guns to entertain the Woodland people.

Then and Now

How was the first Thanksgiving celebration different from a Thanksgiving holiday today?

Answers will vary.

Activity

161

- Direct attention to page 161. Choose a volunteer to read the title of the chart. Point out the chart labels and pictures.

  When we celebrate Thanksgiving Day, we remember the mighty things God did through the Pilgrims who trusted and obeyed Him.

  Our celebration today is different because our culture has changed. The Woodland people had different ways too. During the first Thanksgiving, we think that the Woodland people would have sat in chairs or benches at the table, although their custom was to sit on the ground or floor. In the Pilgrim culture, women would not have eaten with the men. They would have eaten at separate tables. And the children would have stood beside the table. No forks would have been on the table that first Thanksgiving because they did not use forks.

  But nowadays, your parents would not be happy if you did not use your fork. In our culture today, we do not share our drinks or plates. At the first Thanksgiving, you might have shared your cup and plate with all the other children too.

- Guide a comparison of the first Thanksgiving with a modern-day Thanksgiving.

  The first column on the chart shows how meat is prepared. What difference do you see in the preparation of meat? The Pilgrims cooked the meat over a fire, and today meat is cooked in an oven.

  What difference do you see in the way the women are dressed? The Pilgrim is wearing a long dress and a cap; the lady today is wearing a shorter dress and has oven mitts on her hands.

  In the second column of the chart, the guests are being welcomed. Who are the guests in each picture? the Woodland people; a family

  What is the difference in the way the guests are dressed? The Woodland people are dressed in clothing made from deer hide; the family is dressed in modern clothes.

  In the third column, the table is different. How is the table set differently? The Pilgrim table has a man sitting and children standing; the family table has children sitting. The Pilgrim table has very little on it; the family table has flowers, place settings, and lots of food.

- Divide the class into two groups: Pilgrim Family and Family Today. Display a Venn diagram labeled *Pilgrim Family* and *Family Today*.
- List under *Pilgrim Family* the things that the Pilgrims were thankful for. List under *Family Today* the things the students are thankful for. In the overlapping space, list things that both Pilgrims and families today would be thankful for.

Things to Be Thankful For

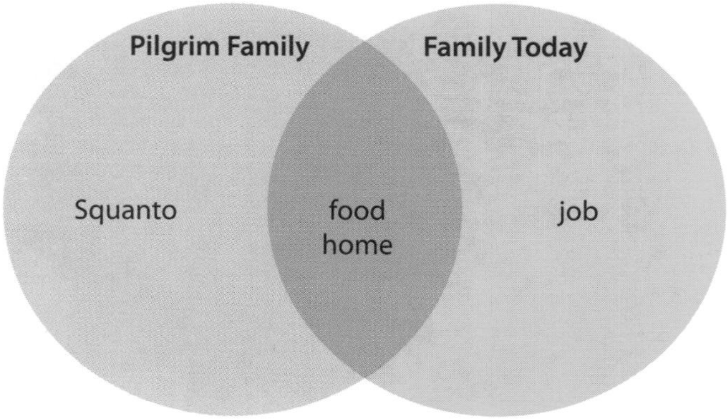

Activity Manual

- Guide completion of page 155.

Lesson 83 Chapter Activity

Objective
- Dramatize the first Thanksgiving

Materials
- *First Thanksgiving of All* (Teacher's Toolkit CD)
- Woodland people dress
- Pilgrim dress
- Thanksgiving food or fun treats

Introduction

- Review the events of the first Thanksgiving celebration by acting out the events.
- Display the title of the poem, "First Thanksgiving of All," and the author's name, Nancy Byrd Turner. Read aloud and discuss the poem.

  What is the title of the poem? "First Thanksgiving of All" The author is the person who wrote the poem. Who is the author of this poem? Nancy Byrd Turner

  What are the names of the Pilgrim children? Peace, Mercy, Jonathan, and Patience

  Are the children standing or sitting? standing

  What are the children thankful for? that their ship had come safely across the sea; for their home, family, food, and flowers

Activity

Encourage the students to dress as a Pilgrim or a Woodland person using the clothing they brought. Organize a Thanksgiving feast or provide a simple treat for the students to enjoy. Plan to have the activity outside as the Pilgrims did.

Optional Activity

Follow Squanto's style of planting corn with fish. Prepare small cups of crushed dark cookies. Distribute fish crackers, candy corn, and the cups with crushed cookies. Direct the students to pretend they are planting corn with fish in the same way that Squanto taught the Pilgrims.

Activity

Lesson 84

Chapter Review
Activity Manual page 157

Objective
- Recall concepts and terms from Chapter 10

Materials
- *Pilgrim Story Cards* (Teacher's Toolkit CD)

Review

- Review the poem on page 144 by reading the stanzas aloud. Stop at the end of each stanza. Invite a student to tell in his own words the account that it is referring to.
- Invite students to read the meanings of the vocabulary words in the Picture Glossary.
- Review Chapter 10 by retelling the events using the Pilgrim Story Cards. Choose volunteers to hold each card. Instruct the student to hold his card in front of him as each one lines up in order of the event. Ask the first student to tell about his card, the *Mayflower*. When he is finished telling all that he knows about the *Mayflower,* encourage him to invite another student to stand with him and add to the story. Summarize the students' information, adding any other important details. Continue until all the cards have been discussed and each student has had an opportunity to tell about one of the story cards.

Activity Manual

- Guide completion of page 157.

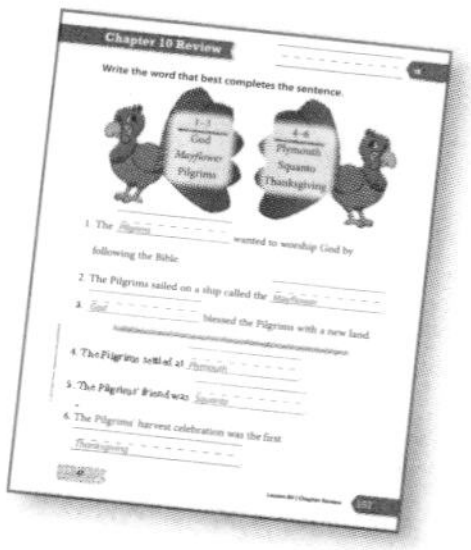

Chapter 10 Test

- Administer Test 10.

Chapter 11

Introduction

The students will learn to distinguish between the past and the present and consider how things change over time. They will learn how new and improved inventions have changed communication. They will examine pictures of early appliances and cars. Objects and pictures from the past will give each student the opportunity to celebrate his family's history.

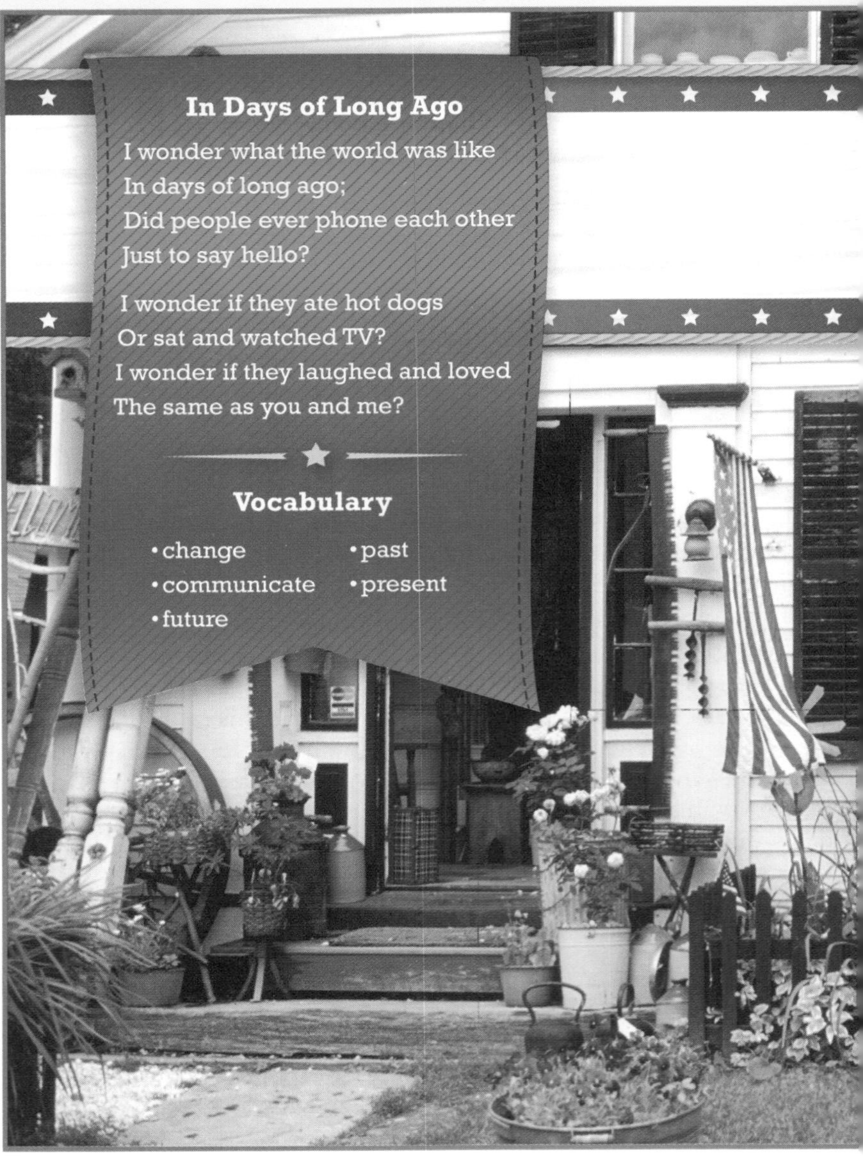
In Days of Long Ago
I wonder what the world was like
In days of long ago;
Did people ever phone each other
Just to say hello?
I wonder if they ate hot dogs
Or sat and watched TV?
I wonder if they laughed and loved
The same as you and me?
Vocabulary
• change
• past
• communicate
• present
• future

Chapter 11 Overview				
Lesson	**ST**	**AM**	**Content**	**Vocabulary**
85	162–65	159	Contrasting the past with the present How things change over time	change past present
86	166–67	161	Communication	communicate
87	168–69	163	Appliances long ago	
88		165	How children's clothing has changed over time	
89	170–71	167	Comparing an early car with cars today	future
90		169	Family History Day; Chapter Review / Test	

Visit bjupress.com/resources for links to enhance the lessons.

Ask students to bring in an object, a photo, or a family story to be presented during Lesson 90.

Today and Long Ago

11

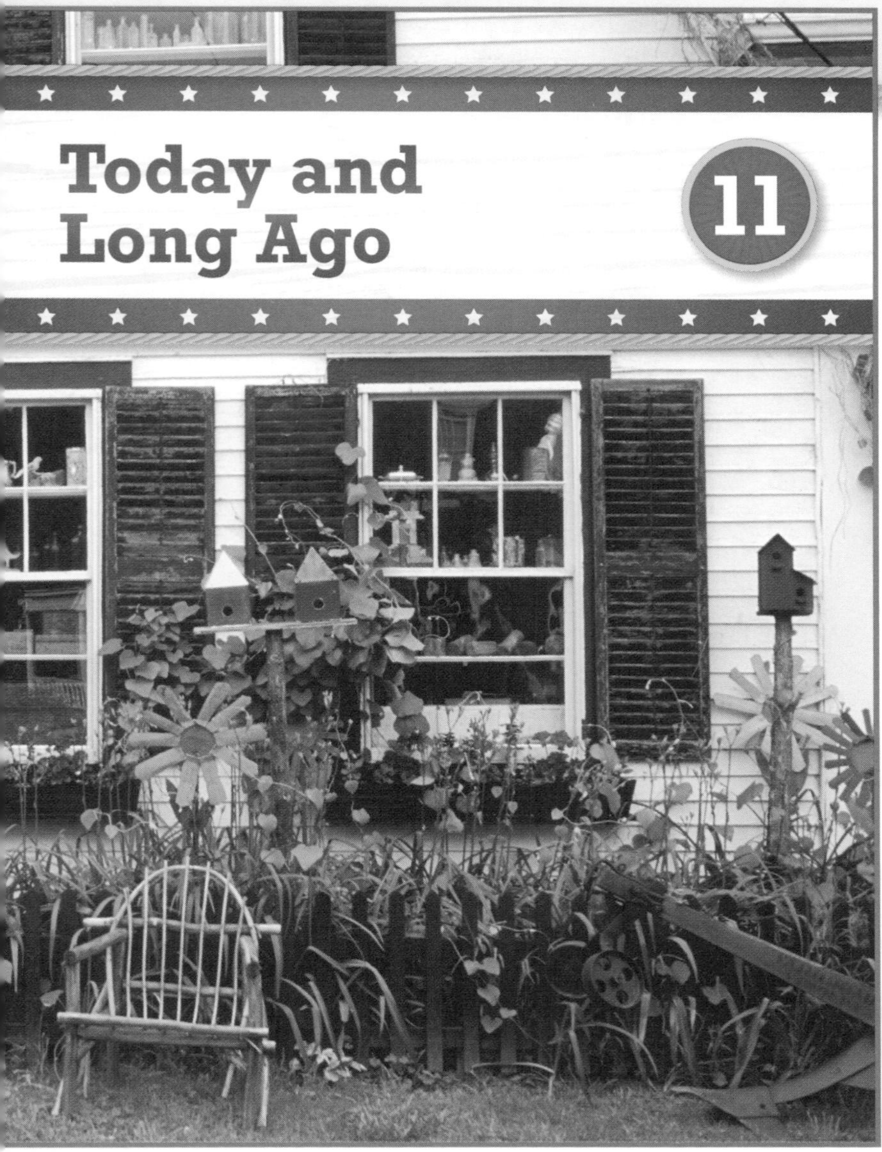

Student Text pages 162–65
Activity Manual page 159

Objectives
- Contrast the past with the present
- Identify ways to learn about the past
- Identify a specific event in his life that occurred in the past
- Explain how God's command to fill and care for the earth leads to change

Materials
- A history trade book marked with several interesting facts
- An object used long ago

Vocabulary
- change
- past
- present

Introduction

- Direct attention to the Contents page.

  We are ready to begin the last chapter of this book. What is the title of Chapter 11? Today and Long Ago

  On what page does the chapter begin? page 162

Teach for Understanding

- Draw attention to the picture on pages 162–63. Ask a volunteer to read the title of the chapter.

  What do you see in the picture? a house with lots of old things in the yard and in the windows

  Someone has turned this old house into a store where old things can be bought.

- Read aloud the poem "In Days of Long Ago."

  Which things in the poem might not have happened long ago? talking on the phone; eating hot dogs; watching TV

  Why do you think Columbus, the Native Americans, and the Pilgrims would not have done these things? Phones, hot dogs, and TVs had not yet been invented in their time.

  Which things in the poem do you think the people of long ago would have done? laughed and loved

  Even though the world changes and people find new ways of doing things, the poem reminds us that some things always stay the same. People will always do important things like enjoying life and loving each other in every time period.

- Draw attention to the vocabulary words the students will learn in this chapter. Remind the students that the words can be found in the Picture Glossary.

JourneyForth

Pulling Together by Dawn L. Watkins

In this early chapter book, Matthew watches his father's steadfast trust in God when a storm brings ruin to their small farm. Matthew determines to do his best to help his family even though he cannot bear to think that Dolly, one of their faithful workhorses, might have to be sold. The rich historical details in the text and illustrations will provide many opportunities to discuss the differences between life in the past and the present.

Lesson

85

- Guide the reading of page 164 to find out what it means to change. to become different

  Have you ever watched workers building a house? It is fun to watch the progress being made on a building project. Things change over time.

  What did God tell people to do on the earth? fill it and care for it

  "Fill the earth" means to get married and have children. It also refers to moving around to different places. We care for the earth by using it to help others and serve God.

  This calling from God leads to change. As people get married and have children, their families change. As people move, their lives change. As people find ways to make God's world more useful, houses change, roads change, and stores change.

  What do we call the time before now? the past

  God made us to work with His world and come up with ways to make it more useful.

- Encourage the students to think about something that happened to them in the past. Invite several students to tell about that event.
- Choose a volunteer to read aloud the caption below the picture.

  Does a grocery store look like this today? no How is this grocery store different from the one you have in your community? It has boxes and barrels of food out front; it is very small.

  What do we call time that is happening now? the present

Change

Things **change** over time.
To change is to become different.
Long ago God told people to fill the earth and care for it.
As people do this, things change.
Your community is different now than it was in the **past**.
The past is the time before now.
The way your community looks now is called the **present**.

This is the way one community's store looked in the past.

164

Learning About the Past

Ask older people about the past.

Read books about the past.

Look at things and pictures from the past.

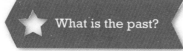

What is the past?

the time before now

165

- Draw attention to the first picture on page 165. Ask a student to read the caption.

  How do older people know things about the past? They have lived a long time and can remember things that happened when they were younger.
- Invite a student to share something he has learned by talking with a grandparent or older family friend.
- Draw attention to the next picture. Choose a volunteer to read the caption.

  We call books about the past history books. These books provide information about things that happened long ago. History books have interesting pictures that help us learn about the past.
- Display the history book. Read aloud the name of the book. Discuss several facts from the book.
- Draw attention to the last picture. Choose a student to read the caption.

  We call objects that were used long ago antiques. There are antique desks, beds, plates, and many other things. The stores where these kinds of items are sold are called antique stores. This picture shows objects that can be found in an antique store.

  What kinds of things do you see in the picture? lamps, bowls, vases

  Many families value their antiques and pass them down from generation to generation.

- Display the object you brought and tell some facts about it.
- Invite students to describe antiques their family might have.
- Review three ways of finding out about the past.

Activity Manual

- Guide completion of page 159.

Activity

Materials

- *In the Past* (Teacher's Toolkit CD)

Give each student a copy of the page from the Teacher's Toolkit CD.

Think of something that happened to you in the past. Draw a picture and write about it.

Allow time for each student to show his picture and read what he wrote. Display the pictures in the room.

Background

Antiques

The definition of the term *antique* varies from place to place and from object to object. People consider objects antiques if they are at least seventy-five to one hundred years old and have unique features that make them collectible. Cars are considered antique if they are twenty-five to thirty years old. Rugs are considered antiques after eighty years.

Lesson 86

Student Text pages 166–67
Activity Manual page 161

Objectives
- Explain how communication has changed over time
- Interpret the order of inventions for communication on a timeline

Materials
- Visual 38: *Communication Timeline*
- Materials for making a string telephone (See the Activity instructions at the end of the lesson.)

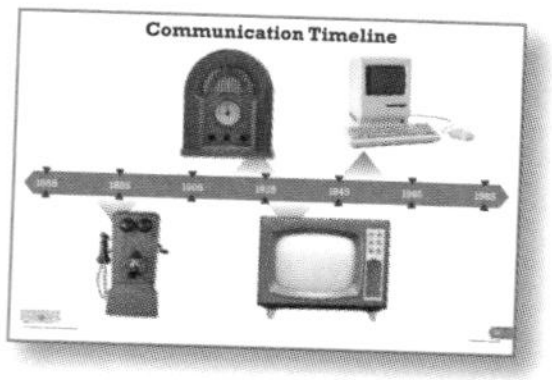

Vocabulary
- communicate

Content Word
- easier

Introduction
- Guide a discussion about communication as you make a string telephone following the Activity instructions.

Teach for Understanding
- Guide the reading of pages 166–67 to find out what has changed over time. the way we communicate
- Display the visual.

This timeline shows the dates of inventions that made communication easier. This timeline is just like the one in your book. The pictures show some of the first inventions that helped people communicate easier and faster.

What do you see on the left side of the timeline? a telephone Does this look like the telephones we use today? no

How is this telephone different from the ones we use today? It has a cord and a handle to put up to your ear. It is bigger than the phones we have today.

How does a telephone help you communicate? It allows you to talk to someone who is far away.

Since the telephone was invented in 1876, it is first on the timeline.

What do you see next on the timeline? a radio Does this look like the radios we use today? no

How is this radio different from the ones we use today? It is bigger. It has knobs instead of buttons.

How does a radio help people communicate? People can hear people talking, singing, and playing instruments.

The radio was invented in 1920.

What do you see next on the timeline? a television Does this look like televisions we use today? no

Sharing Thoughts

The way we **communicate** has changed over time.
To communicate is to share your thoughts.

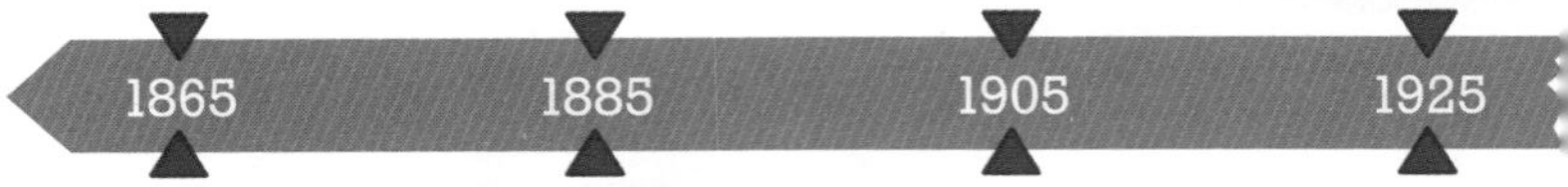

166

How is this television different from the ones we use today? It is not mounted on the wall, does not sit on a stand, and has knobs instead of a remote control.

The early television programs were broadcast in black and white.

How does a television help people communicate? People can see and hear people talking about different subjects and can find out news more quickly.

The television was invented in 1925.

What do you see next on the timeline? a computer Does this look like the computers we use today? no

How is this computer different from the ones we use today? It is bigger and cannot be carried around like laptops and tablets.

How does a computer help people communicate? They can send and receive messages on a computer instantly.

The computer was invented in 1945.

- Conclude the discussion by asking the question on page 167.

We communicate faster and easier today.

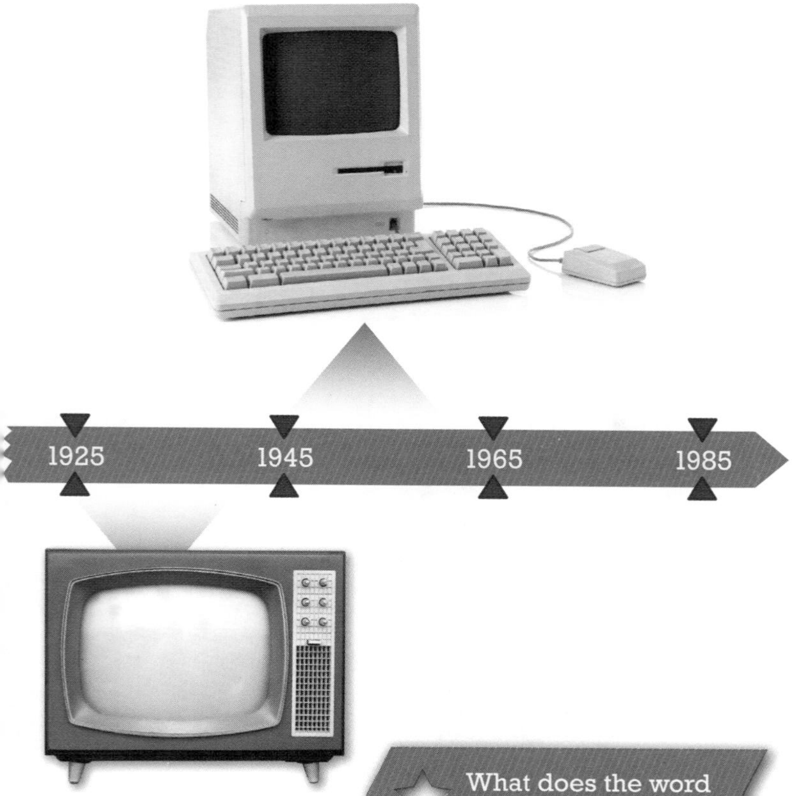

What does the word *communicate* mean?

sharing thoughts

167

Background

Telephone

Alexander Graham Bell thought it might be possible to transmit the human voice over a wire by using electricity. He asked electrician Thomas A. Watson to assist him in his experiments. On June 2, 1875, the men transmitted a sound that resembled a twanging clock spring. The next day, Bell was able to transmit his voice to Watson. A patent was issued for the first telephone on March 7, 1876. By the end of 1880, there were 47,900 telephones in the United States. Early telephones were sold in pairs; the owner was required to install wire to connect them. In 1889 the first pay phones were installed. The first cordless phones appeared in the 1970s.

The first telephone book was published in 1878. It was only one page long and included fifty names. Since the telephone operator connected all of the calls, no phone numbers were listed in the first phone book. The first Yellow Pages were published in 1886.

Radio

By 1876 the telephone had been invented by Alexander Graham Bell. But there was still a need for some kind of communication that could be used on ships and on open areas of land. Ernst Alexanderson was the engineer who gave radio communication its start. He invented a machine and installed it in a station in Brant Rock, Massachusetts, on December 24, 1920. The station transmitted a radio broadcast that included a voice and a violin solo. The first commercial radio station was KDKA in Pittsburgh in 1920.

Television

The inventor of the television was Vladimir Zworykin. He filed two patents in 1923, which formed the basis of the first television. RCA displayed a television at the 1939 World's Fair. People watching the first television viewed the telecast in the RCA Building and on other television sets in New York City. They saw the mayor of New York, a parade, and President Franklin D. Roosevelt. This was the beginning of RCA's first schedule of television programs.

Computer

The abacus, an ancient Chinese adding machine, was one of the original computing machines. Leonardo da Vinci and Blaise Pascal were famous mathematicians who invented more complex calculators. In 1904 the vacuum tube was invented. It is a tube that has all the air and gas removed. Computers before 1950 often had vacuum tubes. In 1947 transistors were developed. They were used to turn circuits on and off. Microprocessors were made that were small enough to fit into the palm of the hand and still perform billions of calculations in a second. The Internet began in 1973. The Internet is a form of communication between computers.

Activity Manual

- Guide completion of page 161.

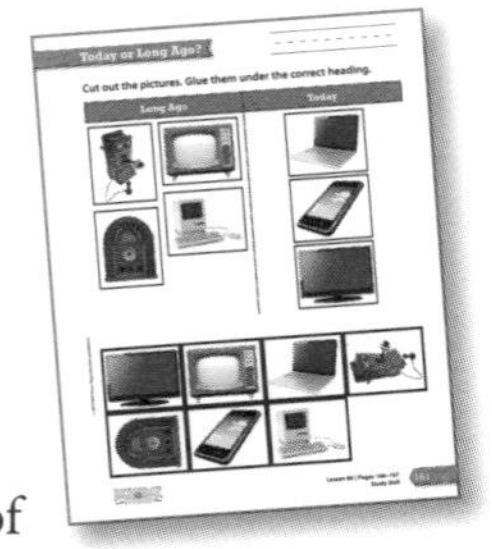

Activity

String Telephone

Step 1: Poke a small hole in the bottom of two plastic cups.

Step 2: Tie a paper clip to one end of a long string.

Step 3: Thread the other end of the string (from the inside of the cup) through the hole in one of the cups. The paper clip will keep the string from going all the way through the hole.

Step 4: Thread the string through the hole in the second cup (from the outside of the cup).

Step 5: Tie a paper clip to the other end of the string. The paper clip should be inside the cup.

Step 6: Pull the cups apart until the string is taut. Choose a student to talk into one cup while another student holds the second cup to his ear.

Lesson

87

Student Text pages 168–69
Activity Manual page 163

Objectives

- Identify tools used in the past
- Explain how tools help get work done

Materials

- Visual 39: *Early Household Appliances*
- A sandwich

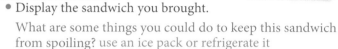

Introduction

- Display the sandwich you brought.

  What are some things you could do to keep this sandwich from spoiling? use an ice pack or refrigerate it

- Use the Background information about refrigeration to guide the discussion.

Teach for Understanding

- Guide the reading of page 168 to find out why people need tools. to help get work done
- Invite several students to name some tools.

  You usually think of a hammer or a screwdriver when you think of tools.

  Do you think tools have changed over time? yes How? Answers will vary.

  Could a refrigerator be a tool? yes How does a refrigerator help people? It keeps food cold.

  Some food must be kept cold so that it will stay fresh and not spoil. Long ago, people used ice to keep food cold.

- Display Visual 39 as you guide a discussion about early household appliances.
- Invite a student to read the caption beside the first picture on page 168.

  This is what one of the first refrigerators looked like.

- Draw attention to the second picture on the page. Invite a student to read the caption.

  Does this look like the stove at your house? no How is it different from your family's stove? Answers will vary.

  How does a stove help us? It is used to cook food.

  What do you think people used to cook food before there were stoves? a campfire; a fireplace

- Draw attention to page 169. Choose a student to read the caption beside the first picture.

  Does the washing machine at your house look like this washing machine? no

  This is a picture of one of the first washing machines. It has a wringer which was used to squeeze the water from the clothes so that they would dry faster.

  Do you have a sewing machine at your house? Does it look like this sewing machine? no

Around Your House

Tools have also changed.
Tools help people get work done.

Used to keep food cold

Used to cook food

168

This sewing machine did not use electricity. The person using this sewing machine had to use her foot to rock the foot pedal.

This is one of the first sewing machines.

- Conclude the discussion by asking the question on page 169.

Lesson 87

Used to clean clothes

Used to make clothes

What did people use to get work done?

tools

169

Activity Manual

- Guide completion of page 163.

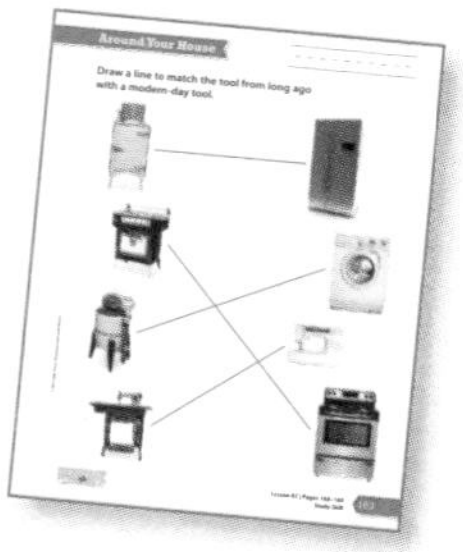

Background

Refrigerator

Before there were refrigerators, people packed their cellars with wood, straw, snow, or ice to keep foods cool. Indians made ice on cold nights by setting water out in earthenware pots and keeping the pots wet. In the eighteenth century, English servants collected ice and put it into icehouses, where the ice was packed in salt, wrapped in flannel, and stored underground to keep it frozen until summer. During the nineteenth century, wooden boxes were lined with tin or zinc and insulated with cork, sawdust, or seaweed to hold ice to keep foods cold. The first practical refrigerating machine was built by Jacob Perkins in 1834. Soon compressor refrigerators were used in many kitchens. Freezers were first used in the 1920s and 1930s when refrigerators with ice-cube compartments became available for home use. Frozen food storage was widely used in homes in the 1940s.

Stove

The first people used open fires to cook their food. Simple ovens were used by the ancient Greeks for baking. Taller brick and mortar hearths with chimneys were used by people in the Middle Ages. People also cooked stews and soups in metal cauldrons that hung over the fire. Inventors began working on building a stove that could contain the fire. Soon cast-iron stoves became available. Coal, kerosene, and gas ovens were built in the 1800s. As soon as electricity was available to power them, electric stoves began to be used.

Washing Machine

Long ago, people used washboards to clean their laundry. Without running water, gas, or electricity, even the most simple hand laundry required much time and labor. When clothes needed to be washed, housewives had to prepare a tub of wash water, a tub of boiling water, and a tub of rinse water. All the water had to be carried from a well or a pump to a stove and tub. Then the wet clothes had to be hung on a line to dry. James King patented a hand-powered washing machine in 1851. Later Hamilton Smith patented the first rotary washing machine. But it was William Blackstone who invented the first washing machine that could be used in the home. The first electric washing machine was introduced in 1908. In the early 1920s, water heaters were added to washing machines. The early washing machines used a wringer to squeeze the water out of the clothes. As clothing was fed into the wringer, often buttons were torn off. Accidents also occurred when hair or fingers got too close to the wringer. A spin-dry feature replaced the wringer in the 1950s.

Sewing Machine

Many people over the years have used hand sewing for mending and making clothes. The first needles were made from bones or animal horns. In the fourth century BC iron needles became available. The first functioning sewing machine was made by Elias Howe in 1846. Isaac Singer built the first successful sewing machine. It was controlled by a foot treadle. The first sewing machine with a zig-zag stitch was patented by Helen Blanchard in 1873. By 1905 most sewing machines used in homes were powered by electricity.

Lesson
88 Activity Manual page 165

Objective
- Explain how children's clothing has changed over time

Materials
- Visual 40: *Clothing Timeline*
- Photos from your childhood showing the kinds of clothing you wore as a child

Introduction

Do you enjoy seeing pictures of your parents when they were children?

What do you notice about the clothes they are wearing in the pictures? How are they different from what you wear?

- Guide a discussion about the photos from your childhood.

Teach for Understanding

- Display the visual as you discuss the clothing on the timeline.

1910s
Younger children wore whites or creams with yoked smocks. Older girls wore softer colors with waist-level sashes. Fabrics had gingham checks or patterns.

1930s
Girls wore short, tailored dresses. Boys wore knickers, vests, trousers, and derby hats. Girls wore party dresses with smocking, tucks, and fine pleating.

1950s
Checkered prints were popular. Poodle skirts, crinoline slips, and bobby socks were in style.

1970s
Floral and bold abstract prints were popular. Girls wore granny dresses trimmed with lace. They also wore solid-colored knee socks with their jumpers and dresses. Bell-bottoms were the fashion.

1990s
Coral, hot pink, and turquoise were popular colors. Hammer pants and athletic clothing were also worn.

2000s
Children's clothing today includes a variety of what was seen in the past with some changes.

Activity Manual

- Guide completion of page 165.

Clothing Long Ago

Color the picture of the children wearing clothing from long ago.

The Future

The **future** is the time that is to come.
Things will keep changing in the future.
Things may change, but we will still work,
share thoughts, and help each other.
God wants us to love and obey Him
and show love to others.
His love will never change.
In the future God will give His people
a perfect world to live in.
That world will never end.

One of the first cars

170

Lesson 89

Student Text pages 170–71
Activity Manual page 167

Objectives

- Identify the things that will remain the same in the future
- Affirm that God is in control and does not change

Materials

- Visual 40: *Clothing Timeline*
- Several pieces of old-style clothing

Vocabulary

- future

Introduction

- Guide a "dress-up" using older-style clothing. Use the visual as you guide a review of the history of children's clothing.

Teach for Understanding

- Guide the reading of page 170 to find out what the future is. the time that is to come

  Even though things change as time goes by, what should stay the same? work, sharing thoughts, and helping others

  Who is in control of the world? God

  Does God change? no
- Read Hebrews 13:8 aloud.

  Everything we know about God is true. He will never change.
- Ask the students what God wants them to do. [BAT: 5a Love] love and obey Him and show love to others

  Will God's love ever change? no

  What will God give His people in the future? a perfect world

  Will the new world in the future ever end? no
- Choose a volunteer to read aloud the caption below the picture.

  Does this car look like your family's car? no

  How is it different from your family's car? Answers will vary.

Lesson 89

- Draw attention to the picture of the car on page 171.

  Does this car look like a car you could see today? yes
- Choose a volunteer to read the caption.

  Cars have changed a lot from the past. Today they are more comfortable, safer, and better designed.
- Conclude the discussion by asking the question on the page.

Activity Manual

- Guide completion of page 167.

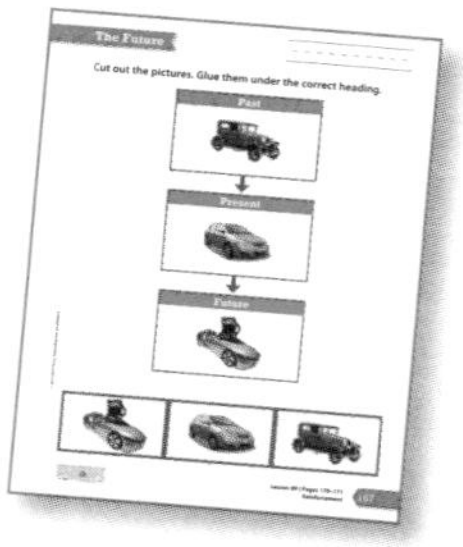

A car we might see today

★ What will cars be like in the future?

Answers will vary.

Activity

171

Lesson 90

Chapter Review and Activity
Activity Manual page 169

Objectives
- Participate in "Family History Day"
- Recall concepts and terms from Chapter 11

Materials
- Objects or photos students brought
- Prepare vocabulary word cards (enough for each student to have a card)

Activity
- Review what the future will hold for the Christian.
- Invite each student to tell about the object or photo he brought or to tell a story from his family's history. (*Variation:* Visit a museum or an antique store.)

Activity

Review
- Review the poem on page 162. Ask the students to name some other things that have changed since the days of long ago.
- Review Chapter 11 vocabulary by inviting the students to look up each word in the Picture Glossary.
- Review Chapter 11 by playing "What's the Word?" Give each student one of the prepared vocabulary cards. Direct the student to stand if the definition you read is the definition of his word.

Activity Manual
- Guide completion of page 169.

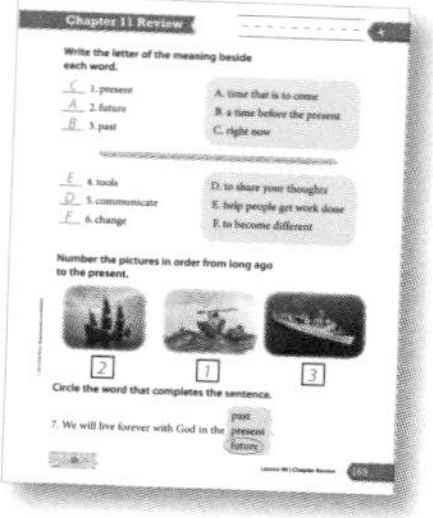
Chapter 11 Review

Write the letter of the meaning beside each word.

C 1. present
A 2. future
B 3. past

A. time that is to come
B. a time before the present
C. right now

E 4. tools
D 5. communicate
F 6. change

D. to share your thoughts
E. help people get work done
F. to become different

Number the pictures in order from long ago to the present.

2 1 3

Circle the word that completes the sentence.

7. We will live forever with God in the past / present / future.

Chapter 11 Test
- Administer Test 11.

Appendix

The BJU Press Heritage Studies texts are developed after reviewing many standards, including the standards from the National Council for the Social Studies (NCSS). The NCSS curriculum standards for social studies are grouped under ten thematic strands. Early grades, middle grades, and high school each have their own performance expectations.

This table provides an overview of the areas in which *Heritage Studies 1* aligns with the NCSS curriculum standards for the early grades. An *X* on the table indicates that at least one component of the standard is addressed in the chapter.

The topics listed in the table are interpreted and discussed in *Heritage Studies 1* according to a Christian worldview.

Bible Action Truths

The quality and consistency of a man's decisions reflect his character. Christian character begins with justification, but it grows throughout the lifelong process of sanctification. God's grace is sufficient for the task, and a major part of God's gracious provision is His Word. The Bible provides the very "words of life" that instruct us in salvation and Christian living. By obeying God's commands and making godly decisions based on His Word, Christians can strengthen their character.

Too often Christians live by only vague guidance—for instance, "do good" to all men. While doing good is desirable, more specific guidance will lead to more consistent decisions.

Man makes consistent decisions when acting on Bible principles—or Bible Action Truths. The thirty-seven Bible Action Truths (listed under eight general principles) provide Christians with specific goals for their actions and attitudes. Study the Scriptures indicated for a fuller understanding of the principles in Bible Action Truths.

Thousands have found this format helpful in identifying and applying principles of behavior. Yet, there is no "magic" in this formula. As you study the Word, you likely will find other truths that speak to you. The key is to study the Scriptures, look for Bible Action Truths, and be sensitive to the leading of the Holy Spirit.

1. **Salvation-Separation Principle**
   Salvation results from God's direct action. Although man is unable to work for this "gift of God," the Christian's reaction to salvation should be to separate himself from the world unto God.
   a. **Understanding Jesus Christ** (Matthew 3:17; 16:16; 1 Corinthians 15:3–4; Philippians 2:9–11) Jesus is the Son of God. He was sent to earth to die on the cross for our sins. He was buried but rose from the dead after three days.
   b. **Repentance and faith** (Luke 13:3; Isaiah 55:7; Acts 5:30–31; Hebrews 11:6; Acts 16:31) If we believe that Jesus died for our sins, we can accept Him as our Savior. We must be sorry for our sins, turn from them, confess them to God, and believe that He will forgive us.
   c. **Separation from the world** (John 17:6, 11, 14, 18; 2 Corinthians 6:14–18; 1 John 2:15–16; James 4:4; Romans 16:17–18; 2 John 10–11) After we are saved, we should live a different life. We should try to be like Christ and not live like those who are unsaved.

2. **Sonship-Servant Principle**
   Only by an act of God the Father could sinful man become a son of God. As a son of God, however, the Christian must realize that he has been "bought with a price"; he is now Christ's servant.
   a. **Authority** (Romans 13:1–7; 1 Peter 2:13–19; 1 Timothy 6:1–5; Hebrews 13:17; Matthew 22:21; 1 Thessalonians 5:12–13) We should respect, honor, and obey those in authority over us. (attentiveness, obedience)
   b. **Servanthood** (Philippians 2:7–8; Ephesians 6:5–8) Just as Christ was a humble servant while He was on earth, we should also be humble and obedient. (attentiveness, helpfulness, promptness, teamwork)
   c. **Faithfulness** (1 Corinthians 4:2; Matthew 25:23; Luke 9:62) We should do our work so that God and others can depend on us. (endurance, responsibility)
   d. **Goal setting** (Proverbs 13:12, 19; Philippians 3:13; Colossians 3:2; 1 Corinthians 9:24) To be faithful servants, we must set goals for our work. We should look forward to finishing a job and going on to something more. (dedication, determination, perseverance)
   e. **Work** (Ephesians 4:28; 2 Thessalonians 3:10–12) God never honors a lazy servant. He wants us to be busy and dependable workers. (cooperativeness, diligence, initiative, industriousness, thoroughness)
   f. **Enthusiasm** (Colossians 3:23; Romans 12:11) We should do all tasks with energy and with a happy, willing spirit. (cheerfulness)

3. **Uniqueness-Unity Principle**
   No one is a mere person; God has created each individual a unique being. But because God has an overall plan for His creation, each unique member must contribute to the unity of the entire body.
   a. **Self-concept** (Psalms 8:3–8; 139; 2 Corinthians 5:17; Ephesians 2:10; 4:1–3, 11–13; 2 Peter 1:10) We are special creatures in God's plan. He has given each of us special abilities to use in our lives for Him.
   b. **Mind** (Philippians 2:5; 4:8; 2 Corinthians 10:5; Proverbs 23:7; Luke 6:45; Proverbs 4:23; Romans 7:23, 25; Daniel 1:8; James 1:8) We should give our hearts and minds to God. What we do and say really begins in our minds. We should try to think humbly of ourselves as Christ did when He lived on earth. (orderliness)
   c. **Emotional control** (Galatians 5:24; Proverbs 16:32; 25:28; 2 Timothy 1:7; Acts 20:24) With the help of God and the power of the Holy Spirit, we should have control over our feelings. We must be careful not to act out of anger. (flexibility, self-control)
   d. **Body as a temple** (1 Corinthians 3:16–17; 6:19–20) We should remember that our bodies are the dwelling place of God's Holy Spirit. We should keep ourselves pure, honest, and dedicated to God's will.
   e. **Unity of Christ and the church** (John 17:21; Ephesians 2:19–22; 5:23–32; 2 Thessalonians 3:6, 14–15) Since we are saved, we are now part of God's family and should unite ourselves with others to worship and grow as Christians. Christ is the head of His church, which includes all believers. He wants us to work together as His church in carrying out His plans, but He forbids us to work in fellowship with disobedient brethren.

4. **Holiness-Habit Principle**
   Believers are declared holy as a result of Christ's finished action on the cross. Daily holiness of life, however, comes from forming godly habits. A Christian must consciously establish godly patterns of action; he must develop habits of holiness.

a. **Sowing and reaping** (Galatians 6:7–8; Hosea 8:7; Matthew 6:1–8) We must remember that we will be rewarded according to the kind of work we have done. If we are faithful, we will be rewarded. If we are unfaithful, we will not be rewarded. We cannot fool God. (thriftiness)

b. **Purity** (1 Thessalonians 4:1–7; 1 Peter 1:22) We should try to live lives that are free from sin. We should keep our minds, words, and deeds clean and pure.

c. **Honesty** (2 Corinthians 8:21; Romans 12:17; Proverbs 16:8; Ephesians 4:25) We should not lie. We should be honest in every way. Even if we could gain more by being dishonest, we should still be honest. God sees all things. (fairness)

d. **Victory** (1 Corinthians 10:13; Romans 8:37; 1 John 5:4; John 16:33; 1 Corinthians 15:57–58) If we constantly try to be pure, honest, and Christlike, with God's help we will be able to overcome temptations.

5. **Love-Life Principle**
We love God because He first loved us. God's action of manifesting His love to us through His Son demonstrates the truth that love must be exercised. Since God acted in love toward us, believers must act likewise by showing godly love to others.

a. **Love** (1 John 3:11, 16–18; 4:7–21; Ephesians 5:2; 1 Corinthians 13; John 15:17) God's love to us was the greatest love possible. We should, in turn, show our love for others by our words and actions. (courtesy, compassion, hospitality, kindness, thankfulness to men, thoughtfulness)

b. **Giving** (2 Corinthians 9:6–8; Proverbs 3:9–10; Luke 6:38) We should give cheerfully to God the first part of all we earn. We should also give to others unselfishly. (hospitality, generosity, sharing, unselfishness)

c. **Evangelism and missions** (Psalm 126:5–6; Matthew 28:18–20; Romans 1:16–17; 2 Corinthians 5:11–21) We should be busy telling others about the love of God and His plan of salvation. We should share in the work of foreign missionaries by our giving and prayers.

d. **Communication** (Ephesians 4:22–29; Colossians 4:6; James 3:2–13; Isaiah 50:4) We should have control of our tongues so that we will not say things displeasing to God. We should encourage others and be kind and helpful in what we say.

e. **Friendliness** (Proverbs 17:17; 18:24; Psalm 119:63) We should be friendly to others, and we should be loyal to those who love and serve God. (loyalty)

6. **Communion-Consecration Principle**
Because sin separates man from God, any communion between man and God must be achieved by God's direct act of removing sin. Once communion is established, the believer's reaction should be to maintain a consciousness of this fellowship by living a consecrated life.

a. **Bible study** (1 Peter 2:2–3; 2 Timothy 2:15; Psalm 119) To grow as Christians, we must spend time with God daily by reading His Word. (reverence for the Bible)

b. **Prayer** (1 Chronicles 16:11; 1 Thessalonians 5:17; John 15:7, 16; 16:24; Psalm 145:18; Romans 8:26–27) We should bring all our requests to God, trusting Him to answer them in His own way.

c. **Spirit-filled** (Ephesians 5:18–19; Galatians 5:16, 22–23; Romans 8:13–14; 1 John 1:7–9) We should let the Holy Spirit rule in our hearts and show us what to say and do. We should not say and do just what we want to, for those things are often wrong and harmful to others. (gentleness, joyfulness, patience)

d. **Clear conscience** (1 Timothy 1:19; Acts 24:16) To be good Christians, we cannot have wrong acts or thoughts or words bothering our consciences. We must confess them to God and to those people against whom we have sinned. We cannot live lives close to God if we have guilty consciences.

e. **Forgiveness** (Ephesians 4:30–32; Luke 17:3–4; Colossians 3:13; Matthew 18:15–17; Mark 11:25–26) We must ask forgiveness of God when we have done wrong. Just as God forgives our sins freely, we should forgive others when they do wrong things to us.

7. **Grace-Gratitude Principle**
Grace is unmerited favor. Man does not deserve God's grace. However, after God bestows His grace, believers should react with an overflow of gratitude.

a. **Grace** (1 Corinthians 15:10; Ephesians 2:8–9) Without God's grace we would be sinners on our way to hell. He loved us when we did not deserve His love and provided for us a way to escape sin's punishment by the death of His Son on the cross.

b. **Exaltation of Christ** (Colossians 1:12–21; Ephesians 1:17–23; Philippians 2:9–11; Galatians 6:14; Hebrews 1:2–3; John 1:1–4, 14; 5:23) We should realize and remember at all times the power, holiness, majesty, and perfection of Christ, and we should give Him the praise and glory for everything that is accomplished through us.

c. **Praise** (Psalm 107:8; Hebrews 13:15; 1 Peter 2:9; Ephesians 1:6; 1 Chronicles 16:23–36; 29:11–13) Remembering God's great love and goodness toward us, we should continually praise His name. (thankfulness to God)

d. **Contentment** (Philippians 4:11; 1 Timothy 6:6–8; Psalm 77:3; Proverbs 15:16; Hebrews 13:5) Money, houses, cars, and all things on earth will last only for a little while. God has given us just what He meant for us to have. We should be happy and content with what we have, knowing that God will provide for us all that we need. We should also be happy wherever God places us.

e. **Humility** (1 Peter 5:5–6; Philippians 2:3–4) We should not be proud and boastful but should be willing to be quiet and in the background. Our reward will come from God on Judgment Day, and men's praise to us here on earth will not matter at all. Christ was humble when He lived on earth, and we should be like Him.

Bible Action Truths

8. **Power-Prevailing Principle**
   Believers can prevail only as God gives the power. "I can do all things through Christ." God is the source of our power used in fighting the good fight of faith.
   a. **Faith in God's promises** (2 Peter 1:4; Philippians 4:6; Romans 4:16–21; 1 Thessalonians 5:18; Romans 8:28; 1 Peter 5:7; Hebrews 3:18; 4:11) God always remains true to His promises. Believing that He will keep all the promises in His Word, we should be determined fighters for Him.
   b. **Faith in the power of the Word of God** (Hebrews 4:12; Jeremiah 23:29; Psalm 119; 1 Peter 1:23–25) God's Word is powerful and endures forever. All other things will pass away, but God's Word shall never pass away because it is written to us from God, and God is eternal.
   c. **Fight** (Ephesians 6:11–17; 2 Timothy 4:7–8; 1 Timothy 6:12; 1 Peter 5:8–9) God does not have any use for lazy or cowardly fighters. We must work and fight against sin, using the Word of God as our weapon against the Devil. What we do for God now will determine how much He will reward us in heaven.
   d. **Courage** (1 Chronicles 28:20; Joshua 1:9; Hebrews 13:6; Ephesians 3:11–12; Acts 4:13, 31) God has promised us that He will not forsake us; therefore, we should not be afraid to speak out against sin. We should remember that we are armed with God's strength.

Bible Promises

A. **Liberty from Sin**—Born into God's spiritual kingdom, a Christian is enabled to live right and gain victory over sin through faith in Christ. (Romans 8:3–4—"For what the law could not do, in that it was weak through the flesh, God sending his own Son in the likeness of sinful flesh, and for sin, condemned sin in the flesh: that the righteousness of the law might be fulfilled in us, who walk not after the flesh, but after the Spirit.")

B. **Guiltless by the Blood**—Cleansed by the blood of Christ, the Christian is pardoned from the guilt of his sins. He does not have to brood or fret over his past because the Lord has declared him righteous. (Romans 8:33—"Who shall lay any thing to the charge of God's elect? It is God that justifieth." Isaiah 45:24—"Surely, shall one say, in the Lord have I righteousness and strength: even to him shall men come; and all that are incensed against him shall be ashamed.")

C. **Basis for Prayer**—Knowing that his righteousness comes entirely from Christ and not from himself, the Christian is free to plead the blood of Christ and to come before God in prayer at any time. (Romans 5:1–2—"Therefore being justified by faith, we have peace with God through our Lord Jesus Christ: by whom also we have access by faith into this grace wherein we stand, and rejoice in hope of the glory of God.")

D. **Identified in Christ**—The Christian has the assurance that God sees him as a son of God, perfectly united with Christ. He also knows that he has access to the strength and the grace of Christ in his daily living. (Galatians 2:20—"I am crucified with Christ: nevertheless I live; yet not I, but Christ liveth in me: and the life which I now live in the flesh I live by the faith of the Son of God, who loved me, and gave himself for me." Ephesians 1:3—"Blessed be the God and Father of our Lord Jesus Christ, who hath blessed us with all spiritual blessings in heavenly places in Christ.")

E. **Christ as Sacrifice**—Christ was a willing sacrifice for the sins of the world. His blood covers every sin of the believer and pardons the Christian for eternity. The purpose of His death and resurrection was to redeem a people to Himself. (Isaiah 53:4–5—"Surely he hath borne our griefs, and carried our sorrows: yet we did esteem him stricken, smitten of God, and afflicted. But he was wounded for our transgressions, he was bruised for our iniquities: the chastisement of our peace was upon him; and with his stripes we are healed." John 10:27–28—"My sheep hear my voice, and I know them, and they follow me: and I give unto them eternal life; and they shall never perish, neither shall any man pluck them out of my hand.")

F. **Christ as Intercessor**—Having pardoned them through His blood, Christ performs the office of High Priest in praying for His people. (Hebrews 7:25—"Wherefore he is able also to save them to the uttermost that come unto God by him, seeing he ever liveth to make intercession for them." John 17:20—"Neither pray I for these alone, but for them also which shall believe on me through their word.")

G. **Christ as Friend**—In giving salvation to the believer, Christ enters a personal, loving relationship with the Christian that cannot be ended. This relationship is understood and enjoyed on the believer's part through fellowship with the Lord through Bible reading and prayer. (Isaiah 54:5—"For thy Maker is thine husband; the Lord of hosts is his name; and thy Redeemer the Holy One of Israel; The God of the whole earth shall he be called." Romans 8:38–39—"For I am persuaded, that neither death, nor life, nor angels, nor principalities, nor powers, nor things present, nor things to come, nor height, nor depth, nor any other creature, shall be able to separate us from the love of God, which is in Christ Jesus our Lord.")

H. **God as Father**—God has appointed Himself to be responsible for the well-being of the Christian. He both protects and nourishes the believer, and it was from Him that salvation originated. (Isaiah 54:17—"No weapon that is formed against thee shall prosper; and every tongue that shall rise against thee in judgment thou shalt condemn. This is the heritage of the servants of the Lord, and their righteousness is of me, saith the Lord." Psalm 103:13—"Like as a father pitieth his children, so the Lord pitieth them that fear him.")

I. **God as Master**—God is sovereign over all creation. He orders the lives of His people for His glory and their good. (Romans 8:28—"And we know that all things work together for good to them that love God, to them who are the called according to his purpose.")

Leading a Child to Christ

One of the greatest desires of Christian teachers is to lead children to the Savior. God has called you to present the gospel to your students so that they may repent and trust Christ, thereby being acceptable to God through Christ.

Relying on the Holy Spirit, take advantage of the opportunities that arise for presenting the good news of Jesus Christ. Ask questions to personally apply the Ten Commandments to your students (e.g., What is sin? Have you ever told a lie or taken something that wasn't yours? Are you a sinner?). You may also ask questions to discern the child's sincerity or any misunderstanding he might have (e.g., What is the gospel? What does it mean to repent? Can you do anything to save yourself?). Read verses from your Bible. You may find the following outline helpful, especially when dealing individually with a child.

1. **I have sinned (Romans 3:23).**
   - Sin is disobeying God's Word (1 John 3:4). I break the Ten Commandments (Exodus 20:2–17) by loving other people or things more than I love God, worshiping other things or people, using God's name lightly, disobeying and dishonoring my parents, lying, stealing, cheating, thinking harmful and sinful thoughts, or wanting something that belongs to somebody else.
   - Therefore, I am a sinner (Psalm 51:5; 58:3; Jeremiah 17:9).
   - God is holy and must punish me for my sin (Isaiah 6:3; Romans 6:23).
   - God hates sin, and there is nothing that I can do to get rid of my sin myself (Titus 3:5; Romans 3:20, 28). I cannot make myself become a good person.
2. **Jesus died for me (Romans 5:8).**
   - God loves me even though I am a sinner.
   - He sent His Son, Jesus Christ, to die on the cross for me. Christ is sinless and did not deserve death. Because of His love for me, Christ took my sin on Himself and was punished in my place (1 Peter 2:24*a*; 1 Corinthians 15:3; John 1:29).
   - God accepted Christ's death as the perfect substitute to take the punishment for my sin (2 Corinthians 5:21).
   - Three days later, God raised Jesus from the dead. Jesus Christ is alive today and offers salvation to all. This is the gospel of Jesus Christ: He died on the cross for our sins according to the Scriptures, and He rose again the third day according to the Scriptures (1 Corinthians 15:1–4; 2 Peter 3:9; 1 Timothy 2:4).
3. **I need to put my trust in Jesus (Romans 10:9–10, 13–14*a*).**
   - I must repent (turn away from my sin) and trust only Jesus Christ for salvation (Mark 1:15).
   - If I repent and believe in what Jesus has done, I am putting my trust in Jesus.
   - Everyone who trusts in Jesus is forgiven of sin (Acts 2:21) and will live forever with God (John 3:16). I am given His righteousness and become a new creation with Christ living in me (2 Corinthians 5:21; Colossians 1:27).

If a child shows genuine interest and readiness, ask, "Are you ready to put your trust in Jesus and depend on only Him for salvation?" If he says yes, then ask him to talk to God about this. Perhaps he will pray something like the following:

> God, I know that I've sinned against You and that You hate sin but that You also love me. I believe that Jesus died to pay for my sin and that He rose from the dead, so I put my trust in Jesus to forgive me and give me a home with You forever. In Jesus' name I pray. Amen.

Show the child how to know from God's Word whether he is in God's family (1 John 5:12–13; John 3:18). Encourage him to follow Jesus by obeying Him each day. Tell the child that whenever he sins, he will be forgiven as soon as he confesses those sins to God (1 John 1:9).

National Curriculum Standards for Social Studies

Standards for Early Grades

	Chapter	1	2	3	4	5	6	7	8	9	10	11
I. Culture												
Knowledge—Learners will understand												
a.	that "culture" refers to the behaviors, beliefs, values, traditions, institutions, and ways of living together of a group of people;	X	X	X	X	X	X	X	X	X	X	X
b.	concepts such as similarities, differences, beliefs, values, cohesion, and diversity;	X	X	X		X		X		X	X	
c.	how cultural beliefs, behaviors, and values allow human groups to solve the problems of daily living;	X	X	X	X	X	X	X	X	X	X	
d.	how culture may change in response to changing needs and concerns;		X	X		X		X		X		X
e.	how individuals learn the elements of their culture through interactions with other members of the culture group;		X	X		X		X	X	X	X	
f.	how people from different cultures develop different values and ways of interpreting experiences.	X		X		X		X	X	X	X	
II. Time, Continuity, and Change												
Knowledge—Learners will understand												
a.	that the study of the past is the story of communities, nations, and the world;	X	X	X	X	X	X	X	X	X	X	X
b.	concepts such as past, present, future, similarity, difference, and change;	X	X	X	X	X	X	X	X	X	X	X
c.	that we can learn our personal past and the past of communities, nations, and the world by means of stories, biographies, interviews, and original sources, such as documents, letters, photographs, and artifacts;	X	X	X	X	X	X	X	X	X	X	X
d.	key people, events, and places associated with the history of the community, nation, and world;	X	X		X	X	X	X	X	X	X	
e.	key symbols and traditions that are carried from the past into the present in the United States and other countries and that reflect diverse cultures;				X	X	X	X	X	X	X	
f.	that people view and interpret historical events differently because of the times in which they live, the experiences they have, and the points of view they hold;	X		X		X	X		X	X		X
g.	that historical events occurred in times that differed from our own but often have lasting consequences for the present and future.	X	X	X			X	X	X	X	X	X
III. People, Places, and Environments												
Knowledge—Learners will understand												
a.	that the theme of people, places, and environments involves the study of location, place, and the interactions of people with their surroundings;	X	X	X	X	X	X	X	X	X	X	
b.	concepts such as location, direction, distance, and scale;	X	X	X			X	X	X	X	X	
c.	physical and human characteristics of the school, community, state, and region and the interactions of people in these places with the environment;	X		X	X	X	X	X		X		
d.	factors influencing various community, state, and regional patterns of human settlement, such as the availability of land and water and places for people to live;	X		X	X	X		X	X	X	X	

	Chapter	1	2	3	4	5	6	7	8	9	10	11
e.	physical changes in the community, state, and region, such as seasons, climate, and weather and their effects on plants and animals;							X		X	X	
f.	cultural patterns and their interactions within and across places, such as migration and settlement and changes in customs or ideas and in the ways people make a living;	X			X	X		X	X	X	X	X
g.	benefits and problems resulting from the discovery and use of resources;	X		X		X		X	X	X		X
h.	factors that contribute to similarities and differences among people locally and in places across the world, including ethnicity, language, and religious beliefs;	X				X	X	X	X	X	X	X
i.	how to use tools such as maps, globes, and geospatial technologies in investigating the relationships among people, places, and environments.	X		X	X	X	X	X	X	X	X	
IV. Individual Development and Identity												
Knowledge—Learners will understand												
a.	that the study of individual development and identity helps us know who we are and how we change;	X	X	X		X				X		X
b.	concepts such as growth, change, learning, self, family, and groups;	X	X	X	X			X	X	X	X	X
c.	that individuals have characteristics that are both distinct from and similar to those of others;	X		X		X		X	X	X	X	X
d.	that individuals bring specific abilities, interests, and talents in working with others to make decisions and solve problems;			X	X			X	X	X	X	
e.	that individuals change over time;			X				X		X	X	X
f.	that physical, intellectual, and emotional growth affects individual identity, growth, and interactions with others;				X				X			X
g.	that people's interactions with their social and physical surroundings influence individual identity and growth;		X	X	X	X		X	X	X	X	X
h.	that individual choices are influenced by personal and social factors.	X	X	X		X	X		X	X		X
V. Individuals, Groups, and Institutions												
Knowledge—Learners will understand												
a.	that this theme helps us know that people belong to groups and institutions which influence them and which are influenced by them;	X	X	X	X	X	X	X		X	X	X
b.	concepts such as community, culture, role, competition, cooperation, rules, and norms;		X	X	X	X	X	X	X	X	X	
c.	characteristics that distinguish individuals;	X			X	X	X	X		X		X
d.	that individuals, groups, and institutions share common elements;	X		X	X	X	X	X		X	X	
e.	the impact of families, schools, religious institutions, government agencies, financial institutions, and civic groups on their lives;			X	X	X	X	X	X	X		
f.	how the rules and norms of groups to which they belong impact their lives.	X	X	X	X	X	X	X	X	X	X	

	Chapter	1	2	3	4	5	6	7	8	9	10	11
VI. Power, Authority, and Governance												
Knowledge—Learners will understand												
a.	that rules and laws can serve to support order and protect individual rights;	X	X	X	X	X	X		X	X	X	
b.	fundamental ideas that are the foundation of American constitutional democracy, including those of the U.S. Constitution, the rule of law, separation of powers, checks and balances, minority rights, and the separation of church and state;	X		X	X	X	X				X	
c.	fundamental values of democracy: the common good, liberty, justice, equality, and individual liberty;	X		X	X	X	X				X	
d.	the basic elements of government in the United States: executive, legislative, and judicial authority;				X	X	X					
e.	the ways in which governments meet the needs and wants of citizens.			X	X	X	X		X	X	X	
VII. Production, Distribution, and Consumption												
Knowledge—Learners will understand												
a.	how people and communities deal with scarcity of resources;		X	X	X	X		X	X	X	X	X
b.	the difference between needs and wants;		X	X					X	X		
c.	what people and communities gain and give up when they make a decision;								X	X		
d.	how economic incentives affect people's behavior;		X	X				X	X	X		
e.	the character and functions of money and its uses;		X						X			
f.	the role of various organizations that help people achieve their individual economic goals (e.g., banks, businesses, and labor unions);								X			
g.	the characteristics of a market economy;											
h.	the difference between the goods and services produced in the market and those produced by the government.			X		X						
VIII. Science, Technology, and Society												
Knowledge—Learners will understand												
a.	that science involves the study of the natural world and technology refers to the tools we use to accomplish tasks;	X	X		X			X	X	X	X	X
b.	how society often turns to science and technology to solve problems;				X				X			X
c.	that media and technology are a part of every aspect of our lives;											X
d.	the ways in which scientific findings and various forms of technology influence our daily lives;				X						X	X
e.	that science often leads to new technology in areas such as communication and transportation and results in change over time;				X				X			X
f.	that science and technology can have both positive and negative impacts on individuals, society, and the globe.								X			

	Chapter	1	2	3	4	5	6	7	8	9	10	11
IX. Global Connections												
Knowledge—Learners will understand												
a.	that global connections may be of various types (e.g., cultural exchange, trade, politics, economics, or travel);					X	X	X	X	X	X	
b.	that global connections affect daily life for individuals and those around them;							X		X	X	
c.	that some global issues have persisted over time while others are more contemporary or emerging (e.g., technology enabling rapid communication across the earth);					X	X		X			
d.	that all cultures have similar needs but meet those needs in different ways that may influence or be influenced by global connections;				X			X	X	X		
e.	that the pace of global change has quickened in recent times.											
X. Civic Ideals and Practices												
Knowledge—Learners will understand												
a.	that the theme of civic ideals and practices helps us know how we can influence the way people live and act together;		X	X	X	X		X		X		
b.	concepts and ideals such as individual dignity, fairness, freedom, the common good, rule of law, civic life, rights, and responsibilities;	X	X	X	X	X	X					
c.	that key practices in a democratic society include civic participation based on studying community issues, planning, decision making, voting, and cooperating to promote civic ideals;			X	X	X	X					
d.	that democratic ideals and practices are often represented in excerpts from contemporary and historical sources, quotations, and stories;						X				X	
e.	the importance of gathering information as the basis for informed civic action.					X						

Index

Student Text

Photograph Credits

The following agencies and individuals have furnished materials to meet the photographic needs of this textbook. We wish to express our gratitude to them for their important contribution.

Alamy	Getty Images
Michael Asire	iStockphoto
Associated Press	Brian Jones
Bigstock	Library of Congress
BJU Photo Services	Preservation Virginia
Brian Collins	SuperStock
Dreamstime	Thinkstock
Fotolia	Wikimedia Commons

Chapter One

Getty Images/Hemera/Thinkstock 6–7; Jose Luis Pelaez/Photographer's Choice/Getty Images 2 (top); © Fancy Collection/SuperStock 2 (bottom); © Steve Vidler/SuperStock 3 (bottom left); © iStockphoto.com/Shawn Gearhart 3 (right); © iStockphoto.com/Chris Bernard 3 (top); Getty Images/Hemera/Thinkstock 4; © iStockphoto.com/DAMIAN KUZDAK 10 (bottom right); © iStockphoto.com/Eduardo Mariano Rivero 10 (bottom right center); © iStockphoto.com/Johannes Kornelius 10 (top right); Getty Images/iStockphoto/Thinkstock 10 (top right center), 10 (top left), 20 (bottom right); © iStockphoto.com/Angelika Stern 10 (bottom left); Jose Luis Pelaez/Iconica/Getty Images 19 (top); BJU Photo Services 19 (bottom); Getty Images/Jupiter Images/Thinkstock 20 (left); Getty Images/Photos.com/Thinkstock 20 (top right)

Chapter Two

© iStockphoto.com/Skip Odonnell 22–23; Getty Images/Stockbyte/Thinkstock 26; Getty Images/iStockphoto/Thinkstock 32; Getty Images/Comstock Images/Thinkstock 33 (top right); Brian Collins 33 (timeline)

Chapter Three

Justin Kase zfivez/Alamy 34–35; Blend Images/Ariel Skelley/the Agency Collection/Getty Images 36; Getty Images/iStockphoto/Thinkstock 37 (top), 40, 45 (bottom), 47 (top right, bottom right, center right); Getty Images/Comstock Images/Thinkstock 37 (bottom), 41 (bottom left); Getty Images/Stockbyte/Thinkstock 38 (left); Getty Images/Comstock Images/Thinkstock 38 (top right); © Tyler Olson/Dreamstime.com 38 (bottom right); Brian Jones 41 (top left); Getty Images/Creatas RF/Thinkstock 41 (right); Getty Images/Fuse 42; Getty Images/Digital Vision/Thinkstock 44; © iStockphoto.com/mathieukor 45 (top); Wikimedia Commons/Public Domain 47 (left), 49 (top); © zsollere - Fotolia.com 47 (center left); Library of Congress 47 (bottom left); BJU Photo Services 49 (bottom)

Chapter Four

Digital Vision/Getty Images 50–51; Getty Images/iStockphoto/Thinkstock 52, 59, 61; ASSOCIATED PRESS 54 (left); AFP/Getty Images 54 (right); © Culver Pictures, Inc./SuperStock 56; Getty Images/Photos.com/Thinkstock 57; Getty Images/Comstock Images/Thinkstock 58; Getty Images/iStockphoto 60; © age fotostock/SuperStock 62; Getty Images/Photodisc/Thinkstock 63; © imagebroker.net/SuperStock 64; Michael Asire 65

Chapter Five

Getty Images/Digital Vision/Thinkstock 66–67; Getty Images/Creatas RF/Thinkstock 68; Getty Images/Comstock Images/Thinkstock 70; © Exactostock/SuperStock 71 © iStockphoto.com/Jeremiah Barber 72 (left); © iStockphoto.com/Peter Spiro 72 (right); Wikimedia Commons/Public Domain 73; © iStockphoto.com/melhi 74 (top); Getty Images/iStockphoto/Thinkstock 74 (bottom), 75–76; ASSOCIATED PRESS 77; Michael Asire 79

Chapter Six

© Charles O. Cecil/age fotostock/SuperStock 80–81; Cameron Davidson/Photographer's Choice/Getty Images 82; Kmccoy/Wikimedia Commons/GFDL/CC-BY-SA_-2.0 83; © Spencer Grant/age fotostock/SuperStock 84; SAUL LOEB/Staff/AFP/Getty Images 85 (right); Getty Images/Stringer/Getty Images Entertainment/Getty Images 85 (left); Library of Congress 85 (center); © Michael S. Nolan/age fotostock/SuperStock 86–87; © Wolfgang Kaehler/SuperStock 88–89; Getty Images/iStockphoto/Thinkstock 90; © iStockphoto.com/Steve Sucsy 91; rrodrickbeiler/Bigstock.com 92 (top); © Hemis/Alamy 92 (bottom); Michael Asire 93

Chapter Seven

© Paul Thompson Images/Alamy 96–97 (girl); Getty Images/iStockphoto/Thinkstock 96–97 (background); Andreas F. Borchert/Wikimedia Commons/GFDL 1.2/CC-BY-SA-3.0 105 (right); © Wolfgang Kaehler/SuperStock 105 (left); Joel Bennet/Peter Arnold/Getty Images 107 (top left); Getty Images/Hemera/Thinkstock 107 (top right); Michael Asire 107 (bottom); © iStockphoto.com/Spiritartist 108 (bottom right); Science & Society Picture Library/Contributor/SSPL/Getty Images 108 (top left); Ernest Amoroso, National Museum of the American Indian/Wikimedia Commons/Public Domain 108 (bottom left); Getty Images/iStockphoto/Thinkstock 108 (top right), 109 (top right); Wikipedia Loves Art at the Brooklyn Museum/Wikimedia Commons/CC-BY 2.5 109 (center); Phil Schermeister/National Geographic/Getty Images 109 (bottom left); © Exactostock/SuperStock 109 (bottom right and top left); © iStockphoto.com/Wellford Tiller 109 (top right)

Chapter Eight

© Mikael Utterstrm/Alamy 110–11; NASA/Wikimedia Commons/Public Domain 114; © Visions of America/SuperStock 118; U.S. Navy/Wikimedia Commons/Public Domain 122; BJU Photo Services 123

Chapter Nine

© David Forbert/SuperStock 124–25; Newport News Daily Press/Contributor/McClatchy-Tribune/Getty Images 128; Courtesy Preservation Virginia 132; Thomas J. Abercrombie/Contributor/National Geographic/Getty Images 137; BJU Photo Services 143

Chapter Ten

© age fotostock/SuperStock 144–45; BJU Photo Services 161

Chapter Eleven

© David Lyons/age fotostock/SuperStock 162–63; Getty Images/Jupiter Images/Thinkstock 164; Getty Images/Hemera/Thinkstock 165 (top), 169 (top); © iStockphoto.com/Cliff Parnell 165 (center); © iStockphoto.com/parema 165 (bottom); Getty Images/Hemera Technologies/Thinkstock 166 (bottom); © iStockphoto.com/Paul Hill 166 (top); © Galló Gusztáv - Fotolia.com 167 (bottom); Getty Images/iStockphoto/Thinkstock 167 (top), 170, 171 (bottom right); Getty Images/iStockphoto/Thinkstock 168 (top); Hemera Technologies/PhotoObjects.net/Thinkstock 168 (bottom); © iStockphoto.com/Elena Butinova 169 (bottom); © Robert Wilson - Fotolia.com 171 (top); Getty Images/Brand X Pictures/Thinkstock 171 (bottom left)

Picture Glossary

Getty Images/Jupiter Images/Thinkstock 181 (center left); ASSOCIATED PRESS 181 (top right), 184 (top right); Blend Images/Ariel Skelley/the Agency Collection/Getty Images 181 (bottom right); Getty Images/iStockphoto/Thinkstock 184 (center left); © iStockphoto.com/Cristina Ciochina 184 (bottom left); Getty Images/Digital Vision/Thinkstock 185 (top left); © Michael S. Nolan/age fotostock/SuperStock 185 (bottom left); © Wolfgang Kaehler/SuperStock 185 (center left); © iStockphoto.com/Peter Spiro 185 (top right); © Galló Gusztáv - Fotolia.com 186 (center left); Getty Images/Stockbyte/Thinkstock 188 (top left); © age fotostock/SuperStock 188 (center right); Getty Images/Hemera/Thinkstock 189 (top left)

Back Matter

© Elenathewise - Fotolia.com 172 (top left); © Silverpics - Fotolia.com 172 (bottom left); Paul_Lewis/Bigstock.com 172 (top right); © Imarc - Fotolia.com 172 (bottom right); Getty Images/Hemera/Thinkstock 172 (center)

Activity Manual

Photograph Credits

The following agencies and individuals have furnished materials to meet the photographic needs of this textbook. We wish to express our gratitude to them for their important contribution.

Fotolia	Thinkstock
iStockphoto	Wikimedia Commons
SuperStock	

Chapter Four

Getty Images/Comstock Images/Thinkstock 63 (Mount Rushmore); Getty Images/iStockphoto/Thinkstock 63 (Grand Canyon); Getty Images/Photodisc/Thinkstock 63 (Statue of Liberty); © age fotostock/SuperStock 63 (Liberty Bell)

Chapter Five

Getty Images/Comstock Images/Thinkstock 69 (American flag); © iStockphoto.com/Jeremiah Barber 69 (bald eagle); © iStockphoto.com/lillisphotography 69 (White House); © iStockphoto.com/Peter Spiro 69 (coin); © iStockphoto.com/melhi 71 (grain); Getty Images/iStockphoto/Thinkstock 71 (ocean and mountains)

Chapter Six

Kmccoy/Wikimedia Commons/GFDL/CC-BY-SA-2.0 91 (Capitol Building); Getty Images/iStockphoto/Thinkstock 91 (George Washington, quarter, Washington Monument); © iStockphoto.com/Steve Sucsy 91 (Lincoln Memorial); Getty Images/Comstock Images/Thinkstock 91 (Mount Rushmore, veteran); Getty Images/Photodisc/Thinkstock 91 (Statue of Liberty); © iStockphoto.com/lillisphotography 91 (White House); © iStockphoto.com/David Hills 91 (Uncle Sam)

Chapter Eleven

Getty Images/Hemera/Thinkstock 159 (bottom right); © iStockphoto.com/Cliff Parnell 159 (top right); © iStockphoto.com/parema 159 (bottom left); Getty Images/Pixland/Jupiter Images/Thinkstock 159 (center right); © iStockphoto.com/Zhang Bo 159 (top left); Getty Images/Hemera Technologies/Thinkstock 161 (early telephone); © iStockphoto.com/Paul Hill 161 (early radio); © Galló Gusztáv-Fotolia.com 161 (early television); Getty Images/iStockphoto/Thinkstock 161, 163, 167 (early computer, cell phone, flat screen television, early refrigerator, modern washing machine, modern sewing machine, early blue car); © iStockphoto.com/Alex Slobodkin 161 (laptop); Hemera Technologies/PhotoObjects.net/Thinkstock 163 (early stove); Getty Images/Hemera/Thinkstock 163 (early washing machine); © iStockphoto.com/Elena Butinova 163 (modern refrigerator); © iStockphoto.com/Daniel Loiselle 163 (modern stove); © Robert Wilson-Fotolia.com 167 (modern car); © imagebroker.net/SuperStock 167 (futuristic car); U.S. Navy/Wikimedia Commons/Public Domain 169 (bottom right); © Visions of America/SuperStock 169 (bottom left)

Visuals

Photograph Credits

The following agencies and individuals have furnished materials to meet the photographic needs of this textbook. We wish to express our gratitude to them for their important contribution.

Bigstock	Thinkstock
Fotolia	Wikimedia Commons
Jim Steinhart of TravelPhotoBase.com	

Chart 6

© Kropic - Fotolia.com (top); © Chris Loft - Fotolia.com (bottom)

Chart 7

Getty Images/Brand X/Thinkstock (left); © Monkey Business - Fotolia.com (right)

Chart 8

© SeanPavonePhoto - Fotolia.com (center); © Monkey Business - Fotolia.com (top) monkeybusinessimages/Bigstock.com (bottom)

Chart 11

Susan ck/Bigstock.com (top right); Honjune/Bigstock.com (top left); © Ciprian Dughir -Fotolia.com (bottom right); SNEHITDESIGN/Bigstock.com (center left); BBS/Bigstock.com (center right); Boris Quintanill/Bigstock.com (bottom left)

Chart 12

© Michael Mill - Fotolia.com (center right); Brian Lasenby - Fotolia.com (bottom left); May Haga/Bigstock.com (top left); © Steve Byland - Fotolia.com (top right); "Brown pelican - natures pics" by Alan D. Wilson/Wikimedia Commons/CC-BY-SA 3.0 (bottom right); "Oregon Department of Fish & Wildlife - 121 ring necked pheasant swart"/Oregon Department of Fish & Wildlife/Wikimedia Commons/CC-BY-SA 3.0 (center left); "Carpodacus purpureus" by Cephas/Wikimedia Commons/CC-BY-SA 3.0 (top center)

Chart 13

Jim Steinhart of TravelPhotoBase.com (left); mush125/Bigstock.com (right)

Chart 15

Beisea/Bigstock.com (top left); Marcy Smith/Bigstock.com (top right); Dolomite Designs/Bigstock.com (bottom left); SamK2/Bigstock.com (bottom right)

Chart 16

© Elenathewise - Fotolia.com (top left); © Silverpics - Fotolia.com (top right); Paul_Lewis/Bigstock.com (bottom left); © lmarc - Fotolia.com (bottom right)

Chart 38

House of Digital/Bigstock.com (telephone); © Paul Hill - Fotolia.com (radio); © Galló Gusztáv - Fotolia.com (early tv); Getty Images/iStockphoto/Thinkstock (early computer)

Chart 39

© James Steidl - Fotolia.com (refrigerator); MargoJH/Bigstock.com (stove); © pmphoto - Fotolia.com (washing machine); flibustier/Bigstock.com (sewing machine)

How to Use the Teacher's Toolkit

Contents

The Teacher's Toolkit CD contains the following materials:

- Activity Manual Answer Key
- Instructional Aids
- Maps
- Visuals

Getting Started

Viewing the Teacher's Toolkit materials requires Adobe® Reader® 7.0 or higher. The most recent version of Adobe Reader may be downloaded at no charge from the Adobe website at www.adobe.com. An Internet connection is required to download Reader.

Windows

Insert the CD. If it does not start automatically, open the CD's file listing and launch the file "Startup.exe." Read and accept the license agreement to begin using the Teacher's Toolkit materials. Navigate within the CD using the bookmarks on the left side of the screen.

Mac

Insert the CD, click on the CD icon, and open the file "main.pdf" to begin using the Teacher's Toolkit materials.

Minimum System Requirements

Processor (CPU): Pentium IV
Operating System: Windows XP; Mac OS Leopard (version 10.5)
RAM: 256MB
Display: 1024 × 768
Application: Adobe Reader 7.0

Additional Help

Additional usage information can be found on the CD in the file "CD_info.pdf." For further assistance, call BJU Press Customer Service at 1-800-845-5731.

WRITING & Grammar 12

Third Edition

Elizabeth Rose
Kimberly Y. Stegall

bju press
Greenville, South Carolina

Advisory Committee
from the administration, faculty, and staff of Bob Jones University
David Fisher, PhD, *Provost*
Steven N. Skaggs, MEd, *Senior Manager of Product Development, BJU Press*
Milton Ashley, MS, *Educational Content Manager, BJU Press*
Brad Batdorf, EdD, *Secondary Authors Supervisor, BJU Press*

WRITING AND GRAMMAR 12 Teacher's Edition
Third Edition

Coordinating Writers
Maisie E. Douglas Hansen
Judith W. Lanier, MA
Elizabeth Rose, MEd, MA
Kimberly Y. Stegall, MEd

Contributing Writers
Seth W. Carper
June W. Cates
Elizabeth R. Cole, MS
Glenda H. Guthrie
Grace Collins Hargis, PhD
Sarah Abigail Stahl Mattos
Rachel S. Matzko, MA
Rebecca A. Osborne, MEd
Michael Pope, MA
Rachel Maes Stewart

Project Coordinator
Benjamin Sinnamon

Bible Integration
Bryan Smith, PhD
Mark L. Ward Jr., PhD

Editors
Rebecca Moore
Elizabeth M. Morgan

Consultants
Will Gray
Grace Collins Hargis, PhD
Chairman Emeritus of the Department of English Education and Chairman of the Department of Linguistics, Bob Jones University

Page Layout
Bonnijean Marley
Kelley Moore

Cover Designer
Drew Fields

Designers
Christy Matias
US Color

Permissions
Sylvia Gass
Brenda Hansen
Ashley Hobbs

Illustrators
Matthew Bjerk
Aaron Dickey
Johanna Ehnis
Cory Godbey
Preston Gravely Jr.
Dyke Habegger
John Roberts

Acknowledgements and Photograph Credits are on page xxvii, which is an extension of this copyright page.

Produced in cooperation with the Bob Jones University Division of English Language and Literature of the College of Arts and Science and the School of Education.

CD-ROM installation instructions appear on page 472.

ISBN 978-1-60682-382-8 (Teacher's Edition with CD-ROM)

15 14 13 12 11 10 9 8 7 6 5 4 3 2

TO THE TEACHER

TO THE TEACHER

WRITING AND GRAMMAR 12, Third Edition, provides students with the tools for deepening their understanding of English grammar and for increasing their proficiency in the use of English. Further, the worktext seeks to present material in an engaging, manageable style. Plentiful examples and exercises cover topics of interest to twelfth-grade students. Special features and a wide variety of writing opportunities enrich the learning experience.

Teachers or students coming to this textbook series for the first time will find that the grammatical terms and concepts are largely familiar. The worktext seeks to emphasize the orderliness of language. This emphasis helps students understand that language, a gift from God, reflects the orderliness of His nature. In addition, the grammar is constructive, not just pulling sentences apart to see how they work but also helping students build clear sentences of their own.

Writing instruction and assignments take students through the writing process as it applies to expository writing, personal narrative, descriptive writing, creative writing, persuasive writing, and research writing.

FEATURES OF THE STUDENT WORKTEXT

The student worktext contains sixteen chapters in four units: **Grammar**, **Usage**, **Composition**, and **Reference**. These are followed by an appendix of spelling rules and by chapter reviews.

In most chapters, every section of new material closes with an **In Summary** review of the concepts, followed by **Practice the Skill**, **Review the Skill**, **Use the Skill**, and/or **Cumulative Review** exercises.

Chapters 1 and 14 (the **Composition** unit) and Chapters 15 and 16 (the **Reference** unit) include information that will benefit students throughout the school year. Teach information from these chapters whenever your students will benefit most.

Chapters 2–13 also include focused **Writing** instruction and assignments that guide students through the writing process. Each of these chapters begins with a professional or student model of the kind of writing taught in that chapter. Discussion questions draw students into the study and call their attention to certain features of the model.

Every chapter concludes with an enrichment section. **From the Written Word** sections present Scripture passages that demonstrate the rhetorical strategies used by the writers of Scripture. **Think About It** pages present critical thinking information and activities. **History of the English Language** sections provide information about our language and the changes it has undergone over time.

Throughout the worktext, **Combine the Skills icons** identify related information that is located elsewhere in the book. The teacher can use these icons to combine instruction of skills from one chapter with related skills from another chapter. A student can use the icons to find information to aid his understanding of the concept he is studying.

A **grammar** icon refers students to corresponding grammar concepts in Chapters 2–5.

A **usage** icon sends students to usage or mechanics concepts in Chapters 6–13.

A **writing** icon directs students to composition concepts in Chapters 1 and 14, in one of the writing activities found throughout the book, or occasionally in *THE WRITER'S TOOLBOX* (see "Additional Resources," p. v).

A **reference** icon points to reference concepts in Chapters 15 and 16 or to special information at the end of a chapter.

Four additional icons appear throughout the student text, providing students with helpful information or opportunities for further study.

ESL **ESL notes** provide in-depth information for the student whose native language is not English. (*ESL* is a widely used abbreviation for *English as a Second Language*.)

tip **Tips**, which appear throughout the worktext, present important advice for student writers.

Thinking Biblically notes challenge students to apply what they are learning to tasks that are significant from a Christian worldview.

The **diagram** icon indicates that students should be able to diagram the sentence elements that they have studied prior to that lesson. Practices not marked with the diagram icon may contain elements that students may not know how to diagram.

Features of the Teacher's Edition

The Teacher's Edition contains several features meant to aid in the preparation and presentation of each lesson. One such feature is the reduced student worktext pages with answers for student practices. To ease classroom instruction, the page numbers of the Teacher's Edition are identical to those of the reduced student pages.

Reference Materials

Representative samples of correlation with the **Common Core State Standards for English Language Arts** appear on pages vi–vii. A comprehensive correlation chart can be found on the Teacher's Toolkit CD and online at bjupress.com/go/ccss-ela. The chart illustrates how *WRITING AND GRAMMAR 12*, Third Edition, complies with English Language Arts standards outlined by the Common Core State Standards Initiative.

A **Scope and Sequence** chart, located on pages viii–xvii, gives an overview of concepts taught in grades 7–12.

The **Lesson Plan Overview** on pages x–xiii offers suggested daily lesson plans for a two-semester course, including the topic, the page numbers, available support materials, and Bible integration for each lesson. For quick reference, a shortened, chapter-specific Lesson Plan Overview appears on the first page of each chapter.

Chapter 8 Overview

Topic	Pages	Support Materials	Days
Pronoun Case	203–13	Bulletin Board 8 Chapter 8 Pretest Practice/ Review/Use the Skill 8.1–8.6 Concept Reinforcements 8A–8C Teaching Help 8	102–4
Video Report	198–202	Writing Rubric 8 Writing Worksheets 8A–8B	105, 110–11
Courtesy Order Reflexive and Intensive Pronouns	213–15	Practice/Review the Skill 8.7–8.8	106
Pronoun Shift Review	215–19 445–47	Practice/Review the Skill 8.9–8.10 Cumulative Review 8.11 Chapter 8 Review	107
Chapter 8 Test			108
From the Written Word	219		109

Lesson Plans

Lesson Plans for each chapter offer inductive teaching strategies, efficient but thorough methods of evaluation, and helpful sources for further information. These plans are subdivided under descriptive headings to make planning easier for the teacher. The subdivisions are as follows:

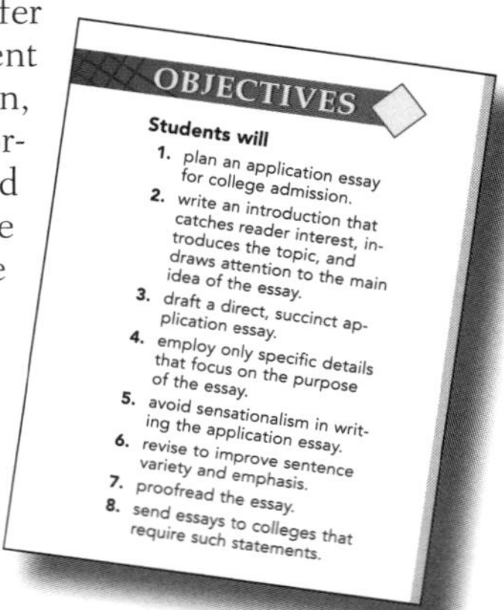

Objectives

A list of **Objectives** appears at the beginning of each lesson. These state the outcome of instruction in terms of student behavior.

Lesson Support

Lesson Support sections list any applicable pages from the student worktext (chapter reviews, for instance) as well as from the Teacher's Edition, Teacher's Toolkit CD, and Tests.

The Teacher's Toolkit CD (inside the back cover of the Teacher's Edition) contains the following reproducibles:

- *Pretests* are diagnostic tools for Chapters 2–13. Evaluating your students' skill levels prior to teaching will allow you to tailor your lessons to the needs of your students.
- *Teaching Helps* accompany specific grammar, usage, and reference lessons. Some are designed to be used for display; others are designed to be used as student worksheets.
- *ESL Helps* accompany specific grammar and usage lessons. These materials give ESL students extra help and practice with difficult concepts.
- *Concept Reinforcements* accompany specific grammar and usage lessons. These worksheets provide students with extra review of certain skills taught in the student worktext. Each set of fifteen questions is divided into three sections, with each group of five questions increasing in difficulty.
- *Writing Worksheets* accompany specific writing assignments in the student worktext. These worksheets guide students through the steps of the writing process.
- *Writing Rubrics* accompany each specific writing assignment in the student worktext. The rubrics inform the students of your expectations and give you a method for evaluating each student's work fairly yet quickly.

Also included on the Teacher's Toolkit are Bulletin Board sketches, Diagram Answers, and a helpful guide entitled *Explaining the Gospel*.

- *Bulletin Board* sketches offer visual ideas for informative displays, interactive reinforcement of concepts, and exhibits of student work.
- *Sentence Diagram Answers* correspond to those sentences in the student worktext marked with the diagram icon. If you choose to teach diagramming, you may wish to refer to "Sentence Diagrams" in The Writer's Toolbox for sample diagrams of sentence elements.

Chapter Tests (a means to evaluate students' understanding of the content and concepts taught in the chapter) are noted in the Lesson Plan Overview and in the Lesson Support section at the beginning of each grammar lesson. A Midterm Examination and a Final Examination are scheduled as well. The teacher should feel free to add, delete, or change any test item in order to create an instrument more suited to individual classroom needs. The Tests and Test Keys may be purchased separately.

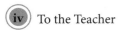

Teaching Strategies

Teaching Strategy sections suggest approaches to and procedures for instruction. These category titles indicate the general emphasis of the information included.

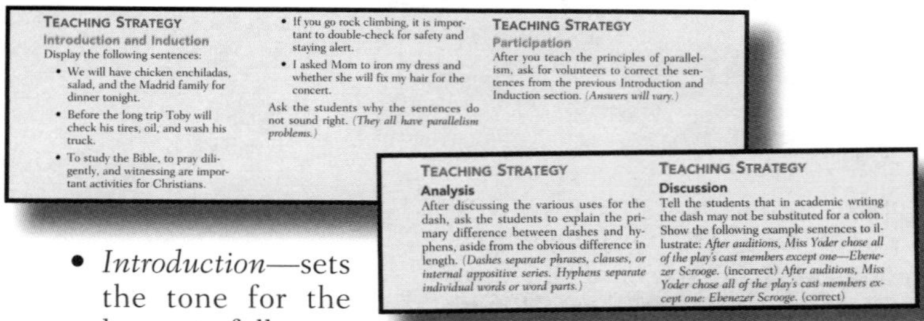

TEACHING STRATEGY
Introduction and Induction
Display the following sentences:

- We will have chicken enchiladas, salad, and the Madrid family for dinner tonight.
- Before the long trip Toby will check his tires, oil, and wash his truck.
- To study the Bible, to pray diligently, and witnessing are important activities for Christians.
- If you go rock climbing, it is important to double-check for safety and staying alert.
- I asked Mom to iron my dress and whether she will fix my hair for the concert.

Ask the students why the sentences do not sound right. *(They all have parallelism problems.)*

TEACHING STRATEGY
Participation
After you teach the principles of parallelism, ask for volunteers to correct the sentences from the previous Introduction and Induction section. *(Answers will vary.)*

TEACHING STRATEGY
Analysis
After discussing the various uses for the dash, ask the students to explain the primary difference between dashes and hyphens, aside from the obvious difference in length. *(Dashes separate phrases, clauses, or internal appositive series. Hyphens separate individual words or word parts.)*

TEACHING STRATEGY
Discussion
Tell the students that in academic writing the dash may not be substituted for a colon. Show the following example sentences to illustrate: *After auditions, Miss Yoder chose all of the play's cast members except one—Ebenezer Scrooge.* (incorrect) *After auditions, Miss Yoder chose all of the play's cast members except one: Ebenezer Scrooge.* (correct)

- *Introduction*—sets the tone for the lesson to follow
- *Motivation*—stimulates the students' interest in the lesson
- *Induction*—challenges students to formulate general principles and practices based on specific examples
- *Discussion*—prompts classwide analysis and discussion of a topic
- *Demonstration*—illustrates the concepts taught in the lesson
- *Participation*—involves the student directly in the lesson
- *Modeling*—offers examples for students to follow
- *Analysis*—examines the specifics of lesson content

Some additional instructional strategies featured in separate sections throughout the lesson plans include the following:

ESL Strategy—offers suggestions for individualized instruction of the student whose native language is not English

Cross-curricular Links—suggest ways to connect the grammar and usage instruction to other disciplines, such as literature, writing, speech, and history

- *Writing Workshop*—alerts the teacher to opportunities for teaching minilessons from the Writing Strategies chapter in conjunction with specific writing assignments

Scriptural Application—points to biblical principles drawn from the lesson content

- *Reinforcement*—offers methods for reinforcing the concepts in the lesson, including homework suggestions
- *Evaluation*—presents ways to assess students' grasp of the material presented
- *Enrichment*—supplements the basic lesson plans with additional enjoyable activities to reinforce lesson concepts

One on One—offers alternative activities for those teachers who have only one student

- *Resources*—recommend supplemental materials to enhance the lesson or the teacher's understanding of the content

Thinking Biblically—provides teaching strategies and answers to questions from the accompanying notes in the student worktext

Creating Writing Assignments

Getting a good writing assignment from a student starts long before the student begins writing. It starts with the teacher's making a thorough plan for the year and then carrying it out, adapting and revising as needs and opportunities arise.

A good textbook, of course, is a solid place to start; but every student, every class, is unique, and only the teacher can really determine what is best. Beyond a general plan, a teacher also needs to make good, specific assignments.

An assignment that gets a good response needs to be focused, inviting, and clear. "Write about your summer vacation" is not going to prompt the kind of polished writing that pleases. It is too general, too broad, and too overwhelming, even for the eager writer. "Write a paragraph describing the most interesting place where you ate on your vacation" is better. It narrows the assignment; it engages the interest of the student; it looks possible, even to the least-eager writer.

In clarifying the topic, it is possible, however, to put too many parameters on the assignment. "Write a five-sentence paragraph using five adjectives to describe the way the restaurant looked" is too limiting. Nor is it advisable to use writing to teach a particular grammar principle. For example, "Write two paragraphs on your favorite sport, using four complex sentences" not only does not teach the grammar well but also engenders poor style.

Writing assignments should prompt good writing—writing that communicates messages that are important to the writer. An assignment given with definition and clarity helps engender writing that has purpose and energy. Then the evaluation of the work is far more enjoyable and useful to both the student and the teacher.

Evaluating Writing Assignments

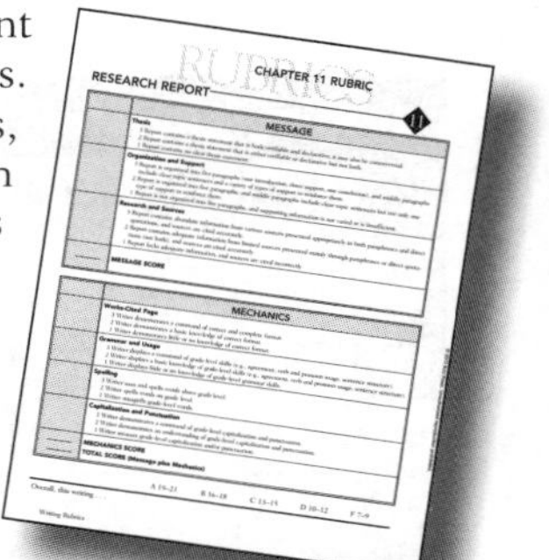

The only thing harder than getting a student to write is grading the writing he produces. The task seems overwhelming. Sometimes, perhaps, it seems easier just to cut back on the amount of writing altogether—less hassle all around.

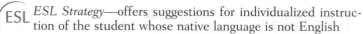

The Writing Rubrics (Teacher's Toolkit) are designed to make the major writing assignments of each chapter manageable for both student and teacher. Rubrics help students understand the teacher's expectations for the assignment, and they assist the teacher in grading the completed compositions impartially and quickly.

Technology Solutions

In our world, technology is inescapable. While the core of sound educational practice remains changeless, every year brings new research and technologies that can improve learning outcomes.

Visit mybjupress.com to discover the latest technological tools to enhance your teaching. Electronic versions of student and teacher resources, editable presentations, test-generating software, and more are available for an additional fee.

Web links provide useful research or supplementary learning opportunities. These links are curated and organized by textbook title at bjupress.com/resources.

Additional Resources

The Writer's Toolbox: A Writing and Grammar Handbook is a valuable supplement for writing and grammar instruction (BJU Press).

For a fuller explanation of the aims of Christian education, consult *Christian Education: Its Mandate and Mission* (BJU Press).

COMMON CORE STATE STANDARDS

The following chart features sample sections of the grade-specific **Common Core State Standards (CCSS) for English Language Arts (Grades 11-12)** outlined by the Common Core State Standards Initiative © 2011 and shows where these are fulfilled in the Student Text (ST) and Teacher's Edition (TE) of *WRITING AND GRAMMAR 12*, Third Edition. As acknowledged by the CCSS, the grade-specific standards correspond to broader College and Career Readiness (CCR) anchor standards, which are amply covered in this text. Both are necessary to ensure that students achieve college readiness. Many of the grade-specific standards included in the table are fulfilled abundantly throughout the text. In those cases, the table may indicate only representative examples. Standards not fulfilled, or fulfilled minimally, in this text are addressed by BJU Press's *BRITISH LITERATURE*; *VOCABULARY LEVEL F*, Third Edition; and *THE WRITER'S TOOLBOX* as indicated in the chart. The complete chart appears on the **Teacher's Toolkit CD** and also online at bjupress.com/go/ccss-ela.

SAMPLE

Reading: Literature (RL)		
Key Ideas and Details		
RL.12.1	Cite strong and thorough textual evidence to support analysis of what the text says explicitly as well as inferences drawn from the text, including determining where the text leaves matters uncertain.	ST: 143, 147, 240, 323–24 TE: 83–85, 143, 145, 238–40 Standard fulfilled primarily by literary texts included in *British Literature*.
RL.12.2	Determine two or more themes or central ideas of a text and analyze their development over the course of the text, including how they interact and build on one another to produce a complex account; provide an objective summary of the text.	ST: 143, 239, 323–24 TE: 143–45, 238–41 Standard fulfilled primarily by literary texts included in *British Literature*.

SAMPLE

Reading: Informational Text (RI)		
Key Ideas and Details		
RI.12.5	Analyze and evaluate the effectiveness of the structure an author uses in his or her exposition or argument, including whether the structure makes points clear, convincing, and engaging.	ST: 113–14, 267, 294 TE: 109, 112–13, 266–67, 291, 294–95 Standard fulfilled primarily by informational texts included in *British Literature*.
RI.12.6	Determine an author's point of view or purpose in a text in which the rhetoric is particularly effective, analyzing how style and content contribute to the power, persuasiveness, or beauty of the text.	ST: 29–30, 33, 61, 64–67, 107, 111–14, 259, 291, 294 TE: 28–30, 65–66, 109, 112–13, 291–92, 293–95 Standard fulfilled primarily by informational texts included in *British Literature*.

COMMON CORE STATE STANDARDS

Writing (W)		
Production and Distribution of Writing		
W.12.4	Produce clear and coherent writing in which the development, organization, and style are appropriate to task, purpose, and audience. (Grade-specific expectations for writing types are defined in standards 1–3 above.)	Standard fulfilled primarily by writing assignments throughout the ST and TE and by Chapter 1: The Writing Process and Chapter 14: Writing Strategies. ST: 1–25, 29–34, 61–68, 81, 83–87, 107, 143–48, 173–77, 199–203, 219, 222–25, 239–42, 257, 262–69, 291–95, 321, 323–28, 353, 355–92 TE: 3, 5–8, 10–11, 15, 18–19, 21–23, 30–34, 49–50, 57, 59, 63–68, 74, 78, 83–87, 91–92, 106, 109–15, 143–48, 156, 160–61, 169, 171, 173–77, 187, 197, 199–204, 215, 219–25, 228, 240–43, 259, 262–69, 272, 283, 289, 291–97, 303, 305, 310, 314, 321, 324–29, 354–55, 358, 360–64, 366–67, 370–73, 378–80, 384–88, 390, 418

Speaking and Listening (SL)		
Comprehension and Collaboration		
SL.12.1c	Initiate and participate effectively in a range of collaborative discussions (one-on-one, in groups, and teacher-led) with diverse partners on grades 11–12 topics, texts, and issues, building on others' ideas and expressing their own clearly and persuasively.	ST: 34, 87, 145, 203, 224–25, 240, 242, 289, 293, 295, 328 TE: xxxii–8, 10, 18–20, 22–23, 25–26, 30–33, 36–37, 41, 44–45, 48–49, 53, 55–56, 59, 61, 63–67, 69–73, 77, 82–84, 88–89, 90–91, 93, 95–97, 100–102, 106–7, 109–12, 116–19, 123, 125, 128, 132, 135, 141, 143–45, 147–48, 154–55, 165–66, 173–76, 187, 192, 197–204, 206–7, 209, 211, 221, 223, 226–27, 229, 232, 237, 239, 241–42, 246, 250–52, 267, 277–78, 282, 289, 291–93, 297, 304, 306–7, 316, 321, 323–32, 335, 338, 348, 354–55, 360, 364, 366, 370–71, 379–80, 390, 396, 405, 408–9, 414, 421, 424

Language (L)		
Conventions of Standard English		
L.12.3	Apply knowledge of language to understand how language functions in different contexts, to make effective choices for meaning or style, and to comprehend more fully when reading or listening.	ST: 4, 6, 8–23, 30–33, 66–67, 84–86, 110, 114–15, 144, 148, 175, 177, 201, 223–24, 239–41, 293, 295, 355–92 TE: 21–22, 30, 34, 37, 55–56, 59, 66–67, 83–84, 86, 104, 109–10, 112–14, 122–23, 126–27, 136, 143, 145, 147, 150, 175–76, 187–88, 197, 224–25, 241–43, 251–52, 266, 269–270, 285, 291–92, 295–96, 307, 315, 327, 332, 334–35, 354–55, 358, 361–64, 366–67, 370–73, 375, 379–80, 386–88, 390

Writing and Grammar Scope and Sequence

	Grade 7 (Third Edition)	Grade 8 (Third Edition)	Grade 9 (Third Edition)	Grade 10 (Third Edition)	Grade 11 (Third Edition)	Grade 12 (Third Edition)
Parts of Speech (and Verbals)	noun; pronoun; verb—*simple and perfect tenses*; adjective; adverb; preposition; conjunction; interjection	review of all from Grade 7 plus the following new material: pronoun—*relative*; verb—*progressive tense, passive voice*; conjunction—*correlative*; verbals—*participle, infinitive, gerund, verbal phrases with modifiers, functions as different parts of speech*	review of all from Grade 8 plus the following new material: noun—*collective*; verb—*indicative and imperative moods*; adjective—*determiner*; adverb—*qualifier, relative*; preposition—*phrasal*; conjunction—*subordinating*; verbals—*verbal phrases with objects*	review of all from Grade 9 plus the following new material: verbs—*subjunctive mood*; pronoun—*indefinite, relative, reciprocal*; adverb—*conjunctive*; verbals—*perfect gerund, passive infinitive*	review of all from Grade 10 plus the following new material: verb—*verb-adverb combinations*; adverb—*indefinite relative, interrogative*; conjunction—*phrasal subordinating*; verbals—*perfect participle, passive gerund, perfect infinitive, progressive infinitive, elliptical infinitive*	review of all from Grade 11 plus the following new material: verbals—*passive participle*
Sentence Structure	sentence patterns—*S-InV, S-TrV-DO, S-TrV-IO-DO, S-LV-PN, S-LV-PA*; introduction to dependent clauses; sentence types—*declarative, interrogative, imperative, exclamatory*; clause structure—*simple, compound, complex*; sentence errors—*fragments, comma splices, fused sentences*	review of all from Grade 7 plus the following new material: dependent clause—*adjective clause*	review of all from Grade 8 plus the following new material: dependent clause—*adverb clause*; clause structure—*compound-complex*	review of all from Grade 9 plus the following new material: sentence patterns—*S-be-Advl, S-TrV-DO-OC*; dependent clause—*noun clause*	review of all from Grade 10 plus the following new material: sentence patterns—*retained object in passive sentence*	review of all from Grade 11 plus the following new material: absolute phrase
Mechanics	capitalization; punctuation; spelling	capitalization; punctuation; spelling	capitalization; punctuation; spelling	capitalization; punctuation; appendix of spelling rules	capitalization; punctuation; appendix of spelling rules	capitalization; punctuation; appendix of spelling rules
Usage	subject/verb agreement; pronoun/antecedent agreement; pronoun reference; troublesome words (homophones, homonyms, etc.)	review of all from Grade 7	review of all from Grade 8 plus the following new material: modifier placement—*misplaced modifier, two-way modifier, dangling modifier*	review of all from Grade 9 plus the following new material: modifier placement—*split infinitive*	review of all from Grade 10 plus the following new material: pronoun shift; verb tense consistency and sequence	review of all from Grade 11 plus the following new material: idiomatic use of prepositions
Writing Skills	writing process—*planning, drafting, revising and proofreading, publishing*; paragraph development—*fact, example, statistic, incident/anecdote, sensory detail, reason*; paragraph organization—*chronological, spatial, order of importance*; style—*precise words, showing not telling*	review of all from Grade 7 plus the following new material: essay—*thesis statement, outlining*; introductory and concluding paragraphs	review of all from Grade 8 plus the following new material: paragraph development—*comparison/contrast*; style—*conciseness, smoothness, fresh words*; sentence variety—*length and complexity, sentence patterns, sentence beginnings*; sentence expansion and reduction—*dependent clauses, phrases, single words*; sentence logic—*misplaced and dangling modifiers; parallelism; avoiding biased language*	review of all from Grade 9 plus the following new material: essay—*choosing a mode*; sentence variety and emphasis—*choosing between constructions, coordination and subordination*; sentence energy—*action verbs, details, accuracy, figurative language*; sentence logic—*logical comparison, clear comparison, subject placement*	review of all from Grade 10 plus the following new material: paragraph organization—*cause-and-effect order, comparison-and-contrast order*; sentence energy—*pauses for breath*; parallelism—*clarity*; sentence logic—*direct expression, logical predication, avoiding mixed constructions, using noun clauses when needed, ending in strength, linking with new information*	review of all from Grade 11 plus the following new material: paragraph development—*quotation, visual aid*

	Grade 7 (Third Edition)	Grade 8 (Third Edition)	Grade 9 (Third Edition)	Grade 10 (Third Edition)	Grade 11 (Third Edition)	Grade 12 (Third Edition)
Examples of Writing Projects	description—*biographical sketch* exposition—*in-class essay, science report evaluation* narration—*family tradition report, drama scene* persuasion—*letter to editor* poetry—*sound poem*	description—*travel brochure, character profile* exposition–*news story, business letter* narration—*autobiography, fable* persuasion—*debate script, print advertisement*	description—*comparison/contrast paper* exposition—*five-paragraph research essay, storyboard (public service announcement)* narration—*personal experience* persuasion—*devotional* poetry—*quatrain, diamante*	description—*eyewitness report* exposition—*research essay, cause-and-effect essay* narration—*short story, oral anecdote* persuasion—*persuasive speech, editorial* poetry—*poetry and metaphor* multimedia—*web-page design*	description—*interview* exposition—*formal research paper, analytical essay, critical response to literature* narration—*narrative poem, folktale* persuasion—*letter to editor* poetry—*hymn*	description—*descriptive essay, comparison/contrast essay* exposition—*research report, response to a dramatic scene (literary analysis)* narration—*dramatic scene, interior monologue* persuasion—*persuasive essay* poetry—*sonnet* multimedia—*video report*
Study & Reference Skills	dictionary—*guide words, entry word, syllabification, pronunciation, definition, function label, etymology*; library—*types of materials, call number, alphabetizing, Dewey decimal system, Library of Congress system, card catalog, computer catalog*; *reference tools; parts of a book; scheduling study time*; *memory techniques*; reading comprehension—*definitions, restatements, examples, word parts*; test-taking strategies—*classroom tests, standardized tests*	review of all from Grade 7 plus the following new material: dictionary—*usage label*	review of all from Grade 8 plus the following new material: dictionary—*inflected forms, variant spellings, field label, stylistic label*; library—*Cutter number*; reference tools—*New York Times Index, subject index, yearbook, Bible commentary*; reading comprehension—*comparison and context*; test-taking strategies—*analogy*	review of all from Grade 9 plus the following new material: library—*website, bibliography, online databases*; reading comprehension—*grammatical context*; test-taking strategies—*essay questions*	review of all from Grade 10 plus the following new material: reference tools—*literary index, literary sources*	review of all from Grade 11

Day(s)	Topic[1]	Pages	Support Materials[2]	Bible Integration
Chapter 1: The Writing Process[3, 4]				
1	Planning	1–4	Bulletin Board 1	Thinking Biblically: Writing well to communicate truth Scriptural Application: A Christian approach to composition (Matt. 22:34–40)
2	Planning	4–8	Practice the Skill 1.1 Practice the Skill 1.2	Scriptural Application: Taking care with the Internet Thinking Biblically: Using biblical discernment to evaluate sources Scriptural Application: Creating an outline for "The Story of Scripture"
3	*Descriptive Essay*	29–32	*Writing Worksheet 2* *Writing Rubric 2*	*Scriptural Application: Lazarus and the rich man (Luke 16:24)* *Description in Esther 1:5–6* *Thinking Biblically: Writing and grammar as a tool for godly purposes*
4	Drafting	8–11		Creationism and the Flood Thinking Biblically: Thesis statements in the Bible and their placements
5	Drafting	11–14	Use the Skill 1.3 Practice the Skill 1.4 Review the Skill 1.5 Use the Skill 1.6	
6	Drafting	15–20	Practice the Skill 1.7 Review the Skill 1.8 Use the Skill 1.9 Teaching Help 1	Gideon and the Midianites (Judges 7)
7	*Descriptive Essay*	33	*Writing Worksheet 2*	
8	Revising	20–24	Use the Skill 1.10 Review the Skill 1.11	Scriptural Application: Words as a reflection of one's heart (Ps. 19:14)
9	Publishing	24–25	Use the Skill 1.12	The Passion of Christ
10	*Descriptive Essay*	34	*Writing Worksheet 2*	
11	History of the English Language *Descriptive Essay*	26–27 *34*	*Writing Worksheet 2* *Writing Rubric 2*	History of the English Language: Translating John 1:1 Thinking Biblically: Language change since the KJV translation Bible translation teams
Chapter 2: Descriptive Essay/Parts of Speech				
12	Nouns	35–37	Bulletin Board 2 Chapter 2 Pretest	
13	*Comparison-and-Contrast Essay*	61–64	*Writing Rubric 3*	*Thinking Biblically: Using the Scriptures as the ultimate standard for evaluation* *Comparison and Contrast in Scripture (Ps. 1:1; Prov. 14:5; Mark 40:30–31; Gal. 5:19–23)* *Scriptural Application: Applying Proverbs 15:1*

[1] The topics in italics refer to writing lessons and assignments within a chapter. Writing lessons for some chapters are used in other chapters as well, to allow enough time for students to complete the assignment.
[2] The following items in the Support Materials column are located in the Teacher's Toolkit: Pretests, Teaching Helps, ESL Worksheets, Concept Reinforcements, Bulletin Boards, Writing Worksheets, and Writing Rubrics.
[3] Chapters 15–16 are reference chapters. Teach material from these chapters throughout the semester whenever it is appropriate for your students.
[4] If necessary, adjust the schedule to teach Chapter 11 (Capitalization) and Chapters 12–13 (Punctuation) before your students take any standardized achievement test.

Day(s)	Topic[1]	Pages	Support Materials[2]	Bible Integration
14	*Comparison-and-Contrast Essay*	64–66	*Writing Worksheet 3*	
15	Pronouns	37–42	Practice the Skill 2.1 Use the Skill 2.2	Scriptural Application: God's power shown through the weather (Job 37)
16	Verbs	42–44		Teen outreach opportunities
17–18	*Comparison-and-Contrast Essay*	66–67	*Writing Worksheet 3*	
19	Verbs	44–47	Practice the Skill 2.3 Use the Skill 2.4	God's use of the weather
20–21	*Comparison-and-Contrast Essay*	67–68	*Writing Worksheet 3* *Writing Rubric 3*	
22	Adjectives and Adverbs	48–53	Practice the Skill 2.5 Review the Skill 2.6 ESL Helps 2A, 2B, 2C, 2D, 2E, 2F, 2G, 2H, 2I Teaching Help 2A	
23	Prepositions, Conjunctions, and Interjections	53–58	Practice the Skill 2.7 Use the Skill 2.8 Review the Skill 2.9 Teaching Help 2B ESL helps 2J, 2K	Christ stills the storm (Matt. 8:23–27; Mark 4:35–41; Luke 8:22–25)
24	From the Written Word Review	59, 431–32	Concept Reinforcement 2 Chapter 2 Review	Rhetorical strategies in the Bible (Ps. 119:44–45; Isa. 40:29–30) Responding to Psalm 78
25	Chapter 2 Test			
Chapter 3: Comparison-and-Contrast Essay/Sentences				
26	*Interior Monologue*	83–84	*Writing Rubric 4*	*Scriptural Application: One's speech reveals his heart (Matt. 12:34; Prov. 4:23)* *What should a Christian's inner thought life be like? Matthew 12:34, Psalm 42:11* *Thinking Biblically: Meditating on the Scriptures to change one's heart and thoughts (Ps. 119:97; 42:5–11)* *Scriptural guidelines for writing (Phil. 4:8; James 3:14–17)*
27	*Interior Monologue*	85–86	*Writing Worksheets 4A, 4B*	
28	Defining Sentences and Kinds of Sentences	69–70	Bulletin Board 3 Chapter 3 Pretest	
29	Finding Subjects and Predicates	70–74	Practice the Skill 3.1 Practice the Skill 3.2 Review the Skill 3.3 ESL Helps 3A, 3B, 3C Concept Reinforcement 3A	Scriptural Application: Modeling Christ (rather than culture) in personal relationships (Gal. 6:10; Eph. 4:3, 32; 1 Tim. 5:1-2; James 1:27)
30–31	*Interior Monologue*	86	*Writing Worksheets 4A, 4B*	
32	Basic Sentence Patterns	74–76		
33	Basic Sentence Patterns	76–78	Practice the Skill 3.4 Teaching Help 3	
34	*Interior Monologue*	86–87	*Writing Worksheets 4A, 4B* *Writing Rubric 4*	

Day(s)	Topic[1]	Pages	Support Materials[2]	Bible Integration
35	Practice and Review	78–80, 433–34	Use the Skill 3.5 Concept Reinforcement 3B Cumulative Review 3.6 Chapter 3 Review	Jesus and the woman at the well
36	Chapter 3 Test			
37	Critical Thinking	80–81		Scriptural Application: The importance of the mind (Mark 12:30; Acts 18:4) Critical thinking—A necessity for believers (Phil. 4:8; Rom. 12:2; 1 Pet. 3:15) Biblical wisdom (1 Cor. 3:19; Ps. 111:10) Responding to Scripture (Mark 12:30; Acts 18:4) Thinking Biblically: Scriptures teach critical thinking
38	*Interior Monologue*	87	*Writing Worksheets 4A, 4B* *Writing Rubric 4*	
Chapter 4: Interior Monologue/Phrases				
39	Nonverbal Phrases	88–92	Bulletin Board 4 Chapter 4 Pretest Teaching Help 4A Practice the Skill 4.1 Practice the Skill 4.2 Use the Skill 4.3	
40	Participial Phrases	92–96	Teaching Help 4B Practice the Skill 4.4 Use the Skill 4.5	
41	Gerund Phrases	96–101	Practice the Skill 4.6 Use the Skill 4.7	Ministry: Homes on the mission field
42	*Persuasive Essay*	109–11		*Thinking Biblically: Importance of correct spelling for the Christian* *Scriptural Application: Persuasion in the Bible (Acts 26:26–28)*
43	Infinitive Phrases	101–3	Practice the Skill 4.8	Scriptural Application: Infinitives in Scripture (Phil. 2:13)
44	*Persuasive Essay*	111–12		
45–46	*Persuasive Essay*	112–14		*Avoiding the offense of stereotypes (Prov. 18:19)*
47	Practice and Review	103–6, 435–36	Use the Skill 4.9 Concept Reinforcement 4B Cumulative Review 4.10 Teaching Help 4C Concept Reinforcement 4A Chapter 4 Review	Moses' home as an Egyptian noble Scriptural Application: Living in one's culture as a pilgrim (Heb. 11:8–10, 24–26)
48	Chapter 4 Test			
49	From the Written Word	107		Descriptions in narratives (Gen. 3; Exod. 25; Josh. 10) Personal Response: Psalm 121 Identifying themes through details in scriptural narratives
50	*Persuasive Essay*	114–15	*Writing Worksheet 5*	Challenge to write a tract
Chapter 5: Persuasive Essay/Clauses				
51	Adjective Clauses	116–18	Bulletin Board 5 Chapter 5 Pretest	
52	*Persuasive Essay*	115	*Writing Worksheet 5* *Writing Rubric 5*	

Day(s)	Topic[1]	Pages	Support Materials[2]	Bible Integration
53	Adjective Clauses	118–21	Practice the Skill 5.1 Use the Skill 5.2	
54	Adverb Clauses	122–23	Teaching Help 5A	
55	Adverb Clauses	124–26	Practice the Skill 5.3 Use the Skill 5.4	Maintaining integrity in public relations (James 5:12; Col. 3:9; Eph. 5:6)
56	Noun Clauses	126–28	Teaching Help 5B	
57	Noun Clauses	129–31	Practice the Skill 5.5 Use the Skill 5.6 Review the Skill 5.7	
58	Using Independent and Dependent Clauses	132–35	ESL Helps 5A, 5B Practice the Skill 5.8 Review the Skill 5.9 Concept Reinforcement 5A	
59	Major Sentence Errors	135–39	Practice the Skill 5.10 Review the Skill 5.11 Concept Reinforcement 5B ESL Help 5C	Ministry: Evangelistic campaigns in the early 1900s Scriptural Application: Evangelism today (John 4:35–36)
60	Review Critical Thinking	140–41, 437–38	Cumulative Review 5.12 Chapter 5 Review	Evaluating an author (1 Sam. 16:7) Scriptural Application: Reflecting Christ (1 Sam. 16:7; Rom. 14:13)
61	Chapter 5 Test			
Chapter 6: Dramatic Scene/Agreement				
62	Subjects and Predicates	148–49	Bulletin Board 6 Chapter 6 Pretest	Scriptural Application: The Bible and language (Eccles. 12:10; Prov. 8:6–9; 15:2; 16:23–24; 23:12)
63	*Dramatic Scene*	143–44	*Writing Rubric 6*	*Words reveal character (Matt. 12:34; Luke 6:45)* *Witnessing to others* *Thinking Biblically: Using biblical themes effectively when writing a drama (James 4:14)* *Scriptural Application: Right speech (Ps. 141: 3)*
64	Subject Identification	150–53	Practice the Skill 6.1 Review the Skill 6.2	
65–66	*Dramatic Scene*	145–46	*Writing Worksheets 6A, 6B*	*Modeling conflict: Finding God's will*
67	Problem Nouns	153–55		
68	Practice	156–57	Practice the Skill 6.3 Review the Skill 6.4	
69	Problem Pronouns	157–59	Concept Reinforcement 6A ESL Helps 6A, 6B	
70–71	*Dramatic Scene*	146–47	*Writing Worksheets 6A, 6B*	
72	Problem Pronouns	159–61	Practice the Skill 6.5 Review the Skill 6.6	
73	Compound Subjects	161–63	Practice the Skill 6.7 Review the Skill 6.8	
74	Nouns as Antecedents	163–66	Practice the Skill 6.9 Review the Skill 6.10	

Day(s)	Topic[1]	Pages	Support Materials[2]	Bible Integration
75	Collective Nouns and Indefinite Pronouns as Antecedents	166–68	Teaching Help 6A Teaching Help 6B Practice the Skill 6.11 Concept Reinforcement 6B	
76	*Dramatic Scene*	147–48	*Writing Worksheets 6A, 6B*	
77	Review	168–70, 439–41	Review the Skill 6.12 Cumulative Review 6.13 Chapter 6 Review	
78	Chapter 6 Test			
79	From the Written Word	171		Elijah and Ahab: Presenting an argument (1 Kings 18) Personal Response: Applying Romans 12:2 Scriptural Application: Obedience to God as the primary argument (Matt. 14:3–4)
80	*Dramatic Scene*	148	*Writing Worksheets 6A, 6B* *Writing Rubric 6*	
Chapter 7: Extemporaneous Essay/Verb Use				
81	*Extemporaneous Essay*	173–75	*Writing Worksheet 7* *Writing Rubric 7*	*Scriptural Application: Friendship (Prov. 17:17)*
82–83	*Extemporaneous Essay*	175–76	*Writing Worksheet 7*	*Thinking Biblically: The importance of skillful extemporaneous writing (Prov. 25:11; 1 Cor. 2:1–5)*
84	Principal Parts and Tenses	177–79	Bulletin Board 7 Chapter 7 Pretest	Verb use: John 2:15
85	Tenses	179–83	ESL Helps 7A, 7B, 7C, 7D Practice the Skill 7.1 Review the Skill 7.2 Concept Reinforcement 7A Use the Skill 7.3	
86	Consistency and Sequence of Tenses *Extemporaneous Essay*	184–87 *176–77*	Teaching Help 7A ESL Helps 7E, 7F Practice the Skill 7.4 Use the Skill 7.5 *Writing Worksheet 7*	
87	Voice	187–88		
88	Voice *Extemporaneous Essay*	188–91 *177*	Teaching Help 7B Practice the Skill 7.6 Use the Skill 7.7 *Writing Worksheet 7* *Writing Rubric 7*	Paul and the New Testament epistles Scriptural Application: Discussing Philippians Missions: Missionary letters
89	Mood Review	192–96, 443–44	Practice the Skill 7.8 Concept Reinforcement 7B Use the Skill 7.9 Cumulative Review 7.10 Chapter 7 Review	Christian writer: Christina Rossetti
90	Chapter 7 Test			
91	Critical Thinking	196–97		Value judgments and Scripture
92–101	Midterm Review and Midterm Examination			

Day(s)	Topic[1]	Pages	Support Materials[2]	Bible Integration
Chapter 8: Video Report/Pronoun Use				
102	Pronoun Case	203–6	Bulletin Board 8 Chapter 8 Pretest Practice the Skill 8.1 Review the Skill 8.2 Concept Reinforcement 8A	Scriptural Application: Grammar and meaning in Jeremiah 7:23
103	Pronoun Case	206–9	Practice the Skill 8.3 Use the Skill 8.4	
104	Pronoun Case	209–13	Practice the Skill 8.5 Review the Skill 8.6 Teaching Help 8 Concept Reinforcements 8B, 8C	Faithful Christian leadership in action Spiritual growth through camp ministries
105	*Video Report*	198–201	*Writing Rubric 8* *Writing Worksheet 8A*	*Scriptural Application: Visual media and the Word (Job 42:5)*
106	Courtesy Order Reflexive and Intensive Pronouns	213–15	Practice the Skill 8.7 Review the Skill 8.8	Scriptural Application: God's provision and protection (1 Kings 19:4; Phil. 4:19; Rom. 8:28)
107	Pronoun Shift Review	215–19, 445–47	Practice the Skill 8.9 Review the Skill 8.10 Cumulative Review 8.11 Chapter 8 Review	Talebearers (Prov. 11:13; 18:8) Hymns : Scriptural truth and "When I See the Blood" God's presence (Ex. 11–12;14)
108	Chapter 8 Test			
109	From the Written Word	219		Comparison and contrast: Cain and Abel (Gen. 4:2–5, 8) Personal Response: Comparison and contrast (1 Sam. 1:1–20; Judg. 13:2–24)
110–11	*Video Report*	201–2	*Writing Worksheets 8A, 8B*	
Chapter 9: College Application Essay/Pronoun Reference				
112	Clear Reference	225–28	Bulletin Board 9 Chapter 9 Pretest Teaching Help 9A Practice the Skill 9.1 Review the Skill 9.2	
113	Referencing Modifiers or Implied Nouns	229–31	Practice the Skill 9.3 Review the Skill 9.4	
114	Indefinite *It*, *They*, and *You*	232–33	Teaching Help 9B	
115–16	*Video Report*	202–3	*Writing Worksheets 8A, 8B*	
117	Broad Reference	233–35	Practice the Skill 9.5 Review the Skill 9.6 Concept Reinforcement 9	Scriptural Application: Evaluating a college's philosophy (2 Peter 2:1–2)
118	Review	236	Cumulative Review 9.7	
119	Critical Thinking Review	237, 449–51	Chapter 9 Review	Think About It: Evaluating arguments for truth Thinking Biblically: Evaluating facts through a biblical worldview
120	Chapter 9 Test			
121	*Video Report*	203	*Writing Worksheets 8A, 8B* *Writing Rubric 8*	

Day(s)	Topic[1]	Pages	Support Materials[2]	Bible Integration
122	*College Application Essay*	221–22	*Writing Rubric 9*	*Model: Serving God through ministry to others* *Scriptural Application: Obeying God (Ezra 7:10)*
123	*College Application Essay*	222–223	*Writing Worksheet 9*	*Scriptural Application: Seeking wisdom about college (Prov. 11:14; 15:22; Eph. 6:1–3; Heb. 13:17)*
Chapter 10: Sonnet/Adjective and Adverb Use				
124	Showing Comparison with Modifiers	243–44	Bulletin Board 10 Chapter 10 Pretest	
125	Showing Comparison with Modifiers	244–46	Practice the Skill 10.1 Review the Skill 10.2 Teaching Help 10A ESL Help 10	David and Mephibosheth (2 Sam. 9)
126	*College Application Essay*	223–24	*Writing Worksheet 9*	
127	Problems with Modifiers	247–50	Practice the Skill 10.3 Review the Skill 10.4 Concept Reinforcement 10A	Joseph's forgiving spirit Scriptural Application: Comparison of presidential pardons with God's pardoning (Isa. 55:6–9)
128	Placement of Modifiers	250–52		
129	*College Application Essay*	224–25	*Writing Worksheet 9* *Writing Rubric 9*	
130	Practice	252–53	Practice the Skill 10.5 Concept Reinforcement 10B	
131	*Sonnet*	238–40	*Writing Rubric 10* *Writing Worksheets 10A, 10B*	*Scriptural Application: Justice and mercy (Rom. 3:20–26; Matt. 18:23–35)* *Literature Link: Metaphors and similes (Gen. 49:22; Prov. 20:5)*
132	Review	254–56, 453–56	Teaching Help 10B Review the Skill 10.6 Cumulative Review 10.7 Chapter 10 Review	Jesus and Stephen: Forgiveness in death (Acts 7:60)
133	Chapter 10 Test From the Written Word	257		Cause and effect in Scripture (Gen. 6:5, 7; Num. 20:2–12) Personal Response: Cause and effect (Judg. 8:1–4; Prov. 15:1–2) Discussion and Participation: God's providence (Ps. 24:1; 115:3; Prov. 16:33; 21:1; Dan. 4:35; Acts 4:27–28)
134	*Sonnet*	240–41	*Writing Worksheet 10A, 10B*	
Chapter 11: Research Report/Capitalization[4]				
135	Personal Names, Religions, Nationalities, and Proper Adjectives	270–73	Bulletin Board 11 Chapter 11 Pretest Practice the Skill 11.1 Review the Skill 11.2	Literature Link: Evaluating Thomas Carlyle's *Sartor Resartus* Scriptural Application: Capitalizing words referring to God (Matt. 12:38)
136–37	*Sonnet*	242–42	*Writing Worksheet 10C*	
138	Place Names, Transportation, and Astronomy Terms	274–77	Practice the Skill 11.3 Review the Skill 11.4	
139	Businesses, Organizations, Cultural and Historical Terms	277–81	Practice the Skill 11.5 Review the Skill 11.6	Science Link: Using God's truth to evaluate observation and reason
140–41	*Sonnet*	242	*Writing Worksheet 10C* *Writing Rubric 10*	

Day(s)	Topic[1]	Pages	Support Materials[2]	Bible Integration
142	Titles First Words and Single Letters	282–87	Practice the Skill 11.7 Review the Skill 11.8 Teaching Help 11 Practice the Skill 11.9 Review the Skill 11.10	Writing Link: Reviewing art (Phil. 4:8) Literature Link: Evaluating E. E. Cummings Arguments for biblical creationism
143	*Research Report*	259–62	*Writing Rubric 11*	*Scriptural Application: Authority and inerrancy of Scripture (Ps. 119:89; John 17:17; 1 Cor. 2:13; 1 Thess. 2:13; 2 Tim. 3:16–17; 2 Pet. 1:21)* *Enrichment: Creation science and the inerrancy of the Bible*
144	*Research Report*	262–65	*Writing Worksheets 11A, 11B, 11C*	*Thinking Biblically: Using biblical discernment when evaluating sources*
145	Review	288–89, 457–58	Concept Reinforcement 11 Cumulative Review 11.11 Chapter 11 Review	
146	Chapter 11 Test Critical Thinking	289		Think About It: Arguing for truth with truth
Chapter 12: Issue Analysis Essay/Punctuation[4]				
147	End Marks and Other Periods	296–301	Bulletin Board 12 Chapter 12 Pretest ESL Helps 12A, 12B Teaching Help 12A Practice the Skill 12.1 Review the Skill 12.2 Concept Reinforcement 12A	
148	Commas	301–10	Teaching Help 12B ESL Helps 12A, 12C Practice the Skill 12.3 Review the Skill 12.4 Practice the Skill 12.5 Review the Skill 12.6 Teaching Help 12C Practice the Skill 12.7 Review the Skill 12.8	
149–50	*Research Report*	265–66	*Writing Worksheets 11B, 11C*	
151	Commas	310–14	Concept Reinforcement 12B Practice the Skill 12.9 Review the Skill 12.10	Scriptural Application: Cultural awareness as a witnessing tool (Acts 17:16–34)
152	Semicolons, Colons Review	315–20, 459–62	Practice the Skill 12.11 Review the Skill 12.12 Concept Reinforcement 12C Cumulative Review 12.13 Chapter 12 Review	Travel as a way to serve the Lord (Jonah, Thomas, Paul) Travel and the Great Commission (Matt. 28:19–20)
153	Chapter 12 Test			
154	From the Written Word	321		Analyzing a plan: Hezekiah (2 Chron. 21:20–21) Personal Response: Reasons to obey (Prov. 3:1–12)
155–56	*Research Report*	266–68	*Writing Worksheets 11B, 11C*	

Day(s)	Topic[1]	Pages	Support Materials[2]	Bible Integration
Chapter 13: Response to a Dramatic Scene/More Punctuation[4]				
157	Quotation Marks	329–34	Chapter 13 Pretest ESL Help 13 Practice the Skill 13.1 Review the Skill 13.2	Favorite Scripture passages and statements of theme
158	*Issue Analysis Essay*	290–94	*Writing Worksheet 12* *Writing Rubric 12*	*Scriptural Application: Analyzing issues carefully to combat relativism (Matt. 28:19–20)* *Christians' obligation to communicate a biblical viewpoint* *Scriptural Application: Thinking biblically about issues (2 Cor. 10:4–5)* *Scriptural Application: Questions to guide biblical analysis*
159	Ellipses, Brackets, and Underlining for Italics	335–40	Practice the Skill 13.3 Practice the Skill 13.4 Review the Skill 13.5 Concept Reinforcement 13A	Protestant migration to America Quoting research: *Free Indeed: Heroes of Black Christian History* Hymns and church history: Isaac Watts Discussing favorite hymns and psalms
160	*Issue Analysis Essay*	294	*Writing Worksheet 12*	
161	Apostrophe and Hyphen	341–46	Concept Reinforcement 13B Practice the Skill 13.6 Practice the Skill 13.7 Review the Skill 13.8	Church history: Hugh Latimer Scriptural Application: Spiritual armor (Eph. 6:10–18) Tudor England and Protestant sermons
162	Dashes and Parentheses	347–51	Teaching Help 13 Practice the Skill 13.9 Review the Skill 13.10 Concept Reinforcement 13C	
163	*Issue Analysis Essay*	295	*Writing Worksheet 12*	
164	*Research Report*	269	*Writing Worksheets 11B, 11C* *Writing Rubric 11*	
165	Review *Issue Analysis Essay*	352, 463–64, *295*	Cumulative Review 13.11 Chapter 13 Review *Writing Worksheet 12* *Writing Rubric 12*	
166	Chapter 13 Test Critical Thinking	353		Scriptural Application: Critical thinking in the believer's life (James 1:5)
167	*Response to a Dramatic Scene*	322–26	*Writing Rubric 13*	*Lady Macbeth and the effects of conscience* *Scriptural Application: The conscience (Eph. 4:19; 1 Tim. 4:2; Rom. 1:18; 2:14–16)*
168	*Response to a Dramatic Scene*	326–27	*Writing Worksheet 13* Bulletin Board 13	
169	*Response to a Dramatic Scene*	328	*Writing Worksheet 13*	
170	*Response to a Dramatic Scene*	328–29	*Writing Worksheet 13* *Writing Rubric 13*	
171–80	Final Review and Final Examination			

TABLE OF CONTENTS

CHAPTER 5

CHAPTER 6

CHAPTER 7

CHAPTER 13

CHAPTER 14

CHAPTER 15

ACKNOWLEDGMENTS

A careful effort has been made to trace the ownership of selections included in this textbook in order to secure permission to reprint copyrighted material and to make full acknowledgment of their use. If any error or omission has occurred, it is unintentional and will be corrected in subsequent editions, provided written notification is made to the publisher.

CHAPTER 3
U.S. Capitol Historical Society: "Grant and Lee: A Study in Contrasts" by Bruce Catton. Copyright © U.S. Capitol Historical Society. Used by permission.

CHAPTER 4
Jamie Langston Turner: Excerpt from *By the Light of a Thousand Stars* by Jamie Langston Turner. Copyright © 1999 Jamie Langston Turner. Bethany House Publishers, a division of Baker Publishing Group. Used by permission of the author.

CHAPTER 5
McGraw-Hill Companies, Inc.: "Signs of the Times: Littering the Verbal Landscape" by Charlotte K. Frank. Copyright © 2002 Charlotte K. Frank. As first appeared in *Education Week*, September 4, 2002. Used by permission. © McGraw-Hill Companies, Inc.

CHAPTER 6
Bob Jones University Museum & Gallery: Excerpt from *This Same Jesus* by David Burke. Copyright © 2002 Bob Jones University Museum & Gallery. Used by permission.

CHAPTER 11
***FrontLine* Magazine:** "Piltdown Chicken" by Stephen Caesar. Copyright © 2002 *FrontLine* Magazine. Used by permission from FrontLine magazine.

CHAPTER 12
Peter Shawn Taylor: "Bringing Some Sanity to Airport Security" **by** Peter Shawn Taylor from *Maclean's* Magazine, May 7, 2012. Used by permission of the author.

PHOTOGRAPH CREDITS

Cover
©iStockphoto.com/Sara Winter

Front Matter
i ©iStockphoto.com/Sara Winter; **xiv** (both) PhotoDisc/Getty Images

xvi, 2, 3, 10, 13, 14, 15, 16, 28, 40, 41, 42, 44, 46, 47, 48, 51, 53, 54, 56, 63, 64, 65, 69, 72, 74, 75, 76, 77, 79, 81, 82, 83, 86, 92, 94, 95, 96, 100, 102, 106, 113, 114, 115, 116, 118, 122, 132, 133, 136 (both), **137, 140, 151, 153, 161, 166, 167, 175, 193, 206, 207, 208, 210, 222, 228, 232, 233, 237** (both), **238, 239, 240, 241, 243, 251, 265, 267, 268, 274, 276, 279, 280, 282, 293, 299, 302, 303, 304, 317, 323, 331, 333, 335, 346, 348, 350, 355, 361, 368, 376, 379, 387, 395, 396, 404, 406, 408, 421, 422** ©2003 Hemera Technologies, Inc. All Rights Reserved; **1, 189, 367** Getty Images/Ron Chapple Studios RF/Thinkstock; **4, 35, 49, 101, 108, 173, 178, 187, 195, 227, 229** (b), **256, 269, 290, 294, 300, 306, 377, 383, 394** Getty Images/iStockphoto/Thinkstock; **7, 59** (t), **98, 329, 401, 411** Brenda Hansen; **8, 34, 36, 38, 39, 43, 52, 55, 59** (b), **70, 71, 78, 89, 104, 105, 107** (b), **107** (t), **109, 112, 125, 142, 145, 147, 154, 158, 171, 179, 180, 197, 202, 212, 214, 217, 218, 219, 252, 257, 258, 259, 286, 287, 295, 301, 305, 307, 308, 309, 312** (all), **313, 320, 321, 325, 330, 334, 337, 340, 342, 343, 349, 354, 362, 363, 364, 369, 375, 378, 380, 386, 398, 409, 415, 416, 417, 418, 420, 424** PhotoDisc/Getty Images; **12, 20** www.arttoday.com; **19** ©Yuri Arcurs-Fotolia.com; **22** ©iStockphoto.com/Rich Legg; **25, 26, 61, 129, 157, 198, 221, 322, 356, 393, 407** (t), **425** (b) Unusual Films; **29** Digital Vision; **31** ©iStockphoto.com/Claudia Dewald; **33** Getty Images/Hemera/Thinkstock; **50** ©iStockphoto.com/dirkr; **57, 68** NOAA; **58** Unusual Films/From the Isabella Stuart Gardener Museum, Boston; **60, 67** National Park Service; **73** ©iStockphoto.com/VikramRaghuvanshi; **80** (t) Unusual Films/From the Bob Jones University Collection; **80** (b), **91, 130, 139, 141, 152, 156, 163, 169, 182, 186, 196** (both), **225, 231, 235, 242, 246, 262, 275, 283, 289, 297, 310, 339, 344, 345, 352, 353, 358, 371, 384, 405, 407** (b) ©2003-www.arttoday.com; **85** ©iStockphoto.com/Catherine Yeulet; **90** Hemera Technologies/Ablestock.com/Thinkstock; **99** Carl Abrams; **110** White House/Tina Hager; **117** www.sporting-heroes.net; **119** (both) National Archives; **138** BJU Press Files; **143** Getty Images/Photodisc/Buccina Studios/Thinkstock; **146, 162, 165, 254, 403** BJU Photo Services; **155** (t) Unusual Films/From the Metropolitan Museum of Art, New York; **155** (b) ©iStockphoto.com/Suprijono Suharjoto; **172** ©iStockphoto.com/kristian sekulic; **174** Getty Images/Brand X/Thinkstock; **177** ©iStockphoto.com/Roberto A Sanchez; **181** Western Union; **192** Getty Images/Photodisc/Thinkstock; **201** ©iStockphoto.com/Wittelsbach bernd; **205** Greg Moss; **213, 229** (t) Getty Images/Digital Vision/Thinkstock; **220** COREL Corporation; **264** ©iStockphoto.com/antony spencer; **271** National Anthropological Archives, Smithsonian Institution 07194100; **273** Richard Lancelyn Green; **284, 390** NASA; **291** Getty Images/Creatas RF/Thinkstock; **311** ©iStockphoto.com/YinYang; **315** ©iStockphoto.com/Nikola Milijkovic; **316** Photo Courtesy of Natasha Vins; **327** Joyce Landis; **328** Corbis; **341** Getty Images/Zoonar RF/Thinkstock; **360** Marian Anderson Collection, Rare Book and Manuscript Library, University of Pennsylvania; **366** ©iStockphoto.com/vichie81; **370** U.S. Navy Photo/Jason Jacobowitz; **372** Ed Richards; **391** Imfolds/Bigstock.com; **397** White House Photo/David Johnson; **399** Bryan Smith; **423** ©iStockphoto.com/EdStock2; **425** (t) ©iStockphoto.com/asiseeit

TO THE STUDENT

Why do we study English? We learn how to understand and how to speak English while we are very young. Why, then, do we spend so much of the rest of our lives studying something we already know?

English is a living language. It changes—constantly. New words appear; obsolete words fade away as they are no longer needed. Usage patterns change; even rules occasionally change. We need to learn to speak and to write so that others can understand. Without a thorough understanding of English, we cannot communicate effectively.

English is also a flexible language. We use different levels of formality for different audiences. We speak to our friends differently than we speak to our pastor or teacher. We use one style for a letter to a friend and another style for an essay to be graded by a teacher.

Writing and Grammar 12, Third Edition, will help you learn to communicate in English more effectively. The first step toward the goal of better speaking and writing is to acquaint yourself with the text. Take a few minutes to look through the book and become familiar with these features:

- **Cross-reference icons** in the margin point you to other pages in the text or to *The Writer's Toolbox: A Writing and Grammar Handbook* with more information about the topic. Each icon indicates the category of material to which that icon refers.

  A **grammar** icon refers you to information in Chapters 2 through 5.

  A **usage** icon sends you to material in Chapters 6 through 13 discussing correct usage or mechanics.

  A **writing** icon indicates that the material is an important writing concept discussed in Chapter 1 or 14 or in one of the writing activities found throughout the book.

  A **reference** icon refers you to the library skills and study skills in Chapters 15 and 16 or to the special information at the end of a chapter.

- **ESL notes** explain in detail the concepts that can be difficult for students from another language background (*ESL* is an abbreviation for *English as a Second Language*). Every student can learn more about the English language from these helpful explanations. ESL
- **Tips** offer advice about using the grammar and usage concepts you are studying to improve your writing. tip

Mastering the concepts in this book will increase your appreciation for language. If you learn to use English correctly and to value the beauty of English, you will enjoy the satisfaction of becoming a more effective communicator.

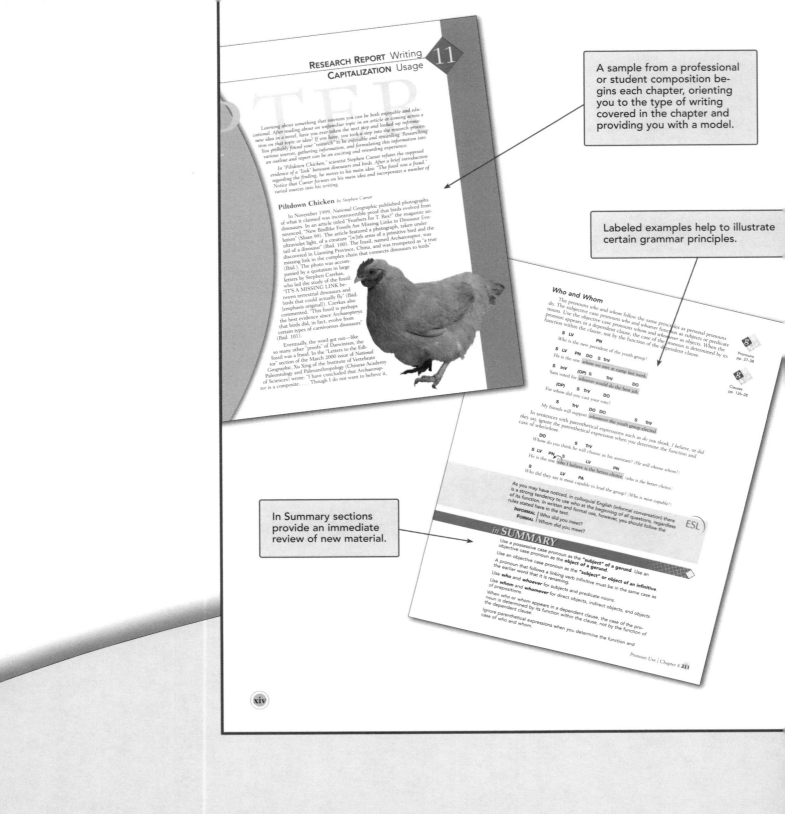

A sample from a professional or student composition begins each chapter, orienting you to the type of writing covered in the chapter and providing you with a model.

Learning about something that interests you can be both enjoyable and educational. After reading about an unfamiliar topic in an article or coming across a new idea in a novel, have you ever taken the next step and looked up information on that topic or idea? If you have, you took a step into the research process. You probably found your "research" to be enjoyable and rewarding. Researching various sources, gathering information, and formulating this information into an outline and report can be an exciting and rewarding experience.

In "Piltdown Chicken," scientist Stephen Caesar refutes the supposed evidence of a "link" between dinosaurs and birds. After a brief introduction regarding the finding, he moves to his main idea: "The fossil was a fraud." Notice that Caesar focuses on his main idea and incorporates a number of varied sources into his writing.

Piltdown Chicken *by Stephen Caesar*

In November 1999, *National Geographic* published photographs of what it claimed was incontrovertible proof that birds evolved from dinosaurs. In an article titled "Feathers for T. Rex?" the magazine announced, "New Birdlike Fossils Are Missing Links in Dinosaur Evolution" (Sloan 99). The article featured a photograph, taken under ultraviolet light, of a creature "[w]ith arms of a primitive bird and the tail of a dinosaur" (Ibid. 100). The fossil, named *Archaeoraptor*, was discovered in Liaoning Province, China, and was trumpeted as "a true missing link in the complex chain that connects dinosaurs to birds" (Ibid.). The photo was accompanied by a quotation in large letters by Stephen Czerkas, who led the study of the fossil: "IT'S A MISSING LINK between terrestrial dinosaurs and birds that could actually fly" (Ibid. [emphasis original]). Czerkas also commented, "This fossil is perhaps the best evidence since *Archaeopteryx* that birds did, in fact, evolve from certain types of carnivorous dinosaurs" (Ibid. 101).

Eventually, the word got out—like so many other "proofs" of Darwinism, the fossil was a fraud. In the "Letters to the Editor" section of the March 2000 issue of *National Geographic*, Xu Xing of the Institute of Vertebrate Paleontology and Paleoanthropology (Chinese Academy of Sciences) wrote: "I have concluded that *Archaeoraptor* is a composite. . . . Though I do not want to believe it,

Labeled examples help to illustrate certain grammar principles.

In Summary sections provide an immediate review of new material.

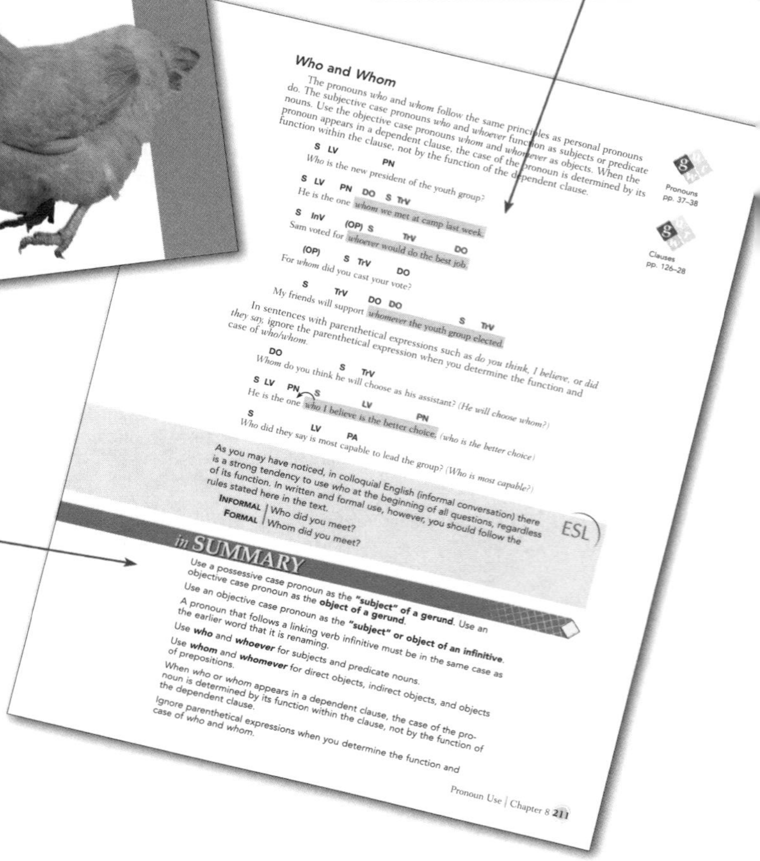

Who and Whom

The pronouns *who* and *whom* follow the same principles as personal pronouns do. The subjective case pronouns *who* and *whoever* function as subjects or predicate nouns. Use the objective case pronouns *whom* and *whomever* as objects. When the pronoun appears in a dependent clause, the case of the pronoun is determined by its function within the clause, not by the function of the dependent clause.

S LV PN
Who is the new president of the youth group?

S LV PN DO S TrV
He is the one whom we met at camp last week.

S InV (OP) S TrV DO
Sam voted for whoever would do the best job.

(OP) S TrV DO
For whom did you cast your vote?

S TrV DO DO S TrV
My friends will support whomever the youth group elected.

In sentences with parenthetical expressions such as *do you think, I believe,* or *did they say,* ignore the parenthetical expression when you determine the function and case of *who/whom.*

DO S TrV
Whom do you think he will choose as his assistant? (He will choose whom?)

S LV PN S LV PN
He is the one who I believe is the better choice. (who is the better choice)

S LV PA
Who did they say is most capable to lead the group? (Who is most capable?)

Pronouns pp. 37–38

Clauses pp. 126–28

ESL

As you may have noticed, in colloquial English (informal conversation) there is a strong tendency to use who at the beginning of all questions, regardless of its function. In written and formal use, however, you should follow the rules stated here in the text.

INFORMAL | Who did you meet?
FORMAL | Whom did you meet?

in SUMMARY

Use a possessive case pronoun as the **"subject" of a gerund.** Use an objective case pronoun as the **object of a gerund.**

Use an objective case pronoun as the **"subject" or object of an infinitive.**

A pronoun that follows a linking verb infinitive must be in the same case as the earlier word that it is renaming.

Use **who** and **whoever** for subjects and predicate nouns.

Use **whom** and **whomever** for direct objects, indirect objects, and objects of prepositions.

When who or whom appears in a dependent clause, the case of the pronoun is determined by its function within the clause, not by the function of the dependent clause.

Ignore parenthetical expressions when you determine the function and case of who and whom.

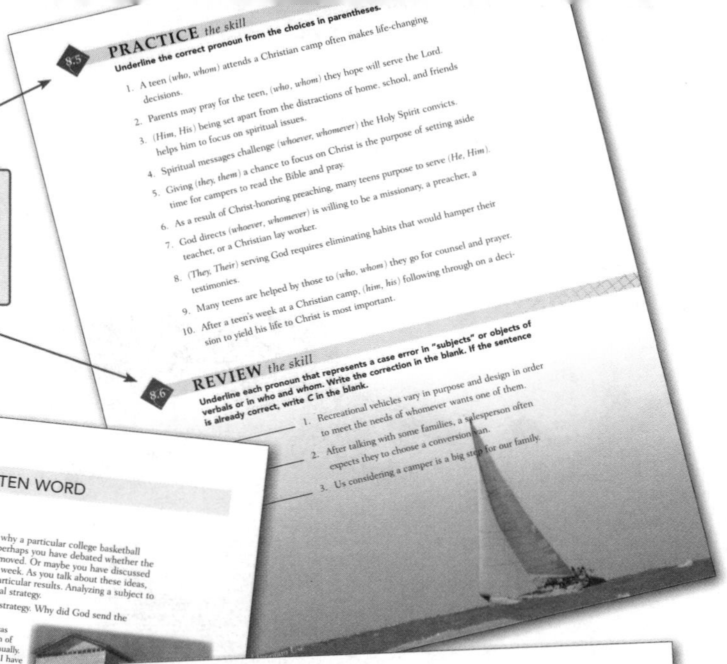
8.5 PRACTICE *the skill*

Underline the correct pronoun from the choices in parentheses.

1. A teen (*who, whom*) attends a Christian camp often makes life-changing decisions.
2. Parents may pray for the teen, (*who, whom*) they hope will serve the Lord.
3. (*Him, His*) being set apart from the distractions of home, school, and friends helps him to focus on spiritual issues.
4. Spiritual messages challenge (*whoever, whomever*) the Holy Spirit convicts.
5. Giving (*they, them*) a chance to focus on Christ is the purpose of setting aside time for campers to read the Bible and pray.
6. As a result of Christ-honoring preaching, many teens purpose to serve (*He, Him*).
7. God directs (*whoever, whomever*) is willing to be a missionary, a preacher, a teacher, or a Christian lay worker.
8. (*They, Their*) serving God requires eliminating habits that would hamper their testimonies.
9. Many teens are helped by those to (*who, whom*) they go for counsel and prayer.
10. After a teen's week at a Christian camp, (*him, his*) following through on a decision to yield his life to Christ is most important.

8.6 REVIEW *the skill*

Underline each pronoun that represents a case error in "subjects" or objects of verbals or in who and whom. Write the correction in the blank. If the sentence is already correct, write *C* in the blank.

_____ 1. Recreational vehicles vary in purpose and design in order to meet the needs of whomever wants one of them.

_____ 2. After talking with some families, a salesperson often expects they to choose a conversion van.

_____ 3. Us considering a camper is a big step for our family.

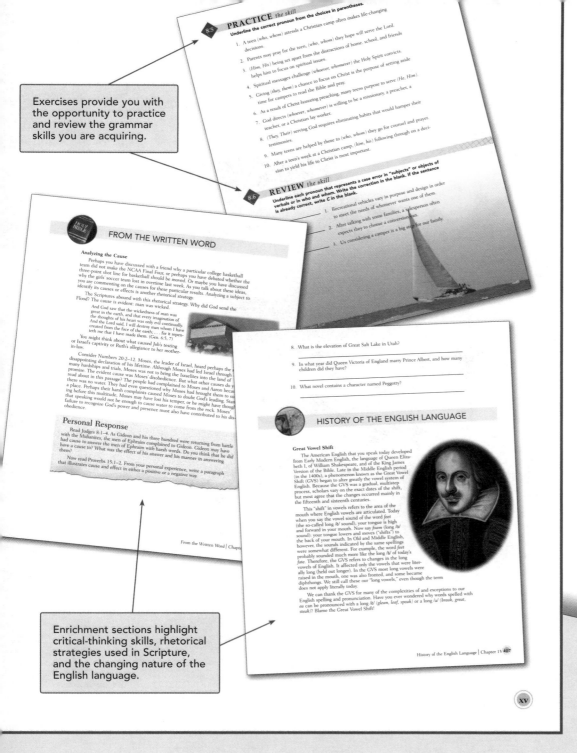

Exercises provide you with the opportunity to practice and review the grammar skills you are acquiring.

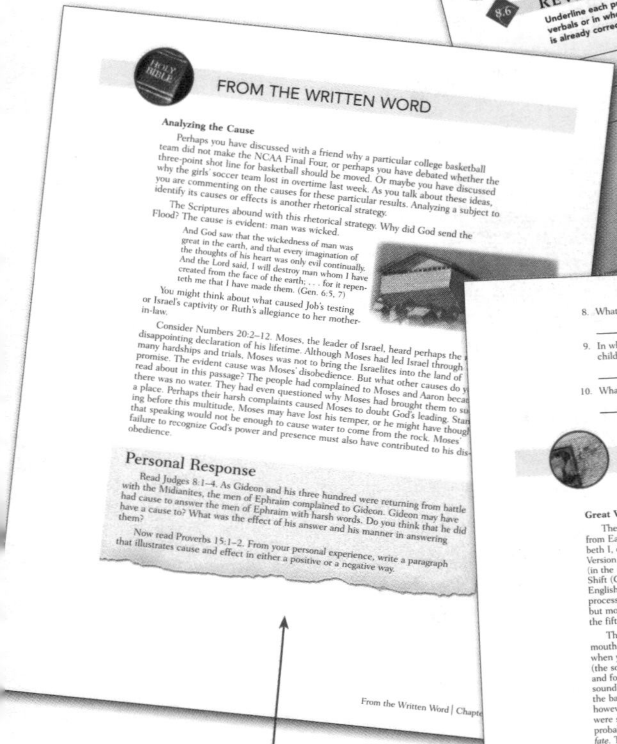
FROM THE WRITTEN WORD

Analyzing the Cause

Perhaps you have discussed with a friend why a particular college basketball team did not make the NCAA Final Four, or perhaps you have debated whether the three-point shot line for basketball should be moved. Or maybe you have discussed why the girls' soccer team lost in overtime last week. As you talk about these ideas, you are commenting on the causes for these particular results. Analyzing a subject to identify its causes or effects is another rhetorical strategy.

The Scriptures abound with this rhetorical strategy. Why did God send the Flood? The cause is evident: man was wicked.

> And God saw that the wickedness of man was great in the earth, and that every imagination of the thoughts of his heart was only evil continually. And the Lord said, I will destroy man whom I have created from the face of the earth; . . . for it repenteth me that I have made them. (Gen. 6:5, 7)

You might think about what caused Job's testing or Israel's captivity or Ruth's allegiance to her mother-in-law.

Consider Numbers 20:2–12. Moses, the leader of Israel, heard perhaps the disappointing declaration of his lifetime. Although Moses had led Israel through many hardships and trials, Moses was not to bring the Israelites into the land of promise. The evident cause was Moses' disobedience. But what other causes do you read about in this passage? The people had complained to Moses and Aaron because there was no water. They had even questioned why Moses had brought them to such a place. Perhaps their harsh complaints caused Moses to doubt God's leading. Standing before this multitude, Moses may have lost his temper, or he might have thought that speaking would not be enough to cause water to come from the rock. Moses' failure to recognize God's power and presence must also have contributed to his disobedience.

Personal Response

Read Judges 8:1–4. As Gideon and his three hundred were returning from battle with the Midianites, the men of Ephraim complained to Gideon. Gideon may have had cause to answer the men of Ephraim with harsh words. Do you think that he did have a cause to? What was the effect of his answer and his manner in answering them?

Now read Proverbs 15:1–2. From your personal experience, write a paragraph that illustrates cause and effect in either a positive or a negative way.

From the Written Word | Chapter

8. What is the elevation of Great Salt Lake in Utah?

9. In what year did Queen Victoria of England marry Prince Albert, and how many children did they have?

10. What novel contains a character named Peggotty?

HISTORY OF THE ENGLISH LANGUAGE

Great Vowel Shift

The American English that you speak today developed from Early Modern English, the language of Queen Elizabeth I, of William Shakespeare, and of the King James Version of the Bible. Late in the Middle English period (in the 1400s), a phenomenon known as the Great Vowel Shift (GVS) began to alter greatly the vowel system of English. Because the GVS was a gradual, multistep process, scholars vary on the exact dates of the shift, but most agree that the changes occurred mainly in the fifteenth and sixteenth centuries.

This "shift" in vowels refers to the area of the mouth where English vowels are articulated. Today when you say the vowel sound of the word *feet* (the so-called long /ē/ sound), your tongue is high and forward in your mouth. Now say *foam* (long /ō/ sound): your tongue lowers and moves ("shifts") to the back of your mouth. In Old and Middle English, however, the sounds indicated by the same spellings were somewhat different. For example, the word *feet* probably sounded much more like the long /ā/ of today's *fate*. Therefore, the GVS refers to changes in the long vowels of English. It affected only the vowels that were literally long (held out longer). In the GVS most long vowels were raised in the mouth, one was also fronted, and some became diphthongs. We still call these our "long vowels," even though the term does not apply literally today.

We can thank the GVS for many of the complexities of and exceptions to our English spelling and pronunciation. Have you ever wondered why words spelled with *ea* can be pronounced with a long /ē/ (*glean, leaf, speak*) or a long /ā/ (*break, great, steak*)? Blame the Great Vowel Shift!

History of the English Language | Chapter 15 407

Enrichment sections highlight critical-thinking skills, rhetorical strategies used in Scripture, and the changing nature of the English language.

xv

OBJECTIVES

Students will

1. write assignments using the stages of the writing process.
2. use various methods to determine a topic for writing.
3. identify an audience.
4. determine a specific purpose for writing.
5. evaluate sources of information.
6. distinguish between topic and sentence outlines.
7. choose a specific mode for a draft.
8. write a thesis statement, topic sentences, and a concluding sentence.
9. identify various methods of paragraph organization.
10. incorporate specific strategies in writing paragraphs of introduction and conclusion.
11. identify different types of essays.
12. draft an in-class essay.
13. edit and revise peers' paragraphs for ideas, style, and correctness.
14. revise their own writing for ideas, style, and correctness.
15. evaluate other revisions for effectiveness.
16. choose appropriate titles for written selections.
17. publish their writing.

Chapter 1 Overview			
Topic	**Pages**	**Support Materials**	**Days**
Planning	1–8	Bulletin Board 1 Practice the Skill 1.1–1.2	1–2
Descriptive Essay	29–34	Writing Worksheet 2 Writing Rubric 2	3, 7, 10, 11
Drafting	8–20	Practice/Use/Review the Skill 1.3–1.9 Teaching Help 1	4–6
Revising	20–24	Use/Review the Skill 1.10–1.11	8
Publishing	24–25	Use the Skill 1.12	9
History of the English Language	26–27		11

THE WRITING PROCESS

Lesson Support

Teacher's Toolkit

Bulletin Board 1
Teaching Help 1

You have not come this far in your academic career without learning at least a little about writing. Essays, reports, and letters are all examples of the types of writing you have most likely already worked on. For some students writing seems to come naturally, as if the words flow from somewhere inside and pour out onto the page (or screen). For others, writing is arduous and therefore something that they dread. Whether writing comes easily or as the result of much labor, the process itself is similar for everyone. It follows a natural progression from the idea to the finished work.

As you have no doubt noticed, the writing process is not strictly linear. In other words, very rarely does a writer complete his research (*planning*), proceed to writing his thoughts (*drafting*), look over what he has written (*revising*), and then submit his work (*publishing*). Rather, the writer does a little research, jots some thoughts down, remembers something he forgot to look up, writes a little more, rereads the first part and crosses most of it out, writes again, reads again, and so on until he arrives at a finished product.

This text will give instruction in the four stages of the writing process (*planning, drafting, revising, publishing*) just described. For each writing project you tackle, you will move through the four steps. Varying amounts of time will be spent on each step, depending on the assignment. That is, some assignments will require extensive planning; some will require very little. Some may be revised repeatedly; others may require only minimal revision. In any case, you, the writer, will follow the four-stage writing process until it becomes second nature, until you are comfortable when you encounter the words "Today's test will be entirely essay."

Thinking Biblically

The *New York Times* website is one of the most visited in the world, let alone the United States. Statistics also reveal that its readers tend to have college and graduate degrees. And what do these accomplished people like to read? The opinion pages are consistently found among the top ten most shared articles on the site. Read a little about the current roster of opinion writers. Check out the opinion pages and see what they say. These are people who can write—but what kinds of ideas are they spreading? Write a comment on one of the articles and share the results with your class. Unless Christians can write and write well, false ideas on the prominent opinion pages of the world will go unchallenged. Writing is an extremely important tool. It is the most prominent tool God Himself chose to communicate truth.

Thinking Biblically

Christians have excellent reasons to learn and hone the communication tool we call writing. Writing is one of the most powerful means of persuasion available, and Christians have many things to communicate to each other and to the world. God (through the apostle Paul) calls believers to "[cast] down imaginations" that oppose the knowledge of Christ—in other words, to destroy anti-Christian arguments (2 Cor. 10:5). This charge is very difficult to carry out without writing. And the ministries of encouragement and teaching that Christians should have with one another often call on believers to write. Finding the opinion pages of the *New York Times* is as easy as going to the homepage (NYTimes.com) and clicking "Opinion" in the menu bar. Direct students to the regular columnists. In addition to commenting on an article, perhaps students can use a topic addressed by a columnist as a springboard for a class discussion or debate or for a persuasive writing assignment.

Planning

For most of the writing tasks you will tackle, the planning stage will be the most important. Work done at the outset will reward the writer later. Planning can involve everything from selecting a topic to interviewing experts in the field to deciding exactly who your audience will be. Remember that the amount of planning you do varies greatly with the task at hand. The following sections will give you plenty of strategies to choose from when planning a piece of writing.

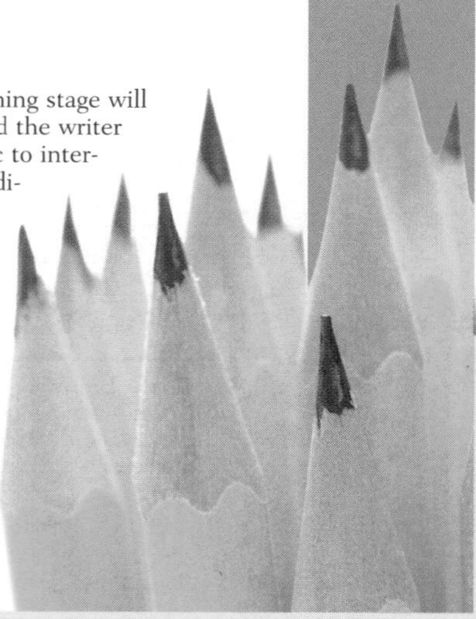

Choosing Your Topic

Some writers know immediately what they will write about. If you are one who has difficulty deciding what course to take, some of the methods listed below may help you find inspiration.

TEACHING STRATEGY

Introduction

Discuss the value of writing as a learning tool. Ask students to give examples that illustrate this idea, such as recording progress toward a goal (charting sit-ups or pushups done in a week), making notes about something that puzzles them (recording a first-person account of a Portuguese man-of-war sting), or writing for pleasure (entering an original poem or paragraph in a journal). Discuss how writing is an essential communication skill that people must use often. Help students understand the benefits that writing skills offer.

TEACHING STRATEGY

Induction and Discussion

Discuss the writing process with students. Ask them to list the steps of the writing process. (*planning, drafting, revising, publishing*) Engage the students in a discussion about their thought processes during each step. Be prepared to offer examples of publishing since this step may be unfamiliar to some students. Discuss the similarities in approach that every writing assignment has. Point out that students may spend different amounts of time on the various steps depending upon the assignment.

TEACHING STRATEGY

Discussion

Direct the students' attention to the statement on page 1, "Today's test will be entirely essay." Discuss the relationship between the steps of the writing process and the steps of writing an in-class essay.

Listing

Keep a running list of ideas and topics in a journal or on your computer. Add to the list whenever you think of a new idea that interests you and consult the list whenever you need inspiration for a writing assignment. Newspapers, magazines, and online articles may also suggest writing ideas to you. Listening to and observing those around you will add many items to your list as well.

palaces of Europe

light bulbs—technology/history

brand/branding (as in advertising)

Bible prophecy

Creationism

popcorn

hairstyles

Questioning

Ask yourself the six journalist's questions (*who? what? where? when? why? how?*) before you start writing. These questions will help you not only to include the important information about your topic but also to expand your ideas as they generate other questions.

- Who/what is in the news right now?
- What issues affect me and my future?
- Where would I like to serve as a missionary, should the Lord send me?
- When is _____ a good idea? When is this same thing a bad idea?
- Why should/shouldn't someone participate in _____?
- How should I handle _____ (person, situation, conflict)?

Going forward or backward in time from the event or item being considered can be another helpful questioning technique. For example, an essay on hairstyles might examine the powdered wigs and intricately woven hairpieces of the past or predict the hairstyles of the future, given trends and the cyclical nature of fashion.

Brainstorming

Brainstorming techniques are used by businesses and organizations when they attempt to create slogans or revamp strategies. Writers use brainstorming to generate ideas for writing. Working alone or in a group, a writer records everything he can think of about a topic. For a Christian, the ideas generated during a brainstorming session should meet the criteria set down in Philippians 4:8. Within those biblical guidelines, a writer should consider no idea unworkable or inane.

tip

Finally, brethren, whatsoever things are true, whatsoever things are honest, whatsoever things are just, whatsoever things are pure, whatsoever things are lovely, whatsoever things are of good report; if there be any virtue, and if there be any praise, think on these things. (Phil. 4:8)

Teaching Strategy

Participation

Using the picture on page 2, ask the students to write down the first word(s) that they think of when they look at the picture. For example, a student might write *wattage of light bulbs, kinds of light fixtures,* or *different kinds of light bulbs.* Ask volunteers to share ideas.

Teaching Strategy

Participation

Direct the students to the list of questions on page 2. Ask them to write down as many answers as they can imagine. Allow the students to work individually or to work in groups of two or three. Remind them that Philippians 4:8 should be the benchmark for their ideas.

Scriptural Application

Encourage students to begin developing a Christian approach to composition. Composition is a tool—like math, spelling, and vocabulary—for achieving God's purposes in the world. And what are God's purposes? Loving God and loving our neighbor are God's design for us (Matt. 22:34–40). Good writing is a way to show love for God by communicating truth in a loving way to our neighbor. Clear, effective writing can, for example, make a personal letter more com-

One brainstorming session produced the following ideas about light bulbs.

- frosted light bulbs
- filaments
- types of bulbs
- Edison
- flashbulbs
- history of streetlights, stoplights, flashlights, refrigerator lights, headlights
- lamps—from gas to electric
- dependence upon
- power outages
- cost of electricity
- ultra long-lasting bulbs
- wattage

Eliminate items from the list that are too far afield (like *Edison* or *cost of electricity*) or re-brainstorm about one of the items (*types of bulbs—incandescent, halogen, fluorescent, black light, infrared*).

Freewriting

Writing on a topic without concern for precise wording, punctuation, or other grammatical issues is called **freewriting.** This technique will enable you to explore aspects of a subject that you have never considered before. To engage in freewriting, set a time limit of four to five minutes and begin writing. Challenge yourself to write without stopping for the time you have. Below is an example of one person's freewriting attempt.

> I have always wanted to learn to scuba dive. I enjoy hearing about the sea adventures of Jacques Cousteau. To me it would be fascinating to see the beautifully colored fish and the intriguing coral formations. A person has to wear a wetsuit, to learn to use oxygen tanks and to function in deep water. Oxygen tanks must be heavy to hold on your back. One danger is going too deep and surfacing too quickly. I have heard that people get the "bends" when this happens. What exactly is the bends? I wonder where there is a good place to learn to scuba dive. Then I wonder where a person would go to dive. The lakes around here are not very clear and I doubt that you would see very many pretty colored fish. I suspect that a person would have to go to the ocean to be able to see the beautiful fish and coral. I wonder how expensive scuba equipment and training is? Then I wonder how much it would cost to go scuba diving at the Great Barrier Reef or in the Cayman Islands.

ESL

Freewriting can be an effective way to develop fluency—a free flow—in writing English. Your goal should be to write out your thoughts without worrying about grammar or word choice. You can edit your writing later, after you have recorded on paper what you want to say about your topic.

Interviewing

For firsthand knowledge about a subject, conduct an **interview** of someone who is an expert in your field of interest. Contact your interview subject and state the purpose of your interview and propose a time to meet. Before meeting your subject, find out as much as possible about him so that you will be able to express interest in him and so that you will not waste time asking questions concerning matters of common knowledge.

ESL Second language students might have a difficult time beginning a writing assignment. Consider offering the students the opportunity to explain to you or another student what they want to say about their subject. Interacting verbally with someone else will help ESL students focus on their ideas.

forting, a newspaper editorial more persuasive, or a speech more memorable.

Teaching Strategy

Demonstration and Modeling

Elicit student ideas for a freewriting topic. After writing four or five ideas for display, model a freewriting activity for the students. Then ask the students to use one of the remaining ideas to complete their own freewriting activity.

Enrichment

Invite someone unfamiliar to the students to be interviewed by them. In advance, give the students a brief biographical sketch of the individual. Ask them to formulate five interview questions based upon the biographical sketch and upon what they would like to find out about the individual. Instruct the students to compose questions that will reveal personal characteristics. Be prepared for spontaneous questions during the interview.

ONE on ONE Arrange for your student to interview a local pastor, political leader, or law enforcement official. In advance, instruct your student to formulate some interview questions. Afterwards, ask your student to write a brief biographical sketch based on the interview. If any newspaper articles have been written about the interviewee, direct your student to read them and to decide whether the articles represent the person fairly.

ESL Use some or all of the following suggestions to modify writing assignments for ESL students (see ESL Strategy on page 5):

- Allow the student to draft the assignment first in his native tongue. This step allows the student freedom to concentrate on the purpose of the writing assignment.
- Tell the student to double-space his draft so that translations or corrections can be more easily written in.
- Recommend that the student write the English words and phrases that he can supply without a dictionary above each line.
- The student can easily use a dictionary to find nouns and adjectives. (Verbs are more difficult because the student must take into account the conjugation in his own language as well as in English. Prepositions are difficult to translate from one language to another. Other aspects of language such as word order, auxiliaries, articles, conjunctions, and some punctuation cannot be determined from normal dictionary use.)
- Set up a conference with the student, allowing him to explain his writing to you in English. This conference allows the student to express the ideas of his writing in English and allows you to see how the student is thinking in his writing process.

(continued on pages 5–6)

Come up with a list of questions that require extended answers (e.g., *How were your findings different each time you conducted the experiment?* is a better question than *How many times did you conduct the experiment?*). Be prepared to use spontaneous follow-up questions in response to the answers given. Consider the following faulty interview:

Interviewer	You conduct fitness seminars in the summer. Tell me about them.
Subject	Over 100,000 people have come to our one- and two-week summer fitness camps.
Interviewer	Why do you prefer ultradistance events to others?

This interviewer should have followed up his first question with another about where the camps are held, what happens at the camps, how campers are challenged, and so on. Instead, the interviewer plowed ahead to the next question on the list and missed an opportunity for more (and better) information.

Narrowing Your Topic

Often you will need to narrow an idea to make it adhere to the length requirements of an assignment or to make it more manageable. As you consider your topic, ask yourself these questions: *What is the length requirement of my paper? Is the topic that I have chosen too broad to be covered adequately in the assigned length?* If you answered yes to the second question, force yourself to focus on one aspect of the topic.

Topic too broad	Light Bulbs: Then and Now
Topic too limited	Uses for Old Light Bulbs
Appropriate topic for brief paper	Advances in Light-Emitting Diode (LED) Technology

Use the ideas generated by listing, questioning, brainstorming, freewriting, and interviewing as you seek to narrow your topic. Sometimes an idea you rejected at first will work well after all.

Considering Your Audience

Before you begin writing, you will need to know more about those to whom you are writing. Are they well educated? Are they adults/children/teens? Are they already familiar with your topic, or are they totally unacquainted with it? A well-educated electrical engineer would not need an explanation of what LED technology is. By the same token, most young children would be unprepared and perhaps unable to read anything more than a very simple explanation of LEDs. In academic writing, you will often be assigned an audience; however, your real-world writing (application essays, school newspaper articles, yearbook copy, letters, e-mails) will require that you choose for whom you write and publish.

Determining Your Purpose

After considering your audience, you will need to determine a purpose for writing. The standard purposes are *to analyze, to describe, to entertain, to inform,* and *to persuade*. Although a single piece of writing may have several purposes within it, the paper's main purpose should be a single one. For example, one student wrote *to inform* his audience of advances in LED technology. As a means of informing the audience of the many uses of LED, the writer told a brief anecdote meant *to entertain*. Another student in the class wrote an article *to persuade* companies to switch to LED lighting as a cost-cutting measure. In order to do this, the writer needed *to analyze* data about traditional fluorescent and incandescent lighting costs versus LED costs. Your answer to the question *What is my purpose?* will narrow your field of inquiry as you begin gathering information and later serve as the basis for your thesis statement. (See page 10.)

Teaching Strategy
Analysis

Ask the students to identify what the interviewer on page 4 has done correctly. *(He has obviously done research since he knows about the fitness seminars. He has also worded his questions to encourage conversation.)*

Teaching Strategy
Discussion and Modeling

Instruct the students to look at the model of freewriting on page 3. Ask them who they think the audience might be for this paragraph. Ask them how a specific audience would affect what information the interviewer would keep or eliminate.

Teaching Strategy
Discussion and Modeling

Display your freewriting sample from the earlier modeling activity. What information would the student use to analyze, inform, or describe? Ask the students how the information would change as the purpose changed.

tip

Force yourself to state your purpose in a single declarative sentence. Then ask the question *What information will best help me accomplish that purpose?*

Gathering Information

In this stage of the process, you will build upon your writing purpose to gather further information about your topic. Writers typically use one of three sources: (1) themselves—by writing about something they already know; (2) others—by interviewing people knowledgeable about their topic; (3) reference materials—by researching books, magazines, newspapers, almanacs, the Internet, and other sources.

Search Tools pp. 399–401

Internet Precaution

Remember that a source is only as reliable as its author; therefore, a good researcher investigates the credentials of any author whose information he chooses to include. Before you use information from a website, investigate the website as thoroughly as possible. Look for information at the top, bottom, or sides of the screen or in a section titled "About This Site" or "Mission Statement." If the site provides a site map or a table of contents, explore it for further information. Try to answer the following questions about each website you visit:

- Who runs the site? Is it a respected academic institution? A government agency? A well-known business? A qualified individual? An interested but possibly uninformed amateur?
- Who wrote the content on the website? What are the author's qualifications? Is he an expert? Does he have experience in this field?
- Are both the sponsoring organization and the author unbiased and trustworthy? Or do they have a financial interest in the subject the website discusses?
- Where did the author get his information? Are his sources reliable?
- Is the information current? Or does the author include outdated information that no longer applies or has since been proved untrue?
- Is the information presented clearly and understandably?
- Do other experts value this website? Does it include links to other respected organizations? Does it display an icon indicating approval from a respected expert or organization?

Thinking Biblically

Overwhelming amounts of information flood us each day. As a result, we need information filters to help us sort the wheat from the chaff and tell us which news is fit to print and which is not worth knowing. We use news sites and search engines for this purpose. But a biblically wise Internet user will understand that every information filter has a bias. A search engine's bias is popularity: sites rise to the top if a lot of people link to them. What does this say about the validity of the information found through a search engine? Does popular equal true? Biblical discernment in an information age requires the ability to evaluate not just information but even the services that filter it for us.

Before you begin your research, list questions that you hope to answer about your topic. These questions should both relate to your purpose and address the needs of your audience. The following questions are one student's list about hair ironing, a topic narrowed from hairstyles under "Listing" above. The student wants to inform his audience, which consists primarily of teenagers in America, about the phenomenon of hair ironing, a process by which a person with curly hair would attempt to straighten his or her hair.

- *What is hair ironing? How was it done?*
- *Were there any harmful effects from hair ironing?*
- *Why would a person iron his hair? How did this relate to his status (perceived or otherwise) in society?*
- *During what period was hair ironing popular?*
- *In what places was hair ironing most popular?*
- *Was hair ironing done only among certain groups or classes of people?*
- *How long did the effects of the ironing last?*
- *Did one need any special equipment for hair ironing?*

ESL continued

- Use conference time to check the accuracy of the English the student has incorporated from his background knowledge and his dictionary use.
- Use conference time to guide the student in writing completely in English. Having you there for immediate feedback should lessen the student's frustration of expressing ideas in a language that is not yet natural to him.

(continued on next page)

Thinking Biblically

Most of the important things a person believes, he believes on authority. If a person believed only the things he saw with his own eyes, his knowledge would be limited to things he had personally experienced. That reality means one's knowledge is only as good as the authorities he trusts, and a large part of one's education is learning who is worth trusting. If students want to use writing as a powerful tool for God's glory, they cannot afford to trust unreliable sources. Educated people will dismiss their ideas. To illustrate the importance of reputable sources, display (or have students share) two articles about the same topic, each of which illustrates the particular bias of its source.

Teaching Strategy

Discussion

Instruct the students to look at the questions about hair ironing on page 5 and to determine whether they are appropriate for the purpose. Point out that in gathering information, writers may come across other ideas that affect their purpose or their point of view.

ESL Strategy

Many ESL students are so concerned, and even defeated, by such things as grammatical correctness, word-by-word translation from their mother tongue, and word choice that the purpose of a writing assignment is hardly considered. Depending on the English proficiency of the ESL student, perhaps use some or all of the suggestions in the side margins on pages 4–6 to modify the process of the writing assignments.

After deciding what modifications to make for ESL students, perhaps delegate some aspects, such as the writing conference, to a teacher's aide.

ESL continued

- When correcting an ESL student's writing, try to group the errors into categories. A student may make fifty errors in his paper. However, most of these errors may fall into only three or four main categories, such as not adding *s* to third person singular present tense verbs *(he climb* instead of *he climbs),* incorrect use of irregular plurals *(mans* for *men),* and so on. If these fifty errors can be grouped into four main categories, then the student can work on mastering three or four concepts as opposed to considering fifty different examples of his lack of ability in English. In addition, you can concentrate on specific areas when grading the mechanics of the paper.
- Ask the student to read his writing aloud. Although your main purpose is not to teach pronunciation, this opportunity will benefit your student.
- Allow the student to revise once or twice after the conference; and, while you consider the whole writing process, grade only the final copy.

1.1 PRACTICE *the skill*

Read the following paragraph and answer the questions at the end. *(Answers may vary.)*

I've never enjoyed eating liver, for I find it difficult to ingest something an animal uses during its digestive process. As I was growing up, my mom served liver on a bimonthly basis. We were always required to eat at least five silver-dollar-sized pieces of liver, and we received extra pieces if we complained about the chunks of liver already on our plates. I believe I never would have survived the ordeal if my mom had not also served mashed potatoes. Five pieces of liver required two large heaps of mashed potatoes; I was always really full at the end of this meal. As we willed down our five pieces, my mom always reviewed the benefits of liver: first, that it was packed full of nutrition and second, that it would put hair on our chests (not a desirable thing for a third-grade girl). Because my mother always told us how good liver is for us, I wonder now why we no longer eat it. Surely if it was good for me when I was in elementary school, it is still beneficial to my health now that I am in high school! I have come to believe that the real reason we ate liver was not because of its nutrition or because of its hair-growing abilities but because eating it instilled character in us—character to endure those things we find unpleasant. It seems to me that my mom could have just made us chop wood.

1. Who is the audience for this paragraph? *anyone who has eaten liver*
2. What is the purpose of this paragraph? *to entertain*
3. What kind of person probably wrote this paragraph? *a high-school student who was made to eat liver*

Outlining the Paper

Often the nature of your writing will necessitate an outline. An outline is simply an organizational plan for your writing. Research reports or essays, issue analyses, and in-class essays require the structure that an outline provides. Perhaps most important, an outline forces the writer to organize his thoughts into a logical sequence, eliminate unnecessary points, and identify any omissions before he begins drafting.

Periods in Outlines pp. 297–98

Sometimes it will be useful for you to write a tentative outline—for brief, informal pieces of writing. A **tentative outline** is one in which the writer does not use numerals or letters and is unconcerned about parallelism of points or making sure that the points are fully developed. Tentative outlines are helpful when jotting down ideas and organization strategies for an in-class essay or a letter. However, if your outline will be published as part of your paper or will be turned in as a separate assignment, you should follow proper outline form. Two forms of outline are considered acceptable: the topic outline and the sentence outline. Although either is correct, you should use the form that your teacher or publication guidelines specify.

Parallelism pp. 379–80

A **topic outline** uses only words or phrases—no complete sentences and no verbs except verbals. Within a numbered or lettered series, each point should have the same grammatical form (e.g., participles or prepositional phrases); that is, all points should be parallel.

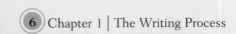

Scriptural Application

Ask students to provide an outline of the topic "The Story of Scripture" using the main headings "Creation," "Fall," and "Redemption." Sample outline subpoints under "Redemption," for example, would include "God's promises to Abraham" and "God's covenant with Israel."

Teaching Strategy

Demonstration

Ask the students to rewrite the paragraph from Practice the Skill 1.1 with a different purpose or for a different audience. Tell them to use the information within the paragraph for the revision. Allow a volunteer to read his paragraph aloud. Ask for comments on the revision from other students.

Teaching Strategy

Discussion and Modeling

Display a list of related ideas. Instruct students to suggest ways of grouping the ideas into both a topic outline and a sentence outline. Respond to the students' answers and offer suggestions as needed. Display both models. Then display a second list of related ideas and direct each student to formulate a topic or sentence outline of the second group of ideas. Using the student outlines, ask the students to discuss the advantages or disadvantages of topic and sentence outlines.

Popcorn

- I. Ways to prepare popcorn
  - A. Air popper
  - B. Microwave
  - C. Oil popper
- II. Varieties of popcorn
  - A. Regular
    - 1. Low fat
    - 2. Extra butter
    - 3. Low sodium
  - B. Caramel
  - C. Cheddar cheese
- III. Uses for popcorn
  - A. Popcorn balls
  - B. Healthful snack
  - C. Stay-awake mechanism
  - D. Holiday decorations

In a **sentence outline,** every point is a complete sentence.

European Palaces

- I. Royalty built many of the European palaces.
  - A. After Maria Theresa established her residence at Schönbrunn, she added many of the 1,440 rooms in existence today.
  - B. Louis XIV built Versailles, the largest palace in Europe.
  - C. King Ludwig II of Bavaria built many fancy and extravagant castles; his most famous is Neuschwanstein.
  - D. The Duke of Buckingham built the original Buckingham House; George IV commissioned a new palace to be built around the old Buckingham House.
- II. Some original palaces were more than a monarch's official residence.
  - A. The Schönbrunn location was originally a hunting estate.
  - B. Versailles, originally a hunting lodge, was Louis XIV's escape from the rebellious people of Paris.
  - C. Neuschwanstein was Ludwig's place to escape reality.
- III. European palaces displayed various artistic accents.
  - A. Most palace areas have beautifully landscaped gardens.
  - B. Many palaces have unique structural features.
    - 1. Schönbrunn exemplifies Baroque architecture.
    - 2. Versailles is famous for its Hall of Mirrors.
    - 3. Neuschwanstein exhibits a fancy design with multiple turrets.
  - C. Many palaces display beautiful sculptures and priceless paintings.

ONE on ONE Write for display a list of related ideas. Ask your student to suggest ways of grouping the ideas into both a topic outline and a sentence outline. Discuss your student's answers and offer ideas for improvement. Model both outlines. Display a second list of related ideas. Instruct your student to write a topic or sentence outline derived from the second group of ideas. Using your student's outline, ask him to discuss the advantages or disadvantages of topic and sentence outlines.

tip

When writing an outline, remember two things: (1) use the same form consistently and (2) be sure that every *I* has a *II* (and every *A* a *B*, and so on).

1.2 PRACTICE *the skill*

Arrange the following list of topics into an outline with three main points. Group the items logically. One item will be the heading for the outline. *(Answers may vary.)*

pollution of environment	preservation of environment
deserts	rainforests
conservation of environment	trash
endangered wildlife	oceans
environmentalism	acid rain
endangered ecosystems	chemicals

Environmentalism

I. Preservation of Environment

A. Endangered wildlife

B. Endangered ecosystems

II. Conservation of Environment

A. Rainforests

B. Deserts

C. Oceans

III. Pollution of Environment

A. Trash

B. Chemicals

C. Acid rain

Drafting

Once the planning is behind you, it is time to put your thoughts and ideas down. The first draft should never be thought of as a finished work: it is rather a work in progress, a preliminary version. The first draft should be written without overmuch concern for grammar, usage, or punctuation. (Do not forget, however, that the work you do now in these areas will save work later in the revision process.) When beginning your draft, try to sustain your writing long enough to get a sense of flow.

tip

Try writing through an entire point in your outline at one sitting.

Writing Exposition

Much of the writing that you will do, not only for the assignments in this text but also for real-life writing, will be expository writing. **Expository writing** is writing that systematically explains, analyzes, or informs about a subject. Most nonfiction is

TEACHING STRATEGY

Discussion

Prompt a discussion about writing by asking students (1) whether writing has any connection to the real world and (2) what kinds of writing are done in the real world. Encourage students to rid themselves of their negative feelings about writing. Ask them in what way they can consider the writing done for this class as "real-life" writing. *(Academics is a part of real life; therefore, an assignment done for class is "real-life" writing.)*

WritingLink

Ask the students to research the topic from the previous Scriptural Application section. Direct them to choose a mode from page 9, create a topic outline, and write a draft based upon their research. Allow students the opportunity to present their drafts to the class.

expository in nature. Narrative or **creative writing** is writing that is characterized by expressiveness, imagination, and originality. Most fiction is considered creative writing. (Of course, as with any dichotomy, exceptions abound. Some expository writing may be quite imaginative; a piece of creative writing may be very informative.) Creative writing does not follow the same set of "rules" that expository writing usually does. For example, the sonnet that you write in Chapter 10 and the interior monologue that you write in Chapter 4 will probably not follow the methods of paragraph development and organization that we will discuss in this chapter. We will focus mainly on writing exposition since you will likely use it most as you continue your education. The individual creative writing assignments in this book will discuss elements of more imaginative writing.

Mode

Mode is the term given to the form or method of writing that you choose. You will study four basic modes: descriptive, expository, narrative, and persuasive. (**Note:** Two of the terms for the modes overlap with the two types of writing described above. These are standard terms, so you should learn to differentiate between type and mode to avoid confusion.) Your stated topic and purpose will influence the mode you choose for your writing, and each has style and organizational patterns particular to it. As you complete the writing assignments in this book, you will note that every piece of writing will fit into one of these modes. For example, the comparison/contrast essay in Chapter 12 will be written in the expository mode. Chapter 4's interior monologue will be written in narrative mode. Sometimes, several modes will be used within one piece of writing, as with the college application you will write for Chapter 9. Often, writers select the mode (or have it selected for them) at the beginning of the writing process; however, some writers wait to see where their research leads them before deciding on a mode. The following chart shows the four basic modes of writing, the purpose of each mode, and an example taken from the literature pieces in this book.

Mode	Purpose	Example
Descriptive	Describes an object, person, or place	"The Encantadas" by Herman Melville
Expository	Informs about a topic; explains or analyzes a process; defines or classifies a topic	"Piltdown Chicken" by Stephan Caesar
Narrative	Relates a story or an event	Sonnet 34 by William Shakespeare
Persuasive	Persuades readers to take action or to change their position on a topic	"Signs of the Times" by Charlotte K. Frank

This writing and grammar series includes two additional modes: academic and personal. Both could be considered subcategories of the four basic modes listed above but have instead been listed separately because of their importance.

Academic	Focuses on demonstrating a specific academic skill	"A Record of Our Journeys" by Ilana Sibley
Personal	Tells an individual's own thoughts or feelings	excerpt from *By the Light of a Thousand Stars* by Jamie Langston Turner

Teaching Strategy

Modeling

Write the following thesis statements for display. Then ask the students to tell what mode a writer might use to develop each thesis statement.

- The Mafia, both in the present and in the past, has involved itself in large-scale crime. *(expository)*
- Niagara Falls is a beautiful but overpowering sight. *(descriptive or persuasive)*
- For the person who wishes to maintain a consistent aerobic routine, jogging meets the requirements. *(expository, narrative, or persuasive)*
- The conduct of high-school students away from school often reflects their true convictions. *(descriptive, expository, or narrative)*
- Participation in athletic competitions builds character. *(expository)*

Thinking Biblically

Sometimes the most effective place to put the thesis is actually at the end of the argument. The thesis of Judges does not appear until chapter 17. It is then repeated several times throughout the book (17:6; 18:1; 19:1; 21:25), including in the last line. Peter's Pentecost sermon also includes a thesis statement at the end: "Therefore let all the house of Israel know assuredly, that God hath made that same Jesus, whom ye have crucified, both Lord and Christ" (Acts 2:36). Ask your students what impact delayed placement of the thesis has on the rhetorical power of a piece. *(It adds suspense and drama to the argumentation, fitting together nicely with a call to action. It also forestalls objections from a hostile audience [as with Stephen in Acts 7]. However, one of the risks of delaying the thesis is maintaining focus: if the writer does not carefully manage his supporting details, the reader can lose track of the main message of the composition.)*

Thinking Biblically

Even the Bible has thesis statements. Proverbs 1:7 is the thesis of the book: "The fear of the Lord is the beginning of knowledge." Likewise, Romans 1:16–18 can be called the thesis statement of Paul's letter to the church at Rome. To clearly communicate your main idea, state your thesis succinctly in a key place in your composition. Placing the thesis statement toward the beginning of your piece, as Solomon and Paul did in the two examples, can be especially helpful to the reader.

Thesis Statements

In the planning stage you asked yourself *What is my purpose?* Your answer to that question will become the basis of the thrust of your writing. That thrust, or main idea, is called the **thesis statement.** The thesis statement is usually expressed in a single declarative sentence. As the term implies, it makes a statement rather than posing a real or rhetorical question. The thesis statement should also be verifiable. In other words, your point should be something that can be substantiated with evidence. In addition, the thesis may indicate what your approach, point of view, and organizational style will be.

In answering the question *What is my purpose?* about an essay on Creationism, one student came up with the following statement:

> My purpose is to inform people about some of the recent scientific findings that support Creationism.

The student researched her topic and interviewed several Creationist scientists doing current research in the field. She found the topic of an ice age particularly interesting. For example, she found that the effects of the Genesis flood could have caused an ice age to occur. This information led her to write the thesis statement below.

> Although it goes almost unnoticed by the media at large, evolutionists cannot adequately explain the causes of the multiple ice ages they posit.

After looking back over her research and her preliminary topic outline, the student realized that her thesis statement did not adequately communicate the approach or the emphasis of her writing. She also wondered whether her opening dependent clause might be unnecessarily inflammatory or might better fit at the end of her piece. She then revised her thesis to read as follows:

> The Genesis flood provides a probable stimulus for a single Temperate Zone ice age and thereby establishes an upper bound on its duration.

The new thesis statement tells how the Genesis flood relates to the ice age, and, further, it gives the implications of that statement.

Introductions

Writers typically use introductions to accomplish several purposes: to capture reader interest, to introduce a topic, and to draw attention to the main idea, the thesis statement. The introduction may be a complete paragraph (as in a research report or a comparison/contrast essay), or the introduction may be a single sentence (as in an in-class essay). Whatever the length, introductions usually accomplish the purposes mentioned above by employing one (or more) of the following methods:

- analogy
- anecdote
- fact or statistic
- question
- quotation

Teaching Strategy

Discussion

Ask the students what makes the examples of introductions on page 11 so effective. *(Both gain the reader's attention either by introducing the main idea or by posing a thoughtful question.)*

Enrichment

Define the term *in medias res* ("in the middle of things") and discuss its use to begin fictional narrative writing but not expository writing. Point out that most epics begin this way, including *Paradise Lost* by John Milton. (See *British Literature,* BJU Press.)

Teaching Strategy

Participation

Ask the students to bring an article to class. Direct them to identify the topic sentences of several paragraphs in the article but not to mark the topic sentences in any way. Instruct the students to place a mark beside each paragraph that they have analyzed before exchanging the article with another student. Direct the students to identify the topic sentences of the selected paragraphs. Discuss their choices of the topic sentences and whether they agree with each other. Then ask them to identify the placement of the topic sentences. *(beginning, middle, or end)*

One on One Ask your student to collect several articles. Instruct him to identify the topic sentences of several paragraphs. Discuss his choice of topic sentences and ask him to

Read the examples of effective introductions below.

Fact No event could have filled me with greater anxieties than that of which the notification was transmitted by your order, and received on the fourteenth day of the present month. On the one hand, I was summoned by my Country, whose voice I can never hear but with veneration and love, from a retreat which I had chosen. . . . On the other hand, the magnitude and difficulty of the trust to which the voice of my Country called me . . . could not but overwhelm . . . one, who inheriting inferior endowments from nature and unpractised in the duties of civil administration, ought to be peculiarly conscious of his own deficiencies. (The introduction of Washington's inaugural address of 1789)

Anecdote Have you seen the effects of HIV? A local islander who had been saved during his twenties was at thirty-five years of age training at a Bible college and planning to assume the pastorate of the local island church that the missionary had established. While trying to study and fulfill his work responsibilities at school, he began to feel ill. After consultation with several physicians, he was diagnosed with AIDS and died within a year. For sixteen years the virus had been dormant, but eventually HIV ravaged his body. The effects of HIV are not always immediate, but they are always devastating.

It should be noted that not all writers write their introductions first. Sometimes a writer will save his introduction for the end of his drafting process and will save an effective quotation or statistic to use in drawing the reader into his piece.

Paragraph Development

Most writing is composed of a series of **paragraphs,** groups of sentences closely related to one another and to the main idea of the piece. Provided you have well-documented research and a well-organized outline, you should be prepared to draft the body of your paper. Your outline from the planning stage should serve as the basis for your paper: Each paragraph will cover one division of your outline.

Topic Sentences

In academic writing, many of the paragraphs you write will contain topic sentences. A **topic sentence** expresses the main idea of a paragraph in a single sentence. Most often, topic sentences are found at the beginnings of paragraphs; however, they may occur anywhere in the paragraph. An opening topic sentence lays the groundwork for what will come next in the paragraph; an ending topic sentence summarizes or reinforces what was said earlier in the paragraph.

The main points of your outline will become the topic sentences of your paragraphs. Of course, you may need to rework the words and phrases (from a topic outline) into complete sentences or to recast the sentences (from a sentence outline) for appropriate transitional expressions and logic.

ESL

Good writing in your native language may follow different patterns and techniques from the ones described here. For effectiveness, observe and use those patterns and techniques when you write in that language.

When you write in English, do your best to follow the patterns and techniques of English writing. For example, English readers will expect to find your main idea (your thesis) stated at the end of your introductory paragraph. Look for these patterns as you read.

identify their placement within the paragraphs. *(beginning, middle, or end)*

Enrichment

As the students work on their own writing, encourage them to develop relevant topic sentences.

Teaching Strategy

Discussion

Draw students' attention to the difference between a thesis statement and a topic sentence. Point out that the thesis statement governs the entire writing while a topic sentence governs an individual paragraph. Remind students that paragraphs must directly support the paper's thesis.

Teaching Strategy

Modeling

Use the articles from the previous participation activity to analyze paragraph development. After reading and analyzing one or two paragraphs yourself, ask the students to read their articles and analyze the developmental strategy of three or four paragraphs.

ESL Strategy

Instruct students to find the thesis in the second introduction example on page 11. *(the final sentence)* Then ask them to identify the topic sentences in the three paragraphs under the heading "Paragraph Development." *(the first, second, and first sentences respectively)*

1.3 USE *the skill*

Write a good beginning topic sentence for the following paragraph. The sentence should express the main idea of the paragraph and indicate what will be said later about the main idea. *(Answers will vary.)*

Dumas lived in France and wrote several historical romances based on French history. He used many characters that are familiar to us from the study of history, characters such as Louis XIV and other French monarchs. Generally, the characters in his works are somewhat larger than life—men who overcome hundreds of guards to gain their freedom and who perform other amazing and heroic feats. Although these and other characters in his stories did exist, most of the events in Dumas's stories never happened. Despite the inaccuracies of Alexandre Dumas's history, his fiction is well written and has captivated audiences from the 1800s until today. Some of his most popular works are *The Three Musketeers*, *The Man in the Iron Mask*, and *The Count of Monte Cristo*.

Alexandre Dumas was a famous writer of the nineteenth century.

Supporting Sentences

As you move through your outline, write each paragraph so that it develops its topic sentence and supports the overall thesis. **Supporting sentences** develop, or support, the topic sentence. Facts and statistics, details and anecdotes—these are some of the ways writers support topic sentences and build paragraphs. Of course, certain types of writing lend themselves to certain strategies. For example, an issue analysis may be best developed using facts and statistics, whereas a personal response essay may draw on sensory details for paragraph development. The chart below shows the various kinds of developmental strategies for supporting sentences.

Developmental Strategy	Definition
Comparison/Contrast	The similarities and differences between two things
Example	An instance or an event that illustrates a point
Fact	A statement that can be proved
Incident/Anecdote	A brief personal account that illustrates a topic
Quotation	The copied words of another person, usually an expert in the field being discussed
Reasons	The explanation of a truth
Sensory Details	The use of sense words—sight, sound, smell, etc.
Statistic	A fact expressed in numbers
Visual Aid	A graphic or pictorial representation of a fact or statistic

tip

Sometimes a combination of several developmental strategies works best for crafting a particular paragraph.

12 Chapter 1 | The Writing Process

Concluding Sentences

Once you have developed a paragraph with a topic sentence and supporting sentences, you are ready to write a **concluding sentence.** If the paragraph is to stand alone (or if it ends a multiparagraph essay), the concluding sentence should summarize your main idea, give a solution to a problem addressed in your paragraph, ask a question of the audience, or make a prediction about an outcome. If the paragraph is to be followed by another paragraph, the concluding sentence should tie the ideas in the paragraph together and provide a transition to the next paragraph. The purpose and the mode of writing you chose to use determine whether your conclusion will describe (descriptive), explain (expository), persuade (persuasive), or relate a story (narrative).

1.4 PRACTICE *the skill*

Identify the type of paragraph development the author used in the following paragraph.

An essential element in maintaining teamwork is trust. Members of a team must trust one another in order to accomplish their goals or assignments successfully. One type of team that particularly needs this element of trust is the military team. Soldiers must be able to trust those with whom they work and fight. They must especially be able to trust their commander, the person who gives them instructions and to whom they must be completely obedient. The commander of a military group makes the final call in every decision. It is he who decides when to wait and when to advance into battle. The soldiers under his command must trust him, or they may hesitate in obeying him. They must be convinced that he has the skills and knowledge to lead them in the right course. Trust is essential for the success of our military.

example

1.5 REVIEW *the skill*

Identify the type of paragraph development the author used in the following paragraph.

For the businessperson who works in New York City, the resident who shops in the city, or the tourist who visits the city, the New York subway system, also called the train system, provides the most efficient means of transportation. Scattered throughout the five boroughs of the city are 468 train stations. In many cases these stations are easily accessible to the five million who commute daily on the trains. Traveling by train eliminates several problems that would be associated with driving a car: commuters avoid bumper-to-bumper traffic, a high risk of accidents on crowded streets, and increased stress levels before the workday begins. The daily commuter can purchase a Metrocard that is both cost-effective and convenient, and the commuter can travel as far as thirty-eight miles one way into the city. The system provides clean stations, well-maintained cars, and safe surroundings for those who choose to commute by train. Certainly, the subway system provides the most efficient means of transportation in and out of New York City.

facts or reasons

The Writing Process | Chapter 1 13

1.6 USE *the skill*

Write an appropriate concluding sentence for the following paragraph. *(Answers will vary.)*

It was dark outside, and rain fell in icy torrents. Inside, the three children sat around their grandfather, the only light in the room coming from an old lantern that sat on the rough, wooden table. The children were captivated by his every word as his low voice poured out tales of pirates, treasure, and the sea. They were certain they could hear the sound of the rough wind hurling the surf against the rocks. Though it was cold and wet outside and in their imaginations, inside it was warm and dry, and one by one the children's eyes began to droop. With gentle hands, the grandfather carried them up to their beds and tucked them in.

Each child sailed quietly off into his own dreamy world filled with high-seas adventure.

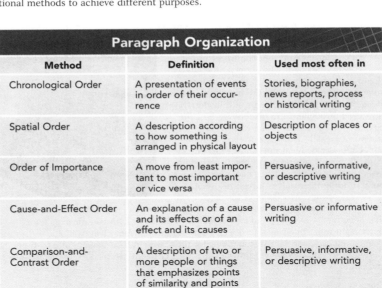

Paragraph Organization

Organizing your ideas within a paragraph is much like organizing your entire paper. You must decide how best to accomplish your purpose using the information that you have gathered. Obviously, certain types of writing lend themselves best to certain organizational methods. For example, news stories most often use chronological order to depict events in the order of their occurrence. The chart below lists the five major methods of paragraph organization as well as the types of writing in which the various methods are used.

Note how the following examples use different organizational methods to achieve different purposes.

Paragraph Organization

Method	Definition	Used most often in
Chronological Order	A presentation of events in order of their occurrence	Stories, biographies, news reports, process or historical writing
Spatial Order	A description according to how something is arranged in physical layout	Description of places or objects
Order of Importance	A move from least important to most important or vice versa	Persuasive, informative, or descriptive writing
Cause-and-Effect Order	An explanation of a cause and its effects or of an effect and its causes	Persuasive or informative writing
Comparison-and-Contrast Order	A description of two or more people or things that emphasizes points of similarity and points of difference	Persuasive, informative, or descriptive writing

14 Chapter 1 | The Writing Process

Chronological Order

One of the most common ordering techniques for writing both expository and creative pieces is chronological order. Writers use words and phrases such as *earlier, not long after,* and *later that afternoon* to indicate that events are being presented in the order of their occurrence. The following paragraph uses chronological order:

> The military career of Colin Powell reveals determination and success. After he graduated from New York City College in 1958, Powell received a commission as an army second lieutenant. He served in Vietnam from 1962 to 1963 and again from 1968 to 1969. Powell received numerous military decorations and civilian awards, including honorary knighthood from the queen of England. Not long after, in 1973, Powell served as battalion commander in Korea. During the interim years from 1974 to 1987, Colin Powell served as a commander in Europe and on bases in the United States. Late in 1987 he became the Assistant to the President for National Security Affairs. In 1989, prior to the first Gulf War, he accepted the appointment as the Chairman of the Joint Chiefs of Staff. Following his retirement from the military in 1993, Colin Powell served as Secretary of State from 2001 to 2004. In his role as chief foreign affairs officer, Powell again worked closely with military leaders.

A variation of the chronological order technique is called flashback. In **flashback**, a writer inserts events out of sequence in order to recall a past event in the middle of narration. The following paragraph uses flashback to tell of Rudi's remembrance of his mother.

> His eyes [Rudi's eyes] eventually came to rest on one cathedral. He then thought back to the first moment he had noticed it. It was on his seventh birthday, the day that he received his mother's first letter. When Rudi's mother had found out that she was dying, Rudi was too young to store up memories of her. So she had decided to write as many letters to him as she could. He had already received five of the seven that she had completed.
> (From *A Father's Promise* by Donnalynn Hess)

Spatial Order

Sometimes a writer wants a reader to visualize the layout of a room or the placement of objects. When such a description is needed, one should write from a single point of view to prevent reader confusion. That single point of view may be from left to right or right to left, top to bottom or bottom to top, or some other system that gives the reader a logical order to follow as he attempts to visualize what the writer is describing.

> The young pastor walked through the center double doors that led into the auditorium. Before him stretched a blue-carpeted aisle that led to the platform where the white wooden pulpit stood. On the left side of the platform was a grand piano and to the right was a large electric organ. Several feet behind the pulpit, forty-eight blue upholstered chairs filled the choir chancel. His eyes looked beyond the chancel to the baptismal pool. The young pastor then observed the rest of the room. On either side of the auditorium were matching stained glass windows that allowed some sunlight to brighten the room. Overhead, track lights and chandeliers provided more light. Twenty rows of white wooden pews with blue upholstered seats were grouped in four sections across the auditorium. As the young pastor assimilated what he saw, he prayed that he would be able to minister to those who would sit in this auditorium.

Enrichment

Encourage the students to read further about Colin Powell and his services to the United States. Ask interested students to present what they learned. Discuss the types of paragraph organization that could be used to convey this information.

Order of Importance

Moving from most important information to least important information (or vice versa) is called order-of-importance writing. Journalists hoping to relay information to readers who have only enough time to scan daily headlines and one or two opening sentences move from most important facts to least important facts (often called the inverted pyramid). Other writers build a case by moving to increasingly important points, building support as they go, thus moving the reader to action. Order-of-importance writing uses terms such as *first, most important,* and *last* to signal what is important to the author.

> In the 1760s and 1770s the emergence of the term *American* reflected a spirit of nationalism among the colonists. One important factor that contributed to an independent spirit was the geographic separation from the Old World. The colonists had to defend themselves; thus they learned self-reliance and independence. In addition to the separation, settlers had the opportunity to own property in this New World, something they had not been able to do in their homeland. Another factor contributing to the development of an American spirit was the diverse backgrounds of the settlers. They had to learn to live together and to blend their cultures. While all of these factors were important, one of the most important influences in the development of nationalism was strong self-government. The colonists were determined to make their own laws, and strong political leaders emerged. These newly named Americans possessed confidence in their role in the New World.

Cause-and-Effect Order

Some writers organize their writing according to a cause-and-effect relationship. Causes and effects create a chain of events: a cause leads to an effect, and then that effect becomes the cause leading to another effect, and so on. For example, neglecting to apply sunscreen can lead to sunburn, which could lead to sun poisoning or even skin cancer. Of course, one cause could have multiple effects: not getting enough sleep might affect your motor skills, your thinking skills, and your general health. The reverse could also be true; that is, one effect could have multiple causes.

> Upon reflection, Charisse discovered that her less-than-desirable chemistry test score resulted from of a variety of causes. During the week before the test, she had missed an important chapter review lesson because of her basketball tournament; she had failed to seek out a study partner or to obtain a copy of the review worksheet. Then, because her tournament game marked the end of a successful basketball season, Charisse celebrated with her teammates by eating all the pizza, sweets, and sodas they had avoided during the sports season. To make matters worse, she tried to compensate for her junk food binge by not eating breakfast the morning of her test. Besides, she felt too exhausted to eat because she had not slept well the night before. While turning in her chemistry test, Charisse realized she had failed to pray for wisdom in preparing for and in taking the test. A lack of academic, physical, and spiritual preparation for her chemistry test resulted in Charisse's poor performance.

Comparison and Contrast pp. 61–63, 66

Comparison-and-Contrast Order

To show similarities and/or differences between two things, writers use comparison-and-contrast order. In this type of order, two arrangements are possible: the block and the point-by-point arrangement. In **block arrangement** the author

16 Chapter 1 | The Writing Process

devotes one paragraph to the characteristics of one item being compared and another paragraph to the characteristics of the second item. **Point-by-point arrangement** makes statements about one item and immediately follows them with statements about the second item—within the same paragraph. The paragraph below shows point-by-point arrangement.

Hotels and motels evidence certain similarities as well as differences. Both provide overnight lodging for travelers. Both target business travelers as well as families. And both may be found in bustling cities and near airports. On the other hand, the word *motel,* a combination of the words *motor* and *hotel,* explains one key difference between these types of accommodations. Motels were first founded in the 1940s and 1950s to meet the lodging needs of American families traversing the new national highway system. Motels therefore have traditionally sought to provide budget lodging with convenient access to parking lots and interstate highways. Hotels, however, with their valet services, on-site restaurants, and conference rooms, appeal to a different clientele. Patrons of hotels can expect a more resortlike atmosphere: services such as complimentary toiletries, room service, and activities for children help the patrons justify spending the extra money required for a hotel stay. As motels and hotels vie for customers, they both tend to offer such amenities as swimming pools and continental breakfasts. How interesting it then appears when these similar yet different institutions try to attract new patrons by advertising to each other's customers!

Note that the paragraph includes terms such as *on the other hand, however, likewise, in the same way,* and so on. Words and phrases like these can tell the reader whether a similarity or a difference is being presented.

1.7 PRACTICE *the skill*

Underline the words or phrases that indicate the type of order used for the following paragraph. In the blank write the type of paragraph organization used.

Although rice is a staple food eaten in almost every country of the world, some people are not aware that white rice and brown rice are different. White rice, the most common type of rice, is milled and polished to produce the shiny white layer. During the milling process the hull or husk is removed. The core is primarily carbohydrate with a lower fiber and oil content. White rice is not a highly nutritious food; therefore, white rice is often enriched to heighten its nutritional value. Brown rice, on the other hand, is the least favorite of the rice varieties. Brown rice is not milled and retains its darker color. The hull or husk has a bran layer of minerals and complex carbohydrates such as fiber and oil. It is not necessary to enrich brown rice since it is a naturally nutritious food. Despite the differences of the varieties, rice remains a food staple for millions of people.

comparison-and-contrast (block arrangement)

The Writing Process | Chapter 1 17

1.8 REVIEW *the skill*

Underline the words or phrases that indicate the type of order. In the blank write the type of paragraph organization used in the following paragraph.

Judges 7 presents Gideon's preparation for battle against the Midianites. God spoke to Gideon and told him that thirty-two thousand men were too many for the army and that Gideon needed to reduce the number of soldiers. First, Gideon told the people that those who were fearful should leave. At this point twenty-two thousand men left the army. Second, Gideon brought the army to water. God commanded that those who knelt down on their knees to drink should not be part of the army, but those who lapped the water from their hands would remain. Gideon retained an army of three hundred men. Next, Gideon divided the three hundred men into three companies and gave each man a trumpet for his right hand and a pitcher containing a lamp for his left hand. When Gideon gave the signal, the men blew their trumpets, broke their pitchers, held their lamps in the air, and cried, "The sword of the Lord, and of Gideon." The Midianites fled from the presence of the army, and God gave the army of three hundred the victory.

chronological order ____________

1.9 USE *the skill*

Write a paragraph using one of the types of paragraph organization discussed in this chapter. Then identify the type of organization you used. Be prepared to explain your reasons for selecting the type of organization you did. *(Answers will vary.)*

____

____

____

____

____

____

____

____

____

____

____

Reinforcement

After the students have completed Use the Skill 1.9, assign writing partners to evaluate the paragraph organization. Tell students to be prepared to explain their answers, particularly if their answers differ from their partners' answers. You may choose to arrange the partners to avoid having close friends work together or having students with the same writing problems work together.

One on One

After your student has completed Use the Skill 1.9, discuss with him his reasons for choosing the specific type of organization.

Teaching Strategy

Discussion and Analysis

Materials

- excerpts from the conclusions of several literary works

After introducing each literary work's theme and objective, read the selected conclusions aloud. Ask for comments on whether the conclusions are effective. Determine whether the conclusions reflect the purpose of each writer.

Conclusions

Strong conclusions are critical to the success of any piece of writing. A conclusion should pull together all of the ideas presented and give the reader a sense of closure on the topic. Several methods for conclusions are listed below.

- call to action
- prediction
- question
- quotation/anecdote
- restatement of thesis
- summary

> Each day the sick and shut-in senior citizens in your community face needless hardships in preparing their own meals. Tasks such as cutting, measuring, and cooking basic ingredients present insurmountable odds for hands crippled with arthritis, eyes dimmed by cataracts, and legs unaccustomed to standing independently. But you can help. Many senior citizens in your community would benefit from an hour or two of your time each week. By agreeing to deliver hot, nutritious meals to these individuals, you can join a community-wide network of people dedicated to strengthening and supporting our community. Won't you invest a few hours each week in serving others by helping our senior citizens maintain the quality of life they enjoy?

In the paragraph above, a call to action concludes a discussion about sick and shut-in senior citizens and their need for hot, nutritious meals. Note how the writer appealed to the reader by employing visual imagery, personal pronouns, and rhetorical questioning. Of course, the purpose of your piece will determine how you conclude your composition.

Writing Essays

Having studied the modes of writing and paragraph development and organization, we turn our attention to the essay form. An **essay** is a composition usually of several paragraphs, all of which deal with the same idea. Similar in form to an individual paragraph, the essay usually contains three parts: introduction, body, and conclusion. A thesis proposes the main idea of the piece and generally appears at the end of the introduction (the major exception being the in-class essay, studied later). Supporting paragraphs develop the thesis statement, and the concluding paragraph unifies the essay, often by a restatement of the thesis.

As you further your academic career this year and in college, you will most likely encounter several types of essay, the most common being the three- and five-paragraph essays and the in-class essay (which you will write in Chapter 7). The form for each type of essay is similar, with the body paragraphs expanding from one to three paragraphs and the introduction and conclusions ranging from a single sentence (in the in-class essay) to a full paragraph (in the three- and five-paragraph essays). In the three-paragraph essay, each part consists of one paragraph: introductory paragraph, body paragraph, and concluding paragraph. In the five-paragraph essay, the body of the piece is expanded to three paragraphs.

Essay Writing
pp. 29–34, 61–68, 109–15, 173–77, 221–25, 291–95

The **in-class essay,** which you will use often in your academic career, may consist of several paragraphs or, sometimes, a single paragraph. In traditional in-class essay form, the thesis and the concluding statements become the first and last sentences of the essay. The thesis begins the first paragraph of the essay, which is followed immediately by the first topic sentence and then the supporting sentences. If the essay consists of multiple paragraphs, the first sentence of each subsequent paragraph is a topic sentence. The conclusion follows the last supporting sentence in the last paragraph. The following example is of a one-paragraph in-class essay.

Teaching Strategy
Participation

Present the students with a question or statement and direct them to write an in-class essay. After they have finished, ask for volunteers to read their essays. Use these student examples to discuss the number of paragraphs needed to write about a topic and the placement of the thesis statement and topic sentences in the paragraphs.

ONE on ONE

Present your student with a question or statement and direct him to write an in-class essay. After he has finished, discuss the number of paragraphs he needed to write about the topic and the placement of the thesis statement and topic sentences in the paragraphs.

Teaching Strategy
Demonstration

Use Teaching Help 1 (Teacher's Toolkit) to demonstrate the form of a five-paragraph essay. Ask students to identify the thesis statement, the topic sentences of each supporting paragraph, and the restated thesis. Then discuss the types of paragraph development and organization evident in the essay.

Some students might avoid revision because they associate it with failure. Avoid identifying their writing as wrong. Rather, impress upon the students that revision is an ongoing process of improving their ideas, organization, and sentence structure. Correction is a part of the revision process.

In Tennyson's "The Lady of Shalott," the mirror into which the isolated woman continually gazes symbolizes her idealized view of life. Daily she weaves and watches the outside world from her island tower, and, while peering into her mirror, she surveys an enchanting cross section of life. Such brilliant and enchanting reflections cause the Lady of Shalott to yearn for life outside of her ivory tower. She cries, "I am half sick of shadows" and takes matters into her own hands. Upon her decision to forsake her dream world, the mirror cracks "from side to side," and the lady senses a deep sense of foreboding. With the mirror ruined, the lady's idealism goes too, leaving a harsh view of life and ultimately leading to tragedy for the Lady of Shalott.

Revising

Thomas Jefferson once wrote, "No [style] of writing is so delightful as that which is all pith, which never omits a necessary word, nor uses an unnecessary one." But few writers compose a perfect draft on the first attempt. Revision is the writer's opportunity to make his writing a delight to read.

The revision stage may well be the most important stage in the writing process. No doubt you did some minor revising—crossing out words, leaving gaps—as you wrote. Now is your chance to look again at the goals you set for yourself in the planning stage: Have you accomplished your purpose for writing? Remember that even professional writers revise—deleting large portions of text or moving paragraphs around. Some writers work directly at the keyboard; others prefer to work from the printed page. However you choose to revise, consider three main areas: ideas, style, and correctness.

Revising for Ideas

Revising for ideas requires that you rethink certain aspects of your paper. The following chart summarizes four specific areas that you need to consider as you revise.

Areas to Consider	Actions to Take
Clarity of Purpose Is your purpose clear from your topic sentence or thesis statement?	Focus on the main idea; eliminate irrelevant information. Check organization.
Interest Does the beginning grab the reader's attention? Do details throughout the piece make the reader want to continue reading?	Change the beginning. Use an interesting fact, question, or anecdote that will interest your audience.
Unity of Ideas Is everything included that needs to be included? Is there anything unnecessary in the piece?	Rewrite or eliminate sentences that do not relate to the topic of the paragraph.
Coherence Is the relationship among ideas, sentences, and paragraphs obvious and logical?	Include transitional expressions to link the various parts of the paper together.

The following paragraphs show how careful revision corrects problems of clarity, interest, unity, and coherence.

20 Chapter 1 | The Writing Process

First Draft

Numerous psychology books discuss color preferences. There are personality tests based on color preferences. Are such tests reliable? Color psychologists generally ascribe outgoing, adventurous, and competitive personalities to those who prefer bold, bright colors. Do these generalizations apply to you? Of course, colors are frequently classified into two broad groups, warm and cool colors. People who prefer softer tones are more likely to exhibit quieter, gentler personas. What about someone whose favorite color is black or white? People from various backgrounds and experiences will gravitate to certain colors and be repelled by others. Color psychology proves an interesting field of study.

Writer's Toolbox

Second Draft

What do color preferences say about people? Some psychologists actually use personality tests based on color preferences. These color psychologists have generally observed that outgoing, adventurous, and competitive people prefer bold, bright colors. Conversely, people who prefer softer tones are more likely to exhibit quieter, gentler personas. While considering such assumptions, one should remember that people from various backgrounds and experiences will gravitate to certain colors and be repelled by others. Therefore, color psychology, although interesting, provides only broad generalizations in analyzing personality types.

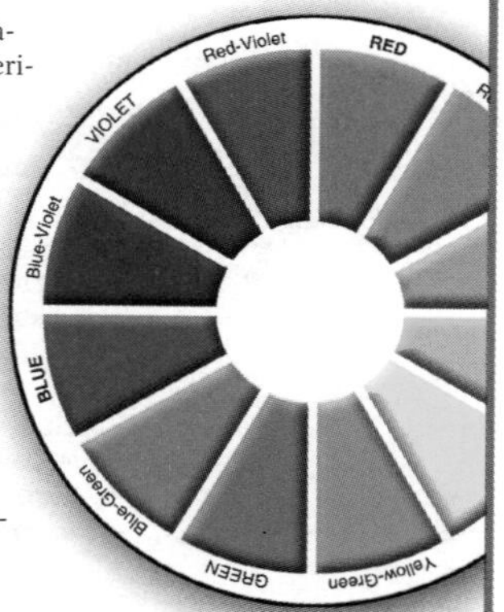

1.10 USE *the skill*

Revise the following paragraph using the checklist on page 20. *(Answers will vary.)*

In the United States photography has been used for many things through the years. Photography began in the early eighteenth century in Europe with the creation of a photosensitive compound. Almost one hundred years later the idea of a photo studio became reality in Paris. In the United States photography was not popularized until the second half of the nineteenth century. The Civil War was the first major war to be photographed. This fact has contributed greatly to historians' knowledge. There were some seven thousand negatives of the Civil War. Shortly after the Civil War, photographers made their way west to document the expansion of the West. Since that time, photography has grown into a major art form, providing a historic treasure trove. Photographs were taken when mankind fought two great world wars and when man walked in space and landed on the moon. Photography enabled man to capture moments in time on film, preserved for generations.

Since the middle of the nineteenth century, photography has been a valuable tool in recording the history of the United States. Although photography was introduced in Europe in the early nineteenth century, it was not popular in the United States until the time of the Civil War. Photographers produced over seven thousand negatives to document the war. Their work has enhanced historians' knowledge of the Civil War era. Shortly after the Civil War, photographers documented the western expansion. Through the years photography has become a major art form as well as a means of historic documentation. Photographers have documented two great world wars, man's walk in space, and man's landing on the moon. Photography has enabled man to capture moments on film for future generations.

Teaching Strategy

Modeling

Direct the students to read the first and second drafts on page 21. Ask them to identify the revisions and group them according to clarity, interest, unity, and coherence. Answers will vary but should include some of the following ideas:

- **Clarity:** The revised second sentence beginning *Some psychologists* is more direct than the original sentence beginning with the expletive *There*.
- **Interest:** The question format of the revised first sentence creates interest in the topic.
- **Unity:** Eliminating unnecessary information, such as a reference to *black* and *white* colors, keeps the focus on the main ideas.
- **Coherence:** Using the transitional word *Conversely* indicates a change of subject and gives coherence to the paragraph. Using the transitional word *Therefore* draws attention to the concluding idea of the paragraph.

Reinforcement

After the students complete Use the Skill 1.10, ask them to exchange papers and to use the checklist on page 20 to evaluate a peer's paragraph.

ONE *on* ONE Use the checklist on page 20 to evaluate your student's paragraph. Then discuss the evaluation with your student.

Individual conferences with students will provide you with the opportunity to focus on specific writing needs. Encourage students to bring any materials that they have accumulated during the planning stage, as well as the writing sample, to the conference.

Revising for Style

As you read the literature pieces that open the chapters in this book, you will find that good writers use emphasis to make certain messages more noticeable to the reader. Manipulating sentence length, type, and structure affects what stands out to a reader and therefore what a reader finds important. Specific, concise words as well as natural expression also influence how a reader interprets a piece of writing. The chart below lists problems and solutions for common stylistic errors. Use these troubleshooting tips as you revise your own writing for style.

Emphasis and Energy pp. 355–69

Areas to Consider	Actions to Take
Emphasis Are the important ideas central or emphasized? Do wrong or unimportant ideas stand out?	Place important ideas at the beginning or end of sentences. (The end is the strongest position in a sentence or paragraph.)
Precise Words Have you chosen nouns and verbs that are imprecise or general? *(The asparagus was not good.)*	Choose specific words. Your thesaurus contains precise words. *(The asparagus was tasteless.)*
Conciseness Is your writing redundant? Are there too many cumbersome dependent clauses?	Use fewer words. Reduce dependent clauses to shorter, simpler phrases.
Smoothness Does your writing contain awkward or rough parts?	Rewrite using language that sounds natural.
Fresh Words Is your writing full of overused words and phrases?	Replace clichéd words and phrases with new comparisons.

1.11 REVIEW *the skill*

Rewrite the following paragraph, correcting any problems of emphasis, precision, conciseness, smoothness, and word choice. *(Answers will vary.)*

Finding a job can often be a real hassle. Sometimes the only jobs available are the ones that not many people want to do. There is definitely an art to finding jobs. You have to be nice to the person interviewing you, and you have to have a good handshake. Otherwise he might not hire you, and if he doesn't hire you, you'll have to work somewhere else. Sometimes people can get good jobs, even though they're only in high school, but other times, they can't. Popular jobs for high schoolers are things like working at grocery stores and restaurants and things like that. The discipline and experience can't hurt even if you aren't pulling down big bucks.

Finding a job can often be difficult for a high school student.
Because many employers are looking for experienced workers,
a high school student will need to convince the employer of
his ability to do the work. To increase the chance of being

Teaching Strategy
Motivation

Read the opening phrase of Franklin D. Roosevelt's original text from his speech to Congress in December 1941: "Yesterday, December 7, 1941, a date which will live in world history." Before delivering the speech to Congress, Roosevelt changed the opening statement to read "Yesterday, December 7, 1941—a date which will live in infamy." Call attention to Roosevelt's choice of words. Read this sentence from the original text: "This reply contained a statement that diplomatic negotiations must be considered at an end, but contained no threat and no hint of an armed attack." Now read Roosevelt's edited sentence: "While this reply stated that it seemed useless to continue the existing diplomatic negotiations, it contained no threat or hint of war or armed attack." Discuss with the students the need to revise for ideas and style.

History Link

Encourage students to investigate the writing and editing skills of President Franklin D. Roosevelt.

Teaching Strategy
Participation

Elicit students' suggestions about style problems in Review the Skill 1.11 before assigning the revision paragraph.

hired, a teenager should try to meet the expectations of prospective employers. His appearance should be neat and professional, and his manners should be polite. He should greet the interviewer with a firm handshake. Even if the job is offered to a more experienced applicant, the experience of applying and interviewing will help the student prepare for the next job opportunity. The discipline and experience of seeking a job can be invaluable in the future.

Revising for Correctness: Proofreading

Proofreading is the final step in the revision process. As you revise for correctness, you will have the opportunity to rid your paper of grammatical and mechanical errors. The chart below presents areas for consideration as you look for specific problems.

Areas to Consider	Actions to Take
Sentence Structure Does your paper contain sentence errors?	Correct comma splices, fused sentences, and all nonstylistic fragments.
Usage Do any subjects and verbs or pronouns and antecedents disagree? Have you used correct pronoun case and reference?	Correct usage problems and agreement—both subject-verb and pronoun-antecedent agreement.
Spelling, Punctuation, Capitalization Do you have any spelling errors? Are sentences punctuated and capitalized correctly?	Use both your computer's spell checker and your own check for spelling errors. Correct punctuation and capitalization errors.

Proofreading skills must be developed. Even professional proofreaders miss errors in the first read-through. The chart of strategies below gives ideas for becoming a better proofreader.

Proofreading Strategies
Read a piece several times. No one finds every error the first time he reads a piece. Read yours three or more times through.
Read slowly. Consider using a blank sheet of paper to cover what you have not read yet so that it does not distract you.
Read aloud. Your ear may hear an error that your eye missed.
Read backwards. This strategy forces you to look at words individually.
Read specifically. Look for a specific error on each read-through. For example, read through once looking only for spelling errors.

Scriptural Application

Remind the students that the Bible contains many verses about words, both positive and negative aspects. Read Psalm 19:14: "Let the words of my mouth, and the meditation of my heart, be acceptable in thy sight, O Lord, my strength, and my redeemer." And Jesus said, "Out of the abundance of the heart the mouth speaketh" (Matt. 12:34). The words that students write on paper are a reflection of the meditations of their heart.

Teaching Strategy

Motivation

Encourage students to compile a list of items to watch for when proofreading and to keep this list with them as they revise.

Teaching Strategy

Discussion

Ask students to share proven proofreading strategies that they have used. Discuss which strategies on page 23 work best.

Use careful proofreading to make your paper the best it can be. After all, the results affect not only your grade but also your effectiveness and your audience's impression of you.

Publishing

After drafting and revising your work, you are ready for the last step in the writing process. **Publishing** is the act of sharing your work with others: fellow students, teachers, friends, or the public at large. In the publishing stage, you may submit your work to someone who will put it in print in a medium such as a periodical or newspaper. More often perhaps, you will publish by allowing someone else to read your work, or you may read it aloud to a group. In any case, you must choose a title and make a neat final copy before you publish in any form.

Choosing a Title

Title selection may affect your reader more than any other writing decision you make. The title of an academic paper, one written primarily for school or for submission to a scholarly publication, should suggest to the reader the subject as well as the approach of the paper (such as "A Dialogue Concerning Heresies and Matters of Religion" by Sir Thomas More). "Signs of the Times," the title of Charlotte K. Frank's persuasive article on the decay of spelling as seen in modern signage, is a clever play on a well-known phrase. Such titles are often appropriate for informal expository writing.

Titles for creative writing assignments differ somewhat from those for academic ones. Creative titles often name the subject directly (as with George Eliot's *Silas Marner*); other titles may merely suggest a topic, prompting the reader to wonder what the title could mean (as with Jamie Langston Turner's *By the Light of a Thousand Stars*).

tip

Titles for academic papers may need to be longer than those for creative works since the writer must give more advance information to the reader.

Making a Neat Copy

Out of respect for your reader, your published work should be as nearly perfect as you can make it. From a technical standpoint no handwritten corrections are acceptable: reprint a single page or the whole piece if need be. For all submissions, pay attention to the accuracy of bibliographic information, margins, and spacing as well as to title page requirements.

For pieces submitted for outside publication, acquaint yourself with the publication guidelines of the journal, newspaper, or magazine to which you are submitting. Follow the guidelines exactly. Not only does this carefulness show respect for the publisher, but it also gives you a better chance of being published, since most publishers immediately reject any piece that does not meet their submission requirements.

REINFORCEMENT
Use Bulletin Board 1 (Teacher's Toolkit) to remind students of the steps in publishing.

1.12 USE *the skill*

Write an appropriate title for each of the paragraphs below. The first is a creative paragraph, and the second is an academic one. Make sure that each title fits the description for a good title as given above. *(Answers will vary.)*

The angry mob surged toward the platform, every face twisted with livid rage and hatred. The multitude of voices rose and combined into one thunderous cry, "Crucify him!" Soldiers stood on either side of the drooping figure that stood before the throng of people. The Roman governor Pilate stood beside Christ and offered a choice to the people. "Will you have me release the King of the Jews?" As he said this, several voices cried out, their voices dripping with hatred, "Release unto us Barabbas!" The crowd took up the cry and began chanting it over and over again, the sound of it like the ocean hurling itself furiously against a rocky shore. "What will you have me do with the King of the Jews?" shouted Pilate over the noise of the people. Before his words had died away, they were drowned in cries of "Crucify him!"

"Crucify him!"

In this paragraph the pronoun *him* is not capitalized in the expression *"Crucify him!"* in order to indicate that those who called for Jesus' crucifixion did not recognize His deity.

Matthew, Mark, Luke and John present four separate accounts of the trial and crucifixion of Christ. Although each Gospel presents a different perspective, each recounts the major events accurately as they appear in the other Gospels, the four together providing a perfect portrayal of the Passion of Christ. This lack of discrepancies among the Gospel accounts reminds us that our Bible is infallible and inerrant. Both together and separately, the Gospels provide us with a vivid picture of the sufferings of our God for His people. The true believer cannot help being stirred as he reads of Christ's sufferings that sinners might be saved from the wrath to come.

The Believer and the Gospels

EVALUATION

Discuss students' answers to Use the Skill 1.12. Allow the students to compare their answers to their peers' responses.

ONE on ONE Compare your student's answers to Use the Skill 1.12 with your answers. Discuss the pros and cons of both sets of answers.

HISTORY OF THE ENGLISH LANGUAGE

Thinking Biblically

The KJV is a good example of language change because it is probably familiar to your students. The following verses demonstrate language change: The first example illustrates change in word meaning alone. The second example illustrates change in both word meaning and grammatical function.

"And when they wanted wine, the mother of Jesus saith unto him, They have no wine" (John 2:3). The early seventeenth-century translators used the word *wanted* here, whereas we would be more likely to use the word *lacked*—or simply to say that the wine "ran out." Today, a person reading that the wedding hosts "wanted" wine would probably think Mary meant they "desired" wine. One preacher of the prosperity gospel, in fact, told his international television audience that this verse means Jesus desires to give you not just what you need but whatever you want!

"Fret not thyself in any wise to do evil" (Ps. 37:8). "Fret not thyself" in 1611 meant something like "to chafe away at one's heart until it is devoured."[1] *Fret* is not often used as a transitive verb today, however. "In any wise" in 1611 meant "in any way." This expression has dropped out of use in contemporary English. The verse is saying that worry tends toward evil. But the English language has changed enough over the centuries that this sentence is almost wholly obscure without a good dictionary.

1. *Oxford English Dictionary*, s.v. "fret," accessed November 5, 2012, http://www.oed.com/view/Entry/74560?rskey=wDi39Z&result=8#eid.

Thinking Biblically

The King James Version was translated between 1607 and 1611. (It was updated in 1769.) No one alive today speaks or writes English in quite the same way the King James translators did, but the KJV definitely belongs to the Modern English period. (If you try to read English from 100 years before the KJV, you will find it very difficult if not impossible.) English has changed even in the modern period, however, and some words now mean the opposite of what they did in 1611. One well-known example is "he who now letteth" (2 Thess. 2:7), which then meant "he who now restrains" and now means "he who now allows." Can you think of any more examples of how language has changed since the King James Version?

Language Differences

Have you ever wondered why there are so many languages and just how many languages there are? Actually, no one knows for sure how many languages exist, partly because some areas of the world are still not very well known. Careful surveys are needed to determine whether certain people speak dialects of the same language or separate languages. We estimate that at least five or six thousand languages are spoken today. Below, John 1:1 is given in a few of these languages, as well as some languages of earlier centuries. Example 3.3 is in Early Modern English, the language of the King James Version of the Bible. The languages are in groups as shown by their first numbers—with all of the languages originating from the same language having the same first number and a different second number: 1.1, 1.2; 2.1, 2.2, 2.3, and so on. Notice what is the same and what is different in each group of languages. (Try to pick out the words for *God* and for *Word* in the verses.)

John 1:1

1.1 Original Greek

En archē ēn ho logos, kai ho logos ēn pros ton theon, kai theos ēn ho logos.

1.2 Modern Greek translation

En archē ēto ho Logos, kai ho Logos ēto para tō theō, kai theos ēto ho Logos.

2.1 Latin translation

In principio erat Verbum, et Verbum erat apud Deum, et Deus erat Verbum.

2.2 Spanish translation

En el principio era el Verbo, y el Verbo era con Dios, y el Verbo era Dios.

2.3 Portuguese translation

No principio era o Verbo, e o Verbo estava com Deus, e o Verbo era Deus.

2.4 French translation

Au commencement était le Verbe; et le Verbe était avec Dieu; et le Verbe était Dieu.

3.1 Old English (Anglo-Saxon) translation

On frymthe wæs Word, and thæt Word wæs mid Gode, and God wæs thæt Word.

Teaching Strategy
Discussion

Explain that people today still derive meaning from older written texts because language is stable enough to support meaning over many years. Ask students how this aspect of language applies to Bible translations.

Teaching Strategy
Participation

Ask students to identify the words for *Word* and *God* in the translations of John 1:1 by underlining the translations of *Word* once and the translations of *God* twice. Ask them to share the clues that they used to identify the words.

Teaching Strategy
Motivation

Talk with students about Bible translation teams, such as those from Bibles International, the Bible Society of Baptist Mid-Missions. Bible translations are nonexistent in many parts of the world, and the goal of translation teams is to provide a trustworthy translation of the Scriptures to those needing the gospel in their language. Ask the students to pray for translation teams. Encourage students to seek God's will for their lives and to follow His leading, perhaps to become Bible translators.

3.2 Middle English translation

In the bygynnynge was the worde (that is goddis sone) and the worde was at god, and god was the worde.

3.3 Early Modern English translation

In the beginning was the Word, and the Word was with God, and the Word was God.

3.4 German translation

Im Anfang war das Wort, und das Wort war bei Gott, und Gott war das Wort.

3.5 Yiddish translation

In anhēb iz givēn das vart, un das vart iz givēn bai gott, un das vart iz givēn gott.

4.1 Welsh translation

In y dechreuad yr oedd y Gair, a'r Gair oedd gyd â Duw, a Duw oedd y Gair.

5.1 Armenian translation

Sgizpēn ēr panə, u panə asdudzo kovn ēr, yev panə asdvadz ēr.

6.1 Hebrew translation

Bərē'shīth hāyāh haddābār, wəhaddābār hāyāh 'eth ha'əlōhīm, wəhū' haddābār hāyāh ə'lōhīm.

6.2 Arabic translation

Fi 'elbed'i kāna 'elkelima, wa 'elkelima kāna ʿanda 'allāh, wa kāna 'elkelimatu 'allāh.

7.1 Tagalog translation

Sa pasimula pa ay naroroon na ang Salita. Ang Salita ay sumasa Diyos at ang Salita ay Diyos.

Notice that some of the languages are very much like one another, and others seem very different. There are two basic reasons for those differences: (1) the confusion of languages at the Tower of Babel as recorded in Genesis 11 and (2) the changeable character of spoken languages. These reasons also explain why there are so many different languages. Over the years, as a language changes differently in its various geographical areas, regional dialect differences develop. Over several centuries these regional differences can become numerous enough to prevent communication. At that point different dialects have become different languages. In Chapter 14 you will learn more about this process.

Enrichment

Consider inviting a missionary who is on furlough to speak to the students about his country's language. Use a bulletin board to announce the missionary's visit and to display materials about the missionary's place of service.

History of the English Language | Chapter 1 27

OBJECTIVES

Students will

1. select a location to describe.
2. list aspects of a location that affect any of the five senses.
3. identify an audience to read a description.
4. choose an organizational method for a descriptive essay.
5. draft a tentative outline based upon the organizational method chosen.
6. identify unique figurative possibilities.
7. select a primary impression to set the tone of the descriptive essay.
8. draft a descriptive essay.
9. revise an essay to include effective figures of speech and to convey a desired impression clearly.
10. publish the essay.

Chapter 2 Overview

Topic	Pages	Support Materials	Days
Nouns	35–37	Bulletin Board 2 Chapter 2 Pretest	12
Comparison/Contrast Essay	61–68	Writing Rubric 3 Writing Worksheet 3	13–14, 17–18, 20–21
Pronouns	37–42	Practice/Use the Skill 2.1–2.2	15
Verbs	42–47	Practice/Use the Skill 2.3–2.4	16, 19
Adjectives and Adverbs	48–53	Practice/Review the Skill 2.5–2.6 ESL Helps 2A–2I Teaching Help 2A	22
Prepositions, Conjunctions, and Interjections	53–58	Practice/Use/Review the Skill 2.7–2.9 Teaching Help 2B ESL Helps 2J–2K	23
From the Written Word Review	59 431–32	Concept Reinforcement 2 Chapter 2 Review	24
Chapter 2 Test			25

DESCRIPTIVE ESSAY

Lesson Support

Teacher's Toolkit

Bulletin Board 2
Writing Worksheet 2
Writing Rubric 2

Literature Link

Ask students to recall from their previous study of American literature some well-known works by Herman Melville. (Moby Dick, *"Bartleby the Scrivener," etc.*) Ask

Before cameras were invented, moments and places could be preserved for posterity only by artists of the brush and of the pen. Great painters captured the sunsets and faces of times past for us with skillful strokes. These masters of the visual arts did not labor alone to record the past, however. Writers painted too, only with words.

Herman Melville, for example, painted a place for us—a place that we will likely never see with our own eyes (today we call this place the Galápagos Islands). He introduces us to this chain of volcanic islands with this description: "Take five-and-twenty heaps of cinders dumped here and there in an outside city lot; imagine some of them magnified into mountains, and the vacant lot the sea; and you will have a fit idea of the general aspect of the Encantadas, or Enchanted Isles."

Do you already "see" this place?

The Encantadas *by Herman Melville*

Take five-and-twenty heaps of cinders dumped here and there in an outside city lot; imagine some of them magnified into mountains, and the vacant lot the sea; and you will have a fit idea of the general aspect of the Encantadas, or Enchanted Isles. . . .

It is to be doubted whether any spot of earth can, in desolateness, furnish a parallel to this group. Abandoned cemeteries of long ago, old cities by piecemeal tumbling to their ruin, these are melancholy enough; but, like all else which has but once been associated with humanity they still awaken in us some thoughts of sympathy, however sad. Hence, even the Dead Sea, along with whatever other emotions it may at times inspire, does not fail to touch in the pilgrim some of his less unpleasurable feelings. . . .

But the special curse, as one may call it, of the Encantadas, that which exalts them in desolation above Idumea and the Pole, is that to them change never comes; neither the change of seasons nor of sorrows. Cut by the Equator, they know not autumn and they know not spring; while already reduced to the lees of fire, ruin itself can work little more upon them. The showers refresh the deserts, but in these isles, rain never falls. Like split Syrian gourds, left withering in the sun, they are cracked by an everlasting drought beneath a torrid sky. "Have mercy upon me," the wailing spirit of the Encantadas seems to cry, "and send Lazarus that he may dip the tip of his finger in water and cool my tongue, for I am tormented in this flame."

Another feature in these isles is their emphatic uninhabitableness. It is deemed a fit type of all-forsaken overthrow, that the jackal should den in the wastes of weedy Babylon; but the Encantadas refuse to harbor even the outcasts of the beasts. Man and

ADDITIONAL INFORMATION

Herman Melville (1819–91) was born the third of eight children to upwardly mobile New York parents. Following his father's bankruptcy and death in the early 1830s, Melville ended his formal education and labored at various occupations before serving as an apprentice seaman aboard the *Highlander*. After a brief stint as a schoolteacher, he again set sail, this time for three and a half years. Melville's service aboard a whaling ship and his adventures in the South Sea Islands proved invaluable to his literary career. The American public responded enthusiastically to his thrilling novels *Typee* (1846), *Omoo* (1847), *Mardi* (1849), *Redburn* (1849), *White Jacket* (1850), and *Moby Dick* (1851). In time, however, readers lost interest in Melville's highly symbolic, ambiguous, and pessimistic style. His finances necessitated a change to short stories, which mirrored elements of his novels. Melville later turned to writing poetry but ended his days quietly as a New York customs inspector.

The Galápagos Islands are a volcanic archipelago belonging to Ecuador, located approximately 650 miles west of Ecuador's mainland.

Idumea was the land inhabited by the Edomites, who refused the Israelites access through their land (Num. 20:14–21). The Bible contains many ominous prophecies about this people.

The *lees of fire* is the residue left after the fire.

The reference to Lazarus comes from Luke 16:24. For the context of this verse, read Luke 16:19–31, where Jesus compares the destinies of the rich man and the beggar Lazarus. The passage climaxes with Abraham's telling the rich man that the witness of Moses and the prophets is sufficient to lead sinners to repentance.

students to describe memorable scenes or images from these works. Emphasize that Melville's richly descriptive writing gives the reader very distinct mental images.

ENRICHMENT

Encourage students to bring to class information about the Galápagos Islands' fascinating history, animal and plant life, society, and tourist interests.

TEACHING STRATEGY

Introduction and Participation

Instruct students to jot down key images that seem especially powerful to them as they read "The Encantadas." After the students read the story excerpt, ask volunteers to read their responses and then to name one of the five senses (*sight, touch, hearing, taste, smell*) that each description prompted.

SCRIPTURAL APPLICATION

Read Luke 16:24 aloud. Remind the students that Melville compared the Galápagos Islands to "split Syrian gourds, left withering in the sun" and to a "wailing spirit" crying for a drop of water from the fingertip of Lazarus. Ask a student to recount the biblical account of the rich man and Lazarus (Luke 16:19–31). Then relate how Melville's vivid description of the Galápagos Islands' torrid and desolate state is nothing compared to the eternal reality of hell. Read Luke 16:27–31 and emphasize the clear testimonies of eternal truth present in the world today but blindly disregarded by many. Emphasize 1 Corinthians 1:18, "For the preaching of the cross is to them that perish foolishness; but unto us which are saved it is the power of God."

Aguano is Melville's misspelling of *iguana*.

Aracama is Melville's misspelling of *Atacama,* a desert in northern Chile that is the driest part of the world.

A *fissure* is a long narrow gap or crevice.

Calcined rock is rock that has been heated to the point where it changes in some physical way.

Clinker is vitrified matter expelled from a volcano.

Vitrified refers to a substance now glassy due to heat fusion.

Plutonian means characterized by a likeness to Pluto, the god of the underworld; relating to death and hell.

Thinking Biblically

The Christian teacher communicates a Christian worldview—a biblical worldview—in writing and grammar by continually showing how the tools handed the students relate to God's purposes in the world. God's major purposes are summed up in the two Great Commandments: love the Lord and love others. So writing and grammar must serve these purposes. Devotional poems to God (like a psalm) or letters of encouragement to suffering people clearly do so. But the very beauty of a descriptive piece or the elegance of a clearly reasoned argument can itself express love to God. And carefulness in grammar and mechanics, in a letter to the editor, for instance, communicates respect for the readers. Part of your job as a teacher is to help students connect the tools in this book to the purposes for which God created them.

wolf alike disown them. Little but reptile life is here found:—tortoises, lizards, immense spiders, snakes, and that strangest anomaly of outlandish Nature, the *aguano.* No voice, no low, no howl is heard; the chief sound of life here is a hiss.

On most of the isles where vegetation is found at all, it is more ungrateful than the blankness of Aracama. Tangled thickets of wiry bushes, without fruit and without a name, springing up among deep fissures of calcined rock, and treacherously masking them; or a parched growth of distorted cactus trees.

In many places the coast is rock-bound, or more properly, clinker-bound; tumbled masses of blackish or greenish stuff like the dross of an iron-furnace, forming dark clefts and caves here and there, into which a ceaseless sea pours a fury of foam; overhanging them with a swirl of grey, haggard mist, amidst which sail screaming flights of unearthly birds heightening the dismal din. However calm the sea without, there is no rest for these swells and those rocks, they lash and are lashed, even when the outer ocean is most at peace with itself. On the oppressive, clouded days such as are peculiar to this part of the watery Equator, the dark vitrified masses, many of which raise themselves among white whirlpools and breakers in detached and perilous places off the shore, present a most Plutonian sight. In no world but a fallen one could such lands exist.

Descriptive Essay

Thinking Biblically

When you think of how writing and grammar fit into the life of a Christian, you should think of the word *tool*. But do not think of the rarely used tools that migrate to the bottom of a toolbox; think hammer and screwdriver, the essential tools used daily. But even these common tools have no value apart from the purposes for which they are used. Hammers help build houses and sheds and a million other useful things. What purposes—and what Christian purposes—can writing and grammar serve? The power of astute description helped Flannery O'Connor, for example, become a memorable and persuasive writer. She seemed incapable of making God's amazing world a boring place through bland writing.

> And when these days were expired, the king made a feast unto all the people that were present in Shushan the palace, both unto great and small, seven days, in the court of the garden of the king's palace;
>
> Where were white, green, and blue, hangings, fastened with cords of fine linen and purple to silver rings and pillars of marble: the beds were of gold and silver, upon a pavement of red, and blue, and white, and black, marble.
>
> *Esther 1:5–6*

Why describe a place? What do you think Melville's purpose was in describing so fully the Encantadas? Why do you think the Bible records in such detail the décor of Ahasuerus's garden court?

Sometimes description serves a scientific purpose, detailing specific features of a place. Sometimes it serves a literary purpose: we have a much better understanding of the power and wealth of the king whom Esther must later petition for the lives of her people. If we had been told only that the king was wealthy and powerful, we might not feel the time and place as strongly and thus would not be as moved by the account.

Sometimes description can serve multiple purposes—but only if it is well done. What makes Melville's description vivid? He appeals to the senses: "like split Syrian gourds, left withering in the sun, they [the islands] are cracked by an everlasting drought beneath a torrid sky"; "tumbled masses of blackish or greenish stuff like the dross of an iron-furnace, forming dark clefts and caves here and there, into which a ceaseless sea pours a fury of foam."

Melville also uses beautiful language. His words sound like poetry, enhancing the meaning. The phrase "ceaseless sea" actually sounds like the hiss of the waves washing a rocky shore. And he chooses keen verbs and adjectives: "swirl of gray, haggard mist" and "they [the swells and the rocks] lash and are lashed."

Teaching Strategy

Introduction and Modeling

Emphasize that various purposes inspire descriptive writing (to inform, record, entertain, inspire, or support a theme or a setting). Display a list of the different motivations. Then create hypothetical situations in which you would need to write descriptively. Display a brief description of each situation. Then describe how you, the writer, would determine your purpose in crafting a descriptive work (examples: a travel brochure on Greece, to inform and to inspire tourists; a report on local pollen levels, to record or to inform residents or scientists; a literary analysis of the seasons in Jane Austen's *Emma,* to support a theme).

Teaching Strategy

Analysis

After discussing the various purposes behind descriptive writing, ask students to identify the purpose of Melville's "The Encantadas." *(to support a theme of desolation and inferno)* Encourage the students to support their answers by providing statements, details, and allusions from "The Encantadas."

Whether the purpose is to inform, record, entertain, inspire, or support a theme or a setting, description must be specific, precisely expressed, clear, and engaging.

Your Turn

Choose a place and write a descriptive essay about it.

Planning

✔ **Choose what you will describe.** Where can you get ideas for this assignment? Perhaps from your memory—is there a place that you like to visit or remember vividly? Perhaps from a picture—did someone send you a postcard from his travels? Perhaps from your everyday surroundings—is there a place you pass going to church that catches your attention? There are advantages to describing a place with which you are quite familiar: you are aware of all of the details and subtleties of the place. On the other hand, a new place offers opportunities to give your initial impressions of a locale, what one sees with fresh eyes.

✔ **Make a list.** Try to account for all of the senses. Are there smells that define this place? What would the description of the corner bakery be without some mention of the aroma of freshly baked bread? What sounds and sights are there? Is it hot? Cold? Mild? Is there a salty taste to the air?

Here is a list one writer made about a trip to the bakery.

irregular brick floor—watch your step!

large brick oven

huge flat wooden paddles for putting bread in oven

clouds of flour

smell of rosemary, yeast, crusty bread

stronger blast of heat the closer you stand to oven

brewing coffee—almost taste the bitter beans

array of creamers, flavors, sugars, condiments for breads

people reading newspapers—business people in suits, folks in exercise clothes, some barely awake

scrape of wooden stools on brick floor

art for sale

✔ **Consider your audience.** When you think first about your audience, you help yourself focus on exactly what kinds of details you should include and which ones you can omit. Will your audience be persons familiar with the place you are describing—like regulars at the bakery described above? Or will they be first-timers entering the place? The two types of audiences will want to know very different things about the place. Remember that looking at a place from a different point of view from your own will help bring different details to your attention.

✔ **Decide how you will organize your description.** Some descriptions are spatially organized; that is, they follow the path your eye would take as you see something for the first time. For example, as you enter a bakery, you might look toward the counter and then toward the board listing the day's specials and then around at the other people and the display cases.

Paragraph Organization pp. 14–17

Other descriptions are organized by the order in which your senses respond (chronological order). Entering a bakery, you would doubtless first be struck by the wonderful smell. Then you might notice the light coming through the

OVERVIEW of the WRITING PROCESS

Planning—choosing a place to describe, making a list of descriptions based on the five senses, considering the audience, choosing an organizational plan, freewriting about the location, and drafting an outline

Drafting—isolating possible comparisons, identifying a primary impression of the place, drafting an opening, and writing a description in one sitting

Revising—placing the writing aside for a while, reading the description aloud, gaining a second reader's feedback, and making changes to the essay

Publishing—holding a contest, creating a travel magazine, drawing a picture, or sending the essay to someone with a special interest in the location

Planning Strategy

Motivation and Participation

Materials

- postcards, travel magazines, etc.

Ask volunteers to tell about interesting vacation spots that they have visited. Pass around the materials that you brought, pointing out interesting features of various sights. Encourage students to ask questions about the locations and to write down their impressions of the locations that interest them.

Planning Strategy

Motivation and Participation

As an additional activity to help students select locations about which to write, ask them to write responses to each of the following:

- Name a place you have visited and wished that others could experience too.
- Name a location you have seen only in pictures or on video but would love to visit.
- What location from your childhood do you remember especially well?
- What interesting places have you visited while participating in extra-curricular activities?

Instruct the students to read their written responses, to add any additional locations that come to mind, and then to select a place that particularly inspires them.

windows and hear the chatter of the customers or the sounds of pans sliding on metal racks. You might notice a baker slicing bread. He might even hand you a piece to taste.

Still other writers arrange the details to produce a single effect (a type of order of importance). They place the details carefully, letting them accrue through the paragraph to achieve a goal. Melville, for example, brings his readers to the Encantadas to overwhelm them with the sublime desolation of the islands.

✔ **Freewrite about your place.** Set a time limit for yourself and write about your topic without stopping. Write whatever comes to your mind—provided it is reasonably on topic and shows biblical restraint. Allow yourself the freedom to write unpolished text; that is, write without worrying about the finer points of grammar or spelling . . . for now. Your freewriting can give you options that might be useful for further exploration or development. Or it may make you realize that you have chosen a topic about which you have little or nothing to say. It is better to find that out now, in the planning stage, than in the middle of a draft. The paragraph below is the result of one writer's freewriting.

> When you enter the bakery, you've gotta watch your step because the floor is made up of irregularly shaped and placed old bricks—red ones that are chipped and flawed and therefore nearly perfect for such a place. If you manage to get yourself two steps inside, you'll *feel* bread baking. I mean, there's flour in the air—not like dust or anything—but like a fine smoky mist. And you smell at once the yeast and flour and coffee beans. Sometimes, if someone's just ground them, the beans are so strong you can taste them. If you're there early enough, the baker is still stoking the brick ovens with wood, and the wood smell mixes with the other smells and seems like winter at my grandparents' cabin. At least, that's what I think of. The baker uses huge wooden paddles, faded and bleached (with flour?) and scorched in places to slide lumps of dough speckled with rosemary—or if you've been especially fortunate, cranberry and white chocolate, into the oven. You can hear the paddles whoosh and scrape against the oven bottom. The ovens cover one whole side of the bakery. Scones fresh from the oven sparkle with sugar. Sometimes I pour cream from the coffee station onto a scone. Yum. At the coffee station there are four flavors of creamer and three types of sugar. Some people use them all. Some don't use any. Matt says people who drink their coffee black have just given up on life.

tip

Let the time limit you set for yourself in freewriting be the minimum amount of time you will spend writing—if you're still inspired at the end of the time, keep writing!

Tentative Outline p. 6

Developmental Strategies pp. 12–13

✔ **List your details in an order appropriate to your organization.** Using the results of your freewriting or your list of details, draft a tentative outline. Be ready to drop some details and add others. After making the outline below, the writer of the bakery piece realized that he needed to include more details on taste. After all, it's a bakery! He also wanted to think more about the senses of touch and hearing, adding information about the sound of beans grinding and coffee perking and people talking in hushed tones.

The Bakery and Senses
- Sight
  - bricks
  - oven
  - paddles
  - lumps of dough, scones

Planning Strategy
Motivation
If time allows, consider conducting a short field trip to an inspiring place. Consider options of historical, scientific, literary, or artistic interest.

Planning Strategy
Motivation
Use Bulletin Board 2 (Teacher's Toolkit) to spark the students' imaginations.

Planning Strategy
Analysis
Ask students what options the writer of the freewriting paragraph has. *(focusing on the layout of the bakery; focusing on the ways the senses respond; focusing on how the details of the bakery lead to a single effect)* Tell them to find details from the paragraph to support each option.

Planning Strategy
Participation
Distribute a copy of Writing Worksheet 2 (Teacher's Toolkit) to each student. Instruct the students to complete the worksheet to begin planning the essay.

Smell
flour
yeast
coffee

Touch
tripping on bricks?
flour

Hearing
scrape of paddles

Taste
scones
coffee

Drafting

✔ **Scan your outline for figurative possibilities.** Melville, for instance, compares the islands to cinder heaps. Is there something in your chosen place that reminds you of something quite different? Do the white crumbs on the bakery counter look like snow? Do the pans going in and out of the oven seem like ships coming and going in a busy harbor? Does the sample of a cinnamon roll taste like Christmas? Avoid the use of clichéd expressions. Try to think of new ways to express your comparisons.

tip

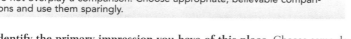

Do not overplay a comparison. Choose appropriate, believable comparisons and use them sparingly.

✔ **Identify the primary impression you have of this place.** Choose some detail or figure of speech that will set the tone for your description. Melville decided that the Encantadas were sere and uninhabitable. He then began his account with a comparison that was not only easy to visualize but also evocative of the emotion he felt as he looked at the islands.

✔ **Draft an opening.** Write your introductory paragraph, keeping in mind the impression you wish to create. Remember that your first paragraph should not only introduce your place but also spark your readers' interest in your description and draw attention to your main idea. Melville immediately draws a brief picture of his place so that we see a generalized picture of the Encantadas as he proceeds with further details. Depending on the length of your essay, you may or may not have a fully developed thesis statement: You may instead just launch into your description. However, some sort of statement of controlling purpose may help your readers adjust to your topic.

tip

Consider placing a thesis statement at the end of your description—especially if you are writing a brief description.

✔ **Write your description in one sitting.** Write with purpose and direction. You can go back later and refine the essay. Keep in mind the overall tone and organization you have chosen. Always be envisioning the place as you write. Try to make the reader feel that he has been there himself.

Drafting Strategy

Discussion

Ask students to decide what the statement of controlling purpose for the freewriting essay might be. *(You can feel the bread baking.)*

Drafting Strategy

Motivation and Participation

To help the students think outside the box, give them the name of an object and ask them to make a comparison that they have never heard before. This activity may be done orally as a class or individually on paper to share later.

Revising

- **Set your writing aside for a while.** If you leave your writing for a few hours or a day, you can get a fresh perspective on it when you return to it. Then pick it up again as though you had not written it. If it were someone else's, what would you think of it? What would you tell him to change? What would you tell him to keep? Take your advice.
- **Read your description aloud.** Does anything sound confusing? Do the sounds of the words help support your meaning in some places? (Remember the "ceaseless sea"?) Do the figures of speech seem appropriate, and do they make your account clearer? If not, you may need to drop them or rework them. The writer of the bakery description eventually dropped his reference to a "fine smoky mist" because he realized that many people would conjure up a negative association with a room filled with cigarette smoke. Be sure that you think about how someone else would read your description.
- **Ask a second reader.** Ask him what his main impression is. Is it the one you intended? Ask him what part was clearest. Ask him whether anything confused him. Ask him whether he can sense this place in his imagination. Use his feedback to make revisions.
- **Make changes to your essay.** You and your reader have implemented revisions for ideas and style. Now proofread the essay for correctness. Check for mistakes in grammar, usage, and spelling. Look also for coherence of transitions, especially if your essay is a chronological one.

Publishing

- **Hold a contest.** Post your essay along with the other essays and ask everyone to vote on which essay is most effective in portraying an impression.
- **Create a travel magazine.** Using computer images or photos or sketches, design a magazine of interesting places to visit.
- **Draw a picture.** Put your own artistic skills to work to illustrate your piece. If you feel you cannot adequately draw or paint your place, take a photograph or make a collage of the impressions you included in your descriptive essay.
- **Send the essay to the owner of the place you described.** The owner of the bakery or produce stand or the pastor of the church—whoever has a special interest in the place you wrote about will certainly appreciate a copy of your work.

Some Ideas to Consider

History

- Write a description as if from a window overlooking a famous place, such as the palace of Versailles.

Literature

- Find good descriptions of places in classic novels or well-known essays. Study the authors' styles and try to use similar techniques in your description.

Science

- Find a factual account of the details of a certain place. Rewrite the information in an expressive way, using figurative language.

Palace of Versailles

Revising Strategy

Analysis

Tell students to scan their writing for bland, overly used expressions, such as "very nice," "lots of fun," "really interesting," and so on. Ask students to suggest more effective phrases and write their responses for display. Discuss the importance of creativity in writing.

Writing Workshop

Conduct a minilesson on the coordination and subordination of sentences (pp. 363–65). Stress that effective writers incorporate a variety of sentence structures in order to convey the relative importance of ideas. Explain that reading a series of short, choppy sentences is just as confusing and distracting as reading a series of long drawn-out ones.

Publishing Strategy

Motivation

Help students begin a writing portfolio or folder. Relate that the writing portfolio is (1) a professional way to store their best writing and (2) a helpful means of tracing their writing development throughout this course.

Evaluation

For help in grading this assignment, see "Grading Student Writing" (p. v) and Writing Rubric 2 (Teacher's Toolkit).

GRAMMAR

Parts of Speech

Words are the means by which we express our thoughts, both spoken and written. The Scriptures give many references concerning words: words that are powerful, words that are comforting, words that are well spoken. Choosing words accurately and correctly depends upon an understanding of the classification of words. In English, words are classified into one of eight parts of speech. However, correct usage goes beyond mere knowledge of the eight parts of speech and includes the understanding that the form and function of a given word can change. In the following sentences, observe how the word *chair* functions and how the form of the word changes.

Noun	His small *chair* remained in good repair.
	Dining room *chairs* come in many different designs.
	Chairing the committee requires many hours of preparation.
Adjective	After years of extended use, the *chair* back broke.
	Chairing the sports committee, he excused himself from participation in the game.
Verb	The senior senator *chairs* the influential committee.
	Tenured congress members *chair* many of the committees.
	His predecessor was *chairing* the committee before he was forced to resign.
Adverb	Because of his leadership ability, he was chosen *to chair* the sports committee.

Determine part of speech by the way the word functions in the sentence.

Nouns

A **noun** names a person, place, or thing. In fact, a noun is the name of anything. A noun can be singular or plural. Nouns function as subjects, direct objects, indirect objects, objects of prepositions, predicate nouns, nouns of direct address, appositives, and objective complements. Notice the first two sentences in the group of example sentences above. In the first sentence *chair* is singular, and in the second sentence *chair* is made plural. Nouns can be made to show possession as well, by adding an apostrophe or an apostrophe plus an *s*.

The *chair's* decorative carving is intricate and beautiful.

The two *chairs'* upholstery matched the décor of the room.

Notice that the first sentence indicates singular possession and the second sentence indicates plural possession.

Nouns are either common or proper. A **common noun** names any person, place, or thing. A **proper noun** names a specific item in one of these categories.

The antique green *chair* broke when the workman dropped it.

Thomasville Chairs manufactures many styles of chairs.

Objectives

Students will

1. identify words in sentences as nouns, pronouns, verbs, auxiliaries, verb-adverb combinations, adjectives, adverbs, prepositions, conjunctions, or interjections.
2. differentiate between nouns and pronouns.
3. write an appropriate noun or pronoun to complete a sentence.
4. differentiate between main verbs and auxiliaries.
5. identify verb-adverb combinations.
6. differentiate between action and state-of-being verbs in sentences.
7. construct sentences using specific verb types correctly.
8. differentiate among adjectives, adverbs, and articles.
9. locate words modified by adjectives and adverbs.
10. distinguish between prepositions, conjunctions, and interjections in sentences.
11. differentiate among coordinating, correlative, and subordinating conjunctions.
12. combine sets of ideas to form one sentence.
13. distinguish among all the eight parts of speech.

PARTS OF SPEECH

Lesson Support

Student Worktext

Chapter 2 Review—pp. 431–32

Teacher's Toolkit

Chapter 2 Pretest
Teaching Help 2A
ESL Helps 2A–2K
Concept Reinforcement 2

Test

Chapter 2 Test

Teaching Strategy

Introduction

Administer Chapter 2 Pretest (Teacher's Toolkit) to ascertain the students' proficiency with the parts of speech. By twelfth grade, some students will need only a brief review.

Reinforcement

Ask students for a random list of words and write them for display. Then ask students to choose one word and to write sentences using that word as various parts of speech (e.g., noun, verb, adverb, adjective). Select a few of the sentences for display. Discuss the results, pointing out how the form of a word changes according to its function in the sentence.

Common nouns can be count nouns or noncount nouns. A **count noun** can be singular or plural (countable). A **noncount noun**, sometimes called a *mass noun,* is singular in form and cannot be counted.

Count	chair, chairs
Noncount	furniture

ESL

Use a determiner, such as an article, before a singular count noun. (See pages 48–49 for more information about determiners.)

Wrong	George returned ~~book~~ to ~~library~~.
Right	George returned **a** *book* to **the** *library.*

Because noncount nouns represent something that cannot be broken up into individual parts, they cannot be preceded by number words such as *a, an,* or *one* or by other determiners that imply counting rather than amount.

Wrong	Would you like ~~a rice~~ with your meal?
Right	Would you like *rice* with your meal?
	Would you like **some** *rice* with your meal?
	Would you like **a serving of** *rice* with your meal?
Wrong	This pitcher holds *~~fewer water~~* than the other pitcher holds.
Right	This pitcher holds **less** *water* than the other pitcher holds.

A common mistake is to use modifiers for noncount nouns as modifiers for count nouns. A list of modifiers for count and noncount nouns appears below.

Singular Count Nouns Only	*Each, every, either, neither*
	Each cow produces milk.
Plural Count Nouns Only	*Many, few/fewer/fewest, a few, several*
	Several gallons of milk are produced.
Noncount Nouns Only	*Much, little/less/least, a little*
Wrong	Much ~~cows~~ produce milk.
Right	Much milk is produced.

Compound nouns combine two or more words in one of three ways: as a closed compound (one word), as an open compound (two words), or as a hyphenated compound (one word).

Closed compound	wheelchair
Open compound	rocking chair
Hyphenated compound	sister-in-law

ESL

Notice the intonation difference between compound nouns and adjectives describing nouns.

- Compound nouns in English have their main stress (their loudest syllable) in the first part of the compound: **high**chair, **blue**bird.
- However, when the same two words appear as an adjective and a noun, the noun receives the main stress: high **chair**, blue **bird**.

Compound Noun	Little Dannie is in his highchair eating cereal.
Adjective and Noun	A double-bass player usually uses a high chair or a high stool.

Evaluation

Ask students to list the noun functions. Check their answers against those listed on page 35. See *The Writer's Toolbox* for additional review and explanation.

Teaching Strategy

Participation

Lead the students in reviewing the multiple functions of a noun (subject, direct object, indirect object, predicate noun, objective complement, object of a preposition, direct address, appositive). Ask the students to write sentences using their own or their classmates' names in each of the different noun functions. Display examples of their sentences to emphasize the variety of noun uses.

Teaching Strategy

Participation

Elicit from the students a list of compound nouns and write their examples for display. Ask the students to indicate whether an example should be written as one word, two words, or with hyphenation. Encourage the students to refer to a dictionary as the final authority for spelling compound nouns.

Collective nouns are words like *majority*, *crowd*, and *audience* that refer to a group. A collective noun, although singular in form, can be considered plural when the individuals of the group act separately.

Agreement p. 154

SINGULAR	The *audience* assumed **its** place near the front of the auditorium.
PLURAL	The *audience* took **their** seats before the orchestra members were seated.

ESL

A number of expressions that name groups of people come from adjectives (including participles): *the talented, the wealthy, the blind*. The following guidelines apply only to collective nouns made from adjectives or participles.

1. Always use the definite article ***the*** before this kind of collective noun.

   Some members of our church minister to ***the*** *homeless* at the local rescue mission.

2. Always use a plural verb when this kind of collective noun is the subject.

   The educated ***are*** likely to obtain good jobs.

3. Use this kind of expression only in reference to a group. To refer to just one such person, use an adjective + noun construction instead.

   A ***visually impaired student*** faces challenges different from those of other students.

Common nouns are either concrete or abstract in meaning. **Concrete nouns**, most of which are count nouns, refer to material things which usually can be experienced by at least one of the five senses. **Abstract nouns**, most of which are noncount nouns, refer to abstract ideas.

CONCRETE NOUNS	apple, flame, rose, bell
ABSTRACT NOUNS	loyalty, truth, purity

Some adjectives may form abstract nouns by the addition of certain noun suffixes, such as *ness, ty,* or *th: goodness, sweetness, purity, sincerity, truth.*

Pronouns

A **pronoun** substitutes for a noun or for a noun and its modifiers. The use of pronouns allows a writer or speaker to employ variety and avoids repetition. The **antecedent** is the word to which the pronoun refers. It usually appears earlier in the sentence or paragraph.

The strict soccer coach said that *he* benched the star player for being late.

The remaining soccer players determined that *they* would be on time.

Personal Pronouns

Personal pronouns are the most common kind of pronoun. They name **three grammatical persons:** first person (the speaker or writer); second person (the person spoken or written to); and third person (any other person or thing). Personal pronouns have three additional characteristics: number, gender, and case. **Number** indicates whether the pronoun is singular or plural. **Gender** indicates whether the pronoun is masculine, feminine, or neuter. **Case** indicates the form of the pronoun based upon its use in the sentence. Personal pronouns have three cases: subjective, objective, and possessive.

TEACHING STRATEGY
Induction and Discussion

Display a list of collective nouns: *jury, team, class, group, company, clergy, committee, family, flock, public*. Using several of these examples, ask the students to provide a sentence in which the noun is singular. Then ask them to provide a sentence in which the noun is plural. Discuss with the students the difference in meaning between the singular and plural usage.

TEACHING STRATEGY
Demonstration and Analysis

Point out several concrete nouns from Melville's essay. Suggest to the students that they read the sentences silently, omitting the concrete nouns. Encourage the students to select other examples of concrete nouns from the essay and to explain what these nouns contribute.

TEACHING STRATEGY
Modeling

Emphasize the importance of using correct pronoun case. The tendency to falsely hypercorrect by inserting the subjective-case *I* in place of the objective-case *me* should be discouraged (e.g., "Between you and I, John gave a present to Mary and I." The *I* in both instances should be replaced by *me*). Learning correct pronoun case will also help students in learning foreign languages.

The professional soccer player played *his* best game in the World Cup championship. *(third person singular, masculine, possessive case)*

His teammates did *their* part in passing the ball effectively. *(third person plural, possessive case)*

He trapped, dribbled, and shot the ball. *(third person singular, masculine, subjective case)*

Did *you* see the ball go in? *(second person singular or plural, subjective case)*

The team congratulated *him* at the end of the game. *(third person singular, masculine, objective case)*

Agreement pp. 148–49

Pronoun Use pp. 203–5

Pronoun Reference pp. 226, 229, 232–33

Singular			
	Subjective	**Objective**	**Possessive**
First person	I	me	my, mine
Second person	you	you	your, yours
Third person			
Neuter	it	it	its
Masculine	he	him	his
Feminine	she	her	her, hers

Plural			
	Subjective	**Objective**	**Possessive**
First person	we	us	our, ours
Second person	you	you	your, yours
Third person	they	them	their, theirs

Indefinite Pronouns

Agreement pp. 157–59

Unlike personal pronouns that refer to specific persons, places, or things, **indefinite pronouns** refer to nonspecific persons, places, or things. For this reason indefinite pronouns do not usually have antecedents.

all	anything	everyone	none	some
any	both	everything	no one	somebody
anybody	each	most	nothing	someone
anyone	everybody	nobody	one	something

Teaching Strategy

Modeling

Point out to the students that in popular writing (newspapers, magazines, brochures) and in everyday speech many indefinite singular pronouns are used incorrectly with plural verbs and plural pronouns as in the sentence, "Everyone must bring their own lunch." Encourage the students, however, to treat these pronouns as singular in their formal writing and speech. Instruct them to avoid the awkward *his or her* structure by rewording the sentence (e.g., instead of *Everyone must bring his or her own lunch,* use *All the students must bring their own lunches*).

Teaching Strategy

Analysis

Point out to the students that frequently the indefinite pronouns *all, any, more, most, none,* and *some* are followed by a prepositional phrase. The number of the object of the preposition will often help determine whether the indefinite pronoun is considered singular or plural. Share the following examples with the students:

- *Some* of the *students* are going to be late.
- *Some* of the *pie* has been eaten.
- *All* of the *book* was carefully supported by research.
- *All* of the *students* are required to take the entrance exam.

Most of the indefinite pronouns shown above are always used with singular verbs.

Anybody *is* able to come.

Each *brings* his own pencil to class.

However, some are always used with plural verbs.

All *are* able to come.

Both *bring* their own pencils to class.

Some indefinite pronouns may be singular or plural, depending on context.

None *is* able to come.

None but her friends *are* here.

ESL

Indefinite pronouns are different from nouns in several ways. Nouns, but not indefinite pronouns, can be made plural and can be preceded by determiners and adjectives. We do not say "somebodies" or "a nice somebody." However, sometimes one of these words can be used idiomatically as a noun: "She thinks that he is **an absolute nobody**." (She thinks that he is not important.) "The coach asked each player to give **his all**." (The coach asked each player to give all of his effort.)

Demonstrative Pronouns

Determiners pp. 48–49

Demonstrative pronouns point out specific persons, places, or things. *This* (singular) and *these* (plural) refer to things that are near. *That* (singular) and *those* (plural) refer to things that are farther away.

That was a well-executed goal by the front line.

The goals scored all season were not as well executed as *these.*

When demonstrative pronouns are used as modifiers, they are determiners, not pronouns.

Adjective Clauses pp. 116–19

Pronoun-Antecedent Agreement pp. 163–68

Relative Pronouns

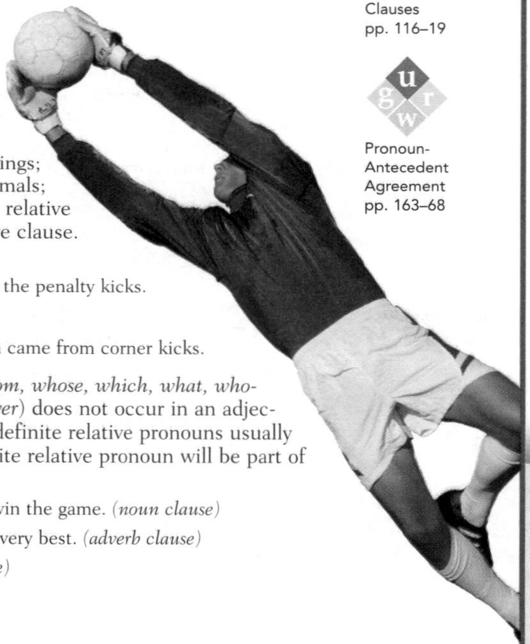

A **relative pronoun** (*who, whom, whose, which, that*) appears in an adjective clause and shows a relationship between itself and its antecedent. The pronouns *who* and *whom* refer to people; *whose* can refer to people, animals, or things; the pronoun *which* refers to things and most animals; the pronoun *that* refers to any type of word. The relative pronoun has a noun function within the adjective clause.

The goalkeeper was the one *who* stopped all the penalty kicks.

The goals *that* were scored by the opposition came from corner kicks.

An **indefinite relative pronoun** (*who, whom, whose, which, what, whoever, whomever, whosoever, whichever,* and *whatever*) does not occur in an adjective clause and does not have an antecedent. Indefinite relative pronouns usually appear in noun clauses. Occasionally, an indefinite relative pronoun will be part of an adverb clause.

[*Whatever* team scores the most goals] will win the game. (*noun clause*)

[*Whoever* comes,] our players will play their very best. (*adverb clause*)

I know [*what* will happen next.] (*noun clause*)

Teaching Strategy

Analysis and Demonstration

Display the example sentences below. Encourage students to use parentheses and brackets to identify adjective clauses that begin with a relative pronoun. Share these two tests: (1) find the antecedent for the relative pronoun by looking for the noun or pronoun immediately preceding the adjective clause; and (2) substitute a personal pronoun for the relative pronoun to show the noun function of the relative pronoun within its clause. Some rewording may be necessary when substituting the personal pronoun.

- The person (*whom* you called yesterday [you called *him* yesterday]) is waiting outside.
- The boy (*whose* dog ran away [*his* dog ran away]) is crying.
- The baseball cap (*that* he bought [he bought *it*]) is bright red.
- The people (*who* arrive early [*they* arrive early]) will get the best seats.

Teaching Strategy

Demonstration

Suggest that the students identify a noun clause by putting brackets around it and replacing it with a personal pronoun.

- [What he wants to do about the problem] is not clear.
- *It* is not clear.
- Give the bonus to [whoever can solve the problem].
- Give the bonus to *him, her,* or *them.*

Interrogative Sentences p. 69

Question Marks p. 296

Interrogative Pronouns

An **interrogative pronoun** (*who, whom, whose, which, what*) asks a question to which a noun or pronoun is the answer. For special emphasis, *ever* may be added to the basic interrogative pronouns.

> *Who* is goalkeeper for the soccer team?
>
> To *whom* did the coach direct his encouraging remarks?
>
> *Whatever* made you think that you could win a game without practice?
>
> Someone left equipment on the field. *Whose* is it?

Appositives p. 206

Commas with Appositives p. 307

Reflexive and Intensive Pronouns

Reflexive and intensive pronouns end in *self* or *selves*. **Reflexive pronouns** are used as objects but refer to the same person or thing as the subject of the sentence. **Intensive pronouns** emphasize a noun or pronoun that is already present in the sentence. Grammatically, an intensive pronoun functions as an appositive; therefore, it can be removed from the sentence without changing the meaning of the sentence. The intensive pronoun may appear at some place in the sentence other than immediately after the noun or pronoun it emphasizes.

Reflexive	The goalkeeper injured *himself* on the corner brace of the goal box.
Intensive	The goalkeeper *himself* stopped the quick, difficult corner kick.
	The goalkeeper stopped the quick, difficult corner kick *himself.*

Reciprocal Pronouns

Reciprocal pronouns express a mutual relationship between or among the persons mentioned in the subject of the sentence. The two reciprocal pronouns, *each other* and *one another,* cannot be separated and usually function as direct objects. Less frequently they function as indirect objects or objects of prepositions.

Direct Object	Defensive players on the soccer team supported *one another* as they practiced for the game.
Indirect Object	The team members gave *each other* encouragement as they jogged their miles in practice.
Object of the Preposition	Both offensive and defensive players gave encouraging words to *each other.*

Reciprocal pronouns can be made into possessive determiners.

> Both defensive and offensive players enjoyed playing *one another's* positions during practice.

in SUMMARY

Nouns name persons, places, or things. Nouns can be singular or plural, and they may be made possessive.

Common nouns name any person, place, or thing. **Proper nouns** name specific persons, places, or things.

Count nouns can be singular or plural. **Noncount nouns** are always singular in form and cannot be counted.

Compound nouns are a combination of two or more words.

Collective nouns refer to a group. A collective noun, although singular in form, can usually be considered plural when the individuals of the group act separately.

40 Chapter 2 | Parts of Speech

Concrete nouns, most of which are count nouns, refer to material things that can be experienced by at least one of the five senses. **Abstract nouns**, most of which are noncount nouns, refer to abstract ideas.

Pronouns substitute for nouns or for a noun and its modifiers. The **antecedent** is the word that a pronoun replaces.

Personal pronouns show **person**, **number**, **gender**, and **case**.

Indefinite pronouns refer to nonspecific persons, places, or things.

Demonstrative pronouns point out specific persons, places, or things.

Relative pronouns show a relationship between themselves and another word in the sentence. **Indefinite relative pronouns** do not have antecedents.

Interrogative pronouns ask a question.

Reflexive pronouns are used as objects but refer to the same person or thing as the subject of the sentence. **Intensive pronouns** emphasize a noun or pronoun that is already present in the sentence.

Reciprocal pronouns express a mutual relationship between or among the persons mentioned in the subject of the sentence.

2.1 PRACTICE *the skill*

Underline each noun once and each pronoun twice. For each pronoun, write the type in the blank (interrogative, indefinite, etc.). If there is no pronoun in the sentence, write *none* in the blank.

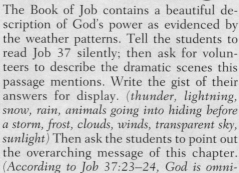

personal 1. I stood watching as the wind tore the remaining leaves from the branches of the oak tree.

personal 2. Like a gymnastics team in slow motion, they tumbled through the air before coming to rest on the cold earth.

relative 3. The tree stood, devoid of leaves, silhouetted starkly against a sky that was a somber gray.

interrogative; personal 4. Icy rain began to fall lightly from the sky. Who knew how long it would last?

intensive 5. The air itself grew colder as the rain fell.

indefinite 6. Rain began to freeze on the tree and on all of the bushes.

none 7. As the ice thickened on the tree, the branches began creaking and groaning beneath the weight.

reciprocal; personal 8. Ice-laden branches rubbed against each other as the wind tossed them about.

demonstrative; relative 9. Bushes and tree branches, especially those that were delicate, were sagging with the weight of the ice.

personal; personal 10. Cautiously, I walked back the way I had come, back to the warm fire and hot chocolate made by Aunt Julie.

SCRIPTURAL APPLICATION

The Book of Job contains a beautiful description of God's power as evidenced by the weather patterns. Tell the students to read Job 37 silently; then ask for volunteers to describe the dramatic scenes this passage mentions. Write the gist of their answers for display. *(thunder, lightning, snow, rain, animals going into hiding before a storm, frost, clouds, winds, transparent sky, sunlight)* Then ask the students to point out the overarching message of this chapter. *(According to Job 37:23–24, God is omniscient, omnipotent, and just. He deserves man's humility and respect.)*

2.2 USE *the skill*

Write an appropriate noun or pronoun to complete each sentence. *(Answers may vary.)*

me 1. The beach glistened, spread like a blanket before ?. *(personal pronoun)*

ocean 2. The ? slowly and rhythmically washed over the sand. *(singular noun)*

each other 3. Shells and rocks in abundance were piled on ? . *(reciprocal pronoun)*

water 4. As the ? swept over the sand, it left behind beautiful patterns. *(noncount noun)*

Someone 5. ? took a few steps forward, looked backwards, and saw footprints. *(indefinite pronoun)*

itself 6. Some shells sparkled beneath the incoming tide ?. *(intensive pronoun)*

Whoever 7. ? steps on the shells will not be happy with the result. *(indefinite relative pronoun)*

What 8. ? scuttled across the sand with its claws waving in the air? *(interrogative pronoun)*

that 9. The crab ? glared angrily at me dodged beneath a rock. *(relative pronoun)*

That 10. ? was a good visit to the beach. *(demonstrative pronoun)*

Verbs

The **verb** is the backbone of a sentence. Verbs combine with nouns and pronouns to form sentences. An **action verb** expresses either an external, observable action that can be perceived by the senses or an inward action that cannot be perceived by the senses. A **state-of-being verb** expresses a state of being or a condition of the subject and is often followed by a complement.

Action	The missionaries *began* a youth group for teenagers in the area.
	The young people's spiritual growth *encouraged* the missionaries.
State of Being	Activities for the teenagers *are* unique.
	The youth group members *remain* fervent in their outreach to friends and other teenagers.

42 Chapter 2 | Parts of Speech

Understanding verbs and their relationships with other words is vital to understanding the meaning of a sentence. Sentence analysis often requires that you identify a verb by one or more of its characteristics. You can determine the person, number, tense, voice, and mood of a verb by examining the verb and its subject.

The muddy *children* **had played** with the new puppy all afternoon.

(third person plural, past perfect, active, indicative)

You can also write a sentence using a verb with certain characteristics.

First person plural, past, linking of *were:*

We **were** sure of the new puppy's welcome.

Verb Use
pp. 178–93

Characteristic	Meaning	Examples
Tense	Time (past, present, future, and so on)	The scavenger *hunt* **begins** at 3:00 p.m. Last month's *activity* **began** too late. Future *activities* **will begin** earlier.
Person	Agreement with the person of the subject	Each *program* **begins** with a time for games. *You* **begin** with opening prayer.
Number	Singular or plural (agreement with the number of the subject)	*Softball* **begins** with one team in the field. Other *games* **begin** after the softball game.
Voice	Active or passive	*All* of the teens **began** the capture-the-flag game. The capture-the-flag *game* **was begun** by all of the teens.
Mood	Indicative, imperative, or subjunctive	*I* **began** that game. If *I* **were beginning** again, I would try harder.

In addition to these characteristics of verbs, verbs can be identified according to the sentence pattern in which they appear. Each sentence pattern has one kind of verb.

Intransitive Verbs

Intransitive Verbs
p. 75

An **intransitive verb** is a verb that, with its subject, is complete in meaning; it has no complement. However, the subject and verb may have modifiers.

Teenagers from the youth group **worked** hard during the car wash.

They **were working** in teams of two or three.

Parts of Speech | Chapter 2 43

Transitive Verbs

Sentence Patterns pp. 76–77

A **transitive verb** is a verb that has a receiver of action to complete the meaning of the verb. The receiver of the action (the complement) is a **direct object**. Some transitive verbs have an additional complement, the **indirect object**, which tells to whom or for whom the verb's action was done. Occasionally, a transitive verb will have an **objective complement** that renames or describes the direct object.

Direct Object	Teenagers and their sponsors *washed* fifty **cars** that Saturday morning.
Indirect Object	Those at the car wash *gave* the mission **fund** their tips.
Objective Complement	The youth group *considered* the car wash a successful **outreach** to the community.

Linking Verbs

Sentence Patterns pp. 75–76

A **linking verb** joins the subject with a complement that either renames the subject—a predicate noun—or describes the subject—a predicate adjective. The most common linking verbs are the forms of *be.*

Predicate Noun	Another successful outreach *was* the community **cleanup**.
Predicate Adjective	Learning to help others *was* **good** for the teens.

Auxiliaries

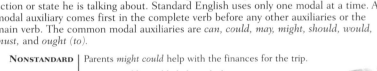

Some grammarians classify auxiliaries as a separate part of speech (not a type of verb) because an auxiliary cannot function alone as a simple predicate.

Auxiliaries, also called helping verbs, combine with the main verb to form the complete verb. They come before the main verb. Forms of *be, have,* and *do* can be used as main verbs or auxiliary verbs. When these are auxiliaries, they will be followed by a main verb.

Main Verb	A youth-group mission trip *is* another outreach.
	The teenagers *have* the opportunity to minister in a different culture.
	In preparation, the teens *do* extensive verse memorization.
Auxiliary	They ***are*** *learning* verses to help them be good witnesses.
	The teenagers ***have*** *worked* hard to earn their support for the trip.
	A mission trip ***does*** *give* the youth group an opportunity to grow spiritually.

Modal auxiliaries indicate something about the speaker's attitude toward the action or state he is talking about. Standard English uses only one modal at a time. A modal auxiliary comes first in the complete verb before any other auxiliaries or the main verb. The common modal auxiliaries are *can, could, may, might, should, would, must,* and *ought (to).*

Nonstandard	Parents *might could* help with the finances for the trip.
Standard	Parents *could* possibly help with the finances for the trip.

Teaching Strategy
Participation and Analysis

Materials
- a newspaper

Distribute the pages of a newspaper among the students. Ask the students to find examples of intransitive, transitive, and linking verbs. One test to determine whether a non-*be* verb is a linking verb is to substitute a form of *be*. Display the following example sentence: *Herb* feels *lonely sometimes.* Ask the students to conduct the linking verb test on the example sentence and to explain their findings. (*Herb* is *lonely sometimes.* Is *can be substituted for* feels *here; therefore* feels *functions as a linking verb.*) Display further representative sentences for each verb type and emphasize the differences among them.

Teaching Strategy
Induction

Instruct the students to write a brief how-to paragraph without using any auxiliary verbs. Ask for several volunteers to read their paragraphs. Discuss the results with the class. Elicit from the students a list of auxiliary verbs and write them for display. Tell the students to add some of these auxiliary verbs to their paragraphs and be prepared to explain what contribution these verbs make to the description.

ESL

Modal auxiliaries are different from other auxiliaries.

- Modals never have an *s* suffix.

Wrong	Takeshi ~~cans~~ run faster than anyone else on the team.
Right	Takeshi **can run** faster than anyone else on the team.

- Except for *ought,* modals are never followed by the *to* of the infinitive.

Wrong	Vivica must not ~~to~~ be late for her appointment.
Right	Vivica **must** not **be** late for her appointment.
	Vivica **ought** not **to be** late for her appointment.
	Vivica **ought** not **be** late for her appointment.

Verb-Adverb Combinations

Adverbs pp. 50–51

A **verb-adverb combination (VAC)** consists of two words, a verb and a following adverb. The verb and the adverb combine to function as the simple predicate in a clause. Often, the two words together produce a meaning different from the meaning of the two words individually. Many VACs are transitive and are followed by direct objects.

In a verb-adverb combination, the adverb may remain with the verb or may move to a position after the direct object. If the meaning of the sentence changes when the adverb is moved, the word is not an adverb but is a preposition instead.

Several teenagers *made up* new games to play with the children.

Several teenagers *made* new games *up* to play with the children.

ESL

Because the meaning of a VAC is often different from the meanings of the two words by themselves, be sure you understand the meaning of a VAC before you use it in your writing. Look in an ESL dictionary or ask your teacher or another native speaker of English for help if necessary.

Your ESL dictionary will probably call VACs *phrasal verbs.* It will include them alphabetically at the end of the verb entry. For example, *make up* will be near the end of the entry for *make; make up* will have its own meaning and sample sentence.

in SUMMARY

A **verb** expresses action or state of being. **Action verbs** express an action by the subject. **State of being verbs** express a state of being or condition of the subject. Verbs have **tense**, **person**, **number**, **voice**, and **mood**.

An **intransitive verb** is complete in meaning with its subject and does not have a complement. A **transitive verb** has a receiver of action to complete the meaning of the verb: the direct object. Transitive verbs may also have an additional complement, either an indirect object or an objective complement.

A **linking verb** links the subject with a complement that either renames the subject or describes the subject.

Auxiliaries combine with the main verb to form the complete verb. **Modal auxiliaries** often indicate the speaker's attitude toward the action or state of being he is relating.

A **verb-adverb combination** consists of a verb and a following adverb. Together these two words produce a meaning different from the meaning of the same two words used individually.

Teaching Strategy

Participation and Discussion

Direct the students to list as many verb-adverb combinations as they can think of in one or two minutes. Then ask volunteers to share some of their answers as you write them for display (e.g., take off, put on, back up, look over). Ask the students to write sentences using several of these combinations. Then instruct them to move the adverb to another part of the sentence. If the meaning of the sentence remains the same even after the adverb is moved, it is a true verb-adverb combination.

2.3 PRACTICE *the skill*

Underline each main verb once and each auxiliary twice. Place parentheses around each verb-adverb combination. In the blank identify each main verb as action (*A*) or state-of-being (*S*).

A 1. Dark thunderclouds had ominously (blotted out) the blue of the summer sky.

A 2. Moving the fields of tall grass like a turbulent sea, the warm winds were blowing over the meadow.

S 3. The sky grew bright with flashing bolts of lightning.

A 4. Like the sounds of cannon fire, the thunder rumbled across the plains.

S 5. Pouring mercilessly out of the sky, the rain was cold against our skin.

A, A 6. To the left and just over the hill, the trees bent and swayed violently in the wind.

S 7. The pond in the middle of the field appeared to boil from the multitude of raindrops.

A 8. The farmer (looked over) the meadow drenched with rain and strewn with hailstones.

S, S 9. After the rain had become less severe, the sky became brighter.

S, A 10. When the storm is over, sunlight will be beaming on the wet ground below.

2.4 USE *the skill*

Answer each question and respond to each statement by writing a sentence using the kind of verb indicated in parentheses. Try to use verbs other than *be* verbs. *(Answers will vary.)*

1. Describe the worst storm that you have experienced. *(third person singular, past, active)*

   A storm tore many branches off the big tree in our front yard last summer.

2. Has your family ever been in a tornado or a hurricane? *(first person plural, present perfect, active)*

   We have weathered a relatively powerful hurricane in Florida.

Enrichment

Encourage students to research and to present answers to basic weather-related questions such as *Why do clouds float? What causes wind?* and *What is lightning?*

3. What is the present weather forecast for your area? *(third person singular, present, active)*

The weatherman predicts sunny skies for today and rain showers for tomorrow.

4. Describe the process of erosion. *(third person plural, present, verb-adverb combination, active)*

Water and wind break down and carry away particles of rock, soil, sand, and other substances.

5. What is one way to prevent erosion? *(second person, modal auxiliary, present, active)*

You could plant trees as a windscreen against erosion.

6. How could the weather damage agricultural crops in ways other than by erosion? *(third person singular, modal auxiliary, present, active)*

The weather can damage crops by means of hail, flood, drought, and a variety of other events.

7. Have lightning and thunder ever scared you? *(first person singular, past, passive)*

I was scared by lightning and thunder when I was eight years old.

8. How has God used weather to bless your life? *(third person singular, past, linking)*

God was good to us by providing rain for our corn crop.

9. How did God use weather in the Bible? *(third person singular, past, active)*

God used hail as one of the plagues on Egypt.

10. Give another example of God's using weather in the Bible. *(third person singular, past, active)*

A flood sent by God destroyed the earth.

Parts of Speech | Chapter 2 47

Point out to the students that capitalizing the first word of elliptical questions—sometimes referred to as a series of questions—is optional. Remind students to consistently apply whichever option they choose.

Adjectives

Adjectives expand, limit, or describe nouns or pronouns. Most adjectives will answer one of the following questions: *which one? what kind? how many? how much? whose?* Adjectives that answer these questions are called descriptive adjectives. Any word that fits into the following test frame can be used as an adjective.

The _____ thing (or person) is very _____.

The *tall* building is very *tall*.

The *feeble* man is very *feeble*.

ESL Adjectives cannot be made plural in English.

WRONG	Patricia picked several ~~fragrants~~ flowers.
	The garden has two ~~elegants~~ gates.
RIGHT	Patricia picked several **fragrant** flowers.
	The garden has two **elegant** gates.

Adjectives can occur in various positions within a sentence. Most adjectives come somewhere before the nouns they modify. An adjective that modifies an indefinite pronoun, however, will appear after the pronoun.

Brian is a *successful* businessman.

His presentation emphasized everything *positive* about the plan.

An adjective that is part of a longer modifying phrase comes after the noun it modifies.

After the meeting, he needed ideas *helpful* for his clients.

Two adjectives joined by a conjunction can come either before or after the noun.

Quiet and *determined*, the businessman planned his strategy.

The client, *calm* and *confident*, waited for the presentation.

A predicate adjective comes after a linking verb and describes the subject. An objective complement follows a direct object and describes the direct object.

Sentence Patterns pp. 75, 77

PREDICATE ADJECTIVE	He was *cautious* about his choice of ideas.
OBJECTIVE COMPLEMENT	He considered his plan *workable* for his clients.

Determiners

A **determiner** is an adjective that points out or limits a following noun. Determiners come before other adjectives that may modify the noun. Unlike descriptive adjectives, determiners do not fit into the adjective test frame and cannot be compared using *er/est* or *more/most*.

Some grammarians classify determiners as a separate part of speech (not as a type of adjective). In that system only those adjectives that can be made comparative or superlative are classified as true adjectives.

ESL STRATEGY

Use ESL Helps 2A and 2B (Teacher's Toolkit) to give ESL students further explanation and practice in putting cumulative adjectives in the correct order in a noun phrase. If your ESL students need help distinguishing between cumulative and coordinate adjectives, consider using ESL Help 12C (Teacher'sToolkit), focusing on the distinctions now and saving the information about comma use for later.

TEACHING STRATEGY

Participation

Assign each paragraph of Melville's essay to a student or group of students. Ask them to list all the adjectives in the paragraph. Lead the students in listing the adjectives that they find under the appropriate headings (determiners, possessives, modifying nouns, articles, etc.). Then discuss the position of each adjective in relation to the noun it modifies.

ONE on ONE

Give your student two or three paragraphs of Melville's essay and ask him to identify and label all the adjectives. Then discuss the position of each adjective in relation to the noun it modifies.

ESL STRATEGY

Use ESL Help 2C (Teacher's Toolkit) to give ESL students more information about how to use determiners.

Articles

Articles are the most common determiners. *A* and *an* are indefinite articles, used to modify general nouns or nouns that have not been previously mentioned. *The* is the only definite article and is used to modify specific nouns or nouns already mentioned.

Brian prepared *a* portfolio for everyone in attendance.

The portfolio explained the retirement benefits.

ESL

Use *a* before a word beginning with a **consonant sound**; use *an* before a word beginning with a **vowel sound**: ***a** tree, **a** university (begins with a y sound), **an** olive, **an** hour (the h is silent).*

Possessives

Independent Possessives p. 204

Possessive nouns or pronouns are determiners when they modify nouns. Possessives always modify a following noun and show ownership or another close relationship. When a possessive noun is modified by at least one other adjective, the possessive and its modifiers form a **possessive phrase**. An **independent possessive** is a possessive that functions as a noun or a pronoun rather than as a modifier.

Possessive Noun	*Brian's* presentation was very informative.
Possessive Pronoun	I could appreciate *his* preparation for the seminar.
Possessive Phrase	*The growing company's* focus was on the individual.
Independent Possessive	*Theirs* was the most comprehensive of the three plans.

Demonstratives

Demonstratives (*this, that, these, those*) can be used as determiners. Demonstrative determiners have the same form and meaning as demonstrative pronouns, but they function as modifiers, not as subjects or objects.

Pronoun	*That* was the most convincing part of the presentation.
Determiner	*That* part of the presentation was the most convincing.

Interrogatives

Interrogative Sentences p. 69

Interrogatives (*what, which, whose*), like demonstratives, can be used as determiners when they modify nouns. They are pronouns when they appear alone.

Pronoun	*What* is the strongest point of the argument?
Determiner	*What* program will you choose to follow?

Indefinites

Question Marks p. 296

Indefinites, like possessives, demonstratives, and interrogatives, can function either as pronouns or as determiners. An indefinite is a determiner when it modifies a noun.

Pronoun	*Some* doubted the success of the program.
Determiner	*Some* workers chose plans to fit their needs.

ESL Strategy

The use of articles is often one of the most difficult concepts for ESL students to grasp. Some languages have no articles at all, and those languages that do often use them differently than English does. ESL students will have a much easier time identifying articles than they will using them. Assign ESL Helps 2D and 2E (Teacher's Toolkit) for more explanation and practice with articles.

Teaching Strategy

Discussion and Induction

Discuss with students the functional difference between possessive adjectives and possessive pronouns. Remind them of the functions of adjectives and pronouns. Ask them to give sentences using possessive adjectives and pronouns and to tell which they used in the sentence.

Teaching Strategy

Participation

Ask the students to bring newspaper and magazine pictures of an item to class. Divide the class into small groups and distribute the pictures among them. Instruct the groups to write a brief descriptive paragraph of one of the items without writing the name of the item. Then ask a representative of each group to read the description aloud as the other students listen and identify the item.

Modifying Nouns

A **modifying noun** is a noun used to modify another noun. A modifying noun follows any other adjectives and appears directly before the noun that it modifies.

Noun	I attended the *seminar* to learn about the new program.
Modifying Noun	I learned about the new program through the *seminar* presentation.

Proper Adjectives

Proper Adjectives pp. 270–71

Proper adjectives are formed from proper nouns. Like the proper nouns, proper adjectives must be capitalized.

The seminar took place in Philadelphia, where we bought *Philly* steak-and-cheese sandwiches from a street vendor.

His ancient portable shop seemed almost *Victorian.*

Adverbs

Adverbs modify verbs, adjectives, or other adverbs. Most adverbs show one of the following meanings: manner (including extent and number), place (including direction and order), time (including frequency), result and logical conclusion, and cause. The adverb *not* has a purely negative meaning.

Adverbs appear in various positions within sentences. An adverb that affects the meaning of the verb is usually movable, able to appear in several positions within the sentence. The negative adverb *not* always appears after the first auxiliary. Furthermore, *not* can be joined to the auxiliary *can* to form a whole word *(cannot)* or to an auxiliary to form a contraction *(haven't, didn't, weren't,* etc.).

Outside, the rain fell.

The rain fell *outside.*

We were *not* prepared for this spring storm.

There was*n't* time to protect the young plants.

Although many adverbs end in *ly,* not all *ly* words are adverbs. Other kinds of words can end in *ly* as well.

Adverb	Gray clouds formed *rapidly* in the sky.
Adjective	The *untimely* storm brought a downpour of chilling rain.
Noun	The *lily* next to the front door couldn't stand up to the force of the rain.

Some grammarians classify qualifiers as a separate part of speech (not a type of adverb). In that system a qualifier modifies only adjectives or adverbs; a true adverb modifies only verbs.

Qualifiers

A **qualifier** is an adverb that modifies an adjective or another adverb. Qualifiers usually appear directly before the adjectives or adverbs that they modify and strengthen or weaken them.

Modifying an Adjective	During the day *really* cold air blew against our skin.
Modifying a Predicate Adjective	The rainfall was *slightly* heavy at times.
Modifying an Adverb	The rain changed to snow *very* soon.

ONE *on* ONE

Ask your student to find newspaper and magazine pictures of an item. Instruct him to write a brief descriptive paragraph of one of the items without writing the name of the item. As he reads the paragraph, try to guess the item described.

Teaching Strategy

Introduction and Participation

Point out to students that relative adverbs and interrogative adverbs differ in function but not always in form. Give students a list of adverbs that can perform either function *(when, where, how, why)* and have them write sentence pairs using each word as a relative adverb and as an interrogative adverb.

Teaching Strategy

Demonstration

Use Teaching Help 2A (Teacher's Toolkit) to elaborate on and show examples of adverb meaning.

ESL Strategy

Use ESL Helps 2F and 2G (Teacher's Toolkit) for a more detailed explanation of and practice with correct adverb placement.

Conjunctive Adverbs

A **conjunctive adverb** shows a meaning connection between two independent clauses that are separated by a period or a semicolon. The conjunctive adverb usually, but not always, appears at the beginning of the second independent clause.

> A spring snowstorm in our area is highly unlikely; *nevertheless,* our three-state area had a severe one last year.
>
> A spring snowstorm in our area is highly unlikely. *Nevertheless,* our three-state area had a severe one last year.
>
> A spring snowstorm in our area is highly unlikely; our three-state area, *nevertheless,* had a severe one last year.

Some common conjunctive adverbs are listed below.

also	however	then
besides	in fact	therefore
for example	instead	
furthermore	nevertheless	

Compound Sentences p. 132

Period or Semicolon pp. 296, 315

Relative Adverbs

A **relative adverb** (*when, where,* or *why*) introduces an adjective clause and relates that dependent clause to the rest of the sentence. An **indefinite relative adverb** introduces a noun clause or, occasionally, an adverb clause. The indefinite relative adverbs *when, where, why,* and *how* introduce noun clauses; *whenever, wherever,* and *however* introduce adverb clauses.

Clauses pp. 116–19

Adjective Clause	During a spring snowstorm, peach farmers spend time in the orchards, *where* they check fragile blossoms.
Noun Clause	Peach farmers know *where* they need to check for damage.
Adverb Clause	The peach farmers realize that a portion of their crop is damaged *whenever* they experience such a storm.

Interrogative Adverbs

An **interrogative adverb** (*when, where, why,* or *how*) asks a question.

> *How* much of the crop was damaged?

Interrogative Sentences p. 69

in SUMMARY

Adjectives expand, limit, or describe nouns or pronouns.

A **determiner** is an adjective that points out or limits a following noun and comes before other adjectives that modify the same noun.

Articles *(a, an,* and *the)* are the most common determiners.

Possessives are nouns or pronouns that modify nouns and show ownership or another close relationship. **Independent possessives** function as nouns or pronouns rather than as modifiers.

Demonstratives, **interrogatives**, and **indefinites** retain their pronoun form but function as determiners when used to modify nouns.

Conjunctive adverbs modify verbs. Explain that in the example sentences, the conjunctive adverbs modify the verbs that follow them.

ESL STRATEGY

Use ESL Helps 2H and 2I (Teacher's Toolkit) for information about the use of *not.*

TEACHING STRATEGY
Analysis and Participation

Materials
- large cards with sentences containing relative and indefinite relative adverbs

Ask a student to select a card and to read it aloud several times as the other students write the relative adverb and its clause on a sheet of paper. The reader then asks a volunteer to read his answer. Discuss the answer with the students. Continue with the rest of the cards, having students take turns as reader. For a more challenging activity, display the cards and ask the students to identify the clause as an adjective, adverb, or noun clause.

ONE *on* ONE

Place the stack of cards facedown and tell your student to be prepared to tell you the relative adverb and its clause from each card. Select a card and hold it up. After your student's verbal response, discuss his answer and continue until all the cards have been read and discussed. For a more challenging activity, ask your student to identify the clause as an adjective, adverb, or noun clause.

A **modifying noun** is a noun used to modify another noun.

Proper adjectives are formed from proper nouns.

Adverbs modify verbs, adjectives, or other adverbs.

A **qualifier** is an adverb that modifies an adjective or another adverb, either strengthening or weakening its meaning.

A **conjunctive adverb** shows a meaning connection between two independent clauses that are separated by a period or a semicolon.

A **relative adverb** introduces an adjective clause. An **indefinite relative adverb** usually introduces a noun clause.

Interrogative adverbs ask questions.

2.5 PRACTICE *the skill*

Underline each adjective once and each adverb twice. Do not underline articles except in a possessive phrase.

1. The tremendous weather elements that accompany hurricanes can cause catastrophic damage to the landscape.
2. Some specialists refer to hurricanes as typhoons or tropical cyclones; however, these terms usually describe less violent storms.
3. Whenever a hurricane reaches land, heavy winds can uproot large trees and can create excessive debris.
4. The hurricane's center, calm and free from clouds, is called the eye.
5. Outside the eye, however, the most violent part of the storm rages.
6. Hurricanes produce abundant rainfall that causes a great risk for flooding.
7. One might wonder how often a hurricane creates favorable conditions for tornadoes.
8. In the coastal regions of the United States, homeowners evacuate quickly whenever hurricane warnings are issued.

9. Tropical storms that become hurricanes usually develop shortly after the peak of summer, when the ocean's waters are the warmest.
10. During these times, advanced technology helps scientists, but sometimes they find accurate prediction difficult.

52 Chapter 2 | Parts of Speech

2.6 REVIEW *the skill*

Underline each adjective once and each adverb twice. Do not underline articles. Then draw an arrow from each adjective or adverb to the word it modifies.

1. When do forest fires usually occur?
2. During the summer months, forest fires can cause damage terrible to see.
3. Often fires are the result of a lengthy drought, but some fires are caused by something tragic—arson or carelessness.
4. These fires begin a process of rebirth; new life springs up in their wake.
5. Some trees produce seedpods that break open and release their seeds in the middle of a raging fire.
6. Which seeds survive the fire and spring up, bringing life to the blackened wilderness, is always an enigma.
7. The Yellowstone National Park fire of 1988 was one event when progress came from apparent destruction.
8. Fighting forest fires is a very dangerous occupation that includes many risks.
9. Firefighters are always extremely careful as they seek to control the inferno.
10. Eventually the firefighters bring the fire under control; then the forest is free to begin rebuilding.

Prepositions

A **preposition** is a word that shows a relationship between its object (usually a noun or pronoun) and another word in the sentence. The **object of a preposition** follows the preposition. A **prepositional phrase** is made up of the preposition, its object, and any modifiers of the object.

Early American settlers used pumpkins (*in* two different **ways**.)

Although there are many one-word prepositions, nine of them occur most frequently: *of, in, to, for, with, on, at, by,* and *from*. In addition to one-word prepositions, multiword prepositions also exist. Some common multiword prepositions are *according to, along with, as well as, because of,* and *in spite of*.

American settlers used pumpkins for food (*as well as* decorative **purposes**.)

gwur
Noun Clauses
pp. 126–28

gwur
Prepositional Phrases
p. 88

Teaching Strategy
Discussion

Explain that the English language contains many idiomatic prepositions. Even native English speakers sometimes overlook these prepositions or are befuddled when trying to classify them as parts of speech. Use Teaching Help 2B (Teacher's Toolkit) to review these tricky prepositions.

Teaching Strategy
Introduction and Participation

Instruct a student to perform a simple task, such as tying shoelaces, putting on a sweater, or taking off a jacket. After the job has been completed, ask the students to write a description of the task without using any prepositions. Discuss the results with the students. Then instruct them to add appropriate prepositions to their descriptions. Ask several students to read their descriptions aloud to the class. Discuss the function of prepositions within sentences.

ESL Strategy

Most ESL students will not have much trouble with concrete prepositions such as those of location and direction. However, since prepositional meanings do not perfectly match from language to language, many ESL students will have problems using prepositions with more abstract meanings. They may find Teaching Help 2B (Teacher's Toolkit) to be helpful.

Prepositions indicate a variety of meanings; here are some examples.

Location	above, across, against, around, at, behind, below, beneath, beside, between, beyond, by, in, in front of, inside, on, outside, over, past, toward(s), under, upon, within
Direction	down, from, into, off, onto, out, out of, through, to, up (*see also* Location)
Time	after, at, before, between, by, during, for, in, on, past, since, until, till, up to
Agency or Means	by, by means of, of (*archaic*), with
Cause	because of, due to, in view of, on account of
Association	about, according to, along with, among, around, as for, besides, for, like, of, with
Opposition or Exception	against, apart from, but (*meaning* "except"), despite, except, except for, in spite of, instead of, without

Prepositional phrases function like adjectives and adverbs to modify another word in the sentence.

Adjectival	Pumpkins (*with* hard **shells** and a bright orange **color**) are ready for harvesting.
Adverbial	(*During* the harvesting **stage**,) one must be sure not to damage or break the pumpkin's stem.

Writer's Toolbox

Many verbs and adjectives and some nouns must be followed by specific prepositions. English speakers and writers usually learn these combinations as they learn the language. However, some of these combinations can cause problems and can be found in dictionary entries that illustrate certain meanings.

Pumpkin farmers *agreed to* the planting proposal for the ten acres. (*to consent*)

Pumpkin farmers *agreed with* the agricultural department about the planting time. (*to be in agreement about an opinion*)

Pumpkin farmers *agreed on* a plan that would produce the most pumpkins. (*to come to terms*)

Conjunctions

All coordinating conjunctions may be used to join words, phrases, and clauses, except *for* and *so*, which may join only clauses.

Conjunctions connect words or groups of words in a sentence. **Coordinating conjunctions** join sentence elements of the same type. The coordinating conjunctions are *and, but, or, nor, for, yet,* and *so*.

Compound and Compound-Complex Sentences pp. 132–33

Subjects	A *maggot,* a *beetle,* **or** a *bore* can damage a pumpkin.
Direct Objects	Pumpkins require *direct sunlight* **and** *well-drained soil.*
Dependent Clauses	A pumpkin farmer considers his yield to be very good *when a small variety yields seven tons per acre* **and** *when a large variety yields thirty tons per acre.*
Independent Clauses	*Connecticut Field pumpkins average about sixteen pounds,* **but** *the Big Mac pumpkins average more than twenty pounds.*

Comma and Semicolon pp. 302, 315

A comma usually precedes a coordinating conjunction that joins two or more independent clauses.

ESL Strategy

Use ESL Helps 2J and 2K (Teacher's Toolkit) for further information about prepositions and practice in the use of prepositions.

Teaching Strategy

Demonstration

Point out to the students that we often use a prepositional phrase instead of an *'s* possessive with furniture, buildings, or inanimate objects in general. Share the following example sentences:

The arm of the chair is wobbly and needs to be replaced.

The large front window of our house was smashed by a vandal.

For expressions of time and measurement, however, the possessive is shown with an *'s*. For example, *After an hour's wait for the concert to begin, the crowd grew restless.*

Correlative conjunctions are coordinating conjunctions that occur in pairs and join equal sentence parts. Correlative conjunctions provide emphasis, let the reader know that a second idea will be added to the first, and make clear the ideas being joined in the sentence. The correlative conjunctions are *either—or, neither—nor, both—and,* and *not only—but also.*

> **Either** *we will go to the pumpkin farm tomorrow,* **or** *we will go on Tuesday.*
>
> **Neither** *the Jack Be Little variety* **nor** *the Munchkin variety* grows much bigger than one pound.
>
> **Both** *the Autumn Gold* **and** *the Jackpot* weigh about twelve pounds.
>
> The farmers enjoy **not only** *planting the pumpkins* **but also** *harvesting a bountiful crop.*

Subordinating conjunctions join dependent clauses to independent clauses. A subordinating conjunction is part of the dependent clause and functions as the introductory word for that clause. The following are some common subordinating conjunctions: *after, although, as, because, before, if, once, since, that, unless, until, when, where, while.* Phrasal subordinating conjunctions include *as if, even though,* and *so that.*

Dependent Clauses pp. 116–28

> *If* it is not raining, we will visit the pumpkin stand tonight.
>
> We will visit the pumpkin stand tomorrow *even though* it may still be raining.

ESL

Don't confuse **because** (a subordinating conjunction followed by a subject and a verb) with **because of** (a preposition followed by a noun or pronoun object.)

Subordinating Conjunction	Lester went to the library **because** his book was due.
Preposition	He avoided a late fine **because of** his carefulness.

Interjections

An **interjection** is a word that can stand alone, punctuated as a sentence, or that can appear along with a sentence in which it takes no real part. Interjections express various meanings, such as strong feeling, agreement or disagreement, greeting or leave-taking, politeness, hesitation, or introduction of a subject.

Exclamation Points and Commas pp. 296, 307

> *Wow!* That pumpkin weighs more than one hundred pounds.
>
> *Yes,* my mother could make many delicious pumpkin pies from that pumpkin.
>
> I cannot eat another piece of that delicious pie. *Thank you.*

Phrases such as *good morning, thank you,* and *you know* may function in the same way as a single-word interjection. An interjection can be followed by a comma, an exclamation point, or a period.

in SUMMARY

A **preposition** shows a relationship between its object and another word in the sentence.

The **object of the preposition** is a noun or pronoun that follows the preposition.

A **conjunction** connects words or groups of words in a sentence.

A **coordinating conjunction** joins sentence elements of the same grammatical type.

Explain that the conjunction *so* may be used as either a coordinating or a subordinating conjunction, depending on the clause that follows it. If *so* is followed by an independent clause, it acts as a coordinating conjunction. If a dependent clause follows *so,* it functions as a subordinating conjunction. Remind students that a comma must precede the word *so* when it is used as a coordinating conjunction.

Teaching Strategy
Analysis

Point out to the students that putting *and* or *but* at the beginning of sentences is not ungrammatical but does draw attention to the conjunction and its transitional purpose. Ask them to consider the following questions about initial usage of *and* or *but:* (1) Is the meaning of the sentence clear without the initial conjunction? (2) Should the sentence with the initial conjunction be connected to the previous sentence?

Teaching Strategy
Demonstration

Then is often incorrectly used as a coordinating conjunction to connect two independent clauses. Emphasize to the students that *then* can be moved around in the sentence, but a true coordinating conjunction, such as *and,* cannot be. Illustrate this principle by writing the following sentences for display:

- Paul stood on a chair, then he raised his voice to make an announcement.
- Paul stood on a chair, he then raised his voice to make an announcement.
- Paul stood on a chair, and he raised his voice to make an announcement.

Each of the first two sentences contains a punctuation error, a comma splice; a semicolon is necessary to separate the two independent clauses.

Correlative conjunctions occur in pairs and join grammatically equal sentence parts.

A **subordinating conjunction** joins a dependent clause to an independent clause.

An **interjection** can stand alone as a sentence or can be part of a regular sentence in which it takes no real part.

2.7 PRACTICE *the skill*

Place parentheses around each prepositional phrase and underline the preposition once. Underline each conjunction twice. Identify each conjunction as *coordinating, correlative,* or *subordinating.* Some sentences may not have both a preposition and a conjunction.

______ 1. (In the distance) a large funnel cloud moved (across the dark sky.)

subordinating 2. Bright flashes (of light) were distinguishable as it approached the farm.

subordinating 3. The neat rows (of corn) started waving noticeably, as if they were fearful.

correlative 4. Not only were the objects flying (around the outer rim) identifiable, but they were also dangerous.

coordinating 5. Wood, metal, and vegetation whirled wildly.

coordinating 6. The deafening sound was (like the sound) (of roaring freight trains or fighter planes.)

______ 7. The tornado also ripped stalks (from the ground,) flinging corn everywhere.

subordinating 8. Then the tornado began tossing cars (into the air,) letting them lie where they fell.

subordinating 9. When the storm began to weaken, it dropped its contents (over the area.)

coordinating 10. The funnel disappeared quickly yet left a disturbed calm behind.

TEACHING STRATEGY
Discussion

Remind the students to use *like* only as a preposition in formal and academic writing, not as a subordinating conjunction to introduce a clause. Encourage them to use *as though, as,* or *as if* instead. Write the following example: *Maria acted* like *she was really angry with us* becomes *Maria acted* as if *she were really angry with us.*

TEACHING STRATEGY
Participation

Ask the students to provide a list of words or phrases that can be used to connect two independent clauses that are separated by a period or semicolon. Write them for display. *(consequently, furthermore, instead, therefore, then, nevertheless, for example, in fact, in addition, meanwhile, etc.)*

Ask the students these questions: What relationships between the clauses do these words show? *(additional information, contrast, cause/effect, time, etc.)* What are these words called? *(conjunctive adverbs)*

Instruct the students to write several sentences using some of these conjunctive adverbs. Write student example sentences for display and discuss the adverb function of the conjunctive adverbs within their clauses. Emphasize that these adverbs can be moved to different positions in their clauses and that they are truly adverbs, not conjunctions.

2.8 USE *the skill*

Combine each set of ideas to form one sentence, using the type of conjunction specified in parentheses. In your answers underline each conjunction and circle each interjection. *(Answers may vary.)*

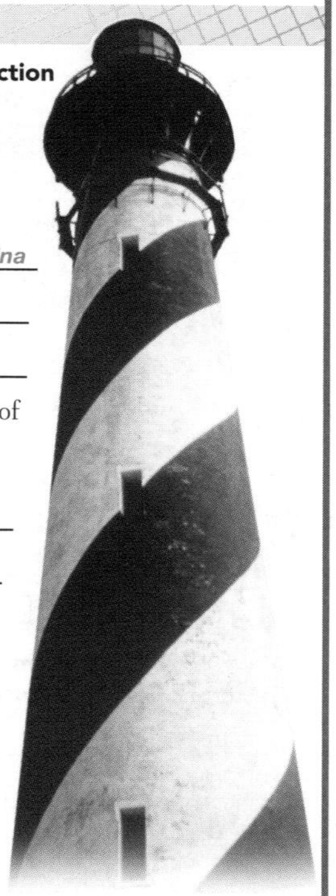

1. The Cape Hatteras Lighthouse was built on the Outer Banks of North Carolina. It could warn ships of the barrier islands. *(subordinating)*

   The Cape Hatteras Lighthouse was built on the Outer Banks of North Carolina so that it could warn ships of the barrier islands.

2. The treacherous waters along the barrier islands are called "the graveyard of the Atlantic." The "graveyard" entombs thousands of seamen and vessels. *(subordinating)*

   The treacherous waters along the barrier islands are called "the graveyard of the Atlantic" because the "graveyard" entombs thousands of seamen and vessels.

3. Erosion had destroyed 1,300 feet of the beach in front of the lighthouse. In the 1900s the lighthouse was within 150 feet of the water. *(subordinating)*

   Since erosion had destroyed 1,300 feet of the beach in front of the lighthouse, in the 1900s the lighthouse was within 150 feet of the water.

4. In 1999 the lighthouse was moved a quarter of a mile inland. It may still be plagued by coastal erosion. *(coordinating)*

   In 1999 the lighthouse was moved a quarter of a mile inland, yet it may still be plagued by coastal erosion.

5. Wow! Beaches and houses are disappearing and cliffs are disintegrating along the coast. Erosion is threatening other parts of the coast. *(correlative)*

   Wow! Not only are beaches and houses disappearing and cliffs disintegrating along the coast, but erosion is also threatening other parts of the coast.

6. Some erosion is desirable. We would have no dunes, bays, or barrier beaches without erosion. *(subordinating)*

   Some erosion is desirable since we would have no dunes, bays, or barrier beaches without it.

7. Many factors contribute to beach erosion. One major factor is that many people want to live near the sea. *(subordinating)*

   Although many factors contribute to beach erosion, one major factor is that many people want to live near the sea.

The *Outer Banks* is a narrow strand of barrier islands off the coast of North Carolina.

Mathematics Link

Students might be interested in knowing that they can decode weather maps by using math skills. Consider inviting a special speaker to discuss the place of mathematics in meteorology.

Writing Link

Encourage students to write original poems concerning weather patterns and containing at least ten prepositional phrases.

History Link

Encourage the students to find out more about the long and fascinating history of the Outer Banks of North Carolina. Allow volunteers to share their findings in class. *(Key ideas: Sir Walter Raleigh; the lost colony at Roanoke Island; Blackbeard the pirate; the first wireless telegraph transmission; the Wright brothers' first successful flight; and Torpedo Junction during World War II)*

8. Major erosion problems must be addressed. New Orleans, already several feet below sea level, could eventually be surrounded by water. *(correlative)*

Either major erosion problems must be addressed, or New Orleans, already several feet below sea level, could eventually be surrounded by water.

9. Efforts have been made to protect the Hamptons in New York from erosion. They could be destroyed if the sea level rises only three feet. *(coordinating)*

Efforts have been made to protect the Hamptons in New York from erosion, but they could be destroyed if the sea level rises only three feet.

10. Oh, no! They are pumping sand from one location to another. Corrections to the erosion problem are not always helpful. *(coordinating)*

Oh, no! They are pumping sand from one location to another, yet corrections to the erosion problem are not always helpful.

See Matthew 8:23–27; Mark 4:35–41; and Luke 8:22–25.

2.9 REVIEW *the skill*

Identify each italicized word or phrase as a *noun, pronoun, verb, adjective, adverb, preposition, conjunction,* or *interjection.*

verb 1. Three New Testament Gospels *record* the events of a storm on the Sea of Galilee.

adverb 2. Often intense storms came up *fast* on the Sea of Galilee.

noun 3. In addition to the strong *wind* and large waves, there may have been a heavy rainstorm.

preposition 4. The disciples rowed a certain distance *into* the strong wind but were unable to reach their destination.

verb 5. The ship *may have had* sails, but the disciples were unable to unfurl the sails because of the strong wind.

conjunction 6. The disciples feared for their lives and their faith failed them *when* shipwreck seemed the certain outcome.

pronoun 7. After the disciples woke Christ, who had been asleep, He spoke, and *all* of the elements of the storm subsided.

adjective 8. Christ showed His *great* power and authority over all creation.

verb 9. *Have* you ever *faced* storms of persecution or rejection in your life?

interjection 10. *Yes,* you can rely on the authority of His words, "Peace, be still."

BJU Living Gallery presentation of the painting *Christ on the Sea of Galilee* by Rembrandt, The Isabella Stewart Gardner Museum, Boston. Photo by Unusual Films.

Reinforcement

Use Chapter 2 Review on pages 431–32 for additional test review.

Evaluation

Use Chapter 2 Test to evaluate students' understanding of the content and concepts of the chapter.

FROM THE WRITTEN WORD

Recognizing the Truth

God uses a variety of rhetorical strategies to communicate truth. God chose the paradox to convey some of the most profound ideas and comforting promises found in the Bible. Have you considered the idea that a person must kneel to conquer? Our initial reaction may be that a person who kneels before another has given up freedom. On the contrary, the person who kneels before God conquers sin and the distresses of this world. Or have you thought about the person who experiences true freedom under the law of God? Often we think of being under the law as a hindrance. Yet the psalmist declared, "So shall I keep thy law continually for ever and ever. And I will walk at liberty: for I seek thy precepts" (Ps. 119:44–45). Law and liberty seem to be opposites, yet here they are not.

God uses what appears to be a contradiction to teach truth. Consider Isaiah 40:29–30.

> He giveth power to the faint; and to them that have no might he increaseth strength. Even the youths shall faint and be weary, and the young men shall utterly fall.

Perhaps you are asking yourself how someone who has fainted or lacks physical strength can have power. Consider the house-church pastor in Russia who was dragged off to prison because he refused to stop holding meetings and preaching the gospel. He endured persecution, separation from his family, dark solitary confinement, and months of malnutrition. In the midst of these circumstances he sang hymns, prayed for his enemies, encouraged other believers, and scratched portions of Bible verses on his prison walls for future prisoners. He experienced power in the midst of weakness. Even in death the house-church pastor was victorious.

Personal Response

Psalm 78 recounts the sinfulness and rebellion of the children of Israel in the wilderness. Read Psalm 78:19. Think about this paradox in relation to your life. Write about a personal experience that illustrates the paradox in this verse.

Teaching Strategy

Discussion

Lead a discussion about rhetorical strategies, particularly the paradox (a seemingly contradictory statement that is true). Ask students to name an example of a paradox in Scripture (e.g., Christ came not to send peace, but a sword; Christians are in the world but not of the world). Then instruct students to read "Recognizing the Truth." Allow students time to read the Scripture passages given.

Teaching Strategy

Discussion and Participation

Ask students to read Isaiah 40:31. Ask students whether they can recognize any paradoxes in this verse. *("They shall run, and not be weary; and they shall walk, and not faint.")*

Instruct students to read Psalm 78:19. If possible, you might share an example from your life that illustrates the paradox of this verse (e.g., "Can God furnish a table in the wilderness?"). Following the discussion period, allow time for students to write a personal experience that illustrates this paradox.

OBJECTIVES

Students will

1. select appropriate subjects for comparison and contrast.
2. evaluate the similarities and differences of ideas and their relevance to the topic.
3. formulate a statement of purpose based on an objective.
4. order ideas to build reader interest.
5. select block or point-by-point arrangement as a method of organization.
6. construct a thesis statement that states each subject and point of comparison.
7. write a comparison-and-contrast essay that includes specific details or examples, a variety of transitional elements, and any concessions about the two subjects.
8. revise the essay for focus, specific details, and transitional elements.
9. proofread the essay for grammatical and mechanical errors.
10. title the essay effectively.
11. publish the essay.

CHA

Chapter 3 Overview			
Topic	**Pages**	**Support Materials**	**Days**
Interior Monologue	83–87	Writing Rubric 4 Writing Worksheets 4A–4B	26–27, 30–31, 34, 38
Defining Sentences and Kinds of Sentences	69–70	Bulletin Board 3 Chapter 3 Pretest	28
Finding Subjects and Predicates	70–74	Practice/Review the Skill 3.1–3.3 ESL Helps 3A–3C Concept Reinforcement 3A	29
Basic Sentence Patterns	74–78	Practice the Skill 3.4 Teaching Help 3	32–33
Practice and Review	78–80, 433–34	Use the Skill 3.5 Concept Reinforcement 3B Cumulative Review 3.6 Chapter 3 Review	35
Chapter 3 Test			36
Critical Thinking	80–81		37

COMPARISON-AND-CONTRAST ESSAY

Lesson Support

Teacher's Toolkit

Writing Worksheet 3
Writing Rubric 3

Bruce Catton, a noted Civil War historian, won both the Pulitzer Prize and the National Book Award for history. The title "Grant and Lee: A Study in Contrasts" reveals the author's purpose. As you read his essay, look for words or phrases that indicate contrast and transition.

Grant and Lee: A Study in Contrasts *by Bruce Catton*

When Ulysses S. Grant and Robert E. Lee met in the parlor of a modest house at Appomattox Court House, Virginia, on April 9, 1865, to work out the terms for the surrender of Lee's Army of Northern Virginia, a great chapter in American life came to a close, and a great new chapter began.

These men were bringing the Civil War to its virtual finish. To be sure, other armies had yet to surrender, and for a few days the fugitive Confederate government would struggle desperately and vainly, trying to find some way to go on living now that its chief support was gone. But in effect it was all over when Grant and Lee signed the papers. And the little room where they wrote out the terms was the scene of one of the poignant, dramatic contrasts in American history.

They were two strong men, these oddly different generals, and they represented the strengths of two conflicting currents that, through them, had come into final collision.

Back of Robert E. Lee was the notion that the old aristocratic concept might somehow survive and be dominant in American life.

Lee was tidewater Virginia, and in his background were family, culture, and tradition . . . the age of chivalry transplanted to a New World which was making its own legends and its own myths. He embodied a way of life that had come down through the age of knighthood and the English country squire. America was a land that was beginning all over again, dedicated to nothing much more complicated than the rather hazy belief that all men had equal rights, and should have an equal chance in the world. In such a land Lee stood for the feeling that it was somehow of advantage to human society to have a pronounced inequality in the social structure. There should be a leisure class, backed by ownership of land; in turn, society itself should be keyed to the land as the chief source of wealth and influence. It would bring forth (according to this ideal) a class of men with a strong sense of obligation to the community; men who lived not to gain advantage for themselves, but to meet the solemn obligations which had been laid on them by the very fact that they were privileged. From them the country would get its leadership; to them it could look for the higher values—of thought, of conduct, of personal deportment—to give it strength and virtue.

ADDITIONAL INFORMATION

Charles Bruce Catton (1899–1978), although known primarily for his exceptional scholarship on the Civil War, also served skillfully as a newspaper reporter, an information director for the U.S. Department of the Interior, and an editor for *American Heritage* magazine. In 1954 Catton was awarded both the Pulitzer Prize in history and the National Book Award for his book *A Stillness at Appomattox*. President Gerald Ford awarded Catton the Presidential Medal of Freedom.

If students question Catton's use of ellipsis marks in this essay, ask them to analyze the sentences in which the ellipsis marks appear. A careful study reveals that Catton uses ellipsis marks to set off a sentence element that he wishes to emphasize. A dash is the more commonly used mark of punctuation for this purpose.

Literature Link

Before you direct the students to read Catton's essay, ask them to share what they already know about Ulysses S. Grant and Robert E. Lee. If time permits, allow the students to read the essay in class and to discuss new things they learned about these men.

Thinking Biblically

Our world is full of competing standards, but people of influence often try to stake out a position supposedly above that competition. They claim to be neutral, to have no fixed standards. They, however, are deceived; everyone draws the line somewhere. The Christian can at least admit it and point directly to the line: our ultimate standard for all evaluations is Scripture. Even when we write comparisons of two poems or two people (like Lee and Grant), our ultimate standard lies as a foundation beneath us. It tells us what things are worth comparing and contrasting. It tells us which side of a contrast, if any, is the better one. Our Christian worldview provides us with a major advantage over the secularist, who will not admit to himself that he, too, has an ultimate standard. Our thinking can be clearer and firmer than his because we have our feet set upon a Rock. This would be a good time to ask your students to write a letter to the editor about an editorial in your local newspaper (or even a national one).

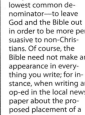

Lee embodied the noblest elements of this aristocratic ideal. Through him, the landed nobility justified itself. For four years, the Southern states had fought a desperate war to uphold the ideals for which Lee stood. In the end, it almost seemed as if the Confederacy fought for Lee; as if he himself was the Confederacy . . . the best thing that the way of life for which the Confederacy stood could ever have to offer. He had passed into legend before Appomattox. Thousands of tired, underfed, poorly clothed Confederate soldiers, long-since past the simple enthusiasm of the early days of the struggle, somehow considered Lee the symbol of everything for which they had been willing to die. But they could not quite put this feeling into words. If the Lost Cause, sanctified by so much heroism and so many deaths, had a living justification, its justification was General Lee.

Grant, the son of a tanner on the Western frontier, was everything Lee was not. He had come up the hard way, and embodied nothing in particular except the eternal toughness and sinewy fiber of the men who grew up beyond the mountains. He was one of a body of men who owed reverence and obeisance to no one, who were self-reliant to a fault, who cared hardly anything for the past but who had a sharp eye for the future.

These frontier men were the precise opposites of the tidewater aristocrats. Back of them, in the great surge that had taken people over the Alleghenies and into the opening Western country, there was a deep, implicit dissatisfaction with a past that had settled into grooves. They stood for democracy, not from any reasoned conclusion about the proper ordering of human society, but simply because they had grown up in the middle of democracy and knew how it worked. Their society might have privileges, but they would be privileges each man had won for himself. Forms and patterns meant nothing. No man was born to anything, except perhaps to a chance to show how far he could rise. Life was competition.

Yet along with this feeling had come a deep sense of belonging to a national community. The Westerner who developed a farm, opened a shop or set up in business as a trader, could hope to prosper only as his own community prospered—and his community ran from the Atlantic to the Pacific and from Canada down to Mexico. If the land was settled, with towns and highways and accessible markets, he could better himself. He saw his fate in terms of the nation's own destiny. As its horizons expanded, so did his. He had, in other words, an acute dollars-and-cents stake in the continued growth and development of his country.

And that, perhaps, is where the contrast between Grant and Lee becomes most striking. The Virginia aristocrat, inevitably, saw himself in relation to his own region. He lived in a static society which could endure almost anything except change. Instinctively, his first loyalty would go to the locality in which that society existed. He would fight to the limit of endurance to defend it, because in defending it he was defending everything that gave his own life its deepest meaning.

The Westerner, on the other hand, would fight with an equal tenacity for the broader concept of society. He fought so because everything he lived by was tied to growth, expansion, and a constantly widening horizon. What he lived by would survive or fall with the nation itself. He could not possibly stand by unmoved in the face of an attempt to destroy the Union. He would combat it with everything he had, because he could only see it as an effort to cut the ground out from under his feet.

So Grant and Lee were in complete contrast, representing two diametrically opposed elements in American life. Grant was the modern man emerging; beyond him, ready to come on the stage, was the great age of steel and machinery, of crowded cities and a restless, burgeoning vitality. Lee might have ridden down from the old age of chivalry, lance in hand, silken banner fluttering over his head. Each man was the perfect champion of his cause, drawing both his strengths and his weaknesses from the people he led.

Yet it was not all contrast, after all. Different as they were—in background, in personality, in underlying aspiration—these two great soldiers had much in common.

Thinking Biblically

Every comparison and contrast you make is made against some standard. When writing for public consumption, Christians may be tempted to write to the lowest common denominator—to leave God and the Bible out in order to be more persuasive to non-Christians. Of course, the Bible need not make an appearance in everything you write; for instance, when writing an op-ed in the local newspaper about the proposed placement of a new sewer line, you may choose to leave the Bible out altogether. But when writing on public issues with strong connections to ultimate questions, Christians cannot afford to leave God out. Neither can they afford to abuse the Bible to support their point. Christians have the right and duty to appeal—carefully—to the eternal, fixed, objective standard of Scripture in public debates. Who else will?

Under everything else, they were marvelous fighters. Furthermore, their fighting qualities were really very much alike.

Each man had, to begin with, the great virtue of utter tenacity and fidelity. Grant fought his way down the Mississippi Valley in spite of acute personal discouragement and profound military handicaps. Lee hung on in the trenches at Petersburg after hope itself had died. In each man there was an indomitable quality . . . the born fighter's refusal to give up as long as he can still remain on his feet and lift his two fists.

Daring and resourcefulness they had, too; the ability to think faster and move faster than the enemy. These were the qualities which gave Lee the dazzling campaigns of Second Manassas and Chancellorsville and won Vicksburg for Grant.

Lastly, and perhaps greatest of all, there was the ability, at the end, to turn quickly from war to peace once the fighting was over. Out of the way these two men behaved at Appomattox came the possibility of a peace of reconciliation. It was a possibility not wholly realized, in the years to come, but which did, in the end, help the two sections to become one nation again . . . after a war whose bitterness might have seemed to make such a reunion wholly impossible. No part of either man's life became him more than the part he played in their brief meeting in the McLean house at Appomattox. Their behavior there put all succeeding generations of Americans in their debt. Two great Americans, Grant and Lee—very different, yet under everything very much alike. Their encounter at Appomattox was one of the great moments of American history.

WRITING

Comparison-and-Contrast Essay

A soft answer turneth away wrath: but grievous words stir up anger.
Proverbs 15:1

The goal of Christian writers should be to learn various kinds of writing techniques and to use their writing skills to good advantage. Comparison-and-contrast writing is a valuable technique to know. When you are determining the ways in which two subjects are alike or different, you are comparing or contrasting based upon certain facts or characteristics. When you make a decision about the purchase of one item over another, you are using comparison or contrast. Comparison shows how two subjects are alike, or similar; contrast, on the other hand, shows how two subjects are different.

Writer's Toolbox

Comparison
pp. 243–44

The Scriptures contain many examples of comparison and contrast. In Psalm 1:1, the blessed man is compared to "a tree planted by the rivers of water." The middle chapters of Proverbs focus entirely on a contrast of good and evil by using the word *but*. "A faithful witness will not lie: but a false witness will utter lies" (Prov. 14:5). In the New Testament, Mark 4:30–31 compares the kingdom of God to a mustard seed, and in Galatians 5:19–23 Paul contrasts the "works of the flesh" and the "fruit of the Spirit." In each of these, specific truths are revealed through the method of comparison and contrast.

Overview of the Writing Process

Planning—choosing subjects, brainstorming, determining and crafting a statement of purpose, choosing an order for the points of comparison, and ordering the most important ideas in the position of strength

Drafting—choosing a method of organization, constructing a thesis, writing a rough draft, introduction, and conclusion, and adding concessions about the two subjects

Revising—reading the essay carefully, marking for revision, revising for correctness, and rewriting the assignment

Publishing—choosing a title and presenting the essay in oral or written format

Scriptural Application

Read Proverbs 15:1 and ask students to talk about times when they saw evidence of this verse in action. Contrast this verse with the world's advice. (*Students will probably comment on the litigious nature of our society and the propensity for wanting to "give as good as one gets."*) Discuss how Christian writers in our society can apply the "soft answer" principle.

Teaching Strategy

Motivation

Materials

- two dissimilar objects

Bring two dissimilar objects to class (e.g., a soft, silky piece of fabric and a hard, sharp rock). Show students one object and ask them to describe it. Write observations for display. Show students the second object and write observations for display. Note with students the differences in the words used to describe each. Additionally, ask students to describe the one in terms of the other (e.g., The fabric is softer than the rock). Challenge students to find similarities between dissimilar objects. Alternatively, you could bring similar objects and ask students to find differences.

In the sample essay, Catton uses words such as *contrasts, different,* and *opposites* to describe Lee's and Grant's characteristics and qualities. In his organization, Catton parallels the points of contrast and the organization of the contrasting points. At the end of the essay, however, Catton acknowledges several similarities between the two men.

Your Turn

Plan and write a two- or four-paragraph comparison or contrast essay on the subjects of your choice.

Planning

Choosing Your Topic pp. 1–4

✔ **Choose your subjects.** As you begin thinking about this assignment, be sure to consider two subjects that are somewhat related and with which you are familiar. Consider your personal interests, or think about articles or stories that you have read, or ask yourself questions about pertinent topics. From these sources determine the subjects for your assignment. You might choose to compare two candidates within the same political party or two candidates from different political parties, two styles of preaching, or two careers. You would not, for example, choose to compare a professional baseball player and a sports car. Although both of these could be temperamental and quite expensive to secure, they are not closely related. As you look back at Catton's essay, notice that he focuses on two related subjects: two men who were both accomplished Civil War leaders and responsible for bringing the war to an end.

Brainstorming pp. 2–3

✔ **Brainstorm on what you know about each topic.** After you have chosen the subjects for the assignment, write them at the top of a piece of paper. On the rest of the paper, write down what you know about each of the subjects, both general and specific ideas. Then sort your ideas according to the subjects they belong with and identify each idea as a similarity or a difference. Some of your ideas will not be relevant and can be eliminated.

Wooden Roller Coaster		Steel Roller Coaster
looping	speed	height
swaying	drops	hills
steep	long runs	fun
scary	above the rail	locations
below the rail	rough	smooth
colors	kinds of seats	sound
single track	double track	

Teaching Strategy

Introduction

Give the students specific guidelines for the length of this essay. If you assign a four-paragraph essay, the introduction can be a short, three- to five-sentence paragraph with a thesis statement as the last sentence. The conclusion will be the same length with a restated thesis as the first sentence. Each middle paragraph should have a topic sentence that gives direction to the paragraph. If the assignment is a two-paragraph essay, the thesis will be the first sentence of the first paragraph followed immediately by the topic sentence. The last sentence of the second paragraph should be a restatement of the thesis.

Additional Note

Encourage your students to choose only two subjects to compare. Inform them that it is possible to compare more than two subjects, but the essay becomes more complex.

Planning Strategy

Motivation

Talk with students about comparisons they have made recently (e.g., sports teams, foods, books). Ask them to comment on why comparisons are helpful in their everyday lives.

Planning Strategy

Discussion

Ask students to suggest topics for the comparison-and-contrast assignment. Display

64 Chapter 3 | Comparison-and-Contrast Essay

✔ **Determine your purpose.** Ask yourself *why* you are writing this essay. Do you propose to show the differences between two subjects such as two modes of transportation, two kinds of cars, or two different sports? Or do you intend to inform your reader about the similarities between two relatives or two concepts by comparing the one to the other one? Catton reveals his purpose when he describes the meeting between Grant and Lee as "one of the . . . dramatic contrasts in American history." Catton's purpose was to show the differences between Grant and Lee.

Determining Your Purpose p. 4

✔ **State your purpose in a single sentence.** At this point, you are ready to write a statement of your purpose. As you formulate this statement, ask yourself what you wish to accomplish in your essay. Here are some ideas you might consider.

What is my purpose?
- To change the reader's opinion about an idea or a product
- To compare solutions to a problem
- To contrast two specific products
- To show readers that one opinion is better than another

Without a clear purpose, your writing assignment may remain a list of facts without any clear direction. Include in this statement of purpose the names of both subjects and the point of comparison or contrast. Catton writes that Grant and Lee were "different generals . . . [who] represented the strengths of two conflicting currents."

✔ **Choose an order for the points of comparison.** Read through your ideas from the Brainstorm step and begin to organize these ideas. Perhaps some of the ideas will fall into a group of observable physical characteristics. Others may form a group of quality characteristics.

Outlining the Paper pp. 6–8

	roller coasters	
wooden		steel
	physical characteristics	
sway		tight
rough		smooth
no loops		loops
above the rail		above and below the rail
176 feet	*longest drop*	418 feet
197 feet	*highest*	456 feet
7,359 feet	*longest*	8,133 feet
70 mph	*fastest*	149 mph
77 degrees	*steepest angle*	121 degrees
	quality characteristics	
loud		quiet
nostalgia (old coasters)		
scary		scary
fun		fun

Notice that there are some ideas from the Brainstorm step that were not used.

their answers. Brainstorm for ways in which suggested topics are similar or different.

Planning Strategy
Participation
After students have selected a topic, allow time to complete the brainstorming activity on page 64. Distribute a copy of Writing Worksheet 3 (Teacher's Toolkit) to each student. Ask them to fill in the two columns as described. Then allow time for students to discuss additional similarities or differences with a peer or in a group.

ONE *on* ONE After your student has filled in his columns, discuss additional similarities or differences that he has not considered, as well as ideas that could be eliminated.

Planning Strategy
Demonstration
Ask students to suggest possible statements of purpose for an essay on the two types of roller coasters. Write answers for display. Require students to write a statement of purpose for their essays.

Planning Strategy
Discussion
Challenge students to find specific paragraphs in "Grant and Lee" in which Catton illustrates background, relationship to country, and vision for future. (Encourage students to number the paragraphs in the "Grant and Lee" essay to facilitate discussion.)

Planning Strategy
Modeling
Using student input, write and display a possible outline for the roller coaster essay.

✔ **Put your most important ideas in the position of strength.** Ordering the facts about your topics is very important. Remember to build the reader's interest. A contrast of wooden and steel roller coasters would capitalize on the difference in their physical characteristics, particularly the height, length, and speed. Therefore, these ideas should be last in the contrast. That way, your reader will remember them best.

In the essay on Lee and Grant, notice the clear organization of ideas as Catton contrasts each man's background and relationship to his country. The point of Catton's essay is to show how the essential qualities of character that Lee and Grant shared outweighed their striking contrasts. Therefore, for Catton, the similarities of the two men are the strongest point. He leaves the men's shared vision for the future to conclude the essay.

Drafting

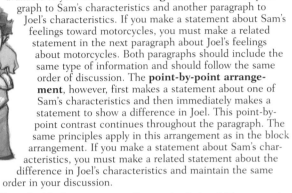

✔ **Choose a method of organization.** Suppose you intend to show the differences between two brothers, Sam and Joel. Two methods of organization are available to you. The **block arrangement** devotes one paragraph to Sam's characteristics and another paragraph to Joel's characteristics. If you make a statement about Sam's feelings toward motorcycles, you must make a related statement in the next paragraph about Joel's feelings about motorcycles. Both paragraphs should include the same type of information and should follow the same order of discussion. The **point-by-point arrangement**, however, first makes a statement about one of Sam's characteristics and then immediately makes a statement to show a difference in Joel. This point-by-point contrast continues throughout the paragraph. The same principles apply in this arrangement as in the block arrangement. If you make a statement about Sam's characteristics, you must make a related statement about the difference in Joel's characteristics and maintain the same order in your discussion.

Catton's essay follows the block arrangement. Paragraphs 4–6 and 10 present the characteristics and qualities of General Lee. Then in paragraphs 7–9 and 11 he describes General Grant. As you survey these paragraphs, you will see that Catton was consistent in the organization of his ideas about each man.

✔ **Construct a thesis.** Using the single sentence that stated the purpose for your writing, develop a thesis statement. The thesis for your assignment will provide organization and give specific direction to your writing. In the thesis statement, state each subject and the point of comparison. Are you going to show that these two subjects are alike or different?

Poor Thesis Statements	I am going to discuss the differences between white sauce vegetable lasagna and red sauce meat lasagna. *(The thesis statement should not announce what you intend to do.)*
	Did you know that the 1927 Cyclone at Coney Island is similar to the 1995 Viper at Six Flags, Great America? *(A thesis should be a statement, not a question.)*
Good Thesis Statements	White sauce vegetable lasagna is quite different from red sauce meat lasagna.
	The 1927 Cyclone at Coney Island and the 1995 Viper at Six Flags, Great America, are similar.

Drafting Strategy
Discussion

Note with students the use of the block arrangement in paragraphs 4–6 and 7–9 of "Grant and Lee" on pages 61–63. Discuss how Catton could have used the point-by-point arrangement.

Drafting Strategy
Modeling

Divide the class into two groups. Ask one group to use the block arrangement to write two brief paragraphs about roller coasters. Ask the other group to write two brief paragraphs using the point-by-point arrangement. Allow a volunteer to read the paragraphs aloud. Ask the class to note the differences between the two arrangements.

ONE on ONE Ask your student to write a brief essay using the block arrangement while you write one using the point-by-point arrangement. Discuss the differences in emphasis and meaning accomplished by each arrangement.

Drafting Strategy
Discussion

Ask students to underline the sentence "In the thesis statement, state each subject and the point of comparison" on page 66. Discuss the importance of having a subject and point of comparison. Direct students to study the example theses on page 66. Discuss the example theses, asking students to note why some are poor and others are good.

✔ **Write a rough draft.** Set aside an amount of time that would allow you to complete the first draft in one sitting. You may wish to postpone writing the introduction and the conclusion until you have written the middle paragraphs of the assignment. Each middle paragraph should have a topic sentence, the main idea of the paragraph. Using your list of organized ideas, compare or contrast the two subjects by using specific details or examples. A variety of transitional elements, both words and phrases, will clarify the points you are making about each subject. Some useful transitional words and phrases follow.

on the other hand	however	also	both
although	similarly	whereas	

tip

Many writers complete the middle paragraphs of an essay before writing the introduction and conclusion.

✔ **Write the introduction and the conclusion of your essay.** The introduction should introduce the two subjects of the paper and should end with the thesis statement. Attention-getting introductions often use quotations or facts and statistics to get the reader thinking about the topic. A conclusion, on the other hand, should begin with a restatement of the thesis. Then make any general closing comments about the two subjects to clinch the main idea and to add finality to the essay.

Introductions pp. 10–11

Conclusions pp. 13

✔ **Consider incorporating both similarities and differences into your essay.** Catton's essay first describes the differences between the two generals. Yet in the closing paragraphs Catton concedes that both Lee and Grant were "marvelous fighters" who had "fighting qualities [that] were really very much alike." He compares their equally successful military skills and emphasizes their similar conduct in their meeting at Appomattox. You may want to both compare and contrast your topics, perhaps in separate paragraphs.

Revising

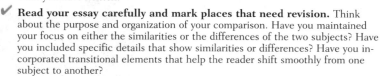

✔ **Let your essay rest.** Allow yourself adequate time, overnight or perhaps a day or two, to put your writing aside before you begin the revising step. When you return to your writing, you will have a fresh perspective from which to evaluate what you have written.

✔ **Read your essay carefully and mark places that need revision.** Think about the purpose and organization of your comparison. Have you maintained your focus on either the similarities or the differences of the two subjects? Have you included specific details that show similarities or differences? Have you incorporated transitional elements that help the reader shift smoothly from one subject to another?

Revising pp. 20–24

Drafting Strategy
Participation

Conduct student conferences about the essays in order to troubleshoot problems regarding purpose, order of points, chosen method of organization, and thesis. Suggest ways to correct any problems.

Writing Workshop

Conduct a minilesson on "Making Clear and Logical Comparisons," pages 384–85. Challenge students to look for faulty comparisons in their own writing.

Drafting Strategy
Discussion

Remind students that the purpose of their essay may be merely to inform. Unless their purpose requires it, they need not issue a judgment about which of the items being compared/contrasted is better.

Drafting Strategy
Discussion

Ask students to suggest possible concessions to the roller coaster topic. *(Although the roller coaster types are very different, they have the same end result: fun. Although the roller coaster types are very different, they have similar safety records.)* Then discuss possible concessions for the topics the students are working on.

Revising Strategy
Peer Response

Allow peers to evaluate student essays using the questions on page 67 about purpose and organization. Allow peers to ask their own questions about possible additions or subtractions.

Proofreading pp. 23–24

✔ **Revise for correctness.** At this point you are carefully checking for accurate sentence structure, for proper usage, and for correct spelling, capitalization, and punctuation. You may use the spell checker on your computer; however, you must remember that the spell checker will not flag all errors. Remember that grammar, spelling, and mechanical errors will distract the reader from the message as well as injure your credibility.

✔ **Rewrite your assignment.** Now you are ready to incorporate the improvements and corrections you have made to your final essay. Before you submit the essay for a grade, be sure to proofread again.

Publishing

Publishing p. 24

✔ **Choose a title.** The title should reveal to the reader the idea of the essay. Be sure that the title is not longer than five or six words.

✔ **Post your essay on a bulletin board entitled "Comparisons and Contrasts."** Your teacher may ask for volunteers to have their works posted in the classroom.

✔ **Submit your essay to the school newspaper.** If the topic of your essay is relevant to a particular section of the school newspaper, the newspaper may want to print it.

✔ **Bind your work for a class display.** Create an attractive cover for your essay and display it in the classroom.

✔ **Read your essay aloud to your family.** If you have chosen to compare or contrast two family members, your family might especially enjoy hearing your essay.

Some Ideas to Consider

History

- Consider a contrast between women of the frontier West and women of the aristocratic South.
- Consider a comparison of the contribution of Chinese immigrants to the building of the transcontinental railroad and the contribution of African Americans to the building of the agricultural South.

Statistics

- Consider a comparison or contrast between essay and objective tests.

Physical Education

- Consider a comparison or contrast of two team sports or two individual sports.

Geography

- Consider a comparison or contrast of the geographic features of the islands of Hawaii and Oahu.

Home Economics

- Consider a comparison or contrast of two diets or cooking styles.

Revising Strategy

Analysis

Consider allowing students to use Writing Rubric 3 (Teacher's Toolkit) to evaluate their own work for correctness.

Publishing Strategy

Discussion

Discuss the title of the Catton essay. Point out that many academic titles use a colon to separate the topic of the paper from its approach.

Art Link

Ask the art teacher to use the art class as a venue for making paper and for illustrating and binding the essays.

ONE on ONE Incorporate art into the lesson by making paper, and then illustrating and binding the essay. Books and articles on papermaking and bookbinding are available at the library, at bookstores, and online.

Evaluation

For help in grading this assignment, see "Grading Student Writing" (p. v) and Writing Rubric 3 (Teacher's Toolkit). Consider distributing a copy of the rubric to each student for use during the revision process.

Sentences

The expression of a complete idea requires more than a random arrangement of words, and successful communication is more than choosing the right kinds of words. Successful communication results from correctly placed and properly related words that create understandable thoughts. In the group of words *the golf course in the mountains,* the words are related but do not express a complete idea. What is there to know about the golf course in the mountains? However, the group of words *The golf course in the mountains presents a challenge to the accomplished golfer* creates a complete thought, a sentence. Successful communication, both spoken and written, depends upon the correct formation of sentences.

Defining Sentences

A **sentence** is a group of related words that has a **subject** (person, place, thing, or idea that the sentence is about) and a **predicate** (a verb and perhaps other words that tell what the subject is doing or what the subject is). A sentence **fragment** is a group of words that may have a subject but no verb, a verb but no subject, or neither a subject nor a verb; or it may have both a subject and a verb but may contain an additional word that makes the thought incomplete. *Because I played the course carefully* has both a subject and a verb, but it does not express a complete thought and is not a sentence. In this example the first word, *Because,* creates a fragment. A sentence, therefore, is a group of words that has a subject and a verb and nothing that makes it a dependent part of a sentence.

Kinds of Sentences

Sentences can be classified according to purpose. A **declarative sentence** makes a statement and ends with a period. An **interrogative sentence** asks a question and ends with a question mark. An **imperative sentence** gives a command or a request and usually ends with a period. An imperative sentence can end with an exclamation point when it expresses strong emotion. An **exclamatory sentence** shows strong emotion and ends with an exclamation point.

End Marks
p. 296

Quotation Marks
pp. 331–32

DECLARATIVE	The mountaintop golf course provides long fairways and difficult greens.
INTERROGATIVE	Have you scored par on a round of golf there?
IMPERATIVE	Take your turn last.
	Watch out for that large rock!
EXCLAMATORY	He made a hole in one on the eighteenth green!

ESL

Imperatives are used in emergencies or with people from whom you expect cooperation or obedience. Requests are often stated as polite questions, not as imperatives.

PLAIN COMMAND	Call an ambulance! (emergency)
POLITE COMMAND	Please repeat your name.
POLITE REQUEST	Could you please repeat your name.

OBJECTIVES

Students will

1. identify the four types of sentences and use appropriate end punctuation for each.
2. compose declarative, exclamatory, interrogative, and imperative sentences.
3. find simple subjects and predicates.
4. label sentences correctly with the seven sentence patterns.
5. write sentences using the seven sentence patterns.
6. identify words in sentences as nouns, pronouns, verbs, auxiliaries, adjectives, adverbs, verb-adverb combinations, prepositions, conjunctions, or interjections.

SENTENCES

Lesson Support

Student Worktext

Chapter 3 Review—pp. 433–34

Teacher's Toolkit

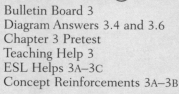

Bulletin Board 3
Diagram Answers 3.4 and 3.6
Chapter 3 Pretest
Teaching Help 3
ESL Helps 3A–3C
Concept Reinforcements 3A–3B

Test

Chapter 3 Test

Teaching Strategy

Introduction and Motivation

Ask students to find examples of sentences in the Catton essay that are difficult to analyze. Respond to their answers. Then assure them that they will find grammatical analysis easier after studying the material in this chapter.

Teaching Strategy

Induction

Ask your students to list the four kinds of sentences. *(declarative, exclamatory, imperative, interrogative)* Ask them what kind of sentence they most often use. *(declarative)* Then elicit situations when your students would use exclamatory, imperative, and interrogative sentences. *(Answers will vary.)*

ESL Consider using the following sentences as examples of intonation differences.

- *Declarative*—The window is open.
- *Interrogative*—Do you see the window?
- *Interrogative with question word*—Why is the window open?
- *Imperative*—Close the window.
- *Exclamatory*—I'm freezing!

ESL In spoken English, one of the major differences in the types of sentences is rising and falling pitch, called ***intonation***. The intonation of a sentence can be a hint about what type the sentence is.

- Declarative sentences have falling intonation at the end.
- Interrogative sentences that expect a *yes* or *no* answer have rising intonation at the end.
- Interrogative sentences that ask for information (using question words like *who, how, where,* and *why*) have falling intonation at the end.
- Imperative sentences have falling intonation at the end.
- Exclamatory sentences are stated at a higher pitch than other sentences or with a greater difference between the high and the low pitches.

Finding Subjects and Predicates

Because sentences have two basic parts, the subject and the predicate, knowing how to identify these parts correctly is important in sentence analysis. The first step is to locate the verb or **predicate**. The predicate tells something about the subject and may include auxiliaries. The **complete predicate** includes the **simple predicate** (or the complete verb) and all other words that relate to the verb.

SIMPLE PREDICATE	The breathtaking panoramic view from the fairway *has drawn* our attention away from the game many times.
COMPLETE PREDICATE	The breathtaking panoramic view from the fairway *has drawn our attention away from the game many times.*

Gerund and Infinitive Phrases pp. 98–99, 101–3

The second step in sentence analysis is to locate the subject of the sentence. Usually, the subject will tell who or what did the action of the verb or who or what was described. The **simple subject** is a noun or a pronoun or a group of words functioning as a noun. The **complete subject** includes the simple subject and any modifiers of the simple subject.

SIMPLE SUBJECT	The breathtaking panoramic *view* from the fairway has drawn our attention away from the game many times.
COMPLETE SUBJECT	*The breathtaking panoramic view from the fairway* has drawn our attention away from the game many times.

ESL In English, the subject of a clause usually comes before the verb (the simple predicate).

S V
When the golfers reached the final hole, the rain began.

Although the subject usually comes before the predicate, the subject of a request or a command may be omitted. In such cases the subject is the **understood subject *you***; the meaning is clearly understood.

(You) Give me my putter, please.

(You) Take your turn at putting.

TEACHING STRATEGY

Demonstration

Remind students that verbals (participles, gerunds, and infinitives) never function as simple predicates. Write the following sentences for display.

- The golf course hosting the tournament is in the next county. *(participial phrase)*
- Kari likes golfing. *(gerund)*
- We drove there to see the golf tournament. *(infinitive as adverb)*

Ask the students to identify the verbals in each sentence. *(hosting, golfing, to see)* Then help the students isolate the sentence patterns *(S-be-Advl, S-TrV-DO, S-InV).*

ESL

The subject *you* can be used with a command for clarity.

Miho, *you* go first.

It can also be used for emphasis, making the command stronger. For example, a mother might say to her careless child, "*You* shut the door right now."

The subject in some sentences may not be immediately apparent because the subject and the verb are in **inverted order**. The inverted order places the verb or a part of the verb before the subject. An interrogative sentence places the subject between the parts of the verb. Inverted order often occurs in sentences that begin with *there* or *here*. (*There* and *here* are almost never the subject of a sentence.)

Sentences p. 69

S/V Agreement, Inverted Order pp. 150–51

V V S
Standing at the tee box *was* my chief **rival.**

V S V
Did **he** *hit* the ball in the fairway?

V S
There *are* two **couples** in the foursome today.

V S
Here *are* the **scores** for today.

ESL

When English inverts the normal word order to form a question (an interrogative sentence), the complete subject changes places with the auxiliary verb, not with the main verb.

Statement	**Grant** and **Lee** *were bringing* the Civil War to its end.
Question	*Were* **Grant** and **Lee** *bringing* the Civil War to its end?

If there are two or more auxiliaries, only the first one occurs before the subject.

Statement	**He** *has been examining* the similarities and differences between these two men.
Question	*Has* **he** *been examining* the similarities and differences between these two men?

Kinds of Sentences pp. 132–33

Subjects and verbs may be compound. **Compound subjects** share the same verb and **compound predicates** share the same subject.

Compound Subjects	My **brother** and **I** *enjoy* playing golf together.
	The **selection** of the club and the **approach** to the tee *are* two important aspects of any golf game.
Compound Predicates	The golf **instructor** *encouraged* me to practice putting and *showed* me how to hold my club.
	James *practiced* his swing and *improved* his game by six strokes.

Teaching Strategy

Induction

Ask students to write several inverted-order sentences. Ask volunteers to share their sentences by writing them for display. Ask students when inverted order most frequently occurs. *(with questions or with statements beginning with* here *or* there*)*

Teaching Strategy

Modeling

Use students' inverted-order sentences to demonstrate how to isolate the simple subject and verb. Rearrange several sentences into regular order (not inverted) while explaining the process.

ESL Strategy

Use ESL Helps 3A, 3B, and 3C (Teacher's Toolkit) to clarify and practice using inverted subjects and verbs.

in SUMMARY

A **sentence** is a group of related words with a subject and a predicate and nothing that makes it dependent on another sentence.

A **fragment** may have a subject but no verb, a verb but no subject, or neither a subject nor a verb. A fragment also may have both a subject and a verb but contain a word that makes it a dependent part of a sentence.

A **subject** is the topic of the sentence. The **predicate** is a verb and perhaps other words that tell what the subject is doing or what the subject is.

A **declarative sentence** makes a statement and is followed by a period. An **interrogative sentence** asks a question and is followed by a question mark. An **imperative sentence** gives a command or a request and is followed by a period. An **exclamatory sentence** shows strong feeling or emotion and is followed by an exclamation point.

The **complete predicate** includes the **simple predicate** (or complete verb) and all other words that relate to the verb. The **complete subject** includes the **simple subject** and any modifiers of the simple subject.

The subject of a request or a command may be the **understood subject *you***.

Inverted order places the subject after the verb or between the parts of the verb.

Compound subjects share the same verb and **compound predicates** share the same subject.

3.1 PRACTICE *the skill*

Identify each sentence as *declarative, interrogative, imperative,* or *exclamatory.* Place an appropriate punctuation mark at the end of each sentence.

declarative 1. Although some cultures approach meal times as a social experience, others view food simply as a necessity.

declarative 2. Japanese culture has developed unique dining traditions.

declarative 3. The Japanese do not talk while eating or drinking.

interrogative 4. Did you know that the Japanese frequently lift their plates or bowls to their mouths when they are eating rice or miso soup?

imperative 5. Watch out for etiquette violations when dining with the emperor!

imperative 6. Never lick your fingers when you are eating a meal in Japan. or !

ENRICHMENT

Encourage students to research the dining traditions and etiquette of foreign cultures. Consider dividing the class into small groups to research a culture, present findings, and provide samples of one authentic dish from that land. Alternatively, invite a guest speaker who has lived in a different nation to present aspects of that nation's particular dining customs.

SpeechLink

Inform students that many corporations with interests overseas pay individuals to speak to their employees about the proper forms of etiquette in foreign countries. Consider hosting a mock "employee training day" on which students present speeches on foreign customs and etiquette as if they were training a corporation's staff members.

declarative 7. Although Korean chopsticks are metal and American chopsticks are plastic, Japanese chopsticks are wooden.

interrogative 8. Why should you learn about Japanese dining?

declarative 9. Knowing some social graces will enhance your Japanese dining experience.

exclamatory/declarative 10. I'm very eager to try these tips when I visit Japan! or .

3.2 PRACTICE *the skill*

Underline the simple subject once and the simple predicate twice. If the subject is understood, write *you* in the blank.

you 1. Compare the family values of different cultures with your own.

_____ 2. Mexicans give their families priority over work.

_____ 3. Unlike people of other cultures, Americans typically concentrate on the nuclear family.

_____ 4. Members of extended families often demonstrate their loyalty and help relatives in need.

_____ 5. The Hawaiian term for the extended family is *o'hana*.

_____ 6. Filipino children and teens are expected to behave well and therefore rarely receive praise in public.

you 7. Notice older Asian children caring for younger siblings.

_____ 8. Native Americans respect elderly family members for their wisdom.

_____ 9. Youthfulness, a quality valued by American culture, receives more respect and attention than age.

_____ 10. There are differences in family relationships from culture to culture.

SCRIPTURAL APPLICATION

Point out the various admirable family values described in Practice the Skill 3.2. Emphasize that every culture has different values. Then ask students to cite scriptural admonitions for Christians to demonstrate respectful and compassionate behavior. *(Gal. 6:10; Eph. 4:3, 32; 1 Tim. 5:1–2; James 1:27; the Good Samaritan; Christ's example)* Encourage your students to go beyond accepted cultural protocol and to follow the supreme example of Christ, the source of all goodness in culture. Emphasize the glory given to God when the lost see Christian teenagers modeling Christlikeness (Matt. 5:16).

3.3 REVIEW *the skill*

Underline the simple subject once and the simple predicate twice. If the subject is understood, write *you* in the blank.

_______ 1. Acadian culture thrives and flourishes in Louisiana.

_______ 2. The French originally settled in an area of Nova Scotia called Acadia.

_______ 3. Did the British king fear the French Acadians?

_______ 4. When did deportees exiled by the British travel to and settle in Louisiana?

_______ 5. Here is a copy of Longfellow's poem *Evangeline*, telling of the struggles and sorrows of a pair of Nova Scotia exiles.

_______ 6. Why is Evangeline's beloved Gabriel forced to leave Acadia?

_______ 7. *Cajun* became the shortened version of *Acadian* and is now the better-known term.

_______ 8. Creole cooking, based on grand cuisine, and Cajun cooking, based on common ingredients, are not the same.

___*you*___ 9. Watch out for the strong seasoning in Cajun cooking!

_______ 10. Found in Cajun cooking is a memorable flavoring: pepper sauce!

Basic Sentence Patterns

All English sentences contain at least a **subject** (sometimes understood *you* in an imperative sentence) and a **verb**. Some sentences need only these two components, but others require more. The kind of verb in the sentence determines whether it will be followed by a complement. A **complement** ("completer") is a word or phrase that completes the thought of the sentence; along with the verb, it is part of the complete predicate. To locate a complement, say the subject and verb of the sentence and then ask yourself *whom?* or *what?* If there is a reasonable answer, then you will have identified a complement. If there is no reasonable answer, then the sentence is probably complete without one. These different combinations of words can be expressed as the **basic sentence patterns** of English. All simple sentences are based upon these patterns, and all other sentences are formed from simple sentences.

Verbs
pp. 43–44

WITHOUT COMPLEMENT	The beautiful oak tree *stands* in the middle of the front yard.
WITH COMPLEMENT	The leaves of the beautiful oak tree *are* bright **orange** and subtle **gold**.
	The artist *drew* a beautiful oak **tree** with orange and gold leaves.

Literature Link

Read an excerpt from Henry Wadsworth Longfellow's poem *Evangeline* and encourage students to research and to present a brief summary of the work.

TEACHING STRATEGY
Participation

Use Bulletin Board 3 (Teacher's Toolkit) to demonstrate the various sentence patterns.

TEACHING STRATEGY
Introduction and Participation

Inform students that behind every sentence is a logical sentence pattern. Explain that the use of language, even by those unaware of the cognitive bases of syntax, is a testament to God's logic and order.

TEACHING STRATEGY
Introduction and Discussion

Ask students to name the sentence patterns. *(S-InV, S-TrV-DO, S-TrV-IO-DO, S-LV-PN, S-LV-PA, S-be-Advl, S-TrV-DO-OC)* Ask how analyzing sentence patterns differs from analyzing parts of speech. *(Parts of speech: examine how an individual word functions in a sentence. Sentence patterns: examine how the verb and any complements relate to the subject and function within the clause.)*

TEACHING STRATEGY
Demonstration

Display these sentences: *Larry watched his brother's baseball game from the dugout. Larry watched as his brother played baseball.*

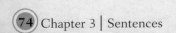

S-InV

The **S-InV** pattern has a subject (S) and an intransitive verb (InV). This pattern does not have a complement. The sentence is complete with only a subject and a verb. Remember, however, that other modifying words may be present in the sentence in addition to the subject and the verb.

S V
The children played.

S InV
The enthusiastic children played in the orange and yellow leaves.

The phrase *in the orange and yellow leaves* modifies the verb *played*, but the phrase is not a complement because it does not receive the action of the verb (i.e., it does not complete the verb).

S-LV-PN

The **S-LV-PN** pattern uses a linking verb (LV) to link the subject (S) with the complement of the sentence, the **predicate noun** (PN). The predicate noun renames or identifies the subject. The forms of the verb *be* are the most common linking verbs when they are used as the main verb in a sentence.

S LV PN
The apple orchard is my favorite place on the farm.

S LV PN
Apple cider became a popular drink at the store.

S-LV-PA

The pattern **S-LV-PA** also uses a linking verb to link the subject with the complement. In this pattern, however, the complement is a word that describes the subject, a **predicate adjective** (PA). Common linking verbs that are completed by

Show the students how to isolate the pattern of each sentence *(S-TrV-DO; S-InV)* by disregarding the possessives, prepositional phrases, and other modifiers. Remind them that transitive verbs will be followed by words answering the questions *who?* or *what?* and that intransitive verbs require no complement.

Teaching Strategy

Analysis

In sentences where the pattern seems debatable between *S-InV* and *S-TrV-DO,* encourage the students to try this simple test: insert an appropriate third-person pronoun for the dubious direct object. If the sentence makes sense, the pattern is *S-TrV-DO,* not *S-InV.*

Teaching Strategy

Analysis

Display these sentences from Catton's essay:

- "These frontier men were the precise opposites of the tidewater aristocrats."
- "Life was competition."
- "Their encounter at Appomattox was one of the great moments of American history."
- "Yet it was not all contrast, after all."

Ask the students what the common pattern is for these sentences. *(S-LV-PN)* Illustrate how linking verbs are like equal signs.

predicate adjectives are *be, appear, become, grow, remain, seem, stay, look, feel, smell, sound,* and *taste.* The last five verbs refer to the five senses.

S LV PA
The apple yield *was* very large in October.

S LV PA
My investment in an apple orchard *became* very profitable.

S LV PA
The samples of ripe red apples *tasted* good to the shoppers in the store.

Either a predicate noun or a predicate adjective can be called a *subjective complement* because either one completes the meaning of the subject.

S-*be*-Advl

Adverbs pp. 50–51

Adverbial Prepositional Phrases p. 54

Interrogative Sentences p. 69

Agreement pp. 150–51

Reflexive Pronouns pp. 213–14

The sentence pattern **S-*be*-Advl** uses only forms of the verb *be*. The complement of the verb is an adverb or an adverbial prepositional phrase showing place or time. The complement is called an **adverbial** (Advl) to show its adverb-like qualities.

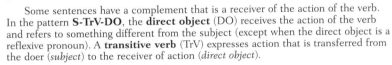

S *be* Advl
The best apples are *there.*

S *be* Advl
Baskets of ripe apples were *in the orchard.*

This pattern often occurs in sentences with inverted order. The interrogative adverbs *where* and *when* may be a part of this pattern as well as other patterns.

The ripened apples are *where?* — *Where* are the ripened apples?

The sale is *when?* — *When* is the sale?

Some sentences use the placeholder *there* to stand in the subject position. In these sentences, *there* is an **expletive** and is not an adverbial. The verb *be* follows the expletive, which is followed by the subject and then the adverbial. Sentences with the expletive *there* typically introduce new topics.

There are twenty bushels of apples in the storage shed.

Twenty bushels of apples are in the storage shed.

S-TrV-DO

Some sentences have a complement that is a receiver of the action of the verb. In the pattern **S-TrV-DO**, the **direct object** (DO) receives the action of the verb and refers to something different from the subject (except when the direct object is a reflexive pronoun). A **transitive verb** (TrV) expresses action that is transferred from the doer (*subject*) to the receiver of action (*direct object*).

S S TrV DO
My brothers and I gathered apples from the orchard.

S TrV DO
Sometimes we ate too many apples.

S-TrV-IO-DO

A transitive verb may have another complement in the sentence in addition to the direct object. An **indirect object** (IO) comes between the verb and the direct object and tells *to whom* or *for whom* the action is done. The indirect object does not follow a preposition. The verb in the **S-TrV-IO-DO** pattern is a transitive verb.

Reinforcement

Remind students that linking verbs such as *appear, become,* and *stay* also function in the *S-LV-PN* sentence pattern. Display these examples: *Todd* seems *the clear winner of the science fair. His experiment* remains *the one the judges most esteemed.*

Teaching Strategy
Discussion

Inform the students that words commonly used as adverbials include adverbs that can be remembered with their opposites, such as *on/off, in/out, before/after, over/under, here/there,* and *now/then.*

Teaching Strategy
Analysis

To test whether a noun functions as a direct object, try replacing it with an objective pronoun and determine whether the meaning stays the same. Display these sentences: *Mrs. Bell believes Charlie. Mrs. Bell believes him.* Because *Charlie* can be replaced with *him, Charlie* is a direct object in this sentence.

Teaching Strategy
Analysis

Display these sentences from Catton's essay:

- "These men were bringing the Civil War to its virtual finish."
- "Lee embodied the noblest elements of this aristocratic ideal."
- "Through him, the landed nobility justified itself."
- "Forms and patterns meant nothing."

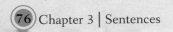

S TrV IO DO
The customers gave Mother the money for the bushel of apples.

S TrV IO DO
Many tourists brought their friends apples from the mountains.

If the indirect object is replaced by a prepositional phrase, the sentence pattern changes. The object of a preposition cannot function as anything else at the same time.

S TrV IO DO
The store clerk took Dad the money for the bushel of apples.

S TrV DO
The store clerk took the money for the bushel of apples to Dad.

S-TrV-DO-OC

Some sentences with a direct object may have an additional complement that renames or describes the direct object. An **objective complement** (OC) is usually a noun or an adjective that completes the idea of what the verb does to the direct object. The **S-TrV-DO-OC** pattern would, of course, have a transitive verb.

S TrV DO OC
The researcher considered our apples the best in the county.

S TrV DO OC
The local farmers elected Dad president of the organization.

Indirect objects and objective complements never occur in the same sentence pattern.

ESL

Notice the close relationship between the direct object and the objective complement. You can usually imagine that there is a form of *be* between them.

S TrV DO OC
The farmers elected Dad (to be) president.

Dad *is* president because the farmers elected him.

in SUMMARY

An **intransitive verb** is a verb that does not have a complement.

A **linking verb** serves as a link, or equal sign, between the subject and a subjective complement.

A **predicate noun** renames or identifies the subject and follows a linking verb.

A **predicate adjective** describes the subject and follows a linking verb.

An **adverbial** is an adverb or adverbial prepositional phrase of time or place that completes the verb *be* in the sentence pattern S-*be*-Advl.

A **transitive verb** has a complement that receives the action of the verb.

A **direct object** receives the action of a transitive verb.

An **indirect object** comes between the verb and the direct object and tells *to whom* or *for whom* the action of the verb is done.

An **objective complement** is a noun or an adjective that follows the direct object and renames or describes the direct object because of the action of the verb.

Ask students to identify the common pattern for these sentences. *(S-TrV-DO)* Point out how the action of the verb is carried across to a receiver, or direct object. (If a student asks about retained objects in passive sentences, consult pages 187–90.)

TEACHING STRATEGY
Participation

Point out to the students that certain verbs, such as *consider, name, elect, declare, call,* and *make,* often take objective complements.

- The coach declared Bianca the most valuable player.
- The grandchildren considered Grandma the best cook.
- Riding in a plane made him nervous.
- Wesley's friends called him Freckles.

Elicit more sentences using these verbs and write them for display. Remind the students that the objective complement can be either an adjective or a noun and that it always follows the direct object. Ask the students to suggest other verbs that frequently take objective complements.

TEACHING STRATEGY
Demonstration

In both *S-TrV-IO-DO* and *S-TrV-DO-OC* sentence patterns, functional verbs for the *TrV* positions are rather limited. For example: *S-TrV-IO-DO—ask, buy, give, offer, pay, sell, tell* and *S-TrV-DO-OC—believe, consider, declare, find, keep, name.*

The terms *Native American* (in sentences 3 and 5) and *eye contact* (in sentence 8) are open compound nouns.

Diagram answers for Practice the Skill 3.4 appear in the Teacher's Toolkit. If you teach sentence diagramming, perhaps consult *The Writer's Toolbox* for sample diagrams.

The words *greeting* in sentence 6 and *greetings* in sentence 7 should be diagrammed as nouns, not gerunds, in this context.

3.4 PRACTICE *the skill*

Label the sentence patterns *S-InV, S-LV-PN, S-LV-PA, S-be-Advl, S-TrV-DO, S-TrV-IO-DO,* or *S-TrV-DO-OC.* If the adverbial is a prepositional phrase, underline it.

1. Within a particular region, various social norms (S) exist (InV).
2. Travel guides (S) give (TrV) tourists (IO) help (DO) with cultural transitions.
3. Native American cultures (S) exhibit (TrV) infrequent use (DO) of hand gestures.
4. However, storytellers (S) are (LV) skillful (PA) with gestures as a means of communicating with their audiences.
5. A Native American storyteller (S) was (be) in the auditorium (Advl) last night.
6. The handshake (S) is (LV) the traditional American greeting (PN).
7. Some cultures (S) include (TrV) more formal greetings (DO) such as bowing or hugging.
8. Direct eye contact (S) is (LV) disrespectful (PA) in many Hispanic cultures.
9. Europeans (S) consider (TrV) eye contact (DO) during a conversation a sign (OC) of respect.
10. Eye contact (S) in Japan and China depends (InV) largely on social status.

3.5 USE *the skill*

Use the given information to write a sentence that has the sentence pattern indicated in parentheses. The new sentence does not need to include all the words from the original sentence(s). You may need to use a new subject or verb. *(Answers may vary.)*

1. There are two areas where the Inuit live. They live in arctic and subarctic regions. (*S-TrV-DO*)

   The Inuit establish their homes in two areas, arctic and subarctic regions.

2. Alaska, Canada, Greenland, and Russia have Inuit communities. (*S-be-Advl*)

   Inuit communities are in Alaska, Canada, Greenland, and Russia.

Evaluation

Instruct the students to freewrite for several minutes on cultural or family traditions important to them. Then direct students to use their freewriting as the basis for seven sentences modeling the seven basic sentence patterns. Check the students' work for accuracy and review any concepts that they do not fully understand.

Enrichment

Distribute a copy of Teaching Help 3 (Teacher's Toolkit) to each student. Use the teaching help as a review of sentence patterns.

3. They are stereotyped as living in igloos; however, this is not the case for most Inuit people. *(S-InV)*

Most Inuit people do not live in igloos.

4. Except for winter hunts, the Inuit rarely use igloos. *(S-InV)*

Except for winter hunts, the Inuit rarely live in igloos.

5. Today, many Inuit live in modern houses with heating systems. *(S-TrV-IO-DO)*

Today, many Inuit build themselves modern houses with heating systems.

6. When it comes to hunting, the Inuit are excellent. *(S-LV-PN)*

The Inuit are excellent hunters.

7. The Inuit often get skins and meat from caribou for protection and nourishment. *(S-TrV-IO-DO)*

Caribou skins and meat provide the Inuit protection and nourishment.

8. The Inuit believe in sharing food and labor with family and friends. *(S-LV-PN)*

Sharing food and labor with family and friends is an Inuit belief.

9. The Inuit religion says that humanity's harmony with nature is a primary concern. *(S-TrV-DO-OC)*

The Inuit religion declares humanity's harmony with nature primary.

10. As they progress through the new millennium, the Inuit depend less and less on the land for their needs. *(S-LV-PA)*

In the new millennium the Inuit are less dependent on the land for their needs.

Sentences | Chapter 3 79

Diagram answers for Cumulative Review 3.6 appear in the Teacher's Toolkit. If you teach sentence diagramming, perhaps consult *The Writer's Toolbox* for sample diagrams.

3.6 CUMULATIVE *review*

Label the sentence patterns *S-InV, S-LV-PN, S-LV-PA, S-be-Advl, S-TrV-DO, S-TrV-IO-DO,* or *S-TrV-DO-OC.* If the adverbial is a prepositional phrase, underline it. In the blank, identify the part of speech of each italicized word.

conjunction 1. The regional conflict (S) between the Jews *and* the Samaritans was (LV) evident (PA) in Christ's encounter with the Samaritan woman at the well.

noun 2. She (S) may have called (TrV) Jesus (DO) a Jew (OC) because of His *manner* of dress.

adverb 3. *Consequently*, she (S) questioned (TrV) Jesus' request (DO) for water.

verb 4. Jesus (S) then *gave* (TrV) the woman (IO) a surprising truth (DO).

adjective 5. The water (S) of *this* well was (LV) not a permanent satisfaction (PN) for her thirst.

verb 6. However, Jesus (S) *could* give (TrV) the woman (IO) the satisfying gift (DO) of God, forgiveness and eternal life.

preposition 7. *In spite of* the conflict between the Jews and the Samaritans, Jesus (S) freely gave (InV).

noun 8. Jesus' gift (S) of *salvation* continues (InV) today.

pronoun 9. Salvation (S) is (be) from God and for *anyone* (Advl).

interjection 10. *Yes,* we (S) can experience (TrV) the same gift (DO) of God, everlasting and abundant life.

BJU Living Gallery presentation of the painting *Chris[t] and the Samaritan Woman* by Francois de Troy, the B[ob] Jones University Collection. Photo by Unusual Films.

THINK ABOUT IT

Thinking Skills

Critical thinking, creative thinking, higher-order thinking—professional educators routinely use these terms to describe what they want their students to be able to do. But what do these terms mean? What do educators mean when they refer to "thinking skills"?

Scriptural Application

Read the words of Jesus Christ in Mark 12:30 and emphasize the importance He places on the mind. Then use Acts 18:4 to show students that thinking is not an end in itself. Rather, believers should use their mental capabilities to try to persuade others of the truth.

Reinforcement

Use Chapter 3 Review on pages 433–34 for additional test review.

Evaluation

Use Chapter 3 Test to evaluate students' understanding of the content and concepts of the chapter.

80 Chapter 3 | Think About It

In the broadest sense, these terms identify not what someone thinks but rather how he thinks. In other words, someone's thinking skills are the procedures that he or she uses to process information. Does he accept the information unquestioningly? Or does he evaluate statements to judge their validity? Does he consider alternatives in order to solve a problem? Is he able to make connections, draw conclusions, and apply what he has learned for use in real-life situations?

Many people focus on what to think. Students want to know what they will be tested over so that they can learn the answers to likely questions. They want to know what they will need to know in order to survive and even prosper in life outside the classroom. Employees may wonder what they are supposed to learn from a presentation or a report. A promotion, a raise, perhaps even job security itself may depend on gleaning the right information. New parents want to know what traits and behaviors they can expect their child to display at every stage of life.

Scripture tells us that God considers what we think to be important too. In fact, the Bible is full of commands about what we are to think on, commands such as Philippians 4:8.

> Finally, brethren, whatsoever things are true, whatsoever things are honest, whatsoever things are just, whatsoever things are pure, whatsoever things are lovely, whatsoever things are of good report; if there be any virtue, and if there be any praise, think on these things.

Clearly, God wants us to know what to think. However, He also wants us to know how to think. Specifically, God wants us to think as He thinks. In Romans 12:2, Paul admonishes other Christians: "And be not conformed to this world: but be ye transformed by the renewing of your mind, that ye may prove what is that good, and acceptable, and perfect, will of God." In this verse and many others, the Bible teaches that true wisdom—both what to think and how to think—is impossible without God.

Of course, an ungodly person can master human reasoning skills. History proves that men and women throughout history have used appeals to logic and emotion in order to sway people toward evil. Human wisdom, nevertheless, can never measure up to God's highest standard. Notice the contrast in these Scripture passages.

> For the wisdom of this world is foolishness with God. (1 Cor. 3:19)

> The fear of the Lord is the beginning of wisdom: a good understanding have all they that do his commandments: his praise endureth for ever. (Ps. 111:10)

Likewise, a Christian who knows what to think (scriptural truths) but does not know how to think (proper reasoning) may be unable to counter the arguments of one who disagrees with God. Each Christian is to "be ready always to give an answer to every man that asketh [him] a reason of the hope that is in [him] with meekness and fear" (1 Pet. 3:15). For the Christian, then, what to think and how to think are equally important because both are important to God.

Thinking Biblically

The very structure of Bible books like Romans says something about the kind of critical thinking God wants to encourage. God could have just handed out a perfect list of rules or a detailed doctrinal statement, but instead He inspired letters. And these letters force you to reason, to push your mind through multiple steps of logic, to draw conclusions. Books like Romans are in the Bible not merely to teach you what to think but also to teach you how to think.

Thinking It Through

Read Mark 12:30 and Acts 18:4. Then write a paragraph concerning what these verses teach about what Christians should think and how they should think.

Thinking Biblically

This insightful quotation from an old book would be worth wading through with your students: "The writer [of NT epistles] does not announce a succession of revelations, or arrest the inquiries which he encounters in men's hearts by the unanswerable formula, 'Thus saith the Lord.' He arouses, he animates, he goes along with the working of men's minds, by showing them the workings of his own. He utters his own convictions, he pours forth his own experience, he appeals to others to 'judge what he says,' and commends his words 'to their conscience in the sight of God.' He confutes by argument rather than by authority, deduces his conclusions by processes of reasoning, and establishes his points by interpretations and applications of the former Scriptures. . . .

. . . Why all this labor in proving what might have been decided by a simple announcement from one entrusted with the Word of God? Would not this apostolic declaration that such a statement was error, and that such another was truth, have sufficed for the settlement of that particular question? Doubtless! but it would not have sufficed to train men's minds to that thoughtfulness whereby truth becomes their own, or to educate them to the living use of the Scriptures as the constituted guide of inquiry."[1]

1. T. D. Bernard, *The Progress of Doctrine in the New Testament* (London: MacMillan and Co., 1864), 157–58.

OBJECTIVES

Students will

1. differentiate between interior monologue and other forms of writing.
2. recognize and describe the characteristics of a Christian's interior monologue.
3. identify examples of interior monologue in outside reading.
4. develop a character for whom to write an interior monologue.
5. express a goal for an interior monologue in a single sentence.
6. write an interior monologue using restraint but including a variety of details.
7. revise an interior monologue for naturalness, details, grammar, usage, and mechanics.
8. balance direct thoughts, indirect thoughts, speech, action, and description in an interior monologue.
9. publish an interior monologue.

Chapter 4 Overview			
Topic	**Pages**	**Support Materials**	**Days**
Nonverbal Phrases	88–92	Bulletin Board 4 Chapter 4 Pretest Teaching Help 4A Practice/Use the Skill 4.1–4.3	39
Participial Phrases	92–96	Teaching Help 4B Practice/Use the Skill 4.4–4.5	40
Gerund Phrases	96–101	Practice/Use the Skill 4.6–4.7	41
Persuasive Essay	109–15	Writing Worksheet 5	42, 44–46, 50
Infinitive Phrases	101–3	Practice the Skill 4.8	43
Practice and Review	103–6, 435–36	Use the Skill 4.9 Concept Reinforcements 4A–4B Cumulative Review 4.10 Teaching Help 4C Chapter 4 Review	47
Chapter 4 Test			48
From the Written Word	107		49

INTERIOR MONOLOGUE

Lesson Support

Teacher's Toolkit

Bulletin Board 4
Writing Worksheets 4A–4B
Writing Rubric 4

SCRIPTURAL APPLICATION

Discuss with students the importance of Matthew 12:34 and ask for examples of

In the novel By the Light of a Thousand Stars, *the main character, Catherine, is a self-absorbed wife and mother who is more interested in the décor of her home than in the welfare of her family. This excerpt follows her after she finds a door open when she returns from shopping. Her son, Hardy, is downstairs listening to loud music and does not know that an intruder could be in the house. In this interior monologue from the book, notice how Catherine's thoughts give us insight into her character. And notice, too, how the monologue builds suspense, although it appears to be only random thinking.*

By the Light of a Thousand Stars by Jamie Langston Turner

[Catherine] yanked a paper towel from the roller, then stooped to pick up the peach with one hand and swipe at the floor with the other. Sparkle Flynn, the cleaning woman she hired once a week, would be in on Friday to do the floors, so a quick wipe-up would do for now. She threw away the paper towel, set the damaged peach on the counter next to the sink, then retrieved her keys from the floor and tossed them on top of her purse.

She had half expected to hear voices coming from the living room or den, but the only thing she heard as she stood in the middle of the kitchen with her hands on her hips was the muffled racket of Hardy's music coming from downstairs. From the kitchen she could see into the dining room, and she moved so that she could admire the new floral table runner with its heavy blue tassels on the mahogany sideboard. She still wondered, though, if burgundy tassels would have looked better with the wallpaper.

She walked from the kitchen through the hallway and into the den. No one was there. She turned and looked across the hallway into the living room. It, too, was empty. She scowled at the open front door, then walked over and closed it firmly. That eucalyptus wreath had cost a small fortune to put together, and it was all for nothing if it couldn't be seen from the street. She had kept telling the floral designer to add another couple of silk roses here, then a few more sprigs of berries there, and then some curly willows, and when she heard the final cost, Catherine had said, "Well, my word, you'd think that stuff was made out of solid gold!"

She moved now toward the draperies and adjusted a tieback, then noticing that a sofa cushion was out of place, she straightened it. Catching sight of herself in the mirror above the fireplace, Catherine turned her head from side to side. Dottie Puckett really knew how to fix hair, she thought.

It suddenly dawned on her that it hadn't even entered her mind to be afraid. Here she was going from room to room, looking for a

ADDITIONAL INFORMATION

A professor of creative writing at Bob Jones University, Jamie Langston Turner makes her home in Greenville, South Carolina, near small southern towns like those she has created as settings for her novels. Turner's works include *Suncatchers, Some Wildflowers in My Heart, By the Light of a Thousand Stars,* and *A Garden to Keep.*

times when someone's speech has revealed his thoughts, perhaps unintentionally (e.g., a politician says something perverse, not realizing the microphones are on). Discuss how students can "keep [their] heart[s] with all diligence" (Prov. 4:23).

Literature Link

Instruct the students to read the excerpt from *By the Light of a Thousand Stars* silently in class. Then ask the students to identify and discuss passages that reveal Catherine's character through her thoughts and actions.

TEACHING STRATEGY
Modeling

Begin this lesson by displaying a brief interior monologue or stream-of-consciousness piece. After a few moments, ask students to describe what kind of writing you are modeling. Then ask students to look at the definitions of *interior monologue* and *stream of consciousness* on page 84. Ask them to identify the model as one of the two and to explain their answers. Remind students that the two techniques often overlap.

TEACHING STRATEGY
Discussion

Discuss the final paragraph of the introduction to interior monologue on page 84. Ask students what the purpose of Catherine's monologue is. *(Answers will vary but should include the author's desire to portray Catherine's extreme self-absorption.)* Discuss what a Christian's interior monologue should reflect. How might Catherine's monologue change if she were a believer? *(Answers will vary but should include a focus on God and people instead of on things.)*

stranger! She was alone in the house for all practical purposes, since Hardy sure couldn't be counted on to be of any help, even when he was home. Well, she *wasn't* afraid. Nobody with ulterior motives was going to leave his umbrella in plain sight and forget to close the front door. Still, she paused and laid a hand across her chest. She briefly imagined herself on stage—the heroine in a suspense drama, unsuspecting of imminent danger.

Thinking Biblically

The powerful Welsh preacher D. Martyn Lloyd-Jones spoke of self-talk in a famous series of sermons called *Spiritual Depression: Its Causes and Its Cure*. He was referencing Psalm 42:5. "Have you realized that most of your unhappiness in life is due to the fact that you are listening to yourself instead of talking to yourself? Take those thoughts that come to you the moment you wake up in the morning. You have not originated them but they are talking to you, they bring back the problems of yesterday, etc. Somebody is talking. Who is talking to you? Your self is talking to you. Now this man's treatment [in this psalm] was this: instead of allowing this self to talk to him, he starts talking to himself. 'Why art thou cast down, O my soul?' he asks. His soul had been depressing him, crushing him. So he stands up and says: 'Self, listen for a moment, I will speak to you.' . . . This self of ours . . . has got to be handled. Do not listen to him; turn on him; speak to him; condemn him; upbraid him; exhort him; encourage him; remind him of what you know, instead of listening placidly to him and allowing him to drag you down and depress you. For that is what he will always do if you allow him to be in control. The devil takes hold of self and uses it in order to depress us. We must stand up as this man did and say: 'Why art thou cast down? Why are thou disquieted within me?' Stop being so! 'Hope thou in God, for I shall yet praise Him.'" [1]

1. (Grand Rapids: Eerdmans Publishing, 1993), pp. 20–21.

WRITING Interior Monologue

For out of the abundance of the heart the mouth speaketh.
Matthew 12:34

Pronouns pp. 37–38

Your brain is never silent. Even when you are sleeping, it continues to generate thoughts and images. It is the part of us that allows us to "talk to ourselves." The psalmist David speaks to himself in Psalm 42:11: "Why art thou cast down, O my soul? And why art thou disquieted within me? hope thou in God: for I shall yet praise him, who is the health of my countenance, and my God."

Thinking Biblically

Controlling your inner thoughts is very difficult. They grow from what you love (out of the abundance of the heart the mind thinks! [cf. Matt. 12:34]), and what you love can't be turned on or off with a switch. But God has given you something to chew on that can renovate your heart and therefore your thoughts: Scripture. This idea sounds ridiculous to people who consider the Bible boring, but to someone who relishes God's words as David did, meditation on the Bible is not a chore. "O how love I thy law! it is my meditation all the day," David said (Ps. 119:97). His thinking was a fruit of his loving.

The **interior monologue** is a narrative technique that presents a character's thoughts and feelings in a way that makes the reader feel that he is seeing the person's true inner self. Of course, the writer controls the monologue and the impressions given to the reader. Interior monologue may be written in either first or third person, depending on the point of view used in the rest of the piece. Interior monologue is closely related to dramatic monologue (poetry) and to soliloquy (drama). Sometimes an author chooses to write in stream of consciousness form. Similar to interior monologue and, in fact, often overlapping and merging with it, **stream of consciousness** is a technique that attempts to record uninterrupted thought. Stream of consciousness writing usually seems irrational and spontaneous, jumpy and disjointed, whereas interior monologue generally flows meaningfully—albeit meanderingly—from point to point. To compose such a monologue, the writer must make the writing appear random but still maintain his purpose.

The interior monologues of Christians should be different from the kind Catherine indulges in. Take a moment to think about what should characterize a Christian's interior monologue.

Your Turn

Choose a specific moment in which someone would be consciously thinking to himself. Think about who the person is. What is his main character trait? His goal? His attitude toward the situation he is in? Then write his interior monologue, using complete sentences.

Teaching Strategy
Discussion

Remind students to keep scriptural guidelines in mind while writing their interior monologues (Phil. 4:8, James 3:14–17, etc.).

Planning Strategy
Motivation

Ask students to keep a journal of conversations they hear or of thoughts they have that might be included in an interior monologue.

Planning Strategy
Participation and Discussion

Challenge students to find two to three examples of interior monologue from outside reading, such as another textbook, a novel, a newspaper, or a magazine. Allow students who bring examples to class to read them aloud. Discuss what makes the examples interior monologue.

One on One

Ask your student to find two to three examples of interior monologue from outside reading and to share the examples with you. Discuss the selections together.

Planning Strategy
Modeling and Participation

Make a character web as a class by choosing someone whom the whole class knows. Write the answers for display. You might also include words or phrases that person says habitually. Write these to the side of

Planning

✔ **Hone your listening skills.** Find a time to listen closely to the people around you. In the mall, at church, in a restaurant—listen to how people talk and how their thoughts flow naturally from one topic to the next. You may find it helpful to write portions of some of the conversations down in a journal so that you can refer to them later. (Be careful about recording anyone without prior consent to do so.)

✔ **Look for examples of interior monologue in your reading.** Once you begin looking for it, you will be surprised at how often you encounter examples of interior monologue in the newspaper, a magazine, or a book you are reading. Notice how and when the writer uses interior monologue. Decide what aspects of the monologue you find especially believable or amusing.

✔ **Decide on a character.** You may want to create a character or choose someone from history for whom you can fill in some fictional details. If you create a character, choose a name for him. Jamie Langston Turner, an author whose fictional characters always seem strikingly real, says, "Writing is such fun because you get to step into so many characters' lives and see what it's like to be all those different people." Make your character real to yourself before attempting to make him real to your audience.

✔ **Make a character web.** Write your character's name in the middle of a sheet of paper. Draw lines extending from the name as shown below. At the end of each line, write words and phrases that describe the character—from likes and dislikes to character qualities. Then circle the one trait that seems to best represent the character or embodies the dominant trait you want your fictional character to possess.

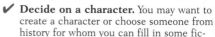

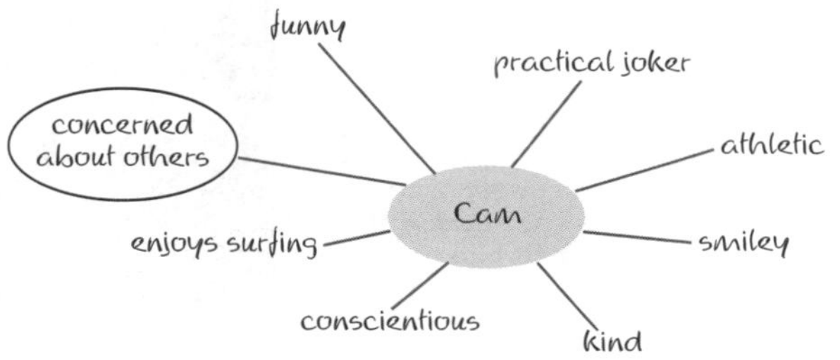

✔ **Decide on a goal for your character.** The discussion of interior monologue on page 84 indicates that good interior monologue appears to be random but in reality has a purpose or a goal. What will the goal of your character's written thoughts be? Will he answer for himself the question of where to attend college or which summer camp to work at? Write your character's goal in one sentence and keep it in mind as you complete your planning.

✔ **Construct a thought train.** At the left side of a sheet of paper, write the character's goal for himself. Draw a box around the sentence. Then draw a line extending to the right and make another box. Write a thought in the box that the character might have about getting to his goal. Continue the thought train. You can branch off on as many tracks as you need to.

OVERVIEW of the WRITING PROCESS

Planning—looking for examples of interior monologue, deciding on a character, making a character web, deciding on a goal, constructing a thought train, choosing a track, and freewriting about a character

Drafting—writing an interior monologue, self-editing when writing, and keeping a goal in mind

Revising—listening for problems while reading monologue aloud; balancing direct thoughts, indirect thoughts, speech, action and description; using peer evaluation; and making changes to monologue

Publishing—dramatizing or posting an interior monologue, developing a monologue into a short story, or recording a monologue

Ask students for sample narrations in first person *(I, me, my, we, us, etc.)* and in third person *(he, she, him, her, they, them, etc.)*.

the web and tell students that these could be worked into an interior monologue about that person.

Planning Strategy
Analysis

Ask students what they think Catherine's character web might look like. If desired, make a web for display using what students know of Catherine.

Planning Strategy
Participation

Ask students to make a character web for the character they are considering for the interior monologue. Encourage them to think of this as a brainstorming activity. Distribute a copy of Writing Worksheet 4A (Teacher's Toolkit) to each student to use for this activity.

Planning Strategy
Participation

After students select a person about whom to write, ask them to decide on a goal for the interior monologue. Remind them that this goal will probably not appear in the monologue but will give focus to their writing.

- ✔ **Choose a track.** With a colored pen or pencil, trace one line of thought through the thought train. Next to each box you have chosen, write some details of action or description that might occur while the character is thinking.
- ✔ **Freewrite about the character you have chosen.** Set a time limit for yourself and write without stopping. This method may be especially helpful for the interior monologue since portraying an impression of free and continuous thought is the effect you want your writing to have.

Drafting

- ✔ **Follow the track.** Using the track you have highlighted and your freewriting, write an interior monologue, filling it out with details of action and description of each thought in the train.
- ✔ **Avoid overindulging yourself.** It can be tempting to allow your character to ramble on too much, making the character say everything you personally would like to say. Realize that a character can follow too many tracks of thought. Turner says of her own process that once "the words . . . start coming out in this new persona's voice, the ideas crowd in on each other, and before long I'm thinking, 'Okay, enough, you've got to stop now. This is getting too long.'" Use the same restraint with your character.

tip

Try to choose actions for the character that either complement what he is thinking or that are ironically opposite of it. For example, when Catherine is trying to discover whether someone has broken into her house, she stops to admire her hair in a mirror.

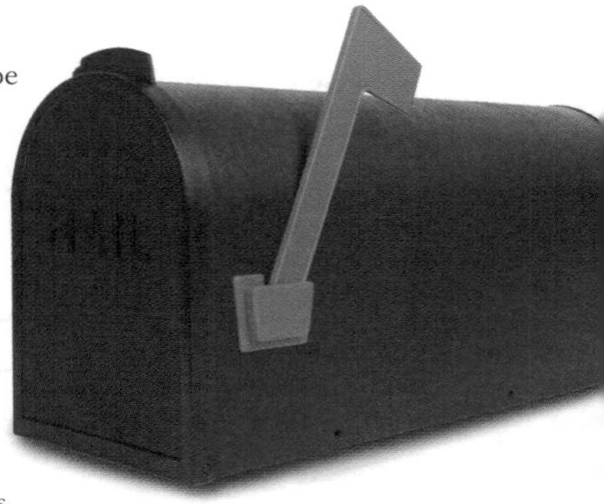

- ✔ **Remember the character's goal.** Although you want the character's goal to be clearly presented, be sure to include some elements that seem random or unplanned in order to maintain a sense of reality. Adding such elements may make your monologue longer, but it will keep the reader believing that the character is real.

  For example, when a character hears a political advertisement on the radio, he begins to think of running for president himself. At the same time, however, an unopened envelope catches his eye and he absently reaches for it. It turns out to be a rejection letter from a law school. Even as he reads it, knowing that it has great bearing on his desire to be president someday, he still pursues his daydream of campaigning.

Revising

Sentence Energy pp. 366–69

- ✔ **Read your monologue aloud.** Does it sound natural? Does it sound as though it is the record of a person's thinking? Do the details you have added to the monologue help or hinder this impression?

Quotation Marks pp. 329–30

- ✔ **Use a balance of direct thoughts, indirect thoughts, speech, action, and description.** In the example about Catherine, the author sometimes lets us hear Catherine speak aloud, sometimes quotes her thoughts directly, sometimes summarizes her thoughts, and intersperses all of these techniques with action and description. How well did you balance these narrative modes in your monologue?

Planning Strategy

Demonstration

Distribute or display Writing Worksheet 4B (Teacher's Toolkit). Discuss the thought train with the students and show them how to make one of their own. Alternatively, construct a thought train using the person in the character web activity.

Drafting Strategy

Participation

Since this assignment is brief and requires no research, students may be able to complete a draft in class.

Writing Workshop

Conduct a minilesson on "Sentence Energy," pages 366–69. Emphasize that vivid verbs, descriptive details, strict accuracy, and figurative language infuse writing with energy. Encourage students to look for ways to incorporate this lesson into their writing.

Drafting Strategy

Discussion

Ask students to look at their monologues for examples of details that seem random or unplanned. Challenge them to include surprising or unusual ideas in their interior monologues to create or maintain a sense of reality.

Revising Strategy

Participation

Instruct students to record their monologues for play back. Ask them to listen for sentences that sound unnatural or that fail to give the impression that they are the record of a person's thoughts. Ask them also to listen for a balance of direct thoughts, indirect thoughts, speech, action, and description.

✔ **Add direct thoughts, indirect thoughts, speech, action, or description where needed.** Try not to have the same narrative mode dominate a section. You want the reader to notice the scene, not your method of creating it.

✔ **Allow a peer to evaluate the monologue.** Ask someone else to read the draft and tell you what he thinks of the character. Does his assessment match your intent? Ask him what questions came to his mind while he read. Listen carefully to his suggestions for making your monologue more interesting and believable.

✔ **Make changes to the monologue.** Compare your peer's comments about your monologue to your own observations about changes you want to make. Which changes are most important to make? Which ones will enhance the reader's enjoyment of the piece? Make changes for clarity and effect. Then proofread the monologue, checking for mistakes in grammar, usage, and spelling.

Publishing

✔ **Dramatize your monologue.** Make two copies of your monologue. Choose someone to act the part of your character. You will read the monologue as the other person pantomimes the scene. He will need to say aloud any lines the character actually speaks. Act out your scene for an audience.

✔ **Post your monologue on a website.** Allow others to share in your character's thoughts by posting the interior monologue either on a personal or class website. Encourage reader feedback to your piece.

✔ **Develop your monologue into a short story.** Use the character you have created to write a short story. Let the reader know whether your character accomplishes his goal.

✔ **Record your monologue.** Make a recording of all of the class monologues. Place the recording somewhere so that others can listen to the readings and then write their impressions of the monologues.

Some Ideas to Consider

History

- Write an interior monologue for a historical person at a crucial moment. For example, what might a soldier have been thinking as he prepared for the battle of Gettysburg? You might also imagine what Lincoln was thinking as he wrote his address to be delivered at Gettysburg after the battle.

Literature

- Write an interior monologue for a character from a classic novel.

Revising Strategy
Discussion

Point out that some writers do not use quotation marks within interior monologue since the technique is a type of discourse. Most agree, however, consistency is the key.

Revising Strategy
Analysis

Ask students to analyze how Turner uses quotation marks in the excerpt from her novel. Point out that the marks are used only when quoting what Catherine has said in the past—not her present thoughts.

Revising Strategy
Peer Response

Instruct students to exchange monologues and to use Writing Rubric 4 (Teacher's Toolkit) or the questions on page 87 for evaluation.

Publishing Strategy
Participation

Pair students for presentation of the interior monologues. Allow students to dramatize their monologues or, if they are uncomfortable performing, simply to read their monologues. If students will be presenting the monologues to an outside audience, direct them to group the pieces by theme or character type or some other organization.

Publishing Strategy
Demonstration

Use Bulletin Board 4 (Teacher's Toolkit) to display students' interior monologues.

Evaluation

For help with grading this assignment, see "Grading Student Writing" (p. v) and Writing Rubric 4 (Teacher's Toolkit).

OBJECTIVES

Students will

1. identify prepositional, absolute, and appositive phrases.
2. compose sentences that contain prepositional, absolute, and appositive phrases.
3. identify participles and participial phrases and the words they modify.
4. label participles as *present, past, perfect, progressive passive,* or *perfect passive.*
5. rewrite a paragraph using participles and participial phrases for conciseness.
6. identify the participles and participial phrases incorporated into a sample paragraph.
7. identify gerunds and gerund phrases and their functions in the sentences.
8. rewrite sentences by inserting gerunds or gerund phrases as needed.
9. identify infinitives and infinitive phrases and their functions in the sentences.
10. combine pairs of sentences using an infinitive phrase as the connector.
11. label infinitives or infinitive phrases as *simple, passive, perfect, perfect passive, progressive,* or *elliptical.*
12. label basic sentence patterns.
13. identify words and phrases as *prepositional, appositive, participial, gerund,* or *infinitive.*
14. identify the function of words and phrases as *noun, adjective,* or *adverb.*

Many English sentences contain groups of words that either add meaning to the subject, verb, or complement or replace a single-word subject or complement. These groups of words, both phrases and clauses, have a function in the sentence. A **phrase** is a group of related words that does not contain both a subject and a verb. Phrases can be divided into two types: **nonverbal phrases** and **verbal phrases.** Phrases may function as nouns, adjectives, or adverbs.

Nonverbal Phrases

Prepositional Phrases

Adjectives and Adverbs pp. 48–51

A **prepositional phrase** (the most frequently used of all the phrases) consists of a preposition, its object, and any modifiers of that object. The preposition shows a relationship between its object and another word in the sentence. Prepositional phrases function either as **adjectival prepositional phrases** that modify nouns or pronouns or as **adverbial prepositional phrases** that modify verbs, adjectives, or adverbs.

The elderly woman *with the tracts* arrived at the street corner.

This faithful woman stood *near the shipyard gate.*

She continued steadfast *in her purpose.*

To this woman, the task *before her* was one *of great importance.*

In some sentences an adjectival prepositional phrase will modify the object of a preceding prepositional phrase. In such sentences the second phrase is part of the first phrase because it is a modifier of the first.

She faithfully fulfilled her mission *(to the workers (of the shipyard)).*

(On a cold winter night,) she handed a salvation tract *(to a shipyard worker (from the local area)).*

Absolute Phrases

Participial Phrase pp. 92–94

An **absolute phrase** consists of a noun followed by a participle or participial phrase. The absolute phrase is independent (absolute) from the rest of the sentence. The phrase indicates a circumstance and loosely modifies the remainder of the sentence; the absolute phrase does not modify a specific word in the sentence.

When an adverb clause has a noun subject and expresses a circumstance, it can be reduced to an absolute phrase by the omission of the subordinating conjunction and replacement of the verb with the related participle.

PHRASES

Lesson Support

Student Worktext

Chapter 4 Review—pp. 435–36

Teacher's Toolkit

Diagram Answers 4.2, 4.4, 4.6, 4.8
Chapter 4 Pretest
Teaching Helps 4A–4C
Concept Reinforcements 4A–4B

Test

Chapter 4 Test

TEACHING STRATEGY
Introduction and Induction

Display these sentences and ask the students for possible words to fill in the blanks:

- The two girls, _?_ and _?_, left the room. *(Janice, Isabell)*
- The teacher _?_ _?_, they left unobserved. *(being distracted)*
- I sat _?_ the front _?_ the room and saw them leave. *(in, of)*

Ask the students to identify the kinds of phrases formed. *(appositive, absolute, and prepositional)*

TEACHING STRATEGY
Discussion and Participation

Point out that some prepositions must be paired with certain words to communicate the proper meaning. Display some examples of these pairings: *agree with, to, on; respon-*

ADVERB CLAUSE	*Because the woman was elderly,* the worker took the tract.
ABSOLUTE PHRASE	*The woman being elderly,* the worker took the tract.
ADVERB CLAUSE	*Because the woman was faithful in prayer,* the Holy Spirit began to work in the life of the shipyard worker.
ABSOLUTE PHRASE	*The woman being faithful in prayer,* the Holy Spirit began to work in the life of the shipyard worker.

Appositive Phrases

An **appositive** is a noun or pronoun that renames or identifies a preceding noun or pronoun. The appositive and its modifiers make up an **appositive phrase**. Most appositives are nouns; however, an appositive may be an intensive pronoun or a personal pronoun.

Dan, *the shipyard worker,* remembered the gospel tract in his pocket.

As he began to read the tract, Dan considered certain things: *God, life, and death.*

Dan *himself* saw his need of salvation.

Two workers, *Dan and he,* read their Bibles together.

Reflexive and Intensive Pronouns pp. 213–14

Although an appositive usually appears immediately after the word it is renaming, an appositive may appear later in the sentence. The sentence, however, could be written so that the appositive immediately follows the noun.

Eventually, all Dan's family members were saved: *Kathy, Matt, and Kara.*

Eventually, all Dan's family members—*Kathy, Matt, and Kara*—were saved.

Colon pp. 315–16

in SUMMARY

A **phrase** is a group of related words that does not contain both a subject and a verb.

A **prepositional phrase** consists of a preposition, its object, and any modifiers of that object. A preposition shows a relationship between its object and another word in the sentence.

Prepositional phrases are either **adjectival** or **adverbial**.

An **absolute phrase** is independent from the rest of the sentence. An absolute phrase consists of a noun followed by a participle or a participial phrase.

An **appositive** is a noun or pronoun that renames or identifies a preceding noun or pronoun.

An **appositive phrase** consists of an appositive and its modifiers.

sible to, for; wait for, at, on. Elicit sentences that use these expressions and ask students to explain the differences in meaning.

TEACHING STRATEGY
Modeling

Tell the students that when the participle of an absolute phrase is a form of *to be,* such as *being* or *having been,* the participle is often omitted from the phrase but understood. Display these sentences and show the students how to distinguish absolute phrases: *The season [being] over, the soccer players packed their uniforms. [Having been] Guests at Grandma's for over a week, the boys were ready to go home.*

REINFORCEMENT

Distribute a copy of Teaching Help 4A (Teacher's Toolkit) to each student for additional practice with absolute phrases.

TEACHING STRATEGY
Discussion

Remind the students that gerund and infinitive phrases can also be appositives. Display and discuss these sentences: *Her hobby, cultivating bonsai and orchids, has brought her much pleasure. Gavin's supreme desire, to win others to Christ, was his constant motivation.*

TEACHING STRATEGY
Discussion

Explain that a close appositive (not set off by commas) is more significant than the noun or pronoun preceding it. For example, *We* tourists *noticed a storm brewing in the distance. Effie is reading a poem by her*

The use of the name *Cape Cod* to describe rectangular steep-gabled houses began in the early to mid-1900s.

Oriel refers to a type of bay window that extends from an upper story and is supported from below by a visible bracket.

Horace Walpole (1717–97) was a scholar of the Renaissance and Medieval ages, an epistolarian, and the key impetus behind the Gothic novel genre. Walpole is also known by his pseudonym *William Marshall.*

4.1 PRACTICE *the skill*

Place parentheses around each prepositional phrase. Draw an arrow from each phrase to the word it modifies. Then label each phrase *Adj* (adjectival) or *Adv* (adverbial).

1. (To the potential homeowner,) the architecture (of a house) can be very important. *Adv, Adj*
2. One style (of house) called Cape Cod has a steep roof, two or more dormer windows, and a door (in the center (of the front wall.)) *Adj, Adj, Adj*
3. Other characteristics (of Cape Cod houses) include a chimney (in the middle (of the house,)) sometimes opening (into several fireplaces (in different rooms,)) and an exterior (of wide clapboard siding) *Adj, Adj, Adj, Adv, Adj, Adj*
4. There are dramatic differences (between Cape Cod houses and Victorian Gothic houses.) *Adj*
5. Victorian Gothic houses have features (like steep roofs, decorative windows, and chimneys) that are grouped (in a cluster.) *Adj, Adv*
6. The owner (of a Victorian Gothic house) could look down (from his pinnacles and battlements,) (past oriel windows) (to a stately lawn.) *Adj, Adv, Adv, Adv*
7. The Victorian Gothic style was begun (by Horace Walpole,) a British writer (of Gothic novels,) who wanted his home to look (like the castles (in his writing.)) *Adv, Adj, Adv, Adj*
8. (In the United States today,) ranch-style houses are quite common (because of their simplicity and relaxed feeling.) *Adv, Adv*
9. (During the 1950s,) ranch houses were built (throughout the country.) *Adv, Adv*
10. Ranch houses, (with open and flexible interior space,) usually have one story (with a low-pitched roof and deep eaves.) *Adj, Adj*

favorite author William Wordsworth. For additional information, see *The Writer's Toolbox.*

TEACHING STRATEGY
Analysis and Participation

Display the following sentences:

- You soccer players know what is needed to win this game.
- Nori's friend Venetia Meyers revealed the secret of Nori's upcoming surprise birthday party.
- Elliot told no one except his teammate Ives Briggs that he was resigning from the team.

Ask the students to identify the appositives in these sentences and what the appositives have in common. *(soccer players, Venetia Meyers, Ives Briggs—close appositives.)* Explain that close appositives are either nouns renaming a personal pronoun or proper names needed to identify the one discussed. Reiterate that close appositives are not set apart with commas.

TEACHING STRATEGY
Reinforcement and Participation

Display the following definitions with their blanks. Direct the students to fill in the blanks with the correct answers.

- A prepositional phrase consists of the preposition, its __ and any __ of the noun or pronoun. *(object, modifiers)*
- An absolute phrase is __ from the rest of the sentence. *(independent)*

4.2 PRACTICE *the skill*

Identify each italicized phrase as *prepositional, absolute,* or *appositive.*

appositive 1. Over the front door of a Georgian Colonial house sits a decorative crown, *an elaborate half-circle of wood or stone.*

appositive 2. Georgian Colonial, *a favorite style of the prosperous,* is the style of many imposing early dwellings.

prepositional 3. The front door stands *between flattened columns.*

absolute 4. *The windows being most noticeable,* Georgian Colonial houses typically have rows of double-hung windows.

prepositional 5. *On either end of a classical Georgian Colonial house* sits one or more chimneys.

appositive 6. One of three kinds of roofs covers a Georgian Colonial: *gabled, hipped, or gambrel style.*

absolute 7. *The roofs typically slanting down to the house with little overhang,* Georgian Colonial houses can easily be spotted.

appositive 8. Stratford, *Robert E. Lee's Virginia home,* exemplifies Georgian Colonial architecture.

prepositional 9. The Old North Church *of Boston, Massachusetts,* is another example of the style.

prepositional 10. *Inside the church* are arched and windowed balconies.

Sentence diagram answers for Practice the Skill 4.2 appear in the Teacher's Toolkit. If you teach sentence diagramming, perhaps consult *The Writer's Toolbox* for sample diagrams.

The term *Georgian Colonial* is treated as an open compound noun in this context; however, if students diagram *Georgian* as modifying *Colonial, accept it as correct.*

4.3 USE *the skill*

Use the given information to write a sentence that contains the kind of phrase indicated in parentheses. *(Answers may vary.)*

1. Every homeowner should take steps to fireproof his home. *(prepositional)*

   Every homeowner should take steps to prevent fires in his home.

2. Gutters easily fill with debris. Potential debris includes leaves, pine needles, seeds, and trash. *(appositive)*

   Gutters easily fill with debris: leaves, pine needles, seeds, and trash.

3. Gutters should be kept clear. The risk of a fire beginning on the roof decreases. *(absolute)*

   Gutters being kept clear, the risk of a fire beginning on the roof decreases.

- An appositive __ a preceding noun. *(renames)*

Literature Link

Materials
- a picture of Horace Walpole's estate Strawberry Hill

Show students the picture of Walpole's estate. Emphasize that Gothic architecture mirrors the tenor of Walpole's famous Gothic novel *The Castle of Otranto* (1764), the first work of its type. Encourage students to research the characteristics of this genre and share their findings with the class. *(a maiden in distress; a dark ominous castle; frightening, mysterious, and supernatural occurrences; a pitiless villain, etc.)* Ask students to search for other works with Gothic elements. *(Charlotte Brontë's* Jane Eyre; *Charles Dickens's* Great Expectations, *etc.)*

Speech Link

Show students that Use the Skill 4.3 presents a thesis (first sentence) and supporting points (additional sentences) for a motivational speech. Ask students to state what the thesis of a speech based on this practice exercise might be. *(Every homeowner should take steps to fireproof his home.)* Encourage students to write an original and supporting points for an outline of a motivational speech. Alternatively, students could write and deliver a motivational

4. A wildfire is very dangerous. Sparks can enter unscreened vents and set a house ablaze. *(prepositional)*

   During a wildfire, sparks can enter unscreened vents and set a house ablaze.

5. A chimney is safer with a cap. Sparks from the chimney will not start a fire in landscaping near the house. *(absolute)*

   A chimney having been capped, sparks from the chimney will not start a fire in landscaping near the house.

6. Faulty connections can spark a fire. Keep furnace and stove electrical plugs well repaired to reduce fire risks. *(prepositional)*

   Keep furnace and stove electrical plugs well repaired to reduce risk of fire from faulty connections.

7. Overhanging tree limbs are a potential means of carrying fire to a house. Prune tree limbs so that they are at least ten feet from the house. *(appositive)*

   Prune overhanging tree limbs, potential fire hazards, so that they are at least ten feet from the house.

8. Firewood is safest stored some distance from the house. A blaze in the woodpile will not spread to the house as easily. *(absolute)*

   Firewood being stored some distance from the house, a blaze in the woodpile will not spread to the house as easily.

9. A messy yard full of tall grass and trailing vines is another fire hazard. Clean up and maintain such a lawn. *(appositive)*

   A messy yard full of tall grass and trailing vines, another fire hazard, should be cleaned up and maintained.

10. An obscured or missing house number is problematic. Firefighters may have trouble finding a house. *(prepositional)*

   Firefighters may have trouble finding a house with an obscured or missing house number.

Verbal Phrases

Parts of Speech pp. 35–37, 42–45, 48–51

A **verbal** is a verb form used as another part of speech—a noun, an adjective, or an adverb. **Participles**, **gerunds**, and **infinitives** can function alone or as part of a phrase. A **verbal phrase** includes the verbal and any subjects, objects, or modifiers of the verbal. A verbal will not function as the simple predicate in a sentence.

Participles and Participial Phrases

Tense pp. 178–79

A **participle** functions as an adjective. A **participial phrase** comprises a participle and any modifiers or complements of the participle. Basic participles use the present form of the verb and add a present- or past-tense ending (*-ing* or *-ed*, usually).

paragraph with a topic sentence and supporting sentences. Instruct students to use a variety of phrases in either activity.

Teaching Strategy

Induction

Before explaining verbals, display the following sentence: *The __ deer bounded into the pathway of the __ car.* Ask for volunteers to fill in the blanks with *-ing* words, most of which will be verbals. *(running, oncoming)* Then explain that verbals intrinsically have attributes of both a verb and another part of speech (in this case, adjectives).

Teaching Strategy

Induction

Ask the students to insert into the blanks of the following sentences the correct word choice from these options: *yelling, dropped, complicated.*

- The __ game became boring to the students. *(complicated)*
- __ with excitement, the team members encouraged Heidi to run faster. *(Yelling)*

Participle	The *approaching* basketball season will provide many opportunities to display school spirit.
	The *planned* schedule still needed some changes.
Participle with Modifiers	The senior cheerleaders *chosen* **earlier in the school year** have prepared for the first pep rally.
Participle with Complements (and modifiers)	*Repeating* the new **cheers** during the pep rally, the student body learned quickly.
	Having finished the **decorations** for the school gym, we were ready for the first game.

Present Participle

A **present participle** has an *-ing* ending attached to the first principal part of the verb. A present participle usually comes before the noun that it modifies and expresses action that is simultaneous with the main verb. A present participial phrase may appear before or after the word that it modifies.

A *cheering* crowd creates a feeling of anticipation.

The team *approaching* the court first was the opponent.

Settling into their offense, the Raiders handled the ball well.

A present participle may look like part of a progressive verb. However, a participle functions as an adjective, not as the predicate in a sentence.

Present Participle	*Dribbling* down the court, the player lost control of the ball.
Progressive Verb	The player *was dribbling* the ball down the court.

ESL

If you have trouble distinguishing a progressive verb from a participle that follows a form of the linking verb *be (is, am, are, was, were)*, try changing the tense. Use *yesterday* and simple past tense, or use *tomorrow* and simple future tense. A progressive verb will lose its *-ing*, but a participle will not.

Progressive Verb	The owner **is welcoming** guests to his restaurant.
	Yesterday the owner **welcomed** guests to his restaurant.
	Tomorrow the owner **will welcome** guests to his restaurant.
Linking Verb + Participle	That restaurant's décor is **welcoming**.
	Yesterday that restaurant's décor was **welcoming**.
	Tomorrow that restaurant's décor will be **welcoming**.

Also, you can sometimes add *very* before a participle: *It's* **very welcoming**. But *very* never modifies a progressive verb—or any other kind of verb. (Check with a native speaker of English if you are not sure whether a sentence sounds right.)

- Having ___ the puzzle, I lost several pieces. *(dropped)*

Call upon a few of them to explain why these words are participles even though the forms are different.

Teaching Strategy

Demonstration

To help students distinguish the present participle (first principal part of the verb ending in *-ing*) from a progressive verb, tell the students to note that the progressive verb will have two components: a form of *to be* as an auxiliary verb plus the present participle. Display the following sentences: Walking *along the trail, we saw a female bear with her cubs.* (present participle) *While we* were walking *along the trail, we saw a female bear with her cubs.* (progressive verb)

Reinforcement

Distribute a copy of Teaching Help 4B (Teacher's Toolkit) to each student for additional practice in distinguishing between present participles and progressive verbs.

Past Participle

A **past participle** is the same as the third principal part of the verb. Past participles usually express a passive meaning. Past participles are formed from transitive verbs, and they modify the noun affected by the verb. On the other hand, when the third principal part of the verb is part of a simple predicate, a form of the helping verb *have (have, has, had)* will accompany the verb.

Past Participle	The *defeated* team soon began practices again.
	The team, *defeated* because of inexperience, soon began practices again.
Passive Meaning	*(The team was defeated because of inexperience.)*
Active Predicate of the Sentence	The opposing team *has defeated* us every year.
Passive Predicate of the Sentence	The team *had been defeated* by their inexperience but soon began practices again.

Perfect Participle

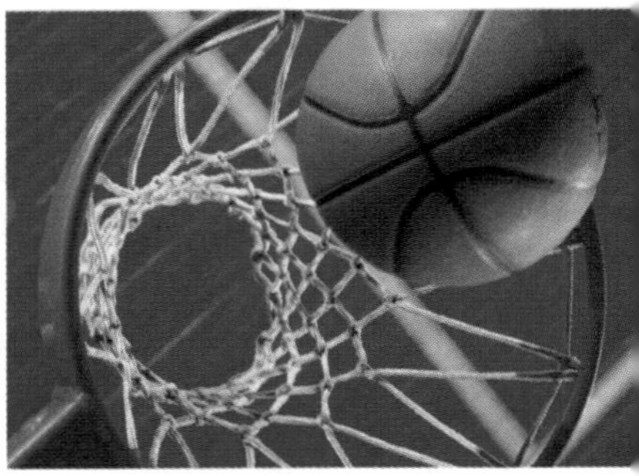

A **perfect participle** uses *having* with the third principal part of the verb. The perfect participle expresses an action that occurred or was completed before the action of the main verb.

> *Having practiced* his free throws, the basketball player made all of his foul shots.
>
> The coach, *having prepared* diligently during the week, substituted players freely.

Other Participles

Other less common participles, the **progressive passive participle** and the **perfect passive participle**, are easily recognized as participles because the first word of the phrase ends in *-ing*. Because these participles are passive, a form of *be* is present in the participial phrase. In the sentences below, the first revision uses a progressive passive participle, and the second revision uses a perfect passive participle, a form of *have* making it perfect. These kinds of participial phrases are helpful in sentence reduction.

Longer	We are just completing a game, and it is our first victory of the season.
Progressive Passive Participle	The game *being completed* will be our first victory of the season.
Longer	The coach was called for an interview, but he did not reveal his game plan.
Perfect Passive Participle	*Having been called* for an interview, the coach did not reveal his game plan.

in SUMMARY

A **verbal** is a verb form used as another part of speech.

A **verbal phrase** includes the verbal and any subjects, objects, or modifiers of the verbal.

A **present participle** has an *-ing* ending attached to the first principal part of the verb.

Teaching Strategy

Induction

Display the following sentences.

- Having ___, Blair persevered to win the race.
- Having ___, Grandmother baked the cookies.
- Maurice, having ___, was exhausted and ready to sleep.
- Having ___, we felt prepared to take the test.

Instruct the students to fill in the blanks with verbs. *(Answers will vary.)* After displaying some of the responses, ask students to identify the form of the verb they supplied after *having. (the third principal part)* Point out to the students that the entire participial phrase states an action that occurred before the action of the main verb.

Teaching Strategy

Participation and Discussion

Display the following sentences, adding *been* to make perfect passive participle examples:

- Having been ___, Blair persevered to win the race.
- Having been ___, Grandmother baked the cookies.
- Maurice, having been ___, was exhausted and ready to sleep.

94 Chapter 4 | Phrases

A **past participle** is the same as the third principal part of the verb.

A **perfect participle** uses *having* plus the third principal part of the verb.

Other participles, such as **progressive passive participle** and **perfect passive participle**, are helpful in sentence reduction.

4.4 PRACTICE *the skill*

Underline each participle or participial phrase. Draw an arrow from each participle to the word it modifies. Then identify the kind of participle as *present, past, perfect, perfect passive,* or *progressive passive.*

present 1. The persevering gardener carefully maintains his hedges.

perfect 2. Having planted the hedges in the ground, he prunes them to six or eight inches.

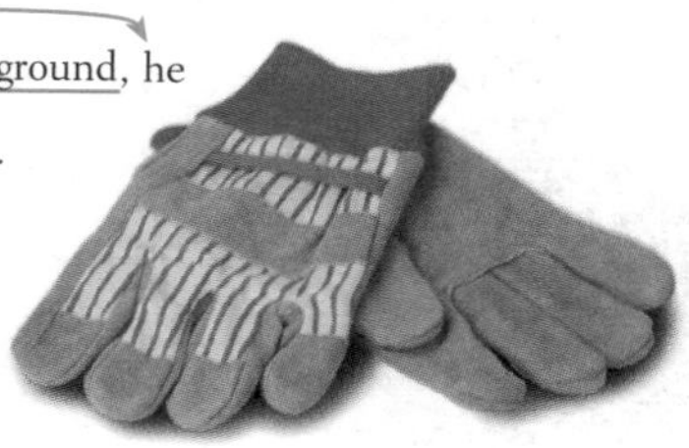

past 3 The pruned plants should develop a number of low branches, the foundation of the hedge.

past 4. Late in the season, the newly grown branches should be cut back about halfway.

perfect passive 5. Having been cut back, the hedge grows with new vigor.

present 6. A hedge with a shape of a descending wedge, widest at the bottom, thrives.

progressive passive 7. Being cut in a wedge-shape, the hedge receives sun and rain on all its branches.

perfect 8. Having flattened the top of a hedge, the gardener may have inadvertently weakened the hedge.

past 9. A rounded hedge has no ledge for heavy snow.

perfect passive 10. Having been carefully nurtured and shaped, a good hedge becomes an elegant screen, wall, or border.

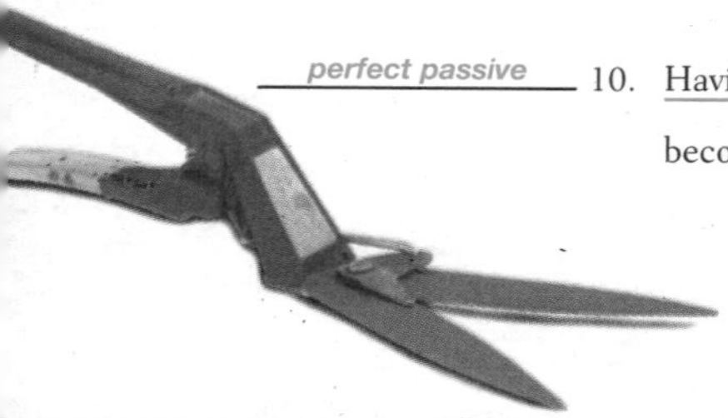

Sentence diagram answers for Practice the Skill 4.4 appear in the Teacher's Toolkit. If you teach diagramming, perhaps consult *The Writer's Toolbox* for sample diagrams.

- Having been ___, we felt prepared to take the test.

Ask students to fill in the blanks with verbs. *(Answers will vary.)* After displaying the responses, ask them to explain the difference in meaning by the addition of *been*. *(The participle becomes passive, and the word described by the participle is acted upon instead of acting.)* Remind them that although this perfect passive participle is not frequently used, it can help condense sentence content.

Reinforcement

Remind students that the entire phrase formed from the perfect participle and the perfect passive participle function as adjectives.

4.5 USE *the skill*

To improve the conciseness of the following paragraph, rewrite the paragraph using eight participles or participial phrases. Underline the new participles or participial phrases. *(Answers may vary.)*

One requirement for roses that bloom beautifully is regular care. After the gardener has planted a bush or shrub rose, he must prune it to only twelve to twenty-four inches in height. Thereafter, he must prune the rosebush every year in order to remove canes that have withered or died and to promote growth. A shrub rose that is pruned correctly should have the canes cut back by one-third of their height. Roses that climb require less care. Once a climbing rose has been trained to grow on its supports, the plant needs only moderate care. Once the gardener has identified any canes that have been damaged, he should cut the canes at least an inch below the damage. A rosebush that is well tended can produce lovely blooms for years.

One requirement for beautifully blooming roses is regular care. Having planted a bush or shrub rose, the gardener must prune it to only twelve to twenty-four inches in height. Thereafter, he must prune the rosebush every year in order to remove withered or dead canes and to promote growth. A correctly pruned shrub rose should have the canes cut back by one-third of their height. Climbing roses require less care. Having been trained to grow on its supports, a climbing rose needs only moderate care. Once the gardener has identified any damaged canes, he should cut the canes at least an inch below the damage. A well-tended rosebush can produce lovely blooms for years.

Gerunds and Gerund Phrases

Nouns pp. 35–37

A **gerund** is a verb form used as a noun. Like nouns, gerunds can be subjects, direct objects, predicate nouns, objects of the preposition, appositives, and occasionally indirect objects.

S **TrV** **DO**
Campaigning will improve a student's ability to interact with others.

S (App.) **TrV** **DO**
His main goal, *winning,* should not affect his principles.

S **TrV** **IO** **DO**
The candidate gave *campaigning* his undivided attention.

TEACHING STRATEGY
Modeling

Model for the students how to change the first sentence in Use the Skill 4.5. Direct them to alter the second sentence. Then ask the students to finish the skill independently.

TEACHING STRATEGY
Introduction

Explain to the students that because the gerund functions as a noun, it will not usually be set off by commas or other punctuation in the sentence. The major exception to that principle is the gerund appositive.

TEACHING STRATEGY
Demonstration and Participation

Display the following sentences: *At Kitty Hawk, North Carolina, the Wright brothers tested their early flying machine. That early flying had to be an exhilarating experience.*

Ask a student to explain how *flying* is used differently in each sentence. *(participle, gerund)* Remind them that both the gerund and the present participle will end in *-ing*.

The *-ing* ending is the indicator for a gerund. Distinguishing a present participle from a gerund depends on discernment of the function of the verbal in the sentence.

Present Participle	The *campaigning* students will have an opportunity to address the student body.
Gerund	*Campaigning* requires time and preparation.

A gerund and its modifiers and complements make up a **gerund phrase**. In a sentence, the gerund phrase functions as a single unit to perform a noun function.

S OP LV PA
The job of *preparing* materials for an election can be overwhelming.

S LV PN
Choosing a campaign committee was a difficult task.

S LV PN
The chairman's task was *determining* an effective plan.

S TrV DO
Early in the campaign, the chairman does his best *planning*.

Because gerunds are verb forms, gerunds can have subjects, complements, and modifiers. The "subject" of a gerund is actually a possessive adjective such as *his, my,* or *Tom's* that identifies the doer of the gerund's action.

The candidate found that *adopting* a friendlier demeanor made people more likely to listen to him.

The candidate found that **his** *adopting* a friendlier demeanor made people more likely to listen to him.

In the first sentence it is unclear whether the candidate or the people adopt a friendlier demeanor. Adding *his* as the subject of the gerund clarifies the meaning.

In addition, the use of a possessive as the "subject" of a gerund avoids confusion between a gerund and a participle that modifies a noun.

Pronouns with Gerunds pp. 209–10

The committee does not approve of that person planning the campaign for me.

The committee does not approve of that **person's** *planning* the campaign for me.

In the first sentence, the disapproval of the person is indicated. However, in the second sentence, the disapproval is of the planning.

A common error occurs when writers use an objective case pronoun as the "subject" of a gerund instead of a possessive case pronoun as the "subject." An understanding of sentence reduction will help to clarify this problem.

S TrV DO
The students understood [that he campaigned vigorously for the position.]

S TrV DO
The students understood his campaigning vigorously for the position.

It would be incorrect to write *The students understood him campaigning vigorously for the position.* The idea is not that the students understood *him* but that they understood his action.

Teaching Strategy

Participation and Induction

Display the following sentences:

- His ___ really angered the voters.
- We could understand their ___.
- Her ___ cannot be explained.
- The coach was not enthusiastic about Marcella's ___.
- Mother does not approve of the children's ___.

Ask the students to supply words that end in *-ing* to fill in the blanks. After displaying the students' responses, ask them what these *-ing* words are called. *(gerunds)* Instruct the students to explain what function the preceding possessive has for each gerund. *(subject of the gerund)* Emphasize the fact that the subject of a gerund should be a possessive in order to communicate the proper meaning. Read these sentences to the students:

- Mother does not approve of the children's jumping up and down on the bed.
- Mother does not approve of the children jumping up and down on the bed.

Ask the students which sentence communicates the proper meaning. *(Supplying the possessive subject of the gerund makes the meaning clear.)*

ESL A gerund is the verb form that can serve as an object of a preposition.
Your goal **of** *running a race each month* is impressive.

Present Gerund

The **present gerund**, like the present participle, is identified by the *-ing* ending on the first principal part of the verb. A present gerund expresses action that occurs simultaneously with that of the main verb.

Running for an important office takes hours of preparation.

The candidate's goal should be *running an ethical campaign.*

When a gerund functions as a modifying noun, it looks very similar to a present participle. Based upon the context of the sentence, a modifying noun has a meaning different from that of a present participle.

PARTICIPLE	The candidate was supported by all his *writing* friends, some of whom wrote excellent letters to the newspaper.
GERUND	Gerald sat at his *writing* desk, working on a new brochure.

Modifying Nouns p. 50

In the first sentence *writing* is a participle that tells what the friends do. In the second sentence *writing* is a gerund functioning as a modifying noun. The desk is not doing the writing; it is "a desk for writing."

Perfect Gerund

The **perfect gerund** uses *having* and the third principal part of the verb. A perfect gerund expresses action that occurred before the action of the main verb.

S LV PN
The candidate's primary accomplishment was *having raised* an enormous amount of money for his campaign.

S TrV IO DO
His *having run* for office in the past gives him valuable experience.

Passive Gerund

Another kind of gerund is the **passive gerund**, which uses a form of *be* just before the third principal part of the verb. The first example sentence contains a **present passive gerund**. The second example sentence contains a **perfect passive gerund**. The action of the perfect passive gerund occurs before the action of the main verb.

S TrV DO
Being coached in debate skills prepared the candidate for the student body debate.

S TrV DO
The slogan's *having been approved* by the faculty advisor created a feeling of anticipation.

TEACHING STRATEGY

Analysis and Discussion

Inform students that the perfect gerund and perfect participle have the same components (*having* + third principal part of the verb) as do the perfect passive gerund and the perfect passive participle (*having* + *been* + third principal part of the verb). Remind the students that they must carefully determine the use of the verbal in the sentence to distinguish the gerund from the participle. Then display the following sentences:

- **Perfect gerund used as subject:** *His having come late for practice every day* put Doug on probation.
- **Perfect participle:** *Having come late for practice every day*, Doug was put on probation.
- **Perfect passive gerund used as predicate noun:** Lucy's downfall was *having been found in the wrong place at the wrong time.*
- **Perfect passive participle:** *Having been found in the wrong place at the wrong time*, Lucy was set for a downfall.

These sentences show similarities in structure but differences in usage between the gerund and the participle. Point out that the participle is set off by a comma but that the gerund is not.

in SUMMARY

A **gerund** is a verb form used as a noun.

The **gerund phrase** consists of a gerund and its modifiers and complements.

A **present gerund** uses the first principal part of the verb and the *-ing* ending.

A **perfect gerund** (*having* plus the third principal part of the verb) expresses action that occurred before the action of the main verb.

Passive gerunds express passive meanings. A **perfect passive gerund** expresses action that occurred before the action of the main verb.

4.6 PRACTICE *the skill*

Underline each gerund or gerund phrase. Identify its function as subject *(S)*, direct object *(DO)*, predicate noun *(PN)*, indirect object *(IO)*, object of the preposition *(OP)*, or appositive *(App)*.

d

S 1. Having moved to a foreign country requires missionaries to adapt to new accomodations.

OP 2. Some missionaries must adjust to hot tropical temperatures without enjoying the luxury of air conditioning.

S 3. Their having built a home indicates the missionaries' commitment to their new culture.

IO 4. Some missionary families give constructing their homes careful attention.

PN 5. In warm climates a necessity is having numerous windows for cross-ventilation.

OP 6. Carpet is often unavailable, so the family must choose between concrete's being poured and tile's being laid.

DO 7. Some families eagerly anticipate having adapted to local wildlife.

DO 8. Some missionaries choose sleeping under mosquito nets for protection from insects; others sleep in hammocks.

App 9. One luxury, having electricity, is limited for many missionaries unless they have generators.

S 10. Using grass mats on the floors and brightly colored tropical decorations on the walls may give the missionary home a local look.

Sentence diagram answers for Practice the Skill 4.6 appear in the Teacher's Toolkit. If you teach diagramming, perhaps consult *The Writer's Toolbox* for sample diagrams.

The verb phrase *is limited* in sentence 9 may be diagrammed as a passive verb or as a linking verb followed by a participle functioning as a predicate adjective.

Phrases | Chapter 4 99

4.7 USE *the skill*

Rewrite each sentence by replacing the italicized word or phrase with a gerund or a gerund phrase and making other changes as needed. *(Answers may vary.)*

1. When I learned that color affects mood, I gave serious consideration *to a redecoration of the rooms of my house.*

   When I learned that color affects mood, I gave redecorating the rooms of my house serious consideration.

2. Color can influence *a person to gain or lose energy or stress.*

   Color can influence a person's gaining or losing energy or stress.

3. *Walls that have been painted a warm color* cause a small room to seem smaller and more confining.

   Painting walls a warm color causes a small room to seem smaller and more confining.

4. *To put cool colors on the walls of small rooms* makes them appear to expand.

   Putting cool colors on the walls of small rooms makes them appear to expand.

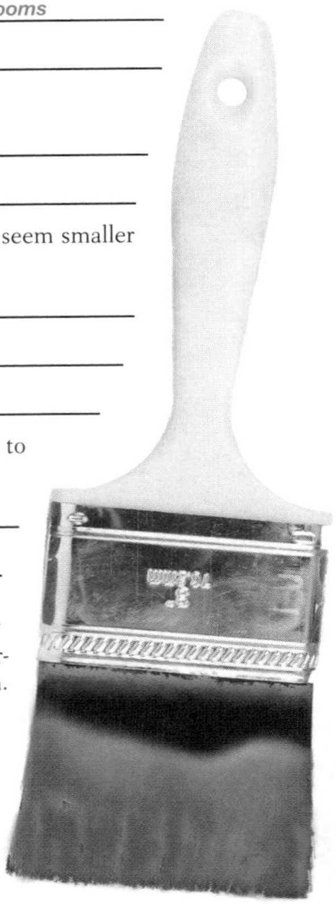

5. *A room that is decorated in hues of red and orange* increases a person's appetite; therefore, these are good colors for a dining room.

   A room's having been decorated in hues of red and orange increases a person's appetite; therefore, these are good colors for a dining room.

6. *It had been painted deep purple*, the color of royalty, and that made my living room appear quite elegant.

   Its having been painted deep purple, the color of royalty, made my living room appear quite elegant.

7. I found that a good way to help me to relax at night was *to have my bedroom painted in blue tones.*

   I found that a good way to help me relax at night was having my bedroom painted in blue tones.

8. *The use of light yellow paint* helped me create a bright, cheerful kitchen.

   Using light yellow paint helped me create a bright, cheerful kitchen.

TEACHING STRATEGY
Introduction and Induction

Display the following sentences and ask the students to supply words that would fit into the blanks. Display a list of the suggested words. *(Answers will vary.)*

- As the pitcher reached the mound, he had every desire to ___ a strike. *(throw)*
- The crowd rose to ___ their hero on. *(cheer)*
- To ___ for the game, the team had practiced daily. *(prepare)*

Then ask the students to identify the part of speech of each word following *to*. *(verb)*

9. *I painted the exterior of the house light brown* because I hoped to convey strength and practicality.

By painting the exterior of the house light brown, I hoped to convey strength and practicality.

10. *The completion of my color scheme* allowed me to relax in a more comfortable environment than before.

My having completed my color scheme allowed me to relax in a more comfortable environment than before.

Infinitives and Infinitive Phrases

Unlike participles and gerunds, which function as only one part of speech, the **infinitive** is a verbal that can function as a noun, as an adjective, or as an adverb. The infinitive consists of the word *to* plus a verb form.

Simple Infinitive

The **simple infinitive** is made up of the word *to* and the first principal part of a verb. The word *to* is considered the "sign" of the infinitive. The word *to* plus an uninflected verb is never a prepositional phrase.

Prepositional Phrase pp. 53–54

INFINITIVE AS NOUN	*To answer* cheerfully is a desired characteristic.
INFINITIVE AS ADJECTIVE	Cheerfulness is a personal quality *to develop*.
INFINITIVE AS ADVERB	A cheerful disposition is important *to encourage* others.
PREPOSITIONAL PHRASE	A cheerful countenance draws people *to you*.

ESL

Do not confuse the *to* of the infinitive with the preposition *to*, especially when the preposition *to* is followed by a gerund as its object.

RIGHT	For daily exercise, Jeannine prefers walking **to running**.
WRONG	For daily exercise, Jeannine prefers walking ~~to run~~.

Infinitives may have "subjects," modifiers, and complements. The "subject" of an infinitive is in the objective case. An **infinitive phrase** includes the infinitive, its "subject" if applicable, and all of its complements and modifiers. The entire infinitive phrase can function as a noun, an adjective, or an adverb.

Pronouns with Infinitives p. 210

S LV PN
My goal is *to drink* only two **cups** of coffee today.

S LV PN
The coffee shop is the place *to buy* good **coffee**.

S TrV DO
The clerk was leaving the counter *to pour* more **coffee**.

S TrV DO
We wanted **him** *to pour* our **coffee**.

TEACHING STRATEGY

Discussion and Participation

Direct students to the four examples of infinitives at the bottom of page 101. Ask them to analyze each infinitive by giving its part of speech and the function of any nouns.

- My goal is *to drink only two cups of coffee today. (noun—predicate noun)*
- The coffee shop is the place *to buy good coffee. (adjective)*
- The clerk was leaving the counter *to pour more coffee. (adverb)*
- We wanted *him to pour our coffee. (noun—direct object)*

SCRIPTURAL APPLICATION

Read Philippians 2:13 aloud and ask the students to locate and identify the use of each infinitive. *(to will, to do; nouns—"It is God which worketh in you* [the desire] *and* [the deed] *of his good pleasure.")* Direct the students to use infinitive phrases to describe ways God works in a person. Identify the use of the infinitive. *(His Word tells me to love others. His Holy Spirit helps me to know the difference between right and wrong.)*

Perfect Infinitive

The auxiliary *have* can also be part of an infinitive. The **perfect infinitive** uses *to,* the auxiliary *have,* and the third principal part of a verb. The perfect infinitive expresses action that takes place before the action of the main verb of the sentence.

Simple Infinitive	I am happy *to meet* you for lunch.
Perfect Infinitive	When you called, I was happy *to have kept* my schedule free for the afternoon.

In the first example, the actions of being happy and meeting the person occur at the same time. The second example means "I am happy (now) because I kept my schedule free (earlier)." A sentence with *have* in both the main verb and the infinitive is usually wrong.

Wrong	I would have liked *to have met* you for coffee and pie.
Right	I would have liked *to meet* you for coffee and pie.
	I would like *to have met* you for coffee and pie.

Like other infinitives, the passive infinitive can be used as an adjective, an adverb, or a noun.

- **Adverb:** Talbot was waiting *to be discovered.*
- **Adjective:** Talbot is the next one *to be discovered.*
- **Noun:** Talbot's goal is *to be discovered.*

Passive Infinitive

Since transitive verbs can be passive, infinitives formed from transitive verbs can also be passive. A **passive infinitive** consists of *to,* the auxiliary *be,* and the third principal part of a verb. A passive infinitive shows that something is being acted upon.

Simple	I want *to greet* you at the coffee shop.
Passive	At the coffee shop, we want *to be greeted.*

A **perfect passive infinitive** adds the auxiliaries *have* (perfect) and *been* (passive) to the simple infinitive. The action of the perfect passive infinitive occurs before that of the main verb.

At the coffee shop, we were pleased *to have been greeted* by many.

Progressive Infinitive

A **progressive infinitive** indicates continuing action. The progressive infinitive consists of the word *to,* the auxiliary *be,* and a verb with an *-ing* ending.

My brother did not want *to be waiting* in line at the coffee shop.

His goal was *to be drinking* his coffee before the crowd arrived.

Elliptical to *in Infinitives*

An infinitive may appear without the sign of the infinitive *(to).* If the *to* in an infinitive sounds awkward, it can be omitted. Sometimes the *to* is included only in more formal English.

Correct	For hot coffee, the best thing to do is *wait until it cools.*
Formal	For hot coffee, the best thing to do is ***to** wait until it cools.*

Teaching Strategy

Induction

Display the following sentence and ask the students when the action of the infinitive takes place in relation to the main verb: *I would like* to have bought a new car for her. *(prior to* would like*)* Then direct the students to change the infinitives in three of the four sentences at the bottom of page 101 to perfect tense. *(My goal was* to have drunk *only two cups of coffee today. The coffee shop was the place* to have bought *good coffee. We wanted him* to have poured *our coffee.)*

Teaching Strategy

Induction and Discussion

Display the following sentences: *I would prefer __. I would have preferred __.* Instruct the students to supply infinitive phrases to fill in the blanks. Tell them to explain the difference in meaning (particularly concerning the time relationship) between the two sentences. Ask whether including *have* in the infinitive and in the main verb at the same time is acceptable. *(no)*

Teaching Strategy

Induction

Ask the students what verb forms are used in a passive infinitive. *(form of* be *+ third principal part of another verb)* Display the following sentence: *Cheerfulness is a personal quality to develop.* Direct students to make the infinitive passive: *(Cheerfulness is a personal quality* to be developed.*)*

ESL

Some verbs are more likely to be followed by a gerund (*enjoy, avoid, admit, finish, risk, consider, appreciate, understand,* and so forth). These verbs often refer to something that has already happened.

Marvin finished **writing** a letter to his grandmother.

Some verbs are more likely to be followed by an infinitive (*want, wish, offer, hope, decide, ask, plan, wait,* and so forth). These verbs often refer to something only wished for or planned but not yet fulfilled.

Marvin plans **to write** her a letter each week.

Some verbs can be used with either meaning.

Marvin likes **writing** letters to his friends and relatives.
He would like **to write** to a missionary family too.

in SUMMARY

An **infinitive** is a verbal that can function as a noun, an adjective, or an adverb.

A **simple infinitive** uses *to,* the sign of the infinitive, in addition to the first principal part of the verb.

An **infinitive phrase** consists of an infinitive, its "subject" if applicable, and any modifiers and complements of the infinitive.

A **perfect infinitive** consists of *to* plus the auxiliary *have* and the third principal part of the verb. The perfect infinitive expresses action that takes place before that of the main verb.

A **passive infinitive** consists of *to* plus the auxiliary *be* and the third principal part of the verb. The passive infinitive expresses action that is done to something.

A **perfect passive infinitive** consists of *to* followed by *have* and *been* and the third principal part of the verb.

A **progressive infinitive** indicates progressive action. A progressive infinitive consists of *to,* a form of *be,* and a verb with an *-ing* ending.

An **elliptical infinitive** is an infinitive in which the *to* is understood and not stated.

4.8 PRACTICE *the skill*

Underline each infinitive phrase. Then identify its function as noun *(N)*, adjective *(Adj)*, or adverb *(Adv)*.

d

Adj 1. An opportunity to visit a traditional Japanese house should not be missed.

Adv 2. The floor of the house, like a very large chair, is intended to be used for sitting.

N 3. The owners of the house wanted the floor to be a pattern of tatami mats (straw and rush floor coverings).

Adj 4. The need to have portable furniture arises from the flexible nature of the house.

Sentence diagram answers for Practice the Skill 4.8 appear in the *Teacher's Toolkit*. If you teach diagramming, perhaps consult *The Writer's Toolbox* for sample diagrams.

The verb phrases *should be missed* in sentence 1, *is used* in sentence 8, and *were thrilled* in sentence 9 may be diagrammed as passive verbs or as linking verbs followed by participles functioning as predicate adjectives.

Teaching Strategy

Induction

Display the following three sentences:

- I did not want to be sleeping when he arrived.
- To be snow skiing right now would be great.
- Dad wants the lawnmower to be working perfectly because he must cut several lawns.

Instruct students to analyze the sentences and explain what they have in common. *(to + be + -ing form of verb)* These are progressive infinitives.

Special Note

For information about the linking-verb infinitive, refer the students to *The Writer's Toolbox* and discuss this special type of infinitive. Although this infinitive has limited usage, students should be aware of it for formal writing or speaking. When a linking-verb infinitive phrase follows a verb such as *believed, thought, considered,* and *assumed,* the predicate nominative of that phrase (the pronoun) should have the same case as the word that it renames (the subject of the phrase). Both the subject of the phrase and the renaming pronoun should be in objective case. For example, *We considered* the best **teacher** to be **her**. *The police assumed* the **thief** to be **him**.

The prepositional phrase *in time-honored Japanese style* may be diagrammed as an adverbial phrase modifying *to have built* or as an adjectival phrase modifying *home.*

N 5. The best way of accommodating guests is to reconfigure the rooms.

Adv 6. Our friends were happy to have built a home in time-honored Japanese style.

N 7. At our visit Akiko and Ken had completed their traditional house; they had not wanted to be finishing the house during our stay.

N 8. Ken and Akiko did little with bamboo in building their house except create a fence surrounding the house and lands; much more bamboo is used inside the house.

Adv 9. We were thrilled to have seen the movable walls, *fusama* and *shoji*.

N 10. To have been invited to a traditional Japanese tea is an honor.

4.9 USE *the skill*

Combine each pair of sentences into one sentence by replacing one of the sentences with an infinitive phrase. Then identify the kind of infinitive in the new sentence as *simple, passive, perfect, perfect passive, progressive,* or *elliptical.* *(Answers may vary.)*

perfect 1. Experts offered families tips for protection against burglars. The experts were pleased that the tips were helpful.

Experts were pleased to have offered families helpful tips for protection against burglars.

simple 2. Many security systems are designed with special features. Some systems provide a link between emergency units and homes.

Many security systems are designed with special features to provide a link between emergency units and homes.

simple 3. When away on vacation, use security lights with motion detectors. Security lights give the appearance that someone is home.

When away on vacation, use security lights with motion detectors to give the appearance that someone is home.

perfect passive 4. We were aware of something suspicious. We were fortunate when we noticed the stranger.

We were fortunate to have been made aware of the suspicious stranger.

Teaching Strategy

Demonstration and Discussion

If possible, avoid putting a modifier, particularly a phrase, between the *to* and the verb of the infinitive, thus creating an awkward structure. Usually a one-word modifier does not cause the same awkwardness.

- **Split infinitive:** She was determined to *all by herself* hike the Appalachian Trail.
- **Improved:** She was determined to hike the Appalachian Trail *all by herself*.

Explain that although some grammarians frown upon all split infinitives, a few situations arise in which mending the split infinitive creates an even more awkward sentence.

- **Awkward wording:** By the end of the semester, Mora was just beginning really to improve her reading skills.
- **Acceptable split infinitive:** By the end of the semester, Mora was just beginning to *really* improve her reading skills.

perfect 5. Burglars watched a house from surrounding shrubbery for several days. This was known.

Burglars were known to have watched a house from surrounding shrubbery for several days.

progressive 6. This door isn't safe. It has only simple door locks rather than deadbolts.

It isn't safe to be using a door that has only simple door locks rather than deadbolts.

progressive 7. Wide-angle peepholes should be installed on the exterior doors. We hope that we can start next month.

We hope to be installing wide-angle peepholes on the exterior doors next month.

simple 8. Lock all doors and windows even when at home. This is another precaution.

Another precaution is to lock all doors and windows even when at home.

elliptical 9. A homeowner could go to the pet store and get a dog. The dog might protect him.

A homeowner could go get a dog for protection.

progressive 10. Emergency responders like house numbers that are visible from the road. Looking for a number during an emergency is not what they want.

During an emergency, responders do not want to be looking for house numbers that aren't visible from the road.

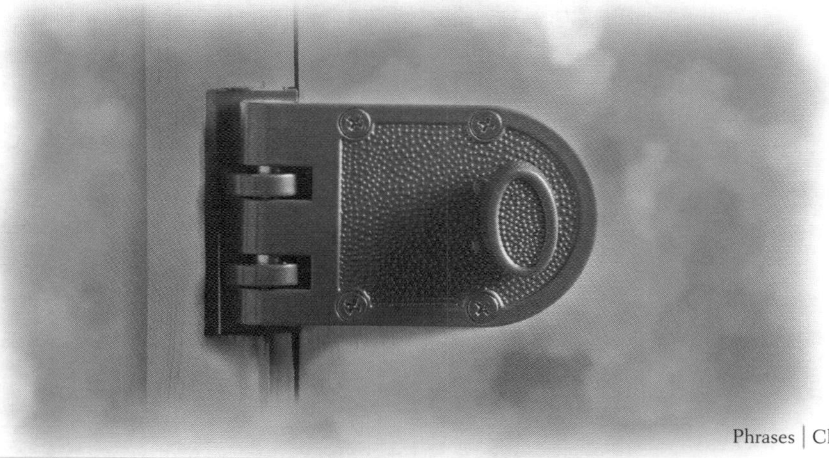

Enrichment

Encourage students to learn more about traditional Japanese homes and the significance of the houses' natural building materials, outdoor gates and paths, and inner moveable partitions. Explain that while Western-style homes are becoming increasingly popular in Japan, the rationale behind traditional Japanese houses is fascinating. Encourage students to share articles about Japan with the class.

See Exodus 2:1–10 for the account of Moses' birth and his adoption into Pharaoh's family.

4.10 CUMULATIVE *review*

Label the sentence patterns in each of the sentences. In the first blank identify the italicized word or phrase as prepositional *(Prep)*, appositive *(App)*, absolute *(Abs)*, participial *(Part)*, gerund *(Ger)*, or infinitive *(Inf)*. Then identify the function of the word or phrase as noun *(N)*, adjective *(Adj)*, or adverb *(Adv)*. (Do not identify a function for an absolute phrase.)

Part Adj 1. Ancient Egyptian houses [S] *made from kiln-dried mud brick* had [TrV] earthen floors [DO] and mud-plaster walls [DO].

Abs ____ 2. *Pharaoh's daughter having rescued Moses from the bulrushes,* the royal household [S] increased [InV] in size.

Ger N 3. For Moses' family, *having a limited amount of wood and living a nomadic existence* [S] made [TrV] owning [DO] furniture unlikely [OC].

App N 4. One piece [S] of furniture, *a stool of three or four legs with animal carvings,* existed [InV] in the homes of commoners and royalty.

Inf N 5. Common people [S] like Moses' family chose [TrV] *to paint the stools and furniture for a more expensive appearance* [DO].

Inf Adv 6. The nobles [S], on the other hand, were [LV] able [PA] *to enjoy fine furniture and decorations.*

Prep Adv 7. People [S] of wealth decorated [TrV] their furniture [DO] by rubbing the furniture *with gold and silver leaf.*

Part Adj 8. Some houses [S] had [TrV] *painted* walls [DO] and leather wall hangings [DO].

Ger N 9. Differing from his previous common surroundings, Moses' daily experience [S] included [TrV] *seeing furniture with gold and silver leaf* [DO].

Inf Adv 10. In spite of these luxurious surroundings, Moses [S] was [LV] determined [PA] *not to forget the God of his fathers.*

Scriptural Application

After emphasizing that Moses never forgot his heritage, ask students to share an aspect of their heritage that is especially meaningful to them. Respond to student answers and read Hebrews 11:24–26. Explain to the students that those who know Christ are pilgrims on this earth and are living for a different time and place (cf. Heb. 11:8–10). Emphasize that although an eternal heavenly heritage motivated Moses to forsake the treasures of Egypt, he did not abandon the culture of his day. Rather his being a pilgrim involved his taking sides in the cultural battle. He "refused to be called the son of Pharaoh's daughter." Moses had a great impact on the culture as a leader of his people and as a lawgiver. Ask students to voice or to write either their impressions of Christianity's heritage or their personal response to their heritage in Christ.

Evaluation

After students have completed Cumulative Review 4.10, use Teaching Help 4C (Teacher's Toolkit) to ascertain the students' knowledge of nonverbal and verbal phrases. Based on the students' results, review specific content areas or proceed with the chapter test.

FROM THE WRITTEN WORD

Formulating the Details

Narration does not often exist as an independent rhetorical strategy but frequently combines with another strategy such as description. A description may be of an idea, an object, or an event. Before Adam and Eve's sin, punishment was nonexistent. After their disobedience to God, however, three punishments were described: the snake's in Genesis 3:14, the woman's in Genesis 3:16, and the man's in Genesis 3:17–19.

Within the narrative warning of the coming Flood is a description of the ark that preserved Noah and his family. The narration regarding the young Moses being hid from the Egyptians includes a description of a smaller, protective ark. Later in Exodus, Moses stands before the people and speaks God's command to build yet another ark with an even greater purpose: to provide the place where God would commune with His people.

> And they shall make an ark of [acacia] wood: two cubits and a half shall be the length thereof, and a cubit and a half the breadth thereof, and a cubit and a half the height thereof. And thou shalt overlay it with pure gold, within and without shalt thou overlay it, and shalt make upon it a crown of gold round about. (Exod. 25:10–11)

Joshua, Israel's new leader after the death of Moses, describes his personal experiences leading Israel. At Jericho he describes victory based on obedience, but at Ai he describes defeat because of one man's disobedience. In Joshua 10:12–13 Joshua describes a momentous occurrence in the lives of the Israelites. Not only does God fight for Israel by causing great stones to fall upon the enemy, but God also allows Joshua to record a miraculous answer to prayer.

> And he [Joshua] said in the sight of Israel, Sun, stand thou still upon Gibeon; and thou, Moon, in the valley of Ajalon. And the sun stood still, and the moon stayed, until the people had avenged themselves upon their enemies. (Josh. 10:12–13)

Personal Response

Read Psalm 121. Reflect upon a time when this or another psalm was of particular encouragement to you. Write a personal narrative that illustrates Psalm 121.

REINFORCEMENT

Use Chapter 4 Review on pages 435–36 for additional test review.

EVALUATION

Use Chapter 4 Test to evaluate students' understanding of the content and concepts of the chapter.

TEACHING STRATEGY

Discussion

Ask a student to read "Formulating the Details" aloud to the class. Challenge students to identify the three biblical themes underlying each narrative account. *(the punishment for sin, the preservation of an ark, and the personal involvement of God with the children of Israel)* Emphasize how the various details of these biblical accounts compose an orderly unit illustrating God's plan. Encourage students to share examples from their own lives when God used a series of events to teach them His truth.

OBJECTIVES

Students will

1. select a current, controversial topic.
2. gather relevant information about the topic.
3. formulate a well-developed thesis statement.
4. develop supporting paragraphs that have a clear topic sentence.
5. give concrete examples and details to support the thesis and topic sentences.
6. use persuasive language effectively.
7. develop a conclusion that reveals the purpose of the essay.
8. revise for content, style, and mechanics.
9. present the essay in the form of a speech or submit the essay for publication.

Chapter 5 Overview			
Topic	**Pages**	**Support Materials**	**Days**
Adjective Clauses	116–21	Bulletin Board 5 Chapter 5 Pretest Practice/Use the Skill 5.1–5.2	51, 53
Persuasive Essay	115	Writing Worksheet 5 Writing Rubric 5	52
Adverb Clauses	122–26	Teaching Help 5A Practice/Use the Skill 5.3–5.4	54–55
Noun Clauses	126–31	Teaching Help 5B Practice/Use/Review the Skill 5.5–5.7	56–57
Using Independent and Dependent Clauses	132–35	ESL Helps 5A–5B Practice/Review the Skill 5.8–5.9 Concept Reinforcement 5A	58
Major Sentence Errors	135–39	Practice/Review the Skill 5.10–5.11 Concept Reinforcement 5B ESL Help 5C	59
Review Critical Thinking	140–41, 437–38	Cumulative Review 5.12 Chapter 5 Review	60
Chapter 5 Test			61

PERSUASIVE ESSAY

Lesson Support

Teacher's Toolkit

Writing Worksheet 5
Writing Rubric 5

PERSUASIVE ESSAY Writing
CLAUSES Grammar

5

A successful persuasive essay presents facts logically and influences the reader to take specific action. Have you ever felt so strongly about a current issue that you have even thought about writing a letter to your local newspaper? Or have you and your friends entered into a lively discussion about some particular idea? In either of these situations, you are trying to persuade someone to accept your position. Notice how Charlotte K. Frank's article "Signs of the Times: Littering the Verbal Landscape" presents specific examples to support her strong outcry against "littering" and urges her readers to take action to correct the problem.

Signs of the Times: Littering the Verbal Landscape *by Charlotte K. Frank*

Why can't kids spell today? While there are no doubt lots of reasons, one may have to do with signs I've been seeing lately on the shops and in the streets of New York.

One large sign on a fence around an empty lot in the Bronx, for example, reads: "Will *Built* to Suit."

Not far from the United Nations, above an art and framing shop, massive block letters advertise: "Jackie Kennedy: An Exhibition of *Photograghs.*"

The sign above a convenience store in Westchester County notes that the establishment sells *"Stationary."* And the awning of a store near Times Square that sells musical instruments announces the availability of *"Harmonica's, Metronome's, Flute's, Trumpet's, Violin's."*

New York is not, of course, alone. I saw this warning posted on a boat docked in Puerto Rico: "Keep *water tight* door *close* at all times."

If I *rote* this *peace* the *weigh* many *sighns* are written, *u wood* understand why many kids can't spell or send grammatically correct letters.

Such mistakes may be worth a laugh—but it's a laugh at the expense of our children. The reason: The signs around us are among the tools that model for children how to use words and spell them—skills they'll need later to get good jobs, support themselves, and become intelligent citizens.

Signs are a time-honored teaching tool. In a kindergarten classroom, simple signs introduce children to the alphabet, the sounds of letters, and the words that identify the objects around them. Can you imagine the reaction of the student whose teacher marks "photograph" wrong on a spelling test and who then sees the same misspelling on a large sign on the corner store?

ADDITIONAL INFORMATION

Charlotte K. Frank has been involved in education all of her life. She earned a PhD in education and served on the New York City Board of Education. She became the executive director of the New York City Board of Education's Division of Curriculum and Instruction. In this position she helped determine what the city's students would study. She also managed a budget of $45 million and a staff of eight hundred employees. At present she is Senior Vice President for Research and Development for McGraw-Hill Education of the McGraw-Hill Companies. Frank has received over sixty awards, including the prestigious Townsend Harris Medal. Her lifelong goal has been excellence in education.

If students question the shortness of the paragraphs in Frank's article, explain that short paragraphs are a feature of journalistic writing, which is often displayed in narrow columns. Academic writing generally features longer paragraphs.

Literature Link

Ask students to explain the purpose of a persuasive essay. Why would someone write a persuasive essay? Continue the discussion by eliciting topics that could be used for persuasion. Instruct students to read "Signs of the Times: Littering the Verbal Landscape" by Charlotte K. Frank. Ask them also to identify the purpose of the essay and discuss whether she accomplished her purpose successfully.

ENRICHMENT

Provide students with additional examples that illustrate the idea of "littering the verbal landscape." Ask them to identify the errors on the signs and correct them.

Thinking Biblically

"Why do I have to learn this stuff?" may be the most common question asked in math class. But its frequency when studying grammar and spelling in English class is not far behind. You know as a teacher that students may use "this stuff" far more than they can imagine, so be sure to have answers ready for that question. These biblical answers may prove helpful: (1) The Bible calls on you to provide for your family (1 Tim. 5:8), and many— if not most—professions require some writing ability. (2) The skill of writing powerful persuasion can be applied to all sorts of Christian purposes: evangelism, edification, even debate in the public square. (3) Writing for the glory of God means, in part, writing as well as you can (Ecc. 9:10). (4) God calls on all humans to "subdue the earth" (Gen. 1:26–28), and writing is one of the many tools He has put in our hands to accomplish this task. (5) Putting your thoughts on paper can help clarify your reasoning, making you a wiser person.

Thinking Biblically

Why learn to spell well? Charlotte Frank points ultimately to two reasons in her essay: spelling is a skill needed to make money and to become an intelligent citizen. These are certainly legitimate reasons for learning to spell, but Christians seek deeper, more lasting purposes in life. For example, good spelling is an essential skill for writing anything persuasive. As Frank contends in her essay, people will ignore ideas—no matter how good they may be—if the writer cannot spell. Since Christians have the most important message in the world, they ought to be "ready always to give an answer" to anyone who asks the reason for the hope in them (1 Pet. 3:15). Some Christians are called to stand and debate—persuasively—with a hostile culture, just as Paul did (Acts 18:4). Some are called to persuade not so much by argument as by offering a compelling and beautiful vision of the way things ought to be. Either of these tasks becomes increasingly difficult for a person who cannot spell.

Businesses with such linguistically challenged signs also do themselves a disservice. When I need notepaper and pass a store that sells "stationary," I unconsciously ask myself, as a former teacher, what quality of notepaper will I find there? I pass it by. Jacqueline Kennedy was a woman dedicated to the quality of furnishings in the White House and protecting the landmark status of buildings in New York City. When I see a display of her "photograghs," I find myself questioning the care and authenticity that went into that exhibit and wonder how Jackie would have reacted. I pass it by. I have no plans to "built" a building on that empty lot—but if I did, I wonder how well I could communicate my ideas with its owner. I would pass it by.

To help ensure properly spelled signs, wouldn't it be nice, the First Amendment notwithstanding, if we could impose a fine on the sign painter or the storeowner who litters the verbal landscape just as others litter the sidewalks? Isn't the damaging of our country's most precious property, the developing minds of our children, a crime? We have a rating system for software and movies to protect our children from inappropriate content. How about demanding a standard of quality for the signs they see in their world?

Legislation and rulemaking aside, there may be a simpler way to get the job done. Each of us can become a one-person "Literacy Squad." When we see a misspelled sign, we can simply walk into that store and, factually and politely, point out the mistake as well as the possibility of the store's losing customers. Some shopkeepers will welcome the information; others may respond with some version of "mind your own business." But I suggest that helping our children learn how to spell properly, to use words correctly, to communicate effectively, and to grow up to be intelligent citizens and neighbors *is* part of our business.

Providing an environment that encourages children to spell, punctuate, and use words and sentences correctly is critical for an educated and literate society. This will help reinforce and extend what they learn in school. Let's leave no sign unscrutinized.

Persuasive Essay

Then Agrippa said unto Paul, Almost thou persuadest me to be a Christian.
Acts 26:28

A persuasive essay asserts that one idea is more legitimate than another idea, motivates the reader to adopt a certain point of view, and urges the reader to take a particular action. Although efforts to persuade are apparent in many areas of our lives, they are quite evident in the political realm. Consider reporters who described President George W. Bush's plans as "divisive" or his speech as "bellicose." What were the reporters trying to do?

Scriptural Application

Read Acts 26:28. Discuss Paul's experience before Agrippa as he methodically recounts his testimony. Point out that Agrippa knew the truth but was not persuaded to act upon that truth (Acts 26:26–27).

Teaching Strategy

Introduction

Read or display several examples from the media that illustrate techniques of persuasion (television commercials, magazine advertisements, newspaper articles). Ask the students what these have in common. (*Answers will vary but should include that all attempt to persuade.*) Discuss with students whether the persuasion is effective and free of biased language.

Another example of persuasive writing is a gospel tract. The tract presents organized facts in the form of a personal testimony or a series of Bible verses. In either case the purpose is to persuade the reader to acknowledge his sin and accept Christ as his personal Savior. In Acts 26 Paul gives his personal testimony to win Agrippa. In fact, Paul speaks directly to Agrippa: "King Agrippa, believest thou the prophets? I know that thou believest" (Acts 26:27). Agrippa had knowledge of these facts, but he failed to act upon that knowledge.

Charlotte K. Frank presents a two-fold discussion of the sign problem. Not only are children affected by the inaccuracies of the signs, but also the businesses compromise their integrity. Frank goes beyond informing the reader of the problem. She admonishes the reader to action: "Each of us can become a one-person 'Literacy Squad.'" She combines factual information and emotional appeal with the purpose of doing something about the situation.

Your Turn

Plan and write a three-paragraph persuasive essay on a topic of your choice.

Planning

New and Improved!
Wonder Shampoo for Pigs
Bring out the pink in your pig!

✔ **Choose a topic.** At this point you are ready to choose a topic for your essay. What current issues do you feel strongly about? Is there a product you believe lives up to its claims? Are there social changes that need to be adopted? Be sure to choose a topic that is controversial. You should be able to state a "pro" and a "con" position about the topic and, keeping Philippians 4:8 in mind, be able to take either position for your essay. For this writing assignment, however, you will be either "pro" or "con," not both.

- Consider some obvious sources that are available to you.
- Consider ideas and issues about which you feel strongly.
- Consult the list of ideas you have compiled in your journal or on your computer.
- Read newspaper or magazine articles on controversial issues.
- Brainstorm with a friend.

As you consider the persuasive essay, keep in mind that Charlotte Frank has been involved in education all of her life. She earned a PhD in education, served on the New York City Board of Education, and became vice president of McGraw-Hill Education. Her life-long goal has been excellence in education. Knowing this background, you find it easy to understand her choice of a topic.

Brainstorming pp. 2–3

You, too, have had experiences that have influenced your life, and you have interests that cause you to feel strongly about certain subjects. You may have been involved in a youth group that participated in a short-term summer mission trip. As a result of your participation on that mission team, your attitude toward being a pastor or youth pastor or a Christian teacher may have changed. Because of the change in your life, you may now feel strongly about the opportunities that a mission trip provides. Or perhaps you know someone with a particular hobby. As you have interacted with that person, you may have seen the enjoyment and education derived from that hobby. You might choose to persuade another person to adopt the same hobby.

OVERVIEW of the WRITING PROCESS

Planning—choosing a topic, establishing the audience, researching the topic, and forming a thesis

Drafting—stating the thesis, organizing the information, writing supporting paragraphs, and using persuasive language effectively

Revising—reevaluating content, reworking style, and proofreading

Publishing—choosing a title, making a neat copy, adapting the information for a speech or a tract, and posting the essay on a website

Planning Strategy
Discussion and Participation

Display a list of topics that students find relevant (e.g., subsidizing local parks, raising the driving age, establishing a savings program). Ask students to comment on these issues and discuss their views.

Planning Strategy
Participation

Instruct students to research their topics. Assist them in accessing articles at the library or through the Internet. Help them to evaluate the breadth of their topic. If it is too broad, guide them to a narrower topic.

Planning Strategy
Motivation

Encourage students to think of their audience as a real group of people (e.g., other students, family members, or concerned citizens), not just the teacher. Direct the students to write a brief description of their audience and under what circumstances their audience will read the essay. Then instruct them to analyze their audience using the questions on page 112 and to record their answers with their descriptions.

Persuasive Essay | Chapter 5 111

✔ **Narrow your topic.** As you consider the three-paragraph assignment, you will need to limit the scope of your topic. For example, three paragraphs would not be sufficient to persuade someone concerning the impact of modern education or the decision for school vouchers.

Broad Idea	Limited Idea
football	compensation for NFL players
education	history class
shopping	Internet shopping (eBay)
collectibles	Byers Carolers

✔ **Consider the audience.** Since the purpose of your writing is to persuade, your audience should have views different from your own. Be careful, though, that the audience is not made too hostile by your confrontation. You must maintain a rational approach in order to persuade your audience. As you consider your audience in relation to your topic, ask yourself these questions.

- How much does my audience know about my topic?
- Is my audience opinionated or apathetic?
- Do I agree on any point with my audience?

The closing paragraphs of Frank's article reveal her audience. "Each of us can become a one-person 'Literacy Squad.'" She emphasizes that helping our children "*is* part of our business."

✔ **Gather information.** Gather information to support your position. Charlotte Frank needed only to observe what was all around her. Depending on the topic, you may find that your surroundings are a source of information. However, it may be necessary for you to go beyond your own knowledge and experience. For current information read magazine articles, newspaper reports, and editorials. You might consider interviewing a person who is an authority on your topic. In the library, consult books that might be helpful to you. Remember that statistics, first-hand observations, and expert testimony must come from credible sources in order to give support to your writing. An interesting example or anecdote is useful in the introduction to gain the reader's attention.

Drafting

✔ **Determine your position and state the thesis clearly.** The thesis is a one-sentence proposition or statement of your main idea and is the guiding sentence for your essay. Remember to be thoughtful and rational as you determine your position and as you choose the language of your essay. Although a subject may have logical arguments for or against it, you must determine your position and hold to it. Do not begin to write the essay without first developing the thesis statement.

You must remember that your primary purpose is to persuade the reader that your thesis is valid. You may have other purposes in your essay, but unless you achieve your primary purpose, all others will fall by the wayside. You must commit yourself to your thesis. Believe that you are right and then prove what you have proposed.

Planning Strategy
Participation

Consider setting aside a class period for students to gather information. Instruct them to bring any research materials they have to class and allow them to look for sources in the library. Encourage students to use the most current sources when possible.

Drafting Strategy
Induction

Ask students what makes the thesis of Frank's essay effective. Show the students that she has a definite opinion about the topic. *("The signs around us are among the tools that model for children how to use words and spell them.")* Discuss student responses and lead them to recognize that a persuasive thesis should be *declarative* and *verifiable.* Allow time for students to draft their thesis statements. Ask volunteers to read their thesis statements aloud. Then lead the students in analyzing their statements for clarity and validity.

Drafting Strategy
Participation

Require students to map their essays using either a formal outline or a general cluster. Instruct them to place the thesis first and to group the information into supporting points under the thesis. Remind them to relate each point to the thesis so that each piece of information supports the argument.

Limited Idea	Thesis Statement
compensation for NFL players	Compensation for NFL players is excessive.
history class	Mrs. Franz's teaching reveals her competence and understanding in World History.
Internet Shopping (eBay)	Internet shopping will not replace mall shopping.
Byers Carolers	Purchasing a Byers Caroler is an investment.

What do you think is the thesis of Frank's article? What idea does she want to prove? Why is she writing this essay?

✔ **Organize information.** If you are making several assertions about your topic, be sure that you have secured adequate information about each point. Avoid presenting an excessive amount of information about one idea and slighting another idea. If your essay contains multiple middle paragraphs, evaluate the material you have about each point and arrange the middle paragraphs so that your strongest point is presented immediately prior to the concluding paragraph.

In the article by Frank, notice how she moves from the importance of signs as a teaching tool for the kindergarten child to the necessity of accuracy in spelling for the older child. Then she moves to the importance of correct signs for businesses. Ultimately she shows how important correctness is in many areas of life.

Organization pp. 14–17

✔ **Develop a successful introductory paragraph.** The introductory paragraph should gain the reader's attention. Perhaps you could use a true story or an anecdote to get the reader thinking about your topic. Storytelling has long been recognized as one of the best ways to get a message across to an audience. In addition to using a story or anecdote, you might present a fact or statistic to gain your reader's attention.

For example, Frank begins her essay with the question "Why can't kids spell today?" Then she uses various examples to show the importance of correctness in signs: "Will *Built* to Suit," *"Harmonica's, Metronome's, Flute's, Trumpet's, Violin's,"* and "Keep *water tight* door *close* at all times." After her various examples, she moves to the thesis of her essay.

The introductory paragraph should close with a well-constructed thesis statement that gives the main idea of the essay. In her essay Frank uses more than one paragraph to gain the reader's attention. Read the last sentence of paragraph seven. Here you will see her purpose for writing.

✔ **Develop supporting middle paragraphs.** Whether you write a single middle paragraph or several, begin the paragraph with a topic sentence that gives direction to the paragraph. Organize your supporting information in such a way that you present your strongest ideas last.

✔ **Develop a strong conclusion.** The concluding paragraph begins with a restatement of the thesis of the essay. Based upon the information that you have presented in the middle paragraph, you are now ready to urge your reader to take some kind of action in relation to your topic.

In the closing paragraph, Charlotte Frank restates her thesis or main purpose for writing: "Providing an environment that encourages children to spell, punctuate, and use words and sentences correctly is critical for an educated and literate society." She admonishes her readers to "leave no sign unscrutinized."

Drafting Strategy

Participation

Instruct the students to draft their essays. Remind them that it is common practice to write the middle paragraphs first, then the introduction and conclusion. Encourage them to spend extra time on the introduction and the conclusion since the introduction must grab the reader's attention and the conclusion must make an effective appeal.

Drafting Strategy

Induction

Ask the students to identify the types of sentences in Frank's beginning statement. *(interrogative, declarative)* Point out that she uses a question to gain the reader's attention and a declarative statement to express the thesis of the essay. Remind students to use active voice in their essays and to remain focused on the subject.

Drafting Strategy

Analysis

Ask students to underline or highlight each of their examples after they have finished their draft. Instruct them to ask two questions: Does each point have an example? Is each example concrete and pertinent to the argument? If the answer to either question is no, instruct students to gather more information and to integrate it into their essay.

Persuasive Essay | Chapter 5 113

Paragraph Development p. 11

✔ **Give concrete examples.** You will increase the credibility of your position by including examples that support your position. Examples are interesting as well as necessary. In Charlotte Frank's article, the examples help support her position. How much clearer it is to show an example of multiple apostrophe errors than to list the rules about the apostrophe.

Remember that you must document any source that you quote, paraphrase, or summarize in your paper.

Document Sources p. 268

✔ **Use persuasive language effectively.** Many words have both a denotative and a connotative meaning. Denotative meanings are their literal definitions, and connotative meanings are their emotional associations. Although both types of word usage may be present in a piece of writing, you must remember not to rely heavily on connotative language but to present sound evidence to persuade your reader.

Consider the following two words: *disappointment* and *dud.* Both of these words have similar definitions. Yet your emotional responses to these words are probably very different. Referring to someone as a *disappointment* conveys the idea of his not meeting certain expectations but does not conjure strong emotional feeling. On the other hand, referring to someone as a *dud* implies strong condemnation and elicits a far different response. Connotative language can be very important because your reader's personal feelings can influence his response to your writing.

Biased Language pp. 390–91

The Christian writer must avoid giving unnecessary offense. One of the most common types of offense is the use of a stereotype. A **stereotype** is an oversimplified generalization of a person or an event—usually based on ignorance, malice, or carelessness. Stereotypes continue because people do not take the time to gather all the information needed for a fair judgment about people or situations. Many generalizations that are based completely on age, cultural or ethnic background, gender, race, or physical characteristics have no place in the Christian's spoken or written communication. The Scriptures warn us that "a brother offended is harder to be won than a strong city: and their contentions are like the bars of a castle" (Prov. 18:19). Do not allow your stereotypical references to hamper your effectiveness in presenting the gospel.

For the examples and the entire paper, be sure to write in active voice.

✔ **Determine the action that the reader should take.** What is your purpose in writing this essay? Do you want the reader simply to read your essay with no motivation to change? Or do you want the reader to take some action? Charlotte Frank is clear in her purpose: The reader must "become a one-person 'Literacy Squad.'" Although the prospect of legislation on the matter of inaccurate signs is highly unlikely, each person can wage his own war against inaccuracies.

In the concluding paragraph of her essay, Frank begins by restating her thesis idea: "Providing an environment . . . is critical for an educated and literate society." She emphasizes again the action that she wants her readers to follow: "Let's leave no sign unscrutinized."

Revising

✔ **Allow yourself time to read your essay carefully.** As you read your essay, ask yourself whether you have presented a clear purpose for your writing and whether you have accomplished that purpose. Does the introductory paragraph compel the reader to go on? Does the middle paragraph present well-organized, accurate information that would persuade the reader to agree with you? Is the conclusion clear about what you want the reader to do?

Drafting Strategy
Participation

Remind the students that their conclusions should clearly state the action that they are encouraging their readers to take.

Revising Strategy
Motivation

Allow the students time to read their essays several times in class. Encourage them to read slowly and thoughtfully to determine whether they are communicating effectively and then to read quickly and smoothly to analyze their style. Provide access to dictionaries and thesauruses (whether in print or online) so that students can check their word choices.

Writing Workshop

Conduct a minilesson using "Achieving Emphasis" (pp. 355–56). Remind students that the choice and placement of words and the use of varied constructions can improve the effectiveness of their writing.

114 Chapter 5 | Persuasive Essay

- ✔ **Evaluate your style.** At this stage of revision, search for opportunities to use precise words and fresh vocabulary that convey your thoughts clearly. Avoiding clichés and overused words will give life and variety to your writing. In addition to these considerations, read for smoothness and conciseness.
- ✔ **Revise for correctness.** As you wrote your essay, you were probably concentrating on content rather than on correctness. Now you have the opportunity to carefully consider sentence structure and usage. Be sure to check for correct spelling, punctuation, and capitalization.

Publishing

- ✔ **Choose a title.** Now that you have polished your writing, you need to choose an appropriate title for your essay. The title should be specific and could suggest the approach of your essay.
- ✔ **Make a neat copy.** Type or print a final copy to submit to your teacher. The copy should be error free and should meet the standards established by your teacher.
- ✔ **Adapt the information for a speech.** If you are taking a speech class, you may be able to use the information in your essay for a persuasive speech. If the topic is a current issue, perhaps you could give the speech at a town meeting.
- ✔ **Consider writing a tract.** If your persuasive essay is based on a Christian topic, you might consider working it into a tract for publication.
- ✔ **Post your writing on your class website.** If your class has a website, you might choose to post your writing there. Be sure that the copy is free of errors.
- ✔ **Include the writing in your writing folder.** Depending on the topic that you have chosen, you might also be able to use the information you researched for a future assignment.

Some Ideas to Consider

History

- Should the United States have a more restrictive policy concerning immigration?
- Should acceptance into a college or university be based on a quota system?

Social Studies

- Should motorcyclists be required by law to wear helmets?
- Should your state require bilingual public education programs?

Mathematics

- Should a high school math program include two years of algebra?
- Should the use of a calculator be accepted in basic math courses?

Health

- Should a high school student use a weight-loss substance?

Revising Strategy

Participation

Distribute a copy of Writing Worksheet 5 (Teacher's Toolkit) to each student. Allow students to exchange papers or to check their own drafts. Encourage them to revise thoroughly.

Publishing Strategy

Discussion

Discuss the effectiveness of Frank's title. Then ask students to suggest another title.

Publishing Strategy

Motivation

Ask volunteers to share responses to their speeches or their published essays.

Publishing Strategy

Motivation

Challenge students who wrote about a Christian topic to write a tract. Encourage them to ask a church leader to read the tracts and to provide feedback for revision. In addition, students could select one tract to revise as a class project and print several copies to give to the class for distribution.

Evaluation

For help in grading this assignment, see "Grading Student Writing" (p. v) and Writing Rubric 5 (Teacher's Toolkit).

OBJECTIVES

Students will

1. identify adjective clauses and what they modify.
2. distinguish between relative pronouns and relative adverbs in adjective clauses.
3. combine sentences by using adjective clauses.
4. identify adverb clauses and what they modify.
5. distinguish between subordinating conjunctions and indefinite relative pronouns in adverb clauses.
6. expand sentences by using adverb clauses.
7. identify noun clauses and their functions within sentences.
8. distinguish between subordinating conjunctions, indefinite relative pronouns, and indefinite relative adverbs in noun clauses.
9. combine sentences by using noun clauses.
10. distinguish between adjective, adverb, and noun clauses.
11. recognize simple, compound, complex, and compound-complex sentences.
12. write sentences using the simple, compound, complex, and compound-complex sentence patterns.
13. identify and correct fragments, comma splices, and fused sentences.
14. edit a paragraph for sentence errors.

g u r w Subjects and Predicates pp. 70–71

g u r w Kinds of Sentences p. 69

g u r w Subordination pp. 364–65

Every sentence consists of at least one clause. A **clause** is a group of related words that contains both a subject and a predicate. An **independent clause** can stand alone as a sentence. A **dependent clause** cannot stand alone; it functions within a sentence as a modifier or in place of a noun. Each dependent clause includes a subordinating word that makes it depend on the independent clause to complete its meaning. Independent clauses are sometimes called main clauses, and dependent clauses are sometimes called subordinate clauses.

INDEPENDENT CLAUSES

The decade of the 1970s was a time of political and social turmoil.

However, technological advances and noteworthy athletic accomplishments also characterize the 1970s.

DEPENDENT CLAUSES

One significant development in a military conflict that had been raging in Southeast Asia for decades was the entry of U.S. troops into Cambodia in April 1970 during the Vietnam War.

After Vietnamese troops regained control of their country from France in 1954, the country was split into noncommunist South Vietnam and communist North Vietnam.

Historians still debate what the role of the United States should have been in Southeast Asia.

Identifying Kinds of Dependent Clauses

There are three kinds of dependent clauses: adjective clauses, adverb clauses, and noun clauses. A dependent clause is named for its function in the sentence. Every dependent clause begins with some kind of subordinating word. These subordinating words signal that the clause is dependent, unable to stand alone as a sentence.

ESL When identifying dependent clauses, look for subject and predicate pairs introduced by words such as relative pronouns *(who, which, that)* and subordinating conjunctions (such as *if, since, because*).

g u r w Adjectives pp. 48–50

Adjective Clauses

An **adjective clause** is a dependent clause that acts like an adjective in a sentence. In other words, it modifies a noun or a pronoun in another clause. An adjective clause may modify a word in the independent clause or a word in another dependent clause. Two different kinds of words can introduce adjective clauses.

CLAUSES

Lesson Support

Student Worktext

Chapter 5 Review—pp. 437–38

Teacher's Toolkit

Bulletin Board 5
Diagram Answers 5.1, 5.7, and 5.8
Chapter 5 Pretest
Teaching Helps 5A–5B
ESL Helps 5A–5C
Concept Reinforcements 5A–5B

Test

Chapter 5 Test

TEACHING STRATEGY

Introduction and Induction

Remind students that there can be two kinds of clauses in a sentence: independent and dependent. Display these groups of words:

- the dark, menacing storm cloud whirled
- that could bring destruction to the area
- the prairie family feared the dark funnel cloud
- whether it travels east or west
- as we took cover in the storm shelter
- will determine the amount of destruction

Ask students which word groups are clauses. *(all)* Ask them how the clauses differ. *(Some are dependent clauses, and some are independent clauses.)* Ask students to

Relative Pronouns

Relative Pronouns p. 39

Most adjective clauses begin with a **relative pronoun**. A relative pronoun communicates several pieces of information.

- It signals that the clause is dependent.
- It *relates* the adjective clause to the word it modifies in another clause.
- It functions as a *pronoun* to replace its antecedent. (The antecedent of the relative pronoun is the noun or pronoun that the adjective clause modifies in the other clause.)
- If nonpossessive, it functions as a subject or an object within the adjective clause. *Whose* can function as a possessive determiner within the adjective clause.

who	whom	whose	which	that

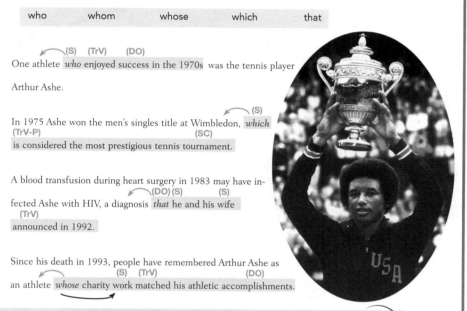

(S) (TrV) (DO)
One athlete *who* enjoyed success in the 1970s was the tennis player Arthur Ashe.

(S) (TrV-P) (SC)
In 1975 Ashe won the men's singles title at Wimbledon, *which* is considered the most prestigious tennis tournament.

(DO) (S) (S) (TrV)
A blood transfusion during heart surgery in 1983 may have infected Ashe with HIV, a diagnosis *that* he and his wife announced in 1992.

(S) (TrV) (DO)
Since his death in 1993, people have remembered Arthur Ashe as an athlete *whose* charity work matched his athletic accomplishments.

ESL

Although most relative pronouns look like interrogative pronouns, there is no subject-verb inversion in clauses introduced by relative pronouns. The relative pronoun comes at the beginning of a clause and functions as the subject or is followed by the subject and verb in normal order.

In some sentences, the adjective clause does not begin with a relative pronoun but with a preposition instead. In these sentences, the relative pronoun *whom* functions as the object of the preposition within the adjective clause. In less formal English, the relative pronoun *that* can replace *whom,* and the preposition appears elsewhere in the adjective clause.

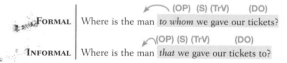

FORMAL	(OP) (S) (TrV) (DO) Where is the man *to whom* we gave our tickets?
INFORMAL	(OP) (S) (TrV) (DO) Where is the man *that* we gave our tickets to?

combine the word groups to form sentences containing both a dependent and an independent clause.

- *The dark, menacing storm cloud whirled as we took cover in the storm shelter.*
- *The prairie family feared the dark funnel cloud that could bring destruction to the area.*
- *Whether it travels east or west will determine the amount of destruction.*

Note that the last sentence contains a noun clause as the subject. Neither group of words is an independent clause, but the two combine to form an independent clause.

REINFORCEMENT

Construct a bulletin board using Bulletin Board 5 (Teacher's Toolkit). Allow students to make various combinations.

TEACHING STRATEGY

Induction and Discussion

Ask students what all clauses have in common and what distinguishes a dependent clause from an independent clause. *(subject and verb; subordinating word)* Display this list of nouns and one pronoun: *restaurant, commercial, Corvette, he.* Ask students to write an adjective clause to modify each noun and pronoun. Remind them that adjective clauses answer the same questions and modify the same parts of speech as adjectives.

Reducing Adjective Clauses pp. 374–75

The relative pronoun *that* is sometimes omitted (simply "understood") when it functions as a direct object or an object of the preposition in the adjective clause.

(OP) (S) (TrV) (DO)
Where is the man [*that*] we gave our tickets to?

(DO) (S) (TrV)
This is the tournament [*that*] we watched on television last year.

To make your writing and speaking clear to your audience, carefully choose the correct relative pronoun. When referring to persons, use *who, whom, whose,* or *that.* When referring to things and most animals, use *which* or *that.*

In 1970 the U.S. government created the Environmental Protection Agency, *which* oversees policies on air, land, and water quality.

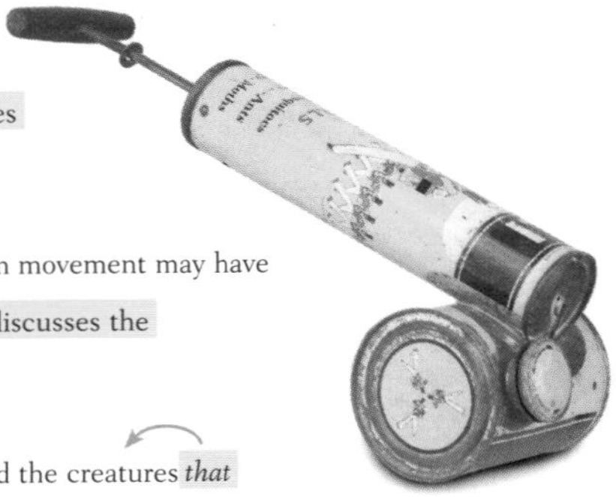

The inspiration for the modern environmentalism movement may have been Rachel Carson, *whose* book *Silent Spring* discusses the effects of pesticides.

As a marine biologist, Rachel Carson had studied the creatures *that* live in the ocean near her home.

Commas p. 308

Whether you are referring to persons, things, or animals, use *that* only for restrictive clauses. A restrictive adjective clause adds information necessary to identify or specify the antecedent and is not set off by a comma. (*Who, whom, whose,* and *which* can be used in either restrictive or nonrestrictive clauses, but many writers prefer to use *which* only in nonrestrictive clauses.)

Restrictive	*Silent Spring* is a controversial book *that* mixes scientific fact with Carson's opinion about the issues.
Nonrestrictive	The public debate sparked by Carson's book, *which* became a bestseller, continues today.

Remind students that restrictive clauses are *essential* to the meaning of the sentence: without them the meaning changes. Nonrestrictive clauses are *nonessential:* the sentence retains its meaning without them.

ESL Never use the relative pronoun *that* after a comma. Instead, use *who, whom,* or *which* as appropriate.

Relative Adverbs

Relative Adverbs p. 51

Some adjective clauses begin with a **relative adverb.** A relative adverb is often a better choice than a relative pronoun when the adjective clause modifies a noun of time, place, or reason in the main clause. Like a relative pronoun, a relative adverb accomplishes several things.

- It signals that the clause is dependent.
- It *relates* the adjective clause to the word that the adjective clause modifies in another clause.
- It functions as an *adverb* to modify the verb in the adjective clause itself.

when	where	why

Teaching Strategy
Participation

Direct students to use adjective clauses to describe a family member. Display their sentences. (*Answers will vary but should follow a pattern similar to this example: My Uncle George,* who lives in New Hampshire, *invites us to visit each summer.*) Then ask students to identify the relative pronoun that introduces each adjective clause. (*Answers will vary.*) Point out that the whole clause functions as a modifier.

Teaching Strategy
Discussion

Advise students to choose relative pronouns carefully. Use *who, whom, whose,* or *that* when referring to persons. Use *which* or *that* when referring to things and most animals. Instruct students to write a representative sentence for each category. Ask for volunteers to read their sentences for the class. Evaluate the relative pronoun in each sentence.

Teaching Strategy
Participation

Consider combining this lesson with a review of comma use. (See p. 308.) Display these sentences, omitting the commas:

- Black caimans live in the tropical waters of the Amazon River, *where they are a major predator.*
- The alligator-like animals, *whose diet consists of vegetation, fish, and water animals,* hunt primarily at night.

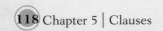

(S) (TrV) (DO)

The year *when* the United States reestablished communication with China after two decades of official silence was 1972.

(S) (InV)

In February President Nixon and his wife, Pat, traveled to China, *where* they met with the leaders of China's communist government.

ESL

An adjective clause beginning with ***when*** modifies a **"time"** noun, such as *day* or *era*. An adjective clause beginning with ***where*** modifies a **"place"** noun, such as *California* or *house*. An adjective clause beginning with ***why*** modifies a **"cause"** noun, usually *reason* or *cause*.

in SUMMARY

A **clause** is a group of related words that contains both a subject and a predicate. An **independent clause** can stand alone as a sentence. A **dependent clause** cannot stand alone; it contains a word that makes it dependent on another clause.

An **adjective clause** is a dependent clause that functions like an adjective in a sentence. It modifies a noun or a pronoun in another clause.

A **relative pronoun** relates an adjective clause to the noun or pronoun that the clause modifies; it functions as a subject, an object, or a possessive determiner within the adjective clause.

A **relative adverb** relates an adjective clause to the noun or pronoun that the clause modifies; it modifies the verb in the adjective clause.

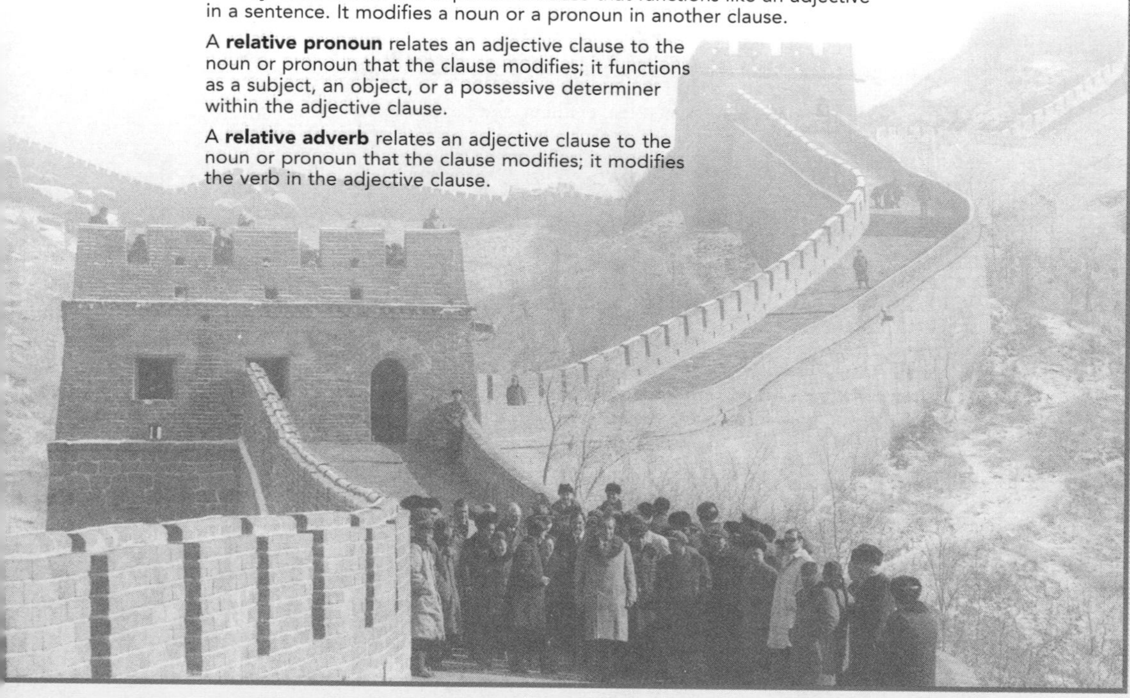

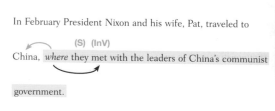

- The black caiman swallows its prey whole in spite of seventy-five sharp teeth *that could chew the prey.*
- The black caimans thrive in the Amazon Basin, *where they find a natural habitat.*
- Hunters *who desire the black alligator skin* have hunted the black caimans to near extinction.
- Reaching lengths of up to twenty feet, the species *that is the largest of the caimans* swims with ease by using its strong tail and webbed feet.

Ask students to identify the adjective clauses. *(the clauses italicized in the list above)* Then ask them to read the sentences aloud to determine whether the clauses are restrictive or nonrestrictive. Instruct students to insert commas accordingly.

TEACHING STRATEGY

Induction

Ask students to identify the relative pronouns and relative adverbs in the sentences from the previous activity. *(relative pronouns—*that *in sentences three and six,* whose *and* who *in sentences two and five; relative adverb—*where *in sentences one and four)*

Sentence diagram answers for Practice the Skill 5.1 appear in the Teacher's Toolkit. If you teach diagramming, perhaps consult *The Writer's Toolbox* for sample diagrams.

Note that *advertising* is a noun in its own right and does not function as a gerund when it refers to the industry that creates and sells advertisements.

5.1 PRACTICE *the skill*

Place parentheses around each adjective clause. Draw an arrow from each adjective clause to the word it modifies. Underline each relative pronoun once and each relative adverb twice.

1. The history of advertising is a subject(that has fascinated many people.)
2. Many Americans,(for whom advertisements are a way of life,)may not know the rich and diverse history of advertising.
3. From the beginning, advertising has been a useful tool for people(who needed to introduce a product, a concept, or a candidate.)
4. The successful advertiser(whose goal is to promote political candidates, new products and services, or new ideas and concepts)uses the strategies for other purposes as well.
5. Encouraging audiences to take certain actions was the reason(why advertising became an art form in itself.)
6. Successful advertising is the means(by which man sells his products or ideas.)
7. One of the first forms of advertising began with people(who were on the street shouting out promotions of their wares.)
8. Eighteenth- and nineteenth-century advertisements,(which were both political and nonpolitical,)promoted tea, clothing, and political parties.
9. Then came the twentieth century,(when advertising took on a new meaning.)
10. One of the most successful advertising campaigns in history began in Atlanta, Georgia,(where the Coca-Cola Company began.)

5.2 USE *the skill*

Combine each set of sentences by changing one sentence into an adjective clause, using an appropriate relative pronoun or relative adverb.

1. Public relations personnel prepare an audience for a message. The message focuses on promises to be fulfilled.

Public relations personnel prepare an audience for a message that focuses on promises to be fulfilled.

120 Chapter 5 | Clauses

2. The use of public relations programs was not common until the twentieth century. During World War II, however, public relations programs became a powerful tool for the Allies.

The use of public relations programs was not common until the twentieth century, when the Allies in World War II used public relations programs as a powerful tool.

3. Public relations is divided into many categories. These include reputation management and public and international affairs.

Public relations is divided into many categories, which include reputation management and public and international affairs.

4. One avenue of public relations focuses on the public's view of a company or an individual. Another focuses on a nation's view of another nation.

Other avenues of public relations focus on the ways in which the public views a company or individual or ways in which a nation views another nation.

5. The popularity and effectiveness of public relations strategies required independent public relations companies. Many companies exist for that reason.

The popularity and effectiveness of public relations strategies are the reasons why many independent public relations companies exist.

6. Corporations and businesses as well as governments have public relations departments. International relations is a division of public relations.

Corporations and businesses as well as governments have public relations departments that include international relations.

7. Government officials attempt to establish amiable international relations. These officials pursue amiable international relations partly to help avoid war.

Government officials who attempt to establish amiable international relations are partly trying to avoid war.

8. Perhaps the hardest public relations job is restoring a company's reputation. At times people have developed negative opinions about a company.

Perhaps the hardest public relations job is restoring a company's reputation at a time when people have developed negative opinions about the company.

9. Now the public relations department is a key part of any organization. It strives to create a good image and to encourage investment.

Now the public relations department, whose tasks are to create a good image and to encourage investment, is a key part of any organization.

10. Public relations skills are a valuable asset. People with these skills are a precious commodity to many companies.

People who have public relations skills are a precious commodity to many companies.

Reinforcement

After the students have completed Use the Skill 5.2, instruct them to underline each relative pronoun once and each relative adverb twice to ensure that they can distinguish between them.

ESL ESL students may find it difficult to decide which subordinating conjunction to use in a sentence. Nuances of meaning do not easily translate from one language to another, and practice is necessary for the ESL student to master these conjunctions.

Adverbs pp. 50–51

Commas p. 304

Conjunctions pp. 54–55

Reducing Adverb Clauses pp. 375–76

Writer's Toolbox

Adverb Clauses

An **adverb clause** is a dependent clause that acts like an adverb in a sentence. Adverb clauses usually modify verbs, but sometimes an adverb clause will modify an entire clause. Adverb clauses can also modify adjectives or other adverbs.

Subordinating Conjunctions

An adverb clause begins with a subordinating conjunction. Like other conjunctions, a **subordinating conjunction** joins two sentence elements, in this case clauses. However, a subordinating conjunction is part of one of the clauses, and it makes its own clause dependent on the other clause. (A subordinating conjunction is only an introducer, having no other function within its clause.) The idea expressed in the dependent clause should be less important than (subordinate to) the idea in the main clause.

Subordinating conjunctions convey a variety of meanings; thus, adverb clauses convey a variety of meanings. Many of these are the same meanings that adverbs themselves convey. A skillful writer chooses the subordinating conjunction that will clearly express the logical relationship between the two clauses. (In the list below, each word in parentheses is a modifier and not a part of the subordinating conjunction.)

Time	when, while, as, before, after, since, now that, once, until, till, whenever
Place	where, wherever
Cause	because, since, as, inasmuch as
Condition	if, on condition that, provided that, unless
Contrast	whereas, while
Manner	as, as if, as though, however
Purpose	so that, so, that, in order that, lest
Concession	although, even though, though, even if
Comparison and Degree	than, (as . . .) as, (so . . .) as
Result	so that, (so . . .) that, (such . . .) that

Margaret Thatcher became Europe's first woman prime minister *after* she gained a momentous 1979 victory for the Conservative Party.

Björn Borg, Swedish tennis legend of the 1970s, still preferred wooden rackets in the 1990s, *as though* the modern types were second-rate.

Even though mechanical difficulties kept her from finishing the 1977 race, Janet Guthrie became the first woman to compete in the Indianapolis 500.

ESL A few of the subordinating conjunctions on this list can also be prepositions, followed only by objects. These are *after, as, before, since, till,* and *until.*

Subordinating Conjunction	Eat supper *before* you go to church.
Preposition	Eat supper *before* six o'clock tonight.

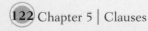

Teaching Strategy

Discussion

Remind students that adverb clauses convey the same meanings adverbs convey. Direct the students to the list of subordinating conjunctions on page 122. Point out the relationship between each group of conjunctions and the meanings that adverbs convey.

Teaching Strategy

Discussion

Remind students that some words can function both as subordinating conjunctions and as prepositions. If the word is a preposition, it is followed only by an object(s). Share the following examples with your students: *You will be responsible for the committee* after the chairman resigns tomorrow. *(subordinating conjunction) You will be responsible for the committee* after the meeting tomorrow. *(preposition)*

Reinforcement

Strengthen students' understanding of the difference between subordinating conjunctions and prepositions by using Teaching Help 5A (Teacher's Toolkit). This exercise could also be used as a quiz if desired.

Teaching Strategy

Discussion and Induction

Display the following sentences: *Our vacation to Chicago was most educational. We visited the aquarium, the planetarium, and*

ESL

When using *whereas, while, although, though,* or *even though* in a dependent clause to contrast or concede something, do not use *but* in the independent clause.

INCORRECT	Even though I do not like milk, ~~but~~ I do like chocolate milk.
CORRECT	Even though I do not like milk, I do like chocolate milk.

When using *because* or *since* in a dependent clause to describe a reason or a cause, do not use *so* in the independent clause.

INCORRECT	Since I have a test tomorrow, ~~so~~ I must study tonight.
CORRECT	Since I have a test tomorrow, I must study tonight.

An **elliptical adverb clause,** which has the same function as a full adverb clause, begins with a subordinating conjunction but omits one or more other words that can be clearly understood from the context. The words omitted from an elliptical adverb clause often include the subject and perhaps the auxiliary or the full verb.

> *While* [she was] dismounting from the uneven bars, gymnast Olga Korbut shocked the judges at the 1972 Olympics by completing a backward somersault.

> At the time, the backward somersault was considered more dangerous *than* other moves [were dangerous].

> *Although* [it was] later banned from Olympic competition, the Korbut Flip has a memorable place in Olympic history.

Whether the subject of the elliptical adverb clause is stated or omitted, it must be the same as the subject of the independent clause (or be a noun or a pronoun standing for the subject). If the subjects of the two clauses are different, the result will be an error called a dangling modifier.

Dangling Modifiers p. 251

Noun Clause, not Adverb Clause p. 386

Indefinite Relative Pronouns

Occasionally, an **indefinite relative pronoun** ending with *-ever* will introduce an adverb clause. An indefinite relative pronoun does not have an antecedent; it refers to something indefinite or unknown in the dependent clause. Although the indefinite relative pronoun fills a noun function in the adverb clause, the clause as a whole still functions adverbially to modify the independent clause as a whole.

Relative Pronouns p. 39

> (S) (InV)
> *Whatever* happens in the world of fashion, you will undoubtedly still see yesterday's fashions recycled as those of today.

> (PN) (S) (LV)
> *Whoever* he is, his appearance certainly reminds me of President Nixon's.

in SUMMARY

An **adverb clause** is a dependent clause that functions like an adverb in a sentence.

A **subordinating conjunction** joins a dependent clause to an independent clause and expresses the relationship between the two clauses.

An **elliptical adverb clause** is a clause that keeps the introductory subordinating conjunction but omits certain other words that are clearly understood from the context.

An **indefinite relative pronoun** ending with *-ever* can introduce an adverb clause.

ESL If ESL students have difficulty with the concept of elliptical adverb clauses, show them the reduced and nonreduced sentences side by side for easier comparison.

two museums. Ask the students to identify the relationship that the second sentence has to the first. *(The second sentence presents the causes that made the first true.)* Then ask the students to combine the two and write the answer for display. *(Our vacation to Chicago was most educational because we visited the aquarium, the planetarium, and two museums.)*

Explain that showing correct relationships between ideas is an important part of successful writing. You could not logically say, "Because our vacation to Chicago was most educational, we visited the aquarium, the planetarium, and two museums."

TEACHING STRATEGY
Discussion and Participation

Remind students that an elliptical clause has the same function as a full adverb clause and that the subject of the elliptical clause must be the same as the subject of the independent clause. Ask the students to write a sentence with an elliptical clause for display. Identify the elliptical clause in several sentences and emphasize the subject of the sentence.

TEACHING STRATEGY
Discussion

Remind students that indefinite relative pronouns *(whoever, whatever)* do not have antecedents and do not occur in adjective clauses. Indefinite relative pronouns occasionally appear in adverb clauses.

5.3 PRACTICE *the skill*

Place parentheses around each adverb clause. Draw an arrow from each adverb clause or elliptical adverb clause to the word it modifies. (Do not draw an arrow from an indefinite relative pronoun to the entire main clause.) Underline each subordinating conjunction once and each indefinite relative pronoun twice.

1. A Christian must be well established in his personal convictions (before he chooses to consider a public relations position.)
2. (Whatever happens,) he must live by biblical commands and standards.
3. Establishing trust is the basis for a successful public relations career (even though one's counterparts may ignore this principle.)
4. (If you do not adopt the command of James 5:12 to "let your yea be yea; and your nay, nay,") you will likely succumb to the manipulation of the world.
5. Despite the temporal cost, God's blessing upon your life is more important (than the world's.)
6. Maintaining honesty and trustworthiness should be paramount in the Christian's life (when he assumes a position in the area of public relations.)
7. Paul's admonition of "lie not one to another" (Colossians 3:9), (although given to the early church,) should be our standard of practice today as well.
8. Success in the public relations area will not materialize (unless a Christian adopts the command of Ephesians 5:6: "Let no man deceive you with vain words.")
9. You must be cautious with your words and promises (since you are obligated to fulfill your promises.)
10. (As you reflect upon the field of public relations,) remember that some Christians have been destroyed because of their departure from biblical standards.

Reinforcement

After the students complete Practice the Skill 5.3, instruct them to identify the meaning of each adverb clause. Direct the students to consult the list of meanings for adverb clauses on page 122.

Enrichment

Ask students to read a recent edition of the local newspaper and to bring an example of a public relations article to class. Allow time in class for the students to share their findings. Note the variety of examples that the students locate.

Reinforcement

After the students have completed Use the Skill 5.4, ask them to identify the relationship between independent and dependent clauses in the sentences. *(time, concession, condition, comparison, cause, manner)* Direct the students to the categories of subordinating conjunctions on page 122 to aid them in their identification.

5.4 USE *the skill*

Expand each sentence by adding an adverb clause, using an appropriate subordinating conjunction or indefinite relative pronoun. Try to vary the location of the adverb clauses and the meanings that they convey. *(Answers may vary.)*

1. Often thought of as limited to press conferences alone, public relations management actually includes a variety of strategies.

   Although some may think of public relations management as only press conferences, public relations management actually includes a variety of strategies.

2. According to some studies, media relations may include news releases, news conferences, and personal letters.

   Media relations, as some studies have shown, may include news releases, news conferences, and personal letters.

3. Special events such as fundraisers, trade shows, or award ceremonies are additional opportunities to improve public relations.

   Whenever an organization participates in special events such as fundraisers, trade shows, or award ceremonies, the company has used another opportunity to improve public relations.

4. Newsletters, whether long or short, can keep clients apprised of new company policies and personnel changes.

   Whatever their length, newsletters can keep clients apprised of new company policies and personnel changes.

5. Information sheets of one or two pages, another public relations tool, are directed at motivating the reader to make a donation or to purchase a product.

   Information sheets of one or two pages, another public relations tool, are successful when they motivate the reader to make a donation or to purchase a product.

6. Tip sheets with bulleted lists of information about a newly released product are sent to customers.

   After a product is available, customers receive tip sheets with bulleted lists of information about the product.

Enrichment

Invite a local public relations professional to speak to the class. Before the lecture, divide the class into groups of three or four students and instruct each group to write three questions about the topic of public relations to ask the lecturer. Allow each group to choose a spokesman to present the group's questions. After the visit, direct the students to use the answers from the public relations representative to incorporate adjective and adverb dependent clauses into three sentences. Allow volunteers to write their sentences for display and to point out adjective and adverb clauses, relative pronouns, relative adverbs, and subordinating conjunctions in the sentences.

ONE *on* ONE Plan a visit to a local organization and interview the public relations representative. Before the visit, ask your student to write some questions about the topic of public relations to ask the representative. After the visit, direct him to use the answers from the public relations representative to incorporate adjective and adverb dependent clauses into three sentences. Then ask the student to point out adjective and adverb clauses, relative pronouns, relative adverbs, and subordinating conjunctions in the sentences.

7. Companies respond to news items about their products through a letter to the editor, another public relations strategy.

Because a letter to the editor is another public relations strategy, companies are able to respond to news items about their products.

8. Sponsoring a local ball team, musical group, or community event is an obvious attempt to improve public relations. However, many companies overlook this opportunity.

Sponsoring a local ball team, musical group, or community event is an obvious attempt to improve public relations, though many companies overlook this opportunity.

9. Consistent—but not always large—contributions to local charities will foster good public relations.

Consistent contributions to local charities, even if the contributions are not large, will foster good public relations.

10. A thank-you note to a customer will often encourage repeat business; many companies, however, fail to write such notes.

Though a thank-you note to a customer will often encourage repeat business, many companies fail to write such notes.

Noun Clauses

Nouns pp. 35–51

A **noun clause** is a dependent clause that functions as a noun in a sentence. Noun clauses appear as subjects, predicate nouns, objects, and appositives in sentences. Three kinds of words can introduce noun clauses.

Subordinating Conjunctions

Most noun clauses begin with the subordinating conjunction *that;* some other noun clauses begin with the subordinating conjunction *whether,* which indicates a choice. The subordinating conjunction introduces the noun clause, but it does not have any other function within the noun clause.

tip

Do not confuse the subordinating conjunction *that* with the relative pronoun *that.* The relative pronoun stands for a noun and has a function in the adjective clause it introduces.

S LV PN (S)
A common assumption once held was *that* King Tut's treasure
(LV) (PA)
was unparalleled among the riches of the ancient world.

Teaching Strategy

Induction

Display the following sentence: *I hope that our visit to the museum will be educational.* Ask the students what answers the question "What?" about *I hope. (that our visit to the museum will be educational)* Ask what is different about this direct object. *(It is a clause.)* Ask what the word *that* accomplishes in the sentence. *(joins the two sentence parts and subordinates the dependent clause)* Ask whether the word *that* has any other function in the clause. *(no)*

Teaching Strategy

Analysis

Use the example sentences on pages 126–28 to analyze the function of the entire noun clause within the sentence and the meaning conveyed by the subordinating conjunction.

Teaching Strategy

Discussion

Students may confuse the relative pronoun *that* and the subordinating conjunction *that.* Emphasize that the difference lies in the function of the word. Relative pronouns relate an adjective clause to a word in the independent clause and have their own function in the dependent clause. For example, *The Egyptian exhibit (that* [relates the adjective clause to *exhibit*; functions as a subject] *was free) contained several interesting artifacts.* Subordinating conjunctions, on the other hand, have no other function within either clause but to introduce noun clauses. For example, *We noticed (that* [no function] *the mummies were quite interest-*

126 Chapter 5 | Clauses

S (S) (TrV) (DO) LV
That a tomb in China's Shanxi province contained great wealth was
PA
unknown.

S TrV DO (S) (TrV)
In 1974 some Chinese farmers wondered *whether* they could dig
(DO) S TrV DO
a better well, but their attempt revealed the burial grounds of Emperor

Qin Shi Huang instead.

Although the Pinyin spelling of Qin Shi Huang used here is currently the preferred spelling, some sources may identify him as Shih Huang-ti, which is the previously preferred Wade-Giles spelling of the name.

The subordinating conjunction *that* is sometimes omitted when the noun clause functions as the direct object of the sentence.

S
Upon unearthing emperor Qin Shi Huang's terra cotta army, archaeologists
TrV DO (S) (LV) (PN)
said *[that]* the former emperor's obsession had been protection.

In designing the thousands of lifelike individualized figurines, Chinese
S TrV DO (S) (TrV) (DO)
artisans hoped *[that]* superior height would indicate superior rank.

When a noun clause functions as the subject of the sentence, a writer can rearrange the sentence, putting the subject last. The word *it* then functions as an **expletive**, a subject substitute that acts as a "placeholder" for the noun clause. When an expletive appears, the reader does not have to read and remember the entire noun clause before he finds out what is being said about it.

S (S) (TrV) (DO)
Whether other archaeological sites surrounded this ancient Chinese tomb
LV PN
became a matter of interest.

S-*be*-Advl
p. 76

LV PN S (S)
It became a matter of interest *whether* other archaeological sites
(TrV) (DO)
surrounded this ancient Chinese tomb.

tip

The subordinating conjunction *if* sometimes substitutes for *whether* in informal speech and writing. In formal English, use *whether*.

Indefinite Relative Pronouns

Another kind of word that can introduce a noun clause is an **indefinite relative pronoun.** Unlike a regular relative pronoun, an indefinite relative pronoun does not have an antecedent in the independent clause. It refers to something indefinite or unknown in the noun clause that it introduces.

Relative
Pronouns
p. 39

S (S) (TrV) (DO) TrV DO
Whoever arranged the terra cotta figures put the emperor's clay soldiers in battle formation.

ing). Clarify with students that although the subordinating conjunction only introduces the noun clause, the entire dependent clause itself still functions as a noun in the sentence.

Reinforcement

Use Teaching Help 5B (Teacher's Toolkit) to identify *that* as a relative pronoun or a subordinating conjunction.

Teaching Strategy

Participation

Display the following: *It is.* Instruct students to complete the sentence with a noun clause. Allow volunteers to write their answers for display. Point out the expletive use of *it* and the noun clauses in the students' sentences.

Then display the following: *I know, Everyone sees.* Tell students to choose one of the beginnings and complete the sentence with a noun clause. Ask volunteers to write their answers for display. Point out how many use *that* elliptically. Tell them that this omission is common when the noun clause is the direct object of the sentence.

Teaching Strategy

Participation

Direct students to the indefinite relative pronoun chart on page 128. Ask them to use several of the indefinite relative pronouns to write sentences for display. Instruct students to label the sentence patterns.

S LV PN (S) (TrV) (DO) (OC)
The 1974 discovery of the terra cotta warriors is *what* made people aware of Chinese culture during the Qin Dynasty.

S TrV-P OP (S) (*be*) (Advl)
The ancient burial site had been vandalized by *whoever* was there immediately following the emperor's committal.

tip

The case of a relative pronoun depends only on its use within its own clause.

Indefinite Relative Pronouns	
who	whoever
whom	whomever
whose	whosever
which	whichever
what	whatever

Indefinite Relative Adverbs

Kinds of Adverbs
pp. 50–51

An **indefinite relative adverb** is another kind of word that can introduce a noun clause. An indefinite relative adverb refers to something unknown and functions as an adverb to modify the verb in the noun clause itself.

S TrV IO DO (S) (LV) (PN)
(You) Please tell me *when* America's speed limit was fifty-five miles per hour.

S (S) (InV) LV PN
Where the world's tallest building stands was the topic of discussion.

S (S) (TrV-P) (RO) LV PA
Why George Washington was posthumously granted the title of six-star general in 1976 seems self-evident.

S TrV DO (S) (InV)
Agnes explained *how* supermarket bar codes work.

in SUMMARY

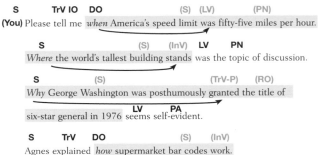

A **noun clause** is a dependent clause that functions like a noun in the sentence.

The **subordinating conjunctions *that*** and ***whether*** can introduce noun clauses.

An **indefinite relative pronoun** or an **indefinite relative adverb** can also introduce a noun clause.

Teaching Strategy

Induction and Participation

Ask the students what each of the following words means: *indefinite, relative,* and *adverb.* (*In grammar something indefinite is something that is unknown. Something that is relative relates two grammatical parts. An adverb modifies a verb, adjective, or another adverb.*) Explain that an indefinite relative adverb performs these functions in addition to introducing a noun clause. Display the following sentences:

- The speaker addressed a very important issue: how college students can study effectively.
- Where I can obtain information about the historical site seems to be eluding me.
- My friends don't seem to understand why I like to read biographies.
- My favorite time of the year is when there is enough snow to go skiing for the first time.

Ask volunteers to identify the indefinite relative adverb and the verb it modifies. Then ask them to identify the noun clause that the indefinite relative adverb introduces and the function of the noun clause in the sentence.

128 Chapter 5 | Clauses

5.5 PRACTICE *the skill*

Place parentheses around each noun clause. Identify the function of each noun clause as subject *(S)*, predicate noun *(PN)*, direct object *(DO)*, indirect object *(IO)*, object of the preposition *(OP)*, or appositive *(App)*. Underline each subordinating conjunction once and each indefinite relative pronoun twice. Circle any indefinite relative adverb.

S 1. It is debatable (whether the success of the Coca-Cola Company comes from the taste of its product or from the talents of its advertising staff.)

DO 2. Did you know (that from 1886 to 1993 the bottling company used thirty-one slogans to promote Coca-Cola?)

App 3. Dr. John S. Pemberton's invention, (what became Coca-Cola,) was marketed as a tonic for brain and nerve problems.

S 4. (Whatever an advertiser spends) should be less than the product's earnings; however, the syrup's marketers spent $73.00 on advertising in 1886 when gross sales were only $50.00.

PN 5. The mixture of Coca-Cola syrup and soda water was (what a patron needed to relieve his headache.)

IO 6. In 1886 Jacob's Pharmacy in Atlanta sold (whoever paid five cents) a glass of fizzy fountain drink called Coca-Cola.

OP 7. Coca-Cola became a marketed item, and soon the company paid dividends to (whoever had become an investor.)

DO 8. Beginning in 1942, advertisers liked (how the "Sprite Boy" promoted the new name, Coke.)

S 9. (That a Coca-Cola advertisement appeared on the cover of *Time* magazine) became an advertising boost.

DO 10. Innovative techniques and strategies reveal (why advertising is important to the success of this industry.)

Clauses | Chapter 5 129

5.6 USE *the skill*

Combine each group of sentences by using a noun clause with an appropriate subordinating conjunction, indefinite relative pronoun, or indefinite relative adverb. *(Answers may vary.)*

1. The history class learned about the New York City mayoral race of 1886. Theodore Roosevelt, Abram Hewett, and Henry George campaigned for the office.

   The history class learned that Theodore Roosevelt, Abram Hewett, and Henry George campaigned in 1886 for the New York City mayoral position.

2. Twenty-eight-year-old Roosevelt had just returned to New York City. Interestingly, he was planning to be married shortly after the election.

   It is interesting to note that twenty-eight-year-old Roosevelt had just returned to New York City and was planning to be married shortly after the election.

3. Abram Hewett was a popular sixty-four-year-old millionaire and philanthropist. He alone could save New York City from socialism and communism, he claimed.

   Abram Hewett's claim, that only he could save New York City from socialism and communism, made the sixty-four-year-old millionaire and philanthropist popular.

4. Redheaded Henry George was forty-seven years old. The supporters of the Central Labor Union considered George a favorite candidate in the mayoral election.

   Henry George, redheaded and forty-seven years old, was a favorite candidate with whoever supported the Central Labor Union.

5. The campaign gained prominence. Active in the election in many ways were labor parties and the nation's most powerful political machine, the Tammany Hall organization.

   The campaign gained prominence through whatever the labor parties and the nation's most powerful political machine, the Tammany Hall organization, did.

6. The Tammany Hall organization had become strong in New York City by achieving its goal. That goal was to get votes from the newly arrived immigrants.

   The Tammany Hall organization's goal in New York City was that it would get votes from the newly arrived immigrants.

7. The opportunities Tammany offered reached all groups of immigrants. Becoming a naturalized citizen was made easy for them.

   Tammany gave whoever wanted to be a naturalized citizen an easy opportunity.

8. On one occasion 40,000 certificates for potential citizens were available in a saloon on Center Street. The certificate read "Naturalize the bearer."

   On one occasion 40,000 certificates reading "Naturalize the bearer" were available in a saloon on Center Street to whoever wanted to be a citizen.

130 Chapter 5 | Clauses

9. By 1870, 44 percent of New York City's population was foreign born. The Tammany Hall political machine sought out the foreigners.

That 44 percent of New York City's population in 1870 was foreign born caused the Tammany Hall political machine to seek out the foreigners.

10. Abram Hewett won the election. George accused Tammany Hall of illegal registrations.

Abram Hewett won the election, but George believed that Tammany Hall cheated him through illegal registrations.

5.7 REVIEW *the skill*

Place parentheses around each dependent clause. Identify each dependent clause as an adjective clause *(Adj)*, an adverb clause *(Adv)*, or a noun clause *(N)*. If it is a noun clause, also identify its noun function. If it is an adjective or adverb clause, underline the word that it modifies.

Adj ______ 1. In the latter part of the nineteenth century, Thomas Nast, (who is most famous for his wood engravings,) drew cartoons about many major events and political issues.

Adv ______ 2. (Because the United States was a booming country with increased industrialization and immigration,) political corruption was everywhere.

_N_ _PN_ 3. One major problem was (that politicians "rigged" elections and bought votes of uninformed immigrants.)

Adj ______ 4. One series of cartoons depicted the corrupt leaders (who controlled New York's Tammany Hall.)

_N_ _S_ 5. (Whomever Nast chose for his cartoon drawings) could not escape the attention of the New Yorkers.

Adv ______ 6. (Although many of the newly arrived immigrants could not read English,) they were able to interpret the cartoon pictures.

Adj ______ 7. Nast directed a series of cartoons against Boss Tweed, (who ruled Tammany Hall for years.)

Adj ______ 8. During the time (when Tweed ruled Tammany Hall,) Tweed and his fellow criminals channeled hundreds of millions of dollars from the city to themselves.

_N_ _DO_ 9. Nast continued his cartoons against Tweed and eventually saw (that Tweed served a sentence in jail.)

Adv ______ 10. Thomas Nast was already a strong influence on politics (before he created the symbols for both the Democratic and Republican parties.)

Sentence diagram answers for Practice the Skill 5.7 appear in the Teacher's Toolkit. If you teach diagramming, perhaps consult *The Writer's Toolbox* for sample diagrams.

The prepositional phrase *in jail* (sentence 9) can be diagrammed as modifying either *served* or *sentence.*

ADDITIONAL RESOURCES

For more information about Thomas Nast and examples of his cartoons, see page 323 of UNITED STATES HISTORY, Fourth Edition, published by BJU Press.

Using Independent and Dependent Clauses

Knowing how to use the various kinds of clauses is an important skill. Effective writers combine different kinds of clauses in different ways to convey different meanings. Analyzing the number and kinds of clauses that a sentence contains is one way to categorize sentences. (Another is to categorize sentences by their purpose, as we did in Chapter 3.)

A **simple sentence** consists of only one independent clause. There are no dependent clauses.

China joined the United Nations in 1971.

The architecture of both the Eiffel Tower and the Centre Pompidou instigated national controversy.

Conjunctions pp. 54–55

A **compound sentence** contains two or more independent clauses but no dependent clauses. The method a writer uses to join the independent clauses often indicates the relationship between the clauses.

- A coordinating conjunction (usually preceded by a comma) can indicate similarity and association *(and, both—and, nor, neither—nor)*, contrast *(but, yet)*, choice *(or, either—or)*, cause or reaction *(for)*, or result or consequence *(so)*.

  The six-story Centre Pompidou in Paris was startlingly revolutionary, *for* all of its pipes were brightly colored and displayed on the structure's exterior.

  Some feared that the avant-garde architecture would be disliked, *but* the Centre Pompidou became overwhelmingly popular.

Commas and Semicolons pp. 302, 315

- A semicolon indicates that the second clause reinforces the first clause. A conjunctive adverb sometimes appears in the second clause (often set off by a comma or a pair of commas) to clarify the exact relationship between the two independent clauses.

  The Nike athletic shoe logo bears mythological import; the "swoosh" was designed to resemble the wing of Nike, a Greek goddess of victory.

  Track coach Bill Bowerman began experimenting with his wife's waffle iron; consequently, Nike's "waffle trainer" entered the shoe market in 1974.

- A colon (which is used only rarely) indicates that the second clause explains the first clause or develops the idea further.

  In 1972 President Richard Nixon made a historic visit to China: prior to his visit, America and China had spent two decades in open opposition.

  The media initially failed to report Secretary of State Henry Kissinger's 1971 visit to China: no word of his secret mission escaped until after the secretary's return.

Coordination and Subordination pp. 363–65

A **complex sentence** contains only one independent clause and at least one dependent clause. The dependent clause can appear before, within, or after the independent clause.

Because supermarkets needed a more efficient checkout system, Bernard Silver and Joseph Woodland began developing the bar code system.

Sentence Expansion and Reduction pp. 371–78

Joseph Woodland tried to develop a method in which ultraviolet lights would scan ink patterns.

The ink that Woodland designed proved too expensive and too unreliable for mass automated use.

Teaching Strategy

Discussion

Remind students not to confuse the compound subject or predicate of a simple sentence with the clauses of a compound sentence. Display the following sentences: *We boarded the airliner in Charlotte and arrived in Vienna ten hours later. We boarded the airliner in Charlotte, and we arrived in Vienna ten hours later.* Ask students to identify the simple sentence and the compound sentence.

Teaching Strategy

Discussion

When studying compound sentences, remind students about the use of conjunctive adverbs as discussed on page 51 in Chapter 2.

Teaching Strategy

Participation

Display two simple sentences: *The soccer team practices every day. The team has not won a championship.* Ask students to combine the two sentences to form a complex sentence. *(Answers will vary.)* Display their answers and then ask the students to identify the independent and the dependent clauses.

ESL Strategy

Use ESL Helps 5A and 5B (Teacher's Toolkit) to help ESL students understand how to combine sentences using dependent and independent clauses.

A **compound-complex sentence** contains two or more independent clauses and at least one dependent clause.

In 1973 George J. Laurer, who worked for IBM, patented the familiar black-lined bar code, but his successors popularized this symbol that now appears on most commercially sold retail products.

Marsh's supermarket, which is located in Troy, Ohio, became the first business to use the bar code; here in June of 1974 a clerk scanned the first purchase bearing this code, a packet of Wrigley's gum.

in SUMMARY

A **simple sentence** consists of only one independent clause.

A **compound sentence** contains two or more independent clauses.

A **complex sentence** contains one independent clause and at least one dependent clause.

A **compound-complex sentence** includes two or more independent clauses and at least one dependent clause.

5.8 PRACTICE *the skill*

Identify each sentence as simple *(S)*, compound *(Cd)*, complex *(Cx)*, or compound-complex *(Cd-Cx)*.

S 1. In 1850 one of the earliest successful advertising campaigns occurred in America.

Cx 2. Phineas T. Barnum, famous circus organizer, decided that Jenny Lind, the Swedish nightingale, should come to America.

Cx 3. After he negotiated a contract to bring her to America, he began a masterful advertising campaign.

Cd-Cx 4. The Swedish singer, although she was very famous on the Continent, was unknown in the United States, and many people questioned Barnum's attempt to bring her to this country.

Cd-Cx 5. Barnum had never heard her sing, but he relied on what others had told him of the young singer.

S 6. Barnum used newspaper ads, handbills, and broadsides, large sheets of paper printed on one side, to advertise the coming of the famous singer.

Cx 7. When she arrived in New York harbor, 30,000 New Yorkers met her at the dock to welcome her to America.

Cd 8. On the wharf was a bower of decorated trees, and two arches welcomed Jenny Lind to New York and America.

Cd-Cx 9. Many people thought that the city of New York had provided these decorations, but the cost of the trees and arches was probably an advertising charge in Barnum's accounting books.

Cd 10. Barnum's successful advertising made Jenny Lind famous in New York, and his advertising spread her fame throughout the country.

Sentence diagram answers for Practice the Skill 5.8 appear in the Teacher's Toolkit. If you teach diagramming, perhaps consult *The Writer's Toolbox* for sample diagrams.

TEACHING STRATEGY

Demonstration

Consider doing sentences 1–4 of Practice the Skill 5.8 orally with the students. Encourage the students to label the sentence pattern of each sentence in the exercise.

5.9 REVIEW *the skill*

Rewrite each sentence or set of sentences to create the kind of sentence indicated in parentheses. *(Answers may vary.)*

1. Advertising is nothing new; it can be traced to ancient times. *(complex)*

   Advertising, which is nothing new, can be traced to ancient times.

2. Some of the earliest advertisements have been found in Rome. Other early advertisements have been found in Pompeii. *(simple)*

   Some of the earliest advertisements have been found in both Rome and Pompeii.

3. Archeologists have discovered some ancient methods of advertising. One of the first known methods of advertising was an outdoor display. The display might once have been a sign painted on the side of a building. *(compound-complex)*

   Archeologists have discovered that one of the ancient methods of advertising was an outdoor display, and the display might once have been a sign painted on the side of a building.

4. Archeologists have found a sign advertisement. One Roman excavation revealed a sign for property for rent. *(complex)*

   In one Roman excavation archeologists have found a sign advertisement that advertised property for rent.

5. Another excavated sign was found on a wall in Pompeii. The advertisement called travelers' attention to a building in another town. *(compound)*

   Another excavated sign was found on a wall in Pompeii, but the advertisement called travelers' attention to a building in another town.

6. During medieval times merchants employed another form of advertising. Town criers walked the streets and shouted the value and praise of a merchant's products. *(complex)*

   During medieval times merchants employed another form of advertising that featured town criers who walked the streets and shouted the value and praise of a merchant's products.

134 Chapter 5 | Clauses

7. Printed advertising was not available prior to 1445. Gutenberg's movable-type printing press provided a means for printed advertising. *(simple)*

In 1445 Gutenberg's movable-type printing press provided a means for printed advertising.

8. Fliers became a popular form of advertising. Sometimes fliers appeared on the walls as posters. *(compound)*

Fliers became a popular form of advertising, and sometimes they even appeared on the walls as posters.

9. Fliers often included the symbols of guild members. Fliers also included the symbols of the tradesmen. *(simple)*

Fliers often included the symbols of guild members and tradesmen.

10. Other forms of advertising followed. In the 1800s in the United States, manufacturers published mail-order catalogs. Catalogs reached many people. *(compound-complex)*

Other forms of advertising followed, and in the 1800s in the United States manufacturers published mail-order catalogs that reached many people.

Avoiding Sentence Errors

Knowing the difference between dependent clauses and independent clauses—and knowing how to combine them correctly—will help you avoid serious sentence errors. The following information will help you develop your ability to find and correct some common problems.

Fragment

A **fragment** is a group of words wrongly punctuated as if it were a complete sentence. A fragment is usually considered a serious error. There are three basic kinds of fragments.

Missing Elements

Every sentence must have both a subject and a predicate. An imperative sentence, which has an understood subject, is the only exception. If a group of words punctuated as a sentence is missing either a subject or a verb, it is a fragment. Correct this kind of fragment by supplying the missing element or by joining the fragment to an adjacent sentence.

Teaching Strategy

Participation

Display the following word groups:

- Effectively campaigning for the office. *(missing subject and verb)*
- Senator James conducted an honest campaign; and won the election. *(wrong punctuation)*
- As though he were the only candidate. *(subordinating words create a dependent clause)*

Ask students to identify the errors of the word groups. *(They are all fragments.)* Ask them what the specific problem of each is. *(See notes following each sentence.)* Ask students to correct each problem to make the word group a sentence. *(Answers will vary.)*

ESL Strategy

To help students identify multiword prepositions, use ESL Help 5c (Teacher's Toolkit).

ESL *Introduced* is past tense, and 1970 is a date in the past. Yet this fragment needs to be in the passive voice because lids are inanimate and cannot themselves introduce anything. *Introduced* is transitive and needs a direct object. Because there is no direct object, one can assume that the phrase is really an incomplete passive sentence: a fragment.

Incorrect	Childproof safety lids introduced in 1970. Opened a subway in its capital city in this same year.
Correct	Childproof safety lids were introduced in 1970. Mexico opened a subway in its capital city in this same year.

ESL Fragments introduced by multiple-word prepositions are difficult to identify. When you use a multiple-word preposition, make sure that the phrase it introduces is attached to an independent clause.

Incorrect	In spite of her desire for convenience.
Correct	In spite of her desire for convenience, her children's safety came first.

Subordinating Words

A sentence must be (or at least contain) an independent clause. A dependent clause standing alone is a fragment. Any group of words that includes both a subject and a predicate but also contains a subordinating word is a dependent clause and cannot stand alone as a sentence.

Incorrect	Since the automotive industry introduced the catalytic converter in 1975. Pollution rates have dropped significantly.
Correct	Pollution rates have dropped significantly since the automotive industry introduced the catalytic converter in 1975.

Wrong Punctuation

Semicolons p. 315

Incorrect use of a semicolon can also produce a fragment. A semicolon can appear only between two grammatically equal groups of words, usually between two independent clauses. When a semicolon appears between an independent clause and a dependent clause, the result is a fragment. The most common way to correct a semicolon fragment is to remove the semicolon, replacing it with a comma if necessary.

Incorrect	Personal grooming became a bit easier in 1975; when the first disposable razor appeared on the market.
Correct	Personal grooming became a bit easier in 1975 when the first disposable razor appeared on the market.

Permissible Fragments

Although fragments are common and acceptable in conversation, they are usually considered errors in writing. However, an effective writer will sometimes choose to use a short fragment to express informality or for special effect, such as emphasis or irony.

Informality	The 1970s brought the first successful crossbreeding of cattle and buffalo. Beefalo burgers, anyone?
Emphasis	In November of 1971 the *Mariner 9* spacecraft failed to transmit highly detailed pictures of Mars back to earth. Only furious red dust storms.
Irony	Scientists discovered an ocean floor garden at the Galápagos Rift in the late 1970s. Plants thriving without photosynthesis!

Teaching Strategy

Participation

Review the guidelines for correctly using semicolons on page 315. Emphasize that a semicolon can be used to join only two independent clauses, not an independent and a dependent clause. Display the following sentences:

- I like to run on trails rather than on street roads; because asphalt is hard on my knees.
- Although you could get hit by lightning during a thunderstorm; you have a better chance of being in a car wreck.
- She recognized the danger of running alone; that someone could attack her.
- While the class president turned red from embarrassment over tripping in front of the entire auditorium; the principal tried to make jokes to divert the crowd's attention.

Instruct the students to correct the fragments. Ask for volunteers to read aloud their corrections.

Teaching Strategy

Discussion

Reinforce the idea that professional writers often use fragments effectively for emphasis or effect; however, students should generally avoid using fragments in their writing.

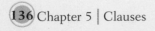

136 Chapter 5 | Clauses

tip

Don't overuse intentional fragments. An occasional fragment can be effective, but too many fragments become tiresome, drawing attention to themselves and distracting the reader from your message.

tip

If you include an intentional fragment in a writing assignment for class, mark it in some way so that your teacher doesn't mistake it for an error.

Comma Splice and Fused Sentence

Conjunctions pp. 54–55

Just as it is incorrect to punctuate a fragment as though it were a complete sentence, it is also incorrect to punctuate two sentences as though they were only one. A **comma splice** is a serious error that occurs when two independent clauses are joined by a comma without a coordinating conjunction. A **fused sentence** is a serious error that occurs when two independent clauses are joined with no punctuation at all. Correct these errors by using the strategy that best expresses the relationship between the two clauses: add a period or a semicolon between the two clauses, combine the two with a comma and a coordinating conjunction, or change one of the independent clauses into a dependent clause.

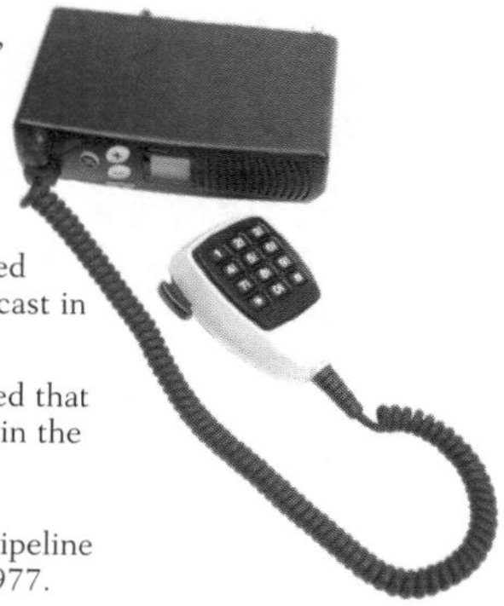

COMMA SPLICE	In 1976 Americans enthusiastic about CB radios discovered that First Lady Ford shared their interest, she often broadcast in the CB world under the name "First Mama."
CORRECT	In 1976 Americans enthusiastic about CB radios discovered that First Lady Ford shared their interest; she often broadcast in the CB world under the name "First Mama."
CORRECT	In 1976 Americans enthusiastic about CB radios discovered that First Lady Ford shared their interest. She often broadcast in the CB world under the name "First Mama."
FUSED SENTENCE	Congress approved the construction of the Trans-Alaska Pipeline System (TAPS) in 1973 oil production began in June of 1977.
CORRECT	Congress approved the construction of the Trans-Alaska Pipeline System (TAPS) in 1973, and oil production began in June of 1977.
CORRECT	After Congress approved the construction of the Trans-Alaska Pipeline System (TAPS) in 1973, oil production began in June of 1977.

tip

Be careful not to correct a fused sentence by inserting only a comma; the resulting comma splice would be no improvement.

in SUMMARY

A **fragment** is a group of words wrongly punctuated as if it were a complete sentence.

A **comma splice** is two independent clauses wrongly joined by a comma only.

A **fused sentence** is two independent clauses wrongly joined without any punctuation.

TEACHING STRATEGY
Analyze

Use the example sentences on page 137 to analyze incorrect and correct punctuation. Point out the sentence errors of comma splice and fused sentence. Ask students to identify why these sentences are wrong.

TEACHING STRATEGY
Discussion

Remind the students that fragments, comma splices, and fused sentences are usually considered to be serious errors in written assignments. Encourage students to proofread carefully in order to avoid these errors.

Clauses | Chapter 5 137

5.10 PRACTICE *the skill*

Identify each group of words as a sentence *(S)*, a fragment *(F)*, a comma splice *(CS)*, or a fused sentence *(FS)*.

Billy Sunday

S 1. Successful evangelistic campaigns in the early 1900s had prayer as their base.

CS 2. Choosing the evangelist for the campaign was most important, the people wanted a man who could "preach the stars down."

F 3. Men such as Bob Jones Sr., Billy Sunday, and others who preached successful campaigns.

FS 4. Local church leaders met together to plan the advertising for the campaign these leaders sought God's blessing on the preaching.

S 5. An advertising committee would oversee the design of signs and fliers that would advertise the dates and times of the preaching services.

F 6. Newspapers from local communities and from distant ones that often sent journalists to the meetings.

FS 7. Journalists would then write an article in the paper telling of the evangelistic meetings this in itself served as a form of advertising for the campaign.

CS 8. Another form of advertising was word of mouth, people who had been saved in the meetings would tell others and invite them to the meetings.

F 9. That these preaching campaigns were successful and effective without loud speakers, radio, or television.

S 10. God honored the prayers of His people who sought revival in their communities.

5.11 REVIEW *the skill*

Identify each group of words as a sentence *(S)*, a fragment *(F)*, a comma splice *(CS)*, or a fused sentence *(FS)*. If the item is a sentence error, rewrite it as a correct sentence. *(Some answers may vary.)*

F 1. The campaign slogan "Tippecanoe and Tyler Too" the rallying cry for the presidential campaign of 1840.

The campaign slogan "Tippecanoe and Tyler Too" became the rallying cry for the presidential campaign of 1840.

S 2. From 1801 to 1812 William Henry Harrison served as governor of the Indiana Territory.

Scriptural Application

After the students have completed Practice the Skill 5.10, read John 4:35–36 to the class and discuss why mass evangelistic campaigns are now rarely used in America. That is, what is it about early twentieth-century American culture that made such campaigns feasible, and what evangelistic methods seem most appropriate today?

FS 3. During that time the Indian tribes rallied behind their leader, Tecumseh, to fight against the white settlers the Indian tribes wanted to protect their hunting lands.

During that time the Indian tribes rallied behind their leader, Tecumseh, to fight against the white settlers; the Indian tribes wanted to protect their hunting lands.

CS 4. On November 7, 1811, the Indians surprised Harrison's army at Tippecanoe, the Americans suffered many casualties.

On November 7, 1811, the Indians surprised Harrison's army at Tippecanoe, and the Americans suffered many casualties.

F 5. Harrison and his army managing to drive the Indians away and later destroying a nearby Indian town.

Harrison and his army managed to drive the Indians away and later destroyed a nearby Indian town.

S 6. Harrison was both praised and condemned for what happened at Tippecanoe.

____

____

CS 7. In 1835 Harrison, who was then unaffiliated with any political party, campaigned for the presidency, he lost the election.

In 1835 Harrison, who was then unaffiliated with any political party, campaigned for the presidency; he lost the election.

F 8. The Log Cabin Campaign of 1840 having placed Harrison against the incumbent President Van Buren.

The Log Cabin Campaign of 1840 placed Harrison against the incumbent President Van Buren.

FS 9. Harrison's running mate for the vice-presidency was John Tyler hence "Tippecanoe and Tyler Too" became their campaign slogan.

Harrison's running mate for the vice-presidency was John Tyler; hence "Tippecanoe and Tyler Too" became their campaign slogan.

CS 10. As a result of a very rigorous campaign, William Henry Harrison became weak and contracted pneumonia, he died after one month in office.

As a result of a very rigorous campaign, William Henry Harrison became weak and contracted pneumonia; he died after one month in office.

Clauses | Chapter 5 139

The types of phrases and clauses in the sentences of the suggested answer paragraph are as follows:

4. Clause—*adjective*
5. Phrase—*infinitive; delayed subject*
7. Phrase—*participle*
8. Phrase—*gerund; object of preposition*
10. Clause—*noun; direct object*
    Phrase—*infinitive; subject*
11. Clause—*adverb*

The sentence patterns of the suggested answer paragraph are as follows:

1. S-TrV-DO
2. S-TrV-DO, TrV-DO, TrV-DO-OC
3. S-InV
4. S-TrV-P (passive)
5. S-LV-PA
6. S-TrV-DO
7. S-LV-PN
8. S-LV-PN
9. S-TrV-P (passive)
10. S-TrV-DO
11. S-TrV-DO
12. S-TrV-DO

5.12 CUMULATIVE *review*

Rewrite the following paragraph, correcting the five sentence errors. Then underline each verbal or verbal phrase and place parentheses around each dependent clause in your answer. (Be prepared to identify the types of phrases and clauses and to label the sentence patterns if your teacher asks for that information.) *(Answers may vary.)*

By the 1880s the United States had entered a new era for advertisements. By this time manufacturers had improved their operations, increased their capabilities, and made more products available. In addition, consumer costs having been decreased. Advertisements were further changed by the telegraph and railroad service that now connected the country, it was possible to have nationwide advertisements and nationwide distribution of goods. Within twenty years ad firms marketing patent medicines, food, soap, cosmetics, and automobiles. Some of the first brand names promoted by nationwide advertisements were Ivory, Colgate, Wrigley, and Coca-Cola. Then in the1920s radio became a chief means of presenting a product to the public its popularity, however, was eclipsed by the advent of television commercials in 1950. Manufacturers knew that to advertise their products on television would be essential. Because advertisers use so many means of communication today, consumers can hardly escape their messages, some people would welcome a return to a simpler world.

By the 1880s the United States had entered a new era for advertisements. By this time manufacturers had improved their operations, increased their capabilities, and made more products available. In addition, consumer costs had decreased. Advertisements were further changed by the telegraph and railroad service (that now connected the country.) It was possible to have nationwide advertisements and nationwide distribution of goods. Within twenty years ad firms marketed patent medicines, food, soap, cosmetics, and automobiles. Some of the first brand names promoted by nationwide advertisements were Ivory, Colgate, Wrigley, and Coca-Cola. Then in the 1920s radio became a chief means of presenting a product to the public. Its popularity, however, was eclipsed by the advent of television commercials in 1950. Manufacturers knew (that to advertise their products on television would be essential.) (Because advertisers use so many means of communication today,) consumers can hardly escape their messages. Some people would welcome a return to a simpler world.

Reinforcement

Use Chapter 5 Review on pages 437–38 for additional test review.

Evaluation

Use Chapter 5 Test to evaluate students' understanding of the content and concepts of the chapter.

140 Chapter 5 | Clauses

THINK ABOUT IT

Authorial Intention

A critical thinker is a person who draws reasonable conclusions from a body of information and then uses those conclusions to make sound judgments about life. But before he can reach these reasonable conclusions from something that he hears or reads, he must analyze it thoroughly.

Sometimes an author's purpose and message are obvious. A book entitled *How to Build a Shed* probably has as its purpose to teach the reader how to build a shed. Sometimes, though, the author's purpose and message are not quite so easy to identify. Most people assume that a novelist's purpose is to entertain his readers. After all, if the novel isn't "a good read," no one will want to buy it. But some novelists want to inform their readers as they entertain them. A historical novel, for example, gives the reader insight into a particular time period. A mystery novel may introduce its readers to the work habits of police detectives. Some novelists go even further, attempting to persuade their readers to adopt a particular belief about their topic. For instance, in *Hard Times,* Charles Dickens condemns utilitarianism.

To analyze what you read, follow these steps.

- Read the passage carefully and completely. You must examine all of the evidence before you can draw a valid conclusion.
- Identify the author's message by pinpointing the most prominent idea that the author emphasizes. Look for key words or phrases that the author repeats.
- Evaluate the writer's attitude as revealed in his writings. Note any emotionally charged language that indicates the author's opinion about the subject, his message, and his audience. Notice how he portrays the characters he creates (in fiction) or the experts that he cites (in nonfiction). Who is presented in a positive light? Who appears in a negative light?
- Does the writer present both sides of an issue? Does he seem especially sympathetic to those on one side of the issue? If he presents just one side, is it presented favorably or unfavorably?
- If possible, investigate the writer's background. What else has he written? Whom does he work for? What experience does he have in this field? Where did he receive his training? The answers to these questions can reveal whether the author is qualified to discuss his topic and whether his opinion may be biased.

One warning: Be careful not to judge any writer too harshly or to approve anyone too readily. Although your observations and evaluations are reliable up to a point, all human reasoning is imperfect. Remember that "man looketh on the outward appearance, but the Lord looketh on the heart" (1 Sam. 16:7).

Thinking It Through

Find a newspaper editorial (not just a letter to the editor but rather an opinion piece written as an article) and analyze it by using the steps described above.

Teaching Strategy

Modeling

Consider analyzing a newspaper editorial with the students. Display an appropriate article or distribute a copy to each student. Lead the students through the steps described in the student worktext. Refer to pages 1–4 and 10 for information on the writing process and a writer's purpose and thesis.

Scriptural Application

Ask a volunteer to read 1 Samuel 16:7 aloud. Discuss the dangers of judging someone and remind the students that no one but God knows motives and thoughts. Challenge the students to speak and act in a manner that will not cause anyone to doubt their sincerity. Ask another volunteer to read Romans 14:13 aloud. Remind the students that a Christian's life should always reflect Christ.

Think About It | Chapter 5 141

OBJECTIVES

Students will

1. select an issue to write about.
2. state a conflict and a resolution in sentences.
3. select a setting, main characters, and stage business for a scene.
4. draft a scene that includes a setting, action, and a climax.
5. evaluate a scene for conflict, resolution, naturalness, and logic.
6. revise a scene for clarity and effect.
7. revise a scene for grammar, usage, spelling, and mechanics.
8. publish a dramatic scene.

Chapter 6 Overview			
Topic	**Pages**	**Support Materials**	**Days**
Subjects and Predicates	148–49	Bulletin Board 6 Chapter 6 Pretest	62
Dramatic Scene	143–48	Writing Rubric 6 Writing Worksheets 6A–6B	63, 65–66, 70–71, 76, 80
Subject Identification	150–53	Practice/Review the Skill 6.1–6.2	64
Problem Nouns	153–55		67
Practice	156–57	Practice/Review the Skill 6.3–6.4	68
Problem Pronouns	157–61	Concept Reinforcement 6A ESL Helps 6A–6B Practice/Review the Skill 6.5–6.6	69, 72
Compound Subjects	161–63	Practice/Review the Skill 6.7–6.8	73
Nouns as Antecedents	163–66	Practice/Review the Skill 6.9–6.10	74
Collective Nouns and Indefinite Pronouns as Antecedents	166–68	Teaching Helps 6A–6B Practice the Skill 6.11 Concept Reinforcement 6B	75
Review	168–70, 439–41	Review the Skill 6.12 Cumulative Review 6.13 Chapter 6 Review	77
Chapter 6 Test			78
From the Written Word	171		79
Midterm Review and Midterm Examination			81–90

DRAMATIC SCENE

Lesson Support

Teacher's Toolkit

Bulletin Board 6
Writing Worksheets 6A–6B
Writing Rubric 6

God's Word teaches that the words a person speaks reveal much about his character. (See Matt. 12:34 and Luke 6:45.) The following excerpt is from This Same Jesus, *a play about a glazier who has allowed events to make him bitter. Dan is the pastor of the church in which Adonis (ad-uh-NEES) is repairing the stained-glass windows. As you read the scene, look for hints about Adonis's and Dan's characters revealed through their dialogue. How does Burke show you other details, such as plot, through the conversation? Later, you will write a dramatic scene in which the characters are developed primarily through dialogue.*

A *glazier* is a person who installs or repairs glass (e.g., windows).

Earlier in the play, Adonis himself tells Dan how to pronounce his name: "add-a-NIECE . . . not add a nephew." Adonis is a Greek name.

This Same Jesus *by David Burke*

DAN Adonis, the windows look better than they have since we moved here. Why don't you come see them tomorrow with the morning sun streaming through?

ADONIS Looks like the storm's finally passed.

DAN We may even get a little sun before the day's over.

ADONIS Hey, I want you to know I appreciate all the talk today. It's been real interesting.

DAN For me too.

(ADONIS *is finishing the bill.*)

ADONIS Second Avenue Baptist Church?

DAN That's right.

ADONIS Hey, you don't have to wait for me. I got this stuff to clean up. I'll leave the invoice and you can send me a check in the mail. Okay?

DAN Okay. . . . Are we finished talking?

ADONIS Well, I don't think I'm gonna' change your mind about anything.

DAN You asked a lot of good questions. Can I ask you one?

ADONIS Yeah, sure.

DAN When you mentioned your wife earlier, you said she used to talk to you about God?

ADONIS You seem like a nice guy, Dan, but I don't think you want me to unload the whole story of my life on you here.

DAN Only if you want to.

ADONIS You know you and your little girl—you two remind me a lot of my wife here today. Charmaine was a genuine, Bible-believing Christian woman.

DAN Sounds like quite a testimony.

ADDITIONAL INFORMATION

David Burke is a teacher, actor, director, and playwright with more than thirty years of experience. Burke earned his PhD in Speech Communication and Theatre with an emphasis in playwriting from Southern Illinois University. Winner of several awards for dramatic writing, Burke takes special interest in Shakespearean and biblical drama as well as experimental theater. In addition to using his abilities in the theater and the classroom, Burke has also written for Christian film and video.

Literature Link

Ask two students to read aloud the roles of Dan and Adonis in the scene from David Burke's *This Same Jesus*. Ask students to discuss how the dialogue reveals details about each man's character, the plot, and other aspects of the play.

REINFORCEMENT

Construct a bulletin board, using Bulletin Board 6 (Teacher's Toolkit). Encourage the students to note all the dramas discussed in the practices throughout Chapter 6.

TEACHING STRATEGY

Introduction

Inform the students that they will not be asked to write an entire play since such a task would be too complex for this assignment. Students will be expected to introduce characters and create a setting and then to write about one point of conflict or one important incident.

Thinking Biblically

Compelling plots, believable dialogue—both are marks of well-written drama and both are tools dramatists use to deliver a powerful message with great subtlety. Part of drama's strength as an art form, in fact, lies in its suggestiveness, its ability to insinuate. But when a drama includes preachy monologues, trite plots, and hackneyed dialogue, it loses its effectiveness. Encourage the writers in your class to read well-crafted drama so that they can absorb its power and use it for Christian purposes.

Thinking Biblically

Dramatic writing can address biblical themes without specifically stating them or becoming overtly didactic. Thornton Wilder's *Our Town* provides a good example. The play explores life and death in the small New Hampshire town of Grover's Corners. Though Wilder himself was not a believer, a Christian who knows Scripture cannot watch the play without thinking of Ecclesiastes and the brevity of life (James 4:14). Drama is a powerful tool for inspiration, edification, even rebuke. It is powerful precisely because (and when) it is not preachy.

Adonis Matter of fact, she's the reason I'm here. This was her church back when it was Methodist. That's why I called to see if I could come fix the windows. She looked out these same windows every week. Used to be in church every time the doors were open. Always volunteered her time with Meals on Wheels—you know to get food to shut-ins?

Dan Is that right?

Adonis Week in and week out when I bring fresh flowers out here, I see your windows. Her grave's at the far end of the cemetery. Near the big oak.

Dan I'm sorry, Adonis. I had no idea.

Adonis Almost four years ago.

Dan I am so sorry.

Adonis Cancer. Like so many. Hadn't been out of the house the last months of her life except in a wheelchair. Even the ladies at Meals on Wheels had stopped coming to see her. Folks from her church came to see her at first. But I guess it got discouraging to see one of their own like that. Or maybe they didn't like to hang around me. I don't know. But I . . . well, I took care of Charmaine. Fed her. Cleaned her. Washed her hair—long brown hair just as fine as when she was a teenager. Clipped her nails. Read to her when she couldn't go to sleep. Sat up with her when she wanted to watch TV. Turned off the TV when she got tired of that. Use to turn off the lights and just talk to her—plain old talk about anything and nothing—windows I was making. Restorations in churches. Long into the night . . .

Dan Adonis, God can fill the void in your heart.

Adonis I wish He could.

WRITING

Dramatic Scene

Set a watch, O Lord, before my mouth; keep the door of my lips.
Psalm 141:3

A play or a dramatic scene is different from most prose in two main ways: (1) it is usually meant to be presented orally, and (2) the elements of character, plot, and setting depend almost entirely on **dialogue**. Dialogue, however much it may sound like ordinary speech, is carefully crafted. If you were to overhear a conversation, it might contain the same information that would be in a dramatic scene, but it would also contain much that the scene would not.

Good dialogue sifts out the distractions of everyday life but leaves the core issues; excellent dialogue presents the issues in such a way that the scene still feels as though you are overhearing an everyday conversation.

The trick to good craftsmanship is not to let it show. Dramatic scenes seem contrived when you can see how the dialogue is being steered toward a topic or an end—they do not convince you that the characters are real people with real concerns. The careful craftsman keeps his audience so engaged in the conversation that the audience arrives at the destination without having bothered to watch the road.

Overview of the Writing Process

Planning—discussing an issue with a peer, narrowing the focus, writing a conflict and a resolution in a sentence, displaying a conflict, choosing setting and characters, deciding on stage business, and mapping out a scene

Drafting—establishing setting, deciding on actions to be included, and deciding on a high point

Revising—re-reading a scene, reading a scene aloud, getting peer input, and refining a scene

Publishing—staging a scene, adapting a scene, or producing a book of scenes

Scriptural Application

Read Psalm 141:3 aloud. Discuss the implications of the verse (prevent us from speaking wrong; encourage us to speak what is right).

Planning Strategy

Discussion

With student input, display a list of possible topics for a dramatic scene. Talk about the advantages of various suggestions.

Planning Strategy

Peer Response

Allow time for students to discuss an issue and to consider the questions on page 145. Meet briefly with each group or pair of students to help focus the discussions toward a single topic.

One on One Discuss the questions on page 145 with your student and help him to focus his ideas on a single topic.

Planning Strategy

Discussion

Ask students to identify the conflict in the scene from *This Same Jesus* in a single sentence. *(Adonis has a void in his life that needs to be filled.)* Discuss how the author makes this conflict evident in the scene.

Your Turn

Think of an issue that is important to you. Have you had conversations about it? What is your viewpoint on the issue? Imagine holding a conversation with people who disagree with you. Turn that conversation into a crafted dramatic scene.

Planning

✔ **Talk with a peer about an issue important to you.** Take notes on your peer's response to the issue. Does he question your reasoning? Does he challenge your opinions? Does he agree too readily? What seems to be the focus of your conversation?

✔ **Narrow your focus.** Looking at your notes, find the crux of your issue. For example, if you are talking about finding God's will for your life and your conversation seems to turn again and again to what your friends think you should do, perhaps your issue is not finding God's will but rather putting God's will before your friends' approval. You might want to write a scene about someone who struggles with trying too hard to please people.

✔ **Write the problem in one sentence.** In a dramatic scene, the problem, or **conflict**, is the struggle between persons (or forces). If you have narrowed your topic and defined it well enough, you should be able to express the problem in one sentence. All of the following are types of conflict:

man vs. man

man vs. himself

man vs. society

man vs. nature

man vs. God or the gods

The conflict in the scene described probably would be one of man against himself (what he knows to be right) and man against God (what God has commanded). The problem might be stated this way: *Trying to please people can cause an individual to violate his own conscience and to weaken his fellowship with God.*

✔ **Decide on a resolution for the problem.** Now that you've stated your problem clearly, consider how your main character will resolve the problem. Will she decide to please her friends or to please God? If she chooses to please God, will she continue to spend time with those friends who don't support her desire? Will she explain her decision to them and try to persuade her friends to change their attitudes? Or will she separate from those friends who might weaken her resolve to obey God? Before you begin writing, have a plan for solving the conflict of your scene.

✔ **Show—don't just tell about—the problem.** You are not writing an essay about the problem. You are presenting a scene that looks much like a moment in real time and characters that seem like real people. The audience should be able to draw the right conclusions about your subject without being told. In the excerpt from *This Same Jesus,* Burke shows us that Adonis is searching for something (seen by his desire to visit the church that his wife attended) and that he is kind and compassionate (apparent through the way he cared for his wife and takes flowers to her grave weekly).

Inform students that this statement of the problem will most likely not occur in sentence form in their scene but will help them to focus their ideas about the scene as they write.

For more information about conflict in literature, see pages 2–3 in *FUNDAMENTALS OF LITERATURE, Second Edition* (BJU Press 2010). Notice that "man vs. society" is a variation of "man vs. man" and that "man vs. nature" and "man vs. God or the gods" are specific types of "man against a greater force."

Planning Strategy

Discussion

Ask students to identify the attributes that the character Dan displays in the scene from *This Same Jesus.* (*He is a good witness; he is caring; he is a good listener.*) Elicit from students how these attributes are clear through the dialogue. (*He is persistent in questioning Adonis; he expresses sorrow at Adonis's disclosure of Charmaine's death; he responds but talks very little in comparison to Adonis.*)

DramaLink

Give students a situation and a setting (e.g., trying to find a lost puppy in the park) and two characters (e.g., an elderly man and a young girl). Ask them to enact the scene, making up dialogue as they go. Change the situation, setting, or characters slightly (e.g., trying to find the elderly man's wallet in the park). Ask another set of students to enact the scene.

Planning Strategy

Discussion

Point out the stage directions in Burke's scene. (There is only one in this excerpt: "Adonis is finishing the bill.") Explain that a minimum of stage directions leaves the interpretation open to a director and an actor. Ask students to speculate on different interpretations of the stage direction.

- ✔ **Choose a setting and main characters.** Do you want the scene to be contemporary or set in another time? How does the place contribute to the effect or meaning of the scene? Remember that this scene is to be staged—settings too exotic will be difficult to represent. How many characters do you need? Usually only two or three characters are needed for a single scene. Getting too many in a scene makes the scene hard to control. Your main character will be your **protagonist**, a character who usually changes in some way. Opposite the protagonist is the **antagonist**, who generally attempts to thwart the actions of the main character. The antagonist may or may not be a **villain**, or an evil character. In Burke's play, Adonis is the protagonist. By the end of his dealings with Dan, the play's antagonist, Adonis changes from an embittered man to one who is willing to choose Christ.

- ✔ **Think about stage business.** Stage business is the movements, gestures, and other physical actions actors use on stage. The best stage business subtly reinforces the meanings of the characters' lines. For example, in the scene before the one you read here, Dan and Adonis are talking. Adonis is tapping on a pane of old glass to see how hard it will be to remove from the leading. Dan is witnessing to Adonis with a series of examples of God's sovereignty—in effect, tapping "the old glass" of Adonis's thinking.
- ✔ **Find a real person to imitate.** When you write dialogue, think of someone you know. Make your character sound like that person. This technique will help your characters sound not only real but also different from each other. Visualize the action and think through the dialogue before you write the rough draft.
- ✔ **Map out your scene.** Use your conflict and resolution, setting, characters, stage business, and any bits of dialogue you have thought about to construct a scene map. Put the first three items (conflict and resolution, setting, and characters) at the top of a page and then make a chart for the beginning, middle, and end of your scene, filling in stage business and dialogue for each part.

tip

Mention only essential stage business. Giving too many stage directions limits the director's and actors' interpretation.

Drafting

- ✔ **Set aside a block of time.** It's best to try to write out the scene all in one sitting. There will be time to refine it later. But you will want to keep the momentum and the tone going in this first effort. Drama depends heavily on the "sweep" (pacing) of the action.
- ✔ **Draft the scene.** You have all the parts of your scene. Now you must drop your characters into your setting and write what they say about the conflict and then move the dialogue toward the resolution. It is generally best to begin at the beginning chronologically; however, some writers begin at the end or somewhere in the middle and then go back to the chronological beginning. As you write, remember that you will rework the scene later, so now you can focus on just getting down on paper what the characters say. Include the following points:
    - Establish your setting. Look at the beginning of your scene map. What do you want to have the audience know within the first few lines? How can the dialogue reveal this information? *This Same Jesus* opens with Pastor Dan standing and practicing a sermon about God's allowing bad things to

PLANNING STRATEGY
Motivation

Challenge students to keep a dialogue journal. Tell them to write down snatches of conversation they hear or interesting quotations that could be woven into their stories.

PLANNING STRATEGY
Modeling

Display Writing Worksheet 6A (Teacher's Toolkit). Discuss the various parts of the scene map. Then distribute a copy of Writing Worksheet 6B (Teacher's Toolkit) and instruct each student to complete a scene map for the scene that he will write.

DRAFTING STRATEGY
Discussion

Some students may want to include a list of characters, commonly called *dramatis personae*. Many lists of characters include brief descriptions of the characters. If desired, display the following excerpt from the dramatis personae of *Macbeth:*

Duncan, *King of Scotland*

Malcolm, Donalbain } *his sons*

Macbeth, Banquo } *generals of the King's army*

happen. As he "preaches," the audience learns that Dan and his family have encountered heartache and yet have found "Peace for the Storm Inside" (the announced title of the message).

- Ask yourself what actions need to be included. Again, do not prescribe too much of the action but include information that is necessary for the success of the scene. Burke's play has Adonis entering midway through Dan's sermon and clearing his throat to get the pastor's attention. Write stage directions into the opening of your scene. Often these instructions will be entrances of one or more main characters.

tip

Avoid burying information essential to move the scene along in the directions outlining stage business.

- Decide on the scene's high point. How can you make the lines of the rising action increasingly energized? Can you feel tension building in the scene? In *This Same Jesus* we begin to feel that Dan is going to confront Adonis about his need for a Savior when Dan says, "Are we finished talking?" and later asks whether he may ask the glazier a question. Burke artfully brings us to the major dramatic question of the play.

tip

As you write, you may find that a line of dialogue or stage business stymies you. Do not get bogged down. Go on with the scene and come back to the sticking point later.

✔ **Check your scene map again.** Where do you want the scene to end? What do you want the audience to carry away from their experience? Because we do not have the ending of Burke's play, we are left wondering what happens to Adonis. Avoid leaving your readers wondering about the outcome of your scene.

Revising

✔ **Read over your scene.** Does the scene sufficiently demonstrate the problem you identified? Does the scene move toward a resolution? Is it convincing? Are the lines natural? Do they follow each other logically and smoothly? Does the scene produce the effect you wanted? Revise to eliminate any problems that you identify.

✔ **Read the scene aloud.** Are the lines easy to articulate? Does each character have a reason (motivation) for the words he says in each line? Are there any awkward combinations of words? (What actor would want to say "All I could remember later was weeping and sleeping"?)

✔ **Ask someone else (or several people) to read the scene aloud.** Watch for places where your readers hesitate or misinterpret lines. Ask the readers how they feel about the lines and how easily they think they could project them to an audience. Are there any changes they would make for clarity or ease of speaking?

DramaLink

Conduct a characterization exercise. Give each student a character from the list below and assign partners. Allow volunteers to perform mini-scenes with dialogue.

- Mr. Matias, missionary to Uruguay
- Mr. Ward, Bible teacher
- Mari, student seeking God's will
- Miss Tunis, school counselor
- Troy, exchange student from Kenya

Drafting Strategy

Analysis

Instruct each student to circle on his scene map the high point of his scene.

Drafting Strategy

Discussion

Tell students that in *This Same Jesus* Adonis eventually accepts Christ as Savior through the witness of Dan and his family. Discuss with the students how this scene helps to prepare the audience for his conversion.

Revising Strategy

Analysis

Ask students to look again at Burke's scene on pages 143–44. Point out the lines about the storm passing and the sunlight shining. Ask students what these lines might be saying about the play's outcome. *(The storm in Adonis's life is passing and the sun [or "Son"] is about to break through.)* Challenge the students to look closely at their scenes for places where they could insert foreshadowing. Remind them that foreshadowing should not be too obvious.

OBJECTIVES

Students will

1. identify the simple subject of a sentence containing intervening phrases, predicate nouns of a different number, and inverted order.
2. choose verb forms that agree in number with their subjects.
3. choose the correct verb for subjects that are nouns of plural form, collective nouns, or titles, quotations, and amounts.
4. select verbs that agree with indefinite or relative pronouns.
5. write a correct verb in sentences containing compound subjects.
6. select a correct pronoun that agrees with a noun or compound antecedent.
7. correct pronoun-antecedent problems in sentences with collective nouns and indefinite pronouns as antecedents.

✔ **Refine your scene.** Make changes for clarity and effect. Then proofread your scene for correctness and consistency in format and for errors in spelling, grammar, usage, and mechanics.

Publishing

✔ **Stage the scene.** Choose your cast members and direct your scene. Rehearse a few times before presenting it to an audience. Get any equipment you will need. (For example, if a line calls for someone to sit down, you will need a chair.)

✔ **Adapt the scene for radio.** Because you will not have the advantage of visual **spectacle**, give the audience auditory clues about the action they cannot see.

✔ **Produce a book of scenes.** Collect the scenes you and your peers have written into a book of scenes. Sell the books as a fundraiser.

Some Ideas to Consider

History

- Read *A Man for All Seasons* and compare the play to historical accounts of the same time period.

Literature

- Compare two plays on a similar topic. Discuss how each reveals and handles the conflict.

Speech and Drama

- Time your scene (using actors and allowing for stage business). Then edit it to make it fit an exact time slot as if it were a commercial or a radio drama limited to a certain number of minutes.

USAGE

Agreement

Achieving the goal of clear communication requires an understanding of and an attention to the rules of agreement. Too often, mistakes in agreement draw our attention away from the communication to the mistake itself. How often have you read a composition littered with pronoun-antecedent agreement errors or heard a speaker err in subject-verb agreement? Written and oral communication, especially that of the gospel message and of biblical principles, should be clear and without error. Mistakes in the areas of agreement can compromise the integrity and effectiveness of our communication.

Subject-Verb Agreement

Subjects and Predicates

Plural Forms of Nouns pp. 35–37

Correct **subject-verb agreement** combines a singular subject with a singular verb and a plural subject with a plural verb. Each verb must agree with its subject in person and in number.

Revising Strategy

Peer Response

Allow time for students to read each others' scenes aloud. Encourage both positive and negative responses.

Writing Workshop

Conduct a minilesson from pages 358–59. Remind students to refine sentences for greater effectiveness.

Publishing Strategy

Participation

Make arrangements for students to perform appropriate scenes for another class.

ONE on ONE Encourage your student to recruit help to perform his scene. Make arrangements for him to present his scene to a children's group or on a ministry activity.

Writing Link

Encourage each student to develop his scene into an act or even a full-length play.

Evaluation

For help in grading this assignment, see "Grading Student Writing" (p. v) and Writing Rubric 6 (Teacher's Toolkit).

Singular

S TrV DO
Plimoth Plantation provides an example of our country's earliest horticulture.

S LV PN
Horticulture is a part of our national history.

S TrV DO
Plimoth Plantation does reflect seventeenth-century life.

Plural

S TrV DO
The *landscapes* of Plimoth Plantation *provide* an insight into the lives of the people.

S LV PN
The *gardens will be* a source of learning for years to come.

S TrV DO
Garden *re-creations do reveal* a part of the settlers' lives.

Present Tense
pp. 178–79

William Bradford (1589–1657) wrote *Of Plymouth Plantation* over approximately twenty-one years (1630–51). Drawing from his memory and various letters, Bradford most likely produced this two-volume work in hope that it would be passed on to his descendants as a record of the Pilgrims' life in Plymouth Colony. However, colonial scholars began using Bradford's notable work for reference, and by 1856—nearly two hundred years after Bradford's death—the work was first printed in its entirety for public use.

Present-tense verbs change form with third-person nouns and pronouns. Except for *was/were,* most past and future tenses stay the same whether singular or plural. As a main verb and as an auxiliary, the irregular verb *be* changes in person and tense. Other auxiliaries, such as *have* and *do,* also change form.

The table below shows the basic forms of *be.* The future tense is always *will be.*

Forms of *Be*

	Present		Past	
	Singular	**Plural**	**Singular**	**Plural**
First Person	I am	we are	I was	we were
Second Person	you are	you are	you were	you were
Third Person	he is	they are	he was	they were

ESL

If a complete verb contains one or more auxiliaries, then the first auxiliary agrees with the subject. Only the first auxiliary shows agreement; auxiliaries that appear later in the complete verb do not change form. However, the only auxiliaries that change form to agree with a singular or plural subject are *be, have,* and *do.* Other auxiliaries do not have different singular and plural forms.

	Singular	Plural
be	I **am looking** for my brother and sister.	My brother and sister **are washing** the car.
have	My father **has been planning** to wash the car for a week.	My parents **have been driving** the same car for several years.
do	My father **does** not **want** to trade in the car for an SUV.	My parents **do** not **want** to trade in the car for an SUV.
will (and all modal auxiliaries)	An SUV **will be** difficult to park.	Eventually, my parents **will buy** a new car of some kind.

AGREEMENT

Lesson Support

Student Worktext

Chapter 6 Review—pp. 439–41

Teacher's Toolkit

Chapter 6 Pretest
Teaching Helps 6A–6B
ESL Helps 6A–6B
Concept Reinforcements 6A–6B

Test

Chapter 6 Test

Scriptural Application

Ask students about the nature of language. Where did language originate? *(God)* What does God say about how language should be used? Does the Bible support the learning of correct grammar? *(Answers will vary but may include references to these passages: Eccles. 12:10; Prov. 8:6–9; 15:2; 16:23–24; 23:12.)*

Teaching Strategy

Demonstration

Display two columns of words. Make the first column singular nouns and the second column present tense plural verbs. Remind students that adding *-s* or *-es* to the end of most nouns makes them plural. Show the opposite situation with the verbs that become singular with the addition of *-s* or *-es.*

Subject Identification

Being able to identify the subject of the sentence correctly will help you avoid using a verb that does not agree with the subject. Certain sentence constructions can make subject identification difficult.

Intervening Phrases

Prepositional Phrases p. 88

Appositive Phrases p. 89

Words that come between the subject and the verb can draw your attention away from the true subject of the sentence. The most common **intervening phrases** are the **prepositional phrase**, the **appositive phrase**, and the **negative phrase**. When analyzing a sentence that contains one of these intervening phrases, first isolate the phrase from the rest of the sentence; then identify the verb and the subject. The true subject of the sentence should agree with the verb.

Prepositional Phrase	**Gardening** *for the early settlers* **was** a difficult task.
	Gardening **tasks** *in certain areas of modern America* **present** problems.
Appositive Phrase	The settlers' **allies** in the gardening process, *the Native American Indians,* **were** willing to help with the work.
	Today, American **farmers**, *men with modern machinery for expansive acreage,* still **have** difficult tasks.
Negative Phrase	American **settlers**, *not the Indian population,* **were** discouraged during the winter.
	Hard **work**, *not just modern machines,* **produces** a successful crop.

ESL Gerunds and infinitives are always treated as singular.

Gerund	**Gardening was** difficult.
	Growing vegetables **was** an important task.
Infinitive	**To grow** vegetables **is** rewarding.

Predicate Nouns of a Different Number

S-LV-PN p. 75

A subject and its predicate noun are usually both singular or both plural. In some sentences, however, the predicate noun will differ in number from the subject. When choosing the correct verb for a sentence, remember that the verb agrees with the subject, the word that precedes the verb, and not with the predicate noun.

The settlers' *gardens* (S) *were* (LV) an area (PN) divided into specific parts.

One *part* (S) of the gardens *was* (LV) medicinal plants (PN).

Inverted Order

Inverted Order p. 71

In most sentences the subject precedes the verb. Occasionally, however, the order of the sentence is **inverted,** placing the subject after the verb. As with any sentence analysis, be sure to identify the verb first and then the true subject of the sentence: The verb must agree with the true subject.

Interrogative Sentences p. 69

Many sentences can show inverted order, but certain sentences indicate that inversion has taken place. In many interrogative sentences, the subject will follow the verb or come between the first auxiliary and the main verb. Another type of inverted sentence begins with *here* or the expletive *there.*

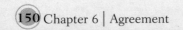

Teaching Strategy

Demonstration

Use the second sample sentence about gardening from page 150 to demonstrate how placing the intervening phrases in parentheses reveals the subject: *Gardening tasks (in certain areas) (of modern America) present problems.*

Evaluation

After teaching the section on intervening phrases, display the following sentences:

- The healthiest kind of vegetables _ found in the fresh produce section. *(is)*
- Canned food, as well as frozen food, _ not as rich in vitamins and minerals. *(is)*
- A farmers' market, in addition to a roadside stand, _ where one finds inexpensive yet quality produce. *(is)*

Ask volunteers to provide a correct verb for each sentence and to explain their answers.

Reinforcement

Remind students that in sentences with predicate nouns, the word preceding the verb is the subject of the sentence. Write these sentences for display: *That charitable organization's backbone is its loyal volunteers. Loyal volunteers are the backbone of that charitable organization.* Show the students how the subject's position in S-LV-PN sentences dictates the number of the verb.

SINGULAR

LV S PN
Was a *garden* a necessity for early settlers?

be
To help maintain the household there *was* a
S Advl
wide *range* of plants **(**in the garden.**)**

Advl be S
Where *is* the *plan* for the flower garden?

PLURAL

Inv
In the garden *grew* many beautiful
S
flowers.

S Inv
When *do* the *flowers* usually *bloom?*

Advl be S
Here *are* several dead *plants* without flowers.

be S Advl
Were there too many *pests* **(**in the garden that year?**)**

in SUMMARY

Subjects and verbs must **agree** in number and in person.

When determining agreement between a subject and a verb, ignore any **intervening phrases.**

In a sentence with a **predicate noun,** the verb agrees with the subject, not the predicate noun.

In some sentences the order of the subject and verb is **inverted.** Identify the true subject and make the verb agree with it.

6.1 PRACTICE *the skill*

Underline the simple subject(s) in each sentence. Then underline the correct verb from the choices in parentheses.

1. John Dryden, one of the seventeenth century's greatest playwrights and authors, *(is, are)* still read today.
2. Dryden's many contributions to literature *(is, are)* one reason for his popularity.
3. According to some critics, Dryden, not his contemporaries, *(deserves, deserve)* the highest accolades.
4. In the Dryden canon *(exists, exist)* multiple plays, poems, satires, and essays.
5. An adaptation of Shakespeare's *Antony and Cleopatra* *(is, are)* among his plays.

John Dryden (1631–1700) was an accomplished dramatist, literary critic, satirist, and poet. He wielded such literary influence in his day that the critics later dubbed his era "the Age of Dryden."

TEACHING STRATEGY
Participation

While teaching subject identification in inverted-order sentences, encourage the students to change the order of the inverted sentences into a more standard form. Ask students to talk through their analyses while you write their sentences for display.

REINFORCEMENT

Ask students to list common indicators of inverted order sentences. *(interrogative sentences, sentences beginning with the expletives* here *and* there*)* Instruct the students to write sentences that illustrate each type of inverted order. Then ask volunteers to share their sentences.

TEACHING STRATEGY
Analysis

Instruct students to find the subject of the following sentence and to supply a correct verb: *Selected from the large fish aquarium — a tetra and a guppy. (were)* Warn students that agreement errors often occur when inverted-order sentences contain a plural subject.

6. Certain common practices in the Restoration era, such as introducing a drastic innovation into an old play, *(outrages, outrage)* some modern readers.

7. Dramatic criticism, one of many areas of literature, *(owes, owe)* much to John Dryden.
8. Analyzing plays and drama through inductive methods *(was, were)* among his contributions to dramatic criticism.
9. In the modern era, opinions on seventeenth-century writing *(has, have)* varied.
10. Even so, his plays and literary criticism *(receives, receive)* acclaim today.

6.2 REVIEW *the skill*

Write the letter of the sentence that shows correct subject-verb agreement.

A 1. A. One famous medieval collection, the York Corpus Christi Cycle of plays, dates from before 1394.
B. One famous medieval collection, the York Corpus Christi Cycle of plays, date from before 1394.

B 2. A. Researchers, not even the best scholar, does not know exactly when the Cycle began.
B. Researchers, not even the best scholar, do not know exactly when the Cycle began.

A 3. A. The sources of the Corpus Christi Cycle are not an area of uncertainty: most details come from the Bible or from tradition.
B. The sources of the Corpus Christi Cycle is not an area of uncertainty: most details come from the Bible or from tradition.

B 4. A. Another realm of dispute are the causes for the season of the Cycle's performance.
B. Another realm of dispute is the causes for the season of the Cycle's performance.

A 5. A. Performance of such plays was reserved for the Easter season.
B. Performance of such plays were reserved for the Easter season.

B 6. A. Why is the plays performed in England on Corpus Christi, which is in late May, rather than at Easter?
B. Why are the plays performed in England on Corpus Christi, which is in late May, rather than at Easter?

B 7. A. The plays of Corpus Christi portrays scenes from the entire Bible.
B. The plays of Corpus Christi portray scenes from the entire Bible.

Teaching Strategy
Discussion

Examine the chart on page 153 with the students. Call on various students to compose sentences using these nouns as subjects with corresponding verbs.

Teaching Strategy
Motivation and Induction

Materials
- a large international map

Display the large international map and ask students to locate plural names of countries and cities. *(the United States, the Azores, the Dardanelles, Coral Gables, Wichita Falls, etc.)* Then ask students to compose sentences using the plural names they have found. Prompt the students to state a grammar rule regarding subject-verb agreement with plural names. *(Plural names of places should be treated as singular entities and linked with singular verbs.)*

Teaching Strategy
Discussion and Participation

Materials
- dictionaries

Emphasize that students may need to consult a dictionary to determine whether some words' meanings necessitate singular

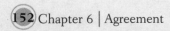

152 Chapter 6 | Agreement

A 8. A. Wagons, one for each play, serve as stages and roll from one town to another for performances.

B. Wagons, one for each play, serves as stages and rolls from one town to another for performances.

B 9. A. There is still performances of these plays in York, England.

B. There are still performances of these plays in York, England.

A 10. A. Of all the Cycle's plays, there remain only forty-eight today.

B. Of all the Cycle's plays, there remains only forty-eight today.

Problem Nouns and Pronouns

Subject-verb agreement is usually easy once you have identified the true subject of the sentence. Some subjects, however, require especially careful analysis.

Nouns of Plural Form

Some nouns have only one form—plural. These nouns may be used just one way; some of them are always singular and others are always plural.

Always Singular	*Molasses* **is** a tasty topping for pancakes.
Always Plural	The *proceeds* from the bake sale **go** toward the school project.

Some of the nouns that are plural in form can be used with *pair of* to indicate how many items are meant. In these sentences the subject is *pair.*

A *pair* of glasses **was found** under the bench in the park.

Two *pairs* of pants **are** necessary for the weekend trip.

The following chart lists some plural-form nouns and categorizes them by their correct usage—as singular or plural. For other words, check the dictionary.

Singular	Plural
billiards	clothes
checkers	(eye)glasses, goggles, contacts [lenses]
measles	pants, slacks (etc.)
molasses	pliers
news	proceeds
Niagara Falls	riches
the United States	shears, scissors
	soapsuds, suds
	thanks
	tights
	tweezers

The names of many teams and organizations exist in the plural form as well. These names require a plural verb.

The *Atlanta Braves* **play** their home games at Turner Field.

The *Rough Riders* **were** led by Theodore Roosevelt.

or plural verbs. Then display the following words: *acoustics, aesthetics, athletics, ethics, mathematics, physics, politics,* and *statistics.* Instruct the students to use these words as both singular and plural nouns, consulting a dictionary if necessary. Consider dividing the class into groups to complete this activity.

Teaching Strategy

Evaluation

Display the following sentences and ask students to identify the correct verb. Based upon their responses, either review nouns of plural form or proceed with the lesson.

- Electronics *(is, are)* what my brother is studying at college. *(is)*
- The politics of the land of Ireland *(is, are)* confusing to many. *(are)*
- The physics of bridge construction *(is, are)* beyond me. *(are)*
- Athletics *(has, have)* never come easily for Oren. *(have)*
- *(Is, Are)* your ethics in accordance with the Bible? *(are)*
- *(Was, Were)* statistics an easy course for you? *(was)*

Agreement | Chapter 6 153

Words ending in *-ics* may be singular or plural, depending on the meaning of the sentence. When the word indicates a field of study, use a singular verb. When the word refers to a characteristic, an activity, or a product, use a plural verb. A dictionary may help you distinguish the singular and plural meanings of words like these.

Singular	*Statistics* **is** a difficult course in his college major.
Plural	The new campaign *statistics* **were** overwhelmingly in his favor.

Collective Nouns

Collective Nouns p. 37

A **collective noun** refers to a group as a unit rather than to the individual people or things in the group. A singular collective noun often requires a singular verb, and a plural collective noun always requires a plural verb. A singular collective noun may require a plural verb if the meaning of the sentence emphasizes the individuals in the group rather than the group as a unit.

Singular Use	The landscape *committee* **is leaving** the assembly room.
	The soccer *team* **has won** all of its games this season.
Plural Use	The landscape *committee* **are arguing** about the decision to plant trees.
	The soccer *team* **have taken** their positions on the playing field.

In the singular sentences, the group is functioning as a unit. In the plural sentences, the members of the group are acting individually.

ESL Americans often reword a sentence to avoid using a collective noun such as *team* with a plural verb.

The political party ***members* vote** for their own candidate.

The British, on the other hand, treat many more words as collective nouns (including singular-sounding names of teams and corporations), and they freely treat these nouns as plural.

The ***political party* are nominating** the candidates that they think can win.

Americans would use *is* in this sentence.

The ***political party* is nominating** the candidates that it thinks can win.

ESL Some nouns always take plural verbs:

1. Some collective nouns derived from adjectives that refer to groups of people
   The ***elderly* are** sometimes neglected by their families.
2. The noun *people* (to indicate singular, use *person*)
   ***People* want** to be remembered, and an elderly ***person* is** no exception.
3. The noun *police* (to indicate one member of the police force, use *police officer*)
   Inner-city ***police* experience** many dangers.
   An inner-city ***police officer* is** constantly alert.

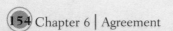

Teaching Strategy

Modeling

Display the following sets of sentences:

- The jury *(is, are)* arguing about the defendant's fine. *(are)*
- After deliberating, the jury *(issues, issue)* a decision. *(issues)*
- The couple *(sings, sing)* solos at the church. *(sing)*
- The couple *(sings, sing)* a beautiful duet. *(sings)*

Talk through how you would select the verb for each sentence. Explain the differences in meaning as each sentence shows either a group acting as a unit or individuals acting independently.

Titles, Quotations, and Amounts as Singular

The **title** of an individual work of art, music, or literature is always singular, even though words in the title may be plural.

BJU Living Gallery presentation of *The Three Crosses* by Rembrandt, The Metropolitan Museum of Art, New York. Photo by Unusual Films.

S LV PN
The Three Crosses is a Baroque-style etching.

S TrV DO
"Trust and Obey" reflects God's promises to us.

S LV PN
Anne of Green Gables is a favorite of many readers.

A **quoted word or phrase** is a single item and needs a singular verb.

S LV PN
Yours is what you meant to write, not *your's*.

S InV
"You can't teach an old dog new tricks" does not apply to my grandfather.

Amounts are considered singular and need a singular verb even when the items that make up the amounts are plural. The principle applies to measured amounts, amounts of money, and periods of time.

S LV PA
Two cups of coffee is sufficient for the morning.

S LV PN
Ten dollars was a reasonable price for the book.

S TrV DO
Three weeks provides plenty of time for rest and relaxation.

in SUMMARY

Certain nouns have only one form, which appears to be plural. Some of these nouns are always used with singular verbs, and some of these nouns are always used with plural verbs.

A **collective noun** refers to a group. Usually, a singular collective noun needs a singular verb. A sentence that emphasizes the individual members of the group, however, needs a plural verb.

Titles, **quoted words or phrases**, and **amounts** are considered singular and need singular verbs.

Teaching Strategy

Induction

Display the following sentences and instruct the students to supply a correct verb for each.

- Two quarters __ a low price for almost anything these days. *(is)*
- Two quarters __ on the floor where Kyle dropped them. *(are, lay, sit)*
- Why __ three bags of apples sitting on the kitchen counter? *(are)*
- Three bags of apples __ more fruit than we need for the pies. *(is, provides)*

Ask the students to explain their verb choices. Lead the students to understand that a measured amount takes a singular verb but counted items take a plural verb. Consider comparing this difference to the difference between a noncount noun *(Some milk is sold by the gallon)* and a plural count noun *(Two gallons of milk are in the refrigerator)*.

6.3 PRACTICE *the skill*

Underline the simple subject(s) of each verb in parentheses. Then underline the correct verb from the choices in parentheses. You may use a dictionary.

1. "All the world's a stage" (*was, were*) the motto of the Globe Theatre, where Shakespeare acted and wrote.
2. The Lord Chamberlain's Men, Shakespeare's company, (*was, were*) occupants of a different playhouse, The Theatre, but by 1598 the lease had lapsed.
3. The troupe (*was, were*) not the owner of the land occupied by The Theatre, and the property owner did not renew the lease.
4. The tactics adopted by the troupe (*was, were*) to dismantle the theater and move it overnight to new property.
5. The news (*was, were*) a shock to the owner, but he could not stop the actors.
6. The poor (*was, were*) delighted by the cheaper admission costs in the yard, which offered standing room for "groundlings."
7. Two hundred pounds (*is, are*) the estimated annual income Shakespeare made from his share in the Globe.
8. *The Merry Wives of Windsor* (*was, were*) performed in the new theater.
9. Acoustics (*was, were*) not a science in Elizabethan times.
10. In fact, the acoustics of the Globe Theatre (*was, were*) likely quite poor.

6.4 REVIEW *the skill*

Rewrite each sentence to correct any errors in subject-verb agreement. If the sentence is already correct, write *C*.

1. *The Romancers* were written by Edmond Rostand.

   ***The Romancers* was written by Edmond Rostand.**

2. Riches are not an issue in the play; rather the conflict concerns love.

   C

3. A pair of young lovers are the focal point of the play.

   A pair of young lovers is the focal point of the play.

ScienceLink

Ask students to investigate the acoustics of the Globe Theatre. Encourage students to make a model Globe Theatre and to present their findings.

4. Many years are the length of the feud between the fathers of Sylvette and Percinet.

Many years is the length of the feud between the fathers of Sylvette and Percinet.

5. Actually, the ethics of the fathers is dubious, because the feud is a pretense to make their children fall in love.

Actually, the ethics of the fathers are dubious, because the feud is a pretense to make their children fall in love.

6. A band of robbers is hired to pretend to kidnap Sylvette.

C

7. Ninety pistoles are the sum the fathers promise to pay the robbers.

Ninety pistoles is the sum the fathers promise to pay the robbers.

8. Percinet's ineffectual athletics seems to frighten the phony brigands.

Percinet's ineffectual athletics seem to frighten the phony brigands.

9. The band hide themselves while the fathers declare that the children can marry.

C

10. "Hatreds always end in marriages" are the statement of Percinet's father.

"Hatreds always end in marriages" is the statement of Percinet's father.

Indefinite Pronouns

Most **indefinite pronouns** do not usually cause problems. Singular indefinite pronouns need singular verbs, and plural indefinite pronouns need plural verbs.

Indefinite Pronouns pp. 38–39

ALWAYS SINGULAR	*Everyone* **is** going to the soccer game.
	No one **wants** to be late.
ALWAYS PLURAL	*Several* **are** injured and cannot play for this game.
	Many **have planned** to stay for the reception afterwards.

TEACHING STRATEGY

Motivation

Materials

- a photograph of several people performing some kind of action or actions

Display a photograph of several people performing some kind of action (e.g., several teens playing soccer). Ask students to look at the picture and to write a brief explanation of the action in the picture, using indefinite pronouns. Remind them to consider singular and plural meanings in their sentences. (Examples: Someone is about to attempt a goal. Nobody is guarding the player running for the ball. Several of the players look confused.)

Always Singular				
another	each	everything	neither	one
anybody	either	less	nobody	somebody
anyone	everybody	little	no one	someone
anything	everyone	much	nothing	something

Always Plural				
both	few	fewer	many	several

Some indefinite pronouns, however, can be either singular or plural. These indefinite pronouns may be understood as singular or plural, depending on what modifies them. These words have a singular meaning when they are modified by an *of* phrase that has a singular object. These same words have a plural meaning when they are modified by an *of* phrase that has a plural object. In some sentences the *of* phrase can be understood.

Singular | Some of my homework is not completed for tomorrow.
I could not find my assignments, so some is not here.

Plural | Some of the assignments were finished on time
I wanted to finish all my assignments, but some were too difficult.

The word *none* follows this rule with one exception. Although *none* is singular when followed by an *of* phrase with a singular object, *none* may be singular or plural when followed by an *of* phrase with a plural object.

None of the turkey dinner *is* left for tomorrow.

None of these recipes *is* a secret.

None of the desserts *are* left from the meal.

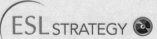

In very formal writing, *none* may be singular even in the third example sentence.

Singular or Plural		
all	more	none
any	most	some

Measure Words

Measure words, such as *half, part,* and *percent,* follow the same guidelines as indefinite pronouns. These words take a singular verb when they are modified by an *of* phrase that has a singular object, but they take a plural verb when they are modified by an *of* phrase that has a plural object.

Singular | Half of the team is in the locker room right now.

Plural | Half of the required hours for graduation are taken in the first two years.

The word *number* follows special rules of agreement. *The number of* (like *the number*) is always singular, but *a number of* (meaning "several") is always plural.

Teaching Strategy

Induction and Analysis

Instruct students to study the first chart on page 158, noting the pronouns in each category. Then ask them to develop a general rule that will help them remember much of the information on this list. (*Pronouns ending in* one, body, *or* thing *are always singular.*)

Reinforcement

Encourage students who have trouble with indefinite pronouns to keep a reference list of the indefinite pronouns that can be either singular or plural.

ESL Strategy

Use ESL Helps 6A and 6B (Teacher's Toolkit) for information about and practice with using *some* correctly.

Teaching Strategy

Induction

Display these sentences and ask the students to supply a correct verb for each and to explain their choices.

- None of the empty boxes __ thrown away. (*was/were*)
- Of the entrées on the menu, only some __ a baked potato. (*include; some refers to plural* entrées)

Singular	Because all five of us in our family can now drive, ***the number** of cars* in our driveway *has increased* to five.
Plural	***A number** of neighbors say* teasingly that my family can start its own used-car business.

Relative Pronouns

A **relative pronoun** *(who, whom, whose, which,* or *that)* does not change form to indicate singular and plural, but we treat a relative pronoun as though it has the same number as its antecedent.

Relative Pronouns p. 39

S InV
He is the player who plays in the goal box.

S InV
The members of the team who have played all year are eligible for the trip.

Before you decide on a singular or a plural verb, consider the meaning of the dependent clause to help you determine the antecedent of the relative pronoun.

Antecedents of Pronouns p. 37

S TrV-P
Here is the roster of players that has been submitted to the school newspaper.

S TrV DO
The list of players who have completed their schoolwork is posted on the bulletin board.

Certain constructions need special attention. A sentence that contains "the only one of the" or "one of the" before a noun and relative pronoun is sometimes a problem. In most cases, use a singular verb after a relative pronoun that follows "the only one of the" and use a plural verb after a relative pronoun that follows "one of the."

S TrV DO
James is the only one of the players who has a perfect score in class.

In this sentence the antecedent of *who* is *one.* Although there were many players in class, James was the only one to achieve a perfect score; the other players did not.

S InV
Charles is one of the players who are practicing diligently for the game.

In this sentence the antecedent of *who* is *players*; a plural verb is necessary. Many players practiced for the game; Charles was a part of that group.

in SUMMARY

Some **indefinite pronouns** used as subjects are always singular; some are always plural; and some can be either singular or plural.

Certain words may be determined as singular or plural depending on what modifies those words. To determine whether to use a singular or a plural verb, consider the object of the following *of* prepositional phrase.

Measure words—*half, part, percent*—take singular or plural verbs according to the same guidelines as indefinite pronouns.

A **relative pronoun** that is the subject of a dependent clause is treated as having the same number as its antecedent.

- Most of the dessert __ whipped cream. *(is;* most *refers to singular* dessert*)*
- Because attendance at the theme park was down, the number of consecutive times that we rode the new roller coaster __ twelve. *(was;* the number *indicates a singular measurement)*
- A number of people __ the roller coaster at the same time. *(ride;* a number *indicates a total of counted people)*

Lead the students to understand that measure words and indefinite pronouns that can be either singular or plural follow the same agreement principle: when the word refers to an amount, use a singular verb; when the word refers to counted items, use a plural verb. Point out that an *of* phrase following an indefinite pronoun can sometimes be a clue to the meaning of the pronoun.

Teaching Strategy

Discussion and Participation

Lead the students in a brief review of the information on page 159 about relative pronouns, antecedents, and adjective clauses. Display a sentence with an adjective clause. Instruct the students to identify the relative pronoun, antecedent, and adjective clause.

6.5 PRACTICE *the skill*

Underline the subject(s) of each verb in parentheses. Then underline the correct verb from the choices in parentheses.

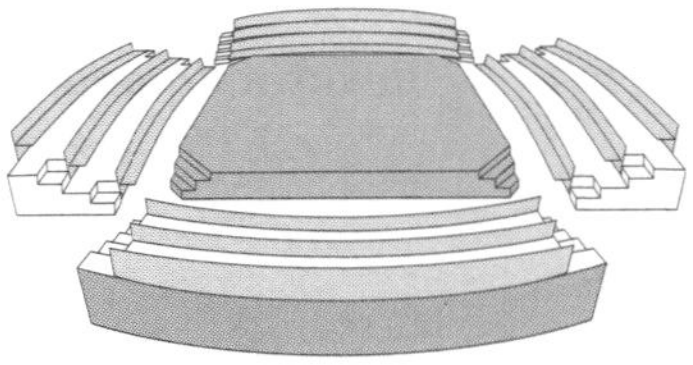

1. There are three types of stages that (*is, are*) in common use.
2. Some (*prefers, prefer*) to use an arena stage for added immediacy.
3. On an arena stage, one hundred percent of the acting area (*is, are*) surrounded by the audience.
4. Many (*chooses, choose*) the thrust stage, which (*extends, extend*) out into the seating area like a peninsula.

5. Theaters come in a variety of configurations, but most (*has, have*) a traditional proscenium stage.
6. Some people think half of the effect (*is, are*) lost if the wrong type of stage is used.

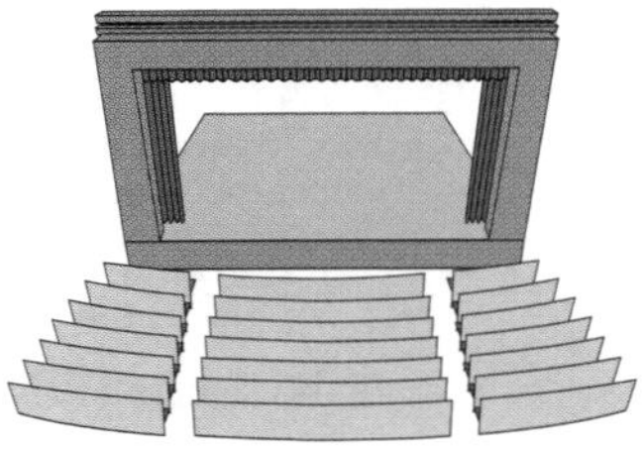

7. The arena stage is the only one of these stage types that (*has, have*) no regular wings.
8. None of these three types (*is, are*) lacking a lip, or edge.
9. The new Globe Theatre, which (*was, were*) opened in 1997, has a thrust stage.
10. Everyone (*forms, form*) his own opinion of his favorite type of stage.

6.6 REVIEW *the skill*

Underline each incorrect verb. Then write the correct verb in the blank. If the sentence is already correct, write *C*.

is 1. One of the forms of drama are the Italian *commedia dell'arte*.

are 2. Some of the major characters is Harlequin, Columbine, and Pierrot.

wears 3. Harlequin, who wear a costume decorated with black-and-white or colored diamond shapes, is sometimes a clown and sometimes the protagonist.

C 4. No one among the actors memorizes the script in advance; the show is improvised around a basic plot.

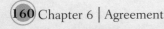

Teaching Strategy

Discussion

Display these sentences: *Nelson is the only one of the runners who* (has, have) *won a marathon. Nelson is one of the runners who* (has, have) *won races.* Ask students to identify the correct verbs and to explain their choices.

Enrichment

Materials

- pictures of the three types of stages: arena, thrust, and proscenium

Display pictures of the three types of stages and discuss each. Encourage students to classify and discuss the type of stage at the school or a local performance hall. Consider taking a field trip to a local theater for a guided tour of the stage.

Enrichment

Ask students to share their experiences in seeing or participating in a dramatic production. Then ask them to identify the type of stage that was used.

History Link

Explain the origin and development of the *commedia dell'arte* movement. Then ask students to find descriptions of the chief characters in *commedia dell'arte:* Harlequin, Pantaloon, Pulcinella, Scaramouch,

C 5. Part of the drama usually involves the tricking of Pantaloon, a bumbling and foolish character.

plague 6. Harlequin is one of the clowns, or *zanni*, who plagues Pantaloon.

C 7. The English word *zany*, which means "clownish or bizarre," comes from the Italian word *zanni*.

is 8. Everyone in *commedia dell'arte* are a stock character, a character with little individuality.

varies 9. The number of characters in a given performance vary.

have 10. Half of Americans has probably never seen an example of *commedia dell'arte*.

Compound Subjects

Determining the correct verb for a compound subject depends upon the conjunction used to join the parts of the subject.

Compound Subjects p. 71

Compound Subjects Joined with And

Compound subjects joined by *and* or *both—and* are usually plural. The sentence requires a plural verb.

Conjunctions pp. 54–55

PLURAL | Overseeding **and** adequate fertilization were necessary for success.

PLURAL | **Both** utilitarian plants **and** flowers decorate our gardens today.

However, two words joined by *and* may refer to the same person or thing or to a single idea. In that case, the subject is considered a singular unit, and the verb is singular to agree with it.

SINGULAR | Today apple pie **and** ice cream is an American tradition.

PLURAL | **Both** apple pie **and** ice cream taste best when homemade.

In the first sentence, the subject looks plural, but the verb is singular. The subject parts refer to one combined thing, a dessert, and so a singular verb is needed. In the second sentence, the subjects refer to two different things, pie and ice cream; therefore, the verb is plural. Usually, though, *and* joins separate things and requires a plural verb.

Compound Subjects Joined with Or

For compound subjects joined with *or* (also *either—or, neither—nor*), the subject nearer to the verb (or to the first auxiliary in a complete verb) determines the form of the verb. Remember that *or* indicates a choice.

Shifts in Person p. 216

Mr. Quinn or *Mr. and Mrs. Adams are* proctoring the test.

Are you or your brother ready for the history test?

Neither James nor his *friends are staying* after school to study.

Is James or his *friends* coming to study tonight?

and Colombine. Direct students to report on their findings and to enhance their presentations with pictures of each character.

Teaching Strategy

Modeling

Before teaching the lesson, instruct the students to write sentences with compound subjects. Ask volunteers to read their sentences aloud or to display them for the class. Evaluate their verb choices and discuss their reasons for using a singular or plural verb. Then review the information about compound subjects on pages 161–62.

Teaching Strategy

Participation

Ask students to suggest other examples of apparent compounds that take a singular verb in certain contexts. *(macaroni and cheese, pride and joy, shirt and tie, founder and president, friend and confidant)*

Teaching Strategy

Discussion

Advise students who have difficulty with subjects joined by *or* and *nor* to consider only the last subject when choosing the correct verb.

Reinforcement

Students often are unaware of subject-verb agreement in their writing. Challenge students to check their own writing for correct subject-verb agreement.

in SUMMARY

Compound subjects joined by *and* or *both—and* are usually plural.

If a compound subject joined by *and* refers to the same idea, person, or entity, the verb should be singular.

For compound subjects joined by *or, either—or,* or *neither—nor,* the verb agrees in number with the subject nearer to the verb or the first auxiliary.

6.7 PRACTICE *the skill*

Underline each incorrect verb. Then write the correct verb in the blank. If the sentence is already correct, write *C*.

have 1. Plays and poems about lovers has often been written.

C 2. In one medieval ballad, a king and a maid fall in love.

end 3. Both *Romeo and Juliet* and *Antony and Cleopatra* ends with the death of the lovers.

threaten 4. Either Tybalt or the Capulets threatens Romeo's life.

commits 5. The Capulets' pride and joy commit suicide at the end.

C 6. Neither Mercutio nor the Capulets were willing to stop the fighting.

have 7. Both the young lovers and the rogue, Autolycus, has double identities in *The Winter's Tale.*

is 8. Are Goethe's Faust or Gretchen aware of the evil of Mephistopheles?

know 9. In "The Eve of St. Agnes," neither the beadsman nor the revelers knows of the lovers' escape.

C 10. Either young lovers or romance in general is a very popular topic for poems and plays.

DramaLink

Consider allowing your students to perform a scene from *Romeo and Juliet* or *Cyrano de Bergerac*. You could divide the class into groups and assign a different scene to each group or allow students to select and perform their favorite scenes.

ONE on ONE

Encourage your student to enlist family members and friends as actors to perform a scene from *Romeo and Juliet* or *Cyrano de Bergerac*.

6.8 REVIEW *the skill*

Correct the ten errors in subject-verb agreement by crossing out each incorrect verb and writing a correct verb above it.

One of the developments of Renaissance drama was the comedy of humours. The main instigator and user of this genre ~~were~~ was Ben Jonson, a contemporary of Shakespeare, who also used elements of it. The basis of the comedy of humours ~~come~~ comes from the Greek idea of four humours, or liquids, corresponding to four personality types. An imbalance of humours ~~cause~~ causes personality differences. Both blood (sanguine) and yellow bile (choleric) ~~is~~ are humours. Either too much blood or too much yellow bile ~~produce~~ produces excess warmth of personality. Falstaff and Autolycus ~~is~~ are examples of the sanguine humour, and Hotspur and Tybalt ~~typifies~~ typify the choleric humour. Another humour is black bile (melancholic). Either Hamlet or Richard II ~~are~~ is a good example of melancholy. The last of the four humours is phlegm (phlegmatic). In *A Midsummer Night's Dream*, neither the lovers nor Titania ~~are~~ is phlegmatic, but both Flute and Starveling ~~is~~ are. As the comedy of humours developed, its characters became dramatic stereotypes, instantly recognizable for their qualities.

Pronoun-Antecedent Agreement

Another important area of correct usage is that of pronoun-antecedent agreement. Just as a subject and a verb must agree, so must a pronoun agree with its antecedent, the word or phrase to which the pronoun refers.

Personal Pronouns pp. 37–38

Nouns as Antecedents

A noun or a noun phrase is the usual antecedent of a pronoun. If the antecedent is singular, the pronoun must be singular; if the antecedent is plural, the pronoun must be plural.

Antecedents of Pronouns p. 37

SINGULAR	The *storm* has destroyed many houses in *its* path.
PLURAL	As a result of the rain, the *rivers* have overrun *their* banks.

Pronouns can also show gender as well as number. The pronoun, therefore, must also agree in gender with its antecedent—masculine, feminine, or neuter.

Shifts in Number p. 216

MASCULINE	*Robert* rescued *his* outdoor animals from the coming storm.
FEMININE	*Dr. Rachel Roth,* the meteorologist, made *her* prediction for the storm's path.
NEUTER	The *storm* made *its* way up the coast in only a few hours.

TEACHING STRATEGY

Discussion

Review singular and plural indefinite pronouns with students, reminding them that most indefinite pronouns are singular. A few indefinite pronouns may be singular or plural *(some, any, more, most, all, none)*. For additional coverage of singular indefinite pronouns and singular nouns modified by indefinite determiners, see *The Writer's Toolbox.*

Agreement | Chapter 6 163

If a singular antecedent does not indicate a specific gender, use a singular masculine pronoun. Do not use a plural personal pronoun if the antecedent is singular.

Right	The *homeowner who* lost *his* house in the storm was able to salvage a few belongings.
Wrong	The *homeowner who* lost *their* house in the storm was able to salvage a few belongings.

tip

To avoid a gender choice, try making the sentence plural.

Each student read his story aloud.
All the students read their stories aloud.

ESL

Some native speakers, in conversation, may insert a pronoun immediately after the antecedent. However, unless you are trying to achieve a colloquial effect, do not use this extra pronoun in your writing.

With the Extra Pronoun	Aiden, ~~he~~ fixed my car.
Without the Extra Pronoun	Aiden fixed my car.

It is incorrect to use both a personal pronoun *(he, her)* and a relative pronoun *(who, whom, whose, which, that)* in the same clause to refer to the same antecedent.

Incorrect	My cat is the one that ~~she~~ clawed up the carpet.
Correct	My cat is the one that clawed up the carpet.

Compound Antecedents

gurw Compound Subjects p. 71

Compound antecedents are determined to be singular or plural in the same way that compound subjects are. Use a plural pronoun when the antecedents are joined by *and* or *both—and.* When the antecedents are joined by *or, either—or,* or *neither—nor,* use a pronoun that agrees with the nearer antecedent.

gurw Conjunctions pp. 54–55

Plural	As a result of the storm's destruction, the *parents and their children* went to *their* relatives' house.
Singular	Either the twin *boys or* their older *brother* will lay out *his* sleeping bag upstairs.
Plural	*Neither Dad nor the children* could close *their* eyes while the wind blew violently.

ESL

Although *either—or* indicates a choice, *neither—nor* is different. The meaning of *neither—nor* is the same as *both—and* plus the negative idea of *not.*

Neither my good deeds ***nor*** my Christian family can get me into heaven.

This sentence means that the speaker's good deeds cannot get him into heaven *and* the speaker's Christian family cannot get him into heaven.

Or works the same way when *not* is present: It makes *not* apply to all the items named.

Salvation is **not** in what I can do **or** in what my family can do; it is in what Jesus has done for me.

In this sentence salvation does not result from what the speaker can do *and* it does not result from what the speaker's family can do.

Teaching Strategy

Participation

Instruct students to compare two or more people—musicians, athletes, or politicians. Instruct them to write sentences that include indefinite pronouns and antecedents. Display student sentences and discuss pronoun-antecedent agreement. (Examples: Each politician presented **his** platform issues clearly. Both began **their** careers in private law practice.)

Reinforcement

Point out to students that a sentence such as "Nobody has their books" displays incorrect pronoun-antecedent agreement. Although this type of error may be common in everyday English, instruct students to use pronoun-antecedent agreement correctly in both their writing and speaking.

Many grammarians have accepted the above usage in the push for gender-neutral language. Thus, many examples the students may see in modern writing stem, not from ignorance, but from political correctness. Instruct students to follow traditional grammar and caution them against adopting poor usage for the sake of being politically correct.

Correcting a sentence with a pronoun-antecedent agreement problem may create an awkward sentence. To avoid the awkwardness, reword the sentence. A plural pronoun is not acceptable for a singular antecedent.

AWKWARD	*Either Susan or Sam* will take *his* turn bailing water.
WRONG	*Either Susan or Sam* will take *their* turn bailing water.
BETTER	*Either Susan* will take *her* turn bailing water, or *Sam* will take *his.*

in SUMMARY

A pronoun must agree with its antecedent in gender and number.

If the singular antecedent does not specify gender when referring to a person, use a singular masculine pronoun.

If a **compound antecedent** is joined by *and* or *both—and,* the pronoun should be plural. If the compound antecedent is joined by *or, nor, either—or,* or *neither—nor,* the pronoun should agree with the antecedent nearer to it.

6.9 PRACTICE *the skill*

Underline the correct pronoun from the choices in parentheses.

1. Does Hamlet have difficulty making up *(his, its)* mind?
2. A reader of the play forms *(his, their)* own opinion.
3. Either Horatio or the guards could have offered Hamlet *(his, their)* advice.
4. Both Hamlet and his mother, Gertrude, mourn the death of *(his, their)* relative.
5. Reynaldo, a servant of Polonius, receives *(his, their)* instructions to spy on Laertes.
6. Neither the players nor Rosencrantz understands *(his, their)* friend's distress.
7. A player recites *(his, their)* speech about the Trojan War.
8. Both Laertes and Claudius scheme against Hamlet in *(his, their)* own ways.
9. Rosencrantz and Guildenstern go to *(his, their)* deaths unknowingly.
10. An ambassador with *(his, their)* entourage brings news of their deaths.

Literature Link

Read several famous lines from *Hamlet* to the students:

- "To be or not to be."
- "What a piece of work is a man."
- "Neither a borrower nor a lender be."
- "To thine own self be true."
- "Brevity is the soul of wit."
- "The play's the thing."

Share a plot summary of *Hamlet* and then lead a discussion about the quotations. Alternatively, ask the students to supply the plot summary and lead the discussion.

Speech Link

Consider assigning a few of the famous soliloquies from *Hamlet* for your students to memorize and perform.

6.10 REVIEW *the skill*

Write an appropriate pronoun to complete each sentence.

his 1. In *A Midsummer Night's Dream,* each character has _?_ own struggles.

them 2. Both Demetrius and Helena are in love with people who do not love _?_.

their 3. Lysander and Hermia abandon _?_ homes and flee into the woods.

her 4. Neither Oberon nor Titania has _?_ priorities straight.

his 5. A player is concerned about memorizing _?_ lines.

he 6. A second player thinks that _?_ should be the one to roar like a lion.

their 7. Either Puck or the fairies are able to use _?_ skills to befuddle the travelers.

their 8. Quince and the other players are nervous about performing _?_ play.

their 9. Both Helena and Hermia are distressed about _?_ situation.

his 10. The reader will find that all _?_ questions are answered at the end.

Collective Nouns as Antecedents

Collective nouns can be singular or plural. A collective noun that emphasizes the group as a unit needs a singular verb and any pronoun referring to it is likewise singular. If the collective noun refers to the individuals of the group, the noun needs a plural verb and any pronoun referring to it is plural. Analyze the sentence for its meaning.

Singular Use	The rescue *unit* does *its* best to rescue an endangered family pet.
	The *team* worked through the night to achieve *its* goal of rescuing the trapped dog.
Plural Use	The rescue *unit* perform *their* jobs with speed and precision.
	The *team* encouraged each other in *their* pursuit of the trapped pet.

In the singular examples, the noun functions as a unit and is referred to by a singular pronoun. The plural examples emphasize the members of the group, and so the collective nouns require plural pronouns. In a sentence with a collective noun, the verb is often a clue, as with the *unit* examples. A past tense verb does not indicate singular or plural, as in the *team* examples.

Teaching Strategy

Discussion

Review material about collective nouns on page 166. Discuss the meanings of the various collective nouns in context. Ask students to write two sentences, one with a singular collective noun antecedent and one with a plural collective noun antecedent. Ask volunteers to read their sentences.

Teaching Strategy

Participation

Ask students to listen to local news broadcasts on radio or television or to read the local newspaper. Encourage them to write down examples of incorrect pronoun-antecedent agreement to read to the class. Discuss how the sentences could be corrected.

Teaching Strategy

Motivation

Challenge students to be alert for agreement errors as they listen to peer conversations. Admonish them that well-educated students want to avoid errors of these kinds.

Reinforcement

Use Teaching Help 6A (Teacher's Toolkit) to strengthen the students' understanding of the agreement rules.

See note about collective noun use in England and America on page 154. ESL

Indefinite Pronouns as Antecedents

Indefinite pronouns can function as antecedents for other pronouns that follow. The later pronoun must agree in number with the indefinite pronoun that precedes it. A prepositional phrase may indicate the true number of the indefinite pronoun.

Indefinite Pronouns pp. 38–39

Singular	*Everybody* put *his* full effort into listening for sounds of life from the dog.
	Part of the rescue was successful when *it* revealed a dusty paw.
Plural	*Most* were eager to show *their* relief when the paw appeared.
	All of the children showed *their* excitement when the freed puppy ran toward them.

Indefinite pronouns do not show gender. The context of the sentence, however, may indicate the correct gender. When the gender is not clear, use the masculine singular pronoun.

Masculine	*Each* of the men on the team took *his* time packing away the rescue gear.
	Did *anyone* leave *his* gear behind the truck?
Feminine	*Neither* of the girls was willing to give up *her* opportunity to play with the puppy.
Neuter	*Another* of the rescue units was ready to give *its* help.

When the gender of a singular indefinite pronoun is not clear, you may also choose to use both masculine and feminine pronouns to refer to it. The sentence, however, may appear awkward. To avoid an awkward sentence, reword the sentence without the personal pronouns. Standard English does not permit a plural personal pronoun to refer to a singular indefinite pronoun.

Awkward	*Everybody* packed *his* or *her* suitcase for the long evacuation trip.
Reworded	*Everybody* packed a suitcase for the long evacuation trip.
Wrong	*Everybody* packed *their* suitcase for the long evacuation trip.

Agreement with nouns modified by indefinite determiners is similar to agreement with indefinite pronouns. A singular noun modified by an indefinite determiner is always singular.

Determiners pp. 48–49

Indefinite Pronoun	The police encouraged *everyone* to bring *his* sleeping bag.
Indefinite Determiner	The police encouraged *every evacuee* to bring *his* sleeping bag.

For a list of indefinite pronouns, see the chart on page 38.

Enrichment

Distribute a copy of Teaching Help 6B (Teacher's Toolkit) to each student. Allow the students to complete the questions and the crossword puzzle to review the agreement rules.

Evaluation

Advise students to read their portfolio or journal entries and to identify any pronoun-antecedent agreement errors.

Teaching Strategy

Motivation

Remind students that errors of pronoun-antecedent agreement are easily overlooked in writing because the errors are heard so often in everyday speech. Encourage the students to pay close attention to proofreading.

in SUMMARY

Collective nouns may be singular or plural. When the group is regarded as a unit, it is singular and needs a singular verb. Any pronoun referring to it must be singular. When the collective noun emphasizes the individuals of the group, it is plural and needs a plural verb. Any pronoun referring to it must be plural.

A pronoun should **agree in number and gender** with an indefinite pronoun that acts as its antecedent.

A **singular indefinite pronoun** does not show gender. Do not refer to a singular indefinite pronoun with a plural personal pronoun. Choose one of these options instead: use a singular masculine pronoun; use both a singular masculine pronoun and a singular feminine pronoun; or reword the sentence to make it plural or to avoid personal pronouns.

A singular noun modified by an **indefinite determiner** is always singular.

6.11 PRACTICE *the skill*

Write the letter of the sentence that shows correct pronoun-antecedent agreement.

__A__ 1. A. All of the plays require appropriate settings to present them well.
B. All of the plays require appropriate settings to present it well.

__B__ 2. A. The team of designers does their best.
B. The team of designers does its best.

__B__ 3. A. The designers divide the work; each tackles their own part.
B. The designers divide the work; each tackles his part.

__B__ 4. A. Everyone must be able to perform their task.
B. Everyone must be able to perform his or her task.

__A__ 5. A. Someone will perform his task of planning the set.
B Someone will perform their task of planning the set.

__B__ 6. A. No one, including the lighting designer and the costume designer, can shirk their responsibilities.
B. No one, including the lighting designer and the costume designer, can shirk his responsibilities.

__A__ 7. A. One arc light is causing a designer some trouble as he tries to fix it.
B. One arc light is causing a designer some trouble as they try to fix it.

__B__ 8. A. Another arc light is doing their job magnificently.
B. Another arc light is doing its job magnificently.

__A__ 9. A. Most of the pieces are finally in their places.
B. Most of the pieces are finally in its place.

__B__ 10. A. The group congratulates itself on its effort.
B. The group congratulate themselves on their efforts.

168 Chapter 6 | Agreement

6.12 REVIEW *the skill*

Underline each incorrect pronoun. Then write the correct pronoun in the blank. If the sentence is already correct, write *C* in the blank.

its 1. In the 1590s the company of the Lord Chamberlain was famous for their actors, as was the company known as the Admiral's Men.

its 2. Each troupe had their own star: Richard Burbage for the Lord Chamberlain's Men and Edward Alleyn for the Admiral's Men.

his 3. Was either of these actors greater than their rival?

his 4. Anyone could enrich their day by watching Alleyn in *Dr. Faustus* or *Tamburlaine*.

C 5. Most said their favorite of Burbage's roles was Richard III.

his 6. Neither of the men focused their career on comic roles.

their 7. Burbage's troupe worked in its various roles to bring success to the Globe Theatre.

C 8. During their lifetimes, few have seen the portraits that the talented Burbage painted.

C 9. Every student of theater can see that Alleyn was esteemed as a great actor if he reads Ben Jonson's tribute to him.

their 10. All in Dulwich were happy when Alleyn retired to its town and built a college and a hospital.

Richard Burbage

Edward Alleyn

LiteratureLink

Ask student volunteers to share brief biographical sketches of Richard Burbage and Edward Alleyn and to share plot summaries of several of the plays in which these actors performed leading roles.

The residents of Oberammergau, Germany, performed their first community-wide Passion play in 1634. These people, having learned that thousands were perishing in Munich from the bubonic plague, promised to produce a play on the Lord's Passion every ten years if God would spare them. The bubonic plague did not enter the city. The tradition continues to this day, with many residents participating in a performance of the Passion play at the start of each decade.

6.13 CUMULATIVE *review*

Rewrite the following paragraph, correcting the ten errors from these categories: fragments, comma splices, fused sentences, subject-verb agreement, and pronoun-antecedent agreement. *(Answers may vary.)*

The Passion play of Oberammergau, Germany, is renowned worldwide. The Passion play depicts scenes from the Bible it focuses on the life of Christ. The play, which is performed every ten years, was first performed in 1634. Nearly half of Oberammergau's five thousand inhabitants takes part, everyone participates eagerly in their hometown's tradition. During the Crucifixion scene there is four hundred actors on stage. However, in the past many have expressed concerns. That the plays are anti-Semitic. Now the director of the plays is attempting to alleviate such concerns by their updated script. Several major changes include the following: Jewish characters are now simply citizens instead of moneygrubbers. Both Hebrew and Greek names are used to show the various layers of Jewish society. Certain negative characters are altered to portray Jews more positively, and some disappears entirely. The crowd before Pilate divides into two parts, those for Jesus and those against Jesus, while Jesus Himself is called "Rabbi" in order to emphasize His Jewish heritage. One of the most significant changes is the deletion of a controversial sentence: "The blood be upon us" have been removed from the text. The goal of the play's director and other reformers are to remove the anti-Jewish stigma and to balance change with tradition.

The Passion play of Oberammergau, Germany, is renowned worldwide. The Passion play depicts scenes from the Bible, focusing on the life of Christ. The play, which is performed every ten years, was first performed in 1634. Nearly half of Oberammergau's five thousand inhabitants take part. Everyone participates eagerly in his hometown's tradition. During the Crucifixion scene there are four hundred actors on stage. However, in the past many have expressed concerns that the plays are anti-Semitic. Now the director of the plays is attempting to alleviate such concerns by his updated script. Several major changes include the following: Jewish characters are now simply citizens instead of moneygrubbers. Both Hebrew and Greek names are used to show the various layers of Jewish society. Certain negative characters are altered to portray Jews more positively, and some disappear entirely. The crowd before Pilate divides into two parts, those for Jesus and those against Jesus, while Jesus Himself is called "Rabbi" in order to emphasize His Jewish heritage. One of the most significant changes is the deletion of a controversial sentence: "The blood be upon us" has been removed from the text. The goal of the play's director and other reformers is to remove the anti-Jewish stigma and to balance change with tradition.

Reinforcement

Use Chapter 6 Review on pages 439–41 for additional test review.

Evaluation

Use Chapter 6 Test to evaluate students' understanding of the content and concepts of the chapter.

Scriptural Application

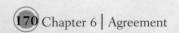

Elijah's supporting arguments would not work with any Gentile in the world in his day—and with very few nonbelievers in ours. Discuss the following questions with your students: Why should it matter that Ahab had forsaken the commandments of Yahweh and followed other gods? Why is that not just "progress"? Should Elijah have changed his strategy? Should he have argued that Ahab's leadership decisions were, for example, economically disastrous? Or that Ahab's corruption damaged

FROM THE WRITTEN WORD

Presenting an Argument

Elijah the prophet and Ahab, the king of Israel, were contemporaries with opposite perspectives and convictions. In spite of his human weaknesses, Elijah determined to serve God. On the other hand, Ahab, influenced by his ungodly heritage and his wicked wife, Jezebel, allowed pagan temples and idols in the land. More than once Elijah feared for his life as he appeared before Ahab. Despite his antagonistic audience, Elijah was able to articulate clearly before Ahab.

What about you when you are confronted by those who disagree with you? How successful are you in expressing logical ideas on the spur of the moment? Are you able to focus on an idea and reason clearly?

In 1 Kings 18 Elijah makes use of one of the most important rhetorical strategies available to a writer or speaker. Successful argumentation depends on the writer's or speaker's ability to formulate logical ideas and organize them effectively. Elijah makes a proposition and sets about to prove that proposition.

> And he answered, I have not troubled Israel; but thou, and thy father's house, in that ye have forsaken the commandments of the Lord, and thou hast followed Baalim. And Elijah came unto all the people, and said, How long halt ye between two opinions? If the Lord be God, follow him: but if Baal, then follow him. And the people answered him not a word.
> (1 Kings 18:18, 21)

Elijah declares his argument: Ahab has provided the wrong leadership for Israel. With this idea in mind, what then are Elijah's proof statements? Ahab has forsaken the law of God; Ahab has followed false gods.

One problem that often appears in argumentation is the use of universal statements. As you argue, avoid statements including *only*, *all,* or *every.* How many times have you argued that everyone was doing a certain thing or that you were the only one who could not participate in an activity? First Kings 19:14 records Elijah's complaint that "I, even I only, am left." Careful reading of 1 Kings 19:18 reveals that seven thousand who had not bowed to idols remained in Israel.

Personal Response

Read Romans 12:2. Imagine yourself in a discussion with another student about some current trend or issue of the day. Remember that an argument could be approached from either the pro or con side. Basing your argument on Romans 12:2, write a paragraph stating your position and the reasons for your position.

the trust necessary to keep a society running smoothly? Point out that though those things probably would have been true, Elijah cuts right to the ultimate issue: Ahab refused to worship the one true God and chose to worship false gods instead. This issue is still the ultimate reason today for problems in society. Though it is not wrong to point to the economic and social results of sinful public policies, such arguments often avoid the primary issue—one's heart allegiance to God. Discuss the following questions: How can a Christian challenge America's political leadership on its real problem—its failure to obey God's commandments? What would that sound like (cf. Matt. 14:3–4)?

Teaching Strategy

Participation

Instruct students to write out their arguments as directed in the "Personal Response" section. Then ask volunteers to present their arguments in class.

OBJECTIVES

Students will

1. specify purpose, identify audience, and choose a topic for an extemporaneous essay.
2. construct a clear thesis statement and position it correctly.
3. write an effective in-class response to an essay prompt.
4. place the strongest point first in the extemporaneous essay.
5. incorporate clear and effective sentences that include facts, examples, and/or illustrations to support the thesis.
6. use an appropriate tone for the essay.
7. use transitional words to move smoothly from one idea to another.
8. develop a concluding sentence and position it correctly.
9. pace writing in order to draft a complete essay within a given time frame.
10. edit for grammatical and mechanical errors.
11. publish the essay.

CHA

Chapter 7 Overview

Topic	Pages	Support Materials	Days
Extemporaneous Essay	173–77	Writing Worksheet 7 Writing Rubric 7	91–93, 96, 98
Principal Parts and Tenses	177–79	Bulletin Board 7 Chapter 7 Pretest	94
Tenses	179–83	ESL Helps 7A–7D Practice/Review/Use the Skill 7.1–7.3 Concept Reinforcement 7A	95
Consistency and Sequence of Tenses	184–87	Teaching Help 7A ESL Helps 7E–7F Practice/Use the Skill 7.4–7.5	96
Voice	187–91	Teaching Help 7B Practice/Use the Skill 7.6–7.7	97–98
Mood Review	192–96, 443–44	Practice/Use the Skill 7.8–7.9 Concept Reinforcement 7B Cumulative Review 7.10 Chapter 7 Review	99
Chapter 7 Test			100
Critical Thinking	196–97		101

EXTEMPORANEOUS ESSAY

Lesson Support

Teacher's Toolkit

Writing Worksheet 7
Writing Rubric 7

Extemporaneous Essay Writing
Verb Use Usage
7

Think for a moment about your friends. How long have you known your closest friend? How have your friendships changed from the time you were young until now? Have you ever lost contact with a friend who moved away? When asked to write an essay about friendship, one student recounted how her relationship with one of her childhood friends has changed over the years. Read her essay and compare her experience to your own.

A Record of Our Journeys *by Ilana Sibley*

As I read the latest message from my friend Nicole, I realized how much our friendship has changed—and yet endured—over the years. We met in kindergarten, where we learned to tie our shoes and write our names. From kindergarten through junior high school, Nicole and I saw each other almost every day. We shared experiences—going to classes, playing softball. We shared discoveries—a new poem, a truth about God. And we shared heartaches—a broken arm, an argument with a classmate.

One summer we spent a month together in Mexico on a youth mission team. Those four weeks of praying, failing, learning, and rejoicing brought us even closer. When the trip was over, we returned—but Nicole went to her new home in another state. At first I missed Mexico and I missed Nicole. Then her first message arrived. She described her new house, her new school, her new church. Although she was sad about leaving her hometown, she enjoyed the adventure of exploring a new city.

Soon the messages flew between us. We shared news about friends, phrases in Spanish, and snatches of poetry. But the letters changed as our high school years passed. Now we discuss college plans, career goals, God's plan for the future. We are learning what really matters in life. What has lasted is the simple faith in God's Word that our parents and our teachers have modeled for us.

"My grandmother has been diagnosed with cancer," my latest message from Nicole reads. "It's so hard for me to be away from her. Please pray for her." I wondered how to answer. I had no advice or poem to meet her need. I turned instead to the Psalms, the only poetry with any real power to comfort.

Through our correspondence, Nicole and I have kept a record of our journeys—of our thinking, of our changing, of our growing in Christ. We have learned this: Even more important than the friendships that we make are the friendships that we keep. They have years to develop and grow, as do the two participants.

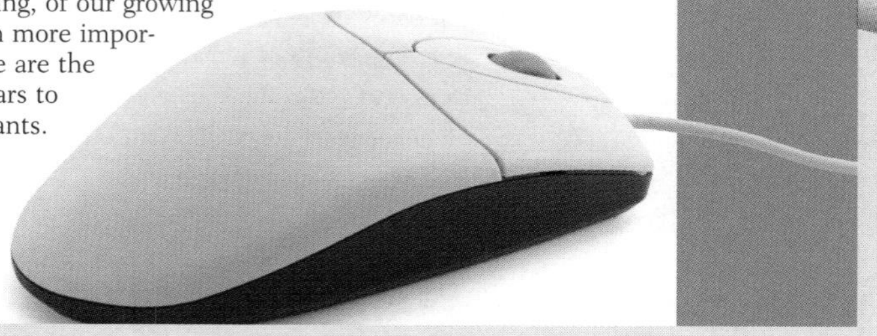

Literature Link

Ask students to reflect upon the friendships they have established. Then ask students to share personal anecdotes about experiences they have had with special friends. *(family vacations, school trips, athletic events, etc.)* Read Ilana Sibley's essay "A Record of Our Journeys." Alternatively, allow students to search for and share other essays or short pieces of literature that have friendship as a theme. Draw comparisons and contrasts between pieces when appropriate.

Enrichment

Encourage any student who has an international pen pal to share letters with the class.

Scriptural Application

Ask a student to read Proverbs 17:17 aloud. Encourage students to establish friendships that are biblical and honoring to Christ.

Teaching Strategy

Participation and Introduction

Ask students how a test essay and an extemporaneous essay are similar. *(Both require the writer to organize his ideas quickly and to write clearly.)*

OVERVIEW of the WRITING PROCESS

Planning—planning for time allotted, analyzing the assignment, generating ideas about the topic, deciding the parameters, creating a thesis and supporting sentences, organizing a rough draft, and sketching a conclusion

Drafting—maintaining a consistent tone, stating the thesis, stating the main points with support, deleting irrelevant information, and stating the conclusion

Revising—proofreading the essay, adding necessary information, and editing for grammar and mechanics

Publishing—reading the essay aloud, adapting the essay for the school newspaper, and expanding the essay into a lesson

EXTEMPORANEOUS ESSAY

A friend loveth at all times, and a brother is born for adversity.
Proverbs 17:17

By this point in your academic life, you have probably encountered an essay test at least once. An essay test measures your knowledge about the subject and your ability to communicate that knowledge clearly in writing. An extemporaneous essay, on the other hand, focuses solely on your ability to express yourself on a given topic. Good essays, whether on a test or extemporaneous, demonstrate your ability to think, to organize your thoughts, and to express those thoughts clearly under time constraints. Even if you are never asked to write an extemporaneous essay outside class, you will be asked to think "on your feet." Memos, business letters, employee evaluations, proposals for new products, applications for funding—all of these are realistic writing projects that must be completed within a prescribed time limit and in addition to the regular workload. Learning to communicate under pressure is a skill that will serve you well in every aspect of life.

Your Turn

Write an extemporaneous essay on a topic your instructor assigns. Your teacher will give you guidelines regarding the length and time limit. Be prepared to identify the purpose, audience, and specific topic that you choose.

Planning

- ✔ **Analyze the assignment.** Be sure that you know exactly what is expected of you. Some assignments will specify what kind of essay you are to write as well as who your intended audience is. This assignment, however, leaves most of the decisions up to the writer.
- ✔ **Generate some ideas about the assigned topic.** Create a brainstorming list or a clustering diagram with all the general ideas and specific details that occur to you. Then examine the results. What groupings appear? Do any themes stand out? Use these notes as you plan your essay. Look at Sibley's original notes to see how she generated ideas on the topic of friendship.

"A man that hath friends must show himself friendly."
"Jesus, What a Friend for Sinners"
Is having friends important?
Nicole
    messages
    meeting in kindergarten
    still friends even though she moved away
How to make new friends
    meeting Jenny at her piano recital
    Dad and his college roommate
    Mom's friendship with her coworkers
Abraham—a friend of God
David and Jonathan

PLANNING STRATEGY
Participation

Distribute a copy of Writing Worksheet 7 (Teacher's Toolkit) to each student. Remind students to record all their work.

PLANNING STRATEGY
Participation and Discussion

Lead a brainstorming session about a topic. Remind students that their ideas are acceptable only if they are biblically appropriate. Display the ideas.

PLANNING STRATEGY
Participation

Ask students what would happen if an author wrote a book without any parameters, such as a purpose or targeted audience. *(The book would be rambling, unfocused, ineffective, etc.)* Relate the importance of setting parameters for an extemporaneous essay. Give the students time to specify their own purposes and intended audience.

PLANNING STRATEGY
Participation

Ask students to identify the thesis statement in "A Record of Our Journeys." *("As I read the latest message from my friend Nicole, I realized how much our friendship has changed—and yet endured—over the years.")* Remind students that the thesis statement should be the first sentence in an essay. Instruct students to write their thesis statements based on the brainstorm ideas. Examine volunteers' thesis statements in light of the topic.

- **Decide on the parameters for your essay.** Now that you have noted some possibilities, you should settle on the specifics. You need to specify a purpose for your essay, identify your intended audience, and choose your specific topic. For example, Sibley chose to discuss her friend and the messages they have shared. But she could just as easily have chosen to persuade teens of the importance of making new friends, to inform children about the influence that one friend can have on another, or to inspire adults to study the friendship between David and Jonathan in the Bible.
- **Create a thesis statement and supporting statements.** Use the ideas you generated earlier to identify the main point that you want to make. State that point as your thesis statement, identifying both your topic and the main thing you intend to say about that topic. Then sketch out the key points you plan to make in support of your thesis. Remember to include such details as facts, examples, and illustrations. Notice that Sibley specifically mentions softball, poetry, and a mission trip to Mexico among the events that she and her friend shared.
- **Organize a rough outline.** Choose an appropriate organizational strategy and then number your points in the order in which they will appear. Note which details you will use to support your main points. Sibley uses chronological order for her essay, recounting the history of her friendship and the changes that their correspondence has recorded.
- **Sketch out a conclusion.** Before you begin to draft your essay, you should know how you want it to end. Your concluding statements are the last thing your readers will see—and probably the first thing they will remember. The conclusion should restate your thesis statement and then show the importance of your point. Examine the sample essay to discover how Sibley uses this strategy.

Drafting

- **Write with revision in mind.** You probably will not have time to rewrite your entire essay before you turn it in. If you write on every other line, you will be able to add words in the spaces between when you revise. Writing on only one side of the paper allows you to make any needed longer revisions on the back.
- **Maintain a consistent tone.** Keep your audience and your purpose in mind as you write. A personal essay can benefit from an informal tone, but an informational essay usually requires some degree of formality. Both word choice and sentence structure contribute to the tone of a piece of writing. In general, reserve first-person and second-person references for essays that are informal or personal in nature.
- **Begin with your thesis statement.** Unless the assignment specifically requires you to write an introduction, your thesis statement should suffice. There is usually little time and no need for a formal introduction to an extemporaneous essay.
- **State each point clearly and provide adequate support.** Because your time is limited, you should begin with your strongest point, leaving less important points for later in the essay. (If you run out of time, your best arguments will be included already.) Depending on the nature of your essay, your first main point will begin a new paragraph or appear immediately after your thesis statement. Support that point with sentences that include the details you identified during the planning stage. Continue stating your points and providing support in subsequent paragraphs. Use transitional words to link ideas together as you move from point to point.

Planning Strategy
Modeling

Lead students in developing a two- or three-point outline for display. Remind them that the outline must be simple enough for the essay to be written within the time constraints for the assignment. Ask students to share personal experiences that would support the outline. Display the ideas.

Planning Strategy
Discussion

Ask students to re-read Sibley's thesis and conclusion and to explain how she restates her thesis statement in the conclusion. *(Sibley reiterates the fusion of development and constancy in long-standing friendships.)*

Drafting Strategy
Demonstration

Explain that using consistent tone while writing saves revision time later. Reiterate that academic writing usually requires third-person pronouns, but first- and second-person pronouns are suitable for informal writing.

Drafting Strategy
Analysis

Ask students whether the support in each paragraph of Sibley's essay is sufficient. *(Answers will vary.)* Ask students to find the transitional words and to suggest additional transitions. *("from then on," "at first," "soon"; additional answers will vary)*

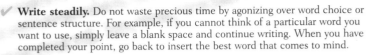

✔ **Write steadily.** Do not waste precious time by agonizing over word choice or sentence structure. For example, if you cannot think of a particular word you want to use, simply leave a blank space and continue writing. When you have completed your point, go back to insert the best word that comes to mind.

✔ **Avoid irrelevant information.** Keep your thesis statement in mind as you draft. Padding your essay with unnecessary details or useless points will take time that would be better spent polishing your key points.

✔ **Draw your essay to a close.** Do not use all your time to draft the body of your essay; save some of your time for your conclusion and for revising. Start with the statement that you sketched in the planning stage. Then reword that statement as necessary to incorporate any changes you made to your essay as you drafted it. An effective conclusion may be as simple as a restatement of your thesis or as complex as a short conclusion paragraph that goes beyond your thesis to show its importance. Ilana Sibley begins her conclusion by restating the connection between letters and her changing yet enduring friendship with Nicole. Sibley then emphasizes the value of maintaining such a friendship over the years: As the friends grow and change, they develop a deeper relationship than newly met friends are able to share.

Revising

✔ **Reserve enough time to read over your essay at least once.** As you read, look for statements that lack adequate support or passages that seem unclear or awkward. You will not have time to rewrite your entire essay, but you should make any minor improvements that are necessary.

✔ **Delete anything that detracts from your focus.** If any off-topic details slipped in to harm the unity or coherence of your essay, cross them out neatly. Notice what Sibley deleted from her first draft in order to keep the focus on what she shared with her friend.

> As I read the latest message from my friend Nicole, I realized how much our friendship has changed—and yet endured—over the years. We met in kindergarten, where we learned to tie our shoes and write our names. ~~Our teacher paired us up when she assigned classroom buddies during recess one day.~~ From then on, Nicole and I saw each other every day. ~~In fact we sometimes spent more time with each other than we spent with our families.~~ We shared experiences—going to classes, playing softball. We shared discoveries—a new poem, a truth about God. And we shared heartaches—a broken arm, an argument with a classmate.

✔ **Add any necessary support or clarification.** Use the space between the lines for additions of only a few words. If you need to insert a longer passage, mark the place with an asterisk and write the new passage at the end of the essay or on the back of your paper. Compare a sentence from Sibley's original draft to the same sentence from her revision to see how even minor changes can clarify the meaning of a passage.

Original	From then on, Nicole and I saw each other every day.
Revision	From kindergarten through junior high school, Nicole and I saw each other almost every day.

Thinking Biblically

The more Bible education you have, the more likely it is that others are going to ask (and expect!) you to share devotional thoughts—sometimes on short notice. Even when you don't have the time to plan a lesson carefully, you may want to write out your thoughts; so the skill of writing extemporaneous essays is important. While you probably will not read your manuscript verbatim, the effort of crafting a few words "fitly spoken" (Prov. 25:11) adds power and memorability to what you say. The apostle Paul did not rely on powerful turns of phrase to make his points; he trusted in the powerful Spirit of God (1 Cor. 2:1-5). But he still very clearly crafted his words.

Thinking Biblically

Return writing assignments from another unit (persuasive essays from Chapter 5 would work nicely) to students if they do not already have them. Tell them that they should prepare to present their essays to the class as if the class were a collection of candidates for political office, a team of Olympic athletes, or a church class full of young children (choose one or make up your own audience). Give the students five minutes to write new introductions and/or conclusions that fit the new audience. Ask them to present their essays as time allows.

Writing Workshop

Teach a minilesson about "Sentence Expansion and Reduction" (pp. 371–72). Point out that these techniques of writing can create clear and meaningful sentences.

Drafting Strategy

Discussion

Remind students that belaboring one's hunt for the perfect word and adding fascinating facts not necessary to the essay's key points waste valuable time. Challenge students to express their points succinctly so that they can finish in the allotted time.

Drafting Strategy

Discussion

Ask students to identify and discuss the effectiveness of Sibley's concluding sentence. Remind students that the concluding sentence must be strong because it may be the only thing the reader remembers about the essay.

Revising Strategy

Discussion

Remind students that they will probably not have time to rewrite their essays. Students should write neatly and make corrections legible.

Revising Strategy

Discussion

Direct students to check their essays for proper form: a thesis statement, supporting paragraphs, and a concluding statement.

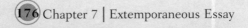

✔ **Edit for grammar and mechanics.** Examine your original essay and any new information that you have added during revision. Look for errors in grammar, usage, word choice, spelling, punctuation, and capitalization. Cross out any mistake neatly and write any necessary correction in the margin or in the spaces between the lines.

Publishing

✔ **Read your essay aloud to an appropriate audience.** For example, consider performing a humorous essay as entertainment at a public gathering.

✔ **Adapt your essay as an article for the school newspaper.** Interview experts on your topic or interested peers and incorporate their comments into an article based on your essay.

✔ **Expand your essay into a lesson with additional support.** An informational essay on an academic topic could become a lesson for younger students. An inspirational essay on a biblical topic may make an excellent lesson for a Sunday school class, a Bible club, or a church youth group.

Some Ideas to Consider

History

- Discuss a notable figure from history. (Since the essay is extemporaneous, any historical topic you pick should be one you already know well and will not have to research.)

Science

- Identify the technological innovation of the past decade (or century) that has affected your life the most.

Bible

- Write an essay about family relationships.

Verb Use

Notice the verbs used by the apostle John to describe the actions of Christ against those who made the temple a place of business. "And when he had made a scourge of small cords, he drove them all out of the temple, and the sheep, and the oxen; and poured out the changers' money, and overthrew the tables" (John 2:15).

Because a verb is considered the backbone or support of a sentence, choosing strong verbs and using those verbs correctly help convey your message clearly. In this passage there is no question as to the Lord's actions and the result of His actions. In the process of choosing and using verbs correctly, the speaker and the writer must understand the varied possibilities of form, function, and type.

OBJECTIVES

Students will

1. recognize the difference between regular and irregular verbs.
2. identify verb tenses in sentences.
3. use verbs in appropriate forms and tenses in sentences.
4. revise incorrect verb tenses.
5. write sentences using verbs correctly in a variety of tenses.
6. employ correct verb sequence in a sentence.
7. distinguish between active and passive voice.
8. identify retained objects and subjective complements.
9. rewrite sentences from passive to active voice.
10. identify verb moods as indicative, imperative, or subjunctive.
11. compose sentences using the indicative, imperative, or subjunctive moods.
12. rewrite a paragraph correcting verb usage errors.

Challenge your students to take an objective approach to their writing and to delete any words or sentences not lending to a concise, coherent whole.

Revising Strategy

Demonstration and Analysis

Materials

- sample paragraph with errors from an extemporaneous essay

Display the sample paragraph with spaces between the lines for inserting corrections into the text. Explain that the original essay and any changes must be examined for errors. Elicit the students' input for the correct revision strategies.

Publishing Strategy

Participation

Encourage students to craft their essays for a particular audience. Allow them to post their essays on the class website or blog.

Publishing Strategy

Participation

Consider grouping the students who have similar topics so that they can expand their essays into lessons for the same audiences. Then assist the students in making arrangements for the lessons to take place.

Evaluation

For help in grading this assignment, see "Grading Student Writing" (p. v) and Writing Rubric 7 (Teacher's Toolkit).

Verb Use | Chapter 7 177

Principal Parts

Verbs
pp. 42–45

English verbs have three **principal parts**. Using these principal (or main) parts, you are able to make any form of those verbs. The principal parts are the present, the past, and the past participle forms.

tip

Use a good dictionary to find the three principal parts of verbs that are unfamiliar to you.

Appendix
Adding Suffixes
pp. 429–30

Verbs that form their second and third principal parts by adding *-d* or *-ed* to the first principal part are **regular verbs**. Most verbs are regular verbs.

oppose	opposed	opposed
play	played	played
hurry	hurried	hurried
occur	occurred	occurred

Some verbs that are otherwise regular substitute a *t* for the *d* of the first principal part instead of adding a suffix.

build	built	built
bend	bent	bent

Irregular verbs form their second and third principal parts in different ways. Some irregular verbs have a different form for each principal part. These differences may appear as vowel changes, ending changes, or a combination of the two.

drink	drank	drunk
know	knew	known
shake	shook	shaken
freeze	froze	frozen

Other irregular verbs have two of their principal parts the same.

Swang is not a word; it is a nonstandard form for the second principal part of *swing*.

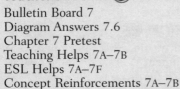

swing	swung	swung
run	ran	run
lead	led	led

Sometimes all three principal parts of the verb are identical.

cost	cost	cost
burst	burst	burst

tip

As you write, look for opportunities to replace *be* verbs with strong action verbs.

Tenses

Tenses are verb forms that suggest the time of an action or of a state or situation. There are three simple tenses as well as perfect and progressive tenses.

Simple Tenses

The three simple tenses are present, past, and future. **Present tense** can indicate a state or a situation that exists in the present. For an action verb, it expresses

VERB USE

Lesson Support

Student Worktext

Chapter 7 Review—pp. 443–44

Teacher's Toolkit

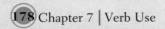

Bulletin Board 7
Diagram Answers 7.6
Chapter 7 Pretest
Teaching Helps 7A–7B
ESL Helps 7A–7F
Concept Reinforcements 7A–7B

Test

Chapter 7 Test

Teaching Strategy

Induction

Ask students to identify the three principal parts of the verb *shake*. *(shake, shook, shaken)* Display the principal parts in three columns. Then ask students to identify other forms of *shake*. *(will shake, has shaken, had shaken, will have shaken, shaking, will be shaking, etc.)* Display these verb forms in the appropriate columns. Inform students that every form of the verb comes from one of the principal parts.

Teaching Strategy

Discussion

Point out that some regular verbs (such as *kneel* and *send*) change spelling in the second and third principal parts. The *-t* substitutes for the *-d* or *-ed*.

habitual action (what normally happens). The present tense uses the first principal part of the verb.

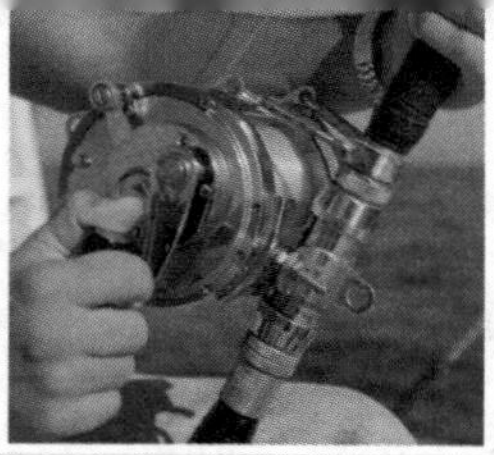

> Numbers of people *enjoy* fishing every year.
>
> My brother *has* an interest in fishing.
>
> Alec usually *fishes* on Lake Erie.
>
> Either he or his wife *cleans* and *fillets* the fish.

ESL The first principal part of nearly every verb is used almost unchanged throughout the present tense, simply adding *s* or *es* to agree with third-person singular subjects (see p. 149). However, three verbs are irregular. As you know, ***be*** uses ***is***, ***am***, and ***are*** instead of a principal part (p. 149). Two other verbs have irregular forms for third-person singular in the present: ***have*** ("he ***has***") and ***do*** ("he ***does***," which is irregular only in pronunciation).

Past tense indicates a state or an action that took place in the past. Past tense verbs use the second principal part of the verb.

> We *watched* our friends fishing from the shore.
>
> Several of our friends *scheduled* a time to fish.

Future tense indicates a state or an action that will take place in the future. The future tense uses the auxiliary *will* (or *shall*) and the first principal part of the verb.

> We *will ask* our friends about their experience.
>
> Next year, I *will take* the opportunity to fish.

Auxiliaries
p. 44

Perfect Tenses

The **perfect tenses** indicate a state of being or an action that is completed. In this sense, *perfect* means "complete." Perfect tenses are formed by using forms of the auxiliary verb *have* and the third principal part of the verb.

The **present perfect tense** indicates a state of being or an action that is completed during the present time or that began in the past and has continued until the present time. Present perfect verbs use the auxiliary *have* or *has.*

> My brother *has read* many articles about parasailing.
>
> Both of my brothers *have planned* to parasail next summer.
>
> Watching them plan this experience *has been* fun.

ESL The present perfect is often used for actions that took place at an indefinite time in the past, especially the recent past. However, if the time of the action is specified, the simple past tense must be used.

PRESENT PERFECT	Yes, I *have read* that article.
SIMPLE PAST	In fact, I *read* it this morning.

The **past perfect tense** indicates a state of being or an action that was completed before a certain time in the past. Past perfect verbs use the auxiliary *had.*

> My friends did not realize that my brothers *had waited* several years to "fly."
>
> Both John and Charles *had* eagerly *anticipated* the experience.

Perfect Participles,
Perfect Gerunds,
Perfect Infinitives
pp. 94, 98, 102

The **future perfect tense** indicates that a state will exist or that an action will be completed before a certain time in the future. Future perfect verbs use the auxiliaries *will have* (or *shall have*).

> They *will have taken* their first ride before Dad arrives at the ocean.
>
> By this evening Dad *will have watched* them parasail several times.

TEACHING STRATEGY
Induction and Participation

Display several examples of irregular verbs: *sink, swim, swing,* and so on. Ask students to identify the principal parts of these verbs. *(sink, sank, sunk; swim, swam, swum; swing, swung, swung)* Direct their attention to the difference in the formation of the principal parts of *swing.* Encourage students to consult a dictionary to identify the principal parts of verbs. Instruct them to write several sentences using these irregular verbs. Ask for volunteers to display several sentences.

REINFORCEMENT

Use Bulletin Board 7 (Teacher's Toolkit) to give students practice using progressive tenses.

TEACHING STRATEGY
Participation

Display the following sentences:

- My older brother ___ on the front row in each of his classes. *(present tense)*
- After he ___ on the front row for six weeks, he plans to request a seat change. *(present perfect)*
- He ___ on the front row of Algebra class before he transferred to Geometry class. *(past perfect)*
- My brother ___ on the front row for the graduation exercises. *(future progressive)*

Ask students to supply the forms of *sit* to complete the sentences. Then ask students to describe the different meanings.

Verb Use | Chapter 7 179

ESL One unusual thing about English is the expression of future time in dependent clauses that begin either with ***if*** or with a time word such as ***when***, ***while***, ***as***, ***before***, and ***after***. Instead of future tense, these dependent clauses use the simple present tense to express future time.

After I ***finish*** my homework, I'll clean my room.

If I ***clean*** my room today, I won't have to clean it tomorrow.

When the verb in the independent clause is in the future perfect tense, the *if* clause or time clause can use either present tense or present perfect to express future time.

When I ***have finished*** *(or:* When I ***finish****)* high school, my sister will have finished four years of college.

Progressive Tenses

Present Participles pp. 92–93

Progressive tenses show continuing action. They use a form of the auxiliary verb *be* and add *-ing* to the first principal part of the main verb. The form of *be* reflects the simple or perfect tense of the verb.

Tense	Meaning	Form of *be*	Example
Present Progressive	Present continuing action	*am, is, are*	I **am learning** a new sport right now.
Past Progressive	Past continuing action	*was, were*	I **was learning** to parasail when I read about the accident.
Future Progressive	Continuing action in the future	*will be*	I **will be learning** new safety techniques this week before I parasail next week.
Present Perfect Progressive	Continuing action performed during the present time period	*has been, have been*	I **have been learning** water safety measures for the past month.
Past Perfect Progressive	Continuing action completed before a certain time in the past	*had been*	Until this summer, I **had been learning** from a book, not from experience.
Future Perfect Progressive	Continuing action that will be completed before a certain time in the future	*will have been (shall have been)*	By noon, we **will have been watching** the parasailers for two hours.

in SUMMARY

The three **principal parts** of verbs are the present, past, and past participle.

A **regular verb** forms its second and third principal parts by adding *-d* or *-ed* to the first principal part. **Irregular verbs** form their second and third principal parts in various ways.

Simple tenses are present, past, and future.

Present tense indicates a state that exists in the present or an action that takes place habitually.

Special Note

Remind students that third-person singular subjects require a verb that has an *-s* or *-es* ending. *(he holds, she teaches, it freezes)*

Teaching Strategy

Participation

While covering each tense, ask students to identify what principal part of the verb forms each tense. (For example, *The present perfect tense uses the third principal part with the auxiliary* have *or* has.)

ESL Strategy

For further explanation about using the auxiliary *do* correctly, see ESL Help 7A (Teacher's Toolkit). For additional help in explaining the English tense system to ESL students, see ESL Helps 7B, 7C, and 7D (Teacher's Toolkit). (Note: If you choose to distribute copies of ESL Help 7D, be prepared to discuss the differences between verb tenses.)

Teaching Strategy

Modeling

Display the following sentences quoted from *Free Indeed: Heroes of Black Christian History* by Mark Sidwell (published by BJU Press). Ask students to identify the tense of each italicized verb.

- Among the most notable of the pastors of these large churches *was* Charles A. Tindley of Philadelphia. (p. 129) *(past)*

Past tense indicates a state or action that occurred in the past.
Future tense indicates a state or action that will occur in the future.
Perfect tenses indicate a state or action that is completed.
Progressive tenses indicate an action that is continuing.

7.1 PRACTICE *the skill*

Underline the complete verb in each independent clause. Then identify its tense.

present progressive 1. As technology improves, new forms of communication are continually developing.

present 2. The electromagnet allows an electrical current to pass through wires that surround a piece of metal and make it magnetic.

future perfect 3. In 2025, electromagnets will have existed for two hundred years.

past 4. Many years ago Samuel Morse realized the potential for this device and invented the telegraph.

present 5. The telegraph consists of a wire through which an electromagnetic current passes and a receptor at the other end that clicks when the current arrives.

past 6. The first message sent by telegraph in America announced the nomination of Henry Clay as a presidential candidate in 1844.

past 7. In May of that year, the telegraph line opened when the first official message was transmitted.

past perfect 8. Samuel Morse had allowed the daughter of a friend to choose the text of the message—Numbers 23:23.

present perfect 9. "What hath God wrought!"

past perfect progressive 10. By 1877, when the telephone was developed, the telegraph had been sending messages worldwide for thirty-three years.

- By 1906 the congregation *had grown* so large that it bought a larger building. (p. 133) *(past perfect)*
- [Tindley once wrote,] "Previous conditions of servitude, in the eyes of our enemies, *have left* its ineffaceable marks of inferiority upon every human being whose veins contain one drop of Negro blood." (p. 137) *(present perfect)*

7.2 REVIEW *the skill*

Write the verb in parentheses in an appropriate tense. Try to use a variety of tenses and be prepared to identify the tense you choose. *(Answers may vary.)*

knows, developed *(present, past)* 1. Not everyone *(know)* the story of the pony express, which began on April 30, 1860, and *(develop)* into one of the greatest legends of the American West.

lost *(past)* 2. Despite the many risks and dangers in the year and a half of its existence, the pony express *(lose)* only one rider and only one mail delivery.

had taken, made *(past perfect, past)* 3. Before the pony express, the trip overland across the United States *(take)* twenty days, but the pony express riders *(make)* the trip in ten days or less.

faced *(past)* 4. On the trail, riders *(face)* many risks, including snowstorms and hostile Indians.

had been hurrying *(past perfect progressive)* 5. One rider, Warren Upson, *(hurry)* through the Sierras when a fierce ice storm forced him to walk his horse many miles.

took, carried *(past, past)* 6. The shortest trip *(take)* seven days and seventeen hours. The riders *(carry)* the inaugural address of the new president, Abraham Lincoln.

was carrying *(past progressive)* 7. "Pony Bob" Haslam *(carry)* Lincoln's speech when he was attacked by Indians; despite wounds, he survived and delivered his message.

had charged *(past perfect)* 8. Initially the pony express *(charge)* five dollars per half ounce of mail, but when financial troubles hit, they lowered the price to one dollar per half ounce—a loss for the company.

had provided *(past perfect)* 9. By the time of its financial failure, the pony express *(provide)* the people of the United States with a series of stories that were the very essence of American culture.

have remembered *(present perfect)* 10. Americans *(remember)* the pony express through the years because of the way it typified perseverance and bravery.

TEACHING STRATEGY

Participation

After students have completed Review the Skill 7.2, ask volunteers to share their answers and to identify the tenses they used.

182 Chapter 7 | Verb Use

7.3 USE *the skill*

Rewrite the following paragraphs, correcting the five verb errors.

Although Samuel F. B. Morse originated the telegraph in America, he did not invent the first working telegraph system. The British inventors William Fothergill Cooke and Charles Wheatstone are making the first usable telegraph system by 1837. In Britain, however, the popularity and usefulness of the telegraph was slow in coming. At first, train stations uses the telegraph to inform other stations of arriving trains.

By 1845 the telegraph had gave essential help in catching two criminals. The men boarded a train from Paddington, London, to Slough. Although the police in London were unable to catch the criminals, they sent a telegram to the police in Slough. When the criminals gotten off the train, the police wait. The publicity created by the spectacular capture and by the telegraph-aided capture of a murderer the next year sent the popularity of the telegram skyrocketing.

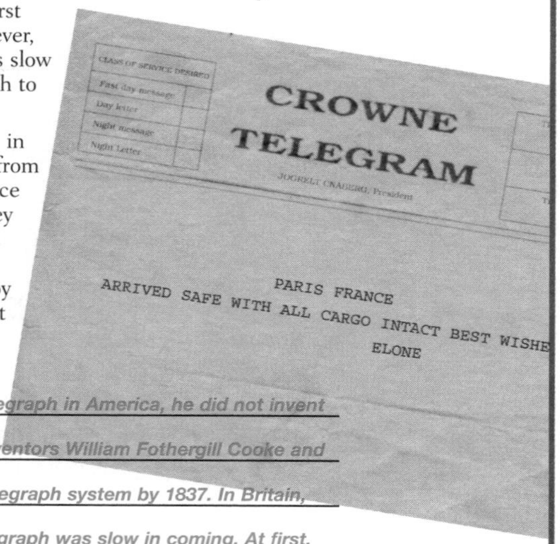

CROWNE
TELEGRAM
PARIS FRANCE
ARRIVED SAFE WITH ALL CARGO INTACT BEST WISHE
ELONE

Although Samuel F. B. Morse originated the telegraph in America, he did not invent the first working telegraph system. The British inventors William Fothergill Cooke and Charles Wheatstone had made the first usable telegraph system by 1837. In Britain, however, the popularity and usefulness of the telegraph was slow in coming. At first, train stations used the telegraph to inform other stations of arriving trains.

By 1845 the telegraph had given essential help in catching two criminals. The men boarded a train from Paddington, London, to Slough. Although the police in London were unable to catch the criminals, they sent a telegram to the police in Slough. When the criminals got off the train, the police were waiting. The publicity created by the spectacular capture and by the telegraph-aided capture of a murderer the next year sent the popularity of the telegram skyrocketing.

Evaluation

Ask students to read aloud several of the sentences they wrote for Use the Skill 7.3. Listen for correct use of the required tense.

Consistency and Sequence of Tenses

Saying Things Consistently p. 384

Using verb tenses correctly enables your reader to have a clear understanding of what you are writing. Have you ever read a lengthy sentence or passage that left you wondering about the sequence of events? Perhaps the problem was inconsistent or inaccurate verb tenses.

Several guidelines govern the use of verb tenses in particular situations. Use present tense to tell about the events in someone's story or another literary work. This "literary present" indicates that the events of the story are considered to exist in the eternal present. In a present-tense passage, use the present perfect for earlier events.

Present	Detective James *takes* his place at the weekly round-table discussion.
Present Perfect	After Detective James *has studied* a case for a while, he *gathers* new information for the investigation.
Literary Present	Hamlet *kills* Polonius mistakenly, thinking that it *is* Claudius behind the arras.

Use the past tense (and past perfect) to tell a story that is not a work of fiction.

Normal Past	Detective Stein *discovered* the truth.
Past Perfect	Before the last incident, however, Detective Stein *had marred* his investigative record.

The present tense may be used in conversation to relay past events and to make the events more vivid. The past tense is expected in written communication.

Oral	Then the assistant *walks* into the room and *throws* the tattered papers on the lawyer's desk.
Written	Then the assistant *walked* into the room and *threw* the tattered papers on the lawyer's desk.

Whether you are speaking or writing, be consistent in the tenses that you use. Avoid mixing the tenses unnecessarily.

Mixed (Incorrect)	When the villain *returned,* he *whispers* furtively to his accomplice.

Accurate tense sequence is particularly important within a sentence. Written English often uses the past perfect for an action that precedes another action in the past. Do not use the plain past when the past perfect is needed.

Imprecise	When the villain *revealed* his identity, he *fled* to a remote villa.
Reworded	When the villain *had revealed* his identity, he *fled* to a remote villa.

If two things took place or were true at the same time in the past, use the past to express both of them. If, however, one of them is a **universal truth**—something still true today—use the present tense for the universal truth.

God *directed* Moses to the Red Sea and *parted* the Sea for the children of Israel.

The Bible *states* that all men *are* sinners.

1. Use the simple past to tell about past actions in their chronological sequence.
2. Set the scene for a flashback by using the past perfect.
3. In a sentence with either subordinating conjunction *after* or *before*, the past perfect is optional for prior actions.

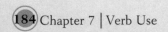

Teaching Strategy
Modeling

Read the following sentences aloud to the students:

- After I had fallen down the stairs, I realized the cause.
- Although men guided by the Holy Spirit wrote the Scriptures many years ago, the Bible remains an infallible book.
- When I was in college, I studied under several interesting professors.

Explain the consistent use of verb tense in each sentence. Point out to the students that using inconsistent verb tenses causes confusion. Ask students to model sentences of their own after yours.

Teaching Strategy
Introduction

To help students think through the sentences thoroughly, perhaps complete the first two or three sentences in Practice the Skill 7.4 together as a class. Ask students to identify the verb tense for each main verb in the sentence and to analyze any consistency or sequence problems.

ESL

Knowing when to shift tenses can be difficult. Here are some common reasons for shifting tenses.

From present tense to past tense or present perfect:

- To provide background information

  Our substitute teacher ***is*** Miss Johnson. She ***studied*** (or ***has studied***) French for seven years and ***lived*** in France for two years.

From present tense to past tense:

- To support a claim with an example from the past

  Sometimes, adverse circumstances ***alter*** a person's plans for the future. The composer Robert Schumann ***wanted*** to become a piano virtuoso. However, when his right hand ***became*** crippled, he ***turned*** instead to composing brilliant music.

- To compare a present situation with a past one

  The choir ***sings*** well this year. Last year they ***sang*** poorly.

From past tense to present tense:

- To express a comment, opinion, or evaluation

  The Schultes recently ***redecorated*** their living room. The result ***is*** lovely.

in SUMMARY

To relate the events in a **literary work**, use the present tense for the main action of the story and the present perfect tense for earlier events.

To relate the events in a **true story**, use the past tense and the past perfect tense, as appropriate. (Although you may use the present tense in ordinary conversation, you should always use the past tense in writing.)

Use the past perfect tense to relate **two past actions** if one of the actions occurred prior to the other.

To state a **universal truth**, use the present tense.

7.4 PRACTICE *the skill*

Underline each verb in incorrect tense. Write the verb in corrected tense in the blank.

determines 1. The man in the telegraph office told Mother, "The number of words in a telegram had determined its cost."

have omitted 2. Conserving words becomes a necessity for any telegram. Through the years people omitted short words such as articles.

is 3. Even auxiliaries such as *do, does, are,* and *is* are absent from a telegram. The result was a savings of several dollars.

REINFORCEMENT

Use Teaching Help 7A (Teacher's Toolkit) to give students additional practice in consistency and sequence of tenses.

have used 4. Through years past, politicians and generals will use telegrams to report news about campaigns or battles.

was 5. Queen Victoria had been the first British monarch to send telegrams; she even used them to congratulate the subjects who reached their one hundredth birthdays.

had 6. After receiving telegrams quite frequently during the early years of the telegraph, British police will have their own address: Handcuffs, London.

understand 7. Through a collection of telegrams from Victorian England, we understood the history of the battle of Mafeking, South Africa.

sent 8. In June 1826 Robert Stephenson, father of the British railroad, sends the first British telegram: "Bravo."

play 9. Telegrams even became part of fiction: they played important roles in many Sherlock Holmes stories.

provides 10. In Mackinlay Kantor's story "The Grave Grass Quivers," a telegram provided confirmation of the murderer's identity.

7.5 USE *the skill*

Write a sentence (or sentences) in response to each prompt. Use the correct tense or sequence of tenses. *(Answers will vary.)*

1. Recount a sequence of two or more actions from a short story or novel.

   In The Pilgrim's Progress, Christian escapes from Doubting Castle and Giant Despair when he remembers that he has the key of Promise.

2. Describe at least two things that you and your family did last week.

   We drove from South Carolina to Massachusetts. Before the trip, we had changed the oil in our car.

3. Pretend to tell someone about a sequence of events that you are observing right now. (Use conversational style.)

   The server drops the tray, and then the customer starts screaming. Now the manager is coming over to the table.

186 Chapter 7 | Verb Use

4. Now write about the same sequence of events as though you observed it yesterday. (Use standard written style).

After the server had dropped the tray, the customer started screaming. Then the manager came over to the table.

5. Write a statement of a scientific universal truth.

Water boils at 212° F.

6. Report an event from history. Describe both the cause and the effect.

Because her own father had died and her uncles had died without legitimate heirs, Victoria became the queen of Great Britain and Ireland in 1837.

7. State a universal truth from Scripture.

God loves a cheerful giver (2 Cor. 9:7).

8. Describe two events that happened at the same time.

Stephanie baked the cake and decorated the room for the birthday party.

9. Retell a short episode from a famous folktale or other fictional story.

While the overconfident hare wastes time by napping, the diligent tortoise takes the lead in the race.

10. Describe a sequence of at least two actions from the life of the prophet Elisha.

After Elijah had been taken to heaven in the whirlwind, Elisha picked up Elijah's mantle and then crossed the river Jordan (2 Kings 2:11–14).

Passive Gerund, Passive Infinitive pp. 98, 102

Voice

Another characteristic that verbs possess is voice. The relationship of the subject and the verb determines voice. If the subject *is* something or is doing something, the verb and the sentence are in **active voice**. If the subject is being acted upon by the verb, the verb and the sentence are in **passive voice**. Passive verbs use a form of the auxiliary *be* before the main verb. Only transitive verbs can be made passive.

Active or Passive pp. 361–62

ACTIVE VOICE	Claudio is a black Labrador retriever.
	Slipper, a small dog, hid under the couch.
	Berkley ate the bowl of dog food.
PASSIVE VOICE	The bowl of dog food was eaten by Berkley.
	Slipper was found by Claudio.

TEACHING STRATEGY

Demonstration and Participation

Display the following two descriptions:

In the ninth inning the sinking fastball was thrown by the pitcher toward the batter. With a three ball and two strike count, the ball was eyed by the batter. The ball was hit over the center field fence.

In the ninth inning the pitcher threw a sinking fastball toward the batter. With a three ball and two strike count, the batter eyed the ball and hit it over the center field fence.

Ask students to identify the subject and verb in each sentence, comparing the two descriptions. Elicit from the students that the first description is wordy and imprecise but that the second is clear and brisk. Instruct students to describe another event using active voice in one description and passive voice in the other. Then ask them to evaluate the effectiveness of their descriptions.

ESL STRATEGY

Use ESL Helps 7E and 7F (Teacher's Toolkit) for an explanation of active and passive voices and to practice changing passive voice to active.

Tense	Active Voice	Passive Voice
Present	Jordan **owns** a book on World War II.	A book on World War II **is owned** by Jordan.
Past	Jordan **owned** a book on World War II.	A book on World War II **was owned** by Jordan.
Future	Jordan **will own** a book on World War II.	A book on World War II **will be owned** by Jordan.
Present Perfect	Jordan **has owned** a book on World War II.	A book on World War II **has been owned** by Jordan.
Past Perfect	Jordan **had owned** a book on World War II.	A book on World War II **had been owned** by Jordan.
Future Perfect	Jordan **will have owned** a book on World War II.	A book on World War II **will have been owned** by Jordan.

Using Active and Passive Sentences

Active voice is more direct and emphasizes the doer of the action. In addition, active sentences are usually shorter. Therefore, active sentences are usually more effective and desirable than passive sentences.

Sometimes, however, passive sentences are useful. For example, a passive verb is necessary in a sentence when the doer is unimportant or unknown. In other sentences, using a passive verb creates a flowing sentence or paragraph that has the same subject for several verbs in a row. A passive verb may also allow you to move certain ideas from the subject position to the end of the sentence for emphasis.

GOOD USE OF PASSIVES	The office doors were locked at five o'clock. The money was donated to the mission fund.
ACCEPTABLE	When *Dad* asked *John* to work on the family farm, *John* accepted the job. Though *Dad* expected John to work extra hours, *John* knew he would learn valuable lessons.
BETTER (CONSISTENT SUBJECTS)	When *John* was asked to work on the family farm, *he* accepted the job. Though *he* was expected to work extra hours, *he* knew he would learn valuable lessons for life.
AWKWARDLY LONG SUBJECT	*Missionaries, senior and associate pastors, choir directors, and Sunday school superintendents* planned the schedule.
BETTER	*The schedule* was planned by missionaries, senior and associate pastors, choir directors, and Sunday school superintendents.

Revising Active and Passive Sentences

In order to change an active voice sentence into a passive sentence, you will need to follow several steps. First, change the transitive verb into the past participle form, if it is not already in that form. Second, add a form of the auxiliary *be* before the main verb. Then, make the direct object (or receiver of action) the subject of the sentence. (Make sure the auxiliary agrees with the subject once all the steps are complete.) The subject (or the doer) of the original sentence may be omitted or may be made the object of the preposition *by* in the passive sentence.

TEACHING STRATEGY
Participation

Ask students to identify the simple predicates, noting the forms of *be,* in the passive section of the chart on page 188. (***is** owned, **was** owned, will **be** owned, has **been** owned, had **been** owned, will have **been** owned*) Direct students to make a chart using another verb. Encourage students to use forms of *be* that were not used on page 188. Allow volunteers to read their charts or to write them for display.

TEACHING STRATEGY
Discussion

Explain that passive voice is useful when the doer of the action is unknown or unimportant. Ask students to consider the following passive sentence: *The used clothing was given to a local charity.* Who or what gave the donation? Ask students to rewrite the sentence in active voice. *(Answers will vary.)*

TEACHING STRATEGY
Participation

Display the following sentences:

- Our lively puppy brought him the ball.
- The committee provided me ample funds for the picnic.
- The science class appointed Stephen their representative.

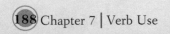

Ask students to rewrite the sentences in passive voice using the same verb. Then ask

ACTIVE	**S TrV-A DO** Joshua *took* the dog for a walk.
PASSIVE	**S TrV-P** The dog *was taken* for a walk.
	S TrV-P OP The dog *was taken* for a walk (by Joshua).

To change a passive voice sentence into an active voice sentence, do the steps in reverse. If there is a *by* phrase in the sentence, make its object the subject of the new sentence. Otherwise, supply a subject (doer) for the active sentence. Make the subject of the passive sentence the direct object of the active sentence. Omit the *be* auxiliary and change the form of the verb to active.

PASSIVE	**S TrV-P** A theme for the banquet was chosen by the senior class.
ACTIVE	**S TrV-A DO** The senior class chose a theme for the banquet.

When the passive sentence does not state the doer, decide who or what the doer is. You may use an indefinite word for the subject.

PASSIVE	**S TrV-P** The books were returned to the library.
ACTIVE	**S TrV-A DO** Somebody returned the books to the library.

In each of the active-voice examples above, the sentence pattern S-TrV-DO appears. Two other sentence patterns, however, use transitive verbs. The sentence pattern S-TrV-IO-DO can be made passive in two ways. When the indirect object becomes the subject, the direct object becomes a **retained object** in the passive voice.

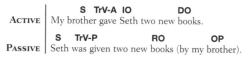

S-TrV-DO
p. 76

ACTIVE	**S TrV-A IO DO** My brother gave Seth two new books.
PASSIVE	**S TrV-P RO OP** Seth was given two new books (by my brother).

S-TrV-IO-DO
p. 76

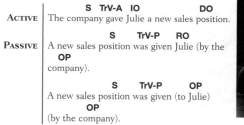

When the direct object becomes the subject, the indirect object may become a retained object or the object in a prepositional phrase.

ACTIVE	**S TrV-A IO DO** The company gave Julie a new sales position.
PASSIVE	**S TrV-P RO** A new sales position was given Julie (by the **OP** company).
	S TrV-P OP A new sales position was given (to Julie) **OP** (by the company).

The sentence pattern S-TrV-DO-OC can also be made passive. In a passive voice sentence, the objective complement, which renames or describes the direct object, becomes a **subjective complement** that renames or describes the subject.

S-TrV-DO-OC
p. 76

ACTIVE	**S TrV-A DO OC** The company made Julie a supervisor.
PASSIVE	**S TrV-P SC OP** Julie was made a supervisor (by the company).

them to identify which of the strategies on pages 188–90 they used to change the sentences. *(Answers will vary.)*

REINFORCEMENT

Use Teaching Help 7B (Teacher's Toolkit) to give the students more practice in rewriting passive sentences as active sentences.

Sentence diagram answers for Practice the Skill 7.6 appear in the Teacher's Toolkit. If you teach diagramming, perhaps consult *The Writer's Toolbox* for sample diagrams.

ESL Most English textbooks for native speakers present only the usual passive forms with *be*, as seen above. However, in spoken English you may also notice a special passive using *get* instead of *be* as the auxiliary.

ACTIVE	The ball ***smashed*** through the glass window.
NORMAL PASSIVE	The glass window ***was smashed*** by the ball.
GET-PASSIVE	The glass window ***got smashed*** by the ball.

As in this example, *get*-passives usually express unfavorable occurrences. Because they tend to be informal, you should usually use the normal *be*-passive in your writing for school or business.

in SUMMARY

A sentence is in the **active voice** when the subject *is* something or is doing something. A sentence is in the **passive voice** when something is being done to the subject.

A **passive verb** includes a form of the auxiliary *be* and the past participle form of a transitive verb.

Although active sentences are clearer and more economical than passive sentences, **passive sentences** are sometimes useful.

7.6 PRACTICE *the skill*

Underline the verb in each independent clause once. Then identify its voice as *active* or *passive*. If the verb is passive, underline any retained objects or subjective complements twice.

passive 1. Many New Testament epistles, or letters, addressed to both churches and individuals, were written by Paul.

active 2. Paul focused his epistles on the person and work of Christ.

active 3. Paul, who was probably in prison in Rome, wrote a letter to the believers in Philippi, a city in western Macedonia.

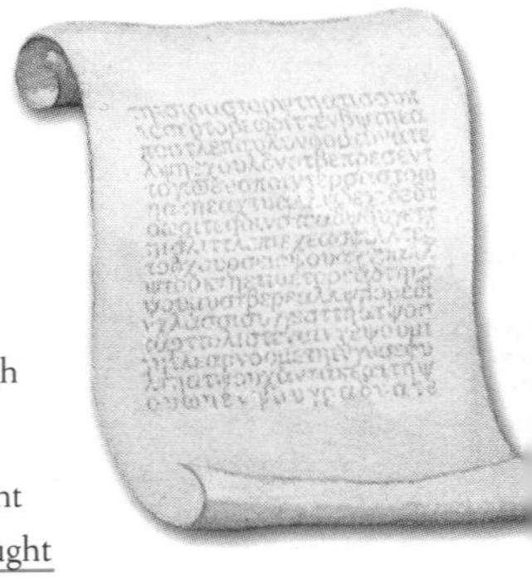

passive 4. The believers in Philippi were given an encouraging letter about God's promises and care.

passive 5. Paul's kindness to the members of the church at Philippi was expressed through his epistle.

active 6. Having faced hardship and imprisonment from hostile people in Philippi, Paul sought to encourage the beloved brethren.

passive 7. Paul was shown kindnesses so that he was not in want.

passive 8. The believers at Philippi were made strong as they grew in sound doctrine.

SCRIPTURAL APPLICATION

After the students have completed Use the Skill 7.6, divide the class into four groups, assigning each group a chapter of Paul's epistle to the Philippians to read. Instruct students to note the ways in which Paul directs the Philippian Christians to cope with the circumstances of life. Discuss the book as a class.

active 9. Paul's letter to the Philippians focuses on Christ's presence within each believer.

passive 10. Spiritual growth is revealed in believers who do all things through Christ.

7.7 USE *the skill*

Underline each passive-voice verb. Then rewrite the paragraph in active voice. *(Answers may vary.)*

Missionary letters, also known as prayer letters, have a multifaceted purpose. First, the reader is informed about the work that is being done on the mission field. Perhaps the missionary was directed by God to be a pastor, a church planter, or a Bible translator. Those who read his letter are informed about his progress on the field. Perhaps the missionary has had the opportunity to lead someone to the Lord, or a major portion of translation was completed. Maybe a children's ministry has been started. Next, the reader is informed about the missionary family. The background for a ladies' ministry may be included in the prayer letter as well as important milestones in the children's lives. Last, the needs that the missionary and his family may have on the field will be placed before the reader. Of utmost importance is the need for the reader to pray diligently for the missionary. Spiritual, financial, or physical needs are presented for special prayer. Through missionary letters Christians learn to pray more effectively for missionaries as they serve the Lord.

Missionary letters, also known as prayer letters, have a multifaceted purpose. First, the prayer letter informs the reader about the missionary's work on the field. Perhaps God has directed the missionary to be a pastor, a church planter, or a Bible translator. Those who read his letter will learn about the missionary's progress on the field. Perhaps the missionary has had the opportunity to lead someone to the Lord, to complete a major portion of translation, or to begin a children's ministry. Next, the reader learns about the missionary family. The prayer letter might include the background for the beginning of a ladies' ministry or important milestones in the children's lives. Last, the missionary may present the needs that he and his family have on the field. Of utmost importance is the need for the reader to pray diligently for the missionary. Other important needs may be spiritual, financial, or physical. Through missionary letters Christians learn to pray more effectively for missionaries as they serve the Lord.

Verb Use | Chapter 7 191

Mood

Kinds of Sentences p. 69

Mood identifies the speaker's attitude toward what he is saying. English verbs have three moods: indicative, imperative, and subjunctive.

The **indicative mood** is the most frequently used mood. The indicative mood makes a factual statement.

The weather in June is usually quite warm.

I enjoy visiting the local ice-cream shop.

Understood Subjects p. 70

The **imperative mood** expresses a direct command. The subject *you* is usually understood (omitted), and the verb is in the simple present-tense form.

Close the kitchen door behind you, please.

Avoid eating too many snacks before meal time.

The **subjunctive mood** expresses the idea that a thing is untrue but desired. It may express a wish, a necessity, or an obligation.

I wish that I were buying the new car today.

The prince's mother insisted that he act his age.

ESL Notice that these subjunctive sentences have a *that* clause, and it is the verb in the *that* clause that is subjunctive. The base form of *be + past participle* (passive) is also possible.

The legislature recommends that the districts be redrawn.

Forms of the Subjunctive

The forms of subjunctive mood verbs may be familiar, but their time references differ from those of verbs in the indicative mood. Use the simple past form of the verb to make a statement about something in the present or future. If the verb is *be*, use *were* (not *was*).

Present	If he *came* late to class, the professor would surely notice.
	If the job *were* completed, we could go home.
Future	If we *arrived* at the restaurant by five o'clock on Friday, we would not have to stand in line.
	If he *were* to leave early Saturday morning, he would arrive in Arizona on Sunday.

Use the past perfect to make a statement about something in the past. Use the simple present without *s* to make a "timeless" statement (of necessity).

Past	After seeing your slides, I wish that I *had detoured* by way of the Grand Canyon.
	If Enrique *had been* with you, he would have pointed out the famous landmarks.
Timeless	The teacher insisted that we *be* in our seats before the bell rings.
	For the job interview, it is necessary that he *come*.

Teaching Strategy

Discussion

Point out that parliamentary procedure uses the subjunctive mood in an expression of recommendation. For example, "I move that this action *be* approved."

Teaching Strategy

Participation

Direct students to write sentences, using the three moods discussed on pages 192–93. Display several of the sentences that use the subjunctive mood and ask students to decide what meaning the subjunctive sentence conveys. *(condition contrary to fact, doubtful future condition, expression of obligation or recommendation, or set expressions)*

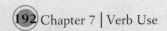

ESL

In conversation you will sometimes hear English speakers use *was* instead of *were* as the present subjunctive of *be*. In written or formal use, however, *was* is considered nonstandard for conditions contrary to fact.

Uses of the Subjunctive

Use the subjunctive mood to express a **condition contrary to fact**. In these sentences the clause begins with *if* (condition clause) and tells of something known to be untrue (contrary to fact). If you are unsure of the truth of the statement, use the indicative mood.

SUBJUNCTIVE (UNTRUE)	If I *were* you, I would study diligently for the test.
	If she *had studied* diligently, she would have earned a higher grade
INDICATIVE (UNKNOWN)	If he *studied* diligently, he probably did well.
	If my sister *comes*, then I will leave early.

Use the subjunctive mood to express a **doubtful future condition**. You could also use the auxiliary *would* in addition to an indicative form of the verb. Using the indicative only, however, eliminates the idea of uncertainty.

SUBJUNCTIVE	If they *were* to leave by seven this evening, they would arrive at the opera on time.
WOULD + INDICATIVE	If they *would leave* by seven this evening, they would arrive at the opera on time.
INDICATIVE	If they *leave* by seven this evening, they will arrive at the opera on time.

Use the subjunctive mood in a clause after an **expression of obligation or recommendation**. The idea of obligation disappears without the subjunctive.

SUBJUNCTIVE (OBLIGATION)	The chairman made the motion that the meeting *be* adjourned.
	The chairman insisted that the committee *be* ready for the presentation.
INDICATIVE (STATEMENT)	The chairman insisted that the committee *is* ready for the presentation.

Use the subjunctive for certain **set expressions**. Notice that some of these express desire.

God be with you.
Long live the king.
Be that as it may, . . .
Thy will be done.
Suffice it to say, . . .
Come what may, . . .

in SUMMARY

The **indicative mood** states a fact or makes a simple statement about something.

The **imperative mood** gives direct commands.

The **subjunctive mood** expresses conditions contrary to fact, doubtful future conditions, and obligation or recommendation; it is also used after expressions of necessity.

Verb Use | Chapter 7 193

7.8 PRACTICE *the skill*

Identify the mood of each italicized verb as *indicative, imperative,* or *subjunctive.*

indicative 1. Letters from soldiers who served at the front line *reveal* many previously undisclosed stories about the D-day activities of 1944.

indicative 2. My story *focuses* on a commanding officer's bodyguard, a fine young man barely out of his teens.

subjunctive 3. After I spent a long day at the frontline gathering statements for my report, my commanding officer insisted that I *be* in his tent immediately.

subjunctive 4. If it *had been* possible, I would have wished to avoid this visit.

indicative 5. The commanding officer *asked* me to speak to a soldier who had just learned that his sister and brother had been killed in the South Pacific.

imperative 6. "*Give* him comfort, but *tell* him that another brother is critically wounded here in France," he admonished.

subjunctive 7. For this kind of confrontation, it was necessary that I *be* well prepared.

imperative 8. "John, *encourage* this young soldier and *help* him return to his duty," my commanding officer said.

subjunctive 9. After the young soldier heard the news, he wished that he *were* home to comfort his mother.

indicative 10. We *have met* the enemy daily; we perform our duties with emptiness and fatigue.

7.9 USE *the skill*

Write a sentence in the mood indicated in parentheses. *(Answers will vary.)*

1. Describe a cost-effective advantage of digital communication. *(indicative)*

   As the cost of paper and postage increases, digital communication provides an inexpensive alternative.

2. Warn the user to write messages that cannot be misinterpreted. *(imperative)*

   Write your messages clearly to avoid any misinterpretation.

3. Your friend is ready to send a message regarding a job problem, but he does not want his boss to misinterpret what he says. What would you advise your friend to do before he sends the message? *(subjunctive)*

   I recommend that he proofread his message carefully before he sends it.

EVALUATION

After students have completed Use the Skill 7.9, ask volunteers to read some of their sentences aloud. Evaluate their answers to determine whether the students understand the differences in moods.

4. Tell your friend that he must be cautious in his message because of the rapid transmission of the messages. *(imperative)*

Choose your words carefully because your message is delivered instantaneously.

5. If you decide to send a digital message, what might be some advantages? *(subjunctive)*

If I were to send a digital message, I would find that it is both efficient and inexpensive.

6. Write a sentence about the role of courtesy phrases such as the words *please* and *thank you* in digital communications. *(indicative)*

Messages should be courteous and should include the words please and thank you as appropriate.

7. Warn a writer that he should avoid including his credit card number in his message. *(imperative)*

Do not give your credit card number as a part of your message.

8. Write a sentence describing the positive value for the corporate traveler of wireless availability in hotels. *(indicative)*

Since most motels and hotels have wireless access, the corporate traveler can keep his business partners informed daily.

9. Your friend sent a message with this idea: "That was a ridiculous statement. How could anyone be so silly!" What is your advice to your friend? *(subjunctive)*

It is necessary that your message be polite to avoid offense.

10. Write a sentence about the positive value of digital communication. *(indicative)*

Digital communication is often more powerful and efficient than traditional print correspondence.

Verb Use | Chapter 7 195

7.10 CUMULATIVE *review*

Rewrite the following paragraph, correcting the ten errors or inconsistencies from these categories: agreement, principal parts, tense, voice, and mood. (Assume that all sentences in this paragraph should have active voice.) *(Answers may vary.)*

Christina Rossetti, accomplished poet and writer, wrote more than 2,100 letters during her lifetime. Through her letters interesting facets of her life are learned by the reader. Rossetti began her letter writing before she reached the age of twenty. Although two-thirds of her letters remain unpublished, many letters to her friends and family is available for reading. If a person was to study the life of Christina Rossetti, they would find that her brother encouraged her in her early writing. In these writings she will be enthusiastic about life and eager for success. During her early forties, however, the tone of her letters had been changed by her. She experienced many personal losses; her writing was affected by these losses. Amid problems with her health and family relationships, Rossetti continued to write. I recommend that a person takes a close look at Rossetti's Christian life. In both her letters and her words, she had spoke of the love of Christ to friends and family. Letter writing was approached by Christina Rossetti as a means of communication when other means failed.

Christina Rossetti, accomplished poet and writer, wrote more than 2,100 letters during her lifetime. Through her letters the reader learns interesting facets of her life. Rossetti began her letter writing before she reached the age of twenty. Although two-thirds of her letters remain unpublished, many letters to her friends and family are available for reading. If he were to study the life of Christina Rossetti, a person would find that her brother encouraged her in her early writing. In these writings she was enthusiastic about life and eager for success. During her early forties, however, she changed the tone of her letters. She experienced many personal losses; these losses affected her writing. Amid problems with her health and family relationships, Rossetti continued to write. I recommend that a person take a close look at Rossetti's Christian life. In both her letters and her words, she had spoken of the love of Christ to friends and family. Christina Rossetti approached letter writing as a means of communication when other means failed.

THINK ABOUT IT

Subjectivity and Objectivity; Fact and Opinion

Before a critical thinker can draw reasonable conclusions and make sound judgments, he must evaluate the information available to him. The soundest decisions are usually those based on objective, factual evidence rather than on feeling or opinion. A

REINFORCEMENT

Use Chapter 7 Review on pages 443–44 for additional test review.

EVALUATION

Use Chapter 7 Test to evaluate the students' understanding of the content and concepts of the chapter.

critical thinker, then, must be able to differentiate between subjective and objective viewpoints and between opinion and fact.

What does it mean to be "objective" or "subjective"? As an example, the winner of a race is determined by an objective measurement: whoever crosses the finish line first wins the contest. The criterion is specific and measurable. The winner of a gymnastics meet, however, is determined by a combination of objective and subjective means. Some criteria are measurable: Did the gymnast finish the routine within the allotted time limit? Did he or she stay within the bounds? Did the gymnast fall or slip? Other criteria are less specific and require the judge to render an opinion. How well did the gymnast execute each skill? Was the routine balanced with a variety of difficult skills?

Similar to objectivity and subjectivity are fact and opinion. A fact is something that can be proved to be true or untrue. An opinion, however, is a belief that has not yet been proved (or cannot be proved) by observation, measurement, or other objective means. Most opinions are based on facts—or at least what someone believes to be a fact. But opinions are not facts themselves.

Use these strategies as you evaluate sources.

- First, evaluate the topic itself. Is it something that can be judged objectively? Or is subjectivity inherent to any discussion of this topic? For instance, the facts of a person's life are objective: the dates when King George III of Great Britain and Ireland was born and died, whom he married, where he lived, who succeeded him after his death. But an evaluation of a person's life must be subjective, for it depends upon one's point of view. Was George III a good king or a bad king? Were his actions regarding the American colonies proper or unjust? Was he or his son responsible for their volatile relationship?
- Search for key words or phrases that indicate opinion. "I think that" or "I feel" or even "This seems" is clearly opinion. But sometimes opinions are harder to spot. Any statement that expresses a value judgment is probably an opinion. Words such as *good, bad, wise, foolish, effective, useless,* and *beautiful* may signal a value judgment. The exception, of course, is a value statement based on a biblical criterion or expressed by God Himself in Scripture.
- When you find a value statement, look for factual support to back it up. A statement of opinion is not necessarily incorrect. If the speaker or writer offers facts and other objective evidence to support the opinion, examine the evidence for truth and validity. Only then should you decide whether to accept or reject the opinion.

Critical thinking allows for both facts and opinions; the key is to be able to distinguish between the two. Basing a decision solely on someone else's opinion is dangerous. Your decision is more likely to be sound if you base it on fact. However, it is sometimes acceptable or even unavoidable to make a decision based on opinion. As long as you recognize that your decision is based on opinion, you will be ready to adjust your plans if that opinion is later proved wrong.

Thinking It Through

Compare a letter to the editor and a newspaper article on the same topic. If possible, examine an encyclopedia article on that topic as well. Evaluate each source for objective and subjective arguments and distinguish the facts from the opinions.

Teaching Strategy

Discussion

Instruct students to offer objective and subjective statements about their town. Objective responses might include the physical characteristics of the town and the number of residents. Subjective responses might include an evaluation of the residents' feelings about the town landmarks. Display their responses. Ask students to differentiate between objective and subjective responses.

Reinforcement

Challenge students to identify examples of biased language in a letter to the editor or a newspaper article.

OBJECTIVES

Students will

1. select an event appropriate in scope to report on.
2. write the main points of a story line.
3. decide on an angle for a video report.
4. script a video report.
5. consider camera movement, editing, framing, lighting, music/sound, and narration while drafting a video report.
6. revise and edit a video report.
7. proofread a script and video text.
8. publish a video report.

Chapter 8 Overview

Topic	Pages	Support Materials	Days
Pronoun Case	203–13	Bulletin Board 8 Chapter 8 Pretest Practice/ Review/Use the Skill 8.1–8.6 Concept Reinforcements 8A–8C Teaching Help 8	102–4
Video Report	198–202	Writing Rubric 8 Writing Worksheets 8A–8B	105, 110–11
Courtesy Order Reflexive and Intensive Pronouns	213–15	Practice/Review the Skill 8.7–8.8	106
Pronoun Shift Review	215–19 445–47	Practice/Review the Skill 8.9–8.10 Cumulative Review 8.11 Chapter 8 Review	107
Chapter 8 Test			108
From the Written Word	219		109

VIDEO REPORT

Lesson Support

Teacher's Toolkit

Writing Worksheets 8A–8B
Writing Rubric 8

Literature Link

Ask volunteers to report on any documentaries they have seen. Discuss the common characteristics of this medium (memorable

Certain types of journalists depend not only on the stories they write but also on the photographs, illustrations, or video clips they incorporate into their reports. Think of the last news story you viewed—probably the text is linked inextricably in your mind with the images you saw. The combination of words and images is extremely powerful. In this chapter's writing assignment, you will combine text with video to present a news story to your high school, youth group, or family.

Invest in Teens

VIDEO	AUDIO
TEEN SLIDING DOWN WATERSLIDE INTO LAKE; TEENS ROASTING HOT DOGS OVER CAMPFIRE; TEEN READING GOD'S WORD WITH MOUNTAINS IN BACKGROUND	music cue—"How Great Thou Art" or "This Is My Father's World"
TEENS PILING ONTO BUS WITH SUITCASES VISIBLE	It's time again for the teens of Mt. Bethel Church to begin planning for summer camp.
TEEN COUNTING MONEY OUT OF WALLET OR CHECKING THE BALANCE IN CHECKBOOK	But before they go, each must raise the $275 needed to attend Camp Sunrise.
TEEN RAKING LEAVES; TEEN SWEEPING PORCH; TEENS SELLING REFRESHMENTS AT SOFTBALL GAME	In the past, teens have gotten money in a variety of ways. Voice: "I collect aluminum cans all year. ~~I even go up and down the highway near my house looking for old cans and stuff that I can recycle.~~ That way, I'm doing something to help better my community *and* raising money for camp."
TEEN THROWING NEWSPAPERS EARLY IN A.M.	Some have even taken on extra work to raise the needed funds for the week of camp.
PASTOR BECKER AND OTHER STAFF MEMBERS IN STAFF CONFERENCE	This year, the church pastoral staff has proposed a new plan
YOUTH WORKERS TALKING WITH TEENS	to alleviate some of the financial strain on teens and their families. The new program is called
INVEST LOGO	Invest.

CONTINUED

video clips, stirring music, sound effects, riveting story line). Then allow students to read through the video script "Invest in Teens" and discuss the format of the script (video on left, audio on right; video in phrases, audio in sentences; video in all capitals).

SCRIPTURAL APPLICATION

Direct the students' attention to Job 42:5 on page 200. Ask a volunteer to read it aloud. Explain that the progression from hearing to seeing has long been used as a symbol of greater understanding. Challenge the students to consider how this truth relates to the power of visual media. Explain that in a world in which God's speech comes through a book (and not through film or some other visual medium), it is important not to allow the sensibilities necessary for careful reasoning to erode. Even someone with a new heart from God can train his brain to expect the constant stimulation of visual media, failing to develop the mindset of an attentive reader. God wants us to "see" Him through hearing and reading His words.

TEACHING STRATEGY

Introduction

Ask students how the video assignment is different from the others in this text. (*It is visual as well as written.*) Discuss the importance of the visual medium by asking students to explain why they agree or disagree with the saying "A picture is worth a thousand words."

VIDEO	AUDIO
TEEN READING BIBLE	Each week teens involved in Invest will give time and energy to reading and memorizing God's Word
TEENS WITNESSING OR WORKING IN THE COMMUNITY	and to witnessing and service projects within the community.
PARENT AND TEEN LISTENING TO ANOTHER TEEN QUOTE SCRIPTURE	Parents and other interested persons will then be asked to reinvest in the teens of the church
ADULT AND TEEN PRAYING TOGETHER	by helping with memorization and partnering with specific teens.
PASTOR BECKER HANDING OUT AWARD CERTIFICATES AND CHECKS	Pastor Becker: "A portion of the church's offerings will be invested in teens who complete the semester-long Invest Program. ~~There are several levels to the program.~~ Teens can earn the registration fee as well as the entire camp sum. ~~Some will obviously earn more than others.~~"
INVEST LOGO	Further information is available in brochures to be handed out following the meeting.

WRITING

Video Report

I have heard of thee by the hearing of the ear: but now mine eye seeth thee.
Job 42:5

Documentaries or news reports like this one about a church's plan to help fund its teens' camp fees can explain many facts briefly and memorably. One's ability to observe closely and to view a topic or event through another's eyes is called upon as he decides both what his audience would *like* to see and what they *should* see about the topic.

Your Turn

Write and produce a two- to three-minute audiovisual report of either an event or a topic of importance to your church, family, or school. You may choose to create your report using video or presentation software. Do your best to capture for your audience the essence of the event or story.

Planning

✔ **Choose an event or topic to feature.** Remember that you have only two or three minutes; therefore, your topic must be something that can be adequately covered in the given time frame. Keep in mind that you must be able to record in person the event you choose, so an event like the Super Bowl or Tour de France is probably out of the question.

ESL An idea for a video report might be to show how to cook a popular food from your country.

OVERVIEW of the WRITING PROCESS

Planning—choosing an event, writing the main points, considering specifics, brainstorming for ideas, deciding on an angle, choosing a frame, and practicing with equipment

Drafting—scripting a report, making informed filming choices, shooting a report, and selecting sound effects

Revising—reviewing a report, rethinking visuals, editing a report, and checking for spelling and mechanical errors

Publishing—arranging for a viewing, hosting a film night, comparing and contrasting reports, or posting a report

Enrichment

View a documentary with students. Ask them to take notes on what makes the documentary memorable.

Note

You may wish to make this video report a class project rather than an individual one. If so, divide the various duties among the students: script writers, sound effects coordinators, narrator, cinematographers, props personnel, editors, and so on.

Planning Strategy

Discussion

Brainstorm together about ideas for the video report. Display all student suggestions. (If doing a class project, ask students to vote for their favorite.) Select one of the topic ideas to use as a model for the students. Display the main points for a story (e.g., science fair: researching the topic, conducting the experiment, making the display, competing in the fair).

Planning Strategy

Peer Response

Allow time for students to meet in small groups and to brainstorm about the report topics. Ask each student to write his topic at the top of a page. Then instruct the groups to brainstorm each of the topics represented by the members of their group. The student whose topic is being discussed should write the group's suggested ideas under his heading.

- ✔ **Jot down the main points of your story line.** For the "Invest in Teens" story, the author decided that the main points were the need, what teens have done in the past to raise money, and how the new plan could help. Listing the main points will help you to focus the details of your report on what is important.

tip

Think about the past (what led up to the event), present (the event), and future (how the event will affect people) when making a video report.

- ✔ **Consider your report.** Think about the main points you want to get across. Will your report proceed chronologically? Or will you need to give your audience some background information in order for them to understand your topic? Will it be possible to get sound bites (short statements edited from longer recordings) or video clips from past events?
- ✔ **Brainstorm for ideas.** Allow peers to assist you in thinking of ideas or facts that your report should include. Write these under the main points you decided upon earlier. Look for holes in the chronology or for places your audience might become confused and decide how to correct these problems.
- ✔ **Decide on an angle for the report.** Will you shoot your footage as an onlooker or as a participant? The "Invest in Teens" story appeared as though written by an impartial observer merely reporting the facts, but many news stories (especially so-called "undercover" stories) use the camera as a first-person eyewitness to or a participant in an event.
- ✔ **Choose a frame of reference for your report.** Decide whether you want to establish yourself as a "reporter" (as in a newscast) or whether you want to film your story more like a documentary. In a typical newscast, the reporter usually appears both at the beginning of the report and at the end—usually on location at the site of the event being recorded. If your equipment has editing capabilities, these segments can be shot at any time and edited into the report.
- ✔ **Practice with your equipment.** Before you go on location, acquaint yourself with the devices you will be using. What special effects can the equipment achieve? What are its limitations? Prepare yourself with extra supplies and make sure that the batteries are charged and the equipment is working correctly. Consider shooting a practice video before the event.

Thinking Biblically

Opera has been called the greatest art form because it combines grand stage drama and impressive music. By that measure, however, movies could be considered much more powerful. Certainly, for many, they are much more entertaining. This popularity of film is largely due to its power as an art form. Movies lift the audience out of their places, push them past the orchestra pit, and put them right into the action. Christians who seek to use this tool for God's glory must consider some current criticism. Christian films have been criticized for being overtly didactic to the point of jeopardizing plot and characterization for the sake of message. A Christian film maker must ask the question, how can I make my film entertaining without sacrificing Christian values? Can a thoroughly Christian movie balance artistry and message, entertainment and Christian worldview? One thing is certain: if such a film can be created, it will start with good writing.

Drafting

- ✔ **Script your report.** With some news stories you will need to write the script before you shoot. Decide what you want to say, and write text to tell your story. Use a format like the one on pages 199–200 for your script and for video ideas. If you will be using sound clips or footage that you already have, write a script that incorporates these smoothly. News stories generally use a more factual, declarative style than other types of writing. You will want to state your ideas directly and logically so that your audience will understand what you mean. The ideas about sentence logic in Chapter 14, pages 383–88, may help you as you script your report.

tip

News scriptwriters sometimes use all capital letters for one column in the script. This can help differentiate between the two columns at a glance.

Thinking Biblically

Here is a question about film writing to stoke class discussion: How can a Christian movie depict sin—like the Bible does—without making it entertaining or salacious? Suggested answer: Film is a very different medium from text; it will have to touch objectionable elements in a less direct way. But our world is fallen, and movies that make it seem otherwise (the story of *Pollyanna* has entered our lexicon as an example of this approach) will seem insipid and unreal.

ONE on ONE Allow time for your student to brainstorm on his topic independently. Then meet with your student, read his ideas, and then work together on his report topic.

Planning Strategy
Participation

Require students to place the ideas from the brainstorming session in chronological order. Instruct them to fill in any gaps.

Planning Strategy
Discussion

Discuss the pros and cons of being a visible or invisible reporter (i.e., one who reports from the field or one who narrates the story from the studio). Ask students to decide which is most appropriate for their report.

Planning Strategy
Demonstration

Allow time in class for students to practice with the equipment they will be using. Encourage them to experiment with the lighting, the zoom feature, the date stamp, and any other features the camera might have.

Discuss flattering and unflattering camera angles. Include information on what various camera angles can convey about a reporter or a subject (e.g., a close-up, in-your-face angle may mean an antagonistic reporter or the pursuit of an elusive subject).

Remind students that a shaky camera often makes obvious an amateur videographer. Encourage students to use a tripod or to steady an arm against something solid in order to keep the camera still.

✔ **Make informed choices.** Use the following chart to make important choices about lighting, framing, and so on, for your report.

Recording Considerations

Camera Movement	Will you hold the camera steady, or will you move it? How will either affect your message?
Editing	Will you use a **montage**, a technique that places a variety of images in close succession? Or will you record steadily through an event?
Framing	What will you include/exclude in your shot? Is there anything that you desire attention taken away from? What will your framing say about your viewpoint—is it neutral or biased?
Lighting	Can you control the lighting of your shot? If so, what will you emphasize or conceal with lighting? What kind of atmosphere will you create?
Music/Sound	What kind of mood do the sounds of your report establish?
Narration	Will you have one narrator or several? What kind of voice is appropriate for your story? Is there any type of voice that would be inappropriate?

✔ **Shoot your report.** Once you have your script, begin shooting footage to tell your story in pictures. Remember to use a variety of close-up and long shots. Avoid placing the camera in one locale and shooting everything from a single vantage point.

✔ **Select sound effects.** Especially if your footage has no sound of its own, include some sounds you either record yourself or locate on a CD or online. (Avoid copyright infringement; some sound effects sources allow you to use the sounds however you wish.) For example, the writer of the "Invest in Teens" report could have added water sounds or sounds of leaves being raked or newspapers hitting the floor to his list of audio effects.

Revising

✔ **Review your report.** Look at your script and your footage again. If possible, get opinions from others, especially eyewitnesses to the event you are covering. Look for places that your story is weak or inaccurate. Make sure that all sound effects and music cues add to, not detract from, the story.

✔ **Rethink the visuals.** Are any of your visuals merely "talking head" visuals? Think of ways that are unusual or interesting to illustrate your report. For example, the "Invest in Teens" report could show a close-up of leaves before pulling back to a shot of the person raking.

Enrichment

Ask an expert to discuss lighting, camera angles, and so on with the students. Ask him to demonstrate proper technique for the type of equipment that will be used.

Drafting Strategy

Modeling

Use Writing Worksheet 8A (Teacher's Toolkit) as a sample template to model a video report script. Distribute copies to the students and complete a sample for display.

Writing Workshop

Conduct a minilesson on sentence logic (pp. 383–84). Discuss the importance of saying things clearly and concisely and placing words correctly in sentences.

Drafting Strategy

Participation

Use Writing Worksheet 8B (Teacher's Toolkit) to help students make informed choices for the video report. Distribute a copy to each student.

Drafting Strategy

Analysis

Ask students to notice when a new shot is called for in the sample video report on pages 199–200. *(at the beginning of a new thought)* Caution the students that switching shots only when there is a new sentence makes the flow of the video very stilted.

✔ **Edit your report.** If the equipment allows for editing, cut and paste your piece after you identify places that need tightening or moving. Add or delete sound cues accordingly. Note that in the "Invest in Teens" script some words have been crossed out. Use this option to help you remember the context of the parts you are keeping should you desire to reconstruct part of the speech later.

tip

Beware of too much cutting and pasting, especially with someone else's words. You might end up misrepresenting a person or an issue.

✔ **Check the spelling of text that appears in the report.** Nothing is more distracting to a viewer than a glaring spelling or punctuation error in giant print on the screen. Read carefully any text—title, quotations, and so on—for mechanical errors.

Publishing

✔ **Arrange for a school-wide viewing.** Allow your principal to preview your report and ask about a showing for the whole school—especially if the event you covered has significance for the students.

✔ **Host a premier night.** Show several of the video reports from your class at a video night. Invite special guests who were involved in the recordings to attend and to answer questions afterwards.

✔ **Compare and contrast reports.** After viewing reports on the same topic, use the guidelines for comparison/contrast writing discussed in Chapter 3 to discuss (or write about) similarities and differences among the reports. Comment on how the point of view changes from report to report.

✔ **Post your report.** If your report is a digital file, post it on a website—yours or your class's.

Some Ideas to Consider

History

- Produce a history of an event in your community, school, or family.

Government

- Cover election night after a local political race.

Art

- Document a visit to a local arts festival.

USAGE

Pronoun Use

Pronoun Case

Pronouns show one or more of four characteristics: person, number, gender, and case. Personal pronouns, the most common, show all four characteristics. Case is probably the characteristic that gives writers the most difficulty. An understanding of the three cases—subjective, objective, and possessive—is important for clear, correct writing.

OBJECTIVES

Students will

1. use subjective, objective, possessive, and independent possessive pronouns correctly.
2. distinguish between subjective, objective, possessive, and independent possessive pronouns.
3. choose the correct case for pronouns functioning as or with appositives.
4. identify the correct pronoun in a construction using *than* or *as*.
5. select the pronoun with the correct case to use with a gerund or an infinitive.
6. choose correctly between *who* and *whom* in sentences.
7. differentiate between the use of reflexive and intensive pronouns.
8. correct sentences exhibiting incorrect reflexive or intensive pronouns or incorrect courtesy order.
9. choose the correct pronoun to avoid shifts in person and number.
10. revise sentences to correct shifts in pronoun person and number.
11. revise a paragraph for agreement, verb usage, and pronoun usage errors.

Revising Strategy

Peer Response

Encourage students to view one another's reports. Instruct the peer responders to comment on whether any sound effects are distracting or confusing and to suggest changes or additions.

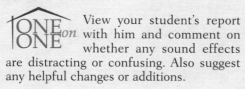

ONE on ONE View your student's report with him and comment on whether any sound effects are distracting or confusing. Also suggest any helpful changes or additions.

Revising Strategy

Discussion

Remind students that refilming some events is not possible. However, they can add still shots or graphic devices.

Revising Strategy

Discussion

Emphasize the tip on page 203. Remind students that honest reporting includes putting a person's deeds and words in context so as not to misrepresent him.

Revising Strategy

Motivation

Display these examples of spelling errors missed by a computer spellchecker: *Her professor's onion was important.* (opinion) *After his fried read the book, John decided to read it to.* (friend *and* too) Emphasize the importance of proofreading.

Evaluation

For help in grading this assignment, see "Grading Student Writing" (p. v) and Writing Rubric 8 (Teacher's Toolkit).

Some grammar textbooks use the term *nominative* in place of *subjective*. If students are familiar with the term *nominative*, explain that the two terms are synonymous when referring to English pronoun case.

ESL Referring ESL students to Sentence Patterns (Chapter 3) might help them to associate *subjective* with *subjects* and *objective* with *objects*. Tying new material together with previously learned material often helps with understanding. Also, seeing the more formulaic sentence patterns and how they relate to subjective and objective pronouns may help them understand the textbook and the exercises.

ESL For Spanish speakers the term *possessive* can be related to *posesivo*, its Spanish counterpart.

General Principles

Pronouns pp. 37–40

Use **subjective case** pronouns—*I, we, you, it, he, she,* and *they*—for subjects and predicate nouns.

We watched a debate between the two gubernatorial candidates.

Tyler and *she* could not stay for the entire debate.

It was *I* who answered the campaign phone.

Informal speech often uses the objective case for a predicate noun. In formal written or spoken English, only the subjective case is acceptable for predicate nouns.

Use the **objective case** pronouns—*me, us, you, it, him, her,* and *them*—for direct objects, indirect objects, and objects of prepositions.

Local reporters called *me* for an interview.

Did they give John and *you* a list of questions before the interview?

Campaign organizers forwarded the list of volunteers to *me*.

As a result of hard work and positive campaigning by *you* and *them,* our candidate won by a large majority.

Gerund Phrases p. 97

Use the **possessive case** to show ownership and other close relationships. Possessive case pronouns can have two forms. The more common forms—*my, our, your, its, his, her,* and *their*—modify nouns.

Your idea to campaign on specific issues was a successful one.

Why did the press dislike *his* approach to the campaign?

ESL The form that shows ownership (possessive) can show a number of other relationships. Here are some of the relationships expressed by possessives.

Ownership	That is *their* dog. (They own it.)
Doer of Action	*Her* sharp words were inappropriate. (She spoke sharp words.)
Producer	I like *his* colorful paintings. (He produced the paintings.)
Object of Action	Praise is *her* reward. (People rewarded her.)
Family Relationship	He will live with *his* cousins this summer.
Representation	I like *your* graduation photo. (It represents you.)
Others	What is *your* address?
	Mr. and Mrs. Hedican watch *their* health.

Pronouns pp. 37–40

Use the **independent possessive** form of a pronoun—*mine, ours, yours, its, his, hers,* and *theirs*—to stand alone as a subject, predicate noun, or object.

Subject	*His* was the best campaign advice to follow.
Predicate Noun	The feeling of skepticism was *mine*.
Direct Object	I thought our plan for education was good, but the newly elected governor chose *theirs* instead.

Publishing Strategy

Participation

Arrange a schoolwide viewing of the video reports. Challenge students to prepare supplemental materials (e.g., a list of sources or website links) for distribution and to develop a survey for viewers' comments.

ONE on ONE Arrange a public viewing of your student's video report. In addition, encourage your student to provide additional information and surveys on the featured event or topic.

Publishing Strategy

Discussion

Arrange for students to view their classmates' video reports and to compare and contrast the reports. Ask students to remark on the various points of view represented by different videographers.

ONE on ONE Invite family or friends to a showing of your student's work. Allow your student to share specific decisions he made and techniques he employed.

PRONOUN USE

Lesson Support

Student Worktext

Chapter 8 Review—pp. 445–47

Teacher's Toolkit

Chapter 8 Pretest
Teaching Help 8
Concept Reinforcements 8A–8C
Bulletin Board 8

ESL

Most possessive modifiers make the noun definite in meaning—that is, the noun refers to a specific person or thing. *Her pencil* is a specific pencil, and *my cousin* is a specific person. However, a special construction with independent possessives enables us to express possession and yet keep the noun indefinite.

I borrowed **a pencil of hers** yesterday (some pencil that she owns).
Jennifer taught piano lessons to **a cousin of mine** (an unspecified one of my cousins).

As you see, this is the construction for possession of indefinite nouns:

a/an + noun + *of* + independent possessive

in SUMMARY

Use **subjective case pronouns** for subjects and predicate nouns. In formal English usage, the objective case is not used for a predicate noun.

Use **objective case pronouns** for direct objects, indirect objects, and objects of prepositions.

Use **possessive case pronouns** to show ownership and other close relationships.

Use the **independent possessive** form of a pronoun to stand alone as a subject, a predicate noun, or an object.

8.1 PRACTICE *the skill*

Underline each personal pronoun and identify it as subjective *(S)*, objective *(O)*, possessive *(P)* or independent possessive *(IP)*.

S 1. Have you ever considered volunteering to help a camp ministry?

IP 2. Uncle Del's favorite ministry is working at the rescue mission; mine is serving at Camp Calvary.

P 3. Camp Calvary's staff needed some help to get the camp ready for its busy summer.

O 4. The Lord gave me a burden to help by doing any job, no matter how small.

S 5. Kevin and I swept the miniature golf course free of fallen leaves.

O 6. The waterslide looked more inviting after several of us cleaned it.

P 7. One teen with artistic ability painted our camp theme onto a mural.

IP 8. For supper the experience of having a lakeside barbecue was ours.

O 9. The camp director, Pastor Reece, thanked us for helping and then shared the history of the camp.

P 10. After the staff had worked all day at the camp, our thoughts turned to the privilege of Christian ministry.

Test

Chapter 8 Test

SCRIPTURAL APPLICATION

Display Jeremiah 7:23 and ask students to find each pronoun and to identify its case. "But this thing commanded I *(sub)* them *(obj)*, saying, Obey my *(poss)* voice, and I *(sub)* will be your *(poss)* God, and ye *(sub)* shall be my *(poss)* people: and walk ye *(sub)* in all the ways that I *(sub)* have commanded you *(obj)*, that it *(sub)* may be well unto you *(obj)*." Point out God's commands and promises and discuss the importance of developing a personal relationship with God. What encouragement and humility result from knowing that He has promised to be our God! Use this opportunity to call attention to inverted order (see p. 71) as displayed in the opening clause of the verse. Point out the archaic use of *ye*, meaning plural *you*, and be prepared to give other examples of archaic pronouns in the Scriptures. *(thou, thee)*

TEACHING STRATEGY

Discussion

Remind students that they must first determine a pronoun's function within the context of a sentence in order to know which case to use.

8.2 REVIEW *the skill*

Write an appropriate personal pronoun in the blank. Then identify the pronoun as subjective *(S)*, objective *(O)*, possessive *(P)*, or independent possessive *(IP)*.

You — *S* — 1. ? are probably familiar with the National Park Service that manages areas designated to the Department of the Interior.

its — *P* — 2 The National Park Service began ? duties in August of 1916.

it — *S* — 3. Since 1916 ? has determined areas to be national parks based on historical or scientific importance.

their — *P* — 4. Other areas have become national parks because of ? recreational importance.

mine — *IP* — 5. What is your favorite park? Glacier National Park is ?.

them — *O* — 6. In some parks, flowers are abundant; a visitor can see ? during several months of the year.

its — *P* — 7. The purpose of the park service is to conserve wildlife, scenery, and natural objects; ? success has been outstanding.

them — *O* — 8. Large numbers of visitors have made the park system successful; many of ? visit year after year.

they — *S* — 9. Park employees have varied responsibilities; ? oversee the more than 83 million acres that make up the park system.

them — *O* — 10. Many of the 375 national parks are open throughout the year; some of ? close in the winter because of weather.

Appositives

Pronouns in subject and object positions may be renamed by appositives. The appositive noun does not affect the case of the pronoun.

> S InV
> At the senior class retreat, we *seniors* listened closely to the evangelist's challenge.

> S TrV DO
> He challenged us *teenagers* about living for Christ.

Pronouns may function as appositives. The case of an appositive pronoun should match the case of the word that it renames.

> S TrV
> The senior class officers—Jim, Sharon, and *I*—appreciated the evangelist's
> DO
> concern for our class.

> S TrV DO
> His enthusiasm for the gospel encouraged several soccer players—Robert, Stephen, and *him*.

Adverb Clauses p. 122

Comparisons Using *Than* or *As*

S-V Agreement pp. 148–61

The subordinating conjunctions *than* and *as* introduce dependent clauses of comparison. Often the second part of the comparison is "understood." In order to choose the correct pronoun case after *than* or *as*, determine how the pronoun would function in the full understood clause.

TEACHING STRATEGY
Participation

Ask students to identify the function of the italicized words in the sentences on page 204. Point out that identifying sentence patterns helps to determine the function of a word in the sentence. *(In the sentence "The history teacher gave us his favorite lecture yesterday,"* us *functions as the indirect object and is in the objective case.)*

TEACHING STRATEGY
Induction

Call attention to the fact that *between* is a preposition. Direct students to supply the missing pronoun in the expression *between you and* ___. *(me)* Ask volunteers to explain their choice. *(Because* between *is a preposition, its object must be in the objective case.)* Lead students to understand that saying *between you and I,* although a widespread practice for many English speakers, is an error of pronoun case. Encourage students to be correct in their usage.

TEACHING STRATEGY
Discussion and Participation

Point out that the pronouns *we* and *us* (as seen in the first two examples on p. 206) are the most common pronouns to be followed by appositives. Tell students to write two sentences incorporating appositives for *we* and *us*. Ask for volunteers to read their sentences aloud.

My closest friend was more eager to work at camp than *I*. (than *I* was [eager to work at camp])

But I am now as happy about working there as *he*. (as *he* is [happy about working there])

In some sentences the meaning of the sentence will determine the pronoun that you use.

The youth sponsor encourages the new converts as much as *I*. (as much as *I* [encourage the new converts])

The youth sponsor encourages the new converts as much as *me*. (as much as [he encourages] *me*)

ESL

English speakers often say the *be* verb or the auxiliary after the subject pronoun of the implied comparison, as in the first two examples above.

My closest friend was more eager to work at camp than **I was.**

Following this practice can help you choose the correct pronoun form.

in SUMMARY

The **appositive noun** does not affect the case of the pronoun it renames.

The case of an appositive pronoun is determined by the case of the noun it renames.

Determine the case of a pronoun after *than* or *as* by determining how the pronoun would function in the full understood clause.

8.3 PRACTICE *the skill*

Underline the correct pronoun from the choices in parentheses.

1. *(We, Us)* campers still rely upon an invention of the late 1800s.
2. During our last camping trip, the flashlight prevented us—Rob, Isaiah, and *(I, me)*—from getting lost when darkness settled more quickly than we had anticipated.
3. During the long hike back to the campsite, Rob entertained *(we, us)*, his audience, with the history of the flashlight.
4. Although inventor David Misell thought he had developed a mere bicycle lamp, his employer, Conrad Hubert, had a better idea than *(he, him)*.
5. Hubert remodeled his employee's patented bicycle lamp into the long torchlike beam so valuable to *(we, us)* today.
6. Isaiah interrupted Rob's lesson to tell how they—his family and *(he, him)*—like to take late night bike rides using modern bike lights.
7. Hubert donated many of his prototype flashlights to New York City policemen because he wanted to make others as interested in his invention as *(he, him)*.
8. Although Hubert failed at selling his earlier inventions (illuminated tie racks and flowerpots), his persistence inspired *(we, us)* boys to pursue our dreams.

TEACHING STRATEGY
Discussion and Participation

Remind students that the correct pronoun case for appositive constructions depends upon whether the appositive construction renames a subject or an object. Display the following sentence: *The orchestra director gave the winning participants, Joel and ___, the trophies.* Ask a volunteer to choose the correct pronoun and to give the reason for the choice. (me; *the appositives rename the indirect object* participants.) Instruct students to write a sentence with a subjective case appositive. Then direct them to evaluate each other's sentences for accuracy.

ONE *on* ONE Instruct your student to write a sentence with a subjective case appositive. Then ask him to explain why his pronoun choice is correct.

TEACHING STRATEGY
Discussion and Participation

Lead a discussion about camping. Ask students to tell about their camping experiences in a tent, in a pop-up trailer, in a travel trailer, or in a motor home. After a discussion of these experiences, instruct students to write a sentence that expresses a comparison between two modes of camping. Direct them to use at least one personal pronoun in a clause beginning with *than* or *as*. Ask volunteers to read their sentences and direct others to explain why the subjective case or the objective case was correct.

9. Because we knew that the first flashlights could not produce a continuous beam of light, (*we, us*) hikers figured out how the flashlight got its name.

10. After Rob gave us—Isaiah and (*I, me*)—a demonstration of the original flashlight, we all were much more thankful for our modern ones.

8.4 USE *the skill*

Rewrite any sentence that contains an error in pronoun usage. If the sentence is already correct, write *C* in the blank. *(Answers may vary.)*

1. My entire family—Mom, Dad, my two sisters, and me—visited Yellowstone National Park.

   My entire family—Mom, Dad, my two sisters, and I—visited Yellowstone National Park.

2. Extending into Idaho, Montana, and Wyoming, the park provided we five a vast expanse for camping and exploration.

   Extending into Idaho, Montana, and Wyoming, the park provided us five a vast expanse for camping and exploration.

3. My sisters did not like the park as much as me.

   My sisters did not like the park as much as I did.

4. Yellowstone, the oldest park in the system, has many activities for we students.

   Yellowstone, the oldest park in the park system, has numerous activities for us students.

5. My sister Julie, who usually has a much shorter attention span than I, enjoyed watching the Old Faithful geyser for forty-five minutes.

   C

208 Chapter 8 | Pronoun Use

6. Several cranes in a nearby pond gave my sister and me an entertaining afternoon.

C

7. My sisters laughed at us when Dad and me imitated the bugle call of an elk.

My sisters laughed at us when Dad and I tried to imitate the bugle call of an elk.

8. One exciting sight for my sisters and I was the grizzly and black bears that we saw in the distance.

One exciting sight for my sisters and me was the grizzly and black bears that we saw in the distance.

9. My sisters needed a storage pole at their backpacking campsite as much as I.

C

10. Boating and hiking were other activities enjoyed by the family—Mom, Dad, my two sisters, and I.

Boating and hiking were other activities enjoyed by the family—Mom, Dad, my two sisters, and me.

- Appositive - noun or pronoun that modifies another noun or pronoun
- Gerund - verb that functions as a noun
  Ex: Sarah enjoys singing.

"Subjects" and Objects of Verbals

Pronouns with Gerunds

A noun or pronoun that precedes a gerund and acts as its "subject," or doer, is in the possessive case. The "subject" of the gerund is the doer of the gerund's verb meaning. A common error places an objective case pronoun rather than a possessive case pronoun before a gerund.

Gerund Phrases p. 97

(S) The *students'* leaving the service early (TrV) discouraged (DO) Pastor Allen.

(S) We students (TrV) noticed *their* (DO) leaving during the invitation.

In these sentences, the students' action of leaving is the focus, not the students themselves. The possessive form before the gerund is correct.

Teaching Strategy

Induction

Display the following sentences:

- The camp counselor was not happy with *(us, our)* coming late to the cabin. *(our)*
- Did you see *(him, his)* waiting for us on the cabin porch? *(him)*
- We were motivated to do better by *(him, his)* recounting of our responsibilities. *(his)*
- During our counselor's devotion time one day, we heard *(him, his)* praying for each of us. *(him)*

Ask students to choose the correct pronoun and to explain their choice. *(In each sentence the student must determine whether emphasis is on the actor or the action.)*

Then display these sentences:

- Carl's most impressive quality is *(he, his)* doing all things as unto the Lord. *(his)*
- Pastor Kent appreciates *(he, his)* looking for ways to serve. *(his)*
- *(He, His)* cleaning the church each Saturday shows Carl's behind-the-scenes devotion. *(His)*

Ask students to choose the correct pronoun and to explain their choice. *(In each sentence the pronoun is the subject of a gerund and, therefore, must be in the possessive case.)*

The "subject" of a gerund is different from a noun or pronoun that is followed and modified by a participial phrase.

S LV PN
Pastor Allen's *preaching* was a challenge to many teens.

S TrV DO
Did you see him preaching to the teens?

The first example shows a possessive acting as the "subject" of a gerund. The main idea of the sentence is *what he was doing*—preaching the gospel. The last example shows a pronoun functioning as the direct object and being modified by a participial phrase. The sentence asks if you saw *him,* not what he was doing.

A pronoun that follows a gerund and acts as its object is in the objective case.

S LV PN S LV PN
Christ was the focus of the sermon; *trusting* ***Him*** is the only way to salvation.

S InV (OP) (OP)
The evangelist had prepared by *praying* earnestly for the students before *teaching* ***them*** this lesson from Scripture.

Pronouns with Infinitives

Infinitive Phrases
pp. 101–2

A pronoun that precedes an infinitive and acts as its "subject," or doer, is in the objective case.

S TrV DO
Pastor Allen wants ***us*** *to withstand* the temptations of the world.

S TrV DO
He urges ***us*** *to read* our Bibles daily.

In both examples the entire infinitive phrase functions as the direct object of the sentence. The objective case pronoun identifies the persons performing the action of the infinitive.

A pronoun that follows an infinitive and acts as its object is in the objective case.

S InV
We will go *to see* ***him*** for encouragement from God's Word.

S TrV DO
Pastor Allen would like *to give* ***them*** some encouragement.

A pronoun that follows a linking-verb infinitive must be in the same case as the earlier word that it is renaming. The pronoun *he* in the following sentence renames the subject of the main verb. The case, then, is subjective in formal usage.

The preacher had to be *he.*

The same pronoun case should be used for both the subject and object of a linking-verb infinitive. Since the subject of the infinitive is in the objective case, the pronoun that renames it must also be in the objective case.

The teens thought *him* to be *me.*

Everyone believed the leader to be *him.*

Teaching Strategy
Demonstration

In the first four example sentences under "Pronouns with Infinitives" on page 210, point out the infinitive phrases and their functions in the sentences. Then point out the pattern of the infinitive phrases themselves. Inform students that both the subject and the object of the infinitive should be in the objective case.

Teaching Strategy
Demonstration

Display the following sentences: *The highway patrolman was thought to be he. The patrolman mistook the criminals to be them.* Ask students to identify each pronoun and its antecedent. *(he/patrolman; them/criminals)* Then ask them to identify the case of the pronoun and the function of the antecedent. *(He is subjective and renames the subject* patrolman; them *is objective and renames* criminals, *the doer of the infinitive.)* Inform them that a pronoun that follows a linking-verb infinitive should be in the same case as the word it renames. Consult *The Writer's Toolbox* for more information.

Who and *Whom*

The pronouns *who* and *whom* follow the same principles as personal pronouns do. The subjective case pronouns *who* and *whoever* function as subjects or predicate nouns. Use the objective case pronouns *whom* and *whomever* as objects. When the pronoun appears in a dependent clause, the case of the pronoun is determined by its function within the clause, not by the function of the dependent clause.

Pronouns
pp. 37–38

Clauses
pp. 126–28

S LV PN
Who is the new president of the youth group?

S LV PN DO S TrV
He is the one *whom* we met at camp last week.

S InV (OP) S TrV DO
Sam voted for *whoever* would do the best job.

(OP) S TrV DO
For *whom* did you cast your vote?

S TrV DO DO S TrV
My friends will support *whomever* the youth group elected.

In sentences with parenthetical expressions such as *do you think, I believe,* or *did they say,* ignore the parenthetical expression when you determine the function and case of *who/whom.*

DO S TrV
Whom do you think he will choose as his assistant? *(He will choose whom?)*

S LV PN S LV PN
He is the one *who* I believe is the better choice. *(who is the better choice)*

S LV PA
Who did they say is most capable to lead the group? *(Who is most capable?)*

ESL

As you may have noticed, in colloquial English (informal conversation) there is a strong tendency to use *who* at the beginning of all questions, regardless of its function. In written and formal use, however, you should follow the rules stated here in the text.

INFORMAL	Who did you meet?
FORMAL	Whom did you meet?

in SUMMARY

Use a possessive case pronoun as the **"subject" of a gerund**. Use an objective case pronoun as the **object of a gerund**.

Use an objective case pronoun as the **"subject" or object of an infinitive**.

A pronoun that follows a linking verb infinitive must be in the same case as the earlier word that it is renaming.

Use ***who*** and ***whoever*** for subjects and predicate nouns.

Use ***whom*** and ***whomever*** for direct objects, indirect objects, and objects of prepositions.

When *who* or *whom* appears in a dependent clause, the case of the pronoun is determined by its function within the clause, not by the function of the dependent clause.

Ignore parenthetical expressions when you determine the function and case of *who* and *whom*.

TEACHING STRATEGY

Discussion

Share with the students the following common aid in determining the correct use of *who* and *whom* in sentences: Isolate the dependent clause of the sentence and insert *he* for *who* and *him* for *whom.* Explain that the correct word *(he* or *him)* will usually "sound" right. (The patrolman asked *who* was driving the car. *He* was driving the car. The speeding ticket is for *whom?* The speeding ticket is for *him.*) Ask the students to explain why this aid typically works in sentences. (Who *and* he *are subjective pronouns and* whom *and* him *are objective pronouns. Each pronoun case occupies its respective role in a sentence: subjects and predicate nouns with subjective case pronouns; direct objects, indirect objects, and objects of the preposition with objective case pronouns.)*

8.5 PRACTICE *the skill*

Underline the correct pronoun from the choices in parentheses.

1. A teen *(who, whom)* attends a Christian camp often makes life-changing decisions.
2. Parents may pray for the teen, *(who, whom)* they hope will serve the Lord.
3. *(Him, His)* being set apart from the distractions of home, school, and friends helps him to focus on spiritual issues.
4. Spiritual messages challenge *(whoever, whomever)* the Holy Spirit convicts.
5. Giving *(they, them)* a chance to focus on Christ is the purpose of setting aside time for campers to read the Bible and pray.
6. As a result of Christ-honoring preaching, many teens purpose to serve *(He, Him)*.
7. God directs *(whoever, whomever)* is willing to be a missionary, a preacher, a teacher, or a Christian lay worker.
8. *(They, Their)* serving God requires eliminating habits that would hamper their testimonies.
9. Many teens are helped by those to *(who, whom)* they go for counsel and prayer.
10. After a teen's week at a Christian camp, *(him, his)* following through on a decision to yield his life to Christ is most important.

8.6 REVIEW *the skill*

Underline each pronoun that represents a case error in "subjects" or objects of verbals or in *who* and *whom*. Write the correction in the blank. If the sentence is already correct, write *C* in the blank. *(Answers may vary.)*

whoever 1. Recreational vehicles vary in purpose and design in order to meet the needs of whomever wants one of them.

them 2. After talking with some families, a salesperson often expects they to choose a conversion van.

Our 3. Us considering a camper is a big step for our family.

212 Chapter 8 | Pronoun Use

Teaching Strategy

Participation

Before students complete Teaching Help 8 (Teacher's Toolkit) or Concept Reinforcement 8C (Teacher's Toolkit), suggest that they mentally change questions into statements where possible. For example, change *To whom did you give the extra books?* to *You gave the extra books to whom?* This strategy can make grammatical analysis of the sentence easier.

Reinforcement

Use Bulletin Board 8 (Teacher's Toolkit) to reinforce the principles of courtesy order.

C ______ 4. Whoever buys a motor home can choose from a variety of designs.

who ______ 5. A boat may be a good choice for the person <u>whom</u> enjoys activities on the water.

Whom ______ 6. <u>Who</u> should the choice of a nonmotorized or motorized boat be given to?

his ______ 7. Dad, viewing the variety of boat choices—speedboats, ski boats, sailboats, and cruising boats—realized that <u>him</u> choosing a boat was going to be difficult.

C ______ 8. Noticing him near the boats was the salesperson's cue to approach us.

C ______ 9. The salesperson told him to buy the most expensive boat because it is, of course, the best.

Whom ______ 10. <u>Who</u> do you think Dad listened to, the salesperson or his own reason?

Pronoun Courtesy Order

Correct courtesy order is necessary when you join a personal pronoun with another personal pronoun or a noun. Be sure to observe these two rules. In a compound construction, mention yourself last.

Say	Senator James wants *Thomas and me* to make campaign calls tonight.
Not	Senator James wants *me and Thomas* to make campaign calls tonight.

Second, mention your hearer before anyone, unless the emphasis of the sentence is otherwise.

Say	*You, Thomas, and I* should help the senator win the election.
Not	*Thomas, you, and I* should help the senator win the election.

Reflexive and Intensive Pronouns

Reflexive and intensive pronouns are personal pronouns that have *-self* or *-selves* as a suffix. A **reflexive pronoun** is used as an object—direct object, indirect object, or object of the preposition—only when it refers to the same person or thing as the subject of the clause. It can never be used as a subject. An **intensive pronoun** is used only as an appositive to emphasize a noun or another pronoun in the sentence. Do not use a reflexive or intensive pronoun in place of a regular personal pronoun.

Wrong	The candidate assured the workers of his commitment to *themselves.*
Right	The candidate assured the workers of his commitment to *them.*
Right	The campaign workers should applaud *themselves* for their efforts.

Pronouns
p. 40

Teaching Strategy

Discussion

Remind students that pronouns ending in *-self* or *-selves* must have antecedents in the same sentence.

Pronoun Use | Chapter 8 213

Appositive Pronouns p. 40

Wrong	Sylvia and *myself* listened to the speech carefully.
Right	Sylvia and *I* listened to the speech carefully.
Right	The candidate *himself* will be visiting our area again tomorrow.

Only certain personal pronouns can have *-self* or *-selves* as a suffix. Words such as *ourself, themself, theirself, theirselves,* and *hisself* are incorrect and should be replaced with the correct forms: *ourselves, themselves, himself.*

Wrong	Senator James made all the campaign arrangements *hisself.*
Right	Senator James made all the campaign arrangements *himself.*

in SUMMARY

In a compound construction, mention your **hearer first** and **yourself last**.

Use a **reflexive pronoun** as an object only when it refers to the same person or thing as the subject of the clause.

Use an **intensive pronoun** as an appositive to emphasize a noun or another pronoun already in the sentence.

8.7 PRACTICE *the skill*

Underline the correct pronoun or pronoun group from the choices in parentheses.

1. While my family was visiting Hawaii, my parents gave (*me and my brother, my brother and me*) the opportunity to visit the Hawaii National Volcano Park.
2. We packed a lunch for (*ourselves, ourself*) and drove to the park, located near Hilo on the big island of Hawaii.
3. The park ranger showed (*ourselves, us*) this place with unusual foliage and land formations that became a national park in 1916.
4. My mother and (*I, me*) enjoyed seeing Mauna Loa, the earth's most massive volcano.
5. In addition to seeing Mauna Loa, my family and (*myself, I*) saw Kilauea, the earth's most active volcano.
6. My family learned for (*theirselves, themselves*) how scientists have gained insight into the formation of the Hawaiian Islands.
7. Since more than half of the park is wilderness area, my brother allowed (*himself, hisself*) several hours to hike some of the trails.
8. A unique opportunity for any visitors is to see for (*themselves, theirself*) that Kilauea still erupts.
9. Between (*me and you, you and me*), hearing that Kilauea is active scared me.
10. Our entire family enjoyed our vacation, even the volcanoes (*theirselves, themselves*).

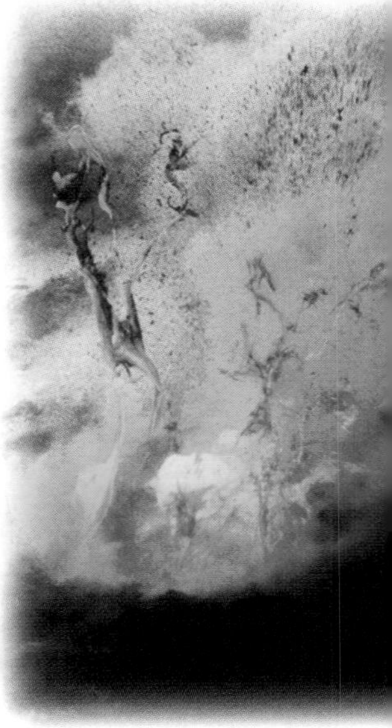

Evaluation

Ask students to identify the *-self* pronouns in Practice the Skill 8.7 as reflexive or intensive and to be prepared to explain their answers. *([2] reflexive, [6] reflexive, [7] reflexive, [8] reflexive, [10] intensive)*

Scriptural Application

Read 1 Kings 19:4. Ask students to identify the *-self* pronouns and their functions in the verse. *(himself, intensive; himself, reflexive)* Discuss the life of Elijah and his condition at this point. Remind students that God is still their provider and protector and has ordained the events of their lives for their good even when the students feel distraught and overwhelmed by circumstances (Phil. 4:19, Rom. 8:28).

Reinforcement

Display a chart illustrating pronoun person and number. Refer to *The Writer's Toolbox* for an example.

8.8 REVIEW *the skill*

Underline the part of the sentence that contains an error in courtesy order or in the use of reflexive or intensive pronouns. Write the correction in the blank. If the sentence is already correct, write *C* in the blank. *(Answers may vary.)*

you and me 1. Another park for me and you to visit is Mount Saint Helens National Park in Washington.

C 2. On May 18, 1980, the eruption that had begun about one mile beneath the earth's surface showed itself and lasted for nine long hours.

they 3. A group of students constructed an elaborate model of Mount Saint Helens based on what themselves had learned about the volcano that had been dormant since 1857.

me 4. A scientist told myself that the eruption caused the north face of the mountain to collapse.

himself 5. One student learned by hisself that almost 150 square miles of forest were destroyed or left dead but standing.

C 6. Thousands of game animals such as deer, elk, and bears had no chance to save themselves.

my friend and me 7. The visiting scientist explained to me and my friend that the volcano destroyed more than twelve million fish-hatchery salmon.

C 8. The eruption itself produced so much debris that the level of Spirit Lake rose sixty meters.

C 9. We learned that mudflows themselves deposited more than ninety-five million cubic yards of sediment in the Cowlitz and Columbia Rivers.

You and the scientist 10. The scientist and you discussed the implications of the Mount Saint Helens incident on the Creation/evolution debate.

Pronoun Shift

Clear writing keeps the reader focused on the writer's intended purpose. Since a shift in the person or number of a pronoun confuses the reader, a careful writer will be consistent in the use of pronouns.

Writing Link

After students complete Review the Skill 8.8, ask them to research another devastating volcano of the twentieth century and to write a four- to five-sentence paragraph on their findings. Tell them to be prepared to read their paragraphs aloud. Some possibilities include Novarupta, Alaska; Lassen Peak, California; Kilauea, Hawaii; Augustine Volcano, Alaska; Kamchatka, Russia; the Rat Islands near Alaska; and the Kuril Islands near eastern Russia.

Teaching Strategy

Discussion

Display the following sentences: *If one hears an unkind rumor, they should not be involved in spreading them further. When a Christian remembers their responsibility not to spread rumors, you will be practicing biblical principles.* Discuss what God has to say about talebearers (Prov. 11:13, 18:8). Then ask students to diagnose the problems in these sentences. *(The first sentence uses the singular subject* one *and the singular object* rumor *but uses* they *and* them *for pronoun reference. The second sentence uses the singular noun* Christian *but uses* their *and* you *for pronoun reference.)* Ask students to rewrite the sentences to make them correct. *(If one hears an unkind rumor, he should not be involved in spreading it further. When a Christian remembers his responsibility not to spread rumors, he will be practicing biblical principles.)*

S-V Agreement pp. 163–65

Shifts in Person

A shift in person often occurs when a writer refers to unnamed people. In these examples, notice the shift from one person to another and the possible corrections.

Shift If a *camper* remembers to bring the camp stove, *you* will be able to cook on the camping trip. *(third person to second person)*

Correction If a *camper* remembers to bring the camp stove, *he* will be able to cook on the camping trip.

If *you* remember to bring the camp stove, *you* will be able to cook on the camping trip.

Shift *Anyone* can forget that *you* need more than a camp stove. *(third person to second person)*

Correction *Anyone* can forget that *he* needs more than a camp stove.

In the last example, the corrected sentence also changes the verb form to match the person of the pronoun.

Shifts in Number

A shift in number occurs when a writer mixes singular and plural in the same general statement. Although most general statements can be either singular or plural, a problem occurs when the two are mixed.

Shift Campers need their sleeping bag for warmth.

Correction Campers need their sleeping bags for warmth.

A camper needs his sleeping bag for warmth.

Shift Anyone can forget their sleeping bag.

Corrections Anyone can forget his sleeping bag.

Campers can forget their sleeping bags.

In each example the shift in number can be corrected by making the sentence singular or plural throughout, depending on which meaning is appropriate.

in SUMMARY

When using pronouns to refer to unnamed people in general statements, avoid shifts in person and number.

8.9 PRACTICE *the skill*

Underline the correct pronoun from the choices in parentheses.

1. As a student reads the Old Testament, *(you, he)* might study Exodus 14, which records the Israelites' encamping between Migdol and the Red Sea.
2. If students could have seen Pharaoh, *(they, he)* would have seen a man who looked upon this encampment as the opportunity to destroy the Israelites.
3. When you read Exodus 11–12 carefully, *(one, you)* will see that Israel had escaped the final plague in Egypt, but the Egyptians had not.

Teaching Strategy

Discussion

Instruct students to analyze some writing excerpts in their journals or portfolios in order to identify problems with shifts in person and number.

Enrichment

After the students have completed Practice the Skill 8.9, share the following information with them. Moses warned the Egyptians that the tenth plague would be the death of the firstborn in every house. In order for the death angel to "pass over," the family had to apply the blood of an unblemished lamb on the doorposts of the house. The firstborn was then delivered from death. When a person accepts the shed blood of Christ on the cross and places his faith in the Savior, Christ delivers from sin and judgment to come.

John G. Foote wrote a gospel song about the Christian's deliverance by the blood of Christ. It includes this chorus: "When I see the blood, / When I see the blood, / When I see the blood, / I will pass, I will pass over you."

Ask students to identify the pronouns and their cases in the stanzas that follow and to be prepared to explain why the pronouns are correct.

Christ our Redeemer died on the cross,
Died for the sinner, paid all his due;
Sprinkle your soul with the blood of the Lamb,
And I will pass, will pass over you.

4. We know that *(we, you)* Christians, like the Israelites, have God's promises.

5. Anyone who reads *(their, his)* Bible can see that God's promise was to destroy the Egyptians.

6. In spite of God's promise, Israel feared when *(you, they)* saw the Egyptians.

7. The angel of the Lord went behind the encamped Israelites to protect *(it, them)*.

8. If you read Moses' account carefully, *(they, you)* will know that the pillar of cloud stood between the camp of Israel and the camp of the Egyptians.

9. Sometimes God asks Christians to encamp in a seemingly dangerous place, but His presence is always with *(you, them)*.

10. God may not always protect the Christian as He did Israel, but He promises to be with *(him, them)* always.

8.10 REVIEW *the skill*

Write the letter of the correct sentence in the blank.

B 1. A. Dad is considering our request for a rafting trip as they survey a vacation place for this year.
B. Dad is considering our request for a rafting trip as he surveys a vacation place for this year.

B 2. A. Not only does he want a cabin on a lake, but you also want a reputable rafting business nearby.
B. Not only does he want a cabin on a lake, but he also wants a reputable rafting business nearby.

A 3. A. When one plans a whitewater rafting adventure, he must choose the raft carefully.
B. When one plans a whitewater rafting adventure, they must choose the raft carefully.

B 4. A. Anyone who chooses a good raft makes their choice based on durability, performance, and safety.
B. Anyone who chooses a good raft makes his choice based on durability, performance, and safety.

A 5. A. If a person chooses fiberglass paddles, he will have paddles that handle the currents well.
B. If a person chooses fiberglass paddles, you will have paddles that handle the currents well.

B 6. A. For the rafter, gloves keep their hands safe and give them a sure grip.
B. For the rafter, gloves keep his hands safe and give him a sure grip.

A 7. A. Remind the rafters to have their life jackets fastened securely.
B. Remind the rafters to have your life jackets fastened securely.

Chiefest of sinners, Jesus will save;
All He has promised, that He will do;
Wash in the fountain opened for sin,
And I will pass, will pass over you.

Judgment is coming, all will be there,
Each one receiving justly his due;
Hide in the saving, sin-cleansing blood,
And I will pass, will pass over you.

O great compassion! O boundless love!
O loving kindness, faithful and true!
Find peace and shelter, under the blood,
And I will pass, will pass over you.

A 8. A. The rafter must choose a good helmet to protect his head.
B. The rafter must choose a good helmet to protect your head.

B 9. A. The novice rafter can choose rubber booties and a wet suit as their optional equipment.
B. The novice rafter can choose rubber booties and a wet suit as his optional equipment.

A 10. A. You must consider a rafting trip for your next vacation.
B. You must consider a rafting trip for one's next vacation.

8.11 CUMULATIVE *review*

Rewrite the following paragraph, correcting the ten errors from the following categories: agreement, verb use, pronoun case, courtesy order, reflexive and intensive pronoun use, and pronoun shift.

Camping along the Blue Ridge Parkway might be the ideal vacation for whomever enjoys the great outdoors. A tent camper's delight is his pitching his tent in a campground along this scenic highway. The Blue Ridge Parkway begin in Shenandoah National Park in Virginia and ends in the Great Smokies. If a person has the time, you can drive the entire distance of 355 miles. The traveler should take their time to see Grandfather Mountain. Just between me and you, the Lincove Viaduct, perhaps the most complicated segmented bridge ever built, is a breathtaking sight. During the spring, flowering plants such as the rhododendron, mountain laurel, and azalea provided a spectacular view for the visitor. Wildflowers also bloom profusely from spring through autumn. The ranger at Grandfather Mountain had given my brother and me a flower guide. I enjoyed seeing the wildflowers more than him. In part of the parkway area, travelers theirselves can pan for precious stones such as garnet, topaz, and sapphire. One might even find a gold nugget. A camper can enrich their mind at educational stops such as gem museums and the Moses H. Cone Memorial.

Camping along the Blue Ridge Parkway might be the ideal vacation for whoever enjoys the great outdoors. A tent camper's delight is his pitching his tent in a campground along this scenic highway. The Blue Ridge Parkway begins in Shenandoah National Park in Virginia and ends in the Great Smokies. If a person has the time, he can drive the entire distance of 355 miles. The traveler should take his time to see Grandfather Mountain. Just between you and me, the Lincove Viaduct, perhaps the most complicated segmented bridge ever built, is a breathtaking sight. During the spring, flowering plants such as the rhododendron, mountain laurel, and azalea provide a spectacular view for the visitor. Wildflowers also bloom profusely from spring through autumn. The ranger at Grandfather Mountain gave my brother and me a flower guide. I enjoyed seeing the wildflowers more than he did. In part of the parkway area, travelers themselves can pan for precious stones such as garnet, topaz,

REINFORCEMENT

Use Chapter 8 Review on pages 445–47 for additional test review.

EVALUATION

Use Chapter 8 Test to evaluate the students' understanding of the content and concepts of the chapter.

218 Chapter 8 | Pronoun Use

and sapphire. One might even find a gold nugget. A camper can enrich his mind at

educational stops such as gem museums and the Moses H. Cone Memorial.

FROM THE WRITTEN WORD

Recognizing the Differences

Think about the following: Abram and Lot, Jacob and Esau, light and darkness, good and evil, belief and unbelief. What comes to your mind? You probably think of these as being contrasting elements. Comparison (showing similarities) or contrast (showing differences) is a writing strategy evidenced throughout the Scriptures.

Consider Genesis 4:2–5, 8.

> And Abel was a keeper of sheep, but Cain was a tiller of the ground. And in process of time it came to pass, that Cain brought of the fruit of the ground an offering unto the Lord. And Abel, he also brought of the firstlings of his flock and of the fat thereof. And the Lord had respect unto Abel and to his offering: But unto Cain and to his offering he had not respect. And Cain was very wroth, and his countenance fell. . . . And Cain talked with Abel his brother: and it came to pass, when they were in the field, that Cain rose up against Abel his brother, and slew him.

When using the contrast writing strategy, you might need to make some concessions. For example, before you focus on the differences between Cain and Abel, you must recognize that they were alike. They had had the same parents and had grown up in the same home. They had observed the giving of animals for the covering of sin. With these concessions made, what do you observe about Cain and Abel?

Notice how the Scriptures show differences between Cain and Abel. Cain was a farmer and brought an offering to God that represented the work of his hands. God did not accept his offering. As a result, Cain was angry, jealous, and proud. Not only did he murder his brother, but he denied the murder and failed to seek forgiveness. Abel, on the other hand, was a shepherd and brought an offering that God accepted, an offering that satisfied God's plan. Abel was sincere, humble, and righteous. The point of contrast was not their occupations or their personalities, for God blesses both farmers and shepherds, and He blesses people of different personalities. The contrast grew out of the ways that these brothers approached redemption.

Personal Response

Read 1 Samuel 1:1–20 and Judges 13:2–24. Write a short paragraph comparing or contrasting the fathers of Samuel and Samson, Elkanah and Manoah, or the two mothers, Hannah and the unidentified mother of Samson.

TEACHING STRATEGY

Participation

Ask two students to read Judges 13:2–14 and 1 Samuel 1:1–20. Direct students to write a six to eight-sentence paragraph comparing and contrasting these passages. Remind students to include a topic sentence that establishes either comparison or contrast. Encourage them to use specific details from the Scriptures to support their topic sentence.

ENRICHMENT

Ask for volunteers to read their paragraphs aloud. Consider posting student writing for display in the classroom or on a class website or blog. Encourage students to share their paragraphs with their family.

OBJECTIVES

Students will

1. plan an application essay for college admission.
2. write an introduction that catches reader interest, introduces the topic, and draws attention to the main idea of the essay.
3. draft a direct, succinct application essay.
4. employ only specific details that focus on the purpose of the essay.
5. avoid sensationalism in writing the application essay.
6. revise to improve sentence variety and emphasis.
7. proofread the essay.
8. send essays to colleges that require such statements.

Chapter 9 Overview

Topic	Pages	Support Materials	Days
Clear Reference	225–28	Bulletin Board 9 Chapter 9 Pretest Teaching Help 9A Practice/Review the Skill 9.1–9.2	112
Referencing Modifiers or Implied Nouns	229–31	Practice/Review the Skill 9.3–9.4	113
Indefinite *It*, *They*, and *You*	232–33	Teaching Help 9B	114
Video Report	202–3	Writing Worksheets 8A–8B Writing Rubric 8	115–16, 121
Broad Reference	233–35	Practice/Review the Skill 9.5–9.6 Concept Reinforcement 9	117
Review	236	Cumulative Review 9.7	118
Critical Thinking Review	237 449–51	Chapter 9 Review	119
Chapter 9 Test			120
College Application Essay	221–23	Writing Rubric 9 Writing Worksheet 9	122–23

COLLEGE APPLICATION ESSAY

Lesson Support

Teacher's Toolkit

Bulletin Board 9
Writing Worksheets 9A–9B
Writing Rubric 9

A prospective college student must present himself in a way that gives the college officials confidence in his ideas and his ability to communicate them. Notice in the essay below how the writer positions himself as a candidate for acceptance in a missionary aviation major.

New Heights *by Dan Berber*

In the past, whenever I thought of my future, I envisioned myself piloting commercial jets across our country and around the world. I wanted an exciting career, and I believed that that profession would provide adventure and fulfillment. It was that same desire for excitement and adventure that prompted me to join others in my church on a mission trip to Kenya. Our trip was indeed exciting, but it was also life changing. I came home with a new sense of purpose and responsibility and a new definition of fulfillment.

In Kenya I saw little children lying helpless on grass mats, their stomachs distended from hunger; they will probably not live to be two years old. I saw adults willing to stand for hours under a blazing sun just to hear the Bible read in their own language. I knew for the first time how selfish I have been. I realized how much I have been given and how little I have given back. My thoughts of becoming a commercial pilot turned to thoughts of getting the gospel to people who have never heard God's Word. As a result I started to pray about being a missionary.

Looking through the catalog of your college, I saw the missionary aviation major. Everything I had been thinking suddenly came together.

I would like to enter the missionary aviation program. If accepted, I believe I would do well. I excel in math and mechanics and have a longstanding but refocused interest in flying. The Bible classes combined with the aviation classes would prepare me for the unique work of a missionary pilot.

Should the Lord lead me there, I would like to go back to Kenya someday to take the gospel to its people. And I would like to be the one flying the plane.

Literature Link

Ask students what they think colleges want in a personal application essay. Discuss with students how they feel writing about themselves. Ask them to discuss such personal kinds of writing experiences in light of their own writing successes and failures. Then read Dan Berber's example essay, "New Heights."

ENRICHMENT

Share these dates in the history of missionary aviation with students:

1943	three World War II pilots discuss missionary aviation
1946	first aircraft purchased for missionary work; first missionary flight (Mexico)
1950s	survey work in several parts of the world
1960s	continued survey work and missionary work around the world
1993	GPS (Global Positioning System) on missionary aircraft

SCRIPTURAL APPLICATION

Ask a student to read Ezra 7:10 aloud. Discuss the importance of being willing to obey God. Point out that Ezra prepared himself not only to recognize God's will but also to obey it. Ezra was both a prophet and a scribe, and God used his speaking and

Planning—looking through college catalogs, praying for God's guidance, narrowing the field of interest, choosing a field of study, making a word web, developing an outline, and thinking of the audience

Drafting—writing an introductory paragraph, drafting the essay, and keeping the goal in mind

Revising—reading the essay aloud, looking for ways to improve the presentation, asking a peer to read the essay, making changes to the essay, and proofreading the essay

Publishing—printing a copy, participating in a role-playing activity, selecting a title, and mailing the essay to a college

College Application Essay

For Ezra had prepared his heart to seek the law of the Lord, and to do it, and to teach in Israel statutes and judgments.

Ezra 7:10

Some colleges to which you apply will require that you write an essay during the application process. Most application essays should reveal something about the applicant: goals, desires, interests, strengths, and so on. When you write an essay as an application to college, you should give an accurate picture of yourself—not boastful but not overly modest either. Too much boldness about yourself will not make a good impression, but not being able to objectively assess your God-given abilities will also make your application less persuasive. Strive for a balance of what you can do and what you need to learn.

Your Turn

Choose a field of study and perhaps a college. Write an application essay, telling why you have made these choices and why you are a good candidate for the program.

Planning

- ✔ **Look through college catalogs.** Read about the programs that interest you. Imagine yourself taking some of the classes. Or investigate colleges online.
- ✔ **Prayerfully consider God's plan for you.** God has promised to lead His children. He often uses parents and other godly counselors, so enlist their help as you research colleges and majors. You will invest a great deal of time and money in the college you select, so your decision is important.
- ✔ **Narrow your field of interest.** Notice which programs you return to and those you pass over quickly. Which studies intrigue you the most? Which ones are you best suited for? Berber recognizes his strengths (math and mechanics). He is also looking ahead at how his strengths could be used for God. Can you think of ministries or careers that would follow the degree you are considering?
- ✔ **Choose a field of study.** For this assignment, settle on one major. If you already know where you want to go to college and what you want to study, this assignment might be used as part of your application. If you are still deciding, this assignment can help you focus your interests and practice for a later application.
- ✔ **Make a word web.** Draw a circle and label it with the major you have chosen. Draw other circles around the outside of the first circle and connect them to the inner circle with lines. In each outer circle, write reasons, examples, and experiences that could be used as support for your choice of that particular field of study.

writing skills to expound the law to the Israelites. Dan Berber in "New Heights" also prepared himself through prayer to recognize God's will. His application essay is evidence of his pursuing God's will. Allow the students to discuss ways they believe the Lord is directing them.

Planning Strategy

Modeling

Guide students in using college publications, including official websites, to learn about particular institutions. Encourage them to read introductory materials, philosophy statements, course listings, and course requirements to identify the true values of the college.

Scriptural Application

Encourage students to seek counsel from their parents and other trusted advisors about college plans. Ask volunteers to read these verses aloud: Proverbs 11:14; 15:22; Ephesians 6:1–3; and Hebrews 13:17.

Planning Strategy

Introduction

Direct students to look at Berber's account of his experience in Kenya. Notice that Berber focused on a single incident that changed his life. Instruct students to choose an appropriate aspect of their lives for the application essay. Personal subjects that are difficult to cover adequately or that are too personal are inappropriate.

Dan Berber's word web looked like this:

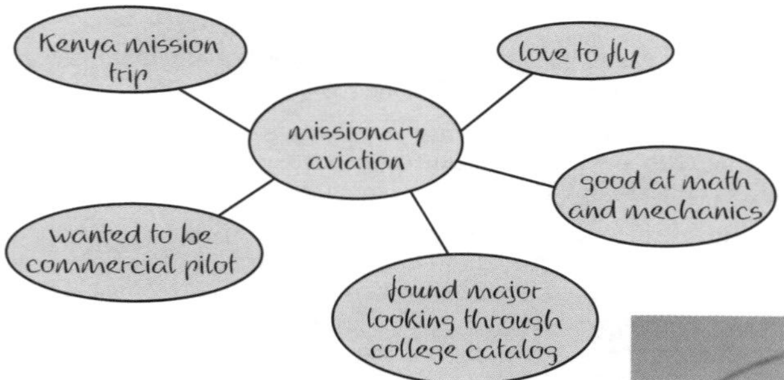

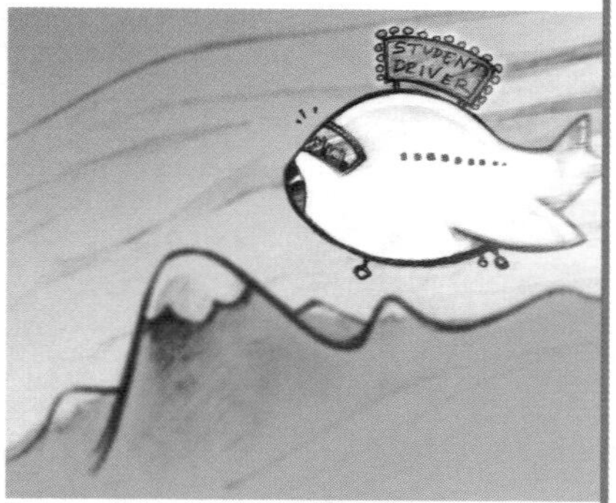

✔ **Develop an outline.** Decide how you will open the essay, how you will arrange the material in your word web, and how you will end the essay.

For example, Dan may have written something like this:

Opening: Change in goal to be a pilot
I. Experiences in Kenya
II. Desire to be a missionary
III. Interest in missionary aviation
Ending: Ultimate goal

tip

Try to end the essay with something that will encourage the reader to take a personal interest in you.

✔ **Think of your audience.** Remember that you are writing to someone who will decide whether you can enter the college. The essay should have a human-interest appeal. For example, do you think you would like Dan Berber? Why? He seems sincere and kind. Suppose he had written his essay as though to his friends? He might have sounded flippant to a college admissions official. Or suppose he had tried to sound more formal. He might have sounded stilted and impersonal, as well as stuffy and conceited.

Drafting

✔ **Write an introductory paragraph.** Remember the purposes of an introduction: to catch the reader's interest, to introduce the topic, and to draw attention to the main idea of the essay. Keep your opening interesting by using an appropriate quotation, a compelling question, or a memorable story. Look at two possibilities for Berber's introductory paragraph below. Which one catches your interest better?

Example 1

Last summer I went on a mission trip to Kenya with my church. When I set out, I was expecting a summer of adventure and new experiences. I came home, however, with a new sense of purpose and responsibility.

Example 2

In the past, whenever I thought of my future, I envisioned myself piloting commercial jets across our country and around the world. I wanted an exciting career, and I believed that that profession would provide adventure and fulfillment. It was that same desire for excitement and adventure that

Thinking Biblically

What role should a biblical worldview and Christian ideas play in a college application essay? In an application to a Christian college, a Christian's faith should obviously play a prominent role. But it should also be present in an application to a local state university if God leads a student there. Choosing to discuss controversial issues such as homosexuality and abortion in a college application is hardly exercising biblical wisdom (Prov. 25:15). But acting as if faith has nothing to do with a Christian's desire to go to college would also be wrong. A believer could state that his search for knowledge is based on the foundation of the fear of the Lord (Prov. 1:7). The applicant could also mention that his pursuit of engineering or nursing has Christian purposes—not just making money, but loving and serving others through his work.

Thinking Biblically

Perhaps have students write a paragraph for their college application essays in which they use Proverbs 1:7 to justify their chosen course of study in college. Students can use several angles, depending on whether they are aiming toward a secular university or a Christian one: (1) Because I fear the Lord, I seek to gain the knowledge I need to glorify Him and serve others with my gifts. (2) Because true knowledge requires accepting God as the foundation of all truth, I want to study in an environment that openly acknowledges Him. Encourage students to articulate specifically Christian reasons for their desire to study.

Planning Strategy
Motivation

Direct students to choose the field of study that they want to pursue in college. Reassure those who are undecided that this assignment will allow them to explore that field and to narrow their choices.

Planning Strategy
Discussion

Distribute copies of Writing Worksheet 9 (Teacher's Toolkit) for students to examine. Discuss the requirements.

Planning Strategy
Modeling and Participation

Ask students to suggest a field of study as an example in a word web. As students suggest supports, add those suggestions to the word web. Discuss the results and allow students to begin their own word webs. Then instruct them to develop an outline using the word web. Ask volunteers to share their outlines. Note any differences among the outlines and discuss their strengths and weaknesses.

ONE on ONE Instruct your student to develop an outline using the word web, while you do the same. Note any differences between the outlines and discuss their strengths and weaknesses.

prompted me to join others in my church on a mission trip to Kenya. Our trip was indeed exciting, but it was also life changing. I came home with a new sense of purpose and responsibility and a new definition of fulfillment.

Notice how the second paragraph makes the opening more interesting and focuses the reader on the main point: his new goal.

- ✔ **Draft your essay.** Be direct and succinct. Using your outline, write your essay in one sitting. Reserve your most convincing statement for your conclusion. What effect do you think Dan Berber's last sentence would have on the reader?
- ✔ **Be specific.** Berber's details about the people he saw will help the reader to envision what Berber saw in Kenya. An image of "children lying helpless" will affect the reader much as it did the writer. Berber struck a good balance between being specific and avoiding sensationalism. Had he continued to describe each detail of the conditions he witnessed, Berber might have alienated his audience.
- ✔ **Keep your goal in mind as you write.** Everything in your essay should advance your goal of being admitted to the college. In this case, less is probably more. If Berber had written three more paragraphs about his time in Kenya, his essay would not have been as focused and effective. Stay close to the topic at hand. Had Berber discussed his passion for spicy foods or his love of soccer, his essay would have been far less effective.

Revising

- ✔ **Read your essay aloud.** Pretend you are speaking to the admissions officer. Does the essay represent you well? Does it sound like your voice? Does it seem sincere? Are there any sentences that distract or confuse?
- ✔ **Look for ways to improve your presentation.** Look again at your opening. Does it make the reader want to read on? Dan Berber's opening has an element of suspense: he says he used to think one way, implying he has changed his position. The reader may be interested to see how. Does the essay flow well, uncluttered by unnecessary details? Does it gain power as it goes, ending with the strongest appeal?
- ✔ **Ask a peer to read the essay.** After he reads it, ask him whether he has any questions. Does he think the essay presents the true you? Get his opinion on your opening and closing. Ask for suggestions on improving the piece.
- ✔ **Make changes to the essay.** Compare your peer's response to your own ideas. Recast sentences or add material (or omit some) to strengthen your writing and improve your chances of being remembered well. Examine the first and second drafts of Berber's second paragraph. Notice the changes made by reworking the sentences and adding or omitting detail.

First Draft

I saw little children who were sick and who were hungry and who probably would not live to be two years old. Some of them had hardly any clothing or toys. I also saw people stand for hours in the heat to listen to someone read the Bible in their language.

Second Draft

In Kenya I saw little children lying helpless on grass mats, their stomachs distended from hunger; they will probably not live to be two years old. I saw adults willing to stand for hours under a blazing sun just to hear the Bible read in their own language. I knew for the first time how selfish I have been. I realized how much I have been given and how little I have given back. My thoughts of becoming a commercial pilot turned to thoughts of getting the gospel to people who have never heard God's Word. As a result I started to pray about being a missionary.

Planning Strategy
Discussion

Materials
- example college application essays

Display example college application essays (perhaps some that colleges post online as good examples) and discuss features that make the essays successful. Draw attention to features such as topic choice, level of diction (formal, semiformal, informal), and tone in light of the intended audience.

Drafting Strategy
Analysis

Ask students to identify the differences between Examples 1 and 2 from pages 223–24. *(Answers will vary.)*

Drafting Strategy
Discussion and Participation

Encourage students to ask themselves *Who? What? When? Where? Why?* and *How?* to develop specific ideas for the application essay. Remind them that an application essay should focus on personal qualities that they would like the college to know about them.

Drafting Strategy
Discussion

Emphasize that successful writing is clear and suited to the audience; therefore, the situation and purpose should determine the writing style. For an application essay, the writer should use a clear, formal style.

✔ **Proofread your paper.** Be sure that the spelling, mechanics, and grammar are impeccable. An error in any of these elements could seriously hinder your goal of being seen as college material.

Publishing

✔ **Print a perfect copy.** Be sure you have followed any guidelines you were given. Following instructions is an important skill that can set you apart.

tip

Avoid odd or hard-to-read fonts for an application essay. A plain serif font is a safe choice.

✔ **Submit your essay to the school counselor or principal.** It would be good to see how these people respond, especially if you are planning to submit it to a college.

✔ **Conduct a mock interview.** Ask another student to play a college admissions officer. Present the material in your essay to him during a mock interview.

✔ **If appropriate, select a title.** Some college admissions policies may require you to title your essay. If so, write one that is interesting and specific. For this type of essay, a short title is probably best. Berber's title, "New Heights," is taken from his essay and applies to the subject of flying as well as to his aspirations to attend college.

✔ **Mail your essay to a college.** If you are planning to apply to a college that asks for an essay, use your revised essay when you apply.

Some Ideas to Consider

History

- Write a college application essay for Abigail Adams or some other famous person. Try to write as that person might have.

Literature

- Write an application for an English or writing major. Tell what pieces of literature have inspired you to study in this field.

All subjects

- Write an application for any major. Tell what qualities you bring to the study and what you plan to do with the degree.

USAGE

Pronoun Reference

Although a few pronouns do not have antecedents (indefinite pronouns, mainly), most pronouns are understood as replacements for other words. The relationship between a pronoun and its antecedent (the noun or other pronoun that it replaces) must be clear if the reader is to understand the sentence. This relationship is often called **pronoun reference**, indicating that the pronoun refers to its antecedent. Follow the principles in this chapter to achieve correct pronoun reference.

OBJECTIVES

Students will

1. recognize pronoun reference problems.
2. rewrite sentences to correct ambiguous and remote pronoun reference.
3. rewrite sentences to correct reference to an implied noun and to a noun that is a modifier.
4. identify an unclear pronoun causing a reference problem.
5. identify sentences containing indefinite reference.
6. rewrite sentences to correct unclear or indefinite pronoun reference.
7. revise a paragraph containing faulty pronoun reference.

See *The Writer's Toolbox*.

Revising Strategy

Discussion

Discuss what Dan Berber's essay reveals about Berber's personality. *(Answers will vary.)* Encourage each student to read his own essay aloud before he revises, checking for tone, sincerity, clarity, and faithfulness to his own personality and interests.

Writing Workshop

Conduct a minilesson on "Placing Words in the Sentence" (pp. 387–89).

Revising Strategy

Peer Response

Instruct students to exchange their essays with peers and to comment on the specific details of the essays they are reading (who? what? when? etc.).

ONE on ONE Instruct your student to share his essay with another analytical reader who will examine his essay for specific details (who? what? when? etc.).

Revising Strategy

Participation

Ask students to compare and contrast the drafts on pages 223–24. Ask volunteers to identify the changes that Berber made and to explain how those changes strengthen the essay.

Evaluation

For help in grading this assignment, see "Grading Student Writing" (p. v) and Writing Rubric 9 (Teacher's Toolkit).

Clear Reference

Pronouns p. 37

Pronoun-Antecedent Agreement pp. 163–65

A pronoun must refer clearly to only one antecedent. If two nearby nouns could be possible antecedents, the sentence will be ambiguous.

AMBIGUOUS	**Mary** told her **sister** that **she** could do anything.
CLEAR	**Mary** told her **sister**, "**You** can do anything."
	Mary told her **sister**, "**I** can do anything."
AMBIGUOUS	Both **Daniel** and **Ben** were running for class president; **he** was the first to congratulate **his** rival when **he** won the election.
CLEAR	Both **Daniel** and **Ben** were running for class president; **Ben** was the first to congratulate **his** rival when **Daniel** won the election.

A pronoun should follow its antecedent closely enough to make the relationship between the two words clear. If the antecedent is too remote, the reader may have trouble following the passage and identifying the word to which the pronoun refers.

REMOTE	In the book *The Plague and I,* **Betty MacDonald** recounts **her** experiences as a tuberculosis patient in the 1930s. At that time TB patients were usually confined to sanatoriums where they endured rigorous treatment programs to enforce rest and healthful habits. The discovery of effective antibiotics in the 1940s drastically changed the standard treatment procedures. Acknowledging the difficult conditions, **she** nevertheless tells **her** story with wit and energy.
CLEAR	In the book *The Plague and I,* **Betty MacDonald** recounts **her** experiences as a tuberculosis patient in the 1930s. At that time TB patients were usually confined to sanatoriums where they endured rigorous treatment programs to enforce rest and healthful habits. The discovery of effective antibiotics in the 1940s drastically changed the standard treatment procedures. Acknowledging the difficult conditions, **MacDonald** nevertheless tells **her** story with wit and energy.

in SUMMARY

Avoid **ambiguous reference** by having a single noun nearby that is the obvious antecedent of the pronoun.

Avoid **remote reference** by not having the antecedent too far away from the pronoun.

9.1 PRACTICE *the skill*

Identify the following sentences as clear *(C)* or unclear *(U)*. If the meaning is unclear, underline the unclear pronoun.

__U__ 1. Andrea met a number of new friends and teachers during her first weeks in college. They were important to her as she adjusted to college life.

__U__ 2. During the wait to register for classes, her roommates made her feel welcome. Their being with her made it seem less difficult.

PUBLISHING STRATEGY
Discussion

Ask students for other title possibilities for Berber's essay besides "New Heights." *(Answers will vary but suggestions are "Kenya: If God Wills" or "Selfless, not Selfish.")*

ENRICHMENT

Use Bulletin Board 9 (Teacher's Toolkit) to display the college application essays.

PRONOUN REFERENCE

Lesson Support

Student Worktext

Chapter 9 Review—pp. 449–51

Teacher's Toolkit

Chapter 9 Pretest
Teaching Helps 9A–9B
Concept Reinforcement 9

Test

Chapter 9 Test

TEACHING STRATEGY
Introduction and Induction

Display these sentences: *The youth group had a car wash to earn money for the mission trip. They washed twenty cars by noon.* Ask students to identify any pronouns in the sentences. *(They)* Ask a volunteer to identify the word from sentence one that means the same thing as *they. (group)* Guide students to the following conclusions: (1) a pronoun

226 Chapter 9 | Pronoun Reference

U 3. Jason moved into the residence hall with the idea of having the bottom bunk. It was the last one on Library Drive.

U 4. Jason bought his chemistry textbook from his roommate. He found it at the bottom of a stack of books.

U 5. Another roommate, Nathaniel, invited Jason to play a game of tennis. He looked everywhere in his room but could not find his racket.

C 6. With a heavy sigh, Andrea asked Susan and Laurie about the homework assignment. They were unable to give Andrea any advice.

U 7. Walking between classes, Julia accidentally dropped her books in front of her friends. They scattered recklessly on the ground.

U 8. Sitting at the computer, Joe asked his roommate some advice about the assignment. He was unable to understand the directions.

C 9. Bryan, my premed roommate, rushed out of the room with his hair uncombed. He was more concerned about the first-hour biology exam.

U 10. While the professor talked about transcendental functions, Cheri drew pictures in the margins of her notes. They were quite interesting.

9.2 REVIEW *the skill*

Rewrite each sentence to correct any unclear pronoun reference. If the sentence is already correct, write *C* in the blank. *(Answers may vary.)*

1. Oxford University, the oldest English-speaking university in the world, continues to excel today. It equips its graduates to perform well in many fields.

   C

2. Oxford grew slowly at first, but after Henry II banned English students from attending the University of Paris, it developed quickly.

   Oxford grew slowly at first, but after Henry II banned English students from attending the University of Paris, Oxford developed quickly.

3. The university's tradition of international scholarship began in 1190. It began with an overseas student from Friesland.

   C

takes the place of a noun, and (2) an antecedent is usually a noun. Then display this sentence: *The youth group told the patrons that they were ready to leave.* Ask students to identify the pronoun. *(they)* Ask a volunteer to identify the antecedent of *they*. (*They could refer either to* group *or to* patrons.) Ask for suggested revisions of the sentence to clarify its meaning.

Teaching Strategy

Discussion

Remind students that some pronouns do not have antecedents (i.e., indefinite pronouns and pronouns in expletive constructions). Most pronouns, however, have antecedents.

Reinforcement

Use Teaching Help 9A (Teacher's Toolkit) to reinforce correct pronoun reference.

Evaluation

Before assigning Review the Skill 9.2, instruct students to correct the sentences in Practice the Skill 9.1 that contain examples of unclear reference. *(Answers will vary.)*

4. The first chancellor of Oxford was a scholar known as Oxonie. According to historical records this individual had been serving it faithfully since 1201.

The first chancellor of Oxford was a scholar known as Oxonie. According to historical records this individual had been serving the university faithfully since 1201.

5. In the thirteenth century, riots between students and townspeople erupted. At this point Oxford leaders established halls for them.

In the thirteenth century, riots between students and townspeople erupted. At this point Oxford leaders established halls for the students.

6. Oxford students lived in dormitory-like halls. Many of them remain notable to this day.

Oxford students lived in dormitory-like halls. Many of these halls remain notable to this day.

7. Early halls of residence focused on particular fields of study. They were under the supervision of masters.

Early halls of residence focused on particular areas of study and were under the supervision of masters.

8. A modern example of this system exists at Wycliffe Hall, with most of its students preparing for ministry as clergy in the Church of England.

C

9. Though academically outstanding, it is a very dark place spiritually.

Though academically outstanding, Oxford is a very dark place spiritually.

10. As one of the best-known colleges in the world, Oxford offers a wide variety of study topics, with some of the most qualified professors in the world teaching them.

C

Enrichment

Inform the students of a few of the many famous people who have attended Oxford University.

1360 John Wycliffe: Bible translator
1492 Sir Thomas More: author of *Utopia*
1572 Sir Walter Raleigh: explorer
1744 Samuel Johnson: writer
1873 Cecil Rhodes: statesman
1926 Theodor Seuss Geisel (Dr. Seuss): author of children's books
1972 Tony Blair: British Prime Minister
1994 Stephanie Cook: 2000 Olympic champion in modern pentathlon

HistoryLink

Ask students to research the life of a famous Oxford University graduate. Ask volunteers to present a short report about their findings.

Reference to a Noun, Not an Implied Noun

A pronoun must refer to a noun that is actually stated, not to an idea only implied by the sentence. To correct a sentence with implied reference, either provide an antecedent for the pronoun or replace the unclear pronoun with a specific noun.

See *The Writer's Toolbox* for more examples of pronoun reference to a stated noun.

Implied | Even though the coach has added morning practices, **they** haven't yet broken **their** season-long losing streak.

Stated | Even though the coach has added morning practices for the **players**, **they** haven't yet broken **their** season-long losing streak.

Even though the coach has added morning practices, the **team** hasn't yet broken **its** season-long losing streak.

Implied | When I got to the desk, **he** told me that I had waited in the wrong line.

Stated | When I got to the desk, the ticket agent told me that I had waited in the wrong line.

Reference to a Noun That Is Not a Modifier

A pronoun should refer to a noun that has a regular noun function, such as a subject or an object. A possessive noun or any other noun that modifies another word is a poor antecedent.

Modifying Nouns p. 50

Weak | Our neighbor's **barn** roof flew off during the storm, but **it** remained standing with no damage to the walls or contents.

Better | Our neighbor's barn roof flew off during the storm, but the **barn** remained standing with no damage to the walls or contents.

Weak | The **museum's** new exhibits brought **it** public acclaim.

Better | The new exhibits at the **museum** brought **it** public acclaim.

Occasionally, the pronoun may precede the antecedent in the sentence.

Clear | **Its** new exhibits brought the **museum** public acclaim.

in SUMMARY

Avoid reference to an implied noun by ensuring that an actual noun is the antecedent of the pronoun.

Avoid reference to a noun that is a modifier.

Teaching Strategy

Analysis

Display the following sentences: *After Brynn graduated from college, they celebrated her accomplishment at the Crusty Lobster. Churchill's leadership in England was vital as he inspired the nation during the dark days of World War II.* Ask students to identify the pronouns and antecedents in each sentence. *(they—none, her—Brynn; he—none)* Ask students what the problem is with these sentences. *(Two of the antecedents are implied.)* Tell students to correct the problem in both sentences. *(After Brynn graduated from college, the family celebrated her accomplishment at the Crusty Lobster. Churchill's leadership in England was vital as Churchill inspired the nation during the dark days of World War II.)*

Pronoun Reference | Chapter 9 229

9.3 PRACTICE *the skill*

Try to match each pronoun (except *you* and *I*) to its antecedent. If a pronoun refers to an implied noun or if its antecedent is a modifier, underline that pronoun and supply an appropriate noun or noun phrase. If the sentence is already correct, write *C* in the blank. *(Answers may vary.)*

a tour guide 1. If you visit a college or university, they will probably let you tour one of the residence halls.

C 2. My sister Elise visited one college residence hall twice, but she never got to stay overnight in it until her freshman year of college.

the welcome center 3. When my sister and I drove on campus, they directed us to the registration building.

Elise 4. Elise's roommate Juanita offered to help carry her luggage when she moved in.

C 5. After getting settled into her room, Elise bought a miniature ladder for her bunk bed so that it would be easily accessible.

Elise 6. Juanita patiently explained each document in Elise's registration packet while she listened.

Elise 7. The supervisor was expecting maximum occupancy in each room, but she had just one roommate as far as I could tell.

memos 8. The new roommates designed a memo board, where they could be posted to inform them of messages while they were out.

her roommate 9. When Elise asked about wireless access, she said it was available.

college 10. As far as I could tell, Elise is adjusting well to her first college experiences, and it will continue to nurture and train her well for life.

9.4 REVIEW *the skill*

Rewrite each sentence to correct any unclear pronoun reference. If the sentence is already correct, write *C* in the blank. *(Answers may vary.)*

1. In America in the early nineteenth century, the opportunity for a woman to become a doctor was nonexistent because they were not accepted in the colleges.

In America in the early nineteenth century, the opportunity for a woman to become a doctor was nonexistent because women were not accepted in the colleges.

HistoryLink

Explain to students that a study of the history of women physicians reveals a long battle to gain acceptance into colleges and then into private practice. At the turn of the twentieth century, African American women met even harsher obstacles, but many, such as Dorothy L. Brown, Mary Edward Chinn, Rebecca J. Cole, and Rebecca Lee Crumpler, persisted until they accomplished their goals.

2. Elizabeth Blackwell knew that women could become teachers, so she received training to be a teacher.

C

3. After Blackwell finished her training, she realized the pressing need for them to become doctors.

After Blackwell finished her training, she realized the pressing need for women to become doctors.

4. Although she tried to meet this need, many medical schools turned down Blackwell's applications because they were not well received.

Although she tried to meet this need, many medical schools turned down Blackwell's applications because women were not well received.

5. In 1849 Elizabeth Blackwell became America's first woman doctor after she graduated from Geneva Medical College in New York.

C

6. Blackwell had gained acceptance as a medical student only because they thought her application was a joke.

Blackwell had gained acceptance as a medical student only because the administrators thought her application was a joke.

7. England's acceptance of Dr. Blackwell became obvious when they admitted her name to the British Medical Register.

England's acceptance of Dr. Blackwell became obvious when English officials admitted her name to the British Medical Register.

8. The Female Medical College of Pennsylvania opened in 1850; it was the first medical school in the world to train only women.

C

9. The college's name has changed several times; it was first renamed the Woman's Medical College of Pennsylvania in 1867.

The college's name has changed several times; the college was first renamed the Woman's Medical College of Pennsylvania in 1867.

10. Since 1969 the school's doors have been open to men, but it maintains a strong commitment to women.

Since 1969 the school's doors have been open to men, but the school maintains a strong commitment to women.

Pronoun Reference | Chapter 9 231

See *The Writer's Toolbox* for more examples of indefinite *they; it,* and *you.*

ESL Because many of these pronoun reference rules are broken in the conversational English surrounding your ESL students, you may have to justify these rules to them.

- Students are graded on their knowledge of the rules.
- Greater care and correctness are expected in written English than in spoken English.
- Correct grammar can help students communicate well enough to overcome their pronunciation and vocabulary limits.
- People judge others by the way they speak. ESL speakers' opinions are more likely to be considered if they speak well.

Definite Reference of Personal Pronouns

Personal Pronouns pp. 37–38

A personal pronoun should refer to a definite individual or group. In formal and academic writing the pronouns *they, it,* and *you* should not be used in an indefinite sense.

Indefinite *They*

Unlike an indefinite pronoun (*anyone, everybody,* etc.), the personal pronoun *they* requires an antecedent. Do not use *they* for indefinite reference.

INDEFINITE	Contrary to the popular image, **they** say that Viking helmets never had horns.
CLEAR	Contrary to the popular image, **historians** say that Viking helmets never had horns.
INDEFINITE	At the café, **they** don't serve breakfast after ten o'clock.
CLEAR	The **café** doesn't serve breakfast after ten o'clock.

Indefinite *It*

Do not use the personal pronoun *it* for indefinite reference in expressions such as *it says.* Replace *it* with the source of information.

INDEFINITE	**It** said in the paper that we can expect snow next week.
CLEAR	The **weather forecast** in the paper reported that we can expect snow next week.
INDEFINITE	In Galatians 6:2 **it** says that we should bear each other's burdens.
CLEAR	In Galatians 6:2 **Paul** says that we should bear each other's burdens.
	Galatians 6:2 says that we should bear each other's burdens.

Certain set expressions use the pronoun *it* in an indefinite sense. These idiomatic expressions are perfectly acceptable even in standard English.

TIME	What time is **it**?
	It is half past eight.
DISTANCE	**It** is only two blocks from our house to the grocery store.
WEATHER	Is **it** still raining?
ENVIRONMENT	Is **it** louder than usual in here today?

Indefinite *You*

Except in casual conversation, avoid using the personal pronoun *you* to refer to people in general. Use a more specific noun or an appropriate indefinite pronoun.

INDEFINITE	In most communities, **you** need a special license to drive a bus.
CLEAR	In most communities, a **bus driver** needs a special license.
	In most communities, **anyone** who drives a bus needs a special license.
	Most communities require a **bus driver** to have a special license.

Although informal writing allows the indefinite *you* in certain idioms, such as folksy proverbs, these expressions are usually out of place in formal discourse.

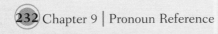

TEACHING STRATEGY

Induction

Display these sentences:

- On many Caribbean islands they drive on the left side of the road.
- In Psalm 7:1 it says, "O Lord my God, in thee do I put my trust."
- For some colleges you must apply more than one year in advance of high-school graduation.
- The application process at some colleges begins quite far in advance to allow time to evaluate it properly.

Ask students to identify and correct the pronoun reference error in each sentence.

- *no noun antecedent*—On many Caribbean islands motorists drive on the left side of the road.
- *no noun antecedent*—Psalm 7:1 says, "O Lord my God, in thee do I put my trust."
- *no noun antecedent*—For some colleges students must apply more than one year in advance of high-school graduation.
- *adjective as antecedent*—The application process at some colleges begins quite far in advance to allow time to evaluate the application properly.

Informal	**You** are what **you** eat.
Formal	The eating habits of a **person** affect **his** health.

Not all uses of the personal pronoun *you* are indefinite. In informal situations, a writer may use *you* when it refers definitely to the reader. When the writer can logically include both himself and the reader in a statement, *we* is acceptable. For very formal situations, however, use the pronoun *one* instead.

Informal	**You** should always remember to thank those who have helped **you** achieve success.
	We should always remember to thank those who have helped **us** achieve success.
Formal	A **person** should always remember to thank those who have helped **him** to achieve success.
	One should always remember to thank those who have helped **him** to achieve success.

Although *he* is an acceptable substitute for the antecedent *one* in North America, British usage, which tends to be more formal, requires *one* in both positions in this example sentence.

Although *you* is appropriate in imperative sentences (such as a set of instructions), some teachers prefer that students avoid all uses of *you* and the imperative mood in academic writing such as research papers and reports.

Informal	Be sure to plug in the machine before **you** turn it on.
Formal or Academic	The **operator** should connect the machine to a power supply before **he** turns it on.

Reference to a Noun, Not a Broad Idea

A pronoun must refer to a specific noun, not to a broad idea stated in a preceding sentence or clause. This rule applies most strongly to *which*. In careful writing it also applies to the demonstratives *this* and *that*.

g u r w
Saying Things Directly
p. 383

Broad Reference	Jason thought a chameleon is an amphibian, **which** is incorrect.
	Jason thought a chameleon is an amphibian, but **this** is incorrect.
Clear	**Jason** thought a chameleon is an amphibian, but **he** is incorrect.
	Jason's belief that a chameleon is an amphibian is incorrect.
Broad Reference	Kangaroos are able to thrive and multiply under even very harsh conditions. **That** creates problems for Australian sheep herders.
Clear	The ability of kangaroos to thrive and multiply under even very harsh conditions creates problems for Australian sheep herders.
	Australian sheep herders have problems with **kangaroos**, **which** are able to thrive and multiply under even very harsh conditions.

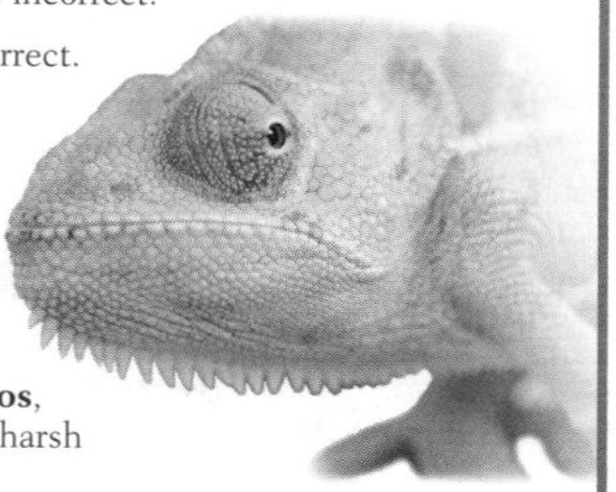

in SUMMARY

Do not use the personal pronoun ***they*** in an indefinite sense to refer to people in general.

Replace the indefinite ***it*** in phrases such as "it says" with a definite source of information.

Reserve the indefinite ***you*** that refers to people in general for conversation and informal writing.

Avoid **broad reference** by making the antecedent of the pronoun a noun, not the general idea of the preceding clause.

Teaching Strategy
Discussion

Discuss with students the correct use of the indefinite *it* in references to time, weather, distance, and environment. Provide a few examples of such references and then ask students to supply additional examples.

Teaching Strategy
Participation

Ask students to check their journals, writing folders, or portfolios for examples of indefinite pronoun reference. Encourage students to correct these problem sentences.

Teaching Strategy
Analysis

Direct the students to compare the examples of broad reference on page 233 to the suggested corrections. For each example, ask the students to identify the pronoun causing the broad reference and the idea that attempts to serve as the antecedent. Then instruct the students to study the suggested corrections and to identify the changes that the writer made. Ask volunteers to suggest other possible corrections.

Instruct students to note that *which* and the demonstrative pronouns can be used correctly or incorrectly; the presence of one of these pronouns does not automatically create broad reference in the sentence.

Consider pointing out that reference to a broad idea is similar to reference to an implied noun and then review the information on page 229.

9.5 PRACTICE *the skill*

Identify each sentence as clear *(C)* or unclear *(U)*. If it is unclear, underline the pronoun causing the indefinite or broad reference. Avoid informal English.

C 1. When looking for a suitable college to attend, someone who is a Christian should consider the opportunities that a Christian college offers.

U 2. In Christian colleges they offer the opportunity for students to grow academically as well as spiritually.

U 3. They will put an emphasis on how the hand of God has worked in history, science, or whatever courses of study you choose.

U 4. One can also make godly friends, and that lasts a lifetime.

U 5. In secular schools, however, you will encounter the ideals and philosophies of the world with little to no biblical guidance.

U 6. It says in this secular college catalog that freshman orientation includes diversity training in religions and alternative lifestyles.

C 7. In many Christian colleges, freshman students receive training in how they can effectively share God's Word with diverse peoples.

U 8. Faculty members at many Christian institutions help their students with academic and spiritual needs, and it really makes a difference.

C 9. One should seriously consider a Christian college or university before making the final decision about where to receive his higher education.

U 10. In making such a life-shaping decision, Christians find assurance in God's Word. In Proverbs 3:5–6 it says, "Trust in the Lord with all thine heart; and lean not unto thine own understanding. In all thy ways acknowledge Him, and He shall direct thy paths."

9.6 REVIEW *the skill*

Rewrite each sentence to correct any unclear or informal pronoun reference. If the sentence is already correct, write *C* in the blank. *(Answers may vary.)*

1. Although many older universities in the United States were begun as theological institutions, you can find little gospel truth in them today.

   Although many older universities in the United States were begun as theological institutions, one can find little gospel truth in them today.

2. When it began, Harvard turned out many Puritan ministers, which greatly furthered the gospel.

   When it began, Harvard turned out many Puritan ministers, and their godly influence greatly furthered the gospel.

REINFORCEMENT

Use Teaching Help 9B (Teacher's Toolkit) to reinforce correct pronoun reference.

SCRIPTURAL APPLICATION

Discuss the importance of choosing a college that will strengthen the moral and religious training that students have received from their parents and church. Remind students to read carefully the philosophy and mission statements of each college they are considering. Ask a student to read 2 Peter 2:1–2. Remind students that Peter knew firsthand what it meant to deny the truth. Discuss the importance of having professors who teach their subjects in light of scriptural truth.

REINFORCEMENT

Instruct students to rewrite unclear sentences in Practice the Skill 9.5. *(Answers will vary.)*

3. In many secular universities they promote worldly philosophy and ideology.

In many secular universities the teachers promote worldly philosophy and ideology.

4. One of the downfalls of religious schools is the election of liberal administrative officers. It weakens the school's underpinnings.

One of the downfalls of religious schools is the election of liberal administrative officers. The leadership of such persons weakens the school's underpinnings.

5. One verse explains the amazing transformation in these institutions of higher learning: in Jude 4 it says, "Certain men crept in unawares."

One verse explains the amazing transformation in these institutions of higher learning: Jude 4 says, "Certain men crept in unawares."

6. If one examines the history of secular universities, he will realize that a single man in an important position can destroy the Christian stand of an institution.

C

7. If only one person questions the validity of the Scriptures upon which the school stands, it can ruin the whole institution.

If only one person questions the validity of the Scriptures upon which the school stands, the resulting disbelief can ruin the whole institution.

8. Strong belief and great faith are necessary for you as well as for an academic institution to remain faithful to Christ and His gospel.

Strong belief and great faith are necessary for a person as well as for an academic institution to remain faithful to Christ and His gospel.

9. It shows throughout academic history that faithfulness cannot be retained through the power of man alone.

Academic history shows that faithfulness cannot be retained through the power of man alone.

10. They must be bathed in the prayers of saints and upheld by the arms of God.

Institutions of learning must be bathed in the prayers of saints and upheld by the arms of God.

Pronoun Reference | Chapter 9 235

9.7 CUMULATIVE *review*

Rewrite the following paragraph, correcting the ten errors from these categories: verb tense, subject-verb agreement, pronoun-antecedent agreement, pronoun use, and pronoun reference. *(Answers will vary.)*

The oldest educational facility still in use in the United States, the Sir Christopher Wren Building at the College of William and Mary, possessed a fascinating history. To begin, no one can say for certain that they know Wren actually designed the building. Only one extant letter refers to him "modeling" the building. However, what you can know for certain about the building proved equally intriguing. Used as the temporary seat of government until the completion of the colonial capitol at Williamsburg, the Wren Building later provided classroom space for three especially notable pupils: Thomas Jefferson, James Monroe, and John Tyler. George Washington hisself even made use of it on numerous occasions when he served as chancellor of the college in 1784. During both the Battle of Yorktown and the American Civil War, the site has served as a makeshift military hospital. Its long history did not continue uninterrupted, though: three times flames engulfed the building and brought terrific damage to its structure. Nevertheless, after they restored the Wren Building to its original grandeur, the facility, complete with both of its original wings, now stands open to whomever desires to tour the building or even to attend college classes there.

The oldest educational facility still in use in the United States, the Sir Christopher Wren Building at the College of William and Mary, possesses a fascinating history. To begin, no one can say for certain that he knows Wren actually designed the building. Only one extant letter refers to his "modeling" the building. However, what one can know for certain about the building proves equally intriguing. Used as the temporary seat of government until the completion of the colonial capitol at Williamsburg, the Wren building later provided classroom space for three especially notable pupils: Thomas Jefferson, James Monroe, and John Tyler. George Washington himself even made use of it on numerous occasions when he served as chancellor of the college in 1784. During both the Battle of Yorktown and the American Civil War, the site served as a makeshift military hospital. The Wren Building's long history did not continue uninterrupted, though: three times flames engulfed the building and brought terrific damage to its structure. Nevertheless, after architects restored the Wren Building to its original grandeur, the facility, complete with both of its original wings, now stands open to whoever desires to tour the building or even to attend college classes there.

REINFORCEMENT

Use Chapter 9 Review on pages 449–51 for additional test review.

EVALUATION

Use Chapter 9 Test to evaluate students' understanding of the content and concepts of the chapter.

THINK ABOUT IT

Truth and Validity

A critical thinker must examine the evidence to evaluate the validity of a speaker's or writer's claims.

Every argument should meet the dual criteria of truth and validity. Truth, of course, depends on the accuracy of the statements themselves. Knowing the difference between fact and opinion will help you to decide whether a statement is true, false, or evaluative (an opinion that cannot be proved or has not yet been proved). If the statements are false, you will probably reject the argument. If the statements are evaluative, you will need to decide whether the opinions on which the argument rests are reasonable opinions.

Validity refers to the form of an argument. If the form of the argument is reasonable, the argument is valid, regardless of its truth or falsity. Study the following examples. Can you explain why they are labeled as they are?

Untrue and Invalid	If a student studies for the test, he will pass it.
	Rick did not study for the test.
	Rick will not pass the test.
	(But Rick already knew the material well enough that he didn't need to study for the test.)
Untrue but Valid	All normal dogs have four feet.
	My cat is a normal dog.
	My cat has four feet.
	(But my cat is a cat, not a dog.)
True and Valid	All people are sinners.
	Marcia is a person.
	Marcia is a sinner.

Only the last argument is completely sound. It is easy to reject arguments based on false premises. But what about validity? If the premises are true, does it matter whether the form of the argument might be invalid? Consider another example.

Possibly True but Invalid	Atheists oppose prayer in schools.
	My senator opposes prayer in schools.
	My senator is an atheist.

Perhaps this last statement is true; the senator under discussion may be an atheist. But perhaps the senator is not an atheist. Some politicians oppose prayer in school because they believe that prayer in schools is unconstitutional. A person is not an atheist simply because he or she shares one particular characteristic with atheists (unless, of course, it is the defining characteristic: rejecting all belief in God). The invalidity of the argument could lead to serious problems if a person were to make decisions about the senator based on these statements. Critical thinkers examine both the truth and the validity of the evidence before they accept any argument.

Thinking It Through

Evaluate current popular arguments, testing them for truth and validity. To find possible topics, examine the editorial pages of a newspaper, listen to a news broadcast, or visit the website of a news organization.

Thinking Biblically

Establishing facts is not as simple as it seems. The evidence a person collects during research needs to be evaluated first. Though such evaluations are made every day, most people do not realize that they are evaluating because their assessments take place at the level of assumptions about the world—at the level of worldview. For example, if an evolutionist encounters a trilobite fossil, he will not see it as evidence for a worldwide flood unless he changes his beliefs (his assumptions) about the earth's origins. Likewise, a creation scientist interprets the same evidence in light of his own beliefs about things he has never witnessed personally (Heb. 11:3). Assumption-based thinking affects more than just scientific evaluations; all evaluations are shaped by worldview. Ultimately, for a statement to be both true and valid, it has to do more than appear to match the facts. It has to be founded on the right assumptions. "The fear of the Lord is the beginning of knowledge" (Prov. 1:7).

Thinking Biblically

The distinction between fact and opinion is useful for anyone, but some non-Christians try to cut an absolute line between the two. If *opinion* means something like *value*—that is, some proposition inaccessible through sense experience—then all facts come with "opinions" attached. Every human being, in other words, has a perspective. Ultimately, each person either loves God or does not, and that fundamental orientation will determine how he reads the facts. If you use the "Thinking It Through" activity suggestion with your students, teach them to question the editorials they read: "Who gets to say what counts as proof?" For example, a science op-ed may argue that belief in the Fall of Adam is fine as a private religious belief, but because it cannot be proved, it does not belong in a science textbook. This scenario is exactly why students should be quick with the question "Who says what counts as proof?"

Enrichment

Materials

- several newspaper articles expressing various viewpoints

Bring a newspaper article for students to read or ask each student to bring an article. Instruct students to read the articles and to discuss whether the arguments used in the articles are valid. Point out the danger of persuasive but invalid arguments.

OBJECTIVES

Students will

1. recognize and explain the English sonnet form.
2. choose a topic or main idea for an original sonnet.
3. organize ideas for a sonnet into a two part structure: part one posing a problem or a question and part two resolving or answering it.
4. use iambic pentameter effectively when drafting a sonnet.
5. practice either the English or Italian rhyme scheme effectively when drafting a sonnet.
6. write a sonnet to achieve a specific desired effect.
7. revise to improve rhyme scheme and clarity of message.
8. proofread a sonnet for grammar, usage, and spelling mistakes.
9. publish a sonnet.

CHA

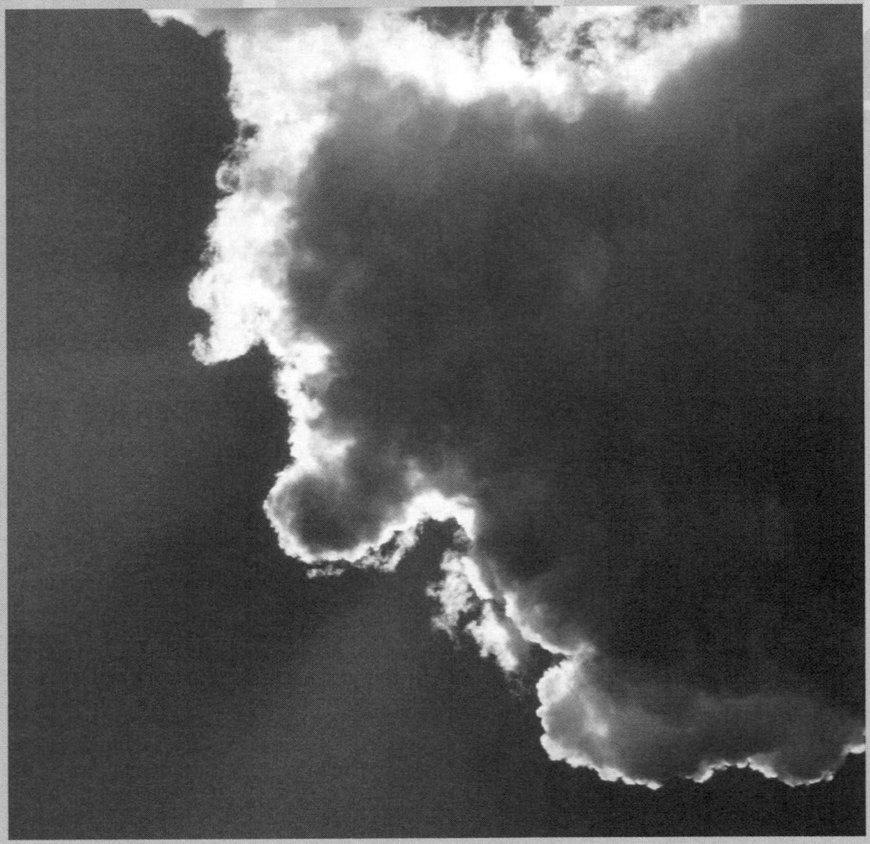

Chapter 10 Overview

Topic	Pages	Support Materials	Days
Showing Comparison with Modifiers	243–46	Bulletin Board 10 Chapter 10 Pretest Practice/Review the Skill 10.1–10.2 Teaching Help 10A ESL Help 10	124–25
College Application Essay	223–25	Writing Worksheet 9 Writing Rubric 9	126, 129
Problems with Modifiers	247–50	Practice/Review the Skill 10.3–10.4 Concept Reinforcement 10A	127
Placement of Modifiers	250–52		128
Practice	252–53	Practice the Skill 10.5 Concept Reinforcement 10B	130
Sonnet	238–41	Writing Rubric 10 Writing Worksheets 10A–10B	131, 134
Review	254–56, 453–56	Teaching Help 10B Review the Skill 10.6 Cumulative Review 10.7 Chapter 10 Review	132
Chapter 10 Test From the Written Word	257		133

SONNET

Lesson Support

Teacher's Toolkit

Writing Worksheet 10
Writing Rubric 10

Literature Link

Read Sonnet 34 to the class. Ask the students what the speaker of the sonnet seems to describe. *(The speaker questions why the*

Sonnet Writing
Adjective and Adverb Use Usage
10

The language of poetry is intensely expressive and emotive. Often a poem uses language that is metaphorical; that is, the words have a meaning other than what is at the surface. In this Shakespearean sonnet, the speaker seems to be addressing the weather. But with only a little imagination, we can see that he is really talking to his love, who hurt him and then felt bad about it. Do you think he forgave her?

Sonnet 34 *by William Shakespeare*

Why didst thou promise such a beauteous day,
And make me travel forth without my cloak,
To let base clouds o'ertake me in my way,
Hiding thy brav'ry in their rotten smoke?
'Tis not enough that through the cloud thou break,
To dry the rain on my storm-beaten face,
For no man well of such a salve can speak
That heals the wound, and cures not the disgrace:
Nor can thy shame give physic to my grief,
Though thou repent, yet have I still the loss,
Th' offender's sorrow lends but weak relief
To him that bears the strong offense's cross.
Ah, but those tears are pearl which thy love sheds,
And they are rich, and ransom all ill deeds.

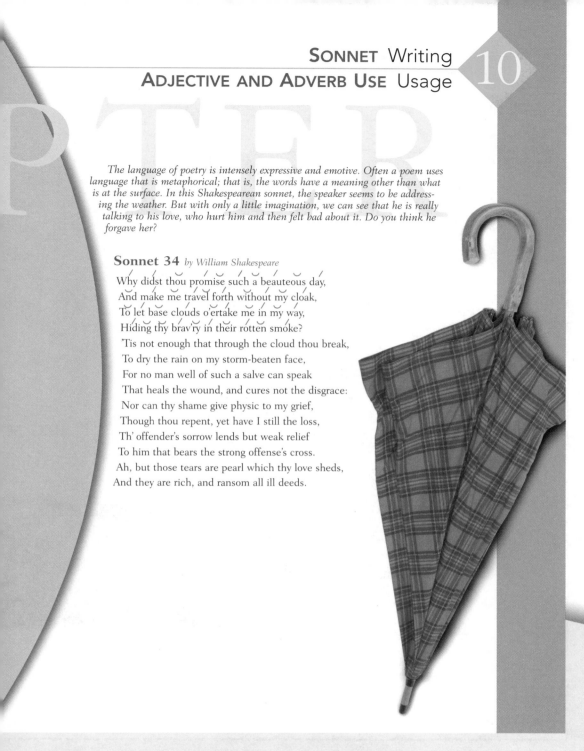

Additional Information
Arguably the most significant dramatist in the history of English literature, William Shakespeare (1564–1616) penned at least thirty-seven dramas. In addition, his sonnet sequence of 1609 showcases his mastery of the sonnet as well.

Additional Resources
For an introduction to Shakespeare and his sonnets, see *British Literature*, published by BJU Press.

weather became stormy.) Instruct students to read the sonnet again and to explain the metaphorical meaning. *(The speaker addresses the love who grieved him but then later regretted that she grieved him.)*

Scriptural Application
Lead a discussion about justice and mercy in Sonnet 34 by asking the students the following questions:

- What gives the speaker the right to forgive his love?
- Ought the offending party give restitution in some way, especially as the speaker still bears the loss? (line 10)
- What about justice? Is the sonnet's ending with forgiveness satisfactory?

After the students have answered, explain that Christianity offers something all the other religions of the world cannot: only Christ's atonement at Calvary combines perfect justice and mercy in one act. Ask a volunteer to read Romans 3:20–26. Explain that a true believer cannot withhold forgiveness when he remembers God's mercy and grace toward him. Instead, moved by the unmerited favor of Christ, the believer can forgive and live a life free of bitterness. (For additional study see Matt. 18:23–35.)

Teaching Strategy
Discussion
Ask students what lines 1–12 of Sonnet 34 imply. *(The speaker refuses to forgive his love.)* Then ask what the closing couplet states. *(The speaker views his love's tears as*

Iambic pentameter is the most common poetic meter in English-language poetry. Each poetic line contains ten syllables that can be broken down into five two-syllable units or "feet" having the accent on the second syllable of each unit. For example, "Shall I compare thee to a summer's day?" (William Shakespeare, Sonnet XVIII).

English sonnets are sometimes called Shakespearean sonnets after their most famous practitioner; likewise, Italian sonnets are sometimes called Petrarchan sonnets, after the Italian poet Petrarch (1304–74). The English poet Edmund Spenser (c.1552–99) created a more complex, interlocking sonnet rhyme scheme, *abab bcbc cdcd ee.*

The quatrain is the most common poetry form in English verse; this four-line stanza may use any of a variety of meters and rhyme schemes.

OVERVIEW of the WRITING PROCESS

Planning—getting an idea, talking the idea over with a peer, and making a brief outline

Drafting—following the outline, using iambic pentameter, remembering the rhyme scheme, and working to produce the sonnet's final effect

Revising—reading the sonnet aloud, checking the rhyme scheme, making certain the message is clear, engaging a peer to evaluate the sonnet, and making final changes to the sonnet

Publishing—holding a poetry reading, making a chapbook, or making an audio recording

SONNET

That which was written was upright, even words of truth.
Ecclesiastes 12:10

As you may have learned in studying literature, a **sonnet** is a fourteen-line poem in iambic pentameter that has one of two main rhyme schemes. The English sonnet rhymes *abab cdcd efef gg;* the Italian sonnet usually rhymes *abba abba cde cde* or *abba abba cdcdcd.*

English sonnets usually make a shift of thought in the last two lines (the **couplet**), and Italian sonnets in the last six (the **sestet**). The speaker in Sonnet 34 implies in the first twelve lines that there is no remedy for his broken heart. But in the closing couplet, he reveals that her tears have mended his wounded feelings.

Most sonnets are serious, but occasionally one is written in jest. For example, Shakespeare wrote a sonnet declaring that his love is no great beauty—and it is a sonnet that seems refreshingly realistic amid the many flowery sonnets of exuberant praise.

Writing a sonnet requires both imagination and discipline. Imagination must find the subject and the approach; discipline must follow the form and choose the precise expression. Together, they should produce a poem that is at once orderly and comprehensible.

Your Turn Think of something that is very important to you right now. Or think of something that amuses you. Compose a sonnet—English or Italian—about your idea.

Planning

✔ **Get an idea.** Some poets get ideas from their observations, some from their reading (the Bible and sermons inspire many Christian poets), and some from conversations or comments or pictures. Wherever your ideas come from, they must compel you to write. It is no good to try to write a poem on a topic you care little about or something you think you should care about but really do not. It will read stiffly—if it gets read at all.

Even humorous poems must spring from a desire to communicate something. In the Shakespearean sonnet in which the speaker states that his ladylove is not especially beautiful, the point is serious (true love is not based on looks), but the presentation is amusing. The formal tone of the sonnet increases the humor, because the form is more elevated than the topic.

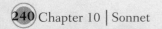

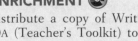

✔ **Talk to a friend.** Explain your idea to someone else. Ask him what he thinks. As you talk to him, you will be refining your own thoughts. Perhaps Shakespeare talked to his friends about how someone had hurt his feelings before he wrote Sonnet 34. Maybe his friends told him that his situation sounded like a nice day that had turned suddenly rainy. Or maybe Shakespeare just happened to be thinking about this topic on such a day. Talking to a friend about your topic will give you another perspective—and perhaps some more ideas.

sufficient payment for "all ill deeds.") Emphasize that the closing couplet of an English sonnet often shows a change in the train of thought.

Literature Link

Ask students to explain the difference between metaphors and similes. *(Metaphors do not state a comparison outright. Similes, however, use* like *or* as *to make a comparison.)* Display the following examples and discuss each:

- Genesis 49:22 "Joseph is a fruitful bough, even a fruitful bough by a well; whose branches run over the wall." *(metaphor)*
- Proverbs 20:5 "Counsel in the heart of man is like deep water; but a man of understanding will draw it out." *(simile)*

Direct students to write three original metaphors and similes each. Encourage students to share their comparisons with the class.

ENRICHMENT

Distribute a copy of Writing Worksheet 10A (Teacher's Toolkit) to each student. Compare and contrast the sonnets with the students. Then either assign or discuss the questions.

PLANNING STRATEGY

Participation

Use Writing Worksheet 10B (Teacher's Toolkit) to help students select a motivating idea for their sonnets.

✔ **Make a brief outline.** Think of your sonnet in two parts: Part One sets up the situation and the speaker's feelings about it, and Part Two (the couplet or the sestet) reveals a new insight and resolves the tension. Here, for example, is how Sonnet 34 might be outlined:

Part One
- A. Quatrain 1—Ask the sun why he allowed bad weather.
- B. Quatrain 2—Complain that the sun is not curing the real problem.
- C. Quatrain 3—Assert that nothing will set this offense right.

Part Two Couplet—Admit that tears from the offender are enough to make up for the hurt.

Drafting

✔ **Follow the outline.** Using the outline you have written, prepare a rough draft of Part One or Part Two. Some people like to write the ending first, finding that it helps them write Part One toward it. Others like to write from beginning to end, letting Part Two arise as a culmination of the previous work.

✔ **Use iambic pentameter.** All spoken English has a rhythm or pattern of stress with weak and strong syllables. Regular recurrence of these stresses is known as **meter**. An **iamb** is a weak stress followed by a strong stress. The sonnet form, which uses iambic pentameter, dictates that the writer compose lines that contain five ("penta") weak-strong stress units, or **feet**.

⌣ / ⌣ / ⌣ / ⌣ / ⌣ /
If ever two were one, then surely we.
⌣ / ⌣ / ⌣ / ⌣ / ⌣ /
If ever man were loved by wife, then thee;
⌣ / ⌣ / ⌣ / ⌣ / ⌣ /
If ever wife was happy in a man,
⌣ / ⌣ / ⌣ / ⌣ / ⌣ /
Compare with me, ye women, if you can.

(from "To My Dear and Loving Husband" by Anne Bradstreet)

tip

Simple—even one-syllable—words carry emotion and meaning better and are easier to work with than complicated ones.

✔ **Remember rhyme scheme.** As you write, be aware of the end words of your lines. Note the choices Bradstreet makes in the excerpt above: *we, thee; man, can.* Choose simple words to end lines; your rhyming will be less forced, more likely to blend into the flow of the ideas naturally. If a line ends with *petition,* it will be difficult to find a pleasing and natural partner for it: *remission, suspicion,* or *fission,* perhaps. But lines ending with *bright, way, song,* or *meet,* for example, will be less troublesome. However, you would not want to choose words only for their ease of making a rhyme. It is never a good idea to let the form overpower the message.

tip

If you use an unusual word as a rhyming word, use it first and later rhyme it with a better-known word. Then the rhyme will not seem forced.

✔ **Keep in mind your goals for the sonnet.** As you write, always remember the final effect you want the poem to have. Think through each line: does it support the big idea? Do the sounds and images contribute to the whole or draw attention away from it? Does it read naturally?

Additional Resources

For more information about meter and rhyme, consult *Elements of Literature,* Second Edition, BJU Press, pages 46–47. For more information about English and Italian sonnets, consult *British Literature,* Second Edition, BJU Press, pages 162–64, 196.

Planning Strategy

Modeling

Model how students can help their partners develop their sonnet ideas. For example, conduct a discussion with a student that leads the student to a more definite (specific) conception of his or her initial ideas.

Planning Strategy

Discussion

Discuss the outline of Sonnet 34 as displayed on page 241, noting the progression of the ideas. Ask students to compare the outline points to the lines of the sonnet. Lead them to see that the outline expresses the poet's message in brief, straightforward statements, whereas the sonnet employs longer, more imaginative expression. Direct the students to follow this model.

Drafting Strategy

Participation

Explain iambic pentameter. Ask students to clap the meter with you as you read the excerpt from Anne Bradstreet's "To My Dear and Loving Husband." Then ask the students to clap and to mark the meter of the first quatrain in Sonnet 34. *(iambic pentameter)* Remind them to use iambic pentameter when drafting their sonnets.

Drafting Strategy

Induction and Analysis

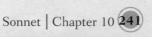

Review how to analyze end rhyme schemes with the alphabetic letters *a, b, c,* and so forth. Demonstrate the process by marking the rhyme scheme of the excerpt from Anne Bradstreet's "To My Dear and Loving

Thinking Biblically

Ask your students to offer several ways to use the sonnet form as a tool for Christian purposes. Here are some suggestions: (1) wooing a godly girl (Prov. 19:14); (2) expressing God's glory directly through artful language (e.g., making God and His glory the subject matter of your poem, as John Donne did in many of his sonnets); (3) expressing God's glory indirectly through artful language (i.e., using language that is so beautiful it points to the Source of all beauty); (4) working out sorrow and grief in a God-dependent way. These reasons (and many others) explain why language is a valuable tool for the Christian.

Thinking Biblically

Do you have a Christian view of adverbs and sonnets? Or is the Christian view of these things the same as the Hindu view, the atheist view, or the Muslim view? Every English speaker on earth uses adverbs and sonnets (well, at least adverbs) in essentially the same way. *Quickly* means the same thing in New York as it does in York. Does that mean that adverbs—and sonnets and essays and interjections and any other literary genre or feature of language—are exempt from God's demand to do all to His glory (1 Cor. 10:31)? No. The key is to view adverbs and sonnets as tools, ready for various purposes. The question is, then, are you using adverbs and sonnets for Christian purposes—to show love to a neighbor, to bring glory to God through the beauty of language? The believer should have a Christian view of everything in the world, even adverbs. The Christian should glorify God in whatever he does and with whatever tool he uses—on purpose!

You must be setting up for the shift in thought and tension, even as you seem to be going in a different direction. For example, in Sonnet 34, the speaker gives you clues that he will not hold a grudge forever. His tone is not angry, but rather incredulous. He asks almost pleading questions. If he had meant never to mend the relationship, would he have not used direct statements, leaving her no room to answer or approach him? Notice in stanza one that he says that base clouds hide the sun's bravery. He seems more upset about the situation (the clouds coming in) than he is with the person (the sun).

Revising

- **Read your sonnet aloud.** Does it read smoothly? Does it produce the effect you want? Does it resolve the tension realistically?
- **Check the rhyme scheme.** Do you have three quatrains and a couplet? Or an octet and a sestet? Do the end-words fall naturally in the sentences? Do any rhyming words seem to stick out, to be there just for the sake of the rhyme?
- **See whether your message is clear.** Even if the rhyme and rhythm are perfect, the poem can still fail. If what you meant to convey is obscured by how you conveyed it, the reader will leave empty-handed. What did you want him to carry away with him?
- **Allow a peer to evaluate the sonnet.** Ask someone else to read the sonnet and tell you what he thinks of it. Does he see the shift in the couplet? Does it convince him? Listen carefully to his comments for making your sonnet more readable and meaningful.
- **Make changes to the sonnet.** Compare your peer's comments about your poem to your own observations about changes you want to make. Which changes are most important to make? Which ones will enhance the reader's enjoyment of it? Make changes for clarity and effect. Then proofread the sonnet, checking for mistakes in grammar, usage, and spelling.

Publishing

- **Hold a poetry reading.** Choose a comfortable place where a small group can meet. Take turns reading the sonnets aloud.
- **Make a chapbook.** Collect sonnets by theme or tone (humorous or serious). Make copies and gather them into a book. Give the book a title.
- **Make an audio recording.** Find a good reader and ask him to record his reading of the sonnets from your chapbook.

Some Ideas to Consider

Math

- Write a sonnet in another iambic line—like iambic heptameter. How does your new iambic line change the sound and effect of the "sonnet"?

History

- Discover other sonneteers. Do not overlook the twentieth-first century.

Literature

- Read Robert Frost's "The Silken Tent." It is one long sentence in perfect sonnet form.

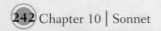

Husband." *(aabb)* Then instruct students to analyze the rhyme scheme of Sonnet 34. *(abab cdcd efef gg)* Remind them to consider rhyme scheme as they draft, remembering that an imperfect rhyme is better than a forced rhyme that distracts from the message.

Drafting Strategy

Discussion

Warn the students against becoming so distracted by form, meter, and rhyme that they ignore the message they want to communicate to the reader.

Revising Strategy

Demonstration

Materials

- Several sonnets by William Shakespeare or Edmund Spenser

Distribute several sonnets by Shakespeare or Spenser. Discuss how the rhyme and meter serve the message of each sonnet. Instruct the students to consider what ideas they can incorporate from the sample sonnets. Suggest additional revision strategies.

Revising Strategy

Participation

Remind students to check their sonnets for proper form (three quatrains and a couplet), correct meter (iambic pentameter), and regular rhyme scheme. Suggest that they mark the stress patterns and rhyme schemes on their drafts. Instruct them to check their sonnets for a clear message. Remind them

Adjective and Adverb Use

As you know, adjectives and adverbs modify other words in sentences. In general, adjectives modify nouns or pronouns; adverbs modify verbs, adjectives, and other adverbs.

Adjectives	He maketh me to lie down in *green* pastures; he leadeth me beside *the still* waters. (Ps. 23:2)
Adverbs	*Then* they *willingly* received him into the ship. (John 6:21)

Sometimes, however, adverbs can modify nouns. These adverbs usually specify time or place and come after the noun.

The leaf cleanup *yesterday* was the best that I have ever seen.

After a hard day at work, the crew will meet in the office *below.*

Adjectives and Adverbs pp. 48–51

On occasion another part of speech may function as an adverb. In meanings of time, place, or manner, nouns (or nouns and their modifiers) can modify verbs. These words that meet the noun test but modify verbs are called **adverbial nouns**.

S-LV-PN, S-LV-PA pp. 75–76

The grounds crew worked *all week* to rake the leaves from the premises.

This Friday they will go *home* early.

The crew has never planned *that way* before.

Showing Comparison with Modifiers

Most adjectives and adverbs show one of three degrees: positive, comparative, or superlative. The **positive degree** describes one person, thing, or action; no comparison is made. The **comparative degree** compares two people, things, or actions. The **superlative degree** compares three or more people, things, or actions.

Adverb Clauses of Comparison pp. 122–23

Positive	The gum tree is *big.*
Comparative	The gum tree is *bigger* than the maple tree.
Superlative	The gum tree is the *biggest* tree in the yard.

ESL

Because the superlative degree indicates an extreme, the definite article *the* usually goes with it.

My friend is *the tallest boy* in our school.

His cousin is *the tallest* in their family.

Objectives

Students will

1. identify adjectives and adverbs that modify nouns.
2. identify adverbs and adverbial nouns.
3. recognize and correct modifiers that cannot be compared, double comparisons, and double negatives.
4. identify and correct misplaced modifiers, two-way modifiers, modifiers that split infinitives, and dangling modifiers.

that proper form is less important than the message the poem conveys to the reader.

Revising Strategy

Participation

Divide the class into pairs and distribute Writing Worksheet 10C (Teacher's Toolkit). Direct the students to exchange sonnets and to use the worksheet to provide helpful feedback. Remind students that the evaluation questions on the Writing Worksheet are similar to the questions you will consider when grading the sonnets.

One on One Use Writing Worksheet 10c (Teacher's Toolkit) to give your student early feedback on his sonnet or consider allowing another adult or student to evaluate his sonnet.

Writing Workshop

Conduct a minilesson on "Parallelism," pages 379–82. Encourage students to examine samples from their writing portfolios or journals to check for proper parallelism.

Evaluation

For help in grading this assignment, see "Grading Student Writing" (p. v) and Writing Rubric 10 (Teacher's Toolkit).

Publishing Strategy

Participation

Give students the opportunity to present their sonnets to the other students and to share the background experience that motivated them to write the sonnet.

Regular Comparison of Adjectives and Adverbs

Regular adjectives and adverbs form the comparative and superlative degrees in one of two ways. One-syllable adjectives and most two-syllable adjectives, particularly those ending in *-y*, *-ly*, and *-le*, form the comparative and superlative degrees by adding *-er* and *-est*. Two-syllable adverbs and most three-syllable adjectives form the comparative and superlative degrees with *more* and *most*. Adverbs made from adjectives by the addition of *-ly* use *more* and *most*.

Positive	Reginald is *tall*.
	Playing the center position on the basketball team is *easy* for him.
	His playing center is *important* to his team.
	He approached the championship game *cautiously*.
Comparative	Reginald is *taller* than his brother Charles.
	Playing the center position on the basketball team is *easier* for him than playing the guard position.
	His playing center is *more important* than his playing forward.
	He approached the championship game *more cautiously* than his brother did.
Superlative	Reginald is the *tallest* of the five brothers.
	Of all positions on the basketball team, the center position is the *easiest* for him to play.
	His position as center is the *most important* of the different positions that he plays.
	Of all the players on the team, he approached the championship game the *most cautiously*.

Absolute Comparative and Superlative of Adjectives

Comparative and superlative degrees of adjectives used without specific comparison to other things are in an **"absolute" sense**. Often, this absolute sense is indicated by certain expressions that have become idioms in English.

Absolute Comparative	Tickets to the basketball game will be provided to the children of *lower-income* families. (*In this context* lower *does not mean "less than low"; it is a general term for "below average."*)
Absolute Superlative	"We had a great time! We had *the best* seats, and the game was exciting." (*The intended meaning is "very good seats."*)

ESL Encourage ESL students to memorize irregular adjective and adverb comparisons because these are frequently used.

Irregular Comparison of Adjectives and Adverbs

Some adjectives and adverbs are irregular in the formation of the comparative and superlative degrees. When you have a question, consult a dictionary.

Adjectives			Adverbs		
bad	worse	worst	badly	worse	worst
good	better	best	well	better	best
	little		less	least	

Publishing Strategy
Participation

Allow the students to practice reading their sonnets aloud with expression and then assist them as they make audio recordings.

ADJECTIVE AND ADVERB USE
Lesson Support

Student Worktext
Chapter 10 Review—pp. 453–56

Teacher's Toolkit
Chapter 10 Pretest
Teaching Helps 10A–10B
ESL Help 10
Concept Reinforcements 10A–10B
Bulletin Board 10

Test
Chapter 10 Test

Teaching Strategy
Discussion

Explain that adverbial nouns are usually noun phrases like *all day, this Tuesday, that way, the next time*. However, some adverbial nouns are single words as in the following sentences: *I am going* home. *Did you feed the goldfish* today? Emphasize that adverbial nouns modify verbs and give information regarding time, place, or manner.

244 Chapter 10 | Adjective and Adverb Use

in SUMMARY

Adverbial nouns are nouns that modify verbs.

Adjectives and adverbs have three degrees of comparison: **positive**, **comparative**, and **superlative**.

One-syllable adjectives and most two-syllable adjectives, particularly those ending in *-y*, *-ly*, and *-le*, form the comparative and superlative degrees by adding *-er* and *-est*. Others use *more* and *most*.

Comparative and superlative degrees of adjectives used without specific comparison to other things are in an **"absolute" sense**.

Some adjectives and adverbs are irregular in the formation of the comparative and superlative degrees.

10.1 PRACTICE *the skill*

Underline each adjective, including the correct choice from the adjectives in parentheses. Double underline each adverb that modifies a noun.

1. The biblical account of Mephibosheth in 2 Samuel 9 illustrates the (*blessed, more blessed*) position of a believer in Christ.
2. After a long war between the houses of Saul and David, the Lord granted David a (*decisive, more decisive*) victory that raised doubts about whether any descendants of Saul remained.
3. Nevertheless, David, because of his past covenant with Jonathan, ordered his men to seek for (*clearer, more clear*) information that would lead to even one descendant.
4. One of the (*most loyal, loyalest*) servants told David about one remaining son.
5. Mephibosheth, the sole surviving descendant, must have wondered whether matters could be (*worse, worst*) for a lame man who had lost all of his kindred.
6. Entering the palace, Mephibosheth bowed before the king, called himself a servant of the (*low, lowest*) degree, and waited for his likely sentence of death.
7. David urged Mephibosheth not to fear, for David wished to honor his covenant with Jonathan and to bless this (*helpless, more helpless*) former enemy.
8. One of the (*great, greatest*) blessings that Mephibosheth received was that he would dine upon the best food and would receive the land of his ancestors.
9. The procedure of conquering kings in the period then was to remove (*seditious, more seditious*) enemies rather than to allow them to renew their plans.
10. Mephibosheth remained in Jerusalem, where he was welcomed in the (*regal, more regal*) court of the king.

Teaching Strategy

Participation

Instruct students to compose sentences with comparative and superlative modifiers and then to find those modifiers in the dictionary. As they work, ask them to explain how dictionary entries for modifiers are formatted. Lead students to see that the positive form is listed as the main entry with the comparative and superlative forms included underneath that entry. If *more* and *most* are added to form the comparative and superlative, only the positive form will be listed in most dictionaries. If students have trouble finding adverbs, point out that *-ly* adverbs are often listed at the end of the entry for the primary word (for example, *quickly* would be listed under the entry for *quick*). Instruct students to use the dictionary whenever they are unsure of the comparative or superlative form of any modifier.

Linguistics Link

Ask students for other idioms (p. 244) that rely on absolute comparative or superlative forms. (*Answers will vary.*) Discuss their suggestions and encourage students to investigate the history of these expressions in order to learn whether any comparison was originally implied and, if so, how the meaning of the expression has changed.

10.2 REVIEW *the skill*

Underline each adverb, including the correct choice from the adverbs in parentheses. Double underline each noun that modifies a verb.

1. An approach that one (*especially, more especially*) notices today is "Do not get mad, get even!"
2. From a worldly perspective, Abraham Lincoln could have (*justifiably, more justifiably*) trounced an old enemy named Edwin Stanton.

3. Prior to Lincoln's election as president of the United States, a group of big-city lawyers abused Lincoln openly and (*hatefully, more hatefully*); Lincoln returned home to Springfield, Illinois, a crestfallen man.
4. Of these lawyers, Edwin Stanton was the one who spoke (*more caustically, most caustically*) of Lincoln.
5. During the presidential election Stanton had even (*maliciously, most maliciously*) spread reports of Lincoln's lowly background, unbecoming appearance, and supposed stupidity around Washington, D.C.
6. However, upon becoming president, Lincoln treated his former enemies amazingly well; instead of treating them the way in which he had been treated, he offered key leadership positions to various lawyers who had treated him (*snobbishly, most snobbishly*).
7. Lincoln's appointment of Edwin Stanton as the secretary of war must have surprised many, for people do not (*often, most often*) respond as Lincoln did.
8. Looking beyond his own personal grievances, Lincoln wanted what was best for the struggling nation: he (*wisely, more wisely*) appointed a man who possessed quite remarkable ability and experience in matters of national import.
9. Interestingly, Stanton became one of Lincoln's closest allies; as time passed, Stanton witnessed Lincoln's amazing leadership ability and (*greatly, most greatly*) regretted his past criticisms of the president.
10. Upon Lincoln's untimely death, Stanton (*clearly, more clearly*) proved his genuine constancy to the memory of his fallen leader; Stanton grieved with Lincoln's family and reportedly uttered the following eulogy: "Now he belongs to the ages."

Writing Link

Explain to students that sometimes a noun or verb communicates a message more effectively than a comparative or superlative modifier could. Ask students to consider the following examples:

- The *tallest* man I've ever seen sat down beside me in the airport terminal. (*adequate*)
- A *Goliath* sat down beside me in the airport terminal. (*more vivid*)
- Just as the game of hide-and-seek began, Avery ran *faster* than I and found a hiding spot in the broom closet. (*adequate*)
- Just as the game of hide-and-seek began, Avery *darted* into the broom closet. (*more vivid*)

History Link

Conduct a discussion of Abraham Lincoln's life, politics, and impact on American government. Encourage students to share what they have learned about Lincoln in their previous studies of American history.

Teaching Strategy

Induction and Discussion

Ask students what the superlative degree of *late* is. (*Students will probably answer* latest.) Tell students that *last* is often used to mean "latest." Ask students to explain the differences between *latest* and *last* and to think of sample sentences to illustrate the use of each. A usage guide may be helpful

Problems with Modifiers

Modifiers That Cannot Be Compared

Certain adjectives cannot be compared. If something is unique, it is the only one of its category; therefore, it cannot be described as more unique or most unique. Other such adjectives that cannot be compared are *perfect, dead,* and *eternal.* Many adverbs, especially qualifiers, cannot have degrees of comparison. Examples of adverbs that cannot be compared include *not, daily, almost, here, very, now, somewhat, really,* and *too.*

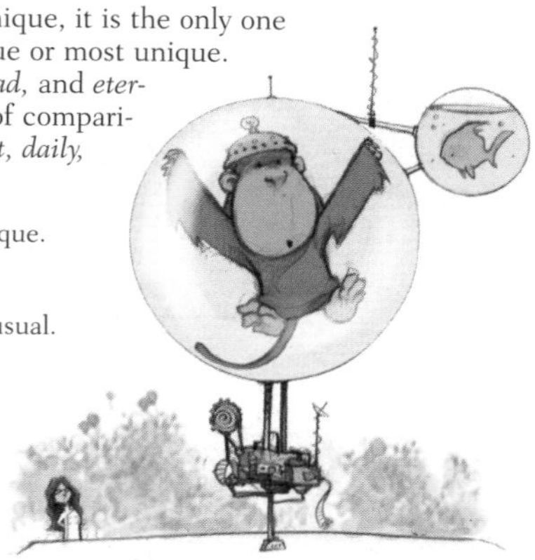

Wrong	Stefanie's science fair project was the most unique.
Right	Stefanie's science fair project was unique.
	Stefanie's science fair project was the most unusual.

Double Comparisons

Do not use both *-er* and *more* to form the comparative degree or both *-est* and *most* to form the superlative degree.

Wrong	She was the *most kindest* student in Mrs. Jenkins's chemistry class.
Right	She was the *kindest* student in Mrs. Jenkins's chemistry class.

Double Negatives

Use only one negative word to give a sentence a negative meaning. When the adverb *not* is used along with another negative word, the **double negative error** occurs. Keep in mind that *no, nothing, no one, never, scarcely, hardly,* and similar words are negative.

Wrong	After a long Christmas vacation, some of the students *did not* have *no* interest in a new class project.
Right	After a long Christmas vacation, some of the students had *no* interest in a new class project.
	After a long Christmas vacation, some of the students *did not* have *any* interest in a new class project.

Adverbs pp. 50–51

ESL

When a sentence with the word *some* is made negative, *some* is replaced by *any.*

Janine opened **some** windows in the house.
Janine did **not** open **any** window in the house.
She said **something**.
She did **not** say **anything**.

in SUMMARY

For modifiers that cannot be compared, do not use *-er*/*-est* or *more*/*most.*

Do not use both *-er* and *more* to form the comparative degree or both *-est* and *most* to form the superlative degree.

Use only one negative word to give the sentence a negative meaning.

Although double negatives are nonstandard in English when used to emphasize a negative meaning ("Nobody said nothing!" actually means that no one refrained from talking), they are acceptable when used to indicate a positive meaning ("She can't not attend her own sister's wedding" means that she must attend).

ESL Some ESL students may speak a language in which double negatives are correct and even used for emphasis. Thus, these students may need extra instruction or practice to master this aspect of English.

when discussing the distinction between the two words

Evaluation

Consider using Teaching Help 10A (Teacher's Toolkit) as a quiz to check the students' understanding of irregular comparison of adjectives and adverbs.

ESL Strategy

For further information and practice in making comparisons involving the four major parts of speech, assign ESL Help 10 (Teacher's Toolkit). (The most common sentence patterns are shown.)

Teaching Strategy

Discussion

Challenge students to think of other adjectives like *perfect, dead,* and *eternal* that cannot be compared. (*favorite, circular, square, round, etc.*) Ask volunteers to explain why these words cannot be compared and to write or state example sentences to illustrate their points.

10.3 PRACTICE *the skill*

Underline each incorrect adjective or adverb and write the correction in the blank. If the sentence is already correct, write *C* in the blank.

unique 1. Joseph's forgiving spirit challenges us to follow his uniquest example.

perfect 2. In spite of his brothers' cruelty toward him, Joseph considered the circumstances to be a part of God's most perfect plan.

C 3. Although Joseph was sold into slavery, was brought into Egypt, and faced almost certain death, he was protected and received a high position in the Egyptian royal court.

C 4. God enabled Joseph to interpret the king's dream; therefore, Joseph was considered the wisest man in the land.

had no 5. As a result of Joseph's wise leadership, Egypt was not in want during the years of famine; Joseph's brothers, however, did not have no stockpile of corn.

C 6. Joseph's brothers and almost all the people of the land came to Egypt to buy corn from Joseph.

perfect 7. Joseph's forgiveness of his brothers found its basis in Joseph's very perfect faith in God's providence.

a unique 8. After Joseph revealed his identity to his brothers and was reunited with his father, Joseph had the most unique opportunity to provide for his family.

C 9. Although Joseph's brothers thought evil against him, God meant it for a good result.

eternal 10. The example of Joseph's forgiveness of his brothers prepares us for the most eternal example of forgiveness, Jesus Christ's forgiveness.

TEACHING STRATEGY
Discussion
Remind students that double comparisons (*e.g., more better*) are nonstandard in today's English and, therefore, have no place in writing or in speech. Some speakers, however, may use double comparisons for humorous effect in informal conversation.

TEACHING STRATEGY
Analysis
Display several words ending in *-n't*. Show students that these words are negatives because they end with a contraction of *not*. Then display the adverbs *barely, hardly,* and *scarcely*. Ask whether combining a negative with any of these words is acceptable (e.g., *he scarcely had no energy left; he couldn't hardly make it back to the campsite*). Explain that these adverbs qualify the meanings of the verbs they modify, functioning like negatives in sentences. Display these examples to illustrate the similar function.

- *Scarcely* have I met a more pleasant person.
- *Never* have I met a more pleasant person.
- She *hardly* cooks from scratch at all.
- She *never* cooks from scratch at all.

10.4 REVIEW *the skill*

Rewrite each sentence, making the modifier clear or correct. If the sentence is already correct, write C in the blank. *(Answers may vary.)*

1. History records some most unique examples of presidential pardons given to those who may or may not have deserved the pardon.

   History records some unique examples of presidential pardons given to those who may or may not have deserved the pardon.

2. Dr. Samuel Mudd was accused of, convicted of, and sent to prison for helping John Wilkes Booth in his most horriblest deed, the assassination of Abraham Lincoln.

   Dr. Samuel Mudd was accused of, convicted of, and sent to prison for helping John Wilkes Booth in his most horrible deed, the assassination of Abraham Lincoln.

3. Dr. Mudd said that he did not have no part in the assassination, but in 1865 a military commission convicted Mudd of aiding Booth because Mudd had treated Booth's broken leg.

   Dr. Mudd said that he did not have any part in the assassination, but in 1865 a military commission convicted Mudd of aiding Booth because Mudd had treated Booth's broken leg.

4. Dr. Mudd claimed that he did not have no idea that Lincoln had been assassinated and that he did not recognize Booth.

   Dr. Mudd claimed that he did not have any idea that Lincoln had been assassinated and that he did not recognize Booth.

5. Mudd's claim that he did not know Booth was not the most smartest declaration since witnesses could testify that these men had met previously.

   Mudd's claim that he did not know Booth was not the smartest declaration since witnesses could testify that these men had met previously.

6. Testimony indicated that Mudd and Booth had met in Washington in March of 1865 and even more earlier, in November of 1864.

   Testimony indicated that Mudd and Booth had met in Washington in March of 1865 and even earlier, in November of 1864.

Literature Link

Point out that during the Medieval and Renaissance periods, writers routinely used double negatives for emphasis. Explain that the emphatic double negative passed from scholarly use in the 1700s.

Foreign Language Link

Double comparisons and double negatives are acceptable in some foreign languages. Encourage students that have studied a foreign language to share some examples of double comparisons and double negatives in that language and to specify whether the expression is used for emphasis or to communicate some other meaning.

SCRIPTURAL APPLICATION

Instruct students to compare presidential pardons to God's pardoning of repentant sinners. *([1] Many seek presidential pardons, but comparatively few seek God's pardon. [2] A presidential pardon is finite in scope, permanence, and power; God's pardon is infinite. [3] Presidential pardons are offered to very few individuals. God, however, has made His pardon available to "whosoever will.")* Read Isaiah 55:6–9, emphasizing the call to repentance and the superiority of God's ways (His righteousness) over man's ways (our sinfulness).

7. The commission did not give in to no pleas; Dr. Mudd was convicted of conspiracy and of harboring Booth.

The commission did not give in to any pleas; Dr. Mudd was convicted of conspiracy and of harboring Booth.

8. A most remarkable decision was rendered; Dr. Mudd escaped the death penalty by one vote and was imprisoned at Fort Jefferson in south Florida.

C

9. At Fort Jefferson soldiers may not have thought that no illness would befall them, but an outbreak of yellow fever took the lives of many, including the resident physician.

At Fort Jefferson soldiers may have thought that no illness would befall them, but an outbreak of yellow fever took the lives of many, including the resident physician.

Or: At Fort Jefferson soldiers may not have thought any illness would befall them, but an outbreak of yellow fever took the lives of many, including the resident physician.

10. Dr. Mudd used his skill as a physician to help. As a result of his outstanding medical help, he received a pardon, but his conviction was not ever overturned.

C

Adjectives and Adverbs pp. 48–51

Prepositional Phrases p. 88

Participial Phrases pp. 92–94

Adjective Clauses pp. 116–19

Placement of Modifiers

Misplaced Modifiers

A word, phrase, or clause modifier that appears to modify the wrong word in a sentence is a **misplaced modifier**. In order to avoid an ambiguous or illogical sentence, move the modifier close to the word that it modifies.

MISPLACED WORD	Charles *almost* studied everything on the study sheet.
CLEAR	Charles studied *almost* everything on the study sheet.
MISPLACED PHRASE	Charles threw the basketball from the middle of the court *with a mighty effort.*
CLEAR	*With a mighty effort,* Charles threw the basketball from the middle of the court.
MISPLACED CLAUSE	The basketball team was ready for the scrimmage game *that appeared on the court.*
CLEAR	The basketball team *that appeared on the court* was ready for the scrimmage game.

TEACHING STRATEGY

Introduction and Demonstration

Materials

- a newspaper or news website

Read news headlines aloud or display several and ask whether any of them catch the students' attention. Then give a few humorous headlines, such as the following: *Two brothers reunited after twelve years in laundry. Lifeguard helps shark bite victim. Mayor wins on urban renewal but more lies ahead. Robber sentenced to five years in cello case.* These headlines catch people's attention because they are rife with modifier errors. Explain that effective communication requires correct placement of modifiers.

REINFORCEMENT

Use Bulletin Board 10 (Teacher's Toolkit) to reinforce correct modifier placement.

TEACHING STRATEGY

Induction

Display the following sentences:

- *Tuesday* Blair arrives in Paris.
- Blair arrives *Tuesday* in Paris.
- Blair arrives in Paris *Tuesday.*

Then ask the students which placement of *Tuesday* is correct. *(all of them)* Ask students whether there can be more than one correct place for a modifier within a sentence. *(yes)* Explain that modifiers should

The following words are likely to cause confusion if they are not placed correctly in a sentence.

almost	just
especially	merely
even	nearly
exactly	only
hardly	simply

Misplaced Charles and Mia *nearly* practiced their scene from the play for an hour.

Charles had *only* memorized half of his lines.

Clear Charles and Mia practiced their scene from the play for *nearly* an hour.

Charles had memorized *only* half of his lines.

Sentences like "Charles had only memorized half his lines" are often heard in conversation, where oral emphasis on *half* provides clarity. In writing, however, a word like *only* should be next to the specific word it modifies.

ESL

Two-Way Modifiers

A **two-way modifier** is one that comes between two sentence elements, either of which it could modify. As a result, the reader cannot determine which of the two it modifies. In order to clarify the sentence, move the modifier or reword the sentence so that its meaning is clear.

Ambiguous Drama students who rehearse *diligently* learn their lines.

Clear Drama students who *diligently* rehearse learn their lines.

Drama students who rehearse learn their lines *diligently*.

Two-way modifiers are sometimes called squinting modifiers.

Modifiers That Split Infinitives

A modifier that comes between the sign of the infinitive, *to,* and the verb form produces a **split infinitive**. Although split infinitives are not ungrammatical, they may be awkward. Correcting a split infinitive often improves the sentence.

Infinitive Phrases
pp. 101–2

Awkward Miguel began *to* with keen interest *practice* the piano.

Better With keen interest, Miguel began *to practice* the piano.

It is, however, better to split an infinitive with a one-word modifier than to create an awkward sentence.

Acceptable To *really* play the piano, he must be prepared to work hard.

Awkward *Really* to play the piano, he must be prepared to work hard.

be placed close to the words they modify. In the example sentences above, every *Tuesday* correctly modifies the verb *arrives.*

Teaching Strategy
Participation

Display the following example sentences containing two-way modifiers:

- The park ranger who had been hiking *cautiously* scanned the trail before him.
- The ranger warned *in the spring* the heavy rains would drive snakes from their normal habitats.
- Many nonpoisonous snake species living in New England *commonly* imitate the scare tactics of their poisonous counterparts.

Ask students to explain the two meanings of each sentence. Then ask them to make the meaning of each sentence clear by either moving or rewording the modifier.

Teaching Strategy
Analysis

Ask students whether modifiers that split infinitives are ungrammatical. *(no)* Share the example of an acceptable split infinitive on page 251. Emphasize, however, that students should avoid splitting infinitives except to prevent awkward sentence structure.

Participial Phrases pp. 92–94

Elliptical Adverb Clauses p. 123

Dangling Modifiers

A **dangling modifier** is a modifier with no logical word to modify. The modifier is not grammatically connected to any word in the sentence. A dangling modifier cannot be corrected by merely moving it to a different place in the sentence; you will need to reword the sentence. Although most dangling modifiers appear at the beginning of the sentence, some appear at the end of the sentence.

Dangling Modifier	Playing the concerto beautifully, the piano lid fell with a bang.
Corrected	While he was playing the concerto beautifully, the piano lid fell with a bang.
Dangling Modifier	Music should be chosen carefully when planning a recital.
Corrected	He should choose the music carefully when planning a recital.
	Music should be chosen carefully when one is planning a recital.

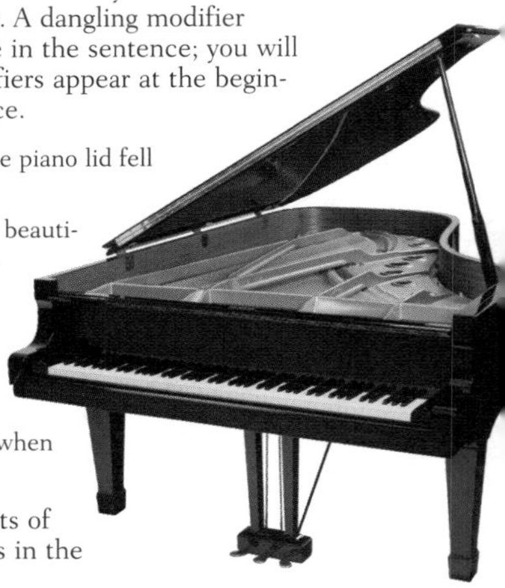

In these examples of dangling modifiers, the implied subjects of *playing* and *planning* are not the same as the stated subjects in the independent clauses.

in SUMMARY

Place each modifier reasonably close to the word it modifies.

Avoid placing a modifier between two elements that it could modify.

In most cases, do not place a modifier between the sign of the infinitive, *to*, and the verb form.

Reword the sentence to correct a **dangling modifier**.

Alexandre Dumas (1802–70) is the French author of such famous works as *The Three Musketeers*, *The Count of Monte Cristo*, and *The Man in the Iron Mask*. He is called Dumas *père* to differentiate him from his son, Alexandre Dumas *fils*, who was also a writer.

The Château d'If, a sixteenth-century castle located on a rocky island off the coast of Marseilles, was first built for the city's protection. Later, however, it became the desolate prison made famous in two of Alexandre Dumas's works, *The Count of Monte Cristo* and *The Man in the Iron Mask*.

10.5 PRACTICE *the skill*

Write the letter of the correct or better sentence in the blank.

__*B*__ 1. A. Providing an outstanding example of how a man's bitterness can destroy himself and others, *The Count of Monte Cristo* was written by Alexander Dumas.
B. Providing an outstanding example of how a man's bitterness can destroy himself and others, Alexander Dumas wrote *The Count of Monte Cristo.*

__*A*__ 2. A. In the story, a character known as Edmond Dantés, a Frenchman, is betrayed by one of his closest friends and is sent to a notorious prison called Château d'If.
B. In the story, a character known as Edmond Dantés, a Frenchman, is sent to a notorious prison called Château d'If, betrayed by one of his closest friends.

__*B*__ 3. A. He determines that he will eventually exact a bitter revenge on those who have betrayed him, dwelling on his bitterness.
B. Dwelling on his bitterness, he determines that he will eventually exact a bitter revenge on those who have betrayed him.

Teaching Strategy

Discussion

Ask students to explain the difference between misplaced and dangling modifiers. *(Misplaced modifiers must be moved closer to the word they modify in the sentence. Dangling modifiers, however, have no word to modify and can be corrected only by rewording the sentence.)*

Reinforcement

Explain that a modifier's sounding correct in a sentence does not guarantee that the modifier has been placed correctly. Remind the students that often writers get carried away with their message and inadvertently use a dangling modifier that sounds logical while the author is writing. Call attention to the examples of dangling modifiers presented on page 252. Ask students to draw arrows to the word each dangling modifier should modify.

Enrichment

Allow students to collect humorous examples of misplaced modifiers. Specify that students diagnose the type of modifier error and provide a correction.

A 4. A. In prison Dantés learns the location of a great treasure.
B. Dantés learns the location of a great treasure in prison.

B 5. A. Dantés escapes, locates the treasure, and elevates himself to a noble position following much hard work and planning.
B. Following much hard work and planning, Dantés escapes, locates the treasure, and elevates himself to a noble position.

B 6. A. Once back in society, he assumes a new identity, "befriends" his old enemies, and proceeds to relentlessly destroy them.
B. Once back in society, he assumes a new identity, "befriends" his old enemies, and proceeds to destroy them relentlessly.

A 7. A. While Edmond Dantés quietly looks on, two of his chief enemies have tragic losses.
B. While quietly looking on, two of his chief enemies have tragic losses.

B 8. A. In the end, however, he almost ruins every one of his enemies, his fiancée, and himself.
B. In the end, however, he ruins almost every one of his enemies, his fiancée, and himself.

B 9. A. Danté did not have to purposefully exact revenge upon his foes: his life would have been much happier had he not.
B. Dantés did not have to exact revenge purposefully upon his foes: his life would have been much happier had he not.

B 10. A. Creating destruction and havoc, *The Count of Monte Cristo* portrays an especially poignant example of a bitter spirit.
B. *The Count of Monte Cristo* portrays an especially poignant example of a bitter spirit's creating destruction and havoc.

Adjective and Adverb Use | Chapter 10 253

10.6 REVIEW *the skill*

Underline each misplaced modifier once and each dangling modifier twice. Then rewrite each sentence, making the modifiers clear or correct. If the sentence is already correct, write *C* in the blank. *(Answers may vary.)*

1. When reading William Shakespeare's *The Tempest*, Prospero emerges at the end of the play as a gracious and forgiving character.

   When reading William Shakespeare's The Tempest, *the reader sees Prospero emerge at the end of the play as a gracious and forgiving character.*

2. He who rules the island powerfully changes his demeanor at the end.

   He who powerfully rules the island changes his demeanor at the end.

3. One character who is to finally be set free is Ariel, Prospero's servant.

   One character who is finally to be set free is Ariel, Prospero's servant.

FineArts Link

To help the students learn more about Shakespeare's *The Tempest,* consider offering one of the following opportunities: (1) allow students to view a production of the play; (2) read a play synopsis and show either sketches or photographs of key characters; or (3) stage a student performance of an act or a scene from the play.

EVALUATION

Use Teaching Help 10B (Teacher's Toolkit) to ascertain student comprehension of key chapter concepts.

4. Prospero often believes that Ariel is not being a willing servant and threatens to imprison Ariel in a tree.

C

5. Having granted Ariel his freedom, Prospero returns home with the other travelers.

C

6. Prospero's forgiveness gives everyone the chance to immediately begin a new life.

Prospero's forgiveness gives everyone the chance to begin a new life immediately.

7. Ariel began to with great fervency fulfill all the duties Prospero required.

With great fervency, Ariel began to fulfill all the duties Prospero required.

8. In the epilogue the character who threatened others repeatedly asks forgiveness from the audience.

In the epilogue the character who repeatedly threatened others asks forgiveness from the audience.

9. Prospero carefully approaches his audience to ask forgiveness.

C

10. Receiving the audience's approval and applause, forgiveness is complete.

When Prospero receives the audience's approval and applause, his forgiveness is complete.

Adjective and Adverb Use | Chapter 10 255

10.7 CUMULATIVE *review*

Rewrite the following paragraph, correcting the ten errors from these categories: pronoun-antecedent agreement, pronoun case, comparison, double negatives, and modifier placement. *(Answers may vary.)*

Jesus' words "Father, forgive them" are beautifully paralleled by the words spoken by Stephen in Acts 7:60. As Stephen was being stoned to death, he too cried out, "Lord, lay not this sin to their charge." How could anyone request forgiveness for those whom were in the act of taking his life? Moreover, in both cases Christ and Stephen had been unjustly accused, condemned, and subjected to sham trials. Then while suffering horrific deaths, their enemies looked on and jeered. Still, Jesus Christ's words and Stephen's dying words demonstrated his concern for the more eternal souls of men. They did not have nothing revengeful to say to their enemies. By comparison, how often are we quick to take offense, to simmer with anger, and to even harbor bitterness toward those who have hurt us? We would do more better to daily remember the dying examples of Christ and his faithful follower Stephen. Forgiving our enemies faithfully fulfills God's command to His children.

Jesus' words "Father, forgive them" are beautifully paralleled by the words spoken by Stephen in Acts 7:60. As Stephen was being stoned to death, he too cried out, "Lord, lay not this sin to their charge." How could anyone request forgiveness for those who were in the act of taking his life? Moreover, in both cases Christ and Stephen had been unjustly accused, condemned, and subjected to sham trials. Then while Christ and Stephen were suffering horrific deaths, their enemies looked on and jeered. Still, Jesus Christ's words and Stephen's dying words demonstrated their concern for the eternal souls of men. They did not have anything revengeful to say to their enemies. By comparison, how often are we quick to take offense, to simmer with anger, and even to harbor bitterness toward those who have hurt us? We would do better to remember daily the examples of Christ and his faithful follower Stephen at death. Faithfully forgiving our enemies fulfills God's command to His children.

Reinforcement

Use Chapter 10 Review on pages 453–56 for additional test review.

Evaluation

Use Chapter 10 Test to evaluate students' understanding of the content and concepts of the chapter.

FROM THE WRITTEN WORD

Analyzing the Cause

Perhaps you have discussed with a friend why a particular college basketball team did not make the NCAA Final Four, or perhaps you have debated whether the three-point shot line for basketball should be moved. Or maybe you have discussed why the girls' soccer team lost in overtime last week. As you talk about these ideas, you are commenting on the causes for these particular results. Analyzing a subject to identify its causes or effects is another rhetorical strategy.

The Scriptures abound with this rhetorical strategy. Why did God send the Flood? The cause is evident: man was wicked.

> And God saw that the wickedness of man was great in the earth, and that every imagination of the thoughts of his heart was only evil continually. And the Lord said, I will destroy man whom I have created from the face of the earth; . . . for it repenteth me that I have made them. (Gen. 6:5, 7)

You might think about what caused Job's testing or Israel's captivity or Ruth's allegiance to her mother-in-law.

Consider Numbers 20:2–12. Moses, the leader of Israel, heard perhaps the most disappointing declaration of his lifetime. Although Moses had led Israel through many hardships and trials, Moses was not to bring the Israelites into the land of promise. The evident cause was Moses' disobedience. But what other causes do you read about in this passage? The people had complained to Moses and Aaron because there was no water. They had even questioned why Moses had brought them to such a place. Perhaps their harsh complaints caused Moses to doubt God's leading. Standing before this multitude, Moses may have lost his temper, or he might have thought that speaking would not be enough to cause water to come from the rock. Moses' failure to recognize God's power and presence must also have contributed to his disobedience.

Personal Response

Read Judges 8:1–4. As Gideon and his three hundred were returning from battle with the Midianites, the men of Ephraim complained to Gideon. Gideon may have had cause to answer the men of Ephraim with harsh words. Do you think that he did have a cause to? What was the effect of his answer and his manner in answering them?

Now read Proverbs 15:1–2. From your personal experience, write a paragraph that illustrates cause and effect in either a positive or a negative way.

Teaching Strategy

Discussion and Participation

Before students write their cause-and-effect paragraphs, help them focus on God's overarching providence by sharing an instance from your own life that corresponds to this theme. If necessary, briefly define God's providence and give historical examples of it. Instruct students to find verses that support the idea that God is sovereign. *(Ps. 24:1; 115:3; Prov. 16:33; 21:1; Dan. 4:35; Acts 4:27–28, etc.)* Then ask students to share events in their own lives that have revealed God's providence.

From the Written Word | Chapter 10 257

OBJECTIVES

Students will

1. research a selected topic.
2. evaluate sources, choosing primary sources over secondary sources.
3. take notes from research.
4. accurately paraphrase from sources.
5. quote sources judiciously and accurately.
6. write a thesis statement that is verifiable and declarative.
7. outline a paper.
8. write a research report comprised of one paragraph of introduction, three of support, and one of conclusion.
9. provide factual evidence to support a claim made about a topic.
10. include a list of works cited with the report.
11. revise for a focused, declarative thesis; supporting topic sentences; well-organized and clear material; and paragraphs that flow smoothly.
12. revise for correct grammar, mechanics, and spelling.
13. publish the paper.

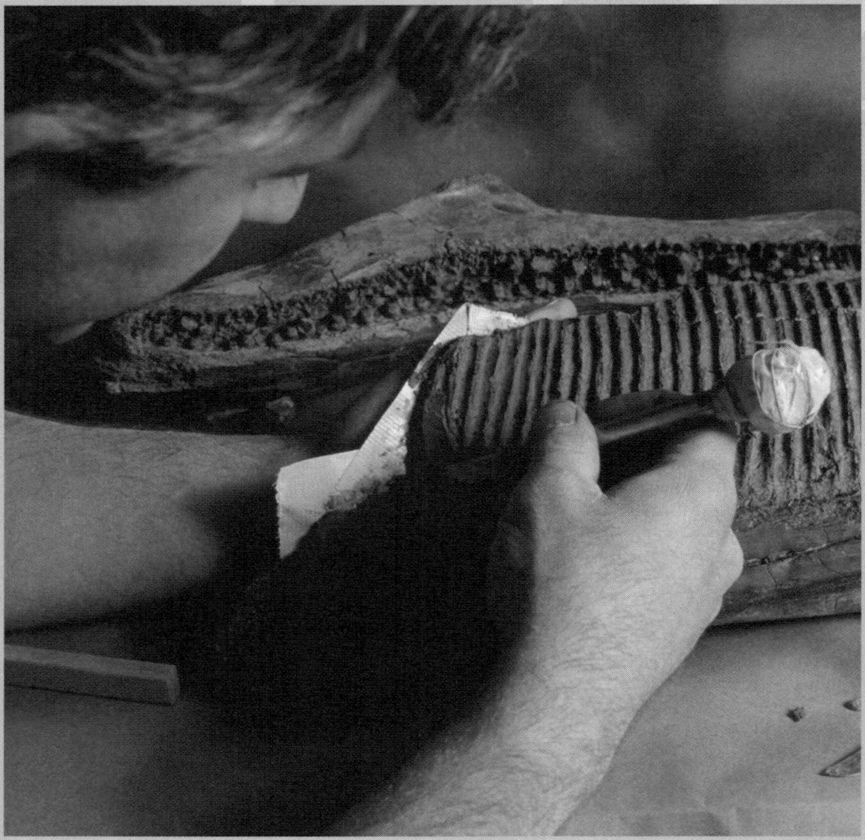

Chapter 11 Overview

Topic	Pages	Support Materials	Days
Personal Names, Religions, Nationalities, and Proper Adjectives	270–73	Bulletin Board 11 Chapter 11 Pretest Practice/Review the Skill 11.1–11.2	135
Sonnet	242	Writing Worksheet 10C Writing Rubric 10	136–37, 140–41
Place Names, Transportation, and Astronomy Terms	274–77	Practice/Review the Skill 11.3–11.4	138
Businesses, Organizations, Cultural and Historical Terms	277–81	Practice/Review the Skill 11.5–11.6	139
Titles First Words and Single Letters	282–87	Practice/Review the Skill 11.7–11.10 Teaching Help 11	142
Research Report	259–65	Writing Worksheets 11A–11C Writing Rubric 11	143–44
Review	288–89, 457–58	Concept Reinforcement 11 Cumulative Review 11.11 Chapter 11 Review	145
Chapter 11 Test Critical Thinking	 289		146

RESEARCH REPORT

Lesson Support

Teacher's Toolkit

Bulletin Board 11
Writing Worksheets 11A–11C
Writing Rubric 11

Learning about something that interests you can be both enjoyable and educational. After reading about an unfamiliar topic in an article or coming across a new idea in a novel, have you ever taken the next step and looked up information on that topic or idea? If you have, you took a step into the research process. You probably found your "research" to be enjoyable and rewarding. Researching various sources, gathering information, and formulating this information into an outline and report can be an exciting and rewarding experience.

In "Piltdown Chicken," scientist Stephen Caesar refutes the supposed evidence of a "link" between dinosaurs and birds. After a brief introduction regarding the finding, he moves to his main idea: "The fossil was a fraud." Notice that Caesar focuses on his main idea and incorporates a number of varied sources into his writing.

Piltdown Chicken *by Stephen Caesar*

In November 1999, *National Geographic* published photographs of what it claimed was incontrovertible proof that birds evolved from dinosaurs. In an article titled "Feathers for T. Rex?" the magazine announced, "New Birdlike Fossils Are Missing Links in Dinosaur Evolution" (Sloan 99). The article featured a photograph, taken under ultraviolet light, of a creature "[w]ith arms of a primitive bird and the tail of a dinosaur" (Ibid. 100). The fossil, named *Archaeoraptor*, was discovered in Liaoning Province, China, and was trumpeted as "a true missing link in the complex chain that connects dinosaurs to birds" (Ibid.). The photo was accompanied by a quotation in large letters by Stephen Czerkas, who led the study of the fossil: "IT'S A MISSING LINK between terrestrial dinosaurs and birds that could actually fly" (Ibid. [emphasis original]). Czerkas also commented, "This fossil is perhaps the best evidence since *Archaeopteryx* that birds did, in fact, evolve from certain types of carnivorous dinosaurs" (Ibid. 101).

Eventually, the word got out—like so many other "proofs" of Darwinism, the fossil was a fraud. In the "Letters to the Editor" section of the March 2000 issue of *National Geographic*, Xu Xing of the Institute of Vertebrate Paleontology and Paleoanthropology (Chinese Academy of Sciences) wrote: "I have concluded that *Archaeoraptor* is a composite. . . . Though I do not want to believe it,

ADDITIONAL INFORMATION

After graduating magna cum laude from Tufts University, Stephen Caesar completed his master's degree in anthropology and archaeology from Harvard University. Caesar continues to use his scientific expertise to write scholarly refutations of alleged evolutionary findings.

Literature Link

Read Stephen Caesar's "Piltdown Chicken" aloud or call on various students to read the essay aloud. Then ask the students whether they have ever (1) read about the discovery of a so-called missing link, (2) heard seemingly reputable scientists discuss evolution as fact, or (3) wondered whether modern science has disproved the Bible. Respond to students' answers: (1) So-called missing links are later found to be fabrications or bad science; (2) even seemingly reputable scientists follow their own biases; and (3) what was "modern science" in the past is often a laughingstock today. Remind your students that God's truth is the one and only certainty in this life and in the next.

SCRIPTURAL APPLICATION

Ask your students whether an unbeliever has ever challenged them to provide biblical proof of the truth or authority of Scripture. Respond by asking students what verses they could offer or how they could follow up with the unbeliever. Remind students that everyone trusts in something, whether it is himself, science, or a religion; however, Christians believe that the Bible is the ultimate, final authority for all of life. Direct students to find Bible verses on the inspiration and inerrancy of Scripture. *(Ps. 119:89; John 17:17; 1 Cor. 2:13; 1 Thess. 2:13; 2 Tim. 3:16–17; 2 Pet. 1:21)*

Consider sharing the following information. As early as the mid-seventeenth century, scholars began using *ibid.* to save space and to avoid confusion. The abbreviation *ibid.* stands for the Latin word *ibidem,* meaning "in the same place." Therefore, a footnote or bibliography entry for the same work and page as the previous entry may be replaced with the abbreviation *ibid.* in some citation styles.

Archaeoraptor appears to be composed of a dromaeosaur [a small, carnivorous dinosaur] tail and a bird body." *National Geographic*'s embarrassment was immense. In its October 2000 issue, it published an article by investigative reporter Lewis Simons, who uncovered the truth behind the hoax. His lengthy investigation, which took him all the way to China, revealed

> a tale of misguided secrecy and misplaced confidence, of rampant egos clashing, self-aggrandizement, wishful thinking, naive assumptions, human error, stubbornness, manipulation, backbiting, lying, corruption, and, most of all, abysmal communication (Simons 128).

Simons learned that a Chinese farmer, eager to sell a fossil to foreigners who would pay top dollar, had dug two fossils out of his land and glued the parts together with homemade paste. He attached the tail from one fossil to the body of the other and then proceeded to add on the legs and feet (Ibid. 128–129). "The result," reported Simons, "was the 'missing link'—the body of a primitive bird with teeth and the tail of a landbound little dinosaur, or dromaeosaur" (Ibid. 129).

The doctored item was bought by a Chinese fossil dealer who "acknowledged that he often sold 'composites'" (Ibid.). The bogus fossil eventually found its way to Stephen Czerkas (quoted above), who, along with his wife, is a dinosaur enthusiast with no scientific qualifications. Upon obtaining the fossil, the Czerkases contacted leading paleontologist Philip J. Currie of the Royal Tyrrell Museum of Paleontology in Alberta. The Canadian scientist didn't spend a lot of time investigating the find; Simons wrote that "Currie was so distracted by other commitments around the world that he gave the *Archaeoraptor* project short shrift" (Ibid. 130).

As it turned out, Currie did have reservations about the fossil but neglected to inform the National Geographic Society's Christopher Sloan, the driving force behind the November 1999 article. Simons referred to this as a "most damaging lapse of responsibility" on Currie's part (Ibid.). Later, Currie and the Czerkases had the fossil examined at the University of Texas High-Resolution X-ray CT Facility in Austin. Professor Timothy Rose, who ran the examination, noticed something wrong and said "there was a chance that it was a fraud" (Ibid.). In response, Currie sent Kevin Aulenback, a fossil technician at the Tyrrell Museum, to investigate the fossil. Aulenback concluded that the fossil "is a composite specimen" (Ibid. 131).

Stephen Czerkas, meanwhile, along with Currie and other scientists, tried to submit a scholarly paper on the "missing link" to the prestigious scientific journals *Nature* and *Science*; both rejected the article due to lack of evidence (Ibid. 131–132). Simons, describing the original draft of the *Nature* submission, wrote:

> On its fifth page the paper stated that the dromaeosaur-like tail on a birdlike creature suggested a previously unknown element in the evolution of birds from landbound dinosaurs. In short, this was what Czerkas would tell National Geographic was "a missing link" (Ibid. 131).

Despite the rejections, the November 1999 issue of *National Geographic* went ahead and published the highly doubtful fossil. Simons referred to the media frenzy that surrounded this alleged proof of evolution as "[a] dog-and-pony show for reporters" (Ibid. 132).

The following month, Xu Xing (who first went public with the fraud) e-mailed Christopher Sloan (the author of the *National Geographic* article) stating, "I am 100% sure . . . we have to admit that *Archaeoraptor* is a faked specimen" (Ibid. 132). Simons describes the less-than-honest way that Xu, who had collaborated in the blunder, tried to cover his tracks: "*National Geographic* published a cleaned-up version of Xu's letter in its March issue [quoted above], at his request changing 'faked' to 'composite'" (Ibid.).

Once the jig was up, those responsible began confessing their foolishness. Czerkas admitted that he and his wife had made "an idiot, bone-stupid mistake." Currie said it was "the greatest mistake of my life." Sloan said, "I was dragging in a monster" (Ibid.). William L. Allen, Editor-in-Chief of *National Geographic*, asked, "How did we get in this mess?" (Ibid. 128). Simons hints at the reason why so many experts fell for the hoax: "To some prominent paleontologists who saw it . . . the little skeleton was a long-sought key to a mystery of evolution" (Ibid.). In other words, they *wanted* to see evidence for dino-to-bird evolution, so that is precisely what they saw. Interestingly, the original article from November 1999 practically admitted as much (without, of course, even realizing it). The article stated that the anatomical features of the *Archaeoraptor* are "exactly what scientists would expect to find in dinosaurs experimenting with flight" (Sloan 101). This is an absolutely golden example of the way in which evolutionists "see" evidence for evolution when there is none—all based on pre-determined assumptions rather than scientific facts.

Criticism of the hoax has been harsh. In its October 2000 issue, *Discover* magazine featured an article titled "Twenty of the Greatest Blunders in Science in the Last Twenty Years." One of the Top 20 was "Piltdown Chicken," a sarcastic term for *National Geographic*'s evolutionary fraud. The term derives from Piltdown Man, the greatest hoax in the history of the theory of human evolution, in which a human skull had been artificially melded with an ape jaw and "discovered" in England in 1912 (Newman 80). For half a century it was used as "proof" of human evolution. The epithet "Piltdown Chicken" was actually coined several months earlier by *U. S. News & World Report*. In February 2000 it reported:

> Imaginations certainly took flight over Archaeoraptor liaoningensis, a bird-like fossil with a meat-eater's tail that was spirited out of northeastern China, "discovered" at a Tucson, Ariz., gem-and-mineral show last year, and displayed at the National Geographic Society in Washington, D.C. Some 110,000 visitors saw the exhibit, which closed January 17; millions more read about the find in November's National Geographic. Now, paleontologists are eating crow (Lord 53).

Storris Olson, curator of birds at the Smithsonian Institution's National Museum of Natural History, had warned the editors at the National Geographic Society about the possible fraudulence of the fossil back in November 1999, when the article was first published. "The public is being completely bamboozled," he said when the scandal broke (Ibid.). Just as earlier paleontologists had embraced Piltdown Man because they were dying for evidence of human evolution, more recent scientists embarrassed themselves by gullibly embracing *Archaeoraptor*—a gullibility stemming from their own overwhelming desire to prove a theory that is incorrect from the start. Yes, Dr. Olson, the public is indeed being bamboozled.

Bamboozle is an informal term meaning "to deceive by elaborate trickery."

References

Lord, Mary. "The Piltdown Chicken." *U.S. News & World Report,* 14 February 2000.

Newman, Judith. (2000). "Twenty of the Greatest Blunders in Science in the Last Twenty Years." *Discover* 21, no. 10.

Simons, Lewis M. (2000). "Archaeoraptor Fossil Trail." *National Geographic* 198, no. 4.

Sloan, Christopher P. (1999). "Feathers for T. Rex?" *National Geographic* 196, no. 5.

Draw attention to the source notes and the reference list in Stephen Caesar's article. Point out that the notes in the article differ from the instructions given to the students because Caesar used a different documentation style. The students will be using the Modern Language Association (MLA) guidelines.

Enrichment

Direct students to compile a list of websites that defend both creation science and the inerrancy of the Bible. Discuss several of the key issues addressed on the websites. Students could also present their findings to the class and afterwards compile a well-organized list of all the sites to keep for ready reference or to share with others. Consider assisting students in designing a website with links to the creation science sites. If your class already has a webpage, consider adding these links to it for students to reference later.

The *Dayton Peace Accords* refers to the 1995 framework agreement for peace in Bosnia and Herzegovina.

T. Edward McCully was one of the five American missionaries killed by the Huaorani Indians, also called Auca Indians, of Ecuador in 1956.

You may wish to specify a word count for the research report in addition to the general requirement that it be two pages long. One standard 8½" × 11" page with one-inch margins holds approximately 250 words in a standard twelve-point font when typed double-spaced.

ESL Not all ESL students will understand the English words *who, what, where, when,* and *why.* Obviously, students need to thoroughly understand these questions before they can write good reports.

Ernest Shackleton (1874–1922) was an Irish explorer famous for his expeditions to the Antarctic.

WRITING

Research Report

But let your communication be, Yea, yea; Nay, nay.
Matthew 5:37

The idea for a research report often begins with a question or two. For example, who was Ernest Shackleton and what did he do? What nations supply the United States with oil? Are the locations of these nations important? What were the Dayton Peace Accords? Who was T. Edward McCully? Questions such as these will lead you to an encyclopedia, library sources, periodicals, or Internet sites. You might also have the opportunity to interview someone who has had a first-person experience relating to your topic. Keep in mind that research of any kind answers questions such as *who? what? where? when?* and *why?*

Your teacher may provide you some general topics that can be springboards to more specific ideas. Take time to think about related ideas and issues as you consider your research report.

Your Turn

Choose a topic and write a two-page printed research report. Since your report will be no more than two pages, you must limit your topic to one that you can treat successfully in a short report. Your report should have a thesis statement that is verifiable and declarative. In addition, you will write a paragraph of introduction, three paragraphs of support, and a paragraph of conclusion. Within your research report, you will want to include factual evidence you have gathered that will support the claim that you make about your topic. Included with your report will be a list of the works cited.

Planning

✔ **Choose a topic.** Now is the time to consult your list of ideas in your journal or notebook or on your computer. If none of these spark your interest, consider reading articles about current events, looking for thought-provoking ideas. If you are still at a loss for ideas, take time to ask yourself a few questions. What am I interested in? Is there a topic that I would like to learn more about? As you consider a topic, determine your audience and keep in mind your desire to communicate evidence that you have discovered.

After reading an article about polar exploration that mentions Ernest Shackleton, you might ask these questions.

- Who was Ernest Shackleton?
- From what country did he come?
- When did he live?
- Where did he explore?
- Why was he important in the history of exploration?
- What was the name of his ship?
- Was he successful in his exploration?
- Did he have some unique experiences?

ESL Strategy

To help ESL students ask the right questions about topics, display the following sentences:

- **Who** asks about people.
- **What** asks about things.
- **Where** asks about places.
- **When** asks about times.
- **Why** asks about reasons or purposes.

Teaching Strategy

Discussion

For this assignment the students should produce three proofs for the argument presented. Emphasize to your students, however, that arguments may have any number of proofs (two, four, five, etc.) so long as they are significant to the argument.

Planning Strategy

Introduction

You might wish to introduce students to the term *heuristics.* A heuristic, from the Greek *heuriskein* (to find), is a list of questions writers use to spur their thinking. Ask students to think of a common heuristic used by journalists. *(the six questions* who? what? where? when? why? *and* how?*)* Ask students whether they can name the ancient Greek rhetorician whose famous work *Rhetoric* outlined various *topoi* (topics) to help the speaker form his argument. *(Aristotle)*

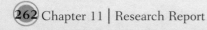

You will probably find that your research is more interesting if you pursue an idea with which you are not familiar. As you consider a topic, remember that you must develop a thesis statement that is verifiable. Your teacher may also ask that you develop a thesis that is controversial.

✔ **Find sources for your report.** Your first consideration for a source is an encyclopedia, either an online copy or a hard copy. This general information will inform you about your topic and will help you focus on more specific ideas. Since the encyclopedia information is only a broad overview, you will not include it in your report. However, the encyclopedia may suggest additional readings that will help you. Once you have some general knowledge about your topic, search the library catalog for more detailed sources. In addition to books and periodicals, be sure to research newspaper, radio, and television transcripts and interviews with authorities on the topic. Your sources of information will be either primary or secondary. Firsthand information such as historical documents, letters, speeches, and journals of the time are considered **primary sources.** Other sources of information from scholars who have studied a subject are **secondary sources.** Secondary sources include most encyclopedia articles and books. You may, on occasion, find a primary source within a secondary source. Information from a primary source is preferred to information from a secondary source.

Library Skills
pp. 399–401

tip

For research writing on the collegiate level, your college instructor may require you to search out several different types of sources. Try branching out some now.

It is important for you to evaluate the trustworthiness of the sources that you consider for your research. In "Piltdown Chicken," notice the quotation from Lewis Simons, a primary source who investigated the hoax. He did not make unfounded accusations; rather he traveled to China and researched firsthand. As you continue in the article, notice the reference to Stephen Czerkas, also a primary source. The reference to Czerkas is far from complimentary and states that he "is a dinosaur enthusiast with no scientific qualifications." Although he is a primary source, his conclusion is faulty and invalid.

✔ **Narrow your topic.** Once you have general knowledge of your subject, you are ready to focus on a specific aspect of that subject. After reading a biographical sketch of Ernest Shackleton, you might focus on his ship the HMS *Endurance,* on the view of a fellow sailor taken from his diary, on an idea taken from an interview with Shackleton's granddaughter, or on Shackleton's strong character in the face of adversity. Consider these suggestions for narrowing your topic.

- Ask yourself questions about what you have read.
- Talk with a friend about your topic. As a result of your conversation, you should be able to determine what really interests you.
- Focus your reading on a specific idea that you would like to know more about.

✔ **Determine whether your topic is narrow enough.** Since this is a two-page report, you must decide whether you can manage your topic within this page limit. If you find that you cannot, keep narrowing.

✔ **Determine the audience to whom you will be writing your research report.** It is important to identify your audience so that you can shape your report to reach that audience.

OVERVIEW of the WRITING PROCESS

Planning—choosing a topic, finding sources for the report, narrowing the topic, taking notes from research, quoting the sources accurately, formulating the thesis, and outlining the paper

Drafting—writing the rough draft, inserting quotations, and accurately documenting words and ideas from sources

Revising—rereading the report, marking points to be revised, making changes to the draft, reading the report again, entering the source notes in correct form, compiling a works-cited list, and proofreading the paper

Publishing—choosing a title for the work, printing a neat copy, presenting the report orally for the class, submitting the report to the school paper or local library, and illustrating the report with appropriate photographs

Planning Strategy
Discussion

You may want to tell your students the number and types of sources that you wish them to consult (e.g., encyclopedias, other printed books, periodicals, and electronic sources). For a two-page report, three different kinds of sources seem appropriate.

Planning Strategy
Analysis

Discuss the differences between primary and secondary sources and the advantages of each kind of source. Then display Writing Worksheet 11A (Teacher's Toolkit). Lead the students in identifying each source as a primary or a secondary source. Encourage students to use appropriate sources for their own research.

Planning Strategy
Discussion

Remind students that evaluating the trustworthiness of sources is an important part of the research process. Draw their attention to the information about Internet sources on page 5.

Planning Strategy
Discussion

Remind students to narrow their topics to an appropriate scope. Refer to the information on page 4 for some examples. Encourage the students to share their tentative topics with you before they spend much time on research. If necessary, assist the students in narrowing their topics.

Thinking Biblically

Provide students with samples of research reports that use a variety of sources, including online sources. Ask students to evaluate each source the report appeals to in light of the information in their Thinking Biblically note.

Thinking Biblically

Since no one can know everything, a research report you write will include ideas from other people and sources. Consequently, trusting the right sources—and not the wrong ones—is extremely important. In some cases, books are more reliable than the Internet. Since online publishing is easy and inexpensive (sometimes free), many people publish their ideas on the Internet. Some of these people may not be credible or may publish content that has not been properly researched or substantiated. For instance, college students have been known to use papers written by seventh graders because the papers turned up in a search engine list. Because books cost more to produce and have a longer shelf life than Internet content, publishers have at least some incentive to insure that they are accurate and therefore salable. But printing something in ink still does not make it true. And the Internet, because it changes rapidly, can have the benefit of being more up-to-date. Knowing which authority to trust takes education, but it also takes wisdom. The worldview a Christian gets from knowing and loving the Bible helps him know whom to trust. Ultimately, the only trustworthy authority on questions of importance is God Himself. The Bible, then, is our ultimate source.

✔ **Take notes from your research.** As you compile information for your report, keep in mind your purpose for writing and write down only information that you will use for your report. Record your research information accurately on your computer or on paper. You will have two kinds of notes: source notes and content notes.

- Source notes include the title (book, article, periodical, electronic database), author/editor, and publication information (publisher, city of publication, date of publication or date on which you accessed a website). You will use these source notes to compile a works-cited list to accompany your paper.
- Content notes record the exact words from the source or summarize in brief phrases the information from the source. Be sure to include page numbers from the source.

Consider this example of paraphrasing.

Original

In 1914 Ernest Shackleton, commander of the HMS *Endurance,* attempted the first transcontinental crossing of Antarctica. After the expedition ship became frozen in ice and sank, Shackleton focused on earning the complete trust of his men, maintaining the morale of his men, and negotiating the safe return of all twenty-seven men.

Brief Notes

- an accomplished seaman
- commander of HMS *Endurance*
- began first transcontinental crossing of Antarctica
- lost ship
- determined to lead and save his men

Paraphrase

Ernest Shackleton saved his crew of twenty-seven men after the HMS *Endurance* sank. Although his mission to cross Antarctica failed, his men remained in high spirits and learned to trust him.

tip

Correct paraphrasing reworks the wording, syntax, and order of the ideas. Writing down just the facts in your own words helps you to paraphrase thoroughly.

✔ **Quote your sources accurately.** Many of your content notes will be a summary or paraphrase of the material that you have read. You may, on occasion, wish to use a brief quotation to emphasize the authority of your source. A quotation is a precise word-for-word copying of the original. When you write a quotation, you must copy the exact words and punctuation of the source. If there is an error of punctuation or a misspelled word in the source, you must copy the mistake and indicate the mistake by inserting [*sic*] after the error.

Original

Almost overpowered by the natural elements, Shackleton remained stationery as he determined a course to save his men.

Quotation

"Almost overpowered by the natural elements, Shackleton remained stationery [*sic*] as he determined a course to save his men."

Planning Strategy

Demonstration

You may wish to ask students to record the source information on 3" × 5" cards and the content information on 4" × 6" cards to turn in as part of the research process. Display several examples of source cards. Additionally, consider specifying a minimum and maximum amount of information to be included on the content cards.

As an alternative to paper cards, digital note and source cards can be especially helpful to students as they organize their information. Online research tools and programs, some of which are free, provide a variety of options and formats for digital cards. In addition, word processing programs can be used to develop templates for note and source cards. Be sure to provide clear instructions regarding how students should format their cards and to demonstrate how to use the program or template you have chosen.

Reinforcement

Use Bulletin Board 11 (Teacher's Toolkit) to remind students of the precautions against plagiarism.

Planning Strategy

Analysis

Discuss the importance of accurate quotations and paraphrases. Then distribute a copy of Writing Worksheet 11B (Teacher's Toolkit) to each student. Encourage the students to use this checklist as a guide

✔ **Formulate your thesis.** The thesis statement is the guiding or controlling statement for your research report. Remember that the thesis of your report is a statement (not a question), is verifiable, and may be controversial.

Brackets pp. 335–36

QUESTION	Who knows about the history of the Iditarod?
STATEMENT	A near tragedy and seemingly insurmountable odds marked the original Iditarod.
UNVERIFIABLE	Many people enjoy hearing about the Iditarod.
VERIFIABLE	Staging the Iditarod requires millions of dollars and hundreds of volunteers each year.
NONCONTROVERSIAL	The Iditarod is a grueling race.
CONTROVERSIAL	Iditarod dogs face inhumane physical conditions.
ANNOUNCEMENT	I want to give you some information about the Iditarod.
STATEMENT	The Iditarod, a complex and multifaceted race, requires careful planning and training.

tip

Avoid hasty generalizations ("All newscasters are liberals"). Instead, be willing to qualify your statement with *most* or *some.*

✔ **Outline your paper.** You are ready to develop an outline that will help you organize your ideas. Your outline is the skeleton for your report; your paragraphs will be the substance of your report. Look at the information you have gathered. Group your related ideas and identify the main idea in each group. The main idea of each group may be the topic sentence for one of the middle paragraphs of your report. Remember that your outline is your guide and that your sentences may change as you write your report.

tip

Topic sentences support the thesis statement. A good topic sentence can often be expressed logically as a dependent clause if attached to the thesis statement with the subordinating conjunction *because.*

Drafting

✔ **Write the rough draft.** Set aside a block of time to write, perhaps an hour, and write your report in one sitting. With your outline and content notes in front of you, strive for clear thinking as you write. Keep in mind that this is a rough draft and will probably not be free of error. Be prepared to use a variety of methods of organization for the middle paragraphs. You may wish to use one or several examples to support a statement about the thesis. You may wish to include statistics or research results. Your goal should be a clear, logical arrangement of complete sentences. Here is how a rough draft copy of a paragraph might look.

> Shackleton's interest in each member of his crew developed a sense of strong loyalty. In dealing with his crew, Shackleton treated everyone eqully. He did not have any favorites. When the men had to desert the *Endurance*, Shackleton announced that they were allowed to take only two pounds of personal things such as books, money, and mementos. Shackleton set the example by throwing away "a handful of gold coins and his gold watch" (Interview with Granddaughter) and his Bible from Queen Alexandra. (Interview with Granddaughter) The Bible was retrieved by a sialor. Another example of his equal treatment of his men was that he would take each sailor's duty at some time during the voyage. One night Sir Ernest rescued a man who had fallen between two ice _______. (*Diary of a Survivor*) Ernest Shackleton was interested in every man.

whenever they use information from outside sources in their writing projects.

PLANNING STRATEGY
Participation

Distribute a copy of Writing Worksheet 11C (Teacher's Toolkit) to each student. Assist the students as they use the worksheet to formulate thesis statements and to identify supporting points.

PLANNING STRATEGY
Motivation

Encourage students to create an outline to give their papers direction. Review the information on pages 6–8 and encourage the students to use Writing Worksheet 11C as they develop their outlines. Consider asking each student to turn in a completed outline before he drafts his report. Evaluate the outlines to help the students correct weak support or poor organization.

DRAFTING STRATEGY
Participation

Ask students to identify the standard placements of a thesis statement, supporting topic sentences, and a thesis restatement in a typical essay. If necessary, review the first paragraph under "Writing Essays" on pages 19–20. Remind the students to use standard placement in their research reports.

Additional Resources

For more information about propaganda devices, see pages 320, 322–23 of *Writing and Grammar 10*, Third Edition (BJU Press).

tip

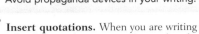

Avoid propaganda devices in your writing.

✔ **Insert quotations.** When you are writing your research report, carefully consider the use of quotations. Remember that quotations should come from reliable sources and should not be overused. If you choose to insert a quotation into your text, be sure to introduce the quotation in such a way that it becomes an integral part of your report. Quoting just a phrase is a helpful technique that enables you to work the quotation into your own sentence. Concerning the description of the creature in "Piltdown Chicken," Caesar writes, "The article featured a photograph, taken under ultraviolet light, of a creature '[w]ith arms of a primitive bird and the tail of a dinosaur.'" Notice how smoothly he incorporates this quotation and others throughout his article.

✔ **Do not plagiarize.** You have a responsibility to handle your sources carefully and correctly. Accurate documentation of words and ideas, whether quoted or paraphrased, insures the credibility of your writing. Whether your inaccurate documentation is intentional or unintentional, you are responsible. Remember—if you plagiarize, you are stealing someone else's work.

tip

If a fact is common knowledge—something mentioned by nearly everyone who writes on the subject—you need not cite your source.

Revising

✔ **Reread your report.** If at all possible, allow yourself a day or two after writing your research report before you reread your work. As you reread, ask yourself the following questions.

- Is the thesis a focused, declarative idea? Do the topic sentences support the thesis statement?
- Is the material well organized and presented clearly? Do the supporting ideas in the paragraphs flow smoothly from one thought to another?
- Are there any grammatical or mechanical mistakes? Are there any misspelled words?
- Have I quoted sources accurately or paraphrased correctly?

✔ **Mark any point of revision.** Do not take time to correct the mistakes or make changes to the draft at this time. You are reading for continuity and clarity.

Sentence Expansion and Reduction pp. 371–78

✔ **Make changes to the draft.** After you have read your report and marked the corrections and points of consideration, you are ready to make changes. You may wish to incorporate the techniques of reduction and expansion to improve your sentence structure. Try a variety of reduction and expansion techniques in your writing.

tip

Joining sentences on an equal basis indicates that the ideas are equal; joining sentences on an unequal basis indicates that some ideas are more important than others.

Now you are ready to determine the most effective arrangement of your middle paragraphs. One helpful strategy is to sandwich the weakest of the arguments between two stronger arguments. Your topic, however, may necessitate a logical or a chronological arrangement. An additional and important strategy is to place the strongest of the arguments just before the conclusion of your paper. By doing so, you leave the reader thinking about the best of your ideas.

Drafting Strategy

Discussion

Encourage students to set aside a block of time for drafting their research reports. Remind them that a rough draft does not need to be polished and free of error.

Enrichment

Explain that propaganda devices are inappropriate persuasion techniques that rely on erroneous reasoning. Review the "Think About It" sections on pages 141, 196–97, 237, and 289 to point out other invalid techniques.

Writing Workshop

Conduct a minilesson using the section "Biased Language" on pages 390–91. Remind students that their message will be more effective if it is void of any unnecessary offense.

Drafting Strategy

Analysis

Instruct students to analyze each quotation in Stephen Caesar's article. Ask them to notice his use of quotation marks, brackets, and ellipses. Lead the students to realize that Caesar usually incorporates the quotations into his own sentences, using long, set-off quotations only twice. Encourage the students to weave useful quotations into their essays smoothly, always placing them carefully into the context of the surrounding sentences. Remind them to quote

tip

On the collegiate level your instructor may refer to the *Nestorian* structure of an argument paper (placing the weakest of the arguments between the two stronger ones).

In "Piltdown Chicken" Caesar follows a chronological arrangement as he presents the refutations for the "fossil." He relays Simons' experience of learning of the Chinese farmer who "glued" it together and the dealer who sold the "composite." Then Caesar moves to Czerkas's published article in *National Geographic*.

✔ **Read your report again.** Now is your opportunity to look very carefully at your writing. Have you used logical transitions between sentences and paragraphs? In addition, do you recognize an overuse of a particular word in your writing? Have you chosen your words carefully?

Here is how a revision of the paragraph on Shackleton might look.

personal crew created a bond of unwavering
Shackleton's interest in each member ~~of his crew developed a sense of~~

had no favorites and equally
~~strong~~ loyalty. ~~In dealing with his crew,~~ Shackleton treated everyone ~~eqully.~~

Shackleton realized was doomed, he planned
~~He did not have any favorites.~~ When ~~the men had to desert~~ the *Endurance*, for survival.

each man was
Shackleton announced that ~~they were~~ allowed to take only two pounds of

personal things such as books, money, and mementos. Shackleton set the

a Bible from Queen Alexandra and
example by throwing away "a handful of gold coins and his gold watch"

(A. Shackleton, p 4).
~~(Interview with granddaughter) and his Bible from Queen Alexandra.~~

sailor, but the other possessions were lost.
~~(Interview with Granddaughter).~~ The Bible was retrieved by a ~~sialor.~~ Another

Shackleton's perform any job.
example of ~~his~~ equal treatment of his men was that he would ~~take each~~

During an encampment on ice
~~sailor's duty at some time during the voyage.~~ ~~O~~ne

night, Sir Ernest rescued a man who had fallen

parts of a floe (Orde-Lees).
between two ~~ice~~ ______ ~~(*Diary of a Survivor*)~~

Not only did Shackleton save the man, but he saved the
~~Ernest Shackleton was interested in every man~~ man's sleeping bag as well.

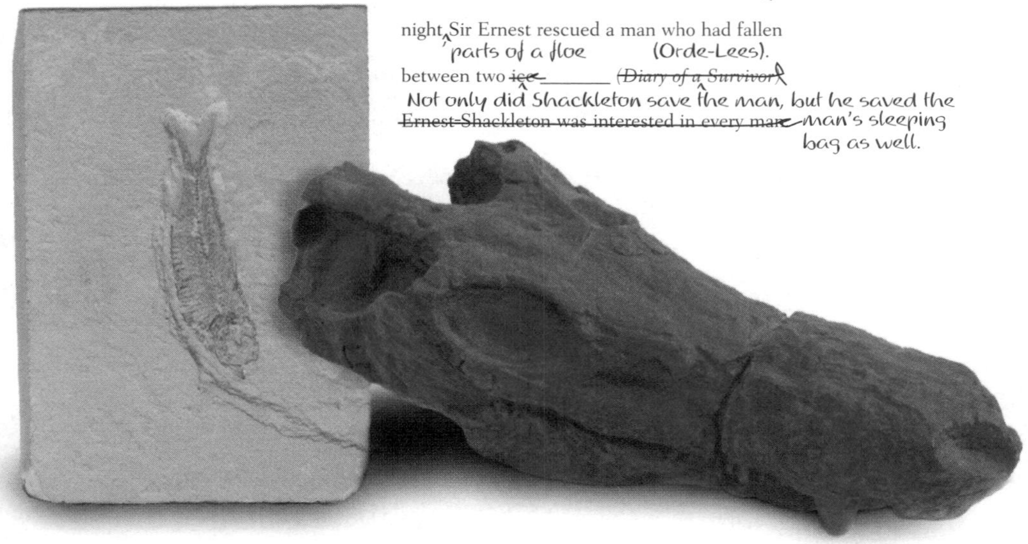

accurately or to paraphrase carefully whenever they use source material in their reports. Encourage them to continue using Writing Worksheet 11B as a guide.

Revising Strategy

Participation

Direct students to reread their reports, asking themselves the questions listed on page 266. Instruct them to mark all the necessary changes before they begin to revise.

Revising Strategy

Demonstration and Discussion

Tell students that just as the sentences within a paragraph should follow some logical organization, the arrangement of paragraphs within an essay should exhibit clear organization too. Review the information about paragraph organization on pages 266–67 and point out the examples of various organizational strategies. Discuss the benefits of using a certain type of paragraph arrangement over another for various topics and purposes.

Revising Strategy

Peer Response

Divide the class into small groups in which the students can read each other's reports, discuss the rationale of the paragraph arrangement, and offer suggestions. Remind the students to offer constructive feedback that explains the reasoning behind any suggestions. Then instruct the students to read their own reports again to determine whether any more revision is necessary.

✔ **Enter your source notes in correct form.** At this point, you are ready to check the accuracy of your parenthetical citations. Parenthetical citations give the source information inside parentheses within the text. These parenthetical notes should be placed at the end of the sentence or at a natural pause within the sentence. The citation should come before any punctuation needed for the sentence.

> The truth of God is eternal and unchanging; truth does not develop, and we do not invent it (Sidwell 71).

The citation above identifies Sidwell as the author of the work from which the statement about the truth of God came; it also specifies that the statement appears on page 71 of that source. The reader can find complete bibliographic information for that source on the works-cited list at the end of the paper.

The entry in the works-cited listing would appear as follows.

> Sidwell, Mark. *The Dividing Line: Understanding and Applying Biblical Separation*. Greenville: Bob Jones UP, 1998. Print.

Parenthetical citations should identify specific sources clearly. When you use two or more works by the same author, add the title, shortened or complete, after the author's name and a comma between author and work.

> Our model for Christianity is to be found in the Bible, not in the history of any nation (Sidwell, *The Dividing Line* 72).

If you include the author's name or the work within the text of your report, you may omit this information from the parenthetical note.

> In his book *The Dividing Line,* Sidwell discusses the influence of Harold Ockenga in the new evangelical movement (114–18).

✔ **Compile a works-cited list.** This page is an alphabetical list of the works that you have cited at least once in your report. Use hanging indentation format: the first line begins at the left margin and the following lines are indented one-half inch or five spaces. Use the author's complete name as it appears on the title page, putting the last name first. If there is more than one author, list the first author putting last name first and succeeding authors putting first name and then last name. If the author is unknown, alphabetize by title and ignore beginning articles.

If you are citing more than one work by the same author, alphabetize by the title of the work and use three hyphens to replace the author's name in all entries after the first.

> Sidwell, Mark. *The Dividing Line: Understanding and Applying Biblical Separation*. Greenville: Bob Jones UP, 1998. Print.
>
> ---. *Free Indeed: Heroes of Black Christian History*. Greenville: Bob Jones UP, 2001. Print.

✔ **Proofread your paper.** After you have incorporated all of your additions and corrections, make a new copy for the final proofreading. As you proofread, be aware of sentence structure errors (fragments, fused sentences, comma splices), usage problems (subject/verb agreement, pronoun/antecedent agreement, pronoun case), and punctuation, capitalization, and spelling errors. A good spell-check program cannot read for context and does not fully replace your ability to catch errors. Your writing should be as clear and appealing to your audience as possible, and the presentation of your report should be without offense.

ONE on ONE Conduct a revision conference with your student and discuss his rationale behind the paragraph organization. Offer your student suggestions for improved clarity or effectiveness and explain your reasons. Then instruct your student to read his report again to determine whether any more revision is necessary.

Revising Strategy

Demonstration

Materials

- three or more sources about one topic (e.g., a book, a periodical article, an encyclopedia article)

Display several quotations from various sources and the bibliographic information for each (list each piece of information—title, author, publisher, etc.—on a separate line as it appears in the source itself). Ask the students to explain the correct form for a source note as you write for display. Lead them to understand that the author's last name and the page number are sufficient for most source notes. Point out that the end punctuation follows the note, with no punctuation preceding the source note (except closing quotation marks when appropriate). Then lead the students in compiling a works-cited list for the same sources. Write the entries for display as the students explain the correct form for each source.

Publishing

✔ **Choose a title for your work.** Follow your teacher's instruction for placement of your title on the page or for preparing a separate title page. The title should suggest the topic of the report.

Too General	Polar Exploration
Good Possibilities	A Story of Polar Survival
	One Man's Determination

✔ **Print a neat copy.** You are ready to submit your final copy to your teacher. This copy should be neat and error free. Be sure to include all necessary ancillary pages, such as the title page, outline, and works-cited page.

✔ **Illustrate your report with appropriate photographs.** Remember that many professional photographs are copyrighted; you must be sure not to violate copyright laws. You might take your own photographs with a standard or digital camera.

✔ **Present your report orally for a class.** If you have written on a current-event topic, you may have opportunity to present your report in a history or government class.

✔ **Submit your report to the school paper or the local library.** You may wish to continue your research and develop your report further for submission to the school paper or the local library.

Some Ideas to Consider

Family and Consumer Science

- Research the effectiveness of vitamin supplements.
- Research a certain diet plan.

History

- Write about the leadership value of a specific general from the Civil War or World War II.

Social Studies

- Write about the impact of a mother's working outside the home.
- Research the impact of imports on the garment industry or the auto industry.

Physical Education

- Research the importance of aerobic exercise for senior citizens.

Revising Strategy

Discussion

Remind students to proofread their research reports carefully. Challenge them to proofread not only for correct grammar, usage, and mechanics but also for correct quotations, complete paraphrases, and proper format for the source notes and the works-cited list.

Evaluation

For help in grading this assignment, see "Grading Student Writing" (p. v) and Writing Rubric 11 (Teacher's Toolkit).

Publishing Strategy

Participation

Ask students why Stephen Caesar chose the title "Piltdown Chicken" for his article. *(He borrowed the term from news reports. It catches the reader's attention and suggests that the article will discuss a hoax about evolution.)* Challenge students to think of alternative titles and then discuss their suggestions. Instruct the students to follow the guidelines for good titles for their own reports.

Publishing Strategy

Motivation

Arrange for students to share their completed research reports with another class in a related subject area. Encourage them to prepare carefully. If time permits, allow the students to present their reports to you and their classmates before visiting the other class.

OBJECTIVES

Students will

1. identify capitalization errors and proper capitalization of personal names, religions, nationalities, and proper adjectives.
2. rewrite sentences containing capitalization errors in place names and transportation and astronomy terms.
3. identify capitalization errors and proper capitalization of businesses, organizations, and cultural and historical terms.
4. differentiate between capitalization errors and proper capitalization of titles.
5. differentiate between capitalization errors and proper capitalization of first words and single letters.
6. rewrite two paragraphs to correct errors in agreement, verb use, pronoun use, adjective and adverb use, and capitalization.

CAPITALIZATION

Common and Proper Nouns pp. 35–36

Languages of the world differ in the use of capitalization. Hebrew does not capitalize to indicate the beginning of a sentence; German capitalizes all nouns; Arabic words are written in reverse order without capitalization. English, of course, capitalizes for various purposes. English capitalization helps readers to identify the beginning of a sentence and to identify proper nouns and titles. Because there has been a recent movement to capitalize fewer words than have been traditionally capitalized, a writer should consult a recent dictionary if he is unsure about the capitalization of a word.

Proper Adjectives p. 50

Personal Names, Religions, Nationalities, & Proper Adjectives

Personal names and initials	Jordan W. Johnson R. W. B. Lewis
Titles used with a name	Prime Minister Cameron General MacArthur Dr. Lydia E. Blackstone Lydia E. Blackstone, DDS
Do not capitalize titles used in place of a person's name.	The general gave an inspiring charge to his soldiers.
Family words used as proper nouns	Aunt Karen Grandma Allen
If the word is modified by an adjective, do not capitalize it.	We are planning a surprise party for Grandpa. Her great-grandmother lives in a small town in New Jersey.
Terms used as descriptive substitutes for proper nouns	Father of our Country (George Washington) the Butcher of Baghdad (Saddam Hussein)
Personifications	Die not, poor Death; nor yet canst thou kill me. (John Donne, "Death, Be Not Proud")
Names of religions	Taoism Baha'i
Nouns and personal pronouns referring to the one true God	After Christ saw their sadness, He called for Lazarus to come forth.
Do not capitalize common nouns or pronouns that refer to pagan gods.	The worship of Diana, goddess of the Ephesians, caused conflict during Paul's missionary journey.
The words *Holy Bible* or *Bible* and parts of the Bible as well as the sacred writings of other religions	New Testament Philippians Koran
Nationalities and languages	Turkish, British, Canadian English, Hmong

CONTINUED

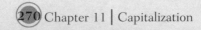

ONE on ONE Arrange for your student to share his research report with family and friends. Encourage him to prepare carefully. Allow time for him to present his report to you before the formal presentation.

CAPITALIZATION

Lesson Support

Student Worktext

Chapter 11 Review—pp. 457–58

Teacher's Toolkit

Chapter 11 Pretest
Teaching Help 11
Concept Reinforcement 11

Test

Chapter 11 Test

Teaching Strategy

Introduction

Ask students what they think of when they hear these sentences: *This is an Apple.* and *He doesn't have Windows.* Discuss possible contexts of these sentences. Then ask students how capitalization affects meaning. *(Without capitalization the terms refer to actual apples and windows; with capitalization the terms pertain to computers.)* Emphasize the importance of using correct capitalization in order to communicate effectively.

Ethnic groups	Caucasian, Asian Kurds, Croats
Proper adjectives *Do not capitalize a word modified by a proper adjective unless the two together form a proper name.* *Some words that were once considered proper adjectives are no longer capitalized when they form part of a compound noun. Check a dictionary if you are unsure of the capitalization of these words.*	Italian marble, Swiss watch British literature includes works written in the British Isles as well as works written elsewhere by British citizens. The Jankowskis have recently installed venetian blinds on every window in their house. Has your family ever owned a car with a diesel engine?

ESL

A proper adjective referring to a certain nationality and language can also be used as a noun (in singular form, always modified by *the*) to refer to persons from that country or area. Words of this type usually end in *ish* or *ese*, such as *Danish, Irish, Spanish, Japanese, Portuguese*, and *Vietnamese*. *French* can also be used this way.

> *The Faroese* speak a language that developed from Old Norse, whereas *the Finnish* speak a Finno-Ugric language.

Many other proper adjectives referring to nationalities can be used as nouns in singular or plural form, according to the meaning of one or more than one person from that country or area. These are mostly words ending in *an*, such as *African(s), Armenian(s), Belgian(s), Laotian(s), Mexican(s)*, and *Russian(s)*.

> *Asians* among the foreign-exchange students included *a Cambodian, two Koreans*, and *a Thai*.

11.1 PRACTICE *the skill*

Underline each word with a capitalization error.

1. One of the greatest scientific hoaxes of all time was perpetrated in the British isles: Piltdown Man.
2. In 1912, charles dawson, an amateur geologist, discovered bones supposedly belonging to a prehistoric british man, as well as other ancient fossils.
3. Dawson recruited several experts to help in the search for and authentication of the bones, including arthur smith woodward and sir arthur keith.
4. The bones were accepted as genuine by many british scientists.
5. The americans and the french, however, tended to be more skeptical.
6. Many were eager to claim Piltdown Man as the ancestor of their Grandfathers.

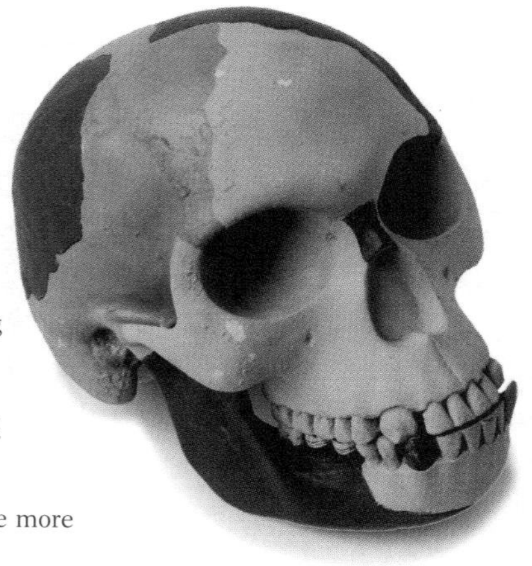

Literature Link

After discussing the use of capitalization in various languages, tell students that the British Victorian author Thomas Carlyle (1795–1881) wrote his famous *Sartor Resartus* with German capitalization because he pretended that the treatise was a translation from a German tailor's writings. Challenge students to discover Carlyle's purpose in writing this treatise and the meaning of the title *Sartor Resartus*. *(During Carlyle's time, attacks on Scripture's authority were eroding England's moral underpinnings. In* Sartor Resartus, *Carlyle tried to create a new system of moral values separate from the Bible. The English translation of the title is* The Tailor Re-tailored.*)*

Additional Resources

For more information about Thomas Carlyle, consult pages 604–8 of *British Literature*, Second Edition (BJU Press).

Teaching Strategy

Discussion

Ask the students whether they should capitalize words such as *president, pastor, senator*, and *queen* when these words are used alone in place of a person's name. *(no)* Inform them that they may see these words capitalized because conventions have changed over time. Emphasize that students should learn the capitalization rules and not rely upon what may "look right."

7. According to some people, Piltdown Man dealt a blow to christianity and the bible. However, as early as 1914 some expressed doubt about Piltdown Man.

8. Captain st. barre and major marriott claimed to have seen dawson in 1913 staining bones to cause them to appear older.

9. The claims of the captain and the Major were not made public for many years, but Dr. j. s. Weiner investigated the structure and makeup of the Piltdown Man.

10. In 1953, forty-one years after dawson announced his find, new scientific tests confirmed that Piltdown Man was a fake: a blend of a medieval human skull and an orangutan jaw.

11.2 REVIEW *the skill*

Rewrite each sentence so that it contains no capitalization errors. If the sentence is already correct, write *C* in the blank.

1. After forty-one years of deception, the truth finally triumphed in the matter of the Piltdown Man.

   C

2. Scientists also concluded that an elephant tooth found at the same site was likely from Tunisia, and a hippopotamus tooth may have been maltese or sicilian.

   Scientists also concluded that an elephant tooth found at the same site was likely from Tunisia, and a hippopotamus tooth may have been Maltese or Sicilian.

3. Who created the hoax about the grandfather of the human race?

   Who created the hoax about the Grandfather of the Human Race?

4. Since the revelation of 1953, accusations of fraud have come from germans, americans, british, french, spanish, and others.

   Since the revelation of 1953, accusations of fraud have come from Germans, Americans, British, French, Spanish, and others.

Evaluation

After teaching the capitalization rules for family words used as proper nouns, direct the students to write a descriptive paragraph about their family. Check the students' capitalization.

SpeechLink

Encourage students to find poems containing personification to read for an oral poetry presentation. Consider specifying a minimum number of poetic lines needed for each person's speech. Then assist the students in writing brief literary analyses of their poems to use as introductions. Assist them in practicing the introduction and delivery of their selections. Conduct a poetry presentation for other students who might learn from and enjoy the performance.

Scriptural Application

Pose the following question for classroom discussion: Is it a sign of disrespect to God that the style practices of many conservative Christian publishing houses no longer capitalize deity pronouns?

Display the following example sentence from a modern translation of Scripture that capitalizes all deity pronouns: "We wish to see a sign from You" (Matt. 12:38, NASB). In this quotation the Pharisees are addressing Jesus Christ, the Son of God. Ask students to suggest what might be wrong,

5. Amateurs and professionals promoted many theories, accusing everyone from dawson, woodward, and keith to sir arthur conan doyle, Author of the sherlock holmes stories.

Amateurs and professionals promoted many theories, accusing everyone from Dawson, Woodward, and Keith to Sir Arthur Conan Doyle, author of the Sherlock Holmes stories.

6. Another helper of dawson was a frenchman who had recently been in the african and mediterranean regions.

Another helper of Dawson was a Frenchman who had recently been in the African and Mediterranean regions.

7. A few people suspect sir arthur conan doyle—the author and amateur paleontologist—of planting the fabricated fossils, but the evidence is not strong.

A few people suspect Sir Arthur Conan Doyle—the author and amateur paleontologist—of planting the fabricated fossils, but the evidence is not strong.

8. One reason so many scientists accepted the discoveries without testing them may have been national pride: Piltdown Man was the first such "discovery" on british soil.

One reason so many scientists accepted the discoveries without testing them may have been national pride: Piltdown Man was the first such "discovery" on British soil.

9. Also, Piltdown Man matched scientists' preconceptions of ancient humans.

C

Sir Arthur Conan Doyle

10. Ultimately, some of the blame falls on human refusal to accept God and his word.

Ultimately, some of the blame falls on human refusal to accept God and His Word.

however, with capitalizing *you* in this instance. (*Capitalizing* you *implies that the Pharisees acknowledged Jesus' divinity, but they did not, as Jesus' response in the next verse makes clear.*)

The rules for English grammar, spelling, and punctuation are not divine. They are human. In some situations an experienced writer may violate a "rule," rather than adhere to it unswervingly in order to communicate his intention more accurately. But violations should take place only with adequate knowledge of established practices and the expectations of one's readership.

Teaching Strategy
Activity and Demonstration

Materials
- an adequate supply of dictionaries or access to an online dictionary

Display the following list of words:

- charley horse
- boston cream pie
- plaster of paris
- india ink
- dutch door
- chinese checkers
- vienna sausage
- french fries
- arabic numeral
- manila envelope

Direct students to consult a dictionary for the correct capitalization of each entry. (Consider allowing the students to work in small groups for this activity.) After students share their findings, explain that various authoritative sources may disagree about the capitalization of words such as these because they are no longer identified with their place of origin. Inform the students that the trend among grammarians is to use lowercase for these terms.

Place Names, Transportation, & Astronomy Terms

Countries Continents	Uzbekistan Asia
Cities States	Evansville Indiana
Sections of a country or the world	Outer Banks, Grand Strand, Amazonia The South is sometimes called the Bible Belt.
Do not capitalize direction words when they refer to compass directions.	We live in the northwest corner of the state. Bill drove south on Interstate 85.
Geographic features and recreational areas	Niagara Falls Grand Canyon National Park
Streets and roads	Pinnacle Drive Sunshine Parkway
Bodies of water	Bay of Fundy, Lake Louise, Caribbean Sea, Pacific Ocean
Do not capitalize a geographical noun unless it is part of a proper noun.	Across the bay several large houses stood tall.
Aircraft	*Spirit of St. Louis*
Spacecraft	*Voyager, Curiosity*
Ships	*H. L. Hunley*
Trains	*Crescent Limited*
Planets, stars, other heavenly bodies	Jupiter, Saturn, Betelgeuse, Orion
Capitalize the word earth *when used as a proper name for our planet, especially when listed with the names of other heavenly bodies that must be capitalized.*	Mercury, Venus, or Mars can be the closest planet to Earth, depending on their locations in their respective orbits.
Do not capitalize earth *when it is preceded by* the.	Water covers approximately seventy percent of the earth.
Capitalize sun *and* moon *only when listed with heavenly bodies that must be capitalized.*	The sun and moon help regulate the ecosystem of the earth. The planet closest to the Sun is Mercury.

Lake Louise

Teaching Strategy
Modeling

Display the following sentences: *After three years of traveling east, Marco Polo arrived in China. Marco Polo spent nearly a quarter century in the East.* Explain that geographic regions must be capitalized (e.g., the American West, America's antebellum South, the Far East), but compass directions should not be capitalized (traveling south of the border, driving northwest, sailing east).

Teaching Strategy
Participation

Help the students master the capitalization of the words *earth, sun,* and *moon* by directing their attention to the last section of rules in the chart on page 274. Discuss how these rules can clear up much error and confusion. Examine the sample sentences. Instruct the students to write five original sentences demonstrating their knowledge of capitalization rules regarding heavenly bodies.

11.3 PRACTICE *the skill*

Underline each word with a capitalization error.

1. Not everyone knows that Edgar Allan Poe, the master of the short story, also enjoyed creating literary hoaxes, including one about a type of early Aircraft.
2. Known as Poe's Great Balloon Hoax, the story was published in the *New York Sun* and told of a balloon flight across the atlantic ocean from europe to north america.
3. The tale claims that balloonists set out from london, england, for paris, France, but were caught in a gale and blown South to charleston, south carolina.
4. The balloon, built in an elliptical shape, bore the name *victoria*.
5. While crossing the ocean, the balloonists passed over many ships, including one called the *atalanta*.
6. Poe claimed the balloon landed at Fort Moultrie in Charleston harbor. Interestingly, Poe himself was once stationed at Fort Moultrie.
7. Another of Poe's newspaper hoaxes told of the first European to cross the rocky mountains, one Julius Rodman, in 1792.
8. According to the story, Rodman and his men crossed the missouri river and then headed North.
9. A third canard concerned the life of Hans Pfaall, a human who flees to the moon in a Balloon in order to escape his creditors.
10. Pfaall keeps a diary in which he records his observations of the earth; the diary is later brought to rotterdam by a native of the moon.

Capitalization | Chapter 11 275

11.4 REVIEW *the skill*

Rewrite each sentence so that it contains no capitalization errors. If the sentence is already correct, write *C* in the blank.

1. One notable hoax said to have occurred on manhattan island in 1824 may itself have been a hoax.

   One notable hoax said to have occurred on Manhattan Island in 1824 may itself have been a hoax.

2. A common meeting place in new york was Centre Market at the intersection of baxter, centre, and grand streets.

   A common meeting place in New York was Centre Market at the intersection of Baxter, Centre, and Grand Streets.

3. At Centre Market, a retired ship's carpenter named Lozier supposedly convinced the people of the island that manhattan was in danger of tipping over into the atlantic ocean.

   At Centre Market, a retired ship's carpenter named Lozier supposedly convinced the people of the island that Manhattan was in danger of tipping over into the Atlantic Ocean.

4. According to the story, Lozier claimed that the weight of buildings in the battery area of the city had unbalanced the Island.

   According to the story, Lozier claimed that the weight of buildings in the Battery area of the city had unbalanced the island.

5. His daring plan for saving the island involved sawing it in half at kingsbridge.

   His daring plan for saving the island involved sawing it in half at Kingsbridge.

276 Chapter 11 | Capitalization

6. Lozier said he had arranged for fifteen hundred boats to tow the half-island into New York Harbor.

C

7. Once out in the Bay, the half-island would be turned around and reattached.

Once out in the bay, the half-island would be turned around and reattached.

8. As part of this great feat, long island would have to be towed out of the way to make room for the turning of manhattan.

As part of this great feat, Long Island would have to be towed out of the way to make room for the turning of Manhattan.

9. More than three hundred men signed up to help. Lozier told half of the men to meet at the corner of broadway and bowery; the other half, on spring street. But Lozier never showed up.

More than three hundred men signed up to help. Lozier told half of the men to meet at the corner of Broadway and Bowery; the other half, on Spring Street. But Lozier never showed up.

10. Retold as fact for decades, there is no proof that the practical joke about saving Manhattan ever really happened.

C

Businesses & Organizations, Cultural & Historical Terms	
Businesses and their abbreviations	Madawaska Hardscapes General Electric (GE)
Do not capitalize the common noun for a business.	Before we finished our yard work, we visited several landscape supply companies.
Brand names of commercial products	Hershey's Kisses Ford Thunderbird
Do not capitalize the product name unless it is part of the brand name.	Timex watch

CONTINUED

Teaching Strategy

Participation

Personalize this lesson's content by asking students for the names of items corresponding to each rule in the chart on pages 277–78. For example, ask the students to list their favorite type of motor vehicle, their favorite birthday present, other schools they have attended, and so on. Display the students' answers but omit all capitalization. Ask the students what words need to begin with a capital letter.

Businesses & Organizations, Cultural & Historical Terms	
Government departments	Department of the Interior Federal Aviation Administration (FAA)
Political parties	Tory Party, Democratic Party
Organizations	United Service Organization Young Republicans
Members of most organizations	a Republican
Do not capitalize the common name of a club or team.	The soccer team practices on Monday afternoons.
Schools	Ironside Middle School Wharton School of Business
Buildings	Metropolitan Auditorium Gaviidae Common
Structures	Hadrian's Wall
Monuments	Washington Monument
Months	January, December
Days	Tuesday, Wednesday
Holidays	Christmas, Mother's Day
Do not capitalize the names of the seasons unless personified.	The first day of summer is usually quite warm.
The abbreviations BC and AD *Notice that BC ("before Christ") is correctly placed after the year and that AD (anno Domini, "in the year of the Lord") is correctly placed before the year.*	Between 2700 and 2500 **BC** the great pyramids of Egypt were constructed. In **AD** 1066 William of Normandy became the first Norman king of England.
The abbreviations a.m./p.m., A.M./P.M. *These abbreviations may be either lowercased or capitalized but should be used consistently.*	10:00 **A.M.**, 5:00 **P.M.** 10:00 **a.m.**, 5:00 **p.m.**
Historical events and periods	Battle of the Bulge Age of Reason
Documents	Treaty of Versailles
Awards	Nobel Peace Prize
Special Events	St. Paul Winter Carnival

ESL To decide whether a name for a business is a proper noun or a common noun, consider whether you could write a check payable to that name. If you could, then you should capitalize the name.

Teaching Strategy
Analysis

Direct the students to find examples of cultural and historical terms in other textbooks. Ask them to compile two lists: terms that are capitalized and terms that are not capitalized. As volunteers share items from their lists, write the items for display. Ask the students to suggest categories for the words and to explain why some categories are capitalized but others are not. Lead them to understand that only specific names of documents, events, and time periods are capitalized as proper nouns. Point out that articles, prepositions, and conjunctions are not usually capitalized unless they begin the name. (Compare with the information about titles on page 282.)

Enrichment

Challenge the students to investigate the history behind the English names for the months of the year, days of the week, and holidays. After the students have presented their findings, lead them to notice that many of these words are derived from proper nouns, which are also capitalized, of course.

11.5 PRACTICE *the skill*

Underline each word with a capitalization error. If the sentence is correct, write *C* in the blank.

_____ 1. Lying near Fossil Butte national monument in Wyoming and extending into Utah and Colorado, the Green River Formation fascinates scientists, both creationist and evolutionist.

_____ 2. On wednesday, october 30, 2002, at the annual meeting of the geological society of America, geologists from Loma Linda university presented a paper on the Green River Formation.

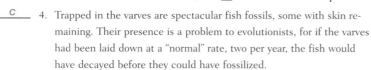

Green River Formation

_____ 3. Evolutionary scientists believe that the Green River Formation gives valuable evidence about the eocene period and the earth's age. They say the number of varves, finely laminated sediment layers, in the formation date it to millions of years bc.

__C__ 4. Trapped in the varves are spectacular fish fossils, some with skin remaining. Their presence is a problem to evolutionists, for if the varves had been laid down at a "normal" rate, two per year, the fish would have decayed before they could have fossilized.

_____ 5. The Chicago natural history museum performed an experiment showing that fish can decay within a week, even in settings with little oxygen.

__C__ 6. In addition, events can change the varve deposit rate; in AD 1960 Hurricane Donna left six inches of varvelike mud in a short time.

_____ 7. Finally, the number of layers is not constant across the formation, varying by over four hundred layers. Scholars from the university of Wisconsin and the Lamont-Doherty earth observatory have studied the formation's age.

_____ 8. The Green River Formation is also a source of oil; in may 2012 a spokesperson for the government accountability office (gao) testified before congress about oil shale deposits in the formation.

_____ 9. Do any geologists hope to receive the day medal for research at Green River?

_____ 10. "Green River blues," a magazine article, is an intriguing look at the formation from a creationist perspective.

If students are unfamiliar with the Green River Formation, explain that *Formation* is capitalized as part of the proper name for this geological feature.

Science Link

After the students complete Practice the Skill 11.5, ask them whether they know of additional scientific evidence supporting the biblical accounts of Creation and the Flood. Respond to student answers and comment that even though God has given us the power of observation and reason, these must be checked constantly by the absolute truth of God's Word. Encourage the students to research and document other geological findings demonstrating the Bible's truth. Then motivate your students to boldly yet graciously combat deception and error.

Capitalization | Chapter 11 279

If ta th it th practice is consistent with capitalizing other specific terms of religious, cultural, and historical importance.

11.6 REVIEW *the skill*

Rewrite each sentence so that it contains no capitalization errors. If the sentence is already correct, write C in the blank.

1. The story of Darwin's deathbed recantation is the basis of an invalid argument for Creation. There is no proof that Darwin, who died in april 1882 during the victorian era, ever made such a statement.

   The story of Darwin's deathbed recantation is the basis of an invalid argument for Creation. There is no proof that Darwin, who died in April 1882 during the Victorian Era, ever made such a statement.

2. Darwin's daughter, Henrietta, stated that the woman who claimed to have heard Darwin's recantation in his house, known as down house, was not present at any time during Darwin's illness.

   Darwin's daughter, Henrietta, stated that the woman who claimed to have heard Darwin's recantation in his house, known as Down House, was not present at any time during Darwin's illness.

3. Another erroneous argument for Creation stems from the national aeronautic and space administration's reported expectation of finding deep layers of dust on the moon, a discovery that would prove an ancient universe.

   Another erroneous argument for Creation stems from the National Aeronautic and Space Administration's reported expectation of finding deep layers of dust on the moon, a discovery that would prove an ancient universe.

280 Chapter 11 | Capitalization

4. Actually, by 1969 evolutionists did not expect thick moon dust, and nasa knew that the early estimates of moon dust had been wrong; much of the public, however, still believed the early estimates.

Actually, by 1969 evolutionists did not expect thick moon dust, and NASA knew that the early estimates of moon dust had been wrong; much of the public, however, still believed the early estimates.

5. Though some think that the great wall of china is visible to the naked eye from the Moon, astronauts reported that all they could see was clouds, ocean, and the occasional patch of desert or greenery.

Though some think that the Great Wall of China is visible to the naked eye from the moon, astronauts reported that all they could see was clouds, ocean, and the occasional patch of desert or greenery.

6. A famous forged document was called the Donation of Constantine.

C

7. Some think that the first thanksgiving took place in late november; actually, it happened sometime between september 21 and november 11 and lasted three days.

Some think that the first Thanksgiving took place in late November; actually, it happened sometime between September 21 and November 11 and lasted three days.

8. Although the first written account of a possible Loch Ness monster episode occurred in ad 565, there is no substantial evidence to prove this supposed hoax.

Although the first written account of a possible Loch Ness monster episode occurred in AD 565, there is no substantial evidence to prove this supposed hoax.

9. In the information age, it seems that rumors and fabrications have only gotten worse.

In the Information Age, it seems that rumors and fabrications have only gotten worse.

10. The Democrats and the Republicans sometimes happily repeat untrue stories about each other, unaware that their information is faulty.

C

Capitalization | Chapter 11 281

Underlining for Italics p. 337

Quotation Marks p. 330

Titles

Capitalize the first and last words in a title as well as all other important words. Do not capitalize an article, a coordinating conjunction, the *to* of the infinitive, or a preposition of fewer than five letters unless it is the first or last word in a title.

Titles

Newspapers and magazines	*Washington Post* *Field and Stream*
Do not capitalize the word the *when referring to a newspaper.*	the *Atlanta Journal-Constitution*
Literary compositions (including books, essays, poems, and plays)	*Jane Eyre* "Prejudice and Intolerance" "The Road Not Taken" *Our Town*
Sections of a book or play	Chapter 12 Index Act 1
Some authorities do not capitalize the parts of a book or play unless they appear as a title.	The drama class performed a cutting of act 1 from *Macbeth.*
Musical compositions (including songs, operas, and instrumental music)	"Silent Night" *Aida* Adagio from the Fifth Symphony
Works of art (including drawings, paintings, and sculptures)	Ed Ruscha's *Self 1967* Baglione's *The Entombment of Christ* Michelangelo's *Pieta*
Television and radio programs	*Dateline NBC* *A Prarie Home Companion*
Specific courses of study	History of Civilization Algebra 1
Do not capitalize the common noun for a course.	Students must bring their textbooks to history class tomorrow.

Teaching Strategy
Participation

Ask students to list their favorite courses of study in high school as well as any courses they might like to take in college. Write the answers for display, some with incorrect capitalization. Then ask students to proofread the list and to explain why some words need changes in their capitalization.

Teaching Strategy
Discussion

You may wish to point out that capitalization conventions vary somewhat among academic and professional disciplines. The rules listed in this section are standard for most printed items. Journalism, however, often requires only the first word of a title to be capitalized in headlines. Furthermore, some styles of documentation that students might encounter in college (e.g., APA or CSE) have different capitalization standards than those used in general practice. Encourage the students to examine headlines and reference notes in magazines or journals and to share their results with the class.

11.7 PRACTICE *the skill*

Underline each word with a capitalization error.

1. In Act 3 of *as you like it,* Touchstone observes, "Honesty coupled to beauty is to have honey a sauce to sugar."
2. Forgery detection might be a good unit for an Art class!
3. In 1945, a painter named van Meegeren ran into serious trouble for his paintings, which included *Christ and the disciples at Emmaus.*
4. Van Meegeren, a native of the Netherlands, had faked Vermeer paintings and sold one, *Christ and the woman taken in adultery,* to the Nazi Hermann Göring.
5. When the war ended, the Dutch government wanted to try van meegeren for treason for selling national treasures to the enemy.
6. No one would believe that paintings like his *the last supper* were frauds, and van Meegeren finally had to paint another "Vermeer" in his cell to avoid conviction for treason.
7. Van Meegeren became a legend in the art world; Radnoti's book *the fake* discusses him, and in 2002, The *Casco Bay Weekly* ran an article referring to van Meegeren.
8. Violinist fritz Kreisler, on the other hand, was guilty of a backward kind of forgery.
9. Kreisler attributed his *tempo di minuetto* and *la précieuse,* as well as other works, to musicians such as Pugnani and Couperin, claiming to be only the arranger.
10. In the 1970s the Canadian Broadcasting Corporation's show *musicamera* presented a profile of this famous violinist.

View of Delft by Vermeer

Writing Link

After teaching the capitalization rules for titles, assist students in creating their own community newsletter. Ask them to pretend to be fine arts connoisseurs writing reviews of various literary works, film documentaries, cultural events, and so forth. Specify that the works and performances they review must meet the requirements given in Philippians 4:8.

Art Link

If the students have written a community newsletter as described in the previous Writing Link, encourage them to use their artistic skills to design elements such as a masthead, headlines, and advertisements. As a class, decide whether to use standard capitalization for design elements or to allow some lowercase letters.

11.8 REVIEW *the skill*

Write the letter of the choice that is capitalized correctly.

__B__ 1. A. One hoax that was not meant to be taken seriously but shocked America concerned H. G. Wells's book *The War Of The Worlds.*
B. One hoax that was not meant to be taken seriously but shocked America concerned H. G. Wells's book *The War of the Worlds.*

__B__ 2. A. On October 30, 1938, the CBS radio Network broadcast *The War Of The Worlds,* a dramatized version of the book.
B. On October 30, 1938, the CBS radio network broadcast *The War of the Worlds,* a dramatized version of the book.

__A__ 3. A. The dramatization begins like any other program, with an orchestra playing music—in this case, "La Cumparsita."
B. The dramatization begins like any other program, with an orchestra playing music—in this case, "La cumparsita."

__A__ 4. A. Next in the show, a reporter interviews a man with great knowledge of astronomy about mysterious explosions on Mars.
B. Next in the show, a reporter interviews a man with great knowledge of Astronomy about mysterious explosions on Mars.

__B__ 5. A. This episode of *Mercury theatre on the air* continues in New Jersey with the attack of the Martians.
B. This episode of *Mercury Theatre on the Air* continues in New Jersey with the attack of the Martians.

__B__ 6. A. Worried inhabitants of Princeton, New Jersey, flooded the campus paper, the *daily Princetonian,* with calls.
B. Worried inhabitants of Princeton, New Jersey, flooded the campus paper, the *Daily Princetonian,* with calls.

__B__ 7. A. In Part two of the program, a man who thinks he is the lone survivor muses on the events.
B. In Part Two of the program, a man who thinks he is the lone survivor muses on the events.

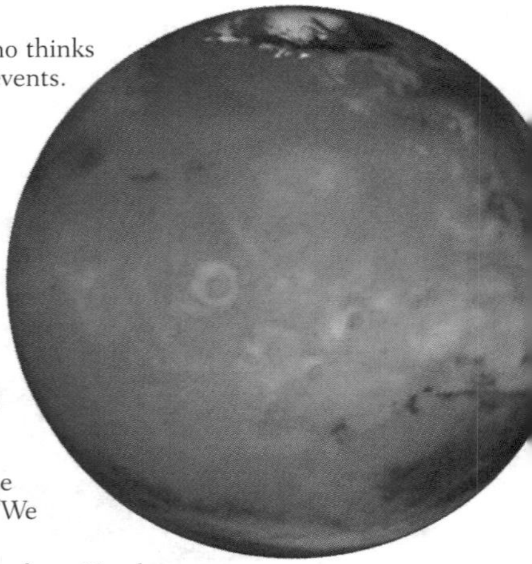

__A__ 8. A. He discovers that the Martians have been killed by natural microbiology (bacteria present on Earth).
B. He discovers that the Martians have been killed by natural Microbiology (bacteria present on earth).

__A__ 9. A. The next day the *New York Times* ran a story on the panic that erupted.
B. The next day *The New York Times* ran a story on the panic that erupted.

__B__ 10. A. The American public could echo a line from *hamlet,* act 3, scene 1, and say, "We were the more deceived."
B. The American public could echo a line from *Hamlet,* Act 3, Scene 1, and say, "We were the more deceived."

Teaching Strategy
Induction

Materials
- recording device

To help students learn to capitalize lines of dialogue correctly, record a series of impromptu questions and answers with the students. After recording several mini-dialogues, play the recording for the class. Direct students to write the dialogue out with correct capitalization. Based upon these written sample dialogues, ask the students to state general rules about capitalizing lines of dialogue. Write the students' answers for display.

ONE *on* ONE Conduct the activity as explained, but record more than one dialogue with your student. Then allow your student to select one of the dialogues to write with correct capitalization.

First Words & Single Letters

First word in a sentence	The nativity scene was lighted beautifully.
Do not capitalize the first word of a sentence in parentheses within another sentence.	The nativity scene (it is a new decoration this year) was lighted beautifully.
First word in a line of dialogue	Josh asked, "Who is your favorite author?"
Do not capitalize the second part of a divided quotation unless the second part is the beginning of a new sentence.	"Dickens," Julie quickly responded, "is definitely my favorite author." "He wrote many great novels," Julie continued. "Sometimes I have trouble deciding which is my favorite."
Do not capitalize quotations integrated into sentences of one's own.	"Do you really think that he wrote 'great novels'?" inquired Josh.
First word in a line of poetry, whether formatted as a poem or quoted in a sentence	In all this place of silence There are no kindred spirits. (Edgar Lee Masters, "Flossie Cabanis") Do you know who wrote the lines "In all this place of silence / There are no kindred spirits"?
Do not capitalize a word that the poet does not capitalize. Many modern poets choose not to capitalize the first word of each line.	
First word (and any proper nouns or proper adjectives) in each item of a formal outline	I. Planning a Christmas party A. Determining a theme B. Choosing the main course C. Deciding on the additional foods
First word in a formal statement or quotation following a colon	Those attending the trial gasped at the jury's verdict: "We, the jury, find the defendant not guilty.
The first word of an explanatory statement following the colon is usually lowercased.	The neighborhood children learned a valuable lesson: don't tease dogs unknown to you.
First word and all nouns in the greeting of a letter	Dear Fellow Students,
First word in the closing of a letter	Yours truly,
Personal pronoun *I*	Joshua and I enjoyed playing board games after dinner.
Archaic address-form *O*	I will love thee, O Lord.

CONTINUED

Commas in Letters pp. 310–11

Literature Link

Ask students whether they can name a modern American poet who abandoned conventional capitalization in his writing. *(E. E. Cummings)* Explain that Edward Estlin Cummings (1894–1962) sought to express his break from traditionalism by creating unconventional poetry. Explain that while something unconventional is not necessarily better or worse than its traditional counterpart, Cummings's disregard for God's truth makes much of his poetry void of true significance. Ask students whether they have experimented with unconventional form in personal correspondence or journal writing. Respond to the students' answers by encouraging their creativity; then discuss what writing situations might allow for more innovation than others. *(journals, poems, and short stories as compared to letters to the editor, resumes, research reports, etc.)* Emphasize that truly effective writing manifests God's truth in a compelling, meaningful fashion. Moreover, innovative forms of writing can complement content that focuses on God.

Additional Resources

For further discussion of E. E. Cummings and samples of his poetry, see pages 593–99 of *American Literature,* Second Edition (BJU Press).

First Words & Single Letters	
Single letters used as words (including academic grades, vitamins, musical notes, and major musical keys)	James earned an A average during his first semester. Recent studies indicate that vitamin K is important for bone strength. During her practice time, she had difficulty with high C.
Letters used to clarify a following word	His T-shirt was hanging out from under his dress shirt. The I-formation is a popular football tactic.

11.9 PRACTICE *the skill*

Underline each word with a capitalization error.

1. Dear members of the Creation Science Society:
2. Yesterday's trip to the Natural History Museum was quite informative. The building is roughly t-shaped, with the entry in the top of the t.
3. When Daniel, Joanna, and i walked through the doors, the first thing we saw was a huge exhibit on the origins of life.
4. sections of the exhibit explained about the Big Bang, DNA, and mutation, and there was even a diagram of an evolutionary "tree." Other ideas were left out: certainly the biblical account got no space.
5. The exhibit credited Darwin with originating the concept of natural selection; Actually, natural selection was first suggested by a creationist twenty years before Darwin wrote.
6. Joanna gives the exhibit an a for graphics and layout and an f for impartiality.
7. Daniel was wearing his Creation Science Society t-shirt, and a man in the tour group asked him whether he really "Believes all that stuff."
8. Daniel replied, "not only do I believe it, but the weight of evidence is for it."
9. "But," the other man said, "How can you believe in Creation when mutation and change are all around?" Daniel pointed out that we know of no examples of mutation that add genetic information in the offspring.
10. In human experience, Mutation involves loss of genetic information in the offspring, which would not lead to a "higher" life form.

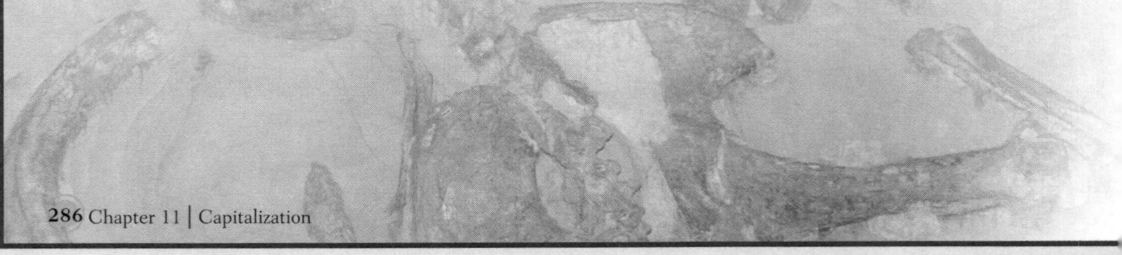

REINFORCEMENT

Distribute a copy of Teaching Help 11 (Teacher's Toolkit) to each student for additional practice with the capitalization rules in this chapter.

REVIEW *the skill*

Write the letter of the choice that is capitalized correctly.

B 1. A. In the meantime, Joanna and i were talking to the guide about evolution's basis of faith.
B. In the meantime, Joanna and I were talking to the guide about evolution's basis of faith.

B 2. A. At one point, the guide said, "a proof for evolution is that all reputable scientists today believe it."
B. At one point, the guide said, "A proof for evolution is that all reputable scientists today believe it."

A 3. A. Joanna commented that truth doesn't depend on who believes it: whether or not a person believes in gravity, it exists.
B. Joanna commented that truth doesn't depend on who believes it: whether or not a person believes in Gravity, it exists.

B 4. A. Saying or hoping a thing doesn't make it true: I can say, "o king, live forever," but my words don't lengthen his life.
B. Saying or hoping a thing doesn't make it true: I can say, "O king, live forever," but my words don't lengthen his life.

B 5. A. Next, the guide stated that the c-14 dating method proves the world to be ancient.
B. Next, the guide stated that the C-14 dating method proves the world to be ancient.

A 6. A. However, the carbon-14 method loses much accuracy when the time span involved exceeds three thousand years.
B. however, the carbon-14 method loses much accuracy when the time span involved exceeds three thousand years.

B 7. A. The guide finally admitted that her presuppositions (She called them "beliefs") have shaped her worldview.
B. The guide finally admitted that her presuppositions (she called them "beliefs") have shaped her worldview.

A 8. A. As we left, I noticed a quotation from Shakespeare above the door: "Truth is truth / To the end of reckoning." How ironic.
B. As we left, I noticed a quotation from Shakespeare above the door: "Truth is truth / to the end of reckoning." How ironic.

B 9. A. We might rather say, "truth is fallen in the street, and equity cannot enter" (Isa. 59:14).
B. We might rather say, "Truth is fallen in the street, and equity cannot enter" (Isa. 59:14).

B 10 A. sincerely yours,
Ginny Avery
B. Sincerely yours,
Ginny Avery

Capitalization | Chapter 11 287

11.11 CUMULATIVE *review*

Rewrite the following paragraphs, correcting the fifteen errors from these categories: subject-verb agreement, pronoun-antecedent agreement, verb use, pronoun use, adjective and adverb use, and capitalization. *(Answers may vary.)*

Literary frauds are produced for many reasons. Some people produce it solely for money and reputation, while others genuinely believe that their work is doing good. One example is W. D. Mahan, an American minister. In 1879, Mahan publishes a volume variously called *The Acts of Pilate*, *the Archko Volume*, or *A Correct Transcript of Pilate's Court*. Mahan claimed that he learned of the historical basis from a German guest. He said the guest (Whose name was Whydaman) later wrote from westphalia, Germany, to give more aid. Mahan supposedly then received documents from the Vatican concerning the trial of Jesus. Mahan later published more documents about Jesus and his life, saying him and other scholars had found additional information at Constantinople's Mosque of st. Sophia.

Unfortunately, the work is a fake. Mahan's claims about these most unique discoveries caused curiosity, and a contemporary attacked the book in the *Boonville Weekly advertiser* in 1885, pointing out various problems in their article. Mahan's church suspended him for a year because of his deception. The circumstances surrounding Mahan's claims are highly dubious. Twyman and McIntosh, the "great scholars" whom supposedly helped him find and translate the documents, is completely unknown. Historical details can be proved untrue: for example, he states that the historian Tacitus wrote a biography in AD 56, though Tacitus was born sometime around ad 55. These facts lead to a sad conclusion—the book by Mahan, though possibly a well-meaning attempt to support Christianity by adding archaeological evidence to the Bible, is a fabrication.

Literary frauds are produced for many reasons. Some people produce them solely for money and reputation, while others genuinely believe that their work is doing good. One example is W. D. Mahan, an American minister. In 1879, Mahan published a volume variously called The Acts of Pilate, The Archko Volume, *or* A Correct Transcript of Pilate's Court. *Mahan claimed that he learned of the historical basis from a German guest. He said the guest (whose name was Whydaman) later wrote from Westphalia, Germany, to give more aid. Mahan supposedly then received documents from the Vatican concerning the trial of Jesus. Mahan later published more documents about Jesus and His life, saying he and other scholars had found additional information at Constantinople's Mosque of St. Sophia.*

Unfortunately, the work is a fake. Mahan's claims about these unique discoveries caused curiosity, and a contemporary attacked the book in the Boonville Weekly Advertiser *in 1885, pointing out various problems in his article. Mahan's church suspended him for a year because of his deception. The circumstances surrounding Mahan's claims are highly dubious. Twyman and McIntosh, the "great scholars" who supposedly helped him find and translate the documents, are completely unknown.*

REINFORCEMENT

Use Chapter 11 Review on pages 457–58 for additional test review.

EVALUATION

Use Chapter 11 Test to evaluate students' understanding of the content and concepts of the chapter.

Historical details can be proved untrue: for example, he states that the historian Tacitus wrote a biography in AD 56, though Tacitus was born sometime around AD 55. These facts lead to a sad conclusion—the book by Mahan, though possibly a well-meaning attempt to support Christianity by adding archaeological evidence to the Bible, is a fabrication.

THINK ABOUT IT

Examine the Evidence!

Many of the hoaxes you have just read about were successful because the so-called evidence appeared to be sound even though it was not. Some hoaxes depended on the credentials or the apparent sincerity of the perpetrator of the hoax. When presented with something they hope to be true, people are often willing to suspend disbelief. They fail to examine the evidence or to question the soundness of the reasoning. They may believe whatever someone says if that person seems to be a sincere expert. A critical thinker, on the other hand, bases his or her decisions on sound reasoning and clear evidence.

Before you make a decision to accept or reject what someone else has proposed, first determine the bases for the statement. What reasons or evidence have been offered as support? Then examine that support, using the tools of critical thinking.

- Is the reasoning valid? Are the premises true?
- Is the evidence presented fact or opinion? If the evidence is merely opinion, is the opinion itself based on facts?
- From what sources is the evidence drawn? Does information come from primary sources, such as original documents or eyewitnesses? Or is the information borrowed from secondary sources, such as reviews of someone else's research or second-hand reports of events ("Mike says that Joyce saw it happen!")? As a general rule, primary sources tend to be the most reliable.
- Are the facts reasonable? Or is it unlikely that they could be true? For example, the claim that Tacitus wrote a biography in AD 56 is unreasonable to one who knows that Tacitus was probably born only a year earlier.

Of course, not all statements need to be tested by this kind of study. Remember that divine revelation is always trustworthy. When God says something in Scripture, we can accept it on His authority. Only human reasoning is subject to error.

Thinking It Through

Find an advertisement that uses what it claims to be facts or statistics to sell a product or a service. Evaluate the ad according to the criteria above. Then discuss your findings with someone and decide together whether you accept the claims.

Teaching Strategy

Discussion and Analysis

After the students have written their advertisement evaluations, select several advertisements that meet the criteria questions given on page 289 and several that do not. Share these advertisements with the rest of the students and ask them to discuss and analyze the products' worth based upon the criteria questions. Assist the students in arriving at the correct conclusions.

Think About It | Chapter 11 289

OBJECTIVES

Students will

1. select an issue to analyze.
2. identify key focus areas for analysis.
3. choose an organizational method for ordering ideas.
4. narrow the topic to a manageable focus.
5. analyze an audience to determine the appropriate level of formality or informality for the essay.
6. complete a topic outline before beginning the drafting stage.
7. write a thesis statement that identifies a problem for analysis or presents a position on a topic.
8. draft an analysis that reflects the outline and organizational method chosen.
9. revise for clear and logical argumentation, grammar and usage correctness, and effective constructions and emphasis.
10. publish the essay.

CHA

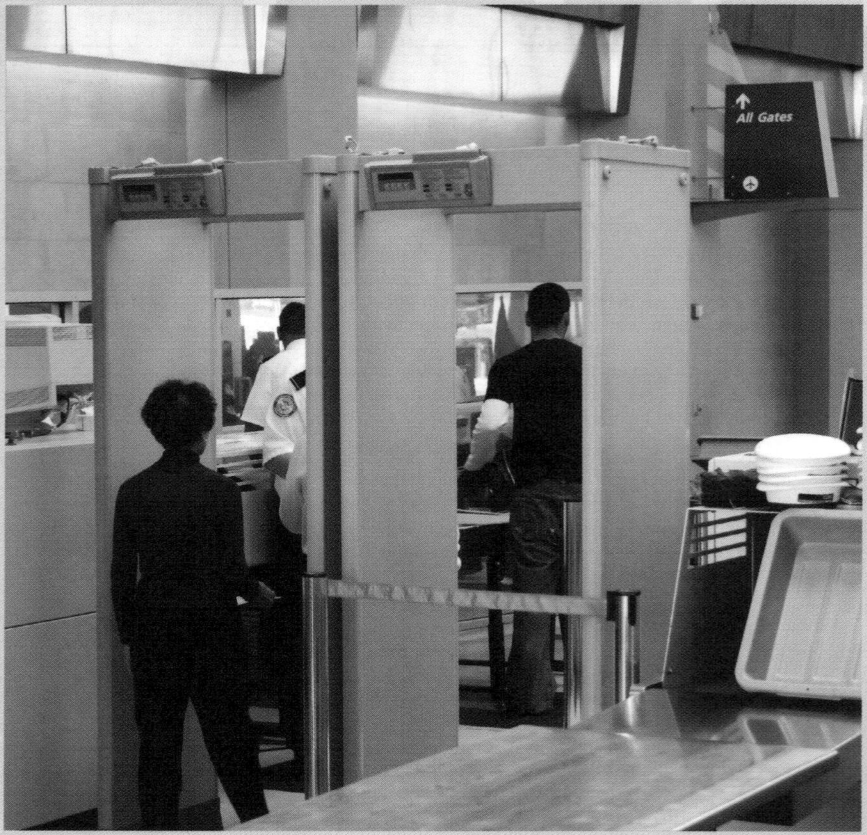

Chapter 12 Overview

Topic	Pages	Support Materials	Days
End Marks and Other Periods	296–301	Bulletin Board 12 Chapter 12 Pretest ESL Helps 12A–12B Teaching Help 12A Practice/Review the Skill 12.1–12.2 Concept Reinforcement 12A	147
Commas	301–14	Teaching Helps 12B–12C ESL Helps 12A, 12C Practice/Review the Skill 12.3–12.10 Concept Reinforcement 12B	148, 151
Research Report	265–68	Writing Worksheets 11B–11C	149–50, 155–56
Semicolons and Colons Review	315–20 459–62	Practice/Review the Skill 12.11–12.12 Concept Reinforcement 12C Cumulative Review 12.13 Chapter 12 Review	152
Chapter 12 Test			153
From the Written Word	321		154

ISSUE ANALYSIS ESSAY

Lesson Support

Teacher's Toolkit
Writing Worksheet 12
Writing Rubric 12

Whenever there are two sides to an issue, careful thought is required of a person as he wades through the facts of the case and decides upon a course of action or a belief to be held. Issues abound—school vouchers, tax cuts, campaign financing, health benefits, food safety—the list is virtually endless. Many writers, mostly journalists, make a living writing opinion pieces in which they give their own opinions about topics or examine the opinions of others. The editors of Maclean's *magazine examine airport security measures in the United States and Canada and proposed changes to the process. They use facts, expert opinion, quotations, and some humor to make a serious point. In your issue analysis, you will write about a topic that interests (or irritates!) you.*

Bringing Some Sanity to Airport Security

by Peter Shawn Taylor

Line up. Liquids in a baggie. Toss your water. Wait. Stuff your jacket in a bin. Empty your pockets. Take off your belt. Wait some more. Walk through slowly. Raise your arms. Stand still.

Is there any modern activity more frustrating, time-consuming and humiliating than the airport security line? Improved vigilance against terrorism may be a necessity in our post–9/11 world. But does it have to be so awkward? And is that bottle of water really a threat to global security?

In what might be considered a welcome breath of fresh air for air travellers, the former head of U.S. airport security is calling for an end to many of the most outrageous and bothersome aspects of airport check-in: liquid of all sizes should be allowed as carry-on, bans on non-weapons such as lighters should be relaxed and, in the name of improved security, airlines should be forbidden from charging checked baggage fees. Could it really be possible to fly like it's 1999?

Kip Hawley was administrator of the U.S. Transportation Security Administration (TSA) from 2005 to 2009. During that time he was responsible for many of the decisions that turned air travel into such a grind, including restrictions on liquids. And that made him a frequent target of public outrage. In 2006, a Milwaukee man was detained by TSA staff when he wrote "Kip Hawley is an idiot" on the baggie holding his miniature vials of liquids at a security check. Hawley now appears to be trying to make amends.

Hawley's book *Permanent Emergency: Inside the TSA and the Fight for the Future of American Security* provides an insider's perspective on how to make airport security a less irritating experience without increasing overall risk. Given the high degree of co-operation between the TSA and the Canadian Air Transportation Security Authority, what Hawley says should resonate with put-upon Canadian flyers as well.

ADDITIONAL INFORMATION

Peter Shawn Taylor is the editor-in-large of *Maclean's* and lives in Waterloo, Ontario. *Maclean's Magazine* is a weekly news publication based in Toronto, Ontario, Canada. Founded in 1905 by John Bayne, it was first known as just *Maclean's*. The publication now reaches more than two million readers each month.

If students question the spelling of words such as *travellers* and *behaviour*, explain that Canadian writers and publications usually follow traditional British spelling

SCRIPTURAL APPLICATION

Introduce the lesson with a discussion of the following question: Why should Christians analyze issues carefully? Encourage students to consider the importance of critical thinking and thorough research when analyzing an issue. Remind them that Christians, as representatives of Christ and witnesses of the gospel, have a responsibility to analyze and evaluate complex issues. Challenge students to view their efforts as more than an academic exercise but rather as work that has real spiritual value. They are not merely holding the line against cultural moral relativism and corruption but advancing into enemy territory. Ask a volunteer to read Matthew 28:19–20. Explain that part of God's mandate in the Great Commission is teaching the world to observe the things that God has commanded.

Literature Link

Tell the students that the key to effective issue analysis writing is tying facts together in a logical and interesting way. Read the unit essay aloud and ask students to write down several points of the essay that grabbed their attention or seemed especially convincing. Respond to the students' answers and discuss why the points they selected are especially potent.

TEACHING STRATEGY

Participation and Discussion

Instruct the students to look for the word pictures in the essay. Direct the students to write down the words, phrases, or clauses rendering powerful images. (*Line up; Toss*

The Shoe Bomber is journalists' nickname for Richard Reid, who in December of 2001 tried but failed to blow up a commercial flight using explosives hidden in his shoes. The Underwear Bomber is a nickname first used for Umar Farouk Abdulmutallab, who failed in a similar attempt in 2009. The nickname has also been used for those involved in another failed plot discovered in 2012.

His most refreshing idea: allow passengers to bring liquids of all sizes in their carry-on luggage. Carry-on liquids and gels are currently limited to 100 ml in Canada and the U.S. But Hawley reports that airport scanners now have the ability to determine if a liquid is an explosive. He suggests specially designated lanes for passengers with "snow globes, beauty products, booze" or any other fluids they might wish to carry on. If you'd rather not buy a microscopic flask of mouthwash for every trip, you could simply pick the "liquids lane" at pre-boarding and bring your bottle from home.

Airline baggage fees should be outlawed as an impediment to security, argues Hawley. Charging for each piece of checked luggage has become commonplace among airlines eager for extra revenue. But this measure encourages passengers to stuff as much as physically possible into their carry-on bags, which are still free. This inevitably slows down pre-boarding inspections. While airlines would have to find other ways to squeeze money out of travellers, the result would be quicker and more thorough inspections.

And Hawley would eliminate the list of forbidden items, beyond the most obvious weapons such as knives and bombs. "Banning certain items gives terrorists a complete list of what not to use in their next attack," he explains in a *Wall Street Journal* column promoting his book. "Lighters are banned? The next attack will use an electric trigger." Both the Shoe Bomber and Underwear Bomber provide evidence of evolving terrorist ingenuity.

Finally, Hawley suggests wholesale reform of the philosophy behind airport security. Instead of rigid protocols, he would give individual officers greater flexibility and discretion to search for possible threats. He would also randomize detailed inspections and institute more interviews to keep terrorists off-balance.

Savvy travellers will recognize Hawley's last point as a modified version of the vaunted Israeli approach to air terrorism, which focuses on the risk posed by individual ticket holders through targeted behaviour recognition. The North American method of obsessing over each and every bag for potential terrorism paraphernalia, on the other hand, wastes everyone's time equally. While this may strike some as equitable, it's wholly illogical and represents a vast waste of resources. It's also worth noting that both the Shoe and Underwear Bombers were thwarted, not by security measures, but by the courageous and spontaneous reactions of passengers and crew. "In attempting to eliminate all risk from flying, we have made air travel an unending nightmare," says Hawley. "Terrorists are adaptive, we need to be adaptive too."

Without much difficulty, and without endangering security, we could return air travel to the modestly pleasurable activity it was 20 years ago. But getting there will require a whole new way of thinking about airport security.

OVERVIEW of the WRITING PROCESS

Planning—looking for an issue to analyze, brainstorming with a partner, making a list of points about the issue, organizing the points, freewriting about a topic, interviewing an expert on the issue, narrowing the topic, considering the audience, and outlining the analysis

Drafting—writing a thesis statement, drafting the analysis, bolstering the ideas with specifics, and paying special attention to the opening and closing paragraphs

Revising—stepping away from the paper, allowing a peer to edit the paper, revising the paper for correctness, and choosing wisely for variety and emphasis

Publishing—submitting the analysis to a journal or magazine, binding the class essays together, mailing the essay to another student, or presenting the essay orally

Issue Analysis Essay

Not that we are sufficient of ourselves to think any thing as of ourselves; but our sufficiency is of God.

2 Corinthians 3:5

Being able to put in writing your thoughts and beliefs about an issue is an important skill—for both now and the future. A Christian writer will be called upon to analyze issues using God's Word as the basis for truth. Learn to think clearly about issues that affect you and your community and to put that thinking into written form.

Your Turn

Write a one- to two-page essay analyzing an issue approved by your teacher.

your water; such a grind; target of public outrage; microscopic flask; outlawed; to squeeze money) Write the students' answers for display, comment on their choices, and encourage discussion on Taylor's choice of certain word structures to convey his meaning. For example, ask students what writing strategy the essay uses when describing the airport security line as "frustrating, time-consuming and humiliating." *(parallelism)*

Literature Link

Ask students to recall from their previous study of literature the name for a question asked to achieve an effect rather than to receive information. *(rhetorical question)* Direct students to find examples of rhetorical questions in the essay. *(most of the sentences in paragraph 2, the last sentence of paragraph 3, "Lighters are banned?" in the quotation from Hawley in paragraph 8)* Explain that this device may be used to catch the reader's attention, to convey irony, or to provoke thought. Encourage students to analyze and discuss the essay's use of rhetorical questions and other literary devices that enhance the analysis.

Scriptural Application

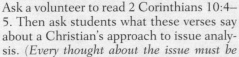

Ask a volunteer to read 2 Corinthians 10:4–5. Then ask students what these verses say about a Christian's approach to issue analysis. *(Every thought about the issue must be brought into captivity to Christ. The Christian should first ask himself, "What does God say about this issue?" Further, Scripture says*

Planning

✔ **Look for an issue to analyze.** Issues, some important and some otherwise, are all around you. Consider some of the following sources as you decide what to write about.

- newspaper
- weekly magazine or journal
- local billboards or notices
- evening news
- sermons from your own pastor or others
- issues before your city or county council

✔ **Brainstorm with a partner.** Talk to your parents, friends, and teachers about issues that are important to them. Discuss varying sides of each issue to consider alternative points of view.

✔ **Make a list of points about your issue.** Answer the following questions to identify the areas you need to focus on in your analysis.

- What is the main point of your analysis?
- How will you support your main point?
- How do you want your readers to respond to your analysis? What action (if any) would you like them to take?
- Are there any objections to your main point? How will you address those?

✔ **Organize your points.** Use one of the methods discussed in Chapter 1 (see pages 14–17 for more information). Two of the five methods, cause-and-effect and order of importance, may be the most helpful as you write your analysis.

- Cause-and-Effect—explanation of a cause and its effects or vice versa
- Order of Importance—presentation of events from least to most or most to least important

✔ **Freewrite about a topic.** Set a time limit for yourself and write without stopping for that length of time. After you have finished, look at your writing for ideas that you need to develop further in order to present an effective analysis.

✔ **Interview an expert on the issue.** Talk to someone who knows a great deal about the subject or issue you want to write about. If possible, obtain permission to record the interview so that you can quote the expert on the record.

tip

It is better to say more about less than to say less about more.

✔ **Narrow your topic.** Be sure that you can cover your topic fully within the length restrictions of your paper. Perhaps Taylor originally wanted to write about the difficulties of air travel in general; if so, he would have quickly found out that the topic was too broad for an article and would have chosen to examine current airport security policies instead. Ask yourself the following questions: *How long will my paper be? Is my topic too broad to be adequately covered in the assigned pages?* If you answer yes to the second, try focusing on just one aspect of your topic.

✔ **Consider your audience.** Analyzing your audience helps you to write the best piece possible for the reader. Taylor's essay is quite informal: it addresses readers directly as though they are passengers going through airport security. Later, it uses contractions and even some fragments instead of only formal sentences. Many journalists use informal language in order to appear to be on the same side as their audience. Use your judgment about how informal your analysis should be.

Thinking Biblically

Learning how to write persuasively is extremely important (Prov. 25:11, 15). To be effective, persuasive writing requires thoughtful, principle-based analysis, but people often fail to evaluate the issues against an objective standard. Instead, they simply choose a position they personally find most appealing. Truly good analysis, however, connects ultimate issues. For example, a debate about the use of excessive force by police raises issues about how much authority God has given to the state. A debate over racially charged issues—affirmative action, racial profiling, ethnic cleansing—is an opportunity to point readers to the only socially leveling force with any authority: the claim of Genesis that all people are made in God's image. As mentioned in Chapter 3, you need not quote a Bible verse every time the Republicans and Democrats disagree over a particular issue. But your reasoning should always return, ultimately, to the basic principles found in the Scriptures.

Thinking Biblically

Elicit some controversial issues from students and ask them to identify the central ideas that make these issues so heated. Rather than asking students to argue for or against one side, ask them to explain why each side takes the matter so seriously. For example, abortion raises questions about the value of human life and the responsibility of human choice. The issue of homosexuality raises questions about whether morality is determined by the cosmos or hinges upon adult consent.

that "the weapons of our warfare are . . . mighty through God to the pulling down of strong holds," i.e., corruption, deceit, and immorality in a godless culture.)

Planning Strategy

Introduction and Motivation

Materials

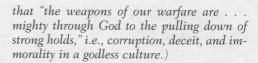

- a newspaper or news magazine (in print or online)

Select one or two highly controversial newspaper stories or letters to the editor. Read portions aloud. Ask students whether they agree with the writer of the article. Follow by asking how many of them feel prepared to write a logical, convincing addendum or rebuttal to the article. Explain the importance of artfully crafting an argument that furthers one's cause rather than discredits it. Ask students whether there are any issues about which they feel strongly; display their responses. Suggest additional sources for finding issues by referring students to the bulleted list on page 293.

Scriptural Application

To help the students develop biblical views on their topics, direct them to answer the following questions:

- What is good about this issue?
- What is bad about this issue as a result of its being touched by the Fall of man? (In other words, how has the good been twisted in the wrong direction?)
- What should be done to redeem this issue to (to bring it under the lordship of) Christ?

Topic Outlines
pp. 6–7

✔ **Outline your analysis.** Complete at least a topic outline before you begin drafting. This will help you identify the main points you hope to cover in your analysis. What follows is one student's attempt at an outline on the topic of year-round school (YRS).

I. YRS and education
  A. Decreased "forgetting time"
  B. Increased review time

II. YRS and economics
  A. Start-up/shut-down costs
  B. Cost of A/C in buildings/buses

III. YRS and family, church, and community events
  A. Difficulty in scheduling events
  B. Extracurricular activities affected

IV. YRS and teachers
  A. Burn-out
  B. Loss of summer education opportunities

Drafting

✔ **Write your thesis statement.** Your thesis should clearly identify a problem for analysis or present your position about your topic. Taylor's essay hints at its thesis in the second paragraph: "Is there any modern activity more frustrating, time-consuming and humiliating than the airport security line?" It states the thesis directly in the last paragraph: "Without much difficulty, and without endangering security, we could return air travel to the modestly pleasurable activity it was 20 years ago." Compose a thesis that you can support well.

Details
p. 367

✔ **Draft your analysis.** Use the ideas you developed in the planning stage to write your analysis. Make sure that your thesis statement is prominent near the opening of the piece. Include any concerns/objections you identified earlier.

✔ **Bolster your ideas with specifics.** Notice how many facts the editorial includes: names, dates, amounts. Your addition of details will make your analysis more credible. Look at these two sentences—the first a quotation from Taylor's piece and the second a rewrite taking out the specific examples. Notice how the first creates a picture that the second does not.

> If you'd rather not buy a microscopic flask of mouthwash for every trip, you could simply pick the "liquids lane" at pre-boarding and bring your bottle from home.
>
> If you'd rather not buy small containers of liquids for every trip, you could simply pick a special lane at pre-boarding and bring regular-sized containers.

✔ **Pay attention to your opening and closing paragraphs.** Do not forget the purposes of your introductory paragraph: to catch reader interest, to introduce the topic, and to draw attention to the main idea. Your conclusion should clinch the main idea, giving a sense of completeness. Taylor's essay does this effectively with its last paragraph. It states the thesis clearly and succinctly and then reminds the reader of what still needs to change: "But getting there will require a whole new way of thinking about airport security." Notice that the last sentence plays upon the travel theme by comparing new policies to a new location.

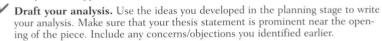

PLANNING STRATEGY
Analysis

After students have brainstormed about an issue, direct them to further analyze the issue by answering the four bulleted focus questions on page 293. Then instruct them to organize their points. If necessary, discuss students' organizational choices in a one-on-one or class setting.

PLANNING STRATEGY
Activity

Encourage your students to freewrite to explore the ideas generated from the brainstorming and focus-point activities.

PLANNING STRATEGY
Motivation

Encourage your students to use their interviews to further focus their topics and to note strong points that will encapsulate their issues and promote their arguments.

PLANNING STRATEGY
Analysis and Modeling

Ask the students to analyze the essay's audience and to write an outline of the essay. Respond to the students' answers. Alternatively, consider modeling for the students how to write an outline for the sample essay. Then allow students time to write their outlines in class.

Revising

✔ **Step away from your paper.** Giving yourself time to think about your topic before revising is often a good idea. Get a good night's sleep and then look at your analysis again. Ask yourself whether your paper makes its point clearly and logically now that you're looking at it with fresh eyes.

✔ **Allow a peer to edit your paper.** Ask another writer to read your paper for you. Ask him to comment specifically on the following questions:

- Is the thesis clear? Could you restate it?
- Is there adequate support for the main points? Do you have any ideas for additional support?
- Do you have any objections to the thesis not addressed in the paper?
- Is there anything in the paper that needs further explanation?

✔ **Revise your paper for correctness.** After you incorporate the changes you have marked and make a fresh copy of your paper, read it over for grammar, mechanics, and usage errors. Use the spell-check feature on your computer but do not depend on it to catch all of your errors. Can you find the error in the sentence below? (The spellchecker cannot.)

Outside, the lightening flashed.

The word *lightening* means "getting or making lighter." The writer probably wanted to use the word *lightning,* which refers to the flashing light in a stormy sky. Careful proofreading can help you catch such errors.

✔ **Choose wisely for variety and emphasis.** As you revise, look again at the various constructions you have chosen. You can improve your writing by making sure that you use the active voice in most instances and the passive voice only when justifiable. Look also at your use of indirect objects and prepositional phrases—do your choices reflect the proper emphasis?

Choosing Between Constructions pp. 361–62

Publishing

✔ **Submit your analysis to a journal or magazine.** Find a publication, either in print or online, that publishes articles on your topic. Research the guidelines for publication and, if necessary, revise your piece to reflect them.

✔ **Bind the class essays together.** Group the analyses by topic and bind them for display. Think of an appropriate title for the collection of essays.

✔ **Mail your essay to another student.** Exchange your essay with another student. Encourage him to comment on the issue you present.

✔ **Present your essay orally.** Read your essay aloud to a group of students and answer questions from your audience.

Some Ideas to Consider

Language

- Write about language changes (e.g., new spellings becoming acceptable, changes in punctuation rules, political correctness in language).

Government

- Analyze a local ordinance that is being considered by your county council.
- Examine efforts to remove the words "under God" from the Pledge of Allegiance.

Drafting Strategy

Participation

Challenge students to compose several thesis statements about a topic that you assign. Point out strengths and suggest improvements to correct weaknesses.

Drafting Strategy

Participation

Caution the students about resorting to propaganda techniques. Using Writing Worksheet 12 (Teacher's Toolkit), discuss each of the common propaganda devices.

Drafting Strategy

Demonstration

Draw the students' attention to the two example sentences about carrying liquids through airport security checks (p. 294). Emphasize the credibility and interest automatically infused into an otherwise bland sentence simply by adding specifics. Then read the first paragraph of the essay to the class. Remind the students of the importance of including interesting specifics in their opening and closing paragraphs.

Revising Strategy

During the peer-editing phase of revision, consider allowing the students to use Writing Rubric 12 (Teacher's Toolkit) in addition to the bulleted questions on page 295.

ONE on ONE Ask another student or adult to edit your student's paper using Writing Rubric 12 (Teacher's Toolkit) and the bulleted questions on page 295.

OBJECTIVES

Students will

1. differentiate between correctly and incorrectly punctuated sentences.
2. insert correct punctuation in sentences needing periods, decimal points, question marks, and exclamation points.
3. insert periods correctly in sentences using initials, abbreviations, outlines, lists, and decimals.
4. add needed commas into a series of three or more items, between coordinate adjectives in a series, and between two independent clauses.
5. insert commas to set off introductory elements.
6. use commas to separate nouns of direct address, parenthetical expressions, interjections, phrases that show contrast, appositives, adjectives after a noun, tag questions, conjunctive adverbs, and restrictive and nonrestrictive elements.
7. insert necessary commas in letters and with quotations, dates, and addresses.
8. use commas to signal special constructions.
9. correct sentences with misused commas.

USAGE

Punctuation

Have you ever walked an unmarked trail in the dark? If you have, you probably remember wondering what you might be stepping on or what might be just ahead of you. On the other hand, you may have walked a well-marked, lighted path and been reassured about where you were stepping and where you were going. Punctuation marks used correctly guide both the writer and reader on a path of clear understanding.

Exclamation Point

Exclamatory Sentences p. 69

An exclamation point follows an exclamatory sentence, a brief exclamation, and some imperative sentences. Be sure to use the exclamation point sparingly.

Exclamatory Sentence	There is a wasp nest under that step!
Brief Exclamation	Oh, no!
Imperative Sentence	Go the other way!

Question Mark

Interrogative Sentences p. 69

A question mark comes at the end of a direct question. A polite request, however, is not usually punctuated with a question mark.

Direct Question	Have you begun a family tradition at your home?
Tag Question	You will begin a tradition soon, won't you?
Elliptical Question	How many traditions do you intend to start each year? one? two?
Polite Request	Would you please consider beginning a patriotic tradition.

Declarative Sentences p. 69

Period

In Sentences

A period is used to indicate the end of declarative sentences, indirect questions, and imperative sentences that do not express strong emotion.

Declarative Sentence	A family tradition can be passed on to succeeding generations.
Indirect Question	He asked us whether we had any family traditions.
Mild Imperative Sentence	Please begin a tradition in your family.

Writing Workshop

Conduct a minilesson using "Choosing Between Constructions" (pp. 361–62).

Evaluation

For help in grading this assignment, see "Grading Student Writing" (p. v) and Writing Rubric 12 (Teacher's Toolkit).

Publishing Strategy

Participation

Provide contact information for government officials and interest groups and encourage students to send their work to relevant audiences.

SpeechLink

Encourage your students to enter their essays in an oratory competition.

PUNCTUATION

Lesson Support

Student Worktext
Chapter 12 Review—pp. 459–62

Teacher's Toolkit
Bulletin Board 12
Chapter 12 Pretest
Teaching Helps 12A–12C
ESL Helps 12A–12C
Concept Reinforcements 12A–12C

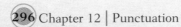

Test
Chapter 12 Test

ESL

In English punctuation, all end marks (periods, question marks, and exclamation points) must follow the last word of the sentence immediately. Do not leave a space before those marks, but leave one or two spaces after them.

Similarly, use no space before a comma or a semicolon, but leave one space after either of these. For any other punctuation, observe the examples carefully. (Expect to use no space before any punctuation except for opening parentheses and opening quotation marks.)

tip

When the period of an abbreviation comes at the end of a sentence, that period also ends the sentence.

For Initials and Abbreviations

A period usually follows a person's initial and often follows an abbreviation.

Initials and Abbreviations	
Personal names and titles	Dr. George Allen Sr.
Periods are usually omitted after academic degrees following a name, after acronyms, and after most abbreviations of the names of governmental agencies, most organizations, and well-known businesses.	James Hall, MD PAC (Political Action Committee) FDA (Food and Drug Administration) USO (United Service Organizations) IBM (International Business Machines)
Parts of an address	Pearlman Dairy Rd. P.O. Box 69875
Periods do not follow state or province postal abbreviations; periods do not follow ZIP codes or other postal codes.	Snow Lake, AK 72379 BWI (British West Indies) Richmond Hill, ON L4B 1B4
Times and dates	10:00 p.m.
Periods are usually omitted in BC and AD.	607 BC; AD 1483
Measurements	6 ft. 3 in. 190 lb. 25 km 80 mg

In Outlines and Lists

A period follows each number or letter division of an outline.

I. Problems building the Panama Canal
  A. Hostile neighbors
  B. Inadequate engineering knowledge
  C. Tropical disease
  D. Topographical elements
    1. Mountainous terrain
    2. Excessive vegetation
    3. Landslides
II. Functions of the Panama Canal
  A. Providing a passageway between the Atlantic and Pacific Oceans
  B. Improving trade routes

Punctuation | Chapter 12 297

OBJECTIVES (Continued)

10. add missing semicolons between two independent clauses, before a conjunction in a long compound sentence, and between word groups containing commas.
11. insert colons in Bible references and expressions of time, after a salutation of a business letter, between a book title and subtitle, before a series at the end of a sentence, before long or formal direct quotations, and between two independent clauses.
12. revise a paragraph to correct incorrect capitalization and to insert missing end marks, commas, semicolons, and colons.

Tell students to check a reliable dictionary if they question whether a business needs periods in its acronym.

Point out that *AD (anno Domini)* should always precede the year cited while *BC* (before Christ) must follow it.

TEACHING STRATEGY

Induction

Display the following sentences:

- Would you please send me your camping equipment catalog.
- Has your company considered opening a store in my city?
- Will you please pass along my request to the proper department.
- Do you have any store locations in my state?

Ask the students to formulate two basic punctuation rules based on the displayed sentences. (*A request made as a polite question should end with a period. A direct question should end with a question mark.*)

History Link

Encourage students to research and report on the controversies associated with the construction and ownership of the Panama Canal. Direct them to use the steps they learned from writing the issue analysis essay to make effective presentations.

ESL STRATEGY

Some ESL students may have difficulty with punctuation, especially those students whose native language uses punctuation marks different from those used in English. Use ESL Helps 12A and 12B (Teacher's Toolkit) for a table of the most common punctuation marks in English and for examples of correct spacing of punctuation marks.

A period follows each number or letter that precedes an item in a vertical list.

1. Determine the number of guests
2. Plan the menu
3. Purchase the groceries
4. Set the table
5. Prepare the food

A period does not follow the number or letter that precedes an item in a list within a sentence. Use pairs of parentheses instead of periods.

In preparation for the Thanksgiving dinner, we must (1) determine the number of guests, (2) plan the menu, (3) purchase the groceries, (4) set the table, and (5) prepare the food.

For Decimals

A period functions as a decimal point in numerical expressions.

$75.00

10.5 feet

94.5° F

12.1 PRACTICE *the skill*

Write the letter of the correctly punctuated sentence.

B 1. A. Our geography teacher, Dr. McGuire, asked us whether we understand the significance of worldwide tourism?
B. Our geography teacher, Dr. McGuire, asked us whether we understand the significance of worldwide tourism.

A 2. A. Would you look at the chart on page 212. There you'll find some statistics from the United Nations World Tourism Organization (UNWTO), which monitors tourism around the globe.
B. Would you look at the chart on page 212? There you'll find some statistics from the United Nations World Tourism Organization (UNWTO), which monitors tourism around the globe.

A 3. A. Wow! During 2010, countries around the world hosted almost 940 million people who crossed their borders as tourists.
B. Wow. During 2010, countries around the world hosted almost 940 million people who crossed their borders as tourists.

A 4. A. Please note the next figure as well. It says that tourists in 2010 spent over $919 billion.
B. Please note the next figure as well! It says that tourists in 2010 spent over 919 billion.

A 5. A. That total means each tourist spent an average of $977.66, doesn't it? Yes, but that's in U.S. dollars.
B. That total means each tourist spent an average of $977.66, doesn't it. Yes, but that's in U.S. dollars.

B 6. A. I think these numbers are staggering, don't you!
B. I think these numbers are staggering, don't you?

Reinforcement

Use Teaching Help 12A (Teacher's Toolkit) to help the students differentiate between direct questions, indirect questions, imperatives, mild imperatives, and polite requests.

Teaching Strategy

Discussion

Point out that people often mistakenly use traditional state or province abbreviations instead of postal abbreviations for addresses. Give the students a few more examples that they might not immediately think of when reading the rule. (For example, *PE,* not *P.E.I.,* for Prince Edward Island and *DC,* not *D.C.,* for the District of Columbia.)

B 7. A. Here's a list of the fifteen most-visited countries. Which country is first, second, third?

B. Here's a list of the fifteen most-visited countries. Which country is first? second? third?

B 8. A. Well, traditionally, the top three nations for attracting tourists are 1. France, 2. the United States, and 3. Spain.

B. Well, traditionally, the top three nations for attracting tourists are (1) France, (2) the United States, and (3) Spain.

B 9. A. I learned a lot about world tourism. My notes look like this:

I. Countries spending the most money as tourists
A Germany
B United States
C China
II. Countries receiving the most money from tourists
A United States
B Spain
C France

B. I learned a lot about world tourism. My notes look like this:

I. Countries spending the most money as tourists
A. Germany
B. United States
C. China
II. Countries receiving the most money from tourists
A. United States
B. Spain
C. France

B 10. A. I took a lot of notes on Dr. McGuire's fascinating lecture. In fact, my notebook probably weighed an extra 5 lb when class ended.

B. I took a lot of notes on Dr. McGuire's fascinating lecture. In fact, my notebook probably weighed an extra 5 lb. when class ended.

Remind students that abbreviations for units of measurement are normally reserved for lists or for use in technical texts. Explain that abbreviations are used here (and in 12.2) in order to test a punctuation rule. Students should usually write out the names of units of measurement.

Punctuation | Chapter 12 299

If students question the hyphens in the name "Mont-Saint-Michel," explain that the hyphens are correct. If you wish, you may share that French tends to use hyphens in names more frequently than English does.

12.2 REVIEW *the skill*

Rewrite the following sentences, adding or deleting periods, decimal points, question marks, and exclamation points as necessary.

1. Mont-Saint-Michel is a popular tourist attraction in France, isn't it

   Mont-Saint-Michel is a popular tourist attraction in France, isn't it?

2. Yes, this site is popular for several reasons:
   A Beautiful architecture
   B Rich history
   C Picturesque landscape

   Yes, this site is popular for several reasons:
   A. Beautiful architecture
   B. Rich history
   C. Picturesque landscape

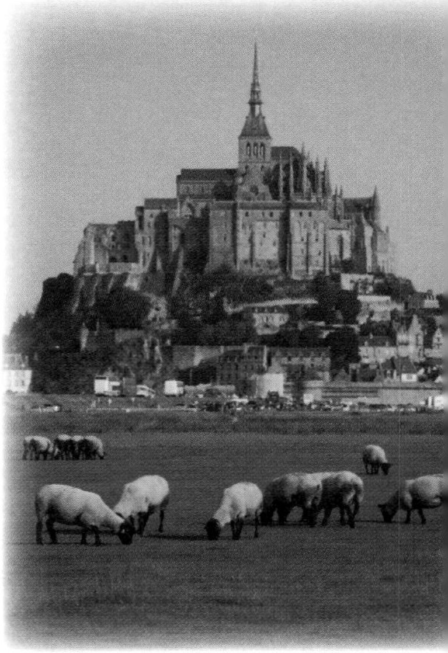

3. Mont-Saint-Michel comprises an abbey and a village mounted atop an enormous rock island with a height of more than 80 m., or 262 ft.

   Mont-Saint-Michel comprises an abbey and a village mounted atop an enormous rock island with a height of more than 80 m, or 262 ft.

4. Listen while I tell you how the first building on this island began in AD 708

   Listen while I tell you how the first building on this island began in AD 708.

5. Did you know that Saint Aubert, a bishop from Avranches, claimed the archangel Michael appeared and told him to build a chapel

   Did you know that Saint Aubert, a bishop from Avranches, claimed the archangel Michael appeared and told him to build a chapel?

6. I wonder why people use the term *La Merveille,* "The Marvel," to speak of Mont-Saint-Michel

   I wonder why people use the term La Merveille, *"The Marvel," to speak of Mont-Saint-Michel.*

300 Chapter 12 | Punctuation

7. How many tourists do you think Mont-Saint-Michel brings to France each year 400,000

How many tourists do you think Mont-Saint-Michel brings to France each year?

400,000?

8. The local AAA might have some brochures about France that would tell us; the nearest agency is located at 56 E Antrim Dr

The local AAA might have some brochures about France that would tell us; the

nearest agency is located at 56 E. Antrim Dr.

9. This view is spectacular

This view is spectacular!

10. Quick, get the camera

Quick, get the camera!

Comma

The comma is the most frequently used mark of punctuation and probably the most frequently misused. Commas that are correctly placed can guide the reader to a clear understanding of the text. Incorrect commas, on the other hand, can create uncertainty. Understanding the following rules will help you write clearly.

In a Series

Commas separate words, phrases, or clauses that appear in a series.

Series of Three or More Items

In a series of three or more items joined by a conjunction, a comma follows each item of the series (except the last item). In less formal writing, such as journalistic writing, the comma before the last item in the series is omitted. In academic writing, however, the comma before the conjunction is expected.

We have chosen Jerry, Tom, and Mark to be the committee chairmen.

Inviting the guests, planning the program, and delegating food preparation responsibilities will be a part of the chairmen's job.

Compound Sentences p. 132

Clauses pp. 116–28

Adjectives p. 48

Participial Phrases pp. 92–94

Coordinate Adjectives in a Series

A comma separates coordinate adjectives (adjectives that modify a noun separately), but a comma does not separate cumulative adjectives (adjectives that build on one another to modify a noun jointly).

COORDINATE	The *howling, swirling* wind whipped through the trees.
	Fall leaves of *vibrant, brilliant* hues began to fall to the ground.
CUMULATIVE	Leaves from the *tall old oak* tree covered the lawn.
	Long green blades of grass poked through the carpet of leaves.

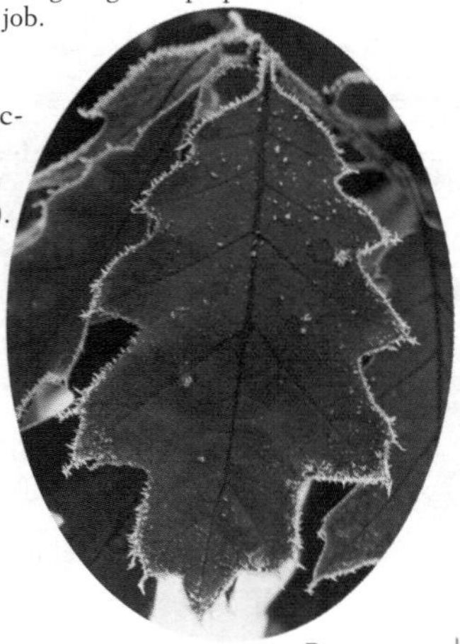

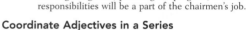

REINFORCEMENT

To check the students' understanding of coordinate and cumulative adjectives and to give them additional practice in differentiating the two, distribute Teaching Help 12B (Teacher's Toolkit). Consider asking the students to share their adjective pairs with the other students and to explain the rationale in their use of commas.

ESL STRATEGY

Use ESL Help 12C (Teacher's Toolkit) to discuss the differences between cumulative and coordinate adjectives. Understanding this distinction is especially important for proper comma placement. Then allow the students to complete the activity at the end of the worksheet. Remind the students to review ESL Help 2A (Teacher's Toolkit) for the correct order of cumulative adjectives in a sentence.

Should a comma precede the coordinating conjunction in a compound imperative sentence? No comma is necessary if the sentence is a simple sentence with a compound predicate. However, a comma can prevent misreading if the first part of the sentence is long or if either element contains other coordinating conjunctions.

Turn out the light and shut the door.

Please shut the window and the door, and don't forget to turn out the light.

g u r w Independent Clauses p. 116

g u r w Compound Sentences p. 132

Two or More Independent Clauses

In a compound sentence, a comma separates the first independent clause from the conjunction. A comma is not used between compound predicates.

> During the storm the night sky filled with dark clouds, and the wind blew violently through the trees.
>
> Did the thunder awaken you, or did you sleep through the storm?
>
> Lightning flashed through the night sky and illuminated the darkness.

Two independent clauses that are very short and closely related in meaning do not require a comma before the conjunction.

> The wind blew and the thunder roared.
>
> The baby cried and the dog barked.

If a compound sentence has three or more short independent clauses, a comma follows each clause except the last one.

> The rain stopped, the sky became clear, and the moon appeared overhead.
>
> The children returned to their beds, the dog stopped barking, and I collapsed into bed.

12.3 PRACTICE *the skill*

Insert any missing commas. If the sentence is already correct, write *C* in the blank.

C 1. The greatest feat of tourism ever imagined might be attributed to Phileas Fogg, the determined, daring hero of Jules Verne's classic story *Around the World in Eighty Days.*

_____ 2. Phileas Fogg is a reserved English gentleman who lives out his existence obsessed with adhering to a predictable, punctual routine.

_____ 3. His daily activities consist of maintaining a respectable personal appearance, taking his meals at the Reform Club, reading the daily papers, and playing whist with his friends at the club.

_____ 4. During a game at the Reform Club, Fogg and his friends begin discussing a recent bank robbery, but a disagreement soon arises.

C 5. Mr. Stuart says the robber can certainly escape capture because the world is so big, and he takes issue with Fogg when the latter asserts that a man could travel around the whole world in a mere eighty days.

TEACHING STRATEGY
Discussion

If students consistently use commas between compound predicates, encourage them to label the subjects and predicates of each clause. Remind students that a clause must have both a subject and a predicate if it is to be separated by a comma and a coordinating conjunction.

TEACHING STRATEGY
Demonstration

Display the following example sentences: *As a result of the city's urban renewal plan, the crime rate is decreasing and the number of residents is increasing. The governor waved and the onlookers cheered.* Explain that these sentences do not need commas because the two independent clauses in each are brief and closely related. In addition, draw attention to the parallel sentence patterns in the sentences above and in the examples given on page 302.

TEACHING STRATEGY
Analysis

Explain that compound sentences of three or more short independent clauses occur relatively seldom in writing. Encourage the students to think of the short independent clauses in these sentences as links that belong together. For example, display the following sentence: *Fog descended over the city, yellow lights appeared, and the pilot searched for the runway.* Explain that the short independent clauses work together

_____ 6. To win a wager and protect his word of honor, Fogg sets out to travel the world in eighty days, taking only his French valet Passepartout, a few articles of clothing, Bradshaw's book of train and steamship schedules, and a carpetbag filled with £20,000.

C 7. On their journey they save an Indian princess from a suttee, they are attacked by Sioux Indians, and they are chased by a detective from England.

_____ 8. Detective Fix believes that Fogg has stolen £55,000 from the Bank of England, and Fix is determined to bring Fogg to justice and win the reward.

_____ 9. Phileas Fogg, Passepartout, and Princess Aouda eventually arrive back in London at the Reform Club just in time to win the wager.

C 10. Phileas Fogg falls in love with Aouda and he marries her.

12.4

REVIEW *the skill*

Insert the ten missing commas in the following paragraph.

When planning a trip, a traveler should think ahead and pack wisely. He needs to determine what the weather will probably be and bring appropriate clothes. Some essentials to remember are an umbrella, a light raincoat, and comfortable shoes. Sample-size bottles of shampoo, conditioner, and hair spray are wonderful space savers. The hotel may have very dry air, and leaving a few wet hand towels around the room at night will allow a traveler to sleep much more comfortably. Clothespins hold hotel curtains shut, detergent wipes are great for stain removal, and hand sanitizer protects from germs. The traveler should always remember to seal liquids and creams in plastic bags, and he shouldn't forget to bring extra bags. A small portable first-aid kit can be a great help. Other handy, useful items include folding scissors, needle and thread, safety pins, and a flashlight with batteries.

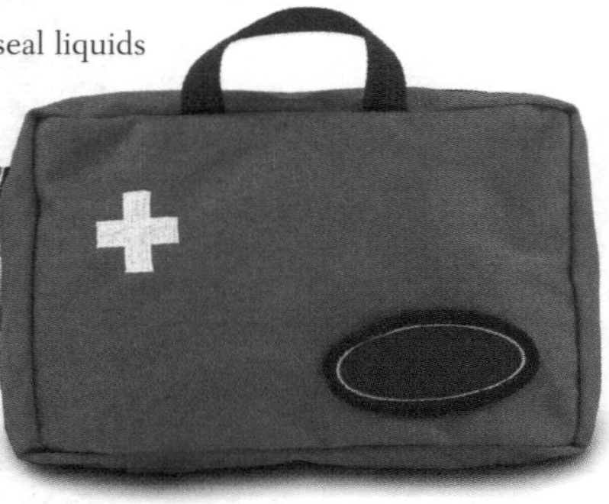

by building toward the final clause and the meaning of the whole compound sentence.

Enrichment

Suggest that interested students research the life and works of Jules Verne (1828–1905) and present their findings to the class. Encourage the students to include a discussion of modern inventions that Verne imagined and wrote about before their time.

Participial Phrase
pp. 92–94

After Introductory Elements

A comma follows certain introductory grammatical elements.

Introductory Participles and Participial Phrases

Use a comma after an introductory participle or participial phrase.

Glistening, the snow lay undisturbed on the fields.

Seizing the sled from its place in the garage, we headed to the slope.

Long Introductory Prepositional Phrases

Prepositional
Phrase
p. 88

Use a comma after a long introductory prepositional phrase (usually five words or more) or after multiple introductory prepositional phrases.

In spite of the bitter temperature, the children played in the snow.

By the side of the old barn, the children built a large snowman.

Introductory Sequencing Words

A comma often follows an introductory sequencing word such as *first, second, next, finally,* or *last.* This comma is optional, but all such words should be treated alike. However, a comma never follows *then* when the word is used in this way.

First, the youngest child chose a floppy wool hat for the snowman.

Next, my brothers created his face.

Last, I wrapped a red plaid scarf around his neck.

Introductory Adverb Clauses

Adverb Clauses
pp. 122–23

Use a comma after an introductory adverb clause.

When the snowman was completed, neighbor children came to see the creation.

After everyone had played in the snow for an hour, Mother served hot chocolate and cookies.

Other Introductory Elements

Use a comma after an element that modifies the sentence as a whole.

To be sure, the children enjoyed their hours of playing outside.

Prepositional
Phrases with
Gerund
pp. 96–97

Use a comma after an introductory element that contains a verbal, even if a comma would not otherwise be necessary.

Before coming inside, the children rode their sled down the slope for a final time.

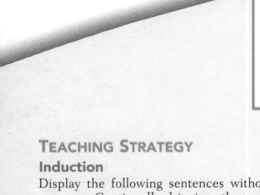

ONE on ONE You may need to explain what a snowman is or elaborate on the traditional ways Americans play in the snow.

Although some usage guides accept both *first* and *firstly* as introductory words, others prohibit adding *ly* to ordinal numbers. Remind students to be consistent when they use sequencing words (instead of *first, secondly, thirdly* use *first, second, third* or *firstly, secondly, thirdly*).

Teaching Strategy

Induction

Display the following sentences without commas: *Continually dripping, the water from the downspout created a puddle in the sand. Having explored the path before, I led the way.* Direct the students to read the sentences and to state whether or not the meanings are perfectly clear. Ask the students to suggest how the sentences might be improved. (*Commas should be added for clarity of reading.*) Tell the students to suggest where the commas should be placed in each sentence and to provide a rationale for their suggestion. (*The commas should be placed after introductory participles and participial phrases.*)

Teaching Strategy

Analysis

To help the students recognize multiple introductory prepositional phrases, direct the students to enclose each prepositional phrase in parentheses:

- (For a while) (after the hike) (to Table Rock), I could not drink enough water.
- (During the grueling climb) (to the top) (of the mountain), we thought we had enough water.
- (Amid the blistering heat) (of the afternoon sun), Yoh examined our nearly empty water jug.
- (At the very bottom) (of my dusty backpack), I found one red apple to augment our dwindling water supply.

12.5 PRACTICE *the skill*

Insert any missing commas. If the sentence is already correct, write *C* in the blank.

__C__ 1. Lying above the river Tauber in northern Bavaria, Rothenburg ob der Tauber remains a medieval city.

_____ 2. Surrounding the city, fully restored and preserved medieval walls create an atmosphere of the Middle Ages.

_____ 3. To be sure, there are modern elements to Rothenburg; it accommodates thousands of tourists yearly.

_____ 4. Among the city's many attractions, the Kriminalmuseum (Criminal Museum) is a collection of medieval punishments; it contains shame flutes for bad musicians, cages for bad bakers, an iron maiden, and an executioner's cloak and ax.

_____ 5. Built in 1395 and later remodeled, the Kriminalmuseum is the only baroque building in the town.

__C__ 6. In the dim, dark cellar of the Kriminalmuseum, one can find a torture rack.

_____ 7. Next, the tourist should visit Käthe Wohlfahrt's Christmas Village.

_____ 8. Open year round, the shop houses a permanent winter wonderland display of Christmas decorations.

__C__ 9. Throughout this entire little city, the feeling of a walk back through time captivates the visitor.

_____ 10. In the twenty-first century, Rothenburg offers both historical and modern cultural opportunities.

ENRICHMENT

Encourage interested students to find out more about the historical town of Rothenburg and to report their findings.

Punctuation | Chapter 12 305

12.6 REVIEW *the skill*

Insert any missing commas. If the sentence is already correct, write *C* in the blank.

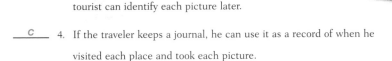

______ 1. While enjoying a trip, many people keep a record of their experiences through photographs.

______ 2. Before leaving home, the traveler should ensure that each camera he brings with him is in good working order.

______ 3. By keeping a journal of pictures taken, the tourist can identify each picture later.

__C__ 4. If the traveler keeps a journal, he can use it as a record of when he visited each place and took each picture.

______ 5. Of course, one way to record information about tourist sites is to take pictures of informative signs on the premises.

______ 6. To get the best photos possible, the traveler should plan each picture for maximum dramatic effect.

__C__ 7. Using people in the foreground to demonstrate scale, a traveler can take pictures that reflect the true size of objects.

______ 8. By stocking up on memory cards and batteries in America, an international traveler can likely save money. Such materials are typically more expensive elsewhere.

______ 9. Finally, a traveler should make sure that he is included in some of his snapshots.

__C__ 10. As reminders of wonderful experiences, photographs are some of the best souvenirs.

Teaching Strategy
Discussion

To help students better understand the idea of parenthetical expression, ask a student to read the definition of *parenthetical* from the dictionary. *(something enclosed in parentheses; something that qualifies or explains)* Suggest that students identify an expression as parenthetical (or not) by determining whether the expression is nonessential to the meaning of the sentence and should therefore be set off with commas.

Teaching Strategy
Analysis

Ask the students to explain the difference between the following two sentences: *Have you met my sister Fiona?* and *Have you met my sister, Fiona?* In the first sentence the name *Fiona* is a restrictive appositive renaming *sister.* In the second sentence, *Fiona* could be either a noun of direct address or a nonrestrictive appositive renaming *sister.* Emphasize to the students that using correct punctuation helps limit misreading.

Teaching Strategy
Participation

Display the following sentences:

- The Hogans, our neighbors, just returned from a trip to Denmark.
- We took care of Gabby, the Hogans' fastidious miniature poodle.
- The Hogans even brought Gabby a souvenir, premium dog food from Denmark.

To Set Off Elements

Commas separate certain words or groups of words from the rest of the sentence. Words or groups of words that come at the beginning of the sentence or at the end of the sentence use only one comma. A pair of commas encloses words or groups of words when they appear in the middle of the sentence.

Nouns of Direct Address

Use commas to separate or enclose a noun of direct address, the name or title of the person being spoken to, from the rest of the sentence.

> *Josh,* did you see the trail through the woods?
>
> I don't know, *Son,* that you should go that far into the woods.

Parenthetical Expressions

Use commas to set off a parenthetical expression, a word or phrase that could be left out of the sentence without damaging its meaning.

> The trail, *as you well know,* is not marked clearly.
>
> *As you well know,* the trail is not marked clearly.
>
> The trail is not marked clearly, *as you well know.*

Adverb Clauses pp. 122–23

Interjections

Use commas to separate a mild interjection from the rest of the sentence.

> *Sure,* there is time to shop for warm clothes.
>
> Be sure to buy a really warm jacket, *please.*

Phrases That Show Contrast

Use commas to set off phrases that show contrast, especially when the phrase begins with a negative word such as *not* or *never.*

> We will be sure to shop tomorrow, *not today.*
>
> A warm coat, *never just a sweater,* is necessary for subzero weather.

Appositives

Use commas to enclose most appositives.

> Jordan, *the boy next door,* wants to sled on the big hill.
>
> He chose the fastest sled, *the one with shiny metal runners.*

A restrictive appositive appears without commas. These short appositives are more specific and more important than the noun before them because they are necessary to identify that noun.

> Have you talked with my brother *Will?*
>
> He recently read J. R. R. Tolkien's novel *The Hobbit.*

Adjectives after a Noun

Use commas to set off a compound adjective or participle that appears after the noun it modifies.

> The children, *tired and cold,* came inside and enjoyed cider.
>
> They quickly gulped the cider, *spicy and warm.*

Participial Phrases pp. 92–94

Tag Questions

Use a comma to separate a tag question from the statement that precedes it.

> You enjoyed the cookies, *didn't you?*
>
> We are going to bake more, *aren't we?*

Adjective and Adverb Use pp. 243–44

Ask the students to identify the words or phrases that rename and further identify other nouns in each sentence. Remind them that these words are called *appositives.*

Teaching Strategy

Demonstration

Remind the students that compound adjectives or participles should appear directly after the nouns they modify. Explain that modifier problems can result from incorrectly placed adjectives or participles. Display these example sentences: *This lemonade, cool and refreshing, readies you to go out and finish the yard work.* (correct) *This lemonade readies you to go out and finish the yard work, cool and refreshing.* (misplaced) Emphasize the importance of placing compound adjectives or participles correctly.

Teaching Strategy

Discussion

Remind the students that the contractions present in tag questions are rarely suitable in academic writing. Point out that writers use written-out tag questions in formal writing: *are you not? did you not? is she not?* Ask the students to suggest times that they might use tag questions in their writing. (*informal writing, dialogue, persuasive essay, special emphasis for a letter to the editor, etc.*)

For a detailed listing of conjunctive adverbs, see *The Writer's Toolbox*.

Compound Sentences p. 132

Conjunctive Adverbs

Use commas to set off a conjunctive adverb from the rest of the sentence.

The chef, *however,* refuses to use prepackaged materials.

Therefore, all of the ingredients for the recipe are fresh.

When the conjunctive adverb appears between two independent clauses, use a period or a semicolon after the first independent clause. Then use a comma after the conjunctive adverb.

The chocolate layered dessert was quite tasty; *however,* it had too many calories for my diet.

The chocolate layered dessert was quite tasty. *However,* it had too many calories for my diet.

Adjective and Adverb Use pp. 243–44

Restrictive and Nonrestrictive Elements

A nonrestrictive modifier gives additional information that is not necessary to identify the thing being modified. The nonrestrictive element is set off from the rest of the sentence with a comma or a pair of commas. A restrictive modifier is necessary for identification; therefore, it is not set off by commas.

NONRESTRICTIVE ADJECTIVE CLAUSE	Walt Disney World, *which is located in Florida,* is a popular vacation spot.
RESTRICTIVE ADJECTIVE CLAUSE	The Disney park *that he likes best* is Walt Disney World.
NONRESTRICTIVE PHRASE	Space Mountain, *with its dark tunnels,* brings smiles to many children's faces.
RESTRICTIVE PHRASE	The roller-coaster ride *with dark surroundings* is Space Mountain.
NONRESTRICTIVE APPOSITIVE	Big Thunder Mountain Railroad, *another roller coaster,* takes its riders through an old mining town.
RESTRICTIVE APPOSITIVE ("CLOSE APPOSITIVE")	The roller coaster *Big Thunder Mountain Railroad* is in the Frontierland section of the park.
NONRESTRICTIVE ADVERB CLAUSE	The children enjoyed other rides at the park, *although the roller coasters were their favorites.*
RESTRICTIVE ADVERB CLAUSE	Sometimes they would get in line again *after they had ridden the roller coaster.*

The Forbidden City, once the location of the Chinese emperors' palaces, is so named because the common people were forbidden to enter it.

Located in southeast Beijing, the Temple of Heaven served as a traditional place of worship for the Chinese emperors. Erected in 1420 and later expanded, the Temple of Heaven stands as a work of architecture free of nails and pegs.

12.7 PRACTICE *the skill*

Write the letter of the correctly punctuated sentence.

__A__ 1. A. Our trip to Beijing, as I may have told you, was very exciting.
B. Our trip to Beijing as I may have told you was very exciting.

__B__ 2. A. Tori did you prefer the Forbidden City or the Temple of Heaven?
B. Tori, did you prefer the Forbidden City or the Temple of Heaven?

__A__ 3. A. We decided that this year, not next year, would be the best time to visit the country.
B. We decided that this year not next year would be the best time to visit the country.

TEACHING STRATEGY
Participation

Ask the students to explain three different uses for the conjunctive adverb, specifying the various types of punctuation accompanying each. Next instruct the students to think of a topic they can write a paragraph about. Instruct them to include three conjunctive adverbs used in three different ways with appropriate punctuation. Allow volunteers to read their paragraphs aloud.

TEACHING STRATEGY
Analysis

To help the students learn to differentiate between restrictive and nonrestrictive elements, distribute a copy of Teaching Help 12C (Teacher's Toolkit) to each student. Consider working through this exercise with your students or grading this worksheet in class. Ask the students to explain their answers. Remind the students to place commas around nonrestrictive clauses.

REINFORCEMENT

Use Bulletin Board 12 (Teacher's Toolkit) to help students understand the difference between restrictive and nonrestrictive elements and how to punctuate them correctly.

A 4. A. Martyn, Tori's brother, wanted to climb the Great Wall of China.
B. Martyn Tori's brother wanted to climb the Great Wall of China.

A 5. A. Oh, the Great Wall has a lot of steps!
B. Oh the Great Wall has a lot of steps!

B 6. A. The Wall massive and gray can be very hot in the summertime.
B. The Wall, massive and gray, can be very hot in the summertime.

A 7. A. Jacinta wanted to buy a pearl necklace, didn't she?
B. Jacinta wanted to buy a pearl necklace didn't she?

B 8. A. However we didn't have time to stop by the marketplace.
B. However, we didn't have time to stop by the marketplace.

B 9. A. The site, that was my favorite, was Tiananmen Square.
B. The site that was my favorite was Tiananmen Square.

A 10. A. Were you aware that the Forbidden City, ancient and grand, opens directly onto Tiananmen Square?
B. Were you aware that the Forbidden City ancient and grand opens directly onto Tiananmen Square?

The longest manmade structure in the world, the Great Wall of China, measures approximately four thousand miles.

Encompassing 122 acres, Beijing's Tiananmen Square can accommodate over one million people. It remains one of the world's largest urban squares.

12.8 REVIEW *the skill*

Insert any missing commas and cross out any unnecessary commas. If the sentence is already correct, write *C* in the blank.

____ 1. When planning a trip, that includes travel abroad, a potential traveler should ensure that he has a valid passport.

____ 2. A passport as many are aware can take several weeks to obtain.

____ 3. Well the process begins at a passport acceptance facility.

C 4. Passport acceptance facilities include many courts, post offices, and libraries, don't they?

____ 5. For the application process which can last some time the applicant should have proof of U.S. citizenship.

____ 6. The applicant must also prove his identity, before he can be granted a passport. A driver's license not a Social Security card, is adequate proof.

Punctuation | Chapter 12 309

_____ 7. However, a previous passport or a naturalization certificate, among other documents, also suffices to demonstrate identity.

_____ 8. Another necessity for the applicant is a pair of passport photographs, pictures of the applicant that are about two inches square.

_____ 9. The passport must be processed; therefore, the applicant must pay a fee.

__C__ 10. The passport, small but powerful, is the prerequisite for travel abroad.

In Letters and with Quotations, Dates, and Addresses

Commas appear in certain locations within letters, dates, and addresses.

Salutations and Closings

Use a comma after the salutation of a friendly letter.

Dear Aunt Jenny and Uncle George,   Dear Charles,

Use a comma after the closing of a friendly letter or business letter.

Yours truly,   Sincerely,
Aunt Elizabeth   John D. Rockman

Direct Quotations

Quotation Marks pp. 329–30

A comma or a pair of commas sets off a quotation tag from the quotation. The comma always appears before the quotation marks—inside closing quotation marks but outside opening quotation marks. A question mark or an exclamation point replaces the comma in sentences such as the third one below.

My brother said, "Let's get in line to ride the roller coaster again."

"I can't," I answered, "until I finish my ice cream."

"Will you please hurry!" he pleaded.

Dates

Use a comma to separate the day from the year in a date of month-day-year order and use one after the year when the date appears within a sentence.

Joshua and Jordan visited Florida on October 15, 2012.

On March 15, 2013, they visited California.

No comma is necessary when the date appears in day-month-year order.

Walt Disney was born 5 December 1901.

Addresses

Commas separate the elements in an address. If the address appears in the middle of a sentence, use a comma after the last element to separate the address from the remainder of the sentence.

Our vacation travels continued from Nags Head, North Carolina, to the picturesque city of Williamsburg, Virginia.

Do not insert a comma between the state, province, or territory and the ZIP code or another postal code.

The old address is 16 South Frederick Street, Evansville, Indiana 47714.

To improve the legibility of addresses on envelopes, the United States Postal Service recommends the following: "Do not use commas or periods." The USPS also recommends that addresses be typed or printed with a pen so that they can be read clearly even from a distance and that both the return address and the delivery address appear on the front of the envelope.

Teaching Strategy

Activity

Materials

- a short literature excerpt with several lines of dialogue

Display the excerpt without punctuation. Ask the students to supply the necessary punctuation marks and to explain why they are needed. Discuss the placement of commas, end punctuation, and quotation marks.

Evaluation

To evaluate the students' understanding of proper punctuation in direct quotations, direct the students to write a short narrative on a topic of their choice. Check the narratives for correct punctuation and for smoothness in the dialogue.

Teaching Strategy

Participation

Direct the students to write five sentences and to include a date in each. (For example, "On December 17, 1999, my sister was born.") Ask students to read their sentences and then to state where they placed the commas. Allow other students to decide whether the date was punctuated correctly. Continue until students demonstrate an understanding of the punctuation rules with days, months, and years.

ONE on ONE Conduct the above activity with your student. Instruct your student to read all five of his sentences. Then check your student's

An address on an envelope uses the standard two-letter abbreviation for the state, province, or territory with no punctuation before or after it and no periods within it.

Miss Christina Jackson
8609 Montebello Road
Charlotte NC 28226

To Signal Special Constructions

Commas can appear in a sentence to signal that the writer has used an unusual sentence construction. These commas do not separate; they alert the reader and prevent misreading.

Transposed Words and Phrases

Use commas to indicate words or phrases that are out of their normal order.

Most of the food at the party was too exotic. *The chocolate cake and pecan pie,* I really liked.

Commas in Place of Omitted Words

Use a comma to indicate the omission of what would otherwise be a repeated word in a parallel construction.

The chef collected wonderful recipes; the maitre d', beautiful menus.

The Hansons enjoyed a round of golf; the Baxters, a day at the museum.

Notice that the comma in the second clause replaces the *verb* of the first clause.

Commas with Certain Additions to Names

Use commas to enclose an abbreviated degree. Do not use a comma before numerals that follow a name.

Jackson Coleman, MD, began his practice in a small rural town.

His brother Dawson Coleman III, MD, joined the practice a year later.

A comma is optional between a name and the abbreviations *Jr.* and *Sr.* If you use a comma between the name and the abbreviation, be sure to use one between the abbreviation and whatever follows as well.

Traditional Practice	Kenneth C. Roberts, Jr., is our new neighbor.
Recent Practice	Kenneth C. Roberts Jr. is our new neighbor.

Incorrect Commas

Commas that are in the wrong places are distracting and can cause confusion. Avoid these comma errors in your writing.

Before a Conjunction Joining Only Two Elements

Avoid using a comma when only two words, phrases, or dependent clauses are joined by a conjunction.

Wrong	Brent, and John are coming for the family reunion.
Right	Brent and John are coming for the family reunion.

After a Conjunction

Do not use a comma after a conjunction unless the comma is necessary for some other reason.

Wrong	Brent arrived by plane this morning, and, John will arrive by train tomorrow.
Right	Brent arrived by plane this morning, and John will arrive by train tomorrow.

punctuation and explain any punctuation rules that give him difficulty.

Teaching Strategy
Demonstration

Display several sentences about journeys that you or your students have taken. Include an address in each sentence. Explain your punctuation choices to the students. Remind the students to place a comma after the last address element if the sentence continues.

Teaching Strategy
Induction

Display some sample envelope addresses. Ask the students to suggest general rules about the punctuation of mailing addresses. Discuss the students' answers. Then display the rules for addresses.

Writing Link

Encourage the students to incorporate the special constructions listed on pages 311–12 into their own writing for variety.

Reinforcement

To give the students additional practice with using the comma rules, distribute a copy of Concept Reinforcement 12B (Teacher's Toolkit) to each student.

Teaching Strategy
Motivation

After teaching the students the rules on avoiding incorrect commas, direct them to review their journals or writing folders for comma errors.

Between a Subject and a Verb

Do not use a comma to separate a subject and a verb. A pair of commas, however, may set off nonrestrictive elements between the subject and the verb.

Wrong	In the late nineteenth century, a Japanese man named Jigoro Kano, developed judo, a sport similar to wrestling.
Right	In the late nineteenth century, a Japanese man named Jigoro Kano developed judo, a sport similar to wrestling.

Avoid using a comma to salvage a sentence that has a long, awkward subject; rewrite the sentence instead.

Poor	That Jigoro Kano studied techniques from many schools of martial art and incorporated them into his judo, is an interesting fact.
Better	An interesting fact is that Jigoro Kano studied techniques from many schools of martial art and incorporated them into his judo.

Integrated Quotations

Do not use a comma to set off a quotation that functions as the subject or predicate noun of a sentence.

Subject	"The sands of time are sinking" is the beginning of a hymn.
Predicate Noun	A favorite invitation hymn is "Just As I Am."

Like other restrictive appositives, a quotation that functions as a restrictive appositive is not enclosed by commas.

The motto "In God We Trust" is stamped on our coins.

Dates

Do not set off a year with commas when it appears with only a month (no date).

Wrong	In May, 2013, James and Susan visited missionaries in Cambodia.
Right	In May 2013 James and Susan visited missionaries in Cambodia.

312 Chapter 12 | Punctuation

12.9 PRACTICE *the skill*

Rewrite the following letter, adding any missing commas and omitting any unnecessary commas.

Dear Crispin

Greetings from the beautiful city of Venice Italy! Tradition says the city was founded on March 25 421. Jean and I are quite thrilled with the atmosphere of romance that fills the hot and busy streets. She actually said "I think we should come back here someday," a statement that is quite encouraging, considering that travel is not always her favorite occupation. I spend my time gazing at scenery and people; my sister at a map and travel brochures. She and I are going to visit Saint Mark's Square tomorrow, and possibly take a gondola ride. Almost everything here is just thrilling! (The humidity I could do without.)

Yesterday we visited the Rialto. I could almost hear that character in *The Merchant of Venice* saying, "What news on the Rialto?" as we walked across. And do you remember how Frank Griswold, MD used to say that the world is being taken over by tourists? Today the famous bridge is covered with stores, mostly souvenir shops. Nonetheless, Jean, and I are thoroughly enjoying our stay.

Sincerely

Gwendolyn

Dear Crispin,

Greetings from the beautiful city of Venice, Italy! Tradition says the city was founded on March 25, 421. Jean and I are quite thrilled with the atmosphere of romance that fills the hot and busy streets. She actually said, "I think we should come back here someday," a statement that is quite encouraging, considering that travel is not always her favorite occupation. I spend my time gazing at scenery and people; my sister, at a map and travel brochures. She and I are going to visit Saint Mark's Square tomorrow and possibly take a gondola ride. Almost everything here is just thrilling! (The humidity, I could do without.)

Yesterday we visited the Rialto. I could almost hear that character in The Merchant of Venice *saying, "What news on the Rialto?" as we walked across. And do you remember how Frank Griswold, MD, used to say that the world is being taken over by tourists? Today the famous bridge is covered with stores, mostly souvenir shops. Nonetheless, Jean and I are thoroughly enjoying our stay.*

Sincerely,

Gwendolyn

Punctuation | Chapter 12 313

12.10 REVIEW *the skill*

Rewrite the following paragraph, omitting any unnecessary commas and adding any missing end marks and commas. There are ten errors.

The history of modern tourism, reaches back several centuries. In Europe it was traditional in the late eighteenth century, and in the nineteenth century for an upper-class young man to tour the Continent upon completing his studies. "Travel . . . is a part of education," was the rationale, as Francis Bacon put it. The Germans called this a *Wanderjahr,* or travel year; the British referred to it as the Grand Tour. As time went on, people began to travel to gain experience, to broaden their knowledge, and to see the world. With the arrival of World War I in June, 1914, many American soldiers found themselves overseas and later took their families to visit the same places. From that point on, there has been no turning back. People have come to love travel. Inexpensive it is not; today the tourism industry grosses about $104 billion yearly for the United States alone, and, Americans spend about $76 billion per year on tourism themselves. Some travel to visit family and friends; others to see new places. Perhaps some travelers feel as R. L. Stevenson did when he said "For my part, I travel not to go anywhere, but to go. I travel for travel's sake"

The history of modern tourism reaches back several centuries. In Europe it was traditional in the late eighteenth century and in the nineteenth century for an upper-class young man to tour the Continent upon completing his studies. "Travel . . . is a part of education" was the rationale, as Francis Bacon put it. The Germans called this a Wanderjahr, *or travel year; the British referred to it as the Grand Tour. As time went on, people began to travel to gain experience, to broaden their knowledge, and to see the world. With the arrival of World War I in June 1914, many American soldiers found themselves overseas and later took their families to visit the same places. From that point on there has been no turning back. People have come to love travel. Inexpensive, it is not; today the tourism industry grosses about $104 billion yearly for the United States alone, and Americans spend about $76 billion per year on tourism themselves. Some travel to visit family and friends; others, to see new places. Perhaps some travelers feel as R. L. Stevenson did when he said, "For my part, I travel not to go anywhere, but to go. I travel for travel's sake."*

Enrichment

Encourage the students to learn whether any church leaders or missionaries of the late 1700s and 1800s took Grand Tours or *Wanderjahrs.* Designate a time for students to share what they learn about the effect travel had on the people studied.

Scriptural Application

Ask the students to imagine what it would be like if educational tours were still the custom for today's youth. Then ask the students to name countries or cities that they would like to tour and how much they know about the cultures of these lands. Begin a discussion about the role of cultural awareness in the life of a Christian. Ask the students whether being equipped as an effective witness involves the capacity to understand the culture of the local people. Direct the students' attention to Acts 17:16–34. Highlight for the students Paul's knowledge of Greek philosophy, religion, and poetry and his use of that knowledge to identify with his audience, gain their attention, and communicate the gospel message effectively. Ask the students what activities they can begin doing today that will further equip them to witness to others. *(Keep abreast of current events and issues around the world, read the classic works of other countries, study the customs of different people groups, etc.)* Emphasize that modern transportation has made the world a global community and that Christians must prepare themselves to witness to diverse peoples.

Semicolon

Use a semicolon to join equal units that require a mark of punctuation stronger than a comma but weaker than a period.

Between Two Independent Clauses

Use a semicolon between two closely related independent clauses not joined by a coordinating conjunction. The second clause often reinforces the first. A transitional word often appears within the second independent clause. When the second clause is introduced by a conjunctive adverb, place a semicolon before the conjunctive adverb and a comma after it.

Compound Sentences p. 132

> The high school cooking class prepared several varieties of pizzas for the reception; pepperoni pizza will probably be everyone's favorite.
>
> The girls in the class assumed many of the preparation duties; the boys, however, also assisted.
>
> The girls in the class assumed many of the preparation duties; however, the boys also assisted.

Independent Clauses p. 116

Before a Conjunction in a Long Compound Sentence

Use a semicolon instead of a comma before a coordinating conjunction that joins two independent clauses when the clauses have interior commas.

> One cookie recipe required a variety of ingredients, including two cups of flour, four eggs, and two cups of chocolate chips; but we had only three eggs.

Comma with Conjunctive Adverb p. 308

Between Word Groups Containing Commas

Use a semicolon to separate a series of coordinate phrases when any of the phrases contain internal commas.

> In the cooking class were the senior class president, Cindy Stormer; the junior class vice president, Jim Meadows; and the junior class treasurer, Adam Miller.

Use semicolons instead of commas when a list is introduced by a colon and has entries that are somewhat long.

> Preparations for the school-wide reception were delegated to a number of people: freshmen and sophomore students made plans and decorated the gymnasium; juniors designed and printed the invitations and decorated the food tables; and seniors planned and prepared the food.

Use a semicolon to separate Bible references whenever a new chapter is mentioned.

> A recent chapel speaker spoke from Titus 2:1–8, 12; and 3:8.

Colon

A colon separates elements almost as definitely as the period. A colon emphasizes what follows as important, explanatory, or more specific. Except in certain expressions, such as Bible references, a complete independent clause must precede the colon.

Teaching Strategy
Introduction

Draw a large pyramid with three divisions. Ask the students to rank in ascending order the potency of the following punctuation marks: the semicolon, the period, and the comma. *(the comma, the semicolon, the period)* Fill in the pyramid with the correct answers as explained by the students. Then discuss the three uses for the semicolon as listed on page 315.

Teaching Strategy
Motivation

Ask the students whether they consider semicolons too formal for everyday writing. Encourage the students to use semicolons by explaining that a correctly placed semicolon communicates a message all its own. First, a semicolon shows the parallel nature of two ideas: it links the connected ideas and shows their logical relationship. Second, using a semicolon shows that the writer is proficient in language and punctuation conventions.

Teaching Strategy
Introduction

Refer the students to the punctuation pyramid used to introduce the semicolon. Ask the students to suggest where the colon would belong on the pyramid. Explain that the colon carries almost as much weight as the period, the most decisive end mark. Tell the students that the period makes a complete break in a sentence, whereas the colon slows the reader down and draws his attention to what follows.

In Bible References and Expressions of Time

Use a colon between the chapter and verse in a Bible reference and between the hour and minutes in an expression of time. Do not put a space after the colon in either case.

1 Timothy 4:12

10:00 p.m.

After a Salutation of a Business Letter

Use a colon after the salutation of a business letter.

Dear Senator Graham:

Between a Book Title and a Subtitle

Underlining for Italics p. 337

When you refer to a book by both its title and its subtitle, use a colon followed by a space between the title and its subtitle even if no punctuation appears on the title page of the book itself.

Children of the Storm: The Autobiography of Natasha Vins

Before a Series at the End of a Sentence

Use a colon to introduce a series that follows a complete independent clause. Do not use a colon when the series is a part of the basic sentence structure, such as a complement or the object of a preposition.

Wrong	The senior class trip will include: the Library of Congress, the Lincoln Memorial, and the Washington Monument.
Right	The senior class trip will include the Library of Congress, the Lincoln Memorial, and the Washington Monument.
Right	The senior class trip will include these popular sites: the Library of Congress, the Lincoln Memorial, and the Washington Monument.
Right	The senior class trip will include the following: the Library of Congress, the Lincoln Memorial, and the Washington Monument.

The words *such as, for example,* and *including* should not be followed by a colon.

They also hope to visit some other interesting places, such as the Smithsonian Institution, the Bureau of Engraving, and the National Archives Building.

Use a colon for emphasis to introduce a single appositive at the end of a sentence.

One of the most interesting exhibits in the Smithsonian Institution's gem section is also one of its most beautiful: the blue Hope diamond.

Before a Long or Formal Direct Quotation

Use a colon before a long or formal direct quotation if the introduction is a formal statement and if the quotation appears at the end of the sentence.

The guidance counselor reiterated the words of Thomas Paine: "Reputation is what men and women think of us; character is what God and angels know of us."

Between Two Independent Clauses

Use a colon between two independent clauses without a coordinating conjunction when the second clause is an explanation of the first independent clause.

The students showed great interest in the Revolutionary War era of America: they chose to read Thomas Paine's *Common Sense.*

Teaching Strategy

Analysis

Ask the students to explain the difference between the semicolon and colon. *(The semicolon precedes a second independent clause that reinforces or supports the first independent clause. The colon precedes a second independent clause that explains the first independent clause.)* Ask the students to suggest sample sentences that illustrate their understanding of this difference between the semicolon and the colon.

316 Chapter 12 | Punctuation

12.11 PRACTICE *the skill*

Write the letter of the sentence that exhibits correct use (or better use) of semicolons and colons.

_B_ 1. A. Dear Travel Light Travel Agency;
B. Dear Travel Light Travel Agency:

_B_ 2. A. I am writing to inquire about your international services for the following reason; my family is planning a trip to Australia.
B. I am writing to inquire about your international services for the following reason: my family is planning a trip to Australia.

_A_ 3. A. The following is a list of our desires for the trip: we would like to stay three weeks in Australia and Tasmania; we wish to stay in comfortable hotels that provide breakfast, a swimming pool, and a hotel safe; and we want to experience as much as possible of Australia's beauty and culture.
B. The following is a list of our desires for the trip; we would like to stay three weeks in Australia and Tasmania, we wish to stay in comfortable hotels that provide breakfast, a swimming pool, and a hotel safe, and we want to experience as much as possible of Australia's beauty and culture.

Tasmania is an Australian island state located southeast of Australia's mainland and across from the Bass Strait.

_A_ 4. A. My wife hopes to see some examples of native crafts; she is especially interested in aboriginal art.
B. My wife hopes to see some examples of native crafts: she is especially interested in aboriginal art.

_B_ 5. A. I understand from the book *Antipodean Splendor, The Wonders of Australia* that Ayers Rock, or Uluru, is a place not to miss: this spectacular red monolith is 9.4 kilometers in circumference.
B. I understand from the book *Antipodean Splendor: The Wonders of Australia* that Ayers Rock, or Uluru, is a place not to miss: this spectacular red monolith is 9.4 kilometers in circumference.

_A_ 6. A. Do tours of Uluru begin as early as 7:00 a.m.?
B. Do tours of Uluru begin as early as 7 : 00 a.m.?

_A_ 7. A. We would also like to visit Shipwreck Coast and see the stones called the Twelve Apostles; however, if that is impossible, we will gladly spend some time on Kangaroo Island.
B. We would also like to visit Shipwreck Coast and see the stones called the Twelve Apostles: however, if that is impossible, we will gladly spend some time on Kangaroo Island.

The Twelve Apostles

Punctuation | Chapter 12 317

__A__ 8. A. During our visit to Tasmania, we hope to see Cradle Mountain-Lake St. Clair National Park, which contains both ancient rainforests and alpine territory; or we could visit Lake St. Clair itself.

B. During our visit to Tasmania, we hope to see Cradle Mountain-Lake St. Clair National Park, which contains both ancient rainforests and alpine territory, or we could visit Lake St. Clair itself.

__B__ 9. A. We plan two specific activities in Sydney, attending a performance at the architecturally wondrous Opera House and climbing the Sydney Harbour Bridge.

B. We plan two specific activities in Sydney: attending a performance at the architecturally wondrous Opera House and climbing the Sydney Harbour Bridge.

__B__ 10. A. For our last stop before leaving the Land Down Under, my family would like to spend a few days sailing and scuba diving in the region of the Great Barrier Reef, diving at the reef has long been a dream of ours.

B. For our last stop before leaving the Land Down Under, my family would like to spend a few days sailing and scuba diving in the region of the Great Barrier Reef: diving at the reef has long been a dream of ours.

12.12 REVIEW *the skill*

Insert any necessary semicolons and colons. If the sentence is correct, write *C* in the blank.

__C__ 1. Travel is not only for sightseeing; it can also be a way of serving the Lord.

______ 2. The Bible includes several instances in which God commanded His servants to travel to spread His Word: Jonah went to Nineveh to deliver God's warning; the young prophet of 1 Kings 13:1–34 came to Jeroboam to prophesy judgment; and Philip went south to Gaza to speak with the Ethiopian eunuch.

______ 3. According to tradition, Thomas went quite far in his efforts to preach Christ crucified (; or :) the tradition says that he arrived in India in AD 52 and preached to some of the leading Brahmin families.

______ 4. Many examples of biblical missionaries exist; however, the apostle Paul's ministry is probably the most obvious example of traveling to spread the gospel.

318 Chapter 12 | Punctuation

______ 5. In Acts 13:46–47; 18:6; and 19:21, Paul expresses his desire and intent to go and preach the gospel among the Gentiles.

______ 6. And in 1 Corinthians 9:16, he makes a dramatic statement about his calling: "Woe is unto me, if I preach not the gospel!"

__C__ 7. On his first three missionary journeys, Paul visited—respectively—Salamis, Paphos, and Iconium; Syria, Cilicia, and Lystra; and Ephesus, Asia, and Troas.

______ 8. He also employed several methods of travel: by foot, by ship, and by basket.

______ 9. Paul even preached during his last recorded journey [; or :] when in a shipwreck on the way to Rome, he testified of God's power to the sailors and soldiers.

__C__ 10. No matter where or how he was traveling, Paul never lost an opportunity to spread the gospel to everyone around.

Punctuation | Chapter 12 319

12.13 CUMULATIVE *review*

Correct the twenty errors in the following paragraphs by crossing out any incorrectly capitalized words and writing the correction above and by inserting any missing end marks, commas, semicolons, and colons. *(Answers may vary.)*

In Matthew 28:19–20 the Lord commands, "Go ye therefore and teach all nations." The ~~greek~~ *Greek* participle for *go* carries the idea of "having gone"; in other words, Christ was telling ~~his~~ *His* disciples and, by extension, all Christians, "Having gone into all the world, preach." It is assumed one has already gone; therefore, in one sense a person does not need to take an explicit missionary trip in order to be a missionary. The ~~International~~ *international* traveler regularly comes into contact with various unsaved people. Before leaving home, the traveler can prepare for the trip spiritually(: or ;) one way to prepare is to gather tracts in the language of the country of destination. Becoming familiar with the culture and language shows the tourist's genuine concern for the people, customs, and nationality of the country; and it often makes citizens more willing to talk to foreigners. Even just letting people know that one is a Christian and behaving in a Christlike manner is a witness. A thoughtful, sensitive traveler will bear in mind the country's customs and laws as he seeks to be a witness for Christ.

¿Cree usted en el infierno?

~~but~~ *But* what kinds of travel include an obligation to witness? Foreign only? No, travel within one's own country also provides opportunities to share the gospel. A seatmate on an airplane, a waitress in a ~~Restaurant~~ *restaurant*, and a person in line at a store or amusement park all need to hear God's Word. Other avenues of witness include the following: a bus, taxi, or shuttle driver; the attendant at a gas station where a traveler fills up; and the cashier at a scenic attraction's gift shop. Whether traveling domestically or abroad, whether for a week or a year, any Christian anywhere can and should reflect to the world the glory of his Lord.

REINFORCEMENT

Use Chapter 12 Review on pages 459–62 for additional test review.

EVALUATION

Use Chapter 12 Test to evaluate students' understanding of the content and concepts of the chapter.

FROM THE WRITTEN WORD

Developing a Plan

Everyone has at some time analyzed a problem or a course of action. If you have spent time in a kitchen producing a chocolate creation that would please any chef only to have the cake fall flat, you were faced with a problem that needed to be analyzed before it could be corrected.

Perhaps you have explained why a particular football play or basketball defense has worked—or not worked—as it was intended. Perhaps you explained why your team tried unsuccessfully to gain possession of the football with an onside kick at the end of the game. Maybe you have explained the success of a box-in-one defense for a basketball game. In either case you were showing how that particular part of the game fit with the other parts of the game.

Analysis seeks to divide a topic or study into its parts and to show how and why these parts contribute to success or failure. By analyzing 2 Chronicles 31, you can discover why Hezekiah was successful as a king.

> And thus did Hezekiah throughout all Judah, and wrought that which was good and right and truth before the Lord his God. And in every work that he began in the service of the house of God, and in the law, and in the commandments, to seek his God, he did it with all his heart, and prospered. (2 Chron. 31:20–21)

How did Hezekiah achieve such success? Why did he do the things that he did? The *why* is explained in a single statement: Hezekiah sought to do that which was right in the sight of the Lord. The *how* involved several ideas. Read carefully 2 Chronicles 31. Then analyze how Hezekiah achieved his purpose.

Personal Response

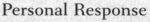

Read Proverbs 3:1–12. The writer admonishes his son to obey. The Scriptures are for our admonition as well. The *why* in Proverbs 3:1–2 is the promise of a peaceful, long life. What, then, are the *how*'s? Based on this passage, write a paragraph that shows how you would secure this promise.

SCRIPTURAL APPLICATION

To get the students thinking about how to obtain a peaceful, long life, read Proverbs 3:1–12 aloud. Ask them to jot down the *how's* found within these verses. *(be faithful to God's commandments, receive guidance from mercy and truth, fear God and avoid evil, respond to God's correction, seek wisdom and understanding, honor God by giving to Him, etc.)* Discuss the students' answers with them, especially how these principles can be enacted in everyday life. Allow students the time to write a personal application paragraph on how they plan to live according to these principles.

OBJECTIVES

Students will

1. choose a scene from a play to analyze.
2. examine the scene by re-reading it in its context, noting key aspects of the play, and deciding on a key feature to evaluate.
3. create an analytical thesis sentence.
4. develop a well-organized outline.
5. draft and arrange concise logical topic sentences.
6. add supporting details to an outline.
7. write a rough draft based upon notes, integrated quotations, and biblical allusions.
8. revise for well-reasoned and well-supported arguments.
9. provide a significant title for the work.
10. publish the response to a dramatic scene.

Chapter 13 Overview

Topic	Pages	Support Materials	Days
Quotation Marks	329–34	Chapter 13 Pretest ESL Help 13 Practice/Review the Skill 13.1–13.2	157
Issue Analysis Essay	290–95	Writing Worksheet 12 Writing Rubric 12	158, 160, 163, 165
Ellipses, Brackets, and Underlining for Italics	335–40	Practice/Review the Skill 13.3–13.5 Concept Reinforcement 13A	159
Apostrophe and Hyphen	341–46	Concept Reinforcement 13B Practice/Review the Skill 13.6–13.8	161
Dashes and Parentheses	347–51	Teaching Help 13 Practice/Review the Skill 13.9–10 Concept Reinforcement 13C	162
Research Report	269	Writing Worksheets 11B–11C Writing Rubric 11	164
Review	352, 463–64	Cumulative Review 13.11 Chapter 13 Review	165
Chapter 13 Test Critical Thinking	353		166
Response to a Dramatic Scene	322–29	Writing Rubric 13 Writing Worksheet 13 Bulletin Board 13	167–70
Final Review and Final Examination			171–80

RESPONSE TO DRAMATIC SCENE

Lesson Support

Teacher's Toolkit

Bulletin Board 13
Writing Worksheet 13
Writing Rubric 13

When you see a play, many elements demand your attention: the sets, the costumes, the actors' voices, the music, the action, perhaps even some smells. Reading a dramatic scene can be a very different experience—no lights or sound cues to pull you in. You, the reader, must respond to the words and ideas themselves. That response can reveal something about you. The following piece was written by a student after a reading of the sleepwalking scene from Macbeth *by William Shakespeare. Notice how the author inserts her own beliefs about Lady Macbeth and her tormented sleep into the response. Later you will respond to a dramatic scene that has made an impression on you.*

Infected Minds *by Lachelle Berkins*

Near the end of Shakespeare's *Macbeth,* Lady Macbeth is awakened by guilt for her part in King Duncan's murder. Her nocturnal wanderings provide some of Shakespeare's most memorable scenes, for who has read her pleas for the removal of the bloodstains and envisioned the wringing of her hands without also feeling the tug of his own conscience for prior deeds? Shakespeare takes pains to make Lady Macbeth's sleepwalking scene especially meaningful. The significance of the scene is found in its use of sensory details, the fitness of the judgment to the crime, and the reminder for the reader that no one can escape the effects of conscience.

Sensory details used throughout make the scene significant: all of the senses but taste are used. Sight imagery—or a lack of sight—is an important part of the sleepwalking scene. Lady Macbeth demands that a light be near her all the time (5.1.20), and she carries a candle, even though she does not see (21–22). The reader watches her rise and write and return to bed through the words of the gentlewoman. Lady Macbeth's voice is the major sound in the scene. One can almost hear the pathos of her haunting "Yet here's a spot" and "Out, I say!" (5.1.26, 29). As Lady Macbeth repeatedly rubs her hands, we both hear and feel the action of the wringing. Her requests for water also seem to force the reader to feel the scouring. The perceived smell of blood on her hands makes Lady Macbeth cry, "All the perfumes of Arabia / will not sweeten this little hand" (5.1.42–43).

Second, I find Lady Macbeth's sleepwalking appropriate to her crime because she has disrupted the sleep of others. In the play sleep represents a respite from worldly cares: Macbeth describes sleep as "innocent" (2.2.33) and "knit[ting] up the ravell'd sleave of care" (2.2.34) and as the "balm of hurt minds" (2.2.36). Banquo, Duncan, and the two attendants—the innocents—all seek sleep or are sleeping in Act 2 before the murder. After Macbeth announces that he has "done the deed" (2.2.14), that is, murdered Duncan as he slept, he predicts that "Macbeth shall sleep no more" (2.2.40). The couple fears the sleepy servants, and Lady Macbeth takes the daggers

Explain to students that they may see older citations in which the capital roman numeral indicates the act, the lowercase roman numeral indicates the scene, and the arabic numeral indicates the specific line(s). This citation format was replaced by a system that uses only arabic numerals separated by periods.

TEACHING STRATEGY

Introduction

If students are unfamiliar with the sleepwalking scene from Shakespeare's *Macbeth,* you may wish to read it with them before assigning "Infected Minds." See *BRITISH LITERATURE,* BJU Press.

Literature Link

Direct the students to read the essay "Infected Minds." After they have read the piece, ask them to explain whether they think Berkins liked or disliked the sleepwalking scene. *(Answers will vary but should include her positive first and last paragraphs.)*

SCRIPTURAL APPLICATION

After the students have read "Infected Minds," discuss what the Bible teaches about the effects of conscience. Read Ephesians 4:19 and 1 Timothy 4:2 aloud or ask a student to read these verses aloud. Ask the students whether these verses support or contradict the essay's statement that "no one can escape the effects of conscience." *(Answers will vary.)* Although these verses teach that some people no longer experience the effects of conscience, this condition is the result of their continued disobedience

Thinking Biblically

Provide a variety of critical essays or articles about films, plays, passages of Scripture, or other creative works. Instruct students to choose one or two to read independently. Allow small groups of students to share the insights they gained from their readings.

OVERVIEW of the WRITING PROCESS

Planning—choosing a scene about which to write, rereading the play or scene for context, taking notes while rereading, selecting an aspect to analyze, formulating a thesis, developing an outline, writing the thesis and topic sentences, organizing the topic sentences, and supplying supporting details in the outline

Drafting—writing a rough draft from the outline, incorporating information from one's notes, integrating quotations into the response, including biblical allusions, abstaining from textual distortion, writing a good opening paragraph, and writing a solid closing paragraph

Revising—checking the rough draft for precise well-supported arguments, and checking for correct mechanics, grammar, and spelling

Publishing—crafting a meaningful title, sharing the essay with the class, and displaying the essay on a bulletin board

Thinking Biblically

Have you ever watched a movie, stage play, or musical and wondered afterwards, "What did that mean?" Sometimes valuable insights and profound themes in a creative work can be difficult to discern. A movie, for instance, may seem merely dark and cynical or hopeful and encouraging on the surface but, when inspected more closely, be complex and full of rich meaning. By examining a creative work closely, critics are able to produce very insightful writing that enhances a reader's understanding. The skill of critical analysis, like any other, requires practice. The Christian critic should be especially interested in developing his abilities because the Bible is a literary work full of dramatic scenes, profound themes, complex characters, and significant symbols. The Bible is not fictional drama, of course, but if "all the world's a stage," Christians know who the Playwright is. And His stories are rich with meaning. The story of Esther, for example, never mentions God by name—but a skilled reader will examine the details that point to Him.

to besmirch them with blood. Lady Macbeth is initially unmoved by the actions of the evening and rebukes her husband for his "brainsickly" thoughts (2.2.43) about the murder. She further determines that "a little water clears us of this deed" (2.2.64). For her part in the king's murder, Lady Macbeth is condemned to "slumb'ry / agitation" (5.1.9–10). And though she pleads with an unseen conversant, "To bed, to bed, to bed" (5.1.58), she will receive no profit from repose.

Lastly, the sleepwalking scene effectively reminds the reader that no one escapes the effects of a guilty conscience. Lady Macbeth seems fearful—of the darkness, of the blood ("who would have thought the old man to have had so much / blood in him?" [5.1.33–34]), of their unmerited royal positions, of her husband's guilty reactions, and of dead Banquo. Guilt for her deed makes her attempt to escape the delusive knocking near the end of the scene ("Come, come, / come, come, give me your hand" [5.1.56–57]), for guilty persons "flee when no man pursueth" (Prov. 28:1). Guilt makes her seek sleep, for there she believes she may "discharge [her] secrets" (5.1.63). But sleep will be as elusive to her as to any other guilty person. Perhaps most effective—and most disturbing for the reader—is the realization that a guilty person is blind to the obviousness of his guilty actions. Lady Macbeth walks in darkness, but she is seen by others in the light. The gentlewoman and the doctor observe her easily and remark openly about her condition. This resembles the guilty person who thinks that no one but he knows what he has done. The Bible comments on man's deeds being seen when it states that "all things are naked and opened unto the eyes of him with whom we have to do" (Heb. 4:13).

Shakespeare's extraordinary deftness with detail and his knowledge of human behavior make him a master storyteller. Our senses are stirred, our demand for justice aroused, and our consciences prodded as we watch Lady Macbeth's nocturnal pacings. Perhaps Shakespeare gave us Lady Macbeth to help us understand what comes from trying to cover up our sin.

WRITING

RESPONSE TO DRAMATIC SCENE

> For the word of God is quick, and powerful, and sharper than any two-edged sword, piercing even to the dividing asunder of soul and spirit, and of the joints and marrow, and is a discerner of the thoughts and intents of the heart.
>
> *Hebrews 4:12*

It's one thing to say that you like something. It's another to be able to say why. And it is important to be able to say why. We should be able to defend our opinions and to make good judgments, judgments based on reason and knowledge as well as emotion. Articulating positions well using textual evidence as support is an important skill not only in writing but also in life. The piece you will write for this chapter will force you to analyze your response to a piece of drama and to support that response from the text of the dramatic scene.

Your Turn

Choose a scene from a play and write a thoughtful response to it. You may choose to respond to the scene from David Burke's "This Same Jesus," found in Chapter 6, or you may respond to part of another play.

and refusal to heed the promptings of their conscience. In other words, their lack of a conscience results from their earlier repudiation of their conscience. Discuss Romans 1:18; 2:14–16. Remind students that God knows everything about them. Encourage them to search the Scriptures earnestly for guidance and help.

TEACHING STRATEGY
Motivation

Materials

- newspaper reviews of plays or books (in print or online)

If possible, bring several play reviews or book reviews from a print or online newspaper to share with students. Pass them around and allow students to comment on various aspects of the reviews: what reviewers found important, interesting, or poorly done.

TEACHING STRATEGY
Discussion

Ask students whether they have ever responded in some way to a written or visual work. Discuss their experiences and encourage them to state exactly what about the piece made them respond—either positively or negatively (e.g., "The ending tied up all of the loose ends" or "I disagreed with the philosophy of the main character").

324 Chapter 13 | Response to Dramatic Scene

Planning

✔ **Choose your scene.** Start with a play you enjoy or are familiar with. Then look for a key moment in the play or a moment that you find especially interesting. The sleepwalking scene from *Macbeth* is a good choice for students who have read the play because of the scene's universal theme and striking imagery.

tip

Make a copy (for personal use only) that you can mark up. Then write impressions and questions in the margins. Underline or circle important images or themes that you notice as you read.

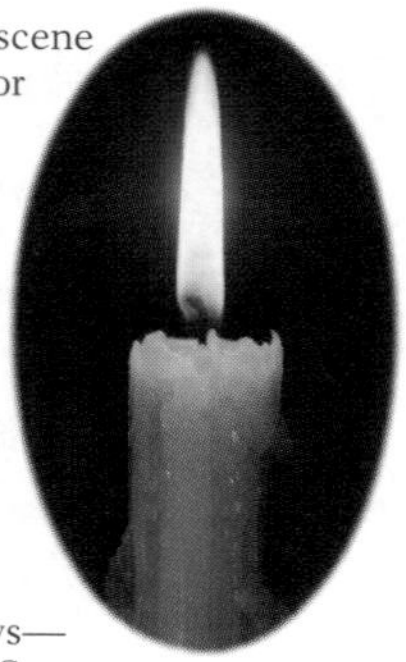

✔ **Re-read the scene.** If you have time, re-read the whole play to set the scene in context. Read the scene itself at least twice: once for flow and again for details. Read as many times as necessary to become familiar with the wording and details.

✔ **Take notes.** As you read, mark or write down anything that stands out to you. In preparing to write her essay on Lady Macbeth, Lachelle Berkins might have noted that Lady Macbeth keeps a candle with her all the time, acts as though she is washing her hands, and speaks of blood. In her notes, then, she could see how many times and in what ways Shakespeare appeals to the senses in the scene.

✔ **Select an aspect to analyze.** Now that you've read the scene several times and taken notes of your impressions, look for common threads among your reflections. One student noticed the significance of windows—both literal [stained glass] and figurative [a person's testimony] in "This Same Jesus" and decided to write about how the scene establishes man as a window to those around him. Think about what you learned in Chapter 6 about characters, conflict and resolution, plot, and setting. Ask yourself about each element: Is there anything unusual or repeated about one or more of these elements? Are any names—places or people—meaningful on a figurative level? What about the various elements might be considered universal? In addition, examine the theme of the piece and decide how the author reveals the theme in that scene. Look at the following notes about the window idea mentioned above.

Windows:

- The whole focus of this scene (and the whole play) is Adonis's fixing the windows. He's just finishing up as the scene starts.
- Both Dan & Adonis admire them.
- comment on storm's passing/getting sun soon
- wife looked out
- noticed windows every time he visited her grave
- Adonis talked to his wife about the windows he was working on.
- uses phrase "restorations in churches"—SIGNIFICANT?

✔ **Decide on a thesis.** Your thesis must state something about the scene that would not be readily apparent to the casual reader. For example, the point this thesis makes may not be obvious to everyone: "The significance of the [sleepwalking] scene is based on its use of sensory details, the fitness of the judgment to the crime, and the reminder for the reader that no one can escape the effects of conscience." On the other hand, a thesis like the following would be so easy to prove that no one would want to read the paper: "Lady Macbeth is guilty of

The assignment for this chapter asks students to respond to one scene from a play. However, if time permits, students should be encouraged to respond to an entire work.

Planning Strategy
Participation

Encourage the students to choose a scene from a familiar play. If they select a play they are unfamiliar with, too much time may be spent reading and not enough time analyzing and responding. Allow students to suggest plays or scenes from plays that they have read or studied recently. Display their suggestions and keep the list to reference for other in-class activities. Emphasize to students the importance of reading the entire play before analyzing a single scene. Note with them that although Berkins responds only to the sleepwalking scene, she pulls in quotations from another scene to support her ideas.

Planning Strategy
Peer Response

Encourage each student to ask a friend to read his chosen scene aloud with him. Reading aloud will bring out images that students do not notice with a silent reading.

Planning Strategy
Modeling and Analysis

Look back at the scene from "This Same Jesus" on pages 143–44. Ask students to mark the places where windows, light, or the sun is mentioned. Briefly review the section on pages 145–46 about characters, conflict and resolution, plot, and setting if necessary. Discuss the students' notes from the previous activity in light of the information and questions on page 325. Ask students to comment on whether the phrase

murder." Anyone who has seen or read the play would certainly yawn at that opening. Your thesis will probably do one of the following:

- analyze a problem in the text
- support an arguable position from the text
- examine a personal view of the text

Outlining pp. 6–8

✔ **Develop an outline.** Look again at your notes. Organize the details into categories of related items. Look at the items within each group. How are they connected? Express those connections in a phrase or a sentence. These ideas will become your topic sentences.

✔ **Write out your thesis and topic sentences.** They should be complete, declarative sentences. The content of the thesis and the topic sentences should be the main ideas of the paper and the paragraphs.

Lachelle Berkins went through several drafts of her thesis before deciding on the one you see above. First, she wrote,

> There are a lot of senses used in the sleepwalking scene, and the judgment fits the crime exactly since Lady Macbeth interrupted the sleep of others, and no one can escape their own conscience.

She decided that the wording of her thesis was weak and that she was presenting some of the information that belonged in the body of the paper too early. She then drafted the following statement:

> The significance of the sleepwalking scene is found in its use of sensory details, the fitness of the judgment to the crime, and reminding the reader that no one can escape the effects of conscience.

After reading her revised thesis, Berkins realized that all that was needed was to make the three points parallel. Her final thesis became

> The significance of the [sleepwalking] scene is found in its use of sensory details, the fitness of the judgment to the crime, and the reminder for the reader that no one can escape the effects of conscience.

✔ **Organize your topic sentences.** Use this strategy: put your strongest point last, your second strongest point first, and any other points between those. You want your paper to end with convincing power. Why do you think Lachelle Berkins chose the order she did for her paper?

✔ **Fill in the outline with supporting details.** Use specifics from the scene. Remember that for your conclusion you will also need a clear restatement of your thesis.

tip

Make your restatement a true restatement—not a simple repeat of the thesis. You can emphasize the purpose of your paper with an effective restatement.

Drafting

✔ **Use your outline to write a rough draft.** Berkins unified her paragraphs by keeping the topic sentences always in mind. She did not add unnecessary details or comments but rather kept directing her proofs and explanations back to the point at hand. Likewise, you should link your sentences together logically, drawing the reader's attention from point to point, adding proof as you go.

✔ **Include information from your notes.** The notes you took in the planning stage will be useful now. If you wrote directly on a copy of the text, consult those notes for quotations and ideas you want to include in your response.

"restorations in churches" is significant. *(Answers will vary.)*

Planning Strategy
Analysis

Conduct a freewriting activity. Challenge students to find a key sentence or passage from the play they have chosen and to explain in writing the importance of the excerpt to the scene. Allow about ten minutes.

Planning Strategy
Participation and Analysis

Ask students to decide on a possible thesis for the window idea presented on page 325. Allow several volunteers to read their theses aloud. Then ask students to identify the purpose of Berkins's essay. *(examines a personal view)* Using the theses from the previous activity, ask students to identify purposes for the window imagery. *(Answers will vary.)*

Planning Strategy
Discussion

Review proper outlining form if necessary. Conduct a minilesson from pages 6–8 for students who need help.

326 Chapter 13 | Response to Dramatic Scene

✔ **Integrate quotations into your response.** To bolster your arguments or analysis, you will need to include direct quotations from your dramatic scene. To do so correctly, you must incorporate the quotation seamlessly into your own text. Look at the following possible use of a quotation.

> Lady Macbeth is initially unmoved by the actions of the evening and rebukes her husband by saying, "Why, worthy thane, / You do unbend your noble strength, to think / So brainsickly of things" (2.2.41–43).

Although technically correct, the incorporated quotation is cumbersome and includes more than Berkins wanted to highlight. Berkins's quotation below takes only the pertinent information—in this case one word—and blends it directly into the text.

> Lady Macbeth is initially unmoved by the actions of the evening and rebukes her husband for his "brainsickly" thoughts (2.2.43) about the murder.

Berkins's first quotation above does show the proper way to quote lines of poetry. (Most of the text of Shakespeare's plays is written in verse.) When quoting lines of poetry (three or fewer) that are incorporated into a paragraph, use a slash mark with a space before and after it to represent line division. The word following a slash mark should be capitalized or lowercased as it appears in the original. For longer quotations (four or more lines), indent the entire quotation and omit the quotation marks. Remember, too, that any changes made to a direct quotation must be noted by brackets.

> There she believes she may "discharge [her] secrets" (5.1.63).

(The original is "discharge their secrets.")

Quotation Marks, Ellipses, and Brackets pp. 329, 335–36

✔ **Include biblical allusions.** Berkins quotes from Hebrews 4:13 in her comments about guilty consciences. An appropriate Bible verse used in context often encapsulates a complex theme and forces the reader to think beyond the actual text.

✔ **Beware of textual distortion.** It is tempting to take quotations and information about the text out of context just to prove a favorite point. Integrity demands that you deal honestly with the text and with the author's intent. Be careful not to twist meanings as you write. Additionally, never take credit for work that is not your own—either in idea or in wording. Doing so makes one guilty of **plagiarism,** a serious offense that is considered to be stealing another's work.

✔ **Write a good opening paragraph.** Notice how Berkins started her paper close to the point she wanted to make. She did not give a summary of the whole play or speak of guilt in general. She began with Lady Macbeth's sleeplessness and referred only to background pertinent to the scene. The opening also engages the reader, giving him reason to read on.

Introductions and Conclusions pp. 10–13

tip

Include in your introduction the title and the author of the piece you will discuss.

✔ **Write a solid closing paragraph.** Do not let the last paragraph be a simple mirror image of the first. The reader no longer needs background; he now needs to understand how this new perspective benefits him. Berkins implies for the reader that, like Lady Macbeth, everyone will be accountable for his sins.

ESL ESL students may not have a strong enough grasp of English to be able to paraphrase. Using direct quotations may be the best course of action. Also, not all countries have plagiarism and copyright laws as strict as those in the United States. Thus, not all students will realize the importance of quotation marks and thorough paraphrasing.

Planning Strategy

Discussion and Analysis

Ask students to examine the revisions of the thesis for Berkins's essay on page 326. What is weak about the first draft? *(opening "There are a lot"; pronoun-antecedent disagreement: "no one"—"their")* What makes draft two not parallel? *(first two ideas are presented using a noun + prepositional phrase, last idea uses gerund + prepositional phrase)* Point out that although a gerund is used as a noun, nongerund nouns are often stronger choices for parallelism.

Planning Strategy

Discussion

Discuss with students the answer to the question under "Organize your topic sentences" on page 326. *(Answers will vary.)*

Drafting Strategy

Analysis

Direct the students to look at Berkins's essay for examples of sentences linked together logically. Ask them to find connecting words. *(second, lastly, further)*

Drafting Strategy

Demonstration

Display the following sentence and quotation: *The distraught parent pleaded with reporters. "Help me! Just help me find my child!"* Ask students to suggest ways to integrate the quotation into the sentence. *(Answers will vary.)* Point out several options. *("Help me!" the distraught parent pleaded with reporters. "Just help me find my child!"* or *The distraught parent pleaded, "Just help me find my child!")* Use this opportunity to review the information on page 327 about

Revising

✔ **Read over your rough draft.** Do you notice any places where the proof or the explanation is missing or weak? Rewrite these passages, making your arguments precise and well supported. You may need to add more details from the scene to prove your points, or you may need to make the explanation clearer or more logical.

Here is the rough draft of Berkins's second paragraph.

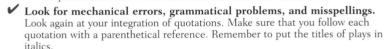

> There are lots of sensory details used throughout to make the scene significant: all of the senses but taste are used in abundance. Sight images—or lack of them—are throughout. Lady Macbeth demands that a light be near her all the time (5.1.20), and she carries a candle (5.1.21–22). The reader watches her get up and write on a paper and go back to bed along with the gentlewoman of the scene. The sound of Lady Macbeth's voice is the major sound in the scene. And her words are haunting when she keeps referring to the spot. Lady Macbeth repeatedly rubs her hands, and it seems as though we both hear and feel the action of the wringing. Her repeated requests for water to wash her hands with. The smell of blood on her hands makes Lady Macbeth cry, "All the perfumes of Arabia will not sweeten this little hand. O, O, O!" (5.1.42–43).

Berkins does not give enough explanation of her points to show the reader how the sensory details of the scene are significant. In her second draft she also corrects several problems of redundancy and lack of precision. Look again at the final draft:

> Sensory details used throughout make the scene significant: all of the senses but taste are used. Sight imagery—or a lack of sight—is an important part of the sleepwalking scene. Lady Macbeth demands that a light be near her all the time (5.1.20), and she carries a candle, even though she does not see (21–22). The reader watches her rise and write and return to bed through the words of the gentlewoman. Lady Macbeth's voice is the major sound in the scene. One can almost hear the pathos of her haunting "Yet here's a spot" and "Out, I say!" (5.1.29). As Lady Macbeth repeatedly rubs her hands, we both hear and feel the action of the wringing. Her requests for water also seem to force the reader to feel the scouring. The perceived smell of blood on her hands makes Lady Macbeth cry, "All the perfumes of Arabia / will not sweeten this little hand" (5.1.42–43).

Quotation Marks and Underlining for Italics pp. 329–30, 337

✔ **Look for mechanical errors, grammatical problems, and misspellings.** Look again at your integration of quotations. Make sure that you follow each quotation with a parenthetical reference. Remember to put the titles of plays in italics.

Publishing

✔ **Title your work.** For this type of essay, the best title ideas often come from the work being studied. Think about your thesis and the message of your response. Then look for a quotation or part of a quotation from the scene that corroborates your message.

✔ **Share your essay with your class.** If possible, obtain a visual recording of a performance of the drama you have discussed and play your topic scene for the class. Following the scene, read your critical response to it.

✔ **Display your essay on a bulletin board.** If your school has a speech and drama room, ask for permission to display your class responses in that room. Near the display, leave a pile of blank note cards and an empty box with a note inviting other students who use the room to read your responses and to write their own comments about particular essays. These comments provide feedback to help you see whether your arguments were convincing to someone else.

integration of quotations. Admonish students to use only those quotations that deal directly with the thesis and supporting points. Remind them that any others, however interesting, detract from the point they are trying to make.

Drafting Strategy

Discussion and Participation

Emphasize the importance of avoiding plagiarism. Use Writing Worksheet 13 (Teacher's Toolkit) for practice.

Drafting Strategy

Modeling

Ask students to find examples of good opening and closing paragraphs in print or online magazines or news stories. Allow them to share examples and to explain what makes each effective. Display examples.

Reinforcement

Use Bulletin Board 13 (Teacher's Toolkit) to encourage students to read and respond to drama.

Revising Strategy

Modeling and Demonstration

Use the paragraphs on page 328 to demonstrate revising. Ask students to underline the problem words or phrases in the rough draft of Berkins's second paragraph. (*Answers will vary but should include the following: "There are lots of" [weak]; "throughout" used twice in close proximity [redundant]; "along with" sounds like Lady Macbeth and gentlewoman retired together; "sound" used twice in close proximity [redundant]; "repeatedly" and "repeated" [redundant].*) Then ask

Some Ideas to Consider

History

- Find a play review from the late 1800s or early 1900s. Compare the style and content to what you might write today.

Journalism

- Write a review of a play for the Arts section of the newspaper.

More Punctuation

End marks and commas, the most frequently used marks of punctuation, aid us in understanding the meanings of sentences. In addition to these, other marks of punctuation further help to clarify meaning for the reader and the writer. Without these additional markers, clear understanding would be difficult.

Quotation Marks

Direct Quotations

Quotation marks indicate the exact words of a speaker or writer. Do not use quotation marks for indirect quotations, words that report the idea of the speaker or writer but not the exact words. Quotation marks always occur in pairs.

Direct	Sunday's sermon text was Philippians 2:25: "Yet I supposed it necessary to send to you Epaphroditus, my brother, and companion in labour, and fellowsoldier."
	I commented as we left, "I had never thought about these ideas before."
	"Yes, Paul must have valued Epaphroditus's friendship greatly," my brother said.
Indirect	Philippians tells us the kind of person that Epaphroditus was.
	I said that I had never thought about these ideas before.
	My brother said that Paul must have valued Epaphroditus's friendship greatly.

tip — Writer's Toolbox

Remember to be accurate and honest when you are quoting another person's work. Place direct quotations in quotation marks. If you are summarizing or paraphrasing, use your own words, your own organization, and your own sentence structure without quotation marks. (See also page 266.)

Objectives

Students will

1. distinguish between correct and incorrect uses of quotation marks with direct quotations, dialogue, titles of short works, words used in a special sense, other marks of punctuation, and single quotation marks.
2. differentiate between correct and incorrect uses of ellipses and brackets.
3. recognize and correctly use underlining for italics.
4. distinguish between correct and incorrect apostrophe usage and insert apostrophes correctly for omissions, possessives, and special plurals.
5. distinguish between correct and incorrect uses of hyphens and insert hyphens correctly in various situations with omission of a connecting word, word division at the end of a line, compound constructions, and words with a common element.
6. insert dashes correctly with interrupting phrases or clauses, with internal appositive series, with introductory lists and summary statements, for emphasis, and to show interrupted speech.
7. insert parentheses correctly to enclose supplementary elements, to use parenthetical material with other marks of punctuation, and to enclose numbers or letters that identify divisions.
8. combine sentences correctly using parentheses or dashes.
9. revise a paragraph to correct capitalization and punctuation errors.

them to suggest revisions for the problems identified and compare their suggestions to Berkins's revisions.

Revising Strategy

Discussion

Discuss special problems associated with the punctuation of titles and with reference citations (pp. 330–32). Conduct a minilesson about these problems if necessary.

Evaluation

For help in grading this assignment, see "Grading Student Writing" (p. v) and Writing Rubric 13 (Teacher's Toolkit).

Publishing Strategy

Discussion

Ask the students to discuss how the title "Infected Minds" relates to Berkins's thesis. *("Brainsickly" thoughts that originally disturb Macbeth work their way into Lady Macbeth's mind and infect her with inescapable guilt over their crime.)*

MORE PUNCTUATION

Lesson Support

Student Worktext

Chapter 13 Review—pp. 463–64

Teacher's Toolkit

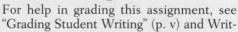

Chapter 13 Pretest
Teaching Help 13
ESL Help 13
Concept Reinforcement 13A–13C

Test

Chapter 13 Test

When the dialogue tag appears in the interior of a sentence, enclose the tag with commas, not with quotation marks. Use quotation marks to enclose the two parts of the quoted material.

> "You can read further about Epaphroditus," the preacher said, "in Philippians chapter four."

Well-known proverbs (including certain biblical sayings) are often not enclosed with quotation marks.

> Jerry remembered his grandmother's admonition to waste not, want not.

tip

A prose quotation that is more than four typed lines or a poetry quotation of more than three lines is not enclosed in quotation marks. Instead, the quotation begins on a new line and is indented one inch. The parenthetical citation occurs at the end of the quotation. If you choose to use one of these long quotations, be sure that the quotation is relevant and fits smoothly into the text of your paper.

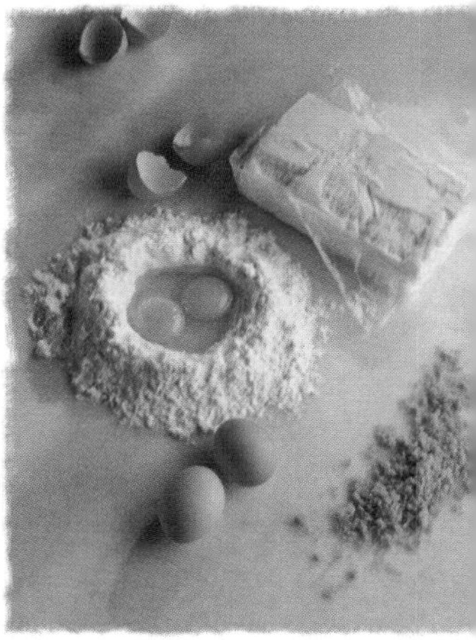

Dialogue

Use quotation marks to enclose the words of each speaker and begin a new paragraph whenever the speaker changes.

> Johanna asked, "Did you purchase all the ingredients that we need for the cookies?"
>
> "I bought everything that I thought we might need," Sheila answered.

Do not use quotation marks for the speeches of characters within a play when the speeches are formatted as a script.

Banquo	How goes the night, boy?
Fleance	The moon is down; I have not heard the clock.
Banquo	And she goes down at twelve.
Fleance	I take't, 'tis later, sir.

William Shakespeare, *Macbeth*, Act 2, Scene 1

Titles of Short Works

Titles
p. 282

Use quotation marks to enclose the titles of short works. A work is considered a short work if it would not stand alone as a published work. Examples of short works are articles, chapters of a book, short stories, essays, songs, and most poems. Use quotation marks for the titles of individual episodes of radio or television programs.

> "Give of Your Best" is an article that challenged me to be more unselfish.
>
> Edgar Allan Poe wrote "The Cask of Amontillado."
>
> John Newton's "Amazing Grace" is a favorite song of many Christians.

Quotation marks are not used to indicate the major subdivisions of the Bible.

> The Sunday morning sermon was from the thirty-second chapter of Genesis in the Old Testament.

The titles of historical or political documents such as the Constitution and the Gettysburg Address are not enclosed in quotation marks. In addition, quotation marks are not used with a title when the title stands as the heading of the work itself.

Teaching Strategy

Introduction and Participation

Ask the students to name situations in which knowledge of quotation marks is essential. *(when composing an e-mail message, when writing a research paper for a class, when reading a newspaper article, etc.)* Display the following:

- By the way, Mona told me you are scheduled to speak at tomorrow's meeting. How exciting!
- By the way, Mona told me, "You are scheduled to speak at tomorrow's meeting." How exciting!

Ask the students to respond to each excerpt as if they were the recipients. Ask the students to explain the difference between the two statements. *(The first contains an indirect quotation; the second, a direct one. The indirect quotation conveys that the recipient is to speak at tomorrow's meeting, the second, that the sender will speak tomorrow.)* Emphasize the importance of using quotations correctly.

ESL Strategy

Because some languages do not have both direct and indirect quotation forms, ESL students may need special help distinguishing between the forms in English. Use ESL Help 13 (Teacher's Toolkit) for examples of indirect and direct quotations.

330 Chapter 13 | More Punctuation

tip

Do not put the title of your own paper in quotation marks on the title page or on the first page of the paper.

Words Used in a Special Sense

Occasionally, it is permissible to use quotation marks to indicate that a word is used in a special sense. It is better, however, to revise the sentence to clarify the meaning. (Do not use quotation marks around a word that is used in its normal sense.)

Acceptable	My favorite "low-calorie" chocolate milk shake was on sale this afternoon.
Better	My favorite chocolate milk shake made with skim milk was on sale this afternoon.

Quotation marks may be used to indicate words or expressions that are noticeably more formal or more informal than the rest of the passage. Although an occasional use of a slang word may seem effective, it is better to avoid slang expressions and maintain a consistent level of usage.

Acceptable	The exhausted college student felt like an "airhead" after a late night of studying.
Better	The college student was mentally exhausted after a late night of studying.

Quotation Marks and Other Punctuation

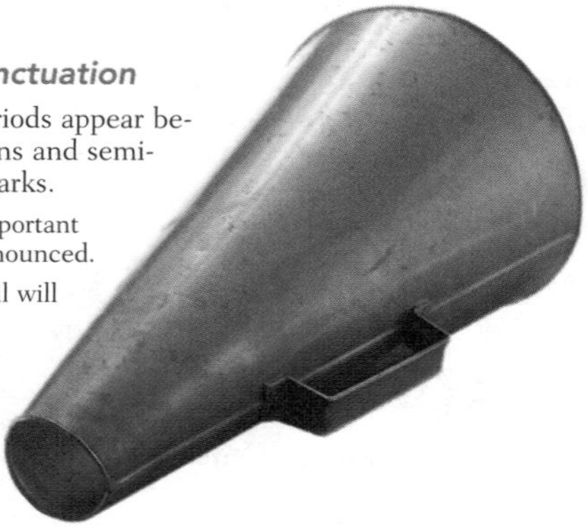

In American usage commas and periods appear before adjacent quotation marks, but colons and semicolons appear after closing quotation marks.

"The players are meeting for an important practice session," the principal announced.

He then said, "The student council will meet as well."

The cheerleaders composed a new closing line for the school song "Fighting Swordsmen": "Give it all your might!"

The student council wrote "Swordsmen Are on the Top"; the new cheer will be introduced at the championship game.

End Marks
pp. 296–98

Commas
pp. 301–12

Semicolon and Colon
pp. 315–16

Question marks and exclamation points may appear inside or outside closing quotation marks, depending upon the meaning of the sentence. If the quotation itself is a question or an exclamation, the mark of punctuation goes inside the closing quotation marks. If the entire sentence, but not the quotation itself, is a question or an exclamation, the mark of punctuation appears outside the closing quotation marks.

Have you read Abraham Lincoln's "Thanksgiving Proclamation"?

"Wasn't Lincoln's thankful spirit during the time of war unusual?" asked the young history student.

"Oh, look at our Thanksgiving dinner!" squealed the child.

ESL

Look carefully at the examples. If a question word (*who, when, where,* etc.) or a subject-verb inversion (*Have you, Was he,* etc.) is inside the quotation marks, then the question mark should also be inside the quotation marks.

Teaching Strategy
Induction

Materials

- newspapers or magazines (print or online)

Distribute print newspapers or magazines to students or provide access to online news or magazine articles. Instruct students to find direct quotations with various types of dialogue tags. Give them several minutes to locate a few examples. Then ask volunteers to display examples. Assist the students in formulating rules on the placement of quotation marks and commas with dialogue tags.

One on One Conduct the above activity by working with your student to locate several examples of quotations with initial, interior, and end dialogue tags. Study the various examples with your student. Then assist your student as he formulates rules on the placement of quotation marks with dialogue tags.

Teaching Strategy
Modeling

Ask the students whether they have ever read dialogue that left them wondering who was speaking to whom. Explain that there is a simple way to remedy the situation. Ask a student for a conversation topic. Then display several lines of dialogue about the topic. Emphasize that the students should use a new paragraph to indicate each change in the speaker. Also demonstrate how to use quotation marks around the words of each speaker.

tip

The placement of the dash in relation to quotation marks follows the same guidelines as given for the question mark and exclamation point.

Only one mark of punctuation appears at a time with quotation marks. When a speaker tag, for example, follows a question, the question mark alone—without a comma—separates the question from the tag.

ESL When a quotation tag follows the quotation, it is spoken with the same rise or fall as the quoted sentence. (See page 70.)

QUOTED STATEMENT	"Thanksgiving is a time to thank God for His blessing," ↘ she said. ↘
QUOTED QUESTION-WORD QUESTION	"When did it begin?" ↘ I asked. ↘
QUOTED YES/NO QUESTION	"Is it always in November?" ↗ I asked. ↗

Single Quotation Marks

Use single quotation marks when quotation marks are necessary within other quotation marks. The rules that govern other marks of punctuation in relation to double quotation marks apply to single quotation marks also.

"Did you hear Brittany say, 'What song should we sing?'" asked Austin.

"Could we sing 'We Gather Together' for our Thanksgiving program?" the children asked.

"Yes, it will fit well with our theme from 1 Thessalonians 5:18: 'In every thing give thanks,'" the teacher answered.

The *Elizabethan period* (1558–1603) refers to the years that Queen Elizabeth I reigned in England.

13.1 PRACTICE *the skill*

Write the letter of the sentence that is correctly punctuated.

A 1. A. "Come, join us; the banquet is prepared," the rich count announced to his guests.
B. "Come, join us; the banquet is prepared", the rich count announced to his guests.

B 2. A. "The table," he exclaimed, "is spread with hundreds of dishes and bowls of fresh fruits"!
B. "The table," he exclaimed, "is spread with hundreds of dishes and bowls of fresh fruits!"

A 3. A. My brother said that he was not sure whether he would thoroughly enjoy a meal without potatoes.
B. My brother said that "he was not sure whether he would thoroughly enjoy a meal without potatoes."

B 4. A. "Loaded" Elizabethans dined twice a day: breakfast at eleven or twelve and supper at five or six.
B. Wealthy Elizabethans dined twice a day: breakfast at eleven or twelve and supper at five or six.

EVALUATION

Display a conversation that is missing quotation marks and paragraph divisions. Direct the students to rewrite the conversation using quotation marks and paragraph divisions correctly.

TEACHING STRATEGY

Activity

Ask students to name their favorite short and long works. Display their answers. Then ask them to decide which titles should be underlined and which should be placed in quotation marks.

TEACHING STRATEGY

Discussion

After reviewing the quotation rules for words used in a special sense, elicit from the students what uses qualify as a special sense. *(words conveying irony; words conveying either greater or lesser formality than their context)* Remind students not to use quotation marks as a crutch; that is, they should use effective diction and syntax to communicate.

TEACHING STRATEGY

Discussion and Analysis

Encourage the students to examine the overall meaning of a sentence to determine the placement of end punctuation in relation to quotation marks. Display the following sentences without end punctuation:

- Didn't Uncle Ross say, "Meet back at the ship by noon"?

B 5. A. "My, my," shouted the guest at a water performance, "look at the actor riding the dolphin"!

B. "My, my," shouted the guest at a water performance, "look at the actor riding the dolphin!"

B 6. A. Singers who sang Rose, Rose, Rose Red and Queen's Round might have provided entertainment for the feasts.

B. Singers who sang "Rose, Rose, Rose Red" and "Queen's Round" might have provided entertainment for the feasts.

A 7. A. Meals of the common man were not nearly as elaborate.

B. Meals of the "common" man were not nearly as elaborate.

B 8. A. "Did you hear the count ask, 'And when do you eat?" asked the servant.

B. "Did you hear the count ask, 'And when do you eat?'" asked the servant.

A 9. A. "Elizabethan noblemen," I read, "loved hospitality and had guests on a regular basis."

B. "Elizabethan noblemen," I read, "loved hospitality and had guests on a regular basis".

A 10. A. The nobleman commanded, "Give the leftovers first to the servants and then to the poor people outside the gates!"

B. The nobleman commanded, "Give the leftovers first to the servants and then to the poor people outside the gates"!

- I panicked when the announcer said, "Leah Wessox, please come to the tourism desk"!
- "Where is the rest of our group?" asked Laurence.
- "Stand back from the gangplank!" said the officer.

Ask the students to analyze and supply punctuation for each sentence.

Teaching Strategy

Demonstration

Display the following sentences and explain that dashes used with quotation marks adhere to the same rules as do question marks and exclamation points. *"I was going to e-mail you, but—" Greer began to say. "I was going to e-mail you, but my laptop crashed for the summer"—a likely story.*

Teaching Strategy

Participation

Display the following sentences without quotation marks. Ask students to supply the appropriate double and single quotation marks and to explain their answers.

- The announcer stated, "We begin today's program with Emily Dickinson's poem, 'There Is No Frigate Like a Book.'"

Marzipan is a candy made from almonds, egg whites, and sugar.

13.2 REVIEW *the skill*

Insert any missing single quotation marks or double quotation marks. Circle any unnecessary quotation marks. Use the transpose symbol (∿) to indicate the correct placement of any misplaced periods, commas, question marks, exclamation points, colons, and semicolons.

1. "Have you ever thought about the kinds of snack foods that existed in Elizabethan England"? the lecturer asked.
2. "Was it John who said, 'They probably didn't have any'?" I asked.
3. I think that chocolate, a thin and bitter drink at the time, had only "medicinal" purposes.
4. The lecturer continued by saying "that at this time the Swiss had not yet added milk and sugar to chocolate."
5. He also said, "The English had delicious marzipan, fruit pies, and puddings."
6. "Did you know that the English enjoyed a cheesecake dessert"? I asked.
7. One student commented, "I can't believe that the English enjoyed, of all things, pretzels and bagels"!
8. "Vanilla was not a flavoring of that time", the lecturer explained, "but almond flavoring was very common."
9. Another student asked, "Was sugar available"?
10. The lecturer answered, "Yes, it was available;" then he explained that it was more expensive than honey.

- "My brother said, 'Only seven of Dickinson's poems were published in her lifetime,'" remarked Margaret.
- "Like Henry David Thoreau at Walden Pond," explained Tom, "this brochure refers to Amherst, Massachusetts, as 'the locale forever Emily Dickinson's.'"

Teaching Strategy
Motivation

Ask the students what type of writing relies on the correct use of ellipses and brackets. *(research, dialogue, literary analysis, etc.)* Encourage the students to pay careful attention to the following lesson, as it will help prevent potential problems in their writing.

Teaching Strategy
Activity

Materials
- A Bible for each student

After teaching the rules for ellipses, instruct the students to find their favorite Scripture passages. Ask several students to share why a certain passage is a particular encouragement to them. Direct all the students to find the essence of their passages and to use their knowledge of ellipses to link at least two partially quoted statements

Ellipses

Ellipsis marks, or points, either indicate the omission of something in a quoted passage or signal halting or unfinished speech. Use three spaced dots or periods with a space before the first and after the last.

Omission of Words in a Quotation

Use ellipses to indicate the omission of one or more words from a quoted passage. Be careful not to change the meaning of the passage when you omit the words.

Original	"Know ye that the Lord he is God: it is he that hath made us, and not we ourselves; we are his people, and the sheep of his pasture. Enter into his gates with thanksgiving, and into his courts with praise: be thankful unto him, and bless his name." (Ps. 100:3–4)
With Omissions	"Know ye that . . . we are his people, and the sheep of his pasture."

When you are quoting from multiple sentences, use a period followed by three spaced dots to indicate the omission of the end of the preceding sentence or the omission of the beginning of the following sentence. The new quotation must be a complete thought, and the first word of the second sentence must be capitalized, regardless of whether it was capitalized in the original.

> The psalmist wrote, "Know ye that the Lord he is God. . . . Be thankful unto him, and bless his name."

Use a full line of spaced dots to indicate the omission of one or more lines of poetry when the poem is formatted in stanzas.

Original	The King of love my Shepherd is, Whose goodness faileth never; I nothing lack if I am His And He is mine forever.
With Omissions	The King of love my Shepherd is, ... I nothing lack if I am His And He is mine forever. From "The King of Love My Shepherd Is" by Henry W. Baker

Halting or Unfinished Speech

Use ellipses to indicate hesitant pauses in speech. Use a period followed by ellipses to indicate unfinished speech that trails off gradually.

> The young child began his part in the program: "'Make a joyful noise unto the Lord' . . . oh . . . I can't remember the next. . . ."

Dashes
p. 347

Brackets

Brackets may resemble parentheses in appearance, but brackets cannot be used interchangeably with parentheses. Brackets indicate an addition to a quotation or a change in a quotation.

to express the theme of the passage. *(For example, "John 1 states that 'in the beginning was the Word . . . and the Word was made flesh.'")* Consider collecting the students' favorite Scripture themes and posting them on a bulletin board.

ONE on ONE Conduct the above activity with your student by asking him to find a favorite Scripture passage. Consider sharing one or two of your favorites as well and then demonstrating how to capture the essence of the passage in one quoted statement using ellipses. Discuss the punctuation needed for each.

Teaching Strategy

Participation

Ask the students to think of instances in their creative writing when they may need to use ellipses to indicate halting or unfinished speech. *(Answers will vary.)* Display several of the students' examples.

Insertion or Replacement in a Quotation

The reader must be able to distinguish your words from the words of the person being quoted. Use brackets to indicate your own words whether they add to, replace, or correct the quoted material.

Original "Many of those who became settlers had been frustrated when the Church of England embraced aspects of the Reformation while continuing several Roman Catholic practices. Christians quickly discovered that their king was not interested in fully implementing the work of the Reformation. As a result, they looked on the New World as a haven where they could establish communities and complete the Reformation. This reason for settlement distinguished the colonial heritage of the United States from that of new colonies established in other regions."
from *United States History*, Fourth Edition, by Timothy Keesee and Mark Sidwell (BJU Press, 2012) [p. 25]

Addition "Christians quickly discovered that their king was not interested in fully implementing the work of the [Protestant] Reformation."

Replacement Keesee and Sidwell write, "As a result, [settlers] looked on [America] as a haven where they could establish communities and complete the Reformation."

Replacing Parentheses Inside Other Parentheses

Though seldom needed, brackets are used as parentheses inside other parentheses. It is better, however, to rewrite the sentence or to give the additional information in a footnote or endnote.

> In the early sixteenth century, Europe saw changes in established religion (the Roman church departed further from some of its basic doctrines [one being the authority of Scripture]) and experienced a spiritual depression.

Error in Original

Underlining for Italics p. 337

At times you may find it necessary to quote a passage that contains an error or some unconventional usage. In order to identify the error or the unconventional usage, you have two options. You may replace the error with your own correction enclosed in brackets or add the Latin word *sic* ("thus" or "such") enclosed in brackets immediately after the word or phrase in question to indicate that you have quoted the text accurately. (Although the word *sic* [a foreign word] has become common in English, documentation standards require it to be italicized.)

Indication of Error "Each believer should read their [*sic*] Bible daily."

"The report identified numerous problems between you and md [*sic*]."

Correction "Each believer should read [his] Bible daily."

"The report identified numerous problems between you and m[e]."

Underlining for Italics

Use italic print to indicate the titles of books or other long works and for other specialized uses. In a handwritten paper, underlining indicates that a word should be italicized.

Handwritten <u>Free Indeed</u> presents biographical sketches of notable black American ministers.

Printed *Free Indeed* presents biographical sketches of notable black American ministers.

Teaching Strategy

Participation

Explain that writers quoting sources must frequently use brackets (1) to clarify the subject or a pronoun reference and (2) to indicate a change in verb tense. Ask the students to name the tense frequently used in literature and in historical narratives for immediacy. *(literary present tense)* Ask them to direct you as you integrate the following sentence into a clear present-tense quotation. This sentence from Mark Sidwell's *Free Indeed: Heroes of Black Christian History* tells of Samuel Morris (1873–93), an African prince originally named Kaboo who converted to Christianity and traveled to America for further Bible training.

"The account of his journey to America was one of drama and adventure, and the story of his brief life in this country was one of inspiration and determination."

According to Mark Sidwell, "The account of his [Samuel Morris's] journey to America [is] one of drama and adventure, and the story of his brief life in this country [is] one of inspiration and determination."

Additional Resources

For an overview of black church history and black Christian leaders, see *Free Indeed: Heroes of Black Christian History* by Mark Sidwell (BJU Press, 2001).

Teaching Strategy

Discussion

Remind the students that they should not place a period after the Latin word *sic;* however, they should italicize or underline it and place it in brackets.

336 Chapter 13 | More Punctuation

Titles of Long Works

Use italics for the titles of long literary or musical works.

Titles
p. 282

Books	My sister enjoyed reading *Suncatchers* by Jamie Langston Turner.
Periodicals	What was today's lead article in the *Wall Street Journal*?
Newspapers	The *Los Angeles Times* reported the newest presidential candidate's bid for the presidency.
Musical Compositions	Donizetti's opera *Lucia di Lammermoor* will be presented at the local university next month.
Television or Radio Series	Do you remember the radio program *The Lone Ranger*?
Epic Poems	The British Library in London houses the epic poem *Beowulf*.
Plays	Does Shakespeare's *Richard III* reveal the problems of England at that time?

Works of Art

Use italics for the names of visual works of art.

The sculpture *Pieta* by Michelangelo can be seen in St. Peter's Basilica in Rome.

Giuseppe Chiari's painting *The Return from the Flight into Egypt* is part of the museum's collection.

Large Vehicles

Use italics for the names of specific large vehicles, but not for a class of vehicles.

Transportation
p. 274

Ships	A visit to the USS *Yorktown* will provide historical insights into the Battle of the Pacific.
Aircraft	The first B-2 or stealth bomber was the *Spirit of Missouri*.
Trains	The *Crescent Limited* follows a route from New York City to New Orleans.
Spacecraft	*Endeavour* has traveled on a mission to the space station.

Words, Letters, and Numerals Being Discussed

Use italics for words, letters, and numerals that you are discussing as words.

The British spelling adds the *a* in *paediatrician*.

Be sure to cross all of your *t*'s to avoid spelling mistakes.

The children practiced dividing by *12*s during math class last week.

Foreign Words and Phrases

Use italics for unfamiliar foreign words or phrases in an English sentence. If the foreign word or phrase is an entry in an English-language dictionary, it does not need italics. Use quotation marks instead of italics if the entire sentence is written in a foreign language.

No Italics	Chef Schopf was a bona fide master in his field.
Italics	Some toddlers are the epitome of an *enfant terrible*.
Quotation Marks	During Sunday school the Spanish children enjoyed singing, "Cristo me ama, me ama a mí."

Enrichment

Tell the students that italic script dates back to the Italian humanists who lived approximately AD 1400. The origin of italic type, however, can be traced more easily. Aldus Manutius, founder of the famous Aldine Press of Venice, Italy, first used an italic font for the 1501 edition of Virgil's works.

Teaching Strategy

Discussion

Explain that in the early days of the press, printers used roman or italic font as they saw fit. Not until more recent times did italic font take on a specialized use. Ask students what modern italic font accomplishes for the reader. *(It calls attention to words used in distinctive ways [e.g., as titles of works, as words themselves, for special emphasis].)* Point out the difference between the titles of works that are considered long or short with regard to italic font.

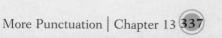

Special Emphasis

Use italics only occasionally to emphasize a particular word or phrase. It is generally better to achieve emphasis by placing the word or phrase at the end of the sentence.

> Many people *think* that politics is a necessary evil.
>
> The idea that politics is a necessary evil has become a part of people's thinking.

13.3 PRACTICE *the skill*

Insert any missing ellipses or brackets in each numbered item. If the item is already punctuated correctly, write *C* in the blank.

From the Reformation until the eighteenth century, English Protestants did not use hymns in their church services. Instead, they sang rhymed settings of the Psalms, believing that church music should be drawn directly from Scripture. Many of these psalm settings, however, were poorly written and hard to sing. Determined to improve the music in his own congregation, a minister named Isaac Watts (1674–1748) began to write hymns. Although at first many Protestants of all denominations rejected this "innovation," Watts persevered in his efforts. He is known today as the Father of English Hymnody.

Churchgoers in the early eighteenth century did not have hymnals; therefore, the pastor or someone else had to read the lines of the psalm or hymn aloud. After each line was read, the congregation would sing it, and then the reader would proceed to the next line. Therefore, Watts ensured that each line of his hymns made sense when read by itself.

> Joy to the world! the Lord is come;
> Let earth receive her King;
> Let every heart prepare him room,
> And heaven and nature sing.

adapted from *World History*, Fourth Edition, by Dennis Bollinger (BJU Press, 2013)

__C__ 1. "From the Reformation until the eighteenth century, English Protestants did not use hymns in their church services."

______ 2. "Instead[English Protestants]sang rhymed settings of the Psalms."

______ 3. "They . . . believ[ed]that church music should be drawn directly from Scripture."

______ 4. "Determined to improve the music in his own congregation, . . . Isaac Watts (1674–1748) began to write hymns."

______ 5. "Although at first many Protestants . . . rejected [his hymns], Watts persevered in his efforts."

__C__ 6. "[Isaac Watts] is known . . . as the Father of English Hymnody."

______ 7. "Churchgoers in the early eighteenth century did not have hymnals. . . . After each line was read, the congregation would sing it."

Teaching Strategy

Motivation and Modeling

Point out that although italics may be used for special emphasis, overuse of this technique can become as distracting as an overuse of exclamation marks. Show the students how to reword sentences in order to eradicate the need for italics.

- Requesting to speak *with* someone on the phone is preferable to simply asking whether he is there.
- When phoning someone, instead of asking whether he is there, ask to speak with him.
- Although Myra has offered to work overtime for the company, the hours of *her* availability are quite limited.
- Although Myra has offered to work overtime for the company, the hours she can work are quite limited because of her schedule.

FineArts Link

After students have read about the history of church music in Practice the Skill 13.3, encourage your students to bring in selections of the Psalms or of Isaac Watts's hymns. Encourage the students to share and discuss the significance of their selections. Then as a group sing several or all of the selections the students have provided.

C 8. "The congregation would sing [one line], and then the reader would proceed to the next line."

____ 9. "Each line of [Watts's] hymns made sense when read by itself."

C 10. "Joy to the world! the Lord is come;
. . . .
Let every heart prepare him room,
And heaven and nature sing."

13.4 PRACTICE *the skill*

Underline each word that should be italicized. If the sentence is already correct, write C in the blank.

____ 1. The Enlightenment, or Aufklärung, encouraged widespread learning in England.

C 2. The eighteenth century Royal Navy consisted of merchant ships that had been equipped for war.

____ 3. One such ship, HMS Northumberland, transported Napoleon into exile on St. Helena.

____ 4. Periodicals such as The Tatler by Richard Steele had an appeal to both men and women and contained essays on various topics.

____ 5. In 1702 the Daily Courant became London's first daily newspaper.

C 6. In addition to these publications that focused on news events, other writing was also popular in England.

____ 7. John Dryden's first play, The Wild Gallant, was a failure, but Dryden soon became a successful writer.

____ 8. John Locke was one of many oil portraits by Sir Godfrey Kneller.

C 9. In England many arts flourished during the eighteenth century.

____ 10. Did you by any chance watch the educational television special entitled The Life of William Shakespeare?

John Locke

The illustration on page 339 is the painting *John Locke* by Sir Godfrey Kneller.

Special Note

Consider using Practice the Skill 13.4 as an opportunity to teach a minilesson from the Library Skills chapter (pp. 394–407). Subjects addressed in the practice, such as politics, periodicals, literature, and art, coincide well with the array of materials students should familiarize themselves with as they develop their library skills.

13.5 REVIEW *the skill*

Write the letter of the sentence that is punctuated correctly.

__B__ 1. A. My brother enjoys listening to "The Lone Ranger" radio program.
B. My brother enjoys listening to *The Lone Ranger* radio program.

__B__ 2. A. Did you know the man who played "Brutus" in Shakespeare's *Julius Caesar*?
B. Did you know the man who played Brutus in Shakespeare's *Julius Caesar*?

__A__ 3. A. In Paris, France, my family enjoyed seeing the *Mona Lisa* in the Louvre Gallery.
B. In Paris, France, my family enjoyed seeing the Mona Lisa in the *Louvre Gallery*.

__B__ 4. A. While we were eating at "Brewster's Bagels," we saw a man reading the *New York Post*.
B. While we were eating at Brewster's Bagels, we saw a man reading the *New York Post*.

__B__ 5. A. The Cub Scouts visited "Patriot's Point," where the aircraft carrier *Yorktown* is located.
B. The Cub Scouts visited Patriot's Point, where the aircraft carrier *Yorktown* is located.

__A__ 6. A. The famous oratorio *Messiah* is often performed during the Christmas season.
B. The famous oratorio "Messiah" is often performed during the Christmas season.

__A__ 7. A. It is sometimes difficult to remember to include the correct number of *s*'s in Mississippi.
B. It is sometimes difficult to remember to include the correct number of *s's* in Mississippi.

__B__ 8. A. The professor stood before the class and said, "Tomorrow we will continue. . . . oh, let's go on to another topic."
B. The professor stood before the class and said, "Tomorrow we will continue . . . oh, let's go on to another topic."

__B__ 9. A. The theme of "Great Expectations," a novel by Charles Dickens, is that love and loyalty are more important than self and ambition.
B. The theme of *Great Expectations,* a novel by Charles Dickens, is that love and loyalty are more important than self and ambition.

__B__ 10. A. "Traditional Home" magazine has many useful and cost-effective tips for home decorating.
B. *Traditional Home* magazine has many useful and cost-effective tips for home decorating.

Teaching Strategy
Participation

Display the following sentences: *Well check whether Sabra phoned and said shed be late. Were hoping shell be here in time for the hayride.* Invite student volunteers to explain how the lack of apostrophes makes these sentences confusing. Then ask them to correct the sentences. *(We'll, she'd; We're, she'll)*

Teaching Strategy
Participation

Ask the students to offer example sentences to demonstrate the difference between *it's* and *its*. *(Answers will vary.)*

340 Chapter 13 | More Punctuation

Apostrophe

Use apostrophes to indicate omissions, possessives, and plurals.

Omission

Use an apostrophe to indicate the omission of letters and numbers in contractions or other shortened forms of words or phrases.

I will	I'll
have not	haven't
class of 2007	class of '07

Be careful to distinguish between the possessive pronoun *its* and the contraction *it's* (for *it is* or *it has*).

Possessive	The new bicycle is not roadworthy; its tire is flat.
Contraction	The new bicycle has a flat tire; it's not roadworthy.

ESL

Some contractions with ***not*** change the spelling of the main word slightly.

will + not = **won't**

can + not = **can't**

Some words, such as *may* and *ought,* are rarely contracted with *not.* The contractions would be understood by a native English speaker, but they would sound formal or old-fashioned. Avoid *mayn't* and perhaps *oughtn't.*

Possession

Possessive Nouns p. 35

Add the *'s* to show possession for most singular nouns and indefinite pronouns. (Use only the apostrophe after the traditional exceptions *Jesus* and *Moses.*)

Terry's motorcycle helmet has a design different from the design on his brother's helmet.

Someone's motorcycle helmet was left in the parking lot of the gymnasium.

Several members of the motorcycle club enjoy reading Dickens's writings.

Add an apostrophe to plural nouns ending in *s* or *es.*

The motorcycle riders' goal was to collect one thousand toys that day.

Several businesses' goal was to help distribute the toys to needy children.

For plural nouns that do not end in *s,* add an *'s.*

Several motorcycle riders saw the children's response of gratitude.

Jessica worked many long hours to prepare the women's part for the program.

If students offer examples of exceptions other than *Jesus'* and *Moses',* explain that some usage guides recommend adding only an apostrophe to a personal name that ends with an *eez* sound, especially if the name is of Greek origin. *(Hippocrates', Sophocles', Socrates', Pericles', Thucydides')*

Enrichment

Explain the historical background behind the contraction *won't* for *will not.* Its origin is the Middle English word *wol,* the earlier version of *will.* Ask the students to recall what two historical events help define the beginning and end of the Middle English period. *(the Norman Conquest of 1066 and the start of the English Renaissance in the early sixteenth century)*

Teaching Strategy

Demonstration

Ask the students to use the word *books* in four complete sentences and in the following positions: subject, object, singular possessive, and plural possessive. Then show the following example sentences.

- Fascinating *books* lined the professor's study. *(subject)*
- Her father had given her many of the *books* upon her completion of college. *(object)*
- One *book's* copyright page showed it was published in London in 1889. *(singular possessive)*
- Beautifully bound, many of the *books'* leather covers had been ornately embellished. *(plural possessive)*

Check their answers to be certain they understand the singular and plural possessive.

To indicate that two or more people own something together, add *'s* to the last noun. To indicate separate possession, an *'s* should be added to each noun or pronoun.

Organizing the distribution of the toys was Mark and John**'s** responsibility.

Brian**'s** and Stephen**'s** ideas for gifts were quite different.

Special Plurals

Plural Nouns
pp. 35–36

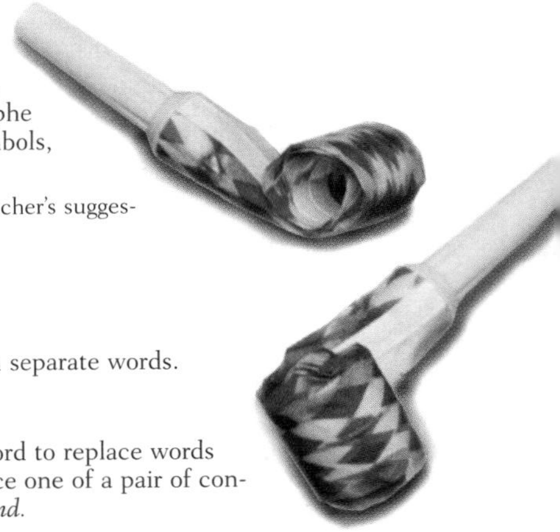

Although regular nouns do not use an apostrophe to indicate plurals, *'s* is used for the plural of an italicized letter or word being discussed. An apostrophe is not necessary to form the plurals of numbers, symbols, and dates.

All the children shouted repeated *yes***'s** to the teacher's suggestion that they have a party.

During the late 1990**s** stock prices advanced.

Hyphen

Use the hyphen to join parts of a word or to join separate words.

Omission of Connecting Words

Use a hyphen in place of a single connecting word to replace words such as *to* or *through*. Do not use a hyphen to replace one of a pair of connecting words such as *from* and *to* or *between* and *and*.

WRONG	This series of messages on Philippians 3:1-7 will last **from** September-November.
RIGHT	This series of messages on Philippians 3:1-7 will last September-November.
	This series of messages on Philippians 3:1-7 will last **from** September **to** November.
WRONG	Pastor Brooks will change the theme of his messages **between** December 1-December 31.
RIGHT	Pastor Brooks will change the theme of his messages December 1-December 31.
	Pastor Brooks will change the theme of his messages **between** December 1 **and** December 31.

Word Division at the End of a Line

Use a hyphen to divide a word at the end of a line. The hyphen appears at the end of the line, not at the beginning of the next line. Do not divide the word unless you can meet all three of these guidelines.

1. Divide a word only between syllables. If the word does not have at least two pronounced syllables, do not divide it.
2. Leave at least two letters and the hyphen on the first line.
3. Carry over at least three letters to the second line.

Listening intently to Pastor Brooks's message, Charles felt deep conviction in his heart.

TEACHING STRATEGY

Discussion

Discuss the rules and example sentences for apostrophes showing possession as listed on pages 341–42. Point out that some singular nouns such as the surname *Fuller* become plural when referring to the individual members of the unit. These plurals then have an apostrophe added to the end when they show possession.

- The *Fuller* family moved to California last year.
- I hope the *Fullers* like their new townhouse.
- Sometimes the *Fullers'* mail still comes to their old address.

Compound Constructions

Use a hyphen in **multiword numbers** from twenty-one through ninety-nine when they are spelled out.

> Luther's *Ninety-Five Theses* challenged the sale of indulgences, calling their sale a corrupt practice.
>
> One hundred sixty-five dollars was the amount on the check.

Use a hyphen in spelled-out **fractions** unless either the numerator or the denominator already contains a hyphen.

> Nearly three-fourths of the team became ill with the flu virus.
>
> Three and one-half cups of flour are necessary for the cake recipe.

Use a hyphen when a **prefix** such as *all-*, *ex-* (meaning "former"), *half-*, or *self-* is added to a word. Prefixes such as *non-* and *anti-* are permissible in either style; however, the trend is toward making these words solid.

> Matthew 28 reveals the all-inclusive task for believers.
>
> Hamilton was an ex-waiter who became the restaurant manager.

Use a hyphen when a prefix comes before a number, a proper adjective, or a proper noun.

> The pre-2002 stock market showed consistent gains.
>
> The post-Christmas day sales offered many desirable bargains.

Hyphens are also necessary to distinguish a word with a prefix from another that is spelled similarly.

> The re-creation of the housing committee made everyone happy.
>
> The recreation building will be completed within six months.

Use a hyphen in certain **compound words**.

> John's father-in-law provided him numerous power tools to aid in building the addition.
>
> The three-year-old tried to act more like his older brother.

Compound Nouns p. 36

Use a hyphen in **multiword modifiers**. When two or more words function as a single unit to modify a following noun, hyphenate the temporary compound.

> His all-or-nothing approach to the game gave him an added competitive edge.
>
> Her tea-length dress was quite appropriate for the reception.

Words with a Common Element

If two or more hyphenated words have the same final element, that element should be omitted from all but the last word. Hyphenate and space the words as follows:

> The fans attended all the pre- and post-game events.
>
> The soccer team hopes to have a first- or second-place finish.

Reinforcement

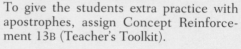

To give the students extra practice with apostrophes, assign Concept Reinforcement 13B (Teacher's Toolkit).

Teaching Strategy

Motivation

Encourage the students to use their dictionaries in order to check (1) the spelling of compound words and (2) the correct location to break a word at the end of a line.

13.6 PRACTICE *the skill*

Underline each word that contains a mistake in the use of apostrophes or hyphens.

Hugh Latimer

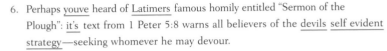

1. Hugh Latimer (c. 1492 1555), a brilliant preacher of the Tudor Renaissance Era, possessed an all consuming desire to proclaim Christ in an England that was still suffering the effects of pre Reformation darkness.
2. It wasnt until Latimer was a thirty year old that he became truly convinced of the theological positions of the Reformers: His Bachelor of Divinity thesis, an anti Reformation treatise, had attacked the doctrines of a prominent reformer named Philip Melanchthon.
3. However, Latimers thesis prompted a godly individual named Thomas Bilney to diligently share the gospels truth with Latimer.
4. Thomas Bilney and Hugh Latimers doctrinal beliefs differed significantly initially; however, Bilneys repeated "What saith the Scripture?" gradually brought Latimer to a full understanding of the gospel.
5. By the mid 1520's Latimer saw the gospel truth as it had been powerfully brought to light again by Martin Luther's *Ninety Five Theses*.
6. Perhaps youve heard of Latimers famous homily entitled "Sermon of the Plough": it's text from 1 Peter 5:8 warns all believers of the devils self evident strategy—seeking whomever he may devour.
7. Ephesians 6:10 18 provides the believer with the spiritual weapons needed not only during Satans attacks but also in pre and post trial living.
8. Latimers work to promote an English translation of the Bible gained him the common citizens's appreciation yet Cardinal Thomas Wolseys censure.
9. In light of the fact that he served under monarch's Henry VIII, Edward VI, and Mary I, its amazing that Latimer never forgot that having Jesus' approval mattered far more than having theirs.
10. Such a strong stance for gospel truth resulted in Latimers imprisonment on various occasions and his eventual martyrs death, but it was because of God's all sufficient might that Latimer endured his tribulations and passed on into glory.

Enrichment

Consider reading several key paragraphs from Hugh Latimer's "Sermon of the Plough" to your students.

Scriptural Application

Ask a volunteer to read Ephesians 6:10–18. Believers often apply this Scripture in the context of fighting temptation. Ask the students what relevancy this passage has to living pre- and post-trial. *(All of the pieces of armor mentioned are meant to be worn before a trial even comes. After a trial the armor must remain as protection for a new trial.)*

13.7 PRACTICE *the skill*

Insert any missing apostrophes or hyphens. If the sentence is already correct, write *C* in the blank.

_____ 1. During the Tudor period, the sermon's literary merit increased drastically.

_____ 2. As language and thought developed in this period, so did man's ability to use that language.

__C__ 3. Though this time period brought great development to the sermon, it brought with it great persecution.

_____ 4. Robert Barnes's sermon against Cardinal Wolsey earned Barnes a conference with Wolsey.

_____ 5. Barnes was persuaded to recant but escaped to Germany 2-3 years later.

__C__ 6. With the support of Henry VIII, Barnes traveled freely between Germany and England pre-1540 until he was executed as a heretic.

_____ 7. Others in the same movement also were outspoken against the pa- pacy.

_____ 8. Hugh Latimer thundered against such vile blasphemies as the venera- tion of images and the practice of indulgences.

_____ 9. He was eventually tried, and he stood powerfully on God's word.

_____ 10. There are several stories of the Reformation and pre-Reformation similar to this one, many written with great power and truth.

Cardinal Wolsey

More Punctuation | Chapter 13 345

13.8 REVIEW *the skill*

Rewrite the paragraph, correcting the ten errors in the use of apostrophes and hyphens.

The tourists couldnt believe that English kitchens had changed very little from the fifteenth-seventeenth centuries. Castle kitchens had any number of unfamiliar cooking utensils or cooking locations. Noblemen had well equipped kitchens, and their's were filled with brass and copper utensils. In the kitchen, most likely, was a posnet, a three legged container with a metal handle, used for boiling. A gridiron was a utensil of parallel metal bars for broiling fresh fish over a fire. Additional rooms were part of the kitchen area. A pastry room had a kneading trough and a baking oven that may have been one half the size of the room. An additional area called the bolting house was a place for sifting bran or coarse meal. The meat room contained ovens with spits for roasting deer, pheasant, wild boar, or rabbit. In addition to the meat-room, there may have been a larder, a closet sized room for storing meat. Some cooking utensils would be familiar to us today. Chafing dishes, graters, mortars and pestles, knives, and frying pans are among the many items in pre and post Elizabethan kitchens.

The tourists couldn't believe that English kitchens had changed very little from the fifteenth to seventeenth centuries. Castle kitchens had any number of unfamiliar cooking utensils or cooking locations. Noblemen had well-equipped kitchens, and theirs were filled with brass and copper utensils. In the kitchen, most likely, was a posnet, a three-legged container with a metal handle, used for boiling. A gridiron was a utensil of parallel metal bars for broiling fresh fish over a fire. Additional rooms were part of the kitchen area. A pastry room had a kneading trough and a baking oven that may have been one-half the size of the room. An additional area called the bolting house was a place for sifting bran or coarse meal. The meat room contained ovens with spits for roasting deer, pheasant, wild boar, or rabbit. In addition to the meat room, there may have been a larder, a closet-sized room for storing meat. Some cooking utensils would be familiar to us today. Chafing dishes, graters, mortars and pestles, knives, and frying pans are among the many items in pre- and post-Elizabethan kitchens.

346 Chapter 13 | More Punctuation

Remind students that when typing a dash they should use two hyphens without a space before, between, or after them.

Dash

The dash—about twice as long as the hyphen—is used to separate, to emphasize, and to indicate an abrupt change in thought. The dash is a rather informal, yet strong, mark and should be used sparingly.

Certain Sentence Elements

Use a pair of dashes to separate an **interrupting phrase or clause** from the remainder of the sentence.

> Her chocolate cake creation—with three kinds of chocolate—won first prize in the baking contest.
>
> A beautiful sight—and I mean beautiful—is the colorful mountain leaves during the fall season.

Commas with Nonrestrictive Elements p. 308

Use a pair of dashes to separate an **internal appositive series** from the remainder of the sentence. When an appositive series contains three or more elements that are separated from each other by commas, a pair of dashes is necessary to signal the beginning and the ending of the appositive.

> My brother's favorite sundae toppings—hot fudge sauce, nuts, and whipped cream—are available at the dessert bar.
>
> Other dessert possibilities—peach pie, sugar cookies, and butterscotch pudding—are also available.

Use a dash to connect an **introductory list** to a grammatically complete **summary statement** after it.

> Hot fudge sauce, nuts, and whipped cream—all are delicious sundae toppings.
>
> Peach pie, sugar cookies, and butterscotch pudding—these are not temptations for me.

Colon Before a Series p. 316

tip

Remember that you do not use a period or comma next to a dash.

Emphasis

On occasion you can use a dash to give special emphasis to a phrase or clause that appears at the end of a sentence. Use dashes sparingly to emphasize material so that they will not lose their effectiveness.

NORMAL PUNCTUATION	My uncle's car is a new production car, a car with style, class, and speed.
EMPHATIC	My uncle's car is a new production car—a car with style, class, and speed.

Interrupted Speech

Use a dash or pair of dashes to indicate various speech interruptions.

FALTERING SPEECH	"Dad, I didn't mean—um—I mean—I will try to do better in the future."
ABRUPT BREAKING OFF OF A SENTENCE	"Son, you must try harder—if you want to use the car," his father said.
	"But, Dad, I—" the young son implored.
ABRUPT CHANGE OF THOUGHT	Looking carefully through his wallet, James said, "But officer, I thought—oh, here, I found it."

Ellipses p. 335

TEACHING STRATEGY

Analysis

After discussing the various uses for the dash, ask the students to explain the primary difference between dashes and hyphens, aside from the obvious difference in length. *(Dashes separate phrases, clauses, or internal appositive series. Hyphens separate individual words or word parts.)*

Parentheses

Like quotation marks, parentheses appear in pairs. Parentheses enclose additional information that is relatively unimportant.

Supplementary Elements

Use a pair of parentheses to enclose additional, or explanatory, information.

His next sermon (the third in the soulwinning series) will be tomorrow.

His last message was his best. (He seemed to reach the hearts of the students.)

Placement of Other Punctuation with Parentheses

Usually end marks, commas, semicolons, and colons go outside parentheses. If the material enclosed by parentheses is a complete thought, the period goes inside the closing parenthesis. If the parenthetical material itself is a question or an exclamation, the question mark or exclamation point goes inside the closing parenthesis.

Tax returns were reviewed by the Internal Revenue Service (IRS).

Our last tax return (did you do yours?) seems to be without error.

We have a refund (how wonderful!) coming this year.

tip

A parenthetical sentence that is not enclosed within another sentence should begin with a capital letter and should have end punctuation inside the final parenthesis.

A parenthetical source note in a paragraph follows the general rules because it is considered to be part of its sentence. However, if the quotation itself is a question or an exclamation, punctuate the quotation appropriately and then place a period after the parenthetical source note.

The preacher reminded us again to "go . . . into all the world, and preach the gospel to every creature" (Mark 16:15).

At Christ's trial before Pilate, Pilate asked, "Shall I crucify your King?" (John 19:15).

Periods with Lists p. 297

Numbers or Letters That Identify Divisions

Use a pair of parentheses to enclose numbers or letters that indicate divisions within a sentence.

Your exercise program should include (1) the warm-up, (2) the workout, and (3) the cooldown.

You should participate in one of the following exercise programs: (a) water aerobics, (b) walking, or (c) low-impact aerobics.

Commas pp. 301–2

tip

Be sure to separate the items of the list within the sentence with commas or semicolons.

Semicolons and Colons pp. 315–16

Comparison of Parentheses with Pairs of Commas and Dashes

Pairs of commas, dashes, and parentheses set off extra information in a sentence. **Commas**, the normal, neutral punctuation, set off short phrases and clauses. **Dashes**, though less formal, indicate to the reader that the enclosed material is important. On the other hand, **parentheses** show the reader that the enclosed material is relatively unimportant. The writer can achieve a particular emphasis by using these marks of punctuation appropriately.

Commas with Restrictive, Nonrestrictive Elements p. 308

Maintaining good health, as I said yesterday, requires an exercise program.

Maintaining good health—as I said yesterday—requires an exercise program.

Maintaining good health (as I said yesterday) requires an exercise program.

TEACHING STRATEGY

Participation

Display the following sentences: *The president's speech (did you listen to it?) outlined his plan for our nation's economy. Following the president's address, the stock market surged. (Do you think a bear market is in store?)* Ask the students to explain why the capitalization differs in the parenthetical expressions. *(The first parenthetical expression is enclosed within another sentence and therefore should not begin with a capital letter. The second parenthetical expression begins with a capital letter because it is a separate sentence.)*

TEACHING STRATEGY

Analysis

Ask the students to explain the difference between using a pair of commas and a pair of parentheses to set off nonessential information. *(Although commas set off information from the rest of the sentence, parentheses de-emphasize the material more than commas do.)*

TEACHING STRATEGY

Discussion

Display the following sentences without end punctuation. Then ask the students to provide the correct end punctuation. *Our pastor's message last night emphasized that it is "God most high . . . that performeth all things for me" (Psalm 57:2). Is your heart's cry to God, "O that my ways were directed to keep thy statutes!" (Psalm 119:5)?* Encourage the students to explain their answers based upon the parenthetical source note rules given on page 348.

13.9 PRACTICE *the skill*

Insert any missing parentheses or dashes. *(Answers may vary.)*

1. Hampton Court Palace — or (it has enclosed tennis courts, a famous garden maze, and paintings from the Royal Collection — or) has a fascinating history.

2. When Cardinal Wolsey built Hampton Court Palace for himself in 1525, he spared no expenses — or (expenses paid out of King Henry VIII's coffers.)

3. In response to Henry VIII's grumbling that Wolsey lived better than he, Wolsey stammered something like "Of course—uh—all these lands belong to thee, O King."

4. Henry VIII took Wolsey at his word and confiscated Hampton Court Palace.(It came with 500 employees and 1,000 rooms.)

5. Catherine of Aragon, Anne Boleyn, Jane Seymour, Catherine Howard, and Catherine Parr—all lived at one time or another at Hampton Court Palace.

6. Inspired by France's Versailles and Louvre, Sir Christopher Wren — or (have you heard of him? — or) remodeled Hampton Court Palace in the late 1600s.

7. The works of various master painters — or (Holbein, Lely, and Tintoretto — or) may now be viewed at Hampton Court, thanks to a more recent addition to the palace: air-conditioned galleries.

8. A turn about the gardens of Hampton Court may provide more horticultural delight than you bargained for—sixty acres' worth!

9. Henry VIII's unique clock—displaying the hours, days, months, lunar phases, and tides at London Bridge—remains a popular attraction at Hampton Court.

10. Although Hampton Court displays some of the finest craftsmanship ever to belong to men, we must remember Scripture's admonition: "For what shall it profit a man, if he shall gain the whole world, and lose his own soul?"(Mark 8:36.)

ESL students may have difficulty with this exercise since such an exercise is more meaning-based. Perhaps pair them with native speakers to do the exercise.

Teaching Strategy

Demonstration

Draw the students' attention to the various meanings communicated by pairs of commas, dashes, or parentheses. Read the example sentences on page 348 with deliberate expression to emphasize the different possible meanings communicated by one sentence using different punctuation. Then explain that such emphasis as the students heard in your voice is automatically communicated to readers who come across the same punctuation marks.

Reinforcement

Use Teaching Help 13 (Teacher's Toolkit) to review correct placement of punctuation marks. Distribute a copy to each student and allow the students to complete the activity in class and discuss their answers. Or display Teaching Help 13 and ask volunteers to answer the questions aloud.

More Punctuation | Chapter 13 349

13.10 REVIEW *the skill*

Combine the following sets of sentences by using commas, parentheses, or dashes. You may reword the sentences slightly and incorporate other punctuation if necessary. *(Answers may vary.)*

1. Much of the music of the Baroque period has an almost dancelike sound to it. It is light, and it is often played on a harpsichord.

   Much of the music of the Baroque period (it is often played on a harpsichord) has a light, almost dancelike sound to it.

2. The major musicians of the Baroque period include Johann Sebastian Bach, Arcangelo Corelli, and Antonio Vivaldi. They all composed in the Baroque style with different emphases.

   The major musicians of the Baroque period—Johann Sebastian Bach, Arcangelo Corelli, and Antonio Vivaldi—all composed in the Baroque style, though with different musical emphases.

3. Many instruments were played during the Baroque period that are not played often today. These include the lute, sackbutt, viol, and harpsichord.

   The lute, the sackbutt, the viol, and the harpsichord—these are among the many instruments played in the Baroque period that are not played often today.

4. The lute is a stringed instrument, similar to the guitar. It is plucked by the player's fingers.

   The lute, a stringed instrument similar to the guitar, is plucked by the player's fingers.

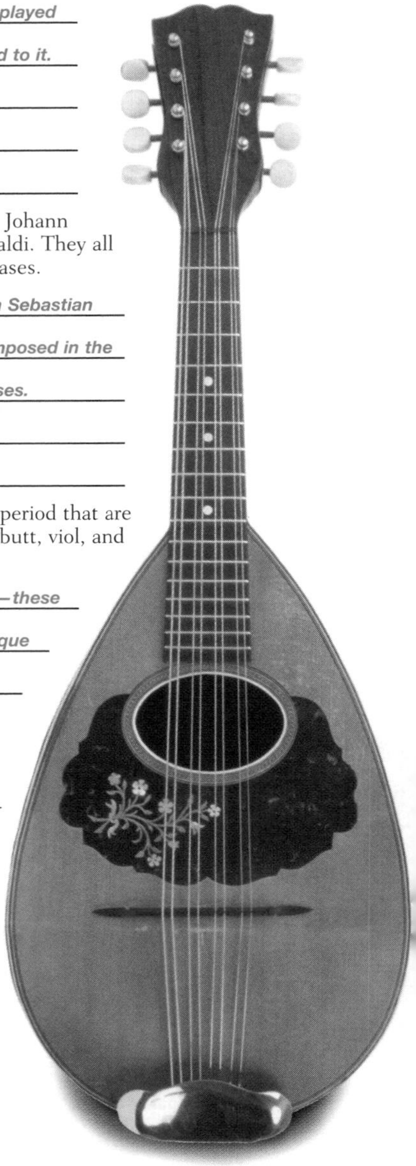

FineArts Link

Consider asking a musician to speak to your students about Baroque music. Encourage the speaker to bring several representative musical recordings for the students to hear.

350 Chapter 13 | More Punctuation

5. The sackbutt is a brass instrument. Although it is similar to the trombone, it produces a softer sound that beautifully complements the harpsichord.

Although the sackbutt (a brass instrument) is similar to the trombone, it produces a softer sound that beautifully complements the harpsichord.

6. The viol is an instrument similar in some respects to the cello, but in many other ways very different. It rests not on the floor but on the knees of the instrumentalist.

The viol is an instrument similar in some respects to the cello, except that it rests not on the floor but on the knees of the instrumentalist.

7. The viol emits a clear, penetrating sound when it is played. The bow of the viol is convex, not concave.

The viol (which has a convex, not concave, bow) emits a clear, penetrating sound when it is played.

8. Another instrument of the Baroque period is the harpsichord. In appearance, the harpsichord is very similar to the piano.

Another instrument of the Baroque period is an instrument resembling the piano—the harpsichord.

9. The strings of the harpsichord are plucked when the keys are pressed. The result is a clear note that can be heard above the other instruments, producing a beautiful effect.

The strings of the harpsichord are plucked when the keys are pressed, producing a clear note—a beautiful effect—that can be heard above the other instruments.

10. The music of the Baroque period utilizes many unfamiliar instruments. The music remains some of the most popular in the world.

The music of the Baroque period, though it utilizes many unfamiliar instruments, remains some of the most popular music in the world.

More Punctuation | Chapter 13 351

13.11 CUMULATIVE *review*

Rewrite the following paragraph, correcting the twenty errors in capitalization and punctuation. (Punctuation marks used as a pair are counted as a single error.)

Catherine Parr the last wife of Henry VIII was possibly the strongest in character of all his wives. She was first offered in marriage to Lord Scropes noble son when she was only twelve years old. However a condition was discovered in the will of her father that prevented her ever marrying him. Eventually she married Edward Lord Borough of Gainsborough but did not live with him until she was fourteen He died in 1529 however, and she returned to the royal court of Henry VIII. She met with her second husband at court functions, and they were married he at the age of forty two and she at the age of nineteen. He was John Neville, lord latimer. The two of them came under suspicion and were almost executed during the controversy over anne Boleyn and Oliver Cromwell. after Neville died, she entered into a relationship with Thomas seymour, brother of the late Queen. This relationship was ended by Henry VIII, who then began his courtship of catherine. Eventually they were married, and Catherine became more like a nurse to the King than a wife for he was by then quite old. She was instrumental in the presentation of the royal family as a strong family; this strength impressed foreign ambassadors when they came to the court. Her great interest in protestantism almost cost her dearly, when she was accused of having ties with heresy. However she avoided prosecution as a heretic by her behavior at a public court function. Of all of Henrys wives, she was perhaps his most loved, and at his death she became a wealthy dowager queen.

Catherine Parr, the last wife of Henry VIII, was possibly the strongest in character of all his wives. She was first offered in marriage to Lord Scrope's noble son when she was only twelve years old. However, a condition was discovered in the will of her father that prevented her ever marrying him. Eventually she married Edward, Lord Borough of Gainsborough, but did not live with him until she was fourteen. He died in 1529, however, and she returned to the royal court of Henry VIII. She met with her second husband at court functions, and they were married—he at the age of forty-two and she at the age of nineteen. He was John Neville, Lord Latimer. The two of them came under suspicion and were almost executed during the controversy over Anne Boleyn and Oliver Cromwell. After Neville died, she entered into a relationship with Thomas Seymour, brother of the late queen. This relationship was ended by Henry VIII, who then began his courtship of Catherine. Eventually they were married, and Catherine became more like a nurse to the king than a wife, for he was by then quite old. She was instrumental in the presentation of the royal family as a strong family; this strength impressed foreign ambassadors when they came to the court. Her great interest in Protestantism almost cost her dearly when she was accused of having ties with heresy. However, she avoided prosecution as a heretic by her behavior at a public court

REINFORCEMENT

Use Chapter 13 Review on pages 463–64 for additional test review.

EVALUATION

Use Chapter 13 Test to evaluate students' understanding of the content and concepts of the chapter.

352 Chapter 13 | More Punctuation

function. Of all of Henry's wives, she was perhaps his most loved, and at his death

she became a wealthy dowager queen.

THINK ABOUT IT

Problem Solving

By now you know much about critical thinking. You know the difference between what to think and how to think. You know how to analyze information to discern the author's or speaker's purpose and message. You can tell the difference between subjective and objective viewpoints and between fact and opinion. You know to evaluate the logic of an argument and to examine the evidence before making a decision. But a critical thinker must do more than just analyze the statements of others. A critical thinker should be able to solve problems in everyday situations.

The ability to solve problems is a skill that relies on the mastery of other thinking skills. Everything you know, every fact you have learned, every skill you have mastered, every talent that you possess—all of these are valuable tools to assist you in your problem-solving efforts.

A key factor in problem solving is the ability to think inductively. The logic problems that we analyzed in an earlier chapter rely on deduction: making a particular application from general principles. Induction, on the other hand, draws a general principle from particular instances. Inductive thinkers begin with what they already know and form principles from that knowledge. For example, scientists employ induction when they draw conclusions (general principles) from the results of observation and experimentation (particular instances).

Likewise, a critical thinker can form a hypothesis and predict what is likely to happen in a given situation. A hypothesis, of course, is more than just a guess; it is an informed opinion, an "educated guess" based on previous observation and experience or knowledge of universal principles. If you know that you usually need thirty minutes to get ready in the morning, you will not arrange your schedule to allow only twenty minutes of preparation. Your experience allows you to predict that twenty minutes will likely be inadequate.

When you are presented with a problem to solve or alternatives from which to choose, consider the situation carefully. What information do you already have about the possible solutions? Are any events from your past similar to the current situation? What universal principles apply? What does Scripture say about the issue? When your analysis is complete, take the information that you have gathered, form a hypothesis for each alternative, and predict the likely outcomes for those alternatives. Then you will be ready to make an informed decision.

Thinking It Through

Are you a critical thinker? Consider a recent decision you have made or a problem you have solved. Analyze the strategies that you used in that situation. Are you satisfied with the outcome? Should you have handled the situation differently? Write about your findings.

Scriptural Application

Sometimes Christians—even mature Christians—find that their Bible reading is dull. They feel as if they are just running their eyes across the page. They may even be led to pray as the psalmist did that God would open their eyes (Ps. 119:18) and incline their hearts toward His Word (Ps. 119:36). But what is God's answer to such a prayer? In part, God's answer is to *think*: "Consider what I say," the Lord says, "and [I will] give thee understanding" (2 Tim. 2:7). Christians are supposed to dig hard for that understanding, to "seek her as silver" (Prov. 2:4). Tell students that the critical thinking skills they acquire in their education will become tools in God's hands to make more truth available to them.

OBJECTIVES

Students will

1. use strategies to achieve proper sentence emphasis.
2. use strategies to achieve proper sentence variety, including varying the length, complexity, patterns, and beginnings.
3. write text using active and passive voices effectively.
4. evaluate and correct sentences containing faulty coordination and subordination.
5. evaluate and combine sentences for correct coordination and subordination.
6. revise text to achieve sentence energy, including action verbs, details, accuracy, and figurative language.
7. expand and reduce sentences using phrases and clauses.
8. revise sentences to correct faulty parallelism.
9. write sentences using correct forms of parallelism.
10. recognize and correct faulty sentence logic.
11. recognize and correct biased language.
12. revise a paragraph using a variety of writing strategies.

CHA

WRITING STRATEGIES

Lesson Support

Teacher's Toolkit
Bulletin Board 14

Literature Link

Ask the students to read Benjamin Franklin's description of how he learned to write logically, clearly, and eloquently. (See *AMERICAN LITERATURE*, BJU Press.) Encourage the students to try Franklin's method.

TEACHING STRATEGY

Modeling and Participation

Materials
- several newspaper and magazine articles (print or online)

Read a portion of a newspaper or magazine article to the students. Point out the words and constructions that the author used to achieve emphasis. Also note any weak strategies and suggest possible improvements. Distribute other articles and

By now you are familiar with the four stages of the writing process. You have written a number of pieces in which you focused on specific writing strategies to help make your writing stronger. In this chapter you will study further the sometimes difficult ideas of variety, emphasis, and logic. Strategies such as these will separate extraordinary writing from that which is ordinary. As you study each topic, take time to look back at the various literary models in Chapters 2–13. Note how each author manipulates words and sentences to make each say exactly what is intended. You too can use language to your advantage when you follow certain guidelines.

Sentence Variety and Emphasis

As a writer, you have the opportunity to create sentences that emphasize (or de-emphasize) whatever you wish and that engage your readers from beginning to end. This chapter will instruct you in methods of manipulating words, phrases, clauses, and sentence types to ensure variety and to achieve emphasis.

Achieving Emphasis

The following general guidelines for achieving emphasis are ordered from least important to most important.

- **Use vivid verbs and strong nouns.** Do not rely on prepositions, adjectives, and adverbs to enliven your writing.

WEAK	Martin's shirt had a garlicky smell.
STRONGER	Martin's shirt reeked of garlic.

Parts of Speech p. 35

- **Place a short sentence before or after a series of longer sentences.** A reader can tire of reading long, complicated sentences, and too many of them in a row can distract him from your message. Brief sentences achieve emphasis. Unusual types of sentences can serve the same purpose. (See page 356.)

Gioacchino Rossini's version of the Cinderella story places the mistreated Cinderella in the household of a greedy stepfather and two pretentious half sisters. Cinderella is made to clean the ashes from the hearth and attend to the vain wishes of each member of the Magnifico family. When she hears of the Prince's upcoming ball, Cinderella begs her stepfather for leave to go, but he refuses her request. Then enters Alidoro. Disguised as a poor beggar, Alidoro, the Prince's own tutor, discovers the kind and beautiful Cinderella and promises her that she will indeed attend the ball.

ask students, as individuals or in groups, to mark emphatic words and constructions. Also instruct them to label the sentences used to achieve emphasis, noting any unusual structures.

REINFORCEMENT

Instruct each student to select a portion of his own writing, possibly a journal entry or a draft of a writing assignment, and evaluate the emphasis of his writing. Instruct the students to rewrite their selections to improve emphasis.

SCRIPTURAL APPLICATION

Remind students to use the methods for achieving emphasis to highlight only valid arguments in their writing. Ask a student to read Job 6:25–30 aloud. In Job 4–6, both Eliphaz and Job use several methods for achieving emphasis discussed in this section, but Eliphaz ultimately draws a faulty conclusion (Job 5:27). Job's response in Chapter 6 demonstrates that skillful use of emphasis can be used to hurt others and to support a false premise.

Thinking Biblically

Read aloud (or have a student read aloud) 1 Corinthians 2:1–5 and ask students what other purpose Paul had for refusing to preach with "enticing words of man's wisdom." Verse 5 answers: "that your faith should not stand in the wisdom of men, but in the power of God."

La Cenerentola means "Cinderella."

Barbiere di Siviglia means "Barber of Seville."

Thinking Biblically

When Paul preached the gospel, he used both rhetorical flourishes and carefully constructed syntax—but he did not trust in these techniques to persuade his hearers (see Rom. 11:36). Paul's letters are full of beautiful, powerful, and often very personal writing. So why did Paul say, "Christ sent me . . . to preach the gospel: not with wisdom of words [or not with words of eloquent wisdom]"? He tells us why himself: "lest the cross of Christ should be made of none effect" (1 Cor. 1:17). Paul recognized that the power of the gospel does not depend upon man's words, no matter how eloquent. No, the gospel itself is powerful—because it is the Word of God. The gospel is His powerful message, which He has given man to deliver. To spread God's message effectively—with clarity and memorability—Christians should practice good writing and speaking, as Paul did. Man's words can be powerful when used well, but only God's Word holds supreme power—the power to save!

Inverted Subject and Predicate p. 71

Fragment pp. 135–37

- **Place the important word or phrase at the end of the sentence for natural emphasis.** Since these are the last words the reader will see, they are the words that he will remember the longest. A writer may accomplish this emphasis by moving phrases and adding clauses to place important ideas in strong positions.

Emphasis on film version	Rossini's *La Cenerentola* differs greatly from the Cinderella story made popular in the children's film version.
Emphasis on *La Cenerentola*	The Cinderella story made popular in the children's film version differs greatly from Rossini's *La Cenerentola.*
Normal Emphasis	The opera *Barbiere di Siviglia* was a great success for Rossini.
Emphasis on *Barbiere di Siviglia*	The opera that was a great success for Rossini was *Barbiere di Siviglia.*

Moving an idea other than the subject to the beginning of the sentence or clause gives a certain amount of emphasis also, albeit to a lesser degree.

The singer saw the conductor, but the falling curtain she missed.

Singing with her eyes closed, the soprano narrowly missed being hit by the weighted curtain.

tip

Do not overuse emphasis strategies: too much emphasis is as tiring as listening to someone shouting all of the time.

- **Include unusual types of sentences in your writing.** The following sentence types should be used only occasionally for effect and emphasis.

Sentence Type	Use	Example Sentence
Inverted sentence	Places a complement or a verb at the front of the sentence	A world-class golfer he was definitely not.
Periodic sentence	Fairly long sentence in which the main idea is not complete until the end	One may find in Prague, in addition to its quaint architecture, soaring cathedrals, numerous bridges, and final resting place of the legendary King Wenceslas, a city truly alive with history.
Rhetorical question	Question not meant to receive an answer	Who would want to eat liver? I prefer a thick, juicy steak.
Short fragment	Expresses emphasis or ironic afterthought	Everyone assumed that Maria knew the way back to the meeting place. Bad assumption.

tip

Avoid using an inverted sentence when the main verb is too far from the rest of the predicate.

14.1 PRACTICE *the skill*

Using the guidelines in parentheses, rewrite each sentence to improve emphasis. *(Answers may vary.)*

1. Poodles come in colors other than the typical white, black, gray, and brown. Poodles' coats sometimes have peach or blue tints to them. *(rhetorical question)*

   Have you ever seen a peach- or blue-tinted poodle? Poodles sometimes come in colors other than the typical white, black, gray, and brown.

2. Poodles can perform a variety of tasks. They often served as water retrievers during the sixteenth century *(important information at the end)*

   Poodles can perform a variety of tasks. During the sixteenth century, they often served as water retrievers.

3. The "Continental" style is the one you may automatically think of when you hear the word *poodle.* In this cut the dog's coat is immaculately styled with little muffs around the legs and the tip of the tail. *(periodic sentence)*

   When you hear the word poodle, you may automatically think of the immaculately cut and styled coat with little muffs around the legs and the tip of the tail as true "Continental" style.

4. Many first-time poodle buyers wrongly suppose that smaller poodles, such as the miniature and toy varieties, have friendlier personalities than larger poodles. *(fragment)*

   Many first-time poodle buyers suppose that smaller poodles, such as the miniature and toy varieties, have friendlier personalities than larger poodles. Wrong idea!

5. This variety of dog may weigh anywhere from three to sixty pounds. *(vivid verbs and strong nouns)*

   The smallest poodles barely qualify for the three-pound weight category, and the largest poodles tip the scales at a whopping sixty pounds.

Writing Strategies | Chapter 14 357

14.2 USE *the skill*

Using the guidelines for proper emphasis, write a paragraph that answers this question: What type of animal makes the best pet? *(Answers will vary.)*

Varying Sentence Length and Complexity

Professional writers use a variety of short, medium, and long sentences to make reading their works easier and more interesting. Often, this strategy involves varying sentence complexity by using simple, compound, complex, and compound-complex sentences.

> Who invented and popularized some of America's favorite icons? Who designed the cartoons of Santa Claus, Uncle Sam, the Democratic donkey, and the Republican elephant? The answer may surprise you. One artist created all of these caricatures. Thomas Nast (1840–1902) was the son of German immigrants. He demonstrated remarkable artistic skill as a young man. He landed his first illustrator's position at the age of fifteen. Nast enjoyed a long and productive career of designing cartoons. This cartoonist was very effective in portraying his political messages. President Abraham Lincoln dubbed Nast the Union's "best recruiting sergeant" during the Civil War. Nast's pictures convey strong impressions. His images continue to communicate distinct messages today.

Though the first paragraph communicates the information, this second paragraph, implementing greater sentence variety, is much easier to read.

> Have you ever wondered who invented and popularized some of America's favorite icons? Consider famous cartoons such as the jolly, stout Santa Claus, the tall tailcoat-wearing Uncle Sam, or the quintessential Democratic donkey and Republican elephant. It may strike you as surprising, but one artist created all of these caricatures. Thomas Nast (1840–1902), the son of German immigrants, demonstrated remarkable artistic skill as a young man and even landed his first illustrator's position at the age of fifteen. Thus began Nast's long and productive career of designing patriotic, whimsical, and even scathing political cartoons. In fact, so effective was this cartoonist in portraying his message that President Abraham Lincoln dubbed Nast the Union's "best recruiting sergeant" during the Civil War. Nast's pictures convey strong impressions that continue to communicate distinct messages today.

EVALUATION

After students have completed Use the Skill 14.2, check their paragraphs for effective emphasis. Check for the following elements in the order of greatest to least importance:

- vivid verbs and strong nouns
- shorter sentences interspersed with longer ones
- important words or phrases placed at the end of sentences
- unusual types of sentences

Evaluate the students' paragraphs and suggest any techniques they might incorporate for more effective emphasis.

Varying Sentence Patterns

What is true of grammatical sentence types is also true for sentence patterns: too much of one type makes for monotonous reading. Use a variety of sentence patterns as you write.

> In the years following World War II, Bette Nesmith Graham was an executive secretary during the heyday of electric typewriters. The trouble with these typewriters was their greater sensitivity to touch than the old manual typewriters. The secretaries were the creators of unsightly company documents covered with erasures. This woman was an amateur painter. She invented a shade of paint that matched her boss's stationery. She began painting over her typing errors with a fluid she dubbed "Mistake Out." The word among the secretaries in Graham's office was that Graham had a new invention. Soon Graham became the supplier for her time- and document-saving invention. She even became the founder of her own Liquid Paper company. She was the one to begin producing and marketing the product. Graham's business became a multimillion-dollar one. Had it not been for her practical problem-solving skills, people would not be the beneficiaries of those handy bottles, pens, and tape dispensers of white correction fluid.

Again, this second paragraph integrates a wider variety of sentence patterns, thereby achieving greater fluidity.

Sentence Patterns pp. 74–77

> In the years following World War II, Bette Nesmith Graham worked as an executive secretary during the heyday of electric typewriters. These typewriters had a greater sensitivity to touch than the old manual typewriters had. As a result, the secretaries kept producing unsightly company documents covered with erasures. Graham, an inventive woman and an amateur painter, simply mixed a shade of paint that matched her boss's stationery and began painting over her typing errors with a fluid she dubbed "Mistake Out." Word spread among the secretaries in Graham's office, and soon Graham began supplying orders of her time- and document-saving invention. In time, she even began her own Liquid Paper company to produce and market her product. What began as one woman's creative solution to a typewriter problem became a multimillion-dollar business. Had it not been for one woman's practical skills, people would not have the benefit of those handy bottles, pens, and tape dispensers of white correction fluid.

Varying Sentence Beginnings

Check your writing for the ways in which you begin your sentences and experiment with changing some of the beginnings for variety and effectiveness.

Phrases pp. 92–102

Clauses pp. 116–28

Possible beginning	Example sentence
Adverb modifiers	*Suddenly* and *noiselessly*, the gate shut.
Prepositional phrase	*Without warning*, a loud buzzing began.
Other phrases	*Trembling at the thought of being seen*, Jason tried to slip through the fence. (participial phrase) *Knees knocking*, he stared down the barrel of a flashlight. (absolute phrase)
Dependent clauses	*After the laughing stopped*, Jason realized *he'd been caught still holding the "Happy Birthday" sign he'd meant to leave on the front door.*

Writing Strategies | Chapter 14 359

14.3 PRACTICE *the skill*

Rewrite the following paragraph, following the suggestions below. *(Answers may vary.)*

[1]Marian Anderson was a pioneer in the field of female music performance. [2]She was African American by birth. [3]Marian Anderson began her musical career by playing the violin. [4]She soon focused on singing. [5]She applied to a music school in order to develop her ability but was denied admission because of her race. [6]With the encouragement and support of a local church, she was able to study under a professional teacher. [7]Her career in the United States met with some disappointments. [8]In 1925 she went to England and then to Europe. [9]During the next ten years she developed into an accomplished performer. [10]She returned to the United States. [11]She became a major box office draw. [12]She, however, continued to meet opposition because of her race. [13]The media's focus on her ability and not on her race was accomplished by her concert on the steps of the Lincoln Memorial in 1939. [14]She eventually became the first African American to sing for the Metropolitan Opera. [15]She is most often remembered for her rich contralto renditions of black spirituals. [16]Dignity and perseverance characterized her career. [17]She was a role model for succeeding generations.

1. Combine sentences 3 and 4 to add complexity.

   Although she began her musical career by playing the violin, Marian Anderson soon focused on singing.

2. Vary the beginning of sentence 5.

   Wishing to develop her ability, she applied to a music school but was denied admission because of her race.

3. Combine sentences 7 and 8 for complexity.

   In 1925, when her career in the United States met with some disappointments, she went to England and then to Europe.

4. Combine sentences 10 and 11 to show coordination of ideas.

   She returned to the United States and became a major box office draw.

5. Change the sentence pattern of sentence 13 to S-TrV-DO.

   Her concert on the steps of the Lincoln Memorial in 1939 shifted the media's focus to her ability, not her race.

TEACHING STRATEGY

Discussion

Ask several volunteers to read their answers to Practice the Skill 14.3. Point out that although there are many possible answers to each practice, each possibility communicates a slightly different meaning. Discuss several possibilities and their meanings.

14.4 USE *the skill*

Write an original paragraph on your own paper. Vary your sentence patterns, sentence beginnings, and the length and complexity of the sentences. When you finish writing, answer the following questions about your paragraph. *(Answers will vary.)*

1. How many sentences did you write? ______________________
2. Write down the number of times you used the following sentence patterns.

S-InV ______	S-LV-PA ______
S-TrV-DO ______	S-LV-PN ______
S-TrV-IO-DO ______	S-be-Advl ______
S-TrV-DO-OC ______	

3. Write down the number of times you used each of the following sentence types.

simple ______	compound ______
complex ______	compound-complex ______

4. List the types of structures that begin your sentences. ______________________

____

5. How many different beginning structures did you use? ______________________

Active and Passive Voice pp. 187–89

Choosing Between Constructions

As you look at a piece of writing, you may wish to make changes to improve variety or to change emphasis.

Active or Passive

Active sentences are stronger and more direct than passive sentences. Where possible, eliminate unnecessary passive verbs from your writing.

Too Many Passives	The first-place medal was awarded to Anja Bronner, whose entry, a pair of ceramic candlesticks, had been sculpted by hand.
Better	Anja Bronner won the first-place medal for her pair of ceramic candlesticks that she had sculpted by hand.

In certain instances (as in the following examples), the passive voice may be a better choice than the active. Know the situation and choose accordingly.

Teaching Strategy

Introduction

Draw students' attention to the section entitled "Choosing Between Constructions." If needed, review the constructions of active and passive voice on pages 187–89. Emphasize to students that active voice is usually preferred but that in some instances the passive is actually the better choice. Direct students to the chart on page 362 for a list of such instances.

Situation	Active Sentence	Passive Sentence
Unknown or unimportant doer of action	Someone tested the water for harmful bacteria.	The water was tested for harmful bacteria.
Inconsistent subjects	The water technician asked how often the manager of the resort checks the pool's pH level. The manager told him that the employees check the pH level weekly.	The water technician was informed by the resort manager that the pool's pH level is checked weekly.
Awkwardly long subjects	Chlorine, chemical test kits, water clarifier, and algae treatments keep pools clean.	Pools are kept clean by chlorine, chemical test kits, water clarifier, and algae treatments.
New or important information not in position of emphasis	The lifeguards quickly noticed and rescued the floundering swimmer.	The floundering swimmer was quickly noticed and rescued by the lifeguards.

tip

An occasional passive is permissible, and in some cases desirable. But when in doubt, use active voice.

Sentence Pattern S-TrV-IO-DO p. 76

Indirect Object or Prepositional Phrase

Any sentence containing an indirect object can be reworded to include a prepositional phrase. Note the change in emphasis between the two sentences.

Prepositional Phrases p. 88

With Indirect Object	Lonnie gave the orphanage two bicycles.
With Prepositional Phrase	Lonnie gave two bicycles to the orphanage.

Interchange these equivalent structures to put last the object that is longer or that you wish to emphasize.

14.5 PRACTICE *the skill*

Rewrite each sentence to give the emphasis indicated in parentheses. *(Answers may vary.)*

1. A visit to the Shedd Aquarium in Chicago will be enjoyed by most families. *(Use active.)*

   Most families will enjoy a visit to the Shedd Aquarium in Chicago.

2. Built in 1929, the Shedd Aquarium offers visitors of every age many updated exhibits. *(Use a prepositional phrase to emphasize the visitors.)*

   Built in 1929, the Shedd Aquarium offers many updated exhibits to visitors of every age.

Teaching Strategy

Analysis

Before students complete Use the Skill 14.6, instruct them to analyze each sentence of the paragraph carefully. Suggest the following questions for their use:

- Did I use any passive sentences?
- Could the passive sentence be better stated in the active voice?
- Did I use an indirect object or prepositional phrase? Why? Does it sound natural? Does it emphasize what I want to emphasize?

3. The Caribbean Reef, a 90,000-gallon aquarium, is inhabited by more than seventy species of animals, including sharks and stingrays. *(Use active instead of passive.)*

   More than seventy species of animals, including sharks and stingrays, inhabit the Caribbean Reef, a 90,000-gallon aquarium.

4. To the enjoyment of the many observers, skilled divers enter the aquarium and feed the fish five times a day. *(Use passive to eliminate the doer of the action.)*

   To the enjoyment of the many observers, the fish are fed five times a day.

5. As the divers feed the fish, the fish swim close to the observation portholes. *(Use passive to have consistent subjects.)*

   As the fish are fed, they swim close to the observation portholes.

14.6 USE *the skill*

Write an original paragraph on your own paper, using active and passive voice, indirect objects, and prepositional phrases appropriately for variety. Answer this question: What was your favorite family vacation and why? *(Answers will vary.)*

Using Coordination and Subordination

The purpose of coordination and subordination is to show how ideas are related to one another within a sentence or paragraph. Proper use of these two strategies results in logical and effective writing.

Coordination

Using equal structure, **coordination** joins ideas that are equal in importance. There are several ways to show that ideas are equal within a sentence: a coordinating conjunction, correlative conjunctions, and a semicolon with a conjunctive adverb.

Coordinating Conjunctions p. 54

Original Sentences	Alfred, Lord Tennyson became England's poet laureate. He became the unofficial spokesman for Victorian England.
Coordinated Sentence	Alfred, Lord Tennyson became England's poet laureate, and he became the unofficial spokesman for Victorian England.
Coordinated Complement	Alfred, Lord Tennyson became England's poet laureate and the unofficial spokesman for Victorian England.

Successful coordination requires that ideas be equal in importance and type and that they be separate. Mixing facts that are unequal or joining statements in which one expands upon the other results in **faulty coordination** of ideas.

Faulty Coordination	Tennyson's *In Memoriam* met with almost instant success, and Tennyson himself compared the structure of this work to Dante's *Divina Commedia.*
Revised for Coordination	Tennyson's *In Memoriam* documents the speaker's journey from despair to elation, and Tennyson himself compared this work's climactic structure to Dante's *Divina Commedia.*

Teaching Strategy

Introduction and Induction

Display the following sentences and ask students to explain what idea(s) each sentence is emphasizing:

- Rachel edged her toe along a miniscule ledge, gracefully transferred her weight onto her foot, and reached her hand to grasp a large pocket in the rock. (*three equally important actions*—edged, transferred, *and* reached)
- Rachel edged her toe along a miniscule ledge and gracefully transferred her weight onto her foot as she reached her hand to grasp a large pocket in the rock. (*two equally important actions*—edged *and* transferred—*and one less important action*—reached)
- Rachel, edging her toe along a miniscule ledge, gracefully transferred her weight onto her foot as she reached to grasp a large pocket in the rock. (*one important action*—transferred—*and two less important actions*—edging *and* reached)

Point out that each of these sentences communicates varying levels of importance through the use of coordination and subordination.

Faulty Coordination	At the age of twelve, Tennyson was engrossed in writing an epic, and he wrote a lengthy narrative poem in formal language.
Revised for Logic (Not Coordinate)	At the age of twelve, Tennyson was engrossed in writing an epic, a lengthy narrative poem in formal language.

Coordination also requires that the parts be similar grammatically.

Faulty Coordination	An excursion to the Pyrenees provided Tennyson with inspiring landscapes for his later poems, a fascination with the isolated village of Cauteretz, and motivating him to return to this location throughout his lifetime.
Correct Coordination	An excursion to the Pyrenees provided Tennyson with inspiring landscapes for his later poems, a fascination with the isolated village of Cauteretz, and the motivation to return to this location throughout his lifetime.

Subordination

Subordinating Conjunctions p. 55

Using unequal structure (structure that emphasizes one idea over another), **subordination** joins ideas that are unequal in importance. In a sentence that evidences appropriate subordination, one idea is less important than another. Subordinate ideas usually appear in dependent clauses or in phrases.

Original Sentences	Tanzanite is a valuable gemstone. It was unknown to the world until 1967.
Subordinated (Dependent Clause)	Tanzanite, which is a valuable gemstone, was unknown to the world until 1967.
Subordinated (Appositive Phrase)	Tanzanite, a valuable gemstone, was unknown to the world until 1967.

tip

When subordinating ideas, try to place at least part of the important idea at the end of the sentence, the position of strength.

Effective subordination joins ideas in such a way that the reader can easily tell which is the more important idea and how it is related to the subordinate idea.

Faulty Coordination	Manuel d' Sousa was a tailor turned prospector, and he became the first to register his discovery of Tanzania's blue sapphire-looking stone.
Appropriate Subordination	Manuel d' Sousa, a tailor turned prospector, became the first to register his discovery of Tanzania's blue sapphire-looking stone.

Notice that the information in the appositive phrase is included as an added detail. The more important information, however, is found in the sentence's independent clause.

Dependent Clauses and Complex Sentences pp. 116, 132–33

Errors in subordination often occur when unequal ideas are joined as if they are equal (faulty coordination) or when the less important idea is emphasized over the more important one (faulty subordination). The less important idea should always be located in the dependent (subordinate) clause or in a phrase.

No Subordination	The bluish gemstone discovered in 1967 could be found only in Tanzania, and Tiffany and Company jewelers named the stone "Tanzanite."

Teaching Strategy

Discussion

Display examples of faulty coordination and subordination from students' previous writing assignments. Ask volunteers to suggest corrections. Display examples of correct coordination and subordination from students' previous writing assignments. Ask volunteers to suggest alternate ways of stating each sentence and to explain the difference in meaning that each alteration produces. Reiterate the need to carefully consider the coordination and subordination that they use in writing assignments.

Faulty Subordination	Since Tiffany and Company jewelers named the bluish gemstone "Tanzanite, " we can guess that this stone discovered in 1967 could be found only in Tanzania.
Better Subordination	Because the bluish gemstone discovered in 1967 could be found only in Tanzania, Tiffany and Company jewelers named the stone "Tanzanite."

14.7 PRACTICE *the skill*

Rewrite each sentence, correcting any faulty coordination or subordination. If the sentence is already correct, write *C* in the blank. *(Answers may vary.)*

1. The Empress Hotel in Victoria, British Columbia, called "The Jewel of the Pacific," is a fine hotel, and people visit throughout the year.

   The Empress Hotel in Victoria, British Columbia, called "The Jewel of the Pacific," is a fine hotel that people visit throughout the year.

2. Built in the Edwardian style, the 460-room hotel offers the visitor quite an historical stay. The hotel was designed by Francis Rattenbury in 1908. Today the hotel continues to be a landmark on Victoria Island.

   Designed by Francis Rattenbury in 1908 and built in the Edwardian style, the 460-room hotel offers the visitor quite an historical stay and continues to be a landmark on Victoria Island.

3. More than 75,000 people per year enjoy the Empress's afternoon tea that includes berries, scones, crumpets, pastries, and sandwiches; and, of course, people drink tea.

   More than 75,000 people per year enjoy the Empress's afternoon tea, which includes berries, scones, crumpets, pastries, sandwiches, and, of course, tea.

4. In 1989 a $45 million project modernized the hotel, but interested parties made sure the hotel retained its historical significance.

   C

5. Past guests to the hotel include members of the monarchy and international leaders, and many famous Americans have stayed there.

   Past guests to the hotel include members of the monarchy, international leaders, and many famous Americans.

Writing Strategies | Chapter 14 365

14.8 REVIEW *the skill*

Correctly combine the following groups of words according to the instructions in parentheses. *(Answers may vary.)*

1. Big Ben is one of London's most famous landmarks. It was named for member of Parliament Sir Benjamin Hall. *(Subordinate one sentence to the other.)*

   Big Ben, named for member of Parliament Sir Benjamin Hall, is one of London's most famous landmarks.

2. The bell tower is most impressive after dark. Each clock is twenty-three feet square. At night the four faces are illuminated. *(Combine the ideas into one sentence.)*

   The bell tower with its four twenty-three foot square illuminated clocks is most impressive after dark.

3. The minute hand on each dial is fourteen feet long. The figures on each clock face are two feet high. *(Coordinate the sentences.)*

   The minute hand on each dial is fourteen feet long, and the figures on each clock face are two feet high.

4. Big Ben is actually the thirteen-ton bell inside the clock tower. Whitechapel Foundry was responsible for casting the bell. *(Combine the ideas into one clause focusing on the casting.)*

   Whitechapel Foundry was responsible for casting Big Ben, the thirteen-ton bell inside the clock tower.

5. The clock tower survived the bombs of World War II. The continued ringing of Big Ben offered hope to the entire world. *(Coordinate the sentences.)*

   The clock tower survived the bombs of World War II, and Big Ben continued to ring, offering hope to the entire world.

Sentence Energy

The words you use make your writing either come alive or fall flat. Vivid verbs, interesting details, strict accuracy, and figurative language infuse your writing with energy.

Action Verbs

Where you can, edit out state-of-being verbs (verbs that show no outward action, e.g., *be, become, seem*), replacing them with strong action verbs.

STATE-OF-BEING VERB	After two hours of snowboarding, Denijer seemed tired.
ACTION VERB	After two hours of snowboarding, Denijer threw himself on top of a snowbank to rest.

TEACHING STRATEGY
Introduction and Participation

Display the following paragraph:

> Last summer my family and I went camping by a lake. The view of the lake and mountains was nice. We tried to swim in the lake, but the water was too cold. Instead of swimming, we went on several hikes. When my sister decided to fish, I skipped rocks on the lake because I get bored fishing, but she got angry with me for scaring away the fish, so I sat under a tree and drew a picture of her fishing. In the evenings my dad made a fire, and we all sat around it and talked. I watched the flames flicker and the smoke rise. I hope we go camping again.

Ask the students for suggestions to make the paragraph more interesting. Add words and details as students suggest changes. Continue eliciting ideas from the students until the paragraph is somewhat ornate. After a volunteer has read the two paragraphs aloud, ask the students which paragraph is more interesting.

TEACHING STRATEGY
Participation

Ask the students to re-read the excerpt from *The Encantadas* (pp. 29–30) and to identify the rich details that Melville uses in the description.

Details

Interesting details give the reader the information needed to imagine a situation.

Few Details	The rain was turning into sleet.
More Details Added	Raindrops pummeled my umbrella for several minutes before I detected faint crunching sounds underfoot.

Accuracy

Pay strict attention to accuracy as you write. Inaccurate words, phrasing, and connotation reflect poorly on the writer and make understanding difficult for the reader. There are four categories of accuracy that you should be aware of as you write.

g u r w
Dictionaries and Thesauruses pp. 404–5

- **Accurate Words**—Choose words carefully. A thesaurus will give you ideas for similar words, and a dictionary will help you determine shades of meaning and differentiate among words with similar meanings.

Wrong Word	A statue of Józef Bem in Budapest, Hungary, bears an *epitaph* recounting the general's motivational words to his troops at Piski.
Correction	A statue of Józef Bem in Budapest, Hungary, bears an *epigraph* recounting the general's motivational words to his troops at Piski.

- **Accurate Phrasing**—Use phrases accurately and idiomatically. Misstated and misused phrases often cause the reader to lose the focus of the message.

Inaccurate Phrasing	As a general *thumb rule* one should not wear plaids and stripes simultaneously.
Correction	As a *rule of thumb,* one should not wear plaids and stripes simultaneously.

- **Appropriate Connotation**—Check the **connotation,** or associated meaning, of a word or phrase when you write. Often the connotation is as important as the **denotation,** what the word names or describes.

Inappropriate Connotation	The *odor* coming from Mom's cooking was amazing!
Appropriate Connotation	The *aroma* coming from Mom's cooking was amazing!

- **Specific, Concrete Words**—Use specific words instead of general or abstract ones where possible.

Abstract	Everyone agreed that the stray cat needed *attention.*
Specific	Everyone agreed that the stray cat needed *warm milk, a soft bed, and plenty of stroking.*
General	Martin was the kind of man whose wardrobe consisted mostly of *work clothes.*
Specific	Martin was the kind of man whose wardrobe consisted mostly of *jeans and T-shirts.*

Teaching Strategy

Motivation

Encourage students to keep a commonplace book in which they can copy quotations from their reading. Explain that these quotations will give them models for their own writing. Point out that passages that catch students' attention most likely exemplify sentence energy.

Enrichment

In his book *De Copia* the Dutch Renaissance scholar Desiderius Erasmus suggests the following type of exercise for developing fresh and lively writing style.

Display the following sentence and variations: *I await your response to my e-mail.*

- A prompt reply to my electronic request is eagerly anticipated.
- I'm on pins and needles in expectation of your speedy response.
- How I long for one small note from you, my most beloved friend!
- A man wandering in the desert could not thirst for water as greatly as I thirst for a letter from you.

Give students a different sentence and instruct them to write variations of the original sentence by substituting their own words and phrases. Tell them that creativity is the key. Then ask volunteers to read their variations aloud.

Pauses for Breath

Long sentences can leave a reader tired and confused. Break a stringy sentence into two or more sentences.

Stringy	In 1824, in order to construct the first rubber balloon, Michael Faraday, a lecturer at the Royal Institution in London, cut and laid out two large sections of rubber sheets that he placed one atop the other before bonding the edges together and dusting the interior with flour to prevent the rubber from sticking and ruining his attempts to fill the balloonlike bag with air and an experimental substance called hydrogen.
Split into Four Sentences	In 1824, in order to construct the first rubber balloon, Michael Faraday, a lecturer at the Royal Institution in London, cut and laid out two large sections of rubber sheets. He then placed one sheet atop the other and bonded the edges together. Next he dusted the interior of the balloon with flour to prevent the rubber from sticking and ruining his experiment. Faraday then filled this rubber balloon with air and an experimental substance called hydrogen.

Figurative Language

Describing one thing in terms of another is called **metaphor**. Metaphors may be stated or implied comparisons.

Stated Comparison	The name of the Lord is a *strong tower:* the righteous runneth into it, and is safe. (Prov. 18:10)
Implied Comparison	For in the time of trouble He shall hide me in His pavilion: in the secret of His tabernacle shall he hide me; he shall set me up upon a rock. (Ps. 27:5)

In Psalm 27 David compares God's comforting nearness during times of trouble to a sheltering pavilion from the blasting heat and other perils of the desert. Further, David likens God's nearness to being protected in God's own dwelling place, His tabernacle. Finally, David compares his stability in the Lord to the security of standing on a block of stone.

A **simile** is a comparison that uses *like* or *as* in the statement of comparison.

And the staff of [Goliath's] spear was **like** a weaver's beam. (1 Sam. 17:7)

tip

Overuse of figurative language can be distracting or annoying to a reader. Use metaphors and similes in moderation.

Mixed metaphors and stretched metaphors often plague the writing of novices (and some professionals!). In a **mixed metaphor** the writer uses two or more metaphors together illogically.

Mixed Metaphor	Having mined the riches of her creativity, Raven reaped a harvest of awards with the publication of her novel.

368 Chapter 14 | Writing Strategies

The phrase "mined the riches" evokes an image of miners working to obtain precious metals from the earth. The phrase "reaped a harvest," on the other hand, is an agricultural description that does not fit logically with the previous metaphor.

Mixed Metaphor	As Ed watched the video advertisement, his interest took flight with no sign of running aground.
Possible Improvement	As Ed watched the video advertisement, his interest set sail with no sign of running aground.

The overly elaborate metaphor also troubles writers. Attempting to apply a metaphor too fully can stretch a metaphor beyond the bounds of proper comparison. In the example below, the basic comparison works well enough, but the comparison begins to break down as the writer continues to use it.

Stretched Metaphor	It does not take a weathered voice coach to tell you that putting a bit of sunshine in your voice goes a long way in cultivating communication. Genuine warmth radiating from your voice can instantly brighten your listener's day, thaw many tensions, and help the friendship to blossom and grow.
Improved	It does not take a voice coach to tell you that putting a bit of sunshine in your voice goes a long way in furthering communication and fostering friendship.

Do not allow your metaphors to hinder your message; avoid stretching them too far.

14.9 PRACTICE *the skill*

Revise each sentence according to the instructions in parentheses. Research the subject and restructure the sentence if necessary. *(Answers may vary.)*

1. Squash is a game played with a racquet and a ball. *(Use more details.)*

   Squash, sometimes called an Ivy League game because it is played primarily in northeastern private clubs, is played with a racquet and a ball.

2. The racquet is almost as long as a tennis racket, but lighter in weight. *(Use an action verb.)*

   The racquet resembles a short, light tennis racket.

3. Since the squash ball is smaller than a golf ball, the squash player should choose approximate eye guards. *(Use an accurate word in place of* approximate.*)*

   Since the squash ball is smaller than a golf ball, the squash player should choose appropriate eye guards.

Writing Strategies | Chapter 14 369

4. The server is the only one to score a point in a game, and the winner is the first one with nine points and a two-point margin. *(Use action verbs.)*

The server scores the points, and the one who reaches nine points first with a two-point margin wins the game.

5. Persons of all years can enjoy playing squash. *(Use an accurate and idiomatic phrase.)*

People of all ages can enjoy playing squash.

14.10 REVIEW *the skill*

Revise the following paragraph to add action verbs, details, accuracy, and figurative language. If necessary, research the subject. *(Answers will vary.)*

Have you ever visited a national cemetery? Although there are many cemeteries, the most beautiful may be the National Memorial Cemetery of the Pacific. The location itself is odd: Puowaina Crater near Honolulu, Hawaii. Many people who fought in different wars are buried in this cemetery. For some visitors, however, it is most closely associated with World War II. Dedicated on September 2, 1949, the cemetery is the resting place for victims of the attacks on Pearl Harbor.

Have you ever visited a national cemetery? Although there are many memorial cemeteries around the world, the most beautiful may be the National Memorial Cemetery of the Pacific. The location itself is unusual: Puowaina Crater, an extinct volcano (called the Punchbowl for its distinctive shape) near Honolulu, Hawaii. More than thirty-three thousand veterans of World War II, the Korean War, and the Vietnam War have been laid to rest in this cemetery. Some visitors, however, most closely associate it with World War II. Dedicated on September 2, 1949, the fourth anniversary of Japan's formal surrender, the cemetery holds the remains of 776 victims of the December 7, 1941, attacks on Pearl Harbor.

Writing Link

As an alternative to Review the Skill 14.10, require students to write a paragraph of their own. Remind them to use action verbs, details, accuracy, and figurative language effectively. Consider allowing students to exchange papers for peer revision.

Teaching Strategy

Analysis

After the students have completed Review the Skill 14.10, ask for volunteers to read their revisions and explain why they made certain changes. Note that the original paragraph, although well written, is bland, and revision can make it much more interesting. Use this exercise to demonstrate that writing with energy may require further research to supply details.

Sentence Expansion and Reduction

You should be aware of two essential techniques as you draft and edit your work. Should you find that you have written simple sentence after simple sentence or only very lengthy sentences, the following expansion and reduction techniques will help you to develop or combine your thoughts logically.

Benjamin Harrison

Expansion of Sentences

Sentence expansion shows connections between ideas and makes your sentences more interesting. Expansion techniques also increase the amount of information that can be contained in a sentence and can change the rhythm of a piece of writing. By adding descriptive clauses and/or phrases, a writer adds interest and meaning to sentences that might otherwise be flat or dull.

Using Clauses

Add adjective, adverb, or noun clauses to increase the variety, clarity, and sophistication of your writing.

Clauses pp. 116–28

Type of Clause	Function	Example Sentence
Adjective	modifies a noun or pronoun	President Benjamin Harrison, **who was our twenty-third president,** held Bible studies in the White House.
Adverb	most often modifies a verb but can modify an adjective or adverb	**Although he was criticized for doing so,** John Ashcroft, attorney general under George W. Bush, held daily Bible studies at the Justice Department.
Noun	functions as a noun (subject, direct object, predicate noun, etc.)	Christians know **that the Bible is the basis of all truth.**

Using Phrases

Descriptive phrases—prepositional and verbal—add complexity of meaning and richness of detail to your sentences.

Phrases pp. 88–102

Original Sentence	Phrase(s) Added	Revised Sentence
Benjamin Harrison requested prayer.	prepositional	In a letter to his wife, Benjamin Harrison requested prayer for himself and for his Civil War regiment.
Harrison regularly shared the gospel.	verbal	Devoted to personal soul-winning, Harrison regularly shared the gospel.

For a more detailed explanation of sentence expansion and reduction, refer to *The Writer's Toolbox*.

Teaching Strategy

Introduction and Induction

Divide the class into two groups. Ask each student in one group to write two or three simple sentences about one topic. Ask each student in the other group to write one long compound sentence. You may want to allow them to work with a partner or in small groups. Encourage the students to be creative with the topic and content of the sentences. Instruct the students to trade sentences—those who wrote short simple sentences should trade with those who wrote long compound sentences. Now direct each student with a compound sentence to reduce it to a simple sentence with compound parts. Instruct each student with the simple sentences to expand one of the sentences using the information from the other sentence(s). Discuss the resulting sentences with the students. If any of the sentences could not be expanded or reduced, offer some explanation.

ONE on ONE With your student write two or three simple sentences about a topic and one long compound sentence about another topic. Encourage your student to be creative with the topics and content of the sentences. Ask him to expand one of the simple sentences using information from the other sentence(s). Then ask him to reduce the compound sentence to a simple sentence with compound parts. Discuss the resulting sentences and explain any problems he might have encountered.

Beware of adding too many descriptive phrases to your writing. The resulting sentences may become stringy and complicated rather than interesting.

> After sticking the brightly colored plastic figurine into the driver's seat of the toy dump truck and cradling his latest acquisition from his Aunt Hazel, two-year-old Braydon squealed with excitement and told everyone what he had decided to name the little construction man included with his new toy: "Me."

14.11 PRACTICE *the skill*

Combine each pair of sentences by making one of the sentences a dependent clause. *(Answers may vary.)*

1. The Maginot Line was to be a protective barrier between France and Germany. The construction of the Maginot Line took place after World War I in France.

   The Maginot Line, which was constructed after World War I in France, was to be a protective barrier between France and Germany.

2. Some historians have called the Maginot Line a fiasco. The Line was a technological success.

   Although some historians have called the Maginot Line a fiasco, the Line was a technological success.

3. The Line, a series of forts and blockhouses, was buried one hundred feet or more in the earth. Access to the forts and blockhouses was by trolleys.

   Because the Line, a series of forts and blockhouses, was buried one hundred feet or more in the earth, access to these was by trolleys.

4. The Maginot Line was a military success. Germany's invasion of France in World War II brought Germany around the line, not through it.

   The Maginot Line was a military success because Germany's invasion of France in World War II brought Germany around the Line, not through it.

5. Reading history reveals an interesting fact. The Line surrendered, but it was not taken militarily.

   Reading history reveals that the Line surrendered but was not taken militarily.

Reinforcement

Direct the students to analyze the sentences of a recent writing assignment. Encourage them to reduce or expand some of their sentences to add greater variety to their writing.

Teaching Strategy

Modeling

Demonstrate expanding the sentences in Practice the Skill 14.11. Show how sentences can be combined in more than one way. Also point out the difference in meaning between the different combinations.

14.12 REVIEW *the skill*

Expand each sentence by adding a clause or phrase to the independent clause provided. You may need to research the subject. *(Answers may vary.)*

1. The Sistine Chapel is most often associated with Michelangelo.

   The Sistine Chapel, which is most often associated with Michelangelo, is an inspiring place to visit.

2. In 1508 Michelangelo was commissioned to repaint the star-covered ceiling.

   Commissioned by the Pope in 1508, Michelangelo began the job of repainting the star-covered ceiling.

3. Before Michelangelo began his work, famous artists such as Botticelli, Signorelli, and others had painted frescoes.

   Before Michelangelo began his work, famous artists such as Botticelli, Signorelli, and others had painted frescoes on the side walls.

4. These fresco cycles portray the lives of Moses and Christ.

   These fresco cycles on the walls portray the lives of Moses and Christ.

5. The side walls show continuity.

   Representing the Old Covenant and the New Covenant, the side walls show continuity.

Reduction of Sentences

Sentence reduction tightens your writing and makes it less complicated. Although it is often desirable to use sentence expansion, sometimes the result is a sentence that is very complicated or lengthy. A writer might then use sentence reduction techniques to make the writing tighter and more understandable. One common way to reduce sentences is to make a compound sentence into a simple sentence with a compound part such as a compound predicate or subject.

Compound Sentence	James M. Barrie lived during the peak of the Victorian Era, and he incorporated all the literary conventions of his age into his writings.
Compound Predicate	James M. Barrie lived during the peak of the Victorian Era and incorporated all the literary conventions of his age into his writings.
Compound Sentence	James M. Barrie used much fantasy in his plays, and W. S. Gilbert of the Gilbert and Sullivan duo did too.
Compound Subject	James M. Barrie and W. S. Gilbert of the Gilbert and Sullivan duo used much fantasy in their plays.

Teaching Strategy
Participation

Materials

- art and history books or pamphlets discussing the art of Michelangelo
- Internet access to sites on Michelangelo

Before assigning Review the Skill 14.12, inform students that sometimes they may need to research a topic before they can expand sentences. Make information about Michelangelo available. Instruct students to work with partners while researching Michelangelo and then to expand the sentences in Review the Skill 14.12.

ONE on ONE

Before assigning Review the Skill 14.12, tell your student that sometimes he may need to research a topic before he can expand sentences. Encourage your student to research Michelangelo's work on the Sistine Chapel. Then expand the sentences in Review the Skill 14.12.

Teaching Strategy
Introduction and Induction

Display the following sentences: *The team ~~that is~~ at the summit began their climb at 3 a.m. The woman ~~who is~~ coiling the rope is the mountain guide.* Ask the students whether the sentences sound natural and understandable without the words that are crossed out. *(yes)* Why? *(The omitted words are understood by the reader.)* Ask the students what the process of eliminating understood words is called. *(ellipsis)*

Writing Strategies | Chapter 14 373

Often, a writer will practice reduction naturally by eliminating words that he knows will be understood by the reader. This process is called **ellipsis**. Ellipsis often results in a simple sentence with a compound part.

> James Barrie gained an appreciation for literature from his mother and [he] vowed to make writing his career.

But sometimes the result is a compound sentence in which some of the words are understood. The sentence below contains an elliptical independent clause.

> People most often associate James Barrie with his play *Peter Pan*, but [they do] not [associate him] with his forty or so other works.

Reducing Adjective Clauses

Writer's Toolbox

Some clauses can be reduced to a brief phrase or a single word. When the subject of an adjective clause is a relative pronoun, you can usually reduce the clause to one of the following:

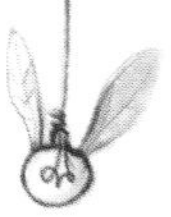

Adjective Clause to Prepositional Phrase

Adjective Clauses pp. 117–18

Prepositional Phrases p. 88

An adjective clause that consists of a relative pronoun, a form of *be*, and a prepositional phrase can be reduced to just the prepositional phrase.

> Many characters ~~which are~~ in *Peter Pan* were modeled after the author's experiences while vacationing with the Davies family.

> Many characters in *Peter Pan* were modeled after the author's experiences while vacationing with the Davies family.

Adjective Clause to Participle or Participial Phrase

An adjective clause can often be reduced to a simple participle or a participial phrase.

> Students ~~who are~~ seeking additional information should stay after the meeting.

> Students seeking additional information should stay after the meeting.

Notice that an adjective clause with an active verb produces a present participle. An adjective clause with a passive verb produces a past participle (more accurately called a "passive participle") as in the sentence below.

> The meeting ~~that was~~ scheduled for tomorrow has been cancelled.

> The meeting scheduled for tomorrow has been cancelled.

So far the phrases we have looked at have remained after the nouns they modify. However, when all that remains of a clause is a simple participle, the participle may move to a position before the noun (much like a regular adjective).

Participles and Participial Phrases pp. 92–94

> No one recognized the importance of the meeting ~~that was~~ cancelled.

> No one recognized the importance of the cancelled meeting.

Note that an entire participial phrase could not be moved; that is, we would not say "*The scheduled for tomorrow meeting* has been cancelled." However, a participle modified only by a preceding adverb can usually be moved.

> No one recognized the importance of the meeting ~~that was~~ suddenly cancelled.

> No one recognized the importance of the suddenly cancelled meeting.

374 Chapter 14 | Writing Strategies

Although it seems that a clause must have a form of *be* in it to be a candidate for reduction, in actuality certain clauses without *be* can be reduced by changing the main verb to a present participle. Note the example below.

students who seek information → students seeking information

Adjective Clause to Single Adjective or Appositive

When an adjective clause contains a relative-pronoun subject and a form of *be* followed by a predicate adjective, that clause can be reduced to the adjective alone.

Appositives p. 89

Jonathan swam in the relay ~~that was~~ arduous.

Jonathan swam in the arduous relay.

An adjective clause that contains a predicate noun after a relative-pronoun subject and a form of the linking verb *be* can be reduced to an appositive or appositive phrase.

Punctuation of Appositives p. 307

Mandy's aunt, ~~who is~~ a doctor, specializes in pediatric medicine.

Mandy's aunt, a doctor, specializes in pediatric medicine.

Reducing Adverb Clauses

Some adverb clauses can be reduced to simpler structures, such as prepositional phrases, verbal phrases, absolute phrases, or elliptical adverb clauses.

Adverb Clause pp. 122–23

Adverb Clause to Prepositional Phrase

Certain adverb clauses can be reduced to prepositional phrases.

After ~~there are~~ rainstorms, the beach looks fresh, smooth, and ready for new footprints and sandcastles.

After rainstorms, the beach looks fresh, smooth, and ready for new footprints and sandcastles.

When the adverb clause does not contain a noun that can become the object of the preposition, sometimes a noun can be made from another part of speech.

When it is cold outside, few people stroll casually along the beach.

During cold weather few people stroll casually along the beach.

Adverb Clause to Verbal Phrase

If an adverb clause has the same subject as the main clause and expresses time, cause, or condition, it may be reduced to a participial phrase.

~~Because you are~~ so tactful, you have been chosen to break the news to the second-place team.

Being so tactful, you have been chosen to break the news to the second-place team.

Note that when reducing a time clause, you use a present participle to indicate the same time as in the main clause. To express prior time, use a perfect participle.

~~After they finished~~ the game, Chad's team reviewed the video.

Having finished the game, Chad's team reviewed the video.

An adverb clause reduced to a participial phrase is considered to be adjectival. Because the subordinating conjunction (*when, after, because,* etc.) is dropped in the reduction, the adverbial meaning of the phrase is also dropped. The resulting participial phrase modifies the noun it tells something about. For a more thorough explanation, see *The Writer's Toolbox.*

If the "purpose" meaning of the infinitive is not clear, *in order to* can make it clear. The purpose infinitive, like the purpose clause, is adverbial and can come in the middle or at the beginning of a sentence (e.g., I hurried with my homework *in order to* have time to play basketball. *In order to* have time to play basketball, I hurried with my homework.).

Writing Strategies | Chapter 14 375

An adverb clause expressing purpose can often be reduced to an infinitive phrase if the adverb clause has the same subject as the main clause.

Eden is going to Camp Hope this weekend ~~so that she can~~ baby-sit the children of those attending the couples' retreat.

Eden is going to Camp Hope this weekend to baby-sit the children of those attending the couple's retreat.

Adverb Clause to Absolute Phrase

Absolute Phrase pp. 88–89

If the subject of the adverb clause is different from that of the main clause, you may be able to turn the adverb clause into an absolute phrase.

being

~~Since~~ her group ~~was~~ late, Sharon decided not to stop for a snack.

Her group being late, Sharon decided not to stop for a snack.

Reduce a clause to an absolute phrase by dropping the subordinating conjunction and changing the verb to a participle. What remains is a typical absolute phrase.

In the example above, the present participle *being* indicates approximately the same time as the verb in the main clause. Note that the reduction could be taken a step further—to a prepositional phrase: "With her group late."

Adverb Clause to Elliptical Adverb Clause

Elliptical Adverb Clause p. 123

Another way to reduce an adverb clause is to keep the subordinating conjunction and simply drop one or more other words that can be understood from context.

Unless ~~he is~~ late for class, Cliff empties the trash cans in the morning.

Unless late for class, Cliff empties the trash cans in the morning.

Because the subordinating conjunction remains in sentence two above, the origin of the word group as an adverb clause is still clear, and we call it an "elliptical clause." Note that an elliptical clause has the same function in the sentence as a full adverb clause.

Elliptical adverb clauses can also include participles, reduced from verbs.

If ~~we are~~ told in advance, our group can bring refreshments.

While ~~she was~~ circling the track, she felt a cramp in her foot.

Elliptical clauses are often used for comparison.

Reena is taller than Jordan is ~~tall~~.

Reena is taller than Jordan ~~is tall~~.

Dangling Modifiers p. 251

tip

Never reduce an adverb clause whose subject is different from that of the main clause. (The result is a dangling modifier.)

ADVERB CLAUSE	Because we arrived early, the hostess was not ready yet.
DANGLING MODIFIER	Arriving early, the hostess was not ready yet.

376 Chapter 14 | Writing Strategies

Reducing Noun Clauses

Many noun clauses cannot be reduced to any simpler construction. When it is possible, though, reducing a noun clause can result in a tighter sentence.

Noun Clause to Verbal Phrase

Noun clauses can sometimes be reduced to gerund phrases or infinitive phrases.

Noun Clause
pp. 126-28

Noun Clause	My choice is *that I would invest the money.*
Gerund	My choice is *investing the money.*
Infinitive	My choice is *to invest the money.*

Verbal Phrases
pp. 92–102

Of the last two sentences above, the infinitive may be preferable, since the gerund could possibly be misread as part of a progressive verb ("is investing"). The last sentence could also be made more concise:

I choose *to invest the money.*

I choose *investing the money.*

Notice how the sentence changes when the subject of the noun clause and the subject of the main clause are different:

S TrV DO

My mother learned that I invested the money wisely.

My mother learned about my investing the money wisely. *(gerund OP)*

In this case (two subjects or actors are different—*mother* and *I*), the subject of the noun clause cannot just be dropped. Instead, it appears as a possessive modifier *(my)*.

When you reduce a noun clause to an infinitive, the subject of the noun clause becomes the "subject" of the infinitive phrase, usually after *for.* If the subject of the noun clause was a personal pronoun, the "subject" of the infinitive must be an objective-case pronoun.

The infinitive phrase is not introduced by *for* when it is the direct object after certain verbs, such as *request.*

S LV PN

The manager's idea is that we participate in the book sale.

The manager's idea is for us to participate in the book sale. *(infinitive PN)*

Noun Clause to Noun Phrase

Sometimes a noun clause can be reduced to a noun and its modifiers (a noun phrase). Usually this reduction is possible only when there exists a noun that is closely related in meaning to the verb of the noun clause.

Clause	I know that he worked as a personal trainer for a time.
Phrase	I know about his vocation as a personal trainer.
Clause	Whom he associates himself with is unknown.
Phrase	His associates are unknown.

Writing Strategies | Chapter 14 377

Reducing Complex Sentences

Complex Sentences p. 132

Certain complex sentences with predicate adjectives can be reduced to simple sentences containing adverbs as sentence modifiers. Notice that the reduced sentence is both shorter and more to the point.

It was providential that no one was hurt in the accident.

Providentially, no one was hurt in the accident.

14.13 PRACTICE *the skill*

Rewrite each sentence to reduce the italicized clause to the shorter construction indicated in parentheses. *(Answers may vary.)*

1. The Western Wall, *which is often called the Wailing Wall*, is located in the old city of Jerusalem. *(participial phrase)*

   The Western Wall, often called the Wailing Wall, is located in the old city of Jerusalem.

2. The Western Wall dates from about the first century, *and the wall is the only remains of the second temple of Jerusalem. (appositive phrase)*

   The Western Wall, the only remains from the second temple of Jerusalem, dates from about the first century.

3. *Because the wall is a sacred place to Jewish people*, prayer and worship often take place at the wall. *(absolute phrase)*

   The wall being a sacred place to Jewish people, prayer and worship often take place at the wall.

4. The Western Wall is also a place *where some participate in Jewish religious or military ceremonies. (infinitive phrase)*

   The Western Wall is also a place to participate in Jewish religious or military ceremonies.

5. Jews *who are mourning* come to the Wailing Place, a part of the Western Wall. *(participle)*

   Mourning Jews come to the Wailing Place, a part of the Western Wall.

TEACHING STRATEGY

Demonstration

Before assigning Review the Skill 14.14, discuss the students' answers to Practice the Skill 14.13. Confirm that the students understand the correct answers and help them to analyze any mistakes they may have made. Complete the first sentence of Review the Skill 14.14 with the students, noting several possible answers.

378 Chapter 14 | Writing Strategies

14.14 REVIEW *the skill*

Reduce each sentence, using the techniques discussed in this section. *(Answers may vary.)*

1. Because Hadrian wanted to mark the northern boundary of his empire, the Romans built Hadrian's Wall in northern Britain.

   To mark the northern boundary of Hadrian's empire, the Romans built Hadrian's Wall in northern Britain.

2. The stone wall, which is considered one of the Roman Empire's greatest engineering feats, is seventy-three modern miles long.

   The stone wall, one of the Roman Empire's greatest engineering feats, is seventy-three modern miles long.

3. During Hadrian's time, a mile castle was located at every Roman mile measurement, and eight soldiers guarded the castle.

   During Hadrian's time, a mile castle, located at every Roman mile measurement, was guarded by eight soldiers.

4. Additional soldiers guarded from turrets that were located equal distances between the mile castles.

   Additional soldiers guarded from turrets located at equal distances between mile castles.

5. After the decline of the Roman Empire, parts of Hadrian's Wall were stolen, and they appeared in houses, churches, and other walls.

   The Roman Empire having declined, stolen parts of Hadrian's Wall appeared in houses, churches, and other walls.

Parallelism

Joining sentence elements of similar form is called **parallelism**. Parallel structures have the same grammatical form and are most often joined by a coordinating conjunction. Effective parallelism shows the relationship between ideas and makes writing flow more smoothly.

ACCEPTABLE	The fisherman says his special today is halibut. He also says there is a special buy on salmon. Additionally, he has a promotional offer on trout.
IMPROVED WITH PARALLELISM	The fisherman's specials today include halibut, salmon, and trout.

TEACHING STRATEGY
Introduction and Induction

Display the following sentences:

- We will have chicken enchiladas, salad, and the Madrid family for dinner tonight.
- Before the long trip Toby will check his tires, oil, and wash his truck.
- To study the Bible, to pray diligently, and witnessing are important activities for Christians.
- If you go rock climbing, it is important to double-check for safety and staying alert.
- I asked Mom to iron my dress and whether she will fix my hair for the concert.

Ask the students why the sentences do not sound right. *(They all have parallelism problems.)*

TEACHING STRATEGY
Participation

After you teach the principles of parallelism, ask volunteers to correct the sentences from the previous Introduction and Induction section. *(Answers will vary.)*

When making verbs parallel, be aware that the coordination should link the more significant subsequent words. Consider the following sentence: *The paint is old and peels easily.* Though this sentence could be interpreted as coordinating *is* and *peels*, the coordination should be on the more important word that follows, *old*. The following sentence is parallel: *The paint is old and easily peeled.*

Using Parallelism Only for Parallel Ideas

Parallelism in writing should be reserved for ideas that are truly of the same type.

Illogical Parallelism	While assessing the Shanghai facility, we noted favorable marketing opportunities, solid first quarter earnings, and *delightful seaport cuisine.*
Correction	While assessing the Shanghai facility, we noted favorable marketing opportunities and solid first quarter earnings.

tip

Make sure that one item in the parallel structure is not more general or less general than the others. For example, write, "We bought seeds for lettuce, carrots, and other garden vegetables," not "for lettuce, carrots, and garden vegetables."

Using the Same Part of Speech

Parts of Speech p. 35

Parallel structures joined by coordinating conjunctions should be of the same grammatical type and part of speech.

Not Parallel	Most first-time home buyers want residences with good resale value, room for an expanding family, and *conveniently located.*
Parallel	Most first-time home buyers want residences with good resale value, room for an expanding family, and *a convenient location.*

Using the Same Type of Structure

Making parallel sentences involves using the same kinds of words, phrases, verbals, or clauses.

Kinds of Words or Phrases

Verbals p. 92

Although verbals function as nouns, adjectives, and adverbs, verbals should not appear in parallel structures with those parts of speech.

Not Parallel	New home buyers often purchase personalized home accessories such as cabinet fixtures, wall hangings, and *installing window treatments.*
Parallel	New home buyers often purchase personalized home accessories such as cabinet fixtures, wall hangings, and *window treatments.*

Prepositional phrases are preferably not mixed with other constructions as in the sentence below.

Not Fully Parallel	Meg finds this project more fulfilling, *of greater importance,* and less stressful.
Parallel	Meg finds this project more fulfilling, *more important,* and less stressful.

Kinds of Verbals

Gerunds, participles, and infinitives should not be mixed in the same construction.

Not Parallel	Research tasks will include *touring* an upholstery manufacturing facility and *to test* product samples for flammability.
Parallel	Research tasks will include *touring* an upholstery manufacturing facility and *testing* product samples for flammability.

Teaching Strategy

Discussion

Direct the students' attention to the example sentences on parallelism of words or phrases (p. 380). Ask students what changes make the second sentences better than the first sentences. *(In the first set, the second sentence changes the gerund into a noun phrase. In the second set, the second sentence changes the prepositional phrase into an adjective.)*

380 Chapter 14 | Writing Strategies

Phrases and Clauses

A phrase and a clause should not be joined with a coordinating conjunction. Rather, make the phrase into a clause or the clause into a phrase.

Conjunctions
pp. 54–55

Not Parallel | The interior designer asked *for* our color preferences and *whether* we had a project budget.

Parallel | The interior designer asked *whether* we had color preferences and *whether* we had a project budget.

Even Better | The interior designer asked *for* our color preferences and *for* our project budget.

With correlative conjunctions (*both—and, neither—nor*), the same type of structure should follow each of the two words.

Not Parallel | Those making matching donations **both** *boosted* the number of charitable gifts **and** *the individual amounts* contributed.

Parallel | Those making matching donations boosted **both** *the number* of charitable gifts **and** *the individual amounts* contributed.

Sometimes adding a subject and an auxiliary makes the two parts parallel.

Not Parallel | **Not only** *has the Christian radio station made* its fundraising goal **but also** *received* enough money to build a better radio tower.

Parallel | **Not only** *has the Christian radio station made* its fundraising goal, **but** *it has* **also** *received* enough money to build a better radio tower.

Kinds of Clauses

A dependent clause and an independent clause should not be joined by a coordinating conjunction.

Not Parallel | All employees must view the safety video, *but when they are not regularly scheduled to work.*

Parallel | All employees must view the safety video, *but they must watch it when they are not regularly scheduled to work.*

Also Good | All employees must view the safety video *when they are not regularly scheduled to work.*

Clarifying Parallelism

A writer may employ several methods to make clear to a reader which sentence parts are intended to be parallel. The methods are listed in the chart below.

Method of Clarification	Example Sentence
Use correlative conjunctions correctly.	Our swim team will compete in freestyle and butterfly or backstroke categories. *(confusing)* Our swim team will compete in either freestyle and butterfly or the backstroke category. Our swim team will compete in the freestyle and either the butterfly or backstroke categories.

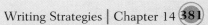

CONTINUED

Writing Strategies | Chapter 14 381

Repeat a key word.	The advanced swimming course offers instruction in interpreting a pace clock, flip turns, and technique drills. *(interpreting flip turns and technique drills?)* The advanced swimming course offers instruction in interpreting a pace clock, in flip turns, and in technical drills.
Reorder joined elements.	The pool's mechanically controlled floor depth and lifeguard staff make this facility an ideal choice for parents with young children. *(mechanically controlled lifeguard staff?)* The pool's lifeguard staff and mechanically controlled floor depth make this facility an ideal choice for parents with young children.

14.15 PRACTICE *the skill*

Rewrite each sentence, correcting any illogical or incorrect parallelism. If the sentence is already correct, write *C* in the blank. *(Answers may vary.)*

1, The Shunammite woman of 2 Kings 4 was a woman of hospitality, perception, and she was content.

The Shunammite woman of 2 Kings 4 was a woman of hospitality, perception, and contentment.

2. Elisha and his servant, Gehazi, visited the woman and her husband on several occasions and when they traveled in that part of Israel.

Elisha and his servant, Gehazi, visited the woman and her husband on several occasions when they traveled in that part of Israel.

3. God directed the Shunammite family not only to build a chamber but also they invited Elisha to use the chamber.

God directed the Shunammite family not only to build a chamber but also to invite Elisha to use the chamber.

4. In the chamber were items necessary for Elisha: a bed, a table, a stool, and there was a candlestick.

In the chamber were items necessary for Elisha: a bed, a table, a stool, and a candlestick.

5. God blessed the Shunammite woman for taking care of both the prophet and the prophet's servant.

C

382 Chapter 14 | Writing Strategies

14.16 USE *the skill*

Write an original sentence using the listed items in parallel ways. Omit or modify items that do not fit with the others logically. Be efficient and logical in word types and constructions. *(Answers will vary.)*

1. high school graduation / going to college / get a job

   After high school graduation Janie began thinking about getting a job and going to college.

2. to work at a summer camp / going on a mission trip / help in Bible school at her church

   She wanted, however, to have the opportunity to work at a summer camp, to go on a mission trip, or to help in Bible school at her church.

3. the payment for her first year in college / to help her sister in need / being her father's assistant in the business

   She also had to consider how she would pay for her first year in college, help her sister in need, and assist her father in the business.

4. praying daily / read God's word / Janie sought wise counsel.

   After praying daily and reading God's word, Janie sought wise counsel.

5. the desire to know God's will / wants to obey God's will

   Janie understands that she must have a desire not only to know God's will but also to obey God's will.

Sentence Logic

Writer's Toolbox

You have no doubt read articles or listened to speeches that caused you to wonder about the logic of the writer or speaker. Sometimes grammatical constructions or meanings do not fit together correctly, and the resulting sentences seem illogical. This section identifies common logic problems and suggests ways to correct them.

Saying Things Directly

Determine to deliver your message in as few words as possible. Look for "built nouns" in your writing—nouns that are formed from simpler words. For example, the noun *separation* comes from the verb *separate; happiness* comes from the adjective *happy.* Many sentences can be simplified by using words in their original part of speech.

Too Wordy (Dense)	To enforce their *warning* that a hurricane was making its *approach,* lifeguards ordered an *evacuation* of the beach.
Revised	Lifeguards *warned* that a hurricane was *approaching* and then *evacuated* the beach.

Writing Strategies | Chapter 14 383

Saying What You Mean

Avoid making your reader unsure of your meaning. Say precisely what you mean by using logical predication and by making sure that your examples are truly examples.

- Make your subjects and verbs work together logically.

Illogical Predication	Lifeguards desiring to take the advanced water safety course will be available next semester.
Correction	Lifeguards who desire advanced training in water safety may take a course next semester.

- Make your examples actual examples. The phrases *for example* and *such as* notify the reader that examples will follow; therefore, the examples should be the main words after those phrases.

Illogical Exemplification	This swimming course emphasizes more advanced skills such as *practicing* diving and rotary breathing.
Correction	This swimming course emphasizes more advanced skills such as *diving* and *rotary breathing*.

Saying Things Consistently

When writing, avoid the tendency to begin a sentence with one construction and mistakenly end with a different one.

Mixed Constructions	When William S. Gilbert wrote the librettos of numerous comic operas were based on plot and character ideas from his earlier contributions to a magazine.
	From studying logic as a law student may have influenced W. S. Gilbert's ability to satirize Victorian England.
Possible Corrections	William S. Gilbert, the librettist of numerous comic operas, drew many plot and character ideas from his earlier contributions to a magazine.
	W. S. Gilbert's ability to satirize Victorian England may have stemmed from his training in logic while a student of law.

Making Clear and Logical Comparisons

When comparing two or more things, state the comparison clearly and logically.

Logical Comparisons

Degrees of Adjectives and Adverbs pp. 243–44

- Things being compared must be separate; one cannot be part of another.

Faulty Comparison	Robert made higher SAT scores than anyone in his senior class. *(Robert is part of the senior class, so he cannot be compared with himself.)*
Correction	Robert made higher SAT scores than anyone *else* in his senior class.

- Things being compared must also be of the same type.

Faulty Comparison	The landscapes of the Hudson River artists are more realistic than most modern painters. *(Landscapes are compared with painters.)*
Correction	The landscapes of the Hudson River artists are more realistic than the landscapes of most modern painters. *(Here landscapes are compared with other landscapes.)*

Peace and Plenty by George Inness

Teaching Strategy

Analysis

Display the following sentences and discuss them along with the examples provided in the text:

Saying Things Directly

- Mrs. Dulaney spent much time in explanation of the historical background of the orchestration. *(Mrs. Dulaney explained the history of the orchestration.)*

Saying What You Mean

- Students hoping to meet the guest soloist will be backstage after the concert. *(The guest soloist will be backstage after the concert so students can meet him.)*
- The concert program includes pieces such as playing Faure's *Romance* and Beethoven's violin *Sonata No. 5*. *(The concert program includes pieces such as Faure's* Romance *and Beethoven's violin* Sonata No. 5.*)*

Saying Things Consistently

- While I practiced the climactic final movement of the concerto has a very technical and difficult cadenza. *(While I practiced the climactic final movement of the concerto, I struggled with the very technical and difficult cadenza.)*

Ask the students why a person may make these mistakes. *(trying to sound knowledgeable)* Point out that simplicity and accuracy are more impressive than large words and elaborate constructions that do not effectively communicate meaning.

384 Chapter 14 | Writing Strategies

Faulty Comparison	Robert's SAT scores were higher than anyone else in his senior class. *(Scores are compared with people.)*
Correction	Robert's SAT scores were higher than those of anyone else in his senior class. *(Scores are compared with other scores.)*

Clear Comparisons

Sometimes the last part of a comparison will be understood from the context.

Jamison has studied longer than Brad. (longer than Brad *has studied*)

He studies chemistry more than physics. (more than *he studies* physics)

Although it is acceptable, even advisable, to leave out the part that will be understood, never leave out anything that is needed for clarity.

Unclear	The teacher heard Ben as well as Liz. *(Is* Liz *the subject of an understood clause? Or is* Liz *the direct object of the understood verb* heard*?)*
Possible Corrections	The teacher heard Ben as well as Liz did.
	The teacher heard Ben as well as she heard Liz.

ESL

Notice the use of *did* in the first "possible correction" above. If a comparison clause (beginning with *than* or *as*) compares subjects of the same verb, English speakers often repeat the first auxiliary in the comparison clause. If there is no auxiliary or *be* verb present, they use the appropriate form of the auxiliary *do*.

First Auxiliary	Jamie has been studying as long as Brad **has**.
***Be* Verb**	I am as tall as he **is**.
Form of *Do*	I finished my homework faster than you **did**.
	He likes drawing more than I **do**.

Completing the Construction Before Or

Some comparisons state that one of the things may be either equivalent or superior with regard to some quality. In such a construction with *or*, *as* is needed before *or*.

Correlative Conjunctions p. 55

Incomplete Construction	Joanie sings this aria *as well* or better than the lead soprano does.
Corrections	Joanie sings this aria *as well as* or better than the lead soprano does.
	Joanie sings this aria *as well as* the lead soprano does, or better.
Incomplete Construction	When Dad hears of Joanie's success, he will be *as happy* or happier than she.
Corrections	When Dad hears of Joanie's success, he will be *as happy as* or happier than she.
	When Dad hears of Joanie's success, he will be *as happy as* she is, or happier.

ESL

Statements of equivalence use an *as . . . as* construction with an adjective or an adverb in the middle.

With Adjective	Dad is *as happy as* Joanie (is).
With Adverb	Joanie sings *as well as* the lead soprano (does).

ESL Strategy

The construction explained in the ESL note on page 385 uses an auxiliary or the main verb *be* (in a strictly ordered set of priorities). See ESL Help 2G or 3A (Teacher's Toolkit) for a fuller explanation. See also ESL Help 7A.

ESL Strategy

See ESL Help 13 (Teacher's Toolkit) for more information about subject-verb inversion in direct questions.

Teaching Strategy

Participation

Use Bulletin Board 14 (Teacher's Toolkit) to help the students demonstrate their knowledge of key chapter objectives. Encourage the students to list the corresponding writing strategies that they employed with each sentence. Then call on various students to share several of their sentences and strategies.

Using Noun Clauses When Needed

Using the wrong type of clause may throw a sentence off course. Learn to use noun clauses correctly.

Noun Clause, Not Adverb Clause

Clauses pp. 122–28

Do not use an adverb clause when a noun or noun clause is required. Either replace the adverb clause with a noun clause or recast the sentence to allow for the original adverb clause.

Adverb Clause as Subject	Because a country signs a treaty is no guarantee it will honor its word.
Correction	That a country signs a treaty is no guarantee that it will honor its word.
Adverb Clause as PN	The time I need to sleep is whenever I'm tired.
Correction	I need to sleep whenever I'm tired.

tip

An adverb clause can never function as a noun: subject, direct object, predicate noun, and so on.

Dependent (Noun) Clause, Not Independent Clause

Never use an independent clause as the subject of a sentence. Rather, convert the independent clause to a noun clause (or noun equivalent) or revise the sentence completely.

Independent Clause as Subject	Spring has come at last was our motive for putting out the patio chairs.
Possible Corrections	The arrival of spring was our motive for putting out the chairs.
	Spring has come at last, so we decided to put out the patio chairs.
	We decided to put out the patio chairs because spring has come at last.

Similarly, a direct question must be changed to an indirect question if it is to be used as a noun clause.

Direct Question as Subject	How do Christians respond to trial is an important question.
Corrections	How Christians respond to trial is an important question.
	An important question is this: How do Christians respond to trial?

ESL Indirect questions do not have subject-verb inversion.

Direct Question	She asked, "How do Christians respond to trial?"
Indirect Question	She asked how Christians respond to trial.

Writing Link

Instruct students to select a piece of writing from their portfolio and to analyze their word placement in each sentence. Instruct them to improve the selection by streamlining the subjects of the sentences and adding strength to the ends of the sentences.

Teaching Strategy

Participation

Assign each student a partner and then give one of the following sentences to each pair of students:

- The Gateway Arch in St. Louis, Missouri, memorializes the expansion into the American West during the nineteenth century.
- Eero Saarinen's design of the Arch won the Jefferson National Expansion Memorial competition and

Placing Words in the Sentence

Create a natural flow from one sentence to another by placing elements strategically at the beginnings and ends of sentences.

Word Placement p. 356

Managing Subjects Within the Sentence

Subjects of sentences or clauses within a paragraph should fit together well. Avoid needless shifting of topics.

Subjects p. 70

Paragraph with Subject Shifts

Shoes with exaggeratedly high soles pass into and out of fashion, but Japan's traditional *geta* shoes existed long before modern platform shoes. During the Heian Period (794–1192) the Japanese developed wooden-soled shoes that rested upon two narrow wooden blocks called *ha*. The word *ha* actually means "teeth." Although *ha* raised the shoe only one or two inches off the ground, the shoes' elevation prevented people from soiling their long kimonos in the dust of the road. The kimono is the traditional formal dress garment of the Japanese. Additionally, on rainy days, people could even wear *geta* water shoes with significantly higher wooden blocks. Another item of traditional Japanese footwear is the *zori*, a sandal made of rush matting or woven brocade. *Geta* are held on the foot by the *hanao*, or "thongs." *Hanao* traditionally come in two colors, red for women and black for men, although more recently, *hanao* have taken on many different colors. In the summer of 1997, *geta* again became popular as a fashion item in Japan.

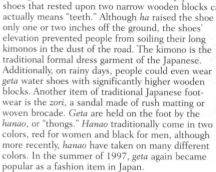

Improved

Shoes with exaggeratedly high soles pass into and out of fashion, but Japan's traditional *geta* shoes existed long before modern platform shoes. *Geta* are wooden-soled shoes that rest on two narrow wooden blocks. Although the blocks, known as *ha* ("teeth") raised the shoe only one or two inches off the ground, the shoes' elevation prevented people from soiling their kimonos in the dirt. *Geta* are held on the foot by *hanao* or "thongs." *Hanao* traditionally come in two colors, red for women and black for men. In the summer of 1997, *geta* shoes again became a popular fashion item.

Notice that the revised paragraph sticks to the topic and does not stray from it. The first paragraph includes several diversions from the original topic, such as the references to kimonos and *zori*. Concise, clear writing depends on the writer's sticking to the topic instead of leading the reader away from the main idea with sentences unrelated to the theme.

Ending in Strength

Final impressions are lasting impressions; therefore, end your sentences with strength.

Important Information

Because we learn inductively (by drawing conclusions from what we already know), it is natural within a sentence or paragraph to progress from familiar information to new information. Good writers take advantage of this natural progression by putting the important information last in their writing. Study the strategies below under "Linking with New Information" for ways to move important information to the end of the sentence.

posed the greatest engineering challenge of the day.

- The Arch, designed as an inverted catenary curve, the shape that a heavy cable would form if suspended from two points, spans 630 feet vertically and horizontally.
- Because the foundation of the Gateway Arch extends 60 feet into the ground, only 18 inches of deflection is possible when winds of 155 miles per hour blow from the east or west.
- The Arch's unique elevator system that carries thousands of visitors to the top each day was designed in only two weeks by Dick Bowser and took six years to build.

Ask students to rearrange the sentences as necessary to strengthen the endings. Remind them that they will have to determine what information is most important. When students are finished, ask them to read the original sentences and their improvements aloud. If more than one pair of students worked on the same sentence, discuss the different changes that each pair made.

ONE on ONE With your student, rewrite one or two of the above sentences to improve its word placement and sentence strength. As you work, point out the various possibilities and the emphasis that each accomplishes within the sentence.

Solid Words

Just as we expect sentences to end with important information, we expect sentences to end with "solid" words. Weak wording dilutes an otherwise strong idea.

Weak	Even if the Victorian Era is not your forte, Gilbert and Sullivan's operettas contain many timeless situations that you will find humor in.
Strong	Even if the Victorian Era is not your forte, Gilbert and Sullivan's operettas contain many timeless and humorous situations.
Adequate	Arthur Sullivan composed masterfully.
Strong	Arthur Sullivan composed with mastery.

Compared with the solid word *situations*, the preposition *in* is a weak word. The noun *mastery* communicates a stronger message than the adverb derived from it. The chart below shows how some parts of speech rank according to their relative strengths.

Strong			**Weak**
nouns	verbs	adjectives, adverbs	prepositions, adverbs that sound like prepositions (such as *in*), pronouns

Not all sentences can or should be manipulated to end with a strong word. Use solid-word endings for your most important information.

Linking with New Information

The end of a sentence is not only the place to put important information but also the place to put information that links ideas together. Good paragraphs contain sentences that lead naturally into one another, often by repeating in one sentence an idea that was introduced briefly in the sentence before. Although this kind of link is not always possible, it is sometimes a good way to tie sentences together. The chart below lists several ways to get new information to the end of the sentence.

Method	Original Sentences	Revised Sentences
Reverse the subject and the predicate noun.	Coins have been made from nonmetals such as porcelain and plastic, as well as from silver, nickel, platinum, and **gold**. By the nineteenth century the worldwide standard was **gold**.	Coins have been made from nonmetals such as porcelain and plastic, as well as from silver, nickel, platinum, and **gold**. **Gold** was the worldwide standard by the nineteenth century.
Move items out of the way at the sentence end.	The United States first used **nickel** to mint coins in 1865. **It** was used to produce a three-cent piece.	In 1865 the United States first minted coins from **nickel**. **It** was used to produce a three-cent piece.
Change active to passive or vice versa.	**Lead** was used by the American colonies to make the continental dollar. Today counterfeiters use **lead** to produce phony coins.	The American colonies made the continental dollar from **lead**. **Lead** is used today by counterfeiters to produce phony coins.

Teaching Strategy

Modeling and Participation

Use the five sentences from the previous exercise to demonstrate the principles of linking new information in sentences. Talk through the first two sentences explaining how you would rearrange them to form a well-organized paragraph. Ask for volunteers to work out the rest of the paragraph.

Certainly not every pair of sentences should be tied together in this way. However, used effectively, this technique will provide the link needed to strengthen your writing.

14.17 PRACTICE *the skill*

Rewrite each sentence, correcting any sentence logic problems. If the sentence is already correct, write C in the blank. *(Answers may vary.)*

1. The reason for the introduction of the Union Pacific Big Boy steam locomotive was because the railroad company needed an engine that could pull a heavy load over a difficult track without assistance.

   The Union Pacific Big Boy steam locomotive was introduced because the railroad company needed an engine that could pull a heavy load over a difficult track without assistance.

2. In the 1930s problems of transporting goods by railroad in the far West were greater than previous years.

   In the 1930s problems of transporting goods by railroad in the far West were greater than they were in previous years.

3. Because their engines were too small is why other trains could not navigate the steep grades of the western mountains of Utah.

   Because their engines were too small, other trains could not navigate the steep grades of the western mountains of Utah.

4. From 1941 to 1944 twenty-five Big Boy engines were built is the reason trains could cross the Wasatch Mountains.

   From 1941 to 1944 twenty-five Big Boy engines were built to cross the Wasatch Mountains.

5. Until their retirement in 1962 Big Boys averaged over one million miles per engine.

   C

Writing Strategies | Chapter 14 389

14.18 USE *the skill*

Rewrite the following paragraph to reduce the number of subject shifts and to end sentences with strength. *(Answers will vary.)*

Guion "Guy" Bluford was the first African American NASA astronaut. In 1979 the desire to be an astronaut became a reality. We read that he traveled on four space flights from 1983 to 1992. The first flight began in August 1983 at Kennedy Space Center in Florida. The last flight landed in December 1992 at Edwards Air Force Base in California. During the four space flights, his participation in a number of scientific experiments was crucial. Dr. Bluford paved the way for future space exploration.

Guion "Guy" Bluford was the first African American NASA astronaut. In 1979 he became an astronaut and fulfilled a lifelong desire. Bluford traveled on four space flights from 1983 to 1992. His first flight began in August 1983 at Kennedy Space Center in Florida, and his last flight ended in December 1992 at Edwards Air Force Base in California. During the flights, he participated in several crucial scientific experiments. Dr. Bluford paved the way for future space exploration.

Biased Language

A Christian's communication must avoid giving unnecessary offense to listeners or readers. Though commanded in Ephesians to "[speak] the truth," Christians are to speak that truth "in love" (4:15). **Stereotypes**, a common vehicle for offense, are oversimplified generalizations about persons or events based on carelessness, ignorance, or even malice, and they often perpetuate inaccurate and unreasonable prejudices against groups of people. Usually a stereotype emphasizes one feature of a person while disregarding other features. Some stereotypes are universally recognized to be negative. Other stereotypes are simplistic or thoughtless statements posing as neutral statements. Offensive generalizations based solely on age, cultural or ethnic background, gender, physical characteristics, or race have no place in the Christian's spoken or written communication.

Today's society increasingly demands strict "political correctness" in all forms of communication. At times, the effort to please everyone ends in sacrifices of accuracy, clarity, or precision. For the informed and thoughtful communicator, three basic guidelines may help as he attempts to balance his writing:

- **If possible, use terms preferred by the group or person that you are writing about.** Many Native Americans prefer being referred to by a specific tribal designation (e.g., *Dakota, Cherokee*).
- **Concentrate on a person's positive qualities or strengths.** Referring to someone as *the girl who runs using a prosthesis* sounds better than *the one-legged runner* or *a prosthesis-wearing runner.*
- **Remember the person foremost and the condition second.** Consider saying *a boy who is blind* instead of *the blind boy* or *the woman using a wheelchair* not *who is wheelchair-bound.*

Many corrections can be made by simply deleting the biased word or phrase or by changing the placement of a given word or phrase. Notice the examples below.

TEACHING STRATEGY
Introduction and Discussion

Ask the students to share some common stereotypes. *(the dumb blond, the unintelligent professional athlete, the dishonest lawyer, etc.)* Discuss the hurtful nature of these stereotypes with the students. Point out that biased language is a manifestation of prejudiced thinking—wrong thinking for a Christian. Encourage the students to eradicate stereotypes from their thinking as well as from their writing.

TEACHING STRATEGY
Discussion

Consider discussing with students whether it is ethical to use a term advocated by one group but offensive or inaccurate according to another group (e.g., pro-choice candidate or pro-abortion candidate).

TEACHING STRATEGY
Analysis

Ask students how stereotypes originate. *(prejudices, hasty judgments, general statements, etc.)* Encourage students to base judgments on facts and the qualities of each individual.

390 Chapter 14 | Writing Strategies

Stereotype	The blond woman driver ignored the stop sign and proceeded through the intersection. *(Failure to stop at a stop sign has nothing to do with the driver's gender or hair color.)*
Correction	The motorist ignored the stop sign and proceeded through the intersection.
Stereotype	Immigrants should attend language school in order to learn the language of their new country. *(Many already know the language of their new country.)*
Correction	Anyone desiring additional language instruction should be able to attend language school.
Stereotype	Just like a typical teenager, he cannot be counted on to mow the grass each week. *(His being a teenager is irrelevant to his choice to be irresponsible.)*
Correction	He cannot be counted on to mow the grass each week.

Inflammatory language reflects poorly on the communicator—it shows that he has not considered the sensitivities of his audience.

14.19 PRACTICE *the skill*

Underline the biased language in the following paragraph. Then rewrite the paragraph, correcting the bias and overall tone. *(Answers will vary.)*

Welcome to Riverdale Driving Academy, our community's leading provider of quality driving instruction. We serve everyone from insecure teenagers to older folks needing a review of state driving rules. For the past twenty-five years our company has led the upstate in making affordable driving instruction available to all. We provide a range of services, including our English- and Spanish-speaking instructors for immigrants, vehicles accessible to the wheelchair-bound, and remedial instruction for the quintessential blond. Please take a moment to examine our brochure and register for the next available class. We thank you in advance for your business.

Welcome to Riverdale Driving Academy, our community's leading provider of quality driving instruction. We serve everyone from first-time drivers to current drivers needing a review of state driving rules. For the past twenty-five years our company has led the upstate in making affordable driving instruction available to all. We provide a range of services, including instruction by speakers of English and Spanish, use of wheelchair-accessible vehicles, and remedial instruction. Please take a moment to examine our brochure and register for the next available class. We thank you in advance for your business.

Writing Strategies | Chapter 14 391

14.20 CUMULATIVE *review*

Revise the following paragraph, using all the skills discussed in this chapter. *(Answers may vary.)*

Buying an automobile for the first time is an exciting event for a teenager. Prior to purchasing an automobile, however, a written driver's test and a road test must be passed and received his driver's license. Don't be afraid to consider several things before you purchase a vehicle. First decide whether you can afford to purchase a new vehicle or a used vehicle. For most teenagers a used car is the better choice. People can often find a very good deal on a used car. Consult the newspaper or a reputable used car dealer. Next you need to consider if you want a truck, a van, or if you want a car that is full-size or compact. There are several additional considerations to be made about the prospective vehicle. What will this vehicle be used for? Some teenagers are buying their first car as a status symbol. Others are buying their first car for transportation to and from work and school. Others are buying their first car just for fun. Then you must consider some other things. Before the car is purchased, a mechanic with good skills and a sound reputation should inspect the car for mechanical problems. How many miles are on the odometer? Has the vehicle been wrecked at any time? Is there any rust on the body of the vehicle? The seats and dashboard should be in good shape with no tears, worn places, or soil marks. Maybe the color of the vehicle is very important to you. Now you are ready to fulfill your dream of purchasing your first vehicle.

Buying an automobile for the first time is an exciting event for a teenager. Prior to purchasing an automobile, however, the teen must pass the written driver's test and road test and must receive his license. The teen should consider several things before he purchases a vehicle. First he must decide whether he can afford to purchase a new vehicle or whether he should consider a used vehicle. For most teenagers a used car is the better choice. By consulting the newspaper or a reputable used car dealer, the teenager can often find a very good deal on a used car. A second consideration is the kind of vehicle to buy: a truck, a van, a full-size car, or a compact car. Once a vehicle has been selected as a possible purchase, the teenager must consider whether it is in good condition mechanically. Having a skilled mechanic with a sound reputation evaluate the car is a necessity. Next are other important considerations such as the number of miles on the odometer and the appearance of the vehicle. An inspection for signs of a wreck and for rust is vital. The seats and dashboard should be in good shape with no tears, worn places, or soil marks. Then the teenager must decide whether the color of the vehicle pleases him. If so, he is ready to fulfill his dream of purchasing his first vehicle.

392 Chapter 14 | Writing Strategies

HISTORY OF THE ENGLISH LANGUAGE

Continual Small Changes

You have read that spoken languages are always changing. Little by little the sounds change, the words change, and even some of the grammar changes. You can see some of these language changes in the Greek examples on pages 26–27 and in the English examples given again below. You would notice even more changes if you heard these translations of John 1:1 pronounced.

Old English (Anglo-Saxon)

On frymthe wæs Word, and thæt Word wæs mid Gode, and God wæs thæt Word.

Middle English

In the bygynnynge was the worde (that is goddis sone) and the worde was at god, and god was the worde.

Early Modern English

In the beginning was the Word, and the Word was with God, and the Word was God.

The examples of Latin and its daughter languages (p. 26, 2.1–2.4) show how one language can slowly split into several languages. Latin, the common language of most of the Roman Empire, was still being spoken in the time of Christ. Although scholars continued to read it and write it in about the same way for centuries, the common people all over Europe spoke it in their own local ways.

After a few hundred years, Latin had changed significantly, with different changes in different parts of Europe. The changes became so great that people from one area could not understand people from another area. When that happens, we say that they speak different languages. In this case, the local varieties of Latin ended up as the languages of Spanish, French, Italian, and so on. Here, then, we see an example of the second reason for language differences: languages are always changing, and a language spoken long enough and over a broad enough area will eventually split into different languages. This same process has occurred all over the world.

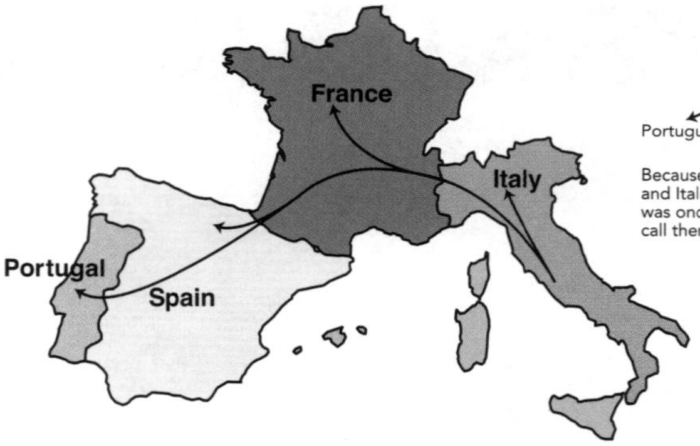

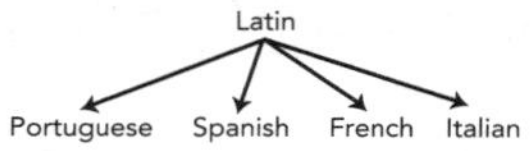

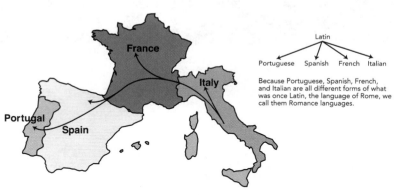

Because Portuguese, Spanish, French, and Italian are all different forms of what was once Latin, the language of Rome, we call them Romance languages.

ENRICHMENT

Materials

- recording of someone reading Old English and Middle English

Either read portions of Old English and Middle English to the students or play a recording for them. If possible, display or distribute a copy of the text so that the class can see how words have changed.

LIBRARY SKILLS

Lesson Support

Teacher's Toolkit
ESL Help 15
Bulletin Board 15

Teaching Strategy

Introduction and Induction

Display the following topics:

- Character Development in *A Tale of Two Cities*
- The Role of Christians in American Government
- Changes in Cinema Equipment Throughout the Last Decade

Ask students to imagine that they have gone to the local library to research one of these topics. When they enter the library, they find stacks of unlabeled books and materials on the floor rather than shelves full of labeled books. Ask students how this disorder would affect their ability to find the information they need for their research papers. Point out that organization in a library is necessary, but unless students understand and use that organization, they will never accomplish their tasks.

ESL Because the use of visuals and real objects in teaching increases comprehension for an ESL student, incorporate actual library books and diagrams of a library into a lesson to illustrate the arrangement and numbering systems used.

Our English word *library* comes to us from a Latin word meaning "of books." That connotation was an appropriate one for thousands of years. Over the past several decades, however, libraries have expanded their holdings to include not only books but also magazines, newspapers, audio-visual recordings, and even artwork. Today's library is a rich depository of valuable resources for education and entertainment.

The Arrangement of Library Materials

In order to use the library to its fullest potential, you need to find the answers to two basic questions. First, how is the library arranged? In other words, what sections or special rooms does it include and where are they located? If the library is small, you can probably figure out the floor plan easily on your own. If the library is large, look for a posted floor plan or ask a library staff member for help. Pay attention to the labels that the library uses to identify its sections and materials. Each item in the library probably carries a label that indicates the room or section to which it belongs.

Kind of Material	Examples	Possible Label
Books	fiction and nonfiction, both hardcover and paperback	FIC, NFIC, PB *(paperback)*, LP *or* LT *(large print or large type)*
Periodicals	newspapers, magazines, journals	PER
Audio-Visual Materials	audiocassettes, CDs, DVDs, videocassettes, filmstrips, works of art	AV, CD, DVD, VHS, CAS *(cassette)*
Reference	encyclopedias and other noncirculating materials that can be used only in the library	R *or* REF
Children / Young Adult	books, periodicals, and audio-visual materials designed especially for children or teens	J *or* JUV *(juvenile) or* YA
Special Collections	local interests, genealogy records, rare books	

SCRIPTURAL APPLICATION

How on the vast Internet does one find the website for a local dentist? Or for the Centers for Disease Control? Or for a reliable manufacturer of fiberglass carnival rides? Without a search engine like Google, such a search would be like trying to find a specific fish in an ocean full of fish. But instead of allowing the sheer volume of information—and the startling rate at which it increases—to overwhelm users, Google has as its mission "to organize the world's information and make it universally accessible and useful." This mission, however, is not original with Google. Libraries had a similar mission long before Larry Page and Sergey Brin founded the company in 1998. The similarity in mission is at least part of the reason Google and some libraries have formed a natural partnership in Google Books. The ramifications of such a partnership and all the information it will generate and organize are staggering. What is all this information—whether found in a library or through a search engine—being used for? Google and libraries leave that answer entirely up to the user.

Unlike an information gathering entity, God provides specific guidance for how to use information. All information in the world should be used for one ultimate end—God's glory—and for one subordinate end—man's good. Libraries and search engines are organizational tools that can help Christians find and then use information for God's purposes.

The second question to answer is this: How are the materials themselves arranged? Finding the fiction or nonfiction section is not enough; you also need to find the specific item that you want. Knowing how the library classifies its materials will save you valuable time as you search for the resources you need. Follow the general principles explained in this chapter. Then look for posted explanations or ask a library staff member if you need further assistance.

Fiction

Parts of a Book pp. 410–11

Fiction books are arranged on the shelf alphabetically according to the authors' last names. If two authors share the same last name, their novels are arranged alphabetically by their first names. If an author has written more than one novel, his books are arranged alphabetically by title, ignoring any initial articles.

No Vacation for Maigret by Georges Simenon
The Manor by Isaac Bashevis Singer
Joy in the Morning by Betty Smith
A Tree Grows in Brooklyn by Betty Smith
The Hundred and One Dalmatians by Dodie Smith

Specialized fiction books might be shelved separately from general fiction. Books in these genres usually carry an extra label that indicates the section to which they belong, such as *MYS* for mystery fiction. Short story collections may be shelved either alphabetically with the novels, in a special section of fiction shelves just for short stories, or in the nonfiction section with other books about literature.

Nonfiction

Nonfiction books are arranged by topic. Most libraries use one of two common classification systems to arrange nonfiction books: the Dewey decimal system and the Library of Congress system. Each book carries a label with the book's **call number**, which represents the subject category to which the book has been assigned. The label might also include a **Cutter number**, which represents the author of the book and may include one or more letters of the author's name or perhaps one or more letters of the title.

Dewey Decimal System

The **Dewey decimal system** is based on units of ten. A three-digit number signifies three levels of division: main category, subcategory, and a further subcategory. Decimal numbers after the three-digit number represent further division into even more specific categories.

Number	Category	Examples
000–099	Computer science, information and general works	encyclopedias, general reference works, computing, journalism
100–199	Philosophy and psychology	metaphysics, logic, ethics
200–299	Religion	Bible, theology, church history
300–399	Social sciences	political science, communications, folklore
400–499	Language	grammar, linguistics
500–599	Science	physics, paleontology, zoology
600–699	Technology	agriculture, chemical engineering, manufacturing

CONTINUED

If necessary, remind students that "initial articles" refers to *A*, *An*, or *The* at the beginning of a title.

ESL Check that your ESL students are familiar with English alphabetical order. If they are not, help them memorize the English alphabet in order and the basic rules of alphabetizing.

Additional Information

Melvil Dewey, born Melville Louis Kossuth Dewey on December 10, 1851, in Adams Center, New York, could be called the Father of Library Science. While a student at Amherst College, Dewey developed a system of classifying books using numbers and decimals. He published a book on his system in 1876, the same year in which he helped found the American Library Association. Dewey was the head librarian at Columbia College (Columbia University) from 1883 to 1888. In 1887, he founded the School for Library Economy to educate librarians. In 1889, he separated his school from Columbia College and moved it to Albany, New York. Today it is known as the New York State Library School. From 1889 to 1906 he served as the director of the New York State Library at Albany, and in 1890 and 1892 he was president of the American Library Association. He died on December 26, 1931, but his influence on the library system is still felt today.

Enrichment

Direct the students' attention to the *special collections* category of library materials. Ask the students a series of questions such as the following: What types of special collections would you like to examine? What special collections have been or are currently offered in our community? Discuss their answers and encourage your students to visit and report on any special collections in your locale.

Teaching Strategy

Discussion

Show your students a call number that represents further category divisions. One example is 822.33 B6233h for the book *Hamlet: Poem Unlimited* by Harold Bloom. (Call numbers may vary from one library to another because each library usually catalogs its own books. However, the call numbers will usually be similar and perhaps identical.)

Enrichment

Direct the students to bring in a variety of their favorite books from the categories of the Dewey decimal system. Consider keeping a list of the books brought in and the categories of the Dewey system that they represent. (This list will help ensure that each category is represented.) Host a book chat in which each student promotes his favorite book. After each presentation, ask the rest of the students to guess in which category of the Dewey decimal system the book belongs.

396 Chapter 15 | Library Skills

700–799	Arts and recreation	sculpture, music, sports, theater
800–899	Literature	novels, short stories, plays, literary essays
900–999	History and geography	travel, biography, genealogy

Most libraries arrange biographies within the 920 section alphabetically by the last names of the subjects. A capital letter *B* may be added to the call number to indicate that the book is a biography or an autobiography. However, some libraries shelve biographies with the appropriate subject area, such as the 780s (music) for a biography of a musician.

Library of Congress System

The **Library of Congress system** uses a combination of letters and numbers. There are twenty-one basic categories, each represented by a letter. These categories can be further subdivided several times. A typical call number usually consists of one or two letters followed by a series of numbers.

A	General works	M	Music and books on music
B	Philosophy, psychology, religion	N	Fine arts
C	Auxiliary sciences of history (such as archaeology, genealogy, biography)	P	Language and literature
D	World history	Q	Science
E	History of the Americas	R	Medicine
F	History of the Americas	S	Agriculture
G	Geography, anthropology, recreation	T	Technology
H	Social sciences	U	Military science
J	Political science	V	Naval science
K	Law	Z	Bibliography, library science, information resources
L	Education		

15.1 PRACTICE *the skill*

Considering the main areas of the library, identify the section in which you would expect to find each item.

1. In which section of the library would you find a novel?

   Books

2. What identifying label would a library use for an encyclopedia?

   R or REF

3. In which library section would you find copies of the *New York Times?*

   Periodicals

4. What identifying label might you find on a biography of Margaret Thatcher?

   NFIC or B

Additional Information

Charles Ammi Cutter, born in Boston, Massachusetts, on March 14, 1837, graduated from Harvard in 1855. In 1856, while he was studying in Harvard Divinity School, he worked as an assistant librarian in Harvard's library. He cataloged the library's books, and from 1861 to 1868, he and the head librarian developed a card catalog of the books for the public to use. From 1868 to 1893, he was the librarian at the Boston Athenaeum, where he compiled a dictionary catalog of all the library's holdings. He standardized the procedure of dictionary cataloging with his book *Rules for a Dictionary Catalog.* He served as president of the American Library Association in 1888 and 1889. During this time, he also developed his book classification system (on which the Library of Congress system is based) by using letters of the author's last name or the book's title. From 1893 until his death in 1903, he was the librarian at Forbes Library in Northampton, Massachusetts.

ONE *on* ONE Instruct your student to compile a variety of his favorite books from his own family collection or from the local public library. Make certain that the books represent each category of the Dewey decimal system. Invite other students to a book chat during which your student presents and promotes books from each category of the Dewey decimal system. Consider sharing the rudiments of the Dewey system with your audience so that they will be better acquainted with the library's method of organization.

Enrichment

Consider adapting the previous enrichment activity to teach the Library of Congress system.

5. A compact disc recording entitled *Gettysburg* would be in what section?

Audio-Visual Materials

6. A large print Bible might have what identifying label?

LP or LT

7. Dr. Seuss's *The Cat in the Hat* would be in what section?

Children

8. In what section of the library would you find a collection of historical records of your city?

Special Collections

9. Some libraries allow patrons to check out works of art. In what section would you find these?

Audio-Visual Materials

10. In what section would you find materials with an indication of "Library Use Only"?

Reference

15.2 PRACTICE *the skill*

Number the following fiction books in the order in which they would appear on a library shelf.

5 1. Milne, A. A. *The Red House Mystery*

3 2. MacInnes, Helen. *Above Suspicion*

1 3. MacDonald, Betty. *Nancy and Plum*

4 4. Milne, A. A. *Now We Are Six*

2 5. MacDonald, George. *The Baronet's Song*

Using the Dewey decimal chart on pages 396–97, identify the number range of the correct category for each item.

400–499 6. *Spanish Made Easy*

900–999 7. *Cayman Islands: A Visitor's Guide*

100–199 8. *Applied Psychology*

700–799 9. *101 Best Sports Stories*

200–299 10. *A Study in Systematic Theology*

398 Chapter 15 | Library Skills

Using the Library of Congress chart on page 397, identify the letter of the correct category for each item.

__N__ 11. *Watercolor Painting Techniques*

__R__ 12. *Heart Disease Diagnosis and Therapy: A Practical Approach*

__C__ 13. *Archaeology in Old Testament Lands*

__K__ 14. *A Compliance Guide to the Family Medical Leave Act*

__Q__ 15. *Transit: When Planets Cross the Sun*

Search Tools and Strategies

Knowing how the library materials are arranged on the shelves is important. But knowing how to search the library's holdings to find exactly the right item you need is important too. Use the following search tools and strategies to find the materials that interest you most or address your research topic best.

Gathering Information p. 5

Library Website

Use the **library website** to plan your library visit before you leave home. Most library websites include the library's hours of operation, its branch locations, its policies, announcements of special activities, information about available resources, and access to the library's online catalog. Patrons can use this access to search the catalog for the materials they need and to check on the availability of those materials. Some online catalogs also allow patrons to reserve or renew library materials, to request materials from interlibrary loan, or to contact the library staff by e-mail for further help or for answers to reference questions.

Library Stacks

Browsing the library stacks—the shelves of circulating materials—is an often-overlooked strategy that may lead you to something that you would never have thought to search for otherwise. Start by using the catalog to find a book about your topic and then browse the shelf where it is located to find additional helpful books. Or simply check the classification table that your library uses and then find the shelves labeled with the number or letter that signals your topic.

tip

Should you ever judge a book by its cover? Sometimes the condition of a book's cover can be a clue that the book is old, perhaps containing out-of-date information. Check the copyright page to find out when a book was first published.

Library Catalog

The library's catalog is a versatile search tool with information about each item that the library owns. Most libraries have online catalogs, sometimes called OPAC (online public access catalog). An **online catalog** allows library patrons to search electronic records that list information about all the library materials. Each electronic record includes the title, the author, the call number, and publication information for that item. Some records also include a summary of the item's contents and a description of the item's physical characteristics, such as the number of pages that the book contains. Most online catalogs also report the status of each item: available, reserved for another patron, or already checked out (and when the book is due to be returned).

Refer to *The Writer's Toolbox* for a sample online catalog entry.

Teaching Strategy

Discussion

Display the website for your local library. Discuss the advantages of using the website information to plan a trip to the library.

Teaching Strategy

Demonstration

Display an online library catalog. Choose your own search criteria and demonstrate how to use the catalog to find the author, title, call number, and publication information for a specific work. If the online catalog shows the status, point out this information as well. Ask the students for the names of authors, book titles, and subject matter for additional practice searches.

Library Skills | Chapter 15 399

Although online catalogs differ somewhat, they generally allow the patron to search the catalog by typing in whatever search criteria the patron has. You can search by author's name, by title, by subject matter, and sometimes by call number or kind of material. The catalog will then display a list of records that match the criteria you typed into it. In addition, some catalogs will allow you to sort the results according to selected criteria (such as publication date or author's name) or to view more detailed information about a particular item by selecting that item from the list.

Some smaller libraries still use card catalogs instead of online catalogs. A **card catalog** is a file of alphabetized cards housed in a cabinet with small drawers. Each item in the library's collection is usually represented by at least three cards: an author card, a title card, and a subject card. Each type of card lists all the basic information for a particular item (author, title, publication information, and call number), but the order of information differs. The author card lists the author's name on the top line, the title card displays the title of the work at the top, and the top line of the subject card shows the subject classification for that item.

Specialized Indexes

The library catalog usually lists only the books, periodicals, and other materials that a library has available but not the various chapters, articles, or stories in those resources. To find a specific article or several articles on a specific topic, use an index or a bibliography. Many of these tools are available in both printed and electronic formats. Consult a librarian for more information about the particular resources available at your library.

Periodical Indexes

Consult a **periodical index** to find a specific article from a newspaper, a magazine, or a professional journal. The most popular periodical index is the ***Readers' Guide to Periodical Literature***, which lists articles from over two hundred magazines by subject and by author. The index is updated regularly throughout the year. Soon after publication, articles are listed in one of the paperback volumes issued during the year. At the end of each year, these volumes are combined and reissued in a single large volume. An online version of the *Readers' Guide* is also available.

To find an article about a particular subject, look up a keyword for your topic. Directly under the subject heading, you may find "see also" entries that suggest related subject headings. The article entries are listed next, sometimes grouped under subheadings. (Some articles may be listed under more than one subheading.) Each individual entry includes the article's subject, its title, its author, the magazine in which it appears, the volume number or date of the magazine, and the page numbers of the article. If the article has illustrations, the entry will include that information too. The listings use several abbreviations explained in the front of each volume.

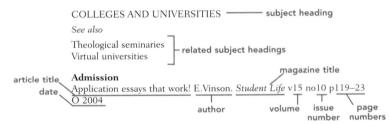

COLLEGES AND UNIVERSITIES — **subject heading**

See also

Theological seminaries
Virtual universities — **related subject headings**

Admission
Application essays that work! E.Vinson. *Student Life* v15 no10 p119–23
O 2004

(labels: **article title**, **date**, **author**, **magazine title**, **volume**, **issue number**, **page numbers**)

400 Chapter 15 | Library Skills

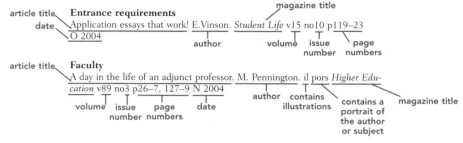

Entrance requirements
Application essays that work! E.Vinson. *Student Life* v15 no10 p119–23
O 2004

article title; date; author; magazine title; volume; issue number; page numbers

Faculty
A day in the life of an adjunct professor. M. Pennington. il pors *Higher Education* v89 no3 p26–7, 127–9 N 2004

article title; volume; issue number; page numbers; date; author; contains illustrations; contains a portrait of the author or subject; magazine title

The ***New York Times Index***, which is available in both print and electronic versions, lists articles that have appeared in that newspaper only. However, by helping you discover the dates of newsworthy events, it can assist your search for information in back issues of other newspapers as well. Some local newspapers also publish indexes, and many newspapers offer searchable archives on their websites.

Consult a **subject index** if you need to find up-to-date scholarly information about your topic. A subject index is more selective than a general periodical index; it usually focuses on detailed articles from scholarly journals. Examples include the *Social Sciences Index* and the *Humanities Index*.

Libraries today carry many electronic databases to index and search encyclopedias, newspapers, periodicals, and books, often giving full texts of newspapers and periodicals. Because these databases select information from reliable sources, they may contain more valuable information than an unknown source accessed through the Internet.

Literary Indexes

Consult a **literary index** to find a particular short work (such as a poem or short story) included in an anthology. A literary index is more useful than the library catalog because the catalog entry for an anthology will often list only partial contents or none at all. A literary index allows you to look up the short work itself for a list of the collections in which it appears. *Granger's Index to Poetry* (also known as *Columbia Granger's World of Poetry* in its electronic format) is especially helpful because it allows you to look up a poem by its title, its author, or its first line. Other useful literary indexes include *Short Story Index, Play Index,* and *Essay and General Literature Index.*

Bibliographies

A valuable source of information that researchers sometimes overlook is a **bibliography**. A bibliography section in the back of a book about your topic can be helpful because it will point you to other sources of information about your subject. Even more helpful may be a book-length bibliography. Many of these longer works (usually compiled by scholars who specialize in the field covered by the bibliography) include annotations for each source listed. The annotation usually includes a summary of the work and a comment on its usefulness or accuracy. After you identify the sources that look most promising, check the library catalog to see which of them are available from your library. If a particular book or article is not available, you may be able to request it through interlibrary loan.

Parts of a Book
pp. 410–11

TEACHING STRATEGY

Reinforcement

After teaching the information about Search Tools and Strategies, arrange a tour of the local library. After the tour, perhaps give your students time to complete Use the Skill 15.3, Use the Skill 15.4, and Use the Skill 15.5 (pp. 402–3).

Since students will need library reference tools to complete Use the Skill 15.7 (pp. 406–7), consider incorporating the Reference Works section (pp. 403–5) into the library field trip

15.3 USE *the skill*

Use the library's catalog to find at least five books and five nonprint items (audio-visual or electronic format) about a topic of your choice. List the title, author, and call number for each item. *(Answers will vary.)*

1. ______________________________
2. ______________________________
3. ______________________________
4. ______________________________
5. ______________________________
6. ______________________________
7. ______________________________
8. ______________________________
9. ______________________________
10. ______________________________

15.4 USE *the skill*

Use the *Readers' Guide to Periodical Literature* to find five articles about a topic of your choice. List the title, author, periodical, and date for each article. *(Answers will vary.)*

1. ______________________________
2. ______________________________
3. ______________________________
4. ______________________________
5. ______________________________

Use the *New York Times Index* or another newspaper index to find five articles about a topic of your choice. List the title, author, newspaper, and date for each article. *(Answers will vary.)*

6. ______________________________
7. ______________________________
8. ______________________________
9. ______________________________
10. ______________________________

402 Chapter 15 | Library Skills

15.5 USE *the skill*

Use an appropriate literary index to answer each question.

1. From what short story is this opening line: "Let us hurry to the walls"?

   "Tale of Jerusalem"

2. What is the first line of Percy B. Shelley's "Ozymandias"?

   "I met a traveler from an antique land"

3. From what play is "Neither a borrower nor a lender be"? Who is the author?

   Hamlet, *William Shakespeare*

4. "Jabberwocky" by Lewis Carroll is part of what larger work?

   Through the Looking Glass and What Alice Found There

5. Who wrote the short story "The Business Man"?

   Edgar Allan Poe

Thinking Biblically

Reference works attempt to be objective, reporting the facts without mixing in opinions. Encyclopedia editors gather experts who are known for their careful work on any given historical, scientific, linguistic, mathematical, or other topic. Even the online community behind Wikipedia aims at what they call NPOV, a neutral point of view. Since many writers—from journalists to authors of pulp fiction—can be deeply and unfairly biased, any effort at evenhanded objectivity is commendable. But Christians must recognize that no one is neutral in the ultimate sense. All truth and all good belong on one side. All lies and all evil belong on the other. Each man retains some good because he is made in God's image; evil nonetheless touches every part of man because of Adam's Fall. The "facts" of a case are always interpreted through a person's worldview; no one is truly neutral. Our goal ought to be to seek GPOV—God's point of view.

Reference Works

General reference works provide an overview of the topics they discuss—and perhaps some detailed information as well—making them excellent sources for someone beginning to research a topic. In addition to the traditional printed reference books, some works are available in microform (such as microfilm or microfiche) or in an electronic format (such as a CD-ROM or an online website). The electronic version makes searching for information fast and easy; some even allow you to print entire articles. Check with a librarian to find out what reference works are available in your library.

Almanacs and Yearbooks

An **almanac** is a yearly publication that includes tables of weights and measures, lists of sports statistics, names of award winners, information about government agencies and programs, summaries of recent events, and other facts. You can find the information you need by looking in the index of the almanac, which may appear at the front of the book like a table of contents.

A **yearbook** is also published annually. It gives current information, such as statistics and events, about a specific subject. Examples include *American Law Yearbook* and *The Shakespearean International Yearbook.*

Atlases and Gazetteers

An **atlas** is a book of collected maps. Most atlases also contain information about weather, geography, population, and other statistics. The index lists the page number for each map in the collection. A **gazetteer** is an index of place names. Some gazetteers include additional information, such as elevation or population, for each place listed.

Thinking Biblically

Search for "NPOV [or neutral point of view] Wikipedia" with your class and explore what you find. (Or give the following questions as a brief assignment in or outside of class.) What issues are being raised on the NPOV Noticeboard? What kinds of issues and topics seem to appear most frequently in NPOV discussions at Wikipedia? Why? Depending on what day your students undertake this exercise, they may find that religion tends to appear often. What seems objective and unbiased to a member of one religion can seem like blasphemy to another.

Refer to *The Writer's Toolbox* for dictionary information and a sample dictionary entry.

Bible Commentaries and Concordances

A **Bible commentary** is a verse-by-verse or section-by-section explanation of Scripture. Some commentaries cover individual books of the Bible; longer works cover the entire Bible.

A **Bible concordance** is an alphabetical index to the words of the Bible, helpful for locating a passage and sometimes for studying a subject through the Bible. Some concordances include the Hebrew or Greek word from which the English word was translated. When you can remember only part of a verse, look up an important word from the verse in the alphabetical list. If the particular passage you want is not listed, try another keyword. Not all keywords or passages will appear in every concordance.

Biographical Sources

Spelling p. 426

Hyphens pp. 342–43

Capitalization pp. 270–86

History of the English Language p. 407

A number of sources provide concise biographical information about prominent people. (For more detailed information, check a book-length biography.) To research someone living today (or just recently deceased), check a current **biographical dictionary**, such as *Current Biography, Contemporary Authors,* or the various *Who's Who* publications. To find information about someone who is no longer living, check an older edition of these works or a source such as the *American National Biography* or the British *Oxford Dictionary of National Biography.* Most of these sources are arranged alphabetically by the subjects' last names; some of the multivolume works may be arranged alphabetically within chronologically arranged sections. Check the index to find the pages that discuss the person you are researching. The index for a multivolume work might be a separate volume.

Dictionaries

Dictionaries contain a wealth of helpful information about words and languages. A typical dictionary entry includes the word's correct spelling (and any acceptable variant spellings), pronunciation, part of speech, inflected forms, definitions, and etymology. Some entries also include labels or notes that indicate proper usage.

A large **unabridged dictionary** contains several hundred thousand words. An abridged dictionary, or **desk dictionary**, is much shorter, but even it contains thousands of words, usually all the words we use on a regular basis. **Special-purpose dictionaries** include Bible dictionaries, dictionaries of synonyms, foreign language dictionaries, dictionaries of English as a second language ("ESL" dictionaries), and dictionaries of subjects like sports, the sciences, and professions such as medicine and law.

ESL

If English is not your first language, you would benefit from having and using an ESL dictionary. In an ESL dictionary, the definitions are easier to understand, and every word meaning has a sample sentence so that you can see the word in use. An ESL dictionary also gives more grammatical information to help you use words correctly. (Ask your teacher to help you understand the features of your ESL dictionary, especially by going through the introductory pages with you.)

Encyclopedias

Encyclopedias contain articles that give brief introductions to many subjects. Electronic versions usually offer keyword-searching options. Printed encyclopedias usually consist of several volumes, each labeled with one or more letters and a numeral. The articles are arranged alphabetically. Guide words at the top of the page

ESL STRATEGY

Assist your ESL students by having at least one ESL dictionary on hand for classroom use. (Order online or from local booksellers.) The *Longman Dictionary of American English*, Fourth Edition, is the most complete, and it includes a number of pictorial pages in color. The *American Heritage ESL Dictionary* is smaller and more convenient for frequent use. The latter is also a good one for the student to own and carry with him. Use the introductory pages to help the students understand the most helpful features of the dictionary, especially those that meet their own needs or relate to what the class is studying.

ESL STRATEGY

To help your ESL students learn about the types of ESL dictionaries available, distribute ESL Help 15 (Teacher's Toolkit). Using the worksheet as a guide, discuss each type of dictionary along with its advantages and disadvantages. Encourage the ESL students to share what types of dictionaries they have found most helpful.

404 Chapter 15 | Library Skills

tell you the topic of the first article on that page. Information on some subjects may be included in several different articles. The index lists all the pages that contain information on a particular subject. Some encyclopedias have an index in each volume; others have a separate volume (usually the last volume) that is the index for the entire set. Many encyclopedia articles list cross-references to other related articles under a heading such as "See also."

Literary Sources

A variety of sources are available to those who are researching literary topics. In-depth research requires more specific information, but these sources can provide an introduction or an overview to those who need only basic information. Both *The Oxford Companion to English Literature* and *The Oxford Companion to American Literature* contain short articles about authors, plots, characters, and related subjects. The *Cyclopedia of Literary Characters* contains brief "biographical" descriptions of characters from famous literary works. *Book Review Index* provides bibliographic entries and excerpts of book reviews that appeared in newspapers, magazines, and journals. A quotation index, such as *Bartlett's Familiar Quotations* or *Columbia World of Quotations,* allows you to find a famous quotation by looking up its author, a keyword, or the topic. Most quotation indexes also list each quotation's source and date.

Thesauruses

Useful with a dictionary is a **thesaurus**, a treasury of synonyms and antonyms. Some thesauruses list the main words alphabetically, and others group all words by meaning, directing you to the meaning groups from a detailed index in the back. In either case, you choose a synonym (or antonym) from the words you find listed. A dictionary and a thesaurus are often used together—the thesaurus to help you think of a word and the dictionary to confirm that the word is in fact the one you need.

ESL ESL students may assume that synonyms have exactly the same meaning. Explain that synonyms normally have different shades of meaning; certain words often have emotional connotations. Encourage all students, especially ESL students, to check the dictionary for the definitions of unfamiliar words.

15.6 PRACTICE *the skill*

Identify the reference tool that would be most useful for finding the answer to each question.

1. What is the population of Cheyenne, Wyoming?

   atlas or gazetteer

2. What was the first published work of the American novelist Sarah Orne Jewett?

   American National Biography

3. Describe the character Mr. Bounderby in Charles Dickens's *Hard Times.*

   Cyclopedia of Literary Characters

4. What did the critics say about Peggy Noonan's book *When Character Was King: A Story of Ronald Reagan*, published in November of 2001?

   Book Review Index

5. Who wrote, "No stile [*sic*] of writing is so delightful as that which is all pith, which never omits a necessary word, nor uses an unnecessary one"?

   Bartlett's Familiar Quotations *or* Columbia World of Quotations

Teaching Strategy

Participation

Materials

- A thesaurus for each group of students
- A dictionary for each group of students
- Access to an online dictionary and thesaurus

Divide the class into groups. Display the following sentences, underlining the appropriate words: *The haughty, young accountant thought himself to be wiser and more proficient than all his colleagues.* Instruct each group to rewrite the sentence, replacing each underlined word with an appropriate synonym from the thesaurus. Remind the students that synonyms often possess different shades of meaning. The students should select synonyms as close as possible to the original word's meaning in the sentence. Allow students to use a dictionary to look up the meanings of unfamiliar synonyms.

ONE *on* ONE Instruct your student to rewrite the sentence, replacing each underlined word with an appropriate synonym from the thesaurus. Allow him to use a dictionary to look up meanings of unfamiliar synonyms.

Evaluation

After students have finished the previous activity, ask one student from each group to read the new sentence aloud. Discuss each rewritten sentence and determine whether the synonyms maintain the sentence's

6. How do electric motors work?

encyclopedia

7. Where would I find a section-by-section explanation of the Bible's book of Job?

commentary

8. Who won the Nobel Peace Prize in the year in which you were born?

almanac

9. Did the International Langland Society hold any sessions in your state last year?

yearbook

10. Where exactly is Londonderry in England?

atlas

Students will need library reference tools to complete Use the Skill 15.7. Consult the Teaching Strategy Reinforcement on page 401

15.7 USE *the skill*

Using standard reference tools, answer the following questions.

1. What is the population of Kingston, Jamaica?

494,000 (atlas or gazetteer)

2. What types of energy sources does Uruguay possess?

Uruguay does not have any natural fuel resources. Instead, it must bring in fuel from other countries. It also harnesses hydroelectric power from the Uruguay River and Río Negro. (encyclopedia)

3. When was the prophecy of Ezekiel 31 pronounced in relation to the fall of Jerusalem?

approximately two months before (Bible commentary)

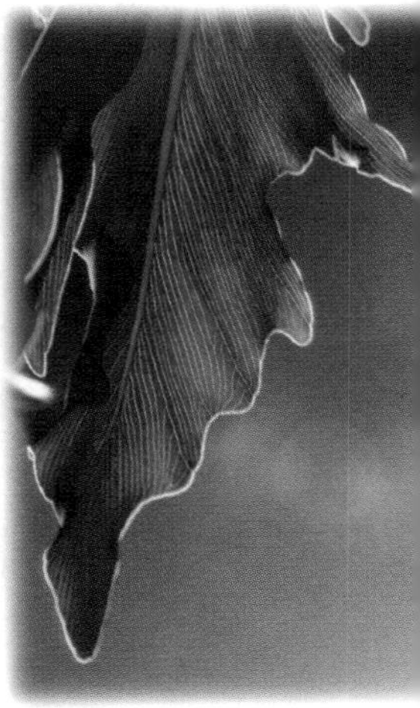

4. List two Old Testament references for uses of the word *leaf.*

Genesis 8:11; Leviticus 26:36; etc. (Bible concordance)

5. Who coined the phrase "the great silent majority"?

Richard M. Nixon (quotation index)

6. What is the area code in Coventry, Connecticut?

860 (almanac)

7. How would one pronounce and define the word *outré?*

pronounced (oo tray); means highly unconventional; eccentric or bizarre (dictionary)

original meaning. Based upon the students' ability to use appropriate synonyms, either give remedial instruction or continue with the lesson.

Teaching Strategy

Participation

Using Bulletin Board 15 (Teacher's Toolkit), make a list of attention-grabbing questions from a variety of subjects. Ask the students to name the types of sources that they would need to consult in order to find the answers. Encourage the students to find the answers to several questions that interest them.

8. What is the elevation of Great Salt Lake in Utah?

4,200 feet above sea level (atlas or gazetteer)

9. In what year did Queen Victoria of England marry Prince Albert, and how many children did they have?

1840; nine (biographical dictionary or encyclopedia)

10. What novel contains a character named Peggotty?

David Copperfield *by Charles Dickens* (Cyclopedia of Literary Characters)

HISTORY OF THE ENGLISH LANGUAGE

Great Vowel Shift

The American English that you speak today developed from Early Modern English, the language of Queen Elizabeth I, of William Shakespeare, and of the King James Version of the Bible. Late in the Middle English period (in the 1400s), a phenomenon known as the Great Vowel Shift (GVS) began to alter greatly the vowel system of English. Because the GVS was a gradual, multistep process, scholars vary on the exact dates of the shift, but most agree that the changes occurred mainly in the fifteenth and sixteenth centuries.

This "shift" in vowels refers to the area of the mouth where English vowels are articulated. Today when you say the vowel sound of the word *feet* (the so-called long /ē/ sound), your tongue is high and forward in your mouth. Now say *foam* (long /ō/ sound): your tongue lowers and moves ("shifts") to the back of your mouth. In Old and Middle English, however, the sounds indicated by the same spellings were somewhat different. For example, the word *feet* probably sounded much more like the long /ā/ of today's *fate*. Therefore, the GVS refers to changes in the long vowels of English. It affected only the vowels that were literally long (held out longer). In the GVS most long vowels were raised in the mouth, one was also fronted, and some became diphthongs. We still call these our "long vowels," even though the term does not apply literally today.

We can thank the GVS for many of the complexities of and exceptions to our English spelling and pronunciation. Have you ever wondered why words spelled with *ea* can be pronounced with a long /ē/ *(glean, leaf, speak)* or a long /a/ *(break, great, steak)*? Blame the Great Vowel Shift!

TEACHING STRATEGY

Participation

Tell students to alternate pronouncing the long /ē/ and long /ō/ sounds in order to understand the difference in mouth and tongue movement for each vowel.

History of the English Language | Chapter 15 407

STUDY SKILLS

Lesson Support

Teacher's Toolkit
Bulletin Board 16

Teaching Strategy

Analysis and Introduction

Ask the students what they remember learning in science class last year and what they remember from their seventh- or eighth-grade science class. *(Answers will vary but will probably include only key concepts, not specific details.)* Then ask the students why studying science each year is important even if they cannot remember all the details of what they studied. *(Answers will vary.)* Point out that all the subjects they study give them a broad range of knowledge and equip them to confront the issues of life with understanding. Emphasize that the process of learning is sometimes more important than the details they learn for tests.

Success in both personal and academic achievements depends upon the ability to set and accomplish goals. Most students find it easy to set goals, but many find it very difficult to accomplish the goals they have set. How many times have you set a goal and within a very short time failed in your efforts to reach that goal? Perhaps you set a personal goal to read your Bible each day and have a specific prayer time. For the first few days, you did well. But then you found that one day you were too involved in other activities to read your Bible and pray. You failed to accomplish the goal, and your first inclination might have been to give up rather than to put the single failure behind you and continue to pursue your goal.

The same may be true for you in academics. You may have tried to do all of your homework, to read all of the outside reading, or to make a passing grade on a test. However, music lessons, basketball practice, work at a fast-food eatery, or myriad other activities took the time you needed for schoolwork. How can you improve this situation? You must learn to set priorities, use time wisely, and develop helpful study skills.

Developing Good Study Skills

Determine a time and place to study. Choose a specific time to study when you plan your daily schedule. Yes, even the weekend should include planned study time. Before you begin studying, pray: ask the Lord for guidance and help for your study time. You may find that fifteen-minute periods of concentrated study may be more effective than a long period of concentrated effort. In addition to a specific time, determine a specific place to study. Your study area should be quiet, well lighted, and free of distractions such as a telephone or television. A computer or tablet can be a highly useful tool for studying; however, limit your use of these devices to academic purposes during your study time. Left unchecked, they too can become distractions.

Organize your study materials. Whether in a notebook or in computer folders as digital files, organized study materials are essential. To organize a multi-subject notebook, designate one division for each subject and use a pocket page to store assignments and related class work. To organize digital files, name them by assignment and sort them into folders named for each subject. In addition to your organized notebook (or computer or tablet), be sure to have other necessary materials, including textbooks, other resource books, and a daily planning calendar (or planning software).

Assess the assignments. Record daily homework assignments in a specific place in your notebook, in a specific assignment notebook, or on planning software. As you evaluate the assignments, designate them as long-term (taking more than a day) or short-term (taking a day or less) and mark them by the day, the week, or the month. Using a calendar to record dates for tests and assignments will give you an overview of times when you will be particularly busy.

SCRIPTURAL APPLICATION

Ask volunteers to read the following Proverbs: 10:4–5; 12:24, 27; 13:4; 21:5; and 22:29. Point out that God would not offer the rewards of diligence in Proverbs 22:29 (and the other passages) unless He meant for them to be motivators. In other words, aspiring to stand before kings is a good thing. This kind of achievement is not the only appropriate motivation for working diligently to gain a skill, but it is one. And it is one given to us by God. God's people can and do gain positions of influence as a result of their writing and other skills.

TEACHING STRATEGY

Introduction

Construct Bulletin Board 16 (Teacher's Toolkit). Direct the students' attention to the bulletin board; then use the "Study Plan" list to introduce a discussion of good study skills.

TEACHING STRATEGY

Participation

Instruct the students to evaluate their own study habits according to the principles in the Developing Good Study Skills section. Encourage them to devise a plan to improve their study habits. Consider asking the students to write a paragraph describing both a weak study habit and a method by which a person can improve his studying.

Thinking Biblically

Remind students that the mature athlete or musician, no matter how driven, takes time to rest from practice. He realizes that not taking time to rest will likely lead to fatigue or even injury. In fact, his times of rest enable him—give him the energy he needs—to make his practice more profitable. Likewise, the mature student must learn to balance study and recreation. Both are necessary to maintaining vitality in one's academic life. Practicing biblical self-control does not mean hours upon hours of endless studying; on the contrary, it means making time for both study and rest.

Thinking Biblically

Developing good study skills requires self-control—a trait that none of us possesses naturally. Naturally, we seek to please ourselves, to avoid work for less demanding activities. In fact, self-control, as the Scriptures remind us, is one of the fruits of the Spirit, the result of a life yielded to Christ (Gal. 5:22–23). In other words, the Holy Spirit is able to empower us to overcome our selfish desires. But the change from selfish to self-controlled does not happen instantly. As the apostle Paul describes, obtaining self-control requires consistent practice (1 Cor. 9:24–27).

Take notes. As you read your assignments, take notes on the material, even if you do not think you will use the notes. Putting ideas that you have read into your own words will help you retain the ideas. Be alert to phrases such as *most important, for example,* and *to review.* Develop a personal abbreviation list for frequently used words or ideas; use these abbreviations to save time as you take notes. At this point, you need to review the notes that you took in class, organize them according to main ideas, and place them in the specific subject area in your notebook or in the appropriate folders on your computer.

Develop study aids. Using vocabulary cards can help you learn vocabulary words and their definitions more quickly. Using cards for Bible verse location and memorization is also helpful. For each subject area, use a different-colored card.

Proofread your work. For written assignments that you will be submitting for a class, allow yourself time to proofread and to review your work several times. As you proofread, be alert to grammatical errors, misspelled words, and inaccurate documentation.

Take personal responsibility for studying. You must remember that no one else can study or take tests for you. It is your responsibility to complete the work independently and punctually. Developing good study habits and using study helps can aid you in reaching your goals. Always precede your study time, your writing endeavors, and your test-taking experiences with prayer for clarity of thought and for God's presence with you.

Using the Parts of a Book

Textbooks and other nonfiction books include information that can help you locate and use information in the book. The chart below gives a summary of features found in a book.

Part of Book	Useful Information
Title Page	Title of book Name of author or editor Name of publisher Place of publication *Look here when you are creating a bibliography.*
Copyright Page	Year of publication Name of copyright holder *A copyright is the legal right to a book—no one can reprint any part of the book without permission from the copyright owner.*
Table of Contents	Main topics Organization of topics *Unit divisions appear in numerical order with page numbers.*
Acknowledgments	Names of people the author or editor wishes to thank for their assistance or contribution
List of Illustrations	Location and sequence of pictures
Introduction or Preface	Purpose of the book or important background information

CONTINUED

Teaching Strategy

Motivation

Encourage the students to complete their work early enough to allow time for thorough proofreading. Consider setting two due dates for one or two writing assignments. Require the students to turn in a rough draft by the first date and then allow them to proofread and to make any necessary corrections before the second date. Then challenge each student to follow your example for future assignments by setting himself a preliminary due date for his rough draft and taking the time to proofread and to correct before the official due date for the final draft. Remind the students that they are responsible to complete their assignments on time.

Text	The main part of the book, usually divided into units or chapters
Bibliography	List of sources that the author used in writing or that would provide additional information about the subject
Appendix	Section of additional information related to the text (may include charts, diagrams, long lists, and notes of explanation)
Glossary	Type of appendix: definitions of important vocabulary in the text
Index	Alphabetical list of key words and phrases in the text with page numbers

16.1 PRACTICE *the skill*

Write the name of the book section that would provide the information necessary to answer each question. (Answers may be used more than once.)

index or table of contents 1. Does this book discuss a certain issue or idea?

list of illustrations 2. On what page does a particular photograph appear?

bibliography 3. Has a certain book been used as a reference in this book?

title page 4. Where was this book published?

copyright page 5. When was the book published?

acknowledgments 6. Whom does the author thank?

glossary 7. What does this unfamiliar term mean?

bibliography 8. Where can I find more information about the topic of this book?

table of contents 9. On what page does the third chapter begin?

introduction or preface 10. What is the author's purpose for this book?

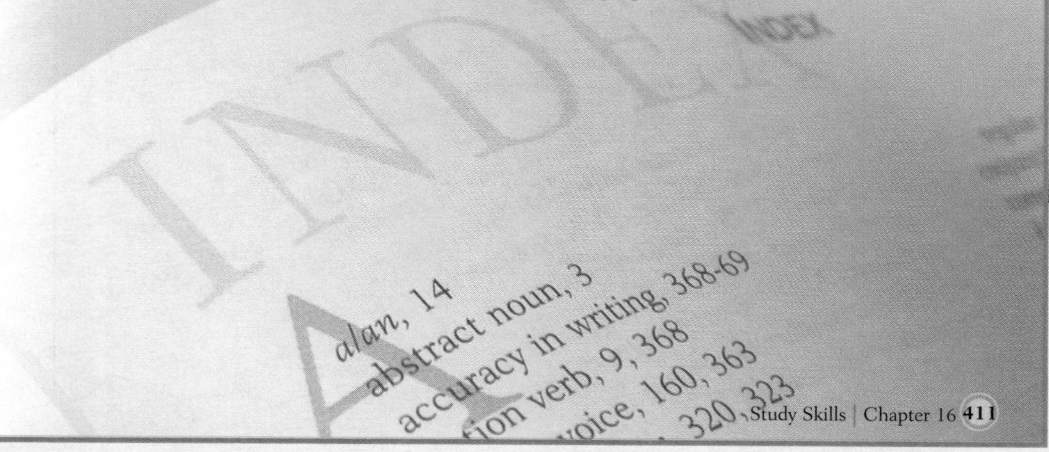

16.2 REVIEW *the skill*

Use the sample table of contents and index pages from *CHEMISTRY*, Third Edition, by Brad R. Batdorf and Rachel Santopietro (BJU Press, 2009) to answer each of these questions.

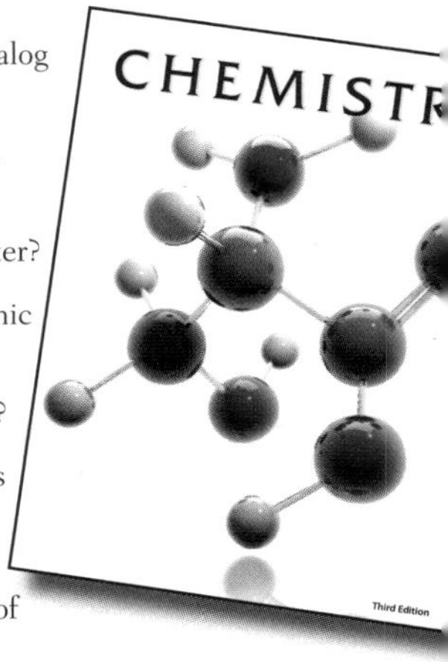

Chapter 3 1. In which chapter could you learn about analog instruments?

129, 484 2. On what pages would you find information about Jons Jakob Berzelius?

Chapter 2 3. Which chapter discusses the states of matter?

yes 4. Would you find information about the atomic theory in Chapter 4?

ix 5. On which page does the introduction start?

no 6. Is Chapter 6 the only chapter that includes information about the Apollo Space program?

143 7. On what page does the discussion of types of chemical bonds begin?

397 8. On which page would you learn about the properties of acid?

2B Energy and Matter 9. In which chapter section would you first find out about absolute zero?

Chapter 1 10. In which chapter might you find a definition of chemical studies?

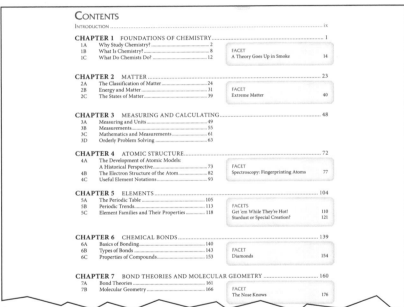

Contents

412 Chapter 16 | Study Skills

Index

Improving Reading Comprehension

As you progress in your academic career, reading will become one of the major contributors to your learning. A good reader takes time nearly every day for recreational reading, such as the newspaper, a trade magazine, or a novel. You will find that recreational reading greatly improves your comprehension, speed, and vocabulary. In the academic realm, the teacher is no longer the primary provider of knowledge. Instead, the student has learned to "dig out" important principles, facts, or truths from the assignments. As you anticipate being a college student, you must realize the importance of improving your reading skills.

Context Clues

Paying attention to the words and sentences that surround an unfamiliar word can help you infer the meaning of that word. The following strategies may help you understand the meaning of an unfamiliar word.

Verbal Context

If the text does not give the meaning of the word, it may use other words from which you can determine the definition.

> Daniel answered in the presence of the king, and said, The secret which the king hath demanded cannot the wise men, the astrologers, the magicians, the *soothsayers,* shew unto the king. (Dan. 2:27)

Although you may not know that *soothsayers* are those who predict the future, you can infer its meaning from surrounding words such as *astrologers.*

Enrichment

Give the students the opportunity to teach useful vocabulary words to their peers. With your prior approval of the word, allow a student to share a new vocabulary word with the other students. Instruct the student to display the word, its etymology, and its definition and then to demonstrate the pronunciation and at least one example of how the word is used in a context. Direct the students to record each new word in their notebooks. Consider incorporating the new vocabulary words into lectures and classroom conversations; repeated exposure to these words may help students to adopt a broader vocabulary.

ONE *on* ONE Give your student the opportunity to broaden his vocabulary. Encourage him to keep a small notebook for recording unfamiliar words he reads or hears. Then conduct a weekly vocabulary minilesson during which your student looks up and writes the definitions of each word, writes a sentence using the word in a proper context, and adds the word to a vocabulary list. Challenge your student to incorporate his new vocabulary words into his everyday writing and speech. Assist your student's efforts by consciously using several of his new vocabulary words in each day's lesson.

An unfamiliar word is often followed immediately by an explanation or a synonym.

> After Daniel interpreted the dream, King Nebuchadnezzar sought to honor Daniel by an *oblation*, the act of offering something to a deity.

From the context you can conclude that an *oblation* was a presentation showing good will to someone who had godlike qualities.

The unfamiliar word in the context may be in a cause-and-effect relationship.

> Because the three Hebrew men would not bow to the golden image, King Nebuchadnezzar became very angry and his *visage* changed toward the men.

When you realize that the king was very angry because the Hebrew men disobeyed his order, you can surmise that *his visage* probably refers to the king's face or appearance.

An unfamiliar word may be compared or contrasted with familiar words.

COMPARISON	The Hebrew men's allegiance to God under King Nebuchadnezzar parallels Daniel's continued *homage* to God under King Darius.
CONTRAST	After learning that Daniel had survived the den of lions unharmed, Darius's *lament* changed to a cry of praise to God.

Were you able to determine that *homage* means a public expression of loyalty and that *lament* is a mournful expression of grief?

ESL

Try all of these strategies and use the ones that are most helpful for you.

- Look at title, chapter, and heading names to discover the topic of the reading.
- Try to read each paragraph or short section without using your dictionary. After reading through the material once, look up any words that keep you from understanding the meaning of the paragraph or short section.
- Do **not** look up in a dictionary every word that you do not know.
- Read a paragraph, write a few words beside it in the margin to summarize it, and keep reading. You can use your marginal words to help you review your reading.
- Do not read everything at once. Read for thirty minutes. Use five minutes to stand up, walk around, or drink some water. Then continue reading for another thirty minutes. Repeat this cycle until you finish your reading.

Grammatical Context

An unfamiliar word may be clarified by the grammatical structure in which it occurs. Look for words that are familiar to you. For example, if a word appears in a series of words, then it probably has something in common with the words in the series.

> Then these men were bound in their coats, their *hosen*, and their hats, and their other garments, and were cast into the midst of the burning fiery furnace. (Dan. 3:21)

Although *hosen* may be an unfamiliar word, you can guess that it must be some article of clothing since it is listed with other articles of clothing.

TEACHING STRATEGY

Induction

Select a passage from a novel that contains several words that the students may not know. Read the passage aloud to the class. Then display several of the difficult words. Read each word again in its context and ask the students to hypothesize definitions for each word. Ask the students what context clues helped them supply their definitions and assist them in fine-tuning their definitions.

Word Parts

Roots, prefixes, and suffixes can help you to determine the meaning of an unfamiliar word. The root is the main part of the word. Common roots appear in many different words. The root *voc* means "to call." You will find this root in many familiar words including *vocal, vocation, vocabulary.* An extension of this root is the word *voice.* An unfamiliar word such as *vocative* becomes easy to understand because you know the meaning of the root word. You can probably guess that *vocative* means "pertaining to or having reference to calling."

g u r w
Dictionaries
p. 404

Prefixes are word parts added to the beginning of a word. The prefix *re-* means "backward or back." To *revoke* means to "call back." Your understanding of both the root word and prefix helps you to determine the meaning of the word. You must remember, however, that some words include more than one prefix. The word *irrevocable* adds an additional prefix to *revoke.* The new prefix means "not," and the new word means "not able to be called back" or "impossible to call back." Using your knowledge of prefix meanings will help you to understand unfamiliar words and to build your working vocabulary.

Suffixes are word parts added to the end of a word. The suffix *-al* means "relating to or characterized by" and is used to form adjectives. The word *vocal* then means "relating to or characterized by calling" or "relating to the voice." The common suffix *-ion* forms nouns; *vocation* then is a person's "calling" or "occupation." *Vocabulary* is the words in a language. By consulting your dictionary, you can trace the etymology of *vocabulary* to the root word *voc.*

g u r w
Adding Suffixes
pp. 429–30

16.3 PRACTICE *the skill*

Write the letter of the word or phrase that most closely matches the meaning of the italicized word. Be prepared to explain what context clues you used.

__B__ 1. The clown entertained the children with feats of *prestidigitation* such as pulling a rabbit from a hat.
A. amusement or entertainment
B. magic or conjuring

__A__ 2. Before the builders can begin the new structure, they must *raze* the abandoned building already on the site.
A. to demolish
B. to renovate

__A__ 3. Troy hurried into the conference room, apparently unaware that his tie was *askew* from the wind outside.
A. crooked
B. flimsy

__A__ 4. That clerk has behaved so badly that his coworkers *ostracize* him, failing even to invite him to eat lunch with them.
A. exclude
B. reject

__B__ 5. Young athletes in training often try to *emulate* successful older athletes.
A. admire
B. imitate

EVALUATION

After students have completed Practice the Skill 16.3, grade the activity in class. Ask volunteers to explain which context clues they used to arrive at their answers. Make certain that all students understand why the correct answer is preferable to the alternative. Based upon the students' performance on this activity, either reteach key concepts or continue with the lesson.

Considering the context of the sentence, write a definition of the italicized word. Be prepared to explain what context clues you used. *(Answers will vary.)*

6. Melanie found the lavishly decorated office very different from the *austere* façade of the municipal building.

   plain or bare

7. The careless student's paper was *replete* with errors.

   full

8. We all admired the *sylvan* setting of the cottage, entirely surrounded by tall trees.

   of or relating to the woods or forest

9. The *stentorian* tones of the speaker, rising above the noise of the crowd, reminded us of a foghorn.

   very loud

10. In his new suit, shirt, and tie, Thomas was the picture of *sartorial* splendor.

   tailored

16.4 REVIEW *the skill*

Use a dictionary to find the meaning of each root, prefix, or suffix. Then write a word that uses the root, prefix, or suffix. *(Answers will vary.)*

1.	de-	*reverse*	*decontaminate*
2.	post-	*after*	*postpone*
3.	anim	*soul, breath*	*animated*
4.	tract	*to draw*	*contract*
5.	in-	*not*	*inconceivable*
6.	-hood	*state of*	*boyhood*
7.	voc	*to call*	*invoke*
8.	arch	*to rule*	*anarchy*
9.	circum-	*around*	*circumvent*
10.	struct	*to build*	*construct*

416 Chapter 16 | Study Skills

Using Memory Techniques

Successful memorization depends upon many factors. One of the most important factors is having confidence in yourself and your ability to memorize. You must realize that the material before you is important, that there is a need for the material, and that you can learn the material.

Read through your notes each day. Regular review will be much more effective than a long study session the night before a test. As you study, make a list of key items you need to remember or mark the most important facts in your notes and review that information daily.

Break down large chunks of information. When studying a large amount of material, try to organize the material into smaller, more manageable units. If you have a long list of items to memorize, separate them into categories and focus on learning one category at a time. If you need to learn facts from maps, charts, or graphs, study only one section at a time, working your way through each section in a regular pattern so that you do not miss any information.

Make flash cards from your notes. Flash cards allow you to quiz yourself or to enlist the help of a family member or friend to quiz you. Write a question on one side of each card and the answer on the other. Note which questions you are unable to answer quickly and then spend extra time studying those flashcards. Digital flashcard programs are also available online.

Create a quiz for yourself as you study. Write down important questions on one sheet of paper and the answers on another. Try to answer the questions a few days later. This strategy will help you know what you need to study more thoroughly.

Use mnemonic [ni-mon´ik] devices to memorize a list. Rhymes, acronyms, and acrostics are convenient ways to remember lists of information. An acronym is a word in which each letter stands for another word. An acrostic is a phrase in which each initial letter stands for a different word or phrase.

Taking Tests

Classroom Tests

Although each test is unique, certain strategies will help you do your best on each test you take. Use these techniques to demonstrate what you have learned.

Arrive early. Be in the classroom and in your seat prior to the beginning of the test. Avoid rushing in at the last minute. Having time to get settled and to arrange your materials for the test will help calm your spirit.

Look over the entire test to determine the number and types of questions. If you are told to write a lengthy essay at the end, you do not want to spend too much time on the first part of the test. Throughout the test, check your watch or a clock to keep track of how much time you have left.

Reinforcement

Encourage students to try each of the Memory Techniques on page 417. As you teach each of the book's chapters, you may want to assign one or two techniques for the students to use. Require the students to give evidence that they implemented specific techniques in their study. Point out that one technique may work well for English class whereas a different technique may work better for history class. Encourage students to be creative in their studying methods and to adapt these techniques to meet their needs.

Scriptural Application

God knows our frame, the psalmist says. He remembers that we are dust (Ps. 103:14). As a result, among many other things God does to aid us, He gives us mnemonic devices. For the Jews, God commanded blue tassels to be placed on their garments as a reminder to keep His other commands (Num. 15:38–39). He also encouraged them to write God's words on their door posts and to talk about them all the time (Deut. 11:18–20). The Jews also had feasts to remind them of God's blessings, preeminently the annual Passover feast. The Christian church has two ordinances that perform a similar function: baptism and the Lord's Supper. In each, a spiritual picture is created by a physical act. In many Protestant churches, a communion table stands in front of the pulpit, bearing the inscription from Jesus' own mouth: "This do in remembrance of me." For people prone to forget, these acts of worship are powerful mnemonics.

Read all directions carefully and listen for any additional instructions from the teacher. You may be tempted to skim the directions and to start right away answering questions, but you can needlessly miss several points by simply failing to follow the exact directions. Don't forget to check the board for additional written instructions. Talk to your teacher if you do not completely understand all of the directions.

Write down from memory any equations, formulas, or rules that you will need. Unless you are allowed to use your textbook or your notes, all of the helps you need to complete the test should be committed to memory. Before you begin answering questions, transfer those helps from your memory to a separate sheet of paper or the margin of the test. Then refer to your jottings as you work through the questions.

Use your time wisely, working through the test in one of three ways:

- **Start at the beginning of the test and keep going.** Answer the questions that you know or that you are reasonably confident about. Mark the questions that you do not know or that you need more time to consider. Then go back to those questions later. Occasionally information in a later part of the test will help you recall other points.
- **Scan the test for the easier questions first and answer them quickly.** Then spend the rest of the time on the difficult questions.
- **Begin by completing the more difficult section of the test.** This strategy is helpful if the difficult questions are worth more credit because it ensures that you will have time to answer those questions before you answer those that will earn you less credit. However, be careful to save enough time to answer the easier questions whose answers you know.

Try to answer every question, even if you have to guess at some.

Think carefully and be selective about what you write. It is better to write a little about what you know than to write a lot about what you do not know.

Allow yourself time to recheck your work. As you review your work, look for any questions that you may have accidentally overlooked. Check for correct spelling and grammar. Careless errors are often identified during this rechecking time.

Write neatly. Correct answers will not count if your teacher cannot read what you have written.

ESL

Your teachers want to help you learn. When you ask your teacher for help, ask specific questions. For example, do not just say, "I don't understand. Can you help me?" You should ask questions like "I do not understand what I must do. Can you explain the directions to me?" or "I do not understand my homework. Can you show me how to do this part?"

Writing Link

Encourage the students to write a short story or dramatic scene on some aspect related to their current studies in literature, history, science, or another discipline. The students' audience may be their classmates, a friend, their parents, or even some acquaintance (such as a store clerk or coworker) that they would like to influence positively. Encourage the students to think critically about the content, to invent characters and narrative that further the content, and to communicate key facts. Emphasize that this writing assignment can not only further one's own study but also teach and minister to others.

Teaching Strategy

Discussion

Some students naturally take tests well. Others clearly struggle to demonstrate their knowledge of the content. Ask the students to share their pretest rituals. Elicit comments concerning the students' morning activities (dress, mindset, last-minute studying, thoughts during the test, etc.). Note the different preparation methods practiced by each student and discuss the effectiveness of each. Encourage students to evaluate their methods and adapt them, if necessary, to be more effective.

Essay Tests

Essays
pp. 19–20

Answering an essay question requires more than simply answering an objective test question. An essay question usually asks you to do more than merely list facts; it gives you an opportunity to demonstrate what you know about the topic and to show connections between ideas. Use these techniques to hone your essay-writing skills.

Read the directions carefully. If you have a list of essay questions to choose from, choose the one you are best prepared to answer.

- **Focus on the main verb in the directions.** Common verbs found in essay questions include *analyze, compare, contrast, discuss, evaluate,* and *explain.* If the question asks you to analyze a situation, merely describing the facts would be insufficient.
- **Notice the important nouns in the question.** If the question asks you to explain how Wyatt and Surrey contributed to the development of the Elizabethan sonnet, you should avoid discussing the sonnets of Shakespeare and Petrarch or the ballads and quatrains of other poets.
- **Understand what format you are to use.** If the directions are unclear, ask the teacher to clarify whether you are to write one well-developed paragraph or a multiparagraph essay, with or without separate introduction and conclusion paragraphs.

On a separate sheet of paper, jot down all the facts you know that are related to the topic. Include names, dates, and important points that you do not want to leave out.

Organize your ideas. Decide which facts are of primary importance and which are subordinate to others. Then group related facts to create a rough outline. To save time, don't write out a formal outline but use arrows and other markings on your idea list instead.

Write a thesis statement. A thesis statement gives the purpose and often indicates the organization of your essay. One useful strategy is to restate the question as a thesis statement.

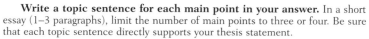

ESSAY QUESTION	Contrast the positions promoted by Lincoln and Douglas in their famous debates.
THESIS	The positions promoted by Abraham Lincoln and Stephen A. Douglas in their famous debates differed in three key respects.

Write a topic sentence for each main point in your answer. In a short essay (1–3 paragraphs), limit the number of main points to three or four. Be sure that each topic sentence directly supports your thesis statement.

Support each topic sentence with specific detail. Provide sufficient proof for each statement but avoid "padding" your essay with interesting but irrelevant information that does not directly support the topic sentence.

Write a conclusion that restates your thesis. A simple rewording of the thesis is usually a sufficient conclusion for a short essay.

Quickly proofread your essay. Correct any factual, grammatical, or mechanical errors and add any necessary clarification. Clearly rewrite any illegible passages.

ESL ESL students will likely profit from the help of a native English speaker in understanding and using proofreading techniques.

Study Skills | Chapter 16 419

Standardized Tests

As you finish high school and prepare for college, you will probably be required to take a standardized test. Since these tests are often different in format from a classroom test, it is important for you to understand the various question formats. Also, be aware that you may not be allowed to write or mark on the test paper but only on an answer sheet.

Reading Comprehension

The reading comprehension section asks you to read a passage and then answer a question or questions about that passage. (If there is just one question, you might read the question first to determine what to look for as you read.)

> After the terrorist attacks of September 11, 2001, U.S. President George W. Bush launched a war on terror. The United States government sent troops to several sensitive locations. Some troops assumed strategic positions in the Persian Gulf. Others found themselves in the mountainous regions of Pakistan and Afghanistan. In the Far East, troops were located in the semideserted island areas.

Example: __**C**__ The main topic of the passage is

A. places in the world.
B. military troops.
C. a global war on terrorism.
D. the president's desire for peace.

Vocabulary

Standardized tests usually contain a vocabulary section. You may be asked to determine the meaning of a word that you do not know. In this case, use the context to help you determine your choice.

Example: __**B**__ United States military troops participate in a number of public operations, but they also execute many **clandestine** operations.

A. daily
B. secretive
C. similar
D. peaceful

Another type of vocabulary question will give a word in a sentence and then ask you to identify another sentence in which the word is used in the same way.

Example: __**D**__ The unusual print on Jessica's scarf is quite striking.

A. The blurred print made the letter difficult to decipher.
B. The investigators were unable to match the suspect's prints to those on the weapon.
C. Keegan has several new prints on display at the art gallery.
D. Does the designer plan to reproduce the original wallpaper print for the restoration project?

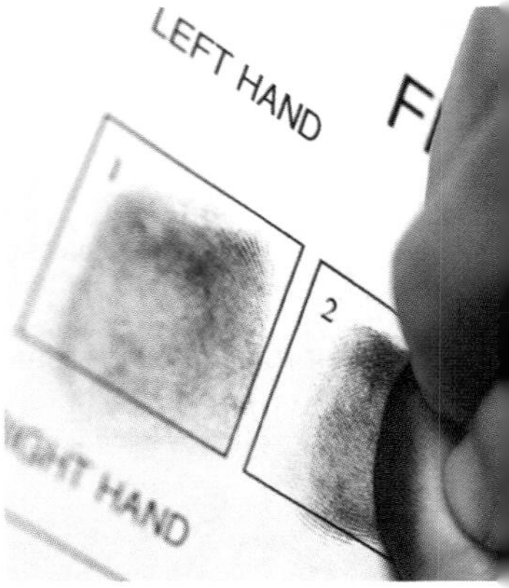

Additional Resources

Further your own knowledge of the standardized tests required for college admittance by researching on the Internet or at the public library. Both the SAT and ACT have official websites that provide detailed information concerning the SAT, ACT, PLAN, and PSAT tests. These sites also provide practice exercises to help students prepare for the tests. Also, most public libraries carry books containing instruction in study methods as well as practice tests. Consider obtaining a few of these books for use in the classroom.

Additional Resources

One way to improve reading, writing, and vocabulary is to study Latin, the basis of the English language. *Latin I* and *Latin II* (BJU Press) offer an inductive approach to learning the language and work well for either independent study or for classroom use. Consider teaching an extracurricular Latin class or encourage your students to study Latin on their own.

Analogy

An analogy is a comparison that shows the similarities or the relationship between two things. Analogy questions ask you to find the relationship between two words by identifying another group of two words that shows the same relationship. The two words in a set are usually separated by a colon that stands for the phrase "is to"; the two sets of words are separated by a double colon that means "as."

Example: **A** artist : brush ::

A. dentist : drill
B. police officer : hat
C. firefighter : fire station
D. commander : flag

Grammar, Usage, and Mechanics

Standardized English tests also include a section on grammar, usage, and mechanics (spelling, capitalization, and punctuation). One type of question will show a sentence with several parts underlined. You are to identify the underlined part that contains an error.

Example: **D** Military personnel (A) were responsible (B)
to organize their equipment (C) in an
orderly fashion. No error (D)

Another type of question will give a sentence with one part underlined. You must choose a replacement part that will make the sentence correct.

Example: **C** The platoon gave lieutenant Johnson's wife a gift for her birthday.

A. lieutenant Johnsons wife
B. Lieutenant Johnsons wife
C. Lieutenant Johnson's wife
D. correct as is

Some tests will divide a sentence into several parts with each part on a separate line. You must choose the line that contains the error in mechanics.

Example: **B**
A. General Thompson invited Tom,
B. Jim, and me, to attend the
C. staff meeting on Friday.
D. no mistakes

Enrichment

Divide the class into groups and ask each group to write several analogy questions. Then direct the groups to trade analogies and to answer the questions.

ONE on ONE Write several analogy questions with your student. Ask another member of the family to answer the questions.

16.5 PRACTICE *the skill*

Reading Comprehension: Read the paragraph and answer the questions that follow it. Write the letter of the best answer.

If you have experienced God's saving grace, you have insight many experienced chemists lack. We cannot properly study chemistry unless we approach it from a Christian perspective. To many people, that statement sounds controversial—even nonsensical. After all, what does Scripture have to do with chemistry? What Bible verses explain the structure of atoms or the nature of chemical bonds?

True, the Bible is not a chemistry textbook. But the Bible confronts humans with a distinct worldview, a perspective from which to see and interpret all of life. Like a corrective lens, the Bible brings into focus every part of the world, including chemistry. As we look at chemistry through the lens of Scripture, we find that the best reasons to study chemistry are biblical ones.

(from *CHEMISTRY*, Third Edition, by Brad R. Batdorf and Rachael Santopietro, BJU Press, 2009)

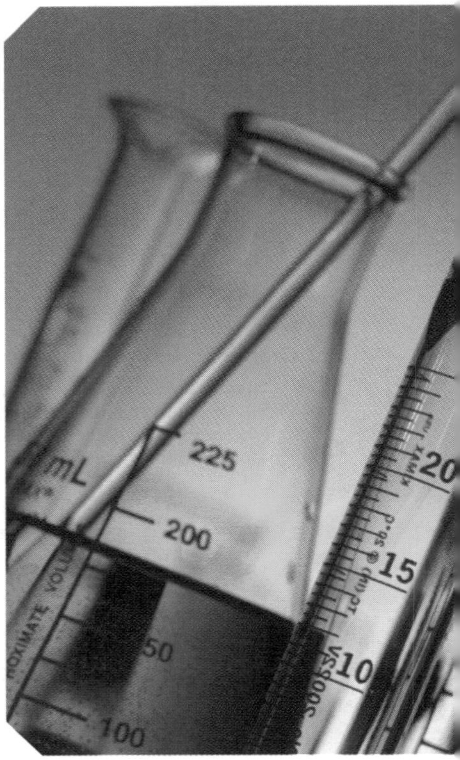

___A___ 1. This passage is mainly about
- A. the biblical study of chemistry.
- B. the development and importance of chemistry.
- C. the philosophical foundations of scientific study.

___C___ 2. According to this passage, the Bible
- A. can be used as a chemistry textbook.
- B. is universally accepted as useful.
- C. provides a necessary perspective for scientific study.

___C___ 3. This passage does not mention
- A. the controversial nature of the biblical worldview.
- B. a justification for chemical study.
- C. the biblical account of Creation.

___C___ 4. A good title for this passage would be
- A. The Development of the Science of Chemistry.
- B. A Definition of Chemistry.
- C. Chemistry in Biblical Focus.

___B___ 5. In this passage the word *nature* means
- A. the physical world.
- B. the characteristics of something.
- C. the human condition without God's grace.

422 Chapter 16 | Study Skills

Vocabulary: Write the letter of the definition that most closely matches the word in bold print.

_B_ 6. The knife's **keen** edge was useful for slicing tomatoes.
A. sensitive
B. sharp
C. quick

_C_ 7. The use of too much makeup may make a person look **ostentatious.**
A. humorous
B. fat
C. showy

_A_ 8. Based on **tenuous** foundations, his argument was unconvincing.
A. flimsy
B. strong
C. wicked

Vocabulary: Write the letter of the sentence in which the definition of the underlined word more closely matches that of the underlined word in the first sentence.

_B_ 9. Who will be giving this year's commencement address?
A Sheila receives her business mail at a separate address.
B. The queen's address to the nation was broadcast live.

_A_ 10. The coach's pep talk galvanized the team in the second half of the game.
A. The editorial in today's newspaper failed to galvanize the council to make a decision.
B. They galvanize both iron and steel at the shop.

Study Skills | Chapter 16 423

16.6 PRACTICE *the skill*

Analogy: Write the letter of the pair of words whose relationship most closely matches the relationship of the original pair of words.

__B__ 1. fur : dog ::
A. dog : dish
B. peel : orange
C. fire : wood

__A__ 2. island : ocean ::
A. moon : space
B. wind : rock
C. sandpaper : wood

__C__ 3. foot : shoe ::
A. page : book
B. nail : board
C. hand : glove

__C__ 4. keys : ignition ::
A. time : clock
B. fan : ceiling
C. pick : lock

__A__ 5. speak : word ::
A. sing : song
B. noise : sound
C. scream : yell

Grammar, Usage, and Mechanics: Write the letter that corresponds to the error in the sentence.

__D__ 6. Everything works (A) together wondrously, (B) yet people (C) still believe that there is no God. No error (D)

__C__ 7. According to Psalm 19, (A) "The heavens declare (B) the glory of God". (C) No error (D)

Grammar, Usage, and Mechanics: Write the letter of the correct replacement for the underlined section of the sentence. If the sentence is correct, choose *D*.

__B__ 8. My brothers enjoys playing the piano, and I often enjoy listening to them play.
A. My brother's enjoys
B. My brothers enjoy
C. My brother's enjoy
D. correct as is

TEACHING STRATEGY

Discussion

Lead a discussion about the information in the student text and in the side-margin note on page 425 of the teacher's edition. Some students may show surprise that grammar rules have not always existed. Some students may conclude that they do not need to follow the rules currently in place. Point out that students do not have to learn the finer points of Latin and Greek grammar as students did in former times, but today's students must conform to established grammar in order to communicate effectively. Also explain that nonstandard grammar may be acceptable in certain instances but that academic writing is rarely, if ever, one of those exceptions.

Grammar, Usage, and Mechanics: Write the letter of the section that contains an error. If the sentence is correct, choose *D*.

B 9. A. Acting is one way
B. to overcome the fear,
C. of speaking to large groups.
D. no mistakes

D 10. A. Many high schools
B. and many colleges
C. offer acting classes.
D. no mistakes

HISTORY OF THE ENGLISH LANGUAGE

Rules for Modern English

The language of the Early Modern English period seemed free and strong, but in the later 1600s some people worried that it was too free. They began looking for rules to guide them as they used English. They already had rules for writing in Latin, and for good reason—for centuries no one had grown up speaking Latin, and so they had to learn it from books. So, they thought, why not also have rules for writing in English? Beginning about 1660, with especially high interest during the eighteenth century, more and more people wanted grammars and dictionaries to tell them how to write and speak. Some people even wanted to regulate the language itself.

People looking for authority tended to accept whatever rules the grammarians made. Some of the rules did describe what good English was like, and we follow most of them today. Other rules were based on Latin (instead of English) or on one person's idea of what English should be.

One example of this kind of rule is the notion that one should never end a sentence with a preposition. However, good English speakers routinely used sentences like the following: *What are you getting at? I don't know what you're talking about. Do you know what rules are for? They didn't know what they were up against.* Because Latin sentences never ended with a preposition, grammarians decided that English sentences should not either. And the rules are seemingly constantly in flux. Your teachers and parents have seen many changes in punctuation rules during their lifetime (e.g., dropping the comma after a short introductory prepositional phrase) as well as in rules of spelling and grammar (e.g., use of *shall* and *will*). It might be easier if we could just forget about all these rules, but some of them have become part of good English—especially formal English. The rules you are taught today reflect how English is used, informally and formally, by educated people in America.

Grammarians of the eighteenth century introduced the rule prohibiting the use of multiple negatives. Before this time multiple negatives emphasized the author's point. For example, Chaucer (fourteenth century) used four negatives to emphasize the courteous behavior of the Knight in the "General Prologue" of the *Canterbury Tales*: "He **nevere** yet **no** vileynye **ne** sayde / In al his lyf unto **no** maner wight." *(He had **never** used wicked or obscene language / Unto any kind of person.)* Shakespeare (seventeenth century) also used multiple negatives: "I have one heart, one bosom and one truth, / And that no woman has; **nor never none** / Shall mistress be of it, save I alone" (*Twelfth Night* 3.1). In this statement Viola, disguised as a man, emphatically states that no woman will ever claim the affections of her heart. The rule prohibiting multiple negatives originated from the desire to make the English language logical. Grammarians of the eighteenth century argued that double negatives logically cancel out, as in algebra, and make a positive. Many people use double negatives, but today such a practice usually communicates the impression of an unprofessional and even uneducated speaker.

Teaching Strategy

Discussion

Ask the students whether they are aware of any other grammar and mechanics rules that have developed or changed since the eighteenth century. *(spelling rules, capitalization rules, etc.)* Share the following titles representing some early American works that demonstrate unconventional spelling:

- *The General History of Virginia* (1624) by John Smith
- *The New England Primer* (c. 1683)
- The Mayflower Compact (1620) by William Bradford

Display a passage from one of these works in order to demonstrate how spelling has changed. (Most student anthologies standardize spellings. Therefore, check college anthologies, old books, and facsimiles for editions of these works that retain the original spellings and capitalization.) Discuss how standardized spelling allows the reader to understand the text more easily.

ESL — ESL students' problems with spelling often arise from the students' transferring of spelling procedures in their native languages to English or from a misunderstanding of English rules. When correcting spelling problems, try to point the students to an English spelling rule and then encourage them to memorize and review it.

Good spelling is an essential writing skill. Whether you are writing a research paper or a personal letter, your message is communicated most clearly by using the right words and spelling them correctly. Use these spelling hints and master these rules so that you will be a competent writer.

Spelling Hints

Pay attention to the spelling of new words.

Make a point of focusing on the spelling of new or unfamiliar words. When you read, you certainly read for meaning; but an occasional focus on spelling can help you become a good speller. (Spell the word softly to yourself and try to learn it.)

Spell by syllables.

Dividing a word into its individual syllables will help you to spell it correctly. Think about prefixes, suffixes, and other word parts as you spell words by syllables.

mis + spell	misspell
over + react	overreact
over + eat	overeat
general + ly	generally

Use a dictionary.

Dictionaries p. 404

Look up the spelling of words when you are unsure of the correct spelling. Keep a good dictionary available when you are writing. Although you might be unsure of a word's exact spelling, you probably know enough of the word to find it in the dictionary.

Keep a list of words that are problems for you.

Whenever you misspell a word and then locate the correct spelling of that word, put it on your list of problem words. Study your list systematically. Begin by writing a word several times, concentrating on its appearance and pronunciation. Repeat this procedure on three or four different days of the next week. Then ask someone to quiz you. If you can write the word correctly without hesitation, transfer it to your "learned" list. If a problem remains, keep working on the word.

Look for possible groupings among your problem words.

If you find a group of similar words, try to formulate or find a rule for that group. For example, you may find that several of your problem words contain *ie* or *ei*. Learning the rules for *ie* and *ei* will allow you to spell an entire group of words correctly.

Compare related words.

The sound of a related word can be a clue to the spelling of an unclear vowel.

Unclear Vowel	*Clear Vowel*	*Unclear Vowel*	*Clear Vowel*
heresy	heretical	similar	similarity
exhibit	exhibition	specify	specific

However, certain related words are spelled differently. Check your dictionary if you are unsure of the spelling of any word.

426 Appendix | Spelling

Spelling Singular Present-Tense Verbs and Plural Nouns

Plural Nouns
pp. 35–37

Present Tense
pp. 178–79

General Principles

If the word ends in *ch, sh, s, x,* or *z,* add *es.*

touch	touches
crash	crashes
pass	passes
annex	annexes
waltz	waltzes

If the word ends in *y* preceded by a consonant, change the final *y* to *i* and add *es.*

casualty	casualties
deny	denies

If the word ends in *y* preceded by a vowel, add *s.*

display	displays
enjoy	enjoys

If the word ends in *f* or *fe,* consult your dictionary. For most, add *s;* for others, change the *f* to *v* and add *es.*

gulf	gulfs
chafe	chafes
cliff	cliffs
self	selves
life	lives

Add *s* to most other words.

parka	parkas
due	dues
boycott	boycotts
eat	eats

If the word ends in *o,* consult your dictionary. For most, add *es;* for others, add *s.*

tomato	tomatoes
archipelago	archipelagos

Musical terms are more likely to require *s* than *es.*

adagio	adagios
piano	pianos

Some nouns have irregular plural forms. Consult your dictionary for nouns with irregular plurals.

man	men
datum	data
parenthesis	parentheses

Spelling | Appendix 427

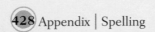

ESL Your ESL students will benefit greatly from your help with the content of this ESL note. At a minimum, pronounce each set of examples, pointing out that the suffixes have the same pronunciation throughout the set. Then you might repeat the words in that set, allowing the students to mimic your pronunciation of each word.

You may also point out this information to your native English speakers. The rules describing our pronunciation habits here are just another example of the highly systematic nature of languages. Every person can communicate easily in his native language because he subconsciously follows a multitude of regularities in grammar, pronunciation, and word usage. (Learning a new language includes learning new sets of regularities.) God's gift of language to us is indeed wonderful.

ESL Voiced sounds are made by the vibration of the vocal cords, producing a humming or buzzing sound. This vibration can be felt by laying the fingertips lightly on the Adam's apple. Use the sounds /s/ and /z/ to help your students hear and feel this difference.

Plurals of Proper Nouns

The plurals of proper nouns are made by adding *s* or *es* according to the preceding rules but without any other spelling changes. Never use an apostrophe in making the plural of a proper name.

the McDonoughs	the Gregorys	the Douglases	the Marches

Some plurals of personal titles are irregular.

General or Formal	*General or Informal*
Messrs. Franklin and Firth	Mr. Franklin and Mr. Firth
Mmes. Proffit and Rood	Mrs. Proffit and Mrs. Rood
Misses Lucy Butler and Frieda Scholtze	Miss Lucy Butler and Miss Frieda Scholtze
Drs. Joseph Markham and Alice Kenney	Dr. Joseph Markham and Dr. Alice Kenney

A plural title can also be used when the same title applies to two or more persons with the same name.

Formal	*General or Informal*
the Misses Pelham	the Miss Pelhams
the Drs. Harvey	the Dr. Harveys

Plurals of Compounds

Attach *s* or *es* to the end of most compounds.

snowboard	snowboards
homestretch	homestretches

Pluralize the first element of certain compound nouns—those in which the first element is felt to be the most important part of the compound. When in doubt, consult your dictionary.

secretary of state	secretaries of state
brother-in-law	brothers-in-law

ESL **Pronunciation of Possessives, Plurals, and Singular Present-Tense Verbs**

The same pronunciation rules apply to three English suffixes—the possessive suffix for nouns (spelled *'s*), the regular plural suffix for nouns (spelled *s* or *es*), and the third-person singular suffix for present-tense verbs (spelled *s* or *es*). The pronunciation of all of these suffixes depends on what kind of sound precedes the suffix.

- These suffixes are pronounced /**əz**/ after **s**, **z**, **sh**, **zh**, **ch**, and **j** sounds (sounds similar to the /s/ and /z/ sounds of the suffixes). These sounds include the **x** and **ge** spellings.

  classes, waxes, glazes, dishes, corsages, matches, badges
- The suffixes are pronounced /**s**/ after other voiceless consonant sounds (sounds that you form with your mouth but do not say with your vocal cords): **f**, voiceless **th**, **p**, **t**, and **k**.

  cuffs, moths, Kip's, Matt's, clocks
- The suffixes are pronounced /**z**/ after other voiced sounds (sounds that you both form with your mouth and say with your vocal cords): **v**, voiced **th**, **b**, **d**, **g**, **m**, **n**, **ng**, **l**, **r**, **w**, **y**, and all vowels.

  knives, clothes, Rob's, Todd's, dogs, hems, tunes, rings, Paul's, hours, tows, toys, fleas, copies, trios, Julia's

Spelling with *ie* and *ei*

When the sound is "long *e*," put *i* before *e* except after *c*.

i* before *e	**except after *c***
believe	ceiling
grief	receipt

Exceptions:

caffeine, leisure, protein, seize, sheik, weird; either and *neither,* in their more common American pronunciation, are also exceptions to this rule.

When the sound is "long *a*," put *e* before *i*.

vein	beige

When the two vowels are pronounced separately, spell according to the pronunciation of the first vowel.

quiet	atheist

We call a vowel "long" when its pronunciation is the same as the name of the letter. For example, the vowel sound in *cake* is "long *a*." ESL

Adding Suffixes

Doubling a Final Consonant

If a one-syllable word ends with a single consonant preceded by a single vowel, double the final consonant before adding a suffix that begins with a vowel.

plot	plott**ed**
stun	stunn**ing**

Similarly, if a multisyllable word with its main accent on the final syllable ends with a single consonant preceded by a single vowel, double the final consonant before adding a suffix that begins with a vowel.

permit	permitt**ed**
refer	referr**ing**

Exceptions:

The consonant does not double when the suffix causes the main accent to shift away from the final syllable: ***con**ference* vs. *con**fer**ring*.

The final *l* sometimes doubles regardless of the location of the main accent, especially in British usage: *counselor* or (mainly British) *counsellor.* Consult your dictionary.

If a word ends with a single consonant preceded by two vowels, do not double the final consonant before adding a suffix.

greet	greet**er**
wait	wait**ing**

Spelling | Appendix 429

Changing the Final *y* to *i*

If a word ends with a consonant and *y*, change the final *y* to *i* before adding a suffix.

cleanly	cleanliness
rely	relied

However, if the suffix itself begins with *i*, do not change final *y* to *i*.

supply	supplying
baby	babyish

Exceptions:

Some words keep the *y*: *babyhood, shyness.*

In a few established spellings, the *y* has become *i* in spite of the preceding vowel: *daily, paid.*

Dropping the Final Silent *e*

Drop the final silent *e* that is preceded by a consonant before adding a suffix beginning with a vowel.

advise	advisable
tune	tuning, tuned

Keep the final silent *e* before adding a suffix beginning with a consonant.

achieve	achievement
tune	tuneful

Exceptions:

The *e* is kept to signal the "soft" pronunciation of *c* or *g* before a suffix beginning with *a* or *o*: *noticeable, courageous.*

A word ending in *ue* normally drops the *e* even when the suffix begins with a consonant: *truly, argument.*

Words ending in *dge* lose their *e* (in American English) before *ment*: *judgment, acknowledgment.*

A few other words are exceptions, some of them to distinguish homonyms: *dyeing* (vs. *dying*), *singeing* (vs. *singing*).

430 Appendix | Spelling

Name

Chapter 2 Review: Parts of Speech

Nouns

Identify each italicized noun as *possessive, proper, compound, collective,* or *abstract.*

collective 1. Hurricanes and typhoons are different names for strong tropical disturbances; the *majority* are often not extremely destructive.

abstract 2. The *truth* of the matter is that both of these can have heavy rain and strong winds.

compound 3. Although all severe weather can be dangerous, hurricanes and typhoons usually cause more damage than *thunderstorms* do.

possessive 4. A number of years ago a Caribbean storm was often named for the *saint's* day on which the storm occurred.

proper 5. Hurricane *Santa Ana* struck Puerto Rico in 1825.

Pronouns

Identify each italicized pronoun as *personal, indefinite, demonstrative, relative,* or *indefinite relative.*

indefinite 6. Before the end of the nineteenth century, an Australian meteorologist began giving women's names to *most* of the tropical storms.

demonstrative 7. For a period of time storm names were given in alphabetical order, but *these* were different in other parts of the world.

indefinite relative 8. In 1979 *whoever* was responsible for naming storms began to alternate men's and women's names for storms in the Western Hemisphere.

personal 9. The name of a storm may be dropped from the list if *its* destruction is very deadly and costly.

relative 10. The committee *that* determines the list of names for a storm season may remove a name and place another name on the list.

Identify each italicized pronoun as *interrogative, reflexive, intensive,* or *reciprocal.*

interrogative 11. *Who* has ever heard of the 1954 hurricane called Hazel?

intensive 12. Hazel *herself* caused the deaths of one thousand people in Haiti.

reflexive 13. As a category-four hurricane, Hazel devastated the North and South Carolina coastlines by *herself.*

interrogative 14. *What* would be the result of such a destructive storm?

reciprocal 15. People asked *each other* whether their lives or property would ever be the same.

Verbs

Identify each italicized verb as *action, state-of-being,* or *auxiliary.*

action 16. Hazel's destructive wind and rain *killed* ninety-five people in the United States.

state-of-being 17. In the Toronto area, hurricane Hazel, accompanied by excessive rainfall, *was* responsible for eighty-one deaths.

action 18. An eighteen-foot storm surge *destroyed* a great part of the coastal region of North Carolina.

state-of-being 19. Because of the extreme destruction of this storm, the name Hazel *is* on the list of retired names.

auxiliary 20. The names Irene, Katrina, and Tomas, among others, *have* been retired as well.

Adjectives and Adverbs

Underline each adjective once and each adverb twice. Do not underline articles.

Southern Hemisphere is a compound proper noun in this context, but some students may identify Southern as an adjective.

21. Tropical cyclones appear predominantly in the Southern Hemisphere, where they get energy from warm tropical oceans.
22. Clockwise winds of a tropical cyclone may whirl unceasingly in excess of 90 km, and storm gusts may exceed 260 km.
23. Very violent storm surges can cause the ocean to rise many feet above high tide.
24. Tropical cyclones may last for many days and follow unpredictable paths.
25. Excessively high winds are a destructive force to vessels at sea and in the harbors.

Prepositions, Conjunctions, and Interjections

Identify each italicized word as a preposition *(prep),* a coordinating conjunction *(coord conj),* a correlative conjunction *(correl conj),* a subordinating conjunction *(sub conj),* or an interjection *(interj).*

correl conj 26. *Not only* do tropical cyclones continue for many days, *but* they *also* follow very unpredictable paths.

coord conj 27. High winds can destroy buildings *and* turn airborne debris into deadly missiles.

interj 28. *Wow!* Did you see the huge pine tree that was blown over by the winds?

sub conj 29. *If* tropical cyclones encounter land or cooler waters, their strength will diminish.

prep 30. Pedestrians should seek substantial protection *during* a tropical cyclone.

432 Chapter 2 Review | Parts of Speech

Name

Chapter 3 Review: Sentences

Kinds of Sentences

Identify each sentence as *declarative, exclamatory, imperative,* or *interrogative.* Place the appropriate punctuation mark at the end of the sentence.

interrogative 1. Have you ever been outside the United States?

declarative 2. International flights are often quite tiring.

declarative 3. Once you arrive at your destination, you will most likely want to sleep.

exclamatory 4. Visiting a foreign country can be a blast!

imperative 5. If you ever have the opportunity to visit a foreign country, take it. or !

Subjects and Predicates

Underline the simple subject once and the simple predicate twice in each independent clause.

6. Juan and Victor flew to Puerto Rico to visit their extended family.
7. As they traveled, they talked excitedly about the events of the upcoming week.
8. After landing, they exited the plane and made their way through the busy airport to the baggage claim area.
9. They claimed their luggage and met their relatives, who were very glad to see them.
10. After an exciting but tiring two weeks, they flew back to the United States with many memories of a different culture.

Underline each complete subject once and each complete predicate twice. If the subject is understood, write *you* to the left of the number.

you 11. Imagine how you would feel leaving your country to live in a foreign country for a long period of time.

12. There are some people who have had that experience.

13. Would you enjoy living outside the United States?

14. Many of the people living outside the country are missionaries.

15. These missionaries sacrifice life in their homeland, financial prosperity, and many other things to spread the gospel of Christ.

Sentences | Chapter 3 Review 433

Sentence Patterns

Label the sentence pattern of each independent clause *S-InV, S-TrV-DO, S-TrV-IO-DO, S-TrV-DO-OC, S-LV-PN, S-LV-PA,* or *S-be-Advl.* If the adverbial is a prepositional phrase, underline it.

S LV PA PA
16. Missionary stories are often extremely exciting and thought provoking for children.

S be Advl
17. Part of the appeal of the missionary story is <u>in its reality</u>.

S TrV IO DO DO
18 In addition to being factual, missionary stories teach children moral values and character qualities.

S InV
19. These stories often come from the missionary's personal experiences.

S TrV DO OC
20. They may make the children more responsive to the needs of others.

S TrV DO
21. Hearing vivid accounts of real needs instills in children a desire to spread the Word and to see God work in their own lives.

S TrV IO DO
22. Many of the stories teach children the power of prayer.

S TrV DO
23. Many young people attending a Bible club have not experienced answers to prayer in their lives.

S LV PN
24. Missionary stories are an interesting, attention-grabbing means of giving the gospel.

S LV PN PN
25. Teaching such a story to children is a wonderful ministry tool and a great responsibility.

434 Chapter 3 Review | Sentences

Name

Chapter 4 Review: Phrases

Prepositional Phrases

Place parentheses around each prepositional phrase and underline the simple object of each preposition. In the blank, write the word or words that each phrase modifies.

advertised 1. (In 1767)the innovative John Webster advertised a new product that proved to be both decorative and practical: wooden blinds.

function 2. Their original name, Wooden Venetian Sun Shades, reveals their primary function(in the home.)

blinds 3. (With the ability to open various degrees,) wooden blinds simultaneously provide privacy and light.

provided, relied, addition 4. (At a time when window decoration relied primarily(on architectural design))wooden blinds provided a welcome addition(to the decorative repertoire.)

was 5. Though today blinds are common, their versatility was a novelty(in the 1700s.)

Appositive Phrases

Underline each appositive phrase. In the blank write the word or words that the appositive renames.

Duke of Gloucester Street 6. In colonial times wooden blinds visible in the homes on Duke of Gloucester Street, a famous avenue in historic Williamsburg, indicated their popularity.

Thomas Jefferson 7. Thomas Jefferson, a most influential man of his day, reportedly had many wooden blinds in his residence.

Edith Wharton 8. Some classicists, such as Edith Wharton, a noted American author and interior decorator, preferred older forms of window coverings such as an inside shutter.

Lawn 9. Wooden blinds are still popular in renovated buildings; those at the Lawn, the historic campus of the University of Virginia, add to the authenticity of the buildings.

miniblinds 10. More popular today are miniblinds, a cheaper alternative to wooden blinds.

Phrases | Chapter 4 Review 435

Participial Phrases

Underline each participle or participial phrase. Then identify the word or phrase as *present, past,* or *perfect.*

past 11. Furniture craftsmen probably developed the first manufactured wooden blinds.

past 12. Boards left from furniture production became blinds.

perfect 13. Having studied Colonial decorating, historians have found that walnut wooden blinds were very prominent.

present 14. Having two-inch wooden slats, these blinds were easily incorporated into Georgian design.

present 15. Painting or staining the wood, manufacturers matched the color of the blind to the color of the room.

Gerund Phrases

Underline each gerund or gerund phrase. Identify its function as subject *(S)*, direct object *(DO)*, predicate noun *(PN)*, indirect object *(IO)*, or object of the preposition *(OP)*.

S 16. Decorating during the Federal Period focused on a classical style.

OP 17. To match the light-colored stone popular in architecture during this period, decorators updated dark blinds by painting them white.

OP 18. Occasionally, a decorator deviated from using the lighter colored blinds and painted them a dark green color instead.

DO 19. Ladies enjoyed working with colorful fabrics and making frilly curtains.

IO 20. These new choices gave decorating a more elegant tone.

Infinitive Phrases

Underline each infinitive and place parentheses around each infinitive phrase. Then identify its function as noun *(noun)*, adjective *(adj)*, or adverb *(adv)*.

noun 21. (To have elaborately decorated homes) became popular during the Victorian Era.

noun 22. Some decorators chose (to replace wooden blinds with movable shutters.)

adv 23. The popularity of wooden blinds declined for a brief time; they became popular again because they are beautiful and easy (to use.)

adj 24. Nearly three centuries have witnessed people's desire (to ornament their windows with wooden blinds.)

noun 25. If you choose (to hang these blinds in your home,) you will continue a long-standing American tradition.

436 Chapter 4 Review | Phrases

Name

Chapter 5 Review: Clauses

Distinguishing Independent and Dependent clauses

Identify each italicized clause as independent *(IC)* or dependent *(DC)*.

IC 1. *What has been your experience with advertising,* if any?

DC 2. You know *you are constantly the target of advertising.*

IC 3. Whenever you see a billboard or a shop, *that is advertising.*

DC 4. Almost everything *that we see* is sending us some sort of message, whether good or bad.

DC 5. Christians must be wise *as they view commercials;* otherwise, they can fall prey to covetousness.

Adjective Clauses

Place parentheses around each adjective clause. In the blank, write the word it modifies. Underline each relative pronoun once; underline each relative adverb twice.

need 6. Often, a local church will have a need for advertising (that you can help with.)

website 7. Perhaps you could help write content for a website (that the church uses for communication with its members and visitors.)

programs 8. Many churches have tract distribution programs, (which aid in the spread of the gospel and acquaint people with the church.)

boards 9. Some churches have boards (where service times and opportunities are listed.)

person 10. You yourself are a form of advertisement, either good or bad, to any person (with whom you speak about your church.)

Adverb Clauses

Place parentheses around each adverb clause, including any elliptical adverb clause. In the blank, write the word or words it modifies. Underline each subordinating conjunction.

keep 11. (When advertising,) keep your message clear and simple.

must settle 12. (Before you prepare an advertisement,) you must first settle on a target audience.

can design 13. You will be glad for your preparation, for you cannot design an advertisement (when you do not know the audience or the objective.)

Clauses | Chapter 5 Review 437

can submit 14. (After you have prepared your advertisement,)you can submit it to the media through which you wish to make it public.

will see 15. (If the message achieved its purpose,)you will see the results.

Noun Clauses

Place parentheses around each noun clause. Identify the function of each noun clause as subject *(S)*, predicate noun *(PN)*, direct object *(DO)*, indirect object *(IO)*, object of the preposition *(OP)*, or appositive *(App)*. Underline each subordinating conjunction, indefinite relative pronoun, and indefinite relative adverb.

S 16. (Where the pretzel comes from) is a question some people may ask.

App 17. The question(whether the pretzel, a creation of a young monk, originated in southern France or northern Italy)became a matter of discussion.

OP 18. After the monk prepared unleavened bread for the Catholic festival of Lent, he shaped small arms folded in prayer from(what was left of the dough.)

PN 19. The recipient of the new pastry was(whoever said his prayers.)

DO 20. We learned(that the creation was named *pretiola,* Latin for "little reward.")

Correcting Sentence Problems

Identify each group of words as a sentence *(S)*, a fragment *(F)*, a comma splice *(CS)*, or a fused sentence *(FS)*.

S 21. Volleyball originated in 1885 at the YMCA in Holyoke, Massachusetts.

F 22. A combination of basketball, baseball, tennis, and handball.

CS 23. William Morgan, a businessman, wanted a game for everyone, people of his status could also play the game.

FS 24. During a demonstration game, someone remarked about the volleying of the ball as a result, Morgan decided to call the game volleyball.

S 25. Since that time volleyball has become a major sport, second only to soccer.

438 Chapter 5 Review | Clauses

Name

Chapter 6 Review: Agreement

Subject-Verb Agreement

Subjects and Predicates

Underline the simple subject(s) of the verb in question. Then underline the correct verb from the choices in parentheses.

1. Although Americans may consider Henry Ford the inventor of the automobile, a study of the history of automobiles *(reveals, reveal)* a different origin.
2. Twenty-seven years *(is, are)* the period of time between Nikolaus Otto's invention and the beginning of the Ford Motor Company.
3. In 1876 neither Nikolaus Otto nor other Germans *(was, were)* aware of the importance of his invention, the gas motor engine.
4. In 1885 both planning and preparation *(was, were)* evidenced in a revolutionary car design.
5. Even today the work of German engineers *(continues, continue)* to bring innovations to the automotive industry.

Subject Identification

Underline the simple subject(s) of the verb in question. Then underline the correct verb from the choices in parentheses.

6. The facts about the German automobile industry *(is, are)* quite fascinating.
7. The invention of the first practical automobiles with internal-combustion engines *(begins, begin)* the story of Karl Benz's influence on the auto industry.
8. Benz's inventive accomplishments, not his skill in business, *(fascinates, fascinate)* anyone who reads about him.
9. In 1894 Benz's first production car, along with many others, *(was, were)* part of the Paris-Rouen Race, the first recorded car race.
10. In addition to his many other accomplishments *(was, were)* the first truck, built in 1895.

Problem Nouns and Pronouns

Underline the simple subject(s) of the verb in question. Then underline the correct verb from the choices in parentheses.

11. In the eyes of German people as well as others, thanks *(goes, go)* to Gottlieb Daimler for being the father of modern automobiles.
12. *The Beaulieu Encyclopedia of the Automobile* *(gives, give)* further information about Daimler.

Agreement | Chapter 6 Review 439

13. All the finishing cars in the Paris-Rouen Race were powered by a Daimler engine, and each team in the race (*was, were*) made up of a driver and mechanic.

14. Germany's economics after World War I (*reveals, reveal*) many problems facing the country.

15. In 1919 twenty-five million marks (*was, were*) needed to purchase an automobile.

Correct any subject-verb disagreement by writing the correct form of the verb in italics. If the sentence is already correct, write *C* in the blank.

realize 16. Few today *realizes* that Wilhelm Maybach contributed greatly to the auto industry.

C 17. He was one of the innovative designers who *were* thriving on the enthusiasm for automobiles.

were 18. In 1889 Maybach, along with Daimler, placed an engine into a carriage; many of the observers of that historical event *was* surprised that the carriage reached a speed of eleven miles per hour.

are 19. Most of those who study in this field *is* surprised that Maybach pioneered the building of the engine for the zeppelin airship.

include 20. Several of the accomplishments attributed to him *includes* an honorary doctorate and a place in the Automotive Hall of Fame.

Pronoun-Antecedent Agreement

Nouns as Antecedents and Compound Antecedents

Underline the correct pronoun from the choices in parentheses.

21. Do you know the person who spent the last years of (*his, their*) career developing dirigible balloons?

22. An individual named Count Ferdinand von Zeppelin spent (*his, its, their*) fortune in expensive experiments to develop an airship.

23. Private donations and contributions from the government made (*its, their*) impact on the further development of the airship.

24. From the earliest experiments until the airship was improved, the dirigible encountered several factors that contributed to (*his, its, their*) destruction.

25. The Germans used the dirigible in World War I to drop bombs on (*its, their*) enemies.

440 Chapter 6 Review | Agreement

Name

Collective Nouns and Indefinite Pronouns as Antecedents

Write an appropriate personal pronoun to complete each sentence.

their 26. Some of the early German dirigibles with ? awkward fuel systems met with failure.

his, its 27. Everyone was interested in ? opportunity to ride in Dr. Hugo Eckner's LZ-127 *Graf Zeppelin* equipped with ? own galley, dining area, and new fuel system.

his 28. The *Graf Zeppelin* was the most successful airship ever built; however, no one in Germany could afford to give enough of ? wealth to keep the ship in the air.

its 29. Dr. Eckner gained support from William Randolph Hearst, an American whose family had made ? wealth in the newspaper business.

his 30. Someone who makes dirigible history ? object of study will find that the *Graf Zeppelin* completed a round-the-world trip in the fastest time recorded up to that point.

Agreement | Chapter 6 Review 441

Name

Chapter 7 Review: Verb Use

Principal Parts and Tenses

Underline the complete verb of each independent clause. Then identify its tense.

present progressive 1. Sam is visiting his Italian grandparents in Chicago this week.

past perfect progressive 2. He had been looking forward to this trip for several weeks.

present perfect progressive 3. His grandmother has been cooking Sam's favorite dishes for days.

present perfect 4. The entire family has always eaten pasta at every family event.

present 5. The history of pasta dates back thousands of years.

present 6. Sources vary concerning the origin of pasta.

present perfect 7. Italians, Chinese, or Arabs could have invented pasta.

past 8. During the American Civil War, macaroni and cheese was a popular dish.

past 9. Italian immigrants in the early 1900s brought with them the popular spaghetti dishes so familiar today.

future 10. Pasta, with its great taste and its variety, will continue to be a popular dish for years.

Consistency and Sequence of Tenses

Underline the verbs in incorrect tense. Write the correct word in the blank. If the sentence is already correct, write *C* in the blank.

C 11. Tracy sits nervously and tightly grips her pencil.

is 12. Trying to remember all that she studied, she is relieved that the precalculus test has not been too difficult.

works 13. She worked quietly and steadily, answering each question carefully.

does 14. A squirrel outside the window entertains Tracy briefly but did not distract her from the test.

marks 15. The bell rings and she marked her final answers on the sheet before setting her pencil down.

Verb Use | Chapter 7 Review 443

Voice

Underline the verb in each independent clause. Then identify its voice as active *(A)* or passive *(P)*. If the verb is passive, double underline any retained objects or subjective complements.

P 16. My first day at college, I was awakened by the sound of leaf blowers outside my window.

A 17. I soon learned the importance of cleaning the sidewalks every day.

A 18. The students whose job it is to clean the sidewalks must remove all debris from the sidewalks.

P 19. Other students would be shown a poor example if leaves or sticks were strewn on the sidewalks.

P 20. Leaf blowers can be ignored when I'm tired enough.

Mood

Identify the mood of each italicized verb as *indicative, imperative,* or *subjunctive.*

indicative 21. Macbeth *is* one of Shakespeare's darkest works.

indicative 22. Driven by intense ambition, Macbeth *dreams* of being king at any cost.

subjunctive 23. If he *had* not *committed* regicide to obtain the throne, he might still have become king one day.

imperative 24. *Notice* Shakespeare's masterful use of particular elements to enhance the mood of the play.

indicative 25. The night setting *presents* a dark mood and *represents* the darkness of the deeds of evil men.

indicative 26. The color red and the blood imagery *permeate* the play to further intensify the mood.

imperative 27. *See* the blood on the king, on the knife, on the hands of the killers, on Banquo, and on Macbeth as he is slain in the end.

subjunctive 28. If you *were wondering* about Shakespeare's source for this play, you would find that similar events actually took place in the year AD 1050.

imperative 29. *Observe* Shakespeare's adaptation of history; historically, Duncan's enemies, not Macbeth, killed Duncan.

indicative 30. Historically and in the play, Duncan's son Malcolm *returns* and *defeats* Macbeth, forcing him to relinquish the throne.

444 Chapter 7 Review | Verb Use

Name

Chapter 8 Review: Pronoun Use

Pronoun Case

Provide an appropriate personal pronoun. Then identify it as subjective *(S)*, objective *(O)*, possessive *(P)*, or independent possessive *(IP)*. *(Answers may vary.)*

mine *IP* 1. My brother's favorite geological features are geysers, but _?_ are volcanoes.

we *S* 2. While visiting Indonesia with our grandparents, _?_ learned of a volcanic island called Krakatau.

our *P* 3. According to _?_ tour guide, the volcanic explosions on Krakatau could be heard in Japan, Australia, and the Philippines!

them *O* 4. Sunsets after the Krakatau disaster were unusual; volcanic dust gave _?_ an eerily unnatural hue.

they *S* 5. People as far away as in England reported that _?_ too witnessed unusual sunsets.

its *P* 6. Following the seismic eruption on Krakatau, two-thirds of _?_ land area vanished into the sea.

us *O* 7. Additionally, the Indonesian guide told _?_ that thirty-six thousand people of Java perished as a result of the Krakatau disaster.

its *P* 8. Devastating tidal waves following the volcanic eruption buffeted the coast of Java and brought devastation to _?_ people.

His *IP* 9. Some survivors wrote about their amazing experiences. One man survived by clinging to an uprooted banana tree floating amid debris from his village. _?_ was a thrilling story.

me *O* 10. To _?_, such an event as Krakatau's eruption serves as a reminder of humanity's absolute dependence on God for sustenance.

Appositives; Comparisons Using *Than* or *As*

Underline the correct pronoun from the choices in parentheses.

11. Reading about the European explorers' search for a route to the Indies caused several students—Takako, Sam, and *(I, me)*—to become curious about what exact land mass the explorers had in mind.
12. *(We, Us)* three learned that the Indies actually encompassed modern day Indonesia in addition to other countries.
13. We students—Takako, Sam, and *(I, me)*—learned that the Indies at one time extended from India to China.

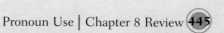

Pronoun Use | Chapter 8 Review 445

14. Takako knew better than *(I, me)* the history of western exploration in Japan.

15. A comparison of colonization attempts in India and Indonesia interested Sam as much as *(I, me)*.

"Subjects" and Objects of Verbals; Using *Who* and *Whom*

Underline the correct noun or pronoun from the choices in parentheses.

16. Have you ever heard of Sir Thomas Stamford Raffles (1781–1826), the politician and colonial official *(who, whom)* wrote the famous *History of Java?*

17. *(He, His)* being born into an English sea captain's family certainly did nothing to discourage the young lad's desire to see new lands.

18. When he was only twenty-three, the East India Company decided to send *(he, him)* to Penang, Malaysia.

19. *(Raffles, Raffles's)* learning the Malay language while traveling to Penang was especially astonishing and made him an invaluable employee to his company.

20. Thomas Raffles learned that it was he *(who, whom)* India's governor-general chose to be a trusted governor.

21. Raffles's wise and judicious social policies enabled *(he, him)* to become the lieutenant governor of Java and later the governor of modern-day Sumatra.

22. Thomas Raffles is also the one *(who, whom)* Singaporeans credit with founding their nation in 1819; they still admire his strong antislavery principles as well as his work to provide education and human rights to the region.

23. Have you heard about *(him, his)* hiring zoologists and botanists to document and study specimens from Java, Sumatra, and Singapore?

24. Often the financier of these costly studies had to be *(he, him)*: with his own savings he would sponsor the collection and study of regional plants and animals.

25. A native named Abdullah was the one *(who, whom)* Raffles relied upon to assist him in the Malay tongue and to manage the various collected plant and animal specimens.

446 Chapter 8 Review | Pronoun Use

Name

Courtesy Order and Use of Reflexive and Intensive

Underline the correct pronoun or pronouns from the choices in parentheses.

26. Grandmother told (*Kasan and me, me and Kasan*) about her girlhood home in Indonesia.
27. She began with describing how all the men of her family labored many long days to construct a *kampong* for (*them, themselves*).
28. Between (*you and me, you and myself*) I had no idea that a *kampong* is a traditional multifamily housing unit in Indonesia.
29. Kasan and I asked (*us, ourselves*) whether we could imagine living in an elevated thatched-roof village with all of our extended family members.
30. Grandmother then explained how refreshingly cool and simple her girlhood home was and how her family planted (*theirselves, themselves*) beautiful fruit and palm trees around the *kampong*.

Pronoun Shift

Underline the correct word from the choices in parentheses.

31. If a tourist to Indonesia enjoys eating rice, (*he, you*) will certainly take pleasure in many of the authentic foods.
32. When comparing the quality of crops in Indonesia, anyone can tell that (*he, you, they*) will reap a much more bountiful harvest from lands near an active volcano, for ash in the soil aids the fruitfulness of the field.
33. Many of the people of Indonesia have chosen Java as (*his, their*) home.
34. Anyone interested in volcanoes must not forget (*his, your, their*) camera when visiting Indonesia; this archipelago contains at least sixty active volcanoes.
35. If you want to see a vast assortment of wildlife, (*we, he, you*) should study Indonesia's reptiles, mammals, marsupials, and birds, for they have both Asian and Australian origins.

Pronoun Use | Chapter 8 Review 447

Name

Chapter 9 Review: Pronoun Reference

Ambiguous Reference and Remote Reference

Identify each sentence or group of sentences as having clear pronoun reference *(C)* or unclear pronoun reference *(U)*.

U 1. Leonardo da Vinci began his trade as an apprentice to Andrea del Verrocchio; he eventually became arguably one of the paramount painters of the Italian Renaissance.

U 2. One distinctive innovation of da Vinci's was a painting technique called *sfumato*. In contrast with del Verrocchio's crisp, obvious lines, da Vinci experimented with shade. Its distinctive trademark is a purposeful blurring of the paint around an image's corners or where shadow is desired.

U 3. Interestingly, when applying for a position under the Duke of Milan, da Vinci told the Duke via letter that he was gifted chiefly in military and civil engineering.

C 4. This same letter closes with da Vinci's casually mentioning his own abilities in painting, sculpting, and architecture.

U 5. People credit da Vinci with helping to usher in the style of the High Renaissance, for he possessed remarkable creativity and was not afraid to try innovative methods. It is characterized by graceful painted images and contrasting areas of dark and light hues.

U 6. *The Last Supper* and *Mona Lisa,* both by da Vinci, possess worldwide eminence, but it has sparked much controversy and debate.

U 7. People still enjoy proposing and speculating about various possible models for *Mona Lisa*. They certainly are interesting.

U 8. *The Last Supper* and *Mona Lisa* paintings both show wear and tear, although it is covered with a lacquer, now turned yellow, designed to preserve the painting's beauty.

C 9. *The Last Supper* shows da Vinci's innovative nature. Another painter might have depicted this scene with a straight row of disciples, according to tradition; yet da Vinci grouped them and depicted their unique personalities.

C 10. Da Vinci also experimented with the mediums he used in conveying his pictures. For example, in painting *The Last Supper,* da Vinci abandoned the usual fresco method that required rapid painting. Instead, he mixed his own special wall coating that permitted slower, more detailed painting. This new medium, however, was not one of his successes.

Pronoun Reference | Chapter 9 Review 449

Reference to an Implied Noun and to a Noun That Is a Modifier

Rewrite each sentence to correct any unclear pronoun reference. If the antecedent is already clear, write *C* in the blank. *(Answers will vary.)*

11. While serving at the court in Milan, da Vinci honed his skills in architecture and designed Milan Cathedral's proposed dome; however, it never received da Vinci's architectural brainchild.

    While serving at the court in Milan, da Vinci honed his skills in architecture and designed Milan Cathedral's proposed dome; however, the cathedral never received da Vinci's architectural brainchild.

12. The Court of Milan's beautiful theatrical productions brought it great popularity.

    The beautiful theatrical productions at the Court of Milan brought it great popularity.

13. Leonardo da Vinci himself designed the costumes, sets, and stage machinery for the productions, which were huge successes for the Court of Milan.

    C

14. After the French attacked Milan, da Vinci sought work as a mapmaker, and they are still regarded as classic masterpieces of this profession.

    After the French attacked Milan, da Vinci sought work as a mapmaker, and his maps are still regarded as classic masterpieces of this profession.

15. During the golden age of High Renaissance art, da Vinci moved to Rome; however, they learned nothing from da Vinci, who chose to spend his days studying other branches of learning.

    During the golden age of High Renaissance art, da Vinci moved to Rome; however, the artists there learned nothing from da Vinci, who chose to spend his days studying other branches of learning.

450 Chapter 9 Review | Pronoun Reference

Name

Indefinite Reference of Personal Pronouns and Reference to a Broad Idea

Identify each sentence as correct *(C)* or incorrect/informal *(I)*.

C 16. What time is it in Italy?

C 17. Art aficionados say that da Vinci was exceedingly proficient as a bronze caster: in fact, this skill landed him his first job at the Court of Milan.

I 18. It says on this website that da Vinci used a technique called aerial perspective: this technique is especially visible in the background of his *Mona Lisa*.

I 19. In 1499, they used a huge clay model of da Vinci's for an archery target.

C 20. How often does it snow in Florence, Italy?

I 21. You should take the opportunity to view da Vinci's *Mona Lisa* should you ever visit Paris's Louvre Museum.

I 22. Da Vinci possessed a great affinity for mathematics, especially geometry, which greatly aided his paintings.

I 23. In fact, da Vinci himself stated that you must be a mathematical scholar to best appreciate his works.

I 24. In Giorgio Vasari's biography of da Vinci it says that the master painter possessed an uncommon assortment of gifts: da Vinci was both immensely handsome and a genius in every discipline to which he applied himself.

I 25. All his life da Vinci felt a great affinity for the natural world. It prompted him to purchase caged birds and then to release them into the wild.

Pronoun Reference | Chapter 9 Review 451

Name

Chapter 10 Review: Adjective and Adverb Use

Modifiers: Comparisons and Functions

Underline each adjective, including the correct adjective choice from the adjectives in parentheses. Double underline each adverb that modifies a noun.

1. While driving toward the historic area of Alexandria, Virginia, one passes (*lower-income, more lower-income*) government housing projects and is suddenly transported back in time with the sight of cobblestone streets and red brick Federal Period buildings.
2. One historic townhouse on Oronoco Street bears (*significant, more significant, most significant*) historical import than all the other traditional red brick residences.
3. The boyhood home of Robert E. Lee was a rather (*unassuming, most unassuming*) dwelling at 607 Oronoco Street.
4. In fact, a (*large, larger*) nursery wing is where Robert's mother cared for her five children: Carter, Ann, Smith, Robert, and Mildred.
5. Before the Lee family's residency here, the previous owners experienced the (*great, greatest*) honor of serving George Washington in their home.

Underline each adverb. Double underline each noun or noun phrase that modifies a verb.

6. My family actually visited Robert E. Lee's boyhood home last year as part of our family vacation.
7. Upon entering the house's foyer, we immediately noticed a gorgeous drawing room now referred to as the Lafayette Room: here the greatly esteemed Revolutionary War general Lafayette had once come to pay his respects to the Lee family.
8. I will always recall feeling somewhat awed as we prepared to ascend the stairs, for five chronological paintings of Robert E. Lee hang majestically along the wall of the staircase.
9. I also learned that day a fact I had not known before: Robert E. Lee's father was the enormously famous General "Light Horse Harry" from the Revolutionary War.
10. My family and I spent the morning leisurely touring Robert E. Lee's boyhood home and totally absorbing ourselves in the period décor and furniture.

Adjective and Adverb Use | Chapter 10 Review 453

Problems with Modifiers

Underline each incorrect adjective or adverb. Write a suitable correction in the blank. If the sentence is already correct, write *C* in the blank.

perfect 11. Henry Lee (1756–1818), Robert E. Lee's father, seemed to naturally possess most perfect military abilities.

better 12. The advent of the Revolutionary War permanently interrupted Henry Lee's plans for law school yet introduced a military career for which he was more better suited.

C 13. One of America's first cavalry soldiers, Henry Lee early proved himself an indispensable leader and arguably became one of George Washington's most trusted military leaders.

C 14. After the Revolutionary War, Lee still enjoyed a close friendship with the commander in chief: Washington even called Lee away from his governing duties in Virginia to quell the Whiskey Rebellion in Texas.

any 15. We do not possess no better epitaph on George Washington than the one penned by Henry Lee: "First in war, first in peace, and first in the hearts of his countrymen."

Placement of Modifiers

Rewrite each sentence, making the modifiers clear or correct. If the sentence is already correct, write *C* in the blank. *(Answers will vary.)*

16. Robert E. Lee most likely almost read all the classic works accessible to him in the original languages, for on his West Point application he mentions his skill in reading classic works in Latin and Greek.

Robert E. Lee most likely read almost all the classic works accessible to him in the original languages, for on his West Point application he mentions his skill in reading classic works in Latin and Greek.

17. Following the death of his father, Henry Lee, young Robert E. Lee took upon himself the duties of caring for his frail mother, who greatly needed individual care.

C

454 Chapter 10 Review | Adjective and Adverb Use

Name

18. Family finances that were depleted drastically dictated the employment of every cost-cutting measure Mrs. Lee could devise.

Family finances, which were drastically depleted, dictated the employment of every cost-cutting measure Mrs. Lee could devise.

19. Robert opted to selflessly receive his higher education at West Point rather than reduce the family finances further by attending a costly university.

Selflessly, Robert opted to receive his higher education at West Point rather than reduce the family finances further by attending a costly university.

20. Attending West Point, not a single demerit blotted his record.

While Robert was attending West Point, not a single demerit blotted his record.

21. Robert E. Lee graduated with the second highest grade average of his class, which demonstrated his unusual discipline and intelligence.

Robert E. Lee's graduating with the second highest grade average of his class demonstrated his unusual discipline and intelligence.

22. A soldier and engineer at Fort Monroe, Virginia, Mary Anna Randolph Custis married Robert E. Lee in her beautiful home called Arlington.

At her beautiful home called Arlington, Mary Anna Randolph Custis married Robert E. Lee, a soldier and engineer at Fort Monroe, Virginia.

23. Only one of Robert and Mary Lee's children was born somewhere other than the family home at Arlington.

C

Adjective and Adverb Use | Chapter 10 Review 455

24. Visitors who observe the Arlington House in detail describe several original oil paintings by the first owner of the home, George Washington Parke Custis.

Visitors who observe the Arlington House describe in detail several original oil paintings by the first owner of the home, George Washington Parke Custis.

25. Touring Arlington House, a gorgeous view of the skyline of Washington, D.C., is a memorable sight for visitors.

A gorgeous view of the skyline of Washington, D.C., is a memorable site for visitors touring Arlington House.

456 Chapter 10 Review | Adjective and Adverb Use

Name

Chapter 11 Review: Capitalization

Personal Names, Religions, and Nationalities

Underline each word that contains a capitalization error.

1. My Grandmother graduated from Central academy.
2. The principal, Horatio Davis, phd, expanded the language program of his school to include german, french, and spanish.
3. At the beginning of each day, dr. Davis led the students in bible reading and prayer.
4. Both my uncle and aunt worked during the Winter as helpers at the school.
5. Neither mother nor uncle Joe graduated from the High School where Grandmother went to school.

Place Names, Transportation, and Astronomy Terms

Underline each word that contains a capitalization error.

6. A trip to Australia aboard a qantas airliner would take the traveler thirty-six hours from san diego to sydney, with much of his flight being over the pacific ocean.
7. After arriving there, the visitor might see a beautiful print of the HMAS *geelong*, a minesweeper built in 1918.
8. A part of a relaxing vacation in australia might include a viewing of the night sky constellations such as the tarantula, which is similar to orion but much larger.
9. Snorkeling north of queensland, a swimmer might see a small jellyfish called an Irukandji.
10. The great barrier reef off the coast of Australia provides some of the most incredible underwater sights in the world.

Businesses and Organizations, Cultural and Historical Terms

Underline each capitalization error. If the sentence is correct, write *C* in the blank.

_______ 11. The spanish club will meet on the Saturday before the fifth of may.

_______ 12. Celebrated primarily as a Regional Holiday in the area of Puebla, that day was chosen to celebrate Mexico's declaration to be independent from Spain.

___C___ 13. Mexico's Independence Day is celebrated later in the calendar year.

Capitalization | Chapter 11 Review 457

_____ 14. Celebrations commemorate Mexico's victories over Spain and other conflicts, including the Mexican civil war.

_____ 15. The hacienda restaurant, where we ate, is a member of the local restaurant owner's association.

Titles, First Words, and Single Letters

Underline each word that contains a capitalization error. If the sentence or phrase is correct, write C in the blank.

_____ 16. Dear aunt Betty and uncle George,
Very Truly Yours,

_____ 17. Next school year I plan to attend the music seminar "A study in hymnology" with Dr. Alan Albert, speaker.

_____ 18. In Dr. Albert's office, I left a piece of sheet music on the t-shaped table.

_____ 19. "There is a fountain filled with blood
drawn from Immanuel's veins;
And sinners, plunged beneath that flood,
lose all their guilty stains."

_____ 20. The male quartet plans to sing "Since I have been Redeemed" and "Rise Up, O Men Of God" next Sunday morning.

_____ 21. Guests on the redeemed radio program are my pastor and youth pastor.

_____ 22. Even our labrador retriever enjoys listening to us practice our music.

_____ 23. Fanny Crosby (She is one of my favorite hymn writers) played the organ at the Bowery Mission in New York City.

_____ 24. I. The Early Life Of Fanny Crosby
A. Hymn Writer at Age Eight
B. School Admission at Age Eleven

_____ 25. On Fanny Crosby's gravestone are the words of a familiar hymn: "Blessed Assurance, Jesus Is Mine! / Oh, what a Foretaste of Glory Divine!"

458 Chapter 11 Review | Capitalization

Name

Chapter 12 Review: Punctuation

End Marks and Other Uses of the Period

Add the correct end mark to each sentence and insert any missing periods or decimal points.

1. How many years does it take to earn a doctoral degree? two? five?
2. Our friend William A. Hindt, MD, earned his degree from the Medical University of South Carolina, known as MUSC, after four years of study.
3. We often asked when he would be done with school.
4. Only family members attended the commencement ceremony, which began at 9:00 a.m.
5. Now he must work as a resident in a hospital—for three more years ! or .

Commas in a Series and After Introductory Elements

Insert any missing commas.

6. To begin meal preparation, a cook should read the entire recipe carefully, assemble all the supplies, and measure all the ingredients.
7. When the diligent, efficient cook has everything ready ahead of time, the meal preparation itself should be easy.
8. Anticipating a delicious meal, the dinner guests may arrive early, but the host should also be prepared for some latecomers.
9. After its time in the oven, a cut of meat may continue to rise in temperature for a few minutes.
10. Finally, the meal is served and the dinner begins.

Punctuation | Chapter 12 Review 459

Commas to Separate

Insert any missing commas.

11. I enjoy studying history, don't you?

12. The study of history, in my opinion, is both useful and enjoyable.

13. Leila, have you ever thought about the benefits of studying history?

14. History teaches us the follies of others; consequently, we are better prepared to avoid their mistakes.

15. One example of failing to learn from others' mistakes happened during World War II, when Hitler attempted to invade Russia.

16. Napoleon Bonaparte, once the emperor of France, had attempted the same thing over a century earlier.

17. Both Napoleon and Hitler, however, failed in their attempts.

18. The Russian winter, cold and severe, was the enemy that defeated them.

19. History teaches lessons relating to almost every field of study, not just warfare.

20. Remind me to finish my history report after dinner, please.

Commas in Letters, Quotations, Dates, Addresses, and Special Constructions

Insert any missing commas.

21. George Bernard Shaw has been credited with saying, "England and America are two countries separated by the same language."

22. Americans have been developing their own expressions and dialect for centuries—even before July 4, 1776.

23. Some words have different meanings in America than they have in Britain. The meanings of *boot* and *bonnet*, I sometimes confuse.

460 Chapter 12 Review | Punctuation

Name

24. Americans call a large four-wheeled vehicle a *truck;* the British, a *lorry.*

25. "We [English] have really everything in common with America these days," Oscar Wilde wrote, "except, of course, language."

26–30. Insert any missing commas in the following letter.

Dear Joyce and Robert,

Thank you so much for hosting the farewell party honoring my sister and me. We have really enjoyed our visit with you and our other cousins these past few weeks. We will visit Uncle Jeff in Portland, Maine, next month. Neither of us has seen him since his graduation from law school; I am still surprised when I think of him as Jeffrey Statz, JD. Theresa and I would love to see you again, and so would Mom and Dad. Perhaps you can come to see us next summer. Thanks again for your hospitality.

Yours truly,

Gary

Incorrect Commas

Circle any incorrect commas. If the sentence is already correct, write C in the blank.

______ 31. Learning how to fish, and learning how to ski are common goals.

______ 32. People can fish and ski in summer and winter, but, I prefer the summer versions.

__C__ 33. Before our last fishing trip, my brother and I tried unsuccessfully to buy some supplies.

______ 34. The slogan "Gone Fishing," was posted on the door of the store.

______ 35. Ralph Samuelson invented water skiing in July, 1922, on Lake Pepin, Minnesota.

Punctuation | Chapter 12 Review 461

Semicolons and Colons

Insert any missing semicolons or colons. If the sentence is already correct, write *C* in the blank.

_______ 36. Did you attend the lecture about Maxwell Perkins at 4:00 yesterday?

_______ 37. The biography *Max Perkins: Editor of Genius* by A. Scott Berg describes how Perkins helped several famous authors of the early twentieth century.

_______ 38. Perkins, a former newspaper reporter, was an editor at Charles Scribner's Sons; he worked with authors such as F. Scott Fitzgerald, Ernest Hemingway, and Marjorie Kinnan Rawlings.

___C___ 39. He died before the publication of Hemingway's book *The Old Man and the Sea;* nevertheless, the author dedicated it to the memory of his friend.

_______ 40. Perkins's ancestors were illustrious too: Roger Sherman, a signer of the Declaration of Independence; William Maxwell Evarts, a United States Senator; and Charles Callahan Perkins, a friend of Browning and Longfellow.

462 Chapter 12 Review | Punctuation

Name

Chapter 13 Review: More Punctuation

Quotation Marks, Ellipses, and Brackets

Read the following paragraph and then determine whether the quotations, ellipses, and brackets in the following items are correct. Identify each item as correct *(C)* or incorrect *(I)*.

A pioneer is someone who launches into the unknown. He might be a settler clearing a wilderness, or he might be a scientist seeking a cure for a deadly disease through a new line of research. In Christian history, a pioneer is one who carries the gospel to an area where the name of Jesus Christ is little known or to a people who are being ignored by the rest of the Christian world. George Liele was a true Christian pioneer. Relatively early in his Christian life, he helped found one of the first black churches in America. Then, forced by necessity to leave his home, he went to Jamaica as a missionary more than ten years before Englishman William Carey launched the modern foreign missions movement.
from *Free Indeed: Heroes of Black Christian History* by Mark Sidwell (BJU Press, 2001)

__C__ 1. "A pioneer . . . launches into the unknown."

__C__ 2. "In Christian history, a pioneer is one who carries the gospel. . . . George Liele was a true Christian pioneer."

__I__ 3. "George Liele found[ed] one of the first black churches in America."

__C__ 4. "Forced by necessity to leave his home, [Liele] went to Jamaica as a missionary."

__I__ 5. "[Liele became] a missionary more than ten years before William Carey, 'the Father of the Modern Missionary Movement,' launched the modern foreign missions movement."

Quotation Marks and Underlining for Italics

Insert any missing quotation marks. Circle any unnecessary quotation marks. Use a transpose sign (∩∪) to indicate the correct placement for any misplaced periods, commas, question marks, colons, and semicolons. Underline any words that should be italicized.

6. James entered the classroom, put his books on his desk, and said, "I have finished reading the novel <u>The Scarlet Letter</u>."

7. "Why did you read an entire book?" asked a classmate; "I read Poe's short story 'The Pit and the Pendulum.' "

8. "According to Miss Stevens, who said, 'You may read either two short stories or one novel' you could do either for the book report," Lauren said.

9. "I thought she told us that "we needed to read just one short story," replied Jack, "so I read only Hawthorne's 'The Minister's Black Veil.' "

10. Lauren remarked in a quiet tone, "Maybe next time you will listen more carefully"

More Punctuation | Chapter 13 Review 463

Apostrophes and Hyphens

Insert any missing apostrophes and hyphens.

11. Preparing one's testimony for presentation at a foreign missions conference requires careful thought and planning.

12. Life verses such as Proverbs 3:5-6 should be a part of the testimony.

13. In addition to someone's life verses, God's direction in leading that person to the mission field should also be a part of the testimony.

14. It's encouraging to others to learn about the problems and blessings associated with preparing to go to the mission field.

15. In the mid-1980s a missionary family, the Moores, left Fairmont, West Virginia, for Fortelaza, Brazil. Their self-sacrificing spirit was an encouragement to many from their home church.

Dashes and Parentheses

Insert any missing dashes or parentheses. *(Some answers may vary.)*

16. "Did you know that no one—at least none that I have talked to—has ever heard of the dessert white fungus with white sugar?" Jacob inquired.

17. "Do you mean—oh, I can't remember the name—yes, tremella, also known as white mushrooms?" Sheila asked.

18. "Yes, the Oriental Cuisine Society (OCS) includes this dessert in their cookbook," chimed in Sylvia.

19. "I'm not sure that—you mean you boil them first?—I would be able to eat mushrooms with sugar," added Jared.

20. "If you want to make the dessert, you have to (1) boil the mushrooms, (2) dry the mushrooms, and (3) mix them with a sugar syrup," said Sylvia.

464 Chapter 13 Review | More Punctuation

Index

Index 465

466 Index

Index 467

468 Index

Index 469

470 Index

Index 471

How to Use the Teacher's Toolkit

Contents

The Teacher's Toolkit contains the following materials:

- Common Core State Standards for the English Language Arts
- Pretests and Answer Keys
- Teaching Helps and Answer Keys
- ESL Helps and Answer Keys
- Concept Reinforcements and Answer Keys
- Writing Worksheets and Answer Keys
- Writing Rubrics
- Bulletin Boards
- Diagram Answers
- Explaining the Gospel

Getting Started

Viewing the Teacher's Tookit materials requires Adobe® Reader® 9.0 or higher. The most recent version of Adobe Reader may be downloaded at no charge from the Adobe website at www.adobe.com. An Internet connection is required to download Reader.

Windows

Insert the CD. The CD is designed to start automatically if your computer is set to allow it. If it does not start automatically, click "Run" if given the option. You may also choose to open the folder to view the CD's files and double-click "Startup.exe" to start the CD. Read and accept the license agreement to begin using the Teacher's Toolkit materials. Navigate within the CD using the bookmarks on the left side of the screen.

Mac

Insert the CD, click on the CD icon, and open the file "main.pdf" to begin using the Teacher's Toolkit materials.

T

U

V

W

Y

Minimum System Requirements

Processor: Pentium IV
Operating System: Windows XP or Mac OS Leopard (version 10.5)
RAM: 256 MB
Display: 1024 × 768
Adobe Reader: version 9.0

Additional Help

For more detailed instructions, including how to print files and insert visuals into presentations, please refer to the usage instructions on the CD. For further assistance, call BJU Press Customer Service at 1-800-845-5731.